INFORMATION SYSTEMS CONTROL AND AUDIT

INFORMATION SYSTEMS CONTROL AND AUDIT

Ron Weber

The University of Queensland

© Prentice Hall, Upper Saddle River, NJ 07458

Executive Editor:	Annie Todd
Editorial Assistant:	Fran Toepfer
Editor-in-Chief:	P. J. Boardman
Executive Marketing Manager:	Beth Toland
Production Editor:	Marc Oliver
Project Manager:	Susan Rifkin
Managing Editor:	Dee Josephson
Manufacturing Buyer:	Lisa DiMaulo
Senior Manufacturing Supervisor:	Paul Smolenski
Manufacturing Manager:	Vincent Scelta
Art Director:	Jayne Conte
Cover Design:	Kiwi Design
Cover Illustration/Photo:	John Martin/Stock Illustration Source
Composition:	UG

Figure 22-8 reprinted by permission, Robert E. Quinn and John R. Rohrbaugh, "A Spatial Model of Organizational Effectiveness," *Management Science*, Volume 29, Number 3, March 1983, and Robert E. Quinn and Kim Cameron, "Organizational Life Cycles and Shifting Criteria of Effectiveness: Some Preliminary Evidence," *Management Science*, Volume 29, Number 1, January 1983. Copyright © 1983, The Institute of Management Sciences (currently INFORMS), 901 Elkridge Landing Road, Suite 400, Linthicum, Maryland 21090-2909 USA.

Library of Congress Cataloging-in-Publication Data
Weber, Ron.
    Information systems control and audit / by Ron Weber.
       p. cm.
    Includes bibliographical references (p.) and index.
    ISBN 0-13-947870-1
    1. Information resources management.   I. Title.
T58.64.W43   1998
658.4′038—dc21   98-25787
                                 CIP

Prentice-Hall International (UK) Limited, London
Prentice-Hall of Australia Pty. Limited, Sydney
Prentice-Hall Canada, Inc., Toronto
Prentice-Hall Hispanoamericana, S.A., Mexico
Prentice-Hall of India Private Limited, New Delhi
Prentice-Hall of Japan, Inc., Tokyo
Prentice-Hall Asia Pte. Ltd., Singapore
Editora Prentice-Hall do Brasil, Ltda., Rio de Janeiro

Printed in the United States of America

10 9

**To my mother
and the memory of my father**

Brief Contents

Contents

How to Use This Book

Before you begin this book, I recommend that you think carefully about the strategies you will use to learn and master its contents. To maximize your learning, you must read it and study it in a purposeful way.

Here are some suggestions:

1. Before commencing each part of the book, read the introduction carefully. You should gain an overall appreciation of the structure and content of the part. In addition, you should understand how the chapters contained within the part fit into the overall structure of the book and help to achieve the overall objectives of the book. Carefully read the chapter summaries contained in the introduction to the part.

2. Before commencing each chapter, carefully study the chapter key points at the start of the chapter. The key points present the most important material covered in the chapter. At a minimum, you must be able to understand and recall the material contained within the key points when you have completed your study of the chapter. Look also at the chapter outline provided at the start of the chapter. It gives you a roadmap for the chapter, and it will help you understand the directions you will be pursuing. Overall, try to understand what you should know by the time you have finished studying the chapter.

3. Next, read the chapter quickly. Skim the content, and try to develop an overall feel for the material contained within the chapter.

4. Then read the chapter carefully. You should try to study the contents actively rather than passively. As you begin each section, think of questions you want answered, and then try to provide answers to these questions based on your reading. The section headings provide some clues about questions you might ask. For example, if you see a subheading called "Separation of Duties" under a major heading called "Effects of Computers on Internal Controls," you might frame the following question: How do computer systems affect the usefulness of separation of duties as an internal control?

5. As you read a section, make brief notes. Try to understand the structure that underlies each section and make notes that reflect this structure. Some examples of typical text structures follow:

   (a) *Definition/example:* The section defines some type of concept and presents examples to illustrate the concept.

   (b) *Description:* The section describes the characteristics of some concept, idea, thing, event, or relationship.

   (c) *Cause–effect–results:* The section describes an event, the causes of the event, and the results of the event.

(d) *Problem–solution–outcomes:* The section describes some type of problem, possible solutions to the problem, the likely outcomes, and the strengths and weaknesses of the proposed solutions.

(e) *Time/order/history:* The section presents a listing of steps in a process or a sequence of events.

(f) *Comparison/contrast:* The section discusses the similarities and differences between concepts, ideas, things, events, or relationships.

6. After reading and making notes on a section, reflect on the section. Try to recall the basic content and structure of the section. Try, also, to see how the detailed material in the section fits into the big picture. See if you can relate the content of the section to prior knowledge or experience.

7. When you've finished the chapter, work on the review questions at the end of the chapter. You do not have to write your answers. Just see if you can provide a quick mental answer to each question. If you cannot, go back to the relevant material in the chapter and read it again.

8. Then do the multiple-choice questions for the chapter. Check your answers against the solutions provided at the end of the chapter. Where you have an incorrect answer, go back again and read the chapter material relevant to the question.

9. Finally, it is important to try some of the exercises and cases at the end of the chapter. They are meant to test your overall understanding of the chapter material and your ability to integrate this material so you can solve problems. Your instructor might assign some of the exercises and cases for you to work on for class discussion purposes. If you discuss and debate your answers with your class colleagues, you should further improve your understanding and recall of the material in the chapter.

Perhaps the most important things to work on while you study this book are your attitude and motivation. Try to be positive about the material and to enjoy your learning. Also, do not lose your self-confidence if the going gets tough. Everyone will find some parts of the book to be difficult. You just need to work a little harder on these parts and perhaps get some assistance from your instructor or your colleagues in class. You will also find that more of the material begins to fit into place as you get further into the book. My experience is that students who keep a positive attitude and work on their motivation find the content of the book challenging and fun. Enjoy it!

Preface

A friend and colleague once said to me: "To be a good auditor, you have to be better at business than your client." I've often pondered that remark. On one hand, it is a compelling notion. On the other hand, it sets an impossible goal for auditors to achieve. Nonetheless, my friend's remark underscores the rich, challenging role that auditors now face. To be successful, they must have a breadth and depth of knowledge that are intellectually daunting. They will perhaps never feel the challenge to their professionalism more keenly than when they enter the domain of information systems control and audit.

The purpose of this book is to provide a solid foundation for the study of information systems auditing, which was established to evaluate whether computer-based information systems safeguard assets, maintain data integrity, achieve organizational objectives effectively, and consume resources efficiently. Safeguarding assets ensures that assets are protected from damage or destruction, unauthorized use, and unauthorized removal. Maintaining data integrity ensures that data is authorized, accurate, complete, non-redundant, timely, and private. Achieving organizational objectives effectively ensures that information systems are developed, implemented, operated, and maintained to meet the needs of their major stakeholders. Achieving resource consumption efficiency ensures that information systems are designed and tuned to minimize the resources they use.

SOME PEDAGOGICAL ISSUES

Before writing this book, I thought long and hard about the approach I should use to present the subject matter of information systems auditing. I found I had to make a choice between two approaches. The first, which I will call the "exposures approach," would have required me to focus primarily on the types of losses that can occur in information systems. I would then have described the controls that might be used to reduce these losses to acceptable levels. The second, which I will call the "controls approach," would have required me to focus primarily on the controls that can be used in information systems to reduce losses to acceptable levels. I would then have described the losses that these controls were designed to mitigate.

Why can't both exposures and controls be the primary focus in a book on information systems auditing? The problem is that exposures and controls do not have a one-to-one relationship with one another. A single control can reduce losses from multiple exposures, and a single exposure can be the subject of multiple controls. If I were to focus on exposures in the book, I would have to repeat some material on controls. On the other hand, if I were to focus on controls, I would have to repeat some material on exposures. If I were to focus on both exposures and controls, the repetition of material would be extensive. When I have tried this approach, my students have been quick to point out that they are bored. There is simply too much repetition for their liking. The only way forward, I therefore believe, is to adopt either an exposures or a controls approach and then to present the material that must be duplicated as efficiently as possible so the presentation of subject matter is complete.

In this book, I have chosen the controls approach for two reasons. First, having tried both approaches, I have concluded after more than 20 years of teaching information systems auditing to tertiary students and to professionals that most prefer the controls approach. I am still unsure why, but I suspect it has to do with controls requiring smaller chunks of understanding than exposures. Second, one of my objectives is to try to integrate the controls literature that appears in computer science and the controls literature that appears in auditing. It dismays me that each area still tends to ignore the other, because each has so much to contribute to our understanding of the information systems audit function.

I need to make one other important point on the subject matter of the book. As a potential reader, you might look for chapters on particular specialized topics within the information systems area—for example, electronic commerce, the World Wide Web, client-server computing, and local area networks. You might be disappointed to find these chapters missing. My choice not to include such chapters, however, is quite deliberate. Through experience, I have found that organizing the subject matter of information systems control and audit around specialized topics undermines students obtaining a deep understanding of the nature of controls and audit procedures. I have worked in the information systems field long enough to know that specialized topics wax and wane. They are "hot" one day, only to cool rapidly the next as some new technological innovation is heralded as the panacea for all our problems. My goal in this book is to expound fundamental concepts—concepts that will be useful in the long run. If students understand these concepts and practice their use with the exercises and cases at the end of each chapter, they should have a sound basis for handling whatever new control and audit situations they ultimately confront.

USING THE BOOK

I intend this book to be useful to three groups of people. The first comprises upper undergraduate and postgraduate students who are seeking to acquire knowledge of information system controls and auditing. The book can be used like any conventional college textbook. The second group comprises information systems audit practitioners. Some might be preparing for professional examinations, such as the Certified Information Systems Auditor examination. I hope this book will assist them with their studies. Some might simply want a reference book. Again, I hope this book will be useful for this purpose. The third group comprises managers and information systems professionals (e.g., analysts and programmers) who are seeking to acquire knowledge about information system controls and auditing. Once more, I hope the book will help them with the knowledge they are seeking.

At The University of Queensland, I teach a semester-long subject based on the content of this book. I have found that students who have either a strong knowledge of auditing and basic knowledge of information systems or a strong knowledge of information systems and basic knowledge of auditing can complete the subject successfully. Of course, the ideal situation is when students have strong knowledge of both fields. The book is not for a beginner, however, who has no knowledge of either information systems or auditing.

At the tertiary level the book provides sufficient material for either a one- or two-semester subject. In a one-semester subject, some chapters will have to be omitted—for example, chapters that deal with system effectiveness and efficiency and management of the information systems audit function. In a two-semester subject, all the chapters can be covered. In addition, more time can be devoted to project work.

At The University of Queensland I have one class session each week lasting four hours. I have taught this session in two ways. First, I've spent half the session giving a mini-lecture on the material assigned for the week. The remainder of the session has been devoted to class discussion of some of the end-of-chapter exercises and cases. The exercises and cases have been designed to force students to think about how they would apply the material they've learned in the chapter in practice. This first approach has always been well-received by students. My best class ratings have been obtained, however, when I've used the second approach whereby the entire session has been devoted to class discussion of the end-of-chapter exercises and cases. I've found it takes some courage not to lecture and to rely entirely on the students to read the text. Nonetheless, my experience is that the students respond most positively. They prepare thoroughly beforehand, and the class discussion is always interesting, enjoyable, and informative.

For the instructor, a supplement to the book is available containing suggested answers to the review questions, multiple-choice questions, and exercises and cases. In addition, it provides additional multiple-choice questions that can be used for quizzes or examination purposes. I recommend that instructors supplement the assignment material in the book with further case studies and computer-based exercises. The additional case studies should be more comprehensive than those in the book so students are forced to integrate material across several chapters. They might also be on specific types of systems—for example, an electronic commerce system, a database system, or some kind of Web-based system. The computer-based exercises might involve using a generalized audit software package to access a file and to evaluate the quality of the data on the file.

ACKNOWLEDGMENTS

This book is based on an earlier book that I published: *EDP Auditing: Conceptual Foundations and Practice*, 2d ed. (New York: McGraw-Hill, 1988). The fundamental structure of this earlier book is manifested in this book, and I also have been able to use some of its content. Seven years ago, however, I began what I thought would be a fairly straightforward revision to this earlier book. What transpired was a task that far exceeded even my most pessimistic estimates of the work that would be required. The technology had gone ahead in leaps and bounds, and I found I had to spend many hours just reading and reflecting to try to ensure that I told the "right" story in what I hoped would be an interesting and informative way. I also found that I wanted to write a more reader-friendly book with better student-support materials by way of exercises and cases. After several thousand hours of work, you are looking at the result.

Throughout the seven years, I am grateful to a large number of colleagues and friends for their support and affirmation. In particular, I want to acknowledge the encouragement given by Professor Gordon Davis, University of Minnesota, and P. J. Boardman and Annie Todd, Prentice Hall, during some especially dark days of writing. They kept their faith in me when I must have seemed a lost cause, and I am deeply indebted to them. My thanks, also, to Marc Oliver of Prentice Hall and Danielle Meckley of UG for the superb assistance they provided to me during the production of this book.

Many colleagues and friends helped in one way or another during the preparation of this book. In particular, I would like to acknowledge Paul Bowen, Lindsay Cardell, Grant Castner, Tony Chew, Roger Clarke, Simon Collyer, Graham Coote, Michael de Crespigny, Brian Cruse, Colin Ferguson, Randall Fletcher, Guy Gable, Peter Green, Jim Hann, Jon Heales, John Marsland, Noela Meier, Karen Morgan, Graeme Peters, Arthur Pool, Phil Procopis, Ian Ritchie, Jeff Scrivener, Peter Seddon, Sia Siew Kien, Roger Simnett, Danny Smith, Ken Trotman, Judy Waugh, and John Wyber. To all these individuals go my sincere thanks.

Finally, to the three women in my life—my wife, Kay, and my daughters, Amy and Georgia—go my deepest thanks. This book has consumed too much time—time that we would otherwise have spent together. The debt I owe them for their love, support, and patience is awesome.

Ron Weber

PART

Introduction

Information systems auditing is a function that has been developed to assess whether computer systems safeguard assets, maintain data integrity, and allow the goals of an organization to be achieved effectively and efficiently. These objectives are important to individuals who work both inside and outside organizations. Within an organization, for example, managers are concerned to use computer systems in such a way that they obtain the best return they can on the shareholders' funds invested in the organization. Outside an organization, groups such as civil rights groups and labor unions often are interested in how an organization uses its computer systems. For example, civil rights groups might be interested if an organization were to develop databases that compromised a person's privacy, and labor unions might be interested if an organization were to implement computer systems that monitored the performance of their members or displaced their members.

The first part of this book comprises two chapters that introduce the information systems audit function. We will examine the reasons why we need to control and audit computer systems, the nature and purposes of the information systems audit function, the way in which computer systems have affected internal controls and the audit function, and the overall approach we use to conduct an information systems audit.

	Chapter	*Overview of Contents*
1	Overview of Information Systems Auditing	Discusses the need for control and audit of computer-based information systems; defines information systems auditing; discusses the objectives of information systems auditing; examines the effects of computers on traditional internal control principles and the auditor's evidence collection and evidence evaluation functions; considers the foundations of information systems auditing.
2	Conducting an Information Systems Audit	Discusses several strategies that information systems auditors can use to deal with complexity; describes the basic steps to be undertaken in the conduct of an information systems audit; examines some of the major decisions that the information systems auditor must make.

Overview of Information Systems Auditing

Chapter Outline

Chapter Key Points

■ An organization must control and audit computer-based information systems because the costs of errors and irregularities that arise in these systems can be high. An organization's ability to survive can be severely undermined through corruption or destruction of its database; decision-making errors caused by poor-quality information systems; losses incurred through computer abuse; loss of valuable computer hardware and software and personnel; the high costs of some types of computer errors; failure to maintain the privacy of individual persons; and failure to control how computers are used within the organization.

■ The information systems audit function has been established to safeguard assets, to maintain data integrity, to achieve system effectiveness, and to achieve system efficiency.

■ Computer-based information systems do not undermine the importance of traditional internal control principles, such as separation of duties. However, these principles must be implemented differently when computer-based as opposed to manual information systems are used.

■ Compared with manual information systems, collecting evidence on the reliability of internal controls in computer-based information systems is often more complex. There are more types of computer controls than manual controls. Furthermore, computer controls are often more critical than manual controls.

■ Evaluating the reliability of controls in computer systems is also often more complex than in manual information systems. There tends to be a greater number of more complex controls to consider.

■ Many of the principles that underlie the practice of information systems auditing have their roots in other disciplines, such as traditional auditing, computer science, management, and behavioral science.

INTRODUCTION

Whereas 50 years ago we fulfilled most of our data processing needs manually, today computers perform much of the data processing required in both the private and public sectors of our economies. As a result, the need to maintain the integrity of data processed by computers now seems to pervade our lives. Many people fear that our substantially increased data-processing capabilities are not well controlled. The media make much of computer abuse. We have concerns about the privacy of data we exchange with organizations such as the tax department, medical authorities, and credit granting institutions. All of us have probably suffered the frustrations of trying to get an organization to update its computer-maintained name and address file.

Uncontrolled use of computers can have a widespread impact on a society. For example, inaccurate information causes misallocation of resources within the economy, and fraud can be perpetrated because of inadequate system controls. Unfortunately, those who suffer most often are those who can least afford to suffer — for example, small shareholders and low-income earners. Perhaps more subtle is the growing distrust of institutions that gather and process large volumes of data. Because computers now seem to be ubiquitous, many people have a sense of lost individuality: The "big brother" of George Orwell's *1984* is upon us.

NEED FOR CONTROL AND AUDIT OF COMPUTERS

Computers are used extensively to process data and to provide information for decision making. Initially, they were available only to large organizations that could afford their high purchase and operation costs. The advent of minicomputers and the rapid decrease in the cost of computer technology then enabled medium-sized organizations to take advantage of computers for their data processing. Nowadays, the widespread availability of powerful microcomputers and their associated packaged software has resulted in the extensive use of computers in the workplace and at home. Given the intensely competitive mar-

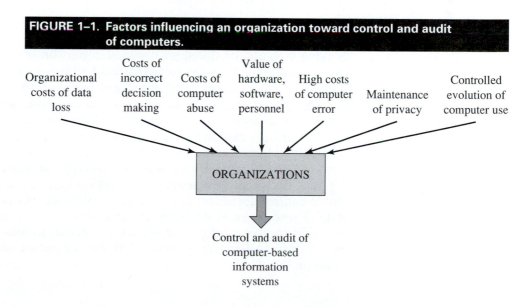

FIGURE 1–1. Factors influencing an organization toward control and audit of computers.

ketplace for computer hardware and software technology, the rapid diffusion of computers in our economies will continue.

Because computers play such a large part in assisting us to process data and to make decisions, it is important that their use be controlled. Figure 1–1 shows seven major reasons for establishing a function to examine controls over computer-based data processing. In the following subsections, we examine these reasons in more detail.

Organizational Costs of Data Loss

Data make up a critical resource necessary for an organization's continuing operations. In this regard, Everest (1985) proposes that data provides the organization with an image of itself, its environment, its history, and its future. If this image is accurate, the organization increases its abilities to adapt and survive in a changing environment. If this image is inaccurate or lost, the organization can incur substantial losses.

For example, consider a large department store whose accounts receivable file has been destroyed. Unless its customers are honest and also remember what they have purchased from the store, the firm can suffer a major loss in cash receipts through customers failing to pay their debts. The department store's long-run survival could be affected. Consider, also, a department store that loses its accounts payable file. Most likely it will be unable to pay its debts on time. As a result, it could suffer a loss of credit rating as well as any discounts available for early payment. If it contacts creditors requesting their assistance, the department store has to rely on the honesty of its creditors in notifying it of the amounts it owes. Furthermore, creditors might now begin to question the competence of the department store's management. As a result, they might be unwilling to extend credit to the department store in the future.

Such losses can occur when existing controls over computers are lax. For example, management might not provide adequate backup for computer files. Thus, the loss of a file through computer program error, sabotage, or natural disaster means the file cannot be recovered, and the organization's continuing operations are thereby impaired.

Incorrect Decision Making

Making high-quality decisions depends in part on the quality of the data and the quality of the decision rules that exist within computer-based information systems. Let's consider the significance of both in turn.

The importance of accurate *data* in a computer system depends on the types of decisions made by persons having some interest in an organization. For example, if managers are making strategic planning decisions, they will probably tolerate some errors in the data, given the long-run nature of strategic planning decisions and the inherent uncertainty surrounding these types of decisions. If managers are making management control and operational control decisions, however, they will probably require highly accurate data. These types of decisions involve detection, investigation, and correction of out-of-control processes. Thus, inaccurate data can cause costly, unnecessary investigations to be undertaken or out-of-control processes to remain undetected.

Besides management, incorrect data can also have an impact on other parties who have an interest in an organization. For example, shareholders might make poor investment decisions if they are provided with inaccurate financial information. Similarly, governments, labor, and lobby groups might make poor decisions if they are provided with inaccurate or incomplete data about an organization. They might begin to make demands on the organization (e.g., for control of greenhouse emissions or higher wages) that the organization cannot sustain.

The importance of having accurate *decision rules* in a computer system also depends on the types of decisions made by persons having some interest in an organization. In some cases, an incorrect decision rule can have minor consequences. For example, a small, inconsequential error can occur in the calculation of depreciation on a low-value asset. In other cases, however, the consequences can be significant. For example, if the algorithm that determines the interest rate to be paid to customers of a bank is incorrect, the bank might make substantial overpayments to its customers. It might not be able to recover these monies without substantial losses of goodwill. Similarly, if a decision rule in an expert system that supports medical diagnosis is incorrect, doctors could prescribe inappropriate treatments for patients, some of which could be fatal.

Costs of Computer Abuse

The major stimulus for development of the information systems audit function within organizations often seems to have been computer abuse. Parker (1976, p. 12) defines computer abuse to be "any incident associated with computer technology in which a victim suffered or could have suffered loss and a perpetrator by intention made or could have made gain."

Some major types of computer abuse that an organization might encounter include the following:

Type of Abuse	*Explanation*
Hacking	A person gains unauthorized access to a computer system to read, modify, or delete programs or data or to disrupt services.
Viruses	Viruses are programs that attach themselves to executable files, system areas on diskettes, or data files that contain macros to cause disruption to computer operations or damage to data and programs (Nachenberg 1997, 1998). They are designed to achieve two objectives: to replicate themselves and to deliver a *payload* that causes disruption of some kind.
Illegal physical access	A person gains unauthorized physical access to computer facilities (e.g., they gain illegal entry to a computer room or a terminal). As a result, they are able to cause physical damage to hardware or make unauthorized copies of programs or data.
Abuse of privileges	A person uses the privileges they have been assigned for unauthorized purposes (e.g., they make unauthorized copies of sensitive data they are permitted to access).

Computer abuse can lead to the following types of consequences:

Consequences of Abuse	*Explanation*
Destruction of assets	Hardware, software, data, facilities, documentation, or supplies can be destroyed.
Theft of assets	Hardware, software, data, documentation, or supplies can be illegally removed.
Modification of assets	Hardware, software, data, or documentation can be modified in an unauthorized way.
Privacy violations	The privacy of data pertaining to a person or an organization can be compromised.
Disruption of operations	The day-to-day operations of the information systems function can cease temporarily.
Unauthorized use of assets	Hardware, software, data, facilities, documentation, or supplies are used for unauthorized purposes (e.g., computer time is used for private consulting purposes).
Physical harm to personnel	Personnel can suffer physical harm.

Computer abuse usually is a less serious problem for organizations than errors and omissions in computer systems or the effects of natural and human-made disasters (such as floods and fires). Nonetheless, organizations now appear to be encountering a high incidence of computer abuse (see, e.g., Benbow 1990; BloomBecker 1990; Evens 1990). Furthermore, the average losses incurred from computer abuse seem to be substantially higher than those incurred from conventional fraud.

In addition, the number and types of threats that lead to computer abuse also seem to be increasing. For example, as of November 1996, Nachenberg (1997) reports that more than 10,000 DOS-based computer viruses had been written. Moreover, more complex, more lethal viruses continue to appear. Similarly, the rapid growth of the Internet has exposed organizations with inadequate security to many threats from outside hostile parties that previously would not have affected them (see, e.g., Vacca 1996).

Unfortunately, surveys continue to indicate that a large number of organizations are not well prepared to deal with computer abuse. For example, Benbow (1990) reports that 80 percent of computer abuse cases investigated in his research were committed by internal employees, but only 20 percent of the organizations he studied performed security reviews of potential employees. Several surveys also have reported that the chances of many organizations surviving a major incident of computer abuse are poor (see, e.g., Evens 1990). A substantial number of organizations could operate for only a few hours without their computer systems, and many would be out of business within a few days.

Yet research by Straub (1990) and Straub and Nance (1990) suggests that deterrent administrative procedures and security countermeasures are often effective in reducing the incidence of computer abuse and the losses incurred when computer abuse arises. These controls are especially important when the laws relating to computer abuse are inadequate in the jurisdiction in which an organization operates. In many countries, the laws covering computer abuse are still evolving. It might be difficult to prosecute a perpetrator of an abuse because of loopholes that still exist in the law. Chapter 7 discusses these matters further.

Value of Computer Hardware, Software, and Personnel

In addition to data, computer hardware, software, and personnel are critical organizational resources. Some organizations have multimillion dollar investments in hardware. Even with adequate insurance, the intentional or unintentional loss of hardware can cause considerable disruption. Similarly, software often constitutes a considerable investment of an organization's resources. If the software is corrupted or destroyed, the organization might be unable to continue operations if it cannot recover the software promptly. If the software is stolen, confidential information could be disclosed to competitors; or, if the software is a proprietary package, lost revenues or lawsuits could arise. Finally, personnel are always a valuable resource, particularly in light of an ongoing scarcity of well-trained computer professionals in many countries.

High Costs of Computer Error

Computers now automatically perform many critical functions within our society. For example, they monitor the condition of patients during surgery, direct the flight of a missile, control a nuclear reactor, and steer a ship on its course. Consequently, the costs of a computer error in terms of loss of life, deprivation of liberty, or damage to the environment can be high. For example, data errors in a computer system used to control flight paths resulted in the death of 257 people when an airplane crashed into a mountain in Antarctica; a person was jailed incorrectly for five months because of erroneous data contained in a computer system.

The costs of computer error in financial terms can also be high. An error in an Australian government computer system resulted in a $126 million overpayment of pharmaceutical benefits. As a result of a human error and deficiencies in its computer systems design, a company had to pay substantial damages for delivering 93,000 barrels of oil to the wrong consignee (Westermeier 1993). Increasingly, it appears that organizations will be held liable for damages that occur as a result of errors in the design, implementation, or operation of their computer systems.

Maintenance of Privacy

Much data is now collected about us as individuals: taxation, credit, medical, educational, employment, residence, and so on. This data was also collected before computers. Nonetheless, the powerful data processing capabilities of computers, particularly their rapid throughput, integration, and retrieval capabilities, cause many people to wonder whether the privacy of individuals (and organizations) has now been eroded beyond acceptable levels. In the United States, for example, civil rights activists have long held substantial concerns about using computer systems for computer-matching purposes (Shattuck 1984). In computer matching, disparate files are merged or compared to build up a profile on a person. A person's taxation data might be compared with data on the social security benefits they receive to detect possible instances of welfare fraud.

Similarly, in Australia, many people were concerned when the then-federal government proposed that it would introduce an Australia card (Graham 1990). Privacy activists argued that use of the Australia card as a universal identifier for each Australian would significantly undermine individual privacy.

More recently, some people have been concerned about the establishment of human genome data banks and the potential to use computers in conjunction with human genetic data to obtain detailed information about a person. They are concerned that knowledge about a person's genetics could be used in decisions about them—for example, whether to give them a job or whether to give them life insurance. Also, some people are concerned about the impact of the Internet on personal privacy (Meeks 1997). For example, they fear that search engines could be used to extract data from large databases that could compromise a person's privacy.

Aside from any constitutional aspect, many nations deem privacy to be a human right. These nations consider it to be the responsibility of those people concerned with computer data processing to ensure that computer use does not evolve to the stage where data about people can be collected, integrated, and retrieved quickly. Furthermore, they consider that computer professionals of all kinds have a responsibility to ensure that data is used only for the purposes intended. Unfortunately, there are now many instances in which computers have been used to abuse the privacy of individuals (Neumann 1995). As a result, computer professionals are now coming under increasing pressure to ensure that this does not happen.

Controlled Evolution of Computer Use

From time to time, major conflicts arise over how computer technology should be used in our societies. For example, some computer scientists continue to be concerned about using computers to support nuclear weapons command and control systems. Many became especially vocal during the debate over the U.S. Strategic Defense Initiative's battle management systems (Borning 1987; Parnas 1987). They argue that the reliability of complex computer systems usually cannot be guaranteed and that the consequences of using unreliable computer systems can be catastrophic.

Similarly, many people are concerned about the effects that use of computers can have on a person's working life. Should computer technology be allowed to displace people from the workforce or to stultify jobs? What effects do computers have on the physical and mental well-being of their users?

It might be argued that technology is neutral—it is neither good nor bad. The *use* of technology, however, can produce major social problems. In this light, important, ongoing decisions must be made about how computers should be used in our societies. Governments, professional bodies, pressure groups, organizations, and individual persons all must be concerned with evaluating and monitoring how we deploy computer technology.

INFORMATION SYSTEMS AUDITING DEFINED

Information systems auditing is the process of collecting and evaluating evidence to determine whether a computer system safeguards assets, maintains data integrity, allows organizational goals to be achieved effectively, and uses resources efficiently. Thus, information systems auditing supports traditional audit objectives: attest objectives (those of the external auditor) that focus on asset safeguarding and data integrity, and management objectives (those of the internal auditor) that encompass not only attest objectives but also effectiveness and efficiency objectives.

Sometimes information systems auditing has another objective—namely, ensuring that an organization complies with some regulation, rule, or condition. For example, a bank might have to comply with a government regulation about how much it can lend; an introduction agency might seek to comply with

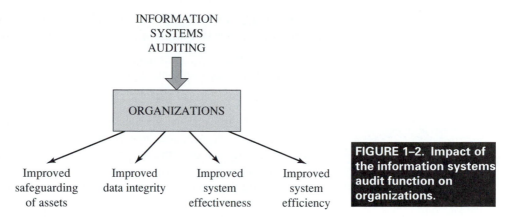

FIGURE 1–2. Impact of the information systems audit function on organizations.

a voluntary code in relation to use of personal data about its clients; or an organization might seek to comply with a covenant in a loan contract that it has with a merchant bank. However, in this book we will not pursue the compliance auditing objective further, for the following reasons: First, we can conceive of compliance concerns within the broader framework of effectiveness objectives. (One goal of an organization is to comply with regulations, rules, and conditions to which it is subject either voluntarily or involuntarily.) Second, in any event, our broad treatment of control and audit within a computer environment should prove useful to auditors who must carry out compliance work. Third, at least in principle the notion of compliance work is straightforward, and it can be incorporated fairly easily within the material we cover in this book.

In this light, Figure 1–2 shows that throughout this book we conceive information systems auditing as being a force that enables organizations to better achieve four major objectives. In the following subsections, we consider each of these objectives in detail.

Asset Safeguarding Objectives

The information system assets of an organization include hardware, software, facilities, people (knowledge), data files, system documentation, and supplies. Like all assets, they must be protected by a system of internal control. Hardware can be damaged maliciously. Proprietary software and the contents of data files can be stolen or destroyed. Supplies of negotiable forms can be used for unauthorized purposes. These assets are often concentrated in one or a small number of locations, such as a single disk. As a result, asset safeguarding becomes an especially important objective for many organizations to achieve.

Data Integrity Objectives

Data integrity is a fundamental concept in information systems auditing. It is a state implying data has certain attributes: completeness, soundness, purity, and veracity. If data integrity is not maintained, an organization no longer has a true representation of itself or of events. Moreover, if the integrity of an organization's data is low, it could suffer from a loss of competitive advantage (see, e.g., Redman 1995 and Strong et al. 1997). Nonetheless, maintaining data integrity can be achieved only at a cost. The benefits obtained should exceed the costs of the control procedures needed.

Three major factors affect the value of a data item to an organization and thus the importance of maintaining the integrity of that data item:

1. *The value of the informational content of the data item for individual decision makers:* The informational content of a data item depends on its ability to change the level of uncertainty surrounding a decision and, as a result, to change the expected payoffs of the decisions that might be made. These notions have been well developed within statistical decision theory.
2. *The extent to which the data item is shared among decision makers:* If data is shared, corruption of data integrity affects not just one user but many. The value of a data item is some aggregate function of the value of the data item to the individual users of the data item. Thus, maintenance of data integrity becomes more critical in a shared data environment.
3. *The value of the data item to competitors:* If a data item is valuable to a competitor, its loss might undermine an organization's position in the marketplace. Competitors could exploit the informational content of the data item to reduce the profitability of the organization and to bring about bankruptcy, liquidation, takeover, or merger.

System Effectiveness Objectives

An effective information system accomplishes its objectives. Evaluating effectiveness implies knowledge of user needs. To evaluate whether a system reports information in a way that facilitates decision making by its users, auditors must know the characteristics of users and the decision-making environment.

Effectiveness auditing often occurs after a system has been running for some time. Management requests a postaudit to determine whether the system is achieving its stated objectives. This evaluation provides input to the decision on whether to scrap the system, continue running it, or modify it in some way.

Effectiveness auditing also can be carried out during the design stages of a system. Users often have difficulty identifying or agreeing on their needs. Moreover, substantial communication problems often occur between system designers and users. If a system is complex and costly to implement, management might want auditors to perform an independent evaluation of whether the design is likely to fulfill user needs.

System Efficiency Objectives

An efficient information system uses minimum resources to achieve its required objectives. Information systems consume various resources: machine time, peripherals, system software, and labor. These resources are scarce, and different application systems usually compete for their use.

The question of whether an information system is efficient often has no clear-cut answer. The efficiency of any particular system cannot be considered in isolation from other systems. Problems of suboptimization occur if one system is "optimized" at the expense of other systems. For example, minimizing an application system's execution time might require dedication of some hardware resource (e.g., a printer) to that system. The system might not use the hardware fully, however, while it undertakes its work. The slack resource will not be available to other application systems if it is dedicated to one system.

System efficiency becomes especially important when a computer no longer has excess capacity. The performance of individual application systems degrades (e.g., slower response times occur), and users can become increasingly frustrated. Management must then decide whether efficiency can be improved or extra resources must be purchased. Because extra hardware and software is a cost issue, management needs to know whether available capacity has been exhausted because individual application systems are inefficient or because existing allocations of computer resources are causing bottlenecks. Because auditors are perceived to be independent, management might ask them to assist with or even perform this evaluation.

EFFECTS OF COMPUTERS ON INTERNAL CONTROLS

The goals of asset safeguarding, data integrity, system effectiveness, and system efficiency can be achieved only if an organization's management sets up a system of internal control. Traditionally, major components of an internal control system include separation of duties, clear delegation of authority and responsibility, recruitment and training of high-quality personnel, a system of authorizations, adequate documents and records, physical control over assets and records, management supervision, independent checks on performance, and periodic comparison of recorded accountability with assets. In a computer system, these components must still exist; however, use of computers affects the implementation of these internal control components in several ways. In essence, they have been adopted and adapted to fit in with a computer environment (Figure 1–3). In the following subsections, we briefly examine some of the major areas of impact.

Separation of Duties

In a manual system, separate persons should be responsible for initiating transactions, recording transactions, and maintaining custody of assets. As a basic control, separation of duties prevents or detects errors and irregularities. In a computer system, however, the traditional notion of separation of duties does not always apply. For example, a program could reconcile a vendor invoice against a receiving document and print a check for the amount owed to a creditor. Thus, the program is performing functions that in manual systems would be considered to be incompatible. Nevertheless, it might be inefficient and, from a control viewpoint, useless to place these functions in separate programs. Instead, separation of duties must exist in a different form. When it has been determined that the program executes correctly, the capability to run the program in production mode and the capability to change the program must be separated.

In minicomputer and microcomputer environments, separation of incompatible functions could be even more difficult to achieve. Some minicomputers and microcomputers allow users to change programs and data easily. Furthermore, they might not provide a record of these changes. Thus, determining whether incompatible functions have been performed by system users can be difficult or impossible.

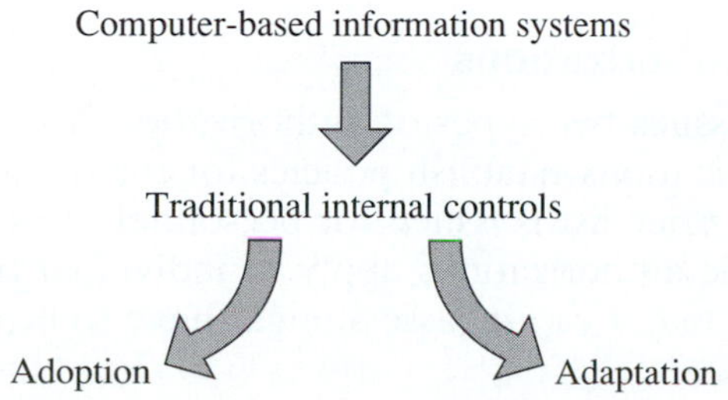

Computer-based information systems

Traditional internal controls

Adoption   Adaptation

FIGURE 1–3. Effects of computer-based information systems on traditional internal controls.

Delegation of Authority and Responsibility

A clear line of authority and responsibility is an essential control in both manual and computer systems. In a computer system, however, delegating authority and responsibility in an unambiguous way might be difficult because some resources are shared among multiple users. For example, one objective of using a database management system is to provide multiple users with access to the same data, thereby reducing the control problems that arise with maintaining redundant data. When multiple users have access to the same data and the integrity of the data is somehow violated, it is not always easy to trace who is responsible for corrupting the data and who is responsible for identifying and correcting the error. Some organizations have attempted to overcome these problems by designating a single user as the *owner* of the data. This user assumes ultimate responsibility for the integrity of the data.

Authority and responsibility lines have also been blurred by the rapid growth in end-user computing. Because high-level languages are more readily available, more users are developing, modifying, operating, and maintaining their own application systems instead of having this work performed by information systems professionals. Although these developments have substantial benefits for the users of computing services in an organization, unfortunately, they exacerbate the problems of exercising overall control over computing use.

Competent and Trustworthy Personnel

Substantial power is often vested in the persons responsible for the computer-based information systems developed, implemented, operated, and maintained within organizations. For example, a systems analyst might be responsible for advising management on the suitability of high-cost, high-technology equipment. Similarly, a computer operator sometimes takes responsibility for safeguarding critical software and critical data during execution of or backup of a system. The power vested in the personnel responsible for computer systems often exceeds the power vested in the personnel responsible for manual systems.

Unfortunately, ensuring that an organization has competent and trustworthy information systems personnel is a difficult task. In many countries and across many years, well-trained and experienced information systems personnel have been in short supply. Therefore, organizations sometimes have been forced to compromise in their choice of staff. Moreover, it is not always easy for organizations to assess the competence and integrity of their information systems staff. High turnover among these staff has been the norm. Therefore, managers have had insufficient time to evaluate them properly. In addition, the rapid evolution of technology inhibits management's ability to evaluate an information systems employee's skills. Some information systems personnel also seem to lack a well-developed sense of ethics, and some seem to delight in subverting controls.

System of Authorizations

Management issues two types of authorizations to execute transactions. First, general authorizations establish policies for the organization to follow. For example, a fixed price list is issued for personnel to use when products are sold. Second, specific authorizations apply to individual transactions. For example, acquisitions of major capital assets might have to be approved by the board of directors.

In a manual system, auditors evaluate the adequacy of procedures for authorization by examining the work of employees. In a computer system, authorization procedures often are embedded within a computer program. For example, the order-entry module in a sales system might determine the price to be charged to a customer. Thus, when evaluating the adequacy of authorization procedures, auditors must examine not only the work of employees but also the veracity of program processing.

In a computer system it is also more difficult to assess whether the authority assigned to individual persons is consistent with management's wishes. For example, it might be hard to determine exactly what data users can access when they are provided with a generalized retrieval language. Users might be able to formulate queries on a database in such a way that they could infer the contents of confidential information. Indeed, substantial research is now being undertaken on controls that prevent violation of the privacy of data. Chapter 15 examines inference controls in more detail.

Adequate Documents and Records

In a manual system, adequate documents and records are needed to provide an audit trail of activities within the system. In computer systems, documents might not be used to support the initiation, execution, and recording of some transactions. For example, in an online order-entry system, customers' orders received by telephone might be entered directly into the system. Similarly, some transactions might be activated automatically by a computer system. For example, an inventory replenishment program could initiate purchase orders when stock levels fall below a set amount. Thus, no visible audit or management trail would be available to trace the transaction.

The absence of a visible audit trail is not a problem for auditors, provided that systems have been designed to maintain a record of all events and the record can be easily accessed. In well-designed computer systems, audit trails are often more extensive than those maintained in manual systems. Unfortunately, not all computer systems are well designed. Some software, for example, does not provide adequate access controls and logging facilities to ensure preservation of an accurate and complete audit trail. When this situation is coupled with a decreased ability to separate incompatible functions, serious control problems can arise.

Physical Control over Assets and Records

Physical control over access to assets and records is critical in both manual systems and computer systems. Computer systems differ from manual systems, however, in the way they concentrate the information systems assets and records of an organization. For example, in a manual system, a person wishing to perpetrate a fraud might need access to records that are maintained at different physical locations. In a computer system, however, all the necessary records can be maintained at a single site—namely, the site where the computer is located. Thus, the perpetrator does not have to go to physically disparate locations to execute the fraud.

This concentration of information systems assets and records also increases the losses that can arise from computer abuse or a disaster. For example, a fire that destroys a computer room could result in the loss of all major master files in an organization. If the organization does not have suitable backup, it might be unable to continue operations.

Adequate Management Supervision

In a manual system, management supervision of employee activities is relatively straightforward because the managers and the employees are often at the same physical location. In computer systems, however, data communications facilities can be used to enable employees to be closer to the customers they service. Thus, supervision of employees might have to be carried out remotely. Supervisory controls must be built into the computer system to compensate for the controls that usually can be exercised through observation and inquiry.

Computer systems also make the activities of employees less visible to management. Because many activities are performed electronically, managers must periodically access the audit trail of employee activities and examine it for unauthorized actions. Again, the effectiveness of observation and inquiry as controls is decreased.

Independent Checks on Performance

In manual systems, independent checks are carried out because employees are likely to forget procedures, make genuine mistakes, become careless, or intentionally fail to follow prescribed procedures. Checks by an independent person help to detect any errors or irregularities. If the program code in a computer system is authorized, accurate, and complete, the system will always follow the designated procedures in the absence of some other type of failure like a hardware or systems software failure. Thus, independent checks on the performance of programs often have little value. Instead, the control emphasis shifts to ensuring the veracity of program code. Insofar as many independent checks on performance are no longer appropriate, auditors must now evaluate the controls established for program development, modification, operation, and maintenance.

Comparing Recorded Accountability with Assets

Data and the assets that the data purports to represent should periodically be compared to determine whether incompleteness or inaccuracies in the data exist or whether shortages or excesses in the assets have occurred. In a manual system, independent staff prepare the basic data used for comparison purposes. In a computer system, however, software is used to prepare this data. For example, a program can be implemented to sort an inventory file by warehouse location and to prepare counts by inventory item at the different warehouses. If unauthorized modifications occur to the program or the data files that the program uses, an irregularity might not be discovered—for example, pilfering of inventory from a particular warehouse bin. Again, internal controls must be implemented to ensure the veracity of program code, because traditional separation of duties no longer applies to the data being prepared for comparison purposes.

EFFECTS OF COMPUTERS ON AUDITING

When computer systems first appeared, many auditors were concerned that the fundamental nature of auditing might have to change to cope with the new technology. It is now clear this is not the case. Auditors must still provide a competent, independent evaluation as to whether a set of economic activities has been recorded and reported according to established standards or criteria.

Nevertheless, computer systems have affected how auditors carry out their two basic functions: evidence collection and evidence evaluation. We examine some of these changes in the following subsections.

Changes to Evidence Collection

Collecting evidence on the reliability of a computer system is often more complex than collecting evidence on the reliability of a manual system. Auditors confront a diverse and sometimes complex range of internal control technology that did not exist in manual systems. For example, accurate and complete operation of a disk drive requires a set of hardware controls not used in a manual system. Similarly, system development controls include procedures for testing programs that would not be found in the development of manual systems. Auditors must understand these controls if they are to be able to collect evidence competently on the reliability of the controls.

Unfortunately, understanding the control technology is not always easy. Hardware and software continue to evolve rapidly. Although some time lag occurs, the associated controls evolve rapidly also. For example, with increasing use of data communications for data transfer, substantial research continues to be undertaken on the development of cryptographic controls to protect the privacy of data. Auditors must keep up with these developments if they are to be able to evaluate the reliability of communications networks competently.

The continuing evolution of control technology also makes it more difficult for auditors to collect evidence on the reliability of controls. Indeed, in some cases auditors might be unable to collect audit evidence using manual means. Thus, they need computer systems themselves if they are to be able to collect the necessary evidence. The development of generalized audit software occurred, for example, because auditors needed access to data maintained on magnetic media. Similarly, new audit tools might be required in due course if auditors are to be able to evaluate the reliability of controls in data communications networks competently. Unfortunately, the development of these audit tools usually lags the development of the technology that must be evaluated. In the meantime, auditors are often forced to compromise in some way when performing the evidence collection function.

Changes to Evidence Evaluation

Given the increased complexity of computer systems and internal control technology, it is also more difficult to evaluate the consequences of control strengths and weaknesses for the overall reliability of systems. First, auditors must understand when a control is acting reliably or malfunctioning. Next, they must be able to trace the consequences of the control strength or weakness through the system. In a shared data environment, for example, this task might be difficult. A single input transaction could update multiple data items that are used by diverse, physically disparate users. Somehow auditors must be able to trace the consequences of an error in the transaction input for all users.

In some ways, auditors are also under greater stress when they perform the evidence evaluation function for computer systems. As noted earlier, the consequences of errors in a computer system can be more serious than the consequences of errors in a manual system. Errors in manual systems tend to occur stochastically; for example, periodically a clerk prices an inventory item incorrectly. Errors in computer systems tend to be deterministic; for example, an erroneous program always will execute incorrectly. Moreover, errors are generated at high speed, and the cost to correct and rerun programs can be high. Whereas fast feedback can be provided to clerks if they make errors, errors in computer programs can involve extensive redesign and reprogramming. Thus, internal controls that ensure that high-quality computer systems are designed, implemented, operated, and maintained are critical. The onus is on auditors to ensure that these controls are sufficient to maintain asset safeguarding, data integrity, system effectiveness, and system efficiency and that they are in place and working reliably.

FOUNDATIONS OF INFORMATION SYSTEMS AUDITING

Information systems auditing is not just a simple extension of traditional auditing. Recognition of the need for an information systems audit function comes from two directions. First, auditors realized that computers had affected their ability to perform the attest function. Second, both corporate and information systems management recognized that computers were valuable resources that needed controlling like any other key resource within an organization.

Figure 1–4 shows that the discipline of information systems auditing has been shaped by knowledge obtained from four other disciplines: traditional auditing, information systems management, behavioral science, and computer science.

Traditional Auditing

Traditional auditing brought to information systems auditing a wealth of knowledge and experience with internal control techniques. This knowledge and experience has had an impact on the design of both the manual and machine components of an information system.

For example, in a computer system, clerical activities, such as data preparation activities, are often a critical component of the system. As with manual systems, these activities should be subject to internal control principles such as separating incompatible duties, having competent and trustworthy personnel, and establishing clear definitions of duties. By applying these principles, management seeks to ensure that the integrity of data is maintained before it is entered into the computer-based components of the information system.

Similarly, traditional auditing concepts like control totals are also relevant to the update and maintenance of files by computer programs. Computer pro-

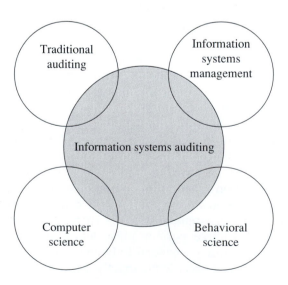

FIGURE 1–4. Information systems auditing as an intersection of other disciplines.

grams must ensure that all transaction data are processed and that they are processed correctly. Control totals have had longstanding use in information systems because these concerns also exist when humans (rather than programs) update and maintain files.

The general methodologies for evidence collection and evidence evaluation used by information system auditors are also based on traditional auditing methodologies (see Chapter 2). The long evolution of and extensive experience gained in traditional auditing highlight the critical importance of having objective, verifiable evidence and an independent evaluation of information systems.

Perhaps most important, traditional auditing brings to information systems auditing a control philosophy. It is difficult to articulate the nature of this philosophy. One can glean elements, however, by reading auditing literature or examining the work of auditors. The philosophy involves examining information systems with a critical mind, always with a view to questioning the capability of an information system to safeguard assets, maintain data integrity, and achieve its objectives effectively and efficiently.

Information Systems Management

The early history of computer-based information systems shows some spectacular disasters. Massive cost overruns occurred, and many systems failed to achieve their stated objectives. As a result, for many years researchers have been concerned with identifying better ways of managing the development and implementation of information systems.

Some important advances have been made. For example, techniques of project management have been carried across into the information systems area with considerable success. Documentation, standards, budgets, and variance investigation are now emphasized. Better ways of developing and implementing systems have been developed. For example, object-oriented analysis, design, and programming have enabled programmers to develop software faster, with fewer errors and easier maintenance characteristics. These advances affect information systems auditing because they ultimately affect asset safeguarding, data integrity, system effectiveness, and system efficiency objectives.

Behavioral Science

Computer systems sometimes fail because their designers do not appreciate the difficult human issues that are often associated with the development and implementation of a system. For example, behavioral resistance to an information system can seriously undermine efforts to meet asset safeguarding, data integrity, system effectiveness, and system efficiency objectives. Disgruntled users could try to sabotage the system or to circumvent controls. Similarly, designers and users could have difficulty communicating with one another because they have different conceptions of the meaning inherent in an application domain (see, e.g., Hirschheim et al. 1995). Because of these difficulties, a system's requirements might be poorly formulated.

Auditors must understand the conditions that can lead to behavioral problems and, as a result, possible system failure. Behavioral scientists, especially organization theorists, have contributed much to our understanding of the "people problems" that can arise within organizations. For some time, several researchers have been applying the findings of organization theory to information systems development and implementation. For example, some researchers now emphasize the need for systems designers to consider concurrently the impact of a computer system on task accomplishment (the technical system) and the quality of work life of persons (the social system) within the organization. Others emphasize the need for information systems designers to understand how users "socially construct" the meaning of the domains in which they work.

Computer Science

Computer scientists also have been concerned with how asset safeguarding, data integrity, system effectiveness, and system efficiency objectives might be better achieved. For example, they have conducted research on how to prove the correctness of software formally, build fault-tolerant computer systems, design secure operating systems, and transmit data securely across a communications link.

The in-depth, technical knowledge that has been developed with the discipline of computer science provides both benefits and problems for auditors' work. On the one hand, they can now be less concerned about the reliability of certain components in a computer system. On the other hand, if this technical knowledge is used improperly, they might have difficulty detecting the abuse. For example, if a skilled systems programmer decides to perpetrate a fraud, it might be almost impossible for auditors to detect the fraud unless they have extensive knowledge of information systems technology.

STRUCTURE AND FOCUS OF THIS BOOK

This book is divided into five parts. The first part is an overview of the audit function. In this first chapter, you should have acquired an understanding of the nature and objectives of the information systems audit function and the way in which computers have changed the audit function. In Chapter 2 we examine the overall approach used to conduct information systems audits.

In the second part, we examine controls over the development, implementation, and operation of information systems in an organization. We then examine the controls that should be in place and working in specific application systems (such as an accounts receivable or a payroll system) in the third part.

The fourth part describes the major types of evidence collection techniques that information systems auditors use and some ways of evaluating the evidence collected to come up with an assessment of the overall reliability of a computer-based information system.

In the final part, we examine how to administer the information system audit function and how the information system audit function is evolving in response to changes in technology and the environment.

Earlier in this chapter, we considered the four objectives of information systems auditing: asset safeguarding, data integrity, system effectiveness, and system efficiency. Throughout this book we focus on the controls organizations must use to help achieve these four objectives and the audit procedures auditors can employ to evaluate whether these controls are in place, have been designed properly, and are operating effectively. At times we will tend to focus more on the traditional attest concerns of auditors: asset safeguarding and data integrity. Always be mindful, however, that failure to achieve system effectiveness or system efficiency objectives can undermine asset safeguarding and data integrity objectives. For example, if a system erodes the quality of a user's working life, the user could sabotage the system, thereby resulting in loss of assets and erosion of data integrity. Similarly, if a system is inefficient, users might try to circumvent controls in the hope they can speed up throughput. In short, though at times we might emphasize asset safeguarding and data integrity in this book, always remember that system effectiveness and system efficiency objectives provide a critical backdrop to traditional audit concerns.

SUMMARY

Information systems auditing is an organizational function that evaluates asset safeguarding, data integrity, system effectiveness, and system efficiency in computer-based information systems. It has arisen for seven major reasons:

1. The consequences of losing the data resource;
2. The possibility of misallocating resources because of decisions based on incorrect data or decision rules;
3. The possibility of computer abuse if computer systems are not controlled;
4. The high value of computer hardware, software, and personnel;
5. The high costs of computer error;
6. The need to maintain the privacy of individual persons; and
7. The need to control the evolutionary use of computers.

Asset safeguarding, data integrity, system effectiveness, and system efficiency can be achieved only if a sound system of internal control exists. Use of computers does not affect the basic objectives of internal control; however, it affects how these objectives must be achieved.

The use of computers affects both the evidence collection and evidence evaluation functions auditors perform. Computer control technology is often more complex than manual system control technology; consequently, it is more difficult to understand controls and collect evidence on the reliability of controls. Similarly, it is more difficult to understand the implications of a control strength or weakness for the overall reliability of a system.

Information systems auditing borrows much of its theory and methodologies from other areas. Traditional auditing contributes knowledge of internal control practices and an overall control philosophy. Information systems management provides methodologies necessary to achieve successful design and implementation of systems. Behavioral science indicates when and why information systems are likely to fail because of people problems. Computer science contributes knowledge about how hardware and software should be designed to be effective and efficient and to safeguard assets and maintain data integrity.

Review Questions

1–1 Why is there a need for control and audit of computer systems?

1–2 For each of the following groups, give a specific example of how incorrect data processing by a company's computer system might lead to incorrect decisions being made:
    a Management
    b Shareholders
    c Labor unions
    d Environmentalists
    e Tax department
    f Affirmative action group

1–3 What are the implications of a company losing its:
    a Personnel master file
    b Inventory master file

1–4 How can inadequate controls in a computer system lead to incorrect decision making?

1–5 Should we be any more concerned about computer fraud and embezzlement versus other forms of business fraud and embezzlement?

1–6 In general, how adequate is the law in terms of being able to prosecute someone who undertakes computer abuse?

1–7 Why are controls still needed to protect hardware, software, and personnel, even though substantial insurance coverage might have been taken out by an organization?

1–8 What characteristics of computer systems often lead to high costs being incurred because of computer-system errors?

1–9 Why does the computer cause us to have increased concerns about the privacy of individuals?

1–10 Give an example of the computer being used for data processing where you consider it to be:
a Socially desirable
b Socially undesirable

1–11 What are the four major objectives of information systems auditing? Briefly explain the meaning of each one of them.

1–12 What are the major assets in an information systems facility?

1–13 Define *data integrity*. What factors affect the importance of data integrity to an organization?

1–14 What is the difference between system effectiveness and system efficiency? Why is the information systems auditor concerned with both system effectiveness and system efficiency?

1–15 Briefly explain the nature of the impact of using computers on the overall objectives of internal control.

1–16 What problems arise for ensuring that incompatible functions are separated in an information systems facility?

1–17 How does resource sharing in a computer system affect the internal control objective of having clear lines of authority and responsibility? Give an example.

1–18 How does the growth of end-user computing affect the internal control objective of having clear lines of authority and responsibility?

1–19 Why is the need for competent and trustworthy personnel even more important when an organization uses computers for its data processing?

1–20 When computer systems are used, how does the auditor evaluate the system of authorizations used by an organization?

1–21 How does the use of computers affect the audit trail within an information system?

1–22 With the increasing use of computers for data processing, is the audit trail disappearing? Explain.

1–23 Briefly explain how assets could be lost by a person having unauthorized access to a payroll program.

1–24 How does a computer system affect the concentration of assets within an organization? What implication does the effect have for internal controls?

1–25 Relative to a manual system, is it easier or harder to implement adequate management supervision of employees using a computer system? Explain.

1–26 How do independent checks on employee performance differ between a manual system and a computer system?

1–27 How does an organization compare recorded accountability with assets when computer systems are used? What controls must be exercised to ensure the veracity of this process?

1–28 How does the continuing evolution of computer hardware and software technology affect an auditor's ability to (a) understand controls, and (b) collect evidence on the reliability of controls?

1–29 What impact does the use of computers have on the nature and conduct of the evidence evaluation function carried out by auditors?

1–30 Briefly explain the contribution of the following areas to information systems auditing:

a Traditional auditing

b Information systems management

c Behavioral science

d Computer science

Multiple-Choice Questions

1–1 Incorrect data in a computer system is likely to have more serious consequences for a(an):

a Strategic planning system

b Expert system

c Personal decision support system

d Management control system

1–2 Loss of which of the following files is likely to have the most serious consequences for a manufacturing organization:

a Inventory file

b Material requirements planning file

c Job routing file

d Bill-of-materials file

1–3 Computer abuse is best defined as:

a Malicious damage carried out to hardware and software

b Any incident associated with computer technology whereby a victim suffered loss and a perpetrator gained

c A fraud perpetrated by modifying software or hardware

d Any incident whereby a hacker breaches controls in a computer system and destroys software or data

1–4 Relative to general fraud and embezzlement, computer fraud and embezzlement seems to be:

a Unaffected by deterrent administrative controls

b Smaller in size

c Larger in size

d Easier to prosecute via the law

1–5 The evolution of technology needs to be controlled because:

a Using new technology always has undesirable consequences unless it is controlled

b It tends to increase the monopolistic power of those companies that can afford to purchase the technology

c Though computer technology is neutral, its use can produce social problems

d It places too much power in the hands of governments

1–6 From an information systems audit perspective, which of the following is the most valuable asset in an information systems facility:

a Hardware

b Database

c Personnel

d Software

1–7 Which of the following information systems audit objectives requires that information systems auditors be concerned about the possibility of proprietary software being stolen:
  a Achieving system effectiveness
  b Preserving data integrity
  c Achieving system efficiency
  d Safeguarding assets

1–8 An effective data processing system:
  a Satisfactorily accomplishes the objectives of its users
  b Maintains data integrity as its primary objective
  c Is the most efficient system that can be implemented
  d Has asset safeguarding as its primary objective

1–9 In a computer-based information system, separation of duties:
  a Can always be attained in the same way as in a manual system
  b Might have to be implemented in different forms compared with manual systems
  c Is less important than in a manual system because programs make fewer errors than clerks
  d Usually is easy to automate, especially in microcomputer systems

1–10 Compared with a manual system, the consequences of error in a computer system often are more serious because:
  a Errors in computer systems tend to be stochastic
  b Computer systems process more data than manual systems
  c Errors in computer systems are generated at high speed, and the cost to correct and rerun programs may be high
  d Users of computer systems place too much faith in the correctness of computer output

1–11 Compared with a manual system, in a computer system:
  a Basic internal control objectives change
  b The methodologies for implementing controls change
  c Control objectives are more difficult to achieve
  d Internal control principles change

1–12 Clear lines of authority and responsibility are sometimes difficult to achieve in a computer system because:
  a Resources are shared and ownership is sometimes difficult to assign
  b Duties constantly change as a result of the rapid evolution of technology
  c Information systems personnel are not organized according to traditional hierarchical principles
  d End-user computing has undermined the usefulness of this internal control principle

1–13 Which of the following statements about information systems personnel is false:
  a Historically, information systems personnel have been in short supply
  b Information systems personnel have lacked a well-developed system of ethics
  c Information systems personnel often perform tasks that are exceedingly complex
  d Information systems personnel have less power vested in them than personnel who work in manual systems

1–14 In a computer system, it is often difficult to evaluate the system of general authorizations because general authorizations have been:
  a Dispersed to more users
  b Combined with specific authorizations

      c Embedded in computer programs

      d Displaced by system software controls

1–15 In a computer system, the audit trail is:

      a Still always present in some type of hard-copy form

      b Disappearing as more online, realtime update systems are used

      c Produced automatically by software during the update process

      d Sometimes more extensive than the audit trail in manual systems if it is designed properly

1–16 Compared with a manual system, the assets and records in a computer-based information system tend to be:

      a More concentrated at a single location

      b Dispersed across many more locations

      c Concentrated to about the same extent

      d More concentrated at different locations but less valuable

1–17 Compared with a manual system, supervision of employee activities in a computer-based information system is:

      a Easier, because observation and inquiry of employee activities is easier

      b Harder, because many activities are performed electronically and remotely

      c Easier, because unauthorized activities can always be detected from the audit trail

      d Harder, because information systems personnel are less tolerant of management supervision

1–18 In a computer system, independent checks on performance are often unnecessary because a procedure is performed by a computer program. Similarly, computer programs rather than independent staff often prepare reports that compare data and assets for accountability purposes. As a result, which of the following controls in a computer system becomes important to the auditor:

      a Equipment controls to ensure that hardware does not malfunction

      b Backup and recovery controls

      c Controls over the development, maintenance, and modification of program code

      d Personnel controls that ensure only high-quality staff are hired

1–19 Which of the following has *not* been an effect of computer-based information systems on auditing:

      a Evidence collection tends to be harder to carry out

      b Understanding the control technology tends to be harder

      c It is often harder to trace the effects of a control weakness

      d The fundamental objectives of auditing have changed

1–20 A major contribution of computer science to the discipline of information systems auditing has been:

      a Insights into how generalized audit software should be developed

      b An understanding of why behavioral problems occur with information systems implementation

      c An understanding of how project management techniques can contribute to information systems success

      d The development of theoretical bases underlying the ways in which software and hardware reliability can be improved

Exercises and Cases

    1–1 **Equity Funding Corporation**

    In 1973, one of the largest single company frauds ever committed was discovered in California. The collapse of the Equity Funding Corporation of America involved an estimated $2 billion fraud. The case was extremely complex, and it took several years before the investigation was complete. However, some of the pertinent findings derived from the Trustee's Bankruptcy report follow.

Equity Funding was a financial institution primarily engaged in life insurance. In 1964, its top management commenced to perpetrate a fraud that would take almost ten years to discover. The intent of the fraud was to inflate earnings so that management could benefit through trading their securities at high prices.

The fraud progressed through three major stages: the "inflated earnings phase," the "foreign phase," and the "insurance phase." The inflated earnings phase involved inflating income with bogus commissions supposedly earned through loans made to customers. Equity Funding had a funded life insurance program whereby customers who bought mutual fund shares could obtain a loan from the company to pay the premium on a life insurance policy. After some years the customer would sell off the mutual fund holdings to repay the loan. The mutual fund shares should have appreciated sufficiently so only a partial sale of shares would be required. Thus, the customer had the cash value of the insurance policy and the remaining mutual fund shares as assets from the investment.

The inflated earnings obtained via bogus commissions were supported by manual entries made on the company's books. Even though supporting documentation did not exist for the entries, the company's auditors failed to detect the fraud. However, the inflated assets did not bring about cash inflows, and the company started to suffer severe cash shortages because of real operating losses.

To remedy the cash shortage situation, the fraud moved into the second stage, the foreign phase. The company acquired foreign subsidiaries and used these subsidiaries in complex transfers of assets. Funds were brought into the parent company to reduce the funded loans asset account and falsely represent customer repayments of their loans. However, even this scheme proved inadequate.

The third stage, the insurance phase, involved the resale of insurance policies to other insurance companies. This practice is not unusual in the insurance business— when one company needs cash immediately and another company has a cash surplus. Equity Funding created bogus policies. In the short run it attempted to solve its cash problems by selling these policies to another insurance company. In the long run, however, the purchasing company expected cash receipts from premiums on the policies. Because the policies were bogus, Equity Funding had to find the cash to pay the premiums. Thus, it was only a matter of time before the fraud could no longer be concealed. Interestingly, the fraud was revealed by a disgruntled employee who was involved in the fraud but had been fired by Equity Funding management.

The computer was not used in the fraud until the insurance phase. The task of creating the bogus policies was too big to be handled manually. Instead, a program was written to generate policies. These policies were coded as the now infamous "Class 99."

The trustee's investigations led to two conclusions. First, the fraud was unsophisticated and doomed to failure. Second, some of the fundamental principles of good auditing were not applied.

Required. Write a brief report outlining some traditional audit procedures that, if they had been used, should have detected the fraud. Be sure to explain why you believe the procedures you recommend would have been successful.

1–2 Jerry Schneider

One of the more famous cases of computer abuse involves a young man named Jerry Schneider. Schneider had a flair for electronics. By the time he left high school, he had already formed his own firm to market his inventions. His firm also sold refurbished Western Electric telephone equipment. In 1970, he devised a scheme whereby Pacific Telephone in Los Angeles would supply him with good equipment—free!

Pacific Telephone used a computerized equipment ordering system. Equipment sites placed orders using a touch-tone card dialer. The orders were subsequently keypunched onto cards. The computer then updated the inventory master file and printed the orders. The orders were supplied to a transportation office that shipped the supplies.

Schneider intended to gain access to the ordering system. He sought to have Pacific Telephone deliver supplies to him as if he were one of its legitimate sites. He used a variety of techniques to find out how the system worked and to breach security: He sifted through trash cans and found discarded documents that provided him with information on the ordering system. He posed as a magazine writer and gathered information directly from Pacific Telephone. To support his activities, he bought a Pacific Telephone delivery van at an auction, "acquired" the master key for supply delivery locations in the Los Angeles area, and bought a touch-tone telephone card dialer with a set of cards similar to those used by the equipment sites to submit orders.

Schneider took advantage of the budgeting system used for ordering sites. Typically, these sites had a budget allocated larger than they needed. Providing this budget was not exceeded, no investigation of equipment ordering took place. Schneider managed to gain access to the online computer system containing information on budgets. He then determined the size of orders that would be tolerated. For seven months Pacific Telephone delivered him equipment that he resold to his customers and to Pacific Telephone. He kept track of the reorder levels for various Pacific Telephone inventories, depleted these inventories with his ordering, and then resold the equipment back to Pacific Telephone.

Schneider's downfall occurred when he revealed his activities to an employee. He was unable to keep up with the pace of his activities. As a result, he confided in an employee to obtain assistance. When the employee asked for a pay raise, Schneider fired him. The employee then went back to Pacific Telephone and told them of the fraud.

There are varying reports on how much Schneider took from Pacific Telephone. Parker (1976) estimates it was possible equipment worth a few million dollars was taken. For the fraud Schneider received a two-month jail sentence followed by three years probation. Interestingly, upon completing the jail term, he set up a consulting firm specializing in computer security.

Required. Write a brief report outlining some basic internal control procedures that, if they had been applied, should have prevented or detected Schneider's activities. Be sure to explain why the application of the internal control procedures you recommend would have been successful.

1–3 Union Dime Savings Bank

Banks seem especially prone to computer abuse. Roswell Steffen used a computer to embezzle $1.5 million of funds at the Union Dime Savings Bank in New York City. In an interview with Miller (1974) after he was discovered, he claimed, "Anyone with a head on his shoulders could successfully embezzle funds from a bank. And many do."

Steffen was a compulsive gambler. He initially "borrowed" $5,000 from a cash box at the bank to support his gambling with the intention of returning the money from his earnings. Unfortunately, he lost the $5,000. He then spent the next three and one-half years trying to replace the money, again by "borrowing" from the bank to gamble at the racetrack.

As the head teller at Union Dime, Steffen had a supervisory terminal in the bank's online computer system that he used for various administrative purposes. He took money from the cash box and used the terminal to manipulate customer account balances so the discrepancies would not be evidenced in the bank's daily proof sheets.

He used several techniques to obtain money. He first concentrated on accounts over $100,000 that had little activity and had interest credited quarterly. He used the supervisory terminal to reduce the balances in these accounts. Occasionally an irate customer complained about the balances. Steffen then faked a telephone call to the data processing department, informed the customer it was a simple error, and corrected the situation by moving funds from another account.

Other sources of funds included two-year certificate accounts and new accounts. With two-year certificate accounts, he prepared the necessary documents but did not record the deposit in the bank's files. Initially he had two years to correct the situation. Matters became more complicated, however, when the bank started to pay quarterly interest on these accounts.

With new accounts, he used two new passbooks from the bank's supply of prenumbered books. Upon opening an account, he entered the transaction using the account number of the first passbook but recorded the entry in the second passbook. He then destroyed the first passbook.

Perpetrating the fraud became very complex, and Steffen made many mistakes. However, the bank's internal control system and audit techniques were sufficiently weak that he could explain away discrepancies and continue. He was caught because police raided Steffen's bookie and noticed a lowly paid bank teller making very large bets.

Required. Write a brief report outlining some basic internal control procedures that, if they had been applied, should have prevented or detected Steffen's activities. Be sure to explain why the application of the control procedures you recommend would have been successful.

1–4 Stanley Rifkin

Stanley Rifkin was a freelance computer consultant who had been employed by a firm that did consulting work for Security Pacific Bank in California. In early October 1978, he visited a diamond broker in Los Angeles and placed an order for about 42,000 carats of polished gemstones. The retail value of the stones was about $13 million; however, Rifkin contracted to pay $8 million as the cash wholesale price. An order was then placed by the broker on Russalmaz, the Soviet government's diamond exporting company.

To finance his purchase, Rifkin decided to defraud Security Pacific. First he gained access to the bank's wire transfer room. He did not arouse the suspicion of employees because he had worked there on earlier consulting assignments. Next he gained access to three critical data items: the security code needed to authorize a particular day's fund transfer orders, the personal identification code used by one of the bank's employees to gain access to the system, and the number of an account that had a substantial deposit balance. At the end of the day, when he knew bank employees would be tired and less likely to detect an impropriety, he initiated the procedures to transfer $10.2 million to a bank account in Zurich. He then authorized the required payment of $8 million to Russalmaz.

After making the payment, Rifkin flew to Zurich under a fake passport to pick up the diamonds. He smuggled them back into the United States and commenced to pawn them. His downfall occurred when he made contact with a lawyer with whom he had been associated in Rochester, New York, during an attempt to sell the remaining diamonds. He disclosed to the lawyer how he had committed "the perfect crime." Ethically, the lawyer was bound to take the matter further with the authorities. The Federal Bureau of Investigation (FBI) traced the sequence of transfers and apprehended Rifkin in a friend's apartment with the diamonds.

Rifkin executed the transfers on October 25. It was not until early November, however, that Security Pacific found out the money was missing, supposedly in response to some inquiries from the FBI. When the fraud was detected, it was easy to identify Rifkin as the culprit because the bank taped all telephone transfer orders. The diamond broker in Los Angeles identified Rifkin's voice on the tape. When questioned about its inability to identify the unauthorized transfer of funds promptly, the bank responded that a $10.2 million transfer was not an unusual occurrence.

Required. It might be argued that the physical access controls in the bank's system were weak. Nevertheless, Rifkin was a skilled, intelligent person who had acquired a position of trust among the bank employees. Consequently, the system might always be vulnerable in spite of strong preventive controls. What *detective* controls would you recommend, therefore, to enable an unauthorized electronic funds transfer to be identified quickly?

Answers to Multiple-Choice Questions

1–1	d	1–6	c	1–11	b	1–16	a
1–2	a	1–7	d	1–12	a	1–17	b
1–3	b	1–8	a	1–13	d	1–18	c
1–4	c	1–9	b	1–14	c	1–19	d
1–5	c	1–10	c	1–15	d	1–20	d

REFERENCES

Abrams, Marshall D., and Harold J. Podell (1995), "Malicious Software," in Marshall D. Abrams, Sushil Jajodia, and Harold J. Podell, eds., *Information Security: An Integrated Collection of Essays.* Los Alamitos, CA: IEEE Computer Society Press, 111–125.

Benbow, Gary (1990), "Computer Abuse in Australia," *The EDP Auditor Journal*, II, 50–57.

Bequai, August (1987), *Technocrimes.* Lexington, MA: D.C. Heath and Company.

Bigelow, Robert (1990), "The Legal Dimension of Computer Crime," *The EDP Auditor Journal*, II, 59–66.

BloomBecker, J. J. Buck (1990), "Computer Crime and Abuse," *The EDP Auditor Journal*, II, 34–41.

Borning, Alan (1987), "Computer System Reliability and Nuclear War," *Communications of the ACM* (February), 112–131.

Brinkley, Donald L., and Roger R. Schell (1995), "What Is There to Worry About? An Introduction to the Computer Security Problem," in Marshall D. Abrams, Sushil Jajodia, and Harold J. Podell, eds., *Information Security: An Integrated Collection of Essays.* Los Alamitos, CA: IEEE Computer Society Press, 11–39.

Burnside, J. W. K. (1990), "Copyright and Computer Software — Autodesk Inc. v. Dyason and Kelly," *The Australian Computer Journal* (November), 140–144.

Clarke, Roger A. (1988), "Information Technology and Dataveillance," *Communications of the ACM* (May), 498–512.

Denning, Peter J., ed. (1990), *Computers Under Attack: Intruders, Worms, and Viruses*. New York: ACM Press Books.

Evens, Mark (1990), "Computer Security: What are the Risks?" *The EDP Auditor Journal*, II, 44–47.

Everest, Gordon C. (1985), *Database Management: Objectives, System Functions and Administration*. New York: McGraw-Hill.

FitzGerald, Jerry (1989), "Detecting and Preventing Computer Viruses in a PC Environment," *EDP Auditing*. Boston: Auerbach Publishers, Portfolio 75–01–40, 1–12.

Forrester, Tom, and Perry Morrison (1990), *Computer Ethics: Cautionary Tales and Ethical Dilemmas in Computing*. Cambridge, MA: The MIT Press.

Gardner, Ella Paton, Linda B. Samuels, Barry Render, and Richard L. Coffinberger (1989), "The Importance of Ethical Standards and Computer Crime Laws for Data Security," *Journal of Information Systems Management* (Fall), 42–50.

Graham, Peter (1990), "A Case Study of Computers in Public Administration: The Australia Card," *The Australian Computer Journal* (May), 51–58.

Hirschheim, Rudy, Heinz K. Klein, and Kalle Lyytinen (1995), *Information Systems Development and Data Modeling: Conceptual and Philosophical Foundations*. Cambridge: Cambridge University Press.

Hughes, Gordon (1990), "Computer Crime: The Liability of Hackers," *The Australian Computer Journal* (May), 47–50.

Hughes, Gordon, ed. (1990), *Essays on Computer Law*. Melbourne: Longman Cheshire.

Jacobson, Robert V. (1990), *The PC Virus Control Handbook*. New York: International Security Technology, Inc.

Joseph, Gilbert W. (1990), "Computer Viruses: How Auditors Can Minimize the Risks," *EDP Auditing*. Boston, MA: Auerbach Publishers, Portfolio 75–01–55, 1–8.

Krauss, Leonard I., and Aileen MacGahan (1979), *Computer Fraud and Countermeasures*. Upper Saddle River, NJ: Prentice-Hall, Inc.

Kusserow, R. P. (1984), "The Government Needs Computer Matching to Root Out Waste and Fraud," *Communications of the ACM* (June), 542–545.

Leveson, Nancy G. (1986), "Software Safety: Why, What, and How," *Computing Surveys* (June), 125–163.

——— (1991), "Software Safety in Embedded Computer Systems," *Communications of the ACM* (February), 34–46.

Laudon, K. C. (1986), "Data Quality and Due Process in Large Interorganizational Information Systems," *Communications of the ACM* (January), 4–11.

Meeks, Brock N. (1997), "Privacy Lost, Anytime, Anywhere," *Communications of the ACM* (August), 11–13.

Miller, Curt. (1973), "Union Dime Picks Up the Pieces in $1.5 Million Embezzlement Case," *Bank Systems and Equipment* (June), 34–35, 92.

——— (1974), "How I Embezzled $1.5 Million— And Nearly Got Away with It," *Bank Systems and Equipment* (June), 26–28.

Nachenberg, Carey (1997), "Computer Virus— Antivirus Evolution," *Communications of the ACM* (January), 46–51.

——— (1998), "The Macro Virus Plague," *EDPACS* (January), 1–8.

Neumann, Peter G. (1995), *Computer-Related Risks*. New York: Addison-Wesley.

Orwell, George (1972), *1984*. New York: Penguin Books. Originally published in 1948.

Parker, Donn B. (1976), *Crime by Computer*. New York: Charles Scribner's Sons.

——— and Susan H. Nycum (1984), "Computer Crime," *Communications of the ACM* (April), 313–315.

Parnas, David Lorge (1985), "Software Aspects of Strategic Defense Systems," *Communications of the ACM* (December), 1326–1335.

Redman, Thomas C. (1995), "Improve Data Quality for Competitive Advantage," *Sloan Management Review* (Winter), 99–107.

Rindfleisch, Thomas C. (1997), "Privacy, Information Technology, and Health Care," *Communications of the ACM* (August), 93–100.

Shattuck, J. (1984), "Computer Matching is a Serious Threat to Individual Rights," *Communications of the ACM* (June), 538–541.

Stoll, Clifford (1988), "Stalking the Wily Hacker," *Communications of the ACM* (May), 484–497.

——— (1991), *The Cuckoo's Egg*. London: Pan Books Ltd.

Straub, Detmar W. (1990), "Effective IS Security: An Empirical Study," *Information Systems Research* (September), 255–276.

Straub, Detmar W., and Rosann Webb Collins (1990), "Key Information Liability Issues Facing Managers: Software Piracy, Proprietary Databases, and Individual Rights to Privacy," *MIS Quarterly* (June), 143–156.

Straub, Detmar W., and William D. Nance (1990), "Discovering and Disciplining Computer Abuse in Organizations: A Field Study," *MIS Quarterly* (March), 45–60.

Strong, Diane M., Yang W. Lee, and Richard Y. Wang (1997), "Data Quality in Context," *Communications of the ACM* (May), 103–110.

Vacca, John R. (1996), *Internet Security Secrets*. Foster City, CA: IDG Books.

Westermeier, J. T. (1993), "Legal Liability for Insufficient Error Controls," *Information Strategy: The Executive's Journal* (Winter), 54–55.

CHAPTER
2

Conducting
an Information
Systems Audit

Chapter Outline

Chapter Key Points

- Usually, auditors cannot examine and evaluate all the data processing carried out within an organization. They need guidelines that will direct them toward those aspects of the information systems function in which material losses or account misstatements are most likely to occur.

- Because ultimately auditors must evaluate the reliability of controls, they need to understand the nature of controls. A *control* is a system that prevents, detects, or corrects unlawful events. It is a system because all components of the control must be in place and working for the control to function reliably.

- Controls reduce expected losses from unlawful events by (a) decreasing the probability of the event occurring in the first place, or (b) limiting the losses that arise if the event occurs.

- Auditors deal with complexity in an information systems audit by dividing systems to be evaluated into subsystems, evaluating the reliability of controls in each subsystem, and then determining the implications of each subsystem's level of reliability for the overall reliability of the system. The objective of factoring is to identify a set of subsystems that can be easily understood and evaluated because they are loosely coupled with other subsystems and internally cohesive in the sense that they perform a single function.

- Two major sets of systems need to be factored as a basis for conducting an information systems audit: *Management systems* provide the stable infrastructure in which information systems can be built and operated on a day-to-day basis, and *application systems* undertake basic transaction processing, management reporting, and decision support.

- Management systems can be factored into subsystems that perform top-level information systems management, systems development management, programming management, data administration, quality assurance, security administration, and operations management. Application systems can be factored into subsystems that perform boundary, input, communication, processing, database, and output functions. An information systems audit involves evaluating the reliability of controls in each of these management and application subsystems.

- During an information systems audit, there is some risk that the audit procedures will fail to detect material losses or account misstatements when they exist. This risk is a function of three factors: (a) inherent risk, which reflects the likelihood that a material loss or account misstatement exists in some segment of the audit before the reliability of internal controls is considered; (b) control risk, which reflects the likelihood that internal controls in some segment of the audit will not prevent, detect, or correct material losses or account misstatements that arise; and (c) detection risk, which reflects that the audit procedures used in some segments of the audit will fail to detect material losses or account misstatements. Because auditors cannot influence inherent risk or control risk, they adjust the nature and extent of audit procedures they carry out to influence detection risk and the overall level of audit risk.

■ Auditors can use five types of audit procedures to obtain evidence on whether assets are safeguarded, data integrity is maintained, and systems are effective and efficient: (a) procedures to obtain an understanding of controls, (b) tests of controls, (c) substantive tests of details of transactions, (d) substantive tests of details of balances or overall results, and (e) analytical review procedures.

■ There are five major steps in an audit: (a) planning the audit, in which the auditor attempts to gain an understanding of the internal controls used within an organization, (b) tests of controls, in which the auditor tests significant controls to evaluate whether they are operating effectively; (c) tests of transactions, in which the auditor undertakes substantive tests to evaluate whether a material loss or account misstatement has occurred or might occur; (d) tests of balances or overall results, in which the auditor seeks to obtain sufficient evidence to make a final judgment on the extent of losses or account misstatements that have occurred or might occur; and (e) completion of the audit, in which the auditor gives an opinion on whether material losses or account misstatements have occurred or might occur.

■ During the tests of controls phase, one of the important decisions that auditors make is whether to test controls by auditing around or through the computer. They might audit around the computer if the application system is simple, its inherent risk is low, and the reliability of the system's internal processing can be easily inferred. They must audit through the computer whenever an application's inherent risk is high and it is difficult to infer the internal processing carried out by the system.

INTRODUCTION

It is a sobering experience to be in charge of the information systems audit of an organization that has several hundred programmers and analysts, many computers, and thousands of files. Obviously, all organizations are not this size. Except for the smallest organizations, however, auditors usually cannot perform a detailed check of all the data processing carried out within the information systems function. Instead, they must rely on a sample of data to determine whether the objectives of information systems auditing are being achieved.

How, then, can we perform information systems audits so that we obtain reasonable assurance that an organization safeguards its data-processing assets, maintains data integrity, and achieves system effectiveness and efficiency? To address this question, this chapter provides an overview of a general approach that we can use to conduct an information systems audit. This material lays much of the groundwork for the remainder of the book.

We start by examining the nature of controls and discussing some techniques for simplifying and providing order to the complexity encountered when making evaluation judgments on computer-based information systems. Next we consider some of the basic risks auditors face, how these risks affect the overall approach to an audit, and the types of audit procedures used to assess or control the level of these risks. We then consider the basic steps to be undertaken in the conduct of an information systems audit. Finally, we examine a major decision auditors must make when planning and conducting an information systems audit—namely, how much do they need to know about the internal workings of a computer-based information system before an effective audit can be conducted?

THE NATURE OF CONTROLS

Information systems auditors ultimately are concerned with evaluating the reliability, or operating effectiveness, of controls. It is important, therefore, that we understand what is meant by a control. Here, then, is the definition we shall adopt for the purposes of this book (see, also, Wand and Weber 1989):

A control is a system that prevents, detects, or corrects unlawful events

There are three key aspects to this definition. First, a control is a *system*. In other words, it comprises a set of interrelated components that function together to achieve some overall purpose. Unfortunately, we tend to name controls by focusing on just one feature of the control. For example, probably all of us are familiar with a password control. A password, per se, however, is not a control. Passwords become a control only in the context of a system that allows secure issue of or choice of passwords, correct validation of passwords, secure storage of passwords, follow-up on illicit use of passwords, and so on. If this system breaks down in some way, passwords will be ineffective as a control. In short, the term "password control" is a notation for the constellation of things that work together to ensure only authorized people use computing resources. When we evaluate a control, therefore, we must consider its reliability from a systems perspective.

Second, the focus of controls is *unlawful events*. An unlawful event can arise if unauthorized, inaccurate, incomplete, redundant, ineffective, or inefficient input enters the system. For example, a data-entry clerk might key incomplete data into the system. An unlawful event can also arise if the system transforms the input in an unauthorized, inaccurate, incomplete, redundant, ineffective, or inefficient way. For example, a program could contain erroneous instructions that result in incorrect computations being performed. Whatever the reason, the system moves into a state that we deem to be unacceptable.

Third, controls are used to *prevent, detect,* or *correct* unlawful events. Consider some examples:

1. *Preventive control:* Instructions are placed on a source document to prevent clerks from filling it out incorrectly. Note that the control works only if the instructions are sufficiently clear and the clerk is sufficiently well trained to understand the instructions. Thus, both the clerk and the instructions are components of the system that constitutes the control. The instructions by themselves are not the control.
2. *Detective control:* An input program identifies incorrect data entered into a system via a terminal. Again, the control is a system because various parts of the program must work together to pinpoint errors.
3. *Corrective control:* A program uses special codes that enable it to correct data corrupted because of noise on a communications line. Once more, the control is a system because various parts of the program must work together in conjunction with the error-correcting codes to rectify the error.

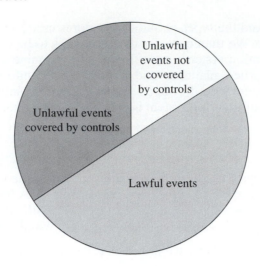

FIGURE 2–1. Lawful and unlawful events in an information system.

The overall purpose of controls is to reduce expected losses from unlawful events that can occur in a system. They do so in two ways. First, preventive controls reduce the probability of unlawful events occurring in the first place. For example, instructions on a source document reduce the likelihood of the clerk who completes the document making an error. Second, detective and corrective controls reduce the amount of the losses that arise if the unlawful event occurs. For example, if a data-entry clerk keys incorrect data into a computer system, an input validation control might detect that the data is in error and halt further processing. A small loss arises from delayed processing, but larger losses associated with a corrupted database do not occur. In addition, the control might be able to determine the nature of the keying error made, perhaps on the basis of past keying errors, and correct the error without the clerk having to intervene. Thus, the losses associated with recovering from the error are also reduced.

The auditor's task is to determine whether controls are in place and working to prevent the unlawful events that might occur within a system. Auditors must be concerned to see that at least one control exists to cover each unlawful event that might occur. Usually, some unlawful events in a system will not be covered because a cost-effective control cannot be found (Figure 2–1). Even if an unlawful event is covered by a control, however, auditors must evaluate whether the control is operating effectively. Moreover, if more than one control covers an unlawful event (i.e., redundant controls exist), auditors must ensure that all operate effectively. Otherwise, losses can be incurred because of reliance on a malfunctioning control instead of a reliable one.

DEALING WITH COMPLEXITY

Conducting an information systems audit is an exercise in dealing with complexity. Auditors somehow must accomplish their objectives given the myriad of systems. Because complexity is a root cause of the problems faced by many professionals (e.g., engineers, architects), researchers have attempted to develop guidelines that reduce complexity (see, e.g., Simon 1981). In the following subsections we consider two major guidelines that underlie the approach taken when conducting an information systems audit:

1. Given the purposes of the information systems audit, factor the system to be evaluated into subsystems.

2. Determine the reliability of each subsystem and the implications of each subsystem's level of reliability for the overall level of reliability in the system.

Subsystem Factoring

The first step in understanding a complex system is breaking it up into subsystems. A *subsystem* is a component of a system that performs some basic function needed by the overall system to enable it to attain its fundamental objectives. Subsystems are logical components rather than physical components. In other words, you cannot "touch" a subsystem. It exists only in the eye of the beholder. For example, we cannot see the input subsystem in a computer system. Instead, we see such things as terminals and data-entry clerks that function to get data into the system, but these things are components of the input subsystem and not the subsystem itself.

The process of decomposing a system into subsystems is called *factoring*. Factoring is an iterative process that terminates when we feel we have broken down the system into parts small enough to be understood and evaluated. In other words, each subsystem is decomposed into its constituent subsystems, which, in turn, are decomposed again until we can sufficiently comprehend the subsystem with which we are dealing. The system to be evaluated can then be described as a *level structure* of subsystems, with each subsystem performing a function needed by some higher-level subsystem (Figure 2–2).

To undertake the factoring process, we need some basis for identifying subsystems. One basis has been suggested already: The essence of a subsystem is the function it performs. Auditors should look first, therefore, for the fundamental functions a system performs to accomplish its overall objectives. Different functions delineate different subsystems. For example, the overall objective of some types of organizational systems is to make a profit. One critical function that must be performed in these systems is the receipt of customer orders. This function delineates the order-entry subsystem, which is distinct from, say, the subsystem that receives and processes customer payments as its basic function. The order-entry subsystem, in turn, can be broken down into further subsystems. These lower-level subsystems are defined on the basis of (sub)functions that must be performed to accomplish the overall objective of getting orders recorded accurately and completely. For example, functions are required to check whether sufficient inventory is available to satisfy an order and determine whether a customer's credit limit has been exceeded.

Besides function, systems theory indicates that two other guidelines should underlie the way in which we identify and delineate subsystems. First,

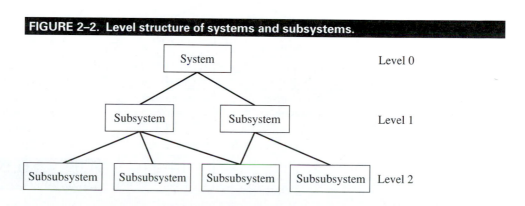

FIGURE 2–2. Level structure of systems and subsystems.

each subsystem should be relatively independent of other subsystems. The objective is for each subsystem to be loosely coupled to other subsystems. If this objective can be achieved, auditors can evaluate the subsystem in relative isolation from other subsystems. In other words, to some extent auditors can disregard the effects of control strengths and weaknesses in other systems.

Second, each subsystem should be internally cohesive. All the activities performed by the subsystem should be directed toward accomplishing a single function. If this objective can be achieved, it will be easier for auditors to understand and evaluate the activities carried out by the subsystem.

The theory of coupling and cohesion has been extensively developed (see, e.g., Yourdon and Constantine 1979; Coase and Yourdon 1991a, 1991b). From an audit viewpoint, however, the pragmatic issue is that subsystems are difficult to understand and their reliability is difficult to evaluate unless they are loosely coupled with other subsystems and internally cohesive. An understanding of complex systems can only be obtained if each of their parts can be studied relatively independently and the activities performed by each part are clear. When we decompose a system into subsystems, therefore, we should evaluate the extent of coupling and cohesion in the subsystems we choose. If the subsystems are not loosely coupled and internally cohesive, we should attempt a different factoring. If no factoring seems to delineate subsystems that possess these characteristics, we will have difficulty evaluating the reliability of the system because its activities are too convoluted. Indeed, auditors have long recognized that some systems cannot be audited. The theory of coupling and cohesion provides the underlying rationale for this conclusion when such systems are encountered.

At least conceptually, auditors might choose to factor systems in several different ways. Over time, however, auditors have found two ways to be especially useful when conducting information systems audits (Figure 2–3). The first is according to the *managerial functions* that must be performed to ensure that development, implementation, operation, and maintenance of information systems proceed in a planned and controlled manner. Managerial systems function to provide a stable infrastructure in which information systems can be built, operated, and maintained on a day-to-day basis. Several types of manage-

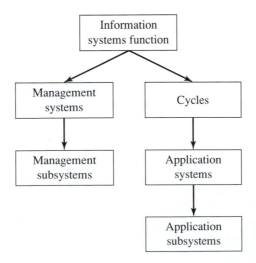

FIGURE 2–3. Decomposition of the information-systems function.

ment subsystems have been identified that correspond to the organizational hierarchy and some of the major tasks performed by the information systems function:

Management Subsystem	Description of Subsystem
Top management	Top management must ensure the information systems function is well managed. It is responsible primarily for long-run policy decisions on how information systems will be used in the organization.
Information systems management	Information systems management has overall responsibility for the planning and control of all information systems activities. It also provides advice to top management in relation to long-run policy decision making and translates long-run policies into short-run goals and objectives.
Systems development management	Systems development management is responsible for the design, implementation, and maintenance of application systems.
Programming management	Programming management is responsible for programming new systems, maintaining old systems, and providing general systems support software.
Data administration	Data administration is responsible for addressing planning and control issues in relation to use of an organization's data.
Quality assurance management	Quality assurance management is responsible for ensuring information systems development, implementation, operation, and maintenance conform to established quality standards.
Security administration	Security administration is responsible for access controls and physical security over the information systems function.
Operations management	Operations management is responsible for planning and control of the day-to-day operations of information systems.

The second factoring is according to the *application functions* that need to be undertaken to accomplish reliable information processing. This factoring corresponds to the "cycles" approach auditors have traditionally used to conduct an audit (see, e.g., Arens and Loebbecke 1997). The information systems supporting an organization are first grouped into cycles. These cycles vary across industries, but a typical set for a commercial or manufacturing enterprise includes (a) sales and collections, (b) payroll and personnel, (c) acquisitions and payments, (d) conversion, inventory, and warehousing, and (e) treasury. Each cycle is then factored into one or more application systems. For example, the sales and collections cycle comprises an order-entry application system, a billing application system, and an accounts-receivable application system. Application systems, in turn, are then factored into subsystems. The set of application subsystems includes the following:

Application Subsystem	Description of Subsystem
Boundary	Comprises the components that establish the interface between the user and the system.
Input	Comprises the components that capture, prepare, and enter commands and data into the system.

(cont.)

Application Subsystem	*Description of Subsystem*
Communications	Comprises the components that transmit data among subsystems and systems.
Processing	Comprises the components that perform decision making, computation, classification, ordering, and summarization of data in the system.
Database	Comprises the components that define, add, access, modify, and delete data in the system.
Output	Comprises the components that retrieve and present data to users of the system.

Neither of these two types of decomposition is irrevocable, and in due course others might prove better (see, e.g., Bell et al. 1997). Nevertheless, they currently underlie the audit approaches advocated by many professional bodies of auditors. They allow us to decrease complexity to a point where we can understand and evaluate the nature of and reliability of subsystems. Throughout the rest of this book, these two factorings will be used in our examination of information systems controls.

Assessing Subsystem Reliability

After we have identified the lowest-level subsystems in our level structure of subsystems, we can evaluate the reliability of controls. Beginning with the lowest-level subsystems, we first attempt to identify all the different types of events that might occur in these subsystems. We must be mindful of both the lawful events and the unlawful events that can occur. Nevertheless, an auditor's primary concern will be with any unlawful events that might arise.

As a basis for identifying lawful and unlawful events in management subsystems, we focus on the major functions each subsystem performs. We consider how each function should be undertaken and then evaluate how well a subsystem complies with our normative views. For example, an important function that should be performed by the top-management subsystem is information systems planning. Given the nature of the organization we are auditing, we might determine that top management should undertake extensive strategic planning but only a moderate level of operational planning if the long-run future of information systems within the organization is to be ensured (see Chapter 3). These views form the basis for determining which information systems planning events are to be deemed lawful and which are to be deemed unlawful. We then identify the information systems planning events that have occurred and classify them as either lawful or unlawful. For example, if no strategic planning has been undertaken, an unlawful event has occurred. Failure to plan ultimately undermines asset safeguarding, data integrity, system effectiveness, and system efficiency objectives. Similarly, if too much operational planning has been undertaken, an unlawful event has occurred because resources have been wasted. As a result, system effectiveness and system efficiency objectives have been undermined.

Perhaps the key aspect of identifying lawful and unlawful events in management subsystems is the decision of how a particular function should be performed within the subsystem. After substantial research on information systems management, it is now clear that the way information systems management functions should be performed in organizations must vary, depending on the particular circumstances faced by each organization. For example, in some organizations, strategic information systems planning is a critical function, but in others it has only minor importance. Auditors must be knowledgeable and astute in determining the ways that management functions should be performed in each organization evaluated. Otherwise, judgments on what events are lawful will be misguided.

As a basis for identifying lawful and unlawful events in application subsystems, we focus on the transactions that can occur as input to the subsystem. All events in an application system must arise from a transaction. The application system initially changes state (an event occurs) when the transaction is first received as an input. For example, an order-entry system must record an order when it is first entered into the system. Further state changes (events) then occur as the application system processes the transaction. For example, after an order-entry system has stored an open order, it then attempts to fill the order. Lawful events will arise if the transaction and subsequent processing are authorized, accurate, complete, nonredundant, effective, and efficient. Otherwise, unlawful events will occur.

To identify all the events that might arise in an application system as a result of a transaction, we must understand how the system is likely to process the transaction. Historically, auditors have used *walk-through techniques* to accomplish this objective: They consider a particular transaction, identify the particular components in the system that process the transaction, and then try to understand each processing step that each component executes. They also consider any errors or irregularities (unlawful events) that might occur along the way. For example, auditors might focus on a credit-sale transaction. After the transaction has been entered into the sales system, they would trace the credit sale through each processing step executed by the order-entry program. They would also consider how the transaction might be entered improperly and how subsequent processing errors or irregularities might arise.

It is often costly to trace each individual transaction through an application system to obtain an understanding of all the different types of events that can occur in the system. For this reason, auditors sometimes focus on *classes* of transactions. In other words, they group transactions together if the transactions undergo similar processing. They then try to understand these transactions and the events that arise as a result of these transactions as a group. In addition, they focus only on those transactions they consider to be material from the viewpoint of their audit objectives. Using these strategies, not all events that can occur in a system are identified. Nevertheless, auditors should examine all those transactions and events that they consider to be important.

When the material events that can occur in a management of application system have been identified, auditors must evaluate whether controls are in place and working to cover the unlawful events. Accordingly, they collect evidence on the existence and reliability of controls to determine whether expected losses from unlawful events have been reduced to an acceptable level. They consider each type of unlawful event that might arise, whether controls cover each of these events, how reliable these controls are, and whether a material error or irregularity can still occur. Lists have been published to assist with this task, showing failings that occur in management subsystems and errors and irregularities that occur for different types of transactions in different types of application systems. These lists also show various controls that can be used to reduce expected losses from these errors and irregularities (see, e.g., Arthur Andersen and Co. 1987 and FitzGerald and FitzGerald 1990). Table 2–1 is an example of one such list for a customer-order transaction in an order-entry application system. The

TABLE 2-1 Some Controls Over the Customer-Order Transaction Class in an Order-Entry System

Errors and Controls Irregularities	Unauthorized customer	Unauthorized terms and credit	Incorrect quantity	Incorrect price	Untimely processing
Order-entry operator well trained	M	M	M	M	M
User-friendly interface			M	M	M
High-quality input validation program	H	H	H	H	
Management review of sales overrides	M	M	L	M	
Daily report on unfilled orders					H
Management review of daily transaction volumes					M

Note: H = high-effectiveness control; M = moderate-effectiveness control; L = low-effectiveness control

table shows a controls matrix in which the columns show errors or irregularities that can occur and the rows show controls that can be set up to reduce expected losses from these errors and irregularities. The elements of the matrix show an auditor's assessment of how effective each control is in reducing expected losses from each type of error or irregularity.

The evaluation of reliability proceeds upwards in the level structure of a system. Lower-level subsystems are components of higher-level systems. When the reliability of a lower-level system has been assessed, its impact on the nature of and frequency of unlawful events in higher-level systems can be evaluated. The evaluation proceeds until the highest-level system (the entire system) has been considered. For every system at every level in the level structure, the evaluation steps are the same. The transactions that might enter the system are first identified. The lawful and unlawful events that can occur as a result are then considered. Finally, the reliability of the controls that cover the unlawful events is assessed.

As we evaluate higher-level systems, we are likely to encounter new controls for three reasons. First, controls in lower-level systems can malfunction. Recall, a control is a system itself, and it can be unreliable like any other system. A higher-level control might be implemented to cover unlawful events that arise when lower-level controls fail to prevent, detect, or correct them. For example, consider a group of clerks that process mail orders. Work might be divided among them based on the first letter of customers' surnames. Thus, several subsystems exist to process orders from different groups of customers. Each clerk might exercise certain controls to prevent, detect, or correct errors. Nevertheless, their manager might also examine the quality of their work. Managers are responsible for the quality of work in all subsystems, and they are exercising a higher-level control in case a lower-level control malfunctions.

Second, it might be more cost-effective to implement controls at higher levels. Again, consider our example of the group of clerks who process mail orders. If they are well trained and diligent, they might not be required to double-check their work. Given the low error rate that is expected to occur, the cost of double-checking might be too high. Their manager periodically might take a sample of their work, however, to assess its quality. The higher-level control is more cost-effective because it is exercised by one person who has greater facility with the control rather than multiple persons, each of whom has less facility with the control.

Third, some events are not manifested as unlawful except in higher-level systems. For example, an employee might query a database to obtain the average salary of female consultants employed within an organization. The subsystem that processes the query might deem this query to be a lawful event. The person might then query the database to obtain the number of female consultants employed within the organization. Again, the subsystem that processes the query might deem it to be lawful. If the organization employs only one female consultant, however, the employee now knows the consultant's salary. A higher-level system control is needed to detect the violation of the confidentiality of her salary. When the two lawful events are considered together, the overall event is unlawful (see Chapter 15).

Clearly, the process of aggregating subsystem reliability assessments to higher levels can be a difficult task. Errors made at one level of assessment will propagate to higher levels of assessment. Auditors must take substantial care with evidence-collection processes and evaluation judgments, especially as they begin to fix evaluation judgments in lower-level subsystems and move to higher-level subsystems and systems.

AUDIT RISKS

Recall that information systems auditors are concerned with four objectives: asset safeguarding, data integrity, system effectiveness, and system efficiency. Both external and internal auditors are concerned with whether errors or irregularities cause material losses to an organization or material misstatements in the financial information prepared by the organization. If you are an internal auditor, it is likely you will also be concerned with material losses that *have* occurred or *might* occur through ineffective or inefficient operations. External auditors, too, might be concerned when ineffective or inefficient operations threaten to undermine the organization. Moreover, many external auditors report such problems as part of their professional services to the management of an organization.

To assess whether an organization achieves the asset safeguarding, data integrity, system effectiveness, and system efficiency objectives, auditors collect evidence. Because of the test nature of auditing, auditors might fail to detect real or potential material losses or account misstatements. The risk of an auditor failing to detect actual or potential material losses or account misstatements at the conclusion of the audit is called the *audit risk*. Auditors choose an audit approach and design audit procedures in an attempt to reduce this risk to a level deemed acceptable.

As a basis for determining the level of desired audit risk, some professional bodies of auditors have adopted the following audit risk model for the external audit function (see, e.g., American Institute of Certified Public Accountants 1988):

$$DAR = IR \times CR \times DR$$

In this model, *DAR* is the desired audit risk (as discussed previously). *IR* is the inherent risk, which reflects the likelihood that a material loss or account misstatement exists in some segment of the audit before the reliability of internal controls is considered. *CR* is the control risk, which reflects the likelihood that internal controls in some segment of the audit will not prevent, detect, or correct material losses or account misstatements that arise. *DR* is the detection risk, which reflects that the audit procedures used in some segment of the audit will fail to detect material losses or account misstatements.

Note that in all cases the risks incorporated into this model are defined to be those associated with the attest objectives of external auditors. We can easily broaden them, however, to include the risks associated with real or potential material losses from ineffective or inefficient operations. In other words, the model is sufficiently general to cover our four objectives for information systems auditing. Throughout the remainder of this book, we assign this broader meaning to the audit risk model.

To apply the model, auditors first choose their level of *desired audit risk*. External auditors consider such factors as the level of reliance external parties are likely to place on the financial statements and the likelihood of the organization encountering financial difficulties subsequent to the audit. Internal auditors also consider these factors. In addition, they assess the short- and long-run consequences for their organizations if they fail to detect real or potential material losses from ineffective or inefficient operations.

Next auditors consider the level of *inherent risk*. Initially auditors consider general factors such as the nature of the organization (e.g., Is it a high flyer?), the industry in which it operates (e.g., Is the industry subject to rapid change?), the characteristics of management (e.g., Is management aggressive and autocratic?), and accounting and auditing concerns (e.g., Are creative accounting practices used?). Auditors then consider the inherent risk associated with different segments of the audit (cycles, application systems, and financial statement accounts). For each segment, auditors consider such factors as the following:

Inherent Risk Factor	*Explanation*
Financial system	Those systems that usually provide financial control over the major assets of an organization—e.g., cash receipts and disbursements, payroll, accounts receivable and payable—often have higher inherent risk. They are frequently the target of fraud and embezzlement.
Strategic system	Those systems that provide an organization with a competitive advantage—e.g., systems that lock in customers or suppliers or embody a patent or trade secret—often have high inherent risk. They might be the target of industrial espionage or retaliatory actions by a competitor.
Critical operational systems	Those systems that could cripple an organization if they fail—e.g., customer reservations systems or production control systems—often have high inherent risk.
Technologically advanced systems	Those systems that use advanced technology often have high inherent risk because they are complex and the organization lacks experience with them.

To assess the level of *control risk* associated with a segment of the audit, auditors consider the reliability of both management and application controls. Auditors usually identify and evaluate controls in management subsystems first. Management (subsystem) controls are *fundamental* controls because they cover all application systems. Thus, the absence of a management control is a serious concern for auditors. Conceptually, management controls constitute protective layers of "onion skins" around applications (Figure 2–4). Forces that erode asset safeguarding, data integrity, system effectiveness, and system efficiency must penetrate each layer to undermine a lower layer. To the extent the outer layers of controls are intact, the inner layers of controls are more likely to be intact. In addition, it is often more efficient if auditors evaluate management controls before application controls. After auditors have evaluated a management control, auditors usually do not have to evaluate it again because it

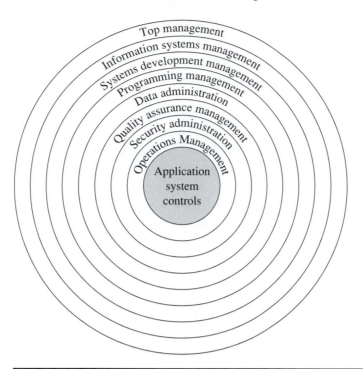

FIGURE 2–4. Management controls as an onion skin around application controls.

should function across all applications. For example, if auditors find that an organization enforces high-quality documentation standards, it is unlikely they will have to review the quality of documentation for each application system.

Next auditors calculate the level of *detection risk* they must attain to achieve their desired audit risk. They then design evidence collection procedures in an attempt to achieve this level of detection risk. To estimate the level of detection risk they might achieve with a set of audit procedures, they must have a good understanding of how likely these audit procedures are to detect a material loss or account misstatement when one exists. Moreover, auditors must evaluate how reliably the audit procedures are likely to be applied. Not only must they choose audit procedures that have the capacity to provide us with a desired level of detection risk, they also must ensure they are properly executed.

In summary, the whole point to our considering the audit risk model is that audit efforts should be focused where they will have the highest payoffs. In most cases auditors cannot collect evidence to the extent they would like. Accordingly, they must be astute in terms of where they apply their audit procedures and how they interpret the evidence they collect. Throughout the audit they must continually make decisions on what to do next. Their notions of materiality and audit risk guide them in making this decision.

TYPES OF AUDIT PROCEDURES

When external auditors gather evidence to determine whether material losses have occurred or financial information has been materially misstated, they use five types of procedures:

1. *Procedures to obtain an understanding of controls:* Inquiries, inspections, and observations can be used to gain an understanding of what controls supposedly

exist, how well they have been designed, and whether they have been placed in operation.

2. *Tests of controls:* Inquiries, inspections, observations, and reperformance of control procedures can be used to evaluate whether controls are operating effectively.

3. *Substantive tests of details of transactions:* These tests are designed to detect dollar errors or irregularities in transactions that would affect the financial statements. For example, an external auditor might verify that purchase and disbursement transactions are correctly recorded in journals and ledgers.

4. *Substantive tests of details of account balances:* These tests focus on the ending general ledger balances in the balance sheet and income statement. For example, an external auditor might circularize a sample of customers to test the existence and valuation of the debtors balance.

5. *Analytical review procedures:* These tests focus on relationships among data items with the objective of identifying areas that require further audit work. For example, an external auditor might examine the level of sales revenue across time to determine whether a material fluctuation that requires further investigation has occurred in the current year.

Auditors can use similar types of procedures if they are concerned with evaluating the effectiveness and efficiency of an organization's operations:

1. *Procedures to obtain an understanding of controls:* Inquiries, inspections, and observations can be used to gain an understanding of the administrative controls set up to achieve effectiveness and efficiency objectives rather than the accounting controls set up to achieve asset safeguarding and data integrity objectives.

2. *Tests of controls:* Tests of controls focus on whether administrative controls have been well designed and whether they are operating effectively. For example, auditors might interview an operations manager to check whether she regularly reviews the response-time performance of a critical online system and, if so, what action she takes when response times are unacceptable.

3. *Substantive tests of details of transactions:* From an effectiveness and efficiency perspective, auditors still have a notion of substantive tests of details of transactions. Using the response-time example discussed previously, auditors might check the response times for a sample of individual transactions to determine whether they are within acceptable bounds.

4. *Substantive tests of overall results:* The notion of account balances does not apply in the context of effectiveness and efficiency concerns. Nevertheless, auditors have a notion of overall effectiveness and efficiency results. For example, management might assert the average response time for an application system over a 12-month period is two seconds. As a substantive test of this claimed overall result, auditors might survey users of the system to determine its validity.

5. *Analytical review procedures:* Analytical review procedures are still relevant in the context of effectiveness and efficiency concerns. For example, auditors might build a queuing model or a simulation model of an application system to evaluate whether the resources consumed by the application system seem reasonable.

Often, the order of tests from the least costly to the most costly is as follows: analytical review procedures, procedures to obtain an understanding of controls, tests of controls, substantive tests of details of transactions, and substantive tests of balances/overall results. On the other hand, the order is reversed when we consider the reliability and information content of the evidence provided by the different audit procedures. Accordingly, auditors usually carry out the less costly audit procedures first in the hope the evidence obtained from these procedures indicates it is unlikely a material loss or material misstatement has occurred or will occur. If this outcome arises, auditors can alter the nature, timing, and extent of the more costly tests used. For example, on the basis of their understanding of controls and tests of controls, auditors might conclude controls are well designed and operating effectively. In this light, they would seek to reduce the costs of substantive testing in the following ways: change the nature of substantive testing by employing less costly substantive tests directed toward internal parties rather than external parties; change the timing of substantive testing by spreading it across a longer period to reduce costs; and change the extent of substantive tests by choosing smaller sample sizes to reduce costs.

OVERVIEW OF STEPS IN AN AUDIT

Keeping in mind the lessons in the previous sections on the nature of controls, the importance of system factoring in reducing complexity, the nature and consequences of audit risks, and the types of audit procedures auditors can carry out, Figure 2–5 flowcharts the major steps to be undertaken in an audit. The general approach shown in the flowchart is representative of the approaches advocated by many professional bodies of auditors (see, e.g., American Institute of Certified Public Accountants 1988b, 1990).

The following subsections briefly describe each step in an audit and highlight those parts of the audit where the information systems auditor often plays an important role. Although Figure 2–5 and the ensuing discussion imply a sequential progression of audit steps, some steps can be carried out concurrently and some iteration of steps can occur. For example, some tests of controls could be carried out as auditors attempt to understand the controls that are supposed to be in place. Furthermore, while both external and internal auditors will follow the general approach shown in Figure 2–5, the decisions they take at each step in the audit might vary because they have different roles. For example, internal auditors might spend more time testing controls because they are more concerned than external auditors about the efficiency of the controls. The following discussion points out how external and internal auditors might differ in the decisions they take at each stage of the audit.

Planning the Audit

Planning is the first phase of an audit. For an external auditor, this means investigating new and continuing clients to determine whether the audit engagement should be accepted, assigning appropriate staff to the audit, obtaining an engagement letter, obtaining background information on the client, understanding the client's legal obligations, and undertaking analytical review procedures to understand the client's business better and identify areas of risk in the audit (see Arens and Loebbecke 1997). For an internal auditor, this means understanding the objectives to be accomplished in the audit, obtaining background information, assigning appropriate staff, and identifying areas of risk.

During the planning phase, auditors must decide on the preliminary materiality level to be set for the audit. An external auditor's concern will be the

FIGURE 2–5. Flowchart of major steps in an IS audit.

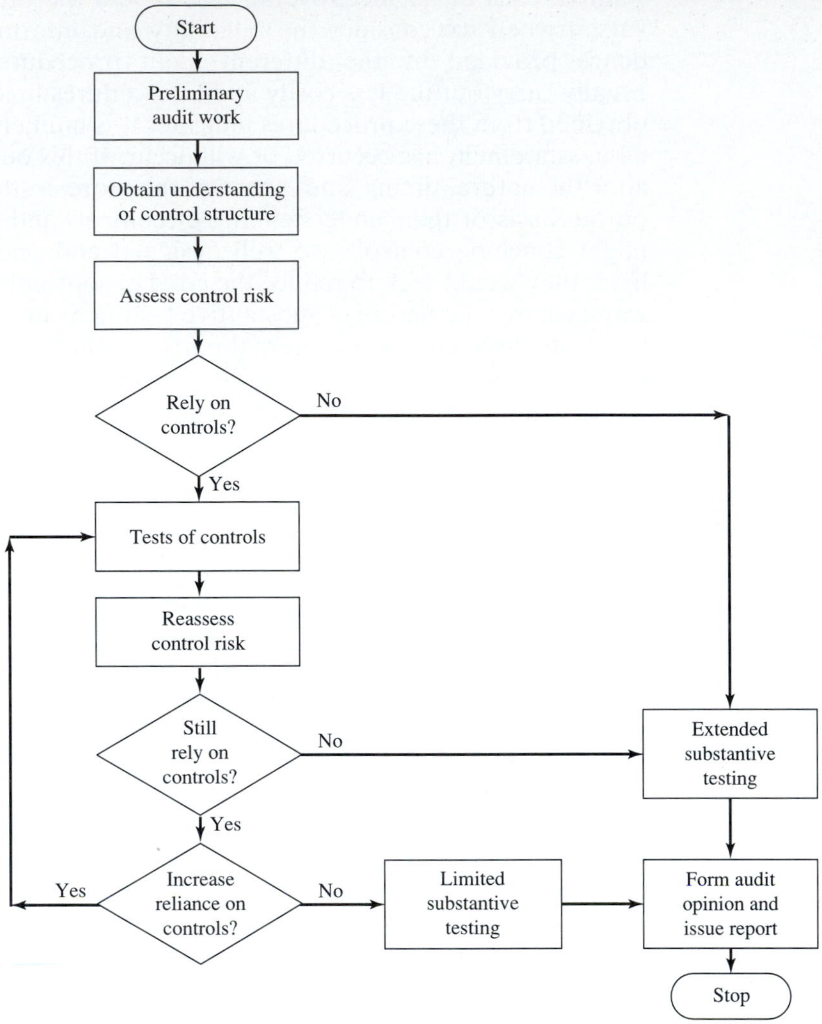

size of misstatements in the financial statements that would affect the decisions of users of the financial statements. Internal auditors might also be concerned about the size of losses that have arisen or might arise through ineffective or inefficient operations.

Auditors must also make a judgment on desired audit risk. Usually the level of desired audit risk is set for the overall audit rather than for segments of it. For external auditors, this reflects the risk they are willing to take to issue an unqualified opinion even though the financial statements are materially in error. For internal auditors, desired audit risk might also reflect the risk they are willing to take to issue an unqualified opinion even though material losses have occurred or might occur through ineffective or inefficient operations.

The levels of inherent risk will vary across different segments of the audit. Some segments are more susceptible to errors, irregularities, ineffectiveness, and inefficiencies. Auditors must consider each segment of the audit in turn and evaluate the factors that lead to inherent risk associated with the segment. For example, systems that involve handling of cash are susceptible to defalcations; technologically complex systems are susceptible to inefficient use of resources.

Perhaps the most difficult decision to make in the planning phase is the judgment on the level of control risk associated with each segment of the audit. When making this judgment, information systems audit skills are especially important. The American Institute of Certified Public Accountants (1995) argues that to decide on the level of control risk, auditors must first understand the *internal controls* used within an organization. Internal controls comprise five interrelated components:

1. *Control environment:* Elements that establish the control context in which specific accounting systems and control procedures must operate. The control environment is manifested in management's philosophy and operating style, the ways authority and responsibility are assigned, the way the audit committee functions, the methods used to plan and monitor performance, and so on.
2. *Risk assessment:* Elements that identify and analyze the risks faced by an organization and the ways these risks can be managed.
3. *Control activities:* Elements that operate to ensure transactions are authorized, duties are segregated, adequate documents and records are maintained, assets and records are safeguarded, and independent checks on performance and valuation of recorded amounts occur. These elements are usually called *accounting* controls. Internal auditors, however, also might be concerned with *administrative* controls established to achieve effectiveness and efficiency objectives.
4. *Information and communication:* Elements in which information is identified, captured, and exchanged in a timely and appropriate form to allow personnel to discharge their responsibilities properly.
5. *Monitoring:* Elements that ensure internal controls operate reliably over time.

In the context of the concepts examined earlier in this chapter and the role information systems auditors perform, understanding internal controls in an organization involves factoring and examining both management controls and application system controls. Auditors can understand the control environment and risk assessment components primarily by examining management controls. For example, when auditors determine whether an information systems steering committee exists, they seek to understand the control environment and risk assessment components of internal control. Auditors can understand specific control activities by reviewing both management controls and application controls. For example, when auditors review those activities associated with production release of programs or entry of data to an application system, they are seeking to understand the control activities undertaken. Auditors can understand the information and communication component by examining both management controls and application controls. For example, when auditors examine how management communicates roles and responsibilities or how transactions are captured, recorded, processed, and summarized within an application system, they are seeking to understand the information and management component. Auditors can understand the monitoring component primarily by examining management controls. For example, when auditors examine the ways management evaluates employee performance, they are seeking to understand the monitoring component.

Management controls can differ substantially from organization to organization. For example, an organization might have all information processing performed at a single site that is under the control of a single information systems department. In this situation, there is only one management system to evaluate—that associated with the information systems department. Auditors would factor this system into various subsystems—top management, systems development management, programming management, and so on—and seek to understand internal controls in the context of each of these subsystems.

On the other hand, another organization's information systems function might be widely dispersed. For example, the organization might have a highly decentralized structure. Divisions might have responsibility for developing, operating, and maintaining their own information systems. Each might have its own computer center and information systems staff. End-user computing also could be substantial. Some end users might be developing, maintaining, and operating their own systems. In these circumstances, auditors must evaluate multiple management systems: one for each divisional site and perhaps one for each major end-user computing site. They must consider each management system in turn, evaluate the risks associated with each, and factor those that are material into their various subsystems. In short, auditors might have to examine multiple top-management subsystems, multiple systems development management subsystems, multiple programming management subsystems, and so on, to understand the internal controls.

Application controls also might be substantially diverse. In a highly centralized organization, there might be only one set of cycles to evaluate. In a highly decentralized organization, however, there might be multiple sets of cycles, each of which must be evaluated. For example, each division might have its own sales and collections cycle, payroll and personnel cycle, acquisitions and payments cycle, conversion, inventory, and warehousing cycle, and treasury cycle. Auditors must identify those cycles that are material to the audit, factor the cycles into application systems and subsystems, understand these systems and subsystems, and identify the controls that have been implemented over each important class of transactions that passes through the different systems and subsystems.

There are several types of evidence collection techniques used to understand the internal controls: review of working papers from prior audits, interviews with top management and information systems personnel, observations of activities carried out within the information systems function, and reviews of information systems documentation. The evidence can be documented by completing questionnaires, constructing high-level flowcharts and decision tables, and preparing narratives. A computer can be helpful to employ these techniques and auditors might use a computer-aided software engineering (CASE) tool to draw flowcharts. Similarly, they might interact with questionnaire software that elicits responses on the status of various types of internal controls (see Chapter 16). Auditors must be careful not to undertake too much work, however, during this phase. The goal is to obtain just enough information to understand internal controls and to decide how to proceed with the audit.

After obtaining a satisfactory understanding of the internal controls, auditors must assess the level of control risk. External auditors assess control risk in terms of each major assertion that management should be prepared to make about material items in the financial statements (Table 2–2). Thus auditors must relate their understanding of internal controls to the impact they ultimately have on the figures presented in the financial statements. In the case of management controls, the relationship usually is indirect and if careful control is exercised over program maintenance, auditors might have

TABLE 2–2 Financial Statement Assertions

Assertion	Explanation
Existence	Assets, liabilities, and equities included in the financial statements actually exist.
Occurrence	All transactions represent events that have actually occurred.
Completeness	All transactions that have occurred have been recorded. All accounts have been presented in the financial statements.
Rights and obligations	Assets are the rights and liabilities are the obligations of the organization at the balance sheet date.
Valuation or allocation	Asset, liability, equity, revenue, and expense accounts have been recorded at the correct amounts.
Presentation and disclosure	Items in the financial statements are properly classified, described, and disclosed.

increased confidence that a specific control in an application system will continue to be exercised properly throughout the financial period. As a result, they would be confident the control supports, say, the completeness assertion for a particular financial statement component. In the case of application controls, the relationship to financial statement components is usually fairly direct. If the control has not been designed properly or has not been operated effectively, the potential impact on a financial statement assertion is usually clear.

Internal auditors can also assess control risk in terms of assertions that management implicitly or explicitly make about the effectiveness and efficiency of systems (see, e.g., Information Systems Audit and Control Foundation 1996). For example, management might say a system achieves a certain throughput rate and that customers of the organization who use the output of the system have a certain level of satisfaction with the performance of the system. Auditors must use their understanding of the internal controls to evaluate whether they have been designed appropriately and whether they have been placed in operation to support management's assertions.

After auditors obtain an understanding of the internal controls, they then must determine the control risk in relation to each assertion:

1. If auditors assess control risk at less than the maximum level, they must then identify the material controls that relate to the assertion and test the controls to evaluate whether they are operating effectively. They work on the assumption that tests will show that if the controls are operating effectively they can reduce the extent of substantive testing needed to reach an audit opinion.
2. If auditors assess control risk at the maximum level, they do not test controls; they might conclude that internal controls are unlikely to be effective and therefore cannot be relied upon or that a more effective and efficient audit can be conducted using a substantive approach.

Tests of Controls

Auditors test controls when they assess the control risk for an assertion at less than the maximum level. They rely on controls as a basis for reducing more costly testing. At this stage in the audit, however, auditors do not know whether the controls identified operate effectively. Tests of controls, therefore, evaluate whether specific, material controls are, in fact, reliable.

This phase usually begins by again focusing first on management controls. If testing shows that, contrary to expectations, management controls are *not* operating reliably, there might be little point to testing application controls. If auditors identify serious management-control weaknesses, they might have to issue an adverse opinion or undertake substantive tests of transactions and balances or overall results. Auditors conduct the evaluation iteratively for each management subsystem and each application subsystem that is material to the assertion.

To illustrate how to test management controls, assume that as auditors came to an understanding of internal controls, they are informed that senior management regularly undertakes information systems planning. To test whether this control is operating effectively, they might examine the minutes of meetings held by senior management to evaluate whether they conscientiously attend to planning on a regular basis. In addition, they might request a copy of the current information systems plan to evaluate its quality.

Assume that as auditors came to an understanding of the internal controls, they have identified standards covering program documentation. In light of their discussions with programmers, they believe programmers comply with these standards when they write programs. To test the control, auditors might identify a sample of programs they consider material to audit objectives. They could then examine the documentation for these programs to determine whether, in fact, documentation exists and whether it complies with the standards.

If auditors conclude that management controls are in place and working satisfactorily, they then would evaluate the reliability of application controls by tracing instances of *material classes of transactions* through each significant control exercised in the various application subsystems. For each transaction considered, auditors evaluate whether the control is operating effectively.

To illustrate how to test application controls, assume that as auditors came to an understanding of internal controls, they identified a control that required an accounts manager to check that her control clerk cleared all errors reported during an update run of a batch application system. Auditors might select a sample of update reports generated during the financial period and check for a signature to indicate that the accounts manager was regularly checking the work of the accounts clerk.

Assume that as auditors came to an understanding of internal controls, they identified a control that required a data-entry operator to enter customer orders only if customers had provided a signed order form. Auditors might select a sample of orders that had been entered throughout the financial period and check to see each entered order is supported by a signed, hard-copy order.

After auditors have completed tests of controls, they again assess control risk. In light of the test results, they might revise the preliminary assessment of control risk downwards or upwards. In other words, auditors might conclude that internal controls are stronger or weaker than initially anticipated. They might also conclude that it is worthwhile to perform more tests of controls with a view to further reducing the substantive testing. Perhaps internal controls are stronger than initially believed. Accordingly, auditors conclude control risk has decreased and seek further evidence to support this assessment.

During the controls-testing phase, internal auditors and external auditors might differ in their approaches to the audit. If internal auditors identify control weaknesses, they might expand their investigations to gain a better understanding of the nature of and implications of these weaknesses. Their objective might be to provide in-depth recommendations to rectify the control weaknesses. External auditors, on the other hand, will tend to cut short their investigations when they identify control weaknesses and proceed to undertake expanded substantive tests in light of the increased control risk they perceive.

Tests of Transactions

From an attest perspective, recall auditors use tests of transactions to evaluate whether erroneous or irregular processing of a transaction has led to a material misstatement of financial information. Typical attest tests of transactions include tracing journal entries to their source documents, examining price files for propriety, and testing computational accuracy. The computer is quite useful to perform these tests, and auditors might use generalized audit software to check whether the interest paid on bank accounts has been calculated correctly.

From an operational perspective, auditors use tests of transactions to evaluate whether transactions or events have been handled effectively and efficiently. For example, to indicate a database system's effectiveness, auditors might examine a sample of queries recorded on a transaction log to evaluate whether the queries have been generated by a wide cross-section of users of the database system. To evaluate efficiency, auditors might examine the turnaround times for a sample of jobs submitted to an application system. Again, the computer can help to carry out these tests. For example, auditors may use generalized audit software to select a sample of database queries from a transaction log for evaluation.

In an attest audit, auditors conduct tests of transactions at interim dates in order to reduce the amount of substantive tests of balances to be done at financial year end and thus to reduce the overall costs of the audit. In an operational audit for effectiveness and efficiency purposes, auditors also use tests of transactions at interim dates in order to reduce the amount of substantive testing of overall results to be done near the reporting date. For example, if the response times for a sample of transactions that occur throughout the period under review are satisfactory, auditors can reduce the number of users surveyed near the report date to determine whether they consider response times to be satisfactory. To follow this strategy, auditors must know an operational audit is required well in advance of the reporting date.

If the results of tests of transactions indicate that material losses have occurred or might occur or that financial information is or might be materially misstated, substantive tests of balances or overall results will be expanded. Auditors can use expanded tests of balances or overall results to obtain a better estimate of the losses or misstatements that have occurred or might occur.

Tests of Balances or Overall Results

Auditors conduct tests of balances or overall results to obtain sufficient evidence for making a final judgment on the extent of losses or account misstatements that occur when the information systems function fails to safeguard assets, maintain data integrity, and achieve system effectiveness and efficiency. In general, tests of balances or overall results are the most expensive of the audit (although Clowes 1988 argues that the costs and benefits of the different types of tests conducted during different phases is changing as the tests become increasingly automated). Thus, auditors should design and execute these tests carefully.

To understand the approach in this phase, consider, first, the asset-safeguarding and data-integrity objectives. Some typical substantive tests of balances used are confirmation of receivables, physical counts of inventory, and recalculation of depreciation on fixed assets. Recall that if auditors believe controls are reliable on the basis of prior audit work, they will limit the number and scope of these tests because material losses or material account misstatements that have arisen through failure to safeguard assets and maintain data integrity are not expected. On the other hand, if auditors believe controls are not reliable, they will need to expand the extent of substantive tests of balances to estimate better the size of the losses and account misstatements.

Consider, now, the system-effectiveness and system-efficiency objectives. The tests conducted to estimate losses from failure to achieve these objectives are less clear cut than those associated with asset safeguarding and data integrity objectives. For example, auditors might work with users of an application system to estimate the losses they believe have arisen because the system does not provide them with the output they require to make high-quality decisions. As another example, auditors might attempt to estimate the costs of inefficiencies that have occurred because failures in information systems planning have resulted in inappropriate hardware purchases. Again, the extent of the audit work performed depends on the auditor's prior assessment of the reliability of administrative controls.

Computer support is often required to undertake substantive tests of balances or overall results effectively and efficiently. For example, generalized audit software can be used to select and print confirmations; an expert system can be used to estimate the likely bad debts that will arise with receivables; a simulation package can be used to estimate how much throughput of work has been lost because a hardware/software platform has been poorly configured. Recall that the focus of the tests is to estimate the size of losses and account misstatements. The computer is a critical tool in these efforts.

As with the prior phases, the nature and conduct of the audit work during this phase can vary considerably, depending on the type of organization auditors are examining. At one extreme the audit could be a small organization that has a single, centralized information systems function. The audit work focuses on the losses and account misstatements that might have arisen from a limited number of sources. At the other extreme, the audit could be of a large, decentralized organization in which the information systems function is widely dispersed. The audit work must be extensive to take into account losses and misstatements that could have arisen from a large number of sources.

Completion of the Audit

In the final phase of the audit, external auditors undertake several additional tests to bring the collection of evidence to a close. For example, they undertake reviews for subsequent events (events that occur subsequent to the financial statement date but that affect the information that should be reported in the financial statements) and contingent liabilities (potential liabilities that must be disclosed in the financial statements). They must then formulate an opinion about whether material losses or account misstatements have occurred and issue a report. The professional standards in many countries require one of four types of opinion be issued:

1. *Disclaimer of opinion:* On the basis of the audit work conducted, the auditor is unable to reach an opinion.
2. *Adverse opinion:* The auditor concludes that material losses have occurred or that the financial statements are materially misstated.
3. *Qualified opinion:* The auditor concludes that losses have occurred or that the financial statements are misstated but that the amounts are not material.
4. *Unqualified opinion:* The auditor believes that no material losses or account misstatements have occurred.

In addition to asset safeguarding and data integrity concerns, internal auditors might also have to decide whether material losses have occurred because the information systems function has failed to achieve system effectiveness and efficiency objectives. Unlike the asset safeguarding and data integrity objectives, the form of the audit opinion relating to system effectiveness and efficiency objectives is not prescribed by professional standards. Therefore, auditors must formulate their wording for the opinion so that it clearly communicates the findings and judgment. Nevertheless, a typical report would include an introduction that describes the audit objectives, scope, and general approach employed, a summary of critical findings, recommendations to address the major issues that arise from the findings, and data to support the critical findings listed in the report (Pondy 1984).

Auditors are also concerned with prognoses about losses and account misstatements. In other words, even though auditors might have concluded no material losses or misstatements have occurred, they might believe control weaknesses exist that mean such losses or misstatements could occur in the future. These weaknesses might motivate a concern about the viability of the organization if a major threat eventuates. In addition, auditors might be concerned about contingent liabilities associated with losses that arise through significant control weaknesses. For example, customers could sue an organization if it cannot provide products or services because its computer systems are not operational. At the conclusion of an audit, therefore, an important function that auditors perform is to provide management with a report documenting any control weaknesses they have identified, the potential consequences of these control weaknesses, and some recommendations for remedial actions.

AUDITING AROUND OR THROUGH THE COMPUTER

When auditors come to the controls testing phase of an information systems audit, one of the major decisions they must make is whether to test controls by auditing around or through the computer. The phrases "auditing around the computer" and "auditing through the computer" are carryovers from the past. They arose during the period when auditors were debating how much technical knowledge was required to audit computer systems. Some argued that little knowledge was needed because auditors could evaluate computer systems simply by checking their input and output. Others contended audits could not be conducted properly unless the internal workings of computer systems were examined and evaluated. Unfortunately, the arguments of the former group were sometimes motivated by their lack of technical knowledge about computers. Thus, among some auditors the phrase "auditing around the computer" had derogatory connotations. Today we recognize that the two approaches each have their merits and limitations and that each must be considered carefully in the context of planning and executing the most cost-effective audit.

Auditing Around the Computer

Auditing around the computer involves arriving at an audit opinion through examining and evaluating management controls and then input and output *only* for application systems. Based on the quality of an application system's input and output, auditors infer the quality of the application system's processing. The application system's processing is not examined directly. Instead, auditors view the computer as a black box.

Auditors should audit around the computer when it is the most cost-effective way to undertake the audit. This circumstance often arises when an application system has three characteristics. First, the system is simple and batch oriented. Sometimes batch computer systems are a straightforward extension of manual systems. They have the following properties:

1. Their inherent risk is low. They are unlikely to be subject to material errors or irregularities or to be associated with significant ineffectiveness or inefficiencies in operations.
2. Their logic is straightforward. No special routines have been developed to allow the computer to process data.
3. Input transactions are batched, and control is maintained using traditional methods—for example, separation of duties and management supervision.
4. Processing primarily consists of sorting the input data and updating the master file sequentially.
5. A clear audit trail exists. Detailed reports are prepared at key points within the system.
6. The task environment is relatively constant and the system is rarely modified.

Second, often it is cost-effective to audit around the computer when an application system uses a generalized package as its software platform. If the package has been provided by a reputable vendor, has received widespread use, and appears error free, auditors might decide not to test the processing aspects of the system directly. Instead they might seek to ensure *(1)* the organization has not modified the package in any way; *(2)* adequate controls exist over the source code, object code, and documentation to prevent unauthorized modification of the package; and *(3)* high-quality controls exist over input to and output from the package.

Note, however, that not all generalized software packages make application systems amenable to auditing around the computer. Some packages provide a set of generalized functions that still must be selected and combined to accomplish application-system purposes. For example, database management system software might provide generalized update functions, but a high-level program still must be written to combine these functions in the required ways. In this situation, auditors are less able to infer the quality of processing from simply examining the system's input and output.

Third, auditors might audit around the computer when a high reliance is placed on user rather than computer controls to safeguard assets, maintain data integrity, and attain effectiveness and efficiency objectives. In testing, the focus is on the reliability of user controls rather than the reliability of computer controls.

Usually auditing around the computer is a simple approach to the conduct of the audit, and it can be performed by auditors who have little technical knowledge of computers. The audit should be managed, however, by someone who has expertise in information systems auditing.

The approach has two major limitations. First, the type of computer system in which it is applicable is very restricted. It should not be used when systems are complex. Otherwise, auditors might fail to understand some aspect of a system that could have a significant effect on the audit approach. Second, it does not provide information about the system's ability to cope with change. Systems can be designed and programs can be written in certain ways to inhibit their degradation when user requirements change (see Chapters 4 and 5). For internal auditors, the system's robustness could be an important concern in light of their effectiveness and efficiency objectives.

Auditing Through the Computer

For the most part, auditors are now involved in auditing through the computer. They use the computer to test *(1)* the processing logic and controls existing within the system and *(2)* the records produced by the system. Depending on the complexity of the application system, the task of auditing through the computer might be fairly simple, or it might require extensive technical competence on the part of the auditor.

Auditing through the computer must be used in the following cases:

1. The inherent risk associated with the application system is high.
2. The application system processes large volumes of input and produces large volumes of output that make extensive, direct examination of the validity of input and output difficult to undertake.
3. Significant parts of the internal control system are embodied in the computer system. For example, in an online banking system, a computer program might batch transactions for individual tellers to provide control totals for reconciliation at the end of the day's processing.
4. The processing logic embedded within the application system is complex. Moreover, large portions of system code are intended to facilitate use of the system or efficient processing.
5. Because of cost-benefit considerations, substantial gaps in the visible audit trail are common in the system.

The primary advantage of auditing through the computer is that auditors have increased power to test an application system effectively. They can expand the range and capability of tests they can perform and thus increase their confidence in the reliability of the evidence collection and evaluation. Furthermore, by directly examining the processing logic embedded within an application system, auditors are better able to assess the system's ability to cope with change and the likelihood of losses or account misstatements arising in the future.

The approach has two disadvantages. First, it can sometimes be costly, especially in terms of the labor hours that must be expended to understand the internal workings of an application system. Second, in some cases we will need extensive technical expertise if we are to understand how the system works. These disadvantages are really spurious, however, if auditing through the computer is the only viable method of carrying out the audit.

SUMMARY

Usually, auditors cannot examine all the data processing carried out by an organization when it reaches an opinion on whether assets have been safeguarded, data integrity has been maintained, and systems have been operating effectively and efficiently. Instead, they must rely on a sample of data to determine whether these objectives have been achieved.

A primary task during the audit is to evaluate whether controls operate effectively. A *control* is a system that prevents, detects, or corrects an unlawful event. Because a control is a system, it will only operate effectively if all its components are in place and working.

Conducting an information systems audit is an exercise in dealing with complexity. To cope with this complexity, auditors factor the system to be evaluated into subsystems, evaluate the reliability of controls over events in the subsystems, and progressively aggregate the judgments on each subsystem to arrive at a global judgment on the overall reliability of the system. To carry out the process of factoring, auditors first identify the management and application systems that are present in the organization and then decompose these subsystems on the basis of the functions they perform.

Auditors should devote most effort to those segments of the audit in which audit risk is highest. Audit risk is determined by considering the inherent risk, control risk, and detection risk associated with a segment of the audit. Auditors evaluate and control these risks using five types of audit procedures: procedures to obtain an understanding of controls, tests of controls, substantive tests of details of transactions, substantive tests of details of account balances or overall results, and analytical review procedures.

There are five major steps to be undertaken during the conduct of an audit. First, auditors must plan the audit. In particular, auditors must reach an overall understanding of internal controls. Second, if auditors expect to rely on internal controls, controls must be tested to evaluate whether they are operating effectively. Third, auditors must carry out substantive tests of details of transactions to evaluate whether a material loss or account misstatement has occurred or might occur. Fourth, auditors must carry out substantive tests of balances or overall results to gather sufficient evidence to make a judgment on the size of the losses or account misstatements that have occurred or might occur. Fifth, based on their evaluation of the evidence collected, auditors issue an audit opinion.

An important decision to be made during an audit is whether to audit around or through the computer. It might be cost-effective to audit around the computer when systems are simple, a clear audit trail exists, and high reliance is placed on user controls. In most cases, however, an audit opinion cannot be reached without auditing through the computer.

Review Questions

2–1 Define the concept of a control.

2–2 Why must auditors focus on controls as a system?

2–3 Briefly explain the differences between a preventive control, a detective control, and a corrective control. Give an example of each.

2–4 Briefly describe the different types of unlawful events that can occur in a system.

2–5 How do controls reduce expected losses?

2–6 What is meant by "subsystem factoring"? Why do auditors factor a system into subsystems? On what basis should auditors factor a system into subsystems?

2–7 What is meant by "loose coupling" and "strong internal cohesion" of subsystems? Why are these desirable goals to achieve in the factoring process?

2–8 Briefly explain the difference between management controls and application controls. Give an example of each type of control, and explain why it is either a management control or an application control.

2–9 For each of the following activities, identify the level of management that has primary responsibility for performing the activity:

  a Control and use of the organization's database

  b Maintenance of old application systems

  c Provision of general systems support software

  d Implementation of long-run information systems policy decisions

2–10 Classify each of the following controls by application subsystem (e.g., input, communications, processing):

  a A control to prevent unauthorized access to computing resources

  b A control to ensure that erroneous data is corrected and reentered into an application system

  c A control to ensure data recorded on a source document is authorized

  d A control to prevent the user of a query language from making unauthorized inferences about private data in the database

  e A control to ensure that messages are not lost when they are transmitted from one computer to another

2–11 Briefly explain the cycles approach to conducting an information systems audit.

2–12 When auditors evaluate application systems, why do they focus on controls over *classes* of transactions rather than on individual transactions?

2–13 Briefly explain the notion of materiality in auditing. Be sure to explain it in the context of traditional attest objectives and effectiveness and efficiency objectives.

2–14 Identify four types of risk that auditors face. Briefly explain the nature of each.

2–15 At the outset of an audit, why do we try to assess the risk we are facing?

2–16 List the five types of audit procedures you can use to collect evidence during an audit. Give two examples of each—one that you would use if your concern was asset safeguarding and data integrity objectives, and one that you would use if your concern was effectiveness and efficiency objectives.

2–17 Briefly describe the five components of internal control that should be established in an organization.

2–18 In what phase of an audit do you evaluate internal controls? Why do you evaluate internal controls during this phase?

2–19 Briefly describe two types of evidence collection procedures you might use to obtain an understanding of internal controls.

2–20 Briefly explain the nature of and importance of management assertions during the conduct of an audit. Be sure to explain them in the context of your four information systems audit objectives: asset safeguarding, data integrity, system effectiveness, and system efficiency.

2–21 What is the purpose of undertaking tests of controls? What is the relationship between tests of controls and control risk?

2–22 Briefly describe two tests of controls you are likely to perform during the conduct of an information systems audit.

2–23 What is the purpose of undertaking tests of transactions? What type of audit risk is affected by the evidence collected from tests of transactions?

2–24 What is the purpose of undertaking tests of balances or overall results? What is the relationship between tests of transactions and tests of balances or overall results?

2–25 Briefly describe two types of tests of balances or overall results you might use—one for asset safeguarding and data integrity objectives; the other for system effectiveness and system efficiency objectives.

2–26 Briefly describe the four types of opinion that an external auditor might give after completing an information systems audit.

2–27 Briefly describe the nature of the report auditors should issue if they conduct an audit of systems effectiveness and systems efficiency.

2–28 Give an example of a system for which auditing around the computer would be appropriate and an example for which auditing through the computer would be necessary. Explain why the approaches are appropriate for the examples you give.

Multiple-Choice Questions

2–1 Which of the following statements about controls is false?
a The primary focus of controls is unlawful events
b Controls are systems of interacting components
c Controls cover all unlawful events in a system
d An unlawful event in a system can be covered by more than one control

2–2 Which of the following is unlikely to be an objective of a control?
a Reduce expected losses from irregularities
b Reduce the probability of an error occurring
c Reduce the amount of loss if an error occurs
d Reduce the normality of the loss distribution

2–3 *Expected losses* are defined as:
a Losses anticipated in the normal course of business
b The losses that arise when an error or irregularity occurs
c The losses that arise when an error or irregularity occurs multiplied by the probability of the error or irregularity occurring
d The losses anticipated when a system does not meet effectiveness and efficiency objectives

2–4 A program check that ensures data entered by a data-entry operator is complete is an example of a:
a Detective control
b Corrective control
c Preventive control
d Redundancy control

2–5 Factoring is the process of:
a Identifying the physical components of a system
b Identifying the interfaces between subsystems
c Decomposing a system into physical component activities
d Decomposing a system into subsystems

2–6 Which of the following is *not* a guideline for the factoring process?
a Focus on functions rather than activities
b Ensure subsystems are tightly coupled
c Proceed in an hierarchical manner
d Ensure subsystems are internally cohesive

2–7 Which of the following is *not* a management subsystem?
a Audit trail subsystem
b Data administration subsystem
c Security administration subsystem
d System development management subsystem

2–8 Which of the following is *not* an application subsystem?
 a Hardware subsystem
 b Boundary subsystem
 c Input subsystem
 d Database subsystem

2–9 When auditors attempt to understand data-processing systems, which order of decomposition are they most likely to follow:
 a Applications, cycles, transactions, controls
 b Cycles, applications, controls, transactions
 c Cycles, applications, transactions, controls
 d Transactions, applications, cycles, controls

2–10 Which of the following is unlikely to be a reason for placing a control in a higher-level system?
 a Controls in lower-level subsystems could malfunction
 b Controls in higher-level systems are easier to put in place
 c Controls in higher-level systems might be more cost-effective
 d Some unlawful events can only be detected by controls in higher-level systems

2–11 Under which circumstance will the level of achieved audit risk decrease?
 a An increase in inherent risk
 b A decrease in detection risk
 c An increase in control risk
 d A decrease in desired audit risk

2–12 Over which type of risk does the auditor have greatest control?
 a Desired audit risk
 b Inherent risk
 c Control risk
 d Detection risk

2–13 Which of the following factors is unlikely to affect the level of inherent risk associated with an application system?
 a The system is strategic
 b Controls over the system appear reliable
 c The system is not a critical operational system
 d The system uses high technology

2–14 If auditors use generalized audit software to recalculate the extensions (price multiplied by quantity) on invoices, they are conducting:
 a Analytical review procedures
 b Procedures to understand internal controls
 c Tests of details of transactions
 d Tests of controls

2–15 Which of the following elements is unlikely to be considered part of the control environment when auditors review internal controls?
 a A requirement for a manager to approve customer orders before they are keyed into an application system
 b The existence of an audit committee
 c The management style used by an organization's executive
 d The existence of a budgeting system

2–16 The *primary* objective of tests of controls is to:
 a Determine whether controls are operating effectively
 b Identify any material errors that have occurred in major classes of transactions
 c Understand whether a control is in place
 d Identify major patterns of errors or irregularities that might exist in final account balances

2–17 Auditors are most likely to undertake tests of controls if, after their evaluation of internal controls, they conclude:

a A substantive approach to the audit will be more cost-effective

b Control risk is less than the maximum level

c The control environment is poor

d Inherent risk is low

2–18 Which of the following is *not* a substantive test?

a A test to compare data with a physical count

b A test to assess the quality of data

c A test to compare data with an outside source

d A test to determine whether source documents have been authorized

2–19 Which of the following statements about the tests of controls phase of an information systems audit is false?

a Management controls are usually tested before application controls

b At the conclusion of the tests of controls phase, auditors reassess control risk

c The auditor focuses on material classes of transactions during the tests of controls phase

d The primary objective of the tests of controls phase is to determine whether material controls exist

2–20 Which of the following statements about the tests of balances/overall results phase is false?

a The primary objective of the tests of balances/overall results phase is to obtain sufficient evidence to make a final audit judgment

b Substantive tests are the most common tests used in the tests of balances/overall results phase to evaluate attainment of asset safeguarding and data integrity objectives

c Tests undertaken during the tests of balances/overall results phase tend to be less costly than those undertaken in other phases of the audit

d Many tests undertaken during the tests of balances/overall results phase require computerized support

2–21 If external auditors concluded no material losses or account misstatements had occurred as a result of a client's information systems activities but that significant *potential* existed for material losses or account misstatements to occur as a result of control weaknesses that existed, they would most likely issue:

a An unqualified opinion

b A disclaimer of opinion

c An adverse opinion

d A qualified opinion

2–22 Auditing around the computer might be used when:

a There are significant gaps in the audit trail in the computer system

b The internal controls in the computer system cannot be relied upon

c Processing consists primarily of sorting the input file and updating the master file sequentially

d The auditor lacks technical expertise to perform a direct evaluation of computer controls

Exercises and Cases

2–1 Consider the personal identification numbers (PINs) that many financial institutions use to control customer access to accounts—for example, withdrawal of funds by customers from their accounts using automatic teller machines (ATMs).

Required.   List all the major functions you can identify that must be performed if PINs are to be an effective control to prevent unauthorized access to an account. Briefly explain why all these functions must be considered as a system if PINs are to operate as an effective control. *Hint:* You might find it helpful to consider the functions to be performed first from the viewpoint of the financial institution and then from the viewpoint of the customer.

2–2 As discussed in the chapter, many audit organizations now follow the "cycles" approach when evaluating an internal control system. This approach involves classifying transactions by cycles, converting the broad objectives of internal control into specific objectives for these classifications of transactions, and evaluating the controls in place in light of these objectives. The following five cycles apply to many organizations: revenue, expenditure, production or conversion, financing, and external financial reporting. For the revenue cycle, the American Institute of Certified Public Accountants (1979) lists the following eight objectives:

a The types of goods and services to be provided, the manner in which they will be provided, and the customer to whom they will be provided should be properly authorized.

b Credit terms and limits should be properly authorized.

c The prices and other terms of sale of goods and services should be properly authorized.

d Sales-related deductions and adjustments should be properly authorized.

e Deliveries of goods and services should result in preparation of accurate and timely billing forms.

f Sales and related transactions should be recorded at the appropriate amounts and in the appropriate period and should be properly classified in the accounts.

g Cash receipts should be accounted for properly on a timely basis.

h Access to cash receipts and cash receipts records, accounts receivable records, and billing and shipping records should be suitably controlled to prevent or detect within a timely period the interception of unrecorded cash receipts or the abstraction of recorded cash receipts.

Required.   For each objective, briefly describe two types of controls that might be used in a computer-based information system to help achieve the objective. Be sure to discuss how each of the two controls would achieve the objective. In particular, point out an unlawful event that each would prevent, detect, or correct.

2–3 You are on the staff of an external audit firm that audits a small to medium-size financial institution. One day you receive a copy of a letter from the president of the financial institution to the partner in charge of the audit. The letter indicates the client is considering replacing its existing minicomputer with 20 desktop computers, connecting these computers via a local area network, and converting all its application systems to run on the new platform. You are alarmed at this "radical" move and its audit implications. As a result, you go to the partner in charge to request time to investigate the proposed changes and, if need be, suggest some design alternatives. The partner in charge hesitates when you make your request. She explains that she believes you should not become involved at this stage because it will affect the firm's independence. She concedes there might be problems with the changes proposed, however, and she asks you to prepare a brief for her.

Required. Write a report to the partner outlining some of the control and audit problems that could arise with the proposed changeover to the desktop computers and local area network. In particular, indicate whether the new platform is likely to affect the inherent risk associated with the client's applications.

2–4 The accounting department of a small company is responsible for payment of creditors. It receives a copy of each purchase order issued, a receiving document when the goods arrive, and the vendor's invoice. All documents are date-stamped upon receipt and filed securely. When the receiving document and vendor's invoice arrive, a clerk matches details and checks the accuracy of items and computations on the documents. A second clerk then prepares a disbursement voucher and a check for payment and gives the check, the voucher, and the supporting documents to a manager who examines them before signing the check.

Required. List the control objectives for these operations. Prepare a controls matrix (see Table 2–1) in which the columns show causes of loss and the rows show the controls in existence to reduce expected losses. The elements of the matrix should show which controls act on the causes of loss (use a tick mark to show which controls relate to a particular cause of loss). How well do the controls allow the control objectives to be accomplished? What controls are likely to change if the system is computerized?

2–5 You are a staff information systems auditor in a public accounting firm. The firm has just acquired a new client—a small manufacturing organization. The client uses a minicomputer for its data processing.

All application systems are straightforward batch systems with well-defined input and output. The client uses a database management system, however, that was purchased initially for its bill-of-materials application system, but all application systems now use the database management system to maintain their associated files. There is only limited sharing of data among applications.

Required. You are undertaking the first audit of the new client. The partner in charge asks you to advise him on whether to plan the audit through the computer or around the computer. He is concerned that the client's use of the database management system could have increased the likelihood of errors and irregularities occurring. Write a short report giving your recommendations and the reasons behind them. In particular, discuss your expectations about the inherent risk and control risk associated with the application systems, and outline how your expectations about the inherent risk and control risk could affect the approach you will recommend to the conduct of the audit.

2–6 You have just been engaged as the external auditor for a medium-sized automotive servicing organization. The organization obtains most of its revenue in three ways: (a) it services motor-vehicle fleets, (b) it sells spare parts, and (c) it converts vehicles from petroleum to liquified petroleum gas (LPG) consumption.

The organization uses a local area network of three microcomputers running the following application software packages:

- General ledger
- Debtor/invoicing
- Creditors
- Payroll
- Spare parts/inventory
- Job costing
- Bill-of-materials

All applications are relatively straightforward. Job costing and bill of materials, for example, are used to support workshop activities. A supervisor specifies the type of service required for a vehicle, and the bill-of-materials application identifies the standard parts and labor required for the job.

The three microcomputers are placed in different locations: (a) workshop—to enter data about a job or inquire about a job, spare part, and so on; (b) accounting—to process data related to debtors, creditors, payroll, and general ledger and to prepare management reports; and (c) spare parts—to provide over-the-counter service to customers and workshop personnel. The operating system used to support the microcomputers allows concurrent but controlled access to a central database. All the software used by the organization is well-known, well-tested, and supplied by a reputable vendor. The general manager assures you that no modifications have been made to the software and indicates there is no one on the staff of the organization with the computer knowledge needed to carry out modifications to the software.

Required. Outline how you would approach the audit of this organization. In particular, indicate how the use of generalized application software that supposedly has not been modified will affect your audit strategy. In this light, consider the levels of inherent risk and control risk that are likely to exist with the applications. Discuss, also, whether you will focus on user controls, computer controls, or both in any audit testing you undertake.

Answers to Multiple-Choice Questions

2–1	c	2–7	a	2–13	b	2–19	d
2–2	d	2–8	a	2–14	c	2–20	c
2–3	c	2–9	c	2–15	a	2–21	a
2–4	a	2–10	b	2–16	a	2–22	c
2–5	d	2–11	b	2–17	b		
2–6	b	2–12	d	2–18	d		

REFERENCES

American Institute of Certified Public Accountants (1979), *Report of the Special Advisory Committee on Internal Accounting Control.* New York: American Institute of Certified Public Accountants.

——— (1988a), *Statement on Auditing Standards No. 47: Audit Risk and Materiality in Conducting an Audit.* New York: American Institute of Certified Public Accountants.

——— (1988b), *Statement on Auditing Standards No. 55: Consideration of the Internal Control*

Structure in a Financial Statement Audit. New York: American Institute of Certified Public Accountants.

——— (1990), *Audit Guide: Statement on Auditing Standards No. 55: Consideration of the Internal Control Structure in a Financial Statement Audit.* New York: American Institute of Certified Public Accountants.

——— (1991), *Statement on Auditing Standards No. 65: The Auditor's Consideration of the Internal Audit Function in an Audit of Financial State-*

ments. New York: American Institute of Certified Public Accountants.

——— (1995), *Statement on Auditing Standards No. 78: Consideration of Internal Control in a Financial Statement Audit: An Amendment to SAS No. 55.* New York: American Institute of Certified Public Accountants.

Arens, Alvin A., and James K. Loebbecke (1997), *Auditing: An Integrated Approach,* 7th ed. Upper Saddle River, NJ: Prentice-Hall.

Arthur Andersen & Co. (1978), *A Guide for Studying and Evaluating Internal Accounting Controls.* Chicago: Arthur Andersen & Co.

Bell, Timothy B., Frank O. Marrs, Ira Solomon, and Howard Thomas (1997), *Auditing Organizations Through a Strategic-Systems Lens: The KPMG Business Measurement Approach.* Montvale, NJ: KPMG Peat Marwick LLP.

Clowes, Kenneth W. (1988), *EDP Auditing.* Toronto: Holt, Rinehart and Winston of Canada.

Coad, Peter, and Edward Yourdon (1991a), *Object-Oriented Analysis*, 2d ed. Upper Saddle River, NJ: Prentice-Hall.

——— (1991b), *Object-Oriented Design.* Upper Saddle River, NJ: Prentice-Hall.

Committee of Sponsoring Organizations of the Treadway Commission (1992), *Internal Control–Integrated Framework: Framework.* New York: Committee of Sponsoring Organizations of the Treadway Commission.

——— (1992), *Internal Control–Integrated Framework: Evaluation Tools.* New York: Committee of Sponsoring Organizations of the Treadway Commission.

FitzGerald, Jerry, and Ardra FitzGerald (1990), *Designing Controls into Computerized Systems*, 2d ed. Redwood City, CA: Jerry FitzGerald and Associates.

Information Systems Audit and Control Foundation (1996), *COBIT: Control Objectives for Information and Related Technology Framework.* Rolling Meadows, IL: Information Systems Audit and Control Foundation.

Warren, J. Donald, Lynn W. Edelson, and Xenia Ley Parker (1997), *Handbook of IT Auditing.* Boston: Warren, Gorham & Lamont.

Pondy, E. H. (1984), "Operational Auditing by CPA Firms," *The CPA Journal* (October), 38, 40, 42, 44, 46, 48, 50.

Simon, Herbert A. (1981), *The Sciences of the Artificial,* 2d ed. Cambridge, MA: The MIT Press.

Steinberg, Richard M., and Raymond N. Johnson (1991), "Implementing SAS No. 55 in a Computer Environment," *Journal of Accountancy* (August), 60–68.

Temkin, Robert H., and Alan J. Winters (1988), "SAS No. 55: The Auditor's New Responsibility for Internal Control," *Journal of Accountancy* (May), 86–98.

Wand, Yair, and Ron Weber (1989), "A Model of Control and Audit Procedure Change in Evolving Data Processing Systems," *The Accounting Review* (January), 87–107.

Watne, Donald A., and Peter B. B. Turney (1990), *Auditing EDP Systems*, 2d ed. Upper Saddle River, NJ: Prentice-Hall.

Wu, Frederick H., and Randall L. Hann (1989), "A Control-Complexity and Control-Point Orientation to the Review of an Entity's Internal Control Structure in the Computer Environment," *Journal of Information Systems* (Spring), 117–131.

Yourdon, Edward, and Larry L. Constantine (1979), *Structured Design: Fundamentals of a Discipline of Computer Program and Systems Design.* Upper Saddle River, NJ: Prentice-Hall.

The Management Control Framework

The auditor's primary objective in examining the management control framework for the information systems function is to evaluate whether management manages well. A recurring theme throughout this book is that the quality of management has a major impact on the extent to which asset safeguarding, data integrity, systems effectiveness, and system efficiency objectives are achieved. If high-quality management controls are not in place and working reliably, application controls are unlikely to be effective. There is little point to examining, testing, and evaluating application controls, therefore, if we have substantial doubts about whether we will be able to rely upon them. Auditors must adjust the plans for the conduct of the remainder of the audit accordingly.

Examining and evaluating the management control framework is important for two reasons. First, at the outset of the audit, an understanding must be reached about the internal control structure of the organization evaluated. Management controls are important components of this overall internal control structure. There must be a good understanding of the management controls that are important to the audit objectives. Second, in light of the understanding of management controls obtained, there must then be a decision made on whether they intend to rely on management controls.

The task of evaluating management controls is not easy, however. Perhaps the greatest difficulty is to know how the presence or absence of a management control might affect asset safeguarding, data integrity, system effectiveness, and system efficiency objectives. If an organization does not have an information systems plan, for example, what are the ramifications for asset safeguarding? Is there any impact? If so, what is it? Does the impact vary across different types of organizations? Even with a little thought, it quickly becomes apparent that the consequences of a missing information systems plan are not always clear-cut. An auditor must develop the ability to work through the implications of reliable or unreliable management controls for asset safeguarding, data integrity, system effectiveness, and system efficiency objectives.

The next seven chapters present the essence of good information systems management practices. We cannot evaluate information systems management unless we know what management *should* be doing. When you have completed your study of the chapters in this part of the book, you should have a good understanding of the fundamentals that will allow you to evaluate the reliability of the management controls you encounter in an organization. In addition, you should understand how your conclusions on the reliability of management controls impact your decisions on how to conduct the remainder of an audit.

Chapter	*Overview of Contents*
3 Top Management Controls	Discusses top management's role in planning, organizing, leading, and controlling the information systems function.
4 Systems Development Management Controls	Provides a contingency perspective on models of the information systems development process that auditors can use as a basis for evidence collection and evaluation.
5 Programming Management Controls	Discusses the major phases in the program life cycle and the important controls that should be exercised in each phase.
6 Data Resource Management Controls	Discusses the roles of the data administrator and the database administrator and the controls that should be exercised over the functions they perform.
7 Security Management Controls	Discusses the major functions performed by security administrators to identify major threats to the information systems function and to design, implement, operate, and maintain controls that reduce expected losses from these threats to an acceptable level.
8 Operations Management Controls	Discusses the major functions performed by operations management to ensure the day-to-day operations of the information systems function are well controlled.
9 Quality Assurance Management Controls	Discusses the major functions that quality assurance management should perform to ensure that the development, implementation, operation, and maintenance of information systems conform to quality standards.

Top Management Controls

Chapter Outline

Chapter Key Points

■ Auditors can evaluate top management by examining how well they perform four major functions: planning—determining the goals of the information systems function and the means of achieving these goals; organizing—gathering, allocating, and coordinating the resources needed to accomplish the goals; leading—motivating, guiding, and communicating with personnel; and controlling—comparing actual performance with planned performance as a basis for taking any corrective actions that are needed.

■ Top management must prepare two types of information systems plans: a long-run strategic plan; and a short-run operational plan.

■ Information systems planning needs will vary depending upon such factors as the importance of existing information systems, the importance of proposed information systems, the extent to which information technology has been integrated into daily operations, and the extent to which information technology has been diffused throughout an organization.

■ An information systems steering committee should take ultimate responsibility for information systems planning. The functions and makeup of the steering committee should vary depending upon how critical information systems are to the success of the organization.

■ As part of the organizing function, top management must ensure that sufficient resources are available to the information systems function for it to be able to fulfil its role.

■ Effective management of information systems personnel requires that controls be established over acquisition of staff, development of staff, and termination of staff.

■ The question of whether the information systems function should be centralized or decentralized depends on decisions that have to be made with respect to control over information systems resources, location of information systems resources, and the information systems functions to be performed at different sites.

■ Jobs within the information systems function should be well defined and documented and preserve separation of duties to the extent possible.

■ The information systems function should be located in the organizational hierarchy so that its independence is preserved.

■ Top management must show it is capable of leading information systems personnel by achieving high levels of motivation among staff, matching appropriate supervisory styles to the circumstances at hand, and ensuring they communicate effectively with staff.

■ Top management must attempt to assess whether it is getting value for money from the information systems function. They must match performance against plans.

■ The level of control exercised over the information systems function needs to vary depending upon whether top management wish to encourage diffusion of new technologies or constrain use of existing technologies.

■ Policies and standards are an important means of exercising control over the information systems function.

■ Users of computer services can be controlled by implementing a review mechanism, such as zero-based budgeting, or a transfer pricing (chargeout) scheme.

INTRODUCTION

The senior managers who take responsibility for the information systems function in an organization face many challenges. Consider some of the problems they encounter. The hardware and software technology that supports information systems is constantly changing. Top management must somehow determine the implications of these changes for the information systems function and the organization. The relationships between the information systems function and other functions in the organization can be difficult to manage. Information systems are critical to the effective performance of many people within the organization. They can become upset if they consider the information systems function is failing to support them properly. In some cases, also, development of innovative information systems might be central to the organization's competitive strategy. As a result, top managers who are responsible for the information systems function have substantial pressures placed on them to ensure they achieve the goals that have been established for them.

How then can an auditor evaluate how well senior management manages the information systems function? One useful way is to consider each of the major functions that senior management must perform: planning—determining the goals of the information systems function and the means of achieving these goals; organizing—gathering, allocating, and coordinating the resources needed to accomplish the goals; leading—motivating, guiding, and communicating with personnel; and controlling—comparing actual performance with planned performance as a basis for taking any corrective actions that are needed.

This chapter outlines the nature of these major functions and describes how they should be performed in the context of the information systems function. If we are to be able to evaluate how well senior managers responsible for the information systems function perform their role, we must understand the fundamentals of good management (see, e.g., Holt 1993). Furthermore, we must understand the special problems that arise when managing the information systems function.

EVALUATING THE PLANNING FUNCTION

Top management is responsible for preparing a master plan for the information systems function. The plan sets both the long-run and short-run directions for information systems within their organization. Preparing the plan involves three tasks (Boynton and Zmud 1987):

1. Recognizing opportunities and problems that confront the organization in which information technology and information systems can be applied cost effectively;
2. Identifying the resources needed to provide the required information technology and information systems; and
3. Formulating strategies and tactics for acquiring the needed resources.

Auditors evaluate whether top management has formulated a high-quality information systems plan appropriate to the needs of their organization. In the absence of a high-quality information systems plan, the information systems function is unlikely to remain effective and efficient. As effectiveness and efficiency decline, controls that preserve asset safeguarding and data integrity may be undermined. For example, poor planning could mean the information systems function has insufficient hardware, software, and personnel resources to handle the available workload. As a result, controls that preserve asset safeguarding and data integrity might be disabled or circumvented to reduce resource consumption.

Poor information systems planning can also result in an organization losing its competitive position within the marketplace. Today, many organizations compete effectively only if information systems support underlies the products and services they offer (Porter and Miller 1985). For this reason, top management continues to report that effective information systems planning is one of their major concerns (Niederman et al. 1991). From an audit perspective, in some organizations auditors' decisions on whether an organization can continue as a going concern might depend upon their assessment of the quality of the organization's information systems plan.

Types of Plans

Top management must prepare two types of information systems plans for the information systems function: a strategic plan and an operational plan. The *strategic plan* is the long-run plan covering, say, the next three to five years of operations. The contents of a strategic plan typically include the following:

1. *Current information assessment:* Existing information systems services provided, current hardware/software platform, existing personnel resources, current technology issues, current strengths and weaknesses, current threats and opportunities.
2. *Strategic directions:* Future information services to be provided, overall strategies for intraorganizational and interorganizational systems.
3. *Development strategy:* Vision statement for information technology, future applications and databases, future hardware/software platform, future personnel resources required, future financial resources required, approach to monitoring the implementation of the strategy.

The *operational plan* is the short-run plan covering, say, the next one to three years of operations. The contents of an operational plan typically include the following:

1. *Progress report:* Current plan initiatives achieved and missed, major hardware/software platform changes, additional initiatives embarked upon.

2. *Initiatives to be undertaken:* Systems to be developed, hardware/software platform changes, personnel resources acquisition and development, financial resources acquisition.

3. *Implementation schedule:* Proposed start and finish dates for each major project, milestones, project control procedures to be adopted.

Both the strategic plan and the operational plan need to be reviewed regularly and updated as the need arises. In particular, their congruency with the overall corporate plan needs to be monitored carefully.

Need for a Contingency Approach to Planning

Information systems planning needs vary across organizations. Some organizations operate in a volatile environment and place heavy reliance on their information systems function to maintain their competitive position within the marketplace. Auditors should expect these organizations to devote substantial effort to information systems planning. In other organizations, however, the environment is relatively stable. Moreover, information systems might not be central to their operations. In these organizations, top management is unlikely to expend much effort on information systems planning. When auditors evaluate how well top management undertakes information systems planning, therefore, they must first determine the nature of and amounts of planning that should be undertaken given their organization's needs.

One model that auditors can use is the strategic-grid model developed by McFarlan et al. (1983). They argue that the nature and amount of information systems planning appropriate to an organization is a function of two important factors: *(1)* the strategic importance of an organization's portfolio of *existing* information systems; and *(2)* the strategic importance of an organization's portfolio of *proposed* systems. They identify four types of organizations, each with different information systems planning needs (Figure 3–1):

Type of Organization	Information Systems Planning Needs
Support	Both existing and proposed information systems have low importance. Only small amounts of planning are needed.
Factory	Although proposed systems are relatively unimportant, existing systems are critical. Moderate amounts of planning will be needed, primarily focusing on the short-run resource needs of the organization.
Turnaround	Although existing systems are relatively unimportant, proposed systems are critical. Moderate to large amounts of planning will be needed, primarily focusing on the long-run application needs of the organization.
Strategic	Both existing systems and future systems are critical. Substantial planning should be undertaken, focusing on both the short- and long-run resource and application needs of the organization.

Sullivan (1985) has developed a similar model to determine the information systems planning needs of an organization. He also focuses on two dimensions: *(1)* infusion—the extent to which information technology and information systems have been integrated into the daily operations of the organization; and *(2)* diffusion—the extent to which information systems and information technology has been dispersed throughout the organization. He identifies four

Importance of Future Systems

		Low	High
Importance of Current Systems	Low	Support organization	Turnaround organization
	High	Factory organization	Strategic organization

types of organizations, each with different information systems planning needs (Figure 3–2):

Type of Organization	*Information Systems Planning Needs*
Traditional	Low infusion and low diffusion of information technology and information systems have occurred. Only small amounts of planning are needed. The planning can be performed by a centralized group.
Federation	Although low infusion has occurred, high diffusion exists. Moderate amounts of planning will be needed. Planning activities will be decentralized, primarily focusing on the needs of divisions and end users. Organizationwide planning activities are likely to be resisted.
Backbone	Although low diffusion has occurred, high infusion exists. Moderate to large amounts of planning will be needed. Planning activities will be centralized, primarily focusing on the needs of the centralized information systems group.
Complex	Both infusion and diffusion of information technology and systems are substantial. Large amounts of planning will be needed. Planning activities will be complex as they try to take into account both the corporate, centralized needs and the needs of individual divisions and end users. Planning must respect divisional autonomy. At the same time, however, it must establish organizationwide directions.

Systems Infusion

		Low	High
Systems Diffusion	Low	Traditional organization	Backbone organization
	High	Federation organization	Complex organization

Both McFarlan et al.'s model and Sullivan's model are useful because they allow auditors to develop an appropriate set of expectations about the ways information systems planning should be conducted within an organization. Auditors must recognize that information systems activities will rightly vary across organizations. At the same time, auditors must be able to identify how organizations should be undertaking information systems planning so they can evaluate how well information systems planning activities are being performed.

Role of a Steering Committee

Ultimate responsibility for information systems planning should be vested in an information systems steering committee. The steering committee should assume overall responsibility for the activities of the information systems function. The information systems plan is a critical tool needed by the steering committee to discharge its responsibilities.

Information systems steering committees seem to work best if they have only a small number of members. Their makeup should vary depending on how critical the information systems function is to the success of the organization. For example, in strategic organizations (see Figure 3–1), the steering committee should be chaired by the chief executive officer. Membership should comprise a broad base of senior users and senior information systems personnel. In support organizations, however, extensive senior representation on the steering committee is not so important. Middle-level management representation is likely to be more appropriate (see Raghunathan and Raghunathan 1990).

Similarly, in those organizations where extensive diffusion of information technology has occurred, the organizationwide steering committee should have broad, divisional representation. Depending on the extent of infusion of information technology and information systems, however, the steering committee could assume a major role or a relatively constrained role in the life of the organization.

EVALUATING THE ORGANIZING FUNCTION

The planning function establishes goals and objectives for information systems within an organization. The organizing function gathers, allocates, and structures resources to enable these goals and objectives to be achieved. Unless top management performs the organizing function properly, the information systems function is unlikely to be effective and efficient. Asset safeguarding and data integrity could then suffer as a result.

Resourcing the Information Systems Function

A major responsibility of top management is to acquire the resources needed to accomplish the goals and objectives set out in the information systems plan. These resources include hardware, software, personnel, finances, and facilities. Adequate funding to support the acquisition and development of resources must first be obtained. The funds must then be expended in a planned, systematic way to ensure adequate resources are available when and where they are needed. For example, if new hardware and software will be required to accomplish the goals set down for the information systems function, top management must raise the capital needed to support the acquisition of these resources. In addition, detailed requirements must be determined, a request for proposals must be prepared and sent to vendors, submissions must be evaluated and a decision made, contracts must be exchanged, the hardware and software must be installed and tested, and any modifications required must be made. All these activities must be carried out on a timely basis.

If top managers are not acquiring needed resources on a timely basis, an auditor might see this problem manifested in several ways. For example, projects set down in the operational plan might not be accomplished, projects might be cancelled when they are partially complete, the morale of information systems users and information systems personnel might be poor, or the organization might be suffering major problems in its day-to-day activities. The auditor should question whether top managers have a good understanding of the role the information systems function should play in their organization. Perhaps they are ascribing too much importance to the function—for example, they mistakenly believe the information systems function is strategic when, in fact, it plays only a support role. Alternatively, in spite of what they might say, top managers might really believe the information systems function plays only a support role when, in fact, it is critical to the competitive position of the organization.

Staffing the Information Systems Function

Auditors should be concerned about how well top management acquires and manages staff resources for three reasons. First, the effectiveness of the information systems function depends primarily on the quality of its staff. The jobs performed are often complex and subject to the vagaries of rapid technological change. Careful planning must be undertaken to ensure that information systems staff remain up to date and motivated in their jobs. Second, historically, high-quality information systems staff have been in short supply. The market for information systems staff has been characterized by intense competition and high turnover. Acquiring and retaining good information systems staff remains a major problem for many organizations. Third, empirical research indicates the employees of an organization are the most likely persons to perpetrate irregularities. For example, Benbow (1990) reports that 80 percent of all documented computer crime in Australia was committed by internal employees.

Staffing the information systems function involves three major activities: *(1)* acquisition of information systems personnel, *(2)* development of information systems personnel, and *(3)* termination of information systems personnel. Auditors must evaluate how well each is performed.

Personnel Acquisition

The information systems plan should set out the staff resources that will be required to accomplish the goals and objectives laid down for the information systems function. If new staff must be hired, top management must ensure high-quality staff with the appropriate skills are hired on a timely basis.

If high-quality staff are to be hired, top management must carefully evaluate the integrity and capabilities of job applicants. Data on applicants can be obtained through interviews, aptitude tests, references, resumes, and scholastic records. Some basic control procedures that should be applied include the following:

1. Background checking of references, resumes, scholastic records, and so on;
2. Screening applicants for mental and physical health;
3. Bonding of key employee;
4. Explanation of organizational protocols to be observed, e.g., matters not to be discussed in public; and
5. General organizational indoctrination.

If staff with the appropriate skills are to be hired, job requirements must first be determined in light of the needs spelled out in the information systems plan. Job descriptions must then be prepared so both management and applicants understand clearly the requirements of the job. These job descriptions form the basis of advertising the job and evaluating applicants for the job.

Personnel Development

Personnel development involves *(1)* establishing promotional and personal growth opportunities for employees and *(2)* education. These activities maintain employee morale and the skill set needed to carry out required tasks.

Providing promotional and personal growth opportunities can be a special problem in the information systems function. On the one hand, employees are often young, have experienced rapid promotion, and are quickly left with few opportunities for advancement. On the other hand, experienced information systems staff are often perceived to be technocrats. As a result, management considers them to be relatively immobile within the organizational hierarchy. These problems have not been well addressed (see, e.g., Ginzberg and Baroudi 1988).

Regular staff reviews should be carried out for three reasons: *(1)* to assess whether an employee warrants promotion, *(2)* to identify opportunities for the employee's personal growth, and *(3)* to identify the employee's strengths and weaknesses. Employees should understand clearly the nature of the review and the bases on which they will be evaluated. They should have the opportunity to discuss their ratings with management and to appeal assessments they believe are unfair. Top management should counsel them in light of the ratings they obtain.

Sometimes staff reviews give insufficient emphasis to identifying opportunities for the employee's personal growth. If promotional opportunities are scarce, personal growth might be the only means of preventing high staff turnover. Top management must seek more responsible and challenging positions for employees. At the same time, top management must evaluate whether employees have earned the necessary trust and acquired the required skills to be appointed to these positions.

Because information technology changes so quickly, training and continuing education are critical to the effective performance of the information systems function. During high-pressure periods or periods when resources are scarce, top management might be tempted to forego training. The long-run implications of this decision can be disastrous for employee morale and for the ability of personnel within the information systems function to cope with new technology.

Training must not be haphazard. Those areas where employee expertise is lacking should be identified. Proposed coursework should be evaluated carefully. Employees attending training sessions should disseminate the knowledge acquired upon their return.

Personnel Termination

Personnel termination can be voluntary or involuntary. In either case, top management should exercise certain control procedures. The severity of these procedures depends on whether the employee is disgruntled. Some examples follow:

1. When an employee gives notice, top management should be informed immediately. The employee's supervisor should be contacted to determine reasons for leaving.
2. Upon termination, a checklist of control procedures should be followed to ensure that (a) keys and ID badges are recovered; (b) the employee's passwords

are cancelled; (c) distribution lists are changed; (d) all reports, books, documentation, and so on are returned; and (e) any equipment issued is returned.

3. If terminating employees are not disgruntled, they should provide training for the replacement employee. If terminating employees are disgruntled, however, they should be assigned to noncritical areas or required to leave the organization immediately.

4. Exit interviews should be given so that (a) any areas of discontent are determined, (b) reminders are given on secrecy oaths, and so on, and (c) potential problems are identified.

Centralization Versus Decentralization of the Information Systems Function

The question of whether the information systems function should be centralized or decentralized has been sorely debated since computers first began to have an important impact on organizations. Typical arguments in support of centralization are that it *(1)* allows better top-management control over the information systems function and *(2)* provides economies of scale in terms of hardware, software, and personnel. Typical arguments in support of decentralization are that it *(1)* improves an organization's capacity to exploit information systems opportunities and *(2)* reduces the costs of communications associated with information systems activities.

The debate over centralization versus decentralization of the information systems function has been fueled, in part, by constant shifting of factors critical to the decision. For example, the economics of computing have changed dramatically over time. Initially, economies of scale accrued if large, centralized, hardware facilities were established. Mendelson (1987) argues, however, that the computer hardware industry is mature and that economies of scale no longer arise when bigger machines are purchased. Thus, arguments for centralization based on economies of scale are weakened. On the other hand, organizations increasingly recognize data is a strategic resource that must be well managed. Accordingly, centralized data management has been advocated as a basis for improved data-resource planning and control. In the early 1980s, another major change was the emergence of low-cost, powerful microcomputers. Many managers used microcomputers to force devolution of information systems activities to their own departments.

When deciding whether to centralize, King (1983) says management should consider three dimensions:

1. *Control:* Responsibility for decision making about the information systems function can be vested in one or a small number of people, or it can be vested in many individuals at different levels and/or locations throughout the organization.

2. *Location:* Hardware/software facilities can be placed at a single site or dispersed to multiple sites throughout the organization.

3. *Function:* Information systems development, operation, and maintenance activities can be undertaken by personnel at a single site or personnel at multiple sites throughout the organization.

These dimensions are only partially independent (Figure 3–3). Decisions on control must be made before decisions on location. Decisions on location, in turn, must be made before decisions on function. Decentralized control is difficult to sustain, for example, if all personnel and all hardware/software facilities

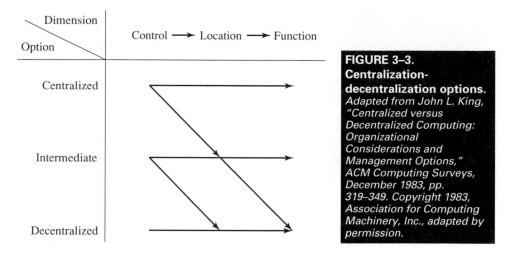

FIGURE 3–3. Centralization-decentralization options. *Adapted from John L. King, "Centralized versus Decentralized Computing: Organizational Considerations and Management Options," ACM Computing Surveys, December 1983, pp. 319–349. Copyright 1983, Association for Computing Machinery, Inc., adapted by permission.*

are located at a single site. Similarly, decentralized systems analysis and design is difficult to sustain if all analysts and designers are located at a single site. Subject to these types of constraints, however, top management have many options in choosing a configuration of control, location, and function for information systems activities.

Auditors must consider whether the particular centralization-decentralization configuration chosen for the information systems function in an organization seems consistent with the organization's history, environment, culture, and structure (see George and King 1991). For example, a centralized information systems function is unlikely to succeed in a highly decentralized organization. Similarly, a decentralized information systems function is unlikely to succeed in an organization where the founder and chief executive officer has dominated decision making over many years. Changed circumstances, however, can significantly affect the centralization-decentralization decision. For example, deregulation of an industry suddenly might force a previously centralized organization to decentralize so it can better respond to market demands. The information systems function might have to change accordingly.

In short, the structure of the information systems function must be congruent with the organization's needs. If congruency does not exist, personnel conflicts are likely to arise. For example, if a centralized information systems function exists in a heavily decentralized organization, divisional managers are likely to strongly resist their loss of control. The effectiveness and efficiency of the information systems function will be undermined as a result. Ultimately, asset safeguarding and data integrity could also be affected.

Internal Organization of the Information Systems Function

Historically, the information systems function was organized internally according to the major technology-based activities that had to be performed. Typically, a centralized data-processing or information systems department was established within organizations. The department usually had a systems-development group, a programming group, an operations group, a data-preparation group, and a general support or control group (Figure 3–4). These groups, in turn, were subdivided further. For example, the programming group might be broken up into a development group and a maintenance group.

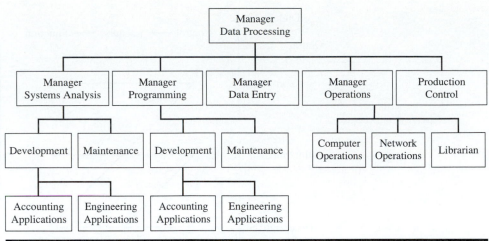

FIGURE 3–4. Traditional data processing organizational structure.

The authority and responsibility structure often had many levels, and each manager's span of control was constrained to a small number of immediate subordinates.

Today, the way the information systems function is organized internally can take many forms. In some organizations, no data-processing or information systems department exists because all information systems activities have been dispersed to user departments. Each user department is responsible for its own hardware/software facilities and the development, operation, and maintenance of its own systems. In these situations, auditors have the difficult task of evaluating the internal structure of an information systems function that is scattered throughout the organization. They should be concerned to see that each user department has established job positions and a reporting and responsibility structure that enable its information-processing needs to be met effectively and efficiently.

If a centralized information systems department does exist, the auditor would not want to see it still structured internally along traditional lines, unless perhaps it plays only a back-office support role. In most organizations today, many important types of information systems activities have devolved to user departments. For example, user departments might take responsibility for their own data entry via microcomputers located on their premises. Similarly, personnel in user departments might be sufficiently skilled to develop some types of computer applications themselves. In this light, effective information systems departments should be set up with a view to servicing the needs of end users who assume some responsibility for their own information-processing activities (see Earl 1989). Such departments tend to be structured around multi-skilled groups that have a customer focus (Figure 3–5). For example, they comprise groups of analysts and programmers who are responsible for particular application areas, client support or call center staff who advise users on personal computing hardware and software, workstation and network specialists who assist users to establish, maintain, and operate workstations, wide area networks, and local area networks. The organizational structures adopted in these departments are often flatter and more diverse than those used in traditional data-processing departments.

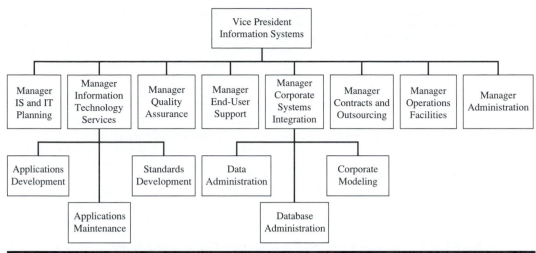

FIGURE 3–5. More recent information systems department organizational structure.

Regardless of the organization structure chosen for the information systems function, some of the typical jobs that must be performed include the following:

Job Title	Position Description
Systems analyst	Elicits information requirements for new and existing applications; designs information systems architectures to meet these requirements; facilitates implementation of information systems; writes procedures and user documentation.
Application programmer	Designs programs to meet information requirements; codes, tests, and debugs programs; documents programs; modifies programs to remove errors, better meet user requirements, and improve efficiency.
Systems programmer	Maintains and enhances operating systems software, network software, library software, and utility software; provides assistance when unusual systems failures occur.
Data administrator	Elicits the data requirements of the users of information systems services; formulates data policies; plans the evolution of the corporate databases; maintains data documentation.
Database administrator	Responsible for the operational efficiency of corporate databases; maintains access control over the database; assists users to use databases better.
Security administrator	Implements and maintains physical and logical security over the information systems function; monitors the status of security over the information systems function; investigates security breaches; assists users to design controls; maintains access control mechanisms.
Network administrator	Responsible for planning, implementing, and maintaining data and voice networks.

(cont.)

Job Title	*Position Description*
Workstation specialist	Advises on the selection, implementation, operation, and maintenance of different types of workstations, e.g., data entry workstations, end-user workstations, computer-aided design workstations.
End-user/client support specialist	Advises end users on analysis, design, and implementation of systems; determines needs for end-user tools; supports use of end-user tools, e.g., high-level languages.
Quality assurance specialist	Establishes quality control standards for the information systems function; ensures all new and modified systems conform with quality assurance requirements before they are released into production.
Executive information systems/decision support systems specialist	Elicits requirements and designs and builds executive information systems and decision support systems; undertakes corporate modeling; determines needs for new executive support and decision support tools.
Expert systems specialist	Elicits requirements; designs, builds, and maintains expert systems; documents expert systems; determines needs for new expert-systems tools.
Operations specialist	Plans and controls day-to-day operations; monitors and improves operational efficiency; assists with capacity planning.
Operator	Operates and maintains computer equipment.
Librarian	Maintains library of magnetic media and documentation.
Data entry operator	Prepares and enters data at workstations or terminals.
Administrative support clerk	Maintains and operates transfer pricing system; acquires consumables needed by the information systems function; registers and follows up on user complaints; maintains and operates information systems function accounting systems; handles user inquiries; collates and distributes reports.

Auditors should be concerned about two matters in terms of the ways information systems jobs are defined. First, the responsibilities of each job position must be clear. Moreover, incumbents must fully understand their duties, authority, and responsibilities. Unless employees have a clear understanding of their roles, the information systems function is unlikely to be effective and efficient. For example, if systems analysts and programmers are confused about their respective application system testing responsibilities, programs could be released into production with unacceptably high levels of errors.

Second, to the extent possible, the jobs performed within the information systems function should preserve separation of duties. Without separation of duties, errors and irregularities might remain undetected. For example, if employees are permitted to undertake both programming and computer operations activities, they can easily make unauthorized modifications to production programs. Asset safeguarding and data integrity objectives are then at risk. Throughout our examination of the different types of management controls in the remaining chapters of this part of the book, we focus on the importance of separation of duties as a means of reducing expected losses from unlawful events. A common theme is the unfortunate demise in separation of duties that occurs when information systems jobs migrate from a centralized information systems department to decentralized groups such as end-user departments. For example, end-user groups might take responsibility for systems analysis, programming, operations, database administration, data entry, and quality assurance. Inevitably, decentralized groups are smaller and, as a result, separation of duties is more difficult to enforce. Moreover, the persons performing critical information systems functions might not be skilled information systems professionals.

Location of the Information Systems Function

The location of the information systems function within the organizational hierarchy potentially has a significant impact on its effectiveness. Auditors first need to determine the importance that should be ascribed to the information systems function within an organization. They then must evaluate whether it is suitably located in the organizational hierarchy to afford it sufficient independence and authority.

One model we can use to help us with these decisions is McFarlan et al.'s (1983) strategic grid (see the section "Need for a Contingency Approach to Planning"). If we deem an organization to be a strategic organization—one in which information systems are important to both the current operations and future operations of the organization—it is likely to have a separate information systems department (or some group) that takes organizationwide responsibility for the information systems function. If this department is to be effective, it must be independent of user groups. It should not, for example, be under the aegis of the controller. Otherwise, its independence will be impaired, and other users will be less inclined to employ its services. Moreover, it should be placed high in the organizational hierarchy so its importance is recognized and its management has access to and influence on top-management decision making (Figure 3–6).

On the other hand, if we deem an organization to be a support organization—one in which information systems are important neither to the organization's current operations nor to its future operations—usually we will be less concerned about the placement of the information systems function. A support organization might not even have a separate information systems department. Instead, all information systems functions could be dispersed to user groups. If the organization does have a separate information systems department, however, it might be under the aegis of the major user department—for example, accounting or manufacturing (Figure 3–7). Other users are unlikely to perceive the department's independence to be a major issue. Therefore, its effectiveness should not suffer. Moreover, the information systems function is unlikely to be placed high in the organizational hierarchy because it does not play a major part in top-management decision making.

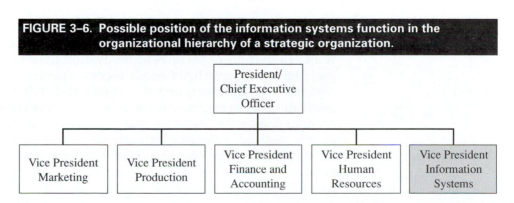

FIGURE 3–6. Possible position of the information systems function in the organizational hierarchy of a strategic organization.

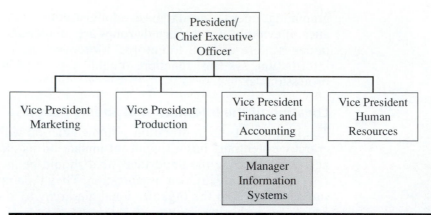

FIGURE 3–7. Possible position of the information systems function in the organizational hierarchy of a support organization.

EVALUATING THE LEADING FUNCTION

Leading is a complex management function designed to influence the behavior of an individual or group. The *purpose* of leading is to achieve harmony of objectives; that is, a person's or group's objectives must not conflict with the organization's objectives. The *process* of leading requires managers to motivate subordinates, direct them, and communicate with them.

Evaluating top management's ability to lead people might seem an abstruse type of activity for information systems auditors to perform. In many cases, auditors might feel they have insufficient training in the behavioral sciences to be able to perform an in-depth evaluation. Nevertheless, they must still attempt to gauge top management's ability to lead the information systems function. Ineffective leadership can result in system failure just as surely as erroneous design specifications can result in system failure: Information systems staff might not understand their overall purposes, they may be poorly motivated, they might not communicate the results they achieve, and so on. Consequently, they perform ineffectively and inefficiently. Poor-quality information systems are the outcome.

How, then, can we evaluate how well top management performs the leading function? We must have a basic understanding of three areas fundamental to effective leadership: how to motivate subordinates, how to match a leadership style with the circumstances of the job, and how to communicate clearly with subordinates.

Motivating Information Systems Personnel

The research and writings on human motivation are immense. Across many years, various major theories of motivation have been proposed—for example, Maslow's hierarchy-of-needs theory, Herzberg's motivator-hygiene theory, and Vroom's expectancy theory (see Holt 1993). Contingency theories of motivation, however, now seem to be the most compelling. These theories are founded on the argument that there is no one best way of motivating all people. Instead, strategies for motivating people need to change depending upon particular characteristics of an individual person and his or her environment.

To illustrate some of the contingency ideas that underlie current motivation theories, consider two well-paid systems analysts. On the basis of some types of unilateral motivation theories, top managers might feel that "challenging" work must be provided to both analysts to motivate them. Contingency theory emphasizes, however, that top managers must take into account individual differences before choosing motivators. One analyst, for example, might have a high propensity for dealing with uncertainty; the other might feel acute stress and anxiety when faced with high uncertainty. Clearly, it would be unwise to assign the latter analyst to a project involving high levels of task uncertainty, even though the project might be a challenging one. If this action were undertaken, the outcome could be a poorly designed and poorly implemented system.

Auditors usually have neither the time nor the expertise to evaluate whether each person who works in the information systems function is properly motivated. What they can do, however, is examine variables that often indicate when motivation problems exist—for example, staff turnover statistics, frequent failure of projects to meet their budget, and absenteeism levels.

Matching Leadership Styles with Information Systems Personnel and Their Jobs

Managers who adopt an effective leadership style exhibit certain characteristics: awareness—they understand the essentials of motivation and leadership; empathy—they can place themselves in the position of others; objectivity—they can examine and evaluate events unemotionally; and self-knowledge—they are aware of the results their actions evoke. They also tend to have a high need for achievement, are self-assured, and possess intelligence and creativity.

Leadership styles vary along a continuum from authoritarian to democratic. As with motivation, many organization theorists now advocate a contingency theory of leadership: There is no one best leadership style for all people and all situations; leadership styles must vary depending upon personalities and tasks. For example, if a project team is developing a decision-support system for strategic planning purposes and a high level of task uncertainty exists, a democratic style of leadership probably will be more successful than other leadership styles. Indeed, at different times, leadership of the group could switch to the person having most expertise with the problem being addressed at that point in time. Even within the group, some persons are likely to require more guidance than others. They might be inexperienced or lack confidence in their abilities. Thus, a more authoritarian style of leadership might be better suited to these personnel.

A thorny issue among researchers on leadership style is the extent to which people can adapt their leadership style to suit the demands of the situation. Some researchers argue that top managers will have difficulty changing lifelong patterns of behavior that affect how they lead. Thus, managers should be chosen who have a leadership style appropriate to the circumstances. Other researchers say that managers can be trained to vary their leadership styles to suit the demands of the job.

Again, auditors usually have neither the time nor the expertise to perform an in-depth evaluation of managers' ability to choose or match the appropriate leadership style for different personnel and different situations. Instead, as with motivation, they must be aware of indicators that suggest poor leadership: staff turnover, projects failing to meet budgets, and so on.

Effectively Communicating with Information Systems Personnel

Because so much work in the information systems function requires precise activities to be undertaken, effective and efficient communications between top management and subordinate staff are critical. Messages must be clearly understood, the integrity of messages must be ensured, and any message sent must obtain the attention of the receiver. In short, effective communications are essential to the conduct of high-quality planning, organizing, and controlling. Effective communications are also essential to promoting good relationships and a sense of trust among work colleagues.

Auditors can use both formal and informal sources of evidence to evaluate how well top managers communicate with their staff. The formal sources include information systems plans, documented standards and policies, the minutes of meetings, and memoranda distributed to information systems staff. We can evaluate this evidence to determine how clearly it communicates top management's intentions. We must be alert to those factors that undermine good communications—for example, messages that have unclear meanings, reflect stereotypical or jaded viewpoints, and have filtered out too much important information.

The informal sources of evidence include interviews with information systems staff about their level of satisfaction with the ways top managers communicate their wishes, observations of whether a sense of purpose seems to exist among members of a project group, and assessments of the general awareness that staff possess of activities being carried out within the information systems function. In interviews with top managers, the auditor will also form an opinion on how well they are likely to communicate with their staff.

Communications problems can sometimes have a direct, immediate effect. For example, the staff working on an information systems project fail to understand the directions given by top management, and a serious error is made in the design of a system. The effects of communications problems, however, could be indirect and long term. For example, over time, senior managers might lose the respect of their staff, and high turnover of information systems personnel could result. Auditors must try to assess both the short-run and long-run consequences of poor communications within the information systems function and to assess the implications for asset safeguarding, data integrity, system effectiveness, and system efficiency.

EVALUATING THE CONTROLLING FUNCTION

The controlling function involves determining when the actual activities of the information systems function deviate from the planned activities. In essence, the remainder of this book addresses the question of how well management performs the controlling function. Nevertheless, when evaluating top management, auditors should focus on only a subset of the control activities that should be performed—namely, those aimed at ensuring that the information systems function accomplishes its objectives at a global level.

Overall Control of the Information Systems Function

When top managers seek to exercise overall control of the information systems function, two questions arise:

1. How much should the organization be spending on the information systems function?

2. Is the organization getting value for money from its information systems function?

Each question concerns the auditor. Like management, we wish to evaluate whether the information systems function is effective. Moreover, we need to evaluate how well top management is monitoring the information systems function.

In terms of the first question, managers often look to industry averages to determine how much they should be spending on the information systems function. This strategy, called *benchmarking*, enables managers to assess how well their own information systems function is performing relative to information systems functions in other organizations. However, benchmarking can be problematic for several reasons. First, it reflects a reactive rather than a proactive stance by top management. It might be appropriate for support and factory organizations but not for turnaround or strategic organizations. Second, organizations might need to deviate purposefully from industry averages. For example, they could be information-technology laggards. High levels of spending may be required to ensure they catch up with industry norms. Third, spending on the information systems function is not tied to the overall corporate strategy. An industry-averages spending strategy reflects that management still see information systems as a back-office function rather than one that might be central to the accomplishment of the corporate mission.

Earl (1989) also argues that an industry-averages spending policy reflects that top management view the information systems function as an expense rather than a capital investment. If the information systems function is conceived as a capital investment, spending should continue while the net present value of returns on the information systems function is zero or positive. Unfortunately, capital-investment analysis of information systems projects is plagued by many problems, such as the large number of intangibles, the high risk of quick obsolescence, and the emergence of unforeseen externalities. (These matters are discussed further in Chapter 23.) Nonetheless, auditors should have more confidence that top managers are exercising careful control over the information systems function if they are making their decisions on how much to spend in light of the overall corporate plan and carefully undertaken capital investment analyses.

In terms of the second question, assessing whether an organization is getting value for money from its information systems function has proved to be notoriously difficult (see, e.g., Hitt and Brynjolfsson 1996). Individual information systems projects can be subjected to a post-audit to evaluate whether their benefits exceed their costs. This approach might be feasible where the information systems function is controlled centrally and development projects are confined to a few well-structured systems. It is more difficult to undertake, however, where the information systems function is dispersed widely throughout the organization, many development projects are in process, the organization's environment is volatile, and many projects have been embarked upon to stimulate innovation and change within the organization. In these situations, top managers are more likely to try to obtain some global assessment of how well the information systems function is performing.

Still another problem is the difficulty associated with sustaining any advantage obtained from information technology. In the case of strategic applications, for example, many organizations have found that their innovations are quickly copied by competitors and their abnormal returns dissipate rapidly.

Even where an organization uses information technology to achieve more moderate goals—say, improved efficiency—any abnormal returns obtained can dissipate quickly; once more, the innovation could be copied by competitors. In addition, new developments in information technology can soon render the innovation obsolete. In short, it is difficult to sustain long-run advantages with information technology. On the other hand, if an organization becomes a technology laggard, it could be forced from the marketplace because it can no longer compete effectively.

In spite of these difficulties, the basis for performing the global assessment should be the information systems strategic and operational plans. Actual performance should be evaluated against the long-run and short-run goals articulated in the plans. In the case of strategic and turnaround organizations, management should see evidence that the information systems function is bringing about the competitive gains and organizational change they deem necessary for the organization to survive. In the case of factory and support organizations, management should see evidence of effectiveness and efficiency improvements in the organization's portfolio of current systems.

Technology Diffusion and Control of the Information Systems Function

To some extent, top management's ability to exercise control over the information systems function depends on the ways different technologies have diffused throughout the organization. Perhaps the first researcher to argue along these lines was Nolan (1973). He proposed that the growth pattern of data-processing expenditures over time follows a sigmoid shape (Figure 3–8). The inflection points on this S-shaped curve represented critical times in the life of a data-processing installation. In the earliest version of his model, Nolan identified four stages:

State	*Characteristics of Stage*
Initiation	Installation of a computer; computer often located in the primary user department; controls are lacking; only a loose budget exists, no transfer pricing scheme is used; projects are assigned priorities on a first-in, first-out basis.
Contagion	Sales-oriented management intent on showing the usefulness of the computer; higher status given to data processing manager; lax controls engender rapid applications development; few standards; informal project control and a loose budget.
Control	Control-oriented management; computer moves out of primary user department; proliferation of controls to contain runaway budget; establishment of steering committee, standards, project control, post-audits; transfer pricing scheme introduced.
Integration	Resource-oriented planning and control; data processing becomes a separate functional area; some decentralization of systems analysts and programmers into user areas; increasing specialization of function within computer installation; advanced systems introduced, e.g., online real-time systems; refinement of controls and transfer pricing scheme; establishment of a master plan.

The data-processing era has clearly passed. Moreover, subsequent empirical research on the stage-growth model has called into question the bases used to identify the various stages (see, e.g., Benbasat et al. 1984). Nevertheless, the

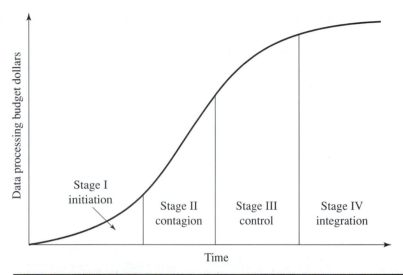

FIGURE 3–8. The S-shaped curve of the stage-growth hypothesis.
From Richard L. Nolan, "Managing the Computer Resource: A Stage Hypothesis,"
Communications of the ACM, July 1973, pp. 399–405. Copyright 1973, Association for
Computing Machinery, Inc., reproduced by permission.

S-shaped curve still seems to provide a good account of how organizations deal with new types of information systems technology—for example, office automation, data communications, and end-user computing (see, e.g., Huff et al. 1988). It appears to reflect the learning processes that organizations experience as they try to assimilate new information technology into their operations.

In this light, top managers and auditors can use the S-shaped curve to determine the appropriate types of control strategies that should be exercised over the information systems function. When new information technologies are introduced into an organization, for example, managers must allow some slack if they want to foster innovation and diffusion of the technologies. When the technologies have matured, however, more control can be exercised. At any time the organization is probably attempting to assimilate a number of information technologies. Accordingly, the control strategies used need to vary depending upon the particular state of assimilation of each technology.

Control of Information Systems Activities

Top managers should seek to achieve control over the activities undertaken by information systems personnel primarily through the establishment and enforcement of policies and standards. Policies provide broad, general guidelines for behavior. Standards provide specific guidelines for behavior. Both policies and standards should be well documented, promulgated widely, reviewed regularly, and updated promptly when the need arises. New staff must be informed of policies and standards as part of their initial indoctrination. Existing staff need to be reminded regularly of the policies and standards that govern their work and to be apprised of any changes to policies and standards that affect them.

The policies that top managers choose to establish depend primarily on the ways the information systems function is organized and the nature of the activities undertaken. If the information systems function is dispersed widely throughout the organization, for example, policies will be needed to provide guidance on the types of work that can be undertaken by divisions or end users and the types of work that should be undertaken by a centralized group of information systems professionals (assuming one exists). Similarly, if the distribution of information systems resources within an organization is an important goal, policies will be needed to provide guidance on the types of hardware and software that can be purchased to ensure compatibility among systems.

Across organizations, fewer variations are likely to exist in the types of information systems standards that will be required. Auditors should expect to see the following standards established, promulgated, and used:

Type of Standard	*Explanation*
Methods standards	Establish uniform practices and procedures to be followed. For example, they govern how analysis, design, and programming practices are to be carried out and how production application systems are to be operated.
Performance standards	Describe the resource usage that should be expected from undertaking different information systems activities and the quality of the results that should be achieved. For example, they specify the time it should take to test certain types of programs and the average response time that should be achieved with online systems.
Documentation standards	Describe how the activities undertaken within and the systems developed by the information systems function are to be documented. For example, they specify the documentation to be provided with programs that are prepared and the types of and quality of documentation that must be provided to users of application systems.
Project-control standards	Describe the ways individual projects undertaken within the information systems function are to be controlled. For example, they specify the major checkpoints at which reviews and sign-offs must be undertaken and the variance-monitoring procedures to be used.
Post-audit standards	Describe the ways in which *ex post* reviews of information systems activities are to be conducted. For example, they specify the makeup of the review team, the activities they must undertake, and the form of the final report that must be prepared.

Some of the specific activities undertaken by the information systems function also can be governed by service agreements written with the users of information services. For example, the service agreement might specify the average response times that online systems must achieve and the levels of assistance to be provided in light of user inquiries. (Chapter 8 discusses these matters further.)

Control over the Users of Information Systems Services

Top managers must develop policies and implement procedures that provide incentives for users to employ information systems services effectively and efficiently. Two basic strategies are commonly used: First, some type of review committee can examine users' requests for services, and second, a transfer pricing or chargeout scheme can be used.

If a review committee evaluates users' requests for computing services, it needs some type of mechanism to evaluate priorities. One approach is to use zero-based budgeting (ZBB). If ZBB is used, the first step is to reduce all information systems activities to a zero base. Next, all potential information systems activities are identified and structured into sequentially dependent incremental service levels. For each service level, estimates must be made of the expected benefits and resource consumption. Finally, the review committee must establish priorities. Cumulative resource consumption can then be calculated. When the level of information systems funding available has been determined, those activities that will be supported can be chosen.

The primary strength of the ZBB approach is that it highlights applications that have outlived their usefulness. Furthermore, it allows strong, centralized control to be exercised over information systems activities without placing onerous requirements on users to quantify the benefits and costs of applications for the review committee. When funding has been approved, users also have reasonable flexibility to expend resources as they see fit. Nevertheless, ZBB's capability to control day-to-day resource consumption is a moot issue; indeed, some type of chargeout mechanism might still be needed. Moreover, ZBB can become complex, perhaps even more complex than chargeout.

If top managers choose to control users via a transfer pricing or chargeout scheme, two decisions must be made. First, they must determine how they wish to view the providers of information systems services. Several options are available:

1. *Cost center:* The providers of information systems services are given the goal of recouping their costs.
2. *Profit center:* The providers of information systems services are given the goal of making a profit on their activities.
3. *Investment center:* The providers of information systems services are given responsibility for their investments in information technology and the goal of making an acceptable return on these investments.
4. *Hybrid center:* Different activities undertaken by the providers of information systems services are given different goals—cost recovery, reasonable profit, or an acceptable rate of return on investment.

Next, a specific transfer price or charge must be determined. Again, several options are available:

Type of Price/ Chargeout Transfer	*Explanation*
Allocated cost	At the conclusion of some time period, the costs for the period are charged to users on the basis of the proportion of services consumed by the users.
Standard cost	The long-run, average cost of providing different services is calculated, assuming (a) the services are provided effectively and efficiently and (b) reasonable levels of demand exist for the different types of services.
Dual price	The prices charged to users and the prices assigned to the providers of information systems services are different. For example, users might be charged on the basis of average cost, and the providers of information systems services might account for their activities on the basis of average cost plus a markup or market price.
Negotiated price	Users of information systems services negotiate a price for the provision of information systems services directly with the providers of the services.
Market price	Users are charged for the provision of services at current market prices for the services.

Information systems auditors must evaluate whether top management's choice of the means of control over the users of information systems services is likely to be effective. They need to adopt a contingency perspective when they carry out this evaluation. Some of the factors they must consider follow:

1. *Is the organization trying to stimulate innovation among users of information systems services or constrain consumption of the services?* If the goal is innovation, clearly oppressive controls are undesirable. Zero-based budgeting or chargeout might be used only for those services that have been assimilated into the organization.
2. *What level of accountability for consumption of information systems services has been assigned to users?* Conflict will arise if users are given accountability for their consumption of information systems services but they cannot control the resources they need to expend or the prices they are charged. A rigid ZBB system is unlikely to work in this situation, nor is an allocated-cost transfer price likely to work.
3. *What level of maturity has the organization attained with respect to information systems services?* If the users and providers of services are not mature, negotiated transfer-pricing schemes or market-pricing schemes, for example, are unlikely to work. The type of transfer-pricing systems chosen must be congruent with the users' abilities to make informed decisions about how they should employ information systems services.

Whatever the control mechanism chosen, users must be able to understand it and predict its effects. Transfer prices, for example, should be based on the number of transactions processed or the number of report pages produced rather than the central-processor cycles consumed or the number of disk input-output operations executed. Users can relate to the former measures; the latter are likely to be incomprehensible to user management.

SUMMARY

Information systems auditors' evaluation of top management is a difficult task. They must have a sound knowledge of the principles of good management. Furthermore, they must be able to determine when and how managerial functions should be performed if asset safeguarding, maintenance of data integrity, system effectiveness, and system efficiency are to be achieved.

A useful way of evaluating top managers is to examine the major functions they must perform: planning, organizing, leading, and controlling. For each of these functions, management theory and empirical research provide normative guidelines that auditors can use as a basis for evaluation. They must first determine what aspects of each function are critical to the organization from a control perspective. They must then evaluate top management's performance of the function against these normative guidelines.

Review Questions

3–1 Why is it important that auditors be capable of evaluating the quality of top management in relation to the information systems function?

3–2 How is the framework of managerial functions—planning, organizing, leading, and controlling—useful to auditors when they carry out an evaluation of top management's performance in relation to the information systems function?

3–3 Briefly describe each of the two types of major plans that must be formulated for the information systems function.

3–4 Why do auditors need to adopt a contingency perspective when they evaluate the quality of information systems planning within an organization?

3–5 Briefly explain how the information systems planning activities of organizations in the four different quadrants of the strategic grid might differ.

3–6 How might the extent of infusion and diffusion of information technology in an organization affect the nature of the information systems planning activities undertaken within the organization?

3–7 What are the functions of an information systems steering committee? Who should comprise the membership of the steering committee?

3–8 Why are auditors concerned about how well the information systems function is resourced?

3–9 For each of the following functions, identify two controls that top management should exercise:
a Personnel acquisition
b Personnel termination

3–10 Why should auditors be concerned about how well information systems staff are developed?

3–11 What impact has the widespread availability of minicomputers and microcomputers had on the decision to centralize or decentralize the information systems function?

3–12 What are the advantages and disadvantages of:
a Decentralizing systems analysis
b Centralizing programming

3–13 What are the three dimensions that need to be considered when deciding whether to centralize or decentralize the information systems function? How are these dimensions related?

3–14 Relative to the traditional ways in which the information systems function tended to be organized internally, how does it now tend to be organized internally?

3–15 Briefly explain two major concerns that we should have as auditors about the way information systems jobs are defined.

3–16 What concerns should auditors have about where the information systems function is located within organizations?

3–17 What are the three primary tasks that top management must perform if they are to provide effective leadership of personnel who work in the information systems function?

3–18 Identify three factors that might indicate that top management is not providing effective leadership of the information systems function.

3–19 Briefly explain two strategies that top management can use to exercise overall control over the information systems function.

3–20 Explain Nolan's stage-growth hypothesis. What is the relevance of the stage-growth hypothesis to the information systems auditor?

3–21 Briefly explain the difference between policies and standards. What are top management's responsibilities with respect to information systems policies and standards?

3–22 Briefly explain the nature of methods standards, performance standards, and documentation standards.

3–23 Briefly explain the nature of ZBB. How might ZBB be used to control users of information systems services?

3–24 Briefly explain the nature of transfer pricing or chargeout. How might transfer pricing or chargeout be used to control users of information systems services?

3–25 Briefly explain three factors that are likely to affect whether a transfer pricing scheme for information systems services is likely to be successful as a control mechanism.

Multiple-Choice Questions

3–1 Which of the following is *most likely* to be a characteristic of an information systems operational plan?

a Focuses on the next five years of information systems activities

b Explains how proposed applications systems will enhance the competitive advantage of the organization

c Identifies the major milestones in the development of major application systems

d Assesses the strengths and weaknesses of the current hardware/software platform

3–2 Which of the following is *most likely* to be a characteristic of the information systems plan for a turnaround organization?

a Primary responsibility for preparing the plan will be vested in staff who work in the information systems function

b The plan will focus primarily on existing application systems

c The link between the information systems plan and the overall corporate plan will be relatively unimportant

d A moderate to large amount of work will be required to prepare the plan

3–3 Which of the following is *most likely* to be a characteristic of the information systems plan prepared for a backbone organization?

a Planning activities will be centralized

b Only small amounts of planning will be needed

c Planning will focus primarily on the needs of end users

d Organizationwide planning activities are likely to be resisted

3–4 Which of the following is *most likely* to be a characteristic of the information systems steering committee established for a support organization?

a The committee will meet frequently to address information systems planning issues

b Middle managers are more likely to be represented on the committee than senior management

c The committee will focus primarily on long-run, strategic issues

d Membership of the committee will comprise a broad base of information systems users

3–5 Careful staff planning within the information systems function is necessary because:

a Information systems staff are much more costly to develop than staff in other functional areas of an organization

b The backlog of information systems work means the information systems function often is attempting more projects than it can handle

c Historically, information systems staff have been in short supply, and acquiring skilled staff can be very difficult

d Unfortunately, information systems personnel have often shown themselves to be unreliable

3–6 If programmers resign because they are disgruntled, they should be:

a Asked to finish their existing projects as soon as possible

b Asked to train a new employee to take over their job so continuity of work is achieved

c Assigned to a noncritical task immediately

d Assigned to maintenance work only and not new development work

3–7 Which of the following controls is *most likely* to ensure that the best person is chosen for a position within the information systems function?

a The existence of up-to-date, well-documented job specifications

b Bonding of the employee

c Indoctrination of the employee

d Screening applicants for mental and physical health

3–8 A disadvantage of decentralizing the information systems function is:

a It is more difficult to standardize and integrate systems within an organization

b Software is less attuned to the needs of individual users

c Substantial hardware diseconomies of scale result

d Data input errors from remote locations increase

3–9 When considering centralization versus decentralization of the information systems function, in which of the following orders will the three major dimensions of the decision most likely be considered?

a Control, function, location

b Control, location, function

c Location, control, function

d Function, location, control

3–10 In an organization in which high infusion and diffusion of information technology has occurred, which of the following is *most likely* to be the best structure for the information systems function?

a A hierarchy with many levels so that information systems personnel can be dispersed throughout the organization but still be centrally controlled

b A flat structure in which information systems personnel take on highly specialized roles

c A hierarchy with many levels so that both functional and project-oriented needs can be accommodated

d A flat structure with multiskilled groups of information systems personnel that have an end-user/customer focus

3–11 Separation of duties would be *most difficult* to enforce between:

a Workstation specialists and systems analysts

b Data administrators and quality assurance specialists

c Decision-support systems specialists and operations specialists

d Systems programmers and network administrators

3–12 In a strategic organization, the information systems function should be located under the:

a Controller

b Chief executive officer

c Marketing vice president

d Production vice president

3–13 Which of the following statements best describes how the information systems auditor will *most likely* evaluate how well top management leads information systems staff?

a The evaluation of how well top management motivates information systems staff will be given higher priority by the information systems auditor than the evaluation of how well top management communicates with them

b The information systems auditor will seek to ensure that top managers always use a democratic style of leadership when they deal with information systems staff

c A behavioral scientist will be employed to provide advice to the information systems auditor on how well top management motivates information systems staff, leads them, and communicates with them

d The information systems auditor will focus on variables such as staff turnover, absenteeism levels, and the frequency with which projects fail to meet deadlines to assess the quality of top management's leadership of the information systems function

3–14 For which type of organization are industry averages *most likely* to be a useful way of determining how much an organization should spend on its information systems function?

a Support organizations

b Factory organizations

c Turnaround organizations

d Strategic organizations

3–15 Which of the following should *not* be a reason given by top managers to account for difficulties they are having in evaluating whether their organization is getting value for money from its information systems function?

a Post-audits of information systems are difficult to conduct because many small development projects are scattered throughout the organization

b Information systems plans are unhelpful as a basis for evaluation because they rarely describe what is actually done in practice

c Many of the important benefits provided by the information systems function are intangible

d The long-run costs and benefits of an information systems are difficult to estimate because they can be quickly eroded through technological obsolescence or strategic moves by a competitor

3–16 Which of the following statements about Nolan's stage-growth model of computing is *true*?

a The contagion phase follows the control phase

b The model is more useful for organizing rather than planning and controlling the information systems function

c It appears to be a good description of information-technology innovation and diffusion in organizations

d The model provides a straightforward way of identifying when control over information systems growth should be exercised

3–17 Which of the following types of standards is *most likely* to act as a preventive control?

a Performance standards

b Post-audit standards

c Methods standards

d Documentation standards

3–18 An advantage of using ZBB as a means of controlling users of computer services is:

a It is easy to use

b It allows control of day-to-day resource consumption

c It is more likely to gain acceptance among user managers than a transfer pricing scheme

d It highlights applications that have outlived their usefulness

3–19 Dual prices are unlikely to be used as a transfer pricing scheme for information systems services where the information systems function is regarded as a:

a Cost center

b Investment center

    c Hybrid center

    d Profit center

3–20 Which of the following means of controlling the users of information systems services is unlikely to work well in an organization where users assume substantial responsibility for their use of computing resources?

    a Standard costs

    b Allocated costs

    c Negotiated prices

    d Market prices

Exercises and Cases

3–1 Innovation, Inc. is a company specializing in research and development. It accepts short-term research and development projects from other companies and aims to obtain results quickly. It has been very successful at achieving this objective (current sales $100 million).

You are a field auditor in a firm of external auditors that has just taken over the audit of Innovation. Because you have information systems audit expertise, you are assigned to evaluate the reliability of controls over the information systems function. Innovation uses computers extensively to support its activities. It has two large machines for both scientific and commercial activities. In addition, several hundred workstations are dispersed throughout the various departments of the company.

Required. (a) Your audit manager assigns you to evaluate the quality of information systems planning processes in Innovation as a basis for reaching an understanding of the internal-control structure used by Innovation. Outline the audit procedures you would use to carry out this task. (b) After completing your audit procedures, assume you find that top management within Innovation undertakes information systems planning on an informal basis only. For example, although they discuss future directions for the information systems function, they do not prepare a formal, documented information systems plan. They argue the costs associated with preparing a formal plan cannot be justified because of the uncertainty surrounding Innovation's activities. What implications does the absence of a plan have for the conduct of the remainder of the audit? How would you now proceed in terms of the audit procedures you recommend the audit team should use to gain an understanding of other elements of the internal-control structure? What are the likely implications for tests of controls and substantive tests that might be conducted during the remainder of the audit?

3–2 Public Funds Transfer Services (PUFTS) Ltd. is a new, rapidly expanding organization that offers public electronic funds transfer facilities to financial institutions. For example, it provides a public data communications network that enables its customers to share automatic teller machines (ATMs) and point-of-sale devices (POSs). Using the network, an account holder in any customer financial institution can enter transactions at a terminal device attached to the network and have these transactions routed to their host institution.

PUFTS is currently undertaking an intensive research and development program to develop new hardware and software to support public electronic funds transfer systems. Approximately 30 percent of current expenditures are devoted to research and development. The projects are high risk, but the potential payoffs are also high. If one of the projects is successful, for example,

PUFTS should be able to diversify its products and services and become an important player in the market for electronic data interchange (EDI) services.

The board of directors of PUFTS comprises representatives from each of the five organizations that are the major shareholders in PUFTS, plus the managing director of PUFTS. The makeup of the board is as follows:

1	John Jones	Director from NBS, a merchant bank
2	Georgia Williams	Director from First National Bank; strong background in accounting
3	Helen Smith	Director from Cost-Less Clothes, a major retailer using POS and with strong interests in EDI; strong background in marketing
4	Ian Reeves	Director from SFSL, a savings and loan association; strong background in accounting
5	Arthur Webb	Director from Second Federal Bank; strong background in general management
6	Amy Coulster	Managing Director of PUFTS; strong background in computer science, especially data communications

To date, PUFTS has not made a profit. After reviewing budgets prepared by Amy Coulster, however, the board is convinced that a profit will be made for the first time in the coming financial year. Coulster has argued that losses have been incurred because of the substantial investments in research and development. Payoffs from these expenditures are only just beginning to occur.

PUFTS has just "gone public," and you are an information systems auditor in the external audit firm hired to perform the audit. During your review of information systems management controls, you note there is no steering committee. When you raise this matter with Coulster, she argues that PUFTS is too small for a steering committee. Moreover, she argues that (a) the board fulfils the role of a steering committee and (b) she is able to brief the board fully on any matters that concern them because most of the technological innovations are her own ideas. Coulster argues emphatically that PUFTS cannot afford to have a steering committee, given its current size, and that she can provide the technical briefings required by the board.

Required. What impact, if any, does the absence of a steering committee have on the way you will approach the audit? What recommendations, if any, would you provide to the board in light of the absence of a steering committee?

3–3 Harrison University is a large university with about 30,000 students offering a wide range of courses in the humanities and the physical, social, behavioral, health, agricultural, biological, and engineering sciences. The existing computing facilities are divided between two groups: an academic computing center and an administrative computing center. Each group has its own hardware, software, personnel, and so on, and each operates independently of the other group. The academic computing center services all teaching and research needs. The administrative computing center services all other computing needs—payroll, student records, budgeting, financial planning, and so on.

Currently the facilities of the administrative computing center are heavily overloaded. A steering committee of the university has been formed to examine the problem. The steering committee has been given wide terms of reference. In recent years, the university has found it increasingly difficult to find sources of private funding and to obtain federal funding. The president of the university has asked the steering group to consider the possibility of amalgamating the academic and administrative computing groups, selling off the existing hardware, and purchasing a large machine that will service both groups. He feels that centralizing computer facilities could produce economies of scale. Because the academic computer will have substantial excess capacity during the interim period, he also questions whether some administrative applications might not be shifted to the academic computer.

Required. You are a member of the internal audit staff of the university. The chair of the steering committee has asked the manager of internal audit for his views on the proposed changes, and he has asked you to brief him. Prepare a memo outlining the advantages and disadvantages of the change from an internal audit viewpoint.

3–4 Autotool Ltd. is a medium-size company that designs and manufactures a range of industrial robots. The company was started 11 years ago by two young entrepreneurial engineers. One had a background in computer engineering. She had a flair for research and design work. The other had a background in mechanical engineering. She had a flair for recognizing the best research ideas in her field and implementing them in practice. Under their guidance, the company obtained a reputation as a high-quality, reliable supplier of industrial robots. It grew steadily, and after its first decade of operations it was in a sound financial position.

A year ago, however, both engineers sold their shares in the company at a substantial profit to a larger competitor. They had decided to start another business that specialized in a niche market for a particular type of industrial robot.

When the new management took over Autotool, they went to tender for audit services. Your audit firm won the tender. You and your colleagues are currently undertaking your first audit of the new client. Because you are the senior information systems auditor within your firm, you are responsible for assessing controls over the information systems function. You are currently undertaking audit activities as a basis for obtaining an understanding of Autotool's internal-control structure.

In the course of your review of top-management controls, you note that high staff turnover has occurred (25 percent) in the previous 12 months. In addition, two Vice Presidents of Information Systems have come and gone over this same period. The current Vice President of Information Systems was appointed only two months ago. He was hired to the position after spending 25 years as the information systems manager of a small retailing company.

When you review staff records, you notice that the current staffing situation differs markedly from the situation that existed during the first ten years. Turnover was low during this period (3 percent), and the same person had been in charge of information systems throughout the entire time. He had left suddenly shortly after the new management took over.

When you conduct interviews with information systems staff, you detect that many appear to have a low commitment to the company. Many seem to be working long hours on a large number of different projects. They seem preoccupied and distracted. Some also appear uncertain about what management and users want in the systems they are designing and implementing. During an interview with a woman who has been there for many years, she comments obliquely that "things aren't what they used to be." She withdraws, however, when you ask her to explain what she means.

You are concerned that your findings could have implications for the conduct of the remainder of the audit. You note, however, that all of Autotool's financial systems are based on software packages that have been purchased from reputable, outside vendors. Internal software development work focuses primarily on engineering applications to support research and the design, implementation, and operation of robots.

Required. Write a brief report outlining what you believe to be the implications of your findings. How will you now proceed with the rest of your examination of the reliability of controls over the information systems function?

3–5 Clayton University is a medium-size, tertiary institution that seeks to offer high-quality graduate education, especially in the professional disciplines. Many of its staff have distinguished research records, and its senior administrative staff continue to emphasize research as a primary goal of the university. Clayton is fortunate to have a substantial endowment that finances many special projects aimed at promoting excellence within the university.

Three years ago, Clayton purchased a powerful mainframe computer to support the work of its academic staff and its graduate students. At that time Clayton's academic staff took the opportunity to argue strongly against the chargeout scheme for mainframe computer services that was in operation within the university. Both academics and students were charged at average costs on a real-money basis. In other words, all users had to pay via research funds, fees, and so on, for the computing services they consumed. Academic staff argued the chargeout system was stifling research and teaching because neither they nor their students could afford the charges that were being levied. The charges were set at the beginning of each academic year based on the expected operational costs that would be incurred in that year, a levy for future capital purchases, and the average level of consumption of services that had occurred over the previous three years. These charges continued to increase, particularly as more users began to employ microcomputers to provide the computing services they needed. Microcomputer costs could be "buried" in general, departmental administrative charges that were funded by block allocations from the central administration to each department. The academics argued, however, that microcomputers were not always the best deployment of resources available to support computing activities.

When the feasibility study for the new mainframe was being undertaken, the academic staff argued that the chargeout scheme should be terminated and that computing should become a free service within the university. They contended that this action would foster innovative research and teaching and that better decisions would be made on whether to use mainframe, minicomputer, or microcomputer services to support different types of research and teaching activities. They argued vehemently about the repressive nature of the chargeout scheme and pointed to slippages in their national research standing as a manifestation of the problem. Their representatives argued that computing services should be funded by an off-the-top allocation of funds to the computing center. In other words, the computing center should receive a grant before funding allocations to departments within the university were made. In light of substantial pressure and discontent, the university administration agreed to abolish the chargeout scheme, fund mainframe computing services via an off-the-top allocation, and make use of the new mainframe free.

The decision to make computing services free was to be reviewed after three years, and the review is currently in progress. The review team has found that many users of mainframe computing services are experiencing substantial difficulties with long response times. Overall, users are expressing acute dissatisfaction and anger with their inability to use mainframe computing services effectively and efficiently.

In light of the users' dissatisfaction, the review team undertook an examination of mainframe usage. One of their major findings was the existence of a large number of unauthorized users of the mainframe. Over the three-year period, academic staff had been careless about removing student accounts from the mainframe. When some students graduated, they continued to use the dial-in facilities on the mainframe to undertake computing activities. For example, they used the mainframe to support their consulting activities. Substantial amounts of computer time have been consumed through unauthorized use of the mainframe.

Another of the review team's findings was the high resource consumption of a few academic users. These users were running long, resource-intensive simulations to support their research. They had devised ways to give their programs high priority, and other users of the mainframe experienced long response times when these simulation programs were running.

Required. You are the internal auditor of Clayton University. The review team has asked your advice about whether a chargeout scheme should be reintroduced to help overcome some of the difficulties being experienced with the mainframe. If you are in favor of a chargeout scheme, they would also like your advice on the type of chargeout scheme you wish to see implemented. If you are not in favor of a chargeout scheme, they would like your suggestions on any control measures they should implement. Write a brief report responding to their request.

Answers to Multiple-Choice Questions

3–1	c	**3–6**	c	**3–11**	d	**3–16**	c
3–2	d	**3–7**	a	**3–12**	b	**3–17**	c
3–3	a	**3–8**	a	**3–13**	d	**3–18**	d
3–4	b	**3–9**	b	**3–14**	a	**3–19**	a
3–5	c	**3–10**	d	**3–15**	b	**3–20**	b

REFERENCES

Benbasat, Izak, Albert S. Dexter, Donald H. Drury, and Robert C. Goldstein (1984), "A Critique of the Stage Hypothesis: Theory and Empirical Evidence," *Communications of the ACM* (May), 476–485.

Benbow, Gary (1990), "Computer Abuse in Australia," *The EDP Auditor Journal,* II, 50–57.

Boynton, Andrew C., and Robert W. Zmud (1987), "Information Technology Planning in the 1990's: Directions for Practice and Research," *MIS Quarterly* (March), 59–71.

Earl, Michael J. (1989), *Management Strategies for Information Technologies.* Hemel Hempstead, Hertfordshire: Prentice Hall International (UK) Ltd.

Ginzberg, Michael J., and Jack J. Baroudi (1988), "MIS Careers—A Theoretical Perspective," *Communications of the ACM* (May), 586–594.

George, Joey F., and John Leslie King (1991), "Examining the Computing and Centralization Debate," *Communications of the ACM* (July), 62–72.

Hitt, Lorin M., and Eric Brynjolfsson (1996), "Productivity, Business Profitability, and Consumer Surplus: Three Different Measures of Information Technology Value," *MIS Quarterly* (June), 121–142.

Holt, David H. (1993), *Management: Principles and Practice*, 3d ed. Upper Saddle River, NJ: Prentice-Hall.

Huff, Sid L., Malcolm C. Munro, and Barbara H. Martin (1988), "Growth Stages of End User Computing," *Communications of the ACM* (May), 542–550.

King, John Leslie (1983), "Centralized versus Decentralized Computing: Organizational Considerations and Management Options," *Computing Surveys* (December), 319–349.

McFarlan, F. Warren, James L. McKenney, and Phillip J. Pyburn (1983), "The Information Archipelago—Plotting a Course," *Harvard Business Review* (January–February), 145–156.

Mendelson, Haim (1987), "Economies of Scale in Computing: Grosch's Law Revisited," *Communications of the ACM* (December), 1066–1072.

Niederman, Fred, James C. Brancheau, and James C. Wetherbe (1991), "Information Systems Management Issues for the 1990s," *MIS Quarterly* (December), 474–500.

Nolan, Richard L. (1973), "Managing the Computer Resource: A Stage Hypothesis," *Communications of the ACM* (July), 399–405.

Porter, Michael E. and Victor E. Millar (1985), "How Information Gives You Competitive Advantage," *Harvard Business Review* (July–August), 149–160.

Raghunathan, Bhanu, and T.S. Raghunathan (1990), "Planning Implications of the Information Systems Strategic Grid: An Empirical Investigation," *Decision Sciences* (Spring), 287–300.

Sullivan, Cornelius H., Jr. (1985), "Systems Planning in the Information Age," *Sloan Management Review* (Winter), 3–12.

Systems Development Management Controls

Chapter Outline

Chapter Key Points

■ Auditors conduct three types of reviews of the systems development process. First, they can *participate* as a member of the systems development team. The objective is to improve the quality of a specific system as it is designed and implemented. Second, they can conduct a *postimplementation review* in which they evaluate a specific system after it has been implemented. The objective is to improve the quality of the systems development process in general and the specific system in particular. Third, they can evaluate the systems development process *in general*. The objective is to determine whether in light of the quality of systems development controls they can reduce the extent of substantive testing needed to reach an audit opinion.

■ To be capable of evaluating the systems development process, auditors need a normative model against which they can compare the systems development practices encountered. They use the model to pinpoint strengths and weaknesses.

■ Six major normative models of the systems development process that have been proposed are (a) the systems development life-cycle approach, which emphasizes the importance of well-controlled work phases; (b) the sociotechnical design approach, which emphasizes the importance of jointly optimizing the technical system as well as the social system; (c) the political approach, which emphasizes the importance of understanding the effects that systems can have on the distribution of organizational power; (d) the soft-systems approach, which provides ways of helping decision makers learn about ill-structured problems; (e) the prototyping approach, which provides ways of helping resolve the uncertainty often surrounding systems-design tasks; and (f) the contingency approach, which emphasizes that the way systems development is undertaken must be adapted in light of the organizational context in which the system is being designed and implemented.

■ In this book, the approach we adopt to selecting a normative model of the systems development process is the contingency approach. Auditors must vary their expectation of the systems development tasks that should be undertaken in light of such factors as the breadth and depth of impact of the system, the uncertainty surrounding the system, and the likely impact on the quality of working life of users.

■ To provide the basis for evaluating the systems development process, the following 13 phases provide an *agenda of issue*s that auditors must consider: (a) problem/opportunity definition, (b) management of the change process, (c) entry and feasibility assessment, (d) analysis of the existing system, (e) formulation of strategic requirements, (f) organizational and job design, (g) information processing systems design, (h) application software acquisition and development, (i) hardware/system software acquisition, (j) procedures development, (k) acceptance testing, (l) conversion, and (m) operation and maintenance.

■ The specific tasks performed in each phase and the ways in which they are performed should vary depending upon the nature of the system to be developed and the specific context in which it is being developed. Both designers and auditors must know how to vary their work practices to reflect these contingencies.

INTRODUCTION

Systems development management has responsibility for those functions concerned with analyzing, designing, building, implementing, and maintaining information systems. In many ways, how we undertake these functions is still an art. Although we have made substantial progress in terms of providing theory and heuristics to guide our practice, good systems development work still relies on the insights, intuition, and experience of individual systems analysts and designers.

This chapter describes how we can undertake an audit of the systems development management subsystem. We begin by considering three different ways to approach the audit: as a participant in the systems development process, a postimplementation reviewer of a specific application system, or a reviewer of the systems development process in general. Next we examine some major approaches intended to provide normative guidelines for systems development. Finally, we consider the major tasks performed during systems development, the controls exercised over these tasks, and the ways we might evaluate the reliability of these controls.

APPROACHES TO AUDITING SYSTEMS DEVELOPMENT

Historically, a major debate among information systems auditors has focused on the question of whether they should become involved as a member of the project team during the systems development process. Those who favor involvement point out that errors are more costly to correct at later stages in the systems development process. Thus, auditors can play a valuable role by indicating where systems development deficiencies exist at an early stage. On the other hand, those who oppose involvement argue their independence will be undermined if they must later evaluate systems they have helped design and implement. They contend that information systems auditors should evaluate the systems development process only in an *ex post* review capacity.

While each of us might have a view on the merits of the respective arguments, we must nevertheless understand both approaches to carrying out an audit of the systems development process. The audit objectives and the ways to undertake evidence collection and evaluation will differ depending on the type of audit conducted.

When we *participate* in the systems development process, we are seeking to ensure the development process employed will lead to the production of a *specific* application system that safeguards assets, maintains data integrity, and achieves systems effectiveness and efficiency. In the context of the specific system to be developed, we must first form a view on how the systems development process should be undertaken. Next we collect evidence on the actual conduct of systems development activities. Our primary means of evidence collection is observation of the activities of the other members of the systems development team. In light of the evidence we collect, we then advise the systems development team of any deficiencies we identify.

When we conduct an *ex post* audit of the systems development process, we can have two objectives. First, we might be seeking to identify what went wrong and what went right during the development of a *specific* system and perhaps how the system should be modified to better meet its objectives. Our review is conducted after the system has been developed and implemented and often after the system has been operational for some time. At the outset we consider the nature of the system and the organizational context in which it has been built and operated. We then determine the systems development process we believe would have been best for the system. Next, we collect evidence on how the system was actually developed so we can compare what occurred against our expectations. In light of this comparison, we can generate hypotheses about the likely strengths and weaknesses of the system. We then collect evidence to test our hypotheses.

We might also carry out an *ex post* audit, however, for another reason. We might be hoping to reduce the extent of substantive testing needed to establish the basis for our audit opinion on the assertions management makes about the financial statements or systems effectiveness and efficiency. The audit proceeds according to the overall approach described in Chapter 2. First, we use interviews, observations, and a review of standards to obtain an understanding of systems development controls in general. Next we evaluate the level of control risk associated with systems development as a management control subsystem. If we do not assess the control risk at the maximum level, we then design and execute tests to evaluate whether the controls on which we wish to rely are operating effectively. For example, we might select a sample of application systems that have recently been developed and check the documentation for these systems to determine whether systems development personnel have complied with design and testing standards.

In summary, therefore, we might conduct three types of audits of the systems development process:

1. *Concurrent audit:* Auditors are members of the systems development team. They assist the team in improving the quality of systems development for the specific system they are building and implementing (Gallegos 1988).
2. *Postimplementation audit:* Auditors seek to help an organization learn from its experiences in the development of a specific application system. In addition,

they might be evaluating whether the system needs to be scrapped, continued, or modified in some way.

3. *General audit:* Auditors evaluate systems development controls overall. They seek to determine whether they can reduce the extent of substantive testing needed to form an audit opinion about management's assertions relating to the financial statements or systems effectiveness and efficiency.

An external auditor is more likely to undertake general audits rather than concurrent or postimplementation audits of the systems development process. Nevertheless, clients might ask external auditors to participate in the systems development process if they believe their involvement will reduce overall audit costs or they value their advice. Similarly, they may ask external auditors to undertake a postimplementation review if they believe they can provide cost-effective advice. For internal auditors, management might require that they participate in the development of material application systems or undertake postimplementation reviews of material application systems as a matter of course.

Both external and internal auditors must strive to preserve their independence. They should not conduct *ex post* reviews of any systems in which they were a member of the systems development team. They cannot independently evaluate their own work! They can also protect their independence by ensuring that they have sufficient knowledge and skills to be able to form independent judgments about the quality of systems development work. With careful planning, auditors can mitigate some of the concerns that arise about participation in the systems development process.

NORMATIVE MODELS OF THE SYSTEMS DEVELOPMENT PROCESS

When we evaluate the systems development process, we need a normative model if we are to be able to undertake the evaluation. We compare actual practice against this model to identify discrepancies and to pinpoint where controls are operating effectively or ineffectively. Life would be simpler for auditors if there was just one normative model. Unfortunately, we now recognize that our normative model must vary, depending on the particular circumstances we confront. For example, the standards applied to a small system developed by a group of end users employing a high-level language must be different from those applied to the development of a large, technologically complex system.

In the following subsections, we briefly examine some of the major factors that have influenced the normative models of the systems development process now used. This background will help you understand why no single model of systems development is adequate as a basis for audit evaluation. It will also help you to understand how to shape the normative model to accommodate the situation at hand.

Systems Development Life-Cycle Approach

Traditionally, systems development personnel have thought about the systems development process in terms of a life cycle comprising various major phases. The life-cycle approach arose from early efforts to apply project management techniques to the systems development process. Historically, many systems were characterized by massive cost overruns, inadequate economic evaluations, inadequate system design, management abdication, poor communications, inadequate direction, and so on. The life-cycle approach was developed to help overcome

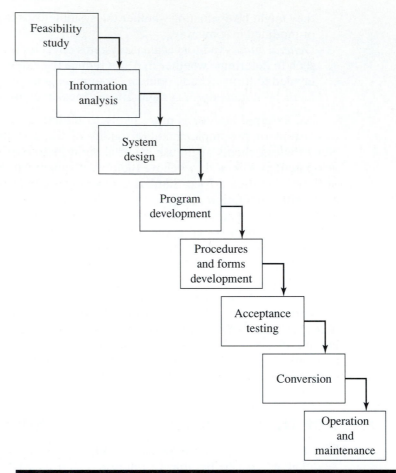

FIGURE 4–1. Traditional life-cycle or waterfall model of systems development.

some of these problems. By clearly defining tasks in terms of the life cycle, project management and control techniques can be applied. To develop high-quality systems, each phase of the life cycle should be planned and controlled, comply with developed standards, be adequately documented, be staffed by competent personnel, have project checkpoints and signoffs, and so on.

There are many forms of the systems development life cycle (see, e.g., Burch 1992). A typical version, however, comprises the following eight phases (Figure 4–1):

Phase	*Explanation*
Feasibility study	Applying cost-benefit criteria to the proposed application.
Information analysis	Determining user information requirements.
System design	Designing the user interface, files to be used, and information processing functions to be performed by the system.
Program development	Designing, coding, compiling, testing, and documenting programs.
Procedures and forms development	Designing and documenting systems procedures and forms for the users of the system.

Phase	*Explanation*
Acceptance testing	Final testing of the system and formal approval and acceptance by management and users.
Conversion	Changeover from the old system to the new system.
Operation and maintenance	Ongoing production running of the system and subsequent modification and maintenance in light of problems detected.

The life-cycle approach does not imply that all these phases must be carried out serially. Some can proceed concurrently; for example, procedures and forms development can occur at the same time program development is undertaken. Moreover, some phases might require several iterations; for example, as programs are developed, the system design might have to be modified to improve processing efficiency. The general notion, however, is that phases "cascade" into new phases—hence, the life-cycle approach is sometimes called the "waterfall model" of systems development.

Sociotechnical Design Approach

After substantial experience with the life-cycle approach to systems development, information systems researchers and practitioners recognized it was not a panacea for the problems encountered during the design and implementation of information systems. In particular, severe behavioral problems sometimes arose when the life-cycle approach was used. Users might show apathy or outright resistance to a proposed system, or they might even attempt to sabotage the system.

In the mid to late 1970s, a new approach emerged that focussed on these persistent behavioral problems (see, e.g., Bostrom and Heinen 1977*a*, 1977*b*). This approach, called the sociotechnical design approach, seeks to optimize two systems jointly: (a) the *technical system*, in which the objective is to maximize task accomplishment; and (b) the *social system*, in which the objective is to maximize the quality of working life of system users (Figure 4–2). Sociotechnical design proponents argued that many problems arose because the life-

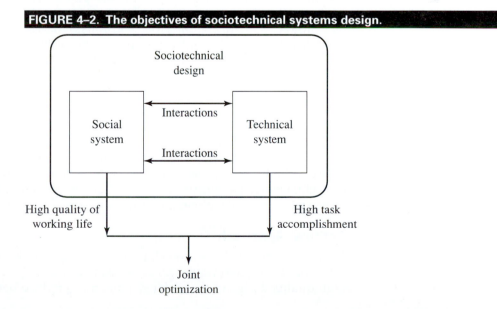

FIGURE 4–2. The objectives of sociotechnical systems design.

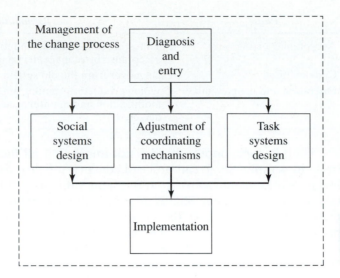

FIGURE 4-3. Major phases in the sociotechnical systems design process.

cycle model had inadequate procedures for dealing with the social system. For example, it did not adequately take into account the impact a system might have on its users via a changed job or organizational structure design. In addition, sociotechnical design proponents argued that systems development personnel were poorly trained in the social aspects of information systems. They contended that designers had limited perceptions of how information systems might affect a user's quality of working life.

Like the life-cycle model, the sociotechnical design approach has several major phases (Figure 4–3):

Phase	Explanation
Diagnosis and entry	Problem identification; determining whether the organization is amenable to change; analysis of the social and technical systems and coordinating mechanisms; determining the strategic requirements for the system.
Management of the change process	Ensuring throughout the design process that the organization is amenable to change; facilitating adaptation to change.
System design	Design of both the technical and social systems.
Adjustment of coordinating mechanisms	Changes in one subsystem might necessitate changes in another subsystem; e.g., a reward system might have to be adjusted because the information processing system supports a new job design.
Implementation	Installation of the new sociotechnical system.

Note from the brief description of these phases that they do not negate the importance of the traditional life-cycle model. Project management techniques and a systematic approach to design, for example, are still critical. The sociotechnical design approach, however, forces designers to take a broader and richer view of the development process.

Political Approach

Early versions of the sociotechnical design approach emphasized the importance of always involving users in the systems development process to promote high-quality design of the social system and to reduce behavioral problems that might arise during implementation. As experience with the approach was gained, however, it became clear that user involvement might be problematical. In some cases, users employed their opportunities to be involved with systems development to undermine progress. For example, if they participated in job redesign, they might procrastinate and vacillate to the point where the systems development process stalled.

In the late 1970s and early 1980s, the political approach to information systems development emerged to try to explain why user involvement was not always an appropriate strategy. It identified the need for designers to take into account the ways in which information systems could change the distribution of power within organizations. For example, Markus (1981) points out a new information system can change existing organizational power structures in three ways. First, systems provide access to information that could facilitate or inhibit a person's decision-making abilities. Because power is a function of decision-making capabilities, changes to information channels can modify the power structure. Second, systems can alter one person's ability to influence the behavior and performance of another. For example, systems can provide access to performance data previously unavailable for evaluation reviews. Third, systems can be used as a source of symbolic power. Managers might promote an image that they can influence outcomes via the system, even if this is not really the case.

When the political approach to information systems development is adopted, a critical task is to study the history of the organization. By studying the organization's history, the designer can evaluate whether the desired system will leave the existing power structure intact or necessitate changes to the power structure. Development and implementation strategies must vary depending on the impact the proposed system will have on the existing power structure (Figure 4–4).

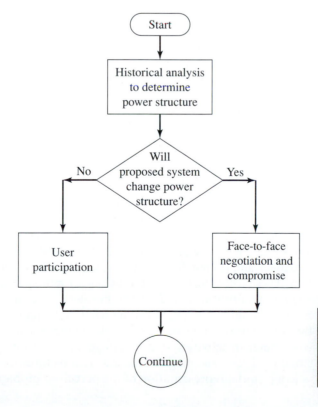

FIGURE 4–4. The political approach and user involvement in the systems-development process.

If the proposed system will leave the existing power structure intact, user participation in the design process is an important means of ensuring congruence between the system and the organization. Users will attempt to have the system design manifest the existing power structure. Serious problems can arise if an important user group is omitted from the design deliberations, because their concerns may not be incorporated into the design.

If the proposed system necessitates changes to the existing power structure, however, design and implementation is more difficult. Indeed, user participation might be counterproductive because users feel they are being manipulated in situations in which the conclusions are foregone. Alternatively, they might attempt to change the design to be congruent with their own political motives. Participation must be replaced by meaningful negotiations between designers and users where compromise is an accepted outcome. In this light, Keen (1981) suggests that explicit contracts for change must be obtained. Moreover, designers must seek out resistance early, build personal rapport, co-opt users from the start, and attempt face-to-face negotiations.

Notwithstanding these tactics, for some systems development projects consensus might be impossible. The designer might confront users who employ counterimplementation strategies to sabotage the system. For example, they might engage in protracted negotiations and meetings in an attempt to increase the costs of building the system and to delay or prevent its implementation. How these difficulties can be overcome successfully is still unclear, but designers might have to invoke their own power base by having a "fixer" who is a senior organizational sponsor.

Soft-Systems Approach

An important tenet underlying traditional approaches to information systems development is that users understood and could articulate their systems requirements. Indeed, users were often denigrated by information systems professionals if they could not communicate their needs.

In the mid to late 1970s, however, Checkland (1981) and his colleagues developed an approach that was designed to assist decision makers to learn about and to better understand ill-structured problems. They called their approach "soft systems methodology" (SSM) because it focused on *learning* and *innovation* in a problem situation (Davies and Ledington 1991). They distinguished their approach from "hard systems" approaches that assumed at the outset that decision makers had specific goals and a substantial understanding of the problem situation.

SSM involves seven steps (Figure 4–5):

1. *Recognize the problem situation:* Someone indicates that a problem situation exists. Three roles must be considered and adopted: (a) the problem solver, who uses SSM to structure discussion, debate, and negotiation about the problem situation; (b) the problem owner, who perceives that the situation is problematical; and (c) the decision taker, who has the power to change the situation. These roles can be adopted by one or more persons.
2. *Express the problem situation:* The problem solver uses SSM to assist stakeholders (problem solver, problem owner, decision taker) to understand better the roles, norms, and values that underlie the problem situation and to uncover "human activity systems" that appear relevant to improving the problem situation. Free-hand diagrams called "rich pictures" are often drawn to provide a pictorial representation of the perceived problem situation.

3. *Produce "root definitions" of relevant systems:* The stakeholders describe each relevant system in terms of customers, actors, transformation, Weltanschauung (underlying world view), owner, and environment—the so-called CATWOE of SSM.
4. *Develop conceptual models of relevant systems:* Using "systems thinking," the stakeholders develop an ideal model of the relevant human activity systems.
5. *Compare conceptual models with perceived problem situation:* The ideal model is compared with the perceived problem situation to identify similarities and differences. The comparison process iterates through exploration, diagnosis, and design as the stakeholders improve their understanding of the problem situation and refine and grow more confident in their conceptual models.
6. *Identify desirable and feasible changes:* The comparison process should allow changes to be identified that will improve the human activity systems. These changes must then be evaluated to determine whether they are feasible.
7. *Take action to improve problem situation:* The stakeholders must take action to implement the desired and feasible changes identified.

SSM initially was not developed specifically to address information systems development needs. Rather, its focus was ill-structured problems in general. In the early 1980s, however, some of its proponents recognized it could assist users to articulate their information systems requirements in situations in which substantial uncertainty surrounded the system to be developed. Accordingly, they adapted existing information systems development approaches to incorporate SSM procedures. These efforts were perhaps the first to recognize formally that uncertainty was an intrinsic part of many information systems development situations and that developers and users needed tools to help resolve the problems that arose when uncertainty existed.

FIGURE 4–5. Major steps in soft-systems methodology.
Adapted from Soft Systems Methodology in Action, by Peter Checkland and Jim Scholes. Copyright John Wiley & Sons Limited, 1990. Reproduced with permission.

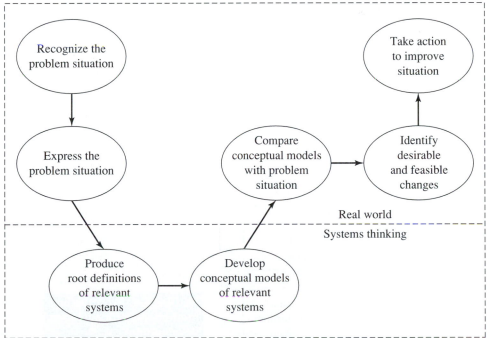

Prototyping Approach

In the mid-1980s, two technological developments had a major impact on the approaches used to develop information systems. First, the appearance of powerful, low-cost microcomputers fueled the diffusion of computing responsibilities away from centralized information systems facilities to end-user areas. Many end-user managers seized the opportunity to develop their own computing capabilities. They were frustrated by major development backlogs and their belief that information systems professionals were not responsive to their needs. In addition, they disliked the loss of organizational power associated with relinquishing control over their information systems to other parties.

Second, powerful, high-level, end-user programming languages began to appear. These languages had a twofold effect. In some cases they allowed end users to develop their own systems. Thus, end users were no longer completely reliant on information systems professionals for their systems development work. In addition, high-level languages facilitated rapid development of information systems prototypes that could be used as a basis for experimentation, refinement, and resolution of uncertainties. These capabilities increased in importance as transaction-processing and management-control systems became commonplace and organizations attempted to build more ambitious systems, such as decision support systems and strategic information systems, where requirements often were poorly understood. In short, consistent with the philosophy underlying the soft-systems approach, the prototyping approach gave users a central role during information systems development. Moreover, the prototyping approach is founded on the assumption that resolution of requirements uncertainty is a legitimate and important task.

At least in principle, the prototyping approach to information systems development is straightforward (see, e.g., Naumann and Jenkins 1982). It involves developing an initial prototype system, gaining experience with the prototype, modifying the prototype in light of this experience, and continuing to iterate through this cycle until an acceptable solution is found (Figure 4–6). High-level

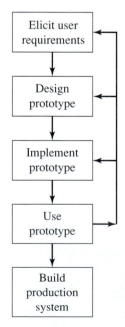

FIGURE 4–6. Prototyping methodology for systems development.

programming languages are used because they facilitate rapid iteration through successive designs. If efficiency is a major problem when the final system is derived, the system can then be programmed in a lower-level language. This action might not be warranted, however, if the ongoing stability of the system is suspect or reprogramming costs more than purchasing additional hardware to support the inefficiencies.

From an audit viewpoint, a significant aspect of the prototyping approach is the transition of responsibility for developmental work that sometimes occurs from information systems professionals to end-user personnel. Using high-level programming languages, end users can undertake their own development work independently of information systems personnel. Auditors must be concerned about whether end users always have sufficient knowledge to design and implement high-quality information systems (Allen 1996).

Contingency Approach

As the different approaches to information systems development have evolved and our understanding of these approaches has improved, it has now become widely accepted that no single approach always works best. The best development approach will vary, depending upon the circumstances at hand.

Proponents of the contingency approach to information systems development seek to identify those factors that affect the effectiveness of different approaches (see, e.g., Gremillion and Pyburn 1983). They argue that the following are important:

1. *Social systems impact:* If a system will have a major impact on jobs, organizational structures, or the distribution of formal and informal power in an organization, the systems development approach must motivate designers to attend to the behavioral issues that arise. For example, it might be important to involve users in the redesign of jobs and to employ strategies for dealing with behavioral conflicts. If a system will have little impact on social systems, however, sociotechnical and political considerations assume less importance.
2. *Task systems impact:* If a system will be central to the ways personnel perform their jobs and the overall effectiveness and efficiency of an organization, professional information systems development personnel must take primary responsibility for the development process. The overall process must be well controlled to ensure effective communications occur among affected parties, high-quality systems development work is undertaken, and quality assurance procedures are exercised. If a system will have a limited, local impact on tasks and an organization, it might be developed by end users.
3. *System size:* The size of a system to be developed is likely to be associated with the extent of its impact on the social and task systems in an organization. The development of large systems should be controlled by information systems development professionals who are capable of undertaking high-quality systems development work and have a good understanding of quality assurance procedures. Small systems might be developed by end users employing high-level languages.
4. *Commonality:* If the system to be developed is relatively common and its requirements are well understood, a software package might be available that will do all or part of the job. If the system will have a limited impact, end users might take primary responsibility for acquiring the package. If the system will have an extensive impact, information systems professionals should play a major role in acquiring the package.

5. *Requirements uncertainty:* As requirements uncertainty increases, soft-systems strategies and prototyping become more important in the development process. If requirements are well understood, however, use of soft-systems strategies and prototyping might add unnecessary overheads to the development process.

6. *Technological uncertainty:* If a system will be developed using information technology with which an organization has little experience, primary responsibility for development should be given to information systems professionals. Knowledge about the technology must be acquired, and development procedures must be adopted that allow for the organization's inexperience with the technology.

If organizations adopt a contingency approach to information systems development, therefore, at the outset a critical task is to identify those factors that might impact the development process and to assess how these factors might influence the development approaches undertaken. Contingency-approach proponents argue the quality of these strategic decisions has an important bearing on the quality of the development process and the resulting systems.

EVALUATING THE MAJOR PHASES IN THE SYSTEMS DEVELOPMENT PROCESS

Given these alternative models of the systems development process, what basis can auditors use, therefore, to evaluate the process? How can they obtain assurance about the quality of systems development, for example, if responsibility for designing and implementing systems is dispersed across many end users employing high-level programming languages? Similarly, how can they rely on controls when in some cases developers and users take for granted they do not fully understand the nature of the systems they are trying to develop?

One approach is to assume that certain phases will always be present in the systems development process, even though the conduct, timing, and sequence of these phases might differ markedly across projects. This approach has proved to be robust in the context of "new" types of systems like knowledge-based systems (see, for example, Weitzel and Kerschberg 1989) and spreadsheet systems (see, for example, Ronen et al. 1989). In essence, the phases define an *agenda of issues* that stakeholders (e.g., designers, users, management) in the systems development process must address. The quality of systems development will depend on how well the stakeholders come to grips with these issues in the context of the project they are undertaking. If auditors are participating in the systems development process, they will be part of the stakeholder group making judgments about how best to address these issues. If, on the other hand, they are conducting an *ex post* review of either a specific system or the systems development process in general, they will be evaluating how well the stakeholders addressed these issues in the context of past systems that have been developed.

In the following subsections we examine the tasks that must be undertaken and the controls that may be important in 13 major systems development phases:

1. Problem/opportunity definition
2. Management of the change process
3. Entry and feasibility assessment
4. Analysis of the existing system
5. Formulation of strategic requirements

6. Organizational and job design
7. Information processing systems design
8. Application software acquisition and development
9. Hardware/system software acquisition
10. Procedures development
11. Acceptance testing
12. Conversion
13. Operation and maintenance

In each phase, we consider how its conduct might vary depending on a system's task and social impact, the size of the system, the commonality of the system, and the requirements and technological uncertainty surrounding the system. We also consider how controls might differ depending upon the levels of these contingent factors. Our objective is to develop some facility in choosing a good normative model of the systems development process that auditors can employ during evidence collection and evaluation tasks.

Problem/Opportunity Definition

Information systems can be developed to help resolve problems or to take advantage of opportunities. Problems and opportunities that might be amenable to information systems support can be recognized in two ways. First, they can be conceived through formal processes associated with the preparation of an information systems plan. Second, they can be conceived fortuitously.

During the problem/opportunity definition phase, the stakeholders must attempt to come to some understanding of the nature of the problem or opportunity they are addressing. Is the problem or opportunity well or ill structured? Does it have implications for a small or a large number of people? Will possible solutions have a large impact on the organizational structure and jobs? Will new technology most likely be needed to support possible solutions?

Auditors should have the following types of concerns about the activities carried out in this phase:

1. If possible information systems solutions to the problem or opportunity will be material in terms of size or impact, have formal terms of reference been prepared? If so, have they been approved by a steering committee or well-constituted project committee?
2. If possible information systems solutions will have a major impact on task systems or social systems, what level of acceptance exists among the stakeholders on the need for change? Do the terms of reference consider the need for consultation and negotiation?
3. If there is a high level of requirements uncertainty or technological uncertainty surrounding possible solutions to the problem or opportunity, do the terms of reference take into account strategies that might help alleviate the uncertainty?
4. Do the stakeholders agree on the definition of the problem or opportunity? If they disagreed at the outset, what approaches were used to try to reach consensus?

During the problem/opportunity definition stage, therefore, auditors are concerned to see that the stakeholders have reached agreement on the problem or opportunity and that they have an understanding of the threats to asset safeguarding, data integrity, system effectiveness, and system efficiency associated with possible solutions. Their concerns will be minor if the problem or opportunity and possible solutions are local and straightforward. They increase, however, as the problem or opportunity becomes more ill structured and possible solutions have a wider impact.

Management of the Change Process

Management of the change process runs parallel to all other phases. The change process starts at the initial conception of the system and continues until the new system is running and the organization has adjusted to the new system.

Management of the change process involves two major tasks: project management and change facilitation (Figure 4–7). Project management involves addressing such matters as budgeting, exception reporting, checkpoints, and user signoffs. The way in which project management is undertaken should vary, however, depending on the type of system to be developed and implemented. For example, if the project is uncertain, McFarlan (1981) points out that external coordination mechanisms must be established to increase the likelihood requirements will be specified correctly. More users might be placed on the design team, for example, to improve communications among the stakeholders. If, on the other hand, the project is straightforward, traditional internal coordination mechanisms should be used. For example, PERT charts might be prepared to help the design team stay on track.

Management of the change-facilitating aspects of systems development becomes more critical as possible solutions are likely to have a greater impact on organizational structures and jobs. Current prescriptive models for facilitating change in the systems development process tend to be some adaptation of the

FIGURE 4–7. Management of the change process during systems development.

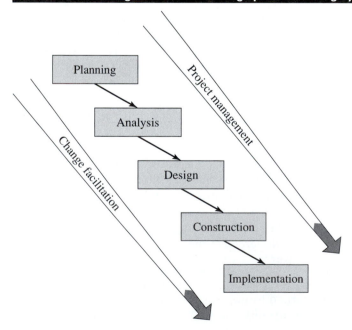

Lewin/Schein or Kolb/Frolman models of organizational change (see Ginzberg 1981). Three major classes of activities are required:

Class of Activities	*Explanation*
Unfreezing the organization	Preparing the organization for change; providing feedback to the organizational members on their attitudes and behaviors; using techniques such as education, participatory decision making, and command to promote the need for change. Unfreezing activities help avoid having to *impose* change on stakeholders.
Moving the organization	Changeover to the new system.
Refreezing the organization	Helping system users adapt to their new roles by providing positive feedback on their changed attitudes and behaviors. Refreezing activities make it more difficult for stakeholders to revert to their old attitudes and behavioral patterns.

Management of change facilitation might also require that stakeholders undertake negotiation and compromise. Recall from our discussion of the political approach to systems development that we must recognize possible solutions sometimes produce important power shifts. Some stakeholders will gain from these power shifts; others will be disadvantaged. Conflict arising from these power shifts could severely undermine systems development unless the nature of and size of these power shifts are addressed.

During this phase, auditors must evaluate the quality of decisions made about project management and change facilitation. Again, they must adopt a contingency perspective. If the proposed system is small, has a localized impact, and will be developed by end users employing a high-level language, project management and change facilitation concerns are unlikely to be material. On the other hand, if the proposed system is large, high levels of requirements and technological uncertainty exist, and organizational structures and jobs will be affected significantly, the decisions made about project management and change facilitation will be a material concern.

Entry and Feasibility Assessment

The purpose of the entry and feasibility assessment phase is to obtain a commitment to change and to evaluate whether cost-effective solutions are available to address the problem or opportunity that has been identified.

Consider, first, a situation in which the problem or opportunity has been recognized by a group of users. They believe they can design and implement a solution themselves using a high-level language. Their proposed system will have little impact on others within the organization, nor will it be material from the viewpoint of the overall organization. In this situation, the users are already motivated to bring about change. Thus, activities to accomplish successful entry are minor or unnecessary.

On the other hand, consider a situation in which potential solutions will have a widespread impact on the overall organization. Activities to accomplish successful entry are now critical. Information systems professionals must seek to establish themselves as legitimate change agents among the stakeholders. Moreover, they must seek to foster among the stakeholders a commitment to change. If potential solutions will have a significant impact on task and social systems, a spirit of collaborative analysis and evaluation among stakeholders must be developed. When significant power shifts are a likely outcome, negotiation and compromise might be required.

If entry is successful, the designer can then carry out a preliminary study to evaluate the feasibility of the new system using four criteria (Figure 4–8):

1. *Technical feasibility:* Is the available technology sufficient to support the proposed project? Can the technology be acquired or developed?
2. *Operational feasibility:* Can the input data be collected for the system? Is the output usable?
3. *Economic feasibility:* Do the benefits of the system exceed the costs?
4. *Behavioral feasibility:* What impact will the system have on the users' quality of working life?

The specific techniques used to evaluate the feasibility of systems should vary depending on the type of system being proposed. For example, if the proposed system is relatively straightforward and the likely benefits and costs are clear, net present value analysis might be used to assess economic feasibility. On the other hand, if substantial uncertainty surrounds the system, an approach such as Keen's (1981) value analysis might be used to assess feasibility. When value analysis is used, seed funding is initially allocated to a system to build a prototype. When users gain experience with the prototype, better estimates of costs and benefits can be obtained. If the anticipated benefits of proceeding further appear to exceed the costs, additional funding is allocated to extend the prototype. In light of experimentation with the extended prototype, additional funding might be provided. This process proceeds iteratively until the benefits no longer appear to exceed the costs.

If auditors are participating in the systems development process, their primary concerns during the entry and feasibility assessment phase will be to ensure that change is not imposed upon stakeholders and that an appropriate approach to feasibility analysis is chosen and undertaken. If change is imposed upon stakeholders, the development process could be undermined by the behavioral problems that arise. If an inappropriate feasibility analysis is chosen or the analysis is poorly done, material losses can be incurred as a result of the development, implementation, operation, or maintenance of the system.

If auditors conduct a postimplementation review or an *ex post* general review, their primary concerns will be *(1)* the processes used historically by systems development personnel to choose an entry strategy and feasibility assessment approach and *(2)* how well entry and feasibility assessment has been done previously. They will then attempt to evaluate the consequences of these past decisions for the quality of systems subsequently developed.

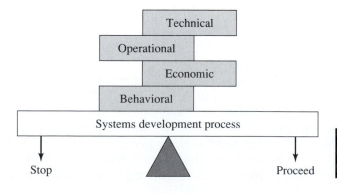

FIGURE 4–8. Feasibility criteria for systems development.

Analysis of the Existing System

When a new system is proposed, in some cases it will replace an existing system. Designers might need to understand the existing system if they are to undertake high-quality work in developing and implementing a new system (Figure 4–9). For example, if they are to avoid the new system being undermined through behavioral conflicts, they might have to appreciate how employees are rewarded under the current system to determine the likely impact the proposed system will have on these rewards. Any redistribution of rewards that arises as a result of the new system might have to be negotiated carefully. Similarly, the strategic requirements for the new system could be based on the existing system's strengths and weaknesses.

Analysis of the existing system usually involves two major tasks: *(1)* studying the existing organizational history, structure, and culture and *(2)* studying the existing product and information flows. The following two subsections provide an overview of these tasks.

Studying the Existing Organizational History, Structure, and Culture

Designers might need to study the existing organizational history, structure, and culture to gain an understanding of the social and task systems in place, the ways these systems are coupled, and the willingness of stakeholders to change. As discussed previously, the proposed system could have a widespread behavioral impact. The greater this potential impact, the more effort designers must expend to understand the present organization. Otherwise, they might propose designs that are problematic either socially or technically. Moreover, they might make poor decisions on how the change process should be managed.

Auditors should be concerned with evaluating designers' decisions on *(1)* whether they needed to study the present organizational history, structure, and culture; *(2)* if so, what aspects they needed to study; and *(3)* given the choice of aspects to study, the extent to which they had to be examined. Like designers, auditors will have to consider the context in which these decisions were made and reflect on the choices they would have made themselves. They can then compare the designers' choices against their own to evaluate the implications of the similarities and differences for the conduct of the remainder of the audit.

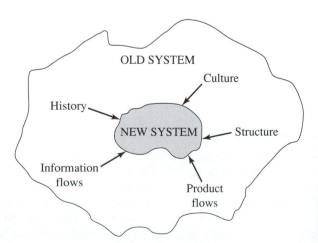

FIGURE 4–9. Shape of existing system can affect new system.

Studying the Existing Product and Information Flows

Studying the existing product and information flows is important for three reasons. First, sometimes the design of the proposed system will be based primarily on current product and information flows. The new system is not intended to be a radical departure from the status quo. Second, designers might need to understand the strengths and weaknesses of the existing product and information flows to determine the new system requirements. In particular, current system weaknesses might have motivated the request for a new system. Third, a good understanding of the existing product and information flows might be required to assess the extent of change needed to implement and operate the new system. Designers can then make better decisions on how to manage the change process.

Several formal methodologies have been developed to assist designers to understand existing product and information flows. One of the more popular is structured analysis (see, e.g., Yourdon 1989). Structured analysis is a top-down, breadth-first approach to studying a system. Although it helps analyze product flows, it is perhaps best known for the set of tools it provides to document data flows, define data, and describe logic and policy. Appendix 4.1 provides an overview of structured analysis.

Object-oriented analysis is also a popular method of analyzing and documenting product and information flows. In contrast to structured analysis, however, it is not a data-driven approach. Instead, designers attempt to understand the system via objects and their classes, structural relationships among these objects, the attributes of these objects, and how the objects interact (see, e.g., Coad and Yourdon 1991; Brown 1997). Appendix 4.2 provides an overview of object-oriented analysis.

Still another approach to use is SSM (see the section "Soft-Systems Approach"). When stakeholders have difficulty describing existing systems, SSM can be used to help them learn about the worlds in which they work. SSM provides procedures and tools that stakeholders can employ to obtain an understanding of and to document existing systems.

When designers study the existing product and information flows, auditors should have three concerns. First, they must evaluate the quality of stakeholders' decisions about the nature and extent of the examination they chose to make. Auditors must consider whether stakeholders made astute decisions in light of the contextual factors that affect their choices. Second, auditors should examine whether stakeholders used a high-quality methodology, such as structured analysis or object-oriented analysis, to guide their examination of the existing product and information flows. Moreover, if designers did employ a formal methodology, auditors must evaluate how well the designers used it. Third, auditors should determine whether designers used computer-aided software-engineering tools (CASE) to support their analysis and documentation of existing product and information flows. If so, the quality of their work is likely to be higher.

Formulating Strategic Requirements

The strategic requirements for a system specify the *overall* goals and objectives the system must accomplish. They might be vague—for example, "increase the wealth of shareholders." Or they might be specific—for example, "reduce staff turnover in the sales area by 30 percent." Strategic requirements are identified based on perceived deficiencies in the existing system or perceived opportunities for enhanced task accomplishment and quality of working life.

Sociotechnical design theorists stress the importance of carefully eliciting a system's strategic requirements *before* design work commences. They say that many system failures can be attributed to inadequate performance of this activity. Fundamental difficulties arise because stakeholders do not recognize they have different and sometimes conflicting strategic requirements for the proposed system. Management's strategic requirements, for example, tend to be task-accomplishment oriented. Users' strategic requirements, on the other hand, tend to focus on quality-of-working-life issues. The two sets of strategic requirements might be incompatible. If subsequent conflict is to be avoided or reduced, the strategic requirements that ultimately guide system-design work will have to be negotiated carefully.

Formulating strategic requirements at the outset recognizes explicitly that information systems technology can be neutral. A given job design, for example, often can be supported via multiple information systems designs. Forcing people, job designs, organization structures, and so on, to fit information systems has been a root cause of behavioral problems. If the strategic requirements for a system are clear, stakeholders are better placed to consider and evaluate alternative designs.

If substantial uncertainty surrounds the proposed system, however, strategic requirements might not be clear at the outset. Methodologies like SSM and prototyping can be used to help clarify strategic requirements. Both methodologies, in particular, help to identify a set of *feasible* strategic requirements. Both also recognize that in some cases the elicitation of strategic requirements and system-design work might have to proceed concurrently.

Auditors should be concerned to see that system designers recognize the importance of articulating strategic requirements for the quality of subsequent design work. If the proposed system will have a substantial behavioral impact, they should examine and evaluate the procedures used by the stakeholders to reach agreement on strategic requirements. If substantial uncertainty surrounds the proposed system, they should examine and evaluate the procedures used to help clarify strategic requirements.

Organizational and Job Design

In some cases, achieving the strategic requirements chosen for a system will necessitate the initial design or redesign of organizational structures and jobs. Recall from our previous discussion, an information processing system design usually can be adapted to whatever organizational structures and job designs are chosen. On the other hand, adapting organizational structures and job designs to fit information processing system designs often leads to behavioral problems among users and, as a result, implementation failure.

In choosing organizational structures and job designs for those parts of the organization that will be affected by the proposed system, many factors should be considered. For example, if substantial uncertainty surrounds the tasks to be accomplished in the proposed system, loose, organic organizational structures and job designs might be successful. These types of organizational structures and job designs promote creativity, innovation, and free flows of information needed to address the stresses and uncertainties that can undermine task performance and quality of working life. Employees perform multiple tasks, require varied skills, assume leadership roles when they are the most able member of the group to address a specific problem, foster interpersonal communications and relationships, and accept responsibility for their own and their work-group's task performance and social growth. In some cases, also, designers might strive to develop organizational structures and job designs that foster emancipation goals. In other words, the organizational structures and job designs provide opportunities for persons to strive to reach their full potential (see, e.g., Hirschheim et al. 1995).

Irrespective of the level of task uncertainty, however, loose, organic organizational structures and job designs might not work if the history of the organization reflects top-level domination by a few people, the culture is autocratic, and jobs traditionally have been rigidly defined. Employees might be unwilling to accept the high levels of responsibility often associated with "enriched" organizational structures and job designs. Moreover, management might be unable to cope with work arrangements in one area that are incongruent with those in other parts of their organization. Traditional, formal, mechanistic organizational structures and jobs that separate thinking from doing might be more appropriate.

In short, the design of organizational structures and jobs can be a complex activity. If auditors assess that a proposed system will impact organizational structures and jobs, they would be concerned to see the systems development team obtained high-quality advice from someone skilled in organizational theory and practice. They would seek evidence, for example, on whether personnel assigned responsibility for organizational structure and job design contained representatives of stakeholder groups, how the design tasks were undertaken, the processes used to resolve conflict and uncertainties, and the level of consensus achieved in relation to the designs finally chosen. If auditors conclude that these types of issues have been resolved satisfactorily, they can reduce the level of control risk associated with systems development. If the issues have not been resolved satisfactorily, however, auditors must revise their assessment of control risk upward and plan increased substantive testing accordingly.

Information Processing Systems Design

If an auditor acts as a participant in the systems development process, the information processing systems design phase is one of major involvement (Gallegos and Dow, 1990). From a systems effectiveness viewpoint, the auditor considers whether the design meets the strategic requirements agreed upon by the stakeholders. From an efficiency viewpoint, the auditor assesses the reasonableness of the resources required to operate the system. From an asset safe-

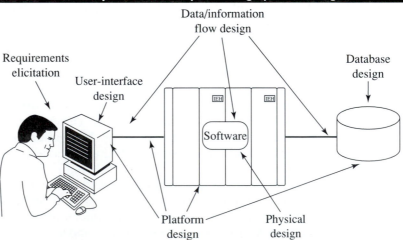

FIGURE 4–10. Major activities in processing systems design.

guarding and data integrity viewpoint, the auditor evaluates the likely reliability of the controls designed into the system.

During this phase, auditors should also evaluate the auditability of the system. They might deem it necessary, for example, to build certain audit capabilities into the system in the form of audit modules. These modules capture data or examine conditions of interest concurrently with production running of the system (see Chapter 18). Auditors might also deem it necessary to purchase certain tools (such as some types of software) in order to audit the system.

When evaluating the information processing system design phase, either as a participant in the design process or in a postimplementation or general *ex post* review capacity, auditors must examine the conduct of six major activities (Figure 4–10):

1. Elicitation of detailed requirements,
2. Design of the data/information flow,
3. Design of the database,
4. Design of the user interface,
5. Physical design, and
6. Design and acquisition of the hardware/system software platform.

As with the previous phases, these activities can vary considerably depending on the type of system being designed and implemented. For example, compared with a large, critical application system, they will be less onerous in a small end-user–developed application system. The following subsections provide an overview of how they might be performed.

Elicitation of Detailed Requirements

To design an information system, designers eventually must understand what information it must provide, the data that must be captured to produce this information, and the transformations that must be undertaken on the data to transform it into information. In addition, they must understand when and where the system must produce the information.

Detailed requirements can be elicited using two fundamental approaches:

1. *Ask the stakeholders what they require:* In some cases, stakeholders know their requirements for the proposed system. For example, the requirements might be clear based on their experience with an existing system or they have a good understanding of what they wish to accomplish with the proposed system.
2. *Discover the requirements through analysis and experimentation:* In other cases, stakeholders might be uncertain about the requirements for the new system. They might have no prior experience with the type of system or the capabilities of the technology proposed, or they might lack understanding of how their proposed organizational and job designs should be supported via an information system. Requirements evolve concurrently as other systems-design work is carried out. Requirements also evolve as users interact with one another to "socially construct" their reality (Hirschheim et al. 1995).

Auditors should evaluate whether designers have chosen appropriate requirements-elicitation strategies in light of the level of uncertainty surrounding the proposed system. If the level of uncertainty is low, they should seek evidence that standard interviewing techniques have been used (see Chapter 19). If the level of uncertainty is high, they should seek evidence that elicitation strategies have been used to help resolve this uncertainty—for example, strategies based on SSM or prototyping approaches. Auditors must assess how well these elicitation strategies have been employed, particularly in terms of the level of consensus and shared understanding of requirements attained among stakeholders and the quality of requirements documentation produced.

Design of the Data/information Flow

The design of the data and information flows is a major step in the *conceptual design* of the new system. It is undertaken in light of any organizational and job design that has occurred and the detailed information requirements that have been elicited. Designers must determine the following:

1. The flow of data and information and the transformation points,
2. The frequency and timing of the data and information flows, and
3. The extent to which data and information flows will be formalized.

The first decision might be influenced by existing flows of data and information, the organizational and job design that has been proposed, the information needs of users expressed during the elicitation process, or the results of experimentation with alternative data and information flows. The flow of data and information through the proposed system must be charted, and the transformations needed to manipulate data or to convert data into information must be specified. Tools such as data flow diagrams and object-oriented notations can be used for these purposes (see Appendices 4.1 and 4.2).

The frequency and timing of the data and information flows affect when data must be submitted to the system, when it must be processed, and when output must be provided. The nature of the job to be supported by the information system is a primary factor influencing these decisions. For example, users monitoring a continuous production process might require immediate input, immediate processing, and immediate output; users answering customer telephone inquiries require immediate output; users facing high levels of task uncertainty might require frequent reports.

The extent to which data and information flows can be formalized affects the assignment of data and information processing to users or the computer. As the level of formalization increases, responsibility can transfer from people to machines. In the past, designers have tended to focus only on the formal data and information flows. In many systems, however, informal information flows might be critical. For example, much of the data needed for a decision support system or an executive information system can be provided via informal data flows. The design challenge is to capture informal data so it can be transformed via a computer into information.

Failure to produce a high-quality design for the data/information flow can seriously undermine a system. For example, poor timing decisions can result in out-of-date data being captured; poor choices about information flows could mean information is directed toward the wrong decision makers. Auditors must carefully evaluate the activities carried out in this phase to determine whether the resulting design meets the requirements established for the system.

Design of the Database

Design of the database involves determining its *scope* (context) and *structure*. The scope of databases ranges from local to global. A major factor affecting scope is the extent of interdependence among organizational units. The greater the interdependence, the greater the need for a global database to prevent suboptimization by subunits. Organizations with highly interdependent subunits also have more incentive to share data resources—for example, by using a database management system. As the database becomes more global, however, the cost of its maintenance and use increases. For example, data integrity becomes more important as data is shared increasingly, and a larger number of controls must be implemented and operated to preserve database integrity.

Choosing the "optimal" structure for the database is a complex decision. Four major activities must be undertaken:

Design Activity	*Explanation*
Conceptual modeling	During conceptual modeling, designers attempt to build a representation of the semantics of the real-world application domain. They describe the application domain via entities/objects, attributes of these entities/objects, relationships among these entities/objects, and static and dynamic constraints on these entities/objects, their attributes, and their relationships.
Data modeling	Conceptual models must be translated into data models so they can be accessed and manipulated by both high-level and low-level programming languages. For example, an entity-relationship model could be transformed into a relational data model that can be accessed and interrogated by a query language.
Storage structure design	Decisions must be made on how to linearize and partition the data structure so it can be stored on some device. For example, tuples in a relational data model must be assigned to records, and relationships among records might be established via symbolic pointer addresses.
Physical layout design	Decisions must be made on how to distribute the storage structure across specific storage media and locations—for example, the cylinders, tracks, and sectors on a disk and the computers in a local area or wide area network.

Auditors should carefully evaluate the decision on database scope to determine whether it is reasonable in the context of the system to be implemented. In particular, the development of too many private databases is a major concern. Private databases often undermine control over and use of data. They can store redundant data, which in due course can become inconsistent and out of date. Moreover, they can be used for private, political purposes, perhaps to the detriment of the overall organization. Public databases, on the other hand, can be costly to maintain and use. They can undermine system effectiveness and efficiency.

The structure of the database should be designed using one of the well-known database design methodologies. For example, semantic data modeling might be undertaken using the entity-relationship model (see Appendix 4.3) or the object-oriented model; data structure design might be undertaken using the relational model (see Appendix 4.4). Auditors should seek evidence that CASE tools have been used to facilitate the design process and, in particular, to document the results of the design process.

Design of the User Interface

Design of the user interface involves determining the ways in which users will interact with a system. Given the diversity of technology now available to support the user interface, the design process can be complex and multifaceted. Some elements that may have to be considered follow:

1. Source documents to capture raw data,
2. Hard-copy output reports,

3. Screen layouts for dedicated source-document input,
4. Inquiry screens for database interrogation,
5. Command languages for decision support systems,
6. Interrogation languages for the database,
7. Graphic and color displays,
8. Voice output to guide users or answer queries,
9. Screen layouts for manipulation by a light pen or mouse, and
10. Icons for pictorial representation of output.

The design process usually begins by identifying system users and classifying them into homogeneous groups. Next the characteristics of the user groups must be understood. For example, are we dealing with a group of novices who will use the system infrequently or a group of experts who will use the system regularly? When the group characteristics are understood, the tasks they wish to perform using the system must be elicited. A preliminary design of the form of interaction that will support these tasks, given the characteristics of the users, can then be commenced. Prototyping tools can often be employed to refine this design with the users.

Auditors often deem the design of the user interface to be a critical activity. In many systems the quality of the user interface affects the extent to which users are likely to make errors when they interact with the system. For example, poorly designed source documents can result in users capturing data incorrectly; poorly designed graphics output can result in users making erroneous decisions. Auditors seek evidence that designers have followed good user-interface design standards. Moreover, they should investigate whether designers have carefully prototyped the interface using, say, CASE tools to resolve problems users might encounter. (Chapters 10, 11, and 15 examine these matters in more detail.)

Physical Design

So far the design activities we have examined primarily address the logical or conceptual aspects of the system. Ultimately, however, the logical design must be converted to a physical design. The physical design process involves breaking up the logical design into units, which in turn can be decomposed further into implementation units such as programs and modules. Various strategies can be used to accomplish this task. For example, if the logical design has been expressed via a logical data flow diagram, Page-Jones (1988) advocates breaking the system into jobs by identifying and drawing three types of physical boundaries on the data flow diagram:

Type of Boundary	Explanation
Hardware	Different parts of the system might be implemented more cost effectively on different machines; e.g., data can be captured and validated using a microcomputer, whereas database update might be better accomplished on a mainframe.
Batch-online/real-time	Some parts of the system might require only periodic actions—e.g., generation of hard-copy reports. Other might require an immediate response—e.g., answers to customer telephone queries on inventory availability. Still others require data to be updated immediately—e.g., funds investment in a system to support short-term money-market operations.
Cycle (periodicity)	Functions to support generation of, say, a monthly report can be separated from functions that update inventory availability.

When boundaries have been identified, jobs can be partitioned into steps. In general, system complexity is reduced as jobs are partitioned into fewer steps. More job steps mean more intermediate files and greater complexity. Figure 4–11 shows job-step partitioning for a sales reporting system. A cycle boundary exists between sales data submission by salespersons and sales report preparation. Sales data submission occurs more frequently than sales report preparation. Thus, data receipt and validation is a separate job from report preparation. Report preparation is then partitioned into two separate job steps. Off-the-shelf sort and report packages are available to place data in the re-

FIGURE 4–11. Packaging of logical system design into jobs.

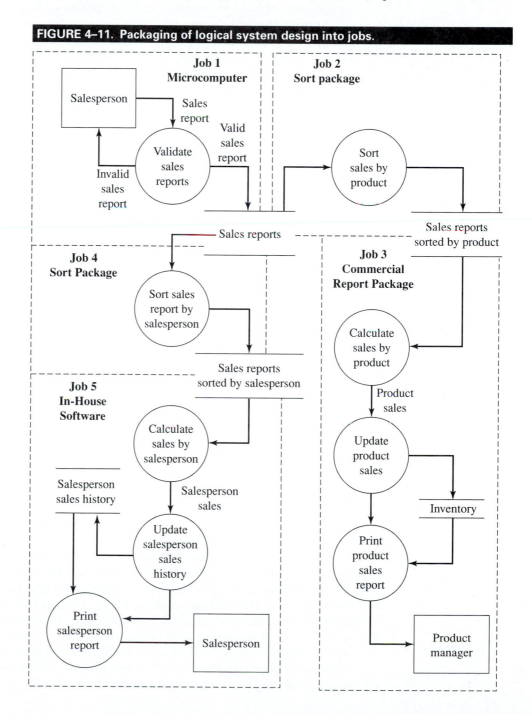

quired order, update files, and prepare reports. Job steps, in turn, are then partitioned into programs and load units.

Other ways of undertaking physical design can be used. For example, if the logical design emerges from experimentation with a high-level language, the physical design might occur by default. If the designer deems it not worthwhile to reprogram the resulting system in a low-level language, the architecture of the high-level language dictates the form of the physical design. Similarly, the logical design might be accommodated using a generalized application package. The architecture of the package dictates the physical design, except to the extent users choose parameter values to configure the package initially.

During physical design, the auditor's primary concerns will be with effectiveness and efficiency issues. If physical design is done poorly, the system could be ineffective because, for example, it does not meet timeliness requirements. The system might also be inefficient because tasks have been assigned to inappropriate hardware and software resources. The auditor should seek evidence that designers follow some type of structured approach when they undertake physical design. Moreover, when physical design is a critical activity, the auditor should seek evidence that designers use CASE tools to assess their relative performance via simulations.

Design of the Hardware/System Software Platform

In some cases the new system requires hardware and system software not currently available in the organization. For example, a decision support system might require high-quality graphics output not supported by the existing hardware and software; user workstations might have to be purchased to support an office automation system; a minicomputer might have to be acquired to provide extra processing resources consumed by a system programmed in a high-level language; a local area network might have to be installed to allow personnel in a work group to communicate with one another. The new hardware/system software platform required to support the application system will have to be designed.

Auditors should be concerned about the extent to which modularity and generality are preserved in the design of the hardware/system software platform. Ideally, different hardware and system software should be able to communicate with each other. Otherwise, subsequent changes to the system will be more difficult to make, and inevitably resources will be expended in trying to overcome communication difficulties that arise. Errors could arise that undermine asset safeguarding and data integrity.

Application Software Acquisition and Development

After the information processing systems design phase is complete, application software might have to be acquired or developed. In some cases generalized software packages can be purchased to perform all or some functions within the system. For example, an order-entry package could be purchased to perform sales functions, or a database management package could be acquired to assist with control and use of data. These packages have to be configured and perhaps modified and adapted. In other cases, the system might exist in a prototype form at the conclusion of the design phase. Work might be undertaken to tune the prototype so it runs more efficiently or to write the prototype in another programming language that will execute more efficiently. In still other cases, new programs must be developed from scratch. Various activities are in-

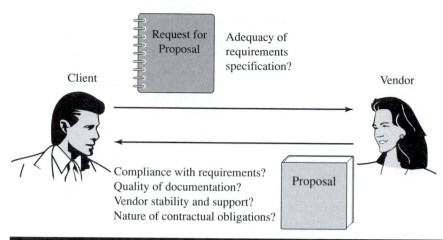

FIGURE 4–12. Audit concerns during hardware/software acquisition.

volved: design, coding, compiling, testing, and documenting. (Chapter 5 discusses these activities further.)

Auditors might have several concerns during the application software acquisition and development phase. If application software is acquired, they should be concerned about the adequacy of the requirements specification provided to vendors, the quality of the procedures used to evaluate the software tendered in terms of such factors as functionality, accuracy and completeness, quality of documentation, vendor stability and support, and the nature of the terms and conditions in the contract exchanged with the vendor. They must evaluate the likely quality of the application software acquired and the adequacy of vendor maintenance and support (Figure 4–12).

If, on the other hand, application software is developed, auditors must be concerned about the procedures undertaken during the design, coding, compiling, testing, and documentation phases. If software development is undertaken by information systems professionals, auditors usually can assess control risk as lower. Skilled programmers, for example, should be aware of the quality-assurance procedures they must follow to reduce the number of errors in the programs they write. On the other hand, if end users are developing material systems, auditors often must assess control risk as higher. In spite of the criticality of systems they sometimes develop, many end users lack knowledge of and experience with the quality assurance procedures needed to produce high-quality programs.

During this phase, auditors could be involved in acquiring or developing software for their own purposes. For example, they might wish to embed certain audit modules in the system so they can continuously monitor the system. They might also seek to acquire generalized software to help audit the system. Auditors must be vigilant in applying the same quality assurance measures expected of the persons audited.

Hardware/System Software Acquisition

If new hardware or system software must be purchased to support the new application system, a request for a proposal must be prepared. Vendor submissions must then be solicited. These submissions must be evaluated and a final selection made.

Auditors have similar concerns during this phase as they do during the application software acquisition and development phase. Auditors should seek evidence that designers carefully prepared a request for proposal for any new hardware/system software needs. The request for proposal should document such matters as transaction volumes, database sizes, turnaround and response time requirements, and vendor support needed. They should evaluate how designers used the request for proposal to assess vendor submissions. For example, auditors might seek evidence on whether simulation models or queuing models were developed to evaluate the merits of different vendor submissions against the response time requirements specified in the request for proposal. Auditors should also evaluate how well the hardware and system software finally chosen enable the overall design goals of modularity and generality to be achieved. Finally, they should be concerned about such matters as vendor viability, ongoing support, the availability of source code and maintenance support in the event of vendor failure, and contractual obligations to the vendor.

Procedures Development

During the procedures development phase, designers specify the activities that users must undertake to support the ongoing operation of the system and to obtain useful output. In general, the objective should be to provide *minimum specification of procedures* (Carroll et al. 1988). Inevitably, many users will disregard instructions and try to develop their own approach to accomplishing a task. From the viewpoint of maintaining control, *what needs to be done* should be clearly specified. Where possible, *how it should be done* should be left to the person responsible for the task. Auditors might provide suggestions, but they must accept that users might not follow these suggestions.

Procedures development involves four major tasks:

Task	*Explanation*
Design of procedures	To the extent procedures must be specified, they must be matched with the job/task design. What triggers the task and the task input and output must be identified.
Testing of procedures	Users and operators must test the adequacy of the procedures design. They might suggest modifications in light of their experience.
Implementation of procedures	Conformity with system procedures represents the most direct way people have to change their behavior when a new system is implemented. Where systems have a substantial behavioral impact, management of the change process can be especially critical during the conduct of this task.
Documentation of procedures	User and operator procedures must be documented formally. Where possible, procedures manuals should be written in a consistent, formal style.

Auditors should have several concerns about the conduct of the procedures development phase. First, they must assess the quality of the procedures design. In particular, they should evaluate whether the principle of minimum specification of procedures has been observed. Second, if the system will have or has had a substantial behavioral impact, they should check to see the procedures design team contained representatives of all important stakeholder groups. As discussed previously, compliance with procedures is an important indicator of users accepting the need for change. For this reason, users might seek to influence the design of the procedures they must eventually employ. Third, auditors should evaluate the approach used to test procedures. The wider the impact of the system, the more critical it is that procedures be tested thoroughly before they are implemented operationally. Fourth, they should evaluate the quality of procedures documentation. Again, documentation becomes increasingly important as the system has a wider impact.

Acceptance Testing

The purpose of acceptance testing is to identify as far as possible any errors and deficiencies in the system prior to its final release into production use. Errors and deficiencies can exist in the software supporting the system, the user interface, procedures manuals, job design, organizational structure design, and so on. Acceptance testing is carried out to identify these errors or deficiencies before they have a widespread impact.

The conduct of acceptance testing can vary considerably, depending on the type of system being implemented and the activities undertaken during systems development. For example, if substantial amounts of program code have been written, acceptance testing must involve ensuring the code is authorized, accurate, and complete. If generalized software has been purchased and the software has an extensive user base, acceptance testing might focus primarily on job designs or user procedures associated with the system. If the system has been developed using a high-level language, testing might be iterative as various system prototypes are tried and either enhanced or discarded.

For several reasons, acceptance testing usually cannot be comprehensive; that is, all system features cannot be tested. First, it is difficult to conceive of every execution path through a system of even moderate complexity. For many systems, the number to be tested is intractable. Second, deficiencies in a system might become apparent only after extensive experience with the system. For example, users might realize they have an inadequate job design or an inadequate procedures manual only after they have used the system for some time. Third, it is difficult to conceive of every condition under which the system must operate. Exceptional circumstances could arise, such as an abnormal system load or a rare combination of transactions, which were not anticipated in the design of acceptance tests. Fourth, in some cases it is difficult to know whether a result is correct, anyway. For example, a complex algorithm might have been implemented in a decision support system. Whether the algorithm is a correct model of reality might be unclear. Fifth, even with the availability of testing tools such as test data generators, acceptance testing can be expensive. At some point the costs of extra testing outweigh the expected benefits. Given these difficulties, information systems professionals now try to design and implement systems without errors or deficiencies in the first place rather than attempt to remove errors during acceptance testing.

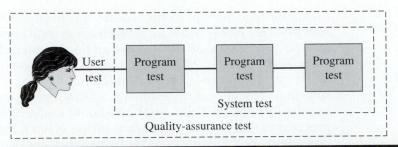

FIGURE 4–13. Domains for different types of testing.

There are four major types of acceptance testing (Figure 4–13):

Type of Testing	*Explanation*
Program testing	Programmers who develop the individual programs in the system must test their programs for accuracy, completeness, and efficiency.
System testing	Some members of the development team must take responsibility for testing the overall system to see especially that the interfaces between the various programs and subsystems work correctly.
User testing	Users must test the total system, including the organizational-structure design, the job design, system interfaces, programs, and procedures.
Quality assurance testing	A quality assurance group is responsible for ensuring the system complies with all standards adopted by the organization.

Auditors should seek to answer the following types of questions when evaluating the conduct of work carried out during the acceptance testing phase:

1. How was the testing process planned?
2. How were test data designed and developed?
3. What test data were used?
4. What test results were obtained?
5. What actions were taken as a result of errors or deficiencies identified?
6. What subsequent modifications to test data were made in light of testing experience?
7. How was control exercised over test data and the acceptance testing process?

Auditors usually strive to obtain high-quality answers to these questions. The way in which acceptance testing is undertaken often has a major bearing on their estimates of the control risk associated with the systems development management subsystem. Good acceptance testing procedures force high-quality work to be undertaken in the other phases of systems development. If acceptance testing procedures are weak, however, controls elsewhere in the systems development process tend to deteriorate. Designers know their work will not be subjected to rigorous evaluation.

Conversion

The conversion phase comprises those activities undertaken to place the new system in operation. In some cases the transition must be made from an existing system. In other cases the system has no predecessor. In all cases, however, conversion requires users to adopt new behaviors. Accordingly, it is often a critical phase within the overall management of the change process.

Depending on the nature of the system being developed and implemented, conversion could be a minor step or it could involve major efforts over an extended period. For example, if users have developed a small decision support system using a high-level programming language, conversion can occur progressively as they experiment with various system prototypes. There might be no existing system aside from informal, private information systems that provide meager support for their decision-making activities. The transition to the new system occurs almost by default. Alternatively, implementation of a major, organizationwide application system often requires extensive planning of and control over the conversion phase. Significant disruption to the organization's day-to-day activities may be unavoidable.

If some type of system exists already, conversion to a new system can occur in one of three ways (Figure 4–14). First, the old system could be stopped abruptly to make way for the new system. This strategy reduces the costs of conversion because no redundant processing occurs. The costs of any deficien-

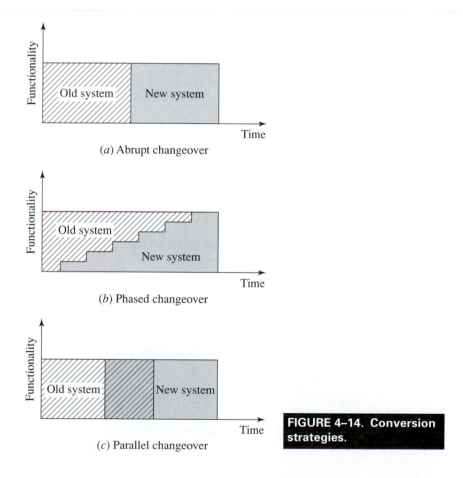

(a) Abrupt changeover

(b) Phased changeover

(c) Parallel changeover

FIGURE 4–14. Conversion strategies.

cies discovered in the new system can be high, however, as the old system is not available as backup. Second, both systems could run in parallel for a period (but performing different functions) with users employing output from both systems. Again, this phase-in conversion strategy reduces conversion costs. Moreover, it permits orderly changeover to the new system. Nevertheless, as with the first strategy, the costs of deficiencies in the new system can be high because no backup is available. Users might also encounter difficulties in having to work with two systems. Third, both systems could run in parallel (performing the same functions) with either the old system output or the new system output being used. In this last case, parallel running provides the basis for validating the design and implementation of the new system. Thus, this strategy reduces the risks associated with conversion. Redundant processing could be costly, however, and users might also encounter difficulties in having to work with both systems.

Changeover to a new system can involve four major activities:

Activity	*Explanation*
Personnel training	Primary and secondary users of the system need training. For example, primary users, such as management, need training in the use of system output. Secondary users, such as clerks, need training in the preparation of input data. Operators and programmers need training if new hardware and software have been purchased.
Installation of new hardware and software	If new hardware and software have been purchased, they must be installed. They also must be tested to evaluate whether they are functioning correctly.
Conversion of files and programs	This process can be complex and lengthy, particularly when a changeover occurs from a manual system. Taking up manual system files can involve many worker hours. Maintaining two systems in parallel can place substantial strains on users.
Scheduling of operations and test running	Scheduling involves timing of input, processing, and output. Schedules should be tested for a period. Any needed adjustments should then be made before the final schedule is approved for production use.

Auditors often pay special attention to several aspects of the conversion phase:

1. If substantial disruption is likely to occur, asset safeguarding, data integrity, system effectiveness, and system efficiency are at risk. For example, a programmer could take advantage of a situation in which managers have insufficient time to review program modifications to install unauthorized code. Likewise, a data-entry clerk could introduce unauthorized transactions into the system when large backlogs of input exist and many data-entry errors have to be corrected.
2. Conversion can be a time when tempers fray and users become severely disillusioned with the system. As a result, they might begin to undermine implementation efforts. Careful management of the change process becomes especially critical when users engage in counterimplementation activities.

3. Often trade-offs must be made between the integrity of data taken up on the new system and the need to get the system running. For example, data-validation criteria might be relaxed because high rejection rates are encountered and the conversion process is stalling. Later correction of data must not be forgotten.
4. Careful planning of the activities to be undertaken during the conversion phase is essential for many systems. Controls to ensure asset safeguarding, data integrity, system effectiveness, and system efficiency must be designed and implemented. For example, control totals might be used to ensure data converted from one storage medium to another is not corrupted or lost. The conversion phase also must be monitored carefully to identify problems and undertake remedial actions promptly.

Operation and Maintenance

During the operation and maintenance phase, the new system is run as a production system. In addition, periodically it is modified to better meet its objectives. Only through day-to-day experience with a system do many of its strengths and weaknesses become apparent.

In light of production experience with a system, three types of changes can be undertaken: *(1) repair maintenance*—logic errors discovered in the system are corrected; *(2) adaptive maintenance*—changes in the system (user) environment might necessitate system modification; and *(3) perfective maintenance*—changes might be made to improve processing efficiency. Repair maintenance and perfective maintenance are more likely to occur early in the life of a system. Adaptive maintenance is more likely to occur at later stages.

Whatever the reason for maintenance, auditors' primary concern is that a formal change process exists to identify and record the need for changes to a system and to authorize and control the implementation of needed changes (Dow and Gallegos 1986). This formal change process is more important in systems that are used widely throughout the organization and which perform basic and critical functions. Nevertheless, even in small systems developed by users for their own purposes, formal change procedures can still be important. Small, localized systems could support users who are making critical decisions affecting the overall welfare of the organization. The introduction of erroneous modifications into these systems can have widespread consequences. In this light, maintenance activities associated with these systems need to be approved and monitored carefully.

SUMMARY

Auditors can become involved in an assessment of the systems development process in three ways. First, in a participative capacity, auditors evaluate the quality of the systems development process for a particular system, ensure that needed controls are built into the system, and design and implement audit modules required to monitor the system. The objective is to ensure that only high-quality systems are released into production use. Second, in a postimplementation review capacity, auditors evaluate the conduct of systems development activities for a specific system that has been placed in production already. They also evaluate its current status in terms of attaining asset safeguarding, data integrity, system effectiveness, and system efficiency objectives. The goals are to enhance learning among stakeholders in the systems development process and to identify any maintenance that needs to be carried out on the production system. Third, in a general review capacity, auditors evaluate the quality of the overall systems development process. This review allows them to make judgments on the likely quality of individual application systems developed by the systems development management subsystem, the control risk associated with this subsystem, and the extent of substantive testing they should carry out to assess how well audit objectives are being met.

During all three types of audit, auditors must choose a normative model of the systems development process to provide the basis for evaluation. Unfortunately, no single normative model exists that is applicable in all situations. Over time, we have come to understand that the ways in which systems development activities should be carried out must vary depending on such factors as the extent of uncertainty surrounding the system, its likely behavioral impact, and the political repercussions it may evoke. Auditors must be able to adopt a contingency perspective of the systems development process so they can determine what activities should be performed, how they should be performed, and when they should be performed.

In spite of this uncertainty surrounding the normative models, auditors still can identify a fairly robust, stable agenda of issues that must be addressed during the systems development process. These issues vary in importance depending upon the system to be developed. Moreover, they vary in terms of the ways they should be addressed in each system to be developed. Nevertheless, they provide a useful framework to guide audit work.

Review Questions

4-1 What are the three ways that auditors can become involved in the systems development process? How do their audit objectives differ? How do their evidence-collection methods differ?

4-2 Why do auditors need a normative model of the systems development process? How might the adequacy of normative models of the systems development process be evaluated?

4-3 Two ways of thinking about the systems development process are the life-cycle approach and the sociotechnical design approach. What are the major *similarities* and *differences* between the two approaches? Can the two approaches be reconciled?

4-4 The sociotechnical design approach negates almost every major feature of the traditional life-cycle approach to systems development. Comment.

4-5 Briefly explain the nature of the political approach to information systems development. If the political approach to information systems development is used, when is it important to have user involvement in the design process? When is it important to have face-to-face negotiation and compromise?

4-6 Briefly explain the nature of soft-systems methodology. List the *seven* major steps in soft-systems methodology.

4-7 How does the prototyping approach to systems development differ from the traditional life-cycle approach? Briefly describe the *five* major phases of the prototyping approach.

4-8 Briefly explain the nature of the contingency approach to information systems development. Give two contextual factors that might affect how systems development is undertaken and explain how they might affect systems development work.

4–9 Why might different normative models of the systems development process be appropriate for auditors to use at different times? Give an example to help your explanation.

4–10 How might the need for a new system be recognized? Give two concerns that auditors should have about the ways information systems projects are initiated.

4–11 Management of the change process involves two major tasks: project management and change facilitation. Briefly explain the nature of each task.

4–12 What are the bases on which the feasibility of an information system should be assessed? What bases are the most important from an audit perspective?

4–13 How might the level of uncertainty surrounding an information system affect the approach taken to assessing its feasibility?

4–14 Under what circumstances should auditors be concerned about whether designers studied an existing system during the development of a new system?

4–15 Briefly describe two matters that auditors might investigate when evaluating how well designers studied existing product and information flows during the development of a new system.

4–16 What is meant by the strategic requirements of a system? How are strategic requirements related to system effectiveness? How might auditors carry out a postimplementation review of how well designers elicited the strategic requirements for a new system to be developed?

4–17 Briefly describe two concerns that auditors might have if a new system required redesign of organizational structures or jobs.

4–18 If an auditor is participating in the systems development process, why is the information processing systems design phase often one of major involvement?

4–19 What types of approaches should auditors expect to see used when designers are attempting to elicit detailed requirements during design of an information processing system?

4–20 Why should auditors investigate whether designers have used tools like data-flow diagrams during design of the data/information flow for a new system?

4–21 From an audit perspective, why are design decisions on the database scope sometimes critical?

4–22 Why do auditors often deem the design of the user interface to be a critical activity?

4–23 Is the physical-design phase of information processing systems design likely to have a greater impact on asset safeguarding and data integrity objectives or system effectiveness and system efficiency objectives? Briefly justify your answer.

4–24 Briefly describe one activity in the design of the hardware/system software platform for an information system that might interest us as auditors when we conduct a postimplementation review.

4–25 Briefly describe two tasks that must be performed during the procedures development phase. How might *internal* auditors evaluate how well these tasks have been undertaken by designers?

4–26 Briefly describe four types of acceptance testing that should be carried out before production release of a new application system. List two concerns that auditors might have about how well these types of testing were performed by designers.

4–27 Briefly describe two types of activities that might be performed during the conversion phase. List two concerns that auditors might have about how well these activities were performed.

4–28 Briefly describe the three types of maintenance that might be carried out on a system. List them in their likely descending order of importance from an auditor's viewpoint.

Multiple-Choice Questions

4–1 In an *ex post* general review audit of the systems development process, the auditor's primary objective is to:

a Evaluate a specific system to determine whether the necessary controls have been included in the design

b Carry out a substantive test of the systems development process for all accounting application systems within the information systems division

c Evaluate the systems development process, in general, as a basis for choosing the extent of substantive testing subsequently needed in the audit

d Determine whether a material accounting application system needs to be modified or maintained

4–2 The auditor uses a normative model of the system development process as a basis for:

a Determining the activities that should be carried out during systems development

b Determining what activities are usually undertaken during systems development

c Describing the activities that are, in fact, performed during systems development

d Predicting the systems development activities undertaken in the organization being audited

4–3 A major difference between the life-cycle approach and the sociotechnical design approach to systems development is:

a The sociotechnical design approach deemphasizes project-control techniques

b The sociotechnical design approach gives more emphasis to joint design of the technical and social systems

c The life-cycle approach is more structured

d The life-cycle approach requires higher levels of user consensus before design is permitted to proceed to the next phase

4–4 Under the political approach to systems development, user participation in the design process is an important means of reducing behavioral implementation problems when:

a The system will alter the existing power structure in the organization

b Face-to-face negotiation has not been successful

c A "fixer" is unable to resolve conflict among users

d The proposed system will leave the existing organizational power structure intact

4–5 Which of the following situations is most conducive to use of the soft-systems approach to eliciting the requirements for an information system?

a Substantial political conflicts exist among users in relation to their requirements

b Users will not agree that a problem exists which needs to be resolved via the system

c Users are willing to engage in self-reflection and learning to tease out their requirements

d Users agree that behavioral and quality-of-working-life issues are more important in the system than task-accomplishment issues

4–6 Design prototyping is more likely to be needed when:
 a The application system to be designed is a traditional accounting system
 b The designer believes users will react negatively to the system to be implemented
 c The life-cycle approach to system development is chosen
 d There is uncertainty surrounding user requirements for the system

4–7 Proponents of the contingency approach to systems development argue:
 a Information processing systems design should not proceed until all user-requirement uncertainties have been resolved
 b No single approach to systems development will work best under all circumstances
 c The key factor affecting the choice of systems development approach is the level of behavioral conflict that might be evoked by the system
 d Although the activities performed in each design phase might vary, the sequence in which design phases will be followed will always be the same

4–8 With respect to the various phases in the systems development life cycle, which of the following is *least likely* to vary?
 a Conduct of each phase
 b Sequence in which the phases are performed
 c Presence of each phase
 d Resources needed to perform each phase

4–9 Which of the following is the *most likely* sequence of phases in the systems development process?
 a Analysis of the existing system, software acquisition and development, organizational and job design
 b Acceptance testing, procedures development, management of the change process
 c Entry and feasibility assessment, organizational and job design, information processing systems design
 d Entry and feasibility assessment, problem definition, analysis of the existing system

4–10 During the problem/opportunity definition phase, which of the following is *least likely* to be described in the terms of reference?
 a Boundaries of the system to be examined
 b Organizational and resource constraints
 c Tentative objectives of the new system
 d Acceptance testing procedures to be followed

4–11 Management of the change process is the phase in the systems development process that:
 a Proceeds concurrently with all other phases
 b Stops after unfreezing has occurred and restarts when refreezing commences
 c Occurs between the problem/opportunity recognition and entry and feasibility assessment phases
 d Distinguishes the sociotechnical design approach from all other approaches to systems development

4–12 During the entry phase, the system designer:
 a Explains to users various alternative designs that can be implemented
 b Determines what problem is the real motivation for the systems development effort
 c Assists users to formulate the strategic design for the proposed system
 d Attempts to obtain a commitment to change among the stakeholders

4–13 If auditors are evaluating how well the entry and feasibility assessment phase was carried out for a material but nevertheless small, localized, straightforward accounting application system developed by end users, they should check to see that:

   a Unfreezing procedures were carried out carefully by an independent design group

   b Primary emphasis was given to economic feasibility in the feasibility assessment

   c Value analysis was used to assess the feasibility of the system

   d The feasibility assessment calculations were checked by the quality assurance group

4–14 Which of the following is *unlikely* to be a purpose of systems designers studying the existing organizational history, structure, and culture?

   a To evaluate whether a proposed system is likely to produce organizational power shifts

   b To determine what types of job designs in the proposed system will most likely be accepted by users as reasonable

   c To better understand how the proposed system will be coupled to other systems in the organization

   d To elicit data and information requirements for the proposed system

4–15 Which of the following is *unlikely* to be a concern of auditors when they evaluate how well system designers studied the existing product and information flows during the design of a new system?

   a Whether designers used a methodology like structured analysis to guide their work

   b Whether designers used CASE tools to document their work

   c Whether designers used prototyping to help them study the existing product and information flows

   d Whether designers needed to study the existing product and information flows in the first place

4–16 Which of the following is *not* an example of a strategic systems requirement?

   a Use a high-level language to program the system

   b Produce a product below a given cost

   c Increase task variety in the jobs supported by the system

   d Maintain the existing organizational power structure

4–17 Which of the following is *unlikely* be a concern of *internal* auditors when evaluating how well systems designers undertook the organizational and job design phase during the development of a new system?

   a Whether designers involved users in the redesign of any jobs affected by the proposed system

   b Whether designers strived to ensure loose, organic, enriched jobs resulted when jobs had to be redesigned

   c Whether designers sought advice from someone skilled in organizational theory and practice

   d How designers resolved conflicts and uncertainties that arose during the design of organizational structures and jobs

4–18 Eliciting detailed information processing system design requirements by asking stakeholders what they require is *most likely* to be successful during the development of which of the following types of systems?

   a An accounts receivable system

   b An electronic data interchange system

    c A decision support system

    d An office automation system

4-19 Which of the following is *unlikely* to be a concern of designers during the design of the data/information flow for the information processing system?

    a The extent to which data and information flows should be formalized

    b The frequency and timing of information flows

    c The medium that will be used to transport the data and information flows

    d The locations where transformations are to be performed on the data

4-20 A global database design is *more likely* to result if:

    a An organization already has a database management system

    b The storage structure design dictates a database is needed

    c Decision making is to be decentralized

    d Subunits within the organization are highly interdependent

4-21 *External* auditors are *most likely* to be concerned about the quality of the user-interface design in an information system because:

    a Most behavioral problems arise with information systems as a result of poor design of the user interface

    b There is a high correlation between the quality of the user interface and the level of inherent risk associated with the audit

    c The quality of the user interface affects the extent to which users are likely to make errors when they enter data into the system

    d Controls in the user interface are among the most difficult to test to determine whether they are operating reliably

4-22 Which of the following tasks usually is not performed during physical design of the information processing system?

    a Breaking the logical design up into implementation units

    b Designing icons to be used on a screen layout

    c Partitioning jobs into job steps

    d Designing intermediate files

4-23 Which of the following is *unlikely* to be a concern of *internal* auditors when they evaluate how well designers undertook the design and acquisition of the hardware/system software platform to be used to support an information processing system:

    a The quality of the request for a proposal prepared for vendors based upon the configuration design

    b The extent to which end users were involved in the choice of the design configuration for the system software

    c The extent to which simulation models or queuing models were used to evaluate different configurations

    d Whether designers have attempted to maintain modularity and generality in the designs they considered

4-24 Which of the following is *unlikely* to be a concern of *external* auditors during the software acquisition and development phase?

    a The resources consumed in compiling programs for the application system

    b The adequacy of requirements specifications provided to generalized software vendors

    c Whether end users are developing software for the application system

    d Whether skilled programmers know the quality assurance procedures that will be used by the quality assurance group

4–25 Which of the following is *most likely* to be an objective during procedures design?

 a Maximum documentation of procedures
 b Maximum differentiation of procedures
 c Minimum specification of procedures
 d Minimum formality in procedures documentation

4–26 The primary difference between program testing and system testing is:

 a System testing focuses on testing the interfaces between programs, whereas program testing focuses on individual programs
 b Program testing is more comprehensive than system testing
 c System testing is concerned with testing all aspects of a system including job designs and reward system designs
 d Programmers have no involvement in system testing, whereas designers are involved in program testing

4–27 During conversion, the primary purpose of parallel running is to:

 a Provide the basis for validating the design and implementation of the new system
 b Determine which of the systems being run in parallel is more effective and efficient
 c Provide the basis for carrying out comprehensive system and user tests
 d Determine whether there are any bugs in the new hardware/system software platform that has been chosen

4–28 The primary focus of repair maintenance is:

 a Reducing the resources consumed by a system
 b Removing logic errors from a system
 c Changing a system to better fit user requirements
 d Improving the quality of the user interface in a system

4–29 In which of the following phases of the systems development process is the auditor *most likely* to have greatest involvement?

 a Conversion
 b Organizational and job design
 c Elicitation of strategic requirements
 d Information processing system design

Exercises and Cases

4–1 NWT Engineering Ltd. is a large consulting engineering firm based in Edmonton, Alberta. It provides services in many areas including mining exploration, environmental management, transportation, water and sewage, civil engineering, waste management, contaminant disposal, and electrical engineering. Each area of specialization is the responsibility of a divisional vice president who operates relatively autonomously of all other areas. Corporate services and accounting, however, come under the control of a single vice president. Although divisions can maintain their own accounting systems, they still must provide data in a standardized form for input to corporate accounting systems.

Your firm has just been appointed as the external auditors for NWT Engineering. You are the partner in charge of the audit, and you are currently planning interim audit work you wish to undertake. In this light you commence to plan the audit of systems development controls in the hope that you can reduce the extent of substantive year-end work.

During an interview with the vice president, corporate services and accounting, you ask about the structure of systems development services within the company. You are told no centralized systems development group exists. Indeed, no centralized information systems facility exists. Although the company once had a centralized data processing facility, in due course it was closed down. Responsibility for information systems was then divested to the individual divisional vice presidents. This arrangement has proved to be very successful. Each division typically now has a local area network of workstations connected to a minicomputer that acts as a server. These divisional minicomputers usually can communicate with one another. Each division also has systems development staff who assist divisional staff with the design, implementation, and operation of information systems within the division. Although systems development staff within the different divisions occasionally meet with one another, primarily they act autonomously. Many end users within the divisions also undertake their own systems development work using high-level design and programming tools that their divisions have purchased or leased.

Required. In light of the information provided to you by the vice president, corporate services and accounting, outline how you plan to approach the audit of systems development controls within NWT Engineering Ltd.

4–2 The vice president of production has requested that top management have the information systems division investigate the feasibility of a computer system to improve the scheduling of production. Though her production managers are extremely competent, she is convinced that because of the complexity of the decision, they do not always make the best judgments.

One of the system designers from the information systems division starts the process of entry by requesting that the production managers participate in a series of workshops that will examine the strengths and weaknesses of the total scheduling system. Even though attendance at the workshop is voluntary, most production managers still attend. After six workshops over a period of four months, the system designer reports to the vice president of production that the production managers believe a computer system will solve many of their problems. Having received this information, the vice president of production is convinced the project should go ahead.

Because top management is uncertain about the eventual success of the system, however, they come to you as the internal audit manager to ask your advice. They value your independence. Your company has been experiencing cash-flow difficulties, and top management is reluctant to embark upon any high-risk systems development projects.

Required. Prepare a brief report advising top management on how they should proceed.

4–3 Sunmatics started out as a small manufacturing firm producing solar energy equipment. With the impending shortage of energy in some countries and greater environmental concerns, demand for its production has grown. The company has trebled in size over a period of five years.

Because of problems experienced with inventory control, a computer system has been designed to facilitate reordering and control over inventory. About 800 components are currently used in the various solar energy equipment manufactured. Currently, inventory records are maintained on bin cards. Inventory levels constantly change as production workers obtain components for their needs.

Required. The systems development team is meeting to consider changeover procedures for the inventory file. You are the internal auditor participating in the systems development effort. How would you recommend the file changeover be accomplished? In particular, what controls would you recommend be set up to maintain data integrity during changeover?

4–4 Finerfoods, Inc., is a large, decentralized and diversified organization that primarily manufactures and sells grocery items. Various divisions of the company are widely dispersed geographically. In the past, divisions have been responsible for all aspects of their information systems operations.

Recently, top management has questioned whether it would be more efficient to have a centralized group of analysts and programmers develop and implement standard systems that could be distributed and used by all divisions within the company. The vice president of information systems, however, is strongly objecting to the proposed change. He argues the primary reason information systems in the company have been so successful is that they have been designed not only to accomplish task objectives but also to achieve a high quality of working life for users. He contends information systems departments in the divisions should be left to develop and implement their own systems as they are best able to develop systems that will support the organization and job design of their users. Top management is questioning whether the costs of having individual divisions develop their own systems, however, can be justified.

Required. The president asks you, the manager of internal audit for the company, to prepare a report outlining your thoughts on the costs and benefits of the proposed change. He asks you to give him your opinion on the validity of the arguments made by the vice president for information systems.

4–5 You are an external auditor undertaking a review of systems development controls in one of your client organizations. Since your last review, the client has converted some of its major accounting applications from batch systems to online, real-time, update systems. They did not notify you of the work they were undertaking. These systems are the first major online systems the company has developed.

During an interview you have with the manager, systems development, you ask about the types of user-interface design standards employed to guide systems development work. The manager indicates the standards are still being developed. She says she is not concerned, however, because all her analysts and programmers who worked on the conversion projects went to a common course where they learned about user-interface design and programming. So far she has not received any complaints from users about the quality of the interface.

Required. In light of the information provided by the manager, systems development, how would you now proceed with your audit work?

4–6 You are the chief internal auditor for Corbault Corporation, a large decentralized, diversified, manufacturing organization. As a result of concerns about controls over hardware and software purchases throughout the corporation, the controller asks you to investigate a major subsidiary of the corporation. Your investigation reveals the subsidiary has purchased over $1 million worth of microcomputer hardware and software and that many managers are actively engaged in developing their own systems. The hardware and software purchases have escaped detection by top management as individual purchases have involved only small expenditures. In total, however, the expenditures are considered to be substantial. Most purchases have occurred during the last three years.

The controller's initial reaction is to prohibit any further purchases of microcomputer hardware and software throughout the corporation. She is concerned about the large expenditures. More importantly, however, she is concerned about the ways in which user-developed systems are being employed in the corporation and their potential impact on operations, especially if the systems are poorly designed. Nevertheless, before taking the matter further, she asks your advice on what should be done to exercise effective control over hardware and software purchases and end-user developed systems in the corporation.

Required. Write a brief report to the controller outlining possible strategies to address her concerns. Your report should list the relative advantages and disadvantages of each strategy you identify.

Answers to Multiple-Choice Questions

4–1	c	**4–8**	c	**4–15**	c	**4–22**	b
4–2	a	**4–9**	c	**4–16**	a	**4–23**	b
4–3	b	**4–10**	d	**4–17**	b	**4–24**	a
4–4	d	**4–11**	a	**4–18**	a	**4–25**	c
4–5	c	**4–12**	d	**4–19**	c	**4–26**	a
4–6	d	**4–13**	b	**4–20**	d	**4–27**	a
4–7	b	**4–14**	d	**4–21**	c	**4–28**	b
						4–29	d

REFERENCES

Allen, Sandra (1996), "Maintaining Realistic End-User Computing Security and Control," *EDPACS* (November), 1–17.

Ambrose, Robert, and Ralph Hessler (1995), "Risk Assessment Approach for Selecting Systems Development Efforts to Audit," *IS Audit & Control Journal*, I, 20–23.

Bostrom, Robert P., and J. Stephen Heinen (1977a), "MIS Problems and Failures: A Socio-Technical Perspective—Part 1: The Causes," *MIS Quarterly* (September), 17–32.

—— and —— (1977b), "MIS Problems and Failures: A Socio-Technical Perspective—Part II: The Application of Socio-Technical Theory," *MIS Quarterly* (December), 11–28.

Brown, David (1997), *An Introduction to Object-Oriented Analysis: Objects in Plain English*. New York: John Wiley & Sons.

Burch, John G. (1992), *Systems Analysis, Design, and Implementation*. Boston: Boyd & Fraser.

Carroll, John M., Penny L. Smith-Kerker, Jim R. Ford, and Sandra A. Mazur-Rimetz (1988), "The Minimal Manual," in Stephen Doheny-Farina, ed., *Effective Documentation: What We Have Learned From Research*. Boston: The MIT Press, 73–102.

Checkland, Peter B. (1981), *Systems Thinking, Systems Practice*. New York: John Wiley & Sons.

Coad, Peter, and Edward Yourdon (1991a), *Object-Oriented Design*. Upper Saddle River, NJ: Prentice-Hall.

—— and —— (1991b), *Object-Oriented Analysis*, 2d ed. Upper Saddle River, NJ: Prentice-Hall.

Chen, Peter P. S. (1976), "The Entity-Relationship Model—Toward a Unified View of Data," *ACM Transactions on Database Systems* (March), 9–36.

Codd, E. F. (1970), "A Relational Model of Data for Large Shared Data Banks," *Communications of the ACM* (June), 377–387.

Davies, Lynda J., and Paul W. J. Ledington (1991), *Information in Action: Soft Systems Methodology*. London: Macmillan.

Doughty, Ken (1996), "Auditing Project Management of Information Systems Development," *EDPACS* (January), 1–14.

Dow, Daniel P., and Frederick Gallegos (1986), "Auditing Systems Maintenance: A How-to Approach," in *EDP Auditing*. Boston: Auerbach, Portfolio 76–07–10, 1–12.

DeMarco, Tom (1978), *Structured Analysis and System Specification*. Upper Saddle River, NJ: Prentice-Hall.

Fabbri, Anthony J., and A. Robert Schwab (1992), *Practical Database Management*. Boston: PWS-Kent.

Gallegos, Frederick (1988), "The EDP Auditor's Role in Systems Development," in *EDP Auditing*. Boston: Auerbach, Portfolio 76–01–30, 1–8.

Gallegos, Frederick, and Daniel P. Dow (1990), "Key Review Points for Auditing Systems Development," in *EDP Auditing*. Boston: Auerbach, Portfolio 74–04–30, 1–20.

Ginzberg, Michael J. (1981) "A Prescriptive Model for System Implementation," *Systems, Objectives, Solutions*, 2(3), 33–46.

Gremillion, Lee L., and Philip Pyburn (1983), "Breaking the Systems Development Bottleneck," *Harvard Business Review* (March–April), 130–137.

Hirschheim, Rudy, Heinz K. Klein, and Kalle Lyytinen (1995), *Information Systems Development and Data Modeling: Conceptual and Philosophical Foundations*. Cambridge: Cambridge University Press.

Keen, Peter W. (1981), "Information Systems and Organizational Changes," *Communications of the ACM* (January), 24–33.

——— (1981), "Value Analysis: Justifying Decision Support Systems," *MIS Quarterly* (March), 1–15.

Markus, M. Lynne (1981), "Implementation Politics: Top Management Support and User Involvement," *Systems, Objectives, Solutions*, 1(4), 203–215.

——— (1983), "Power, Politics, and MIS Implementation," *Communications of the ACM* (June), 430–444.

McFarlan, F. Warren (1981), "Portfolio Approach to Information Systems," *Harvard Business Review* (September–October), 142–150.

Naumann, J. David, and A. Milton Jenkins (1984), "Prototyping: The New Paradigm for Systems Development," *MIS Quarterly* (September), 29–44.

Page-Jones, Meilir (1988), *The Practical Guide to Structured Systems Design*, 2d ed. Upper Saddle River, NJ: Prentice-Hall.

Ronen, Boaz, Michael A. Palley, and Henry C. Lucas, Jr. (1989), "Spreadsheet Analysis and Design," *Communications of the ACM* (January), 84–93.

Weitzel, John R., and Larry Kerschberg (1989), "Developing Knowledge-Based Systems: Reorganizing the System Development Life Cycle," *Communications of the ACM* (April), 482–488.

Yourdon, Edward (1989), *Modern Structured Analysis*. Upper Saddle River, NJ: Prentice-Hall.

TECHNIQUES FOR STUDYING THE EXISTING SYSTEM: STRUCTURED ANALYSIS

The central tool of structured analysis is the data flow diagram (DFD). A DFD is a pictorial representation of the flow of data through a system. It comprises four basic elements: *(1)* data flows—represented by named vectors; *(2)* processes—represented by circles, rounded-edge rectangles, or "bubbles"; *(3)* files or data stores—represented by straight lines or open-ended rectangles; and *(4)* external entities or data sources/sinks—represented by squares.

Constructing a DFD usually involves a two-step process. First, a *physical* DFD is drawn showing how the logical flow of data is currently implemented. Second, a *logical* DFD is derived showing *what* is done and not *how* it is done.

To illustrate how a DFD can be used, consider Figure 4–15, which shows a DFD for an order-entry system. Each bubble in the DFD is decomposed into further levels of detail. For example, Figure 4–16 presents a more detailed de-

FIGURE 4–15. Data flow diagram for order-entry system.

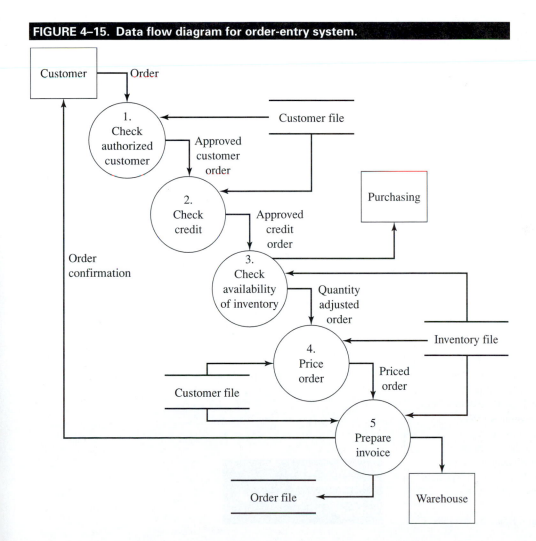

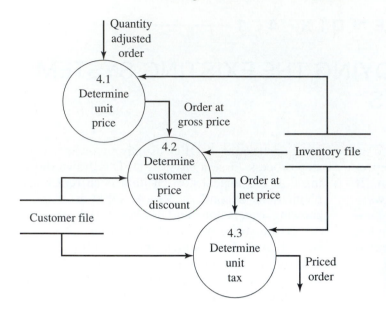

FIGURE 4–16. Lower-level data flow diagram for "price-order" bubble.

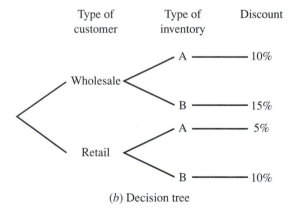

Type of customer	W	W	R	R
Type of inventory	A	B	A	B
Discount	10	15	5	10

(*a*) Decision table

Type of customer   Type of inventory   Discount

Wholesale
   A ——— 10%
   B ——— 15%

Retail
   A ——— 5%
   B ——— 10%

(*b*) Decision tree

```
IF order is from wholesale customer
and IF order is for Type-A inventory item
          THEN item-discount is 10%
      ELSE order is for Type-B inventory item
          SO item-discount is 15%
ELSE order is from retail customer
SO IF order is for Type-A inventory item
          THEN item-disount is 5%
      ELSE order is for Type-B inventory item
          SO item-discount is 10%
```

(*c*) Structured English

FIGURE 4–17. Representation of procedural logic for DFD bubble.

Order	=	Order-Number + Customer-Name
		+ Mailing-Address + Shipping-Address
		+ {Order-Line} + Carrier
		+ Order Date + {Customer-Instruction-Line}
Order-Line	=	Line-Number + Product-Number + Product-Description
		+ Quantity + Unit-of-Measure

FIGURE 4–18. Partial definition of order in data dictionary.

scription of the data flow in bubble 4: Price Order. By recursively breaking down the bubbles into further levels of detail, top-down, breadth-first decomposition occurs—the notion of "leveling" the DFD in structured analysis terms.

The elements in a DFD require further definition if the nature of the system is to be clear. When the bubbles have been "exploded" to their lowest-level bubbles, the logic of these lowest-level bubbles must be described. Three techniques are used: decision tables, decision trees, and structured English. Figure 4–17 shows how the logic for bubble 4.2 in Figure 4–16 might be represented using each of these techniques. Decision tables and decision trees tend to be used when the procedures to be defined primarily de-

scribe conditional logic. Structured English tends to be used when the procedures to be defined describe sequence logic.

The data flows and data stores must also be described in a data dictionary. Figure 4–18 shows how the data flow "order" might be partially described using the data-dictionary conventions given by DeMarco (1978). Before defining the data, however, proponents of structured analysis argue the data flows and data stores should be placed in their "simplest" form using the techniques of "normalization" derived from relational database management systems theory (see Yourdon 1989). In addition, data-structure diagrams might be constructed to show the access paths available to various data items maintained in files in the database.

------------------------------ **A P P E N D I X   4 . 2** ------------------------------

TECHNIQUES FOR STUDYING THE EXISTING SYSTEM: OBJECT-ORIENTED ANALYSIS

Object-oriented analysis is based on the idea that we can model the world in terms of objects and their interactions. *Objects* are the things or entities in the real world that have some meaning for us. They possess attributes, which characterize them. They also interact with each other. In Figure 4–19, for example, the light rounded-rectangle shows that "employee" is an object (the notation used in Figure 4–19 has been proposed by Coad and Yourdon 1991b). It possesses attributes, such as "birth-date" and "address." Another object, "project," interacts with the employee object. When a project is started, it updates the "current-project" attribute of the employee object. In the language of objects, the project sends a *message* to the employee object.

Objects can be organized into two basic structures. First, they can be identified as a member of a *class* or a *subclass* of objects. Classes of objects can be formed whenever different objects possess

FIGURE 4–19. Partial object-oriented representation of application domain.

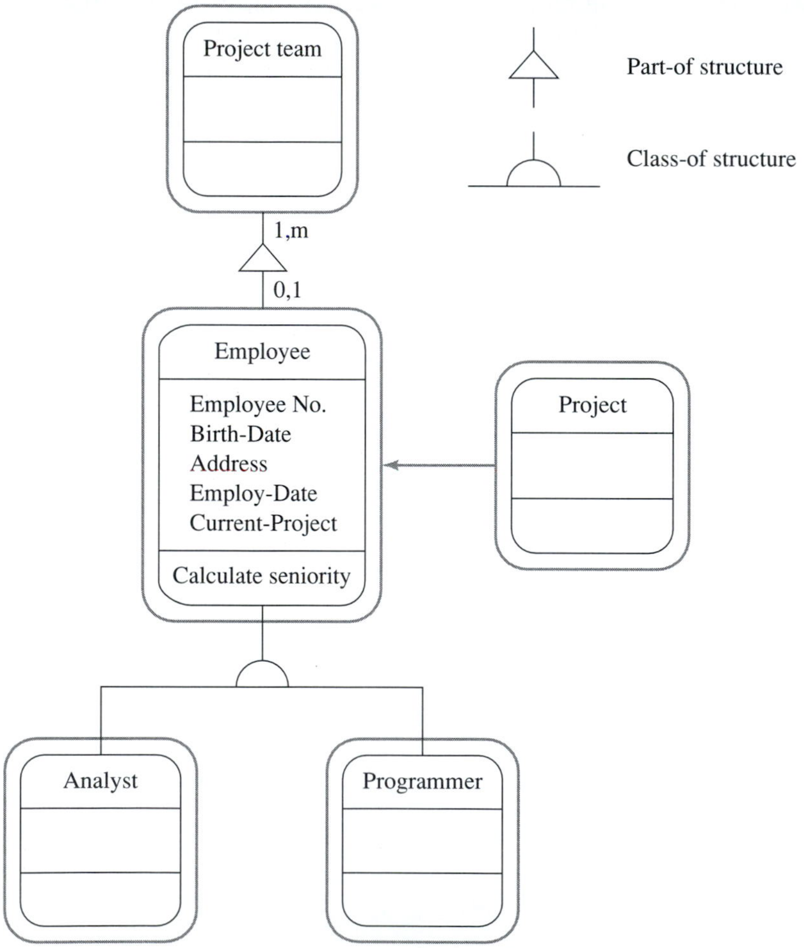

at least one common attribute. In Figure 4–19, for example, the dark rounded-rectangle shows that "employee" is a class. "Analyst" and "programmer" are both subclasses of employee. They possess all the attributes of employee; in addition, each possesses at least one attribute not possessed by employee. Note the semi-circle symbol on the arcs that intersect particular object classes represents the *class-of* structure.

Second, objects can be identified as a *component* of some other object. In Figure 4–19, employees are components of a project team. A project team may have from one to *m* members. An employee, however, may not be a member of any project team and cannot be a member of more than one team. Note the triangle symbol on the arcs that intersect particular object classes represents the *part-of* structure.

Besides attributes, objects can have *methods* or *services* that change their states. For example, the service "calculate-seniority" for the employee object calculates how much seniority employees have in light of the length of time they have been employed with the organization.

Two important goals that have motivated the development of object-oriented analysis and design are *encapsulation* and *inheritance*. Encapsulation means the details of an object are hidden from other objects. In Figure 4–19, for example, only minimal details about the attributes and services of an employee object needs to be known by other objects. By hiding object details, coupling between objects is weakened. Thus, changes to a system are likely to have fewer effects.

Inheritance means the objects in a subclass automatically acquire the attributes and services of their super-classes. For example, the analyst and programmer objects in Figure 4–19 possess all the attributes and services of employee objects. Inheritance promotes reuse of objects and, hopefully, greater system reliability.

------------------------------- **A P P E N D I X   4 . 3** -------------------------------

ENTITY-RELATIONSHIP MODELING

Entity-relationship modeling (ERM) is a technique developed by Chen (1976) to represent certain features of the real world. In particular, ERM focuses on entities, their attributes, and relationships among entities. Using an entity-relationship diagram (ERD), entities are described via rectangles, attributes are described via ellipses, and relationships are described via triangles. ERM is now widely used and supported via computer-aided systems engineering (CASE) tools.

Figure 4–20 shows an ERD that represents some aspects of a student-enrollment system in a university. "Student," "course," and "subject" are entities. The ERD shows a few student attributes, namely, "student ID," "name," and "address." The "enrolled-in" relationship between the student entity and the course entity shows that a student can enroll in only one course (e.g., B.Sc.) whereas many students can enroll in the same course. Similarly, the "registered-in" relationship between the student and subject entities shows a student must be enrolled in one subject but can enroll in no more than four subjects, and a subject can have from zero to m students enrolled in it.

FIGURE 4–20. Entity-relationship diagram.

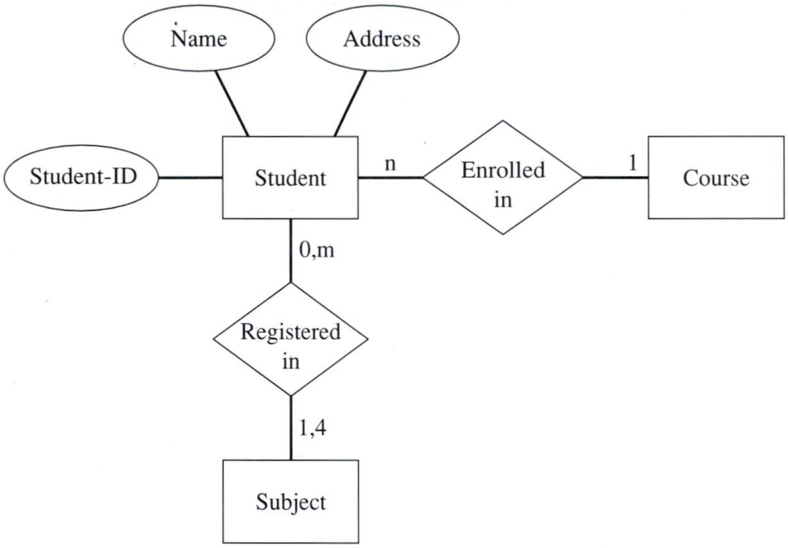

-------------------------------- **A P P E N D I X   4 . 4** --------------------------------

NORMALIZATION

Normalization is a record-design technique developed by Codd (1970) to avoid certain kinds of update anomalies. In essence, it involves breaking a record down into smaller records until the values of all data items in the record depend only on the values of the key(s) in the record.

A number of different types of normal-form records have been identified (see, e.g., Fabbri and Schwab 1992). Here we shall examine the three most commonly-encountered in database design. In *first normal form*, a record contains no repeating groups. Figure 4–21 shows how an unnormalized student record can be converted to a first-normal-form record by removing the repeating group of data items pertaining to grades in various subjects. Of course, multiple instances of the first-normal-form record would now be needed to replace a single instance of the unnormalized record. Nevertheless, the first-normal-form record avoids the problems that arise, for example, when a student takes more subjects than the number of subjects provided for in the repeating group within the unnormalized record.

In a *second-normal-form* record, all nonkey data item values in the record depend only on the values of the key in the record. In Figure 4–21, the key of the first-normal-form record is the concatenation of Stud-ID and Subj-ID. Only one data item depends on this key, namely, Grade. All other data items depend on only part of the key. For example, Subj-Name depends only on Subj-ID.

Three second-normal-form records can be created: the first with a key of Stud-ID; the second with a combined key of Stud-ID and Subj-ID; and the third with a key of Subj-ID. Note how the values of all nonkey data items in these records depend only on the values of their key. Second normal form removes various types of update anomalies that arise with first normal form. For example, consider the problems that arise with the first-normal-form record if we wish to create a new subject in which no student is yet enrolled.

FIGURE 4–21. Normalization of records.

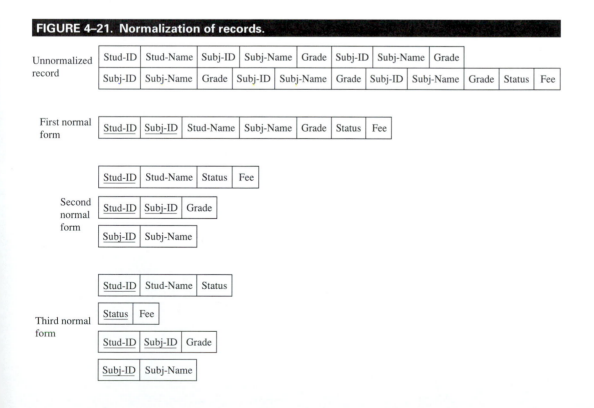

In a *third-normal-form* record, no nonkey data item is *transitively dependent* on another nonkey data item. Assume, for example, that student fee is determined when a student's status is known. Fee is therefore transitively dependent on status. To remove the transitive dependency, the second-normal-form record must be broken up into two third-normal-form records. Again, certain types of update problems are overcome with third normal form. For example, assume the fee for part-time students was increased. If records are in second normal form, the records of all part-time students would have to be located and updated with the new fee. In third normal form, only one record must be located and updated.

Programming Management Controls

Chapter Outline

Chapter Key Points

■ Program development and implementation is a major phase within the systems development life cycle. The primary objectives of this phase are to produce or acquire and to implement high-quality programs.

■ The program development life cycle comprises six major phases: (a) planning, (b) control, (c) design, (d) coding, (e) testing, and (f) operation and maintenance. The control phase is a "phantom" phase that runs in parallel with all other phases.

■ During the planning phase of the program development life cycle, management estimates the resources required to develop or acquire programs. Management must also choose a design approach, an implementation approach, an integration and testing approach, and an organization for the project team.

■ Five major software cost-estimation techniques are (a) algorithmic models, (b) expert judgment, (c) analogy, (d) top-down estimation, and (e) bottom-up estimation.

■ The purpose of the control phase during software development or acquisition is to monitor progress against plan and to ensure software released for production use is authentic, accurate, and complete. Techniques like Work Breakdown Structures, Gantt charts, and PERT charts can be used to monitor progress against plan. To help ensure software is released that is authentic, accurate, and complete, review procedures can be exercised at major milestones in the software development or acquisition process. In addition, manual and automated access controls can be used to restrict access to software to authorized personnel.

■ Programmers should use a systematic approach to program design, such as any of the structured design approaches or object-oriented design.

■ During the coding phase of software development, programmers must choose a module implementation and integration strategy, a coding strategy, and a documentation strategy. Three major module implementation and integration strategies that can be used are (a) top down, (b) bottom up, and (c) threads. The coding strategy should follow the precepts of structured programming. The documentation strategy should be chosen to ensure program code can be easily read and understood.

■ The testing phase of the program development life cycle seeks to ensure a developed or acquired program achieves its specified requirements. Three types of testing can be undertaken: (a) unit testing, which focuses on individual program modules; (b) integration testing, which focuses on groups of program modules; and (c) whole-of-program testing, which focuses on the total program.

■ Unit tests can be classified as either static analysis tests or dynamic analysis tests. Static analysis tests include desk checking, structured walk-throughs, and design and code inspections. Dynamic tests can be classified as either black-box tests, which focus on the overall requirements rather than the internal code of a program, or white-box tests, which focus on the internal code rather than the overall requirements of a program.

■ Three types of integration tests are (a) top-down testing, in which top-level modules are tested first, (b) bottom-up testing, in which low-level modules are tested first, and (c) hybrid testing, in which a combination of top-down and bottom-up testing is used.

■ Whole-of-program tests focus on whether the complete program meets its requirements. In addition, they assess whether the program meets requirements that may not be specified formally, such as fault tolerance, reliability under load, and response time adequacy.

■ Management must establish formal mechanisms to monitor the status of operational programs so maintenance needs can be identified on a timely basis.

■ Three types of program maintenance are (a) repair maintenance, in which program errors are corrected, (b) adaptive maintenance, in which the program is modified to meet changing user requirements, and (c) perfective maintenance, in which the program is tuned to decrease resource consumption.

■ The structure of programming teams can have an important impact on the quality of the resulting software and the resources consumed to produce the software.

■ There are several ways in which programming teams may be organized. Functional teams perform certain types of programming work, such as COBOL coding or maintenance work. Their members are not assigned to particular applications. Project teams are assembled to work on a particular project, such as the development of an application. Chief programmer teams are project teams in which a high level of control and responsibility are assigned to a single programmer assisted by a small group of support staff. Adaptive teams are organic, flexible project teams designed to produce innovative solutions to programming problems. Controlled-decentralized teams have groups of junior programmers reporting to senior programmers, who in turn report to a project leader. They attempt to combine the advantages of both chief programmer teams and adaptive teams.

■ System programmers maintain system software, which is the software that provides generalized functions useful to a wide range of application software. Exercising effective control over system programmers is a difficult task because they are usually highly skilled persons who work alone or in small groups. Moreover, they are often assigned important privileges that they need to perform their work. Because of the high exposures associated with the work of system programmers, controls over their activities must be in place and working reliably.

INTRODUCTION

Recall from Chapter 4 that some outputs from the information processing systems design phase are a physical design showing the program job steps to be accomplished, a design for the user interface, a design for the database, and a hardware/software platform design. In the software development and acquisition phase of the systems development process, working programs must be produced or purchased that are congruent with these designs. Auditors should be mindful of the substantial difficulties encountered in undertaking these tasks and producing high-quality software. After many years of research and experience, the "software crisis" is still with us (Gibbs 1994).

In this chapter we examine those practices that lead to the production or acquisition of high-quality software. We begin by examining the major phases in the program development life cycle. The discussion highlights the types of good practices that should exist and the control concerns that auditors have with respect to each phase. Next we examine alternative ways of organizing and managing programming teams. In particular, from a control perspective we focus on the advantages and disadvantages of the different team structures that can be used. Finally, we examine the special control problems that arise in relation to the activities of system programmers. We consider some approaches that can be used to alleviate these control problems.

THE PROGRAM DEVELOPMENT LIFE CYCLE

As discussed in Chapter 4, program development and acquisition is a major phase within the systems development life cycle. The primary objectives of this phase are to produce or acquire and to implement high-quality programs. Some major characteristics of high-quality programs follow:

1. They perform their functions correctly and completely.
2. They have a high-quality user interface.
3. They work efficiently.
4. They are well designed and well documented.
5. They are easy to maintain.
6. They are robust under abnormal conditions.

If programs are to have these characteristics, development, acquisition, and implementation activities must be well managed. As with systems development, auditors can use a life-cycle model to better understand, plan, and carry out the tasks that must be undertaken to obtain high-quality software. During audits, this model can also guide the conduct of their evidence-collection and evidence-evaluation activities.

The following sections provide normative guidelines for six major phases in the program development life cycle (Figure 5–1): *(1)* planning, *(2)* control, *(3)* design, *(4)* coding, *(5)* testing, and *(6)* operation and maintenance. As with the systems development life cycle, the conduct of these phases can vary considerably, depending on certain contingencies. We examine the effects of such contingencies on each phase and the ways in which the audit approach must be adjusted to take them into account.

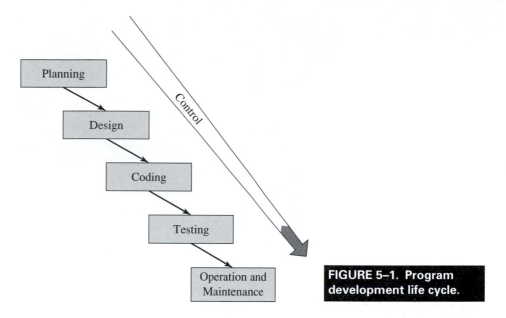

FIGURE 5–1. Program development life cycle.

Planning

Perhaps the major task that management must undertake during the planning phase is to estimate the amount of resources (especially worker hours) required for software development, acquisition, and implementation. If, for example, the software is to be written in house and the development and implementation task is substantial, management might attempt to estimate the lines of source code to be written or the number of function points (see Table 5–1)

TABLE 5–1   Function-Point Computation for Cost-Estimation Purposes

Steps:

1. Estimate the number of domain items (see the following table) for the program.
2. Assign a weight to each domain item (see, e.g., the following table) based on experience and expert advice.
3. Compute $F = \text{Sum } (F_i)$ using the following table.
4. Compute a complexity adjustment C (not shown here) based on such factors as whether data communications or distributed processing functions are required.
5. Compute the function point value, FP, using the following formula:
    $$FP = F * (0.65 + 0.01C)$$
    where the constants 0.65 and 0.01 are determined empirically.

		Weight			
Domain Item	*Count*	*Simple*	*Average*	*Complex*	*F_i*
Distinct input data items		3	4	6	
Output screens or reports		4	5	7	
Types of online queries		3	4	6	
Files		7	10	15	
Interfaces to other systems		5	7	10	
				Total	

to be produced. These estimates might then be extrapolated to the number of worker hours required to produce the software.

If software is to be developed and implemented in house, management should use the five major software cost-estimation techniques identified by Boehm (1984):

1. *Algorithmic models:* These models estimate resources needed based on a set of "cost drivers"—for example, the estimated number of source instructions to be written, the programming language to be used, and the volatility of the requirements definition. A well-known example is Boehm's (1981) COCOMO model.
2. *Expert judgment:* Experts might estimate the resources needed to undertake the programming project. Vicinanza et al.'s (1991) research indicates some experts might be more accurate estimators of resource requirements than algorithmic models.
3. *Analogy:* If a similar software project has been undertaken already, resource requirements can be estimated based on this prior experience.
4. *Top-down estimation:* The project is first subdivided into its various tasks, and resource requirements for each task are then estimated.
5. *Bottom-up estimation:* If the tasks to be undertaken are fairly well defined at the outset, the resource needs for each can be estimated and aggregated to obtain those needed for the entire project.

If software is to be acquired, three major types of costs that will be incurred are purchase costs, the costs associated with contracting for and implementing the software, and the costs of operating and maintaining the software. Potential vendors will provide estimates of purchase costs and operation and maintenance costs. Expert judgment, analogy, top-down estimation, and bottom-up estimation might still be used, however, to predict the costs associated with contracting for and implementing the software.

Besides estimating resource requirements, management must address several other important decisions during the planning phase:

Decision	*Explanation*
Design approach	If the program is to be developed in house, management must choose the design approach to be used, e.g., prototyping or some type of top-down or bottom-up approach.
Implementation approach	The software could be written in house, contractors could be employed, or a package could be purchased. If the software must be coded, decisions must be made on the programming language to use and the coding discipline to be applied.
Integration and testing approach	Testing might require special resources, e.g., simulators or special hardware to monitor performance. Responsibility for integration and testing must be assigned.
Project team organization	If a project team must be formed to develop or acquire the software, the membership and structure of the team must be determined.

The importance and complexity of planning decisions can vary considerably, depending on such factors as the size of the software to be developed or purchased and the uncertainty relating to user requirements or support technology. For example, consider the extent of resource planning needed for a large project involving thousands of lines of programming code versus a small project that can be programmed using a spreadsheet package. Similarly, consider the extent of test and integration planning needed for a large, extensively modified, purchased software package versus a small, off-the-shelf, unaltered, purchased software package. Clearly, the approaches to and effort expended on planning across these cases should not be the same.

Auditors should have two major concerns about the conduct of the planning phase. First, they should evaluate whether the nature of and extent of planning are appropriate to the different types of software that are developed or acquired. They can gather this evidence in the normal ways—for example, interviews, observations, and reviews of documentation. Second, they must evaluate how well the planning work is being undertaken. For example, they might assess how accurately resource requirements have been estimated. If they conclude planning is well done, they should be more confident about the conduct of the remaining phases in the software life cycle. If planning is problematic, however, the conduct of the remaining phases may be undermined.

How difficult it will be to carry out evidence collection and evaluation will vary, depending on the extent to which responsibility for software development, acquisition, and implementation is dispersed throughout the organization. If, for example, end users employ high-level languages to develop programs that are material in the context of audit objectives, auditors must evaluate the quality of the planning work end users are performing, wherever they are located. The audit work will have to extend beyond the boundaries of the information systems department. If, however, responsibility for software development and acquisition is confined to a single, central group, the evidence collection and evaluation tasks are easier.

Control

The control phase has two major purposes. First, task progress in the various software life-cycle phases should be monitored against plan. Any significant deviations detected form the basis for corrective action. Second, control over software development, acquisition, and implementation tasks should be exercised to ensure software released for production use is authentic, accurate, and complete. Note in Figure 5–1 that the control phase is a "phantom" phase that extends in parallel with all other phases of the software life cycle.

To help monitor progress against plan, several techniques can be used (see, e.g., McLeod and Smith 1996). *Work breakdown structures* (WBS) can be prepared to identify the specific tasks that have to be undertaken to develop, acquire, and implement software (Figure 5–2). Detailed resource requirements then can be estimated for each task. These estimates form the basis for monitoring progress.

Gantt charts can be prepared to help schedule tasks (Figure 5–3). They show when tasks should begin and end, what tasks can be undertaken concurrently, and what tasks must proceed serially. They help identify the consequences of early or late completion of a task. The actual progress of a software project can be plotted on a Gantt chart to show pictorially whether the project is on track.

Program evaluation and review technique (PERT) charts show the tasks that have to be undertaken, how they are interrelated, and the resource re-

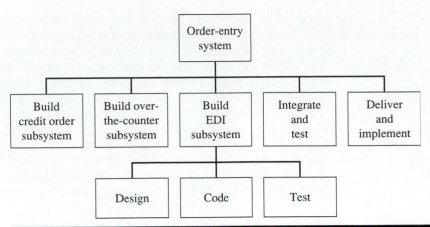

FIGURE 5–2. Partial work breakdown structure for an order-entry system.

quirements for each task (Figure 5–4). They allow the critical path to be determined—that is, the path along which any delay in completion of a task will result in the overall software project being delayed (the bold line in Figure 5–4). Like Gantt charts, therefore, they enable management to determine the consequences of early or late completion of a task.

To help ensure that authentic, accurate, and complete software is released, management must establish review procedures and access controls. Review procedures can be undertaken as each major milestone during software development, acquisition, or implementation is reached. The quality of work per-

FIGURE 5–3. Gantt chart for order-entry system.

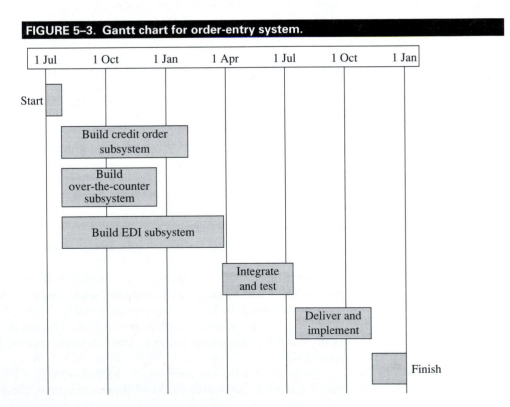

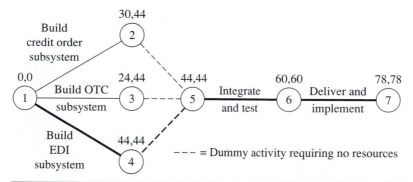

FIGURE 5–4. PERT chart for order-entry system.

formed up to that point should be assessed, and a decision must be made on whether the project should proceed to the next phase. In some cases, a formal review process might be undertaken. For example, in a large software-development project that will have a widespread impact, a review team might be constituted comprising representatives of all the major stakeholder groups. This team is responsible for evaluating the quality of work completed and approving subsequent work. In other cases, the review is somewhat informal. For example, end users might be developing software using fourth-generation languages or acquiring off-the-shelf software that is material from an audit perspective. Nevertheless, the software might have only a localized impact on the organization. In this situation, less onerous review and approval procedures could provide a satisfactory level of control.

Both manual and automated access controls can be established over the development, acquisition, and maintenance of software. Manual controls can be used, for example, to restrict access to hard-copy documentation. Without management approval, a librarian may not permit a programmer to remove program documentation from a library.

Automated controls can be established via program library software. This software permits source and object code files to be established. Access to these files can then be controlled via passwords. The software provides an audit trail of accesses to and changes to source and object files that management can review for propriety. In some cases, program library software can provide a means of ensuring compliance with licensing agreements pertaining to acquired software. For example, access controls in the software reduce the threat of software piracy.

Many organizations also use library software to set up separate test and production libraries of source and object files (Figure 5–5). Programmers are not permitted to access the production library. When a developed or acquired program has been approved for production release, a separate control group transfers the program from the test library to the production library (see Chapter 8). If a program must be maintained, the control group transfers a copy of the program to the test library, where it can be accessed by the programmer authorized to maintain it.

As with the planning phase, the nature of and importance of procedures exercised in the control phase can vary considerably, depending upon the type of software being developed, acquired, or maintained. Consider, for example, the control procedures that should be used in the development of a large electronic data interchange program versus a small spreadsheet application. As the

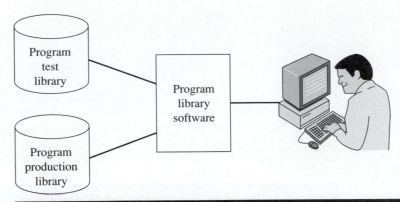

FIGURE 5–5. Program access control via program library software.

materiality of software increases, clearly control procedures become more critical. As materiality decreases, however, less rigorous control procedures can be used.

Auditors should have two concerns about the conduct of the control phase. First, they must evaluate whether the nature of and extent of control activities undertaken are appropriate for the different types of software that are developed or acquired. Auditors should identify those locations in an organization where material software is being produced or purchased and determine whether the control procedures in place are appropriate for the varying levels of materiality of the software.

Second, auditors must gather evidence on whether the control procedures are operating reliably. For example, they might first choose a sample of past and current software development and acquisition projects carried out at different locations in the organization they are auditing. They might then use observations, interviews, and a review of documentation to determine whether management regularly monitors progress against plan. If the organization audited uses program library software, auditors might also choose a sample of programs and examine the audit trail of accesses to and maintenance of these programs to evaluate whether unauthorized activities have occurred.

Design

If programs are to be developed or acquired software is to be modified, design activities must be undertaken. During the design phase, programmers seek to specify the structure and operation of programs that will meet the requirements articulated during the information processing system design phase of systems development. In small systems, a single program might be able to meet these requirements. For example, one spreadsheet program might satisfy the requirements specified for a decision support system application. Larger systems, however, might have been broken up into various job steps (see Chapter 4). Different programs must be designed to satisfy the requirements associated with each job step.

During the design phase, the auditor's primary concern will be to find out whether programmers use some type of systematic approach to design. The auditor must vary expectations depending on such factors as the size and materiality of the program. The need for rigorous, systematic design increases as programs become larger and more material. Auditors must also vary expectations depending on the type of personnel who develop programs. They are likely to have fewer concerns if a centralized, professional information systems group develops programs relative to, say, dispersed, end-user groups.

To some extent, design approaches will also vary depending on the type of programming language that has been or will be used to implement the program. For example, if programmers believe they can develop a program using spreadsheet software, they will think about satisfying requirements in the context of matrices and operations on matrices. Auditors should see design practices that evidence the kinds of ideas shown in Table 5–2.

If, on the other hand, programmers use a third-generation language (such as COBOL), the auditor should check to see whether some type of structured design approach has been used. (Appendices 5.1–5.3 provide an overview of the functional decomposition, data flow, and data structure design approaches.) The relative merits of these different structured design approaches is still a contentious matter, but auditors usually need not be concerned about the debate. Providing at least some type of structured design approach is used, they can have increased confidence in the quality of work performed during the design phase.

If programmers use an object-oriented programming language, they will probably use some type of object-oriented approach to program design. (Appendix 5.4 provides an overview of object-oriented program design approaches.) Again, although object-oriented design approaches might vary, an auditor's primary concern will be to determine whether at least one of the more widely accepted approaches is used.

Systematic design is still important even when fourth-generation languages are used to implement programs. Fourth-generation languages alleviate many of the detailed design issues that must be addressed with third-generation languages—for example, how files will be opened, closed, and accessed. Nevertheless, poor-quality fourth-generation programs will be produced if programmers do not give sufficient thought to the structure and dynamics of the programs they are writing. Design approaches like functional decomposition, data flow design, and data structure design are still useful in a fourth-generation language environment.

Auditors can obtain evidence of the design practices used by undertaking interviews, observations, and reviews of documentation. They can talk with programmers to determine whether they have an understanding of the need for systematic design approaches and, if so, whether and how they use them. Auditors can observe programmers at their work to determine whether they are

---

TABLE 5–2   Some Good Spreadsheet Design Practices

1. Start with a design plan.
2. Separate data-entry areas from calculation areas.
3. Store constants and parameters in a separate area.
4. Design data-capture areas to mirror existing data-capture forms.
5. Enter data in either rows or columns but not both.
6. Place instructions and meaningful names in the spreadsheet itself.
7. Protect critical cells/formulas with the cell-protect feature.
8. To speed up data entry, use the manual recalculation feature for large spreadsheets.
9. Use range names for related cells whenever possible.

using systematic approaches to program design. They can review program documentation to determine whether it contains items like structure charts (see Appendix 5.1) as evidence that programmers are using a systematic approach to design.

Coding

The coding phase is undertaken when software is to be developed or acquired software is to be modified. During the coding phase, programmers write and document source code in some programming language to implement the program design. Sometimes coding can proceed concurrently with the design and testing phases. Some part of a program is designed; it is then implemented and tested.

Programming management must attend to several major issues during the coding phase. Each is discussed briefly in the following subsections, together with some audit implications.

Module Implementation and Integration Strategy

As programs become larger, management must give more consideration to the order in which modules will be coded. Management must also decide how individual modules will eventually be integrated.

Three major module implementation and integration strategies that can be used follow:

Strategy	*Explanation*
Top down	Using this strategy, high-level modules are coded, tested, and integrated before low-level modules. An advantage of this strategy is that errors in high-level module interfaces, which are sometimes the most serious types of errors, are identified early. A disadvantage is that program testing might be difficult when low-level modules perform critical input-output functions.
Bottom up	Using this strategy, lower-level modules are coded, tested, and integrated before higher-level modules. An advantage of this strategy is that low-level modules that are critical to the eventual operation of the program are implemented and tested first. In some cases, modules that have been developed for other applications might be reused or modified. A disadvantage of the approach is that it is difficult to observe the overall operation of the program until late in its implementation.
Threads	Using this strategy, a decision is first made on the order in which program functions should be implemented. The modules that support each function are then determined, and each set is then implemented in decreasing order of functional importance. An advantage of this strategy is that the most important functions are implemented first. A disadvantage is that subsequent integration of modules might be more difficult, compared with a top-down or bottom-up approach.

Auditors should seek evidence on the level of care exercised by programming management in choosing a module implementation and integration strategy. Especially with large programs, use of a poor strategy can seriously undermine the quality of the program produced. Auditors might use interviews, for example, to determine whether management employs a systematic approach to choosing a module implementation and integration strategy. They might also examine program documentation to obtain evidence on the types of strategies that have been adopted.

Coding Strategy

Irrespective of the module implementation and integration strategy chosen, programming management must ensure that program code is written, whenever possible, according to structured programming conventions. These conventions constrain code to three basic control structures, none of which require a "GO TO" mechanism (Figure 5–6):

1. Simple sequence (SEQUENCE);
2. Selection based on a test (IF-THEN-ELSE); and
3. Conditional repetition (DO-WHILE).

In addition, each module in a program should have only one entry and one exit point, the length of modules should be restricted to about 50–100 source statements, and a top-down flow of control should be used.

If structured programming conventions are followed, it is generally believed that programmers write source code that contains fewer errors, is easier to understand, and is easier to maintain. This belief holds irrespective of the type of programming language used. Programs written in a fourth-generation language like SQL, for example, benefit in the same ways as programs written in a third-generation language like COBOL. Even when high-level code must be written in, say, a macro for a spreadsheet application, the code is more likely to be error-free, easier to understand, and easier to maintain if structured programming conventions are followed.

Auditors should seek evidence to determine whether programming management ensures that programmers follow structured programming conventions. They can interview managers and programmers and ask them about the practices they follow, observe programmers at their work, and examine program documentation to determine how code has been written. If high-quality code has been produced, auditors can have increased confidence that programs meet their objectives. If low-quality code has been written, however, auditors might conclude that they have to expand the extent of substantive test procedures.

FIGURE 5–6*(a).* **Simple sequence control structure.** *(b).* **Selection based on test control structure.** *(c).* **Conditional repetition control structure.**

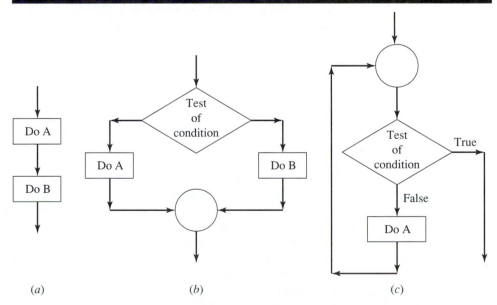

(a)   (b)   (c)

Auditors should also check to see whether programmers employ automated facilities to assist them with their coding work. Some useful types of automated coding facilities follow:

Facility	Explanation
Shorthand preprocessor	Languages such as COBOL are verbose. Shorthand preprocessors allow programmers to write an abbreviated form of code. They can then translate this abbreviated form into full language syntax.
Decision-table preprocessor	Decision-table preprocessors convert decision tables inserted in the text of a program into the source code of the compiler language in which the code is written.
Copy facility	A copy facility allows large sections of code to be copied from a library into a program. Copy facilities allow reuse of code.
Editor	Editors allow code to be created, formatted, and modified easily.
User-interface management system	User-interface management systems facilitate the design of the user interface. For example, they allow fast design and implementation of windows, icons, menus, and dialog boxes.
CASE tool	CASE tools contain several facilities that assist the coding process. For example, they might allow automatic generation of code from design specifications, high-level coding of user-interface designs, and coding standards to be enforced.

If auditors find that programmers are using automated facilities, they can have more confidence in the quality of their coding work. Automated facilities reduce the likelihood of human errors and irregularities, improve programmer productivity, and enhance greater standardization of work.

Documentation Strategy

High-quality source code documentation is an important means of reducing coding errors when a program is initially written and facilitating subsequent maintenance of the program. Some generally accepted guidelines for improving the quality of program documentation follow:

1. Provide charts that show the overall makeup of the program in terms of its major components and the relationships among these components. Appendices 5.1–5.4 give examples of the types of charts that might be part of the program documentation.
2. Use comment lines liberally throughout a program to explain the nature of the program, its various components, and the flow of logic. Program header comments can be used to describe the overall purpose of the program, major functions performed by the program, and important files used. Module comments can be used to explain the function performed by a module and how it fits into the overall program. Line comments can be used to elucidate complex pieces of logic in the program.
3. Use names for variables, constants, types, paragraphs, modules, and sections that are meaningful to the readers of program source code (Figure 5–7). Meaningful names can greatly enhance the self-documenting features of a program.

```
GET-CURR-SALARY SECTION.
START.
        MOVE ZERO TO WS-TOT-SAL.
                FOR SR IN PESYS.SALCD_RATE WITH
                SR.SALCD = WS-SALCD AND
                SR. NOMSC = WS-OLD-SCALE AND
                SR.NOMSP = WS-OLD-SCPOS-3MTH AND
                SR.NOMSD < WS-TRANS-DATE-BIN AND
                SR.NOMED >= WS-TRANS-DATE-BIN
                    GET
                        ON ERROR
                        MOVE 10 TO STATEMENT-ID
                        MOVE 5 TO RELATION-NUMBER
                        PERFORM 9100-PROCESS-ERROR
                        END-ERROR
                        WS-TOT-SAL = SR.NOMRT
                    END-GET
                DISPLAY WS-REFNO,'SALCD ',WS-SALCD,
                ' RATE ' WS-TOT-SAL WITH CONVERSION
                END-FOR
EXIT.
```

FIGURE 5–7. Use of meaningful names to facilitate readability of program code.
Used by permission, The University of Queensland.

4. Lay out program source code so it is easy to read. For example, each sentence should begin on a new line; subsequent lines belonging to a sentence should be indented; statements following conditional tests should be indented; white space should be used to set off related blocks of code.
5. Group related types of code together. For example, in a spreadsheet program, data-entry areas can be separated from areas where computations are performed. In a third-generation language, all the variables and constants relating to a particular module or function can be grouped together.

Several automated tools are available to assist programmers to produce well-documented program code. For example, editors can be used to ensure that data items are named consistently, and pretty-print facilities can be used to make program code more readable. To the extent these types of automated tools are used, higher-quality documentation is likely to be produced.

Perhaps the quickest way for auditors to determine the quality of program documentation is to obtain a sample and to examine it for evidence of high-quality practices. If the documentation quality is low, auditors should have concerns about the care with which software is being developed. In addition, auditors should have concerns about how well subsequent modifications to and maintenance of software can be undertaken. If the quality of documentation is high, they can place increased reliance on the software and decrease the extent of their substantive test procedures.

Testing

During the testing phase, a developed or acquired program is evaluated to determine whether it achieves its specified requirements. Testing can identify program design errors or program coding errors. In some cases, testing may also pinpoint inaccurate or incomplete specifications. Note, however, that testing can identify only the *presence* of errors. It cannot identify their *absence*.

Unless tests are designed specifically to tease out an error, most likely the error will remain undetected.

As with the previous phases of the program development life cycle, the testing phase can vary considerably, depending on such factors as the size of the program and its materiality. Nevertheless, testing often involves *seven* steps:

1. *Select the boundaries of the test:* Testing can focus on an individual module in a program, several modules, or the entire program.
2. *Determine the goals of the test:* Testing can be used to identify unauthorized, inaccurate, incomplete, ineffective, or inefficient code. A particular test should focus on only one (or a small number) of goals—for example, the performance of the program under load stress.
3. *Choose the testing approach:* Several testing approaches have been developed and are now widely used—for example, black-box testing and white-box testing. These approaches are discussed in subsequent sections.
4. *Develop the test:* Test data or test scenarios must be developed that will accomplish the goals of the test. In particular, the expected results of the test must be determined.
5. *Conduct the test:* The conduct of the test can involve, for example, executing test data through a program or performing a hand-simulation of the program's execution pattern under various test scenarios.
6. *Evaluate the test results:* The actual results obtained under the test must be compared against the expected results. The nature of any discrepancies identified must be determined.
7. *Document the test:* All steps in the testing process must be documented.

Auditors usually pay special attention to the testing phase of the program development life cycle. As discussed in Chapter 4, the quality of testing can have a major impact on how well other phases are performed. High-quality testing forces programmers to undertake other phases of the program development life cycle rigorously. Furthermore, in many software projects, experience has shown that testing consumes 40 percent to 70 percent of development and implementation resources. Given audit concerns with effectiveness and efficiency, therefore, testing is often a material item auditors must consider during system development.

Chapter 17 further examines the topic of testing because it is an important means auditors use to gather evidence on the quality of a system they are evaluating. The following sections provide an overview, however, of three levels of testing that can be conducted during program testing: unit testing, integration testing, and whole-of-program testing. They describe the nature of each level of testing, how it might be undertaken, and some concerns auditors should have. They also describe how the conduct of each level of testing might vary depending upon various contingencies, such as the size of the program and whether the program has been developed or acquired.

Unit Testing

Unit testing focuses on evaluating individual modules within a program. Thus, unit testing tends to be undertaken only for large programs in which individual modules constitute substantive pieces of work. If a program is being developed in house or under contract, the applicability of unit testing should always be considered. If an off-the-shelf program has been purchased, however, unit testing is unlikely to be employed unless the program has been modified in some way.

Two major types of unit tests may be undertaken. The first type, *static analysis tests*, evaluates the quality of a module through a direct examination of source code. The module is not executed on a machine, although it might be executed in someone's mind. Some important types of static analysis checks follow:

Type of Test	*Explanation*
Desk checking	Desk checking involves a programmer examining the module's code for evidence of errors or irregularities. For example, the programmer might look for syntax errors, logic errors, deviations from coding standards, or fraudulent code. Desk checking can be performed by the programmer who coded the module or by someone else.
Structured walk-throughs	In a structured walk-through, the programmer responsible for the design and coding of a module leads other programmers through the module with the aim of detecting errors or irregularities. The review group comprises independent programmers, although they might be on the same project team as the programmer who coded the module. The product of the review process is a list of defects to be corrected and not a list detailing how they are to be corrected.
Design and code inspections	In a design and code inspection, a special review team is appointed to review a program module's code. A trained moderator leads the review team through the review. Each review team member must follow defined participant rules. Formal checklists are used to guide the review, and the results are documented using preprinted forms. Follow-up procedures are used to ensure all errors or irregularities identified are rectified. Overall, the procedures used during a design and code inspection are more formal than those used during a structured walk-through.

Some types of static analysis can be undertaken using automated tools. For example, these tools can identify deviations from coding standards, variables that are declared but never initialized or used, module calling sequences, and parameters passed between modules.

The second type of unit testing that can be undertaken is a *dynamic analysis test*. Unlike static tests, dynamic tests require the module to be executed on a machine. Two important types of dynamic tests follow:

Type of Test	*Explanation*
Black-box test	In a black-box test, the internal logic of a module is not examined (Figure 5–8a). Instead, test cases are designed based on the requirements specification for the module. The test cases are then executed to determine deviations from requirements. Black-box testing might not reveal functions performed by a module that are excessive to the requirements specification for the module.
White-box test	In a white-box test, test cases are designed after the internal logic of a module has been examined (Figure 5–8b). The test cases are meant to traverse the different execution paths built into the program. Although a white-box test reveals the internal workings of a module, it might not identify requirements that the module fails to satisfy.

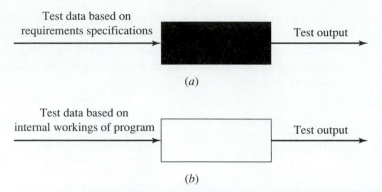

Test data based on requirements specifications → [black box] → Test output

(a)

Test data based on internal workings of program → [white box] → Test output

(b)

FIGURE 5–8 *(a).* **Black-box testing of programs.** *(b).* **White-box testing of programs.**

As with static analysis, automated tools are also available to assist programmers undertake dynamic analysis of a module. For example, tools are available to generate test cases, control the execution of the test, vary the workload under which the module must perform, capture output, identify which execution paths have been traversed by test data, and compare actual output with expected output.

Auditors can use interviews, observations, and examination of documentation to evaluate how well unit testing is conducted. They can ask programmers how they undertake unit testing, observe them at their work, and choose a sample of test documentation to evaluate how well static analysis and dynamic analysis are performed. They should see evidence of automated tools being used to improve the quality of unit testing.

Unless end users are developing large programs, most likely audit concerns about unit testing will focus on the work done by information systems professionals. This latter group typically has responsibility for developing the sorts of programs where unit testing is needed. Furthermore, they typically have responsibility for evaluating acquired software where unit testing is an important facet of the overall contractual process.

Integration Testing

Integration testing focuses on evaluating groups of program modules primarily to determine *(1)* whether their interfaces are defective, and *(2)* overall, whether they fail to meet their requirements specifications. In some cases, integration testing can also be used to determine whether the performance of a set of modules degenerates under high workloads and whether processing is carried out efficiently.

Like unit testing, integration testing is typically undertaken only when larger and more complex programs are being developed either in house or via contractors. Auditors, therefore, will most likely be concerned primarily with the quality of integration testing work carried out by information systems professionals rather than end users. The amount of integration-testing work carried out by end users is likely to be small.

Two different strategies can be used to undertake integration testing: big-bang testing and incremental testing (Figure 5–9). When *big-bang testing* is used, all individual modules are coded, tested individually, and then assembled in total to perform the integration tests. In short, all intermodule dependencies

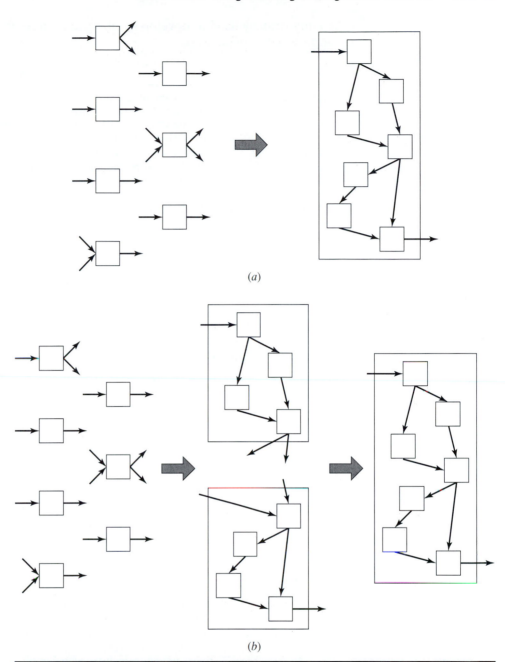

FIGURE 5–9*(a).* **Big-bang testing.** *(b).* **Incremental testing.**

are tested together, and in effect integration testing disappears. The test really becomes a whole-of-program test. Big-bang testing might be an efficient way to proceed in small to moderate-size systems, but it is risky if complex intermodule dependencies exist. Critical errors or irregularities may not be identified on a timely basis.

Incremental testing means subsets of modules are assembled iteratively and tested until the total program is finally in place. Depending on the design and coding strategy used to develop the program, three types of integration-testing approaches may be used:

Type of Test	Explanation
Top-down test	In a top-down integration testing approach, the top-level modules are tested first. Lower-level modules that are not yet implemented are simulated via *stubs*, which are dummy modules that simply confirm the interface is working correctly.
Bottom-up test	In a bottom-up testing approach, the bottom-level modules are tested first. Higher-level modules that are not yet implemented are simulated via *drivers*, which are dummy modules that simply confirm the interface is working correctly.
Hybrid test	A hybrid integration testing approach involves a combination of top-down and bottom-up integration testing. This approach is sometimes called *sandwich testing*.

An auditor's primary concern will be to see that a systematic approach to integration testing has been chosen for those programs where it is applicable and that the approach chosen has been well executed. Auditors can gather evidence via interviews, observations, and reviews of documentation for a sample of programs. They should also check whether automated tools have been used to enhance the quality of integration testing.

Whole-of-Program Testing

Whole-of-program tests focus on the program, in total, to determine whether it meets its requirements. Even when a program is too small to make unit testing or integration testing worthwhile, whole-of-program testing should be undertaken to evaluate its quality. Similarly, if unit testing or integration testing is inappropriate because a program has been purchased, whole-of-program testing should still be undertaken. When programs are acquired, whole-of-program tests are an important means of determining whether developers have fulfilled their part of the contract.

Pfleeger (1991) identifies four types of whole-of-program tests that might be undertaken:

Type of Test	Explanation
Function test	Function tests are used to determine whether the integrated program fulfills its requirements.
Performance test	Performance tests are used to determine whether the integrated program achieves certain performance criteria, some of which might not be formally specified in the requirements: fault tolerance, reliability under load, maintenance of security, response time adequacy, throughput rate adequacy.
Acceptance test	Function tests and performance tests are performed by the programmers responsible for developing the program. Acceptance tests are performed by the end users of a program. Acceptance tests also focus on determining whether the program fulfills its requirements specifications and any general performance requirements.
Installation test	Whereas function tests, performance tests, and acceptance tests can be performed in a test environment, installation tests are performed in the operational environment. For example, the program is executed on the machine that will be used for operational purposes rather than a test machine.

An auditor's primary concerns will be to see that whole-of-program tests have been undertaken for all material programs and that these tests have been well-designed and executed. Whereas unit testing and integration testing might not always be applicable during program development or acquisition, whole-of-program testing should always be undertaken. Auditors can use observations, interviews, and reviews of documentation to assess how well it has been done, expecting that evidence-gathering activities will be dispersed more widely with whole-of-program testing compared with unit and integration testing. Whereas the latter two types of testing primarily will be carried out by information systems professionals, whole-of-program testing could be undertaken by anyone in the organization who has responsibility for the development, implementation, or acquisition of programs. Whole-of-program testing should be undertaken by end users, for example, who develop material programs using high-level programming languages.

Operation and Maintenance

A program becomes operational when it is released for day-to-day use within an organization. From an audit perspective, our primary concern with the operational use of a program is that its performance be monitored properly. Someone must be responsible for identifying when a program needs to be maintained. Otherwise, timely identification of maintenance needs might not occur. As a result, the program might corrupt a database, fail to meet user requirements, or operate inefficiently. Formal mechanisms for monitoring the status of operational programs are especially important when the users of a program are dispersed widely throughout an organization.

As programs carry out their day-to-day work, three types of maintenance might be needed to keep them operational: *(1) repair maintenance*—errors might be discovered that have to be corrected; *(2) adaptive maintenance*—user needs may change and the program has to be altered accordingly; and *(3) perfective maintenance*—the program could be tuned to decrease its resource consumption. Overall, these three types of maintenance tasks often account for a substantial part of the cost of owning software. Some estimates place maintenance costs, on average, at two-thirds of the total cost of owning a program.

The procedures used to carry out maintenance to programs often are a major concern to auditors. If controls over maintenance activities are not exercised, unauthorized, inaccurate, or incomplete code could be introduced into a production program. Controls must exist to ensure changes to production programs are approved formally, and the process of designing, coding, testing, and implementing the modifications required is monitored carefully. Because of the difficulties associated with exercising control over program maintenance activities, some organizations implement *configuration management systems* (Bersoff and Davis 1991). In a configuration management system, maintenance requests must be documented formally and approved by a change control group. In addition, careful control is exercised over each stage of the maintenance process via checkpoints, reviews, and sign-off procedures. To help keep track of the maintenance process and to maintain a record of changes, *configuration management software* is sometimes used. From an audit perspective, effective use of this software provides important evidence of management's commitment to careful control over the maintenance process.

An auditor's primary concerns with the operation and maintenance phase will be to ensure effective and timely reporting of maintenance needs occurs and maintenance is carried out in a well-controlled manner. Auditors should seek evidence that management has implemented a review system and assigned responsibility for monitoring the status of operational programs. Auditors should also seek evidence via interviews, observations, and review of documentation that this system is operating reliably. Next, they should focus on the quality of controls implemented over the maintenance process. As discussed previously, to the extent a configuration management system is in place and working, auditors can have more confidence in the quality of the maintenance process.

Because operations and maintenance activities are often widely dispersed throughout an organization, especially if end users are active participants in the production and use of software, evidence-collection and evaluation efforts could be difficult to carry out. First auditors will have to identify all sites where material software is operated and maintained. They will then have to satisfy themselves that controls over operations and maintenance are operating reliably at each of these sites. In evidence-collection and evaluation activities, auditors should be careful not to focus only on asset safeguarding and data integrity concerns. Given the substantial resource consumption often associated with maintenance activities, they should also consider how effectively and efficiently maintenance activities are being carried out at each of these sites.

ORGANIZING THE PROGRAMMING TEAM

The way in which programmers are organized to undertake their work can have an important effect on the quality of the resulting software and the resources consumed to produce the software. They can be organized functionally, whereby each performs a specialized activity—for example, COBOL coding, maintenance work, or communications programming. Functional structures work best when projects are straightforward and they can be decomposed into relatively self-contained, small- to moderate-sized tasks. They also allow programmers to develop specialist skills and, therefore, can reduce the resource consumption required to complete a task.

Alternatively, programmers can be organized as teams. They work for some period of time on a project. At the conclusion of the project, the team might be disbanded. Teams facilitate communication among their members. Accordingly, they are useful organizational structures when the project to be undertaken is complex and uncertain. On the other hand, team structures incur overheads associated with the high levels of interaction that can occur among their members and the overall management of the team.

Much software development, acquisition, and implementation is now undertaken by teams. In this light, the following subsections examine three major team structures that are used to organize programmers. Each has its advantages and disadvantages. From an audit perspective, the concern is to see that management has chosen a team structure carefully in light of the project size, the level of uncertainty/complexity facing the project, and the level of slack that exists in the project schedule. Moreover, auditors should be concerned to see that management has chosen the team members carefully so their skills and temperament are suited to the team structure in which they must work.

Chief Programmer Teams

In 1971, IBM completed a project for *The New York Times* newspaper. The system developed and implemented was an online retrieval system for the newspaper's file of clippings. Throughout the project, IBM used a program-

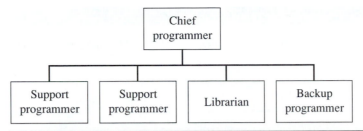

FIGURE 5–10. Chief programmer team organization structure.

ming-team structure that was radically different from the typical ways programming teams were then organized. For the size of the project—about 83,000 lines of source code—the results were impressive: The project was delivered on time with few errors; programmer productivity was very high; errors discovered were easy to correct.

The particular organization structure used by IBM on *The New York Times* project is known as a *chief programmer team*. A chief programmer team is simply a specific form of a project-based organizational structure—one that has a high level of centralized control. Figure 5–10 shows the structure of a chief programmer team. The functions of the various personnel who are members of the team follow:

Team Member	*Functions*
Chief programmer	Ultimately responsible for the system on which the team works; must be an expert, highly productive programmer; responsible for designing, coding, and integrating the critical parts of the system; assigns work to the backup and support programmers.
Backup programmer	A senior programmer responsible for providing full support to the chief programmer; must be capable of assuming the chief programmers' duties at any time.
Support programmer	Needed for large projects that cannot be handled by the chief programmer and backup programmer alone; provides specialist support; assists in coding and testing lower-level modules.
Librarian	Responsible for maintaining the program production library (discussed subsequently); submits input and collects output for programmers; files output from compilations and tests; keeps source-code and object-code libraries up to date.

The chief programmer team structure is designed to reduce the need for information processing among the team members and to increase their capacities to process information. It achieves these objectives in three ways. First, it reduces the number of communications channels needed among team members by minimizing the number of personnel on the team. As a consequence, however, it places more onerous productivity requirements on each team member to compensate for the loss of worker resources.

Second, each member of the chief programmer team performs specialized tasks. The chief programmer primarily is responsible for designing, coding, and testing the system. The backup programmer and support programmers provide specialized support; for example, they might advise the chief programmer on the intricacies of the operating system. The librarian relieves the chief programmer, backup programmer, and support programmers of the routine, cleri-

TABLE 5–3   Choosing a Programming Team Structure

Type of Team	Level of Uncertainty	Level of Complexity	Size of Task	Time Constraints
Chief programmer team	Low–moderate	Low–moderate	Moderate	Tight
Adaptive team	Moderate–high	Moderate–high	Moderate	Loose
Controlled-decentralized team	Moderate–high	Moderate–high	Large	Moderate

cal duties associated with the system. Thus, the structure aims at improving productivity by having team members do what they do best.

Third, the team's capacity to process information is increased by having the librarian perform a lateral, coordinating role. Central to this role is a program production library consisting of two parts: internal and external. The internal part comprises source code, object code, linkage commands, job control statements, and so on. It is maintained solely by the librarian, not the programmers. The external part comprises folders containing compilation results, test results, and other supporting documentation. The programmers work only with the external library, making whatever changes they need on program listings or coding sheets. The librarian then implements these changes. Each team member has access to the external library; thus, code, test results, etc., are public. Programmers are encouraged to examine each other's work so errors or potential interface problems are identified.

Chief programmer teams will be most successful when the task is well defined and moderate in size (Table 5–3). Centralized structures like a chief programmer team inhibit the information flows that are needed to generate innovative alternatives when the task is uncertain. Nevertheless, by controlling interaction among group members, chief programmer teams are more likely to meet tight deadlines than decentralized groups. For large tasks, the productivity requirements placed on members of a chief programmer team become too onerous. Other types of team structures that allow more members need to be adopted.

Adaptive Teams

Weinberg (1971) proposes another type of team structure for programmers: an adaptive team (Figure 5–11). Like chief programmer teams, adaptive teams comprise only a small number of persons, say, 5–10 programmers. The structure of the team is meant to cater for two sets of needs: *(1)* the organization's requirements for quality programs to be produced and *(2)* the social/psychological needs of each programmer in the team.

Adaptive teams differ from chief programmer teams in three ways. First, adaptive teams have no hierarchy of authority. The leadership of the team rotates among its members. The person having greatest skill with the activity undertaken usually assumes the leadership for the duration of that activity. Second, in an adaptive team, tasks are assigned to members of the team rather than defined positions. In the assignment of tasks, the objective is to exploit the strengths and avoid the weaknesses of each team member. Thus, there is no notion of a chief programmer with a defined role, a backup programmer with a defined role, and so on; an adaptive team is a self-organizing entity. Third, an adaptive team has no formal librarian role to perform a lateral coordinating function. Instead, team members are responsible for carefully examining and evaluating one another's work. The intent is to foster a feeling of joint respon-

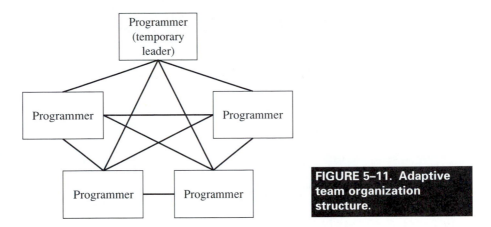

FIGURE 5–11. Adaptive team organization structure.

sibility for the quality of the programming product. At the same time, team members cannot have an ego attachment to the work they perform if open evaluation is to exist; hence, this type of team is sometimes called an "egoless" team.

The structure of an adaptive team is based upon the fact that substantial individual differences exist among programmers in their abilities to perform various types of programming tasks. It is also structured to allow the free flow of information among team members. Thus, adaptive teams are suited to programming tasks where a high level of uncertainty exists (Table 5–3).

Nevertheless, Mantei (1981) points out they have several limitations. First, because an adaptive team is a form of decentralized organization structure, it will generate more communications than a centralized team. Although this increase is an advantage in a long-term, difficult project, it is a disadvantage when a project is subject to tight time constraints. Second, groups engage in riskier behavior than individual people because the effects of failure can be dispersed; thus, an adaptive team might adopt risky solutions to a programming problem. Third, contrary to expectations, adaptive teams sometimes *discourage* innovative programming solutions. Decentralized groups tend to exhibit greater conformity than centralized groups because they enforce uniformity of behavior and punish deviations from the norm.

To overcome some of the problems of adaptive teams, Constantine (1993) advocates using a structured open team for software engineering projects. A structured open team fosters collaborative teamwork and consensus to achieve both innovation and coordination. The team leader adopts a supportive and democratic style with team members, but nevertheless they have full external responsibility for the performance of the team.

Controlled-Decentralized Teams

A fourth type of organization structure for programmers is a controlled-decentralized team (Figure 5–12). This structure has a group of junior programmers reporting to senior programmers who in turn report to a project leader. Information flows occur within a group and upward through the senior programmer to the project leader. Thus, the controlled-decentralized team ideally reaps the benefits of both the chief programmer and adaptive team structures.

Mantei (1981) argues controlled-decentralized teams are best used when the programming task is large and difficult (Table 5–3). Large tasks cannot be accomplished by chief programmer teams, whatever the productivity of the

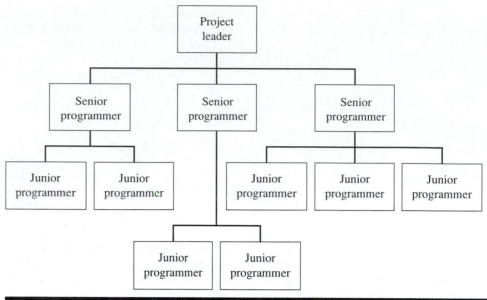

FIGURE 5–12. Controlled-decentralized organization structure.

team members. Moreover, complex problems are best solved by decentralized groups, and the group structure of the controlled-decentralized team facilitates problem solving. Nevertheless, controlled-decentralized teams do not work well when the programming task cannot be subdivided, nor are they suited to projects that must meet tight deadlines.

MANAGING THE SYSTEM PROGRAMMING GROUP

Programmers are often classified as either application programmers or system programmers. The former develop and maintain programs for application systems. The latter develop and maintain system software—that is, software, such as operating systems, database management systems, and communications software, which provides general functions useful to a wide range of application software.

Control Problems

Both the nature of system software and the nature of system programming activities can present substantial control problems for management. System software is a critical, shared resource; thus, errors or irregularities in system software can affect any application systems that use it. Furthermore, system software often must operate in privileged mode to perform its functions; that is, it has a special execution status that enables it to circumvent many standard controls. This privileged status can be abused. For example, system software might be used to gain unauthorized access to private data that can be sold to competitors or to allow jobs to execute without being charged for resource consumption via the normal job accounting software. In the latter case, system programmers could be carrying out private consulting activities, for example, and using the machine as a free resource.

Controlling system programmers is a difficult task. They are usually highly skilled persons who often work alone or in small groups. Thus, exercising traditional controls over their activities, such as separation of duties and independent checks on performance, is difficult. Moreover, they often work in crisis situations in which the need to get a job running overrides the need to maintain established control procedures. For example, the communications software might crash during a peak load period. A system programmer might be required to devise a quick "fix" so terminals can be reactivated and customers once again can be serviced.

Control Measures

In many organizations, management has tended to regard the system programming group as uncontrollable. Indeed, some information systems professionals argue the imposition of controls over system programmers will cause their work to deteriorate: They are sensitive, creative, often erratic persons who do not take kindly to restrictions. They need autonomy if they are to produce their best work, especially if they are subject to tight deadlines.

Auditors, however, should be skeptical of these claims. Organizations that hold to these beliefs run the risk of major losses occurring through system programming errors or irregularities. Well-controlled system programming groups do exist. These groups experience neither high staff turnover nor poor-quality work. Although it is difficult to exercise strong and varied controls over system programmers, some of the following measures can be implemented:

1. *Hire only high-quality system programming staff.* Compared with application programmers, management might undertake more in-depth background checking and interviewing when hiring system programmers.
2. *Separate duties to the extent possible.* If more than one system programmer is employed, duties should be separated to the extent possible. For example, responsibilities for designing and coding a system program might be separated from responsibilities for testing the program.
3. *Develop and document methods and performance standards.* System programmers should know what is expected of them in terms of how they perform their jobs. They should not be left to devise their own approaches, which could run contrary to the organization's control objectives.
4. *Restrict the powers of system programmers.* System programmers should not be allowed to "tinker" with the system software during production time. Moreover, they should be permitted to develop and test system software that runs in privileged mode only during special test periods. During production periods, system programmers usually should have only the same powers as application programmers.
5. *Keep a manual and machine log of system programmer activities.* Independent, secure logs of system programmer activities should be kept. Periodically, these logs should be scrutinized to determine whether unauthorized activities have occurred.
6. *Employ outside consultants to evaluate system programming work.* If internal expertise is not available to evaluate the work of system programmers, outside experts might be hired from time to time to review the work of system programmers.
7. *Have application programmers periodically evaluate system programmers.* Although application programmers might not be capable of writing high-quality system software, they might still be able to evaluate the quality of work performed by the system programming group.

Even with these control measures in place and operating reliably, however, ultimately the best control might be to indoctrinate system programmers in the organization's policies. If system programmers see management exercising high ethical behavior and communicating a clear expectation that all employees must follow this norm, they will find it more difficult to rationalize any abuse of their powers.

Auditors should pay special attention to system programmers because of the high exposure associated with their activities. They should see at least some of the control measures described in this chapter in place and operating reliably. To the extent that controls over system programmers are weak, however, the consequences potentially are widespread. As discussed previously, errors or irregularities in system software can undermine the integrity of all application software that uses the system software. In this light, substantial reliance might have to be placed on compensating controls or the extent of substantive testing conducted may have to be expanded.

SUMMARY

Program development and acquisition is a major phase within the systems development life cycle. The primary objective of this phase is to produce or acquire and to implement high-quality programs. The activities to be conducted during this phase can be managed in the context of a program development life cycle that comprises six phases: *(1)* planning, *(2)* control, *(3)* design, *(4)* coding, *(5)* testing, and *(6)* operation and maintenance. Auditors can use this life-cycle model to determine what types of activities should be conducted in each phase and to collect evidence on and to evaluate the conduct of these activities. Auditors must recognize that the ways in which these activities will be performed will vary, depending on such contingencies as the size of and complexity of the program to be developed. In this light auditors must be able to adjust the audit approach to take into account the effects of these contingent factors.

The way programmers are organized can have an important effect on the quality of the resulting software and the resources consumed to produce the software. If the programming work is small in size and well defined, programmers can be organized functionally, whereby they undertake particular types of programming activities, such as COBOL coding or maintenance work. Alternatively, they can be organized as project teams, whereby they work for some defined period on an application. Besides conventional team structures, programmers are sometimes organized as chief programmer teams, adaptive teams, and controlled-decentralized teams. Chief programmer teams have a high level of centralized control vested in a small number of highly skilled people. They are best suited to moderately sized, relatively straightforward projects that are subject to tight deadlines. Adaptive teams are loosely structured work groups in which leadership rotates among team members and communication among them is intended to be free and open. They are best suited to moderately sized, relatively complex projects that are not subject to tight deadlines. Controlled-decentralized teams seek to combine the advantages of both chief programmer and adaptive teams. Junior programmers report to a senior programmer, who in turn reports to a project leader. They are best suited to large, relatively complex projects that are subject to moderately tight deadlines.

A major problem in programming management is controlling the activities of system programmers. The nature of system programming is such that many opportunities exist to perpetrate frauds. In this light, the work of system programmers must be monitored carefully via a sound system of internal controls.

Given the high exposures that exist with the work of systems programmers, auditors must carefully evaluate whether controls over their activities are in place and working reliably.

Review Questions

5–1 Give three attributes of a high-quality program.

5–2 What are the major phases in the program development life cycle? Which phase is a phantom phase? Briefly explain why it is a phantom phase.

5–3 What is the overall purpose of the planning phase in the program development life cycle? List *four* major decisions that have to be made during the planning phase.

5–4 Briefly describe how the following software cost-estimation techniques differ:
   a Expert judgment versus analogy
   b Top-down estimation versus bottom-up estimation

5–5 Briefly describe *two* concerns auditors might have when evaluating the planning phase of the program development life cycle.

5–6 Briefly describe the *two* major purposes of the control phase of the program development life cycle.

5–7 How do techniques like Work Breakdown Structures, Gantt charts, and PERT charts help during the control phase of the program development life cycle?

5–8 What functions might program library software perform during the control phase of the program development life cycle?

5–9 What evidence-collection techniques might auditors use to determine whether controls are operating reliably in the control phase of the program development life cycle?

5–10 What is likely to be an auditor's primary concern about the ways programmers undertake the design phase of the program development life cycle?

5–11 What concerns should auditors have about the conduct of the program development life cycle design phase in an organization where program development is primarily undertaken by end users who employ high-level programming languages?

5–12 During the coding phase of the program development life cycle, what is meant by the module implementation and integration strategy? Briefly explain the nature of a *threads* module implementation and integration strategy.

5–13 Why should auditors be concerned to see that programmers follow the precepts of structured programming when they undertake program coding? What evidence should we collect to determine whether programmers comply with structured programming precepts?

5–14 Briefly describe *two* types of automated tools that programmers might use to assist them in their coding work. Why should auditors have increased confidence in the quality of the coding process if we find that programmers are using these tools?

5–15 List *two* guidelines that programmers should follow if they are concerned about improving the readability of the program code they write.

5–16 List *seven* major steps in the conduct of program testing.

5–17 Briefly explain the difference between unit testing, integration testing, and whole-of-program testing.

5–18 Briefly explain the difference between static analysis tests and dynamic analysis tests. For each type of test, give two types of automated tools that programmers might use to help them conduct testing.

5–19 Briefly describe the relationship between desk checking, structured walk-throughs, and design and code inspections.

5–20 Briefly explain the difference between:
a black-box testing and white-box testing
b big-bang testing and incremental testing
c top-down testing and bottom-up testing
d acceptance testing and installation testing

5–21 In the context of the program development life cycle, what is the primary concern auditors have about the operational use of programs?

5–22 Briefly explain the difference between repair maintenance, adaptive maintenance, and perfective maintenance. Why are auditors concerned with controls over all types of program maintenance?

5–23 What two factors should have a major impact on the way programming teams are organized?

5–24 Give three advantages that a chief programmer team structure has over traditional organization structures for programming teams. Give one potential disadvantage of the chief programmer team structure.

5–25 Briefly explain the role of the librarian in a chief programmer team. What duties does the librarian have with respect to the program production library? How does the librarian role inhibit unauthorized program modifications?

5–26 Give *two* motivations for organizing programmers as an adaptive team. What are the differences between a chief programmer team and an adaptive team?

5–27 Briefly explain the nature of a controlled-decentralized programming team. Give an example of a programming project in which you think a controlled-decentralized team would be more successful than other types of programming team structures.

5–28 Give *two* reasons why it is difficult to control the work of system programmers.

5–29 List *two* controls that might be used over the activities of system programmers.

Multiple-Choice Questions

5–1 Which of the following phases in the program development life cycle is most likely to be a "phantom" phase?
a Control phase
b Design phase
c Operation and maintenance phase
d Coding phase

5–2 Which of the following cost-estimation techniques depends most on the fact that a similar project has been undertaken already and resource estimates can be based on this previous project?
a Bottom-up estimation
b Analogy
c Algorithmic models
d Top-down estimation

5–3 Which of the following factors should have *least* effect on the ways planning activities are undertaken?
a Whether the software is to be developed or acquired
b The size of the software project

    c The level of uncertainty surrounding the software project

    d Whether the project is to be undertaken by end users or information systems professionals

5–4 Which of the following is *least* likely to be a purpose of using Work Breakdown Structures, Gantt charts, and PERT charts?

    a To identify what tasks must be undertaken in a project

    b To evaluate the consequences of late or early completion of a task

    c To ensure the activities undertaken in a task are authorized

    d To estimate the resources that should be allocated to a task

5–5 Which of the following is *not* a function of program library software?

    a Controlling access to object code via passwords

    b Maintaining an audit trail of changes to source code

    c Testing the accuracy and completeness of acquired software

    d Preserving separation between test and production program files

5–6 From an audit perspective, which of the following statements about the design phase of the program development life cycle is *true*?

    a Program documentation provides little evidence about the quality of the design approach used during software development

    b Object-oriented approaches to design are more useful when low-level programming languages are used to develop programs

    c Formal approaches to design are relatively unimportant when high-level languages are used to develop programs

    d During the design phase, programmers seek to specify the structure and operations of a program that will satisfy a requirements specification

5–7 Which of the following is a *disadvantage* of a bottom-up module implementation and integration strategy?

    a Low-level modules that perform critical input-output functions are not tested first

    b The overall operation of the program is often difficult to observe until late in its implementation

    c The most difficult modules have to be implemented first

    d The approach does not facilitate reuse of software that has already been implemented

5–8 Which of the following is *not* an allowable control structure in structured programming?

    a Conditional repetition

    b Unconditional branch

    c Simple sequence

    d Selection based on a test

5–9 Which of the following automated tools is *unlikely* to be used during the coding phase of the program development life cycle?

    a Execution path monitor

    b User-interface management system

    c Shorthand preprocessor

    d CASE tool

5–10 Which of the following documentation guidelines should *not* be followed during program coding?

    a Use mnemonic names for variables but not constants

    b Indent conditional tests

    c Use program header comments to explain the overall purpose of the program

    d Group related types of code together

5–11 Which of the following statements about design and code inspections is *true*?
  a They are performed by the programmer who coded the program to be tested
  b They are less costly to undertake than desk checking
  c They are a type of dynamic analysis testing procedure
  d They are more formal to carry out than structured walk-throughs

5–12 White-box testing is most often used as a form of:
  a Top-down testing
  b Big-bang testing
  c Unit testing
  d Acceptance testing

5–13 Adaptive maintenance must be undertaken when:
  a Logic errors are discovered in a program
  b The program must be tuned to decrease resource consumption
  c The program's execution time is unacceptable
  d User needs change and the program must be altered

5–14 The purpose of configuration management software is to:
  a Facilitate control over the program maintenance process
  b Allow programmers to be relatively unconcerned about the hardware/software platform on which their programs will run
  c Tune a program to minimize resource consumption
  d Monitor the incidence of operational errors in programs

5–15 A chief programmer team is:
  a A project-based organizational structure
  b A team with decentralized control
  c A team structured to facilitate innovative problem solving
  d A team where each member has low autonomy

5–16 In a chief programmer team, the backup programmer:
  a Ensures that the resources needed for recovery of programs in the event of disaster are working
  b Must be capable of assuming the chief programmer's duties at any time
  c Ensures all program documentation is authentic, complete, and up to date
  d Codes and tests only the lower-level program modules

5–17 In an adaptive team, the leader is:
  a The chief programmer
  b The programming manager
  c The person having most expertise with the task at hand
  d No one—an adaptive team never has a team leader

5–18 Controlled-decentralized teams probably work best when:
  a Information flows must occur from the inside out
  b Only senior programmers participate in the team
  c The programming task is large and difficult
  d The software development project is subject to a tight deadline

5–19 Control problems arise with a system programming group because:
  a It is impossible to enforce separation of duties within the group
  b The group's creativity is undermined when controls are exercised over their work
  c They can only carry out their work when production systems are executing
  d It is difficult to evaluate the authenticity, accuracy, and completeness of their work

5–20 In the long-run, which of the following control measures over system programmers is likely to be the *most* effective?

a Separate duties among system programmers to the extent possible

b Have management lead by example with high ethical behavior and communicate to all employees that they must follow this norm

c Develop and document system programming methods and performance standards

d Have application programmers periodically evaluate the work of system programmers

Exercises and Cases

5–1 Zelta Ltd. is a medium-size company involved in providing a range of specialized products and services for the aerospace industry. Just over a year ago, external consultants undertook a major review of Zelta's information systems function. Consistent with industry trends, the consultants recommended substantial downsizing of the information systems function and greater outsourcing of work. In this light, top management slashed the information systems function from 100 to 50 personnel. They also decided to outsource all programming work for medium- to large-sized projects where specialized programming expertise was required. Top management felt they were employing too many highly skilled programmers who were relatively underutilized, given Zelta's demand for their talents.

Subsequent to the review, Zelta's Board fired the vice president of information systems and went to tender for their external audit services. The Board felt they had been poorly advised by both the vice president and their auditors in that they believed Zelta had invested too heavily in information systems services without an adequate return. A new vice president of information systems was appointed. He had previously been an assistant vice president responsible for accounting and administrative information systems in a large bank. New auditors have also been appointed. You are a manager in the audit firm that has won the contract.

As part of the interim audit work, your partner has asked you to review controls over the programming work that is now outsourced. Over the past year, you find that three major software development projects have been performed by outside contractors. Although Zelta's own information systems staff developed the requirements specifications for each of the three projects, they undertook none of the programming work. In all cases the programming work needed was somewhat specialized, and as a result contractors were employed to do the job.

After making some inquiries about the projects, you conclude none of the software developed is material from the viewpoint of errors or irregularities in the financial statements. You discover, however, that 40 percent of the information systems budget for the past year has been spent on payments to the contractors. Moreover, you find the software has been developed to provide a critical range of new services that will be offered to Zelta's customers. If the software contains errors or improprieties, Zelta's customers could be substantially disadvantaged.

During an interview with the new vice president of information systems, you ask how the contract price for each of the three projects was determined. In particular, you ask him what estimation methods had been used to determine the cost Zelta would likely have to bear to get the work done. He replies that no estimation methods had been used because he believed none were necessary. Because the three software contracts had been let out to tender and the lowest-price bid had been accepted in all cases, he argues Zelta would have been unable to obtain a better deal. In this light he saw little point to having Zelta estimate the cost to undertake each of the projects.

Required. You have been reflecting on your findings for the past few days to try to determine what they mean for the conduct of the remainder of the audit. Write a brief report for your partner recommending any alterations, if any, you believe should be made to the audit plan in light of Zelta's failure to undertake cost estimation for the three projects. Whether you recommend alterations to the audit plan or not, provide a brief justification for your recommendations.

5–2 Makumoney Ltd. is a financial services firm offering a wide range of products and services to its customers. It relies heavily on its information systems to provide up-to-date advice to its customers and to keep abreast of changes in the financial services marketplace, especially new products that might appeal to its customers. Given the volatility of the marketplace, Makumoney spends approximately 70 percent of its information systems budget on maintaining its existing information systems.

You are the senior information systems auditor in a firm of external auditors, and your firm has just won the tender for the audit of Makumoney Ltd. Given the material expenditures of Makumoney on information systems maintenance, during your first interim audit work you interview the programming manager about the procedures in place to undertake maintenance work on programs. She informs you that the following procedures are used:

a. Requests for maintenance to a program must come from users, although users might be acting on the advice of the information systems staff who support their systems. All requests are made on a standard form and submitted to her.

b. Unless the requests are urgent, each week she reviews them and prepares a report for the user who requested the maintenance indicating how much it will cost and the time frame in which the maintenance can be undertaken. She seeks the advice of the programmer with most knowledge of the program to cost the proposed maintenance. Providing the user who requests the maintenance is willing to meet the cost from their budget, the maintenance is then scheduled. She prepares a formal approval of maintenance, which must be countersigned by the user requesting the maintenance before work can proceed.

c. Each month she prepares a report for the vice president of information systems summarizing what maintenance work is being undertaken and the status of the work. The vice president uses this report to brief the information systems steering committee on any matters that may be of interest.

d. When the maintenance work is approved, the programming manager assigns a programmer to do the work. Where possible she chooses the programmer who is most familiar with the program to be modified to undertake the maintenance work. When the programmer has been assigned, she authorizes the operations manager to establish a test copy of the program under the programmer's account.

e. The programmer who undertakes the work is responsible for testing the program and notifying the programming manager when the program is ready for production release. The programming manager then reviews the work undertaken by the programmer to ensure it complies with the quality standards that have been established to govern programming work.

f. When the programming manager is satisfied with the maintenance work, she formally asks the user who requested the maintenance to undertake their own tests of the modified program. Occasionally these tests identify problems with the maintenance work, and the programmer corrects the program accordingly.

g. When the person who requests the change is satisfied with the maintenance work, he or she signs an acceptance form. The programming manager then authorizes the operations manager to release the test version of the program into production use.

When you ask the programming manager whether she is satisfied with these procedures, she indicates she believes they work well. She argues they allow timely maintenance, which is important in a firm like Makumoney. Moreover, she points out the person who requests the maintenance must accept full responsibility for the maintenance because they must pay for the maintenance as well as carry out tests on and sign off on the work. Although users sometimes become disgruntled about the extent of the responsibility they must bear, she believes they nevertheless perceive the information systems department as being responsive to their needs.

Required. To what extent will you rely on controls over program maintenance in planning the remainder of your audit work? Justify your position. What tests of controls, if any, would you undertake?

5–3 You are the manager of internal audit for Do-It-All, Ltd., a large, diversified, decentralized manufacturing company. Over the past two years, the information systems function in Do-It-All has undergone some dramatic changes. In particular, in light of a new strategic plan formulated by top management, it has shifted from a centralized operation to widely dispersed, decentralized operations. After top management had given approval to divisional and departmental managers to pursue their own information systems initiatives (providing projects appeared to be cost-effective), decentralized information systems groups and end-user groups began to proliferate. Indeed, the activities of the centralized information systems group were decimated.

Over a long period of time you had formulated a set of high-quality audit programs to help you evaluate the information systems function. It has become clear to you, however, that these programs badly need updating in light of the decentralization of the information systems function that has occurred. You are currently engaged in the process of systematically updating these programs.

Required. Outline an audit program that will allow you to evaluate the *design* phase of the program development life cycle. Your audit program should start by stating the audit objectives you are seeking to achieve in undertaking an evaluation of the design phase. Next you should list the major controls you would typically test in undertaking an evaluation of the design phase. Finally, you should describe the evidence-collection techniques you would use to test whether the controls are in place and operating reliably. Note that your audit program should take into account the decentralized nature of Do-It-All's information systems function and, in particular, the prominent role played by end users in the development, maintenance, and operation of information systems. Provide sufficient guidance so that one of your junior staff, with adequate supervision, could follow your audit program.

5–4 Daintree Ltd. is a large retailer that operates department stores in all major cities throughout Australia. Recently it has expanded its operations into Southeast Asia. Although each store operates some of its own information systems, all significant information systems are developed and implemented by the corporate information systems staff located in Brisbane. The company's mainframe computers are also sited in Brisbane. These machines are used to support companywide applications, such as point-of-sale processing, corporate sales reporting, and credit-card billing.

You are a manager in the external audit firm that has been carrying out the external audit of Daintree for the past three years. As part of your analytical review procedures, one of the items you have been monitoring is the amounts spent on information systems maintenance across each of Daintree's major application systems. Daintree expends about 65 percent of its information systems budget on maintenance. This percentage has been gradually increasing as new development work has been curtailed by an expenditure cap that top management has placed on the information systems function.

A matter that concerns you is the relative change in the amounts spent on repair maintenance, adaptive maintenance, and perfective maintenance. Three years ago when your firm first commenced the audit of Daintree, total expenditure on maintenance was broken up as follows: repair maintenance—20 percent; adaptive maintenance—70 percent; perfective maintenance—10 percent. In this past year, the figures are 5 percent, 15 percent, and 80 percent respectively. You have pursued the matter with the vice president of information systems, who was appointed in the same year as your audit firm. She claims the change in the percentage allocation across the three categories of maintenance has occurred for two reasons. First, she argues she has improved considerably the professionalism of the information systems staff to the point where the quality of the work they are now undertaking has obviated the need for extensive repair and adaptive maintenance. Second, she argues the previous reporting system for maintenance was inaccurate and, as a result, prior classification of maintenance work was erroneous.

During a further interview with the vice president of information systems, you obtain additional information about how the maintenance reporting system works. The vice president indicates that each programmer who undertakes maintenance must complete a maintenance reporting form that describes the nature of the work done and the resources expended on the work. The programming manager then reviews and classifies the work as either repair maintenance, adaptive maintenance, or perfective maintenance. He enters this data into computer-based maintenance reporting system he developed, and each week he gives a summary report to the vice president. She reviews his work and the overall report. She has high faith in his abilities, however, because they both worked closely together in her previous employment. He was regarded as the best programmer on staff with her previous employer. Indeed, she regards it as a major coup that she managed to attract him to his current position as programming manager, even though she had to offer him a sizable increase in compensation. She considers the maintenance reporting system he developed under her guidance to be an outstanding success. Moreover, the information systems steering committee has been highly complimentary about the reports provided by the system and the overall reduction in repair and adaptive maintenance that has occurred.

Required. Briefly describe any concerns you have, if any, in relation to maintenance expenditures and their classification. If you have some concerns, do they have any implications for the quality of data presented in the financial statements? Do you believe the conduct of the audit needs to be altered in light of your findings about maintenance? If so, how should the audit be altered?

5–5 Slip-up Corporation is a large, decentralized manufacturer of sliding doors and windows. It is based in Auckland, but it services the Southeast Asian market as well as Australia and New Zealand. The company uses information systems technology aggressively, both for its internal data processing requirements and as a strategic means of improving its services to customers. For example, it has a sophisticated manufacturing control system, and it provides a free service to potential customers by using an interactive system to estimate window and door requirements in light of ventilation, insulation, and building capacity needs.

So far the company has purposely restricted use of desktop computers by its managers because top management has feared it will be unable to control systems development within the organization. Nevertheless they recognize substantial benefits can be gained from using desktop computers. As a result, they have authorized a series of studies that will recommend guidelines on how desktop computers should be acquired and used within the corporation.

Required.   You are the chief internal auditor for Slip-up. As part of the series of studies on desktop computers that have been authorized by top management, you have been asked to prepare a set of standards that will govern testing, production release, and maintenance of software developed by end users. These standards will provide guidance to end users who develop their own systems using desk-top computers and high-level software. Prepare an outline of the standards you will recommend in your report to management. *Note:* Be sure to restrict yourself only to the testing, production release, and maintenance phases.

5–6 You are the manager of internal audit of Coverit Corporation, a large insurance company. One day you receive an urgent letter from the controller expressing his concerns about some organizational changes that are about to occur in the information systems department. He has received a memorandum from the vice president of information systems explaining that in the future all new information systems projects will be designed and implemented using the chief programmer team approach. The memorandum describes the nature of chief programmer teams, discusses the benefits of using chief programmer teams to develop information systems, and explains how users will be affected in their interactions with the information systems department during the development of new systems when a chief programmer team is used.

Over the next few years, the controller has several major new information systems scheduled for development. These systems have substantial significance in terms of the underlying data they provide as a basis for preparing Coverit's financial statements. In this light, he is concerned that the organizational structure of the chief programmer team violates a fundamental internal control principle—namely, effective separation of duties. He asks you to advise him on whether his concerns are warranted.

Required.   Prepare a brief report that provides the analysis requested and give a recommendation as to whether you think the organizational change proposed by the vice president of information systems should he allowed to proceed. List, also, some controls that might be used to overcome any exposures you think arise when chief programmer teams are used to develop information systems.

5–7 Supernet Ltd. offers public communications network services. For example, it provides electronic data interchange and electronic funds transfer services to its customers. For over ten years, it has had an excellent reputation for offering high-quality, secure, innovative network services primarily aimed at allowing its customers to develop interorganizational information systems.

During the past year, Supernet has become a public company. Previously it was a private company owned entirely by the current president, Margaret Hawkins, the current controller, Tim Fisher, and the current vice president for research, Anthony Browne. The three now own 30 percent of the company. The remainder is owned in equal parts by two venture capital companies. Hawkins, Fisher, and Browne are now multi-millionaires as a result of the sale of their shares to the venture capital firms.

When Supernet became a public company, your firm was appointed to undertake the external audit. As part of the interim audit work, you are currently interviewing Browne about some of the communications controls that supposedly exist to protect the privacy and integrity of customer data being transmitted over data communications lines. All the controls you are investigating were developed and implemented by Browne in the communications software. Browne is regarded as a technical genius. He is a highly skilled system programmer who almost single-handedly developed the products and services that gave Supernet a competitive edge in the marketplace. He is a quiet, reserved person, however, with few marketing, financial, or managerial skills.

When you ask Browne how some of the controls work, he beckons you to sit beside him at his terminal. He uses a software utility to display a section of internal memory in the main communications machine. The display is unintelligible to you. Browne explains, however, that the display shows that part of the communications program containing the controls that are the subject of your inquiries. He also points to two parts of the display that show an input data buffer and an output data buffer. Browne types vigorously at his terminal for several minutes, and then he issues some commands to print a report. When you ask him what he has done, he explains he has deactivated the controls in the communications program and is printing you a report showing the input and output buffers to illustrate what happens when the controls are not functioning.

You are somewhat perturbed by Browne's actions. When you ask him whether the data being processed is "live" customer data, he indicates it is. He says he is not concerned, however, because other controls in the software most likely will pick up any problems with the data that the deactivated controls are no longer identifying. When you ask him how he deactivated the controls, he indicates he used a utility to alter the program's instructions while it was executing in the communication machine's internal memory. You ask him whether any record of his changes would be kept, and he replies there would be no audit trail. You also ask him whether any programmers on staff could alter the communications program in a similar manner, and he indicates he is the only one with the requisite knowledge. When printing of the report is complete, Brown reactivates the controls, again by altering the program's instructions while it is executing in the communication machine's internal memory.

Required.   In light of the evidence you have collected from interviewing and observing Browne, what exposures, if any, exist in relation to the accuracy and completeness of data in the financial statements? What modifications, if any, would you recommend to year-end audit work? Briefly justify why you would or would not make alterations to the year-end audit work.

Answers to Multiple-Choice Questions

5–1	a	5–6	d	5–11	d	5–16	b
5–2	b	5–7	b	5–12	c	5–17	c
5–3	d	5–8	b	5–13	d	5–18	c
5–4	c	5–9	a	5–14	a	5–19	d
5–5	c	5–10	a	5–15	a	5–20	b

REFERENCES

Albrecht, A. J., and J. Gaffney (1983), "Software Function, Source Lines of Code, and Development Effort Prediction," *IEEE Transactions on Software Engineering* (November), 639–648.

Bersoff, Edward H., and Alan M. Davis (1991), "Impacts of Life Cycle Models on Software Configuration Management," *Communications of the ACM* (August), 104–118.

Boehm, Barry W. (1981), *Software Engineering Economics*. Upper Saddle River, NJ: Prentice-Hall.

——— (1984), "Software Engineering Economics," *IEEE Transactions on Software Engineering* (January), 4–21.

Coad, Peter, and Edward Yourdon (1991), *Object-Oriented Design*. Upper Saddle River, NJ: Prentice-Hall.

Constantine, Larry L. (1991), "Work Organization: Paradigms for Project Management and Organization," *Communications of the ACM* (October), 35–43.

Fagan, M.E. (1976), "Design and Code Inspections to Reduce Errors in Program Development," *IBM Systems Journal*, 15(3), 182–211.

Ghezzi, Carlo, Mehdi Jazayeri, and Dino Mandrioli (1991), *Fundamentals of Software Engineering*. Upper Saddle River, NJ: Prentice-Hall.

Gibbs, W. Wayt (1994), "Software's Chronic Crisis," *Scientific American* (September), 72–81.

Jackson. Michael A. (1975), *Principles of Program Design*. New York: Academic Press.

Mantei, Marilyn (1981), "The Effect of Programming Team Structures on Programming Tasks," *Communications of the ACM* (March), 106–113.

McLeod, Graham, and Derek Smith (1996), *Managing Information Technology Projects*. Danvers, MA: Boyd & Fraser.

Mynatt, Barbee Teasley (1990), *Software Engineering with Student Project Guidance*. Upper Saddle River, NJ: Prentice-Hall.

Page-Jones, Meilir (1988), *The Practical Guide to Structured Systems Design*, 2d ed. Upper Saddle River, NJ: Prentice-Hall.

Pfeeger, Shari Lawrence (1991), *Software Engineering: The Production of Quality Software*, 2d ed. New York: Macmillan.

Pressman, Roger S. (1997), *Software Engineering: A Practitioner's Approach*, 4th ed. New York: McGraw-Hill.

Sage, Andrew P., and James D. Palmer (1990), *Software Systems Engineering*. New York: John Wiley & Sons.

Strauss, Susan H., and Robert G. Ebenau (1994), *Software Inspection Process*. New York: McGraw-Hill.

Vicinanza, Steven S., Tridas Mukhopadhyay, and Michael J. Prietula (1991), "Software Cost Estimation: An Exploratory Study of Expert Performance," *Information Systems Research* (December), 243–262.

Warnier, J. D. (1974), *Logical Construction of Programs*. New York: Van Nostrand Reinhold.

Weinberg, Gerald M. (1971), *The Psychology of Computer Programming*. New York: Van Nostrand Reinhold.

Yourdon, Edward, and Larry L. Constantine (1979), *Structured Design: Fundamentals of a Discipline of Computer Program and Systems Design*. Upper Saddle River, NJ: Prentice-Hall.

------------------------------ A P P E N D I X 5 . 1 ------------------------------

TECHNIQUES FOR PROGRAM DESIGN: FUNCTIONAL DECOMPOSITION

Functional decomposition involves applying the divide-and-conquer technique to programming problems. In other words, the problem is progressively broken up into smaller pieces until the smaller pieces can be solved. The pieces are then reassembled to form the whole. In the programming domain, designers first focus on the overall function to be performed by the program. This function is broken down into subfunctions. The process occurs iteratively until the subfunctions

FIGURE 5–13 (a). System-level functional modules. (b). Program-level function modules. (c). Subprogram-level functional modules.

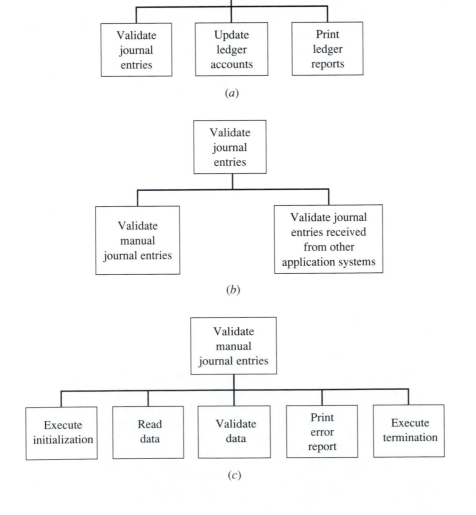

can be understood sufficiently well that they can be translated into programming code. In the programming literature, this technique goes under various names: top-down design, composite design, stepwise refinement, the levels of abstraction approach.

To illustrate functional decomposition, consider a general ledger system. The highest-level function "Update general ledger" might be subdivided into three lower-level functions (Figure 5–13a). Each of these functions can be subdivided again into lower-level functions. For example, "Validate journal entries" might be broken up into a function to validate manually coded entries (adjustments) and a function to validate entries provided as the output of other systems such as accounts receivable, inventory, and order entry (Figure 5–13b). Further subdivision then occurs (Figure 5–13c). Ultimately a hierarchy of functions and subfunctions is produced. The functions and subfunctions then become modules within programs.

There are several guidelines for designers to follow when performing functional decomposition. First, they should focus on *what* is to be done rather than *how* it is to be done. The function description for a program module must contain a verb; thus, "get master record" is valid, but "master record routine" is not. This requirement forces designers to continue to focus on a module's function.

Second, at each level in the hierarchy, designers should focus on only a *small number* of elements or modules. This guideline recognizes the limited capacity of humans to process information. By disregarding other levels, modules, and elements in the hierarchy, designers are better able to define the functions for the small set of modules under consideration.

Third, designers should attempt to conceive modules that have high *strength* or *cohesion*. In other words, the elements in a module should have a singular purpose. The "goodness" of a module can be evaluated by assessing the level of its cohesion.

Fourth, designers should attempt to reduce the extent of *coupling* between modules. The purpose of this guideline is to reduce the effects of changes. If modules are loosely coupled, the effects of changes to one module are unlikely to propagate to another module. Ideally, all modules have only one entry point and one exit point, and entry and exit are accomplished only via receiving or passing data elements.

The primary disadvantage of the functional decomposition approach to program design is that the results are unpredictable. Inevitably multiple ways of undertaking the decomposition can be identified. Consequently, two designers could produce different designs.

-------------------------------- **A P P E N D I X 5 . 2** --------------------------------

TECHNIQUES FOR PROGRAM DESIGN: DATA FLOW DESIGN

Data flow design is simply functional decomposition undertaken with respect to the data flow that occurs in a system (see Yourdon and Constantine 1979). Each module in a data flow design either transforms the structure of data or it transforms the information content of data. For example, it might reformat data items, or it might validate a data item. Thus, the function in a data flow design is always some type of data transformation.

There are two primary strategies for undertaking data flow design. The first is called *transform analysis*. Transform analysis commences by identifying the central transform in a data flow diagram (DFD). The central transform is the bubble, or set of bubbles, that performs the primary function in a DFD. It can be identified by tracing forward the afferent or input data flows to the stage where they are in their most logical form and by tracing backward the efferent or output data flows to the stage where they are in their most logical form. The set of bubbles that links the most logical input form with the most logical output form is the central transform.

By then "picking up" the DFD by its central transform and letting all the other bubbles dangle, the shape of the program structure chart emerges. The central transform constitutes the highest-level module, the modules on the left of the chart deal with input transformations, and the modules on the right deal with output transformations. This first-cut structure chart needs to be refined in various ways. For example, there might be several candidate bubbles in the central transform for the top-level bubble, and other modules might have to be added such as those that handle errors.

To illustrate transform analysis, Figure 5–14*a* shows a DFD for a simple payroll application with the central transform marked. Figure 5–14*b* shows the corresponding program structure chart. Note how the central transform "Calculate Pay" constitutes the top-level module in the structure chart. The left side of the chart shows the afferent or input data stream; the right side shows the efferent or output data stream.

The second data flow design strategy is called *transaction analysis*. Transaction-centered designs tend to be used when systems process many different transaction types, which must be validated in different ways and subsequently could update different master files. This situation often occurs in business systems.

Figure 5–15*a* shows a DFD for part of an order-entry system that will motivate a transaction-centered design. Figure 5–15*b* shows the associated structure chart. Note that the decision diamond at the bottom of the "Determine Transaction Type" module in Figure 5–14*b* signifies that the choice of which lower-level modules to invoke depends on the value of the transaction-type data item.

The data flow approach to program design has been criticized on two bases. First, like the functional decomposition approach, different programmers might not derive the same designs for a problem. Second, it is a moot point as to how well the data flow approach models the problem environment. To the extent the resultant program design is not a good model of the problem environment, small changes in the environment can result in large changes in the program.

FIGURE 5–14*(a)*. Payroll DFD with central transform shown. *(b)*. Structure chart for payroll DFD.

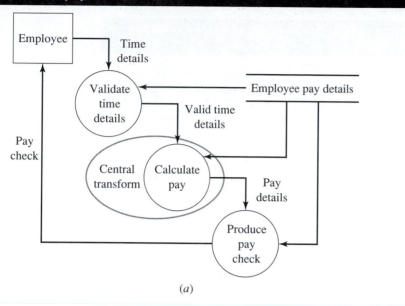

(a)

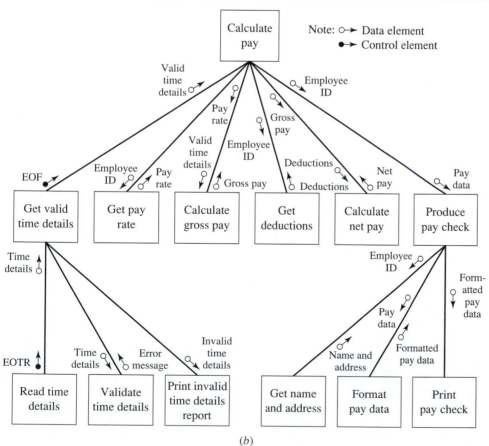

(b)

FIGURE 5–15 (a). Transaction-centered DFD. **(b).** Structure chart for transaction-centered DFD.

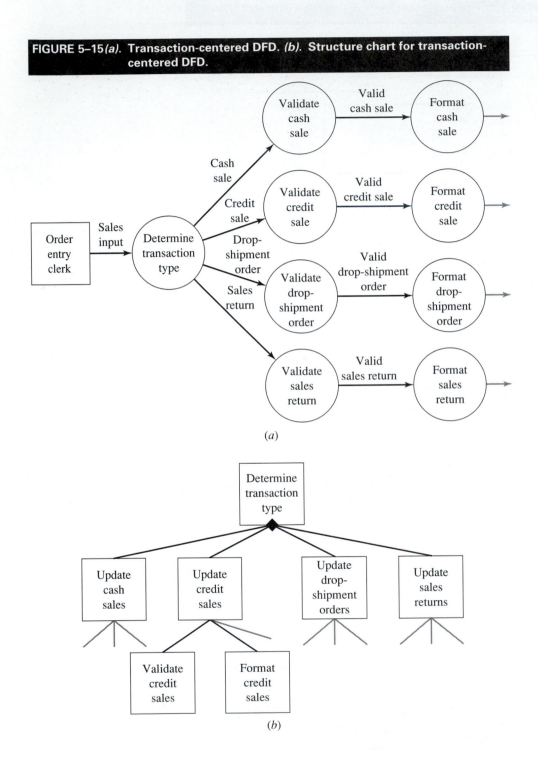

(a)

(b)

---------------------------------- **A P P E N D I X   5 . 3** ----------------------------------

TECHNIQUES FOR PROGRAM DESIGN: DATA STRUCTURE DESIGN

The data structure approach to program design was developed by Jackson (1975) and Warnier (1974). It is founded on the assumption that the "best" program design is one that models its problem domain. The structure of the problem domain is manifested in the data structures that the program must process. Thus, the design of the program should correspond to these data structures.

To establish this correspondence, Jackson (1975) provides a set of four constructs that can be used to show the structure of the data and the structure of the program. The first construct is an *elementary* or *atomic* component—that is, it cannot be decomposed further. A "MOVE" statement or a field declaration via a "PICTURE" clause in COBOL are examples of elementary pro-

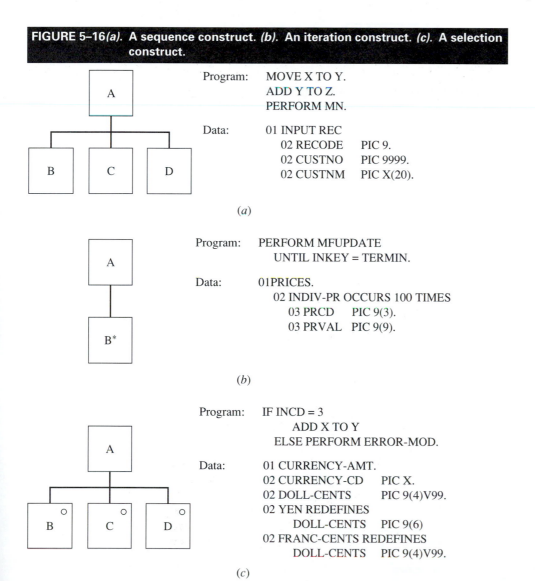

FIGURE 5–16*(a).* A sequence construct. *(b).* An iteration construct. *(c).* A selection construct.

```
Program:   MOVE X TO Y.
           ADD Y TO Z.
           PERFORM MN.

Data:      01 INPUT REC
              02 RECODE    PIC 9.
              02 CUSTNO    PIC 9999.
              02 CUSTNM    PIC X(20).
```
(a)

```
Program:   PERFORM MFUPDATE
              UNTIL INKEY = TERMIN.

Data:      01PRICES.
              02 INDIV-PR OCCURS 100 TIMES
                 03 PRCD    PIC 9(3).
                 03 PRVAL   PIC 9(9).
```
(b)

```
Program:   IF INCD = 3
              ADD X TO Y
              ELSE PERFORM ERROR-MOD.

Data:      01 CURRENCY-AMT.
           02 CURRENCY-CD    PIC X.
           02 DOLL-CENTS     PIC 9(4)V99.
           02 YEN REDEFINES
                 DOLL-CENTS  PIC 9(6)
           02 FRANC-CENTS REDEFINES
                 DOLL-CENTS  PIC 9(4)V99.
```
(c)

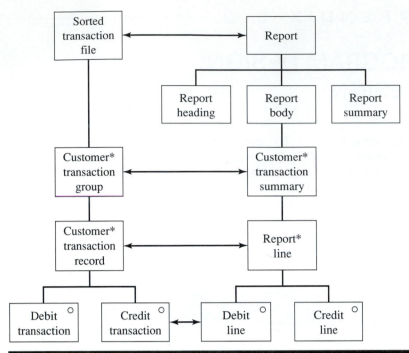

FIGURE 5–17. Correspondence between input and output data structures.

FIGURE 5–18. Program structure for data structures.

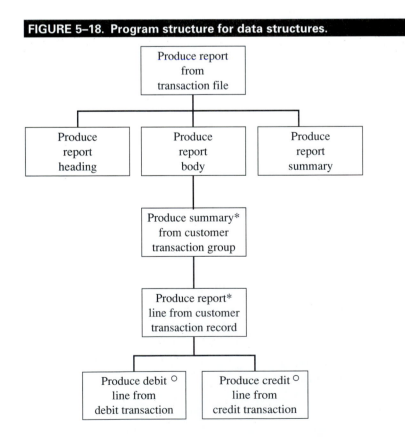

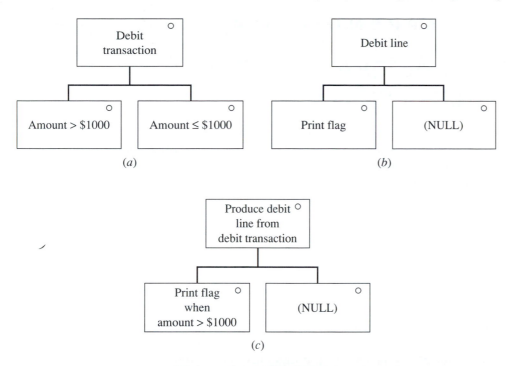

FIGURE 5–19(a). **Modified input data structure.** **(b).** **Modified output data structure.** **(c).** **Modified program structure.**

gram and data structure components, respectively. The remaining three constructs are composite components. Figure 5–16a shows the *sequence* component, which comprises two or more components occurring, once each, in order. Figure 5–16b shows the *iteration* component, which comprises one component that occurs zero or more times for each occurrence of the iteration component. Figure 5–16c shows a *selection* component, which comprises two or more components, only one of which occurs for each instance of the selection component.

To illustrate the data structure design approach, consider a simple accounts receivable application in which a program reads a file of customer charges and payments and updates the customer account. The program produces a report showing the audit trail of transactions, the net amount debited or credited to each account, and the total of debits and credits to all accounts. Figure 5–17 shows the data structure for the input file, the data structure for the report, and the way in which the program structure must establish a one-to-one correspondence between the input and output data structures. Figure 5–18 shows the resulting program structure.

The essence of the data structure approach is the dependence of the data structure on the problem to be solved. If the problem to be solved changes, the data structure must be changed to reflect the new problem structure, and the program structure must be altered accordingly. For example, assume management now wants to flag all debit transactions that exceed $1,000. Figures 5–19a, 5–19b, and 5–19c show the modified input data structure, modified output data structure, and modified program structure, respectively. Note that there has been no alteration to the *physical* form of the input data; nevertheless, the input data structure must be altered to reflect the changed problem structure. As long as the data structures continue to represent the problem structure and the program structure continues to represent the data structures, Jackson (1975) points out that it will be relatively easy to validate and maintain the program.

As with the other approaches to program design, the data structure approach also appears to have limitations. Yourdon and Constantine (1979) argue that the approach seems to work best on relatively small systems. With large systems, some awkward and unwieldy solutions can arise.

------------------------------- **A P P E N D I X   5 . 4** -------------------------------

TECHNIQUES FOR PROGRAM DESIGN: OBJECT-ORIENTED DESIGN

Appendix 4.2 provides a brief introduction to object-oriented analysis. In object-oriented analysis, the real world is modeled in terms of objects and their interactions. Objects have attributes. They can also be organized into two basic structures: class structures and component structures. The state of an object is changed by a method or service.

Object-oriented design develops program architectures that allow the specifications developed in object-oriented analysis to be implemented on hardware/software platforms. Coad and Yourdon (1991) argue four major steps must be undertaken in object-oriented design. First, the Problem Domain Component (PDC) must be designed. The basis for the PDC is the object-oriented analysis results. They describe the existing and conceived real-world phenomena to be represented by an information system. During design of the PDC, the object-oriented analysis results are refined. For example, designers might become aware that user requirements have changed since the analysis work was undertaken. Similarly, a design might have to take into account that a programming language is to be used with limited inheritance capabilities or that performance requirements mean various compromises have to be made in the design of class structures and component structures.

Second, the Human Interaction Component (HIC) must be designed. Again, the HIC is conceived as a set of objects that interact with one another. For example, if a graphical user interface is to be designed, the interface can be conceived in terms of objects like windows, icons, graphics, and fields.

Third, the Task Management Component (TMC) must be designed. A *task* is a set of activities associated with performing some type of job. In many systems, multiple tasks are needed. For example, one task might be responsible for receiving and transmitting data over a data communications line; another task might be responsible for carrying out some type of calculation. Multiple tasks also arise when the HIC permits multiple windows. Each task can be defined as an object. It has attributes, such as its name, description, and priority, and it has services, such as initialization, commencement, and termination services.

Fourth, the Data Management Component (DMC) must be designed. The design approach will depend on what data management facilities are available. If a relational database management system is available, for example, classes containing objects that need to be preserved (stored) first need to be identified. The attributes for these classes are next listed and normalized (see Appendix 4.4). An object-server class and object then needs to be defined to tell each object how to store itself and to retrieve stored objects.

CHAPTER

Data Resource Management Controls

Chapter Outline

Chapter Key Points

■ Many organizations now recognize that data is a critical resource that must be managed properly. Accordingly, they attempt to subject it to centralized planning and control.

■ For data to be managed better, four objectives must be achieved: (a) users must be able to share data; (b) data must be available to users when it is needed, in the location where it is needed, and in the form in which it is needed; (c) it must be possible to modify data fairly easily in light of changing user requirements; and (d) the integrity of data must be preserved.

■ To achieve these four objectives, both technical and administrative solutions are required. Technical solutions are provided by database management systems and data repository systems. These systems allow organizations to define, establish, maintain, and protect the integrity of shared databases. Administrative solutions have come in the form of the data administration and database administration roles. The data administrator handles administrative and policy matters. The database administrator handles technical matters.

■ A major task that data administrators and database administrators perform is to mediate when conflict arises in a shared data environment. In addition, they undertake the following five functions: (a) defining, creating, redefining, and retiring data; (b) making the database available to users, (c) informing and servicing users, (d) maintaining database integrity, and (e) monitoring operations and performance.

■ Auditors need a good understanding of the data administrator's and database administrator's roles. If the incumbents do not perform these roles effectively, the quality of the database environment can be seriously undermined. The incumbents can also provide auditors with important information they need to know about control strengths and weaknesses and the means by which they can access the database for evidence collection and evaluation purposes.

■ If the data administrator and database administrator are to perform their mediation function effectively, they must be placed in the organizational hierarchy so users perceive they have substantial independence and autonomy.

■ In a decentralized organization, corporate standards must be formulated to facilitate management of data that must be shared. Divisional standards must be formulated to facilitate management of data that will only be used locally. Corporate data administrators and database administrators must prepare, promulgate, and enforce corporate standards for data. Divisional data administrators and database administrators have these same responsibilities for divisional standards.

■ Data repository systems are used to provide automated support for managing the data definition in a database environment. Ideally, these systems would maintain a single, authentic, accurate, complete, consistent, and up-to-date definition that all users and programs could access. In practice, multiple data definitions often exist, and multiple data repository systems are often used. As a result, data integrity could be undermined.

∎ Auditors should carefully evaluate an organization's use of and control over its data repository system. If it is used properly, a data repository system can enhance data and application system reliability. It must be controlled carefully, however, because the consequences are serious if the data definition is compromised or destroyed. Auditors can also use a data repository system to assist them to undertake an audit; for example, an auditor could use it to obtain a report showing which programs use a particular data item.

∎ Substantial power is often vested in the data-administration and database-administration roles. The consequences can be serious if the roles are performed incompetently or the incumbents use their power to perpetrate irregularities. Careful control should be exercised over the roles by appointing senior, trustworthy persons, separating duties to the extent possible, and maintaining and monitoring logs of the data administrator's and database administrator's activities.

INTRODUCTION

Increasingly, organizations are recognizing that data is a critical *resource* that must be managed properly. Consequently, they have sought technical and administrative solutions to the problems they face in managing the data resource. Technical solutions have been provided primarily through the acquisition of database management systems (DBMSs) and data repository systems (DRSs). These systems provide hardware-software facilities that enable organizations to define, establish, maintain, and protect the integrity of shared databases. Administrative solutions have centered around the establishment of two new organizational roles: the data administrator (DA) and the database administrator (DBA). Both roles have arisen primarily in response to behavioral problems that have occurred when data must be shared.

In this chapter we discuss the motivations for establishing the DA and DBA roles within organizations. We examine the functions that should be performed by DAs and DBAs and the administrative and technical factors that contribute to effective performance of their roles. Our objective is to obtain sufficient understanding of their roles so we can fulfil our audit responsibilities. In addition, because of the substantial influence that DAs and DBAs have over the quality of the data resource, we also focus on some important implications of their roles for the conduct of audits. Finally, we examine several control problems posed by the existence of the DA and DBA roles and some remedial measures that might be undertaken.

MOTIVATIONS TOWARD THE DA AND DBA ROLES

Historically, few organizations planned their data needs nor exercised careful control over their data use. The strategic importance of data did not become apparent until computers had been widely deployed. Moreover, even if some organizations did recognize data as a critical resource, few had the technical tools and administrative know-how to manage data effectively and efficiently.

When computer systems were first used in organizations, usually the application-development group took responsibility for defining the data needed, establishing the data on machine-readable media, and updating the data definition as user needs evolved. As a result, responsibility for an organization's data was dispersed across many people. Inevitably, difficulties arose: different groups needed the same data but they defined the data differently; multiple versions of the same data item could be found, but they had inconsistent values; resources were wasted when different groups defined and established the same data items; system integration efforts were undermined because data had not been defined in an accurate, complete, and consistent way.

Because of these problems, throughout the 1960s many information systems researchers and practitioners focused their efforts on how to manage data better. Everest (1986, pp. 36–52) argues that their work was motivated by four fundamental objectives:

1. *Sharability:* Different stakeholders in an organization should be permitted to access and use the same data. They should not have to maintain their own separate copies of the same data item.
2. *Availability:* If data were to be shared, different stakeholders should be able to access and use the data whenever they needed it, from the location where they needed it, and in the form that they needed it.
3. *Evolvability:* Facilities had to exist that allowed data and its definition to be modified easily in response to changing stakeholder needs.
4. *Integrity:* If data were to be shared among multiple stakeholders, its authenticity, accuracy, and completeness had to be preserved.

All four objectives have been difficult to achieve. From an administrative viewpoint, however, sharability has been the most problematical objective. When resources are shared, behavioral problems inevitably arise. For example, consider how conflict can arise when several stakeholders need to access and use the same data. At the outset they might disagree over the names and definitions to be assigned to the data items. In an inventory system, for example, one user might want to use the term "part number" and another the term "item number." Should both terms (aliases) be permitted? They might also disagree on the number of characters that should be provided for the part or item number and perhaps the type of coding system that should be used—for example, the manufacturer's code or the distributor's code.

The two users also might wish to access the inventory data differently. For example, one might be concerned primarily with the names of vendors who can supply each inventory item. The other might be concerned about the relationship of each item to other items in a bill of materials. Different access paths to the data might have to be established. Overall performance could degrade as a result of having to accommodate conflicting user needs. Neither user would be happy with the outcome.

These sorts of difficulties are exacerbated as organizations move increasingly to sharing of information both within and across their boundaries. For example, an organization might wish to establish a data warehouse so it can mine its data to identify important trends (see, further, Chapter 24). Most likely the data to be deposited in the warehouse will be gathered from all

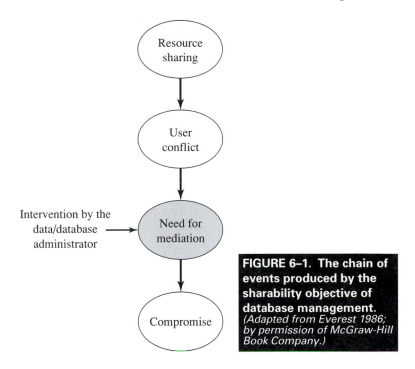

FIGURE 6–1. The chain of events produced by the sharability objective of database management. *(Adapted from Everest 1986; by permission of McGraw-Hill Book Company.)*

over the organization. If those users who mine the data are to be able to assimiliate and process it in useful ways, organizationwide data standards must be developed and enforced—for example, in relation to naming and formatting data.

Similarly, if an organization wishes to participate in an interorganizational information system—for example, an electronic commerce system that links it with its customers and suppliers or some type of World Wide Web–based system that permits it to exchange useful data with other users of the Internet—again, data standards must be developed and enforced. Otherwise, sharing of data across organizational boundaries will not be possible.

In short, sharing produces the chain of events shown in Figure 6–1. When resources must be shared, conflict over resource use inevitably arises. To resolve the conflict, an independent mediator is required who can achieve a satisfactory compromise among the stakeholders involved in the conflict. In the case of data resources, the data administration and database administration roles have emerged to undertake this mediation function.

FUNCTIONS OF THE DA AND DBA

When management first recognized the need for an independent mediator to resolve data-resource conflicts, their response was to create the database administration role. A single role proved inadequate, however, for two reasons. First, it became clear that competency in the role required two different types of skills: A set of administrative skills was needed to handle managerial and policy matters and to interact effectively with database users, and a set of technical skills was also needed to handle the detailed design work and to tune the database so it could be used efficiently. Few people have both sets of skills. Second, over time, the database administrator's workload became excessive. As the amount of end-user computing, decentralized computing, and distributed

TABLE 6–1   Data/Database Administration Responsibilities

Function	DA Responsibilities	DBA Responsibilities
Defining data	Undertaking strategic data planning; determining user needs; specifying conceptual and external schema (user-oriented) definitions.	Specifying internal schema (computer-oriented) definition.
Creating data	Advising users on data-collection procedures; specifying validation and editing criteria.	Preparing programs to create data; assistance in populating database.
Redefining/ restructuring data	Specifying new conceptual . and external schema definitions; advising users on how to conform with new definition.	Specifying new internal schema definition; altering database to conform with new schema definitions.
Retiring data	Specifying retirement policies.	Implementing retirement policies.
Making database available to users	Determining end-user requirements for database tools; testing and evaluating end-user database tools.	Determining programmer requirements for database tools; determining database optimization tools required; testing and evaluating programmer and database optimization tools.
Informing and servicing users	Answering end-user queries; educating end users; establishing and promulgating high-level policy information; providing conceptual schema and external schema information.	Answering programmer queries; educating programmers; establishing and promulgating low-level policy information; providing internal schema information.
Maintaining database integrity	Developing and promulgating organizationwide standards; assisting end users to formulate application controls.	Implementing database controls; assisting programmers to design and implement application controls.
Monitoring operations	Monitoring end-user patterns of database use.	Monitoring programmer patterns of database use; collecting performance statistics; tuning the database.

computing in organizations grew, substantially more support had to be provided, especially to database users who were not information systems professionals. Consequently, the database administration role was split. A new role was created, the data administration role, to handle administrative and policy matters. The database administrator's role was then redefined to focus on technical matters.

Table 6–1 provides an overview of the functions that Everest (1986) says the DA and the DBA should perform in an organization. In the following sections we examine these functions in more detail and discuss some audit procedures we can use to collect evidence on how well they are performed (see also

Weber and Everest 1979). Auditors must have a good understanding of the DA's and DBA's functions for the following reasons:

1. If the DA and DBA do not perform their functions well, asset safeguarding, data integrity, system effectiveness, and system efficiency in a database environment can be severely undermined.
2. The DA and DBA are important sources of information on strengths and weaknesses in a database environment because they are focal points for communications among users of the database.
3. The DA and DBA provide important administrative and technical information auditors need to know to carry out that work. For example, the DA might provide the definition of data the auditor needs to access, and the DBA might assist the auditor to use a database tool to retrieve these data.

Defining, Creating, Redefining, and Retiring Data

When a user requires data that does not currently exist, the life cycle of data commences. The first step is to define the data needed. In a database environment, three types of definition are required. Each reflects a different "view" of the database (Figure 6–2):

Description/view	*Nature*
External schema	An external schema describes a particular user's view of the database in terms of the objects/entities, attributes of these objects/entities, relationships among these objects/entities, and integrity constraints on the objects/entities that interest the user. Because there can be many users, there can be many external schemas. Each defines only a subset of the total database because any particular user is unlikely to be interested in its entire contents. From a control perspective, an external schema can be used to restrict a user's access to only certain parts of the database.
Conceptual schema	The conceptual schema describes the entire contents of the database from a user's perspective. It defines all objects/entities in the database, all attributes of these objects/entities, all relationships among objects/entities, and all integrity constraints on objects/entities. In essence, it is an amalgamation of all external schemas into an accurate, complete, and consistent whole.
Internal schema	The internal schema describes how the contents of the database are mapped onto physical storage media. It defines the records, fields, access paths, and processes used to represent the objects/entities, attributes of objects/entities, relationships among objects/entities, and constraints on objects/entities defined in the conceptual schema.

To illustrate these notions, Figure 6–3 shows the three schemas for a simple database. The external and conceptual schemas have been modeled using a technique called NIAM (see Halpin 1995). A personnel clerk views the database in terms of a person object type and a department object type, an association relating a person object type and a department object type, and a constraint indicating that a person can belong only to one department whereas a department can have many employees. Similarly, a payroll clerk views the database in terms of a person object type, a salary object type, an association

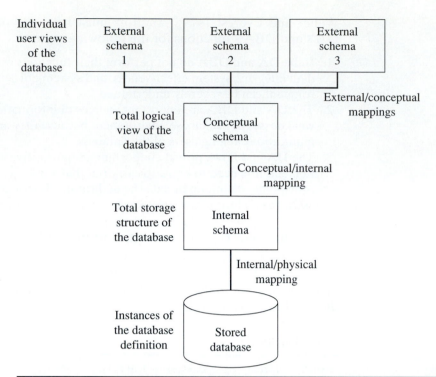

FIGURE 6–2. Database definition: schemas and their mappings.

FIGURE 6–3. Three levels of database definition.

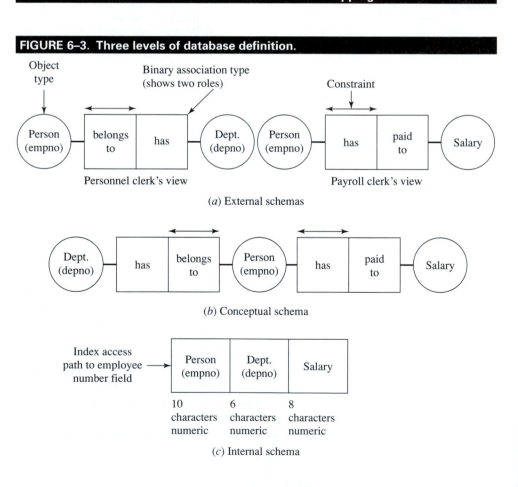

(a) External schemas

(b) Conceptual schema

(c) Internal schema

relating a person object type and a salary object type, and a constraint indicating a person can have only one salary whereas a salary can apply to many employees. These two views are combined into the overall conceptual schema. The conceptual schema, in turn, is mapped into a record structure with three fields: person-number, department-number, and salary. Because person-number is chosen as the primary key of the record, it can be accessed directly via an index.

The DA takes primary responsibility for defining the external schemas and conceptual schema. To define the external schemas, the DA must consult all users of the database so the different object types, attributes, associations, and integrity constraints can be identified. The DA should use a formal methodology to elicit these elements of the definition to resolve semantic ambiguities and to detect inconsistencies and redundancies—for example, NIAM, as illustrated previously, or the object-oriented or entity-relationship methodologies, as illustrated in Appendices 4.2 and 4.3.

Next, the DA must combine these external schemas into an accurate, complete, and consistent whole—the conceptual schema. This step is known as *view integration*. As with the definition of the external schema, view integration and definition of the conceptual schema should be undertaken using a formal methodology (see, further, Batini et al. 1986, 1992). During this step, conflicts among user views will have to be resolved and acceptable compromises reached. The mediation skills of the DA (discussed previously) will be tested.

The DBA then takes primary responsibility for defining the internal schema. Some storage structure decisions may be made automatically by the DBMS; for example, the DBMS may always establish certain kinds of access paths for key fields in records. Nevertheless, usually the DBA has to make several decisions about how the conceptual schema will be mapped onto the internal schema, such as specifying indices for frequently accessed data items, orderings among records, access paths among records, and data compression procedures to be used. Overall, the DBA strives to identify a mapping that will meet performance objectives—for example, acceptable response times and throughput rates. If these objectives cannot be attained, however, the DBA then must work with the DA to determine whether compromises can be reached with the external schema and conceptual schema designs. In short, the process of external schema design, conceptual schema design, and internal schema design usually is iterative.

When the conceptual schema, external schema, and internal schema have been designed, the DA and DBA enter the definitions into the DBMS via its data definition language (DDL). DBMSs vary in terms of how completely they allow the various schemas to be specified in their DDL. For example, one constraint in the conceptual schema might be that a person's salary cannot be increased by more than 5 percent in any 12-month period unless they have been working for the organization for at least six years and they have at least three consecutive "high" performance ratings. Many DBMSs will not allow this type of conditional, dynamic constraint to be defined via their DDL. Instead, the constraint must be enforced via programs that access and use the database. Moreover, to document the constraint, the DA will have to use a means other than the DBMS's definition. For example, the DA could record the constraint using a data repository system (discussed subsequently).

After the new definitions have been established, the database now must be *populated* with data according to these definitions; that is, specific instances of data must be created that conform with the definitions. For example, using the internal schema shown in Figure 6–3, records would be created containing values for the person-number, department-number, and salary fields.

The DA and DBA take joint responsibility for populating the database. The DA advises users on procedures for collecting data and, in particular, validation and editing criteria that should be applied to the data. Where different users have maintained files on the same data item or they have an interest in the same data item, the DA also designates who will be responsible for assembling instances of the data item and how differences between alternative versions of the data item are to be reconciled. The DBA takes responsibility for preparing the programs needed to populate the database. The DBMS might provide facilities in this respect, or special programs might have to be designed and written. During the development of these programs, the DBA should pay special attention to the validation and editing procedures the DA has specified to ensure the database is populated with high-quality data.

As user needs change, existing data definitions might have to be modified. The respective responsibilities of the DA and DBA are much like those described previously for the data definition and creation phases. The DA works primarily with users to determine new external schema and conceptual schema designs and their impact on users. The DBA determines the changes needed to the internal schema, works out the effects of the redefinition on existing data and programs, and establishes how the changes can be accomplished. The redefinition task will be easier if the DA and DBA maintain comprehensive documentation on the database definition.

The final phase in the life cycle of data is retirement. Policies must be formulated to provide guidelines on when data is to be retired and how long it is to be retained. The DA is responsible for consulting users, identifying any relevant legislation on data retention, formulating policies, and advising users on the implications of policies. The DBA is responsible for implementing these policies and executing retirement and retention procedures for specific data items.

Auditors need to assess how well the DA and DBA carry out the functions of database definition, creation, redefinition, and retirement. An auditor could interview the DA and DBA to find out how they perform their work, observe them at their work, and examine a sample of documentation to evaluate such factors as the quality of schema design, control over changes to schemas, and data retirement policies. The auditor could also interview a sample of database users to obtain their views on how well the DA and DBA perform the definition, creation, redefinition, and retirement functions. Because these functions are critical to asset safeguarding, data integrity, system effectiveness, and system efficiency objectives, the auditor should take special care when conducting this evaluation exercise.

Making the Database Available to Users

Database users need various tools to interrogate and update the database. These tools must be purchased or developed. Moreover, because user needs change over time and enhanced or new tools become available, someone must monitor the needs of the user population, remain aware of the current tool technology, and ensure that required tools are available on a timely basis.

Both the DA and DBA have responsibility for making the database available to users. The DA usually has better knowledge of end-user needs. The DBA, on the other hand, usually has better knowledge of programmer needs.

Both must remain aware of tools that might satisfy the needs of their primary stakeholder groups. In addition, both should remain aware of tools that facilitate use of the database generally. For example, the DA should keep abreast of tools that support strategic data planning and schema documentation, and the DBA should keep abreast of tools that would improve the efficiency with which the database can be used.

Irrespective of whether a tool is purchased or developed, it must be evaluated carefully by the DA and DBA. For a start, the initial costs to acquire or build the tool may be high. Even if these costs are minor, however, subsequent costs could be high if use of the tool leads to poor decisions or corruption of the database. Thorough testing of tools used in a shared data environment must be undertaken before production release occurs.

Auditors might evaluate how well the DA and DBA perform this function by first interviewing them to obtain an understanding of the activities they undertake to enhance database availability. If, as a result, auditors intend to rely on controls in this area, they might then confirm they are operating reliably by interviewing users to determine whether they are satisfied with their ability to access and use the database. Auditors can also examine machine logs and manual logs to obtain evidence on how frequently various tools are used and whether problems have been experienced in using particular tools. If they conclude that controls are functioning reliably, they might reduce subsequent testing of application systems that use the database. If database availability is problematic, however, the primary risks are likely to be to effectiveness and efficiency objectives. In this light, they might expand the extent of detailed testing undertaken subsequently on application systems that use the database to determine whether they operate effectively and efficiently.

Informing and Servicing Users

As the focal points in a database environment, the DA and DBA are responsible for informing and assisting users and educating and training users. Users must know the current status of the database. They must be alerted, for example, if a portion of the database is damaged. When users have difficulty accessing or using the database, the DA and DBA must assist them. If a new availability tool has been purchased or developed, the DA and DBA must educate and train users so they can effectively and efficiently employ the tool.

To inform and service users, the DA and DBA must establish good communications with them. There are several means; for example, documentation, memoranda, electronic bulletin boards, Web sites, and electronic mail messages. Nevertheless, the DA and DBA must also develop good personal rapport with users if they are to be effective consultants when users encounter problems.

Auditors might interview the DA and DBA to determine the procedures they employ to inform and service users. They might also examine and evaluate the quality of the communications systems they have in place, such as the documentation and messaging facilities. If auditors conclude that the DA and DBA are performing this function satisfactorily and therefore the controls in place are reliable, they might then interview a sample of users to confirm they are satisfied with the DA's and DBA's performance. If they conclude that the DA and DBA are not performing this function satisfactorily, however, the audit plan must be adjusted to take into account that effectiveness and efficiency objectives, in particular, might have been undermined. They might then expand their detailed examination of specific application systems to determine whether they are meeting their effectiveness and efficiency objectives.

Maintaining Database Integrity

The DA and DBA play a major role in maintaining the integrity of the database. Everest (1986) identifies six areas in which they must undertake control activities:

1. *Definition control:* The DA and DBA establish definition controls to ensure the database always corresponds to its definition. The DA develops and promulgates organizationwide data definition standards and monitors compliance with these standards. For example, users might be precluded from creating new data definitions not approved by the DA. The DBA, on the other hand, takes primary responsibility for the technical aspects of definition control. For example, the DBA tries to ensure programs do not destroy the correspondence between the database and its definition by failing to employ the authorized database definition when they access the database.

2. *Existence control:* The DA and DBA protect the existence of the database by establishing backup and recovery procedures. The DA consults with users to determine backup and recovery requirements. For example, the DA determines how long users can tolerate the whole database or a segment of the database being unavailable. The DBA then implements backup and recovery controls to ensure these requirements are met.

3. *Access control:* Access controls, such as passwords, prevent inadvertent or unauthorized disclosure of data in the database. Various levels of access controls are needed for data items, groups of data items, and files. To prevent irregularities, separation of duties should be applied so that the person who assigns users a level of access authorization is not the same person who implements the access controls. In this light the DA might perform the former function, and the DBA might perform the latter function.

4. *Update control:* Update controls restrict update of the database to authorized users. Update authorization takes two forms. One permits only addition of data to the database. The second allows users to change or delete existing data. Various refinements on these update forms exist. For example, a user might only be permitted to add data to the end of a file. To preserve separation of duties, the DA should determine the level of update authorization that users should possess. The DBA should then implement the level assigned.

5. *Concurrency control:* Data integrity problems can arise when two update processes access the same data item at the same time. For example, an order-entry process and a warehouse-receipts process might be concurrently updating the inventory quantity-on-hand data item. If the two update processes are not controlled, the database can end up in an erroneous state. The DBMS should automatically handle the problems that arise when concurrent processes access a data item. In some cases, however, it could provide only partial solutions. Human intervention might be needed to schedule processes to prevent concurrency problems arising or to implement recovery actions if the database is corrupted. The DA should negotiate with users if applications have to be scheduled to prevent concurrency problems. The DBA should then implement the agreed-upon schedules and devise strategies to recover the database if it is corrupted. (Chapter 14 discusses these matters further.)

6. *Quality control:* Quality controls ensure the accuracy, completeness, and consistency of data maintained in the database. Included within this set of controls

are traditional measures such as program validation of input data and batch controls over data in transit through the organization. Both the DA and DBA share joint responsibility for quality control over the database. The DA tends to address policy matters and to assist end users. For example, the DA might formulate standard check-digit procedures or develop standard validation tests that must always be applied to a particular data item. The DBA assists in implementing quality control policies and monitors the database for compliance with these policies.

Auditors might interview the DA and DBA to determine what controls they exercise to maintain database integrity. Auditors might also interview database users to determine their level of awareness of these controls. Further information on what controls supposedly are in place can be obtained from documentation that should be maintained in the data repository system and from observations of users as they access and update the database. If auditors intend to rely on controls associated with this function, they should test them to see they are operating reliably. For example, auditors might employ test data to evaluate whether access controls and update controls are working. If they conclude that they cannot rely on the controls associated with this function, they must expand the extent of detailed testing associated with the results produced by applications that use the database. Control weaknesses associated with maintenance of database integrity often have significant implications for asset safeguarding and data integrity objectives. In this light, auditors usually pay special attention to how well the DA and DBA perform this function.

Monitoring Operations

Finally, the DA and DBA must monitor operations and performance within the database environment. Ongoing monitoring enables the DA and DBA to identify areas where effectiveness and efficiency can be improved. For example, monitoring user access patterns might allow response times to be improved through redesigning the internal schema. Similarly, changes in the ways users interrogate the database could indicate a new type of interrogation tool is needed.

To monitor the database environment effectively, the DA and DBA must be able to identify areas where changes or difficulties are likely to occur, determine the appropriate performance statistics to be collected, and then devise suitable measurement procedures. In some cases, monitoring simply could involve collecting statistics on the types and frequency of user requests against the database. In other cases, it might involve more complex efforts, such as measuring user satisfaction with the database.

Auditors might interview the DA and DBA to determine the procedures they use to monitor the database environment. They might also examine documentation relating to statistics they have collected and actions they have undertaken to improve performance. If they believe controls relating to this function are operating reliably, they should then test those they intend to rely on. For example, they might interview or administer questionnaires to a sample of users to confirm their systems are operating effectively and efficiently. In some cases, they might submit their own test data to a database application system to confirm, for example, that response times and throughput rates are satisfactory. If they conclude that controls are operating reliably, they can reduce the amount of detailed testing they subsequently carry out to determine whether application systems that use the database are operating effectively and efficiently. If they conclude controls are not operating reliably, however, they must expand their subsequent detailed testing. Auditors should recognize, in particular, that asset safeguarding and data integrity objectives might also be at risk when database application systems are ineffective and inefficient. Users might circumvent controls in an attempt to alleviate the problems caused by ineffective and inefficient systems.

SOME ORGANIZATIONAL ISSUES

The preceding sections adopt a normative perspective of the DA and DBA roles; that is, they discuss what these roles *should* be accomplishing to provide auditors with a basis for evaluating them. Unfortunately, the situation in practice is not as clear-cut as the normative descriptions imply. Both the DA and DBA roles are relatively new, and a number of unresolved difficulties remain. An early study by Kahn (1983), for example, found the DA and DBA roles were only marginally effective, even though they were adequately funded. More recent work by Braithwaite (1988) and Vinden (1990) indicates this situation still persists and is likely to continue for some time.

In this light, the following sections examine two major organizational issues that must be addressed if the DA and DBA roles are to be effective: the placement of the DA and DBA roles in the organizational hierarchy and the impact of decentralization of the information systems function on the DA and DBA. We will see these two issues mean that auditors must evaluate both roles from a contingency perspective.

Placement of the DA and DBA Roles

The DA seems best placed in the organizational hierarchy as either *(1)* a staff function within the offices of top management or *(2)* a staff function reporting to the person responsible for the information systems function (Figure 6–4). If auditors are evaluating which location is likely to be better, they might consider the choice in the context of a model like the strategic grid that we examined in Chapter 3. If the organization is a strategic or turnaround organization—in other words, information systems are critical to the future success of the organization and perhaps to its current operations—the DA is probably better placed as a staff function within the offices of top management. In strategic and turnaround organizations, data is or will be a critical resource that must be managed effectively on an organizationwide basis. The DA must have wide powers, and other functional areas within the organization must perceive that top management considers the DA's role to be important. In particular, the DA needs to be able to undertake effective strategic data planning with all functional areas.

On the other hand, if auditors conclude that the organization is in the support or factory quadrant of the strategic grid, the DA is probably better placed under the control of the person responsible for the information systems function. Recall, in support and factory organizations, information systems are either not critical to the organization's current or future operations or critical only to its current operations. Indeed, in a support organization, auditors might conclude the DA role is not really needed. There will be insufficient work to justify a separate role, and perhaps the DBA can perform DA functions when needed. In a factory organization, however, the DA must continue to manage existing data resources effectively because existing information systems are important to the organization's success.

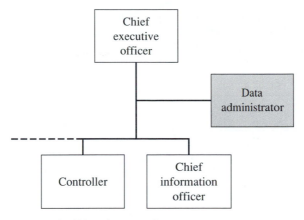

(a) Staff function reporting to top management

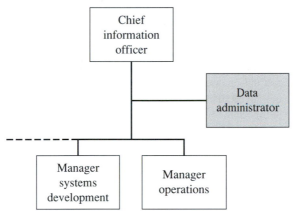

(b) Staff function reporting to chief information officer

FIGURE 6–4. Organizational placement of the data administration role.

Irrespective of an organization's position within the strategic grid, the DBA seems best placed under the person who controls the information systems function. Because DBAs undertake many technical activities, there are advantages to having them located in close proximity to hardware/software resources and to the information systems staff. Nevertheless, the DBA must work closely with the DA. If the DA role is located in the offices of top management, the DBA must be able to communicate directly with the DA and not be constrained by formal lines of reporting within the organization (Figure 6–5a). If the DA role is located in the information systems function, however, the DBA might report directly to the DA (Figure 6–5b). In large factory organizations, both the DA and DBA might even report to a manager who takes overall responsibility for the organization's data resources (Figure 6–5c).

If auditors conclude that the DA and DBA functions are not located appropriately—for example, in a strategic organization they are both located under the manager of systems development—they should assess the risk of ineffective performance of both roles to be higher. As a result, there is a higher risk that the quality of database application systems will be undermined. Accordingly, they will need to expand their detailed testing of these application systems during subsequent stages of the audit.

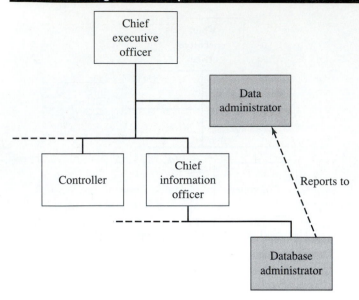

(*a*) Database administrator reports to data administrator
outside IS department

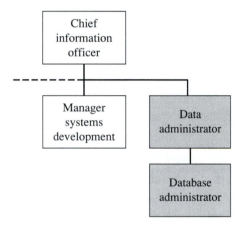

(*b*) Database administrator reports to data
administrator

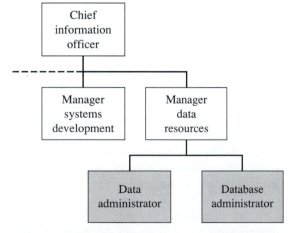

(*c*) Database administrator reports to manager of data resources

Effects of Decentralization of the Information Systems Function

Choosing the location of the DA and DBA roles is more difficult when an organization decentralizes its information systems function. In some ways the objectives of database management and the objectives of decentralizing the information systems function seem in conflict. On the one hand, centralized planning and control of data is the objective with database management. On the other hand, dispersal of information systems functions so they are close to users is the objective with decentralization. A reconciliation is possible, however, if stakeholders recognize that organizationwide standards must apply to data communicated among decentralized groups.

Data should be partitioned, therefore, into two sets: data that will remain strictly within the confines of a localized group, and data that will be communicated to at least one other group within the organization. In the former case, the data can be managed locally. The corporate DA and DBA should have promulgated general data-management guidelines, and the local group should adhere to these guidelines. In the latter case, however, local use of data must comply with the policies and rules established by the corporate DA and DBA. In other words, local users must acquiesce to the corporate DA and DBA so that all users can make effective and efficient use of shared data. This requirement does not imply that shared data must be *stored* centrally. Where the data are stored physically is another matter—one determined primarily by efficiency considerations.

If data in a decentralized organization is managed in this way, some alternatives for locating the DA and DBA roles become clearer (Figure 6–6).

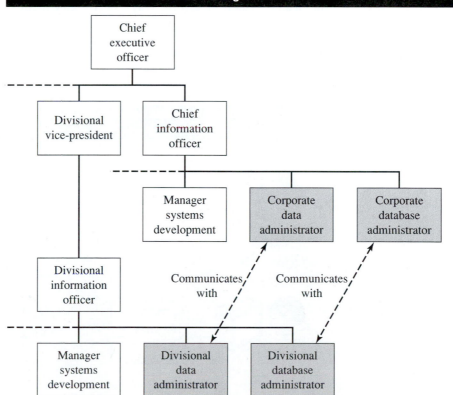

FIGURE 6–6. Placement of the data administration and database administration roles in a decentralized organization.

Large, decentralized groups might have their own DA and DBA to manage local data. These local DAs and DBAs must comply with standards established by the corporate DA and DBA, however, for organizationwide data. Indeed, they should be responsible for enforcing these standards among local users. Alternatively, if local groups are not sufficiently large to support their own DA and DBA functions, the corporate DA and DBA might act in a service role. That is, the corporate DA and DBA act in an advisory role and perform the data management tasks required for local data. In addition, they would be responsible for ensuring the local group understands and complies with standards established for shared data.

Perhaps the most difficult decentralization problems arise when end-user computing is a major facet of an organization's information systems function. If a large number of end users employ high-level tools to design and implement their own databases, the DA and DBA can have difficulty enforcing corporate data standards because monitoring costs will be high. Nevertheless, providing end-user databases have only a localized impact, failure to enforce corporate data standards might not be serious. When many users employ the same data, however, failure to enforce corporate data standards is a serious concern. Multiple, conflicting versions of data can arise, which in turn can lead to erroneous decision making. A critical but difficult function of the DA and DBA, therefore, is to develop and promulgate data standards for end users and to ensure compliance by end users with these standards.

DATA REPOSITORY SYSTEMS

Recall that two major objectives of database management are to facilitate evolution of the database and to maintain database integrity. These objectives can be accomplished in several ways. A primary means, however, is to maintain a single, complete, automated definition of the data and to separate this definition from the data itself and from the programs that use that data (Figure 6–7). If a single, complete, automated definition is maintained, all users and programs have access to a common, consistent, up-to-date description of the data.

FIGURE 6–7. Using a separate data definition to achieve the objectives of database management.

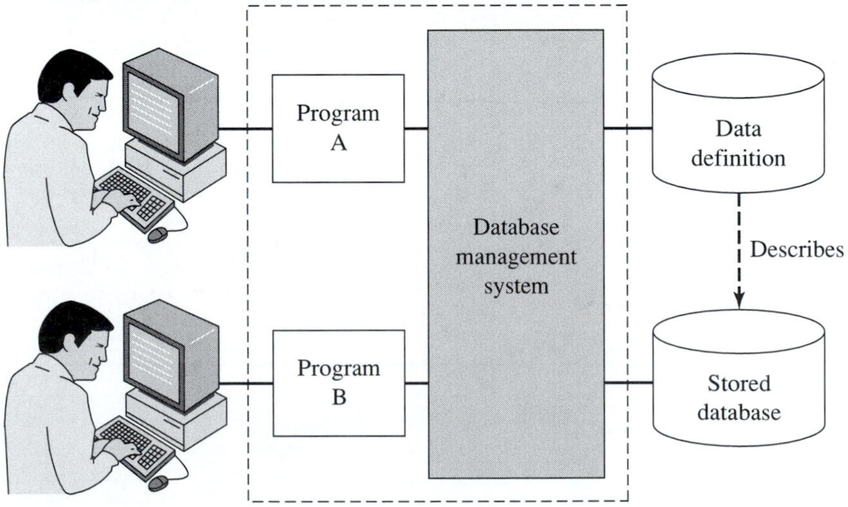

Moreover, by separating the definition of data from instances of the data, certain types of changes can be made to the definition without affecting the stored data. For example, in some cases a user's view of the data can be altered without modifying the stored data. Similarly, certain types of changes can be made to the definition without affecting the programs that use the data. For example, the internal schema can be changed without having to alter program source code and to recompile programs.

The facility used to maintain an automated definition of the data is called a data dictionary system, data directory system, or more recently a data repository system (DRS). Auditors must be familiar with the nature and functions of a DRS and its importance for the audit conducted. In this light, the following three sections review the basic functions of a DRS, some problems with DRSs that can undermine controls, and the relevance of DRSs for the auditor's work.

Basic Functions of a DRS

As discussed previously, the primary function of a DRS is to store the database definition. Recall that three types of definition are required to provide a complete description of the database: a conceptual schema definition, an external schema definition, and an internal schema definition. Because these definitions are data themselves, they are sometimes called "metadata"; they are data about data. This metadata should provide an authentic, accurate, complete, consistent, and up-to-date description of the database that can be employed by (1) programs that must access and manipulate the database and (2) users who must carry out their day-to-day activities as well as plan and provide for their future activities.

To support these needs, Figure 6–8 shows the major functional capabilities that a DRS must provide. A data definition language processor allows the DA/DBA to create or modify a data definition. It performs validation tests on the definition entered by the DA/DBA to ensure the integrity of the metadata

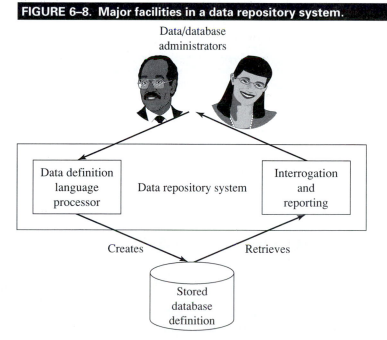

FIGURE 6–8. Major facilities in a data repository system.

ATTRIBUTES WHERE USED REPORT
Entity Name

Attribute Name	Data Element
ACTIVE	
Date-Card-Expires	Date-Card-Expires
ID	Borrower-ID
APPLICANT	
ID	Borrower-ID
References	References
BOOK LOCATION	
Copy-ID	Copy-ID
Current-Copy-Location	Current-Copy-Location
Date-Borrowed	Date-Borrowed
Days-May-Keep	Days-May-Keep
ID	Borrower-ID
ISBN	ISBN
Owning-Branch-ID	Owning-Branch-ID
BORROWER	
Address-Block	Borrower-Address-Block
Caution-Flags	Caution-Flags
ID	Borrower-ID
Name	Borrower-Name
Status	Borrower-Status
FORM LETTER	
ID	Form-Letter-ID
Text	Form-Letter-Text
INACTIVE	
ID	Borrower-ID
Inactive-Date	Inactive-Date
Reason-For-Inactive	Reason-For-Inactive
INVENTORY	
Copies-Being-Repaired	Copies-Being-Repaired
Copies-Borrowed	Copies-Borrowed
Copies-In-Stacks	Copies-In-Stacks
Copies-On-Order	Copies-On-Order
Copies-Owned	Copies-Owned
ISBN	ISBN

FIGURE 6–9. Where-used report produced by Data Repository System.
Used by permission, Popkin Software and Systems.

is preserved. It also exercises controls to prevent unauthorized access to or manipulation of the metadata. An interrogation and reporting language allows users or the DA/DBA to make enquiries on the data definition. For example, one report provided via the interrogation and reporting facility is a where-used report showing which data elements are associated with each entity (Figure 6–9). A programming facility allows programs to read the data definition so they can then access the database.

Some Problems with DRSs

Ideally, there would be a single, complete database definition that all users and programs could access. If this situation existed, auditors could be more confident about the consistency and currency of the data definition. Moreover, they should be able to assess control risk as lower. Access controls and backup and recovery controls, for example, could be focused on a single definition rather than multiple definitions. Accordingly, auditors would expect that the controls should be more reliable.

Unfortunately, DRS implementations are sometimes problematic in several ways. First, a DRS is often embedded within other software, such as a DBMS, a CASE tool, a high-level language, an application generator, or in-house developed software. The specific functional capabilities incorporated within the DRS tend to support the specific needs of the host software. For example, if a DRS is embedded within a DBMS, the internal schema capabilities probably will be stronger than the conceptual schema capabilities. The DBMS must be capable of accessing and manipulating the database, so the definitional needs of users are likely to be compromised. Similarly, if a DBMS is embedded within a CASE tool, the conceptual schema capabilities probably will be stronger than the internal schema capabilities. Many CASE tools primarily support user needs to document an existing system or a new system design rather than program access to a database. Multiple data definitions are required, therefore, to support the needs of different software. Unfortunately, the definitions cannot always be easily integrated or reconciled. For this reason, efforts have been made to formulate a standard for an information resource dictionary system (IRDS) (see Prabandham et al. 1990). One objective of these standardization efforts is to allow metadata created by different tools to be stored within a single repository so it can be shared. In other words, one tool ought to be able to access and use metadata created by another tool.

Second, maintaining a single, complete data definition becomes more difficult as information processing functions are distributed. If distributed information systems are to be effective and efficient, the data definition will also have to be distributed. Programs located remotely, for example, might provide unacceptable response times if they have to access a central definition. Inevitably, the data definition must be either partitioned or replicated. It is often difficult to integrate and reconcile multiple, distributed descriptions of the data.

Third, technically it has been and continues to be difficult to build a DRS that supports all types of usage needs in a database environment effectively and efficiently. As a result, historically two types of DRSs have existed: *active* DRSs and *passive* DRSs (Figure 6–10). The former primarily support program development (active in development) and in some cases program access to the database (active in production) (see Tannebaum 1994). They have strong internal schema definition capabilities and weak conceptual schema and external schema definition capabilities. The latter primarily support users of the database. They facilitate documentation of conceptual schemas and external schemas, but their internal schema capabilities are weak. More recent DRSs usually have been classified as *hybrid* systems. Although they tend to support either internal schema definition or conceptual schema and external schema definition, nevertheless they provide broader definitional support than earlier DRSs.

Auditors must be aware of how the problems associated with DRSs can undermine the objectives of asset safeguarding, data integrity, system effectiveness, and system efficiency. They must identify where data is defined and how data definitions are used, integrated, and reconciled. Control risk increases as data definitions become more diffuse and more disparate. For example, usually auditors can place less reliance on the controls that seek to maintain correspondence between a database and its definition when a passive DRS is used or when the definition is distributed widely. As control risk increases, they must expand the extent of their detailed testing of database application systems. For example, if auditors have an inventory system that employs a distributed data-

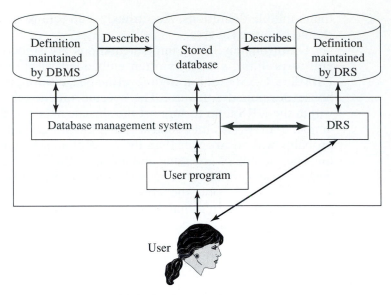

(*a*) Active data repository system

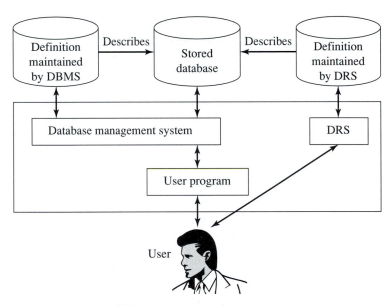

(*b*) Passive data repository system

FIGURE 6–10. Types of data repository systems.

base and a passive DRS, they might conclude that they cannot rely on data validation controls being applied uniformly throughout the system. Accordingly, they might expand the extent of physical inventory work undertaken.

Audit Aspects of a DRS

There are three implications for auditors when an organization uses a DRS. First, if the organization uses the DRS properly, they can have increased confidence in the reliability of controls over data and application systems. Second, by establishing a centralized data definition using a DRS, the organization faces a new set of exposures that could have serious consequences if the data definition or the DRS is lost or corrupted. Thus, controls must be established over the data definition and the DRS. Third, the existence of a DRS facilitates the audit process. The following three sections briefly discuss each of these implications.

Enhanced Data and Application System Reliability

By allowing centralized control to be exercised over data, a DRS should enhance the quality of data and application systems. Responsibility for data-definition functions is not dispersed across the individuals who are accountable for various application systems. Instead, the DA and DBA take responsibility for determining the data definition. They use the DRS to enforce the definition across individual application systems. Because the data definition is not embedded in individual application programs, the authenticity, accuracy, completeness, consistency, and currency of the data definition should be enhanced. As a consequence, the integrity of data should increase.

Use of a common database definition and DRS also enhances control over the systems development process. Some benefits obtained follow:

1. It assists planning, requirements analysis, database design, and maintenance through being able to determine the effects of change on users, programs, and data.
2. It facilitates programming by reducing the effort required to establish the data definition. The data definition might be copied into programs, or a program might access the data definition directly.
3. It enhances documentation of data and systems through the dictionary capabilities of the DRS.
4. It improves data integrity because data validation criteria can be enforced via the DRS rather than having individuals program these criteria.

Control over the Data Definition and DRS

The data definition is a critical master file within an organization, and the DRS is a critical system. Both should be subjected to rigorous security, backup, and recovery controls. If the data definition or DRS were lost or destroyed, the operations of the organization could be severely impaired. Moreover, if unauthorized access were obtained to the DRS, the data definition could be corrupted. The integrity of the database could be violated as a result. Duplicate copies of the data definition and DRS need to be stored off site. A log of changes to the data definition also must be maintained for backup and recovery purposes. To protect the integrity of the data definition, access controls and input validation rules should be established via the DRS. To protect the integrity of the DRS itself, access controls can be established via program library software. Program change controls should also be exercised over any modifications to the DRS (see Chapter 5).

If an organization is committed to establishing and maintaining a database and to employing a DRS to support database use, auditors must evaluate whether this commitment is accepted by all stakeholders. A major cost of centralized control is that individual users often have to compromise their own needs to achieve organizationwide goals. They must be willing to accept common protocols such as data-item naming and numbering conventions. If they are not willing to compromise and to accept common protocols, often they will seek ways to circumvent controls. The integrity of the data definition and the database may be undermined as a result. If auditors find that users are disgruntled with the standards imposed upon them or the mediation capabilities of the DA and DBA, they might need to expand detailed testing of the database application systems associated with these users.

Audit Use of the Data Definition and DRS

Auditors most likely will be users of the data definition and the DRS as they carry out evidence-collection and evaluation work. For example, auditors might use them in the following ways:

1. The data definition might be accessed to determine the layout of records that auditors wish to retrieve and manipulate via generalized audit software.
2. Auditors might retrieve the validation criteria associated with data items considered material to the audit so they can evaluate whether these items are likely to be accurate and complete.
3. If auditors discover that a data item has been corrupted, they might use the DRS to find out which files will be affected and the likely impact on the financial statements.
4. Auditors might access the data definition to determine the backup and recovery procedures associated with particular files so they can evaluate the adequacy of these procedures.

In some cases, the data definition also contains identification and authentication information that is used to enforce access controls. For example, a DBMS, a CASE tool, an application generator, or a high-level language can access the data definition to determine whether to permit or deny access by a user to some part of the database. Auditors might wish to examine this information to evaluate the likelihood of privacy violations or unauthorized data modifications occurring.

CONTROL OVER THE DA AND DBA

Even a cursory examination of the functions performed by the DA and DBA shows that substantial power can be vested in these roles, particularly in turnaround and strategic organizations in which information systems are critical to the organization's success. This power can be used with propriety; alternatively, it can be abused. On the one hand, centralizing certain functions to be performed in a database environment improves communication, coordination, and control. On the other hand, vesting substantial power in the DA and DBA roles runs contrary to fundamental principles of sound internal control.

Auditors must understand how the powers vested in the DA and DBA roles can be used to undermine control. They must understand, also, how the exposures that arise can be reduced. In this light, the following sections briefly examine the nature of the exposures and some remedial measures that can be used to reduce expected losses from these exposures (Figure 6–11).

FIGURE 6–11. Control over data administration/database administration exposures.

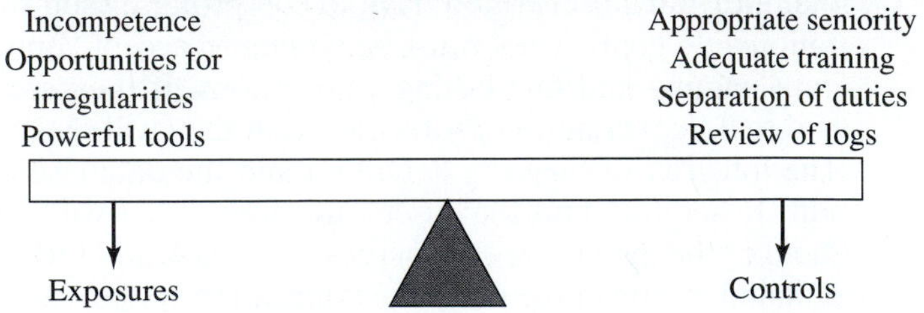

Incompetence
Opportunities for
  irregularities
Powerful tools

Appropriate seniority
Adequate training
Separation of duties
Review of logs

Exposures   Controls

Some Exposures

Three types of exposure arise by virtue of the nature of and existence of the DA and DBA roles:

1. *Incompetent performance of roles:* In some organizations (e.g., strategic organizations), the functions performed by the DA and DBA can be complex and demanding. For example, the DA must be a visionary to foresee long-term data needs and an astute diplomat to perform mediation functions effectively. The DBA must excel technically if the database is to be used efficiently and the inevitable user conflicts are to be mitigated. Because the DA and DBA play pivotal roles in a database environment, poor performance by the incumbents can quickly undermine asset safeguarding, data integrity, system effectiveness, and system efficiency objectives.

2. *Opportunities to perpetrate irregularities:* On the one hand, centralization of power in the DA and DBA roles simplifies complex communication and coordination functions that must be performed in a database environment. On the other hand, it provides opportunities to perpetrate irregularities. The powers vested in the DA and DBA might violate the fundamental internal control principle of separation of duties. For example, the DA might have the power to authorize user access privileges and to set up these privileges in the DBMS via the access control mechanism. Thus, the DA both authorizes and executes the activity. If no one subsequently checks the DA's work, improper access privileges could be granted to a user such that irregularities can then be perpetrated.

3. *Availability of tools to override controls:* Both the DA and DBA have available powerful tools that they need to establish and monitor controls in a database environment. For example, they can set up various levels of access and update authorizations, perhaps find out user passwords, and possibly gain access to and change audit trails and log files. Improper use of these tools can undermine asset safeguarding and data integrity objectives. For example, the DA or DBA might increase funds in a friend's bank account and then alter the audit trail to remove any trace of the unauthorized activity.

If only a DBA position exists in an organization, these exposures become more salient. The DBA's work will not be monitored by a DA. Consequently, there are more opportunities for improprieties and undetected errors. Even if a DA position exists, however, auditors must be alert to the possibility of collusion between the DA and the DBA.

Some Remedial Measures

The remedial measures an organization adopts to reduce exposures associated with the DA and DBA roles should depend on the power vested in these positions. In turnaround and strategic organizations, the DA and DBA are likely to have substantial power. Accordingly, controls will need to be stringent. In support and factory organizations, however, exposures are likely to be attenuated. Less costly controls might be satisfactory.

Perhaps the most effective control is to assign appropriate seniority to the DA and DBA roles and to appoint competent and trustworthy persons to these positions. If an organization appoints long-standing employees with known records to the DA and DBA roles, exposures are reduced. If persons must be hired to fill the positions, however, standard control procedures should be applied, such as background checking and interviewing. As the power of the DA and DBA increases, employee bonding might also be used to reduce expected losses from improprieties.

Whoever is appointed to the DA and DBA roles, they must receive adequate training to ensure they are effective and efficient and to reduce the likelihood of their making errors. The technology supporting management of databases is constantly changing. The DA and DBA must keep up to date with these changes. Moreover, the nature of user requirements is continuing to change. For example, many organizations are now participating in the development of interorganizational information systems—systems that cross the boundaries of multiple organizations. The DA and DBA face a new set of challenges when management of data must be considered not only within the context of their own organization but also within the context of other organizations.

Careful thought should be given to how the duties of the DA and DBA can be separated without unduly impairing their work. In large organizations, the DA and DBA roles might be undertaken by several people rather than a single person. Different functions could be assigned to different members of the DA and DBA groups. For example, one person in the DA group might authorize changes to the data definition. Another might implement the changes. The first person could then check the work of the second for authenticity, accuracy, and completeness. DA and DBA groups also facilitate rotation of duties to enhance control.

Another basis for separating duties is to divide authority to use a database tool from the authority to keep custody of and to maintain the tool. Table 6–2 shows one possible breakdown of authority and responsibility that might be used for a critical, high-exposure tool. Control over the tool's source code (if it is available) and object code can be exercised via a program library system under the control of a program librarian. Control over the tool's documentation might be exercised by a documentation librarian. The DA could be responsible for authorizing the DBA's use of the tool and its documentation and the programming manager's maintenance of the tool. The DA should be prevented from using or maintaining the tool, however. The operations manager might have responsibility for safeguarding machine logs associated with the DBA's use of the tool. Periodically, the DA might provide a log of tool-use authorizations to the operations manager, who might then reconcile this manual log against the machine log of tool use.

Manual and machine logs provide an important means of exercising control over the activities of the DA and DBA. Manual logs record such activities as a

TABLE 6–2 Possible Breakdown to Authority and Responsibility for High-Exposure Database Servicing Tools	
Function	*Person Responsible*
Storage of source code and object code	Program librarian
Storage of documentation	Documentation librarian
Authorization to use tool and to maintain tool	Data administrator
Usage of tool	Database administrator
Maintenance of tool	Programming manager
Safeguarding machine logs of tool use	Operations manager
Reconciling manual and machine logs of tool use	Operations manager

user's request to change an external schema, authorization of user access privileges by the DA, the DBA's request for access to a high-exposure database tool, and the DA's request to the DBA to retire certain parts of the database. Where possible, secure machine logs should also be kept that allow an independent check to be carried out on the veracity of activities recorded in manual logs. For example, a machine log should show what sections of the database were retired at a certain date and time by the DBA. An independent person should check the actions undertaken by the DBA to retire data were those authorized by the DA. When conducting an audit of the activities of the DA and DBA, auditors should seek the record of reconciliations carried out between the manual and machine logs.

SUMMARY

The DA and DBA perform five major functions: *(1)* defining, creating, redefining, and retiring data; *(2)* making the database available to users; *(3)* informing and servicing users; *(4)* maintaining database integrity; and *(5)* monitoring operations and performance. These functions manifest an organization's recognition that data is a critical resource which must be subject to centralized planning and control.

The existence of DA and DBA roles affects the auditor's work in several ways. First, the auditor is concerned to see that the DA and DBA perform their functions well. Otherwise, asset safeguarding, data integrity, systems effectiveness, and system efficiency will be undermined. Second, the DA and DBA provide the auditor with important information on strengths and weaknesses within a database environment. This information allows auditors to better plan an audit. Third, the DA and DBA provide administrative and technical information needed if auditors are to be able to perform evidence collection and evaluation functions properly.

A major function of the DA and DBA is to act as mediators when sharing of data produces conflict among users. If they are to perform this mediation role effectively, users must perceive that they can act independently. In this light, the DA's and DBA's positions within the organizational hierarchy must allow them substantial autonomy.

Data repository systems facilitate control over the definition of data in a database environment. Ideally, they provide a single, complete, consistent, accurate, up-to-date definition of data that all users and programs can access. In practice, however, difficulties arise because multiple data definitions must be maintained. Existing DD/DSs often support only partial data definitions, and multiple, distributed definitions must be maintained to facilitate use of data at remote locations.

Substantial power is often vested in the DA and DBA roles. For example, they are provided with software tools that can be used to compromise asset safeguarding and data integrity. Remedial steps must be undertaken to exercise control of the DA and DBA—for example, appointing senior, trustworthy persons to perform the roles, separating duties to the extent possible, and maintaining logs to record activities they undertake.

Review Questions

6–1 What are the objectives of database management? Why are data administrators and database administrators needed to help accomplish these objectives?

6–2 Is it necessary for an organization to be using a database management system before it institutes data-administration and database-administration roles? Support your answer.

6–3   Sharing of data among multiple users inevitably produces conflict among the users. What roles do the DA and the DBA play when conflict arises?

6–4   Why have both data-administration and database-administration roles emerged in some organizations that seek to manage their data resources instead of just one role? Do you think both roles will continue, or will they be combined or disappear?

6–5   What implications does the existence of either a data-administration role or a database-administration role have for the conduct of an audit? Is either role more important than the other from the viewpoint of auditors?

6–6   Briefly describe the differences among the conceptual schema, the internal schema, and the external schema. For each type of schema, identify whether it will be the data administrator or the database administrator who takes primary responsibility for its definition.

6–7   Why are auditors concerned to see that the data administrator uses a formal methodology to undertake view integration when defining or redefining an organization's conceptual schema?

6–8   What is meant by populating the database? What steps should the data administrator and the database administrator take to preserve data integrity when the database is being populated?

6–9   When data redefinition is undertaken, what are the respective responsibilities of the data administrator and the database administrator?

6–10   How might the database administrator "comprehensively test" a new availability tool acquired for database users?

6–11   Why should the DA and the DBA be responsible for informing and servicing users and not someone else be responsible for this function in a database environment?

6–12   Briefly explain the DA's and the DBA's responsibilities with respect to:
    a Definition control
    b Existence control
    c Access control
    d Update control
    e Concurrency control
    f Quality control

6–13   Give three performance statistics that the database administrator might collect to improve performance within a database environment.

6–14   In the context of the strategic-grid model, why might we expect to see only a database-administration role in some organizations rather than both data-administration and database-administration roles?

6–15   In a turnaround or strategic organization, why should the data administrator report to top management in a staff function capacity rather than report to the controller?

6–16   To maintain independence, the data administrator must hold a senior position within the organizational hierarchy of the information systems function. Briefly explain.

6–17   What impact does decentralization of the information systems function have on the roles of the data administrator and the database administrator?

6–18   What impact might the existence of end-user computing in an organization have on the roles of the data administrator and the database administrator?

6–19   Briefly explain the nature and functions of a data repository system. What is the relationship between a data repository system and the database definition?

6–20 Briefly explain the nature of metadata. Why is it critical that a database management system have strong capabilities for defining metadata?

6–21 What is the difference between an active data repository system and a passive data repository system? Why should auditors be concerned with whether an organization is using an active or a passive data repository system?

6–22 How can a centralized database definition and a data repository system enhance control over the systems development process?

6–23 Why is it important to exercise control over a data repository system? List three control procedures that might be used.

6–24 Why is obtaining support from programmers and systems analysts for a data repository system sometimes difficult? Why is it important to obtain their support? How might their support be obtained?

6–25 How might auditors be users of a data repository system? How might auditors' use of the data repository system give insight into the problems of other users?

6–26 Explain how the roles of both the data administrator and the database administrator both strengthen and weaken control. Briefly explain the nature of the trade-offs involved.

6–27 Give three examples of tools that DAs and DBAs need to perform their functions but which can also be used to override database integrity.

6–28 There are two types of remedial measures that can be used to increase control over the DA and the DBA: (a) administrative controls, and (b) technical controls. Explain the nature of each set of controls, and give an example of each. Which set of controls do you think will be the more effective and why?

6–29 Briefly explain how separation of duties can be used to increase control over the DA and the DBA.

6–30 What types of logs should be kept on activities relating to the functions of the data administrator and the database administrator?

6–31 How can auditors use logs to evaluate the propriety of work carried out by the data administrator and the database administrator?

Multiple-Choice Questions

6–1 Data-administration and database-administration roles are usually established when:
a Management recognizes data is a critical organizational resource
b A database management system is purchased
c Management decides to integrate application system files
d Application project managers begin to make suboptimal decisions with respect to data

6–2 Which of the following is *not* a reason why the data-administration role emerged subsequent to the database-administration role?
a It is difficult to find people who have both managerial and policy skills as well as technical skills
b The amount of work the DBA had to perform was often too great for a single role
c DBA had proved to be unsuccessful at working out suitable backup and recovery strategies for the database
d With the growth in end-user computing, more support had to be provided to database users who were not skilled information systems professionals

6–3 Which of the following is *not* a way in which the DA and the DBA affect the auditor?

a They provide administrative and technical information that the auditor needs to know

b They provide database tools that the auditor needs to use

c They act as a mediator when conflict arises between management and the auditor over database issues

d They are a source of information on control strengths and weaknesses in the database environment

6–4 The schema that defines the entire contents of the database from a user's perspective is the:

a Internal schema

b Logical schema

c External schema

d Conceptual schema

6–5 The DBA has primary responsibility for defining the:

a Internal schema

b Logical schema

c External schema

d Conceptual schema

6–6 When the DA performs the data-definition function, the first step is to:

a Determine whether some database users have already established in the database at least some of the data items needed

b Design a logical structure that attempts to mirror the user's real-world view of the data

c Use the data definition language to model the data structure needed

d Formulate the storage structure needed

6–7 Which of the following functions is *most likely* to be performed by the DA?

a Determining the effects of database redefinition on the internal schema

b Formulating data retention and retirement policies

c Preparing the data validation programs needed to populate the database

d Implementing backup and recovery procedures

6–8 Which of the following functions is the DA and DBA *most likely* to perform with the aim of making the database available to users?

a Ensuring data retirement policies comply with any applicable legislation

b Implementing database access and update controls

c Mediation in conflicts between end users and programming users of the database

d Monitoring changing user needs with respect to interrogation and update facilities needed

6–9 A memorandum system in a database environment should document:

a Semantic descriptions of database elements

b Data-retention information

c Potential short-term hazards that have arisen for users of the database

d Storage-structure designs that have been used

6–10 In a database environment, traditional program validation of input data is an example of:

a A quality control

b An existence control

  c A concurrency control

  d An access control

6–11 Which of the following control functions is *most likely* to be performed by the DA rather than the DBA?

  a Ensuring that neither a program nor a procedure could destroy the correspondence between the database and its definition

  b Determining backup and recovery requirements

  c Implementing access privileges that have been assigned to database users

  d Ensuring concurrency controls are in place and working

6–12 Which of the following is *least likely* to be a reason for the DBA to monitor performance in a database environment?

  a To identify changes that need to be made to the internal schema

  b To prevent controls being compromised as users attempt to circumvent the overheads associated with controls

  c To identify whether some part of the database may have been corrupted

  d To determine whether the functionality provided in an applications system that uses the database is needed

6–13 Using the strategic-grid model, in which of the following types of organization is an auditor *most likely* to see only a DBA role in existence?

  a Strategic organization

  b Support organization

  c Turnaround organization

  d Factory organization

6–14 In a strategic organization, DAs are *more likely* to be successful in their role if they report to:

  a Top management in a staff capacity

  b The controller in a staff capacity

  c The manager of the information systems function in a line capacity

  d The manager of the systems development function in a line capacity

6–15 In a factory organization, the DBA should be responsible to:

  a Top management in a staff capacity

  b The manager of programming in a line capacity

  c The manager of the information systems function in a staff capacity

  d The controller in a line capacity

6–16 Which of the following guidelines should apply to the DA and DBA roles in a large, strategic, decentralized organization that performs a diverse range of activities?

  a The DA and DBA in each division should be completely autonomous

  b The DBA should assume a more important role than the DA

  c The DA role should always be centralized but the DBA role can be decentralized

  d Data-management standards should be developed for shared data and promulgated throughout the organization

6–17 Which of the following best describes the concept of metadata?

  a Data about data

  b Logical definitions of data that are not stored in the database

  c Definitional information that applies to shared databases but not to partitioned localized databases

  d Logical constraints that apply to the conceptual schema

6–18 A *passive* data repository system is one that is used:

    a By the database management system to retrieve and manipulate data but not to define data

    b Only by the centralized data-administration group and not by any decentralized data-administration groups

    c As an optional facility that is made available to users of the database

    d To define data only but not to gain access to and to manipulate data when the database management system is being used

6–19 Which of the following is *least likely* to be an advantage of using a data repository system?

    a Facilitates programming by reducing the effort required to establish the data definition

    b Helps to enforce common validation criteria

    c Optimizes the storage structure to use for the conceptual schema

    d Facilitates data requirements analysis for a new application

6–20 Which of the following should *not* be a control exercised over use of the data repository:

    a Ensure that a numbering and naming convention is adopted for data items even in decentralized organizations

    b To increase security, use separate data repository packages for the different types of database schemas

    c Implement passwords to ensure that only authorized users access metadata

    d Make backup copies of the data definition and store them off site

6–21 The existence of the DA and DBA roles tends to violate the traditional internal-control principle of having:

    a Clear lines of authority and responsibility

    b Proper procedures for authorization

    c Physical control over assets and records

    d Adequate segregation of duties

6–22 Match each of the following functions relating to high-exposure database servicing tools with the role that should be assigned responsibility for the function:

I	Control over documentation	A Database administrator
II	Machine log of tool use	B Librarian
III	Use of tool	C Programming manager
IV	Tool update and maintenance	D Operations manager

    a I-B, II-D, III-A, IV-C

    b I-C, II-B, III-A, IV-D

    c I-D, II-C, III-B, IV-A

    d I-B, II-A, III-C, IV-D

6–23 Which of the following activities carried out by the DA is unlikely to be recorded on a machine log maintained by an operating system or by a database management system?

    a Access to the database

    b Change of a password

    c Disclosure of a password to an unauthorized user

    d Deletion of a database record

Exercises and Cases

6–1 Wowem Corporation manufactures a wide range of clothing apparel. It is a decentralized organization in which different divisions have responsibility for the manufacture and distribution of major product lines—sporting apparel, leisure wear, country-and-western gear, maternity wear, industrial clothing, uniforms, evening wear, and so on. Each division has several line and staff departments: design, purchasing, production, marketing, accounting, information systems, and so on. In addition, Wowem has several corporate departments that undertake overall planning and control functions and provide staff assistance to divisions. A small corporate information systems department exists. It supports corporate information systems, develops and promulgates companywide information systems standards, and provides consulting advice to divisions.

In line with its decentralized operations, Wowem operates a responsibility accounting system that allows top management to track the performance of different divisions and departments and to cost the products that Wowem manufactures. All divisions have used a common database management system to implement the responsibility accounting system. Providing the divisions comply with corporate information requirements for the responsibility accounting system, however, the design, implementation, maintenance, and operation of the system has been and continues to be the prerogative of the divisions.

Over the past five years, Wowem has suffered a major decline in profitability. In light of the difficulties that have arisen, the old company president has resigned, and a new one has been appointed. In an effort to revitalize the company, she decides to undertake an extensive reorganization of the company. The changes include elimination of some divisions, reallocation of products to different divisions, migration of some staff functions to corporate headquarters, and extensive downsizing of personnel who work in a staff capacity. Because of Wowem's precarious financial position, she indicates she wishes to put these changes in place quickly. Moreover, she underscores the need to modify the responsibility accounting system urgently to reflect the new responsibility structure. She sees the responsibility accounting systems as being critical to her monitoring the success of the changes and to taking timely action if problems arise.

Required. Wowem's corporate data administrator has been made responsible for preparing an overall plan to redefine the corporate and divisional databases to reflect the new lines of responsibility. As the manager of internal audit for Wowem, the company president has asked you to review and evaluate the plan prepared by the data administrator. Given the intense scrutiny that Wowem is under from its shareholders and its external auditor, she is particularly concerned that the accounting changes be made accurately and completely. At the same time, she is concerned to see that the changes are implemented as smoothly as possible. Make a list of the major items you think should exist in the plan if data integrity is to be preserved during the redefinition process.

6–2 Savers Surety is a large investment house that provides a wide range of investment services for its clients. For some years, Savers has been a pioneering and innovative user of a high-level programming language that has allowed its staff to interact directly with the company's centralized database. For example, investment managers have used the language to prepare various types of analyses on client portfolios or market trends.

In spite of the encouragement given to end users by management in their use of the high-level language, management has restricted use of the language in two important ways. First, users have not been permitted to download copies of the database (or sections of the database), perform update and retrieval operations and then upload the database with the data on which they have been working. Second, users have not been permitted to define new data items and store them in the database without the express permission of the data administrator.

Savers has now embarked upon a policy of providing its staff with powerful microcomputers in an attempt to improve productivity. As a consequence, top management has been under substantial pressure to relax the restrictions on downloading/uploading data and defining data because many users are now arguing the real payoffs will occur if they can work on localized copies of data and establish and maintain their own specialized, localized databases.

Required. Top management has asked Saver's DA to prepare a report outlining the costs and benefits of allowing users to upload data to and download data from the centralized database. The issue is to be considered at a forthcoming meeting of the information systems steering committee. As the internal audit manager for Savers, the DA approaches you to seek your assistance. He asks you to advise him on any concerns you have if uploading and downloading activities are permitted to go ahead. Prepare brief notes outlining the matters you will address in your report to the DA.

6–3 To improve access times to its database and increase its storage capacity, an organization purchases higher-density disks. The database administrator is given the responsibility of preparing a plan to convert the database from the old disks to the new disks.

Required. As the internal auditor for the organization, what items would you look for in the conversion plan proposed by the database administrator? Highlight any differences you would expect to see between the conversion plan prepared for the database and the conversion plan that might have been prepared if the organization was converting traditional application system files to higher-density disks.

6–4 Cassowary Castings Limited (CCL) is an Adelaide-based major manufacturer of motor-vehicle components—for example, engine blocks, chassis, axles, and differential gears. It relies extensively on its existing computer systems for such functions as production control, materials requirements planning, bill-of-materials, sales forecasting, order entry, inventory control, and design. Indeed, much of its production facilities are automated, and it relies heavily on robotics.

For several years, CCL has been involved in electronic data interchange (EDI) with some of its major suppliers and customers. EDI has been used in a fairly straightforward way—exchange of invoices and shipping notices, order transmittal, price quotations, and so on. Recently, however, CCL has been asked by some of its smaller competitors to join a cooperative arrangement whereby the participants will undertake joint marketing of their products to try to gain a greater share of the international market for motor-vehicle components. Although the participants will still compete against one another in some respects, the overall goal is to have each participant begin to specialize in certain products so they can obtain economies of scope and scale. They will cooperate to present a full product line of motor-vehicle components to prospective customers.

Top management of CCL have greeted the cooperative arrangements proposal enthusiastically. They perceive they can break some of the boundaries to sales growth imposed by the limited size of the Australian market. When the company president discusses the proposal with the chief information officer for CCL, however, she finds he is lukewarm. He complains bitterly that for several years he has asked top managers to fund a data-administration position within CCL. For alleged cost-containment reasons, however, top management have refused to fund the position. They have pointed out that the information systems function already has a DBA position and, given their perceptions of the company's needs, they see no reason to also establish a data-administration role. As a result of this decision, the chief information officer argues that data within CCL is now poorly integrated because no one has had responsibility for overall data planning and control. He contends that multiple conflicting definitions of data exist and, as a result, CCL is poorly placed strategically to enter the proposed cooperative arrangements. He refuses to give an assurance to the president that CCL's information systems can be modified appropriately to support the interorganizational information systems that will be needed under a cooperative arrangement.

You are the partner-in-charge of the audit of CCL. Your firm has just taken over the audit, having won the tender for audit services from the previous auditor. In light of the chief information officer's reaction to the cooperative arrangements proposal, the president seeks your advice. If the cooperative arrangements proposal were to fail, she believes CCL's financial position could be irrevocably damaged. She asks you to prepare a report to advise her on whether the chief information officer's concerns have substance.

Required.   What information will you gather as a basis for preparing your report? Outline the steps you will undertake to gather this information.

6–5   Maple Leaf Distributors Limited (MLDL) is a large, diversified, Toronto-based distributor of perishable and durable goods to small- to medium-sized retail outlets. It has 12 divisions organized along product lines, each of which operates relatively independently. MLDL is an extensive user of information systems to support its data-processing and management-reporting needs. Each division has its own information systems department that operates autonomously of the other divisions. Nevertheless, the divisions provide common information to the corporate information systems department to enable the company to prepare consolidated financial reports.

Your firm has just taken over the external audit of MLDL. As part of the interim audit work, your partner asks you to assess how well MLDL manages its data resources. During your preliminary investigations, you find that MLDL uses four different database management systems. This situation has arisen because the divisions could not agree on a single system that would meet their needs.

When you conduct further investigations, you find that two of the database management systems have data repository facilities that are primarily passive, and two have data repository facilities that are primarily active. In addition, end users are employing a large number of high-level query and update languages, some of which use their own active data repository facilities to access and manipulate MLDL's databases.

Required.   Write a brief report for your partner outlining how you believe your findings should affect the conduct of the remainder of the audit.

6–6   You are the external auditor for Dumpadollar National Bank, a large bank within the Dallas metropolitan area. Dumpadollar has an extensive online real-time update database system. One of the controls exercised by the information systems management of Dumpadollar is to print out each day a listing of all sensitive utility programs used. This data is obtained from the operating-system log. The listing is checked to detect any unauthorized use of these utility programs.

During a review of this log, you notice that Delores Sleek, Dumpadollar's DBA, had used a pointer-maintenance utility on the database. This utility is capable of adding, deleting, or modifying the pointers that establish the logical relationships between records on the database. You recall that the pointer fields in a record are important because they contain the addresses of other records that are logically related in some way to the current record. For example, they might chain transaction records to a customer-account record.

You are concerned about unauthorized use of this utility, and you express your concern to Harry Thompson, the information systems manager. He explains that sometimes a pointer in the database is corrupted and that Delores is the only person with sufficient knowledge of the database to be able to correct the pointer. When you ask how often a corrupted pointer occurs, Harry informs you that Delores reports the occurrence of one about once a month. When you ask why a corrupted pointer occurs, Harry says he does not know and that you will have to talk with Delores.

Required. Write a brief report to your supervisor documenting why you are concerned about the current situation and informing him what action you now intend to take.

Answers to Multiple-Choice Questions

6–1	a	**6–7**	b	**6–13**	b	**6–19**	c
6–2	c	**6–8**	d	**6–14**	a	**6–20**	b
6–3	c	**6–9**	c	**6–15**	c	**6–21**	d
6–4	d	**6–10**	a	**6–16**	d	**6–22**	a
6–5	a	**6–11**	b	**6–17**	a	**6–23**	c
6–6	b	**6–12**	d	**6–18**	d		

REFERENCES

Allen, Frank W., Mary E. S. Loomis, and Michael Y. Mannino (1982), "The Integrated Dictionary/Directory System," *Computing Surveys* (June), 245–286.

Batini, C., S. Ceri, and S. B. Navathe (1992), *Conceptual Database Design: An Entity-Relationship Approach*. Redwood City, CA: Benjamin/Cummings.

———, M. Lenzerini, and S. B. Navathe (1986), "Comparison of Methodologies for Database Schema Integration," *Computing Surveys* (December), 323–364.

Braithwaite, Ken S. (1988), *Analysis, Design, and Implementation of Data Dictionaries*. New York: McGraw-Hill.

Elmasri, R., and S. B. Navathe (1994), *Fundamentals of Database Systems*, 2d ed. Redwood City, CA: Benjamin/Cummings.

Everest, Gordon C. (1976), "Database Management Systems Tutorial," in Gordon B. Davis and Gordon C. Everest, eds., *Readings in Management Information Systems*. New York: McGraw-Hill, 164–187.

——— (1986), *Database Management: Objectives, System Functions, & Administration*. New York: McGraw-Hill.

Gillenson, Mark L. (1982), "The State of Data Administration—1981," *Communications of the ACM* (October), 699–706.

——— (1985), "Trends in Data Administration," *MIS Quarterly* (December), 317–325.

Goodhue, Dale L., Laurie J. Kirsch, Judith A. Quillard, and Michael D. Wybo, (1992), "Strategic Data Planning: Lessons from the Field," *MIS Quarterly* (March), 11–34.

Halpin, T.A. (1995), *Conceptual Schema and Relational Database Design*, 2d ed. Sydney: Prentice-Hall.

Hazzah, A. (1989), "Data Dictionaries: Paths to a Standard," *Database Programming and Design*, 2(8), 26–35.

Kahn, Beverly K. (1983), "Some Realities of Data Administration," *Communications of the ACM* (October), 794–799.

Leong-Hong, Belkis W., and Bernard K. Plagman (1982), *Data Dictionary/Directory Systems: Administration, Implementation and Usage*. New York: John Wiley & Sons.

March, Salvatore T., and Young-Gul Kim (1992), "Information Resource Management: Integrating the Pieces," *Database* (Summer), 27–38.

McCririck, Ian B., and Robert C. Goldstein (1980), "What Do Data Administrators Really Do," *Datamation* (August), 131–134.

McFadden, Fred, and Jeffrey A. Hoffer (1994), *Modern Database Management*, 4th ed. Reading, MA: Addison-Wesley.

Narayan, Rom (1988), *Data Dictionary: Implementation, Use, and Maintenance*. Upper Saddle River, NJ: Prentice-Hall.

Prabandham, Mohan, William J. Selfridge, and Douglas G. Mann (1990), "A View of the IRDS Reference Model," *Database Programming and Design* (March), 40–53.

Tannenbaum, Adrienne (1994), *Implementing a Corporate Repository: The Models Meet Reality*. New York: John Wiley & Sons.

Vanecek, Michael T., Ira Solomon, and Michael V. Mannino (1983), "The Data Dictionary: An Evaluation from the EDP Audit Perspective," *MIS Quarterly* (March), 15–27.

Vinden, Robert J. (1990), *Data Dictionaries for Database Administrators*. Blue Ridge, PA: TAB Books.

Weber, Ron, and Gordon C. Everest (1979), "Database Administration: Functional, Organizational, and Control Perspectives," *EDPACS* (January), 1–10.

Weldon, Jay-Louise (1981), *Data Base Administration*. New York: Plenum Press.

Wertz, Charles J. (1993), *The Data Dictionary: Concepts and Uses*, 2d ed. New York: John Wiley & Sons.

Security Management Controls

Chapter Outline

Multiple-Choice Questions

Exercises and Cases

Answers to Multiple-Choice Questions

References

Chapter Key Points

■ Information security administrators are responsible for ensuring that information systems assets are secure. Assets are secure when the expected losses that will occur over some time are at an acceptable level.

■ There are two types of information systems security. Physical security protects the physical information systems assets of an organization—personnel, hardware, facilities, supplies, and documentation. Logical security protects data/information and software. Security administrators tend to have responsibility for controls over (a) malicious and nonmalicious threats to physical security and (b) malicious threats to logical security.

■ A major task of security administrators is to conduct a security program. A security program is a series of ongoing, regular, periodic reviews conducted to ensure that assets associated with the information systems function are safeguarded adequately.

■ Security programs comprise eight steps: (a) preparation of a project plan, (b) identification of assets, (c) valuation of assets, (d) threats identification, (e) threats likelihood assessment, (f) exposures analysis, (g) controls adjustment, and (h) report preparation.

■ Nine major threats to the security of information systems assets are (a) fire—well-designed, reliable fire-protection systems must be implemented; (b) water—facilities must be designed and sited to mitigate losses from water damage; (c) energy variations—voltage regulators, circuit breakers, and uninterruptible power supplies can be used; (d) structural damage—facilities must be designed to withstand structural damage; (e) pollution—regular cleaning of facilities and equipment should occur; (f) unauthorized intrusion—physical intrusion and eavesdropping can be prevented via physical access controls, prevention of electromagnetic emissions, and proper siting of facilities; (g) viruses and worms—controls should be implemented to prevent use of virus-infected programs and to close security loopholes that allow worms to propagate; (h) misuse of software, data, and services—a code of conduct should govern the actions of information systems employees; and (i) hackers—strong, logical access controls mitigate expected losses from the activities of hackers.

■ Controls of last resort take effect when the information systems function suffers a disaster. A backup and recovery plan specifies how normal operations are to be restored. Insurance mitigates the losses associated with the disaster.

■ Where security administrators are placed within the organizational hierarchy depends on the size of an organization and the extent of its reliance on information systems. In small organizations that use turnkey systems, the organization's president or accountant might perform the security-administration role. In moderate-size organizations, the computer operations manager might perform the security-administration role. In large organizations that depend substantially on their information systems, a security administrator might report to the chief information officer. Alternatively, the information systems security administrator might report to the person responsible for overall security within the organization.

■ Security administration becomes more difficult as organizations decentralize and distribute their information systems function. Security procedures must be adapted to take into account the dispersal of information systems resources and the different circumstances under which information systems resources are used. Moreover, more people must take responsibility for executing and maintaining the controls needed to preserve information systems security.

INTRODUCTION

Information systems security administrators are responsible for ensuring that information systems assets are secure. Assets are *secure* when the expected losses that will occur from threats eventuating over some time period are at an acceptable level. Note three important aspects of this definition of security. First, we accept that some losses *will inevitably occur*. Eliminating all possible losses is either impossible or too costly. Second, we specify some level of *ac-*

FIGURE 7–1. Categories of information systems assets.

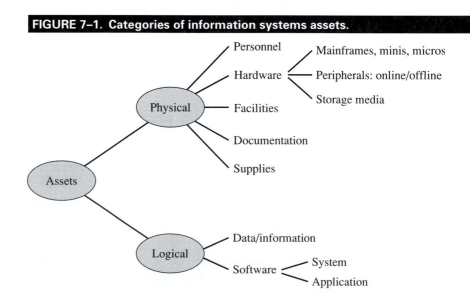

	Physical assets	Logical assets
Malicious threats	Responsibility of security administrator	Responsibility of security administrator
Nonmalicious threats	Responsibility of security administrator	

FIGURE 7–2. IS security-administration responsibilities.

ceptable losses. This level will dictate how much we are willing to spend on controls. Third, we must choose a *time period*. We determine what level of loss we would be willing to bear during this time period.

The information systems assets we must protect via security measures can be classified in two ways (Figure 7–1). The physical assets comprise personnel, hardware (including storage media and peripherals), facilities, supplies, and documentation. The logical assets comprise data/information and software. In a sense, this entire book deals with measures auditors can use to ensure these assets are secure. For example, Chapters 5 and 6 discuss controls auditors can use to prevent unauthorized changes to programs and databases. Later chapters, such as Chapter 10 on boundary controls and Chapter 11 on input controls, discuss measures auditors can use to protect the integrity of application systems.

In this chapter, however, we focus on the work usually performed by information systems security administrators. Although their specific functions vary across organizations, they tend to be responsible for controls over *(1)* both malicious and nonmalicious threats to physical assets and *(2)* malicious threats to logical assets (Figure 7–2). In addition, they often are responsible for controls of last resort. These controls comprise backup and recovery procedures and insurance. They are invoked when all else fails.

We begin our discussion of security administration by examining the major functions that security administrators perform during the conduct of a security program. Next we consider some major threats to security that security administrators must consider and some controls they might implement to reduce expected losses from these threats. We then examine controls of last resort. Finally, we consider where information systems security administrators should be placed within the organizational hierarchy if they are to be able to perform their role effectively and efficiently.

CONDUCTING A SECURITY PROGRAM

A security program is a series of ongoing, regular, periodic reviews conducted to ensure that assets associated with the information systems function are safeguarded adequately. The first security review conducted is often a major exercise. Security administrators have to consider an extensive list of possible threats to the assets associated with the information systems function, prepare an inventory of assets, evaluate the adequacy of controls over assets, and perhaps modify existing controls or implement new controls. One outcome of the initial security review might be a *security policy* to guide security practices within an organization and to provide a basis for subsequent evaluation of these practices (Henderson 1996). Subsequent security reviews might focus only on changes that have occurred—for example, acquisition of a new mainframe computer, distribution of microcomputers to more sites, construction of new facilities, establishment of a new local area or wide area network, or the emergence of a new security threat. A security policy, if one exists, might need to be updated in light of these subsequent reviews.

Several formalized approaches have been proposed to undertake security reviews. For example, the United Kingdom Government's Central Computer and Telecommunications Agency has developed an approach called CRAMM (CCTA's Risk Analysis and Management Methodology), which is used as a governmentwide, standard approach to risk analysis and security management (see, e.g., McLean and Watts 1996). Software also has been designed and implemented to support each stage of the approach. Baskerville (1993) provides an overview of the different security-evaluation approaches and their associated decision support software.

FIGURE 7–3. Major steps in the conduct of a security program.

Auditors must evaluate whether security administrators are conducting on-going, high-quality security reviews. If the security of information systems assets is at risk, asset safeguarding and data integrity objectives can be undermined. For example, fire could destroy a mainframe facility, or employees might damage storage media to cover up evidence associated with frauds they have perpetrated. Similarly, system effectiveness and efficiency objectives can be undermined. For example, the destruction of an application system's documentation might mean programmers have difficulty modifying the system to accommodate changing user needs. Likewise, the destruction of hardware could mean required system response times cannot be achieved until the hardware is replaced.

In this light, the following sections describe eight major steps to be undertaken when conducting a security review (Figure 7–3): *(1)* preparation of a project plan, *(2)* identification of assets, *(3)* valuation of assets, *(4)* threats identification, *(5)* threats likelihood assessment, *(6)* exposures analysis, *(7)* controls adjustment, and *(8)* report preparation. As we study these sections, our objective is to gain sufficient understanding of the steps in a security review for us to be able to evaluate how well they are performed by security administrators.

Preparation of a Project Plan

It might seem an obvious requirement that security reviews should commence with the preparation of a project plan. Unfortunately, security reviews are a mine field for the unwary. Security administrators, and any project team established to assist them, can get bogged down in detail unless strict constraints are imposed on the conduct of the review. If the review's objectives are not kept clearly in mind, too much work will be undertaken that has only marginal benefits. In due course this detail might be appropriate, but at the outset security administrators might wish to adopt a phased approach to the conduct of the overall security review program. Initial reviews focus on critical areas; subsequent reviews then address lesser concerns.

The project plan for a security review should encompass the following items:

Project Plan Component	*Explanation*
Objectives of the review	The objectives of the security review can be broadly based or narrowly defined. For example, the review might be undertaken to improve physical security over mainframe hardware in a particular division or to examine the adequacy of controls in light of a new threat to logical security that has emerged.
Scope of the review	The objectives of the review define, in part, the scope of the review. Defining scope is especially important, however, if the information systems function is widely dispersed throughout an organization. For example, if the adequacy of controls over hardware is to be evaluated, the scope of the review might or might not include all sites where microcomputers are located.
Tasks to be accomplished	Although the overall tasks to be undertaken will be known, specific tasks must be defined. For example, the project plan might specify the tasks to be undertaken to compile an inventory of hardware at end-user sites.

(cont.)

Project Plan Component	Explanation
Organization of the project team	Depending on the size and complexity of the review, the security administrator might have to enlist the assistance of consultants or staff who have detailed knowledge of the areas to be evaluated.
Resources budget	The resources budget will be affected by the size and complexity of the review. It must specify the labor hours, materials, and money required to complete the review.
Schedule for task completion	The plan must specify which tasks must be completed by what dates if the objectives of the security review are to be accomplished on a timely basis.

The security-review plan should be documented formally to provide working guidelines for the project team. Standard tools such as Gantt charts and PERT charts can be used to assist the documentation and communication processes (see Chapter 5). As the project progresses, security administrators must monitor progress of the review against the plan.

Identification of Assets

The second major step in a security review is to identify the assets associated with the information systems function. This step can be difficult for two reasons. First, some organizations possess a substantial number of information systems assets. For example, a large organization might have several mainframe computers, hundreds of microcomputers, a wide-area communications network, many local area communication networks, and thousands of files and programs. Second, the information systems assets might be widely distributed throughout an organization. For example, they could be scattered across different divisions and departments, and many might be located with end users.

One way to identify assets is to seek out *instances* within various general categories. For example, security administrators might use the categories shown in Figure 7–1:

Asset Category	Examples
Personnel	End users, analysts, programmers, operators, clerks, guards.
Hardware	Mainframe computers, minicomputers, microcomputers, disks, printers, communications lines, concentrators, terminals.
Facilities	Furniture, office space, computer rooms, tape storage racks.
Documentation	Systems and program documentation, database documentation, standards, plans, insurance policies, contracts.
Supplies	Negotiable instruments, preprinted forms, paper, tapes, cassettes.
Data/information	Master files, transactions files, archival files.
Applications software	Debtors, creditors, payroll, bill-of-materials, sales, inventory.
Systems software	Compilers, utilities, database management systems, operating systems, communications software, spreadsheets.

Within each category, the review team must prepare a comprehensive list of assets. The difficult part is knowing the level of aggregation at which to work. For example, consider the problem of preparing an inventory of application programs in a large organization that has several thousand programs. On the one hand, for backup purposes a complete inventory of these programs will be needed. On the other hand, from the viewpoint of deciding what controls should be exercised over the disks on which they are stored, it might be possible to consider groups of programs rather than individual programs.

Similar problems exist with data files. Do data assets need to be identified at the data item, group, record, or file level? Clearly, the finer the level of asset identification required, the more costly will be the review process.

Valuation of Assets

The third step in a security review, valuing the assets, is also a difficult step. Parker (1981) points out that the valuation might differ depending on who is asked to give the valuation, the way in which the asset could be lost, the period of time for which it is lost, and the age of the asset (Figure 7–4). In terms of who values the asset, an asset might be more useful to some people than to others. For example, end users who employ a generalized retrieval package more frequently than programmers are more likely to assign a higher value to the package. In terms of how the asset is lost, accidental loss might be less serious than loss that arises through an irregularity. For example, although the accidental destruction of a customer master file might be serious, management might be more concerned if it is stolen by a competitor. In terms of the time period of loss, for most assets the loss becomes more serious as use of the asset is denied for a longer period. For example, if it is difficult to replace a piece of hardware quickly, management might value it more highly than other hardware that has a higher capital cost but that, nonetheless, can be replaced immediately. In terms of the age of the asset, most assets deteriorate with age. For example, management might be less concerned about a competitor gaining access to an old customer master file.

Valuation of physical assets also cannot be considered in isolation from valuation of logical assets. The reason is that the value of physical assets often must be considered in light of the logical assets they store. For example, consider the value of a microcomputer's hard disk. The replacement value of the physical disk might be only a few hundred dollars. Its contents, however, might be worth thousands, even millions of dollars. The project team must take care, therefore, to prepare an inventory of all material *physical and logical* assets that fall within the scope of the review. Otherwise, the team might fail to identify significant exposures.

Several techniques can be used to assign a value to an asset. In some cases, users might be able to provide a direct dollar valuation for the asset. For example, if an item of hardware can be replaced quickly, they simply might value it

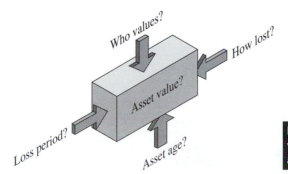

FIGURE 7–4. Factors that affect the valuation of information systems assets.

at its acquisition cost, assuming the item does not store logical assets whose value must also be taken into account. Often, however, precise dollar valuations are hard to assign to assets. For example, it can be difficult to determine the loss of customer goodwill that occurs when system failure leads to a degradation in service or to estimate the lost revenues that result when a competitor steals proprietary software. In these types of situations, the following sorts of indirect valuation techniques might be used:

1. A formal procedure, such as the Delphi method, can be used to try to get stakeholder consensus on an asset valuation. The Delphi method employs successive rounds of confidential questionnaires to elicit the respondents' opinions on some matter. Feedback is provided after the results of each round are obtained in case respondents then wish to revise their views.

2. Users can be asked to value an asset on some type of scale where, say, a score of 1 represents a low value and a score of 10 represents a high value. This approach might help users rank assets in order of importance.

3. Courtney (1977) suggests that users be asked to value assets on a logarithmic scale. They assign a rating, v, to an asset based on their estimate of the dollar value as a function of the base 10. Thus, an asset valued around \$100 would be assigned a v of 2; an asset valued around \$1 million would be assigned a v of 6. Using this technique, respondents are not forced into making fine discriminations between assets based on value.

When undertaking the asset-valuation task, security administrators must be careful that the evaluation does not flounder because it becomes too onerous. The primary objectives of asset valuation are to develop users' sensitivity to the possible consequences of a threat that eventuates and ultimately to enable an estimate to be made of the amount that can be justified as expenditure on safeguards. The task of asset valuation should be pursued only to the extent that these objectives can be accomplished satisfactorily.

Threats Identification

A threat is some action or event that can lead to a loss. During the threats-identification phase, security administrators attempt to flesh out all material threats that can eventuate and result in information systems assets being exposed, removed either temporarily or permanently, lost, damaged, destroyed, or used for unauthorized purposes.

One useful way to identify threats is first to consider possible *sources* of threats and then to consider the *types* of threats these sources might initiate (Figure 7–5) (see also Cohen 1997). When considering the types of threats, it is

	Nature of threat	
	Accidental	Deliberate
External	e.g., Acts of God	e.g., Hackers
Internal	e.g., Pollution	e.g., Sabotage

Source of threat

FIGURE 7–5. Types of threats facing information systems assets.

also useful to categorize threats as malicious (intent to do harm) or nonmalicious (accidental). For example, the following threats arise from sources that are *external* to the organization:

Source of Threat	*Examples of Threat Types*
Nature/Acts of God	Earthquake, flood, fire, mud, gases, projectiles, living organisms, extreme temperatures, electromagnetic radiation.
Hardware suppliers	Unreliable hardware, ineffective hardware, incompatible hardware, improper maintenance, lawsuits.
Software suppliers	Erroneous software, ineffective software, poor documentation, improper maintenance, lawsuits.
Contractors	Erroneous software, ineffective software, improper hardware/software maintenance, untimely provision of services, disclosure of confidential information.
Other resource suppliers	Power outages, disruption to communication services, untimely provision of resources.
Competitors	Sabotage, espionage, lawsuits, financial distress through fair or unfair competition.
Debt and equity holders	Financial distress though foreclosure on claims.
Unions	Strikes, sabotage, harassment.
Governments	Financial distress through onerous regulations.
Environmentalists	Harassment, unfavorable publicity.
Criminals/hackers	Theft, sabotage, espionage, extortion.

Similarly, the following threats arise from sources that are *internal* to the organization:

Source of Threats	*Examples of Threat Types*
Management	Failure to provide resources, inadequate planning and control.
Employees	Errors, theft, fraud, sabotage, extortion, improper use of services.
Unreliable systems	Hardware failure, software failure, facilities failure.

Some types of threats are clear because their consequences are immediate and obvious. For example, the nature of and impact of fire on information systems assets usually will be readily apparent. Other types of threats are more subtle. For example, astute actions by a competitor can undermine the financial viability of an organization. As a result, controls might not be maintained because management initiates cost-cutting measures.

Threats Likelihood Assessment

Having identified the threats that face the information systems function, security administrators must next attempt to estimate their likelihood of occurrence of each threat over a specified time period. In some cases, statistical data might be available. For example, an insurance company might be able to provide information on the probability of a fire occurring over varying time periods. Similarly, analyses have been undertaken on cases of computer abuse that give insights into their likelihood of occurrence (e.g., BloomBecker 1990; Loch et al. 1992).

Often, however, prior data is not available. Security administrators must then elicit the likelihood of occurrence of a threat from the stakeholders associated with an information system. For example, users can probably best estimate the likelihood of erroneous data leading to decisions that incur significant losses, and management can probably best estimate the likelihood of controls being compromised because financial distress has arisen. As with asset valuation, security administrators can use formal elicitation techniques like the Delphi method to obtain estimates of the likelihood of occurrence of a threat.

To some extent, the nature and value of the assets associated with the information systems function affect the likelihood of occurrence of a threat. If the information systems function has many high-value, proprietary software packages, for example, it is a prime target for piracy attempts. Thus, the identification and valuation of assets also assists with the identification of threats and their likelihood of occurrence.

Periodically, we must reassess the likelihood of a threat occurring. Changes can occur in the structure, direction, and environment of an organization that produce changes in the threat profile that face an organization (Bannan 1996).

Exposures Analysis

The exposures analysis phase comprises four tasks: *(1)* identification of the controls in place; *(2)* assessment of the reliability of the controls in place; *(3)* evaluation of the likelihood that a threat incident will be successful, given the set of controls in place and their reliability; and *(4)* assessment of the loss that will result if a threat incident circumvents the controls in place (Figure 7–6). When these tasks are accomplished, the exposures associated with the information systems function can be determined. An exposure is simply the expected loss that will occur over some time period, given the reliability of the controls in place. Exposures arise because either *(1)* there is no control to cover the threat incident or *(2)* there is some probability that the control in place will not operate reliably for the particular threat incident that occurs (Figure 7–7).

Consider, then, the first task: identifying the controls in place. Perhaps the easiest way to perform this task is to use one of the many questionnaires designed to assess security (e.g., FitzGerald and FitzGerald 1990). These questionnaires contain extensive control checklists that security administrators can use to determine systematically whether a control is missing. Like auditors, security administrators can use interviews, observations, and documentation to obtain information about the controls in place.

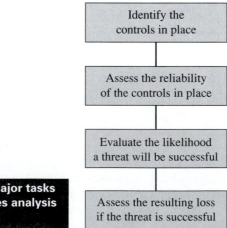

FIGURE 7–6. Major tasks in the exposures analysis phase.

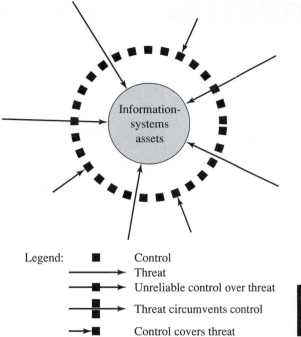

Legend: ∎   Control
          ——————→   Threat
          ———∎—→   Unreliable control over threat
          ——∎—→   Threat circumvents control
          —→∎   Control covers threat

FIGURE 7–7. Threats, control reliability, control coverage, and exposures.

To assess the reliability of these controls, security administrators must test them. In some cases, tests are straightforward. For example, usually it is easy to determine whether locked doors prevent unauthorized access to a computer room. Some types of controls, however, are difficult to test. For example, to check whether fire extinguishers work, usually one would not start a fire and then discharge the extinguisher to evaluate its effectiveness. Instead, auditors must rely on assurances given by the manufacturer and examine the extinguisher's servicing tag to see whether it has been maintained regularly. Similarly, testing whether the fire extinguisher system for a computer room works can cost many thousands of dollars. In some high-exposure situations auditors might periodically simulate a fire in the computer room to determine whether the system extinguishes the fire. Usually, however, auditors rely on maintenance records and the manufacturer's assurances that the system will operate effectively.

To evaluate the likelihood of a threat incident circumventing a control, the security administrator considers each of the assets or categories of assets identified during the second phase of the review, considers each of the threats identified during the fourth phase of the review, determines whether a control exists to cover the threat incident, and, if so, evaluates the probability of the control operating effectively to eliminate or mitigate the effects of the threat incident. To aid in this task, Parker (1981) recommends that security administrators write scenarios to describe how threat incidents could compromise controls. These scenarios then can be considered by stakeholders to assess their realism (Table 7–1).

To determine the losses that will be incurred from a threat incident that circumvents controls, the effect of the threat incident should first be determined. Will the asset be lost, damaged, exposed, removed, destroyed, or used for unauthorized purposes? Next, a value must be assigned to the effect. The value of the asset determined in the third phase of the review provides the basis for

TABLE 7–1 Scenario Analysis of Exposures	
Threat:	Malicious damage to mainframe computer by operator.
Existing controls:	1. Two operators always present.
	2. Background check carried out before hiring operators.
Control weaknesses:	Ongoing psychological stability of operators is not assessed regularly in a formal way.
Scenario:	An operator who becomes psychologically unstable could destroy the mainframe when the other operator leaves the computer room temporarily. Alternatively, the unstable operator might be able to overpower the other operator to carry out the damage.
Probability of occurrence:	Less than 1 in 10,000 a year.
Loss that would occur:	$600,000 replacement cost of machine. Backup exists for software and data.
Assessment:	Exposure is acceptable as costs of carrying out psychological testing exceed $60 per year. The effect of this type of testing on employee morale is also a serious concern.

this assessment. Security administrators must determine whether the full value of the asset will be lost if the threat is successful or whether the loss will be partial.

For each asset and each threat, the expected loss can then be calculated using the following formula:

$$EL = p_t \times p_f \times L$$

where:

EL = expected loss associated with asset (exposure)
p_t = probability of threat incident occurring
p_f = probability of control failure
L = resulting loss if threat is successful

For example, given the controls that exist, if the likelihood, p_t, that a fire will occur in a corporation's computer room in any one year is .001, the probability, p_f, of controls failing to detect and extinguish the fire is .1, and the loss, L, that will occur as a result is $4 million, the expected loss each year, EL, with respect to the fire threat and the computer room assets is $400; that is, $EL = .001 \times .1 \times \$4,000,000$. The exposure, therefore, is $400.

If security administrators have not chosen the right level of aggregation in their identification of assets and threats, the exposures-analysis phase may falter badly. Clearly, substantial work can be involved in carrying out an exposures analysis. Too much detail will undermine the analysis. Security administrators need to devote most effort to material assets and material threats. In this regard, the choices they make during prior phases of a security review about the assets and threats that are important have significant implications for the conduct of the exposures-analysis phase.

Controls Adjustment

Subsequent to the exposures analysis, security administrators must evaluate whether the level of each exposure is acceptable. Formally, this evaluation means they must determine whether over some time period any control can be designed, implemented, and operated such that the cost of the control is less than the reduction in expected losses that occurs by virtue of having the control in place and working to cover one or more threats. In other words, the benefits of a control that arise because it reduces expected losses from threats must exceed the costs of designing, implementing, and operating the control (see also Chapter 21).

How security administrators make this decision is in large part a matter of judgment, experience, and training. To some extent, guidance can be obtained from the control questionnaires used to identify missing controls during the exposures-analysis phase. These controls are candidates for inclusion in a revised controls system. Security administrators also might consult their colleagues in other organizations to determine control profiles that are used commonly. These profiles represent the combined experience and judgments of others who have faced similar problems. As such, they could provide important insights into controls that will be cost-effective.

Still another strategy for identifying new controls needed is to analyze the scenarios developed during the exposures analysis phase. These scenarios can motivate insights into the types of controls that will be cost-effective against a threat. In addition, they provide a tangible basis for considering how the control will work to reduce exposures, thereby making the cost-benefit analysis more concrete.

Finally, Parker (1981) proposes 20 "principles" that he argues should provide the formal basis for selecting controls. For example, he says that controls should place minimum reliance on real-time human intervention, have failsafe defaults, and should not rely on design secrecy for their effectiveness. Proposed safeguards can be evaluated against these principles to determine their likelihood of success.

The controls adjustment phase also includes consideration of existing controls. Security administrators must examine whether existing controls should be terminated or modified in some way to improve their cost effectiveness. The bases used for selecting new controls also can be employed to evaluate the status of existing controls. For example, scenario analyses might show deficiencies in procedures for evacuating a computer room in the event of fire. Security administrators might see ways to improve evacuation procedures after studying these deficiencies.

Report Preparation

The final phase in a security review is the preparation of a management report. This report documents the findings of the review and, in particular, makes recommendations as to new safeguards that should be implemented and existing safeguards that should be terminated or modified.

Like all reports to management, often the most difficult part is getting the recommendations accepted. The level of acceptance depends on the extent to which management agrees with the criticality of the exposures identified and whether they perceive the recommended safeguards are economically, technically, and operationally feasible. Again, scenarios are a useful technique for increasing management's sensitivity to the exposures identified. They provide a tangible basis for management to evaluate how concerned they should be about an exposure. With respect to the feasibility of the safeguards recommended, the onus is on security administrators to demonstrate that the safeguards are within the information systems function's capabilities to design, implement, and operate.

The security report also must include a plan for implementing the safeguards recommended. Both the seriousness of the exposure to be rectified and the difficulty of implementing the remedial safeguards must be considered. The most serious exposures should be addressed first, but then the ease with which a safeguard can be installed or modified should determine the order of implementation. To the extent some safeguards are interdependent and management decides not to implement them all, the report must consider alternative control configurations.

MAJOR SECURITY THREATS AND REMEDIAL MEASURES

The previous section describes a general methodology for evaluating security over information systems assets and selecting and implementing controls. This section briefly discusses some of the major security threats that face the information systems function (Figure 7–8) and safeguards that can be implemented. Auditors must understand the nature and potential consequences of these

FIGURE 7–8. Major threats to the information systems function.

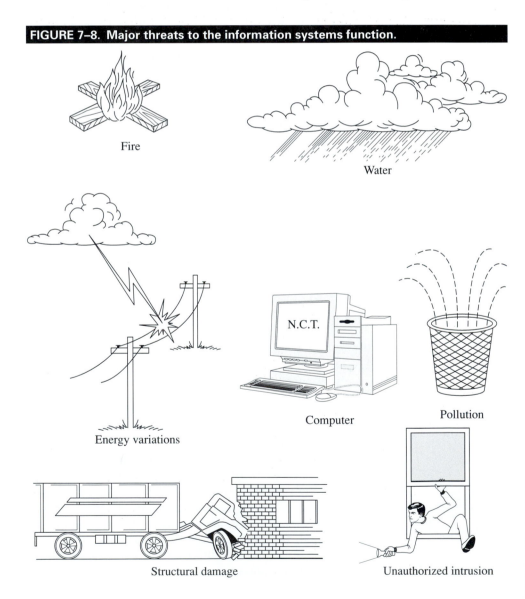

Fire

Water

Energy variations

Computer

N.C.T.

Pollution

Structural damage

Unauthorized intrusion

threats for audit objectives and the controls that are likely to be effective. If an auditor deems controls over these threats to be inadequate or unreliable, the extent of substantive testing will have to be expanded, especially in relation to asset safeguarding and data integrity objectives.

Fire Damage

Fire is often the most serious threat to the physical security of information systems assets. Indeed, Toigo (1992) reports that National Fire Protection Association statistics indicate on average a fire occurs in a computer room within the United States every 10 minutes.

Loss from fire can also be substantial. A fire in the Pentagon, for example, destroyed $6.7 million worth of hardware and more than 7,000 magnetic tapes. Similarly, a fire in First Data Corporation's computer room in New York City destroyed more than $2 million worth of hardware.

Some countries have various public service and governmental organizations that provide advice on fire-protection measures. Nevertheless, implementing a specific fire-protection system usually requires specialist advice. Some major features of a well-designed fire-protection system follow:

1. Both automatic and manual fire alarms are placed at strategic locations throughout those parts of the organization where material information systems assets are sited.
2. Automatic fire-extinguisher systems exist at strategic locations that dispense the appropriate suppressant: water, carbon dioxide, or halon. Water is the least harmful suppressant for humans; however, it can damage equipment. Carbon dioxide is relatively cheap, but it can debilitate a person in seconds. Halon gas is a widely used suppressant because it is safe and effective. Personnel will not be debilitated by halon, for example, providing only short-term exposure occurs. Moreover, it is noncorrosive, nonconductive, highly compressible, and chemically stable. In some countries, however, production of halon gas is now prohibited because of its detrimental effect on the earth's ozone layer (Gibbs 1993). Alternative suppressants are being sought.
3. Appropriate types of manual fire extinguishers exist at strategic locations throughout those parts of the organization where material information systems assets are sited.
4. A control panel shows where in the organization an automatic or a manual alarm has been triggered.
5. Beside the control panel, master switches exist for power (including air conditioning) and automatic extinguisher systems.
6. Buildings where material information systems assets are sited have been constructed from fire-resistant materials, and they are structurally stable when fire damage occurs.
7. Fire extinguishers and fire exits are marked clearly and can be accessed easily by staff.
8. When a fire alarm is activated, a signal is sent automatically to a control station that is always staffed.
9. Good housekeeping procedures ensure that combustible pollutants and materials are minimized around high-value information systems assets—for example, computer rooms are cleaned regularly to remove paper lint, and printer paper supplies are kept in a separate room.
10. To reduce the risk of extensive damage from electrical fires, electrical wiring should be placed in fire-resistant panels and conduit.

Security administrators should arrange regular inspections and tests of all fire protection systems and ensure that they are properly serviced. Proper use of these systems also requires staff training and periodic drills. The procedures to be followed during an emergency also should be documented.

Water Damage

Water damage to information systems assets can be the outcome of a fire; for example, an extinguisher system sprays water that enters hardware, or water pipes could burst. Water damage can result, however, from other sources: cyclones, tornadoes, ice, and torrential rains. In 1974, for example, the city of Brisbane experienced freak flooding after torrential rains. As a result, the Brisbane River burst its banks. One mainframe computer room in close proximity to the river was submerged completely.

Some major ways of protecting information systems assets against water damage follow:

1. Where possible, have waterproof ceilings, walls, and floors.
2. Ensure that an adequate drainage system exists.
3. Install alarms at strategic points where material information systems assets are located.
4. In flood areas, have all material information systems assets located above the high-water level.
5. Have a master switch for all water mains.
6. Use a dry-pipe automatic sprinkler system that is charged by an alarm and activated by the fire.
7. Cover hardware with a protective fabric when it is not in use.
8. To prevent flooding, locate information systems assets above the ground floor of the buildings in which they are housed.
9. Have a dry moat around buildings where material information systems assets are housed.

Again, regular inspections, tests, and drills are essential if the disaster plan is to be operational when a situation of potential water damage arises.

Energy Variations

Energy variations take the form of increases in power (surges or spikes), decreases in power (sags or brownouts), or loss of power (blackouts). They can disrupt not only hardware operations but also the systems needed to maintain an acceptable operational environment—one that is dust free and relatively constant with respect to temperature and humidity. Thus, careful assessment of the likelihood of unacceptable energy variations occurring is essential to the ongoing operations of the information systems function. Moreover, energy sources must be monitored constantly to ensure their continuing adequacy and reliability.

To protect hardware against *temporary* increases in power, voltage regulators can be used. To protect hardware against *sustained* increases in power, circuit breakers can be used. A wide range of voltage regulators and circuit breakers can now be purchased for mainframe computers, minicomputers, and microcomputers.

To protect hardware against power loss, if possible, two independent supply sources should exist so that one can be used if the other fails. In addition, uninterruptible power supply systems (UPSs) can be installed. Three types are available. *Static* UPSs rely primarily on batteries and are intended as short-term backup. *Rotary* UPSs provide a generator as backup. Usually they are driven by diesel engines and are intended for longer-term power loss. *Hybrid* UPSs employ both batteries to provide power initially and a generator that takes over when the batteries run low. Like rotary UPSs, they are intended for longer-term power loss. Unless sustained operation of a microcomputer is critical to an organization's operations, usually UPSs are purchased to support only mainframe computers and minicomputers.

The design of security for the information systems function must provide for the possibility of total loss of power. For example, certain controls such as doors can fail-safe on a power loss. It must be possible to deactivate these controls manually should staff need to exit the building quickly. Other safeguards such as alarms and extinguisher systems also might fail to operate in the event of power loss. Alternative controls must then be used. For example, buildings might be evacuated and locked to protect personnel and to reduce the likelihood of unauthorized access to and use of hardware, software, and data.

Structural Damage

Structural damage to information systems assets can occur in several ways: earthquake, wind, mud, snow, avalanche, and mishap. Structural damage can also be an outcome of some other disaster. For example, fire might weaken the floor of a room in which mainframe computers and their associated peripherals are housed. Eventually the floor might collapse, and hardware might be damaged as a result.

Some information systems assets are more prone to structural damage than others. Those located in an earthquake region, for example, face a higher risk. Similarly, smaller assets, like microcomputers, are prone to mishap. A microcomputer might be dropped, for example, as it is carried from one desk to another. The microcomputer's hard disk drive, as well as other components, could be damaged.

Preventing disaster from occurring through structural damage is often an engineering problem. In the design of a building, for example, the engineers will consider the structural stresses the building might endure. They should be notified, however, if significant computer hardware is to be housed in the building. They can then take this fact into consideration when they prepare their building plans and strengthen, say, the floor areas where equipment will be located.

If there is some choice as to where information systems assets are to be located, the site chosen should be the least prone to structural damage—for example, away from a floodplain or an earthquake region. Similarly, information systems assets should be located, if possible, on an upper floor of a building. They are less susceptible to damage by floods.

Information systems assets also should be secured so they will not dislodge or tip easily. For example, microcomputers should be placed on stable desks that are not located near major thoroughfares. Similarly, mainframe hardware and storage cabinets should be secured so they will not overturn if structural stress is placed on a building during, say, an earthquake.

Pollution

The ongoing operations of much of the equipment used by the information systems function depend on having an environment that is relatively unpolluted. Pollution can damage a disk drive, for example, and as a result critical data could be lost. Valuable time also could be lost while the damaged equipment is repaired. Pollution can also cause fires. Toigo (1992) reports that one major information systems insurer attributes a significant percentage of fires to pollution-related spontaneous internal combustion associated with hardware components.

The major pollutant is dust. Dust can become a problem if the air passing through the air conditioning system is filtered inadequately or if it is allowed to accumulate on, say, floors and ceilings. More subtle forms of pollution exist, however. For example, coffee is a pollutant if it is spilled in a microcomputer keyboard or printer, thereby rendering the keyboard or printer inoperable.

Several steps can be taken to reduce losses from pollution. Ceilings, walls, floors, storage cabinets, and equipment should be cleaned regularly. Vacuuming is especially important, particularly in areas where dust collects, such as under raised floors. Dust collecting rugs can be placed at entrances. Floors can be treated with special antistatic compounds. Dust generating activities—for example, paper shredding, decollation, or bursting—should be carried out well away from dust-sensitive equipment. Foodstuffs can be prohibited in certain areas such as mainframe computer rooms or microcomputer work areas, especially where pests such as rodents and insects can cause problems. Regular emptying of wastepaper baskets also prevents dust and combustible materials from collecting.

Unauthorized Intrusion

Unauthorized intrusion takes two forms. The intruder physically could enter an organization to steal information systems assets or carry out sabotage or extortion. For example, intruders might be seeking to remove magnetic tapes, disk and tape cartridges, or diskettes or to plant a bomb. Alternatively, the intruder might eavesdrop by wiretapping, installing an electronic bug, or using a receiver that picks up electromagnetic signals. One other form of eavesdropping is visual eavesdropping. The intruder might photograph sensitive information or use a telescope to view the information.

Physical intrusion can be inhibited or prevented by erecting various barriers. Buildings that house information systems assets can be protected by a wall, a fence, or a dry moat. Doors and windows should be secured. Some type of card locking system might then be used, for example, to restrict entry to authorized personnel. Sometimes air conditioning ducts allow unauthorized entry to buildings. Intruders simply have to gain access to the roof of the building (perhaps via the fire escape) and crawl through the ducts. Thus, security administrators must ensure that air conditioning ducts are secure. Buildings that house high-value information systems assets, such as an organization's mainframe computer installation, might be disguised to reduce the likelihood of unauthorized intrusion occurring.

Alarms and guards can be used to detect unauthorized intruders. Various types of security devices and systems can be installed that signal the presence of an intruder. Nevertheless, these defences can be compromised: a guard could be bribed or a security device improperly deactivated. The last lines of protection are then safes, vaults, filing cabinets, or locks. For example, magnetic tapes, disk and tape cartridges, and diskettes can be locked in filing cabinets, microcomputer components can be secured using lockdown devices, and check stationery (negotiable instruments) can be stored in a safe. Nonetheless, even these controls might not withstand the threats posed by a saboteur or terrorist intent on destruction.

Intruders also could pose as visitors or employees to attempt unauthorized entry to buildings that house information systems assets. Receptionists or guards can challenge unidentified visitors and provide advance warning of unauthorized intrusion. A badge system can be used to identify the status of personnel within the building: permanent staff or visitors. All visitors should be escorted by a permanent staff member. Unescorted visitors or persons without a badge should be questioned about their presence in the building. A security check might be performed before visitors are issued a badge.

Eavesdropping breaches the privacy of data. Intruders seek access to sensitive information such as passwords, sales information, geological survey information, and engineering design information.

Controls must be implemented to prevent eavesdropping via the electromagnetic emanations that computer equipment produces. For example, eavesdropping devices can be used to pick up emissions from microcomputers or printers. Some manufacturers shield their computer equipment against electromagnetic emanations. Alternatively, equipment must be housed in buildings that are designed to inhibit emissions. For example, specially screened rooms can be built to prevent emanations from equipment that processes highly sensitive data.

Eavesdropping can also be undertaken via bugs that are installed by intruders. Various devices are available to detect the presence of bugs. Security administrators periodically might employ a security firm that possesses these devices to check whether bugs are present.

In a communications network the points most likely to be wiretapped are the junction boxes and the private branch exchange. It is difficult to wiretap a communications line after it leaves the building in which the computer is housed; the line might be underground, signals might be sent via microwave, several thousand channels might be multiplexed together. Thus, security administrators should ensure that the junction boxes and private branch exchange are secure.

Visual eavesdropping can be prevented in several ways. Cameras should not be allowed in buildings where security is a concern. Some buildings have no windows; however, staff might object to the absence of natural light. If windows do exist, they can be shielded by blinds or curtains. Visual display units can also be placed strategically so intruders outside a building cannot use telescopes or cameras with a telescopic lens to view or photograph output.

Viruses and Worms

A *virus* is a program that requests the operating system of a computer to append it to other programs (Figure 7–9). In this way the virus propagates to other programs. Viruses can be easily transmitted, for example, via files that contain macros that are sent as attachments to electronic mail messages. For example, macros in word processing files can be infected with viruses. When recipients open these infected files with their own copies of the word processing software, their system will be infected unless their word processing software first checks for the presence of these viruses.

A virus can be relatively benign; for example, it can cause minor disruptions by printing humorous messages or drawing diagrams on visual-display screens. Alternatively, it might be malignant; for example, it could delete files, corrupt other programs so they are unusable, or severely disrupt the operations of application systems.

FIGURE 7–9. Program corruption through viruses.

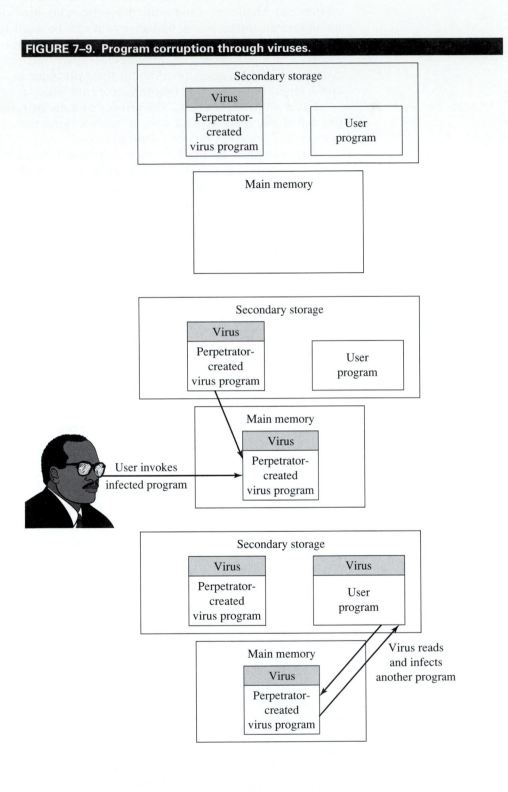

To reduce expected losses from viruses, security administrators can implement the following types of controls:

Type of Control	*Examples*
Preventive	Use only "clean," certified copies of software files or files that contain macros.
	Do not use public domain/shareware software or files that might contain macros that are prepared by others unless they have been checked for viruses.
	Download software or files that contain macros only from reputable bulletin boards or Web sites or avoid downloading from bulletin boards or Web sites altogether.
	Implement read-only access over software.
	Check new software with antivirus software before it is installed.
	Check new files with antivirus software before they are used.
	Educate users about the dangers of viruses and the means of preventing infection.
Detective	Regularly run antivirus software to detect infections. Undertake file size comparisons to determine whether the size of programs has changed. Undertake date/time stamp comparisons to determine whether unauthorized modifications have been made to software.
Corrective	Ensure "clean" backup is maintained.
	Have a documented plan for recovery from virus infections.
	Run antivirus software to remove infections.

Like viruses, *worms* propagate copies of themselves with benign or malignant intent. Whereas viruses attach themselves to other legitimate programs, however, worms usually exist as separate, independent programs. Worms use operating system services as their means of replication. Often they exploit some type of bug or security weakness in the operating system to infiltrate other systems. For example, a worm introduced into the Internet computer network in 1988 exploited a bug and a security weakness in the Unix operating system and e-mail facilities to propagate rapidly to machines connected to the network (Denning 1990). The worm caused major disruption as machines in the network labored to execute the worm's many replicas. Machines had to be taken off line and purged of all copies of the worm.

Threats from worms arise when an organization connects its computers to an open network—one that users can join relatively easily and one in which they are not subjected to rigorous security requirements. Use of open networks is likely to increase because many advantages accrue from easy access to other computers—for example, facilitating use of e-mail, electronic commerce, and the World Wide Web.

Unfortunately, establishing effective controls over worms is often more difficult than establishing effective controls over viruses. Exposures that arise from viruses can be controlled to a large extent by actions the organization takes itself. Exposures that arise from worms, however, must be addressed by all users of a network. Otherwise, control weaknesses in one user's system can undermine security in another user's system.

If security administrators work for organizations that participate in open networks, they should undertake the following types of control steps:

1. Actively lobby to establish network security administration groups that will take responsibility for security in the networks in which their organization participates.
2. Participate in efforts to establish control protocols for network users to follow to reduce exposures from threats like worms.
3. Be aware of weaknesses in network resources that can undermine security. Implement any remedial measures that can cost-effectively reduce exposures from these weaknesses. For example, change any system default passwords and remove "visitor" accounts.
4. Ensure that strong access controls exist over those resources that are the security administrator's responsibility. For example, inform users of the importance of choosing passwords that are difficult to guess.
5. Educate users so they are aware of the importance of controls, the need for backup, and the actions they should take when they suspect a security violation has occurred.

Misuse of Software, Data, and Services

Organizations can incur losses because software, data, and services they own are misused. For example, the following types of abuses can arise:

1. Generalized software and proprietary databases that the organization develops are stolen by employees or competitors. The organization loses the revenue it would otherwise obtain from sales of the software and databases.
2. The organization fails to protect the personal privacy of individuals about whom it stores data in its databases. It may incur losses because of legislative breaches or unfavorable publicity.
3. Employees use information systems services to support their own personal activities. For example, they may use computer time for private consulting purposes or have the organization acquire resources (e.g., microcomputer hardware and software) for their own private use.

Security administrators can implement various controls to reduce expected losses from these types of abuses. In some countries (e.g., Australia, the United States, the United Kingdom), software is protected via copyright laws. Also, software sometimes can be protected via patents, licensing agreements, or trade-secret laws (Yoches 1989). Moreover, when the name of a software package is deemed important to its marketing, protection might be available through a trademark. Security administrators must evaluate each piece of software to determine whether it needs to be protected, the form of protection needed, and the best means of providing protection.

In many countries the laws governing proprietary databases are problematic. Either they do not exist or the protection they afford is uncertain. For example, a proprietary database might not pass the test of "originality" that is typically required under copyright law. As a result, licensing agreements are often employed to govern the conditions under which other parties may use a proprietary database. Security administrators might find that enforcing licensing restrictions, however, is difficult.

Many countries now have laws that seek to protect personal privacy (e.g., Australia, Canada, France, Germany, Norway, Sweden, the United

States, the United Kingdom). Some laws apply only to personal data maintained by public-sector organizations; other laws apply also to private-sector organizations. Security administrators must ensure that controls (e.g., access controls and encryption controls) are in place and working to enforce compliance with these laws. Management and employees also need to be informed about the nature of these laws and their implications for the organization. Even if there are no applicable laws, however, preservation of personal privacy may be important to maintenance of an organization's reputation and goodwill.

Security administrators should regularly scrutinize hardware and software purchases and use of information systems services for evidence of abuse. All employees should be informed about actions that are deemed inappropriate. Penalties should be enforced in the event of an abuse. Compliance might be taken into account, for example, in promotion decisions.

Security administrators must also consider exposures that can arise because members of their own organization abuse the software, data, and services provided by other organizations. For example, employees might use pirated software, violate the licensing agreements associated with third-party software and proprietary databases, and circumvent billing controls when they are using another organization's computing resources. Lawsuits can arise as a result of these actions. As a result, severe damage can be done to the organization's reputation and goodwill.

In consultation with management, security administrators should prepare a code of conduct to govern the actions of employees within the organization with respect to information systems resources and activities. Table 7–2 shows the types of matters a code of conduct might address. Top managers must also show by example that they consider compliance with the code to be important.

Control can also be enhanced if security administrators take responsibility for or are informed about acquisition of hardware/software and enforcement of licensing agreements. Centralized control over hardware, software, data, and services reduces organizational flexibility, but it might be necessary to reduce expected losses from abuse to an acceptable level.

TABLE 7–2 Example Code of Conduct for Information Systems Personnel

Information systems personnel will:

1. Be honest, fair, and trustworthy.
2. Honor property rights with respect to information systems assets and take steps to preserve these property rights.
3. Respect a person's, group's, or organization's right to privacy and take steps to preserve privacy.
4. Respect confidentiality requirements and take steps to preserve confidentiality.
5. Respect the work of others and give proper credit when using the work of others.
6. Maintain professional competence.
7. Exercise due care when developing, implementing, and operating information systems.
8. Carefully evaluate the potential impact of systems.
9. Act ethically where deleterious impacts might arise from information systems work.
10. Seek and provide appropriate peer review of information systems work.
11. Respect access privileges assigned to information systems assets.
12. Keep management fully informed of material issues relating to information systems assets or the conduct of information systems work.

Hacking

A computer hacker is a person who attempts to gain unauthorized entry to a computer system by circumventing the system's access controls. Hackers can have benign or malignant intent. They simply might explore the capabilities of the system they hack or read files without changing them (computer trespass). Alternatively, they could wreak havoc by deleting critical files, disrupting system operations, or stealing sensitive data and programs.

In some countries, laws have been changed specifically to cover the activities of hackers (e.g., Australia, the United States). Because laws might not provide adequate remedial damages, however, it is better to prevent hacking in the first place. In this light, the primary preventive safeguards that security administrators can employ are access controls, especially logical access controls such as hard-to-determine passwords. (Chapter 10 discusses these controls in some detail.) In addition, security administrators must be aware of security weaknesses in systems software that hackers can exploit. As discussed previously, guest accounts with easy-to-determine passwords can be a major exposure.

Detective controls are also important in reducing expected losses from hacking activities. Accordingly, security administrators should regularly monitor system use for evidence of suspicious events. In the hacking incident described by Stoll (1988), for example, investigations of a minor billing discrepancy led to the discovery of major security violations having occurred through the activities of hackers.

CONTROLS OF LAST RESORT

In spite of safeguards that might be implemented, the information systems function still could suffer a disaster. A control might fail, or a threat might occur that management has not considered or that management has decided to accept as an exposure that cannot be covered via cost-effective controls. When disaster strikes, it still must be possible to recover operations and mitigate losses. In this situation, two controls of last resort must take effect: *(1)* a disaster recovery plan and *(2)* insurance.

Disaster Recovery Plan

The purpose of a disaster recovery plan or contingency plan is to enable the information systems function to restore operations in the event of some type of disaster. The impact of a disaster might be localized; for example, a personal-computer user might accidentally delete critical data stored on a hard disk. The impact, however, might be widespread; for example, an organization's mainframe computer installation might be destroyed by fire.

Periodically, surveys have been undertaken of organizations to assess the adequacy of their disaster recovery plans. A common, recurring finding is that the quality of disaster recovery plans, if an organization even has one, is low. This situation exists even though other surveys report that on average the length of time organizations can survive in the event their information-processing function is lost is decreasing. Perhaps these findings reflect that disaster recovery plans are costly and difficult to prepare, maintain, and test. In organizations that have extensive decentralization and distribution of computing resources, for example, disaster recovery planning will be an onerous activity. For a start, security administrators are likely to have difficulty obtaining a commitment from large numbers of microcomputer users to maintaining effective backup.

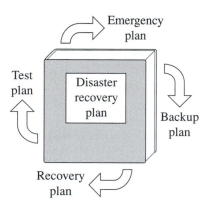

FIGURE 7–10. **Disaster recovery plan and its components.**

Auditors are concerned to see that the organizations audited have appropriate, high-quality disaster recovery plans in place (Salzman 1997, 1998). Because the preparation, maintenance, and ongoing testing of disaster recovery plans is often costly, the plan should be appropriate to the needs of the organization. Clearly, organizations that depend more on computers to support their operations will have greater needs. External auditors will be especially interested in a client's ability to continue as a going concern in the event disaster strikes and recovery cannot be effected quickly. They must also consider whether contingent claims might arise because contractual agreements the client has with other parties specify an appropriate, high-quality, regularly tested disaster recovery plan must be in place. Indeed, in some cases, clients might be governed by legislation that requires that they have appropriate, high-quality disaster recovery plans. Internal auditors will have the same concerns. In addition, they might also evaluate whether preparation, maintenance, and testing of the plan is carried out efficiently.

Comprehensive disaster recovery plan comprise four parts (Cerullo 1981): *(1)* an emergency plan, *(2)* a backup plan, *(3)* a recovery plan, and *(4)* a test plan (Figure 7–10). The plan lays down the policies, guidelines, and procedures for all personnel who have responsibility for the information systems function to follow. For example, it specifies the daily backup procedures that microcomputer users should follow and the site where recovery of mainframe operations is to be effected in the event of a fire. As a basis for assisting the audit evaluation, the following subsections briefly examine the nature, content, and preparation of each of the four parts of the plan.

Emergency Plan

The emergency plan specifies the actions to be undertaken immediately when a disaster occurs. Management must identify those situations that require the plan to be invoked—for example, major fire, major structural damage, and terrorist attack. The actions to be initiated can vary somewhat depending on the nature of the disaster that occurs. For example, some disasters require that all personnel leave the information systems facilities immediately; others require a few select personnel remain behind for a short period to sound alarms, shut down equipment, and so on.

If an organization undertakes a comprehensive security review program, the threats identification and exposures analysis phases involve identifying those situations that require the emergency plan to be invoked. Each situation will be an exposure; that is, it will be a threat that eventuates and brings about losses because controls have failed or none exist to cover the threat.

When the situations that evoke the plan have been identified, Cerullo (1981) points out that four aspects of the emergency plan must be articulated. First, the plan must show who is to be notified immediately when the disaster occurs—management, police, fire department, medicos, and so on. Second, the plan must show any actions to be undertaken, such as shutdown of equipment, removal of files, and termination of power. Third, any evacuation procedures required must be specified. Fourth, return procedures (e.g., conditions that must be met before the site is considered safe) must be designated. In all cases, the personnel responsible for the actions must be identified, and the protocols to be followed must be specified clearly.

Backup Plan

The backup plan specifies the type of backup to be kept, the frequency with which backup is to be undertaken, the procedures for making backup, the location of backup resources, the site where these resources can be assembled and operations restarted, the personnel who are responsible for gathering backup resources and restarting operations, the priorities to be assigned to re-covering the various systems, and a time frame in which recovery of each sys-tem must be effected. For some resources, the procedures specified in the backup plan might be straightforward. For example, microcomputer users might be admonished to make backup copies of critical files and store them off site. In other cases, the procedures specified in the backup plan could be com-plex and somewhat uncertain. For example, it might be difficult to specify ex-actly how an organization's mainframe facility will be recovered in the event of a fire.

The backup plan needs continuous updating as change occurs. For exam-ple, as personnel with key responsibilities in executing the plan leave the orga-nization, the plan must be modified accordingly. Indeed, it is prudent to have more than one person knowledgeable in a backup task in case someone is in-jured when a disaster occurs. Similarly, lists of hardware and software must be updated to reflect acquisitions and disposals.

Perhaps the most difficult part in preparing a backup plan is to ensure that all critical resources are backed up. The following resources must be considered:

Resource	Nature of Backup
Personnel	Training and rotation of duties among information systems staff so they can take the place of others. Arrangements with another company for provision of staff.
Hardware	Arrangements with another company for provision of hardware.
Facilities	Arrangements with another company for provision of facilities.
Documentation	Inventory of documentation stored securely on site and off site.
Supplies	Inventory of critical supplies stored securely on site and off site with list of vendors who provide all supplies.
Data/information	Inventory of files stored securely on site and off site.
Applications software	Inventory of application software stored securely on site and off site.
Systems software	Inventory of systems software stored securely on site and off site.

The selection of backup sites is an important decision. These sites must be close enough to enable easy pickup and delivery of backup resources. They must be sufficiently distant, however, so it is unlikely that both the organization's information systems facilities and the backup-site facilities will be destroyed as the result of a single disaster. In some cases, this objective might be difficult to achieve. For example, if a major earthquake were to occur, nearby backup sites might also be destroyed.

Provision of suitable backup for mainframe computers usually is a more difficult task than provision of suitable backup for minicomputers and micro-computers. Replacement minicomputers and microcomputers often can be obtained quickly. Furthermore, usually they have minimum requirements in terms of an appropriate operating environment. Mainframe computers, on the other hand, typically require specialized operational facilities. Security administrators should consider the following backup options:

1. *Cold site:* If an organization can tolerate some downtime, cold-site backup might be appropriate. A cold site has all the facilities needed to install a mainframe system—raised floors, air conditioning, power, communications lines, and so on. The mainframe is not present, however, and it must be provided by the organization wanting to use the cold site. An organization can establish its own cold-site facility or enter into an agreement with another organization to provide a cold-site facility.
2. *Hot site:* If fast recovery is critical, an organization might need hot-site backup. All hardware and operations facilities will be available at the hot site. In some cases, software, data, and supplies might also be stored there. Hot sites are expensive to maintain. They usually are shared with other organizations that have hot-site needs.
3. *Warm site:* A warm site provides an intermediate level of backup. It has all cold-site facilities plus hardware that might be difficult to obtain or install. For example, a warm site might contain selected peripheral equipment plus a small mainframe with sufficient power to handle critical applications in the short run.
4. *Reciprocal agreement:* Two or more organizations might agree to provide backup facilities to each other in the event of one suffering a disaster. This backup option is relatively cheap, but each participant must maintain sufficient capacity to operate another's critical systems. Reciprocal agreements are often informal in nature.

If a third-party site is to be used for backup and recovery purposes, security administrators must ensure that a contract is written to cover such issues as *(1)* how soon the site will be made available subsequent to a disaster, *(2)* the number of organizations that will be allowed to use the site concurrently in the event of a disaster, *(3)* the priority to be given to concurrent users of the site in the event of a common disaster, *(4)* the period during which the site can be used, *(5)* the conditions under which the site can be used, *(6)* the facilities and services the site provider agrees to make available, and *(7)* what controls will be in place and working at the off-site facility. These issues are often poorly specified in reciprocal agreements. Moreover, they can be difficult to enforce under a reciprocal agreement because of the informal nature of the agreement.

The need for backup highlights the value of using hardware and system software that conform to widely accepted standards and developing portable application systems. Specialized hardware and software might be more effective and more efficient, but they undermine an organization's ability to recover from a disaster quickly.

The recovery component of the backup plan needs careful consideration. In the event of a disaster, personnel will be responsible for tasks they undertake infrequently. Furthermore, they might be working under stress in an unfamiliar environment. The backup plan must assist them by providing concise, complete, clear instructions on recovery procedures they must follow.

Recovery Plan

Whereas the backup plan is intended to restore operations quickly so the information systems function can continue to service an organization, recovery plans set out procedures to restore full information systems capabilities. The specifics of how recovery is to be effected are often difficult to articulate. They depend on the circumstances of the disaster. For example, they will depend on whether the disaster is global or localized and, if localized, the nature of the machine (e.g., microcomputer, minicomputer, mainframe), the applications, and the data to be recovered. In this light, recovery plans should identify a recovery committee that will be responsible for working out the specifics of the recovery to be undertaken. The plan should specify the responsibilities of the committee and provide guidelines on priorities to be followed. For example, certain members of the committee could be responsible for hardware replacement. The plan might also indicate which applications are to be recovered first.

Members of a recovery committee must understand their responsibilities. Again, the problem is that they will be required to undertake unfamiliar tasks. Periodically, they must review and practice executing their responsibilities so they are prepared should a disaster occur. If committee members leave the organization, new members must be appointed immediately and briefed as to their responsibilities.

Test Plan

The final component of a disaster recovery plan is a test plan. The purpose of the test plan is to identify deficiencies in the emergency, backup, or recovery plans or in the preparedness of an organization and its personnel in the event of a disaster. It must enable a range of disasters to be simulated and specify the criteria by which the emergency, backup, and recovery plans can be deemed satisfactory.

Periodically, test plans must be invoked; that is, a disaster must be simulated and information systems personnel required to follow backup and recovery procedures. Unfortunately, top managers are often unwilling to carry out a test because daily operations are disrupted. They also fear a real disaster could arise as a result of the test procedures.

To facilitate testing, a phased approach can be adopted. First, the disaster recovery plan can be tested by desk checking and inspection and walkthroughs, much like the validation procedures adopted for programs (see Chapter 5). Next, a disaster can be simulated at a convenient time—for example, during a slow period in the day. Anyone who will be affected by the test (e.g., personnel and customers) also might be given prior notice of the test so they are prepared. Finally, disasters could be simulated without warning at any time. These are the acid tests of the organization's ability to recover from a real catastrophe.

Insurance

Insurance sometimes can be used to mitigate losses that arise when disasters eventuate. Policies usually can be obtained to cover the following resources:

Insurance Area	Explanation
Equipment	Covers repair or acquisition of hardware. Varies depending on whether the equipment is purchased or leased.
Facilities	Covers items such as reconstruction of a computer room, raised floors, special furniture.
Storage media	Covers the replacement of the storage media plus their contents—data files, programs, documentation.
Business interruption	Covers loss in business income because an organization is unable to trade.
Extra expenses	Covers additional costs incurred because an organization is not operating from its normal facilities.
Valuable papers and records	Covers source documents, preprinted reports, documentation, and other valuable papers.
Accounts receivable	Covers cash-flow problems that arise because an organization cannot collect its accounts receivable promptly.
Media transportation	Covers damage to media in transit.
Malpractice, errors, and omissions	Covers claims against an organization by its customers, e.g., claims and omissions made by the clients of an outsourcing vendor or service bureau.

Insurance coverage for certain types of losses, however, might be difficult, if not impossible, to obtain. For example, security administrators might be unable to purchase insurance to mitigate losses from some types of computer crime, such as, destruction of critical files by a virus. Information systems insurance is still a reasonably new area, and the types of policies that are available are continuing to evolve.

When an insurance policy has been written, security administrators must ensure that their organizations fulfil any obligations under the policy. For example, some policies require the insured have an up-to-date, comprehensive disaster recovery plan. In addition, usually the insurer must be notified of any substantive change in risk. Just what constitutes a substantive change in risk might be unclear. Usually it includes changes to hardware, but the position with respect to changes to software and data files may be uncertain.

If organizations act as an outsourcing vendor or a service bureau or use an outsourcing vendor or a service bureau to perform some of their information systems functions, special care must be taken to establish responsibilities for safeguards as a basis for determining the types of insurance that are then needed. The following matters must be considered:

1. What liability does the outsourcing vendor or service bureau have for malpractice, errors, and omissions?
2. What liability does the outsourcing vendor or service bureau have for failure to deliver promised services?
3. Who owns each of the programs and data files maintained by the outsourcing vendor or service bureau?

4. What are the respective responsibilities of the outsourcing vendor or service bureau and customers with respect to backup and recovery?

Each of these matters needs to be addressed contractually. If possible, residual exposures should then be covered by insurance.

SOME ORGANIZATIONAL ISSUES

Depending on the size of an organization and its reliance on its information systems function, the security-administration role can occupy four possible positions within the organizational hierarchy (Figure 7–11). In small organizations that use turnkey systems—that is, hardware and software systems that have been purchased as a package rather than developed in house—there might be no full-time professional information systems staff. As a consequence, no one obvious might be available to assume the security-administration role. Nonetheless, even in a small organization, security administration is still important. A small business that processes all its accounting records on a microcomputer could be forced into liquidation, for example, if a malicious employee or

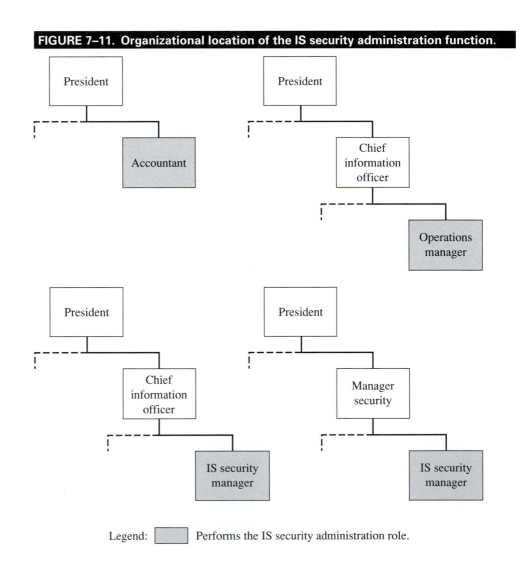

FIGURE 7–11. Organizational location of the IS security administration function.

Legend: Performs the IS security administration role.

a virus were to destroy its critical master files. Someone, therefore, must take responsibility for security. Possibly the organization's president or accountant might assume this role.

If an organization has its own information systems staff but insufficient work to justify an ongoing, separate security administration position, responsibility for security matters might be vested in the operations manager (see Chapter 8). Because operations managers are responsible for the day-to-day running of hardware and software systems, security-administration functions seem a natural extension of their responsibilities. A concern with this approach, however, is that operations managers then have direct access to systems as well as responsibility for security over these systems. A dishonest or malicious operations manager could easily compromise security.

Large organizations might have sufficient work to justify a separate security-administration position. In some cases the security administrator might report directly to the chief information officer. In other cases, the *information systems* security administrator might report to a manager who has *overall* responsibility for security matters with the organization. The advantage of the former structure is that responsibility for security matters is vested in persons who are close to the information systems function. The advantage of the latter structure is that computer security is more likely to be well integrated into the overall security measures adopted by the organization.

Security administrators often have to work closely with other information systems personnel. For example, if an organization has a data administrator and a database administrator, security administrators will have to liaise with them to establish access controls over data resources. Recall from Chapter 6 that the data administrator might assign access privileges to database users. The database administrator might then implement these privileges using the database management system's access control mechanism. Users might be able to circumvent these access controls, however, if the security administrator were to give them access to a powerful utility program that could access the database directly.

Similarly, security administrators usually have to work closely with operations managers. Operations managers often are responsible for the day-to-day functioning of physical access controls and backup and recovery controls. They need to understand the security administrator's control requirements. Security administrators, in turn, need to understand the difficulties operations managers might face when seeking to comply with these requirements.

Perhaps the most difficult organizational problems arise as the information systems function becomes increasingly distributed throughout an organization. Consider, for example, the implications for security as microcomputers proliferate through an organization. Security policies and procedures must be adapted to take into account the dispersal of sometimes critical information systems resources and the different circumstances in which microcomputers might be used. Moreover, if the organization is not to sustain unacceptable losses from threats that eventuate, the security administrator must now rely on a larger number of people to comply with security policies and procedures.

Whatever the particular organizational circumstances in which security administrators must function, however, top management must define its authority and allocate its responsibilities carefully. Auditors must evaluate whether management has given proper consideration to the security administrator's role.

They must also assess whether the way in which the role has been established allows incumbents to fulfil their responsibilities effectively and efficiently. Finally, auditors must consider whether the incumbent is competent and trustworthy.

SUMMARY

Information systems security administrators are responsible for ensuring that information systems assets are secure. Assets are secure when the expected losses that will occur from threats eventuating over some time period are at an acceptable level.

Controls must protect the security of physical information systems assets (personnel, hardware, facilities, supplies, and documentation) and logical assets (data/information and software). Security administrators tend to have responsibility for controls that guard against malicious and nonmalicious threats to physical assets and malicious threats to logical assets.

A major task of security administrators is to conduct a security program. A security program is a series of ongoing, regular, periodic reviews conducted to ensure that assets associated with the information systems function are safeguarded adequately. It comprises eight steps: *(1)* preparation of a project plan, *(2)* identification of assets, *(3)* valuation of assets, *(4)* threats identification, *(5)* threats likelihood assessment, *(6)* exposures analysis, *(7)* controls adjustment, and *(8)* report preparation.

Nine major threats to the security of information systems assets are *(1)* fire—well-designed, reliable fire-protection systems must be implemented; *(2)* water—facilities must be designed and sited to mitigate losses from water damage; *(3)* energy variations—voltage regulators, circuit breakers, and uninterruptible power supplies can be used; *(4)* structural damage—facilities must be designed to withstand structural damage; *(5)* pollution—regular cleaning of facilities and equipment should occur; *(6)* unauthorized intrusion—physical intrusion and eavesdropping can be prevented via physical access controls, prevention of electromagnetic emissions, and proper siting of facilities; *(7)* viruses and worms—controls should be implemented to prevent use of virus-infected programs and to close security loopholes that allow worms to propagate; *(8)* misuse of software, data, and services—a code of conduct should govern the actions of information systems employees; and *(9)* hackers—strong, logical access controls should mitigate expected losses from the activities of hackers.

In small organizations that use turnkey systems, the president or accountant might assume responsibility for security-administration functions. In medium-sized organizations, the security-administration role might be performed by the computer operations manager. In large organizations, the security administrator might report to the chief information officer or the manager who has responsibility for overall organizational security.

In the event security is compromised, two controls of last resort must exist to restore operations and to mitigate losses from the disaster that occurs. A disaster recovery plan specifies backup and recovery procedures to be undertaken when disaster strikes. Adequate insurance also must be available to replace information systems assets and to cover the extra costs associated with restoring normal operations.

Security administration becomes more difficult when the information systems function is decentralized and distributed. Information systems assets are dispersed across a greater number of sites. Controls must be in place and working to preserve security at each of these sites. Moreover, reliance must be placed on a greater number of people to perform security functions.

Review Questions

7-1 When is an information systems asset *secure*?

7-2 In the context of information systems assets, briefly explain the difference between physical security and logical security.

7-3 Briefly define what is meant by a security program. What are the eight major steps that must be undertaken during the conduct of a security program?

7-4 Why is it important that a project plan be prepared for a security program? Who should be responsible for preparing the plan? Who should be responsible for approving the plan?

7-5 Briefly explain the nature of the "aggregation" problem during the assets identification phase of a security program. What basis can be used to choose the "right" level of aggregation?

7-6 Why might the value of an asset differ depending on who is undertaking the valuation? If different values are assigned to the same asset, which value should security administrators use when valuing the asset?

7-7 Briefly describe two techniques that can be used to value assets. What are the relative strengths and limitations of the techniques you identify?

7-8 What is meant by a threat? In the context of information systems assets, identify two sources of threats that are external to an organization and two sources of threats that are internal to an organization. Give an example of a threat that might eventuate from each source.

7-9 Give two techniques that security administrators can use to estimate the likelihood of the occurrence of a threat. Under what situations would one of these techniques be used in preference to the other?

7-10 Briefly describe the *four* major tasks that must be undertaken during the exposures analysis phase of a security program.

7-11 How are internal control questionnaires useful during the exposures analysis phase of a security program?

7-12 Briefly explain how scenarios analysis might be used in the exposures analysis phase of a security program. Under what circumstance is scenarios analysis likely to be most useful?

7-13 Using probability theory, briefly explain how security administrators calculate the expected losses from an exposure.

7-14 What activities are undertaken during the controls adjustment phase of a security program?

7-15 Briefly describe the contents of the security report prepared at the conclusion of a security program. From the viewpoint of having recommendations accepted, what is the most critical aspect of the security report?

7-16 List the major points that should be covered during an audit of security controls over the information systems function to assess the adequacy of hand-held fire extinguishers.

7-17 What is the purpose of covering hardware with a protective fabric when it is not in use?

7-18 Briefly discuss the responsibilities of security administrators with respect to maintenance of the supply of energy to the information systems function.

7-19 Outline the steps you might undertake as an auditor to determine whether a mainframe computer facility could withstand structural damage.

7–20 Briefly describe *two* problems that can be caused by the presence of dust within a computer facility. What controls can be exercised to limit the effects of pollutants in (a) a mainframe computer room, and (b) a microcomputer work area?

7–21 From a security viewpoint, what advantages accrue from having no windows in a computer facility, providing only one entrance to the facility, and placing the facility on an upper floor of a building?

7–22 Briefly describe two ways in which data integrity can be violated using an electronic bug. Where in a computer facility are bugs most likely to be placed?

7–23 What are the most vulnerable points in a data communications network with respect to wiretapping? What actions can security administrators take to prevent or inhibit wiretapping?

7–24 Briefly distinguish between viruses and worms. List two controls over viruses and worms (one for viruses and one for worms) that security administrators might implement to reduce exposures.

7–25 For each of the following threats, give a control that might reduce exposures:
a Pirated software
b Violation of the licensing conditions pertaining to a proprietary database
c Employee use of an organization's computer time for private purposes

7–26 Give one preventive control and one detective control over the activities of computer hackers.

7–27 What are the controls of last resort? Briefly explain the nature of each.

7–28 Briefly describe the major components of an emergency plan.

7–29 Briefly describe the major components of a backup plan.

7–30 What considerations affect the choice of a backup site?

7–31 Briefly describe the major components of a recovery plan. Why are the responsibilities of the recovery committee an important component of the plan?

7–32 What are the purposes of the test-plan component of a disaster recovery plan? How does a "phased approach" facilitate testing of disaster recovery procedures?

7–33 Briefly explain the difference between a hot-site and cold-site backup and recovery facility.

7–34 Identify *nine* major aspects of the information systems function that must be covered by an insurance policy. What are the security administrator's responsibilities after the insurance policy has been agreed upon and signed?

7–35 For the following types of organizations, who is likely to perform the role of the security administrator?
a A medium-sized organization that has its own data processing facility
b A small organization that uses a microcomputer for its data processing
c A large organization that has multiple data processing facilities

Multiple-Choice Questions

7–1 Security administrators are *least likely* to have responsibility for:
a Malicious threats to physical assets
b Nonmalicious threats to logical assets
c Malicious threats to logical assets
d Nonmalicious threats to physical assets

7–2 An information systems security program is:

    a A one-shot investigation to determine the state of logical and physical security

    b A specialized piece of software used to monitor and control access to information systems assets

    c The evidence collection and evidence evaluation procedures auditors use to evaluate how well hardware and software are safeguarded

    d A series of ongoing, regular, periodic evaluations conducted to ensure information systems assets are safeguarded adequately

7–3 For the following steps in a security program, what is the *most likely* sequence in which they will be conducted?

    I   Controls identification

    II Exposures analysis

    III Assets valuation

    IV Threats identification

    a I, III, IV, II

    b IV, III, II, I

    c III, IV, I, II

    d I, IV, II, III

7–4 Which of the following is *least likely* to be a component of a security evaluation project plan?

    a Organization of the project team

    b Risk-analysis method to be used

    c Resources budget

    d Schedule for task completion

7–5 When valuing an information systems asset for security evaluation purposes, which of the following statements is *most likely* to be *false*?

    a Accidental loss of an asset will be more serious than a loss that arises through an irregularity

    b Losses become more serious as use of the asset is denied for a longer period

    c The value of an asset varies across users of the asset

    d Management will be less concerned about competitors gaining access to an old version of a master file

7–6 The primary objective of the asset-valuation phase in a security evaluation is to:

    a Develop users' sensitivity to the possible consequences of a threat

    b Determine an accurate monetary value for all assets

    c Obtain consensus among users about the losses that will arise from a threat that eventuates

    d Determine the controls needed to protect assets

7–7 A threat from which of the following sources is *most likely* to affect the *logical* security of information systems assets?

    a Hardware suppliers

    b Utility suppliers

    c Environmentalists

    d Hackers

7–8 Which of the following is *most likely* to be able to provide information on the likelihood of a fire destroying a mainframe computer facility?

    a The facility's operations manager

    b Users of the facility

    c The facility's insurer

    d Top management

7–9 An exposure is:
  a Any threat that may eventuate
  b Any threat for which no controls have been implemented
  c The expected loss that will occur over some time period, given the reliability of the controls in place
  d The expected loss that will occur prior to implementing any controls

7–10 Which of the following activities is *not* a task during the exposures-analysis phase of a security program?
  a Identifying the source of threats to the assets
  b Assessing the losses that will result if a threat circumvents the controls that are in place
  c Assessing the reliability of the controls that are in place
  d Evaluating the likelihood that a threat will be successful given the controls that are in place

7–11 During a security evaluation, an internal control questionnaire is *most* useful in undertaking which of the following tasks?
  a Assessing the reliability of the controls that are in place
  b Identifying the new controls needed to enhance security over the information systems function
  c Identifying the exposures that exist
  d Identifying the controls that are in place

7–12 Which of the following tasks is *most* facilitated by scenario analyses?
  a Identifying controls and their associated level of reliability
  b Identifying how threats can circumvent controls
  c Determining the assets to be protected
  d Calculating the probability of threat occurrence

7–13 Reducing exposures to an acceptable level means:
  a All controls implemented are reliable
  b Residual losses have been eliminated
  c Threats for which no control exists have a low probability of occurrence
  d The costs of implementing and operating further controls exceed the reduction in expected losses that will occur

7–14 Which of the following should *not* be used as a basis for determining new controls that might be implemented over information systems assets?
  a Choose controls that emphasize design secrecy
  b Examine the types of controls used over the same types of information systems assets in other organizations
  c Analyze the scenarios developed during the exposures analysis phase
  d Review the answers to questions on the internal control questionnaires completed during the exposures analysis phase

7–15 Which of the following is *not* a component of the final security report presented to management?
  a Recommendations on existing safeguards that should be changed
  b A recommendation on the single control configuration that, in the opinion of the project team, must be implemented
  c A plan for implementing the safeguards recommended
  d Scenarios describing the nature of some exposures identified

7–16 Which of the following statements about halon gas as a fire suppressant is *false*?
  a It is relatively safe for humans
  b It has detrimental effects on the earth's ozone layer

      c It is chemically unstable

      d It is noncorrosive

7–17 Which of the following controls is *least likely* to reduce the likelihood of losses to information systems assets arising from water damage that occurs as the result of a cyclone or hurricane?

      a Have a dry moat around buildings

      b Use a dry-pipe automatic sprinkler system

      c Cover hardware with protective fabric

      d Locate hardware above the ground floor

7–18 The purpose of a voltage regulator is to:

      a Protect hardware against temporary increases in power

      b Protect hardware against sustained power surges

      c Compensate when brownouts occur

      d Protect the contents of memory when a blackout occurs

7–19 Which of the following controls is likely to be *most* effective at *preventing* losses that result from structural damage to the building in which a mainframe computer facility is housed?

      a Voltage regulator

      b Reinforced floors

      c Failsafe doors

      d Halon gas system

7–20 Which of the following is *not* a control to prevent pollution?

      a Prohibition of food in the computer room

      b Filters on air conditioning

      c Confining decollation to the computer room only

      d Placing antistatic rugs at doorways

7–21 The unchecked emission of electromagnetic signals is a concern because:

      a The signals can be picked up and printed on a remote device

      b The signals interfere with the correct functioning of the central processor

      c Noise pollution levels increase as a result

      d They facilitate visual eavesdropping

7–22 Which of the following is the *most likely* source of a worm program?

      a Another computer connected to the same communications network as the infected computer

      b Public domain software obtained by a personal computer user from a reputable bulletin board

      c A third-party, multi-user operating system for a standalone minicomputer

      d A proprietary database purchased for use on a local area network

7–23 Which of the following controls is *most likely* to protect an organization's investment in developing and maintaining a proprietary database?

      a Copyright laws

      b A registered trademark

      c Clauses in the licensing agreement

      d A patent

7–24 Which of the following controls is *most likely* to protect an organization's information systems from computer hackers?

      a Card-key locks

      b A virus detection program

      c Encryption of programs

      d Hard-to-determine passwords

7–25 Which of the following is *not* a component of the emergency plan?
   a Personnel to be notified upon the occurrence of a disaster
   b Evacuation procedures
   c Restart priorities
   d Equipment shutdown protocols

7–26 Which of the following is *not* a component of the backup plan?
   a Site where resources can be assembled and operations restarted
   b Procedures for periodically testing that recovery can be effected
   c Priorities to be assigned to recovering the various systems
   d Personnel who are responsible for gathering the backup resources

7–27 The *primary* purpose of the recovery plan is to:
   a Specify precisely how recovery will be effected
   b Identify which applications are to be recovered immediately
   c Identify a recovery committee that will be responsible for working out the specifics of the recovery to be undertaken
   d Specify how backup is to be assembled for recovery purposes

7–28 Which of the following types of backup facilities rely *most* heavily on an organization's hardware vendor to effect recovery?
   a Reciprocal agreement
   b Warm site
   c Cold site
   d Hot site

7–29 Business interruption insurance covers:
   a Additional costs incurred because the organization is not operating from its normal facilities
   b Costs involved in reconstructing the computer facility
   c Claims made by customers because the organization cannot service its customers
   d Loss in business income because the organization is unable to trade

7–30 If an organization has its own information systems staff but insufficient security work exists to justify a separate security administration position, responsibility for security matters might be vested in the:
   a Controller
   b Computer operations manager
   c Systems analysis manager
   d Internal auditor

Exercises and Cases

7–1 Kiwi Kapers Limited (KKL) is a New Zealand-based manufacturer and retailer of sports clothing with headquarters in Dunedin. Although its manufacturing facilities are all located in Dunedin, its retail facilities are scattered throughout Southeast Asia, especially in Australia, Singapore, and Indonesia.

   KKL is an aggressive and innovative user of information systems to support its manufacturing and retail activities. It has a large mainframe computer in Dunedin as well as minicomputers in each of its overseas offices. The minicomputers are linked to the mainframe via communications lines. They fully support the information processing needs of the local offices (e.g., debtors, creditors, general ledger). In addition, they are used to transmit electronic mail and summary information to Dunedin and to receive electronic mail and information on shipments, inventory levels, budgets, and so on from head office.

Microcomputers are also used throughout the company. Some are connected to local area networks which in turn are connected to local office minicomputers or the head office mainframe. Some, however, are used as stand-alone personal computers. In several of the larger overseas offices, the minicomputer provides a gateway to the head office mainframe and in turn to microcomputers connected to other local area networks.

You are a member of the external audit firm that has just taken over the audit of KKL. Your partner has asked you to undertake a review of the security-administration function. In this light, you interview the information systems security administrator of KKL to determine whether he undertakes regular security reviews. He informs you that he undertakes an annual evaluation of information systems security within KKL and that he involves management and users in this review. You ask whether he has any documentation on the recent reviews, and he hands you reports covering the past three years' security reviews.

When you examine the three security review reports, you find they address security only within the Dunedin mainframe facility. They do not cover security over computer facilities within the overseas offices. Moreover, apart from a limited examination of one local area network of microcomputers connected to the Dunedin mainframe, they do not address security over KKL's microcomputer facilities.

When you ask the security administrator about the limited scope of the security reviews that have been conducted, he indicates that so far he has had neither the time nor the resources to evaluate security over computer facilities other than the mainframe. He points out, however, that two years ago he developed security policies and guidelines for all overseas offices. The managers in charge of overseas offices understand that they must ensure compliance with these guidelines in their offices. Moreover, in conjunction with some of the major microcomputer users in Dunedin, he is currently developing security policies and guidelines for microcomputer facilities.

Required.   In light of your findings, write a brief report for your partner advising him how you believe the audit of KKL should now proceed.

7–2 You are a security consultant who has been employed by First Singaporean, a large bank based in Singapore, to examine the adequacy of security controls over a new site that it established nine months ago to house its mainframe computer facilities.

At first glance, the new facilities seem impressive. The bank has purchased an old warehouse. To disguise the purpose of the warehouse, its wooden facade remains, but internally it has been extensively refurbished in an attempt to set up a secure facility. The location of the warehouse and its purpose are known to only a small number of people who are employees of the bank. These persons have signed a secrecy agreement in relation to the operations and location of the warehouse.

As part of your review of physical controls, you examine the adequacy of controls to prevent and detect fire. When you tour the computer room, you notice that there are no hand-held fire extinguishers placed at strategic locations throughout the room. You question the operations manager about this apparent weakness. He assures you that this is not a control weakness. He informs you that a sophisticated heat-detection system has been set up in the computer room that will detect even the smallest fire. As soon as a fire is detected, an extinguisher system will dump a gas suppressant into the room after a 30-second delay. Operators have been instructed to clear the room immediately when the alarm sounds because the suppressant is somewhat toxic. Consequently, he argues, hand-held extinguishers are not needed. Indeed, he contends they would be dangerous as they might cause operators to delay their exit from the computer room when the alarm sounds.

When you interview several operators about the fire evacuation procedures outlined by the operations manager, it is clear they are familiar with the procedures and that they are practiced regularly. One operations supervisor also points out that six months ago there was an electrical fire in the computer room. The evacuation procedures worked smoothly, and the fire alarm and suppressant system worked perfectly. Only minor damage was incurred as a result of the fire, and no one was injured.

Required. At this stage, what are your conclusions about the adequacy of the controls described by the operations manager? How will you now proceed in terms of your investigation of fire prevention and detection controls for the computer room?

7–3 Assemblit, Inc., is a medium-sized parts manufacturing company based in London with distribution outlets in the major cities throughout Great Britain. It has a mainframe computer in its London headquarters. Distribution outlets all have microcomputers that are connected via communications lines to the London mainframe.

As a member of the external audit team of the company, you have gathered the following information on its operations:

1 All the company's major application systems are computerized; some are online real-time update systems, and some are batch systems.

2 The company uses a database management system. The system was purchased initially to aid bill-of-materials processing (online real-time update system), but now it is used extensively with other application systems.

3 All application source data is captured at microcomputer terminals in head-office branches and each distribution outlet.

4 The mainframe runs six days a week, two shifts a day. Sunday and the third shift are available for "hands-on" development and testing of application systems by programmers and analysts. During normal operations, however, only the operators and the system programmer have access to the computer room. Access is controlled using a card lock system.

5 Assemblit's mainframe computer facility is located in the basement of its head office. A floor plan is attached (see Figure 7–12).

6 The following information systems staff are employed:
   a An information systems manager
   b Six analysts
   c 15 programmers
   d Five operators (one–two per shift; shifts rotated)
   e One control clerk (day shift only)
   f One system programmer
   g One librarian (day shift only)

7 The control clerk and the analysts set up daily processing schedules a day in advance.

8 During the week, programmers and analysts use microcomputer terminals for development and maintenance work. The company has purchased powerful software to support online programming work.

9 Program development and maintenance work must be authorized by the analyst in charge of an application system.

10 Copies of all disk files are taken twice a week for backup purposes. The backup files are stored on site in a special fire-resistant vault room.

11 The vendor has promised to provide backup hardware within a few days if an emergency occurs.

12 Output is placed in trays just outside the computer room. Every hour the control clerk picks up output and forwards it to users. Users reconcile input to output and notify the control clerk if there are any discrepancies.

Required.   On the basis of the information you have so far, write a short report for your manager indicating suspected control weaknesses.

FIGURE 7–12. Floor plan — Assemblit mainframe facility.

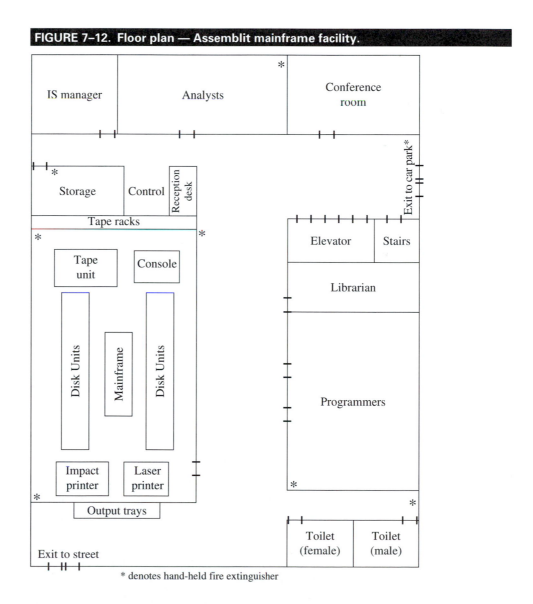

* denotes hand-held fire extinguisher

7–4 Orchard Enterprises Limited (OEL) is a medium-sized Miami-based distributor of leisureware fashion garments. It has a mainframe computer in its Miami headquarters to process its major application systems. In addition, it has a large number of microcomputers to provide personal support for its staff. These microcomputers are connected to various local area networks which are in turn connected to the mainframe.

You are the partner in charge of the external audit of OEL. One day, as you are working with one of your audit managers to plan OEL's year-end audit work, you receive a telephone call from OEL's managing director. He is extremely distressed. One of his executives had been using her personal computer. As she commenced her work, she found many of her critical files had been deleted. When she tried to recover her files from backup copies, she found the backup had been corrupted. The situation was investigated by one of OEL's programmers, and he believes that a virus has been introduced into the system. Although he has no proof, he suspects the virus has been planted by a programmer who was fired six months earlier after repeated counseling about his poor performance. It appears the programmer introduced the virus shortly before he was fired. The virus has remained relatively dormant, however, until it was triggered by the date on which the executive used her machine. Over the six-month period, however, it has been progressively corrupting backup files. The damage done to backup has increased as time has passed.

The managing director indicates that he has ordered all computers to be shut down pending further investigations. He asks your advice on how he should now proceed. He also asks whether the discovery of the virus will mean the costs of the year-end audit work will increase significantly and what implications it will have for the audit opinion you issue.

Required. Write some brief notes in preparation for an urgent meeting with the managing director where you will attempt to answer his questions.

7–5 Money Mover (MM) is a public electronic funds transfer network with its head office and major computer switch based in Melbourne. The company has computer switches in each capital city throughout Australia that are linked into a national communications network. Approximately 150 financial institutions—banks, building societies, credit unions—use the network to provide automatic teller machine and point-of-sale services to their customers.

MM has been in operation for only a few years, but during this time it has been very successful. It has used cutting-edge technology, high-quality innovative services, and aggressive pricing to attract customers away from other electronic funds transfer networks. Moreover, any new financial institutions that have entered the Australian market have inevitably selected MM to provide their electronic funds transfer services in preference to other network vendors.

As a consultant specializing in computer controls and audit, you have been hired by the managing director of MM to examine the state of controls within the electronic funds transfer system. She explains to you that an increasing number of potential customers are requesting some type of independent assurance that controls within the system are reliable. Accordingly, the board of directors of MM has decided to initiate a controls review of the entire system so that a third-party "letter of comfort" can be provided to potential customers.

The initial part of your controls review focuses on the main switch in Melbourne. As part of your review of physical access controls, you note one day during a visit that one of MM's system programmers has a card key that provides him with access to the computer room. You interview the supervising operator, and he informs you that all system programmers have similar keys.

As a result of this finding, you interview the managing director to find out why systems programmers have access to the computer room. She argues that they need this access because they are often called in at any hour of the day or night to correct problems "on the fly" that customers are experiencing with the system. For example, customers might be having problems with a communications line, and the system programmer has to diagnose the problem and correct it as soon as possible so that continuous service can be maintained.

You explain to the managing director that you are concerned about the possibility of system programmers undertaking unauthorized activities, particularly if they come in during the middle of the night when no one else is present in the computer room. She laughs and says that system programmers can carry out unauthorized activities any time they want because of their in-depth knowledge of the system. Accordingly, she says that it is useless to exercise any type of physical access controls over them. Besides, she argues there are certain compensating controls over system programmers. First, she has pointed out to the system programmers their responsibility for preserving system security and that they will be fired immediately if any breach of security is discovered. Second, because MM employs only four system programmers, it will not be hard to pinpoint responsibility if any type of irregularity occurs.

Required. In light of the managing director's responses, how will you now proceed with your investigation? What will be the likely implications, if any, of your current findings for the report you will present to the board of directors?

7–6 Read the description for Case 7–5. The following details apply to the review you are conducting on the state of controls within the company.

As part of your review of the Melbourne switch site, you examine the status of disaster recovery planning. In terms of short-term recovery, controls appear to be in place and working. Backup tapes for all data and programs are stored both on and off site to enable recovery if programs and data are lost for some reason. In addition, protocols for short-term recovery are well documented. Operators seem to be familiar with and well trained in these protocols. From time to time they have to exercise these protocols because some temporary system failure occurs. Because MM claims to offer its customers 24-hour service, all personnel recognize the criticality of being able to recover the system accurately and completely on a timely basis.

When you examine controls over long-term disaster recovery, however, the situation is different. There is no long-term disaster recovery plan, nor are operators and other personnel trained in recovery protocols for a major disaster. For example, it is uncertain how MM would recover from a fire that destroyed the switch or an event that caused major structural damage to the switch.

As a result of your findings, you meet with the managing director to find out why controls in this area are so weak when controls in other areas seem strong. She is surprised by your concern about long-term disaster recovery. She argues that for three reasons it is not cost-effective to prepare a long-term disaster recovery plan and to practice recovery protocols on a regular basis. First, she believes it is useless having a long-term disaster recovery plan because, in the event of a major disaster, timely recovery would be impossible anyway. She points out that it would take several days for the telephone company to reconfigure all the data communications lines to another site. Even if MM had another switch available immediately, it could not operate during this period. Second, she argues that long-term disaster recovery cannot be practiced because MM's customers would not tolerate a decrease in their service levels while disaster recovery exercises were carried out. Unless the recovery protocols are practiced regularly, she points out, they are useless. Third, she contends that eventual recovery will not be a problem anyway. Operations can simply be transferred to another switch in one of the other capital cities. While the telephone company reconfigures data communications lines to the other switch, backup files can be flown to the site with plenty of time to spare. She argues that the customers of MM recognize they will not be able to use their electronic funds transfer facilities during the recovery period, but they accept this situation as a risk of doing business. The only other alternative, she argues, is to replicate all switching facilities in each capital city, and multiple hot sites for backup and recovery purposes are clearly not cost-effective.

Required. Outline how you intend to respond to the managing director's comments in your report to the board of directors on the state of controls in MM's computer operations.

Answers to Multiple-Choice Questions

7–1	b	7–9	c	7–17	b	7–25	c
7–2	d	7–10	a	7–18	a	7–26	b
7–3	c	7–11	d	7–19	b	7–27	c
7–4	b	7–12	b	7–20	c	7–28	c
7–5	a	7–13	d	7–21	a	7–29	d
7–6	a	7–14	a	7–22	a	7–30	b
7–7	d	7–15	b	7–23	c		
7–8	c	7–16	c	7–24	d		

REFERENCES

Anderson, Ronald E., Deborah G. Johnson, Donald Gotterbarn, and Judith Perrolle (1993), "Using the New ACM Code of Ethics in Decision Making," *Communications of the ACM* (February), 98–107.

Bailey, David (1995), "A Philosophy of Security Management," in Marshall D. Abrams, Sushil Jajodia, and Harold J. Podell, eds., *Information Security: An Integrated Collection of Essays.* Los Alamitos, CA: IEEE Computer Society Press, 98–110.

Bannan, John (1996), "Needs Analysis Considerations," *EDPACS* (March), 8–13.

Baskerville, Richard (1988), *Designing Information Systems Security.* New York: John Wiley & Sons.

Baskerville, Richard (1993), "Information Systems Security Design Methods: Implications for Information Systems Development," *ACM Computing Surveys* (December), 375–414.

Bigelow, Robert (1993), "The Legal Dimension of Computer Crime," *The EDP Auditor Journal*, II, 59–66.

Brinkley, Donald L., and Roger R. Schell (1995), "Concepts and Terminology for Computer Security," in Marshall D. Abrams, Sushil Jajodia, and Harold J. Podell, eds., *Information Security: An Integrated Collection of Essays.* Los Alamitos, CA: IEEE Computer Society Press, 40–97.

Caelli, William, Dennis Longley, and Michael Shain (1989), *Information Security for Managers.* New York: Macmillan Stockton.

—— (1991), *Information Security Handbook* New York: Macmillan Stockton.

Cerullo, Michael J. (1981), "Accountants' Role in Computer Contingency Planning," *The CPA Journal* (January), 22–26.

Ciechanowicz, Zbigniew (1997), "Risk Analysis: Requirements, Conflicts and Problems," *Computers & Security*, 16(3), 223–232.

Clarke, Roger A. (1988), "Information Technology and Dataveillance," *Communications of the ACM* (May), 498–512.

Cohen, Fred (1997), "Information System Attacks: A Preliminary Classification Scheme," *Computers & Security*, 16(1), 29–46.

Courtney, Robert H., Jr. (1977), "Security Risk Assessment in Electronic Data Processing Systems," *Proceedings of the 1977 National Computer Conference.* Montvale, NJ: AFIPS Press, 97–104.

Denning, Peter J., ed. (1990), *Computers under Attack: Intruders, Worms, and Viruses.* New York: ACM Press.

Fites, Philip, and Martin P. J. Kratz (1993), *Information Systems Security: A Practitioner's Reference.* New York: Van Nostrand Reinhold.

FitzGerald, Jerry, and Ardra F. FitzGerald (1990), *Designing Controls into Computerized Systems.* Redwood City, CA: Jerry FitzGerald & Associates.

Gardner, Ella Paton, Linda B. Samuels, Barry Render, and Richard L. Coffinberger (1989), "The Importance of Ethical Standards and Computer Crime Laws for Data Security," *Journal of Information Systems Management* (Fall), 42–50.

Gibbs, W. Wayt (1996), "Extinguished," *Scientific American* (June), 104.

Henderson, Stuart (1996), "The Information Systems Security Policy Statement," *EDPACS* (June), 9–18.

Hughes, G. (1990), "Computer Crime: The Liability of Hackers," *The Australian Computer Journal* (May), 47–50.

Kovacich, Gerald (1997), "ISSO Career Development," *Computers & Security*, 16(6), 455–468.

Loch, Karen D., Houston H. Carr, and Merrill E. Warkentin (1992), "Threats to Information Systems: Today's Reality, Yesterday's Understanding," *MIS Quarterly* (June), 173–186.

Longley, Dennis, Michael Shain, and William Caelli (1992), *Information Security: Dictionary of Concepts, Standards and Terms.* New York: Macmillan Stockton.

McLean, Kevin, and Len Watts. (1996),"Evolution of a UK-Sponsored Risk Analysis Methodology," *IS Audit & Control Journal*, III, 32–36.

Parker, Donn B. (1981), *Computer Security Management.* Reston, VA: Reston Publishing Company.

Roberts, D. W. (1990), *Computer Security: Policy, Planning and Practice.* London: Blenheim.

Saddinton, Tricia, ed. (1988), *Security for Small Computer Systems: A Practical Guide for Users.* Oxford: Elsevier Advanced Technology.

Salzman, Thomas (1997), "An Audit Work Program for Reviewing IS Disaster Recovery Plans," *EDPACS* (December), 9–18.

—— (1998), "An Audit Work Program for Reviewing IS Disaster Recovery Plans (Conclusion)," *EDPACS* (January), 8–20.

Stoll, Clifford (1988), "Stalking the Wily Hacker," *Communications of the ACM* (May), 484-497.

Straub, Detmar, and Rosann Webb Collins (1990), "Key Information Liability Issues Facing Managers: Software Piracy, Proprietary Databases, and Individual Rights to Privacy," *MIS Quarterly* (June), 142–156.

Toigo, Jon William (1992), "Auditing and Controlling Environmental Contamination," *EDP Auditing* Boston: Auerbach, Portfolio 76–02–20, 1–10.

Yokes, E. Robert (1989), "Legal Protection for Computer Software," *Communications of the ACM* (February), 169–171.

Operations
Management
Controls

Chapter Outline

Chapter Key Points

■ Operations management is responsible for the daily running of
hardware and software facilities so that (a) production
application systems can accomplish their work and
(b) development staff can design, implement, and maintain
application systems.

■ Operations management typically exercises controls over
the following functions: (a) computer operations,
(b) communications network control, (c) data preparation and
entry, (d) production control, (e) file library, (f) documentation
and program library, (g) help desk/technical support,
(h) capacity planning and performance monitoring, and
(i) outsourced operations.

■ Controls over computer operations govern the activities that
support the day-to-day execution of either test or production
systems. Three types of controls must exist: (a) those that
prescribe the functions that either human operators or
automated operations facilities must perform; (b) those
that prescribe how jobs are to be scheduled on the
hardware/software platform; and (c) those that prescribe how
hardware is to be maintained in good operating order.

■ Network operations govern the activities of wide area and
local area networks. In wide area networks, careful control
should be exercised over network control terminals. These
terminals allow powerful access and action privileges to be
executed to monitor and maintain a network. In local area
networks, file servers must be secured. Unauthorized access to
a file server can allow an intruder to disrupt the operations of
a local area network or compromise data integrity within the
network.

■ Data preparation and data entry facilities should be designed to
promote speed and accuracy and to maintain the well-being of
keyboard operators. Keyboard operators should also be well
trained to perform data preparation and data entry tasks.
Suitable backup must exist for input data and data preparation
and data entry devices.

■ The production control section under operations management performs five major functions: (a) receipt and dispatch of input and output, (b) job scheduling, (c) management of service-level agreements with users, (d) transfer pricing/chargeout control, and (e) acquisition of computer consumables. Careful control must be exercised over receipt of input and dispatch of output to ensure input is accepted only from authorized parties, input is submitted on a timely basis, and output is provided only to authorized parties. Job schedules must be established to ensure only authorized production jobs are executed. Production control staff establish and test the job control files that manage production execution of systems. If a computer operations facility signs service-level agreements with its users, production control staff monitor compliance with the agreements. When users are charged for their consumption of information-processing resources, production control staff are responsible for billing users, collecting receipts, and following up on unpaid accounts and complaints. Production control staff are also responsible for acquiring and managing consumables (such as printer paper) that the computer operations facility uses.

■ The file-library function within the operations area takes responsibility for the management of an organization's machine-readable storage media. Four functions must be undertaken: (a) ensuring that removable storage media are stored securely in a clean environment; (b) ensuring that storage media are used only for authorized purposes; (c) maintaining storage media in good working order; and (d) locating storage media appropriately at either on-site or off-site facilities.

■ The documentation and program library function takes responsibility for maintaining the documentation needed to support computer operations and managing the inventory of acquired or licensed software. Documentation should be kept up-to-date and be used only by authorized parties. Acquired or licensed software should be carefully managed so it is not lost or stolen, its documentation is not lost or stolen, illegal copies of the software are not made, use of the software complies with the terms and conditions of the licensing agreement, and suitable backup for the software is maintained.

■ The help desk/technical support function in the operations area has two primary responsibilities: (a) assisting end users to employ end-user hardware and software, such as microcomputers, spreadsheet packages, database management packages, and local area networks and (b) providing technical support for production systems by assisting with problem resolution. If the help desk/technical support area is to function effectively and efficiently, it must be staffed by competent and trustworthy personnel and be supported by a logging and reporting mechanism to help manage user queries and complaints.

■ Operations management must continuously monitor the performance of the hardware/software platform to ensure that systems are executing efficiently, an acceptable response time or turnaround time is being achieved, and an acceptable level of uptime is occurring. Performance statistics can be used to determine whether (a) unauthorized activities are occurring, (b) systems performance is acceptable, and (c) more hardware and software resources are needed.

■ Operations management often has responsibility for managing the day-to-day activities associated with an outsourcing contract. Four types of controls must be exercised: (a) ongoing evaluation of the financial viability of the outsourcing vendor, (b) ensuring compliance with the outsourcing contract's terms and conditions, (c) ensuring the ongoing reliability of controls in the outsourcing vendor's operations, and (d) maintaining procedures for disaster recovery with the outsourcing vendor.

INTRODUCTION

Operations management is responsible for the daily running of hardware and software facilities so that *(1)* production application systems can accomplish their work and *(2)* development staff can design, implement, and maintain application systems. Given the criticality of information systems to many organizations, many operations managers consider they run and maintain the "engine" of their organizations. The tasks they perform are often straightforward; nevertheless, their work can be critical to an organization's success.

In the late 1980s and early 1990s, major changes occurred to the operations function. From an auditor's perspective, four were especially significant. First, many operations tasks were automated. As a result, some significant concerns auditors previously had about the authenticity, accuracy, completeness, effectiveness, and efficiency of actions undertaken by operations personnel dissipated. Second, in many organizations the operations function became increasingly decentralized. For example, as microcomputers and minicomputers proliferated, end users took responsibility for some operations functions (such as the maintenance of backup for their files). As a result, audits of the operations function became more difficult to undertake because they were no longer localized to a single, central site. Third, conflicting pressures emerged with respect to operations efficiency. On the one hand, hardware had become relatively cheap, so efficiency was less of a concern. On the other hand, users became more demanding in terms of their performance expectations for the operations function. As a result, many internal auditors found increasingly they had to monitor how well the operations function met the service-level agreements made between the operations function and end users. Fourth, many organizations began to outsource their operations function. They believed they should focus their efforts on those tasks they performed best and those that contributed most to their primary mission. They contracted out those they believed others could perform better and those that were subsidiary to their primary mission. As a result, auditors became increasingly concerned about the control implications of contractual agreements with third parties.

In this chapter we examine the controls that should exist over eight functions that are the responsibility of operations management: *(1)* computer operations, *(2)* communications network control, *(3)* data preparation and entry, *(4)* production control, *(5)* file library, *(6)* documentation and program library, *(7)* help desk/technical support, and *(8)* capacity planning and performance monitoring. In addition, we examine the control issues that arise when organizations outsource their operations function. Our objectives are to understand good practice in the operations area and to be able to determine the implications of control weaknesses for the conduct of our audits.

COMPUTER OPERATIONS

Controls over computer operations govern the activities that directly support the day-to-day execution of either test or production systems on the hardware/software platforms available. Three types of controls must exist: *(1)* those that prescribe the functions that either human operators or automated operations facilities must perform, *(2)* those that prescribe how jobs are to be scheduled on a hardware/software platform, and *(3)* those that prescribe how hardware is to be maintained in good operating order. The following subsections discuss each type of control and their implications for audits.

Operations Controls

Many types of activities need to be undertaken to support the execution of programs on a computer; for example, programs have to be started and terminated, storage media have to be loaded onto their read/write units, appropriate forms and documents must be loaded onto a printer, and output must be retrieved and distributed to users. A large number of general housekeeping activities also must be performed; for example, storage space must be retrieved from files whose useful life has expired, backup files must be made routinely, and disk storage space must be reorganized to promote more efficient retrieval of data. From time to time, emergency actions also must be undertaken; for example, files must be recovered after a disk crash, machines must be powered down when air conditioning units fail, and printers must be serviced when paper jams occur.

Historically, all these activities were undertaken or initiated by computer operators. They used a console terminal to start and stop programs according to a run schedule, loaded tapes and removable disks onto their respective drives, did backup at a certain time, and so on. Nowadays, most activities previously performed by computer operators have been automated. In many organizations, for example, operators no longer have to load and unload storage media. Only fixed disk storage is used. Alternatively, robotics facilities might exist that load and unload removable storage media such as tapes or cartridges. In addition, *automated operations facilities* (AOFs) might have been implemented to start and stop programs according to a predetermined schedule, make backup, respond to system messages, restart operations in the event of some types of failure, retrieve storage space from expired files, and so on. In these so-called lights-out facilities, human intervention is rarely needed.

Where human intervention is required in operations activities, the primary control to be used is specification of and compliance with a set of standard procedures (Figure 8–1). For example, if operators have to undertake backup activities, the procedures they should follow must be determined and documented. Operators should then be trained to follow these procedures. Documentation and training is especially important when operations procedures are executed infrequently. For example, having to recover from a disk crash should be a rare event. When this type of disaster occurs, however, cor-

Backup Activities	Notes
1. Monitor and respond to requests on the NSR admin screen.	Check screen at least every ten minutes. Restore requests are to be mounted in the single drive. Restore requests to be logged in the "Recovery Tape Mounts Log." Recently recycled tapes may need to be relabelled. Record system faults in Operations Shift Message Log and report to the System Administrator.
2. Review system logs and report problems.	Successful backup reports can be deleted immediately. Unsuccessful backup reports include details about the problem and client contact information. Unless it is a known ongoing problem, unsuccessful backups should be reported to the contact by phone; then the reports may be deleted. Bootstrap reports need to be printed and filed, as well as being filed electronically. The daily Service Reports are filed electronically.

FIGURE 8–1. Some standard operations procedures.
Used by permission, The University of Queensland.

rect actions by operators are essential to complete recovery. They must have high-quality, documented procedures to follow.

Traditional controls like separation of duties, effective supervision, and rotation of duties also reduce the exposures associated with operator activities. For example, operators should not be allowed to perform programming work. Because they have direct access to files, documents, and printers, they might modify programs to perpetrate an impropriety—for example, alter a payroll program and print an unauthorized check. In this light, controls should restrict the access operators have to programs and data files. Similarly, improprieties are less likely to occur if two or more operators work a shift and shifts are rotated. A malicious operator has fewer opportunities, for example, to erase critical backup or physically damage hardware.

Where operations activities are automated, auditors must be concerned about the authenticity, accuracy, and completeness of the automated operations. The following sorts of questions must be addressed:

1. Who authorizes the design, implementation, and maintenance of AOF parameters?
2. Are there standards to guide the design, implementation, and maintenance of AOF parameters?
3. Are AOF parameters maintained in a secure file?
4. How are new or modified AOF parameters tested?
5. Is there ongoing monitoring of the authenticity, accuracy, and completeness of AOF operations?
6. How well are AOF parameters documented?
7. Is an up-to-date copy of AOF parameters stored off site?

An AOF can also present problems for backup and recovery. In the event an AOF fails and human intervention is required, operations staff might no longer have the knowledge and experience needed to sustain operations in manual mode. Moreover, slight differences in the hardware/software platform at a backup site could render the AOF inoperable until parameters are modified appropriately. It might not be possible to carry out these modifications quickly, particularly in times of stress.

Auditors' evaluation of operations controls is further complicated by the diversity of hardware/software platforms encountered and the extensive decentralization of the operations function that has occurred in many organizations. Auditors might find, for example, that an AOF can support some of the platforms used by an organization but not all of them. As a result, they must evaluate both automated and manual operations and, in particular, the quality of the interface between automated and manual operations. In a mixed automated-manual operations environment, whether recovery can be effected in the event of a disaster should be a particular concern.

As another example of the diverse audit approaches that might be needed, consider operations control requirements for a large mainframe computer versus a microcomputer. The mainframe might support a lights-out facility. Accordingly, the auditor would address the kinds of control concerns described previously. The microcomputer, on the other hand, might be operated by an end user. If no disaster eventuates, there might be few concerns about operations controls over the microcomputer. Assume, however, that critical applications and files are stored on the microcomputer's hard disk and that one day the end user accidentally executes a command that erases the hard disk. The end user might recognize the error and halt processing before the entire disk is erased. In an attempt to recover the situation, he or she might then try to employ utilities to restore deleted files. The end user's inexperience with the utilities, however, could exacerbate the situation. In short, auditors must consider the need for operations controls across all hardware/software platforms.

As still another example of the diversity of audit approaches that might be needed, consider some impacts of decentralization on the operations function. In a mainframe environment, for example, backup might be made regularly as a feature of the daily schedule. If minicomputers and microcomputers are dispersed throughout the organization, however, auditors must rely on large numbers of people to be knowledgeable about and be responsible for backup of critical files. Auditors have a more difficult task of collecting evidence on and evaluating the quality of operations controls.

To collect evidence on the quality of operations controls, auditors can examine documentation, undertake interviews, and make observations. In this regard, an important source of evidence is the operating systems log. The log should record all important operations events. Auditors can examine the log for completeness and interview the operations manager to determine whether the log is reviewed regularly for evidence of irregularities. Such reviews should be documented.

Scheduling Controls

Scheduling controls seek to ensure that computers are used only for authorized purposes and that consumption of system resources is efficient. With small computers, these objectives are often difficult to achieve. For example, microcomputers might be given to people to improve their personal productivity. How they then use their microcomputers can be difficult to determine and to control. Contrary to organizational policies, for example, at times they might use them for private consulting purposes. The expected losses that arise from this type of exposure, however, are unlikely to justify a requirement for all microcomputer users to submit schedules of daily jobs they intend to run and to monitor compliance with these schedules.

With large computers, the expected losses from executing unauthorized jobs and poor workload balancing can be high. Production systems should run according to a predetermined schedule set up by applications project managers and the operations manager. The purpose of the schedule is to authorize use of hardware and system software resources by application systems. In addition, where possible the schedule should seek to time the execution of application systems so conflicting resource demands are minimized.

AOFs enforce compliance with an authorized production schedule. Where AOFs are not used, however, the operations manager must monitor compliance with the production schedule. An operating system will provide an audit trail of jobs executed on a machine, and this audit trail can then be checked against the authorized schedule. The overriding concern is for the operations manager always to be alert for evidence of irregularities in the daily execution of jobs. This concern exists even if an organization uses an AOF.

Auditors should check for the existence of and enforcement of a production schedule. If a schedule does not exist or one exists but it is not enforced, the auditor's effectiveness and efficiency objectives are primarily at risk. Jobs might not be completed on time or hardware and software resources might not be used efficiently. The auditor should expand substantive testing to determine, for example, whether users are satisfied with application systems and whether various types of machine resources have high utilization rates.

The asset safeguarding and data integrity objectives might also be at risk. Failure to enforce a production schedule could mean a computer is used for unauthorized purposes, such as the execution of private consulting jobs or unauthorized production of duplicate payroll checks. Again, auditors must expand substantive testing if they assess control risk relating to production scheduling to be high.

Maintenance Controls

Maintenance of computer hardware is either preventive or remedial in nature. Preventive maintenance is undertaken to avoid hardware failure in the first place. Repair maintenance occurs on demand when machine components no longer function properly.

Preventive maintenance is more likely to be undertaken with mainframes than minicomputers and microcomputers. Mainframe vendors recommend preventive maintenance schedules that include routine tests and inspections as well as component replacement. Preventive maintenance with minicomputers and microcomputers, however, usually is minimal. For example, with a microcomputer it involves cleaning a mouse, wiping component covers with a damp, soft, lint-free cloth, and cleaning diskette drives.

The relative amounts of preventive and repair maintenance can always be traded off against each other. More frequent preventive maintenance usually means less frequent repair maintenance. Management's problem is to minimize the total cost of both types of maintenance (Figure 8–2).

Two factors that affect the decision on how much preventive versus repair maintenance should be undertaken are *(1)* the location of the hardware and *(2)* the criticality of the hardware to the operations of an organization. If the hardware is sited at a remote location (e.g., a mining site) where ready access to maintenance engineers is not available, more preventive maintenance work might be undertaken. Similarly, if the hardware is critical to ongoing operations (e.g., a minicomputer acting as a front-end processor in a major financial communications network), more preventive maintenance might be undertaken.

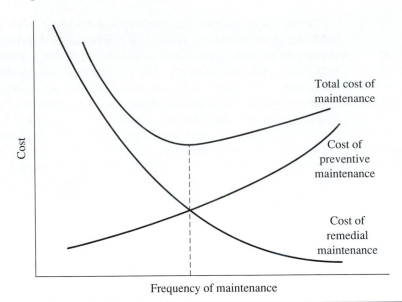

FIGURE 8–2. Trade-off between preventive and remedial maintenance.

In a mainframe and minicomputer environment, performance monitoring software should be used to prepare regular reports on hardware reliability. For example, the operations manager should be able to determine the downtime that has occurred with a particular central processing unit or the number of read/write errors that have occurred with a particular disk drive. The operations manager should also review maintenance reports prepared by maintenance engineers to evaluate whether the levels of preventive and repair maintenance being undertaken are at acceptable levels.

Like system programmers, maintenance engineers can cause some difficult control problems for management. Maintenance engineers have available to them hardware and software tools that allow them to bypass controls. These tools are needed if maintenance is to be carried out effectively and efficiently. Their misuse, however, could mean integrity violations occur.

Depending on the levels of exposure, several basic controls can be exercised over maintenance engineers. Periodically, another engineer might be hired (perhaps a consultant engineer) to evaluate the work of the primary engineer. If more than one engineer is employed to carry out maintenance work, duties can be rotated. Sensitive programs and data might be removed from a machine while it is being maintained. Engineers also might be required to sign a nondisclosure agreement in the event that sensitive data is exposed in the normal course of duties. Management can carry out background checking to assess the likely integrity of engineers.

An auditor's primary concerns about hardware maintenance relate to effectiveness and efficiency objectives. If hardware is unreliable, timely output might not be obtained. Moreover, excessive hardware resources might be needed to accomplish a task. Asset safeguarding and data integrity objectives can also be at risk. Unreliable hardware might corrupt data. Corrupted data, in turn, can present opportunities for misappropriation of assets.

To evaluate how well the maintenance function relating to mainframes and minicomputers is managed, auditors can interview the operations manager, engineers, and operators to determine what maintenance activities are performed and how. They can also observe maintenance engineers and operators undertake their work and examine documentation such as maintenance reports and logs to assess how well the maintenance function is carried out. In the case of microcomputer maintenance, auditors should first identify those machines that carry out critical functions. They can then interview personnel responsible for these machines to evaluate the adequacy of the maintenance function.

NETWORK OPERATIONS

Operations managers have responsibility for the day-to-day operations of any wide area or local area communications networks their organizations use. To discharge this responsibility, they must start and stop network operations and monitor the performance of network communications channels, network devices, and network programs and files.

Wide Area Network Controls

In a wide area network, many different types of incidents require human intervention. For example, a communications line might fail, a program might terminate abnormally, message queues might consume all the storage space available, unauthorized messages on a communications line might be identified, and unacceptable line error rates could occur. Operators must be able to identify when these events occur and reconfigure the network to accommodate them.

An important tool that operators use to manage a wide area network is a *network control terminal* (Figure 8–3). A network control terminal provides access to specialized systems software that allows the following types of functions to be performed:

1. Starting and stopping lines and processes,
2. Monitoring network activity levels,
3. Renaming communications lines,
4. Generating system statistics,
5. Resetting queue lengths,
6. Increasing backup frequency,
7. Inquiring as to system status,
8. Transmitting system warning and status messages, and
9. Examining data traversing a communications line.

Network control terminals can also be used to execute similar functions with respect to the individual devices that are connected to a network. For example, the following types of functions can be executed:

1. Starting up or closing down a terminal,
2. Inquiring as to a terminal's status,
3. Down-line loading of data or programs,
4. Generating control totals for terminal devices such as automatic teller machines (ATMs) and point-of-sale devices, and
5. Sending and receiving terminal warning and error messages.

A network control terminal also allows operators to access and maintain various data files required by communications software. For example, a terminal identification file designates which terminals are legitimate devices within the network. It enables the communications software to check the authenticity of a terminal when it attempts to send or to receive messages. If new terminals are added to the network or existing terminals are removed, this file must be

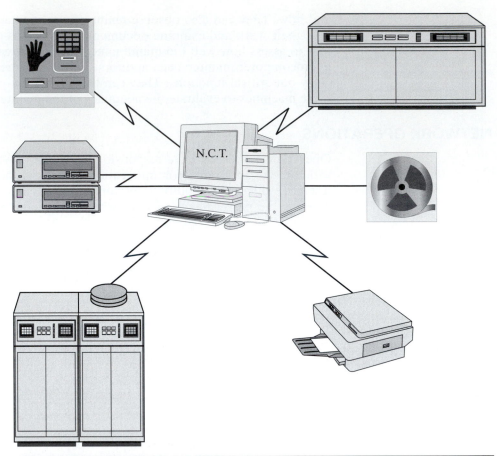

FIGURE 8–3. Management of a communication network using a network control terminal.

updated by a network operator. Similarly, a network control terminal can allow access to various transaction logs. The operator can determine the events surrounding a particular incident in the network. For example, a transaction might have been submitted at an ATM but not received at a mainframe that updates customer accounts. A network control terminal can be used to access logs and to trace the passage of the transaction through the network to the point of its disappearance.

From an asset safeguarding and data integrity perspective, the network control terminal is a critical component within the network. Its misuse could result in substantial disruption to the system or in unauthorized activities going undetected. Accordingly, several controls must be exercised over operator use of a network control terminal:

1. Only senior operators who are well trained and have a sound employment history should perform network control functions.
2. To the extent possible, network control functions should be separated and duties rotated on a regular basis.
3. The network control software must allow access controls to be enforced so that each operator is restricted to performing only certain functions.
4. The network control software must maintain a secure audit trail of all operator activities.

5. Operations management must regularly review the audit trail to determine whether unauthorized network operator activities have occurred.
6. If multiple network control terminals are used, network control functions should be partitioned and restricted to a particular terminal.
7. Documented standards and protocols must exist for network operators.
8. Operations management must regularly review network operator activities for compliance with standards and protocols.

The need for control also applies to the activities of engineers who maintain the network. As with mainframe maintenance, engineers have available to them special hardware and software that enables them to bypass the controls implemented in the network. It is difficult to prevent them from undertaking unauthorized activities and to detect any unauthorized activities when they do occur. The types of compensating controls described earlier—rotation of duties, supervision, and so on—must also be exercised over network engineers. In addition to these asset safeguarding and data integrity concerns, proper management of the network is essential to attaining system effectiveness and system efficiency objectives. If, for example, workloads are not balanced throughout the network, response times might be slow, which in turn can undermine management decision-making effectiveness.

Auditors can evaluate the reliability of controls over the operations of wide area networks using interviews, observations, and review of documentation. For example, auditors can use interviews to evaluate whether network operations staff appear competent and to determine the procedures supposedly used to grant access to network control terminals. They can observe network operators as they carry out their work to determine, for example, whether they are carrying out work in compliance with the access and action privileges they have been granted. They can review reports prepared on the basis of network control terminal logs to evaluate whether the operations manager has identified and followed up on possible irregularities.

Local Area Network Controls

Operations management of local area networks occurs via the facilities provided on file servers. A file server is a computer on which a local area network operating system resides and executes. In addition, shared files and programs (e.g., commercial databases, spreadsheet software) are also stored on a file server, and the operating system maintains its own files (e.g., authorization and configuration files) on a file server.

A file server plays an important role in supporting the access control mechanisms used in a local area network. (Chapter 10 discusses the access control functions provided by a file server further.) From an operational viewpoint, however, operating system utilities that reside on a file server enable operations staff to manage the day-to-day and long-term operations of the network better. For example, the following types of functions can be performed:

1. Available disk space on a file server can be monitored. If a shortage of disk space occurs, the performance of the network can become erratic. Moreover, errors can occur that compromise asset safeguarding and data integrity within the network.
2. Utilization activity and traffic patterns within the network can be monitored. This information can allow operators to reconfigure the network to improve performance, identify users who are using network resources inappropriately, and identify the level of interactions with other networks connected to the

local area network via a gateway or bridge. Moreover, it may allow management to better plan network expansion to accommodate the future needs of network users.

3. Levels of corrupted data within the network can be monitored. This information can allow operators to identify faulty transmission media or sources of interference. Transmission media might have to be replaced or the network reconfigured to reduce noise and cross-talk on transmission media.

4. Special network cards are often employed to connect workstations to a local area network. These cards provide the functionality to allow a workstation to communicate with file servers and other workstations in the network. The network operating system might provide a utility that enables faulty workstation cards to be identified.

5. A file server can be used to execute software that prevents, detects, and removes viruses. In this way, the likelihood of corruption to network resources or to resources in other networks that are connected to the local area network can be reduced.

Besides the utilities provided in the network operating system, other utilities and devices are available to assist with operations management of a local area network. For example, *cable scanners* can be used to identify shorts, breaks, kinks, and intermittent faults within transmission media. The cable scanner will provide a report showing the location of, say, the break in terms of distance from the file server.

Like network control terminals in a wide area network, file servers are critical control components within a local area network. They contain sensitive data and programs that can be used to compromise the security and integrity of the network. For example, access to a file server might enable the network to be reconfigured to include an unauthorized workstation or to read sensitive data that is being transmitted over a communications line. In this light, file servers should

FIGURE 8–4. File server in secure area.

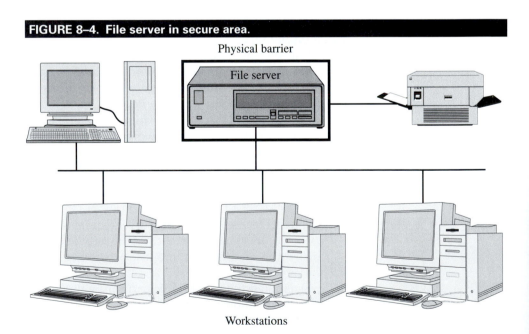

be located in a secure area (Figure 8–4). Furthermore, access to file servers should be restricted to authorized operators who are trustworthy and competent.

Auditors can use interviews, observations, and reviews of documentation to evaluate the reliability of controls over the operations of local area networks. For example, an auditor can interview the operations staff responsible for a local area network to determine the procedures they use to monitor the adequacy of the network hardware and software resources needed to support network users. The auditor can observe whether file servers are located in a secure area and whether access to file servers appears to be restricted to authorized personnel. Reports on available disk storage space in file servers are reviewed to evaluate whether management identifies deficiencies in a timely manner.

DATA PREPARATION AND ENTRY

Historically, all source data for application systems were sent to a data preparation section for keying and verification before it was entered into a computer system. It was keyed, for example, to punched cards or magnetic tape. Nowadays, much source data is keyed into a microcomputer located close to the point of data capture or in the end-user department that takes responsibility for the application system that processes the source data. Much is also entered directly using some type of device like a supermarket scanner or a mouse. Nevertheless, some types of specialized data preparation and entry activities still occur. For example, some financial institutions encode amounts on checks using a magnetic ink character inscribing device (others now read the check with a magnetic ink character reader and key in the amount at a terminal). The checks are subsequently read by a magnetic ink character reader to create a tape file or disk file, which is then used as input to various check processing applications systems.

If data must be keyed from source documents, operations management must ensure keying tasks are well designed. Otherwise, the work of keyboard operators will be slow and error-prone. Major bottlenecks might occur. As a result, keyboard operators could experience high job stress and job-related illnesses. These in turn can lead to high keyboard operator turnover.

Chapter 11 discusses how source documents and input screens can be designed to facilitate keyboarding of source documents. Overall, however, to relieve operator boredom, source document keyboard tasks should be designed so they are no longer than an hour. Keyboard operators also must be able to perceive an end to a task. If source documents continue to arrive unrelentingly, keyboard operators might be unable to cope with the work volume. They might experience frustration and loss of confidence, which in turn can lead to inaccuracies and decreased keying speed.

Irrespective of whether data is obtained indirectly from source documents or directly from, say, customers, keyboard environments and facilities should be designed to promote speed and accuracy and to maintain the well-being of keyboard operators. Poor design can have costly consequences. In the United States, for example, losses from repetition strain injury (RSI) or Occupational Overuse Syndrome (OSS) are now estimated to exceed $50 billion per year

(*Australian Financial Review*, 4 March 1992). The following sorts of factors should be considered:

1. Lighting in a keyboard area should be adequate without causing glare. This factor is especially important when operators have to read poorly prepared source documents or look at display screens for prolonged periods.
2. Acoustically the environment must be neither too noisy nor too quiet. On the one hand, careful choice of carpets, paneling, screens, and flooring reduces noise levels that could distract or irritate. On the other hand, keyboard operators might find it hard to maintain concentration and rhythm in a noise-free environment.
3. The layout of the work area should be uncluttered to facilitate the work flow. Layout considerations include space, amenities, and the position of keyboard devices.
4. Ergonomically designed office equipment should be used to reduce the likelihood of, say, back injury or repetition strain injury. For example, display screens should be nonreflective and positioned at a comfortable viewing distance. Likewise, chairs and tables should be adjustable to allow operators to maintain good posture (Figure 8–5).

Keyboard operator training can be an important means of improving the speed and accuracy with which data is entered into a computer system. Operations management sometimes takes the view that data preparation and entry tasks are straightforward and require little training. In some cases, this assumption might be reasonable. In other cases, however, significant benefits can accrue from training.

Some types of data preparation and entry equipment require regular maintenance. In particular, equipment with substantial mechanical components, like automatic teller machines, have to be serviced regularly if they are to operate reliably.

FIGURE 8–5. Ergonomically designed furniture.

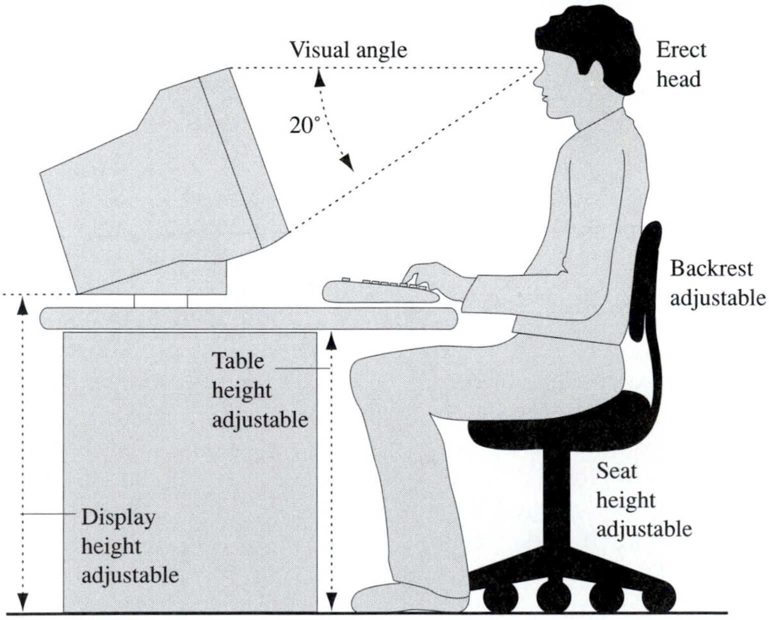

Operations management must ensure that backup exists for both input data and data preparation and entry devices. Source documents should be stored securely until they are no longer required for backup purposes. Their retention period might also be governed by law. Data entered directly into computer systems (no source documents) should be backed up as part of the normal file backup system. Any programs stored locally on microcomputers for data preparation and entry purposes must also be backed up.

Because responsibility for data preparation and entry is now dispersed so extensively in many organizations, auditors' evidence collection and evidence evaluation tasks can be difficult. Auditors might first enquire whether an organization has a set of standards to govern data preparation and entry activities— for example, standards relating to the design of keyboard tasks and keyboard environments. If such standards exist, they might then determine where material data preparation and entry activities are undertaken and use enquiries, observation, and review of documentation to evaluate compliance with these standards. If standards do not exist, auditors must consider how extensively they wish to revise control risk upwards and the effect on subsequent tests of controls and substantive testing. Weak controls over data preparation and entry can have a fairly direct impact on the four objectives of asset safeguarding, data integrity, system effectiveness, and system efficiency.

PRODUCTION CONTROL

The production control section under operations management performs five major functions: *(1)* receipt and dispatch of input and output, *(2)* job scheduling, *(3)* management of service-level agreements with users, *(4)* transfer pricing/chargeout control, and *(5)* acquisition of computer consumables. These functions are usually straightforward. Their proper execution, however, is often essential to the smooth running of the day-to-day activities of the information systems function. Moreover, they are assigned to production control to implement some important forms of separation of duties. The following subsections briefly describe each function and their importance from the viewpoint of auditors.

Input/Output Controls

In many cases, operations personnel have no contact with the input provided to or the output obtained from application systems. Users submit input to an application system directly via a terminal. Similarly, they either display or print output on devices located in their workplace and directly under their control.

In some cases, however, input for an application system can be submitted to the operations function for processing. For example, an outside organization or a remote user may provide a tape cartridge or diskette as input to an application system (Figure 8–6). Production control personnel have responsibility for ensuring that they accept input only from authorized parties, receiving and logging the input, safe custody of the input, timely submission of the input for processing, and safe retention of the processed input until it is no longer required or alternatively it is returned to the parties who provided it. By having production control personnel undertake these duties rather than operators, less scope for errors and irregularities exists. For example, production control should follow up to see that operators have processed all input received on a timely basis.

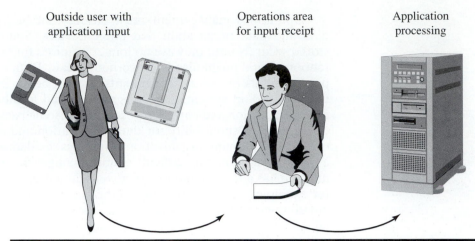

Outside user with application input Operations area for input receipt Application processing

FIGURE 8–6. Outside input to an application system.

Similarly, in some cases, production control personnel are responsible for receipt of and dispatch of output to outside parties and users. For example, a tape cartridge could be prepared for another organization, or lengthy reports could be prepared for a user on a high-speed, high-volume laser printer located in the computer room. In these situations, production control personnel might have several responsibilities. First, they might need to ensure that output is prepared on a timely basis. For example, if an outside organization picks up output at a regular time each day, production control personnel might be responsible for ensuring that the output is ready. Second, production control personnel might perform some types of basic quality assurance checks on any output received on behalf of outside parties or users. For example, they might scan reports prepared on a laser printer to ensure that the print is dark enough to be legible. Third, production control personnel might be responsible for safe custody of and dispatch of output. For example, some reports could contain sensitive information. Production control personnel might be responsible for storing these reports safely and ensuring that they are collected only by an authorized user.

Job Scheduling Controls

In the computer operations environment, a job comprises one or more programs that are to be executed and the resources needed to support the programs (e.g., printers, data files, terminals). Jobs can be activated in one of two ways. First, users can start jobs via commands given at a terminal. This approach is usually followed when the work performed is relevant only to the user and the job has little impact on other jobs that are executing. Alternatively, jobs can be started using either console commands or automated scheduling facilities. This approach is usually followed when the job performs work on behalf of many users or its resource consumption has a major impact on other jobs. For example, batch jobs like a payroll run or large online applications are usually initiated by operations staff.

When jobs are to be initiated by operations staff or an automated operations facility, the production control section should have responsibility for establishing the operations schedule and preparing and testing the job control file needed for each job. The job control file contains job control commands that specify, for example, when programs in a job are to be run, the order in which programs in a job are to be run, the data files they will need, the printers they will use, the priorities to be assigned to the programs, and what procedures are to be invoked in the event a program terminates abnormally.

Job control files can be complex. Auditors should investigate whether the files have been prepared and documented according to a set of standards, whether they have been tested before they are placed in operation, and whether they are controlled to ensure they are not subject to unauthorized changes. They should be concerned, for example, about the controls exercised over changes to job control files that are made in light of last-minute modifications to daily job schedules. Such changes arise through mishaps or delays. Auditors should also review the log of jobs actually executed to evaluate compliance with the job schedule. They should be concerned, for example, about jobs that have been executed that are not on the authorized schedule or jobs that have been rerun where the rerun has not been authorized. Such incidents could manifest errors or irregularities—for example, unauthorized production of a confidential report.

Backup of job control files is also important. If job control files are corrupted or lost through some type of disaster, continuity of operations could be severely impaired if they cannot be recovered quickly. Moreover, if operations have to be restored at an alternative site, management must evaluate whether job control files will have to be modified to accommodate hardware-software differences at the backup site. As computer operations become increasingly automated, less reliance can be placed on operators to provide accurate and complete manual backup in the event of a disaster.

Management of Service-Level Agreements

As the focus on providing effective and efficient computer services to users becomes sharper, many organizations are now implementing service-level agreements between users and the computer operations facility. These service-level agreements specify, for example, the turnaround and response time that users can expect from the operations facility, the level of maintenance support they will have, the costs they will incur for the services they use, and the penalties that will apply in the event that either users or the operations facility fail to meet the terms of the agreement (Figure 8–7).

The production control section often has responsibility for managing service-level agreements. For example, production control personnel might have responsibility for ensuring that service-level agreements are current, documentation is up-to-date and stored securely, and users and the operations facility comply with the terms of an agreement. An important control is to have user complaints about service levels directed to the production control section rather than to systems analysis, programming, or operations staff. A complaint can manifest errors or irregularities. It should be handled by an independent party rather than a person who might be the source of the error or irregularity. Otherwise, the person responsible for an error or irregularity may take actions to disguise the problem.

Auditors can evaluate how well the production control section is managing service-level agreements by interviewing users and operations personnel, examining the documentation supporting service-level agreements, examining logs of complaints and evaluating the adequacy of follow-up actions, and observing how production control staff interact with users and operations personnel. Their primary concerns will be with effectiveness and efficiency objectives.

PRODUCT/SERVICE:

    Workstation Procurement

PRODUCT MANAGER:

    Jean Jones
    Extension: 56555
    Fax: 56556
    E-mail: j.jones@isd.com

DESCRIPTION:

    Service relates to procurement, delivery, and installation of workstation hardware and software. ISD will operate a centralized purchasing facility to reduce corporate costs through arrangements with preferred suppliers.

AVAILABILITY:

    8.00 am to 6.00 pm, Monday to Friday (except public holidays)

RESPONSE TIME:

    Ordered items will be delivered and installed within 5 working days. End user will be notified within 2 working days if item is out of stock.

REPORTING:

    A catalog of current products and prices will be maintained on ISD's Web pages at: http://www.isd.cat.fict.co.au.

USER RESPONSIBILITY:

    End users will complete procurement form and transmit promptly to ISD product manager.

ISD RESPONSIBILITY:

    ISD will provide advice about the price, availability, and suitability of products requested.

PAYMENT:

    Upon installation, end user will be invoiced. Payment to ISD within 30 days of invoicing.

VARIATIONS:

    Must be placed in writing and negotiated with ISD product manager.

FIGURE 8–7. Example of a service-level agreement.

Nevertheless, their evaluation of how well complaints and disputes are handled also should affect their judgment on whether asset safeguarding and data integrity objectives are being achieved satisfactorily.

Transfer Pricing/Chargeout Control

If the computer operations facility uses a transfer pricing or chargeout system, the production control section often has responsibility for billing users, collecting receipts (or initiating internal transfers of funds), and following up on unpaid accounts. In this light, production control personnel must carefully monitor the chargeout system to ensure that charges are authorized, accurate, complete, and understandable by users (see also Chapter 3). In addition, production control personnel must be able to answer user queries on any charges made.

Because of the important role production control personnel play in the operations of the chargeout system, they might be able to alert management when transfer prices are not motivating users to employ computer resources efficiently or when dissatisfaction is rising among the user community with the level of charges incurred or the transfer-pricing scheme used. Production control personnel should also notify management when the level of charges incurred by users begins to deviate from the norm. Such deviations could reflect that abnormal error rates are occurring or irregularities are being perpetrated. For example, charges might be abnormally high because data-entry personnel are having to spend more time correcting erroneous source data. Charges also might be abnormally high because computer resources are being used for unauthorized purposes.

If the computer operations facility outsources some of its activities, it will incur charges itself. Production control personnel might be responsible for checking the authenticity, accuracy, and completeness of the invoices received from the outsourcing vendor. Again, because production control personnel play an important role in monitoring these charges, they should alert management if they believe the charges are unreasonable or if they believe better outsourcing opportunities exist elsewhere.

Auditors can evaluate how well the production control section is managing the transfer-pricing function by interviewing users to determine whether they are satisfied with the level of service provided, interviewing production control personnel to determine the nature of the duties they perform, examining documentation associated with the transfer-pricing function to determine whether it is current, accurate, complete, and secure, examining logs of complaints for evidence of errors or irregularities and the adequacy of follow-up procedures, and observing the ways production control personnel carry out their duties. Their primary concern will be with effectiveness and efficiency objectives. Nevertheless, auditors must be mindful that transfer-pricing abnormalities can manifest problems that will undermine asset safeguarding and data integrity objectives.

Acquisition of Consumables

The computer operations facility often uses substantial amounts of consumables—for example, printer paper, diskettes, magnetic tapes, toner cartridges for laser printers, and preprinted stationery. These items can often be a material component of the operations budget. In addition, operations schedules can be disrupted if consumables are not provided on a timely basis. For example, a billing run might have to be deferred because insufficient preprinted invoicing stationery is in stock.

Production control personnel often have responsibility for acquiring and managing consumables that the computer operations facility uses. They should ensure that adequate (but not excessive) stocks of consumables are available, monitor the price and quality of consumables acquired, ensure that consumables are stored securely, and control use of consumables. Poor control over purchasing of consumables can result in excessive stock, excessive prices, and low-quality stock. Poor inventory control over consumables can result in excessive losses through theft or misuse.

Auditors should follow the usual evidence collection and evaluation procedures employed for purchasing and inventory activities (see, e.g., Arthur Andersen 1987). For example, they can interview production control personnel to determine the controls they exercise over purchasing and storage of consumables, examine documentation for evidence of senior management's monitoring of the purchasing function, observe whether consumables are stored securely, and interview operations staff to determine whether high-quality consumables are being provided on a timely basis. As with any purchasing and inventory activities, the four objectives of asset safeguarding, data integrity, system effectiveness, and system efficiency will be salient during auditors' evidence collection and evaluation work.

FILE LIBRARY

The file-library function within the operations area takes responsibility for the management of an organization's machine-readable storage media. Usually, most work is expended on managing *removable* storage media, such as magnetic tapes, cartridges, and optical disks. Nevertheless, fixed storage media must also be managed; for example, the reliability of fixed disks must be monitored.

Historically, a reasonably high level of resources had to be devoted to the file-library function. Organizations often had extensive collections of magnetic tapes and removable disks. These collections required substantial storage space, clean environments, and careful control over their maintenance and use. Nowadays, fewer storage media are needed because storage densities have increased considerably. Moreover, use of removable storage media has decreased markedly. Most storage is now on fixed disk or disk and tape cartridges that are managed automatically via robotics devices. Nevertheless, many organizations continue to use magnetic tapes or cartridges for backup purposes or to transfer data to another department or organization. In addition, microcomputer users might still use diskettes to store copies of critical files. In both cases, storage-media controls must be exercised.

Managing the organization's collection of machine-readable removable storage media involves four functions: First, storage media must be kept in a secure facility; second, it must be used only for authorized purposes; third, it must be maintained in good working order; and fourth, it must be suitably located, and transit to and from the facility must be controlled. The following subsections briefly discuss each of these functions.

Storage of Storage Media

Because storage media might contain critical files, they should be housed securely. In the case of mainframe operations, a separate room should be constructed adjacent to the computer room to house storage media needed during daily operations. Access to this room should be restricted. If possible, it should be under the control of a file librarian. In the case of off-site backup storage, again a secure facility should be used, and access to the facility should be restricted. Both off-site and on-site facilities also should maintain a constant-temperature, dust-free environment to reduce the likelihood of damage to the media and, as a result, to the data they contain. Like removable mainframe storage media, removable microcomputer storage media (e.g., diskettes, optical disks) must be kept securely, and access to them must be restricted. Diskettes that contain important files should not be kept, for example, in unlocked desk drawers.

To manage a large number of removable storage media effectively, usually some type of automated library system is needed. Such systems typically record the following:

1. An identifier for each storage medium;
2. Place where each storage medium is currently located;
3. Name of the person who has ultimate responsibility for the storage medium;
4. Name of the person who currently has the storage medium;
5. Files stored on each medium;
6. Persons authorized to access each storage medium;
7. Date when the storage medium was purchased;
8. History of use of the storage medium (e.g., persons who obtained access to it and dates of access);
9. History of difficulties experienced with the medium (e.g., read/write errors);
10. Dates when contents of the storage medium can be deleted;
11. Date when storage medium last released from file library;
12. Date when storage medium last returned to file library.

Auditors can use interviews and observations to check whether storage media are housed securely. They can ask the file librarian, operators, production control personnel, and microcomputer users where removable storage media are located. To evaluate security, they can then observe the facilities employed to house the storage media at both on-site and off-site locations. If an automated library system exists, auditors can undertake basic inventory audit procedures to check whether the locations of storage media match records within the system. In addition, they should be alert to the possibility of an organization holding excessive storage media (e.g., magnetic tapes) for its needs. Aside from the costs associated with holding excessive storage media, poor management of files on the media can result. For example, sensitive files might not be deleted on a timely basis, thereby increasing the risks of exposure of the files.

Use of Storage Media

Use of storage media should be controlled carefully. In mainframe environments, file librarians should issue removable storage media in accordance with an authorized production schedule. Ideally they will transport the storage media needed to the computer room and collect the media after production runs have been completed. In all other cases, file librarians should issue removable storage media only if the person requesting the media presents a properly authorized requisition. Records of removable storage media use also need to be maintained.

In microcomputer environments, the extent of control exercised over use of removable storage media should depend on the criticality of data maintained on the media. For example, if a diskette contains highly confidential data, the person responsible for the diskette should issue it only to authorized persons. As with mainframe environments, a record of media use should be maintained. Less formal controls can be exercised if the data stored on media has lower materiality.

Personnel at off-site locations should receive and issue backup files only in accordance with an authorized schedule or a signed requisition. Asset safeguarding and data integrity objectives can be seriously compromised, for example, if they issue critical master-file backup to a competitor. Because off-site personnel often work for a vendor who specializes in providing backup facilities, they might not have sufficient personal knowledge of customer organizations to determine who is authorized to access storage media. Compliance with formal authorization procedures, therefore, is essential.

Care should be taken when multiple files are assigned to a single storage medium. Unless proper controls exist, an application system reading one file might be able to enter the space of another file and read it, thereby exposing sensitive data. Ideally, sensitive files should exist alone on a storage medium. If a storage medium contains multiple sensitive files, however, auditors should investigate how the integrity of individual files is safeguarded. For example, they should check whether the operating system exercises sufficient control over an application system to restrict access only to the files the application system is authorized to use.

As the retention dates of files expire, the files should be expunged from storage media. This procedure reduces the likelihood of sensitive data being exposed at some future time. In addition, the media can then be used to store other files, and inventory requirements are reduced. Care should be taken, however, in relation to how files are deleted. In some cases, operating systems delete files simply by changing file header information. The data in the file is not deleted, however, and programs that subsequently use the storage medium might be able to read the data. When a file contains sensitive data, controls must exist to ensure that the data is overwritten completely before the storage medium is used by another program. In microcomputer systems, for example, utility programs are available that ensure that all data in a file is overwritten when the file is deleted.

Auditors can use interviews, observations, and reviews of documentation to evaluate the reliability of controls over storage media use. For example, they can interview on-site and off-site file librarians to determine the procedures they follow before they will issue storage media. They can also observe them at their work. If a log of storage media use is maintained, auditors can review the log to evaluate whether only authorized personnel accessed storage media. To the extent that improper use of storage media might be occurring, asset safeguarding and data integrity objectives could be undermined.

Maintenance and Disposal of Storage Media

Many types of storage media are reliable over long periods of time, but in general their reliability decreases with age. For example, usually an increasing number of read/write errors occurs as magnetic tapes and diskettes become older and more used. In this light, the reliability of storage media should be monitored, especially those storage media that are used to store critical files. Records should be kept of difficulties experienced with storage media. Some file management systems can be used, for example, to read an operating system log, retrieve information pertaining to the reliability of storage media operations (e.g., number of read/write errors encountered with the media), and update reliability information in their databases for each storage medium used (Figure 8–8). Reports can then be generated automatically to warn of impending problems with a storage medium.

Storage media should not remain unused for long periods of time. Otherwise, the risk of a read/write error occurring with the media increases. With a magnetic tape, for example, pressure builds up over time toward the center of

TAPE-E Seq 72. at 18-Jan-1998 14:16:58.40, Out-of band 000705
Tape Formatter connected to Requestor 2. Port 1.
Has been declared Inoperative intervention required
TAPE-E Seq 73. at 18-Jan-1998 14:17:44.80, Out-of-band 000345
Tape unit number 0. connected to Requestor 2. Port 1.
Dropped state clock while Online

FIGURE 8–8. Report on media reliability.
Used by permission, The University of Queensland.

the tape on its hub. This pressure causes bonding and compacting of the materials from which the tape is made. As a result, the tape could become unreadable. In this light, backup storage media need to be managed carefully. If backup must be stored for long periods, backup media should be retrieved, say, every six months and backup files rewritten to another medium. Whereas mainframe operations staff are often aware of this exposure, many microcomputer users often leave removable storage media unused for long periods of time. Recovery of accidentally deleted or damaged files then cannot be effected from these media because they are unreadable.

When storage media become unreliable, it is usually best to discard them. Care should be taken to ensure that all sensitive data is removed from discarded media. Simply deleting the files on the media does not achieve this objective. Deletion alters the file header, but the data on the media is left intact. Even bulk erasure of media might be ineffective. A residual signal could still be left on the media that can be recovered with the appropriate equipment. It might be necessary to carry out bulk erasure, then write random bits to the media, and then carry out bulk erasure again. These procedures take time, however, and in some cases it might be easier to destroy the media.

In some cases, unreliable storage media can be repaired satisfactorily. For example, magnetic tapes can be cleaned to improve their reliability and to increase their life. Cleaning also relieves pressure on the tape hub and alleviates the types of problems mentioned previously. Various types of utilities are also available that can be used to repair some types of diskette damage. Nevertheless, clearly it is unwise to store critical files on storage media whose reliability is suspect.

If storage media must be sent outside an organization for cleaning or repair, care must be taken to erase any sensitive data contained on the media. The information on magnetic tapes, for example, can be erased through a process called degaussing. Moreover, if the worn ends of magnetic tapes are to be clipped or damaged portions of a tape are to be cut back, degaussing again should be undertaken in case the clippings or tape cuttings contain sensitive information. An unauthorized person might retrieve the clippings or cuttings from a trash can, for example, and examine the data recorded on the clippings or cuttings.

Auditors can evaluate the reliability of controls over maintenance of storage media through interviews, observations, and reviews of documentation. For example, they can interview file librarians and microcomputer users about the procedures they use to ensure storage media are reliable. They can observe any work they undertake to evaluate the likely reliability of storage media. If an organization uses a media management system, auditors can review reports produced by the system to determine whether the file librarian is apprised of unreliable media. They can then evaluate the adequacy of any follow-up actions taken by the file librarian.

Location of Storage Media

Removable storage media are located either on site or off site. They should be located on site if they are intended primarily to support production running of application systems. They should be located off site if they are intended primarily for backup and recovery purposes.

In a mainframe environment, file librarians are responsible for managing the transport of removable storage media to and from off-site locations. Such movements should comply with backup schedules prepared by a team comprising the security administrator, the data administrator, application project managers, the manager responsible for systems development, the operations manager, and the file librarian. The operations manager is then responsible for ensuring backup is made according to the schedule. The file librarian, in turn, takes responsibility for ensuring that backup is moved on a timely and secure basis to off-site facilities.

In a minicomputer or microcomputer environment, someone must still perform file librarian duties with respect to on-site and off-site movement of storage media. Backup has to be prepared for minicomputer disk storage, local area network file server storage, and material microcomputer files. Stronger controls are likely to exist if these responsibilities are vested in a single person—for example, the file librarian who takes responsibility for mainframe backup. Both operations staff (who manage minicomputers and local area networks) and microcomputer users can then provide backup to this person for transport to off-site storage. If the mainframe file librarian does not perform this function, however, minicomputer and microcomputer users must perform it themselves. Management can help by having standards formulated and then promulgating these standards to guide minicomputer and microcomputer users in the backup activities they undertake.

Auditors can use interviews, observations, and review of documentation to evaluate whether removable storage media are suitably located. For example, they can ask file librarians and microcomputer users about the procedures they follow to determine where removable storage media should be located. They can also observe how they dispatch backup to and receive backup from off-site storage locations. If documented backup schedules exist, they can then be checked as to the existence of and location of backup storage media for compliance with these schedules.

DOCUMENTATION AND PROGRAM LIBRARY

Many types of documentation are needed to support the information systems function within an organization: strategic and operational plans; application systems documentation; application program documentation; systems-software and utility program documentation; database documentation; operations manuals; user manuals; and standards manuals. In addition, ancillary documentation such as memoranda, books, and journals must also be kept. Much of this documentation is now kept in automated form. For example, systems analysts use computer-aided systems engineering (CASE) tools to produce machine-readable versions of dataflow diagrams and entity-relationship diagrams. Similarly, some software vendors now provide the documentation supporting their products on optical disks (CD-ROM). Nevertheless, much documentation is still kept in hard-copy form. Indeed, Galitz (1993, pp. 52–53) reports the results of several studies that indicate that hard-copy documentation still has several advantages over online documentation. It is unlikely, therefore, that the need to maintain hard-copy documentation will disappear in the near future.

Effective management of information systems documentation can be difficult for several reasons. First, responsibility for documentation is often dispersed throughout an organization. A librarian might be appointed to manage documentation supporting mainframe and minicomputer systems. Responsibility for managing documentation supporting microcomputer systems, however, might be vested in all users of microcomputers. Second, the documentation can be kept in multiple forms and in multiple locations. It might exist only in magnetic form, only in hard-copy form, only in microform, or in some combination of forms. Copies of documentation could be distributed to many users. Third, given the diversity of and dispersion of documentation, ensuring that documentation is kept up-to-date and accessible only to authorized users can be difficult. Ensuring adequate backup for documentation exists also can be difficult.

Documentation librarians have responsibility for managing the documentation supporting the information systems function. Their functions include *(1)* ensuring that documentation is stored securely, *(2)* ensuring that only authorized personnel gain access to documentation, *(3)* ensuring that documentation is kept up-to-date, and *(4)* ensuring that adequate backup exists for documentation. The documentation librarian function might have to be dispersed to multiple persons. For example, someone could be appointed to perform this function for centralized information systems activities. In addition, documentation librarians could be appointed in each major user area to manage the documentation supporting use of microcomputers and local area networks. When documentation is maintained on magnetic media, documentation librarians might have to liaise with the security administrator and the data administrator to ensure that adequate access controls are in place and working to restrict access to documentation only to authorized personnel.

Documentation librarians might also take responsibility for managing an organization's inventory of acquired software or licensed software. For example, many organizations acquire a large number of packages to support their microcomputer operations. If this inventory of software is not managed properly, several problems often arise such as the following: *(1)* too many copies of the software are purchased for the use made of the software; *(2)* the software is lost or stolen; *(3)* the documentation is lost or stolen; *(4)* illegal copying of the software occurs; *(5)* use of the software does not comply with terms and conditions of the licensing agreement; or *(6)* the software is not backed up properly. These types of problems are mitigated if someone takes responsibility for maintaining records of purchase, distribution, and use of software and its associated documentation, and for ensuring that users comply with the terms of licensing agreements. Various types of software are available to support this function. For instance, some local area network operating systems provide a utility that generates a report listing all software stored on workstations or file servers within the network. This report can then be reviewed, for example, for evidence of illegal copies of software. Similarly, some software metering packages will produce a report of the use made of licensed software (Figure 8–9). This report can then be reviewed to detect whether too many software licenses have been purchased.

File Server: QA Accounting
Requested by: Supervisor
Print Date: 16 December 1998

Report Date: 1 January 1998 through 16 December 1998

License Name	Owned	Cost/Lic	Total Cost	Max InUse	Unused	Saving
Fastspread	100	$275	$27500	91	9	$2475
GoodWP	100	$290	$29000	75	25	$7250
ClearGraphs	75	$150	$11250	16	59	$8850
EasyMoney	50	$399	$19950	22	28	$11172
SuperStats	10	$649	$6490	3	7	$4543

FIGURE 8–9. Report on licensed software use.
Used by permission, Elron Software.

Auditors can use interviews, observations, and review of documentation to evaluate the activities of documentation librarians. For example, they can ask documentation librarians about the nature of the tasks they perform, observe the ways in which they maintain a library of acquired software and documentation, and review records of documentation use to evaluate the adequacy and completeness of these records. Auditors should be concerned to see that documentation is maintained securely and that it is issued only to authorized personnel. Otherwise, improper use of or modifications to software could arise, or the documentation might not be available when the software must be maintained.

HELP DESK/TECHNICAL SUPPORT

The help desk/technical support function in the operations area has two primary responsibilities. First, it assists end users to employ end-user hardware and software, such as microcomputers, spreadsheet packages, database management packages, and local area networks. Second, it provides technical support for production systems by assisting with problem resolution. Some typical functions of the help desk/technical support area follow:

1. Acquisition of hardware and software on behalf of end users;
2. Assisting end users with hardware and software difficulties;
3. Training end users to use hardware, software, and databases;
4. Answering end-user queries;
5. Monitoring technological developments and informing end users of developments that might be pertinent to them;
6. Determining the source of problems with production systems and initiating corrective actions;
7. Informing end users of problems with hardware, software, or databases that could affect them;
8. Controlling the installation of hardware and software upgrades; and
9. Initiating changes to improve efficiency.

For the help desk/technical support area to function effectively and efficiently, there are two critical requirements. First, competent and trustworthy personnel are essential. Support staff must be knowledgeable about the diverse range of systems used throughout their organization. Otherwise, they will be unable to provide accurate, complete, and timely answers to queries. Moreover, they must have a high level of interpersonal skills so that they can interact effectively with users. They must show empathy, for example, when users encounter problems.

Assigned To Individual : Mary Manager
Short Description : Win 3.1 User tool not working well under Win 95
Escalate Time : 26 November 1997 11:21:24 PM
Case ID : 000864
Status : Escalated

Assigned To Individual : Mary Manager
Short Description : keyboard not working
Escalate Time : 26 November 1997 15:02:34 PM
Case ID : 000265
Status : Escalated

Assigned To Individual : Mary Manager
Short Description : Unable to access any drives from any machine
Escalate Time : 19 December 1997 13:23:12 PM
Case ID : 000176
Status : Escalated

Assigned To Individual : Mary Manager
Short Description : information on move from Unix 10.10 to Unix 10.20
Escalate Time : 22 December 1997 11:35:11 PM
Case ID : 000275
Status : Escalated

FIGURE 8–10. Help-desk exception report.
Used by permission, Remedy Corporation.

Second, a problem management system that provides inventory, logging, and reporting capabilities must be available to support the activities of the help desk/technical support area. When users report some type of difficulty or request some type of advice, their report or request must be logged immediately into the system. Support personnel must then be assigned to investigate the difficulty or to respond to the request for advice. They can access the inventory database maintained in the system to determine what hardware and software the user who requests the help possesses. This knowledge can assist them to resolve the problem. If a response is not provided within a designated time period, the system should alert the manager of the help desk/technical support area that there is an outstanding problem (Figure 8–10). The manager should then take follow-up action. The system should also maintain a log of all activities undertaken relating to the difficulty reported or the advice requested. This log can be used to determine whether problems are occurring in a particular area (e.g., a particular application system). Corrective actions can then be taken. The log also provides a record of the actions taken to fix a problem. Help-desk staff can access the log to find out how a particular type of problem has been fixed in the past. They do not have to determine a problem solution from scratch.

Auditors can evaluate how well the help desk/technical support area undertakes its work via interviews, observations, and review of documentation. For example, they can interview end users to determine their level of satisfaction with the service provided by the help desk/technical support area. They can observe help desk/technical support personnel to see how they respond to user queries. They can review logs maintained by the help desk/technical support reporting system to determine whether personnel provide accurate, complete, and timely responses to user queries.

CAPACITY PLANNING AND PERFORMANCE MONITORING

A primary objective of the information systems function is to satisfactorily achieve the goals of information systems users at minimum cost. To some extent, this goal is achieved by high-quality system design and implementation. Nevertheless, achieving it also depends on providing a suitable hardware/software platform on which systems can run. In this respect, operations management must continuously monitor the performance of the hardware/software platform to ensure that systems are executing efficiently, acceptable response times or turnaround times are being achieved, and acceptable levels of uptime are occurring. This monitoring extends not only to the hardware/software platform existing within a centralized facility but also to other platforms (such as minicomputers and microcomputers) dispersed throughout the organization. Although the costs of inefficiency might be small for an individual machine, the aggregate costs of inefficiency for the organization may be substantial. These overall costs must be evaluated carefully.

Chapter 20 provides a detailed discussion of some of the instruments that can be used to monitor the performance of hardware/software platforms and the various measurements that might be taken. Chapter 23 discusses how the measurements can then be assimilated to evaluate overall system efficiency. Operations management has responsibility, however, for devising a plan for monitoring system performance, identifying the data that must be captured to accomplish the plan, choosing the instruments needed to capture the data, and ensuring that the instruments are correctly implemented. The performance monitoring plan and its execution varies considerably depending on many factors—for example, whether large mainframes or microcomputers are being evaluated. Moreover, the plan and its implementation must be reconsidered periodically in light of changes to hardware/software platforms or changed patterns of system use.

On the basis of the performance monitoring statistics calculated, operations managers must make three decisions. First, they must evaluate whether the performance profiles indicate unauthorized activities might have occurred. For example, abnormal workloads during a night shift might reflect the fact that an analyst or programmer has used system resources for private consulting purposes. Second, in light of user needs, they must determine whether system performance is acceptable. If system performance is not acceptable, they must diagnose why performance is problematic. Poor job scheduling might be occurring that is resulting in undesirable job mixes being executed. Hardware and system software might also need to be reconfigured to avoid particular resource bottlenecks. Finally, more hardware and system software resources might be needed. In this respect, careful, regular monitoring of performance facilitates capacity planning. Given the substantial leadtimes that can exist in acquiring and implementing some hardware and system software resources, resource deficiencies must be identified early if the resources are to be available when they are needed.

Auditors are concerned to see that operations management monitors performance properly and makes competent hardware and system software decisions on the basis of the statistics collected. Recall from Chapter 1 that poor system performance can undermine asset safeguarding and data integrity controls. If users are frustrated by inadequate system performance, they might circumvent controls in an attempt to decrease resource consumption. As controls degrade, asset safeguarding and data integrity objectives are threatened. Auditors should use interviews, observations, and review of documentation to evaluate how well operations management undertakes the capacity planning and performance monitoring function. They can ask operations management what activities they undertake, observe how they review and act on performance monitoring statistics, and examine past statistics and the actions they have undertaken in light of these statistics.

MANAGEMENT OF OUTSOURCED OPERATIONS

Many organizations now outsource some of their information systems functions. A major reason is that they wish to focus more on the functions that represent their core business and to acquire products and services from the outside marketplace in those areas where they have no comparative advantage. Where an organization outsources some of its information systems functions, operations management often has responsibility for carrying out the day-to-day monitoring of the outsourcing contract.

In spite of its current popularity, outsourcing is not a new phenomenon. Over many years, organizations have used service bureaus to undertake some part of their information-processing work. What is different with outsourcing, however, is the extent to which information-processing functions are performed by an outside party. Generally more information-processing functions are performed externally under an outsourcing contract compared with a service-bureau contract. Nevertheless, the same types of control concerns that traditionally applied to service-bureau contracts also apply to outsourcing contracts. The reliability of controls under outsourcing contracts becomes more important, however, because the exposures faced are often higher.

Operations management should focus on four types of controls in their monitoring of outsourcing contracts: *(1)* ongoing evaluation of the financial viability of the outsourcing vendor, *(2)* ensuring compliance with the outsourcing contract's terms and conditions, *(3)* ensuring the ongoing reliability of controls in the outsourcing vendor's operations, and *(4)* maintaining procedures for disaster recovery with the outsourcing vendor. The following subsections address each of these types of controls and the procedures auditors should use to evaluate their reliability.

Financial Viability of the Outsourcing Vendor

Prior to entering an outsourcing contract, senior management should carefully assess the long-term financial viability of the outsourcing vendor with whom they wish to contract. The greater the importance of the information systems functions assigned to the outsourcing vendor, the more critical is the ability of the outsourcing vendor to survive in the long run. If the outsourcing vendor were to fail, the operations of any organization that employs its services can be impaired irrevocably.

When an outsourcing contract is in force, operations management must continuously monitor the financial viability of the outsourcing vendor. Long time delays can be encountered before an organization can disengage successfully from an outsourcing contract. For example, the organization might have lost its in-house source of systems-development expertise because of reliance on the outsourcing vendor. If the outsourcing vendor were to fail, it might not be possible to reestablish this expertise quickly. Accordingly, senior management will need substantial warning of any problems with financial viability that the outsourcing vendor is encountering. Otherwise, it might not be possible to establish needed expertise on a timely basis.

Operations management should regularly review the outsourcing vendor's financial statements. This information should be provided promptly as part of the outsourcing contract. The contract should also allow operations management to undertake further in-depth inquiries if concerns surface about financial aspects of the outsourcing vendor's operations.

Auditors should use interviews, observations, and reviews of documentation to evaluate whether operations management regularly assesses the financial viability of any outsourcing vendors that an organization uses. They can interview operations management to determine the procedures they follow, observe them at their work, and review financial information obtained from outsourcing vendors for evidence of timely and proper review by operations management.

Compliance with the Outsourcing Contract's Terms and Conditions

Before an outsourcing contract is signed, senior managers should ensure that the rights and responsibilities of both the outsourcing vendor and their organization are clearly specified. For example, the contract should specify precisely the goods and services to be provided by both parties, the quality and timing objectives that both parties must achieve, the cost of goods and services to be provided by the outsourcing vendor, the confidentiality requirements to be met by both parties, the ownership of goods and services produced under the contract, and the procedures for terminating the contract.

When the contract is exchanged, however, operations management must monitor compliance with the contract. For example, operations managers should ensure that outsourcing invoices for work done are accurate, their organization provides timely, high-quality input data to the outsourcing vendor, the work done by the outsourcing vendor is authentic, accurate, complete, and timely, and confidentiality requirements are being achieved. If the outsourcing vendor fails to comply with the terms and conditions of the contract, operations management must provide timely notification to senior management so that corrective actions can be undertaken.

Auditors can use interviews, observations, and reviews of documentation to evaluate whether operations management is monitoring compliance with the outsourcing contract. They can ask operations management about the procedures they use to monitor compliance with the contract, observe them exercise these procedures, and search for evidence that, say, operations management has checked the accuracy of invoices submitted by the outsourcing vendor.

Reliability of Outsourcing Vendor's Controls

An outsourcing contract must provide for some means of regularly reviewing the reliability of controls used by the outsourcing vendor. Two strategies might be followed. First, the outsourcing vendor might be required periodically to provide a third-party audit report attesting to the reliability of controls implemented by the vendor. The outsourcing contract should require that the third-party auditor is acceptable to both the outsourcing vendor and its clients. Second, the outsourcing vendor might permit a review of its controls to be undertaken periodically by its clients' internal and external auditors. Clearly, this second approach would be followed only if the outsourcing vendor has a small number of clients. Otherwise, the overheads associated with control reviews undertaken by client auditors are likely to be unacceptable.

If an organization uses an outsourcing vendor, it should ensure that the outsourcing contract specifies penalties in the event that losses arise because the outsourcing vendor has unreliable controls. For example, if the outsourcing vendor has poor system development controls, application systems could be developed that are ineffective and inefficient. As a result, the organization might suffer a loss of market share. Similarly, if the outsourcing vendor has poor access controls, the organization's confidential data could be exposed to other clients of the outsourcing vendor. Again, the organization could suffer a loss of market share. Unfortunately, determining the size of the losses that arise from such incidents can be difficult. Moreover, the long-term relationships that are so important to effective outsourcing of information systems functions could be damaged irrevocably. Prevention of losses from unreliable controls in an outsourcing relationship is far better than detection and correction.

Operations management can have several responsibilities with respect to ensuring the controls used by an outsourcing vendor are reliable. First, it might collect any third-party audit reports periodically prepared on the reliability of controls used by the outsourcing vendor. It should distribute these reports to the organization's internal and external auditors for perusal. Second, it might organize periodic audits of the outsourcing vendor by the organization's own internal and external auditors. Third, it should ensure that any control concerns noted in third-party audit reports or in reports prepared by the organization's own internal or external auditors are followed up by senior management.

Auditors can evaluate how well operations management monitors the reliability of outsourcing vendor controls through interviews, observations, and reviews of documentation. They can ask operations management about the procedures they use to evaluate whether outsourcing vendor controls are reliable. They can then observe how they undertake these procedures. Auditors can also obtain a copy of recent audit reports prepared on the reliability of outsourcing vendor controls to determine what actions, if any, have been undertaken by operations management in light of any control concerns noted in the reports.

Outsourcing Disaster Recovery Controls

When an organization exchanges a contract with an outsourcing vendor, it becomes dependent on the outsourcing vendor for the ongoing availability of some or all of its information systems functions. If the outsourcing vendor experiences a disaster, the organization as a client of the outsourcing vendor will in turn be affected.

An outsourcing contract should specify the disaster recovery controls that the outsourcing vendor will have in place and working. These controls should be evaluated periodically (as discussed in the previous subsection). Client organizations should develop their own disaster recovery procedures, however, in the event their outsourcing vendor experiences a disaster. These controls should be coordinated with the outsourcing vendor's disaster recovery controls. In addition, controls might be established to reduce exposures in the event that some or all of the outsourcing vendor's disaster recovery controls fail. Client organizations must consider the possibility that they will have to recover information systems functions themselves.

An organization's security administrator should be responsible for the design and implementation of disaster recovery controls associated with an outsourcing contract. Operations management might be responsible, however, for the day-to-day operation of these controls. They must monitor the adequacy of these controls as the exposures facing the organization change and notify the security administrator if they believe modifications to the controls are needed. In addition, periodically they must test the controls to ensure that they are functioning reliably. These tests might have to be carried out in conjunction with the outsourcing vendor.

Auditors can evaluate how well operations management monitors the reliability of outsourcing disaster recovery controls through interviews, observations, and reviews of documentation. They can ask operations management about the procedures they use to ensure outsourcing disaster recovery controls are in place and operating reliably. They can observe how operations management carries out periodic tests of outsourcing disaster recovery controls. Auditors can also review documentation pertaining to past tests of outsourcing disaster recovery controls to determine whether appropriate follow-up actions were undertaken by operations management.

SUMMARY

Operations management is responsible for the daily running of hardware and software facilities so that *(1)* production application systems can accomplish their work and *(2)* development staff can design, implement, and maintain application systems. Specifically, operations management performs nine major functions: *(1)* managing the day-to-day operations of an organization's hardware/software platforms; *(2)* managing wide area and local area network operations; *(3)* managing data preparation and entry; *(4)* operating a production control section to manage input/output, schedule jobs, manage user service-level agreements, manage chargeout, and acquire consumables; *(5)* managing an organization's library of machine-readable files; *(6)* managing the documentation that supports the information systems function and the inventory of acquired and licensed software held by an organization; *(7)* operating a help desk and technical support function for users of the information systems function; *(8)* monitoring performance and ensuring adequate hardware/software capacity is available; and *(9)* managing operations that are outsourced.

Many of these functions appear somewhat mundane and routine. Nevertheless, if they are not performed properly and well controlled, asset safeguarding, data integrity, system effectiveness, and system efficiency objectives can be undermined severely. Operations management must ensure that methods and performance standards exist for each function, high-quality personnel are hired to perform each function, and operations personnel are trained and managed properly.

Review Questions

8–1 What is the primary role of operations management?

8–2 Briefly describe two changes that have occurred in recent years that have had an impact on how the operations function is audited. Outline the nature of the effect that has occurred.

8–3 What is an AOF? Briefly explain the relationship between an AOF and a lights-out facility.

8–4 Briefly describe *three* controls that should be exercised over computer operators.

8–5 Briefly explain why it is undesirable to allow operators to authorize reruns of application systems.

8–6 Briefly describe *three* control concerns that auditors should have with automated operations facilities.

8–7 Briefly describe *two* implications that use of microcomputers and decentralization of the information systems function have on the reliability of controls over computer operations.

8–8 What is the purpose of computer operations scheduling controls?

8–9 For the following activities, briefly indicate who should be responsible for authorizing the availability of machine resources to undertake them and why:

   a Regular execution of a production application system
   b Program testing
   c Production application system reruns
   d Program compilations

8–10 Briefly explain the difference between preventive and repair maintenance. Why might an operations manager decide to increase the amount of preventive maintenance undertaken on a machine?

8–11 Give a decision that operations management might make on the basis of data recorded on the maintenance log prepared for a machine.

8–12 Briefly describe how a maintenance engineer might violate data integrity during the maintenance of hardware. Give *two* controls that might be exercised over the engineer to inhibit or prevent the integrity violation you describe.

8–13 What is the overall purpose of a network control terminal in a wide area communications network? Give three specific functions that can be performed by an operator using a network control terminal.

8–14 Why is a network control terminal a threat to the overall security of a communications network? What controls should be exercised to try to ensure that a network control terminal is used only for its intended purposes?

8–15 List two aspects of the operations of a local area network that need to be monitored to ensure that data integrity within the network is maintained. Briefly explain why these two aspects need to be monitored.

8–16 Why do file servers within a local area network need to be physically secured?

8–17 Briefly describe some guidelines that should be followed to reduce operator boredom in the design of keying tasks undertaken in the data preparation function.

8–18 What responsibilities does operations management have with respect to backup and recovery in the data preparation function?

8–19 Briefly describe the production control section's responsibilities with respect to receipt of input from and dispatch of output to external users of the information systems function.

8–20 Briefly describe the production control section's responsibilities with respect to job scheduling.

8–21 From a control perspective, why is it important to have user complaints about information systems services directed to production control personnel?

8–22 What are the production control section's responsibilities with respect to transfer-pricing charges in terms of:

   a Internal users of the information systems function's services?
   b The information systems function as a user of an outside service bureau's services?

8–23 What are the production control section's responsibilities with respect to acquisition of consumables used by the information systems function?

8–11 Which of the following guidelines applies to the design of keying tasks to increase the effectiveness and efficiency of the data preparation function?

 a Keying tasks should be no longer than an hour

 b To the extent possible, operators should always key the same application system's data

 c Keying tasks should be precisely defined

 d To reduce distractions, no noise should be permitted in the data preparation area

8–12 Which of the following design guidelines should be followed to reduce the likelihood of repetition strain injury?

 a Ensure that the data preparation area is brightly lit so keyboard operators can read source documents easily

 b Ensure that all seats are at a uniform height so all keyboard operators get used to a common position

 c Choose keyboards that require some pressure to activate so operators can hear an audible click

 d Choose a workstation table that has been ergonomically designed

8–13 Which of the following is *not* a function of the production control section?

 a Dispatching input received from an outside party to the computer room

 b Scheduling of production jobs

 c Follow-up on unpaid accounts if the information systems function uses a transfer-pricing scheme

 d Altering source data to correct input errors

8–14 Which of the following activities should *not* be performed by control section personnel when they collect the output of a batch application system from the computer room?

 a Checking to see the output has been produced according to the production schedule

 b One-to-one reconciliation of input with output

 c Checking to see whether any programs terminated abnormally

 d Scanning the output for obvious errors

8–15 Which of the following is *not* a function of production control personnel in terms of production scheduling?

 a Assisting with the establishment of the production schedule

 b Preparing job control files

 c Establishing access controls over job control files

 d Testing job control files

8–16 Which of the following is *unlikely* to be a responsibility of the production control section with respect to the management of service-level agreements?

 a Ensuring that documentation of service-level agreements is up-to-date

 b Monitoring user complaints relating to noncompliance with service-level agreements

 c Specifying the terms of a service-level agreement

 d Providing advice to user management and information systems management on where service-level agreements can be improved

8–17 Which of the following is *not* a responsibility of the production control section with respect to transfer pricing of information systems services?

 a Determining the prices to be charged for information systems development work

 b Following up with users on unpaid accounts

    c Monitoring user complaints about a transfer pricing system

    d Ensuring that charges made to users are authorized, accurate, and complete

8–18 Which of the following is *not* a responsibility of the production control section with respect to acquisition of consumables that the information systems function uses?

    a Ensuring that consumables are stored securely

    b Monitoring the price and quality of consumables used

    c Issuing consumables only to authorized personnel

    d Performing credit control checks on vendors who provide consumables

8–19 Which of the following is *unlikely* to be a capability of an automated library system for removable storage media?

    a Preparing reports indicating times when the temperature and dust levels in the room where storage media are stored reached unacceptable levels

    b Recording the history of read/write errors that occur with storage media

    c Recording the dates when the contents of storage media can be deleted

    d Preparing reports on the history of uses of storage media

8–20 Which of the following reflects *good* control over use of removable storage media?

    a Only computer operators should remove storage media from the file library

    b Sensitive files and nonsensitive files should not be stored on the same removable storage medium

    c Project managers should maintain records of media use associated with the application systems over which they have responsibility

    d Backup for all media except diskettes should be kept off site

8–21 Which of the following decisions *most likely* could *not* be made on the basis of file management reports prepared from the storage media maintenance log?

    a Whether to move files from one storage medium to another to reduce read/write errors

    b Whether a storage medium should be retired

    c Whether a master file should be stored on a particular storage medium

    d Whether a program has updated the correct version of a master file

8–22 Which of the following actions should be undertaken when a file retention date expires?

    a The storage medium on which the file resides should be retired from use

    b The file should be removed to archival storage

    c The file should be purged

    d The file should be retrieved from backup storage

8–23 Removable storage media should not remain unused for long periods of time because:

    a The data they contain will become out-of-date

    b The risk of read/write errors occurring with the media increases

    c The likelihood of unauthorized access occurring to the media increases

    d It becomes more difficult to back up the media

8–24 The purpose of deleting data from magnetic tapes before the ends are clipped is to:

    a Indicate which section of the tape should be clipped

    b Protect the privacy of data

    c Prevent damage to the data on the tape

    d Relieve pressure from the tape hub

8–25 With respect to off-site storage of backup files, which of the following tasks is *most likely* to be undertaken by the operations manager:
  a Transporting backup files to off-site storage
  b Determining the frequency of backup for an application system
  c Choosing the site for off-site storage of backup
  d Ensuring that backup is made according to a predetermined schedule

8–26 Which of the following is *least likely* to be a function of a documentation librarian:
  a Ensuring that access rights to documentation are given only to the appropriate personnel
  b Ensuring that documentation is stored securely
  c Ensuring that adequate backup exists for documentation
  d Ensuring that only authorized person get access to documentation

8–27 Which of the following is *least likely* to be a function of a documentation librarian with respect to an organization's inventory of acquired or licensed software?
  a Ensuring that the software is backed up properly
  b Ensuring that use of licensed software complies with the terms of the agreement in relation to copying
  c Ensuring that user benefits from acquiring software exceed the costs
  d Ensuring that the software is not stolen

8–28 Which of the following is *least likely* to be a function performed by the help desk/technical support area?
  a Modifying end-user databases to correct errors and irregularities
  b Acquiring hardware and software on behalf of end users
  c Determining the source of problems with production systems and initiating corrective actions
  d Controlling the implementation of software upgrades

8–29 Which of the following decisions *most likely* could *not* be made on the basis of performance monitoring statistics that are calculated:
  a Whether the system being monitored has provided users with a strategic advantage over their competitors
  b Whether new hardware/system software resources are needed
  c Whether unauthorized use is being made of hardware/system software resources
  d Whether resource bottlenecks are occurring

8–30 Which of the following is *unlikely* to be a function performed by operations management with respect to the outsourcing contracts entered into by an organization:
  a Ensuring compliance with the outsourcing contract's terms and conditions
  b Choosing the outsourcing vendor to be used by the organization
  c Regular testing of disaster recovery procedures associated with the outsourcing vendor
  d Monitoring the outsourcing vendor for evidence of any financial difficulties

Exercises and Cases

8–1 Savers-Surety is a large, Brisbane-based credit union. Twelve months ago it purchased and implemented an automated operations facility (AOF) to control its mainframe operations. Prior to the purchase and implementation of the AOF, operators worked during three eight-hour shifts, seven days a week to support the mainframe. Savers-Surety had experienced several problems with this arrangement, however. First, operators often made costly mistakes in the jobs they performed. For some time, Savers-Surety had been unable to retain its operators, and inevitably critical jobs had to be performed by newly hired, inexperienced operators. Second, to reduce costs, only one operator had been working the graveyard shift (midnight to 8:00 AM). Management suspected that a previously employed operator who worked this shift had been making copies of critical data and selling the data to other financial institutions who were competitors. Third, management believed the mainframe was being used inefficiently because operators took little time to balance workloads on the machine.

You are an information systems auditor with a firm of chartered accountants that has just been appointed to take over the audit of Savers-Surety. During your evaluation of operations management controls, you question the information systems manager about the AOF. She explains that Savers-Surety has been delighted with the AOF. The credit union now operates a lights-out facility that the information systems manager believes has enhanced the security of information systems. In addition, the credit union no longer employs operators. As a result, she argues, all the previous problems associated with the operators have gone.

When you ask how the AOF parameters were prepared, she explains that Savers-Surety hired a new programmer who already had experience with the AOF that was purchased. He developed and implemented the parameters. In addition, the programmer had previously been an operator, so he had a good understanding of operations procedures. Indeed, his operations experience was useful because he could provide manual backup support when the AOF failed. On a few occasions he had operated the machine when the credit union had encountered problems with the AOF.

When you ask for documentation on the AOF parameters and the tests carried out on them before they were released into production, the information systems manager explains that you will have to interview the programmer. No one else within the credit union has knowledge of the AOF nor the nature of the parameters used to run the AOF.

Required. On the basis of the information you have collected so far, what are your conclusions about the reliability of controls over computer operations in Savers-Surety? Are there any exposures that concern you from the viewpoint of the opinion your firm must ultimately give on the financial statements? How would you now proceed with the audit?

8–2 Meridian Manufacturing Ltd. is a large, multidivisional Singapore-based manufacturer of electronic components and products. Over the past few years, Meridian has progressively implemented local area networks throughout its divisions. Currently, eight local area networks exist. Each can communicate with the others through bridges installed in their file servers. All local area networks also provide the platform for accounting information systems that are material from the viewpoint of Meredian's financial statements.

You are an information systems auditor in a firm of certified public accountants that has just taken over the external audit of Meridian. The partner in charge of the audit asks you to examine controls over the local area networks. You encounter the following situations during your investigations:

1. The file servers supporting the eight local area networks sit on a long desk outside Meredian's mainframe computer room. When you point out to the operations manager that you are concerned about the security of the file servers, she retorts that access to the information system facilities

is restricted to information systems staff. In addition, she informs you that the file-server keyboards are locked via a password. The keyboards can be unlocked only if the correct password is first keyed in to the file server.

2. One of the local area networks in an engineering division provides a gateway to a public wide area network. When you ask the divisional manager about the purposes of the gateway, he informs you that his staff uses the gateway to exchange electronic mail with their colleagues in other companies and in several research institutes. In addition, they sometimes exchange software and data files that they have found helpful in their jobs.

3. Maintenance of the local area networks is undertaken under contract by a small firm that specializes in selling and supporting local area networks for manufacturing organizations. The operations manager comments that she is very happy with the service provided by the person who undertakes the maintenance work. The networks have very little downtime. More-over, the person who undertakes maintenance work is happy to work on the networks after hours so that disruption to network users is minimized.

4. When you ask the operations manager about future plans for the networks, she informs you that the person who undertakes maintenance periodically makes recommendations about how the networks should be reconfigured and expanded. He has several utilities that he employs to monitor network usage, and in the past he has provided timely information on new hardware and software that should be purchased to support the networks.

Required.   From the viewpoint of the external audit, do any of the situations described here constitute exposures? If so, write a brief report for the partner in charge of the audit informing him how the situation constitutes an exposure and what controls should be implemented to eliminate the exposure or to reduce expected losses from the exposure to an acceptable level. In addition, provide suggestions on how the conduct of the remainder of the audit should be modified in light of your concerns.

8–3 You are the chief internal auditor for a large public utility that has used computer systems for many years in most areas of its operations. One day you are called to a meeting with the general manager and the information systems manager. The general manager indicates that she has called the meeting to discuss major difficulties that are being experienced with respect to data preparation and data entry activities within the utility. She provides statistics that show there has been a threefold increase in workers compensation claims paid by the utility to data preparation and data entry staff over the past five years because of repetition strain injury (office trauma). In addition, she indicates that morale among keyboard operators is at an all-time low be-cause several operators who have been with the utility for more than ten years have been forced to give up their jobs as a result of RSI.

Other difficulties have also arisen: the utility is in conflict with several unions over the RSI problems; there has been a major loss in productivity in the data preparation and data entry area; the error rate for keyed data has risen dramatically; and customers are complaining vociferously about poor turnaround time and errors in their accounts.

The general manager points out that part of the problem lies in the poor office environment in which many keyboard operators work. Several years ago data preparation and data entry activities were removed from the infor-mation systems facility and dispersed to user departments. Unfortunately several departmental managers now responsible for data preparation and data entry activities have been negligent in their management of these activities. Keyboard operators have been working for too long with poorly designed furniture, improper lighting, too few rest breaks, and so on. She also argues that some departmental managers have adopted an intolerant attitude toward workers who have shown symptoms of RSI, thereby aggravating relationships with their staff and the unions.

In an attempt to overcome the problems that have arisen, the general manager indicates she has called in a consultant to advise her on office and task redesign. She points out, however, that the consultant has been asked to focus only on long-run solutions to the problems that have arisen. It will take some time to implement any of the consultant's recommendations, such as purchasing new equipment, redesigning office layouts, and redesigning data preparation and data entry tasks. In the meantime, some action must be undertaken to restore productivity levels and to reduce data preparation and data entry error rates. In this light she seeks your advice on short-run strategies that might be followed to help alleviate the problems that have arisen.

Required. Prepare a brief report for the general manager outlining the courses of action you recommend to help increase productivity and to reduce error rates in the data preparation and data preparation function. What advice, if any, will you provide to your external auditors about the problems that have arisen with respect to data preparation and data entry?

8–4 In Australia, many financial institutions participate in a clearinghouse system for direct credit and direct debit transactions. For example, the employees of an organization can request that their pay be credited directly to their account in a financial institution. A typical situation is that the employer will prepare a magnetic tape or diskette with the payroll credits and then deliver this tape or diskette to the computer operations facility of some financial institution. The financial institution will read the tape or diskette and transmit the direct credits to a clearinghouse computer. At the clearinghouse computer, the transactions are split according to financial institution. The transactions are then transmitted to the respective financial institutions for posting to the employees' accounts.

Direct debit transactions are processed in a similar way. For example, a utility supplier might prepare a tape of debit transactions to be charged directly to the accounts of its customers. It will deliver the tape to the computer operations facility of some financial institution. The tape will then be read and the contents transmitted to a clearinghouse computer. The clearinghouse computer will split the transactions by financial institution and then transmit batches of debit charges to the respective financial institutions for posting to the accounts of the utility's customers.

The financial institutions that receive direct credit or direct debit transactions from employer or supplier organizations play a straightforward but critical role in the clearinghouse system. In particular, it is usually the production control groups in their computer operations facilities that are responsible for achieving the following objectives:

1. Only authorized direct credit and direct debit transactions must be submitted to the clearinghouse computer (authenticity objective).
2. Direct credit transactions received from employers and direct debit transactions received from suppliers must not be altered (accuracy objective).

3. All direct credit transactions received from employers and all direct debit transactions received from suppliers must be transmitted to the clearing-house computer (completeness objective).

4. All direct credit transactions received from employers and all direct debit transactions received from suppliers must be transmitted to the clearing-house computer on a timely basis (timeliness objective).

Required. For *each* of these four objectives, briefly describe the following:

1. An error or irregularity that would result in the objective not being achieved;

2. An exposure that would arise from the error or irregularity you identify;

3. A control exercised by production control personnel in the operations area that would reduce expected losses from the error or irregularity you identify;

4. An audit procedure you would use to determine whether the control is operating reliably.

8–5 You are an information systems auditor in a firm of external auditors that has just been appointed to undertake the audit of Second Sunstate, a medium-sized bank located in Orlando, Florida. As part of your efforts to gain familiarity with Second Sunstate's computer systems, you are currently investigating backup and recovery controls. In particular, you are seeking information on off-site storage of backup.

When you question the information systems manager about backup procedures, he informs you that the operations staff makes a full backup of files each day on magnetic tape. The backup is commenced around 11:00 PM during a quiet period of operations. Operators store the backup in the tape library, which is a locked room close to the computer room. The library is managed by a part-time clerk, who also works part-time for the bank's loans department. Each day the clerk collects the backup and takes it to another bank located several miles away. This bank in turn brings its backup each day to Second Sunstate for safe storage in the file library. They give their backup to an operator who places it in the file library.

When you ask if you can see the file library, the information systems manager gives you a key and says to "help yourself." Upon entering the file library room, you discover it is in a very untidy state. A large number of tapes have been stacked on the floor. When you look at these tapes, they appear to contain backup files created on various days over the past two weeks. In addition, the other bank's backup tapes are intermingled with Second Sunstate's backup tapes. There are also a large number of unlabeled tapes in tape racks and on the floor.

On a desk, you also notice a folder which seems to be a record of all tapes held by Second Sunstate and their location. Upon inspecting entries in the folder, you find that many are incomplete. Moreover, no entries seem to have been made in the past few days.

Subsequently you interview the clerk responsible for the file library and express concerns about your findings. He shrugs at your concerns and complains that he is overworked. He says he has had to work large amounts of overtime in the loans department and that he does not have time to attend to his file library functions each day. He has informed the loans manager about the problem, but nothing has been done. In any event, he points out that the backup tapes have never had to be used to his knowledge, so he considers his file librarian duties to be a lower priority than his loans duties.

Required. In light of your findings so far, what exposures does Second Sunstate face? What recommendations, if any, would you give to your partner in terms of how the current audit of Second Sunstate should be altered to take into account your findings?

Answers to Multiple-Choice Questions

8–1	b	8–9	c	8–17	a	8–25	d
8–2	d	8–10	b	8–18	d	8–26	a
8–3	c	8–11	a	8–19	a	8–27	c
8–4	a	8–12	d	8–20	b	8–28	a
8–5	a	8–13	d	8–21	d	8–29	a
8–6	d	8–14	b	8–22	c	8–30	b
8–7	b	8–15	c	8–23	b		
8–8	c	8–16	c	8–24	b		

REFERENCES

Arthur Andersen & Co. (1987), *Evaluation of Internal Controls: A Guide for Studying and Evaluating Internal Accounting Controls*. Chicago: Arthur Andersen & Co.

Cash, Jr., James I., F. Warren McFarlan, James L. McKenney, and Lynda M. Applegate (1992), *Corporate Information Systems Management: Text and Cases*, 3rd ed. Homewood, IL: Richard D. Irwin.

Dykman, Charlene A., and Charles K. Davis, eds. (1992), *Control Objectives*, 4th ed. Carol Stream, IL: The EDP Auditors Foundation, Inc.

Galitz, Wilbert O. (1993), *User-Interface Screen Design*. Wellesley, MA: QED Information Sciences, Inc.

Hoffman, Paul S. (1992), "What a Service Bureau Contract Should Contain," *EDP Auditing*. Boston: Auerbach Publications, Portfolio 76–01–20, 1–12.

Information Systems Audit and Control Foundation (1996), *COBIT: Audit Guidelines*. Rolling Meadows, IL: Information Systems Audit and Control Foundation.

King, Jonathan R. (1990), "Auditing the Lights-Out Operations Facility," *EDP Auditing*. Boston: Auerbach Publications, Portfolio 76–01–90, 1–12.

Loh, L., and N. Venkatraman (1992), "Diffusion of Information Technology Outsourcing: Influence Sources and the Kodak Effect," *Information Systems Research* (December), 334–358.

McCreary, Henry S., and Ellen M. Birch (1990), "Computer Capacity Planning from an Auditing Perspective," *EDP Auditing*. Boston: Auerbach Publications, Portfolio 76–02–85, 1–12.

McLean, Ephraim R., and Ronald Wilkes (1990), "Computer Operations: A Case of Management Neglect," *Journal of Information Systems Management* (Spring), 73–76.

McNurlin, Barbara C., and Ralph H. Sprague, Jr., eds. (1989), *Information Systems Management in Practice*, 2d ed. Upper Saddle River, NJ: Prentice-Hall.

Murphy, Michael A., and Xenia Ley Parker (1989), *Handbook of EDP Auditing*, 2d ed. Boston: Warren, Gorham & Lamont.

Rini, Nick C. (1990), "Cost Justifying an Automated Change Control System," *Journal of Information Systems Management* (Winter), 73–75.

Quality Assurance Management Controls

Chapter Outline

Chapter Key Points

■ Quality assurance (QA) management involves ensuring that the information systems produced by the information systems function achieve certain quality goals and that development, implementation, operation, and maintenance of information systems comply with a set of quality standards.

■ There are six reasons why the information systems QA role has emerged in many organizations: (a) increasingly organizations are producing safety-critical systems; (b) users are becoming more demanding in terms of the quality of the software they employ to undertake their work; (c) organizations are undertaking more ambitious information systems projects that have more stringent quality requirements; (d) organizations are becoming increasingly concerned about their liabilities if they produce and sell defective software; (e) poor control over the production, implementation, operation, and maintenance of software can be costly; (f) improving the quality of software is part of a worldwide trend among organizations to improve the quality of the goods and services they sell.

■ The first function of QA personnel is to develop quality goals for the information systems function overall and to assist in the development of quality goals for specific information systems. Obtaining consensus on quality goals can be difficult because different stakeholders have differing perspectives on quality, quality goals might need to vary across information systems, and at times quality goals may conflict with one another.

■ The second function of QA personnel is to develop, promulgate, and maintain information systems standards. Standards are the backbone of planning and control activities in the information systems function. QA personnel are in the best position to be responsible for standards because they should be the most knowledgeable about standards, they should be perceived as independent, and they have incentives to keep standards up to date.

■ The third function of QA personnel is to monitor compliance with standards. Monitoring must be undertaken in terms of *general* standards that govern the overall information systems function and *specific* standards that govern a particular information system.

■ The fourth function of QA personnel is to identify areas for improvement. Identifying areas for improvement should be part of an ongoing process that leads to higher-quality information systems being produced. QA personnel should make recommendations for improvement based on facts rather than intuition or experience.

■ The fifth function of QA personnel is to report to management. Regular reports on compliance with *general* standards and *specific* standards must be prepared. Reports must be positive in nature, contain no surprises, and be based on sound analyses that are supported by concrete facts.

■ The sixth function of QA personnel is to train all other information systems personnel in quality assurance standards and procedures. One type of training focuses on general knowledge about standards and procedures. Another type focuses on specific training that is needed to support the development, implementation, operation, and maintenance of a specific application system.

■ The QA function should be placed in the organizational hierarchy of the information systems function so that it can operate independently of other information systems activities. The manager of the QA function should report directly to the executive who is in charge of the information systems function. QA personnel should be afforded sufficient status so they can operate effectively.

■ Properly staffing the QA function can be difficult to accomplish. QA personnel need to be well trained and competent, and their skills must be up to date. They must also have a high level of interpersonal skills. Many information systems personnel prefer to engage in development work rather than quality assurance work. Consequently, management must sometimes work hard to attract high-quality staff into QA positions.

■ In many ways, the objectives of and functions of QA personnel and auditors are the same. Both are concerned with ensuring high-quality information systems are developed, implemented, operated, and maintained. Both also are concerned with collecting evidence on and evaluating the reliability of information systems controls. As a result, auditors often can place greater reliance on controls and reduce the extent of substantive testing work when a QA function is in place and working reliably.

INTRODUCTION

Quality assurance (QA) management is concerned with ensuring that *(1)* the information systems produced by the information systems function achieve certain quality goals and *(2)* development, implementation, operation, and maintenance of information systems comply with a set of quality standards. The QA function has come into existence because many organizations now recognize they can no longer compete effectively unless they emphasize quality throughout all their operations. Moreover, they also recognize the need for independent review of the work done by information systems development, maintenance, and operations staff. Even with the best intentions, people cannot properly evaluate the quality of their own work. Independent, objective assessments are required.

Like the data administration function (see Chapter 6), the information systems QA function is relatively new. Auditors might not find it in all organizations. It is more likely to exist in those organizations where the information systems function is large and those that produce software where the quality of the software is a paramount requirement. Where a QA function does exist, however, it can have an important impact on the conduct of audit work. QA personnel are concerned with controls compliance in the same way that auditors have this focus. If auditors find a high-quality QA function in place, most likely greater reliance can be placed on controls, and the extent of substantive testing during the audit can be reduced.

In this chapter we first address the motivations for establishing an information systems QA role within organizations. Next we examine the various functions that QA personnel should perform. We then discuss some organizational issues that relate to where the QA function should be placed within the organizational hierarchy and how it should be staffed. Finally, we examine briefly how the existence of a QA function impacts the audit function.

MOTIVATIONS TOWARD THE QA ROLE

There are six reasons why the information systems QA role has emerged in many organizations (Figure 9–1). First, increasingly organizations are producing safety-critical information systems. For example, software is now used to support air traffic control, weapon guidance systems, ship guidance systems, nuclear reactors, radiation therapy equipment, heart pacemakers, and drug infusion systems (Leveson 1986, 1991). Errors in these systems can have devastating effects, such as loss of life, extensive destruction of property, and widespread damage to the environment. Organizations that produce safety-critical software must strive to ensure it is error free.

Second, users are becoming more demanding in terms of their expectations about the quality of software they employ to undertake their work. Many organizations that produce software now believe they will not be able to compete effectively in the marketplace unless their software meets stringent quality control standards. Otherwise their customers will simply switch to competitors who produce higher-quality software. Some customers also require that software developers meet certain quality standards. In Australia, for example, in the absence of mitigating circumstances, the Queensland State Government will not purchase software from developers unless they have been certified by a third party as meeting Australian Standard AS3563—Software Quality Management System.

Third, organizations are undertaking more ambitious projects when they build software. As information systems development skills, tools, and methodologies improve and the needs of more straightforward applications have been addressed, organizations are looking to pioneering and innovative applications for software in an attempt to gain a competitive advantage. These applications are often large and complex. As a result, their development, implementation, operation, and maintenance is difficult. If these applications are to accomplish their objectives, they must meet stringent quality control standards.

Fourth, organizations are becoming increasingly concerned about their liabilities if they produce and sell defective software. Although the law relating to

FIGURE 9–1. Motivations toward implementation of the information systems quality assurance function.

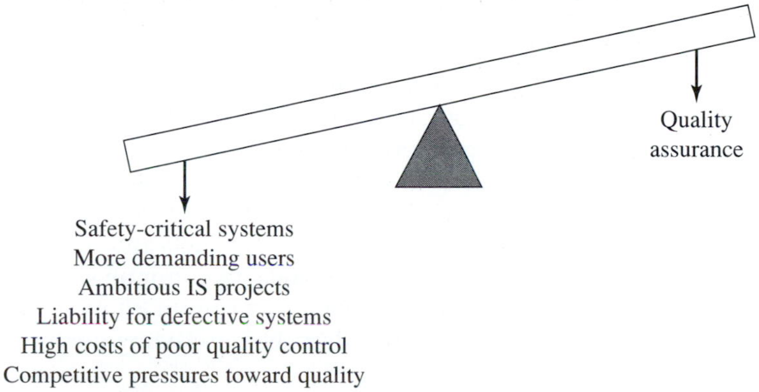

Quality
assurance

Safety-critical systems
More demanding users
Ambitious IS projects
Liability for defective systems
High costs of poor quality control
Competitive pressures toward quality

this area is still evolving, there are signs that companies might be liable for losses caused by defective software unless they have taken reasonable and prudent steps to ensure the quality of the software they market (Chmiel and Wilson 1993). In any event, even if eventually a company is not found liable for defective software it has produced and sold, the loss of customer goodwill that might arise could severely undermine its profitability.

Fifth, poor quality control over the production, implementation, operation, and maintenance of software can be costly in terms of missed deadlines, dissatisfied users and customers, lower morale among information systems staff, higher maintenance, and strategic projects that must be abandoned. In some cases the senior management of organizations have had to explain to shareholders why software development debacles have severely affected profits, dividends, and share prices. In short, high-quality information systems and high profitability are inextricably bound in some organizations. Indeed, many proponents of quality management argue it is free (see, e.g., Crosby 1979 and Deming 1986): The benefits of quality management exceed its costs.

Sixth, improving the quality of information systems is part of a worldwide trend among organizations to improve the quality of the goods and services they sell. Many Western organizations, for example, are seeking to emulate the success of Japanese companies which have had an unbending focus on customer needs, continuous quality improvement, and the production of zero-defect goods and services. Total quality management (TQM) is now a major driving force in many organizations because of their need to compete effectively in international marketplaces.

QA FUNCTIONS

QA personnel should work closely with information systems personnel to improve the quality of information systems produced, implemented, operated, and maintained in an organization. They perform a *monitoring* role for management to ensure that *(1)* quality goals are established and understood clearly by all stakeholders and *(2)* compliance occurs with the standards that are in place to attain quality information systems. Like auditors, QA personnel should not assume responsibility for performing development, implementation, operations, or maintenance work. Otherwise, they will lose their independence. Moreover, they will become embroiled in costly, time-consuming disputes over specific issues and lose perspective on whether the information systems function overall is striving to meet quality goals.

In some organizations, QA personnel also play the critical role of preparing an organization to be accredited as being in compliance with a certain set of quality standards and then maintaining accreditation once it has been achieved initially. For example, in the United Kingdom, organizations may seek accreditation from the British Standards Institute that they comply with the International Organization for Standardization's (ISO's) 9000 series of standards on quality (Ince 1994). These organizations will be subject to an initial audit for compliance with the standards and then regular ongoing audits for compliance. Obtaining a certificate of compliance with the ISO 9000 standards can be critical to their being able to sell their software products and services in the marketplace.

In the following subsections we examine six specific functions that QA personnel should perform. Auditors should know enough about these functions to be able to evaluate whether they are being performed reliably by QA personnel. Moreover, if QA personnel are not performing these functions reliably, auditors must understand the implications for the conduct of the audit. We assume that auditors are auditing organizations that are not seeking accreditation on compliance with quality standards from some official body. In this light, the organizations audited will have some flexibility in the choice of approach they take to quality assurance.

Developing Quality Goals

One of the more difficult tasks that QA personnel must undertake is to develop quality goals for the information systems function and to develop or approve quality goals for specific information systems. Three problems arise. The first is that quality can have a different meaning depending on whose perspective is adopted. Top management, for example, might evaluate quality in terms of whether an information system allows their organization to compete better in a marketplace. Programmers, on the other hand, might evaluate quality in terms of whether the program code for an information system is well structured. Customers might evaluate quality in terms of the level of functionality the system provides. Many different notions of quality might have to be taken into account, therefore, when formulating quality goals.

The second problem is that quality goals might need to vary across information systems. In safety-critical systems, for example, accuracy and completeness may be paramount objectives. In a strategic planning system, however, achieving timely reporting could override data accuracy and completeness goals. In short, quality goals can vary, depending on the nature of the system to be developed, operated, and maintained.

The third problem is that quality goals could be in conflict with one another. For example, one quality goal for an information system might be a fast response time. This goal might be achieved, however, only by writing complex algorithms that are difficult for programmers to understand and maintain. Specifying the goals for information systems, therefore, sometimes requires that decisions be made on how one goal will be traded off against another.

At the overall level of the information systems function, there now seems to be general agreement that quality encompasses notions like "fitness for purpose," "having information systems meet the objectives and standards in place," and "having information systems support the goals of the organization" (see, e.g., Chmiel and Wilson 1993 and Ragozzino 1990). In many organizations, a focus on customer needs also pervades the overall quality goals established for the information systems function (Brinkworth 1992). This focus reflects a move from traditional quality systems to modern quality systems. Whereas traditional quality systems emphasize detecting and correcting defects in software, modern quality systems also emphasize maximizing customer satisfaction with the resulting product. In this regard, Zultner (1993, pp. 80–81) points out that achieving zero-defect software does not necessarily mean customers are happy with the software.

At the level of specific information systems, however, articulating quality goals is more difficult. If QA personnel are responsible for preparing the quality plan, they must work with the stakeholders in an information system to elicit the quality goals they deem important. These goals can differ across information systems. For example, as discussed previously, in some cases the goals of an information system may focus on accuracy and completeness; in other cases timeliness goals may mean that accuracy and completeness goals have to be compromised.

TABLE 9–1 Software Quality Characteristics

Quality Characteristic	Explanation
Functionality	Extent to which the software contains the functions needed to satisfy user needs.
Reliability	Extent to which the software sustains its level of performance under stated conditions for some defined time period.
Usability	Level of effort needed for users to exploit the functionality of the software.
Efficiency	Level of resources consumed by the software to perform its functions.
Maintainability	Level of effort needed to modify the software.
Portability	Extent to which software can be transferred from one hardware/software platform to another.

Table 9-1 shows six quality characteristics that the International Organization for Standardization has adopted in their standard for Software Product Evaluation (ISO 9126, 1991). QA personnel can use these characteristics to articulate quality goals for *individual* information systems. The six characteristics provide a checklist that QA personnel can use during their interviews with stakeholders to determine quality goals. The levels required for each characteristic can be evaluated, and trade-offs that need to be made among the characteristics can be considered.

When formulating or evaluating the quality goals for a specific information system, QA personnel must take care to ensure the specific goals are not in conflict with the overall goals of the organization. For example, to achieve certain strategic goals for the organization, management might require that information systems not be sold to customers if the likelihood of a system containing a defect is above a certain level. It might be impossible to achieve this goal, however, if a particular system is to be developed within a time frame that is acceptable to its customers. Either management must relinquish the overall quality goal, or customers must compromise with respect to the development time frame. If neither of these alternatives is acceptable, the organization may have to desist from developing the system.

Similarly, the goals of individual information systems can be in conflict. For example, to achieve the desired response time for an information system, substantial operational resources (e.g., the amount of memory and disk space) might have to be allocated to the system. As a result, response times for other systems that operate concurrently with the system may decline to unacceptable levels. QA personnel must be mindful of quality goals for a specific information system in the context of quality goals that exist for other information systems.

Gaining acceptance among stakeholders of the quality goals for a specific information system can be difficult. In the case of system-development staff, for example, they might consider that quality goals place unwanted constraints on the ways they work. Only token acceptance of quality goals might occur. As a result, quality goals are compromised quickly when problems are encountered during system development. For this reason, some organizations require that the quality plan for a specific information system be prepared by a quality-control group within the project team. These organizations believe quality goals are more likely to be *owned* by the project team if team members have responsibility for preparing the quality plan. QA personnel then play the role of ap-

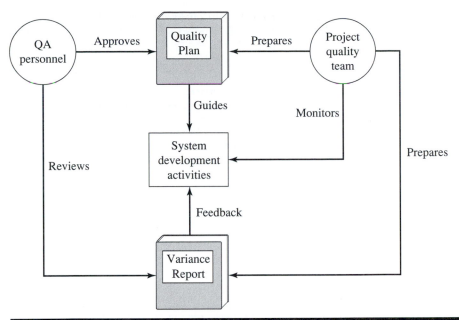

FIGURE 9–2. Using a project quality plan to attain quality goals.

proving the quality plan prepared by the project team and monitoring how the project team uses the plan to achieve quality goals (Figure 9–2).

When quality goals have been determined for a specific information system, it is important that quality metrics be chosen. Quality goals are unlikely to be accomplished satisfactorily unless information systems personnel know the criteria to be used to determine whether quality goals have been met. Because the adequacy of various quality measures can be a contentious area, it is important that QA personnel again consult all stakeholders and try to negotiate agreement on the quality metrics to be used.

There are several ways in which auditors can check how well QA personnel formulate quality goals for the information systems function and for specific systems. First, they can check whether a charter has been established for the QA function and, if so, whether this charter contains a statement of overall quality goals for the information systems function. Second, auditors can check whether quality goals and quality metrics have been established for specific information systems by examining the quality plan that should have been prepared for each information system. Third, auditors can interview and observe QA personnel and information systems personnel to determine their level of awareness about overall quality goals for the information systems function and the approaches they use to formulate quality goals for specific information systems. Finally, auditors can interview stakeholders (including management) to obtain their opinion on how well they believe QA personnel discharge their duties with respect to formulating quality goals for the information systems function and for specific information systems.

If, on the basis of evidence-collection activities, auditors conclude that QA personnel are formulating quality goals satisfactorily, most likely it will be worthwhile to proceed to evaluate other QA functions with a view to reducing the extent of substantive testing. On the other hand, if auditors conclude that QA personnel are not formulating quality goals satisfactorily, they should consider carefully whether it is worthwhile proceeding further to evaluate other controls that should be exercised by the QA function. If quality goals are missing or poorly formulated, it is unlikely that other QA controls can be exercised satisfactorily.

Developing, Promulgating, and Maintaining Standards for the Information Systems Function

As discussed in Chapter 3, information systems standards are an important means of achieving asset safeguarding, data integrity, system effectiveness, and system efficiency objectives. They must cover all major tasks performed within the information systems function—for example, requirements analysis, design, programming, testing, documentation, operations, and maintenance. They must also recognize that substantial diversity exists in the ways the information systems function is now performed. For example, they must take into account that information systems are developed under varying levels of uncertainty, that information systems functions are sometimes performed on mainframe computers and sometimes performed on microcomputers, and that information systems are sometimes developed by information systems professionals and sometimes by end users. In general, the objective is to provide *minimal specification of standards*: The standards should enable quality objectives to be attained, but they should not stultify the ways in which information systems personnel must work to accomplish their jobs.

There are four advantages to having QA personnel assume responsibility for the development, promulgation, and maintenance of information systems standards. First, QA personnel are charged with being knowledgeable about and remaining up to date with best practice in information systems standards. They should be familiar with the types of standards that have been adopted by organizations that are similar to their own. Furthermore, they should be knowledgeable about standards that are being developed or those that have been adopted by national or international standards organizations. Given the substantial work that is now being undertaken worldwide on information systems standards, organizations must make a major commitment to keep up to date with developments and to understand the potential impacts that standards may have on their own activities.

Second, within an organization, decisions on standards can often be a political issue that evokes strong, emotive reactions. Standards can have a major impact on the ways work is done. Some people perceive that standards will inhibit their work; others will argue that standards allow too much freedom; still others will be concerned about how standards affect the formal or informal power they hold. Consequently, many people have a vested interest in the outcome of standards decisions. Of all stakeholders, QA personnel are likely to be perceived as the most independent if they assume responsibility for the development, promulgation, and maintenance of information systems standards. QA personnel are charged with adopting an organizationwide view on standards. To the extent they do not adopt this broad perspective, their position within the organizations is likely to become untenable.

Third, QA personnel are supposed to undertake analyses of the reasons when an organization fails to achieve its information systems quality goals (see the following section). In this light, they should obtain insights and understanding that will allow them to make good judgments on the characteristics of standards that are best suited to their organizations. They should be able to identify any new standards that need to be developed or any existing standards that need to be modified based upon the follow-up analyses of information systems problems that they undertake. Again, they are likely to be better placed than any other stakeholder to make judgments on standards because their work allows them to obtain a broad overview of information systems activities within their organizations.

Fourth, QA personnel should have incentives to ensure that their organization adopts and complies with the best set of information systems standards possible. No other personnel within the organization are likely to have their performance evaluated on the basis of attainment of quality goals to the extent that QA personnel are evaluated on this basis. Moreover, other personnel inevitably face dilemmas because quality goals conflict with other goals that are more central to their role. For example, development personnel might face a situation in which deadlines will be missed if they comply with documentation standards. If senior management establishes the correct incentives for the QA function, it should always be in the best interests of QA personnel to seek to achieve both the short- and long-term quality goals of the organization.

QA personnel have an important role to play in *monitoring* national and international information systems standards that could affect their organization. These standards should inform the process of developing the overall standards to be used by an organization's information systems function and any specific standards that are needed to support the work conducted in relation to a particular information system project (Figure 9–3).

QA personnel also might want to actively *participate* in the development of national or international standards. In some cases, these standards can be exceedingly helpful to an organization attaining its goals. For example, agreement on some type of data communication standard can allow an organization to interact better electronically with its customers and to strengthen its position within the marketplace. In other cases, however, standards could undermine an organization's competitive position. For example, the organization may have invested heavily in systems that are at odds with the standards eventually adopted. By participating in the standard-setting process, QA personnel can seek to safeguard the interests of their organizations and provide timely warning when adverse standards are likely to be adopted.

QA personnel also have an important role to play in monitoring *best practices* in other organizations. As with national and international standards, best

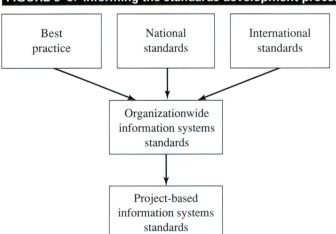

FIGURE 9–3. Informing the standards development process.

practices can affect the specific information system processes that are adopted and enforced as standards within an organization. In some cases, knowledge about best practice can be obtained via publications. For example, the *clean-room method* of software development is widely accepted as best practice in producing software with known and certified mean time to failure (MTTF). It involves relying heavily on software practitioners using formal specifications, formal verification, formal design and code inspections, independent software product testing, and statistical process control. The processes associated with the cleanroom method are now well documented (see, e.g., Dyer 1992). In other cases, however, knowledge about best practice is not readily available. It can be obtained only by QA personnel fostering a network of professional contacts and attending conferences and professional meetings.

Whatever standards or practices are chosen, QA personnel must take care to match the capabilities of their organization with the demands that arise from seeking to adhere to different types of standards or practices. In this regard, the Software Engineering Institute at Carnegie Mellon University has developed a Capability Maturity Model (CMM) that defines five levels of organizational maturity and the software quality processes associated with each of these levels (Figure 9–4). Organizations are admonished not to try to jump levels. Rather, they are urged to undertake continuous process improvement and to move through these levels in an evolutionary way (see, e.g., Paulk et al. 1993 and Chrissis et al. 1995). Only by mastering the software quality processes associated with lower levels in the CMM is an organization likely to be able to implement successfully the software quality processes associated with higher levels in the CMM.

Auditors can use interviews, observations, and reviews of documentation to evaluate how well QA personnel develop, promulgate, and maintain standards for the information systems function. They can ask QA personnel about

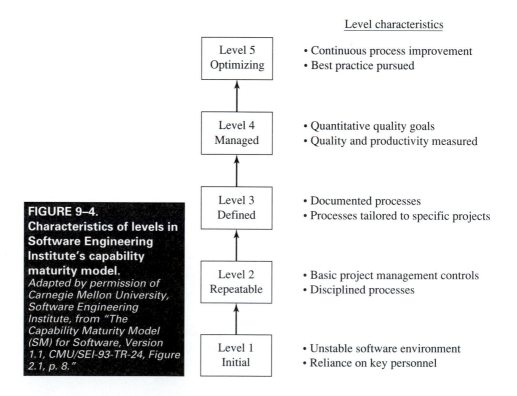

FIGURE 9–4. Characteristics of levels in Software Engineering Institute's capability maturity model.
Adapted by permission of Carnegie Mellon University, Software Engineering Institute, from "The Capability Maturity Model (SM) for Software, Version 1.1, CMU/SEI-93-TR-24, Figure 2.1, p. 8."

Level characteristics

Level 5 Optimizing
• Continuous process improvement
• Best practice pursued

Level 4 Managed
• Quantitative quality goals
• Quality and productivity measured

Level 3 Defined
• Documented processes
• Processes tailored to specific projects

Level 2 Repeatable
• Basic project management controls
• Disciplined processes

Level 1 Initial
• Unstable software environment
• Reliance on key personnel

the procedures they use to develop, promulgate, and maintain standards. Similarly, they can ask stakeholders to evaluate how well QA personnel undertake these activities. By attending meetings where QA personnel focus on standards, auditors can observe how they undertake standards work. Because standards should be documented, they can review this documentation to assess the quality of the standards work carried out by QA personnel.

To the extent that auditors see high-quality standards being developed, promulgated, and maintained, they can have more confidence that QA personnel are performing their functions reliably. Moreover, they can have more confidence that other information systems personnel are performing their functions reliably because they have good standards to guide their work. In this light, auditors should be able to reduce the extent of their substantive testing. If QA personnel do not develop, promulgate, and maintain high-quality standards, however, many other QA functions are undermined. For example, in the absence of high-quality standards, monitoring for compliance with standards is likely to be ineffective. As a result, the work performed by other information systems personnel is likely to deteriorate. To assess the effects on audit objectives, auditors will need to expand the extent of their substantive testing.

Monitoring Compliance with QA Standards

QA personnel undertake two types of monitoring of compliance with QA standards. First, they monitor compliance with the QA plan prepared for a *specific* system. In this regard they focus on development, implementation, operations, and maintenance activities associated with that system. In their compliance monitoring role, they might participate as moderators during design and code inspections, evaluate whether test data has been properly documented, and participate in review meetings when important milestones occur. They should also check to see that project personnel are themselves monitoring compliance with the quality plan prepared for the project. In this regard, they should see project personnel actively using standard quality-control tools that allow deviations from plans to be identified and improvements in project activities to be effected. For example, fishbone diagrams should be used to diagnose the causes of problems and to identify ways to mitigate these problems in future software projects (Figure 9–5).

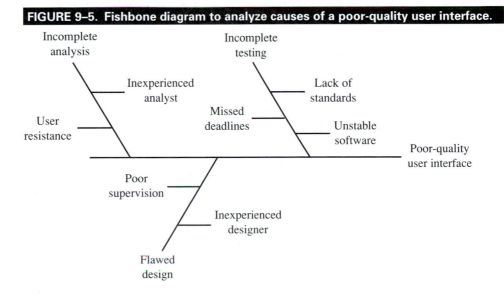

FIGURE 9–5. Fishbone diagram to analyze causes of a poor-quality user interface.

QA personnel also should monitor compliance with *general* standards (standards that do not focus on a specific system). For example, an organization might have standards relating to the amount of ongoing professional development training that information systems staff must undertake. Certain managers might be responsible for ensuring that staff undertake the requisite training. QA personnel, in turn, should evaluate whether both staff and management are complying with the training standard.

Two principles govern how compliance monitoring should be undertaken by QA personnel. First, they must remember that their role is to facilitate rather than to inhibit information systems development, implementation, operations, and maintenance. In this light they must be constructive and positive in their monitoring role. If they adopt an arbitrary, antagonistic, negative stance, they will lose credibility, and they no longer will be able to play an effective role.

Second, QA personnel should seek to avoid disputes over detail. Instead, their role should be to notify management when compliance with standards has not occurred. Management is then responsible for resolving specific difficulties that have ensued or may ensue. Ultimately, management must decide whether it wishes to insist that compliance with standards occurs. If QA personnel engage in disputes over details and petitions to enforce compliance, they will lose the confidence of information systems staff and management.

When a compliance failure occurs, QA personnel should seek to understand the reasons for the failure so they can advise management. In some cases, there could be good reasons for noncompliance. Such reasons could motivate reconsideration of standards and ultimately bring about improved standards. In other cases, noncompliance could reflect a breakdown in a process, in which case corrective action will be needed.

QA personnel should also consider the consequences of compliance failure and brief management on these consequences. The repercussions could be serious if, for example, the failure results in a breach of contract with a customer or the potential arises for a substantial liability associated with a defective software product. On the other hand, the consequences might not be serious, at least in the short run, and urgent action might not be required.

When compliance failure occurs, QA personnel should consider appropriate corrective actions so they can make recommendations to management. Better recommendations can be made if QA personnel have a sound understanding of the reasons for the failure and the potential consequences of the failure. The recommendations are likely to be more concrete, more specific, and more compelling. Whether management acts on the recommendations, however, is their prerogative. Again, QA personnel should seek to avoid becoming involved in specific debates.

Compliance monitoring can be an important element of any certification that the organization has been given with respect to software quality. When the organization is being recertified, the certifying party might look to see that monitoring is carried out rigorously and that management takes appropriate actions in light of advice received on the basis of the monitoring process.

Auditors can use interviews, observations, and reviews of documentation to evaluate how well QA personnel perform their monitoring role. They can ask QA personnel what monitoring procedures they follow, talk with stakeholders to determine their experience of the QA monitoring process, observe QA personnel as they undertake the monitoring process, and review reports produced as a result of the monitoring process. Auditors should also seek to determine what actions have been undertaken as a result of the monitoring process to reach a decision on whether it is effective.

If auditors conclude that the monitoring process is not in place or that it is not being conducted reliably, they should have grave concerns about the overall effectiveness of the QA function. Without proper monitoring, an organization does not demonstrate a commitment to quality. As a result, its staff are unlikely to take quality seriously. Accordingly, auditors would have to place less reliance on controls and expand the extent of substantive testing.

Identifying Areas for Improvement

An important outcome of QA personnel's monitoring role is that they should identify areas where the activities of the information systems function can be improved. As discussed previously, noncompliance with quality standards means either the standards have to be revised because they are deficient or a development, implementation, operations, or maintenance process has to be improved because there has been a genuine breakdown. In either case, noncompliance should lead to improved standards or processes.

For two reasons, QA personnel should have responsibility for identifying areas where the information systems function can be improved. First, given their overarching concern with quality assurance, they are in the best position to offer *independent* advice. Other stakeholders, such as programmers and users, have vested interests. As a result, their recommendations will tend to lack credibility. For example, to reduce the number of missed development deadlines, programmers might argue that users have to be more diligent when they provide requirements specifications. Given the conflicts of interest that often exist between users and programmers, however, users are likely to be skeptical about such views. QA personnel, on the other hand, have no allegiance to a particular stakeholder group. Thus, their recommendations are more likely to be accepted. Nevertheless, they must be mindful that they will be given this trust only if they both act independently and are perceived to act independently. Like auditors, independence "in fact" and "in mind" are essential to the effective discharge of their duties.

Second, QA personnel should have the knowledge and experience to make the best recommendations for improvements to information systems standards or processes. QA personnel are supposed to keep up-to-date with the types of difficulties that all stakeholders in the information systems function encounter. Moreover, they should be aware of the best practice to overcome or to mitigate these difficulties. Given their duties, they also should have a broad appreciation of activities across all stakeholder groups. In this light, they should be able to address issues such as *(1)* the likelihood that information systems activities can be improved cost effectively, *(2)* the appropriateness of changes to information systems standards, *(3)* the impact that changes to standards or processes will have on all stakeholder groups, *(4)* the likelihood that changes to standards or processes will evoke behavioral resistance, and *(5)* the support that is likely be forthcoming from management if standards or processes are changed.

As discussed previously, regular monitoring for compliance of information systems activities against standards provides an important basis for QA personnel identifying areas where the information system function can be improved. In addition, material information systems *errors* that occur should also be reported routinely to QA personnel. For example, QA personnel should be informed when an application program updates a database incorrectly or an application program aborts prematurely during production execution. An error-management system should be in place to record these types of errors and to report them to QA personnel on a timely basis. QA personnel should then analyze the errors to identify their causes and to determine whether standards or processes need to be improved. For example, in the short run, QA personnel might be able to alert programmers that certain types of errors have been made frequently in programs that update distributed databases. In the long run, program testing standards may be modified to detect these errors before programs are released into production.

As with recommendations for corrective actions when noncompliance with standards occurs, recommendations for improved standards or processes will be more compelling if they are based on analyses of particular deficiencies that have occurred, a sound understanding of the reasons for these deficiencies, and careful argumentation as to why the recommendations will overcome or mitigate the deficiencies. Stakeholders, especially management, are unlikely to be convinced by abstract arguments. Consequently, QA personnel should strive to be specific and concrete in the recommendations they make.

When conducting activities to identify areas for improvement, QA personnel should be guided by the Japanese notion of *Kaizen* (Imai 1986). *Kaizen* means "ongoing improvement." It involves everyone in an organization (managers and workers), and it has been fundamental to Japan's success with TQM. It stresses the need for a continuous, process-oriented cycle of planning, approval, execution, monitoring, and evaluation (Figure 9–6). In this light, QA personnel must regard the identification of areas for improvement as an ongoing activity rather than a periodic activity. Furthermore, *Kaizen* focuses on the need to base improvement decisions on *facts* rather than experience or intuition. QA personnel should seek, therefore, to make recommendations for improvement only if they have a substantive empirical basis to back up their recommendations.

Auditors can evaluate how well QA personnel make recommendations for improved standards or processes through interviews, observations, and reviews of documentation. For example, they can interview stakeholders in the information systems function to obtain their opinions on the quality of advice provided by QA personnel with respect to improvement in standards and processes. They can observe the procedures followed to report material errors to QA personnel and the actions they follow upon being notified of material errors. Auditors can review reports to assess the quality of the recommendations provided by QA personnel with respect to improvements in standards and

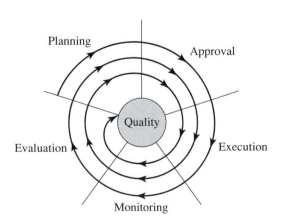

FIGURE 9–6. The quality spiral.

processes. In particular, auditors should seek to determine what actions were taken by management in light of the recommendations. If they conclude that QA personnel function effectively to provide advice on improved standards and processes, they can have greater confidence in the overall reliability of information systems controls. Accordingly, it is likely auditors will be able to reduce the extent of substantive testing. If they do not function effectively, however, most likely the extent of substantive testing will have to be increased.

Reporting to Management

QA reporting is an important but difficult undertaking. Given the nature of the QA function, stakeholders could be quick to take umbrage with the contents of reports. As a result, political difficulties can ensue. Moreover, it is sometimes difficult to identify who should receive a QA report in order to achieve the greatest impact.

QA personnel must take great care in preparing their reports. The reports must not degenerate into a long list of defects that have been identified. Otherwise, they will cause anger among stakeholders, and conflict will arise. Instead, the reports must focus on major findings and fundamental issues that need to be addressed. Recommendations must be backed up by sound analyses based on concrete facts. The reports also must be positive in nature, and they should contain no surprises. Otherwise the reports will evoke protracted escalation meetings where stakeholders seek to defend their positions. When this outcome arises, inevitably QA personnel lose their credibility, and the effectiveness of the QA function is undermined.

Regular reports on compliance with *general* information systems standards should be provided to the manager of the information systems function. Those who should be the recipients of *project-based* reports, however, are less clear-cut. Project managers need to receive copies of these reports because they provide the basis for better management of their projects. Moreover, they have a right to know the contents of reports about projects under their control. Project managers have vested interests in projects under their control, however, and as a result they may resist recommendations for change. In this light, QA reports must be provided to stakeholders who have opposing interests. The views of one group who oppose the changes can then be counterbalanced by another group who support the changes. Nevertheless, lines of reporting must be agreed on at the outset of a project so recipients are not altered midstream to further some group of stakeholder's political ends.

Auditors can evaluate how well QA personnel undertake the reporting function through interviews, observations, and reviews of documentation. For example, auditors can interview QA personnel to determine the approaches they use to report their findings. They can also interview stakeholders to determine their levels of satisfaction with the QA reporting process. When meetings are called to discuss the contents of reports, auditors can attend to see how the reports are received and what changes they evoke. They can also review a sample of QA reports to obtain evidence to make a judgement on their quality.

If auditors conclude that QA personnel are carrying out the reporting function effectively, they can have greater confidence in the likelihood that QA efforts are having a material impact on the quality of information systems that are being developed, implemented, and maintained. Accordingly, auditors can reduce the extent of substantive testing. If, on the other hand, the reporting function is not being carried out effectively, QA activities are likely to have little impact on information systems practices. Even if all other QA functions are well carried out, poor reporting can negate their impact. As a result, auditors will have to increase the extent of substantive testing.

Training in QA Standards and Procedures

Training is an essential element to maintenance of and compliance with QA standards and procedures. Indeed, Deutsch and Willis (1988, p. 19) argue that "the cornerstone of quality is skilled and motivated people." Without training, QA standards and procedures are likely to fall into disuse because they are not updated or due to either ignorance or apathy on the part of stakeholders.

QA personnel have responsibility for training all stakeholders in the information systems function in QA standards and procedures. They must undertake two types of training. The first focuses on providing *general* knowledge about quality assurance. It addresses the nature of and motivations for quality assurance. It also examines the general standards and procedures established to attain QA objectives. For example, stakeholders would be apprised of systems-development milestones that require formal approval and sign-off and requirements for user documentation that must be met before software will be released for production use.

The second type of training focuses on standards and procedures that will be *specific* to an application system. For example, because a particular application to be developed will support life-critical activities, a third party might be employed to undertake independent verification and validation of the system. In the normal course of events, an organization might not develop life-critical applications. As a result, specific QA standards and procedures might have to be formulated for the application. These specific standards and procedures should be identified when the QA plan for the application is prepared. Information systems personnel associated with the development, operation, and maintenance of the system then must be apprised of these standards and procedures.

QA training should be focused. A personal development plan should exist for each information systems employee. This plan should reflect both the organization's and the employee's goals and a development strategy for the employee to attain these goals. In relation to quality assurance, it should specify general education that the employee should acquire, specific training that the employee should undertake, and work experience that the employee should obtain. By analyzing the needs manifested in these personal development plans, QA personnel can formulate an overall QA training program for their organization.

QA training should also be ongoing. New employees must be inducted in the QA goals, standards, and procedures that have been adopted by the information systems function. Such induction is especially important when new employees are experienced information systems professionals who have *not* worked previously in organizations where quality is a paramount goal. Breaking undesirable work habits among experienced professionals can be a difficult problem to overcome. Subsequent training must be undertaken regularly. If a QA program is to work effectively, all stakeholders must be constantly reminded of its importance. Moreover, through regular training they can be admonished to achieve QA goals and objectives and reminded how they can achieve these goals and objectives.

QA personnel can use in-service training as an important means of discernment in relation to QA standards and procedures. Stakeholders have an oppor-

FIGURE 9–7. Quality assurance in-service training as a discernment process.

tunity to articulate the problems they have experienced in complying with QA standards and procedures. Discussion and debate can ensue. Furthermore, the shared wisdom of the group can be brought to bear to help resolve problems that people might be experiencing and to provide feedback on ways in which QA standards and procedures can be improved. In short, QA personnel should actively use in-service training opportunities to enact two-way communication: from themselves to stakeholders, and from stakeholders to themselves (Figure 9–7).

The quality of QA training is an important indicator of management's level of commitment to the production of quality information systems products and services. In the absence of management providing adequate resources for training, stakeholders are likely to become skeptical about management's commitment to quality. Quality goals will not be accomplished if stakeholders are not provided with the knowledge and experience to attain them.

Auditors can evaluate how well QA personnel manage training by using interviews, observations, and reviews of documentation. They can interview QA personnel to obtain an understanding of the approach they follow to undertake QA training within their organization. Another option is to interview stakeholders to obtain their views on whether the nature, scope, and frequency of QA training are satisfactory. By observing QA training sessions in progress, auditors obtain evidence on how well they are conducted. Reviews of training schedules and training materials also provide evidence on whether QA training is being carried out satisfactorily. Moreover, auditors can examine personnel records to determine whether QA training is being properly directed to meet the needs of individual stakeholders.

If auditors conclude that QA personnel are carrying out the training function reliably, they can reduce the extent of substantive testing. If they conclude that training is not being carried out reliably, however, in the absence of compensating controls substantive testing must be expanded. Inadequate training usually means breakdowns in other areas. For example, monitoring for compliance with QA standards and procedures becomes problematic when stakeholders are not fully apprised of the standards and procedures in the first place. In short, the quality of training is likely to be an important indicator of how well QA personnel are carrying out other QA functions. It is also an important indicator of management's commitment to the QA function.

ORGANIZATIONAL CONSIDERATIONS

If the QA function is to be effective, it must be properly established within the organizational hierarchy of the information systems function. Moreover, it must be staffed properly.

Placement of the QA Function

The QA function must be placed within the organizational hierarchy of the information systems function so that it can act independently of other information systems activities. In this light, it cannot report to a manager responsible for development, maintenance, or operations. Otherwise, it will not be perceived as independent, and its activities also will be too easily subject to duress. Instead, it must report directly to the executive who has overall responsibility for the information systems function (Figure 9–8). Moreover, managers responsible for the QA function must be given appropriate seniority to enable them to maintain their independence and to ensure their arguments carry sufficient weight in any disputes that arise.

To operate effectively, the QA function must also have a properly approved charter. This charter should be prepared in consultation with information systems stakeholders. When the final form of the charter has been negotiated, it should be endorsed by senior management so it has force in terms of the ways information systems personnel conduct their activities. To avoid confusion and disputation, the charter should lay out clearly the rights and responsibilities of the QA function. Job positions must also be defined to fulfill responsibilities under the charter. Authority and accountability commensurate with the activities that have to be performed in each job should be specified. If the charter is to continue to have force, senior management will need to affirm periodically the importance of the charter. Moreover, they will have to provide adequate resources so the QA function can discharge its responsibilities under the charter.

Auditors must evaluate whether the QA function has been placed within the organizational hierarchy of the information systems function such that it can perform an independent evaluative role. They should determine that it re-

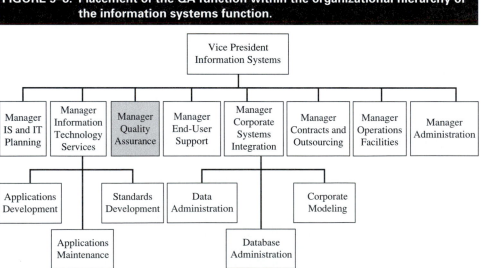

FIGURE 9–8. Placement of the QA function within the organizational hierarchy of the information systems function.

ports directly to the executive in charge of the information systems function. Moreover, they should determine that a properly approved charter exists that documents the rights and responsibilities of the QA personnel. The charter should be supplemented by job descriptions that allow the charter to be fulfilled. Auditors can interview QA staff, information systems staff, and information systems users to determine the scope and depth of QA work and to assess whether funding of the QA function is adequate. They can also review documentation to evaluate whether the work that has been undertaken by QA personnel is consistent with their charter.

Staffing the QA Function

The QA function poses some special problems in terms of staffing. QA personnel must be well trained and competent, and their skills must be kept up to date. Otherwise, they will not command the respect of the information systems personnel whose work they must evaluate.

QA personnel also require a high level of interpersonal skills because the potential for conflict between QA personnel and information systems personnel is high. If interactions are not handled tactfully, the level of disputation is likely to become pathological. Senior management should have to become involved in disputes only on an infrequent basis. When they do, often the pressures to finish a job mean that senior management will support the development staff in a dispute rather than the QA staff. Long-term goals can be compromised to meet short-term objectives.

Many organizations report difficulties in attracting competent staff to QA positions. In general, information systems professionals prefer to develop, implement, and operate systems rather than to evaluate them for quality. Indeed, quality assurance work often is afforded lower prestige than other types of information systems work. If QA responsibilities are to be discharged effectively, however, competent, experienced personnel must be attracted to QA positions. Senior management must engender a culture that sees the QA role as important.

Auditors should evaluate whether QA personnel have adequate knowledge of information systems development, implementation, and operations procedures. They should also evaluate whether they receive ongoing, regular training. Through interviews with information systems users and information systems staff, auditors can determine whether QA staff are considered to be competent. They can also use these interviews to determine whether QA staff exercise a high level of interpersonal skills. If auditors conclude that QA staff lack required knowledge or their level of interpersonal skills is not high, they must place less reliance on QA controls when planning the remainder of the audit.

RELATIONSHIP BETWEEN QUALITY ASSURANCE AND AUDITING

In many ways, the objectives of and functions performed by QA personnel and auditors are the same. Both QA personnel and auditors are concerned with the existence of information systems standards, compliance with these standards, and timely, corrective actions when deviations from standards occur. Prior to the existence of the QA function, auditors performed many of the checks that QA personnel now perform. For example, they sought evidence on whether systems-development practices followed prescribed standards.

The existence of a QA function might change how both internal auditors and external auditors perform their work in several ways. First, if a QA function is in place and working reliably, auditors most likely can reduce the extent of substantive testing they undertake. The existence of a QA function manifests an organization's commitment to quality. Moreover, the functions performed by QA personnel provide greater assurance that high-quality controls are in place and working over the information systems function. As a result, auditors can place greater reliance on controls during the conduct of their audits.

Second, QA personnel most likely will undertake more comprehensive checking of information systems controls than auditors. Although both QA personnel and auditors inevitably rely on sampling for their evidence-collection purposes, QA personnel probably will examine more extensive samples. As a result, auditors usually can place higher reliance on information systems controls and reduce the extent of their substantive testing.

Third, auditors can now focus primarily on ensuring the QA function works reliably rather than undertaking direct tests of information systems controls. Providing auditors have confidence in the QA function, they can rely on the conclusions reached by QA personnel in relation to information systems controls and plan the conduct of their audit accordingly. Auditors should have less work to undertake because QA personnel should be able to provide them with much of the evidence they need to plan an audit and to reach an audit opinion.

In short, auditors should welcome the existence of a QA function in any organization. The control risk associated with the organization should be lower, and less work should be required to gather the evidential matter needed to reach an audit opinion. With proper planning, auditors can work hand in hand with QA personnel to achieve the four objectives of asset safeguarding, maintenance of data integrity, system effectiveness, and system efficiency.

SUMMARY

Quality assurance personnel within the information systems function are concerned with ensuring that the information systems produced achieve certain quality goals and that development, implementation, operation, and maintenance of information systems comply with a set of quality standards.

The QA function associated with the information systems function has arisen for six reasons. First, increasingly organizations are producing safety-critical systems where high levels of quality must be achieved. Second, users are becoming more demanding about the quality of software they use to undertake their work. Third, organizations are undertaking more ambitious projects when they build software. Fourth, organizations have become more worried about their liabilities if they produce and sell defective software. Fifth, poor control over the development, implementation, operation, and maintenance of information systems can be costly. Sixth, improving the quality of information systems is part of a worldwide trend among organizations to improve the quality of the goods and services they sell so they can compete more effectively in marketplaces.

Quality assurance personnel perform six major functions: *(1)* developing quality goals for the information systems function overall and for individual information systems projects; *(2)* developing, promulgating, and maintaining standards for the information systems function; *(3)* monitoring compliance with QA standards; *(4)* identifying areas for improvement; *(5)* reporting to management; and *(6)* training personnel in QA standards and procedures.

The QA function must be placed within the organizational hierarchy of the information systems function so that it can act independently of other information systems activities. Both the QA manager and QA staff must have sufficient seniority so that their arguments carry weight in any disputes that arise.

Staffing the QA function properly can be difficult. QA personnel must be well trained and competent, and their skills must be kept up to date. They must also have a high level of interpersonal skills. Finding suitable people with the range of skills required can be hard. Furthermore, many information systems professionals prefer to work in development rather than quality assurance roles.

Auditors usually can place more reliance on controls when a QA function exists. Like auditors, QA personnel have a substantial interest in seeing that controls are in place and working reliably. In this light, auditors often can reduce the extent of substantive testing they would otherwise undertake in the absence of a QA function.

Review Questions

9–1 What is the primary role of quality assurance management as it operates within the information systems function?

9–2 Give *three* reasons why the QA function has emerged in organizations.

9–3 Why should QA personnel *not* undertake information systems development, implementation, operations, and maintenance work?

9–4 What is an information systems quality assurance project plan? Who should prepare the plan?

9–5 Briefly describe two problems that arise when preparing an information systems quality assurance project plan.

9–6 Why is it important to include quality metrics in an information systems quality assurance project plan?

9–7 Why would auditors be concerned about whether a charter has been established for the information systems QA function in an organization?

9–8 Why is it best to have QA personnel develop, promulgate, and maintain information systems standards rather than other stakeholders in the information systems function undertake these tasks?

9–9 Why is it best to strive for minimal specification of standards when preparing information systems standards?

9–10 Why do QA personnel need to monitor national and international information systems standards?

9–11 Why should QA personnel seek to avoid disputes over detail when monitoring compliance with the quality assurance plan prepared for a specific information systems project?

9–12 What actions should QA personnel take when they identify a compliance failure in terms of a project's quality assurance plan?

9–13 Relative to other stakeholders, why should QA personnel have primary responsibility for identifying where the information systems function can be improved?

9–14 Briefly explain the Japanese notion of *Kaizen*. Describe two principles on which *Kaizen* is based.

9–15 Why should QA personnel be notified routinely of errors or irregularities that occur in information systems?

9–16 Briefly describe *two* principles that should guide how QA personnel report to management.

9–17 Briefly distinguish between the general types of training and the specific types of training that QA personnel should provide to information systems personnel.

9–18 Why should QA training be based on personal development plans prepared for each information systems employee?

9–19 Why is QA training an important means of discernment for QA personnel in relation to QA standards and procedures?

9–20 Briefly describe where the QA function should be placed in the organizational hierarchy of the information systems function.

9–21 Outline the nature of the charter that should be prepared for the QA function.

9–22 Give *two* problems frequently encountered when seeking to staff the QA function.

9–23 Briefly describe *two* ways in which the existence of a QA function may change the work of both internal and external auditors.

Multiple-Choice Questions

9–1 Which of the following *best* describes the role of QA management with respect to the information systems function?

a Testing a system subsequent to its development to determine whether system effectiveness and system efficiency objectives have been achieved

b Advising information systems development staff on the quality of the requirements specification and design specification that they have prepared

c Working with internal auditors to devise a program of compliance testing and substantive testing activities for the information systems function

d Monitoring information systems activities for compliance with information systems standards

9–2 Which of the following is *least likely* to be a motivation to establish a QA role within the information systems function?

a A QA role will substantially decrease the costs of review work and testing work associated with the development and implementation of an information system

b An organization might face substantial liabilities if it produces and sells defective software

c A QA role facilitates organizations successfully undertaking more ambitious information systems projects

d An organization may not be able to sell some of its information systems products and services unless it can show its customers that it has a viable QA function

9–3 Which of the following is *not* a problem that undermines the establishment of quality goals for an information systems project?

a Quality can have different meanings for different stakeholders in the information system

b There are no widely accepted quality goals for information systems

c The quality goals chosen for the information system can be in conflict with the quality goals chosen for another information system

d Quality goals can vary, depending on the nature of the information system to be developed, implemented, and maintained

9–4 A major way in which modern quality systems used to support the information systems function differ from traditional quality systems is:

a Modern quality systems focus on the production of zero-defect software as the primary goal

b Traditional quality systems fail to recognize the inherent conflict that can exist among some goals established for an information systems project

c Modern quality systems focus on customer satisfaction as the primary goal

d Traditional quality systems require more extensive involvement by stakeholders in formulating quality goals for the information systems function

9–5 If possible, the quality goals for a specific information systems project should be formulated by:

a An internal audit team

b QA personnel

c The project's quality control group

d The project manager

9–6 The *major* reason why quality metrics need to be chosen for a specific information systems project is:

a To alleviate conflict between stakeholders

b To clarify the basis on which QA personnel will evaluate whether quality goals have been met

c To provide a basis for the design of test data for the system

d To reduce the amount of monitoring of compliance with standards that QA personnel will have to undertake

9–7 Which of the following is *most unlikely* to be a reason for having QA personnel responsible for formulating, promulgating, and maintaining standards for the information systems function?

a QA personnel should have the most knowledge about the impact of national and international quality standards on their organizations

b QA personnel should have most experience of information systems development, implementation, operations, and maintenance activities

c QA personnel will be perceived by stakeholders to be independent when they formulate, promulgate, and maintain standards

d QA personnel should have incentives to ensure their organization adopts the best set of quality assurance standards possible

9–8 Which of the following statements about national and international information systems standards is *true*?

a Widespread acceptance of national and international information systems standards can undermine an organization's competitive position

b The adoption of national and international information systems standards will reduce the cost of the QA function

c QA personnel lose their ability to think critically when their organization adopts national and international information systems standards

d The adoption of national and international information systems standards reduces the scope for conflict among stakeholders

9–9 Which of the following principles should guide the ways in which QA personnel monitor compliance with information systems standards?

a QA personnel should seek to understand the reasons for a compliance failure so they can advise management

b QA personnel should focus on the detailed facts in any disputes they have with information systems staff

c QA personnel should alert management on a timely basis when they suspect a compliance deviation has occurred

d QA personnel should avoid making comments to management about the consequences of compliance failures

9–10 When a compliance failure occurs, QA personnel should:
- **a** Notify external auditors because it may affect the audit plan
- **b** Consider appropriate corrective actions so they can make recommendations to management
- **c** Determine who must shoulder responsibility for the compliance failure
- **d** Take action to mitigate the effects of the compliance failure on stakeholders

9–11 Which of the following principles underlies the Japanese notion of *Kaizen*?
- **a** Regular, periodic monitoring and evaluation of processes is essential to quality improvement
- **b** Improvement efforts are the primary responsibility of top management
- **c** Quality improvement decisions should be based only on facts and not experience and intuition
- **d** The quality of the product should be the primary focus of quality improvement efforts

9–12 Which of the following is *least likely* to be a reason for making QA personnel responsible for identifying areas where quality improvements can be made?
- **a** QA personnel are in the best position to decide whether quality improvements will result in better achievement of the organization's overall corporate strategy
- **b** QA personnel are in the best position to offer independent advice on quality improvements that should be made
- **c** QA personnel should have most knowledge about best practice in terms of information systems standards
- **d** QA personnel should have the greatest incentives to effect improvements to information systems standards

9–13 Which of the following principles should *not* guide the way in which QA personnel report to management?
- **a** The recommendations that QA personnel make should be backed up by concrete facts
- **b** Stakeholders should be informed of the contents of reports before they are released to management
- **c** QA personnel should ensure they list all information systems process defects they identify
- **d** The recipients of project-based reports should be agreed upon at the start of a project

9–14 Which of the following statements about personnel training in QA standards and procedures is *false*?
- **a** A personal development plan with respect to QA training should exist for each employee in the information systems function
- **b** The quality of QA training is an important indicator of top management's commitment to the attainment of quality assurance within the information systems function
- **c** Training is an important means of discernment for QA personnel in relation to the quality of information systems standards and procedures
- **d** Training in general QA standards should be provided by QA personnel whereas training in specific QA standards should be provided by project managers

9–15 The manager of the information systems QA function should report to the:
- **a** Manager in charge of the information systems function
- **b** Controller of the organization
- **c** Manager responsible for systems development
- **d** Manager responsible for the internal-audit function

9–16 Staffing the QA function is often difficult because:

    a High levels of interpersonal conflict often arise among QA personnel

    b Information systems personnel tend to prefer a development role to a monitoring role

    c Incumbents have little opportunity to exercise high-level information systems skills

    d QA personnel have fewer opportunities to keep up to date with technological developments relative to development staff

9–17 Which of the following statements about the relationship between quality assurance and auditing is most likely to be *false*?

    a Auditors can most likely reduce the extent of their substantive testing when the QA function is working reliably

    b The inherent risk associated with an organization decreases considerably when an organization has an information systems QA function

    c QA personnel are likely to undertake more comprehensive checking of information systems controls than auditors

    d External auditors are more likely to focus on whether the QA function works reliably rather than undertaking direct tests of information systems controls

Exercises and Cases

9–1 You are an external auditor in a firm that undertakes the audit of Canadian Life and Mutual (CLM), a large, Montreal-based financial institution. CLM relies heavily on its computer-based information systems to maintain its competitive position within the marketplace.

Currently you are undertaking interim audit work. You have been assigned by your partner to review the quality assurance function within CLM's information systems department. The QA function was established about one year ago, and your firm was notified of this fact. Indeed, your partner had consultations with CLM's chief information officer, and she indicated her strong support for the QA proposals that were made.

During an interview with the manager of the QA function, you ask whether project quality plans have been established for CLM's information systems. The QA manager replies that at this time QA plans have been developed only for new information systems; in other words, those commenced during the last financial year. He explains that QA plans will be developed for existing information systems when the QA function becomes better established and better resourced. You ask whether you might review a sample of these plans, and the QA manager readily agrees.

CLM has commenced the development of 17 new information systems during this past year. When you review the project documentation associated with these information systems, however, you find QA plans for only 6 of the information systems. The remaining 11 have no QA plans, and you note that 5 of the 11 systems are financial information systems of some sort.

You take this matter up with the QA manager. He explains that QA plans have been developed only for those systems that satisfy two requirements: *(1)* the system had to be material and *(2)* stakeholders had to reach agreement on quality goals for the system in a reasonable period of time. During this startup year for the QA function, he argues that he had neither the time nor resources to have his staff develop QA plans for systems that were not material nor systems where stakeholders could not reach agreement in a reasonable period of time on the quality goals to be set for the system. As his staff gain more experience with the QA function and he is better resourced, QA plans will be established for all new information systems.

Required. On the basis of the information you have collected so far, what are your conclusions about the reliability of controls associated with CLM's information systems QA function? Are there any exposures that concern you from the viewpoint of the opinion your firm ultimately must give on the financial statements? How would you advise your partner to now proceed with the audit?

9–2 Ferntree Products Limited (FPL) is a large New Zealand–based manufacturer of diverse products with headquarters in Auckland. It uses information technology extensively to support all aspects of its operations. For example, it uses robotics throughout its manufacturing processes and distributed information systems to assist its widely dispersed sales force.

You are the manager of internal audit for FPL. One day you are called suddenly to a meeting with the general manager. When you arrive at the meeting, you find the information systems manager and the QA manager in attendance. The general manager explains that some difficulties have arisen with respect to some quality assurance strategies the information systems department is proposing to undertake in the future. In particular, he indicates that the information systems manager and the QA manager are proposing to change the way in which information systems standards and QA standards are formulated in FPL. He asks the information systems manager to elaborate.

The information systems manager explains that in the past information systems standards and QA standards have been formulated by a committee comprising representatives of all stakeholder groups potentially affected by the standards. In the case of QA standards, for example, the committee might comprise representatives from user groups as well as representatives from the information systems department. These committees are always chaired by the QA manager.

The information systems manager indicates that this committee process has broken down. She informs you that inevitably committee deliberations degenerate into bitter fights over the appropriate standards to adopt. As a result, poor-quality standards are produced, and important milestones for the production of standards are being missed. Relationships among professionals within the information systems department have deteriorated, and relationships with user groups also are not good. QA personnel are finding they can no longer work effectively with the IS staff or users because a lack of trust exists. Moreover, information systems staff are complaining about the uncertainty they face in the ways they must work. She then asks the QA manager to outline a solution they are proposing to adopt.

The QA manager explains that he and the information systems manager believe the committee structure used to develop standards should be terminated. He argues strongly that too much time is lost and that the whole process is unproductive. In its place, he indicates that he and the information systems manager believe the standards-development process should become the prerogative of the QA group. When standards must be developed or maintained, the QA manager and some of his group will seek the opinion of stakeholders, but ultimate responsibility for the standards adopted will be given to the QA manager.

The information systems manager then indicates she will require all her staff to comply with the standards. The reason for the current meeting is that they are seeking the support of the general manager to enforce compliance with standards by other groups throughout the organization.

Required. The general manager explains that he has some concerns about the standards-formulation process being proposed by the information systems manager and the QA manager. Nevertheless, he understands the difficulties associated with the current process, and he wants resolution of these difficulties. He asks your opinion on the proposed changes to the standards-formulation process. All eyes turn eagerly to you. What advice will you give your colleagues in the meeting?

9–3 Dayton Deliveries (DD) Plc. is a large Manchester-based distribution company with an extensive and diverse customer base scattered throughout England. DD is regarded as a market leader in the distribution industry. Senior management have stated publicly that DD maintains its competitive edge in an aggressive marketplace through innovative use of information technology.

For several years, DD has had a QA function in its information systems department. As an information systems auditor working for the firm that conducts the external audit of DD, you have had responsibility for evaluating the reliability of controls in the QA function. Overall, you have been satisfied with the ways in which QA personnel have discharged their duties. Indeed, at the conclusion of all control reviews of the QA function you have conducted, you have recommended to your partner that reliance be placed upon controls and that substantive testing be reduced as a result.

One day you are called to an urgent meeting with your partner. He is somewhat agitated because he has received a telephone call from the chief executive officer (CEO) of DD. The CEO is upset about difficulties that DD is experiencing with a major new warehousing system that it has implemented recently. The CEO has been besieged by complaints from irate users of the system. Apparently information that is being produced by the system contains significant errors. Moreover, reports produced by the system do not contain some important information that users need to make decisions about where to locate inventory within warehouses. DD's CEO has asked why these problems were not identified in the most recent audit. Your partner, in turn, has asked you about the basis you have used to recommend that reliance be placed on QA controls, which led to his deciding to reduce the extent of substantive testing during the remainder of the audit.

In light of the problems that have arisen, you visit DD and review the QA file on the warehousing system. You are surprised to find that there is little evidence of problems that have been encountered during development and testing of the system. In particular, you note that the relevant users, project team members, and QA personnel have signed off at various milestones during system development. When you interview the project team leader about this fact, however, she dismisses the sign-off documents. She tells you that senior management had demanded the new warehousing system be implemented as part of their overall strategic plan for DD. Moreover, they had imposed a deadline for the system that was almost impossible to achieve. Because of the significant way that their jobs would be affected, users had been against the system from the outset. When the project team and QA team first reported to senior management that there were major problems with the system, they were told to "stop finding obstacles and get on with the system." As a result, compliance monitoring by users, project-team members, and QA personnel had become a meaningless activity. Sign-offs at various milestones were a token affair. She comments that the current complaints by users are their "last-ditch efforts to get their own back on senior management before the job changes and job losses occur."

Required. What recommendations would you make to your partner in terms of (a) the response he should provide to the DD's CEO, and (b) any audit work that should now be undertaken? In terms of your own approach to the audit, are there any lessons to be learned?

9–4 You are an information systems auditor in the firm of external auditors for Black Snake Breweries (BSB) Ltd., a large Brisbane-based manufacturer and supplier of beer to Australia, New Zealand, Papua New Guinea, and several countries in Southeast Asia. BSB is considered to be one of the most modern, up-to-date brewers in the southern hemisphere. It has always been an extensive user of computer systems to support all facets of it activities.

Currently you are carrying out interim audit work. One of your tasks is to evaluate the quality of controls in the information systems department's QA function. In your opinion, BSB has had an excellent QA function for many years. It was established by the previous manager of internal audit. She appointed one of her best and most senior internal auditors to manage the QA function. He, in turn, did an outstanding job in setting up the QA function and gaining respect for and recognition of the importance of QA activities across a broad range of stakeholders.

Shortly after you completed your audit work last year, the QA manager retired. A new QA manager was appointed from a small list of applicants for the job. He was previously a senior internal auditor for a major bank. BSB's management decided to hire him because he had extensive experience with a new hardware-software platform to be implemented throughout BSB. Although he had several years experience as an internal auditor, previously he had been a systems programmer. He had graduated with a master's degree in computer science, and he was considered to be an excellent technician. He had been appointed to the bank's internal audit department primarily to provide advice on how data integrity, asset safeguarding, system effectiveness, and system efficiency could be improved in the bank's data communications system. The bank's management considered that he had done an outstanding job.

As you carry out your audit work, however, you find some discontent over the performance of BSB's QA function since the new QA manager was appointed. In particular, two major new financial information systems have been commenced since he took up the position. Both are still in the requirements determination stage. The managers of the functional areas that will use the systems are unhappy, however, about several disputes they have had with the QA manager. The disputes relate to reports that the QA manager has provided to senior management. In their view, the QA manager has made a "mountain out of a molehill" in relation to some areas of noncompliance with standards. When you interview the QA manager about the disputes, however, he tells you that the areas of noncompliance are unacceptable because they relate to user involvement in the requirements determination phase for data communications controls in the new systems. He points out that this is his area of expertise, and he knows what users should be doing. He remarks to you in confidence that he also believes the previous QA manager had been in his position too long and that he had compromised his independence with users. When you interview senior management, they are somewhat bewildered about the way in which the disputes have escalated so quickly. They indicate that they are confused and concerned because they are unable to evaluate whether the areas on noncompliance are serious or minor. They lack the expertise to make this judgement.

Required. What is your assessment of the situation? How would you now proceed with the remainder of your interim audit work? What impact, if any, might your findings have on year-end audit work?

9–5 Hunger-Payne (HP) Inc. is a medium-sized Atlanta-based manufacturer and distributor of snack-foods. It has sought to establish a niche in the marketplace by developing products aimed at health-conscious consumers. Over the past few years, its sales have grown rapidly. Demand for its products by middle-aged consumers, in particular, has been high.

To support its operations, HP has had to develop and implement new computer systems quickly. Because much of the work has been done in haste and several major problems have arisen with the systems, the manager of internal audit has convinced management that a QA group should be established within the information systems department. The internal audit manager has received only lukewarm support from the information systems manager, who is a powerful person within HP. Initially the information systems manager opposed the establishment of a QA group because he argued it would add unnecessary overheads to systems-development work. He pointed out that the information systems department had been continually subjected to extremely tight deadlines and that the establishment of a QA group would simply create further obstacles to meeting these deadlines. When it became apparent that the internal audit manager would win the argument with management, however, he reluctantly gave backing to the QA group, providing he was permitted to have a major say in choosing staff for the QA group. In an effort to resolve the conflict that had arisen, the QA manager and senior management agreed to allow the information systems manager to choose those personnel who would staff the QA function.

You are an information systems auditor in the firm that undertakes the external audit of HP. Currently your firm is undertaking interim audit work, and your partner has asked you to evaluate the reliability of controls in the QA function. Given that the QA function is new, there is little by way of a track record that can be examined. Nevertheless, you decide to undertake interviews with the QA manager and her two staff.

Prior to assuming her current position, the QA manager was a project leader in the systems-development group. She was responsible for managing the development of systems that were subject to the most critical deadlines. She had acquired a reputation as being a tough-minded professional who rammed work through to a conclusion in the face of significant opposition from difficult users. She indicated she was now exhausted, however, and that the information systems manager had promoted her to QA manager as a reward for her prior work and to provide her with some respite from the pressures to which she had been subjected. Most likely she would return to systems-development work in two years when the current manager of systems development retired. The information systems manager had promised her she would be appointed to the position vacated by the manager of systems development.

The second QA staff member had previously been a systems analyst in the information systems department. You found him to be shy and retiring in your interview with him. Indeed, he indicates he disliked systems analysis work because he found it difficult to interact well with users. He much preferred his previous programming job within the department. He believes he was appointed to the QA position for two reasons. First, several years ago he developed several programming standards for the information systems department. He believes this experience was considered useful to his effectively discharging a QA role. Second, he was supposed to have returned to programming work. The programming manager had indicated to the information systems manager, however, that he had no suitable position available for him at this time. Perhaps later a suitable position could be found.

The third QA staff member is a newly-appointed computer-science graduate. He is an outgoing, self-confident person. Although his grade-point average in college was low, he is quick to point out that he found most of his subjects poorly designed for and poorly matched to the needs of a computer-science practitioner. He indicates he was the best mathematics student in his final year of high school, and he found college subjects had not provided him with the intellectual challenge he should have encountered. Although he was initially disappointed with his assignment to the QA job, he says he is now excited by the prospects of the job. The information systems manager has told him that he will be responsible for recommending how compliance failures will be fixed. If he can demonstrate his diagnostic skills in the QA job, he has been told he will quickly be appointed to a senior systems programming position that would otherwise be reserved for someone who had several years experience in programming with HP.

Required. In light of your interviews, what are your prognoses for controls within the QA function? How would you advise your partner to plan the remainder of the audit?

Answers to Multiple-Choice Questions

9–1	d	**9–5**	c	**9–9**	a	**9–13**	c
9–2	a	**9–6**	d	**9–10**	b	**9–14**	d
9–3	b	**9–7**	b	**9–11**	c	**9–15**	a
9–4	c	**9–8**	a	**9–12**	a	**9–16**	b
						9–17	b

REFERENCES

Abel, D. E., and T. P. Rout (1993), "Defining and Specifying the Quality Attributes of Software Products," *The Australian Computer Journal* (August), 105–112.

Brinkworth, John W. O. (1992), *Software Quality Management: A Pro-Active Approach.* Upper Saddle River, NJ: Prentice-Hall.

Chmiel, Walter F., and David N. Wilson (1993), "Software Quality Assurance: Now is the Time, Australia," *The Australian Computer Journal* (August), 94–97.

Chrissis, Mary Beth, Bill Curtis, Mark C. Paulk, and Charles V. Weber (1995), *The Capability Maturity Model: Guidelines for Improving the Software Process.* Reading, MA: Addison-Wesley.

Clapp, Judith A., D.R. Wallace, Saul F. Stanten, Deborah A. Cerino, W.W. Peng, and Roger J. Dziegiel, Jr. (1995), *Software Quality Control, Error Analysis, and Testing.* Park Ridge, NJ: Noyes Data Corporation.

Crosby, P. (1979), *Quality Is Free: The Art of Making Quality Certain.* New York: McGraw-Hill.

Deming, W. Edwards (1986), *Out of Crisis.* Cambridge, MA: MIT Press.

Deutsch, Michael. S., and Ronald R. Willis (1988), *Software Quality Engineering: A Total Technical and Management Approach.* Upper Saddle River, NJ: Prentice-Hall.

Dunn, Robert H., and Richard S. Ullman (1994), *TQM for Computer Software*, 2d ed. New York: McGraw-Hill.

Dyer, Michael (1992), *The Cleanroom Approach to Quality Software Development.* New York: John Wiley & Sons.

Humphrey, Watts S. (1989), *Managing the Software Process.* Reading, MA: Addison-Wesley.

Imai, M. (1986), *KAIZEN (Ky'zen): The Key to Japan's Competitive Success.* New York: Mc-Graw-Hill.

Ince, Darrel (1994), *ISO 9001 and Software Quality Assurance.* London: McGraw-Hill.

International Organization for Standardization (1991a), *ISO 9000–3: Quality Management and Quality Assurance Standards—Part 3: Guidelines for Application of ISO 9001 to the Development, Supply and Maintenance of Software.* Geneva: International Organization for Standardization.

——— (1991b), *ISO 9126: Software Product Evaluation—Quality Characteristics and Guidelines for Their Use.* Geneva: International Organization for Standardization.

Ishikawa, Kaoru (1989), *Guide to Quality Control.* White Plains, NY: Quality Resource.

Jobber, David, John Saunders, Brian Gilding, Graham Hooley, and Jon Hatton-Smooker (1989), "Assessing the Value of a Quality Assurance Certificate for Software: An Exploratory Investigation," *MIS Quarterly* (March), 18–31.

Kan, Stephen H. (1995), *Metrics and Models in Software Quality Engineering.* Reading, MA: Addison-Wesley.

Leveson, Nancy G. (1986), "Software Safety: What, Why, and How," *Computing Surveys* (June), 125–163.

——— (1991), "Software Safety in Embedded Computer Systems," *Communications of the ACM* (February), 34–46.

Paulk, Mark C., Bill Curtis, Mary Beth Chrissis, and Charles V. Weber (1993), "Capability Maturity Model, Version 1.1," *IEEE Software* (July), 18–27.

Perry, William E. (1987), *Effective Methods of Quality Assurance*, 2d ed. Wellesley, MA: QED Information Sciences.

Ragozzino, Pat P. (1990), "IS Quality — What Is It?" *Journal of Systems Management* (November), 15–16.

Schulmeyer, G. Gordon (1990), *Zero Defect Software.* New York: McGraw-Hill.

———, and James I. McManus, eds. (1993), *Total Quality Management for Software.* New York: Van Nostrand Reinhold.

Standards Association of Australia (1991), *Standard AS3563: Software Quality Management Systems.* Sydney: Standards Association of Australia.

Strong, Diane M., Yang W. Lee, and Richard W. Wang (1997), "Data Quality in Context," *Communications of the ACM* (May), 101–110.

Te-eni, Dov (1993), "Behavioral Aspects of Data Production and Their Impact on Data Quality," *Journal of Database Management*, 4(2), 30–38.

Wand, Yair, and Richard Y. Wang (1996), "Anchoring Data Quality Dimensions in Ontological Foundations," *Communications of the ACM* (November), 86–95.

Wang, Richard Y., and Diane M. Strong (1996), "Beyond Accuracy: What Data Quality Means to Data Consumers," *Journal of Management Information Systems* (Spring), 5–33.

———, M.P. Reddy, and Henry B. Kon (1995), "Toward Quality Data: An Attribute-Based Approach," *Decision Support Systems*, 13, 349–372.

Zultner, Richard E. (1993), "TQM for Technical Teams," *Communications of the ACM* (October), 79–91.

The Application Control Framework

Application system controls involve ensuring that individual application systems safeguard assets, maintain data integrity, and achieve their objectives effectively and efficiently. Application system controls differ from management controls in four ways. First, they are usually exercised by hardware and software rather than people. Second, they apply to data and the processing of data rather than to system development, maintenance, and operation processes. Third, their existence in *each* application system is a cost-benefit question. The existence of management controls, on the other hand, depends on a cost-benefit analysis of the whole set of application systems. Fourth, they tend to focus on safeguarding assets (reducing expected losses from unauthorized or inadvertent removal or destruction of assets) and maintaining data integrity (ensuring that data is authorized, complete, accurate, and not redundant). Nevertheless, system effectiveness and efficiency concerns are not irrelevant. For example, an output distribution control might exist to ensure that an application system meets a timeliness requirement, and an audit trail control might exist to enable users to obtain data on resource consumption by an application system.

On the basis of their evaluation of management controls over the information systems function in an organization, auditors might decide to evaluate application system controls for two reasons. First, external auditors might have concluded that management controls are reliable. As a result, they might have decided to proceed to test the controls in material application systems with a view to relying on these controls and reducing the extent of substantive testing. Second, internal auditors, based on an evaluation of management controls, might wish to test an hypothesis about the strengths or weaknesses in specific types of controls within an application system. For example, they might have concluded that system testing standards are deficient. They might then seek to determine whether these deficient standards result in weak application controls.

The next six chapters examine in detail the application control framework. The chapters follow a natural sequence: the flow of data from its source through processing to storage to its eventual output.

Chapter	Overview of Contents
10 Boundary Controls	Discusses the nature and functions of access controls, the use of cryptography in access controls, personal identification numbers, digital signatures, plastic cards, audit trail controls, and existence controls.
11 Input Controls	Discusses the different kinds of data input methods, input control via good source-document design and data-entry screen design, check digits, batch controls, validation of data input and instruction input, audit trail controls, and existence controls.

Boundary Controls

Chapter Outline

Chapter Key Points

- The boundary subsystem establishes the interface between the would-be user of a computer system and the computer system itself.

- Controls in the boundary subsystem have three purposes: (a) to establish the identity and authenticity of would-be users; (b) to establish the identity and authenticity of computer-system resources that users wish to employ; and (c) to restrict the actions undertaken by users who obtain computer resources to an authorized set.

- Cryptographic controls are used extensively throughout the boundary subsystem. Cryptographic controls protect the privacy of data and prevent unauthorized modifications of data. They achieve this goal by scrambling data so it is not meaningful to anyone who does not have the means to unscramble it.

- There are three classes of techniques used to transform cleartext data into ciphertext data: (a) transposition ciphers, (b) substitution ciphers, and (c) product ciphers. Most modern cryptographic systems use a product cipher because it is the most difficult to break (it has the highest work factor). The U.S. National Bureau of Standards' Data Encryption Standard (DES) uses a product cipher.

- A major disadvantage of conventional or private-key cryptosystems is that the parties who wish to exchange information must share a private, secret key. To overcome this disadvantage, public-key cryptosystems have been developed. Public-key cryptosystems use two different keys to encrypt data and to decrypt data. One key can be made public, and the other key is kept private.

- From an audit perspective, the most important aspect of cryptosystems is often the way in which cryptographic keys are managed. Cryptographic key management must address three functions: (a) how keys will be generated; (b) how they will be distributed to users; and (c) how they will be installed in cryptographic facilities.

■ Access controls restrict use of computer system resources to authorized users, limit the actions users can undertake with respect to those resources, and ensure that users obtain only authentic computer resources. They perform these functions in three steps: (a) they authenticate users who identify themselves to the system; (b) they authenticate the resources requested by the user; and (c) they confine users' actions to those that have been authorized.

■ Users can provide three classes of authentication information to an access control mechanism: (a) remembered information (e.g., passwords); (b) possessed objects (e.g., plastic cards); and (c) personal characteristics (e.g., fingerprints). Remembered information is the most commonly used form of authentication information. Its major limitation is that it can be forgotten. As a result, users employ strategies to help them remember the information that can lead to the information being compromised (e.g., they write down a password).

■ Users employ four types of resources in a computer system: hardware, software, commodities (e.g., processor time), and data. The most complex actions they take (and the most difficult to control) relate to data resources.

■ An access control mechanism can be used to enforce two types of access control policy. Under a discretionary access control policy, users can specify to the access control mechanism who can access their resources. Under a mandatory access control policy, both users and resources are assigned fixed security attributes. Mandatory access control policies are easier to enforce but they are less flexible.

■ Discretionary access control policies can be implemented via a ticket-oriented approach or a list-oriented approach. With a ticket-oriented approach (or capability approach), the access control mechanism stores information about users and the resources they are permitted to access. With a list-oriented approach, the access control mechanism stores information about each resource and the users who can access each resource.

■ Access controls should enforce the principle of least privilege: Users should be assigned only the minimum set of resources and action privileges that they need to accomplish their work.

■ Personal identification numbers (PINs) are a form of remembered information used to authenticate users of electronic funds transfer systems. Controls need to be in place and working to reduce exposures to an acceptable level at several phases in the life cycle of PINs: (a) generation of the PIN; (b) issuance and delivery of the PIN to users; (c) validation of the PIN upon entry at a terminal device (e.g., an automatic teller machine); (d) transmission of the PIN across communication lines; (e) processing of the PIN; (f) storage of the PIN; (g) change of the PIN; (h) replacement of the PIN; and (i) termination of the PIN.

■ A digital signature is a string of 0s and 1s used to authenticate a user. It is the equivalent of the analog signature that humans use to sign documents. Unlike analog signatures, however, digital signatures should be impossible to forge.

■ The most common way to implement digital signatures is via public-key cryptosystems. The sender of a message signs the message with their private key, and receivers of the message verify the signature by decrypting the message using the sender's public key.

■ Sometimes arbitrators must be used with digital-signature systems to prevent the sender of a message reneging or disavowing the message. The arbitrator acts as an intermediary between the sender and the receiver. In essence, the arbitrator is a witness to the contract between the sender and the receiver.

■ Plastic cards are primarily a means of identifying individuals who wish to use a computer system. Controls need to be in place and working to reduce exposures to an acceptable level at a number of phases in the life cycle of plastic cards: (a) application by the user for a card; (b) preparation of the card; (c) issue of the card; (d) use of the card; (e) return of the card; and (f) destruction of the card.

■ The audit trail should record all material events that occur within the boundary subsystem. It can be analyzed to search for errors or irregularities. It can also be analyzed for evidence of ineffective or inefficient resource consumption.

■ Existence controls in the boundary subsystem are usually straightforward. If the subsystem fails, existence controls usually do not attempt to restore the subsystem to the point of failure. Instead, the user is simply asked to undertake sign-on procedures again.

INTRODUCTION

The boundary subsystem establishes the interface between the would-be user of a computer system and the computer system itself. When a user sits down at a terminal, switches the terminal on, and begins the initial handshaking procedures with an operating system, boundary subsystem functions are being performed. Similarly, when a customer walks up to an automatic teller machine (ATM), inserts a plastic card, and keys in a personal identification number (PIN), the boundary subsystem is in operation.

Controls in the boundary subsystem have three major purposes:

1. To establish the identity and authenticity of would-be users of a computer system. (The system must ensure that it has an authentic user.)

2. To establish the identity and authenticity of the resources that users wish to employ. (Users must ensure that they are given authentic resources.)

3. To restrict the actions taken by users who obtain computer resources to a set of authorized actions. (Users may be allowed to employ resources only in restricted ways.)

Historically, boundary controls were considered relatively unimportant. Either none were used, or some limited form of password system tended to be used.

Two factors, however, have led to a marked increase in the use of and strength of boundary controls. First, widespread deployment of distributed systems has resulted in many users being dispersed physically—for example, via wide area networks, local area networks, and client-server computing. As a result, it is more difficult to rely on close contact with users and separation of duties to exercise control over the actions they take. Instead, increased reliance must be placed on computer-based controls to limit and monitor the actions that users take. Second, the rapid growth of electronic commerce systems has resulted in substantial work being undertaken on measures to identify and authenticate the parties who exchange monies via these systems. Today, therefore, boundary controls are some of the most complex controls auditors may encounter in computer systems.

In this chapter we examine some major types of controls exercised in the boundary subsystem. We begin our discussion by examining cryptographic controls. These types of controls are used in several subsystems, but typically auditors encounter them first in the boundary subsystem. Next we study the general characteristics of an access control mechanism. Like cryptographic controls, access controls are also used in several application subsystems. Once again, however, auditors are likely to encounter them first in the boundary subsystem. We then focus on several controls that are critical in the boundary subsystems of electronic funds transfer systems and distributed systems. Specifically, we examine PINs, digital signatures, and plastic cards. By studying these types of controls, we can obtain a better understanding of the nature of and problems associated with boundary-subsystem controls. Finally, we consider the types of audit trail and existence controls that can be used within the boundary subsystem.

CRYPTOGRAPHIC CONTROLS

Cryptographic controls are designed to protect the privacy of data and to prevent unauthorized modifications of data. They achieve this goal by scrambling data so it is meaningless to anyone who does not possess the means to unscramble it.

Cryptographic controls are becoming increasingly important controls in computer systems as it becomes more difficult to prevent unauthorized access to data. They are used in several subsystems. Because they underlie several important boundary controls like passwords, PINs, and digital signatures, however, we examine them here. When you study Chapters 12 and 14, you will also see how cryptographic controls are used in the communications and database subsystems.

Nature of Cryptography

Cryptology is the science of secret codes (Figure 10–1). It incorporates the study of cryptography and cryptanalysis. *Cryptography* deals with systems for transforming data into codes (cryptograms) that are meaningless to anyone who does not possess the system for recovering the initial data. *Cryptanalysis* deals with techniques for illegitimately recovering the critical data from cryptograms. The person who designs a cryptographic system (*cryptosystem*) is called a *cryptographer*. A *cryptanalyst* is the antagonist or opponent of a cryptographer.

Cryptographic Techniques

A cryptographic technique transforms (encrypts) data (known as *cleartext*) into cryptograms (known as *ciphertext*). The strength of a cryptographic technique is measured via its work factor. The work factor is a function of the time and cost needed for a cryptanalyst to decipher the ciphertext.

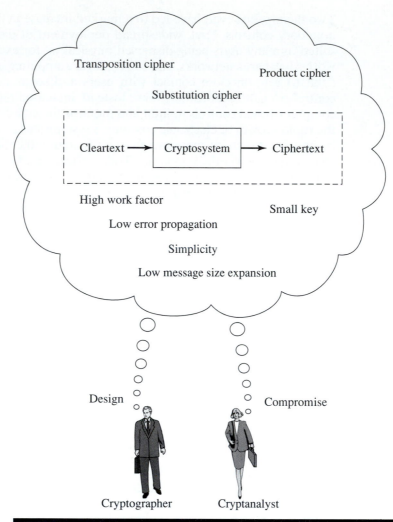

FIGURE 10–1. Science of cryptology.

There are three classes of encipherment techniques: *(1)* transposition ciphers, *(2)* substitution ciphers, and *(3)* product ciphers. We briefly examine each in the next subsections.

Transposition Ciphers

Transposition ciphers use some rule to permute the order of characters within a string of data. For example, a simple transposition rule is to swap the position of characters in consecutive pairs. Thus, this message

PEACE IS OUR OBJECTIVE

would be coded as

EPCA ESIO RUO JBCEITEV

Note that spaces have been counted within a character pair.

Even the more complex transposition ciphers are an easy target for the cryptanalyst. They protect the integrity of data only against the casual browser. When the integrity of data is critical, transposition methods should not be used.

Substitution Ciphers

Substitution ciphers retain the position of characters within a message and hide the identity of the characters by replacing them with other characters according to some rule. The key-word Caesar alphabet is an example of a substitution cipher. Using this cipher, a key first must be chosen that has no duplicate letters—say, IDEOGRAPHY. Given the 26 letters of the alphabet, the ciphertext for each letter is derived in the following manner. The first 10 letters of the alphabet are replaced by the key letters. The remaining 16 letters are replaced by those letters not contained in the key, proceeding from the beginning of the alphabet to the end. Thus the alphabet and its corresponding ciphertext are:

Cleartext: A B C D E F G H I J K L M N O P Q R S T U V W X Y Z
Ciphertext: I D E O G R A P H Y B C F J K L M N Q S T U V W X Z

In this light the message

PEACE IS OUR OBJECTIVE

would be coded as

LGIEG HQ KTN KDYGESHUG

Many other substitution ciphers (such as the much stronger vigenère and Vernam systems) were used widely before the advent of computers (see Kahn 1996). These systems can be broken fairly easily using a computer, however, and they are of little use as a means of protecting data integrity.

Product Ciphers

Product ciphers use a combination of transposition and substitution methods. Research has shown they can be designed so they are resistant to cryptanalysis. As a result, product ciphers are now the major method of encryption used. The remaining discussion assumes we are using only this class of ciphers.

Choosing a Cipher System

A cipher system has two components (Figure 10–2): *(1)* an encipherment method or algorithm that constitutes the basic cryptographic technique and *(2)* a cryptographic key upon which the algorithm operates in conjunction with cleartext to produce ciphertext.

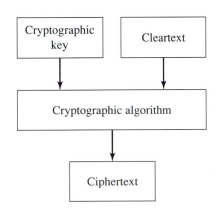

FIGURE 10–2. A cryptographic system.

Shannon (1949) lists five desirable properties of a cipher system:

Property	Explanation
High work factor	The cipher should be difficult for the cryptanalyst to break.
Small key	The cryptographic key should be small so it can be changed frequently and easily.
Simplicity	Complex cipher systems can be costly.
Low error propagation	Some types of ciphertext depend on previous ciphertext generated for a message. If a chained encryption method is used, corruption of a single bit of ciphertext will cause subsequent decryption to be in error.
Little expansion of message size	Some cipher systems introduce noise into a message to hinder use of statistical techniques to break a code. These techniques examine single-letter frequencies, double-letter frequencies, and so on.

Unfortunately, Shannon shows these properties cannot all be achieved simultaneously when encrypting natural language. Computer cryptographic methods have traded off either smallness in the key or simplicity in the algorithm. Those cipher systems that use a simple algorithm and a long key are called *long-key systems*. Those that rely on a known algorithm for their strength are called *strong-algorithm systems*.

Perhaps the best-known computer cryptographic system emerged in 1977 when the National Bureau of Standards (NBS) in the United States accepted as a standard an algorithm developed by IBM. This algorithm is known as the data encryption standard (DES). The DES is a strong-algorithm cipher system. Although long-key systems cannot be broken by a cryptanalyst if the key is random and equal in length to the number of characters in the message to be encrypted, in most commercial information systems they are impractical. The volume of data traffic that occurs requires keys to be relatively short, of fixed length, and capable of repeated use. For these reasons the NBS chose the strong-algorithm approach. The DES uses a 64-bit key: the algorithm uses 56 bits, and 8 bits are parity. The algorithm converts a 64-bit (8-character) block into a 64-bit block of ciphertext by passing through 16 rounds of encipherment (Figure 10–3). Several modes of encryption are available with the DES

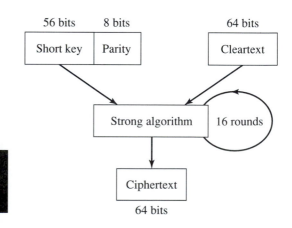

FIGURE 10–3. National Bureau of Standards data encryption standard (NBS-DES).

depending on whether we want to encrypt blocks of cleartext independently or chain the encrypted blocks together in some way. We examine these encryption modes in Chapter 12.

Public-Key Cryptosystems

A major disadvantage of conventional or private-key cryptosystems is that the parties who wish to exchange information must share a common, secret key. The key is used for both encryption and decryption purposes. Ensuring secure distribution of the key to all parties who need it is a difficult task.

To help overcome this problem, Diffie and Hellman (1976) proposed a new cryptosystem in which the encryption and decryption processes were asymmetric; that is, different keys were needed to encrypt and decrypt a message. Moreover, the keys were reversible in the sense that either could be used to encrypt a message and the other could be used to decrypt the message. By allowing one key to be public and keeping the other private, a sender S could transmit a message to a receiver R under R's public key, and R could then decrypt the message under R's private key (Figure 10–4). Security efforts, therefore, focus only on the private key that does not have to be distributed.

Several public-key cryptosystems have been proposed. The most widely known is a scheme proposed by Rivest, Shamir, and Adleman (1978), now called the RSA scheme after its founders. The major disadvantage of all public-key cryptosystems, however, is that they encrypt and decrypt slowly relative to private-key (symmetric) cryptosystems. Nevertheless, we demonstrate later in the chapter during our discussion of digital signatures that their application is becoming more widespread, and faster systems are emerging.

Key Management

In both strong-algorithm and long-key cryptosystems, maintaining the secrecy of the cryptographic key is of paramount importance. We cannot assume the algorithm will remain secure. Indeed, in the case of the DES, the algorithm is publicly known.

Cryptographic keys must be carefully managed if they are to remain secure. Key management involves three functions: *(1)* key generation, *(2)* key distribution, and *(3)* key installation. From the auditor's perspective, evaluating the key-management system is often the most critical factor affecting judgment

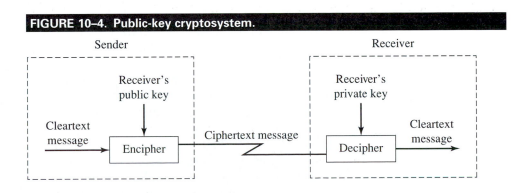

FIGURE 10–4. Public-key cryptosystem.

on whether a cryptosystem is reliable. In this light, we briefly examine the three functions of key management in the subsections that follow.

Key Generation

Three questions must be addressed by personnel who perform the key-generation function. First, what keys must be generated? Second, how should these keys be generated? Third, how long must the keys be?

Maintaining a secure cryptosystem usually means multiple cryptographic keys have to be used. To see why multiple keys are often needed, consider an information technology platform that has a shared database and communications facilities. At one extreme, only one cryptographic key might be used throughout the entire platform. All data could be routed through a cryptographic facility, and system users would not even have to concern themselves with encryption processes.

This approach clearly has the advantage of simplicity. Unfortunately, it also has several disadvantages. First, it protects the privacy of data only against unauthorized parties who are external to the system. If internal users gain unauthorized access to another user's data, they can decipher the ciphertext because they have access to the cryptographic facility for their own data encryption and decryption purposes. Second, the risk of key compromise is high. A large number of people have access to the cleartext and ciphertext generated via the key, and thus they might be able to deduce the key. When the cryptographic key is compromised, all data within the system is exposed. Third, the approach does not guard against hardware or software faults that cause, for example, a message to be misrouted during data transmission. The incorrect recipient of a confidential message will still be able to decipher the message because they have access to the cryptographic facility.

For these reasons, cryptographic systems often use multiple keys. In an electronic funds transfer system, for example, the key used to encrypt a PIN will be different from the key used to encrypt other data within a transaction. Similarly, different keys can be used to encrypt data sent to and received from different terminals, such as ATMs and point-of-sale terminals. Australian Standard 2805, for example, specifies a hierarchy of cryptographic keys that should be used in electronic funds transfer systems if the privacy and integrity of data is to be maintained (Standards Association of Australia 1988). Besides having different keys for different data, some keys are used to encrypt other keys.

When a decision has been made on what keys must be generated, a decision can then be made on how the keys will be generated. The most critical keys should be generated via a completely random process. For example, a die could be tossed. Less critical keys can be generated via a pseudorandom number generator. Various security devices have been developed that can be used to generate cryptographic keys securely.

Deciding on the length of a cryptographic key involves making a trade-off between the overheads incurred in processing longer keys against the extra security provided by longer keys. As computers become faster and more powerful, the keys must be lengthened to protect them against brute force attacks (Highland 1997a). Some cryptographic experts now recommend using 75-bit and 90-bit keys if the long-standing security of data is a major concern.

Key Distribution

Some cryptographic keys must be distributed to different locations in an information system because the place where they are generated and the place where they are to be used are not the same. For example, a bank generates a cryptographic key when it installs a new ATM. The key somehow must be distributed to the ATM so communications between the ATM and a terminal controller or (or perhaps a mainframe) can occur.

The key might be carried physically by someone to the point of installation. For example, a trusted employee or a courier might be used to transport the key. Sometimes the key is broken into fragments, and different employees or different couriers used to transport the different fragments. In this way, security over the key is enhanced because no single employee or courier has access to the whole key. Collusion would be needed to compromise the key.

A key can also be distributed electronically. For example, when a new ATM is purchased, a bank might initially install a key encrypting key (KEK). This key is not used for transmission of transactions between the ATM and a controller or mainframe. Instead the KEK is used to encrypt various data encrypting keys, such as the key used to encrypt PINs during transmission. When the bank wants to change a data encrypting key, it transmits the new key encrypted under the KEK to the ATM.

Public-key cryptosystems also provide an important means of distributing keys securely. The sender of a key simply transmits the key encrypted under the receiver's public key. Only the receiver can decrypt the message containing the key because they alone should know their private key.

Key Installation

If a key is not generated internally to a cryptographic facility, it must be installed from an external source. The method used depends on the architecture of the cryptographic facility where the key is to be installed. For example, the key might be entered by setting switches or turning dials. Alternatively, it might be entered via a keypad or transmitted over a communications line and stored in temporary memory in the cryptographic facility. A special command might then be invoked to install the key as the working key.

The key installation process must be secure. If the key is entered via a keypad, for example, it must not be possible to wiretap the line between the keypad and the cryptographic facility. Moreover, any attempt to access a device's memory where the key is stored either temporarily or in the longer term should result in the key being destroyed.

Mindful of the problems associated with ensuring keys are generated and installed securely, some organizations have developed cryptographic devices that can be used to generate and install keys in another device. The key is first generated by the device and held within its secure memory. The device is then transported physically to another device that is to receive the key. The cryptographic device is "plugged into" the recipient device, and a special command is given to the cryptographic device to transfer the key to the recipient device. At no time does the key exist in the clear.

Because a cryptographic facility should prevent direct reading of a key when it has been installed, tests sometimes must be undertaken to ensure that the correct key resides in the facility. If the key is entered via a keypad, for example, the facility might require the person who typed in the key to enter the key a second time. The facility then compares the first key entered with the second key entered and signals any discrepancy that exists. If the key is installed electronically, the device that transmitted the key might undertake some type of handshaking procedure with the device that received the key to ensure both devices hold the same key.

ACCESS CONTROLS

The most common type of control encountered in the boundary subsystem are access controls. Access controls restrict use of computer system resources to authorized users, limit the actions authorized users can take with these resources, and ensure that users obtain only authentic computer system resources. At the outset, it is useful to establish a clear understanding of why we need access controls to perform these functions in many computer systems.

Access controls are straightforward when only one person employs the resources of a computer system. We can simply use physical barriers to limit access to the system to that user only. In some cases, computing resources are so critical that they justify this form of access control. Certain military computer resources, for example, fall into this category. Given the processing power of current computing systems, however, typically a single person can use only a small proportion of the available capabilities. Absolute access control of the type described above, therefore, is an expensive strategy.

Most current computer systems are designed to allow users to share their resources. This goal is achieved by having a single computer system simulate the operations of several computer systems. Each of the simulated computer systems is called a *virtual machine*. Virtual machines allow more efficient use of resources by decreasing the "real" computer system's idle capacity. In a virtual machine environment, however, a major design problem is to ensure that each virtual machine operates as though it were completely unaware of the operations of other virtual machines. Unfortunately, with virtual machines, increased scope exists for unintentional or malicious damage to computer system resources or a user's actions. For example, a design flaw could result in one virtual machine unintentionally violating the integrity of processes and data belonging to another virtual machine. Moreover, because it is difficult to isolate virtual machines from one another, one virtual machine could be used intentionally to gain unauthorized access to another virtual machine. In short, sharing resources via virtual machines leads to more efficient use of computer resources, but difficult control problems arise as a result (Figure 10–5).

In a shared resource environment, auditors should have two concerns about access controls. First, they need to determine how well any access control mechanism uses safeguards assets and preserves data integrity. Second, given the capabilities of the access control mechanisms that are available, for any particular application system auditors must determine whether the access

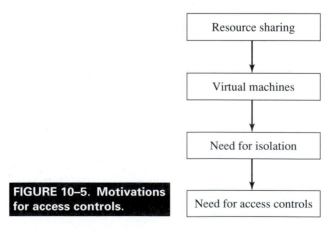

FIGURE 10–5. Motivations for access controls.

Resource sharing

Virtual machines

Need for isolation

Need for access controls

controls chosen for that system suffice. To assist you to understand how auditors might undertake these evaluations, the following subsections discuss the major features that should exist in an access control mechanism.

Functions of an Access Control Mechanism

Access controls are implemented via an access control mechanism. An access control mechanism associates with authentic users the resources they are permitted to access and the action privileges they have with respect to those resources. Access control mechanisms are often implemented as part of the operating system used by an organization. Sometimes, however, special access control software is used to implement an access control system (see, e.g., West 1993). In addition, special systems, called *firewalls*, are now often used to protect trusted computer networks from untrusted computer networks (see, e.g., Cobb 1996, Vacca 1996, and Oppliger 1997).

An access control mechanism processes users' requests for resources in three steps (Figure 10–6). First, users identify themselves to the mechanism, thereby indicating their intent to request system resources. Second, users must authenticate themselves, and the mechanism in turn must authenticate itself.

FIGURE 10–6(*a*). Identification process. (*b*). Authentication process. (*c*). Authorization process.

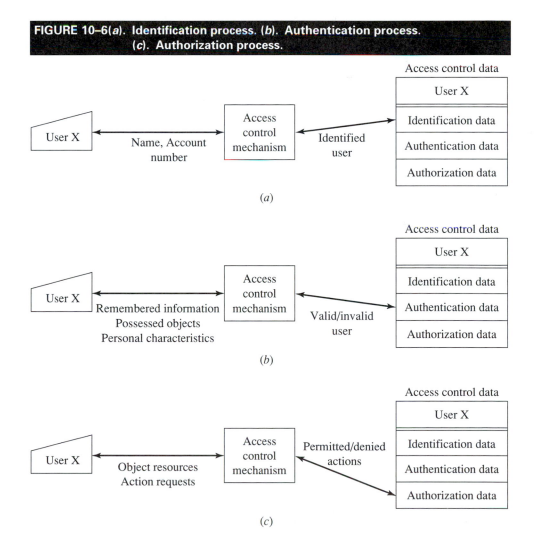

(*a*)

(*b*)

(*c*)

Authentication is a two-way process. Not only must the mechanism be sure it has a valid user, users also must be sure they have a valid mechanism. Third, users request specific resources and specify the actions they intend to take with the resources. The mechanism accesses previously stored information about users, the resources they can access, and the action privileges they have with respect to those resources. It then permits or denies the request.

Identification and Authentication

Users identify themselves to an access control mechanism by providing information such as a name or account number. This identification information enables the mechanism to select from its file of authentication information the entry corresponding to the user. The authentication process then proceeds on the basis of the information contained in the entry. Thus, the user must be able to indicate prior knowledge of this information to be deemed an authentic user. In this light, the privacy of authentication information must be preserved when it is stored or transmitted (for example, it should be encrypted). Otherwise, unauthorized parties can read the information and use it to gain access to information system resources (Figure 10–7).

Users can provide three classes of authentication information:

Class of Information	Examples
Remembered information	Name, birthdate, account number, password, PIN.
Possessed objects	Badge, plastic card, key, finger ring.
Personal characteristics	Fingerprint, voiceprint, hand size, signature, retinal pattern.

Each class has its inherent weaknesses. The primary problem with remembered information is that it can be forgotten. As a result, users tend to choose information that can be guessed easily by another party, or they write the information down somewhere that is not secure. Protecting the secrecy of passwords as the most commonly used form of remembered information, for example, is notoriously difficult. Users employ all sorts of strategies to help them remember passwords. As a result, their passwords often become compromised (see, e.g., Pipkin 1997). Table 10–1 describes a scheme proposed by Barton and Barton (1984) to help users choose secure passwords that also are easy to recall. Table 10–2 shows some of the major problems with passwords, and Table 10–3 shows some ways to manage passwords better.

The primary problem with possessed objects as a means of authentication is that they can be lost or stolen. Reliance must be placed on the user to pro-

FIGURE 10–7. Encryption of authentication information when it is transmitted or stored.

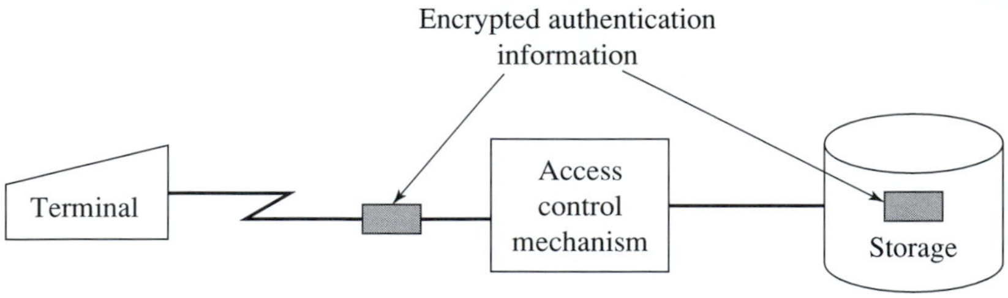

TABLE 10–1   A Scheme for Choosing Hard-to-Guess but Memorable Passwords

Think of the title of one of your favorite poems or songs. For example, say you tried out your songwriting skills at one time and penned a very memorable melody called:

DON'T KNOW WHY I'VE GOT THESE INFORMATION
SYSTEMS AUDIT BLUES

The password is generated by choosing the first letter of each word in the title of your song. Thus your password will be:

DKWIGTISAB

To make your password even more secure, place one of the special characters after, say, every three letters of your password. For example, you might alternate the ampersand and asterisk special characters. Thus your password will now be:

DKW&IGT*ISA&B

When you have to enter your password to an access control mechanism, you simply recall the title of your song and key in the first letter of each word in the title. A casual observer of your keying is unlikely to see any memorable pattern.

---

vide timely notification that they no longer have the object. For example, they must tell their financial institution they have lost their card and that further transactions using the card should be denied. The access control mechanism then should be instructed to reject all requests for resources made using the object. Moreover, it should log any attempts to use the object, activate an alarm, and perhaps retain the object in the reading device.

The primary problem with personal characteristics as a means of authentication is that the devices needed to verify personal characteristics are more costly than the other methods. Nevertheless, personal characteristics are difficult if not impossible to forge. The additional costs might be offset by the benefits of improved authentication.

During the authentication process, users also must be sure they are interacting with an authentic access control mechanism. An unauthorized party might write a program that "masquerades" as the system's access control mechanism, for example, to capture a user's password. When the user signs onto the system, the program simulates the sequence of steps undertaken by the authentic access control mechanism. As soon as the user provides the password, the program simulates a system crash. It then asks the user to sign on again. This

---

TABLE 10–2   Some Problems with Passwords

1. To remember passwords, users write them down.
2. Users choose easy-to-guess passwords, such as the name of a family member or the month in which their birthday occurs.
3. Users do not change passwords for prolonged periods.
4. Users fail to appreciate the importance of passwords.
5. Users disclose their passwords to friends or work colleagues.
6. Some access control mechanisms require users to remember multiple passwords.
7. Some access control mechanisms do not store passwords in encrypted form.
8. Passwords are not changed when a person leaves an organization.
9. Passwords are transmitted over communications lines in cleartext form.

TABLE 10–3 Some Password Management Principles

The U.S. National Bureau of Standards (1985) and the U.S. Department of Defense (1985) have published comprehensive guidelines for the generation and management of passwords. Some major principles of good password management, however, are as follows:

1. A large set of passwords should be acceptable to an access control mechanism.
2. An access control mechanism should not permit passwords to be chosen that are below a minimum length.
3. An access control mechanism should not permit users to choose weak passwords—for example, words that are found in a dictionary or words containing minimum variation in the letters chosen.
4. Users should be forced to change their passwords periodically.
5. Users should not be permitted to reuse passwords that they have used during, say, the past 12 months.
6. Passwords should be encrypted via a one-way function whenever they are stored or transmitted.
7. Users should be educated about the importance of password security, the procedures they can use to choose secure passwords, and the procedures they should follow to keep passwords secure.
8. Passwords should be changed immediately if there is a possibility they have been compromised.
9. An access control mechanism should limit the number of password entry attempts.

time the user interacts with the authentic access control mechanism. The user's password has been compromised, however, and the unauthorized party now has access to their resources.

The type of exposure described above is sometimes called a *Trojan horse*. In general, it arises because one resource cannot always be sure it is using another resource that is authentic. A Trojan horse appears to be authentic, but unfortunately it is camouflaging unauthorized activities that are also being undertaken (such as capturing a password or making an illegal copy of a sensitive file).

Preventing or detecting Trojan horses has proved to be difficult (see, e.g., Gasser 1988). Public-key cryptography, however, offers some hope of overcoming or at least mitigating the problem. If each resource had to provide an identifier that was encrypted under its private key to another resource that requested it, the requesting resource could then check the identity of the resource requested by decrypting the identifier under the public key to determine whether the identifier was valid.

Object Resources

The resources that users seek to employ in a computer-based information system can be classified into four types:

Resource Classification	Examples
Hardware	Terminals, printers, processors, disks, communication lines.
Software	Application system programs, generalized system software.
Commodities	Processor time, storage space.
Data	Files, groups, data items (includes images and sound).

Each resource must be named, because a generalized access control mechanism must be able to couple users with the resources they request. As with the identities of users and the access control mechanism, it is important that the identity of object resources cannot be forged. Otherwise, the access control mechanism is again subject to a Trojan-horse threat. For example, assume a manager requests access to an audit trail file to examine whether any unauthorized transactions have been posted to an account. Somehow the access control mechanism must ensure that it gains access to the correct file and not another file with the same name set up by a person who has perpetrated a fraud. The perpetrator might have deleted audit trail transactions that show the fraud from the Trojan-horse file.

Action Privileges

The action privileges assigned to a user depend on the user's authority level and the type of resource requested for use. In terms of hardware resources, a user usually is or is not permitted to use a resource. Action privileges can be refined in various ways. For example, users might be permitted to use a terminal only in display mode or only during specified time intervals.

In terms of software resources, again, a user usually is or is not permitted to use a resource. Once more, various refinements exist. Some users might be permitted to make copies of a program's source or object code. Some might only be permitted to view the source code at a terminal. Others might only be allowed to execute the program.

Commodity resources are measured quantitatively. If a user has permission to use a commodity, the amount of the commodity the user can consume must be specified. Thus, a user might be assigned so many seconds of processor time, so many tracks of disk space, a certain number of input/output channels that can be used at one time, and so on. Again, various refinements exist. For example, commodity resources might be assigned to users only if they request them during a specified time interval or request them only from a specified terminal.

The most complex action privileges relate to the use of data resources. Some of the action privileges needed follow:

1. Read
   - Direct read
   - Statistical or aggregate data read only
2. Add
   - Insert
   - Append
3. Modify (write)

Ideally, the access control mechanism can enforce these action privileges at both an aggregate level and a detailed level. For example, they should apply at the level of a file so that all the contents of the file are subject to the action privileges assigned to the file. Alternatively, they could apply to data items (fields within records) within a file, thereby allowing different data items to have different action privileges assigned to them.

Certain kinds of conditional action privileges may apply to data. For example, a user might be permitted access to an employee's record only if the employee's salary is under $25,000 per year, or the user might be permitted to access the employee's record only between the hours of 9:00 AM and 5:00 PM. Similarly, a user might not be provided with the results of a query on a database if the results will compromise the privacy of persons about whom the database contains information. We examine this type of conditional action privilege in more detail in Chapter 15.

Access Control Policies

An access control mechanism is used to enforce an access control policy. Two types of access control policies exist: *(1)* discretionary access control policies and *(2)* mandatory access control policies. We examine the nature of each and their relative strengths and limitations in the following subsections.

Discretionary Access Control

If an organization adopts a discretionary access control policy, users are permitted to specify to the access control mechanism who can access their files. Thus, users can choose whether they wish to share their files with other users or restrict access to these files to themselves.

To help us understand a discretionary access control policy better, consider the authorization matrix shown in Figure 10–8. The rows of the matrix show a system's users, the columns show a system's resources, and the elements show the action privileges that each user has with respect to each resource. Thus, User A can read file X and enter the Editor. User A has no action privileges, however, with respect to File Y and Program 5.

Under a discretionary access control policy, usually only a system administrator can add rows to or delete rows from the matrix—in other words, authorize additional users to have access to the system or remove existing users from the system. Also, only a system administrator might be permitted to add certain types of columns to the matrix or delete certain types of columns from the matrix—for example, those that represent system software. Other users of the system, however, can add or delete columns that represent programs or data files they have created or own. Moreover, the user who has created or has ownership of the resource can then specify the contents of the elements of the matrix; in other words, they can specify the action privileges that every other user has with respect to the resource they have created or the resource they own. These privileges can be given or revoked at the user's discretion.

Clearly, a discretionary access control policy provides substantial flexibility in a system and enhances sharing of resources. This type of access control policy is needed in many commercial computing environments.

Unfortunately, however, discretionary access control policies are subject to two kinds of threats that can undermine system security and integrity. The first is a Trojan horse. Recall that a Trojan horse is a resource (e.g., a program) that undertakes an unauthorized action without the user's knowledge. In a discretionary access control system, users can request the access control mechanism to modify the action privileges associated with resources they have created or own. Unfortunately, the access control mechanism might not be able to detect whether the request has been made by a genuine user or a Trojan horse. If the

FIGURE 10–8. Authorization matrix in an access control mechanism.

Resource / User	File X	Editor	File Y	Program 5
User A	Read	Enter		
User B	Statistical read only	Enter		Enter
User C		Enter	Append only	
User D		Enter		Read source code only

FIGURE 10–9. Access control problem resulting from authorization dynamics.

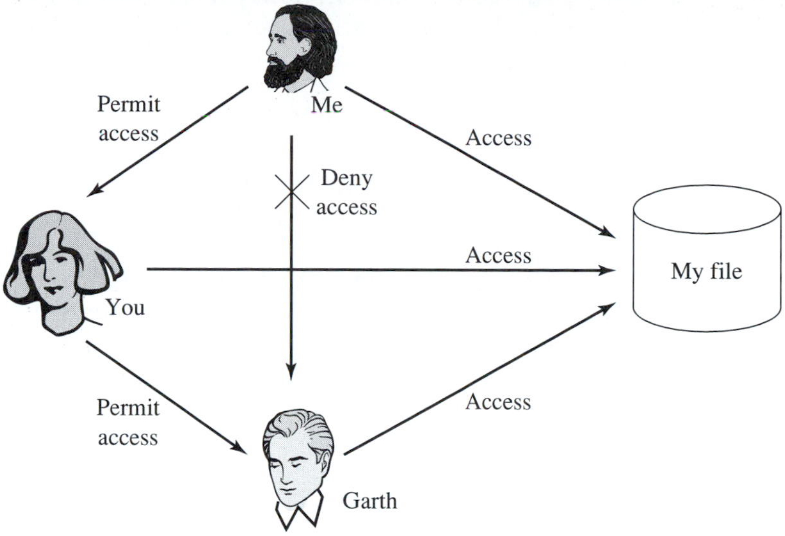

request has been made by a Trojan horse, the user's resources will be compromised.

The second threat arises because the dynamics of access controls sometimes can be complex. As a result, we are not sure how well access controls will be enforced. To give you a feel for this complexity, assume I do not want a person called Garth to get access to my files (Figure 10–9). I am quite happy, however, to give you access to my files. Assume, also, that I allow you to allocate access to my files to other people. I do not realize, however, that you are friends with Garth. Furthermore, I fail to tell you I do not want Garth to access my files. As a result, without my knowledge, you give Garth access to my files.

Mandatory Access Controls

Because of the problems associated with discretionary access control policies, organizations sometimes adopt mandatory access control policies: Both users and resources are assigned fixed security attributes. An access control mechanism uses these attributes to determine which users can access which resources. Only a system administrator can change the security attributes of a user or a resource.

To illustrate a mandatory access control policy, consider the U.S. Department of Defense's military security policy. Under this policy, a security administrator assigns all information (resources) a *classification* and all users a *clearance*. A classification or clearance has two components:

1. A security level, chosen from a small number of levels such as unclassified, confidential, secret, and top secret.

2. A category or compartment, chosen from a larger number of categories (relative to the number of security levels) such as nato, nuclear, pacific, and shuttle.

A classification or clearance can then be conceived as an n-tuple, where the first element is the security level and the remaining elements are categories—for example, {top secret: nuclear; shuttle}.

First consider the conditions we would have to satisfy to protect the *privacy* or *confidentiality* of data. If we do not wish to disclose data to unauthorized parties, users should be permitted to access information (resources) only if they satisfy two conditions. First, they must possess a security level that is equal to or greater than the security level assigned the information, where the following ordering applies:

UNCLASSIFED < CONFIDENTIAL < SECRET < TOP SECRET

Second, their clearance must at least have all the categories assigned to the classification of the information they wish to access. When these two conditions are satisfied, we say the user's clearance level *dominates* the information's classification level.

For example, assume a piece of information has the following classification: {secret: nuclear; pacific}. The following two users could *not* access the information: user A with clearance {confidential: nato; nuclear; pacific}, and user B with clearance {top secret: nato, pacific, shuttle}. User A's security level is too low, and user B's set of categories does not include all categories assigned to the piece of information. On the other hand, user C with clearance {secret: nuclear; pacific} and user D with clearance {top secret: nuclear; pacific; shuttle} could access the information. Their clearance levels dominate the information's classification level.

The security policy rule for *reading* information, therefore, is fairly straightforward. What rule should apply, however, if a user wants to *write* information? This issue has been addressed in a security model developed by Bell and LaPadula (1973). Their rule for writing information is the following:

> A user cannot *write* information unless their clearance level *is dominated by* the classification level of the information they wish to write.

To see why this rule is needed, consider Figure 10–10, which shows two databases classified as unclassified and secret and two users (processes) with clearance levels of unclassified and secret (assume no categories apply to the

FIGURE 10–10. Read and write privileges under simple security property and confinement property.

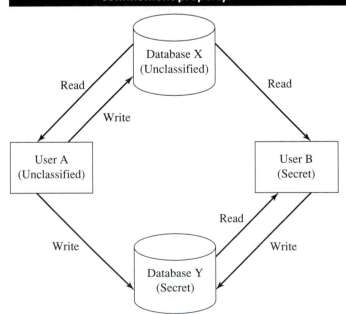

security levels). Under our security policy for reading information, both users can access the unclassified database, but only the secret user can access the secret database. Assume, however, that both users can write to the unclassified and secret databases. This results in the following security weakness. The secret user could read the secret database and write the information obtained to the unclassified database (either accidentally or deliberately). The unclassified user could then access the unclassified database and read this secret information. In effect, the secret user has *downgraded* information obtained from the secret database. By only allowing the secret user to write to a database that is classified as secret or top secret, however, we overcome the problem. Remember, our concern is with the privacy or confidentiality of data only.

In the jargon of Bell and LaPadula's (1973) model, the read policy examined previously is called the *simple security property*. The write policy is called the **-property* ("star property"). Given its relatively uninformative name, Gasser (1988, p. 67) prefers to call the *-property the "confinement property" to reflect that it prevents a user from downgrading information.

Unfortunately, from the viewpoint of modifying data, Figure 10–10 shows that there is a security weakness. Under Bell and LaPadula's security rules, both the unclassified user and the secret user can write to the secret database. Because the unclassified user has not been subjected to the evaluation required of a secret user, however, he or she could accidentally or deliberately contaminate the secret database. Moreover, the secret user could also accidentally contaminate the secret database. For example, an unclassified user might deliberately write erroneous information to the unclassified database knowing that the secret user will read this information and write it to the secret database.

This security weakness has been addressed specifically in a security model developed by Biba (1977) to address *integrity* concerns—that is, concerns about improper modification of data. Like Bell and LaPadula's model, his model also has two rules. His first rule precludes users from *writing* to a database unless their clearance level dominates the classification level of the database they wish to modify. Under this rule, the unclassified user in Figure 10–10 could not write to the secret database. His second rule precludes users from *reading* from a database unless the classification level of the database they wish to read dominates their clearance level. Under this rule, the secret user in Figure 10–10 cannot read the unclassified database. As a result, the user cannot read a lower-level contaminated database and write its contents to a higher-level database.

Figure 10–11 shows the effects of both Bell and LaPadula's and Biba's security rules. The net effect is that users can read from and write data to a database only when their clearance level equals the classification level of the database. This outcome might be too restrictive. As a result, some access control mechanisms assign separate *confidentiality labels* and *integrity labels* to the object they must protect. They then enforce the following combined mandatory controls (see, further, Sandu 1993):

1. Users cannot read an object unless their confidentiality clearance level dominates the confidentiality classification level of the object and their integrity classification level is dominated by the integrity clearance level of the object.
2. Users cannot write an object unless their confidentiality clearance level is dominated by the confidentiality classification level of the object and their integrity classification level dominates the integrity clearance level of the object.

At first glance, it might not be clear why it is sometimes reasonable to permit confidentiality and integrity labels to be different. Consider an audit trail,

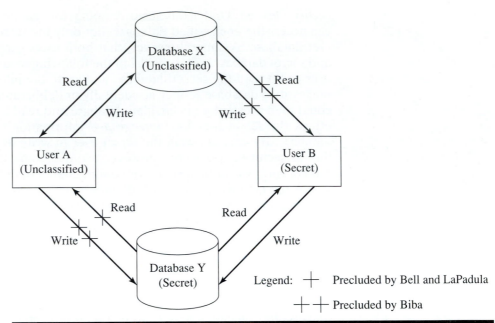

FIGURE 10–11. Read and write privileges under Bell and LaPadula's (1973) and Biba's (1977) security models.

however. In some cases we might wish to permit users with only the highest clearance level to read the data. We want all users to be able to write to the audit trail, however, at least by way of appending data to the audit trail. In short, the confidentiality label and the integrity label for the audit trail will be different.

Implementing an Access Control Mechanism

So far we have examined how an ideal access control mechanism would function. Unfortunately, in practice, we will rarely, if ever, encounter one. Designers and implementers of access control mechanisms inevitably have to make trade-offs between enforcing controls and attaining acceptable levels of performance. As a result, users of access control mechanisms often have to employ other means to cover control deficiencies.

In the following subsections, we briefly examine some of the problems that arise when implementing access control mechanisms. You should then be better able to identify where some of the weaknesses with access control mechanisms are likely to exist and to adjust your audit approaches to take these weaknesses into account.

Open Versus Closed Environment

Under a discretionary access control policy, access controls can operate in either an open or a closed environment. In an open environment, users can access resources unless authorization data specifies otherwise. In a closed environment, users cannot access resources unless they have been assigned the necessary action privileges.

An open environment is easier to implement via an access control mechanism. Less authorization information needs to be maintained and managed. There are also lower system overheads associated with the enforcement of access controls. On the other hand, higher exposures exist. At the outset, users who pose threats to a system might not be recognized. Thus, authorization information that would restrict their activities is not put in place.

Approaches to Authorization

Under a mandatory access control policy, recall that a system administrator assigns fixed clearance levels and classification levels to users and resources. The access control mechanism stores information about these levels with identification and authentication information relating to users and resources. When users seek to undertake some action on a resource, the access control mechanism simply compares user clearance levels with resource classification levels to determine whether the actions requested will be permitted.

Implementing a discretionary access control policy, however, is more complex. Historically, two alternative approaches have been used: *(1)* a "ticket-oriented" approach and *(2)* a "list-oriented" approach. We can see the differences between the two approaches by once again considering the authorization matrix shown in Figure 10–8. Using a *ticket-oriented* approach, the access control mechanism assigns users a ticket for each resource they are permitted to access. Conceptually, it operates via a row of the authorization matrix shown in Figure 10–8. This approach is also sometimes called a *capability* system to indicate users possess capabilities with respect to each resource. Using a *list-oriented* approach, the access control mechanism associates with each resource a list of users who can access the resource and the action privileges they have with respect to the resource. Conceptually, it operates via a column of the authorization matrix shown in Figure 10–8.

Each implementation approach has its advantages and disadvantages. With a ticket-oriented or capability system, the primary advantage is run-time efficiency. When a user process executes, its capability list can be stored in some type of fast-memory device. When the process seeks access to a resource, the access control mechanism simply looks up the capability list to determine whether the resource is present in the list and, if so, whether the action the user wants to undertake has been authorized.

Managing the assignment of action privileges in ticket-oriented systems, however, can be difficult. For example, initially resource owners might allow other users to access one of their resources. These other users in turn could pass on the action privileges they possess to still more users. The resource owner might then decide to revoke the action privileges assigned initially to some user. (The resource owner might be concerned, for example, that the user is no longer trustworthy.) The resource owner might also want to revoke any action privileges assigned by that user to other users. How does the resource owner find out, therefore, which users have access to the resource? Unfortunately, the capability lists for all users must be searched to determine whether an entry exists for the resource.

List-oriented systems, on the other hand, facilitate efficient administration of capabilities. To determine who has access to a resource, for example, the access control list for the resource simply has to be examined. Recall, entries in the list identify which users can access the resource and what action privileges they possess. If a particular user's access to a resource is then to be revoked, their entry in the access control list simply has to be deleted.

Unfortunately, list-oriented systems are inefficient during process execution. Each time a process seeks access to some resource, the access control list for the resource must be examined. The overheads associated with having to reference access control lists each time a resource is requested can be high.

To overcome this problem, access control mechanisms can use a combination of ticket-oriented and list-oriented techniques. Capabilities are stored permanently in access control lists so they can be administered efficiently. As a process executes, however, a temporary capability list is created in memory. When a process requests access to a resource, the access control mechanism first examines the temporary capability list to see whether the capability is present. If the capability is not present, the mechanism then examines the access control list for the resource. If the capability is present in the access control list, the mechanism loads the capability into the temporary capability list so further access to the access control list is not required.

Auditors need to understand which approach has been used to implement access controls so that they can predict the likely problems they will encounter in the application systems they are evaluating. If a ticket-oriented approach has been used, they should expect that revocation of action privileges might be problematical. On the other hand, if a list-oriented approach has been used, auditors should expect that access controls could be weaker to reduce the overheads associated with execution of user processes.

Size of Protection Domains

The level of protection that an access control mechanism affords a system depends on the size of the protection domain it enforces. The protection domain can be conceived as the elements (the intersections of the rows and columns) of the authorization matrix shown in Figure 10-8. The size of a protection domain depends on how "finely" the rows and columns can be specified. If, for example, we can define a data resource only at the level of a file, the action privileges we specify will be the same for all elements (records and fields in records) of the file. Clearly we have only a coarse level of definition. On the other hand, if we can define data resources at the level of a field in a record, we have a fine level of definition. Different actions privileges may be assigned to different fields in the same record.

Small protection domains are a desirable goal in access control mechanisms. They allow the *principle of least privilege* to be enforced; that is, at any time a process has been assigned only the necessary and sufficient set of privileges it needs to be able to accomplish its purpose. Thus, the risk of user processes performing unauthorized actions on resources is reduced.

Achieving small protection domains, however, is a difficult design problem. As we permit the rows and columns of the authorization matrix to be specified more finely, the size of the matrix grows as a result. Efficient implementation of the matrix becomes more difficult. Moreover, as user processes execute, the access control mechanism now must provide a means to achieve *fast switching* between protection domains.

Auditors should seek to determine the size of the protection domain that an access control mechanism enforces. When they know the size of the protection domain enforced, they can estimate the risk of user processes carrying out unauthorized actions on resources. They can then alter the conduct of the audit to take this risk into account. For example, if the risk is low, auditors might test the access control mechanism is working reliably and reduce the extent of substantive testing of application systems that use the access control mechanism.

Access Control Packages

Because the access control mechanisms incorporated in some major operating systems, communications systems, and database management systems have weaknesses, several software packages have now been developed to provide supplementary access controls (see, e.g., Perry 1994). In essence, these so-called access control or data security software packages extend and enhance the access controls provided in, say, the operating system used by an organization.

Auditors should be circumspect, however, when they encounter these packages during audit work. On the one hand, their use indicates an organization is clearly concerned about security and integrity. On the other hand, their use also indicates that access control weaknesses exist in some area. Use of the package might rectify these weaknesses. Sometimes, however, the package might introduce other access control weaknesses. For example, when multiple software components must be used to enforce access controls, inevitably some loophole exists because the components do not enforce controls consistently. During review of access controls, therefore, auditors must not only consider whether access controls exist to cover the major threats, they must also ensure that access controls are enforced consistently across multiple access control mechanisms.

PERSONAL IDENTIFICATION NUMBERS

So far we have examined some fundamental concepts relating to cryptographic controls and access control mechanisms. In this section and the next two sections, we examine how these concepts underlie two important means of *authenticating* people (PINs and digital signatures) and one important means of *identifying* people (plastic cards). If you have a good understanding of these types of boundary controls, you should be able to grasp fairly easily the characteristics of other types of boundary controls we might encounter in an audit.

We begin, then, with an examination of PINs as a widely used technique for authenticating people. A PIN is simply a type of password. It is a secret number assigned to a person that, in conjunction with some means of identifying the person, serves to verify the person's authenticity. PINs have been adopted by financial institutions as the primary means of verifying customers in an electronic funds transfer system (EFTS). Typically, customers insert a plastic credit or debit card in some device (identification) and then enter their PIN via a PIN keypad (authentication).

Maintaining the privacy of PINs is critical. In an EFTS, for example, privacy violations can have disastrous consequences. Assume someone wiretaps a communications line and somehow manages to discover many customers' PINs. The person could produce counterfeit plastic cards and, using the PINs obtained, make unauthorized withdrawals or charges to customer accounts. Customers would not discover the situation until they inquired on their account balance, received a statement, or received an account overdrawn notification. The initial loss would be the large sums of money that could be removed from the system. The consequential losses, however, could be more serious. When the fraud became public, customers might deny transactions recorded in the system. These denials could be genuine because customers had forgotten transactions they had undertaken, or they could be fraudulent as dishonest cardholders attempted to take advantage of the chaos. In addition, major administrative costs would be associated with discovering the extent of the fraud and handling customer inquiries and complaints. The loss of customer goodwill might be irreparable.

In the following subsections we examine various types of controls over PINs. We can structure our understanding of these controls if we recognize that PINs have a life cycle. Different controls apply at different stages in the PIN's life cycle. This type of structure applies to other types of boundary controls. For example, recall that PINs are just a form of password. As you study the following subsections, therefore, consider the life cycle of a password and the controls that would apply at various stages.

PIN Generation

There are three methods of generating PINs (Figure 10–12): The first two methods have the institution generating the PIN and conveying it to the customer; the third has the customer generating the PIN and conveying it to the institution.

1. *Derived PIN.* The institution generates a PIN based on the customer's account number (or some other identifier). The account number is transformed via the cryptographic algorithm and cryptographic key to produce a PIN of fixed length. The primary advantage of this method is that the PIN need not be stored. When customers enter their PINs, the reference PIN is regenerated based on the entered account number so the validity of the entered PIN can be assessed. The disadvantage is that new account numbers must be issued to customers if their PINs are lost or compromised. Moreover, the cryptographic key cannot be changed without changing all customers' PINs.
2. *Random PIN.* The institution generates a random number of fixed length to be the PIN. The advantage of this method is that PINs are not tied to account numbers; thus, PINs can be replaced without having to change account numbers. The disadvantage is that the encrypted PIN must be stored for reference purposes in the issuer's database. Thus, the database must be secure against unauthorized access.
3. *Customer-selected PIN.* Customers choose their own PINs. The advantage is they can choose PINs that are easy to remember. Unfortunately, this characteristic is also a shortcoming. Customers tend to select words or numbers that are significant—for example, a spouse's name or a birthdate. In addition, as with random PINs, the PIN must be stored somewhere.

Besides choosing the PIN-generation method, the institution also must decide on the nature and length of the PIN to be used. PINs can be numeric, alphabetic, or a combination of both. Alphabetics are more useful when customer-selected PINs are employed because a meaningful combination of characters can be chosen.

As a PIN's length increases, it is more difficult to determine by trial and error. Longer PINs slow down the PIN entry process, however, and increase the overheads associated with PIN verification. If the number of PIN entry attempts is limited before the card is retained and the account closed, the likelihood of successfully guessing a PIN of, say, four characters is low.

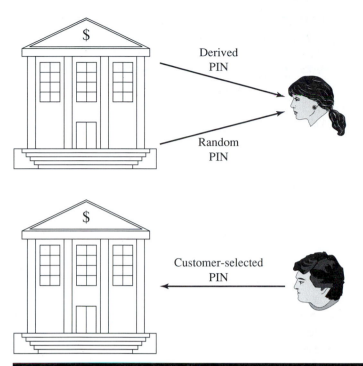

FIGURE 10–12. Personal identification number generation methods.

PIN Issuance and Delivery

The method of PIN issuance and delivery depends in part on the method used to generate PINs. If the institution generates either a derived PIN or a random PIN, a PIN mailer is often used to convey the PIN to the customer. PIN mailers are two-part forms in which the first part contains only the customer's name and address for mailing or identification purposes and the second part contains only the customer's PIN (Figure 10–13). PIN mailers are either given to customers when they open their accounts or mailed to customers subsequently. If they are mailed subsequently, they should not be mailed with the customer's card in case the PIN mailer and card are intercepted.

If customers select their PINs, there are four ways in which they can convey their PINs to the institution:

1. *Mail solicitation.* The institution mails a PIN mailer plus an opaque return-address envelope to the customer. The customer tears off and discards the first part of the PIN mailer. The second part contains a reference number cryptographically generated from the customer's account number plus a box in which customers are instructed to write their chosen PIN. Customers insert the completed second part of the PIN mailer in the return-address envelope and mail it back to the institution. They are admonished not to put their name and address or account number on the envelope or the PIN mailer. Upon receipt of the envelope at the institution, at least two employees who were not responsible for the initial mailing open the envelope and enter the encrypted reference number plus the chosen PIN into the system via a secure terminal. The PIN mailer is then destroyed. At no stage can the chosen PIN be associated with a customer's account number.

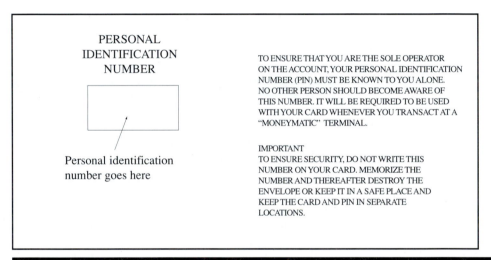

FIGURE 10–13(*a*). First part of two-part PIN mailer. (*b*). Second part of two-part PIN mailer (by permission, Suncorp-Metway Ltd.)

2. *Telephone solicitation.* Customers call a telephone number after they have received their PIN mailer and selected a PIN. The encrypted reference number provided on the second part of the PIN mailer plus the PIN are keyed in or spoken to an audio-response system. Again, customers are admonished to provide only their reference number and their chosen PIN. At the institution, at least two employees who were not responsible for the initial mailing listen to the recorded PINs, enter them at a secure terminal, and then erase the recording.

3. *PIN entry via a secure terminal.* Customers present themselves at the institution and enter their chosen PIN at a secure terminal. Their cards are mailed or given to them initially. When they request PIN entry, they must prove their identity to an official, who then activates the terminal into PIN-selection mode. Customer identification is required in case the card has been stolen. Alternatively, the institution can issue an initial PIN that can be changed by the customer. Using this method, intervention by an official is not required because knowledge of the initial PIN is taken as proof of identity.

4. *PIN entry at the issuer's facility.* To simplify the PIN solicitation process, customers could be required to select a PIN at the time they open an account. This approach also enables the encrypted PIN to be stored on the card prior to its issue. Again, a PIN mailer can be used, only this time the first part contains the customer's account number in cleartext form and the second part contains the cryptographically derived reference number plus a space for inserting the chosen PIN. The customer privately chooses a PIN, places the second part in an opaque envelope, and deposits it in a special mailbox provided for this purpose. The first part containing the account number is submitted with the account application. Later, the system decrypts the reference number, associates the chosen PIN with the account number, encrypts the PIN, and stores it securely with the account number. Alternatively, customers can enter their chosen PINs themselves via a secure terminal at the issuer's facility.

Whatever the PIN issuance and delivery technique used, careful control must be exercised over PIN mailers. Ideally, the PIN mailer printer will be an integral part of a secure cryptographic facility. To activate the printer, two independent employees should have to submit their own secret identification number to the facility. In addition, dual control must be exercised over the dispatch and receipt of PIN mailers.

Customers also should be notified when a PIN has been established for their account number, though they should not be notified of the PIN itself. If customers have not taken any actions to establish a PIN and they receive such notification, they should be told to contact the issuer institution immediately.

PIN Validation

Upon PIN entry, customers usually are allowed a certain number of attempts to submit a valid PIN before the card is retained and the account is closed. This procedure is problematic. With a four-digit PIN, on average it would take considerable time to obtain the PIN through trial and error. If the card is retained, procedures must be established for safeguarding and returning the card to reduce the likelihood of employee irregularities. Moreover, cards can be reproduced; thus, a determined imposter would not be deterred. From the customer's viewpoint, it is frustrating to have a card retained after two or three attempts at PIN entry. Customers might have a temporary memory loss, which might be overcome if they were allowed more attempts at PIN entry. If only a small number of attempts are allowed, customers have an incentive to write the PIN down somewhere as a memory aid. It seems best to allow a reasonable number of PIN entry attempts (say, five to ten), to close the account after the limit has been reached, and not to retain the card. A further control is to limit the amount of money that can be transacted in any one day under the PIN.

There are two ways of validating a PIN upon entry: local PIN validation and interchange PIN validation. Local PIN validation occurs when the PIN is entered at a terminal controlled by the PIN issuer. Interchange PIN validation occurs when the PIN is entered at a terminal controlled by an institution other than the PIN issuer (assuming this institution is a participant in the EFTS). The following subsections describe how each type can be undertaken.

Local PIN Validation

Local PIN validation can be undertaken in either online or offline mode. In online mode, validation occurs at the issuing institution's host computer; that is, the terminal transmits the PIN to the host for verification purposes. Two options are available. First, the terminal encrypts the entered PIN and sends it to the host. The host decrypts the PIN under the terminal key, encrypts the PIN under the host key, and then compares it with either a stored PIN or a PIN derived cryptographically from the account number. Second, if the PIN encrypted under the host key is stored on the card used for identification purposes, the stored encrypted PIN and the entered PIN encrypted under the terminal key can be transmitted to the host. The host decrypts the entered PIN under the terminal key and then encrypts it under the host key for comparison with the encrypted PIN obtained from the card.

In offline mode, the terminal validates the entered PIN. This means that either the encrypted PIN must be stored on the card or the PIN must be a cryptographic function of the account number. In both cases, the terminal must have the master key under which PINs are encrypted by the institution. Consequently, offline validation creates greater exposures for the institution because the master key must be distributed to each terminal, and compromise of one terminal puts all PINs at risk.

Use of smart cards mitigates the exposures associated with offline local PIN validation. *Smart cards* are plastic cards that have a tamper-proof microprocessor embedded in their plastic layers. The microprocessor can be used to store an encrypted PIN and an encryption key. When the customer enters a PIN at a smart-card terminal, the PIN is read into the microprocessor, encrypted by the microprocessor using its encryption key, and compared against the stored encrypted PIN. If a customer wants to withdraw money or pay for a purchase, the card could also have a store of funds that it decreases when it authorizes an ATM to dispense cash or initiates an electronic transfer of funds to a vendor's account. Periodically, customers have to replenish these funds by using a special terminal to update the amount available on the card (either in exchange for cash or via a transfer of funds from one of their accounts) (see, further, Fancher 1996).

Interchange PIN Validation

In an interchange environment, a fundamental principle is that PINs must be validated by the issuing institution and not the acquiring institution. Otherwise, compromise of any terminal in the EFTS exposes the PINs of all participants in the network. Thus, the acquiring terminal must encrypt the PIN under its own key and send the transaction to a switch for routing to the issuing institution. Because the transaction can pass through several nodes before it reaches its destination, the PIN can be decrypted and encrypted several times under various interchange keys. To identify genuine PIN entry errors, a PIN "checkdigit" could be used that can be validated by the acquiring terminal. In this way, a miskeying, for example, can be identified quickly.

PIN Transmission

Unless the privacy of a PIN can be assumed when it is transmitted over some medium, it must be encrypted prior to transmission. The cipher generated must be unique for each transmission of the PIN; otherwise, imposters who wiretap a communication line can substitute the encrypted PIN in a transaction they generate on an account number with an invalid PIN. Similarly, imposters could open a valid account and passively wiretap the communication line to determine the ciphertext generated upon submission of their PIN. When another customer's PIN generates the same ciphertext, they could use their own PIN against that customer's account number to initiate fraudulent transactions.

A unique cipher can be obtained by making the encrypted PIN value a function of some data item that changes with each transaction—for example, a terminal-generated sequence number. Alternatively, a different cryptographic key can be used for each transmission. The new cryptographic key can be generated cryptographically as a function of the old key. Because the host knows the initial key and the cryptographic generation function, it can update the terminal key upon each transmission from the terminal.

PIN Processing

The only kind of processing that needs to be undertaken on a PIN is encryption and decryption of the PIN and comparison of an entered PIN with a reference PIN. When entered, the PIN should be encrypted immediately by a secure cryptographic facility. Thenceforth, it should never exist in the clear except inside a secure cryptographic facility. Whenever an entered PIN must be compared with a reference PIN, the encrypted versions rather than the clear versions of the PINs should be compared.

PIN Storage

If a PIN is not a cryptographic function of the account number and the cryptographic key, it must be stored for reference purposes. In addition, it might be necessary to store a PIN as part of the audit trail maintained at a terminal or a node in a network. The audit trail might be required to enable the transit of transactions between network nodes to be verified at a later stage, or it could be part of a store-and-forward facility in a communication network.

Whenever a PIN is stored, it must be encrypted. To prevent substitution of the PIN, it must be encrypted as a function of some card- or account-related data (such as the account number). That is, the encrypted PIN is derived from the cleartext PIN, the cryptographic key, and, say, the account number.

Either reversible or irreversible encryption can be used on the PIN. Reversible encryption has two advantages. First, the cryptographic key can be changed periodically to reduce the likelihood of compromise. Second, customers' PINs can be reissued if they forget them. The disadvantage is that the cleartext PIN can be determined from the ciphertext PIN if the cryptographic key is compromised. This disadvantage is overcome by irreversible encryption. Forgotten PINs cannot be recovered, however, when irreversible encryption is used. Moreover, the cryptographic key used in irreversible encryption must be retained for the life of the PIN, which increases the risk of compromise. To make compromise more difficult, reversible encryption might be applied to the ciphertext PIN generated via irreversible encryption.

When short- or long-term storage of a PIN is complete, the storage medium should be degaussed or overwritten immediately. This cannot be accomplished unless careful records are kept of the locations where PINs are stored. The goal is, however, to make it impossible to recover either cleartext or ciphertext PINs by scavenging the residue on storage media.

PIN Change

Customers can be permitted to change their PINs. In an interchange environment, the change must be performed through the issuer's system and not any acquiring system. As discussed earlier, other systems or networks simply should provide a secure means of transmitting a transaction to the institution that issued the customer's card and PIN.

PIN change can be accomplished using the same techniques (described previously) for PIN generation, issuance, and delivery. In the case of a derived PIN, the issuer must change one of the parameters used to generate the PIN. In the case of a random PIN, a new random number must be generated. In the case of a customer-selected PIN, the customer simply chooses a new PIN.

If the PIN is stored on the identification card used, the card must be reissued. In all cases the customer should be notified independently that a PIN change has occurred. Clear instructions should be printed on the notification letter advising the customer to inform the issuer immediately if they have not requested a PIN change.

PIN Replacement

PIN replacement occurs when PINs are forgotten or compromised. If PINs are forgotten, it is better to reissue the same PIN because customers find it easier to recall the old PIN rather than to memorize a new one. Moreover, identification cards do not have to be reissued if PINs are stored on the cards. Customers are reminded of their PINs by sending out a PIN mailer prepared and dispatched under the secure conditions described previously.

If a PIN is exposed, the extent of the exposure determines the actions that must be taken. If all PINs are at risk, a new cryptographic key must be chosen and new PINs issued to every customer. Clearly, the consequences are serious when all PINs are exposed. If only a single PIN is exposed, however, a new PIN has to be issued. The procedures for issuing a new PIN are the same as those for a PIN change.

PIN Termination

PIN termination occurs when customers close their accounts, new PINs are issued, or PINs are destroyed accidentally. Whenever accounts are closed or new PINs are issued, all traces of the deactivated PINs should be removed from the system. If PINs are destroyed accidentally through, say, a hardware failure, a backup copy of the PIN file is required to restore the system. The backup copy of the PIN file must be kept secure.

DIGITAL SIGNATURES

When two people exchange letters or write a contract, the sender of the letter and the parties to the contract sign their names to the documents used. The signature serves two important purposes. First, it establishes the authenticity of the persons involved. Of course, signatures can be forged. As a result, additional measures to establish authenticity often must be used. Second, it prevents the sender of a letter or a party to a contract disavowing the letter or denying their participation in the contract.

Establishing the authenticity of persons and preventing the disavowal of messages or contracts are still critical requirements when data is exchanged in electronic form. Indeed, given that the parties are often physically remote and sometimes in conflict with each other, these requirements become even more important. A counterpart is needed for the analog signature used on documents. In computer systems, this counterpart is the *digital signature*. Unlike an analog signature, however, a digital signature is simply a string of 0s and 1s rather than an inscription on a page. Furthermore, digital signatures are not constant like analog signatures—they vary across messages; and, unlike analog signatures, it should be impossible to forge a digital signature.

Public-Key Approaches

Digital signatures can be established using either private-key (symmetric) or public-key (asymmetric) cryptosystems. For example, the Kerberos system uses a private-key digital signature scheme to distribute tickets (capabilities) to workstations in a network so they can access services on servers distributed throughout the network (see, further, Schiller 1994). As discussed earlier, however, maintaining the privacy of keys with symmetric cryptosystems is often difficult. For this reason, digital signature schemes are often based on public-key cryptosystems.

In this light, consider how public-key cryptosystems can be used to establish secret messages, signed messages, and signed, secret messages (see Denning 1983). Chapter 12 examines secret messages in more detail. It is useful to see the transition from secret messages to signed messages to appreciate how public-key cryptosystems can be used to establish digital signatures.

If a sender S wants to send a secret message M to a receiver R using a public-key cryptosystem, S first obtains the public key Pu_R of R. Next S encrypts the message M under R's public key and sends the encrypted message $Pu_R(M)$ to R. R decrypts $Pu_R(M)$ using R's private key Pr_R. Thus, $Pr_R[Pu_R(M)] \rightarrow M$. Because Pu_R is known, there must be enough uncertainty about M for the secrecy of M to be maintained. Otherwise, M can be discovered by enciphering various candidates for M under Pu_R until the ciphertext matches that produced for M. A variable quantity, such as a random number generated by S, can be appended to M and stripped off after M is deciphered.

To send a *signed* message to R, S encrypts M under S's private key Pr_S. The encrypted message $Pr_S(M)$ can be deciphered by R using S's public key. Thus, $Pu_S[Pr_S(M)] \rightarrow M$. It is difficult for R to forge a message and claim that it was sent from S because, without knowing Pr_S, it is impossible to produce ciphertext which, when decrypted under Pu_S, will be meaningful. Thus, Pr_S attaches a digital signature to M that authenticates S as the originator of the message. Note, however, that because Pu_S is public, the cleartext M can be recovered by anyone, and so the secrecy of M is not preserved.

To send a signed, secret message to R, S undertakes the following steps (Figure 10–14):

1. Encrypts the message under S's private key. The ciphertext $Pr_S(M)$ is produced. This action attaches a digital signature to the message.
2. Encrypts the ciphertext $Pr_S(M)$ under R's public key. The ciphertext $Pu_R[Pr_S(M)]$ is produced. This action preserves the secrecy of the signed message because only R can decipher the message using R's private key.

To retrieve the message, R undertakes the following steps:

1. Deciphers $Pu_R[Pr_S(M)]$ under R's private key. Thus, $Pr_R(Pu_R[Pr_S(M)]) \rightarrow Pr_S(M)$.
2. Deciphers $Pr_S(M)$ under S's public key. Thus, $Pu_S[Pr_S(M)] \rightarrow (M)$.

Only if M is meaningful is the authenticity of S as the sender of the message established. Moreover, only if M is meaningful is R assured the message has not been altered in transit. Again, R cannot forge a message from S. If a dis-

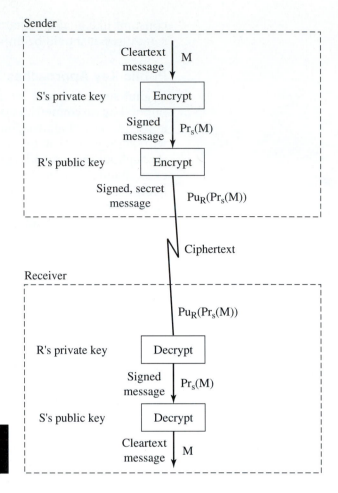

FIGURE 10–14.
Cryptosystem for signed,
secret messages.

pute over message authenticity arises, R must reveal Pr_R to an arbitrator and demonstrate that a ciphertext message decrypted under Pr_R is then meaningful when decrypted under Pu_S. For this outcome to occur, the message must have been encrypted under Pr_S, which only S supposedly knows.

Unfortunately, this scheme for sending signed, secret messages has two limitations. First, as discussed earlier, public-key cryptosystems are still slow compared with private-key cryptosystems. To help overcome this problem, a combination of private-key cryptosystems and public-key cryptosystems can be used. For example, S can send a session key to R encrypted under R's public key. R can decrypt the session key under R's private key. Exchange of messages then occurs using the session key. Similarly, rather than use a public-key cryptosystem to calculate a digital signature on the entire message, a hash code (message digest) for the message is first calculated using a fast algorithm. This hash code, which is shorter than the message, is then encrypted under the public-key cryptosystem to sign the message. The receiver decrypts the signature using the sender's public key, recalculates the hash code, and checks the value against the value sent in the message. These types of strategies are used, for example, in schemes devised to protect the privacy of electronic mail, such as the Pretty Good Privacy (PGP) scheme and the Privacy-Enhanced Mail (PEM) scheme (see, further, Stallings 1995 and Vacca 1996).

Second, in case a dispute arises over message authenticity, R must maintain a copy of $Pu_R[Pr_S(M)]$. Note that R cannot reproduce the message because R does not know Pr_S. If the audit trail of messages must be accessed frequently—say, for inquiry purposes—decryption operations will introduce high overheads. R can reduce these overheads by storing the cleartext M, but storage overheads are now incurred because both M and $Pu_R[Pr_S(M)]$ must be retained. Various proposals have been made to overcome both these problems. These matters are left, however, for further study (see, e.g., Davies 1983).

Arbitrated Schemes

Even with digital signatures, a sender S wishing to renege or disavow a contract can simply make his or her private key Pr_S public and claim the message has been forged. To prevent S from adopting this strategy, an arbitrator A can be introduced as a mediator when S sends a message M to a receiver R. The arbitrator fulfils the role of a witness in a conventional contract.

Arbitrated schemes are left for further study (see, e.g., Akl 1983 and Mitchell, Piper, and Wild 1992). To give you a sense of how arbitrated schemes work, however, the following is a protocol that can be used:

1. A sender prepares a signed, secret message for a receiver.
2. The sender then attaches an identifier to the signed, secret message. The sender next encrypts the identifier plus the signed, secret message under their private key. He or she then sends the encrypted message to an arbitrator.
3. Upon receipt, the arbitrator decrypts the message under the sender's public key. The arbitrator checks that the identifier in the message does, indeed, belong to the sender. The arbitrator thus confirms that the sender is the true source of the signed, secret message.
4. The arbitrator then attaches a time stamp and a verification stamp to the signed, secret message and identifier sent by the sender. The arbitrator next encrypts all this information under his or her private key (the arbitrator's private key) and sends it to the receiver.
5. Upon receipt, the receiver decrypts the information using the arbitrator's public key. He or she checks the time stamp and verification stamp provided by the arbitrator.
6. Next the receiver decrypts the signed, secret message sent by the sender in the manner described in the previous subsection.

Using this protocol, the arbitrator does not need to know the contents of the message sent between the sender and the receiver. The arbitrator can act as an independent witness, however, to confirm that the sender did indeed send the message to the receiver.

Some Exposures

Digital signatures are exposed when fake public keys are used. For example, assume a perpetrator P actively wiretapped a communications line, intercepted a request from a sender S to a key server K for receiver R's public key, and returned a fake public key to S. As a result, P could decipher messages sent by S enciphered under the fake public key. P would then encipher the message under R's true public key before forwarding the message on to R.

Two countermeasures can be used to help overcome the problem of fake public keys. The first requires a key server to issue public keys inside a signed certificate (similar to the protocol described previously for an arbitrator). The second requires mass distribution of public keys. For example, keys might be published in an official directory or newspaper. These matters are left for further study (see, e.g., Denning 1983 and Diffie 1992).

Digital signatures are also exposed when private keys are compromised. This situation could occur, for example, through poor key management: The private key might not be generated and installed using a secure cryptographic facility. To mitigate expected losses from this exposure, the good key-management practices described earlier in this chapter should be followed.

PLASTIC CARDS

Whereas PINs and digital signatures are used for authentication purposes, plastic cards are used primarily for identification purposes. (Cards also can be used to store information required in the authentication process.) Control over plastic cards, therefore, is an essential element of the overall set of boundary controls exercised in some types of systems—for example, electronic funds transfer systems.

The following subsections briefly examine controls over different phases in the life cycle of a card. Throughout the discussion, remember that cards are just an example of a means of identifying users. Other means of identification might be used (e.g., badges), and they should be subjected to similar controls. By understanding the types of controls that should be exercised over cards, however, you should be able to work out appropriate controls for other possessed objects that are used to identify users (and sometimes to authenticate users).

Application for a Card

Unsolicited cards should never be mailed to a customer. The risk of interception and improper use of the card is too high. Instead, cards should be issued only on the basis of a properly completed application form. The application form must state clearly the duties and responsibilities of the customer who holds the card and the issuing institution. Customers must understand fully the liabilities they incur when possessing a card before they make application for a card.

Upon receipt of the signed application form, the veracity of the customer must be checked—creditworthiness, previous credit card refusals, and so on. When all relevant information has been gathered, a supervisor either approves or refuses the issue of a card to the customer.

Preparation of the Card

After an application has been approved, a card can be prepared. This step involves embossing name, account number, and expiration date information on the card, and writing similar information on the magnetic stripes on the back of the card. In the case of smart cards, cryptographic keys and PINs also might have to be installed in the card's microprocessor.

Basic inventory control procedures should be exercised over the stock of cards. Blank cards must be effectively controlled. The number of blank cards issued must correspond to the number of approved applications. Spoiled cards should be destroyed under dual control and the event properly documented as a basis for issuing another blank card. Encoding equipment must also be controlled. If an outside card vendor prepares the cards, some assurance should be obtained that the vendor exercises effective controls over card preparation. In this light, a third-party audit report might be required. When an outside vendor is used, shipment of applications and receipt of cards must be carefully controlled.

Issue of the Card

Controls over the issue of cards seek to ensure the card arrives safely in the hands of the authorized customer. At the outset, mailing of cards must be carefully controlled to ensure that all cards that have been prepared on the basis of an authorized application are dispatched to customers. Dishonest employees should not be able to intercept cards prior to their mailing.

Three controls can be used to help ensure that cards reach customers after they have been mailed. First, premailers might be dispatched first to detect invalid addresses. Second, registered or certified mail might be used to those postal areas that have high rates of mail loss or mail theft. Third, when a large number of cards is to be mailed, postal authorities might be notified so they can ensure effective control exists over the mailing.

Controls also must exist over returned cards. Cards should be mailed in envelopes with a return address that does not identify the issuing institution. Returned cards should be controlled and investigated by a group not responsible for the initial mailing of the cards nor the day-to-day operations of the system. If, after some period, the address of a customer cannot be identified, the card must be destroyed under supervision.

Use of the Card

Controls over card use seek to ensure that customers safeguard their card so it does not fall into unauthorized hands. If a card is lost or stolen, the information on the card can be "skimmed"; that is, the information on the magnetic stripe can be read and a fraudulent card produced with the same information. If the authorized card is then returned to the customer, the existence of a fraudulent card might not be identified until unauthorized withdrawals of monies have occurred.

The primary control to be exercised over card use is customer education. The issuing institution must make substantial efforts to alert customers to the importance of safeguarding their cards. The issuing institution must also show, by example, that it regards security over cards as an important matter. If customers perceive the issuing institution takes card security seriously, they might be motivated to exercise careful control over their cards themselves.

Card Return/Destruction

Although the policy might be difficult to enforce, some organizations require customers to return their cards if they wish to close their accounts. Subsequent to account closure, the card then cannot be used to undertake unauthorized debit and credit transactions.

To avoid the inconvenience of returning cards, customers might withdraw all monies from their accounts and leave the accounts dormant. Thus, having customers return their cards when they wish to close their accounts could be an ineffective control against subsequent improper use of the card. A better control is to have online verification of any transaction undertaken using the card. To some extent, losses from improper use of the card subsequent to account closure can also be mitigated by having an expiry date on the card.

If cards are returned upon account closure, proper records must be kept of the return, and careful control must be kept over the destruction of cards. It should not be possible for an employee to remove a returned card and use it for unauthorized purposes.

AUDIT TRAIL CONTROLS

Recall that Chapter 2 identified two types of audit trails that should exist in each subsystem: *(1)* an accounting audit trail to maintain a record of events within the subsystem and *(2)* an operations audit trail to maintain a record of the resource consumption associated with each event in the subsystem. The following subsections briefly discuss each type of audit trail for the boundary subsystem.

Accounting Audit Trail

All material application-oriented events that occur within the boundary subsystem should be recorded in the accounting audit trail. The following sorts of data associated with an event might be kept:

1. Identity of the would-be user of the system,
2. Authentication information supplied,
3. Resources requested,
4. Action privileges requested,
5. Terminal identifier,
6. Start and finish time,
7. Number of sign-on attempts,
8. Resources provided/denied, and
9. Action privileges allowed/denied.

This data allows management or auditors to re-create the time series of events that occurs when a user attempts to gain access to and employ system resources.

Periodically the audit trail should be analyzed to detect any control weaknesses in the system. Either manual or automated analyses can be undertaken. For example, management might scan the audit trail for unusual events. Alternatively, a program, such as an intrusion-detection system, might be used. These systems monitor users to determine whether current behavior conforms with past behavior (see, e.g., O'Leary 1992). The audit trail is the primary source for building a profile of past behavior.

Public audit trails are an important control in systems that use digital signatures for authentication purposes. Denning (1983) identifies three events that should be recorded in the public audit trail:

1. Registration of public keys,
2. Registration of signatures, and
3. Notification of key compromises.

Only the key server can record these events. Moreover, although all parties to the system can access the audit trail, they can do so only via the key server. As an additional control to prevent unauthorized modifications to the audit trail, Denning (1983) recommends that it be stored sequentially on a write-once device such as an optical disk. Each event is time stamped by the key server, and entries are recorded in ascending order by time.

The public audit trail is used in the following ways. First, any user can register a public key with the key server. The server validates this registration by sending the public key back to the user encrypted under the server's private key. The user decrypts the certificate under the server's public key to check the validity of the public key received by the server. The server records the registration of the public key on the audit trail. Second, any user can request another user's public key. The server simply obtains the latest public key from the audit trail and sends it inside a certificate to the user who requests the key. Third, signature certificates provided by the key server are recorded in the audit trail so a particular private key is bound to a public key at a point in time. Finally, users notify the key server when their private keys are compromised, and the key server writes a key-compromise message to the audit trail. The user's liability for messages signed under the compromised key is then limited.

Operations Audit Trail

Much of the data collected in the accounting audit trail also serves the purposes of the operations audit trail. For example, recording start and finish times and resources requested also facilitates analyses of resource usage within the subsystem. As with the accounting audit trail, certain types of resource consumption might also be of interest as a basis for detecting unauthorized activities. For example, an intrusion-detection system might monitor the amount of processor time consumed by a user to detect unusual deviations from the amount of processor time requested by the user in the past.

EXISTENCE CONTROLS

If the boundary subsystem fails, would-be users of a computer system cannot establish an interface to the system. Failure can occur in any boundary subsystem component; for example, circuitry in a terminal could malfunction, the access control software could fail, an ATM or point-of-sale device might malfunction, a dial-up modem could fail, and a cryptographic facility could start to operate incorrectly.

In some ways, boundary subsystem existence controls are simpler than those in other subsystems. If failure occurs, boundary subsystem existence controls usually do not attempt to restore processing to the point of failure. Instead, users must commence the sign-on process again. This requirement usually imposes little cost on users because boundary subsystem functions often can be accomplished quickly. Furthermore, it protects against a situation in which the original user has left the terminal device and been replaced by another user.

If a hardware component fails, often a duplicate component can be made available; for example, another terminal or ATM can be used. Where duplicate hardware is not readily available, however, regular maintenance acts as a preventive control. In some cases, careful control must be exercised over maintenance activities. For example, if an ATM fails late at night in a high-crime area, perhaps maintenance should not be undertaken until the following day.

SUMMARY

The boundary subsystem establishes the interface between a would-be user of a system and the system itself. The primary purpose of controls in the boundary subsystem is to identify and authenticate users and to assign them action privileges.

Several major types of controls are used in the boundary subsystem. First, cryptographic controls can be used to protect the integrity of data used within the boundary subsystem. Second, access controls can be used to prevent unauthorized access to and use of resources. For example, plastic cards and PINs are a primary means of identifying and authenticating users in electronic funds transfer systems. Digital signatures can also be used to prevent electronic messages being forged or disavowed. Third, as with all subsystems, events in the boundary subsystem must be recorded in an audit trail. An accounting audit trail records application-oriented events. An operations audit trail records resource-oriented events. Finally, existence controls must be provided to restore the boundary subsystem in the event of failure.

Review Questions

10–1 Briefly describe the functions of the boundary subsystem. Give two components that perform basic activities in the boundary subsystem.

10–2 Why are boundary subsystem controls becoming more important? Do you expect this trend to continue? If so, why?

10–3 Define the following terms:
   a Cryptology
   b Cryptography
   c Cryptanalysis
   d Cryptogram

10–4 Briefly explain the difference between transposition ciphers, substitution ciphers, and product ciphers. Which type of cipher is used most often in modern cryptosystems? Why?

10–5 What is meant by the "work factor" associated with a cipher system? Explain the relationship between the work factor and the size of the cryptographic key.

10–6 Briefly explain the difference between a strong-algorithm cryptosystem and a long-key cryptosystem. Why did the U.S. National Bureau of Standards choose a strong-algorithm cryptosystem for the data encryption standard?

10–7 Briefly explain the nature of public-key cryptography.

10–8 What functions must be carried out in cryptographic key management? Why is the evaluation of key management probably the most important aspect of evaluating an information system function's use of cryptography?

10–9 How does the architecture of a cryptographic facility affect the method used to install cryptographic keys?

10–10 What is meant by an access control? Why are access controls needed in most computer systems? Can you think of any computer systems that might purposely decrease the level of access control they exercise?

10–11 What functions should an access control mechanism perform? Give two components in a computer system in which auditors are likely to find an access control mechanism. Describe the types of resources the access control mechanism is likely to protect.

10–12 Distinguish between identification and authentication. Is there a relationship between the two? In setting up an authentication scheme, what would be the major factor(s) influencing you to choose personal characteristics in preference to possessed objects as a means of authentication?

10–13 Explain why authentication should be a two-way process: the access control mechanism authenticating itself and users authenticating themselves.

10–14 What are the three classes of authentication information? Give an example of each.

10–15 In the context of boundary-subsystem controls, what is a Trojan-horse threat?

10–16 Why is it important that object resources be identified uniquely in a computer system and that the identity of each object resource cannot be forged?

10–17 Which object resource typically has the most complex action privileges applying to its use? Briefly explain why this is the case.

10–18 Briefly explain the difference between conditional and unconditional action privileges. Give two examples of fields in an accounts receivable file where conditional action privileges might be required.

10–19 What is the difference between a discretionary access control policy and a mandatory access control policy? In commercial information systems environments, which type of access control policy is most likely to be used? Why?

10–20 Briefly explain the nature of the simple security property and the confinement property associated with access controls under a mandatory access control policy.

10–21 What is the difference between a closed access control environment and an open access control environment?

10–22 Briefly explain the difference between a "ticket-oriented approach" and a "list-oriented" approach to access authorization. Outline the relative advantages and disadvantages of each approach.

10–23 What is meant by a "protection domain"? Why are small protection domains desirable? What performance requirement does the implementation of small protection domains place on an access control mechanism? How are small protection domains related to the principle of least privilege?

10–24 Briefly explain the difference between derived PINs, random PINs, and customer-selected PINs. What are the relative advantages and disadvantages of each type of PIN?

10–25 How does the method of PIN issuance and delivery differ depending on the method used to generate PINs?

10–26 Briefly explain the nature of each of the following methods for eliciting PINs from customers:
  a Mail solicitation
  b Telephone solicitation
  c PIN entry via a secure terminal
  d PIN entry at the issuer's facility

10–27 Briefly explain the difference between local PIN validation and interchange PIN validation. Why is a PIN checkdigit useful when interchange PIN validation must be used?

10–28 Why is it important that a unique cipher be generated each time a PIN is transmitted over a communications line? How might this objective be accomplished?

10–29 When an encrypted PIN must be stored for reference purposes, why must it be stored as a function of the account number to which it applies? Briefly discuss the relative advantages of using reversible versus irreversible encryption for storing the PIN.

10–30 What is a digital signature? Why are digital signatures needed in data communication systems? How are digital signatures used to send signed, secret messages?

10–31 Why are arbitrated digital signature schemes sometimes needed?

10–32 In terms of the access control mechanism used in an electronic funds transfer system, what function does a plastic debit or credit card fulfil? Why should cards be issued only after a formal application has been received and approved?

10–33 Why must basic inventory control procedures be used over the stock of plastic cards? If cards are produced by an outside vendor, what can auditors do to obtain some assurance about the reliability of control procedures over cards?

10–34 Why should plastic cards and PIN mailers never be mailed at the same time to a customer? What is the purpose of using premailers prior to mailing a PIN or a card? What actions should be taken by the issuing institution when a card is returned because the customer's address is no longer current?

10–35 Why is customer education such a critical control in the use of plastic cards in an electronic funds transfer system?

10–36 Give four data items that might be recorded in the accounting audit trail and two items that might be recorded in the operations audit trail for the boundary subsystem. Briefly explain why these data items might be recorded.

10–37 Why are existence controls in the boundary subsystem often somewhat simpler than existence controls in other subsystems?

Multiple-Choice Questions

10–1 Which of the following is *not* a function of controls in the boundary subsystem?
a To restrict the actions taken by users of computer resources to a set of authorized actions
b To validate the identification information submitted by would-be users of a computer system
c To establish the identity of would-be users of a computer system
d To establish the authenticity of computer-systems resources that users wish to employ

10–2 The person who designs a cryptosystem is called a:
a Cryptographer
b Cryptanalyst
c Cryptologist
d Cryptogenist

10–3 The type of cipher having the *highest* work factor is the:
a Substitution cipher
b Transposition cipher
c Product cipher
d Transcription cipher

10–4 Which of the following is *not* a desirable property of a cipher system?
a Simplicity
b Small key
c Low error propagation
d Low work factor

10–5 The DES is an example of a:
a Short-key cipher system
b Weak-algorithm cipher system
c Long-key cipher system
d Non-parity cipher system

10–6 A public-key cryptosystem uses:
a Two public keys
b A private key and a public key
c Two private keys and a public key
d Two public keys and a private key

10–7 The class of authentication information to which a password belongs is:
a Possessed objects
b Personal information

    c Remembered information

    d Dialog information

10–8 Trojan-horse threats arise in the boundary subsystem when:

    a Users do not change their passwords frequently

    b It is difficult to guarantee the authenticity of object resources requested by users

    c A mandatory access control policy is enforced

    d Personal characteristics are used as a means of authentication

10–9 The most complex action privileges relate to:

    a Hardware resources

    b Commodity resources

    c Software resources

    d Data resources

10–10 Which of the following statements about a mandatory access control policy is *true*?

    a It is less likely to be used in a business-systems environment than a discretionary access control policy

    b Users can change their clearance levels but not their classification levels

    c Compared with a discretionary access control policy, it must be enforced by a more complex access control mechanism

    d An audit trail is not required with a mandatory access control policy

10–11 If an access control mechanism is implemented in an open environment, it allows users to access a resource:

    a Unless authorization information specifies users cannot access the resource

    b Only if authorization information specifies users can access the resource

    c Without having to supply authentication information

    d With all action privileges always being assigned

10–12 Which of the following statements applies to a capability-based approach to authorization?

    a The mechanism associates with each resource a list of users who can access the resource together with the action privileges that each user has with respect to the resource

    b The mechanism assigns capabilities to a user as a function of the class into which the user's password falls

    c The mechanism assigns privileges to users only if they know the password for each resource

    d The mechanism associates with each user the resources they can access together with the action privileges they have with respect to each resource

10–13 Relative to the ticket-oriented approach to authorization, the primary *advantage* of the list-oriented approach to authorization is that:

    a It allows efficient administration of capabilities

    b It is efficient during process execution

    c Access control lists can be stored on some type of fast memory device to facilitate access to the list

    d It permits smaller protection domains

10–14 To be able to implement the principle of least privilege effectively, it is necessary to have:

    a A ticket-oriented approach to authorization

    b Small protection domains

    c A list-oriented approach to authorization

    d An open environment as the basis of granting access privileges

You are a member of the external audit team examining access and communications controls within the reservation and ticketing system. Your firm has just taken over the audit of Global Airways in light of a successful tender bid. You are amazed to find the system does not use passwords to prevent unauthorized access to the system. When you question the information systems manager why this is the case, he informs you that passwords are unnecessary. He explains that each terminal connected to the computer is given a unique identification number. This number is stored in a table within a secure area of the operating system. A terminal must supply this identification number with each message it sends, and the system will respond only to a valid identification number. The identification number is sent automatically by a terminal because it is hard-wired into the terminal.

He further explains that a password system had been tried previously and abandoned. Each reservation and ticketing clerk had been given a unique password. Because multiple clerks often used a single terminal, however, the system was too awkward and unwieldy as clerks had to continuously sign on and sign off the system. Major problems occurred with the system during rush periods.

Finally, the information systems manager is surprised about your concerns. Under the current system, he argues unauthorized removal of assets cannot occur. Moreover, he points out that the previous auditor had never expressed concerns about the system.

Required: Write a brief report identifying what could go wrong, if anything, with the current system that would result in the company losing assets or violation of data integrity occurring in the system. In light of your report, what advice will you give to the partner in charge of the audit in terms of how the remainder of the audit should proceed.

10–3 First International Bankco of Illinois is a large Chicago-based bank. As the manager of internal audit, you are called one day to a meeting with the controller. He is concerned about the operation of the bank's ATMs. Several major problems have arisen with customers' use of the ATMs. In particular, the following difficulties have occurred:

a Currently the bank issues a plastic card to each customer containing the customer's account number (magnetically encoded) and a PIN. Unfortunately, customers have been writing their PINs on their cards. Consequently, when customers have lost their card or their card has been stolen, unauthorized withdrawals of funds have occurred. The number of unauthorized withdrawals is increasing.

b The ATMs allow a customer three attempts to enter the current PIN. They then lock the card in the machine. Many customers seem to forget their PINs. Recently, an irate customer tried to retrieve his card using a crowbar.

c The bank currently mails cards and PINs to new customers. Recently, mail has been stolen, and unauthorized withdrawals of funds have occurred.

Required: The controller asks you to consider the problems and to propose some solutions. Write a brief report outlining your recommendations.

10–4 The following situation happened to a friend of mine.

One weekend she was leaving to go to a beach resort with her husband. Because she was short of money, she asked her husband to stop at an ATM belonging to a building society so she could withdraw money from her account. When she arrived at the ATM, she had a memory lapse and was uncertain about her PIN. She tried one number, which failed. She tried a second number, and this number failed, also. To her surprise, however, the ATM then informed her that it was retaining her plastic account card. It then provided her with a telephone number to call to report her difficulties.

Because neither she nor her husband had much cash on them and they were entertaining a guest for the weekend, she was somewhat annoyed and distressed. Upon arriving home, she called the telephone number given to her by the ATM. A recorded message asked her to state her name and telephone number and to report her problem. The recorded message also indicated that a representative of the building society would return her call as soon as possible.

Prior to calling the telephone number given to her, my friend had looked up her correct PIN in a file that she maintained. In her confusion and frustration over having lost her card, she disclosed her PIN upon reporting her difficulty. After hanging up, she realized that she no longer had her card, nor was her PIN secure.

When no one returned her call after an hour, she borrowed some money from her parents and left for the coast. On Monday morning, she was waiting as the building society branch opened its doors. She asked immediately to see the manager, and she told her what had happened. The manager then went through a tray containing some 25 cards that had suffered the same fate that weekend. She informed my friend that her card was not in the tray of captured cards. After further searching, my friend's card still could not be found.

My friend then indicated the problem that existed because she had disclosed her PIN and asked why no one had returned her telephone call. She was told it was the building society's policy to assist people on a weekend only when an ATM malfunctioned. Customers who lost their card because they had forgotten their PIN had to wait till the Monday.

Required:

a Upon discovering her card was "lost," my friend initiated a series of steps to protect her account. What steps would you have advised her to undertake?

b Do you think the building society's system provides reasonable protection over customer accounts? If not, what changes would you recommend, and why?

10–5 Monash Manufacturing Limited (MML) is a large, Melbourne-based manufacturer and retailer of pipes and pipe fittings. For some time it has had electronic-data-interchange (EDI) links with all its major suppliers and a good number of its smaller suppliers. The EDI system has been used in a fairly straightforward way—for example, to exchange orders, invoices, bills of lading, and credit notes.

You are an information systems auditor in a firm of chartered accountants that has just taken over the audit of MML. The partner in charge of the audit has asked you to review controls over the EDI system and report to him on their likely reliability. In this light, you are currently documenting internal controls within the system.

You decide to start your review by examining procedures that MML uses to authenticate trading partners within its EDI system. In this light, you interview MML's chief accountant. She informs you that the following procedures are in place:

a Trading-partner information is maintained in a secure file. When an EDI transaction (e.g., an invoice) is received from a trading partner, the trading-partner identifier in the transaction is checked against the file of authorized trading partners. If a match is not obtained, the transaction is rejected and written to an error file. An exception report is printed and given each morning to the chief accountant so that she can scrutinize the nature of rejected transactions and, if need be, undertake follow-up actions.

b The trading-partner identifier (plus other sensitive information) is encrypted before transmission within the EDI system. MML and its trading partners use a private-key cryptosystem. At the end of each month, MML distributes a cryptographic key to each of its trading partners. The same key is used by all trading partners (although the trading partners are not aware of this fact). The key is distributed by downloading the new key to all trading partners encrypted under the old key. The new key is decrypted and then installed automatically in each trading partner's system.

c Before new trading partners are approved, they are screened extensively. MML is concerned about the honesty of their management, their financial viability, their reliability in terms of the provision of goods and services, and so on. The chief accountant undertakes this screening, although she sometimes relies on an outside firm that specializes in screening activities.

d Only the chief accountant and a trading-partners clerk are authorized to establish new trading partners on the trading partners file. Only they have the action privileges assigned to enable them to add, delete, or modify data on the trading-partners file.

e All accesses to the trading-partners file are recorded in an audit trail. A summary report is prepared each month on the basis of the audit trail, and a copy of this report is given to both the chief accountant and the controller (to whom the chief accountant reports).

Required: On the basis of the information you have obtained so far, what are your conclusions about the likely reliability of controls over authenticating trading partners within the system? What further evidence would you now collect? Depending on your findings, what advice are you likely to give the partner in charge of the audit as to how the remainder of the audit should proceed?

Answers to Multiple-Choice Questions

10–1 b	**10–8** b	**10–15** b	**10–21** a
10–2 a	**10–9** d	**10–16** a	**10–22** b
10–3 c	**10–10** a	**10–17** b	**10–23** c
10–4 d	**10–11** a	**10–18** c	**10–24** d
10–5 a	**10–12** d	**10–19** a	**10–25** b
10–6 b	**10–13** a	**10–20** d	**10–26** d
10–7 c	**10–14** b		

REFERENCES

Abrams, Marshall D., and Harold J. Podell (1995), "Cryptography," in Marshall D. Abrams, Sushil Jajodia, and Harold J. Podell, eds., *Information Security: An Integrated Collection of Essays*. Los Alamitos, CA: IEEE Computer Society Press, 350–384.

Akl, Selim G. (1983), "Digital Signatures: A Tutorial Survey," *Computer* (February), 15–24.

Barton, Ben F., and Mathalee S. Barton (1984), "User-Friendly Password Methods for Computer-Mediated Information Systems," *Computers & Security*, 3, 186–195.

Bayuk, Jennifer (1996), "Security Controls for a Client/Server Environment," *EDPACS* (June), 1–9.

Bell, D.E., and L.J. LaPadula (1973), "Secure Computer Systems: A Mathematical Model," ESD-TR-73–278, Vol. 2, ESD/AFSC, Hanscom AFB, Bedford, MA, MTR-2574, Vol. 2, Mitre Corporation, Bedford, MA, November.

Biba, K. J. (1977), *Integrity Considerations for Secure Computer Systems*. Springfield, VA: National Technical Information Service. NTIS AD-A039324.

Chokhani, Santosh (1992), "Trusted Products Evaluation," *Communications of the ACM* (July), 64–76.

Cobb, Stephen (1996), "Auditor, Firefighter, Lumberjack," *IS Audit & Control Journal*, I, 36–39.

Davies, Donald W. (1983), "Applying the RSA Digital Signature to Electronic Mail," *Communications of the ACM* (February), 55–62.

Denning, Dorothy E. (1983), "Protecting Public Keys and Signature Keys," *Computer* (February), 27–35.

——— (1984), "Digital Signatures with RSA and Other Public-Key Cryptosystems," *Communications of the ACM* (April), 388–392.

Diffie, W. (1992), "The First Ten Years of Public Key Cryptography," in Gustavas J. Simmons, ed., *Contemporary Cryptology: The Science of Information Integrity*. New York: The Institute of Electrical and Electronic Engineers, 135–175.

——— and M.E. Hellman (1976), "New Directions in Cryptography," *IEEE Transactions on Information Theory* (November), 644–654.

EDI Council of Australia and the EDP Auditors Association (1990), *EDI Control Guide: Make Your Business More Competitive*. Sydney: EDI Council of Australia.

Fancher, Carol H. (1996), "Smart Cards," *Scientific American* (August), 24–29.

Gasser, Morrie (1988), *Building a Secure Computer System*. New York: Van Nostrand Reinhold.

Gauntt, Ann (1995), "Windows NT™ Security and Auditing," *IS Audit & Control Journal*, IV, 42–47.

Highland, Harold Joseph (1997), "Rocke Verser and the Death of DES," *Computers & Security*, 16(4), 266–268.

——— (1997), "Data Encryption: A Non-Mathematical Approach," *Computers & Security*, 16(5), 369–386.

Joyce, Rick, and Gopal Gupta (1990), "Identity Authentication Based on Keystroke Latency," *Communications of the ACM* (February), 168–176.

Kahn, David (1996), *The Codebreakers—Revised and Updated*. New York: Scribner.

Kalakota, Ravi, and Andrew B. Whinston (1996), *Frontiers of Electronic Commerce*. Reading, MA: Addison-Wesley.

——— and ——— (1997), *Electronic Commerce: A Manager's Guide*. Reading, MA: Addison-Wesley.

Lokan, Christopher J. (1991), "The Design and Applications of Smart Cards," *The Australian Computer Journal* (November), 159–164.

Matyas, Stephen M., and Carl H. Meyer (1978), "Generation, Distribution, and Installation of Cryptographic Keys," *IBM Systems Journal*, 17(2), 126–137.

Menkus, Belden (1996), "Various User Authentication Mechanisms," *EDPACS* (March), 14–17.

Meyer, Carl H., and Stephen M. Matyas (1982), *Cryptography: A New Dimension in Computer Data Security*. New York: John Wiley & Sons.

McLean, John (1990), "The Specification and Modeling of Computer Security," *Computer* (January), 9–16.

Mitchell, C.J., F. Piper, and P. Wild (1992), "Digital Signatures," in Gustavas J. Simmons, ed., *Contemporary Cryptology: The Science of Information Integrity*. New York: The Institute of Electrical and Electronic Engineers, 325–378.

O'Leary, Daniel E. (1992), "Intrusion-Detection Systems," *Journal of Information Systems* (Spring), 63–74.

Oppliger, Rolf (1997), "Internet Security: Firewalls and Beyond," *Communications of the ACM* (May), 92–102.

Perry, William E. (1994), "Reviewing the Selection of Data Security Software," *EDP Auditing*. Boston, Warren Gorham Lamont, Portfolio 75–01-10.1, 1–15.

Pipkin, Donald L. (1997), *Halting the Hacker: A Practical Guide to Computer Security*. Upper Saddle River, NJ: Prentice-Hall.

Rivest, R.L., A. Shamir, and L. Adleman (1978), "A Method for Obtaining Digital Signatures and Public-Key Cryptosystems," *Communications of the ACM* (February), 120–126.

Sandhu, Ravi S. (1993), "Lattice-Based Access Control Models," *Computer* (November), 9–19.

Schiller, Jeffrey I. (1994), "Secure Distributed Computing," *Scientific American* (November), 54–58.

Serpell, Stephen C. (1985), "Cryptographic Equipment Security: A Code of Practice," *Computers & Security*, 4, 47–64.

Shannon, Claude E. (1949), "Communication Theory of Secrecy Systems," *Bell System Technical Journal* (October), 656–715.

Simmons, Gustavas J., ed. (1992), *Contemporary Cryptology: The Science of Information Integrity*. New York: The Institute of Electrical and Electronic Engineers.

Stallings, William (1995), *Network and Internetwork Security: Principles and Practice*. Upper Saddle River, NJ: Prentice-Hall.

Standards Association of Australia (1988), *Australian Standard® 2805.6.2–1988: Electronic Funds Transfer—Requirements for Interfaces: Part 6.2—Key Management-Transaction Keys*. Sydney: Standards Association of Australia.

U.S. Department of Defense (1985), *Password Management Guideline*. Ft. Meade, MD: National Computer Security Center, CSC-STD-002–85.

U.S. National Bureau of Standards (1985), *Password Usage Standard*. Gaithersburg, MD: National Bureau of Standards. FIPS PUB 112.

U.S. National Institute of Standards and Technology (1992), "The Digital Signature Standard," *Communications of the ACM* (July), 36–40. (Note, this publication is an edited version of the full standard.)

Vacca, John R. (1996), *Internet Security Secrets*. Foster City, CA: IDG Books.

West, David J. (1993), "Auditing CA-ACF2," *EDP Auditing*. Boston: Auerbach Publication, Portfolio 75–01–80.1.

Zajac, Jr., Bernard P. (1988), "Dial-up Communication Lines: Can They Be Secured?" *Computers & Security*, 7, 35–36.

Input Controls

Chapter Outline

Chapter Key Points

- ■ Components in the input subsystem are responsible for bringing both data and instructions into the information system.
- ■ Data can be input into an information system in diverse ways. For example, it can be entered directly into an information system via a keyboard, a touch screen, or a mouse. Alternatively, it can be recorded first on some medium, such as a source document, and later keyed into an information system at a terminal or read via some type of optical scanner.
- ■ The type of data input method used in an information system affects asset safeguarding, data integrity, system effectiveness, and system efficiency objectives. For example, as more human intervention is required to input data into an information system, the likelihood of error occurring rises.
- ■ Where source documents are used to capture input data, good source document design is important to achieving asset safeguarding, data integrity, system effectiveness, and system efficiency objectives. For example, the choice of a source document's layout and style affects the likelihood of the person completing the source document making an error.
- ■ If data is keyed into an information system via a terminal, high-quality screen design is important to minimizing input errors and to achieving effective and efficient input of data. Data-entry screens should be designed so they are uncluttered and symmetrically balanced. Captions should be separated clearly from their associated data-entry fields. The data to be entered in a data-entry field should be clear. To maintain the rhythm of keyboard operators, manual tabbing between fields should be required. Color should be used sparingly and consistently. The

response time and display rate for screens should be fast. Prompting and Help facilities should be provided to assist the keyboard operator.

∎ The most important factor affecting data-entry screen design is whether the screen is used for direct-entry input of data or whether the screen is used to key data from a source document. In the former case, the screen should mirror the way in which the data is obtained during the data-capture task. In the latter case, the screen should mirror the source document on which the data is first captured and transcribed.

∎ Data codes are used to identify an entity uniquely. Poorly designed data codes cause recording and keying errors. Error rates increase as the code becomes longer, a mix of alphabetic and numeric characters is used, error-prone characters such as B, I, 1, and 2 are used, uppercase and lowercase fonts are mixed, and unpredictable character sequences are used.

∎ Four types of coding systems used are (a) serial codes, which assign consecutive numbers or alphabetics to an entity, (b) block sequence codes, which assign blocks of numbers to particular categories of an entity, (c) hierarchical codes, which assign codes on the basis of an assigned order of importance of the attributes of an entity, and (d) association codes, which are a concatenation of codes assigned to different attributes of an entity. Each of these coding systems have their strengths and weaknesses in terms of their error proneness and their effectiveness and efficiency.

∎ A check digit is a redundant digit added to a code that enables the accuracy of other characters in the code to be checked. Because overheads arise from using check digits, they should be used only to verify the accuracy of critical codes—for example, customer numbers or product numbers.

∎ Batching is the process of grouping together transactions that bear some type of relationship to each other. Two types of batches are used. Physical batches are groups of transactions that constitute a physical unit—e.g., a batch of source documents. Logical batches are groups of transactions bound together on some logical basis—e.g., transactions entered directly into a terminal during some time period. Various types of control totals can be calculated for batches to ensure data entered into an information system is authorized, accurate, and complete.

∎ Four types of validation checks can be exercised over input data: (a) field checks, which do not depend on the values of other fields in the input record; (b) record checks, which depend on the values of other fields in the input record; (c) batch checks, which depend on the characteristics of a batch of input records; and (d) file checks, which test whether the characteristics of a file used during input are congruent with the expected characteristics of the file.

∎ Errors identified by the input validation program should be reported in a clear, concise, courteous, and neutral manner. Errors that cannot be corrected immediately should be written to an error file so the data in error is not lost. Users should be reminded of any errors that they do not clear promptly from the error file.

■ There are six major ways in which instructions can be entered into an information system: (a) menu-driven languages, which ask users to select from a list of options with which they are presented; (b) question-answer dialogs, which ask users to respond to questions presented by the application system; (c) command languages, which require users to recall and initiate instructions for the application system; (d) forms-based languages, which require users to specify commands in the context of some input or output form; (e) natural languages, which allow users to instruct an application system via free-form input; and (f) direct-manipulation interfaces, which allow users to enter instructions to an application system via direct manipulation of objects on a screen. Each of these methods of instruction input have their strengths and weaknesses in terms of data integrity, system effectiveness, and system efficiency objectives.

■ Three types of validation checks can be exercised over instruction input: (a) lexical validation, which evaluates whether commands contain valid commands; (b) syntactic validation, which evaluates whether commands contain a string of valid operations; and (c) semantic validation, which evaluates whether the actions to be invoked by a command are meaningful.

■ The accounting audit trail in the input subsystem must record the origin, contents, and timing of the data and instructions entered into an application system. The operations audit trail in the input subsystem records the resources consumed to process data and instruction input.

■ Existence controls relating to data input are critical. It might be necessary to reprocess input data in the event master files are lost, corrupted, or destroyed. Existence controls relating to instruction input usually are less critical. The actions invoked by instructions are often manifested in changes to data, which are recorded in the audit trail. Thus, recovering the instructions themselves may not be necessary.

INTRODUCTION

Components in the input subsystem are responsible for bringing both data and instructions into an application system. Both types of input must be validated. Moreover, any errors detected must be controlled so input resubmission is accurate, complete, unique, and timely.

This chapter examines controls over the input subsystem. From an auditor's viewpoint, input controls are critical for three reasons. First, in many information systems the largest number of controls exists in the input subsystem. Consequently, auditors will often spend substantial time assessing the reliability of input controls. Second, input subsystem activities sometimes involve large amounts of routine, monotonous human intervention. Thus, they are error-prone. Third, the input subsystem is often the target of fraud. Many irregularities that have been discovered involve addition, deletion, or alteration of input transactions.

DATA INPUT METHODS

Recall that a typical way auditors evaluate controls in an application system is to trace instances of material transaction types through the system. If they are to undertake this task, however, they must first understand how the application system obtains its data input.

Figure 11–1 provides an overview of the diverse ways in which data input can be entered into an application system. In all cases, auditors are interested in recording the *state* of some object or thing or an *event* that has occurred to some object or thing. For example, auditors might want to record a person's pay rate (a state) or an order placed by a customer (an event).

In many cases, data about the state or event will be input directly to a system (the lower branch of Figure 11–1). For example, a customer might approach a sales counter and place an order, and an order-entry clerk might then key data about the order into a terminal. Beside keyboard-based input devices, many other types now exist that allow direct-entry input of data—for example, touch screens, mice, joysticks, trackballs, voice, video, and sound. Some types of devices will even track eye movements and gestures that a person makes with their hands (see, e.g., Nielsen 1993).

Data about a state or event might also be recorded on some medium before it is entered into a system (the upper branch of Figure 11–1). For example,

FIGURE 11–1. Input methods.

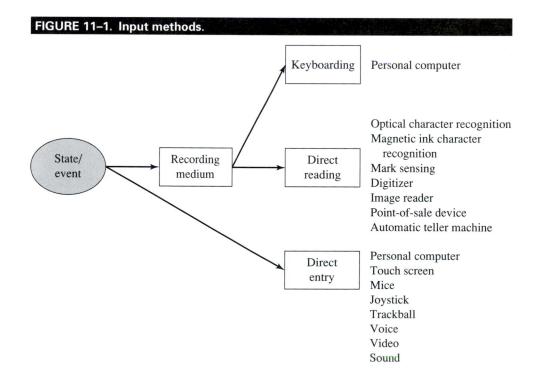

a salesperson might transcribe data about a sale onto a source document; data about a person's account number might be recorded on the magnetic strip on the back of a plastic credit card; a universal product code (UPC) might be printed on the packaging material for some product. In some cases, the medium then might be read directly by an input device—for example, an optical character reader or imaging device. In other cases, data recorded on the medium might be keyed into a terminal—for example, a data-entry operator keys data off source documents into a microcomputer. When this input method is used, *data preparation activities* are often undertaken prior to entering the data into the system. For example, source documents might be scanned for authenticity, accuracy, and completeness prior to their being keyed at a terminal. Similarly, annotations and notes might need to be erased and paper clips and staples might need to be removed before documents are read by an imaging device. The documents might then be sorted and assembled into batches.

When data is recorded on some medium prior to input to an application system, either prerecording or postrecording of the state or event can occur. Under *prerecording*, the state or event is recorded on the medium before the existence of the state is detected or the event has occurred. For example, an organization might record on a plastic credit card that one of its customers is always entitled to a discount when the customer purchases goods (prerecording of a state), or the characteristics of a clothing item and its price might be recorded on a tag so that these data can be read using an optical wand at the time of sale (prerecording of an event). Under *postrecording*, the state or event is recorded on the medium after the existence of the state has been detected or the event has occurred. For example, a person's marital status might be recorded on a source document during an interview (postrecording of a state), or a sale might be recorded on a source document after it has occurred (postrecording of an event).

Combinations of data input methods can also be used. For example, when customers use an automatic teller machine (ATM), the machine reads data from the plastic card (e.g., an account number) that customers insert into the machine (prerecorded, medium-based data entry). Customers also use the machine's keypad to enter the amount they wish to withdraw from their accounts (direct entry).

By understanding the types of data input methods used within an application system, auditors can develop expectations about the probable control strengths and weaknesses in the input subsystem. Consider, for example, the

---

TABLE 11–1 Control Advantages of Using Point-of-Sale Terminals

1. Optical scanning of a premarked code improves pricing accuracy.
2. Customers can verify accuracy and completeness of a sale because they can be provided with a detailed receipt.
3. Improved control over tender because the terminal controls the cash drawer, automatically dispenses change and stamps, and handles any types of tender—cash, checks, coupons, food stamps.
4. Automatic check authorization or credit-card authorization. Customers can also enter PINs to authorize funds transfer from their accounts to the vendor's account.
5. Maintenance of independent records of transactions undertaken via journal tapes.
6. Better inventory control through more timely information on item sales.

TABLE 11–2 Control Advantages of Using Automatic Teller Machines

1. Physical security over cash. Many have antitheft features like alarms, camera surveillance, movement indicators, and heat detectors.
2. Maintenance of independent records of transactions undertaken via journal tapes and control counters.
3. Cryptographic facilities to preserve the privacy of data entered.
4. Software to guide customers through the input process, thereby minimizing errors or omissions.

following three aspects of input methods and how they are likely to affect auditors' assessment of control strengths and weaknesses:

1. As the amount of human intervention in the data input method increases, the likelihood of errors or irregularities occurring increases. For example, if sales data is first recorded onto a source document and then keyed into an application system, there is a greater chance of errors occurring than if the data is keyed immediately into a microcomputer or scanned from a tag. In the former case, errors can occur during transcription as well as during keying, whereas in the latter two cases, errors can occur only during keying or scanning. In general, relative to direct-entry input or prerecorded, medium-based input methods, postrecorded, medium-based input methods are more prone to errors and irregularities because they are more labor intensive.
2. As the time interval between detecting the existence of a state or event and input of the state or event to an application system increases, the likelihood of errors or irregularities occurring increases. Data about the state or event could be forgotten; or the person who enters the data might not be the person who observed the state or event, and thus he or she might be less able to respond to queries about the validity of the data. As the time interval lengthens, more opportunities also arise for data about the state or event to be altered improperly.
3. Use of certain types of input devices facilitates control within the input subsystem because they possess characteristics that mitigate against errors or irregularities. For example, Tables 11–1 and 11–2 list some of the major control advantages that arise when point-of-sale terminals and automatic teller machines are used as input devices.

SOURCE DOCUMENT DESIGN

Some data-input methods use source documents to record data that will be entered into a computer system. Source documents are often used when there will be a delay between capturing the data about a state or event and input of that data into a computer system. For example, sales data might be captured remotely and mailed to the head office of an organization for input to an order-entry system. Source documents are also used as turnaround documents. For example, a computer-prepared remittance advice could be sent to customers with their invoices. Customers are asked to return the remittance advice along with their payment. The remittance advice is then read optically into an accounts receivable system.

From a control viewpoint, a well-designed source document achieves several purposes:

1. It reduces the likelihood of data recording errors;
2. It increases the speed with which data can be recorded;
3. It controls the work flow;

4. It facilitates data entry into a computer system;
5. For pattern recognition devices, it increases the speed and accuracy with which data can be read; and
6. It facilitates subsequent reference checking.

Auditors, therefore, must understand the fundamentals of good source document design. Source document design begins after carrying out source document analysis. Source document analysis determines what data will be captured, how the data will be captured, who will capture the data, how the data will be prepared and entered into a computer system, and how the document will be handled, stored, and filed.

After these requirements have been determined, two decisions can be made. First, the characteristics of the paper medium to be used for the source document can be chosen. This decision involves selecting the length and width of the paper, its grade and weight, and whether single-part or multipart paper will be used. If the wrong length and width is chosen, for example, the source document might be difficult to handle or to read via some type of scanning device. If the wrong grade and weight are chosen, the paper could smudge or tear under adverse conditions. If the wrong decision is made on whether to use single- or multipart paper, multiple recordings of the same source data could have to be made, or alternatively the multipart paper chosen to avoid multiple recordings could tear because it is too thin.

The second decision relates to the layout and style that will be used for the source document. The choice of layout and style has an important impact on the number of input errors that will be made using the source document. Some important design guidelines follow:

1. *Preprint wherever possible.* Preprint all constant information on a source document. If only a limited number of responses to a question is appropriate, preprint the responses and have the user tick or circle the correct responses or delete those that are inappropriate.
2. *Provide titles, headings, notes, and instructions.* A title clearly identifies the purpose of the source document. Headings break up the document into logical sections. Notes and instructions assist the user to complete the document. Where codes are used, preprint their meaning on the form so the user does not have to rely on memory or waste time looking up reference manuals.
3. *Use techniques for emphasis and to highlight differences.* Different type fonts such as italics and boldface give emphasis to different parts of the source document. Heavy thick lines or hatching highlight important fields or sections of the source document. Different colors facilitate distribution of different copies of the source document. Background colors emphasize special sections of the source document—for example, those for office use only.
4. *Arrange fields for ease of use.* Design the source document to be completed in a natural sequence from left to right, top to bottom. Group related items together. The sequence of fields should follow the work flow: The most used fields on the left of the document; those usually used in the center; and those seldom used on the right.
5. *Use the "caption above fill-in area" approach for captions and data fields.* Figure 11–2a shows three approaches to designing the layout of captions and fields on a source document: caption preceding the fill-in area, caption within the fill-in area, and caption above the fill-in area (floating box). Galitz (1993) argues that the "caption above fill-in area" or floating-box approach is the best. The caption should be centered above the fill-in area or left justified above the fill-in area if the fill-in area is long.

to be more e
screen is like

All the i
still should l
multiple scre
broken at so
ments togeth
ensuring elen
gically.

If a scree
the screen mu
ture task. If t
screen must b
tured and trar
data-capture p
on the source
screen only wh

An import
ity with a pa
should be used
screen should a
error messages.

Caption Desig

Captions indica
Design consider
mat, alignment,
the design of ca
data or input of

Captions mu
capture. Because
the meaning of t
source documen
refer to the sourc

Captions mu
field. For examp
lowercase type fc
tor. To further dif
tensities can be
entry, they shoul
users. Alternative
ferent colors.

Captions shou
same line as the d
tiple data-entry fie
fields should be sta

SALESPERSON: _

6. *When possible, provide multiple-choice answers to questions to avoid omissions.* Figure 11–2b shows how this technique can be used with the floating-box approach. Rather than ask users to remember all the business subjects they studied, provide a list they can check.
7. *Use tick marks or indicator values to identify field-size errors.* Figure 11–2c shows how these techniques highlight field overflow or underflow. Tick marks can be used when a field must contain a fixed number of characters. Indicator values can be used to show the maximum when a variable number of characters can be inserted in the field.
8. *Combine instructions with questions.* Figure 11–2d shows how this technique overcomes possible confusion about the format for a date.
9. *Space items appropriately on forms.* Correct spacing of fields on forms is particularly important if responses are to be typewritten (e.g., the form is input to a laser printer to receive output from a word processing package).
10. *Design for ease of keying.* Have the order in which fields are keyed follow the order of field placement.
11. *Prenumber source documents.* Prenumber source documents so users can account for every document. If each document has a unique serial number, input transactions can be sorted by serial number and breaks in the sequence of numbers identified.
12. *Conform to organizational standards.* An organization should have a forms control section responsible for overall forms design standards; for example, numbering and color conventions, placement of the organization's logos, retention requirements, and ordering and stockkeeping requirements. Ensure the source document design conforms with these standards.

FIGURE 11–2(a). Caption preceding fill-in area, caption within fill-in area, and caption above fill-in area source-document design approaches. (b). Using multiple choice to prevent omissions. (c). Using tick marks and indicator values to identify field-size errors. (d). Combining instructions with questions.

LAST NAME:

LAST NAME:

LAST NAME: _____

(a)

PRIOR SUBJECT STUDIED

| Accounting | Taxation | Economics | Statistics |
| □ AC | □ TX | □ EC | □ ST |

(b)

PRODUCT CODE

SUPPLIER NUMBER

10

(c)

DATE

Y Y M M D D

(d)

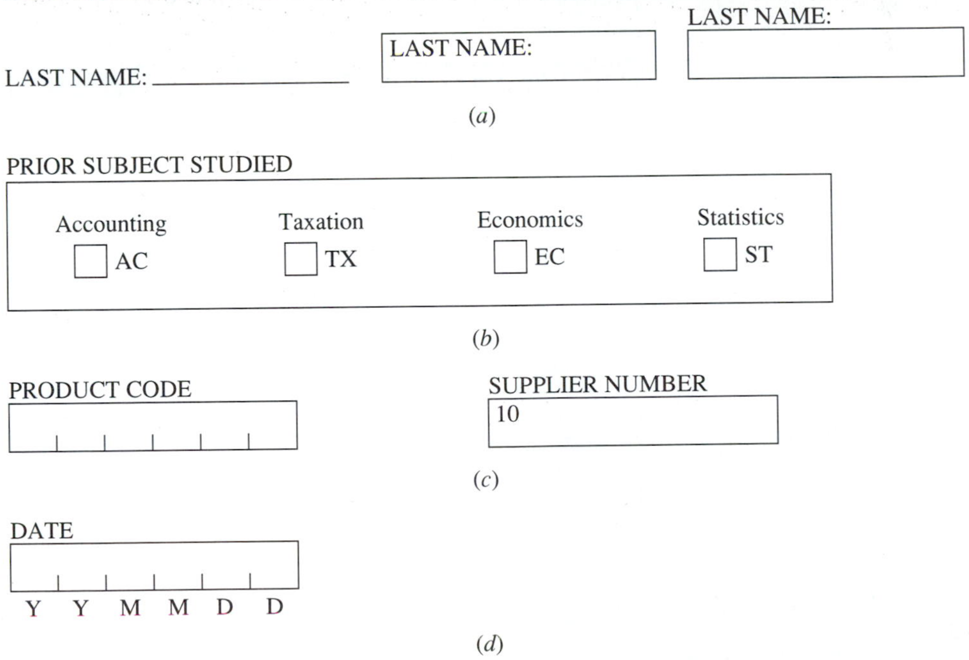

DATA-ENTRY SCREEN DE

If data
portar
input s
in an
which
sign ei
affect t

Th
sues ai
Mullet
all type
the scre
source
mendai
recomn
ommen
caption
aligned
must m
fronted.
are no f

Screen

Screens
anced.
groups.

As t
screen i
complex
more coi

FIGURE

XXXXXX
XXXXXX
XXXXXX
XXXXXX
XXXXXX

XX
XX
XX
XX

Mori
• 9 rc
• 5 v
• 23

Where the caption and data-entry field appear on the same line, the caption should be followed immediately by a colon. At least one space also should exist between the colon and the data-entry field. Where the data-entry fields are stacked, however, a colon is not needed before each data-entry field (providing underscores indicate the field position and size).

If direct-entry input of data is used, captions should be aligned vertically in columns. Within a column, Galitz (1993, p. 97) argues that either (1) both captions and data-entry fields should be left justified or (2) captions should be right justified and data-entry fields should be left justified. For example:

```
NAME:   _____          NAME: _____
AGE:      _____          AGE: _____
POSITION:_____          POSITION: _____
```

If the screen is used for entry of data already captured on a source document, however, alignment and justification are dictated by the source document. The screen design should be an image of the source document.

Both horizontal and vertical spacing around captions are important to attaining an uncluttered screen. For horizontal spacing, direct-entry data capture screens should have a minimum of five spaces between the longest data entry field in a column and the leftmost caption in an adjacent column. Source document screens should have a minimum of three spaces between a data-entry field and the following caption. For vertical spacing, direct-entry data capture screens should have a blank line every fifth row; that is, captions and the associated data-entry fields should be clustered in groups of five. Source-document screens, on the other hand, should mirror the vertical spacing found on the source document.

Data-Entry Field Design

Data-entry fields should immediately follow their associated caption either on the same line or, in the case of a repeating field, on several lines immediately below the caption. The size of a field should be indicated by using an underscore character or some other character. As each new character is entered into the field, the existing character is replaced. Alternatively, the size of a field can be indicated by using a lined box filled in with a contrasting color or background (see, for example, Weinschenk and Yeo 1995). Galitz (1993, p. 138) reports, however, that empirical studies have shown the underscore character is the best means of indicating field size.

Where direct-entry data capture screens are used, completion aids can be used to reduce keying errors. For example, if a date must be entered, either the caption or the field-size characters can be used to indicate the date format:

```
DATE (YYMMDD): _____          DATE: YYMMDD
```

On the other hand, where source-document screens are used, completion aids are not needed because the keyboard operator can refer to the source document for completion instructions.

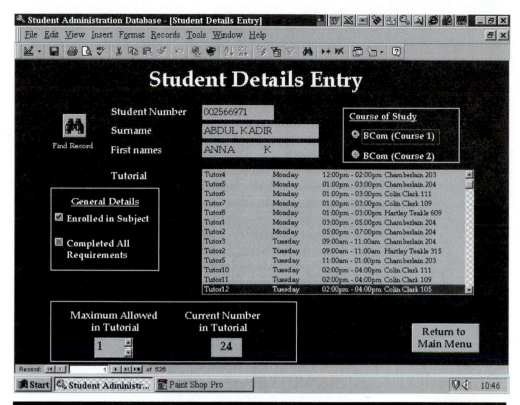

FIGURE 11–4. Screen illustrating use of radio buttons, check boxes, list boxes, and spin boxes.
Courtesy of The University of Queensland, and screenshot reprinted by permission from Microsoft Corporation.

Radio buttons, check boxes, list boxes, and spin boxes are now frequently used for direct-entry data capture (Figure 11–4) (see, e.g., Weinschenk and Yeo 1995). Radio buttons and check boxes should be used only if one or a small number of options exists. With long lists of options, list boxes can be used. Spin boxes can be used to cycle through a limited number of options.

Tabbing and Skipping

Galitz (1993, pp. 133–135) argues that automatic skipping to a new field should be avoided in data-entry screen design for two reasons. First, with an automatic skip feature, keyboard operators might make a field-size error that remains undetected because the cursor simply skips to a new field. The additional character inadvertently added to the field will affect the character positions of all other fields, thereby causing them to be in error. Second, in many applications, data-entry fields often are not filled anyway. Thus, keyboard operators must still tab to the next field. Rather than having keyboard operators decide whether tabbing is needed, it is simpler to require them always to tab to the next field. Although the tab requires an additional keystroke, the operator's keying rhythm is maintained.

Color

In a data-entry screen design, color can be used to aid in locating a particular caption or data item, to separate areas on the display, or to indicate a changed status (e.g., an error situation). Color appears to reduce search time for an item on a screen and to motivate users better because the screen is more interesting. Nonetheless, poor use of color can distract or confuse users by implying that similarities or differences exist among captions or data items on the display when this is not the case. Good color data-entry screen designs will

1. Use color sparingly and consistently;
2. Use only a few colors that are widely spaced along the visual spectrum, e.g., red, yellow, green, and blue;
3. Use colors that are visible in the context of the environment in which data entry will occur, e.g., the glare of overhead lighting;
4. Avoid overuse of bright colors that cause fatigue when the screens must be used for prolonged periods;
5. Use colors to denote meaning that is congruent with the users' experience— for example, red for an icon associated with an error message;
6. Accommodate users who are color blind—for example, by using other means, such as uppercase and lowercase text, to differentiate captions from data entered by a user; and
7. Recognize that different colors may have different meanings in different cultures (see, e.g., Nielsen 1990*b*).

Response Time

During data entry, the response time is the interval that elapses between entry of a data item and the system's indication it is ready to accept a new data item. As with all types of interactive tasks, the response time for data entry should be reasonably constant and sufficiently fast to sustain continuity in the task being performed by the user.

Within a transaction, response time should be fast—say, two to four seconds. When data entry for a transaction has been completed, users will tolerate a longer response time. Fast response times are required if data is keyed from a source document because the user will not want their keying rhythm broken by response delays. If a dedicated source document is not used, however, users will tolerate a slower response time as they move from one data item to another.

Display Rate

The display rate is the rate at which characters or images on a screen are displayed. It is a function of the speed with which data can be communicated between the terminal and the computer (baud rate).

Data-entry screens require a fast display rate. Users are unwilling to wait long periods for captions and images to appear on a screen. They seek to enter data quickly into the system, especially if it is keyed from a dedicated source document. If the display rate is slow or variable, a higher rate of data-entry errors will occur.

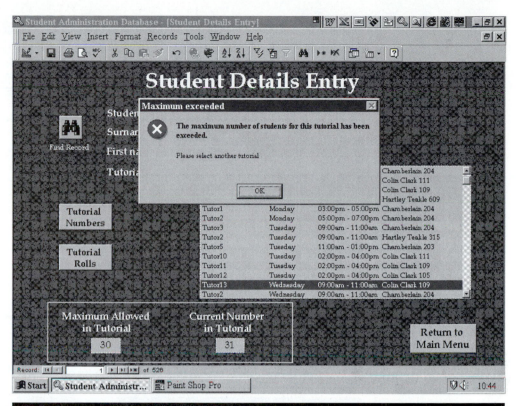

FIGURE 11–5. Pop-up window to prompt user on error condition.
Courtesy of The University of Queensland, and screenshot reprinted by permission from Microsoft Corporation.

Prompting and Help Facilities

A prompting facility provides *immediate* advice or information about actions users should take when they work with a data-entry screen. A prompt often takes the form of a pop-up window containing an instructional message that appears automatically when a user moves the cursor to a particular field (Figure 11–5). The advice or information provided must be brief and easily comprehended—for example, the range of values that can be keyed into a data-entry field. Hypertext links can also be provided that enable users to access quickly other information related to the topic about which they are seeking information (see, also, Horton 1994).

A Help facility provides look-up advice or information about actions users should take when they work with a data-entry screen. Unlike a prompt, users must invoke a Help facility by accessing a menu, keying a command, or pressing a function key (Figure 11–6). Thus, the advice or information provided to users is delayed. In this light, Help facilities are appropriate when *(1)* longer or more complex advice or information must be provided to users or *(2)* the advice or information will be needed infrequently. For example, users might access a Help facility to obtain more details on an error message they have not encountered before, or they could use a Help facility to assist their recall on how to enter data required only at the end of a financial year.

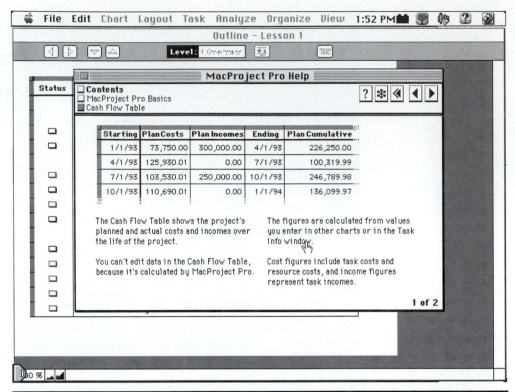

FIGURE 11–6. Help facility.
Courtesy of FileMaker, Inc.

Prompting and Help facilities are more likely to be useful when data entry is not based upon a dedicated source document. Nonetheless, even if users key data from a source document, the source document might not provide the answers to all questions they might have—for example, the validation rules that apply to a data item. Thus, prompting and Help facilities can still be useful even when source document-based data entry occurs.

Prompting and Help facilities are also more likely to be useful to novice users or at times when users undertake infrequently occurring data-entry tasks. In this regard, users should be able to turn prompting facilities on and off. They inhibit data entry by expert users, but expert users should still be able to invoke them when they encounter a difficult or infrequent data-entry task.

The design of effective prompting and Help facilities can be difficult. Designers must first determine the types of prompting and help that users will need during data-entry tasks. They must then write text that contains information, instructions, and examples that are succinct, meaningful, and task oriented. Users also must be able to interact easily with the prompting and Help facilities provided.

DATA CODE CONTROLS

Data codes have two purposes. First, they uniquely identify an entity or identify an entity as a member of a group or set. Textual or narrative description does not always uniquely identify an entity; for example, two people could have the same name. Second, for identification purposes, codes often are more compact than textual or narrative description because they require fewer characters to carry a given amount of information.

Poorly designed codes affect the input process in two ways: They are error prone, and they cause recording and keying processes to be inefficient. Auditors, therefore, must evaluate the quality of the coding systems used in application systems to determine their likely impact on data integrity, effectiveness, and efficiency objectives.

Data Coding Errors

There are five types of data coding errors:

1. *Addition.* An extra character is added to the code, e.g., 87942 coded as 879142.
2. *Truncation.* A character is omitted from the code, e.g., 87942 coded as 8792.
3. *Transcription.* A wrong character is recorded, e.g., 87942 coded as 81942.
4. *Transposition.* Adjacent characters of the code are reversed, e.g., 87942 coded as 78942.
5. *Double transposition.* Characters separated by one or more characters are reversed, e.g., 87942 coded as 84972.

Five factors affect the frequency with which these coding errors are made:

1. *Length of the code.* Longer codes are more error prone. The notion that length could be important derives from the work of Miller (1956). He argues that humans effectively can hold only about five to nine (average seven) "chunks" of information in short-term memory. In this light, long codes should be broken up into chunks by using, for example, hyphens, slashes, or spaces to reduce coding errors.
2. *Alphabetic/numeric mix.* If alphabetic and numeric characters are to be mixed in a code, the error rate is lower if the alphabetics are grouped together and the numerics are grouped together. Thus, a code such as ABN653 is less error prone than the code A6BS3N. The latter code is also harder to key because it breaks the keying rhythm by interchanging alphabetics and numerics.
3. *Choice of characters.* If possible, the characters B, I, O, S, V, and Z should be avoided in codes because they are frequently confused with the characters 8, 1, 0, 5, U, and 2. Also, the letters Y and N often are illegible when they must be handwritten.
4. *Mixing uppercase/lowercase fonts.* Having to use the shift key during keying of a code breaks the keying rhythm and increases the likelihood of error. If possible, only an uppercase or a lowercase font should be used for a code. Special characters, such as @, *, and # also cause problems because the shift key must be used.
5. *Predictability of character sequence.* Some character sequences are more predictable than others and, as such, are less error prone. For example, the character sequence THE is more predictable than the character sequence ZXQ.

Types of Coding Systems

Specific codes are chosen within the context of a coding system. Ideally, a coding system achieves five objectives:

Objective	Explanation
Flexibility	A code should allow easy addition of new items or categories.
Meaningfulness	Where possible, a code should indicate the values of the attributes of the entity.
Compactness	A code should convey maximum information conveyed with the minimum number of characters.
Convenience	A code should be easy to encode, decode, and key.
Evolvability	Where possible, a code can be adapted to changing user requirements.

Unfortunately, it is impossible to achieve all these objectives simultaneously. The following subsections briefly examine four types of coding systems that auditors will encounter frequently and the extent to which they achieve these objectives.

Serial Codes

Serial coding systems assign consecutive numbers (or alphabetics) to an entity, irrespective of the attributes of the entity. Thus, a serial code uniquely identifies an entity. The code indicates nothing further about the entity, however, such as the category of items to which it belongs.

The major advantages of a serial code are the ease with which a new item can be added and conciseness. The low mnemonic value of serial codes can also be an advantage in some circumstances. For example, consider a database environment in which extensive sharing of data occurs and the number and types of users and their needs are in a state of flux. Different users might wish to view data differently. A code that presumes one view of data might be inappropriate for certain users. Thus, a serial coding system might contribute better to the evolution of the system.

The code presents problems when the file of items is volatile—that is, significant numbers of additions and deletions occur. Deleted items must have their codes reassigned to new items; otherwise, significant gaps in the sequence occur, and the code is no longer concise. Users can become confused if the codes are constantly reassigned to new entities. Because the codes have no mnemonic value, they are also difficult to remember.

Block Sequence Codes

Block sequence codes assign blocks of numbers to particular categories of an entity. The primary attribute on which entities are to be categorized must be chosen, and blocks of numbers must be assigned for each value of the attribute. For example, if account numbers are assigned to customers on the basis of the discount allowed each customer, a block sequence code would look like this:

101 R. Allen
102 J. Smith   } 3% discount allowed
103 M. Clarke

.
.
.

201 S. Elders
202 M. Ball   } 3½% discount allowed

.
.
.

301 K. Kline
302 G. Brown   } 4% discount allowed
303 F. Water

Block sequence codes have the advantage of giving some mnemonic value to the code. Nevertheless, choosing the size of the block needed can be difficult (and the remedy if overflow occurs). If the block sizes are too large, characters are wasted, and the code is no longer concise. Long codes are more difficult to remember.

Hierarchical Codes

Hierarchical codes require selection of the set of attributes of the entity to be coded and their ordering by importance. The value of the code is a combination of the values of the codes for each attribute of the entity. For example, the following hierarchical code for an account has three components (expenditure within departments within divisions):

C65	/	423	/	3956
Division number		Department number		Type of expenditure

Hierarchical codes are more meaningful than serial or block sequence codes because they describe more attributes of the entities to which they apply. Thus, they should be easier to recall. Nevertheless, they are not always concise. As a result, their length undermines recall accuracy. Sometimes they also mix alphabetics and numerics, which again undermines recall accuracy.

Hierarchical codes sometimes present problems when change occurs. In the example given previously, consider the implications of a change to the organizational structure—for example, department 423 might be assigned to a different division C25. The codes for many items might have to be altered, and in some cases extensive resequencing of master files might have to occur.

Association Codes

With an association code, the attributes of the entity to be coded are selected, and unique codes are then assigned to each attribute value. The codes can be numeric, alphabetic, or alphanumeric. The code for the entity is simply the concatenation of the different codes assigned to the attributes of the entity. Unlike an hierarchical code, however, the order in which the codes for the attributes occur in the overall code does not necessarily imply some type of hierarchical relationship.

The following is an example of an association code assigned to a shirt:

$$SHM32DRCOT$$

where SH = shirt
M = male
32 = 32 centimeters, the neck size
DR = dress shirt
COT = cotton fabric

Association codes have high mnemonic value. They can be error-prone, however, if they are not concise or they contain too much of a mixture of alphabetic and numeric characters. Error-prone characters, such as I, O, and S, also might have to be used if the code is to have mnemonic value.

CHECK DIGITS

In some cases, errors made in transcribing and keying data can have serious consequences. For example, keying the wrong stock number can result in a large quantity of the wrong inventory being dispatched to a customer. Aside from the costs of retrieving the inventory and replacing it with the correct inventory, customer goodwill can be lost. One control used to guard against these types of errors is a check digit. Check digits are now used as a means of detecting errors in many applications—for example, airline ticketing, credit card processing, bank account processing, blood bank item processing, and driver's license processing (see, e.g., Gallian 1996).

Nature of Check Digits

A *check digit* is a redundant digit(s) added to a code that enables the accuracy of other characters in the code to be checked. The check digit can act as a prefix or suffix character, or it can be placed somewhere in the middle of the code. When the code is entered, a program recalculates the check digit to determine whether the entered check digit and the calculated check digit are the same. If they are the same, the code is most likely to be correct. If they differ, the code is most likely to be in error.

Calculating Check Digits

There are many ways of calculating check digits. A simple way is to add up the digits in a number and assign the result as a suffix character. For example, if the code is 2148, the check digit is $2 + 1 + 4 + 8 = 15$. Dropping the tens digit, the check digit will be 5 and the code 21485. This check digit does not detect a very common kind of coding error, however—namely, a transposition error. The incorrect code 2814 still produces the correct check digit.

To overcome this problem a different method of calculating a check digit can be used. The approach assigns different weights to different digits in the code. Given, again, the code 2148, the steps are as follows:

1. Multiply each digit by a weight. Assume the weight used will be 5–4–3–2; that is, 2 for the units digit, 3 for the tens digit, 4 for the hundreds digit, and 5 the thousands digit, viz:

$$8 \times 2 = 16$$
$$4 \times 3 = 12$$

$$1 \times 4 = 4$$
$$2 \times 5 = 10$$

2. Sum the products = 42.
3. Divide by a modulus. In this case, assume we choose the modulus 11:

$$\frac{42}{11} = 3 \text{ with remainder } 9$$

4. Subtract the remainder from the modulus and the result constitutes the check digit.

$$11 - 9 = 2$$

5. Add the check digit to the code as a suffix. The result is 21482.

The check digit can be recalculated upon keying to detect a coding or keying error, or upon reading the data into the computer. The recalculation for this code proceeds as follows:

1. Multiply each digit by its corresponding weight. The check digit takes a weight of 1.

$$2 \times 1 = 2$$
$$8 \times 2 = 16$$
$$4 \times 3 = 12$$
$$1 \times 4 = 4$$
$$2 \times 5 = 10$$

2. Sum the products = 44.
3. Divide by the modulus

$$\frac{44}{11} = 4$$

4. If the remainder is zero, there is a high probability the code is correct.

If the code contains alphabetics or a special character (such as a hyphen), a check digit can still be calculated. Each alphabetic or special character must be assigned a number according to some rule.

Efficiency Of Check Digit Methods

Table 11–3 shows the relative efficiency of different check digit methods at detecting various types of errors. The percentages given refer only to the combination of digits that can produce an erroneous code that the check digit will detect. In practice, the different types of errors are unlikely to occur with the same frequency. For example, Beckley (1967) reports one study found the frequency of errors to be as follows:

Transcription	86%
Single transposition	8%
Double transposition and random	6%

He points out, however, that other factors affect error frequency—for example, whether codes are typed or handwritten.

TABLE 11–3 Efficiency of Different Moduli for Check Digits

					Percentage errors detected			
Modulus	Range weights that may be used	Max. length of number without repeating weight	Weights used	Trans-cription	Single trans-position	Double trans-position	Other trans-position	Random
10	1–9	8	1-2-1-2-1	94.5	100	Nil	50.0	90.0
			1-3-1-3-1	100	88.9	Nil	44.5	90.0
			7-6-5-4-3-2	88.2	100	88.9	89.8	90.0
			9-8-7-4-3-2	94.5	100	88.9	72.2	90.0
			1-3-7-1-3-7	100	88.9	88.9	88.9	90.0
11	1–10	9	10-9-8.....2	100	100	100	100	90.9
			1-2-4-8-16, etc.	100	100	100	100	90.9
13	1–12	11	Any	100	100	100	100	92.3
17	1–16	15	Any	100	100	100	100	94.1
19	1–18	17	Any	100	100	100	100	94.7
23	1–22	21	Any	100	100	100	100	95.6
31	1–30	29	Any	100	100	100	100	96.8
37	1–36	35	Any	100	100	100	100	97.3

Source: Adapted from Daniels and Yeates [1971]. Used by permission. NCC Education Services Ltd.

One difficulty that arises when choosing a check digit system with modulus 11 or greater is that two check digits rather than one are required. For example, if modulus 11 produces a remainder of 1, a check digit of 10 is required. The overhead of having a two-character versus a one-character check digit might be unacceptable. There are several solutions to the problem. First, codes generating a check digit of 10 or more are declared illegal and cannot be used. With modulus 11, for example, 9 percent of possible codes are then unavailable. Second, a special character (say, an alphabetic) can be used to represent a check digit that exceeds nine. This approach is problematic if only numeric codes are desired. Finally, Campbell (1970) suggests a scheme whereby two sets of weights are used. When a check digit of 10 or more results using the first set of weights, an alternative check digit is calculated using the second set of weights. When the check digit is validated and a nonzero remainder is obtained, the second set of weights must then be used to see whether the check digit is valid according to this set of weights.

When to Use Check Digits

Overheads arise from using check digits because a redundant character must be carried at least partially through the system. Extra computation is also needed to calculate and validate the check digit. Therefore, use of check digits should be limited to critical fields.

Manual calculation of or checking of check digits should be avoided. The process is time-consuming and error-prone. For new codes, the check digit should be precalculated automatically and assigned as part of the code.

Validation of check digits should be undertaken only by a machine—for example, during keying or by an input program. To save storage space, the check digit can be dropped after it has been read by an input program and re-calculated upon output. The trade-off here is storage space versus processing time.

BATCH CONTROLS

Some of the simplest and most effective controls over data capture and entry activities are batch controls. Batching is the process of grouping together transactions that bear some type of relationship to each other. Various controls then can be exercised over the batch to prevent or detect errors or irregularities.

Types of Batches

There are two types of batches: physical batches and logical batches. *Physical batches* are groups of transactions that constitute a physical unit. For example, source documents might be obtained via the mail, assembled into batches, spiked and tied together, and then given to a data-entry clerk to be entered into an application system at a terminal. Similarly, documents that are to be input to an electronic imaging system might be assembled into batches before they are scanned or filmed.

Logical batches are groups of transactions bound together on some logical basis, rather than being physically contiguous. For example, different clerks might use the same terminal to enter transactions into an application system. Clerks keep control totals of the transactions that they have entered. The input program logically groups transactions entered on the basis of the clerk's identification number. After some period has elapsed, it prepares control totals for reconciliation with the clerk's control totals.

Means of Batch Control

Two documents are needed to help exercise control over physical batches: a batch cover sheet and a batch control register. A batch cover sheet (Figure 11–7) contains the following types of information:

1. A unique batch number;
2. Control totals for the batch;
3. Data common to the various transactions in the batch, e.g., transaction type;
4. Date when the batch was prepared;
5. Information on errors detected in the batch; and
6. Space for signatures of personnel who have handled the batch in some way, e.g., the person who prepared the batch and the person who keyed the batch.

A batch control register (Figure 11–8) records the transit of physical batches between various locations within an organization. Each person responsible for handling batches has a batch register. The register is signed each time a batch is received or dispatched. The person who brings the batch or takes it away countersigns the register. In some cases the person taking over responsibility for the batch also checks its contents. If a dispute arises over the location of a batch, the batch control registers can be consulted.

FIGURE 11–7. Batch cover sheet.
Courtesy of The University of Queensland.

BATCH NUMBER: 6511

THE UNIVERSITY OF QUEENSLAND
ACCOUNTS PAYABLE BATCH TRANSMITTAL FORM
PROCESSING MONTH OF JANUARY 19 98

VOUCHER NUMBERS	
FROM	TO
251867	251896

SOURCE DOCUMENTS ATTACHED. PLACE X IN RELEVANT BOX.

TRANSACTION TYPE

RE	X	UNPAID VOUCHERS (Regular Vouchers)
MA		PAID VOUCHERS (Manual Vouchers)
CM		VENDOR CREDIT MEMO

DOCUMENT COUNT: 30
RECORD COUNT: 36

DOCUMENT TYPE

RE	X	AP VOUCHERS
CM		CREDIT MEMO
GC		GENERAL CLAIMS

DATA PREPARATION TO COMPLETE
ENTERED IN AP BATCH CONTROL LOG

JOB NO. 81

ENTERED BY: DATE:

VERIFIED BY: DATE:

TOTAL: 385245 95 CR

BATCH DATE: 220198

BANK NO.: 01

Vouchers checked and batched by: SW

Batches checked and passed for payment by:

O'Baheer
Expenditure Accountant

22/ 1 /98
Date

I certify that the payments are in order and have been properly authorised.

Cheque signatory/Operations Accountant

/ /
Date

ERROR MESSAGES

MICROFILMING COMPLETE
OPERATOR:
DATE:

FIGURE 11-8. Batch control register.
Courtesy of The University of Queensland.

BS155 2/93

BUSINESS SERVICES – ACCOUNTS PAYABLE TRANSIT LOG

for the Accounting Month of _January_ 199_8_

CLERK	M T H	BATCH NO	DATE	VOUCHER NO RANGE FROM	TO	RUN NO	RUN DATE	VOUCHERS NOT IN BALANCE	RELEASE DATE	RE/MA/CM	BATCH TOTAL	DOC CNT	REC CNT	ORIG INIT	FILM COMP-LETE	BOX NO
E2	A	6469	13/1	250947 – 250976		VR114	14/1/98	250949, 250955	16/1/98	RE	4495.65	30	32	A.W.		
	R															
E2	A	6470	13/1	250977 – 251002		VR114	14/1/98		16/1/98	RE	4748.65	26	29	A.W.		
	R															
E2	A	6471	13/1	251003 – 251032		VR114	14/1/98	251013	19/1/98	RE	53803.83	30	55	A.W.		
	R															
E2	A	6472	14/1	251033 – 251062		VR114	14/1/98	251034, 251050	19/1/98	RE	5680.43	30	31	A.W.		
	R															
	R															
	R															
	R															
	R															
	R															
	R															

To identify errors or irregularities in either a physical or a logical batch, three type of control totals can be calculated:

Control Total Type	Explanation
Financial totals	Grand totals calculated for each field containing money amounts.
Hash totals	Grand totals calculated for any code on a document in the batch, e.g., the source document serial numbers can be totaled.
Document/record counts	Grand totals for the number of documents or records in the batch.

In the case of a physical batch, these totals can be written on to the batch cover sheet and keyed into the application system prior to key entry of the transactions in the batch. The input program then computes the batch totals as the transactions are entered. When keying of all transactions in the batch has been completed, it compares the computed total against the entered total and signals any discrepancy.

In the case of a logical batch, the person responsible for keying data must keep an independent record of transactions entered into the application system. Periodically, the batch totals calculated by the input program must then be compared against the batch totals calculated on the basis of these independent records.

Design of Batches

Batch design involves choosing the size and nature of the batches to be used. Three major design guidelines should be followed:

1. The batch should be small enough to facilitate locating errors if control totals do not balance.
2. The batch should be large enough to constitute a reasonably sized unit of work.
3. The batch should constitute a logical unit—for example, a group of documents all containing a single transaction type.

VALIDATION OF DATA INPUT

Data submitted as input to an application system should be validated as soon as possible after it has been captured and as close as possible to its source. Errors then can be corrected by persons who are likely to have most knowledge about them and while the circumstances surrounding the data are still fresh in their minds. Sometimes this objective cannot be achieved. For example, the data in error might have been received from a remote organization via an electronic data interchange system. Some time could elapse before the receiving organization resolves the error with the sending organization.

Any errors identified that are not corrected immediately should be written to an error file (Figure 11–9). Otherwise, users might forget to correct the errors. The input subsystem should use the error file to remind users when they have not corrected errors on a timely basis. Reminder messages can be displayed on screens or printed on hard-copy reports.

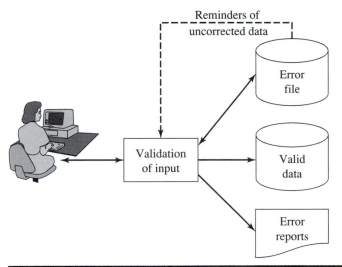

FIGURE 11-9. Use of an error file for data validation.

Types of Data Input Validation Checks

To some extent the types of data input validation checks undertaken depend on the nature of the data input method used. For example, if documents are scanned via an imaging device, a quality-control person should be responsible for examining document images, comparing them against the original documents, and rejecting the image or undertaking cleanup work if its quality is unacceptable.

To illustrate the nature of data input validation checks, however, consider four types that can be undertaken when input data that is keyed in at a terminal: *(1)* field checks, *(2)* record checks, *(3)* batch checks, and *(4)* file checks. Each is discussed briefly in the following subsections.

Field checks

With a field check, the validation tests applied to the field do not depend on other fields within the input record or within other input records. For example, we can check whether a field that is supposed to contain numeric data only does, in fact, contain only numeric characters. The following types of field checks can be applied:

Type of Field Check	*Explanation*
Missing data/blanks	Is there any missing data in the field? For example, if a code should contain two hyphens, though they might be in a variable position, can only one be detected? Does the field contain blanks when data always should be present?
Alphabetics/numerics	Does a field that should contain only alphabetics or numerics contain alphanumeric characters?
Range	Does the data for a field fall within its allowable value range?
Set membership	If a permissible set of values is defined for a field, is the data in the field one of these values—for example, one of six valid sales discount codes?
Check digit	Is the check digit valid for the value in the field?

(cont.)

Type of Field Check	Explanation
Master reference	If the master file can be referenced at the same time input data is read, is there a master file match for the key field—for example, customer number?
Size	If variable-length fields are used and a set of permissible sizes is defined, does the field delimiter show the field to be one of these valid sizes?
Format mask	Data entered into a field might have to conform to a particular format. For example, a date might have to be entered as year followed by month followed by day, i.e., yymmdd.

When data entry is not based on a source document, it is usually best to notify data-entry operators immediately (e.g., via a "beep") when a field-check error arises. Operators can then attempt to correct the error before moving to the next field. If data is keyed from a source document, however, it might be better to wait until operators complete and attempt to dispose of a screen before notifying them of field-check errors. Otherwise, their keying rhythm might become too disrupted. Fields in error can be shown by, say, flashing their contents or using a different color to display their contents. When the operator moves the cursor to the field in error, the relevant error message(s) can be displayed.

Record Checks

With a record check, the validation tests applied to a field depend on the field's logical interrelationships with other fields in a record. For example, auditors can check whether the range of salary values in one field is reasonable given the value of another field that indicates a person's seniority. The following types of record checks can be applied:

Type of Record Check	Explanation
Reasonableness	Even though a field value might pass a range check, the contents of another field might determine what is a reasonable value for the field. For example, the range of valid salaries for employees might depend on their position within the organizational hierarchy.
Valid sign–numerics	The contents of one field might determine which sign is valid for a numeric field. For example, if a transaction type field indicates a cash payment has been received from a customer, the amount field should have, say, a positive sign.
Size	If variable-length records are used, the size of the record is a function of the sizes of the variable-length fields or the sizes of fields that optionally might be omitted from the record. The permissible size of fixed- and variable-length records also might depend on a field indicating the record type.
Sequence check	A logical record might comprise more than one physical record. For example, multiple screens might be required to enter all data about an event, and the data from each screen might be stored as a physical record. The input program might check the sequence of the physical records it receives.

When data entry is not based on a source document, like field checks it is usually best to notify data-entry operators immediately when a record-check error arises. If data is keyed from a source document, however, again like field checks, it might be better to wait until operators complete and attempt to dispose of a screen before notifying them of record-check errors.

Correcting errors identified during record checks is more difficult when cross-screen validation occurs. If the values in one field depend on the values in another field that is located on a different screen, operators might have to page back and forth between screens to identify the cause of the error. For this reason, it is better to have data that is logically related grouped together on a single screen.

Batch Checks

With a batch check, the validation tests examine whether the characteristics of a batch of records entered are congruent with the stated characteristics of the batch. For example, auditors can check whether the total of all financial fields in the batch of records equals the grand total given for the batch. The following types of batch checks can be applied:

Type of Batch Check	Explanation
Control totals	Does the accumulation of a field across all records in a batch or the number of records in the batch reconcile with the number specified for the batch?
Transaction type	All input records in a batch might have to be a particular type.
Batch serial number	All input records in a batch might have to include a serial number that has been assigned to the batch.
Sequence check	The input records in a batch might have to follow a particular order.

Some batch errors cannot be identified until all records pertaining to the batch have been entered—for example, a calculated control total does not equal its expected value. Other types can be identified immediately after the data is entered into a field—for example, an incorrect transaction type for the batch.

File Checks

With a file check, the validation tests examine whether the characteristics of a file used during data entry are congruent with the stated characteristics of the file. For example, if auditors validate some of the characteristics of data that is keyed into an application system against a master file, they can check whether they are using the latest version of the master file. The following types of file checks can be applied:

Type of File Check	Explanation
Internal label	The input validation program checks to see that it is accessing a file having the correct name.
Generation number	The input validation program checks to see that it is accessing the correct generation of any file it uses.
Retention date	The input validation program checks to see that it is not using a file whose retention date has expired.
Control totals	Control totals can be calculated for a file on the basis of the contents of the file. The input validation program checks to see that it is using a file with the correct control totals.

File-check errors usually can be identified immediately after a file is accessed. For example, the internal label of a file can be checked immediately after the file is accessed by the input validation program.

Reporting Data Input Errors

Errors must be reported by the input validation program in a way that facilitates fast and accurate correction of the errors. Errors can be signaled via a buzzer or bell. The cursor also can be made to flash to show the data item in error. An error message should then be displayed to indicate the nature of the error and possible corrective actions that might be undertaken.

Error messages must be designed carefully to be

1. *Clear and concise.* Messages should use short, meaningful, and familiar words, avoid the passive voice, avoid contractions and abbreviations, and issue instructions in the sequence to be followed.
2. *Courteous and neutral.* Messages should avoid familiarity, be polite and instructive, avoid humor or condemnation, and assist the user to solve the problem even if repeated errors are made.

The input validation program also might provide various levels of error messages, such as short-form messages for experienced users and more detailed explanations for novice or infrequent users. Users should be able to instruct the program to display the level of error messages they require.

INSTRUCTION INPUT

Ensuring the quality of instruction input to an application system is a more difficult objective to achieve than ensuring the quality of data input. Data input tends to follow standardized patterns. The errors or irregularities that are likely to occur usually can be anticipated. During instruction input, however, users often attempt to communicate complex actions that they want the system to undertake. On the one hand, the input subsystem must provide considerable flexibility so users can accomplish their processing objectives. On the other hand, it must exercise careful control over the actions they undertake. The approaches used to communicate instructions to an application system tend to trade off flexibility with control.

Menu-Driven Languages

The simplest way for users to provide instructions to an application system is via a menu. The system presents users with a list of options (Figure 11–10). Users then choose an option in some way—for example, by typing a number or letter to indicate their choice, positioning the cursor on the selection and pressing the return key, pressing or releasing a button on a mouse, using a light pen, or touching the screen with their finger.

Different types of menus can be used. Menu bars contain items that always appear on a screen. They provide major guidance for users when interacting with a screen. Pull-down menus contain items that are used less frequently. They disappear, for example, when users release a mouse button. Pull-down menus often lead into cascading menus where highlighting one menu item leads to a list of subsidiary menu items then being displayed. Pop-up menus are used to provide users with a limited set of actions specific to a certain place where they are located on a screen or a particular action they are taking.

Increasingly, menus are being composed from icons rather than words—for example, an icon with a "scissors" picture to activate the "cut" command

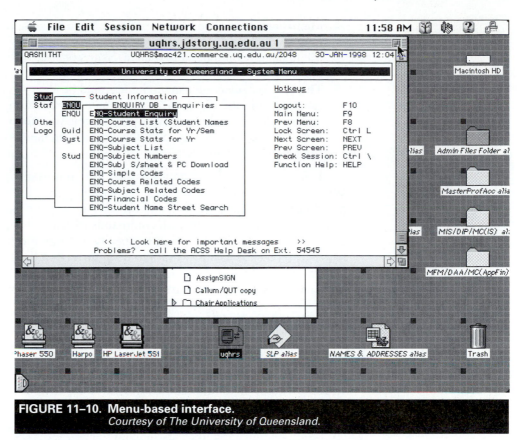

FIGURE 11–10. Menu-based interface.
Courtesy of The University of Queensland.

rather than the word "cut" in a list of menu items. The choice of icons to use in menus must be made carefully so their meaning is communicated clearly to users of a system. Sometimes they are chosen because they have become widely recognized as standing for a certain action to be taken—for example, a button displaying a printer to indicate it activates the print command. Sometimes, however, they are designed in the context of a particular *metaphor* that has been chosen to ease a user's interaction with the system—for example, a set of index cards and actions on them to represent storage and manipulation of data in a database. Whenever metaphors are used, however, like icons, they must be designed carefully and tested thoroughly to ensure that they assist rather than hinder users' interaction with a system (see, e.g., Weinschenk and Yeo 1995).

The following guidelines should reduce the number of errors that are likely to occur using menu input (see, further, Shneiderman 1992):

1. Menu items should be grouped logically so they are meaningful and memorable.
2. Menus with greater breadth and less depth are usually faster to use and less error prone than menus with greater depth and less breadth.
3. Menu items should follow any natural order that exists. If no natural order exists, short menus are often best ordered by frequency of occurrence and long menus by alphabetical order.

4. Menu items that appear in more than one menu should retain the same position within the different menus.

5. Menu items should be fully spelled, clear, concise, verbs or nouns or verb-noun pairs.

6. The basis for selecting a menu item should be clear—for example, numbers (starting with one, not zero), a mnemonic abbreviation, or a radio button.

7. Where other output is displayed on a screen, the menu should be clearly differentiated. Alternatively, pull-down or pop-up menus can be used to hide some or all of the menu.

Effectiveness and efficiency issues are important when menus are used. Whereas menus facilitate novices' use of an application system, they inhibit experts' fast use of the system. There are various ways to assist expert users. Menus can be used in conjunction with commands (discussed subsequently). Users then can select either a menu option or specify a command name. A menu of menu names can be used to allow users to drop through a hierarchy of menus to a particular menu. Backtracking features should exist to enable users to return to higher-level menus, particularly when they wish to restart a series of choices.

Question-Answer Dialogs

Question-answer dialogs are used primarily to obtain data input. The application system asks a question about the value of some data item, and the user responds. Nevertheless, question-answer dialogs also can be used to obtain instruction input in conjunction with data input. For example, Figure 11–11

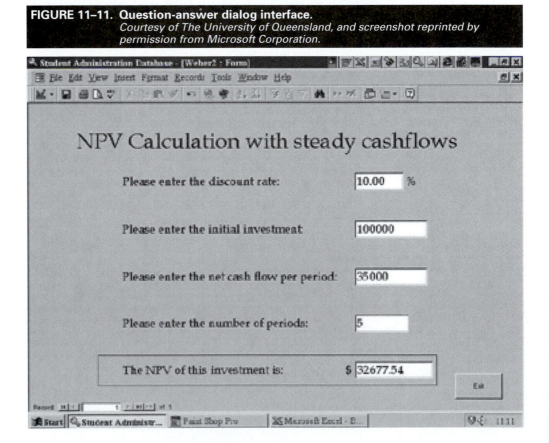

FIGURE 11–11. Question-answer dialog interface.
Courtesy of The University of Queensland, and screenshot reprinted by permission from Microsoft Corporation.

shows that the user wants a project to be evaluated using the net present value technique. The entry of "NPV" then directs the system to ask for particular types of data input.

If the answers to be provided in a question-answer dialog are not clear, users could make errors when they provide instruction (or data) input. A well-designed question-answer dialog makes clear the set of answers that are valid. In those cases in which the required answers are not obvious, a help facility can be used to assist inexperienced users.

As with menus, effectiveness and efficiency issues are a primary concern with question-answer dialogs. They are most useful when users are moderately experienced. For inexperienced users, however, the answer to be provided might not always be obvious. Moreover, for experienced users, the alternating sequence of question and answer might be tedious. The dialog might permit experienced users to stack answers—that is, provide multiple answers at the same time—or to change to another language mode.

Command Languages

Command languages require users to specify commands to invoke some process and a set of arguments that specify precisely how the process should be executed. For example, SQL is a database interrogation language that uses a command-language format. To print the customer numbers of those customers who had more than ten transactions over $200, the following SQL command sequence might be specified:

> SELECT CUSTNO
> FROM TRANS
> WHERE AMOUNT > '200'
> GROUP BY CUSTNO
> HAVING COUNT (*) > '10';

In this example, "SELECT" is a command, and "CUSTNO" is an argument.

Two major decisions must be made in the design of command languages: first, whether to use a large number of commands with a small number of arguments or a small number of commands with a large number of arguments; and second, whether to use keywords or position to specify the arguments. These decisions affect how easy the language is to use and the number of errors users are likely to make.

In most situations, it appears better to use command languages with a small number of commands and a large number of arguments. Inevitably, users seem to employ only a small subset of the commands available in a command language—perhaps because they have difficulty remembering all the commands. Thus, it seems better to make these commands powerful by providing an extensive list of arguments.

Whether arguments should be specified by keywords or position seems to depend on the user's expertise with the command language. With a little experience, presumably most users would prefer to type the following:

> COPY MYFILE YOURFILE

instead of

> COPY FROM = MYFILE TO = YOURFILE

Nevertheless, as argument lists become longer, remembering the position of each argument and whether it is mandatory or optional becomes more difficult. Keyword specification of arguments might then be preferred.

To facilitate recall of commands, command names should be meaningful. Moreover, commands that specify opposite actions should be congruent with one another in the sense of everyday usage of the commands. For example, when users wish to add characters to or remove them from a file, they are likely to prefer the commands INSERT/DELETE to the commands INSERT/OMIT (Carroll 1982).

To reduce typing effort, it should be possible to truncate commands. This strategy is easier to implement when only a small number of commands are used because truncations are likely to be unique. There are several ways to truncate commands—for example, use the first and last letter of the command or delete vowels from the command. Whatever the truncation strategy used, it should be applied consistently across all commands (Benbasat and Wand 1984).

Prompts and defaults reduce the number of errors made using a command language. For example, if users cannot remember the arguments associated with a command, they should be able to type a "?" or press some other key to obtain a prompt from the language on each argument required. Similarly, a command language reduces typing effort if it supplies the likely value of an argument as a default. For example, some spreadsheet command languages use the position of the current cell as the default value in many commands. The default can simply be overwritten if it is not the value required.

Forms-Based Languages

Forms-based languages require users to specify commands and data in the context of either some input or output form. For example, Figure 11–12 shows a command issued in the Query-by-Example database interrogation language to print details on students with the surname "Smith" who scored more than 40 on their second assignment. Note how the input commands are provided in the context of an input form that mirrors the relation in the database. Similarly, if the output were some type of graph, users might employ a light pen to select a command that indicates they want the scales of the axes to be changed.

Forms-based languages can be successful if users solve problems in the context of input and output forms. In these cases the syntax of the language corresponds to the ways users think about the problem. As a result, input errors are reduced, and the language tends to be used effectively and efficiently. When the functions to be performed do not map easily into the context of input and output forms, however, forms-based languages tend to be awkward and unwieldy to use.

Natural Languages

Natural language interfaces are still primarily the subject of substantial research and development efforts. Nevertheless, a few commercial products are now available. Auditors, therefore, might confront them increasingly in selected application domains and be required to evaluate their capabilities.

The ultimate goal of research on natural language interfaces is to enable relatively free-form natural language interaction to occur between users and an

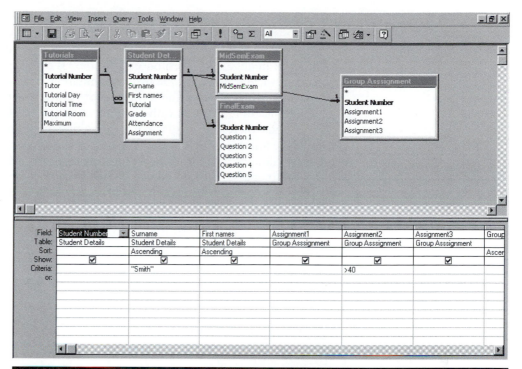

FIGURE 11–12. Forms-based language interface.
Courtesy of The University of Queensland, and screenshot reprinted by permission from Microsoft Corporation.

application system, perhaps via a speech production/recognition device. For certain types of applications, this objective might be laudable. Natural language might not be the best form of interface, however, for all types of applications. In particular, many of the sorts of applications that tend to concern auditors might not be suited to natural language interfaces.

Current natural language interfaces have several limitations:

1. They do not always cope well with the ambiguity and redundancy present in natural language. For example, the meaning of the sentence "Time flies." is different depending on whether "time" is the noun and "flies" is the verb or vice versa.

2. Substantial effort sometimes must be expended to establish the lexicon for the natural language interface. Users must define all possible words they could use, and this work must be redone each time a new application domain is to be accessed via natural language.

3. Even minor deviations outside the lexicon established for the application domain can cause problems. Users might be unaware of the precise boundaries of the domain and be inhibited in the commands they issue in case they traverse these boundaries.

4. If the database with which users interact is subject to frequent definitional changes, natural language interfaces can quickly become problematic.
The lexicon must be able to evolve in light of definitional changes.
Current lexicons do not always adapt well to changes in the database definition.

5. Users might be unaware of the ambiguity that can exist in natural language responses that the system gives to the commands they issue. For example, the query "How many stores in Tasmania had price overrides for sales of windsurfers?" might evoke a response of "none." If no stores in Tasmania are selling windsurfers, however, the response might be misleading.

6. It is still unclear whether the wordiness of natural language leads to ineffective and inefficient interaction with an application system. If users wish to express commands, therefore, in a formal, constrained, or abbreviated way, a natural language interface should be able to accept this form of input.

7. Users still need some training when they employ natural language interfaces. Otherwise, they might ask queries that a natural language interface with even an extensive lexicon might not be able to interpret (Dekleva 1994).

Until these technical problems have been overcome, auditors should be cautious in their evaluation of natural language interfaces. If it is critical that absolute precision be attained in the command and data input supplied to an application system and in the responses obtained from the system, other types of interfaces might be better.

Direct Manipulation Interfaces

Some user interfaces to application systems employ direct manipulation to enter commands and data. Shneiderman (1992) identifies three attributes of a direct manipulation interface: *(1)* visibility of the object of interest, *(2)* rapid, reversible, incremental actions, and *(3)* use of direct manipulation devices (e.g., a mouse) rather than command language syntax to manipulate the objects of interest.

Some examples of direct manipulation interfaces follow:

1. *Electronic spreadsheet.* Users see a visual image of the spreadsheet and its associated cell values. They can alter cell values by using a mouse to move the cursor to the cell to be altered and then keying in the new value. The results of the change are immediately apparent as all dependent cell values adjust.

2. *Spatial data manager.* Users see a graph or a map at one level of detail. They can "zoom" to lower or higher levels of detail using a joystick.

3. *Electronic desktops.* Users see an image of a desktop with an in-basket, an out-basket, a trash basket, a set of files, a Rolodex name-and-address file, and so on. They can manipulate these objects using a mouse, a joystick, or some type of pointing device. For example, files to be deleted can be moved to the trash basket.

Direct manipulation interfaces offer substantial advantages: Users often are highly motivated to master the system; they enjoy learning and exploring the more powerful aspects of the system; they work effectively and efficiently; and they quickly gain confidence in using the system. Perhaps the most substantial drawback is finding the appropriate image or icon of the object to be manipulated, particularly where an application system has a large number of objects to be manipulated. For many types of accounting data, for example, it is difficult to think of an appropriate icon to use: How should the payment of an accounts receivable be portrayed pictorially? Nevertheless, whenever direct manipulation can be used, it often provides a more error-free, effective, and efficient interface than traditional menu- or command-oriented interfaces.

VALIDATION OF INSTRUCTION INPUT

Like data input, instruction input entered into an application system also must be validated. Auditors might have little concern about the validity of instruction input when *(1)* the instructions are provided as part of a widely used application software package (e.g., the menu in an accounts receivable package) or *(2)* the instructions are interpreted via a high-level programming language (e.g., SQL commands in a database management system package). Where instruction input is designed and implemented specifically for a particular application system, however, auditors must evaluate the ways instructions are validated more carefully.

Types of Instruction Input Validation Checks

Three types of validation checks can be undertaken on input instructions: *(1)* lexical checks, *(2)* syntactic checks, and *(3)* semantic checks. Each is discussed briefly in the following subsections.

Lexical Validation

During lexical validation, the system evaluates each "word" entered by a user. Three types of words can be encountered: *(1)* identifiers (labels, variables), *(2)* terminals (operators, reserved words), and *(3)* literals (numerical constants, strings). Because words are formed from characters, the system must establish rules whereby strings of characters are recognized as discrete words. Usually this recognition occurs via boundary characters and delimiters. For example, a space or an operator (*, /, +, −) might delimit a word.

To illustrate lexical analysis, assume the following SQL command is entered by a user:

> SELECT name
> FROM employee
> WHERE salary > '15000'

The lexical analyzer in the system would read the command, character by character, and attempt to identify the words entered. For example, it would see that a space terminates the characters S, E, L, E, C, and T and that the character string "SELECT" is a reserved word within the language. Similarly, a space terminates the variable "salary," the constant "15000" is delimited by the quotes symbol, and the variable "salary" and the constant " '15000' " are separated by an operator ">." If the lexical analyzer cannot recognize a valid word, it must print or display an error message so users can undertake corrective action.

Syntactic Validation

During syntactic validation, the system reads the string of words identified and validated by the lexical analyzer and attempts to determine the sequence of operations that the string of words is intended to invoke. For example, an instruction issued in an interactive command language might be the following:

INTEARN = (OLDBAL + DEPOSITS − WITHDRAWS)*INTEREST

The parentheses imply a particular sequence of operations, namely:

Add DEPOSITS to OLDBAL
Subtract WITHDRAWS from the result
Multiply the results by INTEREST
Store the result in INTEARN (interest earned)

Without the parentheses, the first action invoked might be to multiply WITH-DRAWS by INTEREST.

The syntax analyzer validates the syntax of an instruction by *parsing* the string of words entered to determine whether it conforms to a particular rule in the grammar of the language. Thus, the quality of syntactic validation depends on having a formal and complete description of the grammar on which the language is based and on making a good choice with respect to the parsing scheme chosen. Otherwise, errors in an instruction entered might not be identified or the error message displayed or printed might not be meaningful.

Semantic Validation

During semantic validation, the system completes its analysis of the meaning of the instruction entered. The boundary between syntactic validation and semantic validation is often obscure. During semantic validation, however, the language might check, for example, whether two variables that are to be multiplied together are numeric types and not alphabetic or alphanumeric types. Similarly, the system might prevent a comparison of two numeric values that would be meaningless—for example, the salaries of employees with their weight.

The quality of semantic analysis depends on how well the constraints that relate to the data on which the instructions operate can be expressed. Database management systems that provide extensive data definition facilities, for example, allow high-quality semantic validation to be performed. The system can check that the operations to be undertaken on data items or the results produced conform to the constraints expressed in relation to the data items in the data definition.

Reporting Instruction Input Errors

The guidelines for reporting errors discussed earlier for data validation apply also to instruction validation. Error messages must communicate to users as completely and meaningfully as possible the nature of errors made during instruction input. Because the instructions that users enter could be variable and complex, substantial time can be lost if error messages do not allow users to pinpoint errors quickly. Multiple levels of error messages might be provided to cater for different levels of user expertise. Furthermore, if the system fails to identify an error, unbeknown to users, meaningless results can be produced.

AUDIT TRAIL CONTROLS

The audit trail in the input subsystem maintains the chronology of events from the time data and instructions are captured and entered into an application system until the time they are deemed valid and passed onto other subsystems within the application system (e.g., the communications subsystem or the processing subsystem).

Accounting Audit Trail

In the case of data input, the accounting audit trail must record the origin of, contents of, and timing of the transaction entered into an application system. The types of data collected include the following:

1. The identity of the person (organization) who was the source of the data,
2. The identity of the person (organization) who entered the data into the system,
3. The time and date when the data was captured,
4. The identifier of the physical device used to enter the data into the system,
5. The account or record to be updated by the transaction,
6. The standing data to be updated by the transaction,
7. The details of the transaction, and
8. The number of the physical or logical batch to which the transaction belongs.

This data must be collected irrespective of whether the data was first captured on source documents, entered or read directly into the application system, or received from another organization via some type of interorganizational information system (say, an electronic data interchange system).

When input data is validated, a time and date stamp should be attached so the timing of data validation, error correction, and error resubmission subsequently can be determined. In some cases, a processing reference might be attached to the input data to indicate the program that performed the validation tests. In a distributed system, for example, input validation software could be replicated and executed at multiple sites. It might be important to know which instance of the software performed the validation tests, particularly if doubts exist about consistency among replications.

If the input validation program identifies an error that cannot be corrected immediately, it must generate and attach a unique error number to the data in error. This error number must be associated with the data until it is corrected. It must be printed out or displayed on reports, entered on source documents used to correct the error, or keyed in at a terminal if the data is subsequently retrieved from the error file and corrected interactively. In this way the history of the erroneous data can be traced until the time of its correction.

In the case of instruction input, the audit trail might record the following types of data:

1. The identity of the originator of the instruction,
2. The time and date when the instruction was entered,
3. The identifier of the physical device used to enter the instruction,
4. The type of instruction entered and its arguments, and
5. The results produced in light of the instruction.

Like data, instructions entered in error can also be assigned a unique error number by the program that undertakes the validation. Unlike data, however, erroneous instructions often are not recorded on an error file that must be cleared. Instead, users simply reenter the instruction when they have determined the nature of the error they have made. If they do not reenter the instruction, the instruction is "lost." Any record of the instruction error typically is used for other purposes—for example, analysis of the frequency with which different types of instruction errors are made.

Operations Audit Trail

Because the input subsystem often involves labor-intensive activities, operations audit trail data is an important means of improving the effectiveness and efficiency of the subsystem. Some of the types of operations audit trail data that might be collected follow:

1. Time to key in a source document or an instruction at a terminal,
2. Number of read errors made by an optical scanning device,
3. Number of keying errors identified during verification,
4. Frequency with which an instruction in a command language is used, and
5. Time taken to invoke an instruction using a light pen versus a mouse.

By analyzing this data, error-prone or inefficient input activities can be identified and remedial action taken. For example, the time taken to enter data via a screen could indicate that more user training is needed or that screen redesign is necessary. Similarly, a comparison of times taken to enter the same data or instruction using different devices could be used to encourage users to employ the more efficient device.

EXISTENCE CONTROLS

Existence controls that relate to data in the input subsystem are critical. If an application system's master files are destroyed or corrupted, recovery could involve going back to a previous version of the master files and reprocessing input against these files. Recovery cannot be effected unless the input files are available. Therefore, input files must be stored securely, and backup copies should be maintained at an off-site location.

In a worst-case situation in which input files are also destroyed or corrupted along with the application system's master files, recovery might have to be effected from source documents if they are available or hard-copy transaction listings if they are available. Thus, source documents or transaction listings should be stored securely until they are no longer needed for backup purposes. Note, they might have to be stored securely for longer periods for other reasons—for example, compliance with statutory requirements.

Existence controls for instruction input usually are less critical than those required for data input. If, say, an instruction evokes an update to the database, it will be recorded anyway as part of the input transaction log. If it does not affect the database—for example, it is simply an interrogation of a data item value—recovering the record of the instruction input might be less important. Nonetheless, recovering instruction input should not be dismissed as unnecessary. Sometimes it is important to identify who interrogated a database when possible security problems are being investigated or when the database is found to be in an erroneous state.

SUMMARY

Components in the input subsystem are responsible for bringing both data and instructions into an application system. Both types of input must be validated. Moreover, any errors detected must be controlled so input resubmission is accurate, complete, unique, and timely.

Auditors must understand the different types of approaches used to enter data into an application system and their relative strengths and weaknesses.

Some rely on immediate entry of data into an application system. Others rely on recording the data on some type of medium prior to the data being entered into an application system.

Good source document design and good data-entry screen design lead to reduced data input errors and to more effective and more efficient input of data into an application system. Auditors must understand the principles of good source document design and good data-entry screen design. Otherwise, they will not be able to evaluate properly the likelihood of input errors arising and ineffective and inefficient input occurring.

Data codes are used to identify an entity uniquely or to identify an entity as a member of a group or set. Poorly designed codes are error prone. Moreover, poorly designed codes cause recording and keying processes to be inefficient.

Check digits are redundant digits added to data codes that enable the accuracy of other digits in the code to be checked. When the code is entered, a program recalculates the check digit to determine whether the entered check digit and the calculated check digit are the same.

Batching is the grouping together of transactions that bear some type of relationship to each other. Two types of batches can be used: *(1)* physical batches, in which the transactions in the batch constitute some type of physical unit; and *(2)* logical batches, in which the transactions in the group bear some type of logical rather than physical relationship to one another. Controls can be exercised over batches to identify unauthorized, inaccurate, and incomplete data.

Four types of validation checks can be exercised over data input: *(1)* field checks, which can be applied independently of other fields in an input record; *(2)* record checks, which depend upon the values of other fields in an input record; *(3)* batch checks, which determine whether the characteristics of a batch of records entered are congruent with the stated characteristics; and *(4)* file checks, which examine whether the actual characteristics of a file used as input are congruent with the stated characteristics.

Six approaches can be used to enter instructions into an application system: *(1)* menu-driven languages require users to select an instruction from a list of options; *(2)* question-answer dialogs require users to indicate what instruction they want invoked in response to a question asked by the application system; *(3)* command languages require users to recall and issue an instruction to invoke it; *(4)* forms-based languages require users to specify instructions in the context of some input or output form; *(5)* natural-language interfaces allow users to invoke instructions via free-form interaction with the application system; and *(6)* direct-manipulation interfaces allow users to invoke instructions via manipulation of some object on a screen.

Three types of validation checks can be exercised over instruction input: *(1)* lexical validation checks the validity of each word that users enter; *(2)* syntactic validation checks the validity of a string of words that users enter; and *(3)* semantic validation checks the validity of the meaning implied by the string of words that users enter.

The accounting audit trail in the input subsystem records the nature of, contents of, and timing of data and instruction input. The operations audit trail in the input subsystem records the resources consumed to enter data and instruction input.

Existence controls must be able to recover data and instructions that have been entered into the input subsystem. Existence controls for data are usually more important than existence controls for instructions because the effects of the latter are often manifested in changes to data.

Review Questions

11–1 From an audit perspective, why are controls over the input subsystem critical?

11–2 Briefly distinguish between direct entry of input data and medium-based entry of input data. Why must auditors understand the different types of methods used to input data into an application system?

11–3 What impact can the following source document design decisions have on the level of data integrity achieved in an application system?
  a Choice of the medium to be used
  b Choice of the layout to be used

11–4 From a control perspective, briefly explain the importance of each of the following source document design guidelines for layout and style:
  a Arrange fields for ease of use during data capture
  b Where possible, use tick marks to identify field-size errors
  c Prenumber source documents
  d Combine instructions with questions
  e Where possible, provide multiple-choice answers to questions

11–5 What is the primary factor affecting the design of data-entry screens? Explain why this factor is important. How, for example, does it affect the organization of a screen?

11–6 Briefly explain the design guidelines that apply to captions in terms of:
  a Structure and size
  b Type font and display intensity
  c Format
  d Alignment
  e Justification
  f Spacing

11–7 What techniques can be used to indicate the size of a field on a data-entry screen?

11–8 From a data integrity perspective, why is it desirable to have a data-entry operator always tab to a new field on a data-entry screen rather than having the cursor automatically skip to a new field when the previous field is full?

11–9 Briefly explain the advantages of using color in the design of data-entry screens. What design guidelines apply to:
  a The number of colors that should be used
  b The spacing of colors on the visual spectrum
  c The choice of bright colors versus muted colors

11–10 Distinguish between the response time and the display rate for a data-entry screen. How does the use of a dedicated source document in data-entry screen design affect the display rate and response time that must be achieved?

11–11 If data-entry screen design is based upon a dedicated source document, how useful is a Help facility likely to be?

11–12 What attributes of a data code affect the likelihood of a recording error being made by a user of the code? Briefly outline some strategies to reduce error rates that occur with data codes.

11–13 Distinguish between the following types of data coding errors:
  a Truncation and transcription
  b Transposition and double transposition

11–14 List the four types of data codes—serial, block sequence, hierarchical, and association—in increasing order of:
  a Mnemonic value
  b Compactness
  c Flexibility for expansion

11–15 What is a check digit? Calculate the check digit for the number 82942 using the weights 1–2–1–2–1 and modulus 10. Show, also, that the check digit you have calculated is correct.

11–16 Briefly describe three solutions to the problem of having a check digit result that is greater than one digit—that is, a check digit that is greater than 9. Point out any disadvantages to the solutions you suggest.

11–17 Briefly discuss the distinction between a physical batch and a logical batch. Are there any differences between the controls that can be exercised over physical and logical batches?

11–18 Briefly explain the difference between the following types of batch control totals:
   a Document count
   b Hash total
   c Financial total

11–19 List four types of information typically placed on a batch cover sheet. Briefly explain the purpose of each piece of information you list for the overall control of the batch.

11–20 Without giving examples, briefly explain the nature of the following types of data input validation checks:
   a Field checks
   b Record checks
   c Batch checks
   d File checks

11–21 Distinguish between a range check and a reasonableness check. Why is a reasonableness check not a field-level check?

11–22 Why is the check for a valid sign on a numeric field not a field-level check?

11–23 Why is correcting errors based on cross-screen validation of input data sometimes difficult?

11–24 How might the timing of reporting input errors differ between a direct-entry screen and a screen based on a dedicated source document?

11–25 Give three design guidelines for reporting of data input errors.

11–26 Are novice users of an application system more likely to make errors entering instructions via a menu-driven language or a question-answer dialog? Briefly explain your answer.

11–27 Why does it seem better to use a command language with a small number of commands and a large number of arguments? How can errors in the specification of arguments then be reduced?

11–28 What is the major limitation of using a forms-based language as a means of entering instructions to an application system?

11–29 Briefly explain the limitations of natural-language interfaces to an application system with respect to:
   a Ambiguity of commands
   b Establishing the lexicon
   c Ambiguity in responses
   d Changes to the database definition

11–30 What is meant by a direct manipulation interface? What is the major advantage of using a direct manipulation interface as a means of providing instruction input to an application system?

11–31 Briefly explain the nature of lexical validation of instruction input. How does the lexical analyzer handle:
   a Identifiers
   b Terminals
   c Literals

11–32 Briefly explain the nature of semantic validation during instruction input. What factors govern the quality of semantic validation during instruction input?

11–33 Give five items that might be captured on the accounting audit trail in relation to data input in the input subsystem.

11–34 Why is the operations audit trail for the input subsystem an important resource in improving the effectiveness and efficiency of an application system?

11–35 Existence controls for instruction input are often less critical than existence controls for data input. Briefly explain.

Multiple-Choice Questions

11–1 Which of the following actions is most likely to *increase* the number of errors made during data input to an application system:

  a Direct entry of data captured during interaction between a clerk and a customer rather than source document-based data entry

  b Prerecording of information about a customer on a plastic credit card's magnetic stripe

  c Increasing the time interval between detecting an event and entry of the event into the application system

  d Using a point-of-sale terminal rather than an automatic teller machine to make a payment to a vendor

11–2 The factor *most likely* to affect the grade and weight of paper chosen for a source document is:

  a The conditions under which the source document will be completed

  b Whether the documents will be inserted in window envelopes

  c Whether a dropout color is to be used on the source document

  d The amount of data to be captured on the source document

11–3 In the layout of a source document:

  a To prevent users from being confused, keying instructions should not appear on the form

  b Instructions should not be combined with questions

  c Fields should be sequenced from left to right and top to bottom

  d Instructions should always be printed in a dropout color

11–4 The primary factor affecting the design of a data-entry screen is:

  a The amount of data to be collected on the screen

  b The expertise and experience of the keyboard operator

  c How frequently the screen will be used

  d Whether or not the screen is to be based on a dedicated source document

11–5 If a screen is used for direct entry of input data, it should be organized to:

  a Maximize the number of vertical alignment points to decrease screen complexity

  b Mirror the way in which data is to be obtained during the data capture task

  c Place alphabetic information to the top of the screen and numeric information to the bottom of the screen

  d Use asymmetry to minimize the number of screens required for data input

11–6 Which of the following is *not* a design guideline for captions on a data-entry screen?

  a Use uppercase type font for captions and lowercase type font for data-entry fields

  b Fully spell out captions if direct data entry is to be used

  c Captions should always precede their associated data-entry field

  d Always right justify captions

11–7 Which of the following is *not* a design guideline for data-entry field design on a screen?
  a Tab automatically to the next field when the current field is full of data
  b In the case of a repeating field, stack each instance of the field below the caption
  c Identify at least the start of each field with a special character
  d Provide completion aids when direct entry data capture is used

11–8 Which of the following is *not* a design guideline for using color on a data-entry screen?
  a Use colors sparingly
  b Use bright colors so differences are highlighted
  c Use colors that are widely spaced along the visual spectrum
  d Do not use red for error messages

11–9 Under what circumstances will a data-entry screen keyboard operator tolerate the slowest response time?
  a The transition between one screen and the next screen
  b The transition between one field and the next field
  c When data entry for a transaction has been completed
  d When keying is based on a dedicated source document

11–10 If the product number A5723 is coded as A2753, this is an example of a:
  a Truncation error
  b Double transposition error
  c Random error
  d Transcription error

11–11 A strategy for reducing coding errors is to:
  a Have only numeric codes
  b Group more characters in a chunk of information
  c If a mixed alphabetic-numeric code is used, group alphabetics together and numerics together
  d Use frequently occurring character pairs like B8 and S5

11–12 The code AJB/156/7G is *most likely* to be an example of a(n):
  a Hierarchical code
  b Block sequence code
  c Alphabetic derivation code
  d Serial code

11–13 Given the code 7215, modulus 13, and the weights 2–1–2–1, the check digit is:
  a 1
  b 10
  c 0
  d 3

11–14 Which of the following guidelines should *not* be used when designing a batch?
  a Have only one type of document in the batch
  b Have the batch small enough to facilitate locating errors
  c Have the batch large enough to constitute a reasonable size unit of work
  d Minimize the amount of information that is recorded on the batch cover sheet

11–15 A check for missing data/blanks is an example of a:
  a Record check
  b Set membership check
  c Field check
  d Batch check

11–16 A check for a valid sign (numerics) is an example of:
  a Record check
  b Batch check
  c Field check
  d Alphabetics/numerics check

11–17 The purpose of an input validation sequence check is to:
  a Check that input files are loaded in the correct order
  b Check that multiple physical records for a single logical record follow the required order
  c Check that the transaction type is always the first item in a record in a batch
  d Check that the batch serial number is in ascending order

11–18 The purpose of a file retention date is to:
  a Enable files with the same generation number to be distinguished
  b Indicate when the file should be recovered from production activities
  c Prevent the file from being overwritten before the expiry of the retention date
  d Prevent the file from being read before expiry of the retention date

11–19 Novice users are *most likely* to make errors when they use a:
  a Menu-driven language
  b Command language
  c Question-answer language
  d Forms-based language

11–20 To reduce errors, it is better to use a command language that has:
  a Specification of arguments without having to use keywords
  b A small number of commands with a large number of arguments
  c A large number of commands with a small number of arguments
  d Few default values in the argument list

11–21 Which of the following is a *strength* of using a natural-language interface to an application system?
  a It copes well with the ambiguity and redundancy inherent in natural language
  b The lexicon provides an easy means of coping with new words that different users might employ
  c Changes to the database have minimal effects on lexicon
  d Users require minimal training to use the interface

11–22 Which of the following is a *limitation* in the use of direct manipulation interfaces to application systems?
  a They are error-prone, even with experienced users, because they are not precise
  b It is sometimes difficult to choose an appropriate icon for objects to be manipulated
  c Users take some time to gain confidence in their interactions with the system
  d It is difficult to work efficiently using a direct manipulation interface

11–23 During lexical validation of instruction input, which of the following "words" would be classified as a literal?
  a A reserved word
  b A mathematical operator
  c A label
  d A numerical constant

11–24 Which of the following is *not* a function of the syntax analyzer during instruction input?
a Identifies the sequence of operations to be performed
b Classifies identifiers as either labels or variables
c Identifies whether the string of words entered conforms to a grammatical rule
d Executes a parsing rule on the instructions entered as input by a user

11–25 Which of the following would be identified as an error during semantic validation of instruction input?
a Use of a reserved word as a literal
b A missing parenthesis in a mathematical equation
c Addition of a numeric variable and an alphabetic string
d Failure to delimit a numerical constant by a quotes symbol

11–26 Which of the following data items is likely to be most useful as part of the operations audit trail (rather than the accounting audit trail) for the input subsystem?
a The identity of the person who prepared a source document
b The logical batch number of a direct-entry transaction
c The number of keying errors identified during verification
d The identifier of a terminal at which a transaction was entered

11–27 Which of the following statements about existence controls in the input subsystem is most likely to be *false*?
a Existence controls for instruction input are more important than existence controls for data input
b Backup copies of input files should be maintained at an off-site location
c Source documents should be retained for some time as a means of backup
d During the recovery of a corrupted database, records of which users queried the database might be important

Exercises and Cases

11–1 Orchard Distributions Pte. Ltd. is a large, Singaporean-based distributor of clothing products to other companies throughout Southeast Asia. Orders are received from customers either by telephone, facsimile, or mail. In the case of telephone orders, order-entry operators key the order directly into the order-entry system while they speak with customers. In the case of facsimile or mail orders, regular customers usually complete one of Orchard's order forms and send it to Orchard. In some cases, however, occasional customers will send orders on their own stationery. An order-entry clerk then transcribes the order onto one of Orchard's order forms. If necessary, the clerk follows up missing information with the customer by telephone to complete the form. The mail and facsimile orders are then batched and given to operators to be keyed into the order-entry system.

You are an information systems auditor in the external audit firm that has just been appointed to carry out the audit of Orchard. The partner in charge of the audit has asked you to review controls over the input subsystem of the order-entry system. During your review of controls, you note the order-entry system is a 10-year-old system. Although it has been maintained regularly over the years, the source-document and order-entry screen designs have remained relatively constant. In your opinion, both are in urgent need of redesign. For example, over the years Orchard has needed to collect more data items during order entry. Rather than undertake redesign of source documents or screens, it has simply added the new items to the end of a source document and reproduced the new version of the source document or reprogrammed the application to add the new items to the end of an existing screen.

When you indicate your concern to the sales manager, he replies that he knows the source documents and screens are no longer well designed. He points out, however, that there is little turnover among the existing order-entry staff. Most of the staff have worked with Orchard for many years, and as a result they have learned and adapted to the idiosyncrasies of the system. He also argues that customers will soon point out any errors made in orders to Orchard. Although he knows the source documents and screens could be improved, he is not especially concerned about their deficiencies. He believes there are higher priorities in terms of systems development work and maintenance work that need to be undertaken within Orchard.

Required: In light of your findings, what would you recommend to your partner in terms of how the audit should now proceed? In particular, discuss whether there are any implications of your findings for control risk, the tests of controls you might undertake, and the substantive tests you might undertake.

11–2 Chang & Co. is a Malaysian civil engineering firm based in Kuala Lumpur. It performs construction work throughout Southeast Asia. The firm employs 1,000 people at various offices and construction sites. Many construction sites are small and remotely located.

As the newly appointed internal auditor for the firm, you are investigating controls over personnel change-of-status processing in the payroll system. The various offices and sites send change-of-status source documents to the personnel department at the head office. A clerk in the personnel department checks the source documents for completeness. She then assembles the source documents into batches and prepares a batch cover sheet. She calculates two batch control totals: a hash total of the employee numbers in the batch and a document count. Periodically another clerk collects the batches and takes them to a data-entry operator who works in the personnel department. He keys the change-of-status information into the payroll system at a terminal located in the personnel department.

The input program performs a comprehensive set of validation checks. The input program also prepares a report that shows *(1)* any transaction in error, the nature of the error, and the batch number in which the transaction occurs and *(2)* any batches in error because the control total calculated for the batch by the input program does not match the control total on the batch cover sheet. The data-entry operator stamps the batch cover sheet as keyed when the batch has been entered into the payroll system. A clerk periodically collects the keyed batches plus the input validation reports and returns them to the clerk responsible for assembling the batches. This latter clerk then corrects the transactions and batches and resubmits them for data entry. She initials each item on the error report once she has corrected it. Periodically the personnel manager reviews a sample of the input validation reports.

Required: Prepare your audit working papers and indicate
a any control weaknesses that exist
b the possible consequences of these control weaknesses
c some remedial measures

11–3 You are the internal auditor for a large distributor participating in the design of a new order-filling system. The programmer responsible for the design of the input validation program asks your opinion on whether the tests he proposes to undertake with respect to customer orders are satisfactory. The customer base is large, and most customers are small retailers. Orders are received either via the mail or via telephone.

The validation tests proposed are as follows:

Field	Missing Data	Must be Numeric	Must be Alphabetic	Valid Range	Check Digit	Valid Code	Valid Sign
Record code						X	
Customer number		X		X	X		
Salesperson number		X				X	
Sales order number	X						
Part number	X				X		
Quantity ordered	X	X					X
Price instructions				X		X	

The following data on the fields is relevant to your decision:

Field	Description
Record code	Must be the value "04."
Customer number	Numeric value that must range between 01000 and 90000.
Salesperson number	Must be one of 50 numeric values.
Sales order number	Five-character field: first character is alphabetic; last four are numeric.
Part number	Alphanumeric field.
Quantity ordered	Four-character numeric field.
Price instructions	Alphabetic: only four codes are valid.

Required: Write the programmer a brief report with your comments on the validation tests he proposes to undertake.

11–4 Refer to case 10–1. Using the bill-payment-by-telephone system, customers enter the following data:
  a customer number
  b account number
  c creditor number
  d amount to be paid to creditor in cents
  e date when amount is to be paid

An automated teller requests each data item on a step-by-step basis. After the date when the amount is to be paid has been entered, the teller asks for a new creditor number. Note, creditor numbers must be authorized for customers. They must write or telephone the savings and loan association at a prior time, and new creditor numbers for the customer will be entered into the system. Customers also have special instructions that they can enter using the TouchTone telephone—for example:

a by entering #9# when a creditor number is requested, the customer terminates data entry

b by entering #8# they can obtain their account balance

c by entering #4# the automated teller will repeat the last transaction entered

Required: Identify the types of input errors that a customer could make when using the system. What controls could be used to prevent, detect, or correct these errors?

11–5 Keep-on-Truckin Corporation (KOTC) is a manufacturer and distributor of shoes. It has established electronic data interchange (EDI) links with most of its customers.

The sequence of electronic transactions that occurs when a customer sub-mits an order to KOTC is as follows:

1 The customer sends a purchase-order transaction to KOTC.

2 KOTC sends a functional acknowledgment transaction to the customer to indicate the purchase-order transaction received complies with the agreed-upon EDI standards.

3 KOTC sends a purchase-order acknowledgment transaction to the cus-tomer to confirm the details of the order received.

4 The customer sends a functional acknowledgment transaction to KOTC to confirm proper receipt of the purchase-order acknowledgment transaction.

5 If the customer wishes to change an order they have placed, they send a purchase-order change request transaction to KOTC.

6 KOTC sends a functional acknowledgment transaction to the customer to confirm proper receipt of the purchase-order change request transaction.

7 KOTC sends a purchase-order change request acknowledgment to the customer to confirm the details of changes to an order.

8 The customer sends a functional acknowledgment transaction to KOTC to confirm proper receipt of the purchase-order change request acknowledg-ment transaction.

When KOTC receives a purchase-order transaction from a customer, the customer is first authenticated. Customers use passwords that are encrypted before they are transmitted over communications lines to authenticate them-selves. Providing the password is valid, the order-entry system then deter-mines whether the purchase order should be authorized, depending on such factors as the dollar value of the purchase order and the customer's level of existing indebtedness to KOTC.

You are the newly appointed internal auditor to KOTC. During a re-view of application system controls, you ask the information systems man-ager about the input validation controls exercised over the order-entry sys-tem. The information systems manager responds that only one is exercised—namely, that the customer has ordered a product that has a valid product code. Moreover, he believes that no other validation tests are neces-sary for two reasons. First, customers exercise their own input validation controls over orders when they enter them into their purchase-order sys-tems. Second, customers are sent purchase-order acknowledgments immedi-ately after their orders are received at KOTC. If the purchase order is in error, customers will respond with a purchase-order change request transaction.

Required: As the internal auditor for KOTC, what is your evaluation of the information systems manager's arguments? You should consider his response in terms of the four objectives of asset safeguarding, data integrity, system effectiveness, and system efficiency.

11–6 Canterbury Convenience Stores (CCS) is a newly formed organization in Christchurch, New Zealand. It comprises 10 moderately sized convenience stores that previously operated independently of each other. Each store has from three to six checkout lanes.

The owners of the stores have decided to establish CCS as a cooperative to take advantage of discounts they can obtain from bulk buying and to reduce the administrative and advertising costs associated with their operations. The prices for products sold will be set by the central administration for CCS, although the manager of each store will have the option of varying prices within their store if they so wish. On average, it is expected that managers will decide upon price variations from the centrally set price for less than 12 percent of items offered in each store. The managers will still retain substantial autonomy over how they run their stores, however, because they are concerned to preserve the local-neighborhood characteristics of their stores.

One matter considered at a joint meeting of the store managers is whether they should replace their existing cash registers with point-of-sale equipment. Several of the younger managers have argued that CCS should establish a central price file and inventory file that can be accessed by point-of-sale terminals in each of the stores. They believe this approach will result in reduced overheads, more accurate pricing, and improved inventory control in their stores. A few of the older managers are reluctant to proceed in this way, however. They are concerned that prices will no longer appear on the products they sell. Moreover, they question what will happen if the system fails at any time. They argue they compete effectively against the larger supermarkets only because they offer better service to their customers. They wonder what will happen if they have a system failure and they then have difficulties transacting business with their customers. If they cannot input sales because the system is down, what will happen to their local-neighborhood, high-quality personalized service image?

Required: You are an information systems auditor in the accounting firm that CCS has retained to provide financial services. CCS has asked your firm to provide advice on whether a suitable point-of-sale system can be designed that will allow each store to continue to transact business in the event of system failure. Can you devise a design for the system that will mitigate their concerns?

Answers to Multiple-Choice Questions

11–1	c	**11–8**	b	**11–15**	c	**11–22**	b
11–2	a	**11–9**	c	**11–16**	a	**11–23**	d
11–3	c	**11–10**	b	**11–17**	b	**11–24**	b
11–4	d	**11–11**	c	**11–18**	c	**11–25**	c
11–5	b	**11–12**	a	**11–19**	b	**11–26**	c
11–6	d	**11–13**	d	**11–20**	b	**11–27**	a
11–7	a	**11–14**	d	**11–21**	d		

REFERENCES

Beckley, D. F. (1967), "An Optimum System with 'Modulus 11'," *The Computer Bulletin* (December), 213–215.

Benbasat, Izak, and Yair Wand (1984), "Command Abbreviation Behavior in Human-Computer Interaction," *Communications of the ACM* (May), 376–382.

Bogusky, Clay, and Stan Halper (1991), "Control and Security Issues in Electronic Document Imaging Systems," *The EDP Auditor Journal*, IV, 33–47.

Campbell, D. V. A. (1970), "A Modulus 11 Check Digit System for a Given System of Codes," *The Computer Bulletin* (January), 12–13.

Carroll, John M. (1982), "Learning, Using and Designing Command Paradigms," *Human Interaction*, 1(1), 31–62.

Daniel, Alan, and Donald Yeates (1971), *Systems Analysis*. Palo Alto, CA: Science Research Associates.

Dekleva, Sasa M. (1994), "Is Natural Language Querying Practical?" *Data Base* (May), 24–36.

Galitz, Wilbert O. (1993), *User-Interface Screen Design*. Wellesley, MA: QED Information Sciences, Inc.

Gallian, Joseph A. (1996), "Error Detection Methods," *ACM Computing Surveys* (September), 504–517.

Hansen, James V., and Ned C. Hill (1989), "Control and Audit of Electronic Interchange," *MIS Quarterly* (December), 403–413.

Horton, William (1994), *Designing and Writing Online Documentation*, 2d ed. New York: John Wiley & Sons.

Iannella, Renato (1992), "Designing 'Safe' User Interfaces," *The Australian Computer Journal* (August), 92–97.

Lacis, Chris (1994), "Auditing the Digital Imaging System," *EDP Auditing*. Boston: Auerbach Publications, Portfolio 74–01–56, 1–15.

Miller, George A. (1956), "The Magical Number Seven, Plus or Minus Two: Some Limitations on Our Capability for Processing Information," *The Psychological Review* (March), 81–97.

Morse, Alan, and George Reynolds (1993), "Overcoming Current Growth Limits in UI Development," *Communications of the ACM* (April), 73–81.

Mullet, Kevin, and Darrell Sano (1995), *Designing Visual Interfaces*. Englewood Cliffs, NJ: SunSoft Press.

Nielsen, Jakob (1990a), "Traditional Dialogue Design Applied to Modern User Interfaces," *Communications of the ACM* (October), 109–118.

———, ed. (1990b) *Designing User Interfaces for International Use*. Amsterdam: Elsevier Science.

——— (1993), "Noncommand User Interfaces," *Communications of the ACM* (April), 83–99.

Norman, Kent L. (1991), *The Psychology of Menu Selection: Designing Cognitive Control of the Human/Computer Interface*. Norwood, NJ: Ablex Publishing.

Shneiderman, Ben (1992), *Designing the User Interface: Strategies for Effective Human-Computer Interaction*. Reading, MA: Addison-Wesley.

Weinschenk, Susan, and Sarah C. Yeo (1995), *Guidelines for Enterprise-Wide GUI Design*. New York: John Wiley & Sons.

Communication Controls

Chapter Outline

transmitted concurrently with the receiver processing earlier frames that it received. Thus, the sliding-window protocol makes better use of line capacity.

■ In wide area networks, line error controls and flow controls are incorporated into link protocols. If an organization uses a major link protocol like the Higher-level Data Link Control protocol or the Synchronous Data Link Control protocol, reliable error controls and flow controls most likely will be in place and working.

■ A communication network topology specifies the location of nodes within a network, the ways in which these nodes will be linked, and the data transmission capabilities of the links between the nodes. Four types of network topology are used within local area networks: (a) bus topology—all nodes are connected in parallel to a single communication line, and messages are broadcast over the line; (b) tree topology—nodes are connected to a branching communication line that has no closed loops; (c) ring topology—nodes are connected to a communication line that is configured as a closed loop; and (d) star topology—nodes in a network are connected in a point-to-point configuration to a central hub. Tree, ring, and star topologies are also used in wide area networks. In addition, mesh topologies are also employed, which conceptually permit every node in a network to be connected to every other node.

■ Whenever two or more nodes compete to use a communication channel, some type of channel access control technique must be used. Polling (noncontention) techniques establish an order in which nodes can gain access to channel capacity. Two common polling methods are (a) centralized polling, in which a master node polls subordinate nodes, and (b) distributed polling, in which each node takes some responsibility for control over channel access. A common form of distributed polling is token passing, in which a token is passed among nodes to give them authority to access the channel. Using contention access control techniques, nodes in a network compete with each other to use a channel. A common contention method is carrier sense multiple access with collision detection (CSMA/CD). With CSMA/CD, nodes broadcast onto a channel at any time. They then listen to whether their message has collided with any other message that has been broadcast onto the channel by another node.

■ Seven types of controls are used over subversive threats in the communication subsystem: (a) link encryption, which protects data traversing a communication line between two nodes; (b) end-to-end encryption, which protects data traversing a communication line between a sender and a receiver; (c) stream ciphers, which create interbit dependencies in ciphertext messages to make them less susceptible to attack; (d) error propagation codes, which are sensitive to the order of blocks used to transmit a message and therefore inhibit undetected changes to the order of blocks; (e) message authentication codes, which are encrypted checksums that can be used to detect alterations to a message; (f) message sequence numbers, which can be used to check changes to the order of messages; and (g) request-response mechanisms, which detect when communication between a sender and a receiver has been broken.

■ *Internetworking* is the process of connecting two or more communication networks together so the users of one network can communicate with the users of another network. Three types of devices are used to connect different networks: (a) bridges, which connect similar local area networks; (b) routers, which connect heterogeneous local area networks; and (c) gateways, which perform protocol conversion to allow networks that employ different types of communication architecture to communicate with one another. These devices improve the reliability of the total network because they allow subnetworks to be relatively independent of each other. Thus, failure in a subnetwork should not affect operations in another subnetwork. Moreover, sensitive data can be restricted to a subnetwork where highly reliable but costly controls have been installed.

■ Communication functions can be conceived and organized within the layers of a communication architecture. Within each layer of the architecture, protocols can be defined that specify the functions and controls that components in the layer must execute. Three major architectures that are currently used are the International Organization for Standardization's open-systems interconnection architecture, IBM's systems network architecture, and the transmission control protocol/internet protocol architecture.

■ The accounting audit trail in the communication subsystem must record the contents of and passage of each message that passes through a network. The operations audit trail in the communication subsystem records the resources consumed to transport data through a network.

■ Existence controls must be capable of restoring the communication subsystem if it fails. High-quality components should be deployed throughout the network, and backup components should be available. Hardware and software should be properly maintained. High-quality test and diagnostic equipment should be available to monitor the operations of the network. Adequate logs should be maintained to effect prompt recovery when the communication subsystem fails.

INTRODUCTION

The communication subsystem is responsible for transporting data among all the other subsystems within a system and for transporting data to or receiving data from another system. Its physical manifestation could be a cable (channel or bus) linking a disk drive with a central processor, or it could be a complex configuration of minicomputers, microcomputers, and communication lines linking remote computers that must interact with one another.

Auditors are likely to spend increasing amounts of time evaluating controls relating to the communication subsystem. The worldwide growth in communications traffic associated with computer systems has been dramatic, and it is likely to continue unabated for some time yet. Indeed, many organizations now could not survive in the absence of secure, effective, and efficient computer communication networks. We are also moving progressively toward information superhighways that will provide enormous capacity to transmit large volumes of voice, image, video, and data communications. Many organizations will have to make use of these superhighways if they are to survive competitively.

In this chapter we examine the types of controls that can be established within the communication subsystem to preserve asset safeguarding and data integrity. Although effectiveness and efficiency objectives are critical, we are able to consider them only in passing because they involve complex issues that warrant separate volumes. We focus, instead, on controls to reduce losses from failure in the subsystem components and deliberate attempts to subvert the authenticity and privacy of data traversing the subsystem components.

COMMUNICATION SUBSYSTEM EXPOSURES

Three major types of exposure arise in the communication subsystem: First, transmission impairments can cause differences between the data sent and the data received; second, data can be lost or corrupted through component failure; and third, a hostile party could seek to subvert data that is transmitted through the subsystem. The following subsections briefly examine each type of exposure.

Transmission Impairments

When data is transported across a transmission medium, three types of impairments can arise: attenuation, delay distortion, and noise. *Attenuation* is the weakening of a signal that occurs as it traverses a medium. It increases as the distance traveled by the signal increases. In the case of analog signals, *amplifiers* must be used after a signal has traveled a certain distance to boost the signal to a higher strength (amplitude). Otherwise, the receiver will not be able to detect and interpret the signal, or it will be corrupted by noise. In the case of digital signals, *repeaters* are used to boost the signal strength periodically as the signal traverses the medium. Attenuation can also cause *distortion* of analog signals. An analog signal is made up of a number of frequencies, and the amount of attenuation suffered varies across frequencies. Digital signals also suffer from attenuation distortion. They use a narrower range of frequencies, however, and thus the attenuation distortion that arises is less.

Delay distortion occurs when a signal is transmitted through bounded media (twisted-pair wire, coaxial cable, optical fiber). It does not occur when the signal is transmitted through air or space (free-space transmission). Different signal frequencies traverse bounded media with different velocities. Thus, signals are distorted because their different frequency components are subject to different delays. Delay distortion can have a marked effect on digital data because the signal energy in one bit position can spill over into another bit position.

Noise is the random electric signals that degrade performance in the transmission medium. There are four types of noise: white noise, intermodulation noise, crosstalk, and impulse noise. *White noise* (thermal noise) arises through the motion of electrons. It increases as a function of absolute temperature. *Intermodulation noise* arises when the output from a component in the communication subsystem is not a linear function of its input. It can arise because of component malfunctioning. *Crosstalk* arises because signal paths become coupled. Bounded media are placed too close to each other, or the signal emitted by antennas used with unbounded media overlap. *Impulse noise* arises for a variety of reasons: atmospheric conditions (e.g., lightning), faulty switching gear, and poor contacts.

Noise increases as more data is transmitted over a medium. If the public telephone exchange network is used for data transmission, for example, line errors increase during peak periods because the increased traffic produces additional noise. Aside from the problems that arise with transmission errors caused by noise, wiretappers also can use noise to mask unauthorized activities.

Component Failure

The primary components in the communication subsystem are *(1)* transmission media—for example, twisted-pair wire, optical fiber, and microwave; *(2)* hardware—for example, ports, modems, amplifiers, repeaters, multiplexors, switches, concentrators; and *(3)* software—for example, packet switching software, polling software, data compression software. Each of these components may fail. As a result, data in the communication subsystem may be lost, corrupted, or routed incorrectly through the network and perhaps displayed to a person who is unauthorized to view the data.

As discussed previously, transmission media suffer from various kinds of impairments when data is transported across them. Other types of failure can occur, however. For example, a cable could become crimped or broken, or an antenna could become corroded. Transmission of data across the medium then can no longer be accomplished.

Hardware and software failure can occur for many reasons—for example, failure in an integrated circuit, a disk crash, a power surge, insufficient temporary storage for a queue, or program bugs. The failure can be either temporary or permanent. For example, an intermittent failure in a modem could corrupt a bit pattern only in short bursts—a temporary failure. Or an operating system could crash for some unknown reason, however, and the operator might be unable to restart it on a timely basis—a permanent failure. The failure also can be either local or global. For example, the failure of a microcomputer terminal affects only the users of the terminal—a local failure. Failure in a concentrator, however, affects all users connected to the concentrator—a global failure.

Subversive Threats

In a subversive attack on the communication subsystem, an intruder attempts to violate the integrity of some component in the subsystem. For example, invasive or inductive taps can be installed on telephone lines using, say, a data scope. An *invasive tap* enables the intruder either to read or to modify the data being transmitted over the line. An *inductive tap* monitors electromagnetic transmissions from the line and allows the data to be read only. Similarly, satellite signals propagated in broadcast mode can be read by a ground receiver over a wide geographic area. Modifying satellite transmissions, on the other hand, is more difficult.

Subversive attacks can be either passive or active (Figure 12–1). In a *passive* attack, intruders attempt to learn some characteristic of the data being

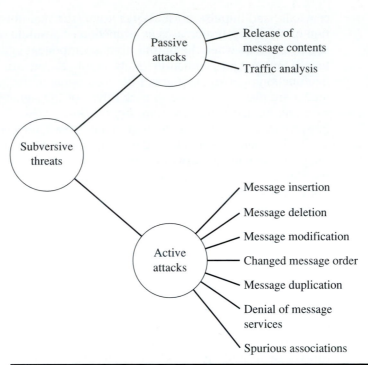

FIGURE 12–1. Subversive threats to the communication subsystem.

transmitted. They might be able to read the contents of the data so the privacy of the data is violated. Alternatively, although the content of the data itself might remain secure, intruders could read and analyze the cleartext source and destination identifiers attached to a message for routing purposes. They also could examine the lengths and frequency of messages that are transmitted. These latter attacks are known as *traffic analysis*. They can provide an intruder with important information about messages being transmitted. For example, analysis of source and destination identifiers can provide insights into troop movements in a military application, or they could provide sales information in a commercial application. Similarly, the lengths and frequency of messages could indicate the types of messages being transmitted.

There are seven types of *active* attack:

1. Intruders could *insert* a message in the message stream being transmitted. For example, in an electronic funds transfer system (EFTS), they could add a deposit transaction for their account to the message stream being transmitted.
2. Intruders could *delete* a message being transmitted. For example, they could remove an account withdrawal transaction from the message stream being transmitted.
3. Intruders could *modify* the contents of a message being transmitted. For example, they could increase the amount field in a deposit transaction.
4. Intruders could *alter the order* of messages in a message stream. For example, they could change the sequence of deposit and withdrawal transactions to affect penalties incurred or interest charged or earned on their account.
5. Intruders could *duplicate* messages in a message stream. For example, they could copy deposit transactions for their account.

6. Intruders could *deny* message services between a sender and a receiver by corrupting (jamming), discarding, or delaying messages. This attack is similar to a message deletion attack. Message deletion is a transient attack on an established association between a sender and a receiver, however, whereas an attack that denies message services prevents the association from being established in the first place. It might be used by a competitor to severely impair the day-to-day operations of an organization.

7. Intruders could use techniques to establish *spurious associations* so they are regarded as legitimate users of a system. For example, they could play back a handshaking sequence previously used by a legitimate user of the system. Chapter 10 discusses this type of attack as part of our consideration of boundary subsystem controls.

PHYSICAL COMPONENT CONTROLS

One way to reduce expected losses in the communications subsystem is to choose physical components that have characteristics that make them reliable and that incorporate features or provide controls that mitigate the possible effects of exposures. The following subsections give an overview of how physical components can affect communication subsystem reliability.

Transmission Media

A transmission medium is a physical path along which a signal can be transported between a sender and a receiver. Figure 12–2 shows the various types of transmission media that can be used in the communications subsystem. With *bounded* (or guided) media, the signals are transported along an enclosed physical path. Bounded media comprise twisted-pair wire, coaxial cable, and optical fiber. With unbounded (unguided) media, the signals propagate via free-space

FIGURE 12–2. Types of transmission media.

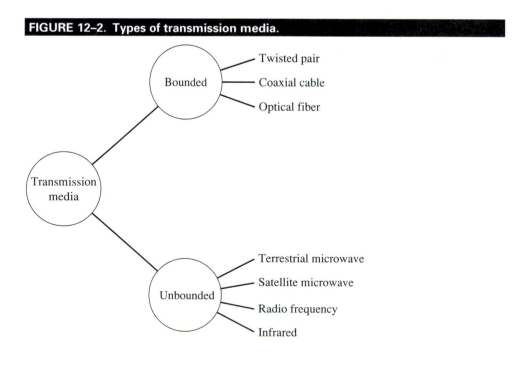

TABLE 12–1(*a*).	Characteristics of Bounded Transmission Media		
Characteristic	*Twisted Pair*	*Coaxial Cable*	*Optical Fiber*
Data rate	Low	Moderate	High
Expense	Low	Moderate	Moderate
Distance	Moderate	Low–Moderate	High
Line of sight	No	No	No
Interference	High susceptibility	Moderate susceptibility	Low susceptibility
Wiretapping	High susceptibility	Moderate susceptibility	Low susceptibility

emission rather than along an enclosed physical path. Unbounded media comprise terrestrial and satellite microwave, radio frequency, and infrared.

Tables 12–1*a* and 12–1*b* provide an overview of the capabilities of the various transmission media and their relative strengths and weaknesses in relation to the various exposures that can arise in the communication subsystem. *Twisted-pair* wire permits only a low rate of data transmission. Amplifiers for analog signals or repeaters for digital signals must be placed every few kilometers if data is to be transmitted over long distances. Unfortunately, amplifiers also increase distortion on the line. Moreover, by increasing the strength of the signal, both amplifiers and repeaters increase free-space emanations that can be picked up via an inductive wiretap. Indeed, wiretaps can be installed easily on twisted pair. Twisted pair is also highly susceptible to interference such as crosstalk and noise. These problems are offset to some extent, however, by the low cost of twisted pair.

Coaxial cable permits a moderate rate of data transmission over relatively short distances. If data is to be transmitted over long distances, amplifiers or repeaters must be installed more frequently than for twisted pair. Coaxial cable is moderately susceptible to various forms of interference, although less so than twisted-pair wire. It is relatively easy to install a wiretap on coaxial cable, although more difficult than with twisted pair. Coaxial cable is also more expensive to install than twisted pair.

Optical fiber permits very high rates of data transmission over relatively long distances before repeaters must be used. Although signals transmitted over optical fiber suffer from attenuation, nonetheless, they are immune to other forms of interference such as noise and crosstalk. Moreover, it is difficult to install a wiretap on optical fiber. Chao (1990) describes two methods of wiretapping that can be used, both of which are expensive. Under the *bending method*, the fiber is bent such that some light loss occurs at the bend. Sensitive equipment is needed to pick up the light loss that results. Under the *insertion method*, the fiber is first broken.

TABLE 12–1(*b*).	Characteristics of Unbounded Transmission Media		
Characteristic	*Terrestrial Microwave*	*Satellite Microwave*	*Radio Frequency*	*Infrared*
Data rate	Moderate	Moderate	Moderate	Low
Expense	Moderate	High	Moderate	Moderate
Distance	High	High	Moderate	Low
Line of sight	Yes	Yes	No	Yes
Interference	High susceptibility	High susceptibility	High susceptibility	High susceptibility
Wiretapping	High susceptibility	High susceptibility	High susceptibility	High susceptibility

A tapping device and transmitter with a light source are then inserted. Providing a continuous flow of data is maintained over the fiber, installation of the insertion wiretap will be detected because the link will go down for a short period.

Terrestrial microwave permits moderate rates of data transmission over relatively long distances. Line-of-sight transmission is required, however; thus, a microwave station is needed about every 40 kilometers because of the earth's curvature. Microwave transmission is highly susceptible to various forms of interference. For example, rain causes signal attenuation. It is also relatively easy to install a wiretap. The wiretap will break the line-of-sight transmission, however, and therefore it should be easy to detect.

Satellite microwave permits moderate rates of data transmission over long distances. Line-of-sight transmission is maintained by having the satellite orbit the earth so it remains stationary with respect to its earth stations (achieved by having the satellite at a height of approximately 35,800 kilometers). Like terrestrial microwave, satellite microwave is highly susceptible to interference, and it can be wiretapped easily. If point-to-point transmission is used, installation of the wiretap should be detected because the signal will be broken. If the satellite is operating in broadcast mode (point-to-multipoint transmission), however, the wiretap will not be detected. Any earth station within the area of broadcast will be able to pick up the satellite's transmission.

Radio frequency permits moderate rates of data transmission over moderate distances. Like microwave transmission, it is highly susceptible to interference. Radio frequency is omnidirectional, however; that is, the signal is transmitted in all directions. Thus, it is easy to wiretap, and the wiretap will not be detected.

Infrared permits moderate rates of data transmission over short distances. It is highly susceptible to interference, and it requires line-of-sight transmission. Like microwave and radio frequency, it is easy to wiretap. The wiretap will break the line-of-sight transmission, however, and therefore it should be easy to detect.

Communication Lines

The reliability of data transmission can be improved by choosing a private (leased) communication line rather than a public communication line. Public lines use the normal public switching exchange facilities. As a result, users often have no control over the lines allocated to them for data transmission purposes. In some cases, however, users can specify the characteristics of the lines they require. The switching center will then allocate them a line having those characteristics. For small amounts of data transmission (generally, less than a few hours per day), public lines are cheaper than private lines.

Private lines are lines that are dedicated to service a particular user. In terms of transmission reliability, they have two advantages. First, they allow higher rates of data transmission. Thus, they are better able to accommodate the overheads associated with controls that might be implemented over transmitted data (e.g., encryption controls). Second, private lines can be conditioned; that is, the carrier ensures the line has certain quality attributes. A conditioned line limits the amounts of attenuation, distortion, and noise that its users will encounter.

Modems

Computer hardware uses and generates discrete binary signals (Figure 12–3a). For transmission purposes, these signals are sometimes converted to analog signals (Figure 12–3b). The device that accomplishes this conversion is called a modem or data set.

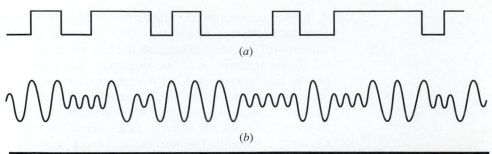

FIGURE 12–3(*a*). Digital signal. (*b*). Analog signal.

FIGURE 12–4(*a*). Wave form characteristics. (*b*). Modulation techniques.

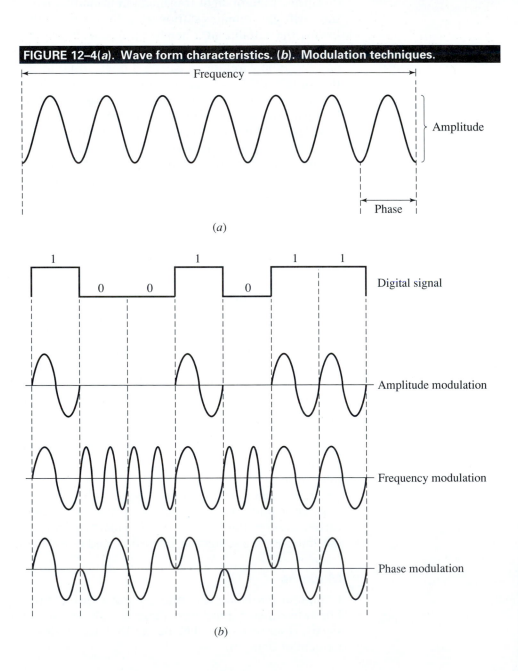

Modems undertake three other functions that affect the reliability of the communication subsystem. First, they increase the speed with which data can be transmitted over a communication line. They accomplish this objective by using some type of multiplexing technique (discussed subsequently). Higher rates of data transmission mean the overheads associated with controls have less impact. Higher rates of data transmission also mean that someone who successfully wiretaps a line gets access to more data.

Second, modems can reduce the number of line errors that arise through distortion if they use a process called *equalization*. If a modem has dynamic equalization capabilities, it will continuously measure the characteristics of a line and perform automatic adjustments for attenuation and delay distortion. Dynamic equalization is especially useful when public, unconditioned lines are used. Recall, that users have no prior knowledge of the characteristics of these lines.

Third, modems can reduce the number of line errors that arise through noise. To compensate for noise, a variable-speed modem will decrease the rate of data transmission as higher levels of noise are encountered. Recall that as transmission speeds increase, the effects of noise are more pronounced.

Modems work by varying either the amplitude, frequency, or phase of an analog signal to represent a digital signal (Figure 12–4, see page 480). Noise affects the performance of the three modulation methods differently. Phase modulation outperforms frequency modulation, which in turn outperforms amplitude modulation. The high-speed modems now in use sometimes employ a combination of methods to increase the speed of data transmission—for example, amplitude and phase modulation.

Port-Protection Devices

Port-protection devices are used to mitigate exposures associated with dial-up access to a computer system. When users place a call to the system they seek to access, a connection is established with the port-protection device rather than the host system. The port-protection device then performs various security functions to authenticate users. Some examples of these security functions follow:

1. Users could be permitted to place calls to the host system only from authorized telephone numbers. When they dial the host system's telephone number, the port-protection device could disconnect them and then dial them back at their authorized number to ensure that they are calling from an authorized location.
2. A port-protection device could eliminate the telltale modem tone that autodialer routines can detect. It might respond to a call with a synthesized voice message or with silence as it awaits further user input.
3. Users could be required to provide passwords before the port-protection device will allow them access to the host system. The host system might in turn exercise its own user authentication functions.
4. Port-protection devices could maintain an audit trail of all successful and unsuccessful accesses to the host system. In addition, they might record the times when different activities occurred and the duration of each activity.

Some of the security functions performed by port-protection devices might also be available in modems. For example, modems might provide a disconnect-and-callback feature. Modems are unlikely to provide the extensive password and logging functions often incorporated into port-protection devices, however.

Multiplexors and Concentrators

Multiplexing and concentration techniques allow the bandwidth or capacity of a communication line to be used more effectively. The common objective is to share the use of a high-cost transmission line among many messages that arrive at the multiplexor or concentration point from multiple low-cost source lines.

Multiplexing techniques use static channel derivation schemes to assign transmission capacity on a fixed, predetermined basis. Each data source shares a common transmission medium, but each has its own channel.

The two common multiplexing techniques used are frequency-division multiplexing and time-division multiplexing. The former divides a single bandwidth into several smaller bandwidths that are used as independent frequency channels (Figure 12–5a). The latter assigns small, fixed time slots to a user during which the user transmits the whole or part of a message (Figure 12–5b). Thus, channels are defined in terms of either a frequency band or a time slot.

Two types of time-division multiplexing are used. *Synchronous* time-division multiplexing assigns time slots to each signal source on a round-robin basis. If the source has no data to transmit when its turn arrives, its corresponding time slot will be empty. *Statistical* or *asynchronous* multiplexing assigns time slots on a needs basis. Each signal source has an input buffer, and the multiplexor scans the input buffers collecting input data to fill a frame. The multiplexor sends the frame when it is full. In this light, statistical time-division multiplexing is more efficient than either frequency-division or synchronous time-division multiplexing because frequency bands and time slots are not wasted if a source has no data to send.

Concentration techniques use schemes whereby some number of input channels dynamically share a smaller number of output channels on a demand basis. Three common concentration techniques are message switching, packet

FIGURE 12–5(a). Frequency division multiplexing. (b). Time division multiplexing.

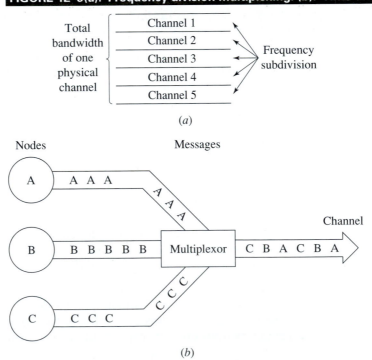

switching, and line switching. In *message switching*, a complete message is sent to the concentration point and stored until a communication path can be established with the destination node. In *packet switching*, a message is broken up into small, fixed-length packets. The packets are routed individually through the network depending on the availability of a channel for each packet. In *line switching* or *circuit switching*, a device establishes temporary connections between input channels and output channels where the number of input channels exceeds the number of output channels.

Multiplexing and concentration techniques affect system reliability in several ways:

1. Both allow more efficient use to be made of available channel capacity. As a result, some channel capacity can often be used for backup purposes.
2. Concentration techniques can route a message over a different path if a particular channel fails.
3. Multiplexing and concentration functions often are incorporated into an intelligent front-end processor that performs other functions such as message validation and protocol conversion. These functions would otherwise be performed by the host processor, thereby increasing the workload of and reliance that must be placed on the host processor.
4. Both techniques help to protect data against subversive attacks. Wiretappers have greater difficulty disentangling the myriad of messages passing over a channel connected to a multiplexor or concentrator. Conversely, sophisticated intruders gain access to more data if they have suitable hardware and software and can determine the multiplexing or concentration techniques used.
5. Multiplexors and concentrators are critical components in a network. Thus, they should have a high mean-time-between-failure (MTBF).

LINE ERROR CONTROLS

Whenever data is transmitted over a communication line, recall that it can be received in error because of attenuation, distortion, or noise that occurs on the line. These errors must be detected and corrected. In the following subsections, we examine some major methods used to detect and correct transmission errors.

Error Detection

Line errors can be detected by either using a loop (echo) check or building some form of redundancy into the message transmitted. A *loop check* involves the receiver of a message sending back the message received to the sender (Figure 12–6). The sender checks the correctness of the message received by

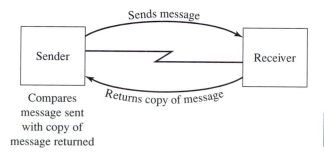

FIGURE 12–6. Loop check on communications line.

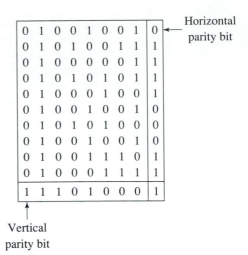

FIGURE 12–7. Horizontal and vertical odd parity check.

the receiver by comparing it with a stored copy of the message sent. If a difference exists, the message is retransmitted with suitable line protocol data to indicate the previous message received was in error. On some occasions, the message received might have been correct. The receiver's retransmission of the message back to the sender might have been corrupted, however, and hence a difference exists.

Because a loop check at least halves the throughput on communication lines, normally it is used on full-duplex (simultaneous two-way communication) lines or where communication lines are short. If lines are short, the high protection afforded data transmission using a loop check could justify the costs of the extra channel capacity needed. On full-duplex lines, the return path is often underused anyway. In this light, it can be used productively for error detection purposes.

Redundancy involves attaching extra data to a message that will allow corrupted data to be detected. Two common forms of redundancy-based error detection methods are parity checks and cyclic redundancy checks.

Parity checking involves adding an extra bit to a string of bits. Figure 12–7 shows the use of both horizontal parity bits and vertical parity bits on a 10-character block of data. Each horizontal parity bit is used to detect whether a character in the block has been corrupted. Nevertheless, if a burst of noise on a line causes two bits in a character to flip from, say, zero to one, a horizontal parity check will not detect the error. A vertical or block parity check will detect the error, however.

With *cyclic redundancy checks* (CRCs), the block of data to be transmitted is treated as a binary number. This number is then divided by a prime binary number. The remainder is attached to the block to be transmitted. The receiver recalculates the remainder to check whether any data in the block has been corrupted.

Parity checks are employed when *asynchronous* data transmission is used—that is, when data is transmitted one character at a time. CRCs can also be used with asynchronous transmission, but they tend to be used with *synchronous* transmission—that is, where data is sent as a continuous stream of bits.

Error Correction

When line errors have been detected, they must then be corrected. Two methods used are *(1)* forward error correcting codes, and *(2)* retransmission of data in error (backward error correction).

Forward error correcting codes enable line errors to be corrected at the receiving station. To determine what the correct data should be, redundant data must be added to the data transmitted. If line errors are infrequent, this redundant data can impose high overheads on the communication subsystem. Moreover, even with redundant data, there is always a risk that an attempted correction to an error will be carried out incorrectly. For these reasons, retransmission of erroneous data is often the error correction strategy chosen in preference to forward error correcting codes.

Nonetheless, forward error correcting codes have their place. For example, retransmission is costly when propagation times are long, such as in satellite transmission. Similarly, retransmission might be impractical in broadcast situations where multiple receivers exist. The sender would have to wait for multiple receivers to acknowledge correct receipt of the data. Moreover, only some receivers might receive corrupted data. Rebroadcasting the data would therefore impose overheads on receivers who received the data correctly.

With *retransmission*, the sender sends the data again if the receiver indicates the data has been received in error. An agreed-upon protocol is used to indicate correct or incorrect receipt of the message. In the ASCII ACK-NAK protocol, for example, an ACK signal is transmitted by the receiver if the message received is correct, and a NAK signal is transmitted by the receiver if the message received is incorrect. In some protocols, the sender waits for either an ACK or a NAK signal before transmitting the next message (stop and wait). In other cases, the sender continues to transmit messages while awaiting an ACK or NAK signal. If a NAK signal is received, the sender goes back to the message sent in error and retransmits messages from that point (go back N).

Noise also can corrupt the control characters used for retransmission in an error detection and correction system. An odd-even record count enables such errors to be detected. For example, consider a situation in which control characters are corrupted and two messages appear to the receiver to be a single message. Assume the control character for the first message was odd. The control character for the second message, an even number, has been corrupted. Thus, when the receiver identifies a third message having an odd-numbered control character, it will recognize a message is missing and an error has occurred.

FLOW CONTROLS

Flow controls are needed because two nodes in a network can differ in terms of the rate at which they can send, receive, and process data. For example, a mainframe can transmit data to a microcomputer terminal. The microcomputer cannot display data on its screen at the same rate the data arrives from the mainframe. Moreover, the microcomputer will have limited buffer space. Thus, it cannot continue to receive data from the mainframe and to store the data in its buffer pending display of the data on its screen. Flow controls will be used, therefore, to prevent the mainframe swamping the microcomputer and, as a result, data being lost.

The simplest form of flow control is *stop-and-wait* flow control. Using this approach, the sender transmits a frame of data. When the receiver is ready to accept another frame, it transmits an acknowledgment to the sender. The sender will not transmit another frame until it receives an acknowledgment from the receiver. Thus, the receiver controls the rate at which data reaches it.

The stop-and-wait flow control protocol is inefficient because the communication channel remains unused for periods of time while the receiver is processing the frames received. For this reason, the *sliding-window* flow control approach has been developed. Using this approach, both the sender and receiver have buffers that hold multiple frames of data which allow them to overlap transmission and processing of data.

Figure 12–8 provides an overview of a sliding-window control protocol. Assume the sender and receiver both have windows of seven frames (the shaded boxes at time t_1). Think of the data to be sent and received, also, as an endless sequence of data that will be broken up and allocated to one of eight windows in a sending or receiving buffer. The protocol works as follows:

1. At time t_1, the sender sends frames F0 and F1 to the receiver.
2. At time t_2, the sender's window shrinks by two frames to indicate frames F0 and F1 have been sent.
3. At time t_3, the receiver receives frames F0 and F1. The receiver's window shrinks by two frames to indicate receipt of the frames.
4. At time t_4, the receiver sends an acknowledgment to the sender indicating readiness to receive frame F2 (thereby signalling that F0 and F1 have been received safely). It then expands its window by two frames.
5. At time t_5, the sender receives the acknowledgment from the receiver and expands its window by two frames. It then sends four frames—F2, F3, F4, and F5—to the receiver.
6. At time t_6, the sender's window shrinks by four frames to indicate frames F2, F3, F4, and F5 have been sent.
7. At time t_7, the receiver receives frames F2, F3, F4, and F5. The receiver's window shrinks by four frames to indicate receipt of the frames.

And so the process goes on. At any time, the receiver can also send a Receive-Not-Ready (RNR) frame. This type of frame acknowledges receipt of prior frames but forbids the sender from transmitting any more frames until a further instruction is issued.

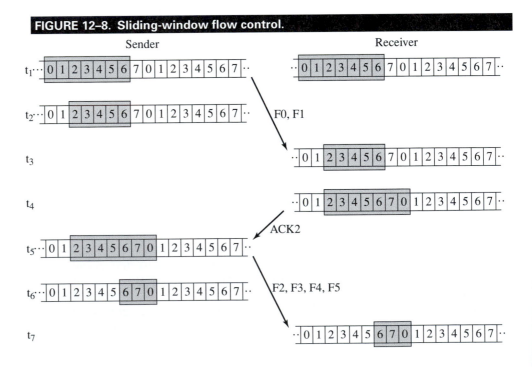

FIGURE 12–8. Sliding-window flow control.

LINK CONTROLS

In wide area networks, line error control and flow control are important functions in the component that manages the link between two nodes in a network. The way these link-management components operate is specified via a protocol. Two common protocols that are used are the International Organization for Standardization's Higher-level Data Link Control (HDLC) protocol and IBM's Synchronous Data Link Control (SDLC) protocol. Both are packet protocols developed specifically for computer communications. A newer packet protocol is Asynchronous Transfer Mode (ATM), which has been designed to handle a wider variety of data rates and data types than HDLC and SDLC. It is used commonly with broadband integrated services digital networks (B-ISDN), which have been developed to support high-speed communication of all types of data—for example, sound and video as well as computer data.

A discussion of the details of the HDLC, SDLC, and ATM protocols is beyond the scope of this book (see, further, Stallings 1997). From an auditors' viewpoint, however, they can have increased confidence in the likelihood of data being transferred accurately and completely between two nodes in a wide area network if well-developed and well-accepted protocols like HDLC, SDLC, and ATM are being used. To the extent that little-known or idiosyncratic data link protocols are being used, auditors must expand their evidence-collection work to obtain assurance that data are being transferred accurately and completely between two nodes in a wide area network.

TOPOLOGICAL CONTROLS

A communication network topology specifies the location of nodes within a network, the ways in which these nodes will be linked, and the data transmission capabilities of the links between the nodes. Specifying the optimum topology for a network can be a problem of immense complexity. Consider some of the design constraints that must be taken into account. First, an overall cost ceiling will apply, perhaps expressed as a limit on the cost per bit of information to be transmitted. Second, throughput and response time constraints exist. Communication of messages between different points in the network must be achieved within a certain time. Third, availability and reliability constraints exist. The network must be available for use at any one time by a given number of users. If a component of the network fails, alternative routing of messages or alternative hardware and software might be needed.

In the following two subsections, we examine the topologies that are commonly used in local and wide area networks. We briefly examine the nature of each topology and their strengths and weaknesses from a controls viewpoint.

Local Area Network Topologies

Local area networks tend to have three characteristics: *(1)* they are privately owned networks; *(2)* they provide high-speed communication among nodes; and *(3)* they are confined to limited geographic areas (for example, a single floor or building or locations within a few kilometers of each other). They are implemented using four basic types of topologies: *(1)* bus topology, *(2)* tree topology, *(3)* ring topology, and *(4)* star topology. Hybrid topologies like the star-ring topology and the star-bus topology are also used.

Bus Topology

In a bus topology, nodes in the network are connected in parallel to a single communication line (Figure 12–9). Each node in the network is passive. A tap is used to transmit data onto and receive data from the bus. Data is broadcast in both directions along the bus. At each end of the bus is a terminator that absorbs a signal on the bus, thereby removing it from the bus. A bus is a *multipoint* topology because more than two nodes share the same communication line.

Two types of bus are used. A *baseband bus* uses digital signaling. The signal consumes the entire bandwidth of the transmission medium. Thus, frequency division multiplexing is not possible. Transmission is bidirectional over short distances. Repeaters must be used to increase the length of the network. Each repeater joins different segments of the communication line. A baseband bus is susceptible to wiretapping because only a single signal is traversing the bus.

A *broadband bus* uses analog signaling. Thus, frequency division multiplexing can be used to support different types of traffic on the network. Transmission is unidirectional because the amplifiers used in broadband bus networks are unidirectional devices. Thus, an inbound and an outbound path are required in the network. This objective is achieved by using either two cables (one for each path) or using different frequencies on the same cable. One end of the bus is designated as the head end. The head end then either acts as a passive conductor between the inbound and outbound cable, or it converts inbound frequencies to outbound frequencies on a single cable. Broadband buses cover longer distances than baseband buses because analog signals suffer less from attenuation, distortion, and noise than digital signals. A broadband bus is also less susceptible to wiretapping than a baseband bus because multiple signals are traversing the bus.

From the auditors' perspective, the following control considerations arise with a bus topology:

1. Relative to other topologies like the ring, a bus degrades the performance of the transmission medium because the taps that connect each node to the bus introduce attenuation and distortion to the signal being transmitted.
2. Because the taps that connect each node to the network are passive, the network will not fail if a node fails. Thus, bus networks are fairly robust when node failures occur.
3. Because all nodes have access to traffic on the network, messages not intended for a particular node can be accessed either deliberately or accidentally by the node. Thus, controls must be implemented to protect the privacy of sensitive data (e.g., encryption controls).

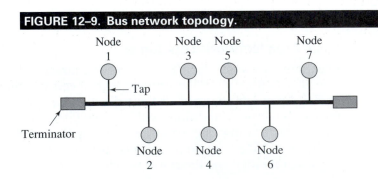

FIGURE 12–9. Bus network topology.

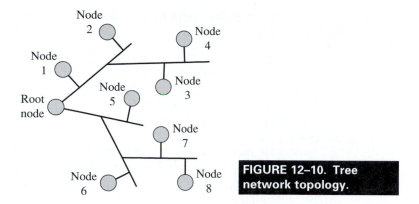

FIGURE 12–10. Tree network topology.

Tree Topology

In a tree topology, nodes in the network are connected to a branching communication line that has no closed loops (Figure 12–10). In this regard, a tree topology is simply a generalization of a bus topology. As with a bus, messages are broadcast along the transmission medium. Moreover, as with a bus, each node uses a passive tap to broadcast data onto and receive data from the communication line.

It is difficult to propagate digital signals through the branching points that exist in a tree topology. Thus, tree topologies use analog signaling rather than digital signaling. Each node broadcasts messages in the direction of the root of the tree (which constitutes the head end). The root then propagates messages along the outbound path.

From the auditors' perspective, the control considerations that apply to a bus topology also apply to a tree topology.

Ring Topology

In a ring topology, nodes in the network are connected via repeaters to a communication line that is configured as a closed loop (Figure 12–11). The repeater is an active device: It inserts data onto a line, receives data from a line, and removes data from a line. In many ring networks, data is transmitted only in one direction on the ring (either clockwise or counterclockwise). A node often breaks a message up into packets of data and then inserts each packet on the ring. A ring is an example of a point-to-point (rather than a multipoint) topology. Each node is connected directly to another node; no intermediate node has to be traversed.

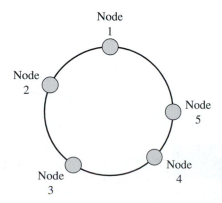

FIGURE 12–11. Ring network topology.

From the auditors' perspective, the following control considerations arise with a ring topology:

1. Unlike the taps used in a bus network, repeaters do not introduce attenuation and distortion to the signal being transmitted. Indeed, repeaters retransmit a clean signal after the signal has been received. Timing errors arise, however, as bits of data are transmitted around the network. These timing errors accumulate and effectively limit the number of repeaters that can be used in the network.
2. Because repeaters are active components in a ring topology, they will bring the network down if they fail. Repeaters might have a bypass mode, which is useful if their node is down.
3. Because all traffic on the network must be routed through each node's repeater, messages not intended for a particular node can be accessed either deliberately or accidentally by the node. As with bus networks, controls must be implemented to protect the privacy of sensitive data (e.g., encryption controls).

Star Topology

In a star topology, nodes in the network are connected in a point-to-point configuration to a central hub (Figure 12–12). The central hub can act as a switch. It can route messages from one outlying node to another outlying node. Alternatively, it can broadcast messages from one node to all other nodes or some subset of nodes.

From the auditors' perspective, the following control considerations arise with a star topology:

1. The reliability of the central hub is critical in a star network. If the central hub fails, the entire network will be brought down.
2. Failure in an outlying node or in a communication line linking a node to the hub has only a limited effect on the network. The remaining nodes can still transmit data to each other.
3. The security of the central hub is critical. All data must be transmitted through the hub. Therefore, compromise of the hub can mean all messages are compromised.
4. Servicing and maintenance of a star network are relatively easy. Diagnosis of problems can be performed from the central hub, and faults usually can be located quickly.

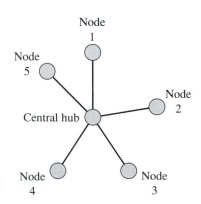

FIGURE 12–12. Star network topology.

Hybrid Topologies

Various types of hybrid topologies are also used in local area networks. For example, in the star-bus topology, nodes are connected via relatively long communication lines to a short bus that is usually housed in a wiring closet. Star-bus networks can be expanded easily, simply by connecting another drop cable to the bus. They have the control advantages and disadvantages of a bus. Nevertheless, they have an additional advantage because physically the short-length bus can be easily secured.

In the star-ring topology, nodes are connected via relatively long communication lines to a short-diameter ring. Again, this type of topology allows the network to be expanded relatively easily. From a control viewpoint, star-ring topologies have the advantages and disadvantages of a ring. They have an additional advantage, however, in that physically the short-diameter ring can be easily secured.

Wide Area Network Topologies

Wide area networks have the following characteristics: *(1)* they often encompass components that are owned by other parties (e.g., a telephone company); *(2)* they provide relatively low-speed communication among nodes; and *(3)* they span large geographic areas.

With the exception of the bus topology, all other topologies that are used to implement local area networks can also be used to implement wide area networks. The most commonly used topology in a wide area network, however, is a *mesh* topology. In a mesh topology, conceptually every node in the network can have a point-to-point connection with every other node (a fully connected network). This topology is usually too expensive, however, and one node often must communicate with another node through intermediate nodes (Figure 12–13). A path between nodes is established using any of the concentration techniques discussed previously: message switching, packet switching, and line switching.

From a controls viewpoint, a mesh topology is inherently reliable because data can be routed via alternative paths through the network. If one path fails, the concentration methods used allow the data to be routed via another path. A major concern, however, is that reliance often must be placed on other parties to ensure the security, integrity, and reliability of the network. If, for example, a node that is owned and managed by another party is compromised, all

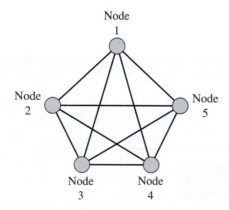

FIGURE 12–13. Mesh (fully connected) network topology.

data passing through this node is at risk. These concerns motivate the use of encryption controls in wide area networks (discussed later in the chapter).

CHANNEL ACCESS CONTROLS

Two different nodes in a network can compete to use a communication channel. Whenever the possibility of contention for the channel exists, some type of channel access control technique must be used. These techniques fall into two classes: polling methods and contention methods. The following subsections provide a brief description of each class of techniques.

Polling Methods

Polling (noncontention) techniques establish an order in which a node can gain access to channel capacity. There are two forms of polling: centralized polling and distributed polling. In *centralized polling*, one node within the network is designated as the control node or master node. This node takes responsibility for asking each other node in turn whether they wish to use the channel. For example, in the bus topology shown in Figure 12–14, the control node polls each other node according to a preset polling list: first node 1, then node 2, then node 3, then node 4, and so on, until it returns again to poll node 1. If a node has no message to send, the control node polls the next node on the list. If a node has a message to send, however, channel access is given to the node until its message or packet is sent. The next node on the polling list is then polled.

In *distributed polling*, each node takes some responsibility for control over channel access. For example, a common form of distributed polling is *token passing*. A token is a special packet of information that traverses the channel. When a node wants to transmit data, it must first obtain the token and remove it from the channel. A common approach is to change a bit in the token so that it becomes a start-of-packet header. In Figure 12–15, for example, assume node 1 on the ring wants to send a message to node 4. Node 1 will "grab" the token as soon as it passes, "attach" its message to the token, and insert it onto the ring. The address of the message will be read by each node as it passes along the ring. Node 4 will recognize that it is the intended recipient and read the message. It will not remove the message, however, from the ring. Instead, it will allow it to return to node 1 (the sender). Node 1 can then determine that the message has reached its intended destination. It will remove the message from the ring and then return the token to the ring.

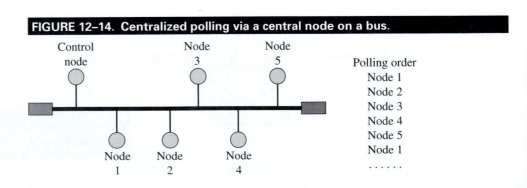

FIGURE 12–14. Centralized polling via a central node on a bus.

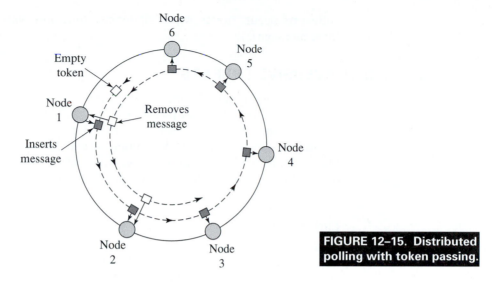

FIGURE 12–15. Distributed polling with token passing.

Several types of problems can arise with token passing techniques:

1. A token can be corrupted as it traverses the communications line. As a result, nodes in the network that wish to send data will not be able to detect the token. Some type of protocol must exist whereby one of the nodes will introduce a new token on the channel if it does not detect a token within some time period. If that node fails to enter a token within some time period, another node might then enter a token onto the channel.
2. A node could fail to release the token after capturing it to read a message. Again, other nodes in the network that wish to send data will not be able to detect the token, and so a protocol must exist to reintroduce a token onto the channel.
3. The receiving node's address in a message could be corrupted. As a result, the receiving node might not detect a message intended for it. The sending node must recognize that the token has returned without the message having been read by the intended receiver. The message must then be resent.
4. The sending node's address could be corrupted.

Contention Methods

Using contention methods, nodes in a network must compete with each other to gain access to a channel. Each node is given immediate right of access to the channel. Whether the node can use the channel successfully, however, depends on the actions of other nodes connected to the channel.

Although several different types of contention methods have been proposed, one commonly used with bus local area networks is called carrier sense multiple access with collision detection (CSMA/CD). With CSMA/CD, a node wishing to send a message first "listens" to the channel. If the channel is clear, it transmits the message to be sent. If another node also sends a message at the same time, however, a collision between the two messages will occur as they traverse the channel. To detect collisions, each node that sends a message must continue to listen to the channel. If a sending node "hears" a collision, it knows it must retransmit its message. To try to reduce the possibility of a further collision, a node will wait for some time interval before retransmitting its message. Different nodes will wait for different time intervals. If further collisions occur, nodes will wait longer time intervals before retransmitting their messages.

CONTROLS OVER SUBVERSIVE THREATS

There are two types of control over subversive threats to the communication subsystem. The first seeks to establish *physical* barriers to the data traversing the subsystem. Recall that we examined this type of control in Chapter 7. The second accepts that an intruder somehow will gain access to the data and seeks, therefore, to render the data useless when access occurs. We examine this type of control in the following subsections. Table 12–2 provides an overview of the controls discussed.

Link Encryption

Link encryption protects data traversing a communication channel connecting two nodes in a network (Figure 12–16). The sending node encrypts data it receives and then transmits the data in encrypted form to the receiving node. The receiving node subsequently decrypts the data, reads the destination address from the data, determines the next channel over which to transmit the data, and encrypts the data under the key that applies to the channel over which the data will next be sent.

With link encryption, the cryptographic key might be common to all nodes in the network—in which case it is easy to establish a communication session between any two nodes, but it is difficult to protect the privacy of the key. Alternatively, each node must know the cryptographic keys of all other nodes with which it communicates—in which case the keys are more secure, but key management is more difficult.

Link encryption reduces expected losses from traffic analysis. With link encryption, the message and its associated source and destination identifiers can be encrypted. Thus, a wiretapper has difficulty determining the identity of the sender and receiver of the message. In addition, frequency and length patterns in data can be masked by maintaining a continuous stream of ciphertext between two nodes.

TABLE 12–2 Controls over Subversive Threats

Type of Attack	*Control*
Release of message contents	Link encryption
	End-to-end encryption
Traffic analysis	Link encryption
Message insertion	Message sequence numbers
Message deletion	Message sequence numbers
Message modification	Stream ciphers
	Error propagation codes
	Message authentication codes
Changed message order	Message sequence numbers
Message duplication	Unique session identifiers
	Message sequence numbers
Denial of message services	Request-response mechanism
Spurious association	Secure authentication

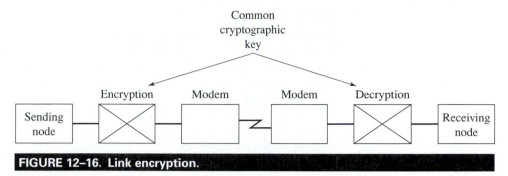

FIGURE 12–16. Link encryption.

Because each node must be able to decrypt a message to determine where it should be forwarded, link encryption cannot protect the integrity of data if a node in the network is subverted. In this light, encryption and decryption should be performed by a tamperproof cryptographic facility. Thus, even if intruders subvert a node in the network, the integrity of cryptographic operations is still protected.

End-to-End Encryption

Link encryption has several limitations (see, further, Voydock and Kent 1983):

1. If an intermediate node in the network is subverted, all traffic passing through the node is exposed. As a result, high costs might have to be incurred to protect the security of each node in the network. For example, security personnel might have to be present, physical barriers might have to be constructed, and regular security reviews might have to be undertaken.
2. Users of a public network might rely on link encryption to protect their data. In this light, the owners of the network could incur high insurance costs to protect themselves against damages resulting from security violations.
3. It can be difficult to work out a transfer-pricing scheme for allocating link encryption costs to users, particularly if some users argue that they do not need protection.

To help overcome these problems, end-to-end encryption can be used. End-to-end encryption protects the integrity of data passing between a sender and a receiver, independently of the nodes the data traverses. Thus, a cryptographic facility must be available to each sender and receiver because each now takes responsibility for implementing cryptographic protection. The sender encrypts data before it is given to the network for transmission to the receiver. The data traverses each node and each communication channel in encrypted form. It is not decrypted until it reaches the receiver.

Although end-to-end encryption reduces expected losses from active or passive attacks when an intermediate node is subverted, it provides only limited protection against traffic analysis. Recall that with end-to-end encryption, intermediate nodes that the data traverses do not possess the key under which the data has been encrypted. If intermediate nodes are to send data over the correct route, therefore, the source and destination identifiers attached to a message must exist in the clear. In this light, link encryption can be used in conjunction with end-to-end encryption to reduce exposures from traffic analysis.

Stream Ciphers

There are two types of ciphers: block ciphers and stream ciphers. With *block* ciphers, fixed-length blocks of cleartext are transformed under a constant fixed-length key (Figure 12–17). The Data Encryption Standard (DES) provides this mode of encryption via its electronic code book (ECB) mode. With *stream* ciphers, however, cleartext is transformed on a bit-by-bit basis under the control of a stream of key bits. The stream can be generated in various ways. A widely used technique, however, is to make the key bit stream a function of an initialization value, an encryption key, and generated ciphertext. Figure 12-18 shows this method as implemented in the DES cipher block chaining (CBC) mode. The cleartext is first partitioned into fixed-length blocks. Next, the first cleartext block is added (modulus 2) to this block. The result is enciphered, and the ciphertext produced is added (modulus 2) to the next cleartext block to be enciphered once more. The process continues iteratively.

Stream ciphers have two important characteristics. First, they make it more difficult to analyze patterns in ciphertext. In block mode, each enciphered block is independent of each other block. A cryptanalyst can examine

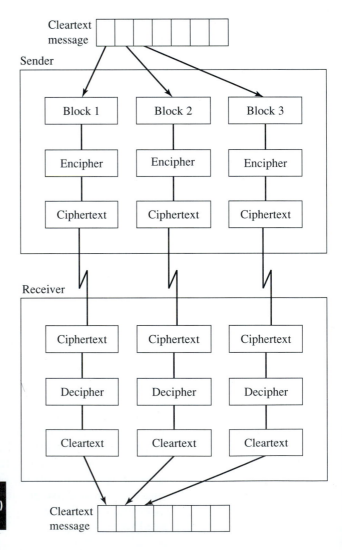

FIGURE 12–17. DES electronic code book (ECB) mode.

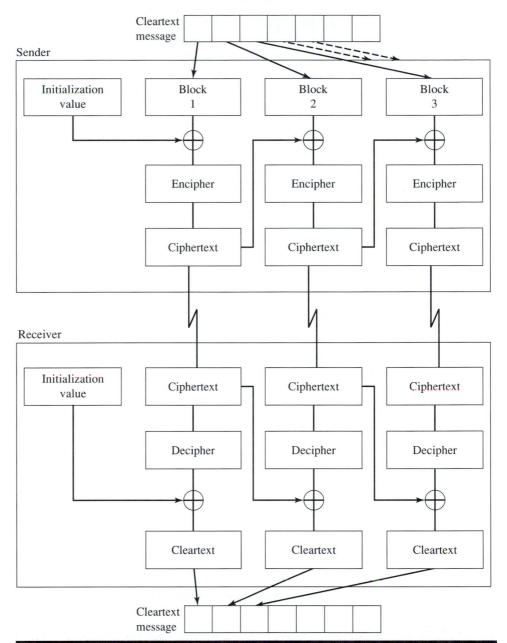

FIGURE 12–18. DES cipher block chaining (CBC) mode.

character frequency patterns, which can lead to the cipher being broken. Stream ciphers, however, create interbit dependencies. Thus, patterns are masked from the cryptanalyst. Second, because interbit dependencies exist, changes to ciphertext propagate to subsequent ciphertext. If data is corrupted via a burst of noise on a line, at least some of the subsequent ciphertext will be unreadable. Similarly, if a wiretapper undertakes an active attack and modifies data in transit, at least some of the subsequent ciphertext will be affected. In this light, stream ciphers reduce expected losses from both active attacks and passive attacks.

Error Propagation Codes

Unfortunately, using stream ciphers alone is not sufficient to prevent all types of message modification. Even if messages are partitioned into fixed-length blocks and the CBC mode of encryption is used, cryptanalysts might still be able to make changes that will not be detected to the order of blocks within messages. This type of attack can also be undertaken successfully on other types of stream ciphers. The procedures to implement the attack are fairly complex, and we do not examine them here. Voydock and Kent (1983) provide an overview, however, of ways they can be undertaken.

To protect the integrity of messages, a suitable error propagation code must be used. The code must be sensitive to the order of bits in a message so that a change to the order of blocks has a high probability of being detected. Several common error propagation codes, such as longitudinal parity checks, are unsuitable for this purpose because cryptanalysts can fairly easily determine changes to the ciphertext that will produce the same error detection code. Peterson and Weldon (1972) describe some error detection codes that are suitable because they are sensitive to bit order. The auditors' primary concern is to see that suitable error propagation codes have been chosen and implemented whenever attacks on message order could produce material losses.

Message Authentication Codes

In electronic funds transfer systems, a control used to identify changes to a message in transit is a message authentication code (MAC). The MAC is calculated by applying the DES algorithm and a secret key to selected data items in a message or to the entire message. Think of a MAC as an encrypted checksum calculated on the basis of some or all of the fields in a message. The MAC is then appended to the message and sent to the receiver, who recalculates the MAC on the basis of the message received to determine whether the calculated MAC and the received MAC are equal. If the calculated MAC and the received MAC are not equal, the message has been altered in some way during transit. The transmitted message could be in the clear, or only selected data items in the message (such as the personal identification number) might be encrypted.

Message Sequence Numbers

Message sequence numbers are used to detect an attack on the order of messages that are transmitted between a sender and a receiver. An intruder could delete messages from a stream of messages, change the order of messages in a stream, or duplicate legitimate messages. In each case the receiver does not obtain messages in the order generated by the sender.

If each message contains a sequence number and the order of sequence numbers is checked, these attacks will not be successful. It must be impossible, however, for the intruder to alter the sequence number in a message. Controls to prevent message modification have been discussed already: stream ciphers, error propagation codes, and message authentication codes. Furthermore, to prevent message duplication (playback), sequence numbers must not be reused during a communication session between a sender and a receiver. A unique identification number must be established for each communication session, and within this identification number each message sequence number must be unique.

Request-Response Mechanisms

A request-response mechanism is used to identify attacks by an intruder aimed at denying message services to a sender and a receiver. Recall that this type of attack is a form of message stream modification whereby the intruder deletes messages passing over a communication line or delays them for an extended period. If the parties to a communication session are not continuously communicating with each other, the receiver cannot detect that a message should have arrived from the sender. The sender might realize that the receiver has not obtained the message because no acknowledgment has been returned by the receiver. In some cases, however, the sender might have no means of notifying the receiver that the communication channel has been broken. For example, in certain high-security applications, the sender might not be able to place a telephone call to the receiver to notify the receiver of the attack.

With a request-response mechanism, a timer is placed with the sender and receiver. The timer periodically triggers a control message from the sender. Because the timer at the receiver is synchronized with the sender, the receiver must respond to show that the communication link has not been broken. Providing that the timing signals can be generated with a pattern that is difficult to determine, the intruder will find it hard to undertake temporary undetected attacks that deny message service. In addition, the intruder must not be able to provide valid responses to the control messages. Otherwise, the sender will believe the channel is still open, and the receiver will be unaware that message services have been denied. Thus, those controls that establish the authenticity of the response (discussed in Chapter 10 and earlier in this chapter) must be applied to the request-response mechanism.

INTERNETWORKING CONTROLS

Internetworking is the process of connecting two or more communication networks together to allow the users of one network to communicate with the users of other networks. The networks connected to each other might or might not employ the same underlying hardware-software platform. In other words, internetworking might be based on either homogeneous networks or heterogeneous networks. The overall set of interconnected networks is called an *internet*. An individual network within an internet is called a *subnetwork*.

Three types of devices are used to connect subnetworks in an internet:

Device	*Functions*
Bridge	A bridge connects similar local area networks (e.g., one token ring network to another token ring network).
Router	A router performs all the functions of a bridge. In addition, it can connect heterogeneous local area networks (e.g., a bus network to a token ring network) and direct network traffic over the fastest channel between two nodes that reside in different subnetworks (e.g., by examining traffic patterns within a network and between different networks to determine channel availability).
Gateway	Gateways are the most complex of the three network connection devices. Their primary function is to perform protocol conversion to allow different types of communication architectures to communicate with one another. The gateway maps the functions performed in an application on one computer to the functions performed by a different application with similar functions on another computer.

Bridges, routers, and gateways perform several useful control functions. First, because they allow the total network to be broken up into several smaller networks, they improve the overall reliability of the network. Failure in a node or communication line within a subnetwork, for example, will not disable all nodes in an internet. Second, for security reasons it might be desirable to keep different types of applications on different subnetworks. For example, high-exposure electronic funds transfer messages might be routed over a high-security, high-cost subnetwork. Low-exposure administrative messages, on the other hand, might be routed over a relatively insecure, low-cost subnetwork. Bridges, routers, and gateways might allow users of an internet to specify the subnetworks they wish their messages to traverse. Third, bridges, routers, and gateways may provide access control mechanisms to restrict access to subnetworks only to authorized users (Popalzai 1996). Not all users in a local area network, for example, may be allowed to access other subnetworks in an internet.

COMMUNICATION ARCHITECTURES AND CONTROLS

So far we have examined the functions and controls performed within the communication subsystem in a somewhat disjointed fashion. In an effort to provide an integrated view of these functions and controls, many people have developed coherent models of the communication subsystem. These models, or *architectures*, classify communication functions into a hierarchy of layers. Protocols for each layer are then defined, which are the set of syntactic, semantic, and timing rules governing the behavior of the components that provide the functions in each layer. Researchers have tried to show how various types of communication controls map onto the different layers in an architecture.

Although a fair number of architectures have been proposed, three that have achieved prominence are the open-systems interconnection (OSI) architecture, IBM's system network architecture (SNA), and the transmission control protocol/internet protocol (TCP/IP) architecture. To illustrate the nature of these architectures and the placement of controls within them, we examine only the OSI model. Stallings (1997) provides a good discussion of the SNA and TCP/IP architectures.

The OSI architecture has been proposed by the International Organization for Standardization (ISO). The purpose of the architecture is to allow heterogeneous hardware/software platforms to communicate with one another across local area networks or wide area networks, providing they conform with the architecture. The architecture has seven layers of functions, each of which has associated controls:

Layer	*Name*	*Functions and Controls*
1	Physical	A hardware layer specifying both the mechanical features (transmission media and connectors) and electromagnetic features (voltage, signal strength, signalling method, amplification, modulation) of the connection between devices and the transmission medium. Receives data from some device and sends an unstructured bit stream over a transmission medium. The network topology (e.g., star) is part of the physical layer.
2	Data link	Primarily a hardware layer. Specifies channel access control method (e.g., HDLC, token ring). Ensures reliable transfer of data across the transmission medium. The bit stream is divided into blocks or frames of data. These blocks are then

Layer	Name	Functions and Controls
		subjected to synchronization, error control, and flow control. Link encryption used at this level.
3	Network	Chooses the physical route through which a message packet is sent through the network. Creates a virtual circuit for the upper layers so they are independent of the data transmission and switching technologies used to connect nodes. Establishes, maintains, and terminates connections between nodes. Ensures correct routing of data through the network.
4	Transport	Ensures reliable end-to-end transfer of data between user processes. Assembly and disassembly of message packets. Provides end-to-end error recovery and flow control. Multiplexing and end-to-end encryption undertaken at this level.
5	Session	Establishes, maintains, and terminates sessions (interactions) between user processes. Identification and authentication undertaken at this level. Might provide a checkpoint mechanism (see Chapter 13) so that recovery can be effected by retransmitting data from the last checkpoint.
6	Presentation	Controls how data appears on a screen. Transforms data to provide a standarized application interface. Encryption and data compression may also be performed at this level.
7	Application	Provides services to users—e.g., file sharing, file transfer, electronic mail. Database concurrency and deadlock controls may be performed at this level (see Chapter 14).

Figure 12–19 shows how two nodes using the OSI architecture communicate with each other via an intermediate node that also uses the OSI architecture. The sending node passes a message it wants to transmit down through the various layers. Hardware, firmware, or software perform the various functions assigned to each layer. When data reaches the physical layer, it is finally entered onto and sent over the transmission medium. Intermediate nodes will perform functions associated with layers 1–3 to ensure that the data is routed accurately, completely, and securely to its correct destination. The receiving node then passes the data it receives up through the various layers until it reappears to users at the application level. In effect, each layer in the sending node communicates with its peer layer in the receiving node (and vice versa)—although the actual transmission of data occurs only at the physical layer level.

Auditors can organize their examination and evaluation of controls in the communication subsystem in terms of the various layers in the communication

FIGURE 12–19. Transmission of data through the OSI layers.

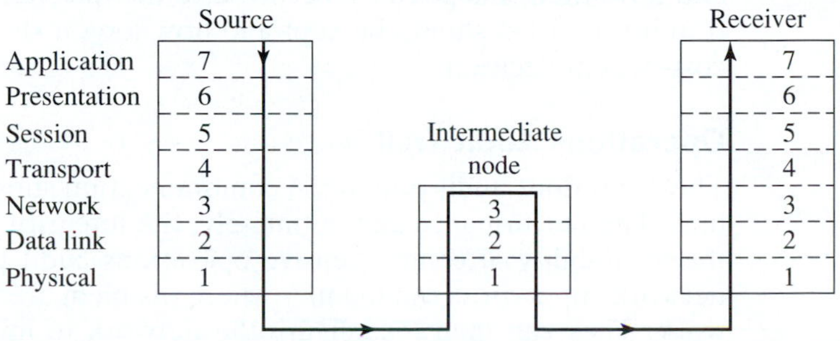

architecture they encounter. Unfortunately, the placement of controls within the various layers of a particular architecture is not always clear-cut. Indeed, the relationship of different controls to different layers is still a research issue with a number of communication architectures. In spite of these difficulties, however, the layers still provide a compelling way of thinking about controls in the communication subsystem.

AUDIT TRAIL CONTROLS

The audit trail in the communication subsystem maintains the chronology of events from the time a sender dispatches a message to the time a receiver obtains the message. With the rapid growth in the use of data communications technology, the audit trail in the communication subsystem has become increasingly important. In an electronic data interchange system, for example, the absence of paper documents to support business transactions might mean that data contained in the audit trail is essential to the resolution of disputes that arise and the enforcement of contracts. Similarly, past messages dispatched via an e-mail system might be subpoenaed in the event of a dispute between parties to an electronic exchange of information.

Accounting Audit Trail

The accounting audit trail must allow a message to be traced through each node in a network. Some examples of data items that might be kept in the accounting audit trail follow:

1. Unique identifier of the source node,
2. Unique identifier of the person or process authorizing dispatch of the message,
3. Time and date at which message dispatched,
4. Message sequence number,
5. Unique identifier of each node in the network that the message traversed,
6. Time and date at which each node in the network was traversed by the message,
7. Unique identifier of the sink node,
8. Time and date at which the message was received by the sink node, and
9. Image of message received at each node traversed in the network.

Given that a message should not be changed as it traverses a node in the network, keeping all this information might seem pointless. Indeed, if a message traverses a public network or interchange network, the owner of the network might not be willing to maintain or supply the audit trail information. Nevertheless, the audit trail information is needed if *(1)* a message is lost in the network or *(2)* a node has been compromised or it has been malfunctioning and unwanted changes have occurred to the message. Nevertheless, what audit trail information should be kept and how long it should be kept as always is a cost-benefit decision.

Operations Audit Trail

The operations audit trail in the communication subsystem is especially important. The performance and, ultimately, the integrity of the network depend on the availability of comprehensive operations audit trail data. Using this data, network supervisors can identify where problem areas are occurring in the network. They can then reconfigure the network to mitigate the impact of these problems. Some examples of data items that might be kept in the operations audit trail follow:

1. Number of messages that have traversed each link,
2. Number of messages that have traversed each node,
3. Queue lengths at each node,
4. Number of errors occurring on each link or at each node,
5. Number of retransmissions that have occurred across each link,
6. Log of errors to identify locations and patterns of errors,
7. Log of system restarts, and
8. Message transit times between nodes and at nodes.

The availability of high-quality network control software is essential to network supervisors being able to make effective use of the operations audit trail (see Chapter 8). Although substantial operations audit trail data might be available, often it is not readily accessible or presented in a form that permits effective decision making. Good network control software will access the relevant operations audit trail data and provide reports that allow network supervisors to maintain or improve the performance of the network.

EXISTENCE CONTROLS

Recovering a communication network if it fails can be problematical. Some components might be complex, and determining the location and nature of a failure is often difficult. The status of the network upon failure also can be hard to assess. Message fragments might be dispersed throughout the network at various stages of processing. Ensuring complete and accurate recovery of these in-flight messages can be difficult. It is also hard to provide backup for all network components. Some might be remote geographically. High costs could be incurred if redundant components are to be provided at these remote locations. Yet the network could be severely disrupted if long lead times are required to recover operations in these remote components.

Some backup and recovery controls that should be implemented in a communication network are discussed earlier in this chapter when network reliability was considered: automatic line speed adjustment by modems based on differing noise levels, modems on private lines having automatic or semiautomatic dial-up capabilities for the public network, choice of a network topology that provides alternative routes between the source node and the sink node, and acquisition and use of high-quality network control software. Some additional backup and recovery controls follow:

1. Where possible, place redundant components (e.g., modems) and spare parts throughout the network.
2. Use equipment with in-built fault diagnosis capabilities.
3. Acquire high-quality test equipment (e.g., data scopes with extensive diagnostic capabilities).
4. Ensure adequate maintenance of hardware and software, especially at remote sites.
5. Ensure that adequate logging facilities exist for recovery purposes, especially where store-and-forward operations must be carried out in the network.

Because recovery can be a highly complex process that must be executed under severe time pressures, it is essential that well-trained, technically competent personnel operate the network. They must be provided with well-documented backup and recovery procedures either for a warm start (partial failure) or for a cold start (total failure). Given that multiple, physically dispersed components might have to be recovered in a coordinated way, a control site must exist for reporting all problems in the network and for managing personnel involved in the recovery process. Network backup and recovery procedures must be practiced regularly.

SUMMARY

The communication subsystem is responsible for transmitting data among all the other subsystems within a system or for transmitting data to or receiving data from another system. The integrity of data within the subsystem can be undermined by impairments in transmission media (attenuation, distortion, and noise), hardware and software component failure, passive subversive threats (release of message contents and traffic analysis), and active subversive threats (insertion, deletion, modification, and duplication of messages, changes to the order of messages, denial of messages services, and establishment of spurious associations).

One way to reduce expected losses from exposures in the subsystem is to choose reliable components. Different types of transmission media vary in terms of their susceptibility to interference and wiretapping. Private conditioned communication lines can be chosen, which are more reliable than public lines. Modems vary in terms of their speed and their ability to accommodate errors on a communication line. Port-protection devices can be used to restrict unauthorized access via the communication subsystem. Multiplexing and concentration techniques can be used to free channel capacity for control purposes.

Two important controls that must be executed within the communication subsystems are line error controls and flow controls. Line errors can be detected via loop checks, parity checks, and cyclic redundancy checks. They can be corrected using forward error correction techniques or retransmission. Flow controls are needed because two nodes in a network could differ in terms of the rate at which they can receive and process data. The simplest form of flow control is stop-and-wait flow control. The sliding-window flow control method is more complex, but it makes better use of the available channel capacity. Line controls and flow controls are combined within the link management protocols exercised over a communication line. Three widely used link protocols are the HDLC, the SDLC, and the ATM protocols.

A network topology specifies the location of nodes within a network, how they will be linked, and the data transmission capabilities of the links between nodes. Four types of topology that are used in local area networks are the bus, tree, ring, and star topologies. From a control viewpoint, each has strengths and weaknesses. Wide area networks can also use tree, ring, and star topologies. Often they use a mesh topology, however, in which conceptually every node can have a point-to-point connection with every other node.

Two different nodes in a network can compete to use the same channel. Access to a channel is controlled via a channel access control method. The methods can use noncontention (centralized or distributed polling) or contention techniques (e.g., carrier sense multiple access with collision detection).

Seven types of control can be used in the communication subsystem to reduce exposures from subversive threats. First, link encryption can be used to protect the integrity of data traversing a communication line between two nodes. Second, end-to-end encryption can be used to protect the integrity of data passing between a sender and a receiver. Third, stream ciphers can be used to make it more difficult to analyze patterns in ciphertext. Fourth, error propagation codes can be used to detect unauthorized changes to blocks of data in a message. Fifth, message authentication codes can be used to identify changes to the content of a message. Sixth, message sequence numbers can be used to identify changes to the order of messages. Seventh, request-response mechanisms can be used to identify subversive attacks that deny message services.

Different types of networks can be connected to each other to form an internet. Bridges are used to connect similar local area networks. Routers are used to connect heterogeneous local area networks. Gateways are used to perform protocol conversions to allow heterogenous networks to be linked. Breaking up an internet into subnetworks has control advantages because different types of controls can be implemented to address the specific needs of the subnetwork.

The functions performed and controls executed within the communication subsystem can be organized within the layers of a communication architecture. Auditors can use an architecture to structure their approach to the examination and evaluation of controls in the communication subsystem. Some major architectures are the International Organization for Standardization's OSI architecture, IBM's SNA, and the TCP/IP architecture.

The audit trail in the communication subsystem maintains the chronology of events from the time a sender dispatches a message to the time a receiver obtains the message. The accounting audit trail must allow a message and its contents to be traced through each node in the network. The operations audit trail must permit the performance of the communication subsystem to be monitored.

Existence controls must allow the communication subsystem to be restored in the event of failure. Where possible, redundancy should be built into a network so alternative paths are available for messages in the event of failure. The network also must be monitored continuously to obtain early warning of problems that may undermine the availability of the network.

Review Questions

12–1 Briefly describe the three major types of exposure in the communication subsystem.

12–2 What is meant by noise on a communication line? What factors affect the amount of noise that exists on a line? What are the effects of noise?

12–3 Briefly distinguish between a passive threat and an active threat to the communication subsystem. Identify each of the following as active threats or passive threats:
   a Traffic analysis
   b Denial of message service
   c Release of message contents
   d Changed message order
   e Message insertion

12–4 From a control viewpoint, do bounded transmission media or unbounded transmission media pose more of a problem? Why?

12–5 What control advantages do private communication lines offer over public communication lines?

12–6 How can modems improve the reliability of the communication subsystem?

12–7 Briefly describe three security functions performed by a port-protection device.

12–8   Briefly explain the difference between multiplexing and concentration techniques. How do they improve the reliability of the communication subsystem?

12–9   Briefly explain the difference between a loop check and redundancy as a means of detecting errors on a communication line. What are the relative advantages and disadvantages of each approach?

12–10 Briefly explain the difference between a parity check and a cyclic redundancy check.

12–11 Give an example of where forward error correcting codes might be chosen in preference to retransmission as a means of error correction.

12–12 What is the purpose of flow controls in the communication subsystem? Briefly explain the difference between the stop-and-wait flow control protocol and the sliding-window flow control protocol.

12–13 What is the purpose of link controls in the communication subsystem?

12–14 What is meant by the topology of a network? List *three* factors that should be considered when choosing a network topology.

12–15 From a control perspective, list the advantages and disadvantages of the following topologies: (a) ring, (b) mesh, and (c) star.

12–16 Briefly explain the function that channel access controls perform within the communication subsystem. What is the difference between polling methods and contention methods as a means of channel access control?

12–17 Briefly describe *two* problems that can arise with token passing techniques as a means of channel access control.

12–18 Why is encryption an important means of protecting the integrity of data passing over public communication lines? Is encryption also useful as a means of protecting data passing over private communication lines?

12–19 Distinguish between link encryption and end-to-end encryption. What are the relative strengths and limitations of link encryption versus end-to-end encryption?

12–20 Distinguish between block ciphers and stream ciphers. What are the relative strengths and limitations of block ciphers versus stream ciphers?

12–21 Explain the nature of a message authentication code (MAC). Why are message authentication codes often used in electronic funds transfer systems?

12–22 Expected losses from which types of threats can be reduced by using message sequence numbers? Why must encryption controls be used in conjunction with message sequence numbers?

12–23 Briefly explain the nature of a request-response mechanism. Why is it unlikely that request-response mechanisms would be used extensively in commercial data communication systems?

12–24 Briefly explain the difference between a bridge, a router, and a gateway. Why are these devices useful from a control viewpoint?

12–25 What is a communication architecture? How is the concept of a communication architecture useful to us as auditors?

12–26 What is the purpose of the accounting audit trail in the communication subsystem? List *four* items that might be contained in the accounting audit trail in the communication subsystem.

12–27 How does the operations audit trail in the communication subsystem assist network supervisors in their decisions on how to reconfigure the network to improve efficiency? List *three* data items that network supervisors might retrieve from the operations audit trail.

12–28 Why is it difficult to provide backup for all components that might be used in a communication network?

12–29 Why is it especially important that operations personnel be well-trained with respect to backup and recovery procedures for a communication network?

Multiple-Choice Questions

12–1 Which of the following statements about transmission impairments is *true*?
a Delay distortion is the weakening of a signal as it traverses some transmission medium
b Digital signals are subject to more attenuation distortion than analog signals
c Amplifiers increase free-space emissions that can be picked up by an inductive wiretap
d Noise is less likely to occur when the data transmission medium is used to its full capacity

12–2 Which of the following conditions is *most likely* to lead to an increase in white noise?
a Faulty switching gear
b Atmospheric conditions
c Poor contacts
d Temperature increases

12–3 Which of the following types of subversive attacks on a communication network is a *passive* attack?
a Message modification
b Denial of message service
c Traffic analysis
d Changed message order

12–4 Which of the following transmission media is *most* resistant to wiretapping?
a Optical fiber
b Satellite microwave
c Twisted-pair wire
d Infrared

12–5 Which of the following transmission media is *most* resistant to interference?
a Radio frequency
b Coaxial cable
c Terrestrial microwave
d Satellite microwave

12–6 As a control, line conditioning is likely to be *least* effective against which of the following threats?
a Noise
b Wiretapping
c Attenuation
d Distortion

12–7 Which of the following usually is *not* a purpose of a modem?
a Reduce line errors caused by noise
b Produce encrypted messages
c Convert digital signals to analog signals
d Increase the speed of data transmission

12–8 Which of the following is *not* a desirable control feature in a modem?
a Dynamic equalization
b Automatic dial-up capabilities
c Multiple transmission speeds
d Attenuation amplification

12–9 Which of the following functions is *unlikely* to be performed by a port-protection device?

    a Forward error correction of line errors that arise through noise and distortion

    b Limiting calls to a host system only to authorized telephone numbers

    c Maintenance of an audit trail of unsuccessful attempts to access the host computer system

    d Elimination of the modem tone that can be detected by autodialers

12–10 Packet switching is an example of a:

    a Multiplexing technique

    b Line conditioning technique

    c Concentration technique

    d Modulation technique

12–11 Which of the following is *not* a control benefit that arises as a result of using concentration techniques in a communication network?

    a There is a reduction in the amount of data available to a wiretapper

    b Messages can be routed over a different path if a link in the network fails

    c More channel capacity is available for backup purposes

    d It is more difficult to disentangle messages passing over a communication channel

12–12 Which of the following error detection controls has the *most* impact on the throughput of a communication line?

    a Horizontal parity check

    b Cyclic redundancy code

    c Vertical parity check

    d Loop check

12–13 Forward error correcting codes are *most likely* to be used to detect line errors with which of the following transmission media?

    a Coaxial cable

    b Infrared

    c Optical fiber

    d Satellite microwave

12–14 The *primary* purpose of flow controls is to:

    a Detect and correct errors on a communication line caused by excessive traffic on the line

    b Regulate the rate at which a node in a communication network sends data to another node

    c Allow two nodes in a network that use different error detection and correction techniques to communicate with each other

    d Reduce the rate at which data is communicated over a line when the level of noise becomes excessive

12–15 In choosing a network topology, maximum reliability can be achieved using a:

    a Star network

    b Ring network

    c Mesh network

    d Multidrop line network

12–16 Which of the following statements about bus topologies versus ring topologies is *false*?

    a Encryption is a more important control in a bus topology compared with a ring topology

    b The taps used in a bus topology introduce attenuation and distortion to a signal, whereas the repeaters used in a ring network do not

    c Failure in the taps used in a bus topology will not bring the network down, whereas failure in the repeaters used in a ring topology will bring the network down

    d A bus is a multipoint topology whereas a ring is a point-to-point topology

12–17 Which of the following statements about star topologies is *false*?

    a A star topology is more reliable than a mesh topology

    b The hub is the most critical node in a star network

    c Servicing and maintenance of a star network is relatively easy

    d Failure in an outlying node in a star network usually will not bring the network down

12–18 Which of the following problems is *unlikely* to undermine the reliability of a token ring local area network?

    a A node could fail to release the token after capturing it to read a message

    b Tokens could be broadcast over the communication line at the same time and a collision may occur

    c The token could return to the sender without the receiver having read the message

    d The token could be corrupted as it traverses a communication line

12–19 Which of the following is an *advantage* of using link encryption?

    a Individual nodes in the network do not have to be protected

    b The exposure that results from compromise of an encryption key is restricted to a single user to whom the key applies

    c It protects messages against traffic analysis

    d The costs of using link encryption can be easily assigned to the users of the network

12–20 End-to-end encryption provides only limited protection against a subversive attack that uses:

    a Message insertion

    b Spurious associations

    c Change of message order

    d Traffic analysis

12–21 A characteristic of a stream cipher is that it:

    a Transforms variable-length blocks of cleartext to ciphertext

    b Uses a constant fixed-length key to produce ciphertext

    c Transforms cleartext on a bit-by-bit basis to ciphertext

    d Produces ciphertext blocks that are independent of one another

12–22 When encryption is used in the communication subsystem, the primary purpose of an error propagation code is to protect against:

    a Release of message contents

    b Spurious associations

    c Change of message order

    d Denial of message services

12–23 A message authentication code is used to protect against:

    a Changes to the content of a message

    b Traffic analysis

    c Release of message contents

    d Exposures that arise when PINs are transmitted in the clear

12–24 Which of the following controls does *not* protect against message sequence numbers being altered?
  a Error propagation codes
  b Cyclic redundancy check
  c Message authentication codes
  d Stream ciphers

12–25 A request-response mechanism is *most* likely to be used in a:
  a System where the receiver and sender are in constant communication with each other
  b Military data communication system where data transmission is spasmodic
  c Commercial data communication system that transmits sensitive data
  d Data communication system that does not use encryption to protect the data being transmitted

12–26 Which of the following is *not* a reason for establishing an internet?
  a To improve the overall reliability of the network
  b To better exercise access controls over the various subnetworks
  c To confine high-exposure messages to particular parts of the network
  d To minimize the high-risk protocol conversion functions that gateways perform

12–27 In the context of the OSI communication architecture, in which of the following layers are encryption controls *unlikely* to be exercised?
  a Presentation
  b Data link
  c Physical
  d Transport

12–28 Which of the following data items is *most likely* to appear in the operations audit trail and not the accounting audit trail for the communication subsystem?
  a Time and date at which the message was dispatched
  b Unique identifier of the source node
  c Queue length at each network node traversed by the message
  d Message sequence number

Exercises and Cases

12–1 You are the external auditor for Centnet Pty. Ltd., a public electronic funds transfer network that operates switches in the capital cities of all states in Australia. Because Centnet has a large number of customers that transmit large volumes of data, it has been cost-effective to link the switches via private communication lines. In addition, Centnet has several customers that use point-of-sale facilities, and the private lines are needed to reduce the occurrence of line errors and speed up data communications traffic.

One day you are called to a meeting with the managing director of Centnet. He informs you that he is considering purchasing some data communications capacity on one of Australia's communication satellites. In particular, he is seeking to establish a link between Sydney and Perth as a backup for the terrestrial link. If the terrestrial link fails, communications can be switched to the satellite so that services to customers can be maintained.

Although his initial investigations indicate that the satellite backup link will be cost-effective, the managing director is concerned that there might be some significant control issues that he has not considered. Because he knows you have recently spent substantial time studying the implications of satellite communications for auditing, he asks you to advise him on any control matters that he should take into account. In addition, he is concerned about any implications of the proposed move for the audit of Centnet, especially any increased costs that will occur.

Required: Write a brief report for the managing director advising him of the effects of his proposal to use satellite communications as backup for the Perth–Sydney link on (a) controls, and (b) the audit.

12–2 Centnet Pty. Ltd. is a public electronic funds transfer network that operates switches in the capital cities of all states in Australia (see case 12–1). Because much of the data transmitted throughout the network is sensitive, the data must be encrypted to preserve its privacy and to prevent and detect any unauthorized alterations to the data.

To implement encryption facilities throughout the network, Centnet uses secure encryption devices. These devices are placed at each end of a communication line. They store the encryption key, and they perform encryption and decryption functions. Before a new customer can use the network, Centnet must install a black box at the customer's site. Thus, when the customer transmits data to a Centnet switch, it is encrypted by the black box before transmission. Similarly, when the customer receives data from a Centnet switch, it is decrypted before it is processed on the customer's computer.

Each customer in the network chooses his or her own encryption key. During the initial installation of a customer on the network, the customer is asked to generate randomly a 16-digit key. The customer is advised strongly to generate the key as two separate 8-digit parts. Each part should be known only by one customer employee, that is, no customer employee should be privy to the full key. When the key has been generated, each part should be securely stored at different locations by the customer.

To install the key in the black boxes, the two customer employees who know the separate parts of the key must attend a Centnet office. The key is installed using a secure terminal to which a black box is first attached. Behind closed doors, one customer employee enters the first part of the key into the secure terminal. After the entry is completed, the second customer employee enters the second part of the key in the same manner. Thus, Centnet employees do not know the keys entered by customers, nor does any customer employee know the full key.

After key entry has been completed, the contents of the black box are copied securely into two other black boxes. Thus, three black boxes ultimately hold the encryption key. One is then installed at the Centnet switch, the second is installed at the customer site, and the third is kept for backup purposes.

Required: You have just been hired as the external auditor of Centnet. As a basis for undertaking your first audit, write a brief report outlining (a) the exposures you will consider in your evaluation of the key management system and (b) the tests you will undertake to evaluate the reliability of controls within the key management system.

12–3 During 1984–85, the credit union industry in Australia considered various ways of improving the electronic funds transfer services that it offered to its members. Most credit unions already provided automatic teller machines (ATMs) for their members to use. The ATMs were connected only to the local mainframe machine, however, at the credit union's head office. Thus, members could transact business only at an ATM owned by their credit union. If a member traveled elsewhere within Australia, therefore, credit union services were limited.

In an attempt to remedy this situation, many credit unions decided to connect their ATMs to a public electronic funds transfer network. In addition, they agreed to share ATM facilities throughout Australia. In principle, therefore, a member could go to any ATM in Australia owned by a credit union, use their membership card to gain access to the ATM, and carry out deposit or withdrawal transactions. Because the ATM was controlled by the public electronic funds transfer system, a switch in the system would identify the credit union to which the member belonged and route the transaction to the member's own credit union computer for approval and processing. Although the topology of the public electronic funds transfer network changed from time to time in light of cost-benefit considerations, Figure 12–20 shows one configuration that was used.

To illustrate processing, assume that you belonged to the XYZ credit union in Brisbane. If you wanted money while you were visiting Sydney, you would go to any ATM connected to the credit union network. Using your membership card, you would activate the ATM, enter your PIN, and then key in a withdrawal transaction. The ATM would then send the transaction to a switch in the public electronic funds transfer network which, in turn, would route the transaction to the XYZ credit union computer in Brisbane for approval and processing. The XYZ credit union computer would identify and authenticate you, examine whether you had sufficient funds in your account to cover the withdrawal amount, and send a message back to the switch either approving or denying withdrawal of the funds. The switch would then send a message to the ATM that you had used to initiate the transaction.

Required: Identify *four* exposures that arise as a result of the shared ATM configuration. Identify some controls that you believe should be present to reduce expected losses from these exposures to an acceptable level. Note, do *not* list exposures that existed before the use of the shared ATM configuration.

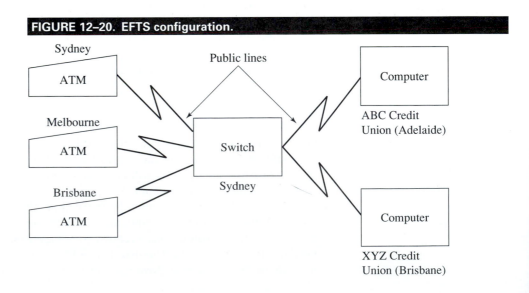

FIGURE 12–20. EFTS configuration.

12–4 To provide more extensive services to their customers, financial institutions in some countries are becoming increasingly involved in using interchange network facilities. In an interchange network environment, one network agrees to receive data from and to pass on the data to another network. For example, a group of financial institutions connected to a common communications network may agree to have their network connected to a second communications network that services another group of financial institutions. Communications between the networks will occur across a gateway switch. In this way, the facilities offered by both groups of financial institutions can be used by the customers of any institution that is a member of either group. For example, a customer of a financial institution in one group can use the ATM facilities of a financial institution in the other group (see case 12–3). The network to which the transaction receiving institution belongs will then route the transaction to the gateway switch, which, in turn, will route the transaction to the customer's own financial institution. A transaction authorization or denial message will then be routed back via both networks to the transaction receiving institution.

A significant problem with interchange network environments is the reliance that each individual network in the interchange must place on the reliability of controls in each other network in the interchange. If controls are weak in one network, the integrity of data in all other networks participating in the interchange is at risk. For example, if encryption controls in one member network are weak, the PINs of the customers of financial institutions belonging to other member networks could be compromised. Aside from the possible monetary losses, the damage done to the goodwill of each financial institution that participates in the interchange may be irreparable.

Required: Assume you are the external auditor for a financial institution belonging to a network that is about to be connected to another network in an interchange environment. If the integrity of data in your client's systems is partially dependent on the reliability of controls in other institutions and networks that are not your client's, how will you formulate an audit opinion? Note: It is unrealistic to expect that other institutions and networks will allow you to visit them to collect evidence on the reliability of their controls.

12–5 You are the partner-in-charge of information systems auditing for a large public accounting firm. One of your clients is a major insurance company that is a mature user of computer-based information systems. The company has its headquarters in Minneapolis, but it has offices scattered throughout the United States. You receive an invitation from the chairman of the company's audit committee to participate in a meeting relating to the company's proposed move to distributed information systems. The company is contemplating distributing both its database and its processing.

The primary reason for the meeting is a debate that has arisen between the vice president of internal audit and the vice president of information systems about whether the move to distributed information systems is beneficial from a control perspective. The vice president of information systems argues that the major security problem facing the company is the risk of wiretapping by unknown parties. Substantial information is sent to the head office via different forms of transmission media from terminals located in the company's offices. Similarly, the head office sends substantial information to its various remote offices. He argues that a distributed information system will minimize the amount of information that must be communicated, thereby reducing the expected losses from data integrity violations. The vice president of internal audit argues, on the other hand, that the primary security problems are likely to arise from within the company in the form of unauthorized actions by employees. He argues a single centralized site is much easier to control.

Required: The chair of the audit committee asks you to prepare for him a report outlining your own feelings on this matter. He also asks you to identify the types of information the committee should have to obtain to try to resolve the debate.

Answers to Multiple-Choice Questions

12–1	c	**12–8**	d	**12–15**	c	**12–22**	c
12–2	d	**12–9**	a	**12–16**	a	**12–23**	a
12–3	c	**12–10**	c	**12–17**	a	**12–24**	b
12–4	a	**12–11**	a	**12–18**	b	**12–25**	b
12–5	b	**12–12**	d	**12–19**	c	**12–26**	d
12–6	b	**12–13**	d	**12–20**	d	**12–27**	c
12–7	b	**12–14**	b	**12–21**	c	**12–28**	c

REFERENCES

Abrams, Marshall D., and Harold J. Podell (1987), *Tutorial: Computer and Network Security.* Los Alamitos, CA: IEEE Computer Society Press.

Abrams, Marshall D., and Harold J. Podell (1995), "Local Area Networks," in Marshall D. Abrams, Sushil Jajodia, and Harold J. Podell, eds., *Information Security: An Integrated Collection of Essays.* Los Alamitos, CA: IEEE Computer Society Press, 385–404.

Berson, T. A., and T. Beth (eds.) (1989), *Local Area Network Security.* Berlin: Springer-Verlag.

Chao, Joseph C. (1990), "Interception Controls of Data Communication Systems," *Journal of Information Systems* (Spring), 69–80.

Cooper, James Arlin (1989), *Computer & Communications Security: Strategies for the 1990s.* New York: McGraw-Hill.

Crowell, David A. (1993), "PBX Security," *The EDP Auditor Journal*, II, 37–46.

Davidson, Robert P., and N. J. Muller (1990), *LANs to WANs: Network Management in the 1990s.* Norwood, MA: Artech House.

Davies, D. W., and W. L. Price (1989), *Security for Computer Networks: An Introduction to Data Security in Teleprocessing and Electronic Funds Transfer*, 2d ed. Chichester: John Wiley & Sons.

Denning, Dorothy E. (1982), *Cryptography and Data Security.* Reading, MA: Addison-Wesley.

Ewer, Sid R., Harold E. Wills, and Richard L. Nichols (1993), "How Safe Are Your Data Transmissions?" *Journal of Accountancy* (September), 66–70.

Ford, Warwick, and Michael S. Baum (1997), *Secure Electronic Commerce: Building the Infrastructure for Digital Signatures and Encryption.* Upper Saddle River, NJ: Prentice-Hall.

Gallegos, Frederick, and Thomas R. Halsell (1991), "An Overview of Microcomputer Network Controls and Security," in *Data Center Operations Management.* New York: Auerbach.

——— and ——— (1993a), "Microcomputer Network Controls and Security: Part 1," *Data Security Management.* New York: Auerbach.

——— and ——— (1993b), "Microcomputer Network Controls and Security: Part 2," *Data Security Management.* New York: Auerbach.

Gasser, Morrie (1988), *Building a Secure Computer System.* New York: Van Nostrand Reinhold.

Humphreys, Ted (1995), "Electronic Data Interchange (EDI) Messaging Security," in Marshall D. Abrams, Sushil Jajodia, and Harold J. Podell, eds., *Information Security: An Integrated Collection of Essays.* Los Alamitos, CA: IEEE Computer Society Press, 423–438.

Institute of Internal Auditors Research Foundation (1991), *Systems Auditability and Control: Module*

8: Telecommunications. Altamonte Springs, FL: Institute of Internal Auditors Research Foundation.

Kovacich, Gerald L. (1996), "Establishing a Network Security Programme," *Computers & Security*, 15(6), 486–498.

Lamb, Jason, Stanley R. Jarocki, and Ana M. Seijas (1991), *NetWare Security: Configuring and Auditing a Trusted Environment*. Provo, UT: Novell.

Leiman, Amin, and Martin Miller (1993), "Security of Wireless Local Area Networks," in *Data Security Management*. New York: Auerbach.

Meyer, Carl H., and Stephen M. Matyas (1982), *Cryptography: A New Dimension in Computer Data Security*. New York: John Wiley & Sons.

McCarthy, Linda (1998), *Intranet Security — Stories from the Trenches*. Upper Saddle River, NJ: Prentice-Hall.

Nelson, Karen (1992), "Auditing a Telecommunications System—A Primer," *The EDP Auditor Journal*, II, 61–76.

Peterson, W., and E. Weldon (1972), *Error Correcting Codes*, 2d ed. Cambridge, MA: The MIT Press.

Popalzai, Azam (1996), "Internetworking Security," *EDPACS* (July), 1–13.

Rotenberg, Marc (1993), "Communications Privacy: Implications for Network Design," *Communications of the ACM* (August), 61–68.

Russell, Selwyn (1995), "Avoiding an Impersonation Attack on a Communications Network," *EDPACS* (July), 1–16.

Seberry, J., and J. Pieprzyk (1989), *Cryptography: An Introduction to Computer Security*. Sydney: Prentice-Hall.

Stallings, William (1990), *Tutorial: Local Area Network Technology*, 3d ed. Los Alamitos, CA: IEEE Computer Society.

——— (1995), *Network and Internetwork Security: Principles and Practice*. Upper Saddle River, NJ: Prentice-Hall.

——— (1997), *Data and Computer Communications*, 5th ed. Upper Saddle River, NJ: Prentice-Hall.

——— (1998), *High Speed Networks: TCP/IP and ATM Design Principles*. Upper Saddle River, NJ: Prentice-Hall.

——— and Richard Van Slyke (1998), *Business Data Communications*, 3d ed. Upper Saddle River, NJ: Prentice-Hall.

Voydock, V. L., and S. T. Kent (1983), "Security Mechanisms in High-Level Network Protocols," *Computing Surveys* (June), 135–171.

Processing Controls

Chapter Outline

Chapter Key Points

■ The processing subsystem is responsible for computing, sorting, classifying, and summarizing data. The major components in the processing subsystem are the central processor on which programs are executed, the real or virtual memory in which program instructions and data are stored, the operating system that manages system resources, and the application programs that execute instructions to achieve specific user requirements.

■ Four types of controls are used to reduce expected losses from errors and irregularities associated with central processors. First, errors in processors can be detected via parity checks or instruction validity checks. If the errors are transient, they can be corrected by attempting to execute failed instructions again. Second, to prevent irregularities, privileged instructions can be executed only if the processor is in a special supervisor state. Third, timing controls can be used to prevent the processor remaining in an endless loop because of a program error. Fourth, processor components can be replicated to allow processing to continue in the event that a processor component fails.

■ Two types of controls are used to reduce expected losses from errors and irregularities associated with real memory. First, memory errors can be detected via parity checks and Hamming codes. Hamming codes also allow errors to be corrected. Second, access controls, which are implemented via boundary registers, can be used to ensure one process does not gain unauthorized access to the real memory assigned to another process.

■ Virtual memory exists when the addressable storage space is larger than the available real memory space. Two types of controls can be exercised over blocks of virtual memory. First, the addressing mechanism should check that the memory reference is within the bounds of the block allocated to the process. Second, an access control mechanism should check to see that the actions a process wants to exercise on a block are within its allowed set of privileges.

■ A reliable operating system achieves five goals: (a) It protects itself from user processes; (b) it protects users from one another; (c) it protects users from themselves; (d) it protects itself from itself; and (e) it brings operations to an orderly halt in the event of environmental failure.

■ There are four types of threats to operating system integrity: (a) Privileged personnel abuse their powers; (b) would-be penetrators deceive privileged personnel into giving them special powers; (c) special devices are used to detect electromagnetic radiation, emit electromagnetic radiation, or wiretap communication lines; and (d) would-be penetrators interact with an operating system to determine and exploit a flaw in the system.

■ Operating system integrity can be breached via two types of covert channel. First, a process can communicate confidential information to another process by changing the values of any state variables in the system (e.g., a file name). Second, a process can communicate confidential information to another process by changing the time that the system takes to complete a function.

■ Operating system flaws arise for two reasons. First, the access control policy designed for the system is defective. Second, the access control policy is implemented incorrectly in the operating system.

■ To improve the design and implementation of the security features in an operating system, reference monitors are sometimes used. A reference monitor is an abstract mechanism that checks each request by a subject to use an object complies with a security policy. A reference monitor is implemented via a security kernel, which is a mechanism supported by either hardware, firmware, or software.

■ Because operating systems are complex, critical pieces of software, they need to be carefully designed and implemented. Top-down design and structured programming principles should be followed. The system should be designed and specified as a hierarchy of layers corresponding to different levels of abstraction of the functions to be performed.

■ Several different organizations and countries have specified criteria that can be used to design, implement, and evaluate operating system integrity. Perhaps the best-known criteria are those specified by the U.S. Department of Defense. Using these criteria, operating systems are assigned to one of four categories: (a) Division D—those that fail to meet the criteria of a higher division; (b) Division C—those that support discretionary access control; (c) Division B—those that support mandatory access control; and (d) Division A—those that use formal methods to support specification, design, modelling, and analysis of the system.

■ Application software can exercise three levels of checks in the processing subsystem: (a) field checks, which evaluate whether field overflow or out-of-range values have occurred; (b) record checks, which evaluate whether the contents of a field are reasonable or whether a field has the correct sign; and (c) file checks, which employ crossfooting and control totals to check overall processing is accurate and complete.

■ The reliability of application software can be improved if programmers use good programming style in the software they write. They should (a) handle rounding correctly when the level of precision required for an arithmetic calculation is less than the level of precision actually calculated; (b) print run-to-run control totals to allow users to check the accuracy and completeness of application program processing; (c) minimize human intervention in providing parameter values to determine the type of processing to be undertaken; (d) understand hardware/software numerical hazards when writing programs that undertake complex numerical calculations; (e) use redundant routines to cross-check the accuracy of complex numerical calculations; and (f) avoid closed routines that assume the existence of a value when the tests for all other values fail.

■ The accounting audit trail in the processing subsystem must allow processing to be traced and replicated. If transactions are triggered by some event—e.g., inventory falls below a reorder point—the audit trail must show the event that triggered the transaction and the nature of the processing undertaken as a result.

■ Of all subsystems, perhaps the most extensive operations audit trail is maintained in the processing subsystem. Logging facilities in the operating system can be used to record (a) resource consumption data, (b) security-sensitive events, (c) hardware malfunctions, and (d) user-specified events. Special software is often available to interrogate the operations audit trail.

■ An important existence control in the processing subsystem is a checkpoint/restart facility. Checkpoint/restart facilities allow programs to be reestablished at some prior, valid intermediate point in their processing and restarted from that point. Data does not have to be reprocessed from scratch. Careful control must be exercised over checkpoint/restart logs, however, because unauthorized changes to a log can result in integrity breaches.

INTRODUCTION

The processing subsystem is responsible for computing, sorting, classifying, and summarizing data. Its major components are the central processor in which programs are executed, the real or virtual memory in which program instructions and data are stored, the operating system that manages system resources, and the application programs that execute instructions to achieve specific user requirements.

Historically, most auditors have been concerned about the reliability of application program processing. Few have been concerned, however, about the reliability of central processors, real memory, virtual memory, and operating systems. Perhaps auditors have lacked the knowledge to be able to evaluate competently the reliability of these processing subsystem components. Perhaps they have believed these components are highly reliable anyway and accordingly warrant little audit attention.

In this chapter we examine controls associated with central processors, real memory, virtual memory, and operating systems. Auditors need to understand the types of controls that can be exercised over these processing subsystem components. Otherwise, they cannot evaluate what exposures are covered by controls within a particular computer system and what exposures remain. We also review various application program controls, audit trail controls, and existence controls that can be exercised in the processing subsystem.

PROCESSOR CONTROLS

The central processing unit is the most important resource to allocate in a computer system. It executes program instructions that are fetched from primary memory. The processor has three components (Figure 13–1): (a) a control unit, which fetches programs from memory and determines their type; (b) an arithmetic and logical unit, which performs operations, like addition and a Boolean "OR," that are needed to be able to execute instructions; and (c) registers, which are small high-speed memories that the processor uses to store temporary results and control information such as the address of the next instruction to be executed. The processor is connected to main memory and input/output devices via a high-speed bus.

Four types of controls that can be used to reduce expected losses from errors and irregularities associated with central processors are (a) error detection and correction, (b) multiple execution states, (c) timer controls, and (d) component replication. The following subsections provide an overview of each type of control.

Error Detection and Correction

Processors are highly reliable components in a computer system. Auditors usually can have substantial confidence in their working properly. Nonetheless, occasionally processors malfunction. The causes are factors like design errors, manufacturing defects, damage, fatigue, electromagnetic interference, and ionizing radiation. The failure might be transient (it disappears after a short period), intermittent (it reoccurs periodically), or permanent (it does not correct with time). Transient and intermittent failures usually occur more frequently

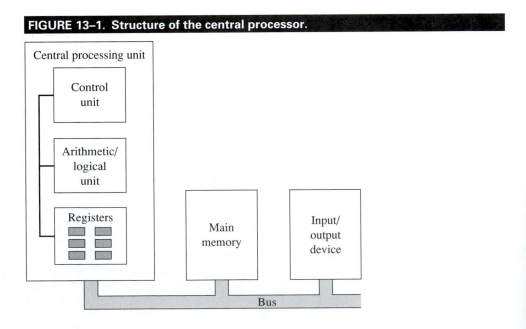

FIGURE 13–1. Structure of the central processor.

than permanent failures. Moreover, they tend to be more difficult to diagnose because they disappear after an error has happened.

One problem that can occur in the processor is that the control unit might fetch an instruction from main memory that it finds is not within the set of instructions it "knows" how to execute. This outcome might occur, for example, because the bit pattern representing the instruction has been corrupted in some way. The control unit can refetch the instruction (perhaps multiple times) and evaluate once again whether it is within the valid set. If the error is transient or intermittent, retries might be successful. Otherwise, the processor will have to halt and report the error.

A second problem that can occur is that execution of an instruction fails. Various types of codes can be used, for example, to detect errors that originate in the arithmetic and logic unit. If the error is transient or intermittent, reexecution of the instruction can result in a successful outcome. Otherwise, the processor must halt and report the error.

A third problem that can occur is that data in a register is corrupted. Simple parity checks are often used to detect an error in a register. These checks will succeed, providing an odd number of bits are corrupted. If an even number of bits are corrupted, pairs of corrupted bits will compensate one another and the check will fail. If an error is detected, various types of error correction strategies might be used. For example, the processor might refetch and reexecute the instruction.

Multiple Execution States

Instructions usually are invoked sequentially in the central processor by increasing order of memory address. Instructions can be skipped or repeated, however, using special branching instructions that cause the processor to execute an instruction that is not the next in sequence by memory address. In this way a program can call subroutines, undertake logical tests, and perform loops. Similarly, the operating system can transfer use of the processor to another program residing elsewhere within memory.

Breaks in the strict sequence of executing instructions by increasing order of memory address also occur as a result of interrupts. *Interrupts* are special events that cause the processor to halt and to transfer control to the operating system. They are triggered by hardware or software to indicate some situation has occurred that requires functions to be performed by an *interrupt service routine*.

For example, a process (a program in execution) might want to write data to a disk. For various reasons, usually the process is not permitted to write data directly to the disk. For example, we do not want the process to have the capability of deliberately or accidentally writing data to an unauthorized area on the disk, thereby overwriting another user's data. As a result, to write data to a disk, the process is forced to issue a system call that leads to an interrupt. The processor halts when the interrupt occurs and invokes the operating system. The operating system then determines the nature of the interrupt (a disk write request), saves the state of the process that has requested data be written to disk, and invokes the appropriate interrupt service routine. The interrupt service routine will then write the data to disk on behalf of the process. When it is done, it will in turn issue an interrupt that causes the processor to halt and to invoke the operating system. The operating system will then restore the original process that requested the data be written to disk. The process can then continue its work.

Processors often restrict the set of instructions they will execute for a process depending upon the *state* that applies to the process. For example, from a security perspective an instruction that causes the system to load a register with a new value is critical. It could be used by a process to change the contents of a boundary register to enable the process to gain unauthorized access to memory locations belonging to another process. Accordingly, use of this instruction needs to be restricted to trusted processes.

Many processors operate on the basis of two states to determine whether they will execute an instruction: *(1)* a *supervisor state* for privileged users, such as the operating system, that allows any instruction to be executed and *(2)* a *problem state* that typically applies to user programs in which only a restricted set of instructions can be used. The processor determines the state of the program it is executing by referencing some type of secure indicator such as a privilege state bit. This bit is set by a trusted process (or the processor itself) when transitions between states occur. For example, if a user process issues a supervisor call, the trusted process hands control of the processor over to the operating system and sets the privilege state bit to "on." When the operating system returns control to the user program, the trusted process reinstates the user process in the processor and sets the privilege state bit to "off."

To illustrate how this control works, consider the example we examined previously in which a user process wanted to write data to a disk. The processor would not permit the process to write data to the disk controller's registers because the user process is not executing in supervisor state. When the user process made a system call, however, the resulting interrupt would cause the trusted process to switch the privilege state bit "on." The interrupt service routine could then do its work of writing to the disk because it is in supervisor state. When the trusted process returned control to the user process, it would turn the privilege state bit "off." The user process is thereby prevented from loading data into the disk controller's registers that would cause the disk to write data to addresses that have not been assigned to the user process.

Some computer systems now use more than two execution states to assess the legitimacy of an instruction. For example, a *multiple-state machine* might have a kernel state, a supervisor state, and a problem state. The *kernel state* is the most trusted state. It is reserved for a small nucleus or core of the operating system that performs the most sensitive functions. (We examine the concept of a kernel again later in this chapter.) In the conduct of the auditors' work, however, they should determine the number of and nature of the execution states enforced by the processor. This information is important because it will allow auditors to determine whether user processes will be able to carry out unauthorized activities, such as gaining access to sensitive data maintained in memory regions assigned to the operating system or other user processes.

Timing Controls

A problem that can arise with the processor is that a user program can get stuck in an infinite loop. In the absence of some type of control, the program will retain use of the processor and prevent other programs from undertaking their work. The operating system will simply sit and wait for the user program to issue a system call. Because no interrupt occurs, the operating system will wait indefinitely.

A control used to prevent this situation occurring is a *timer*. A timer allows a user program to run for a fixed time period. If the user program has not issued a system call before the time period has elapsed, the timer will generate an interrupt to return control to the operating system. The operating system must then decide whether to allocate another time slice to the user program. If too many time periods elapse without the user program issuing a system call, at some point the operating system will terminate the program and generate an error message.

Component Replication

In some cases, processor failure can result in significant losses. For example, the processor might support a safety-critical application such as an airplane navigation system or a nuclear reactor's control system. Even if lives will not be lost through processor failure, however, substantial disruption and loss of customer goodwill can result. For example, customers will become disgruntled quickly if an electronic funds system or an airline reservation system goes down even for a short period. For some types of applications, therefore, component replication strategies are used to mask the effects of processor failure. The losses from failure outweigh the costs of replication.

Two types of component replication strategies involve use of multiple processors (Siewiorek 1990) (Figure 13–2). First, in a *multicomputer* architecture, uniprocessors, which are composed of a processor, memory, and input/output devices, are replicated and connected to one another via a high-speed backplane. Each uniprocessor has its own copy of the operating system. Second, in a *multiprocessor* architecture, the processor is replicated, but

FIGURE 13–2. Fault tolerance through component replication.

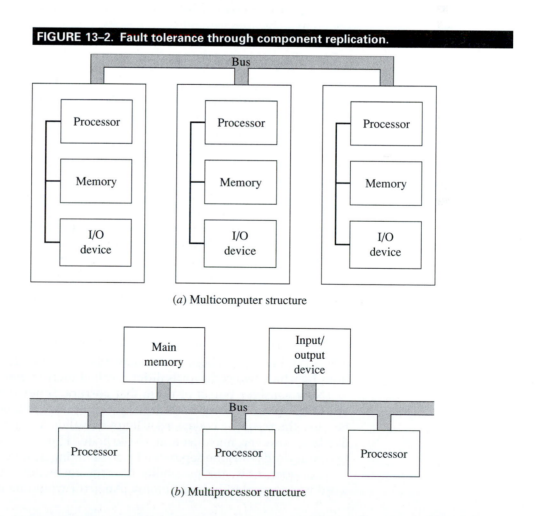

(*a*) Multicomputer structure

(*b*) Multiprocessor structure

memory and input/output devices are shared. All processors have equal access to the shared resources.

Redundant processors allow errors to be detected and corrected. For example, the outputs of two processors operating in lockstep can be compared to determine whether an error has occurred. If their outputs are not the same, an error has arisen, although the processor that is in error will not be known. If three or more processors exist, some type of voting procedure can be used to designate which processors have functioned correctly when an error is detected. For example, the processor that produces a different output in a three-processor system will be the processor deemed to be in error.

If processor failure is permanent in multicomputer or multiprocessor architectures, the system might reconfigure itself to isolate the failed processor. An engineer or technician can then replace the failed processor while the other processors continue to process the workload. The system will then reconfigure itself once again when the replacement processor has been installed.

REAL MEMORY CONTROLS

The real memory of a computer system comprises the fixed amount of primary storage in which programs or data must reside for them to be executed or referenced by the central processor. Controls over real memory seek to detect and correct errors that occur in memory cells and to protect areas of memory assigned to a program from illegal access by another program.

Error Detection and Correction

In the same way that the operation of processors can be corrupted by factors like electromagnetic interference and deterioration, the contents of real memory cells also can be corrupted. For this reason, many computer systems employ controls to detect and correct errors in real memory.

The simplest type of control used to detect errors in a memory cell is a parity bit. Each time the contents of the cell are referenced, the parity of the contents is computed and compared with the stored parity bit. If the computed and the stored parity bit differ, an error is signaled. Recall, simple parity bits will detect errors only when an odd number of bits have been corrupted.

Many computer systems also employ parity-based Hamming codes (named after their developer, Richard Hamming) to detect and correct errors in real memory. To get an intuitive grasp for the nature of Hamming codes, consider the following two eight-bit valid codewords that can be stored in a memory cell:

$$10101000$$
$$10010110$$

Note that the two codewords differ by five bits. Moreover, assume no codewords "in between" these two codewords are valid. The number of bit positions by which two codewords differ is called their *Hamming distance*.

Now consider bursts of noise that corrupt either one, two, three, or four bits in these codewords. Each of these corruptions will be detected as an error because the resulting codeword will not be valid. A burst of noise that corrupts five bits, however, may result in a valid code. Thus to detect d single-bit errors, two codewords must be separated by a Hamming distance of $d + 1$.

Consider, now, the possibility of error correction. Assume the first codeword was corrupted by one bit only. An error would be detected. Moreover, it is fairly straightforward to determine that the resulting invalid codeword is "closest" to the first codeword (they differ only by one bit position). Thus, we would correctly conclude that the correct codeword prior to the burst of noise was the first and not the second. Similarly, if a burst of noise corrupted two bits in the first codeword, again we would conclude correctly that the first codeword was the correct codeword because it is closest to the invalid codeword.

When a burst of noise corrupts three bits, however, we are in trouble. The corrupted codeword is now equidistant from the first and second codewords. If we simply try to guess the correct codeword, we have a 50 percent chance of being wrong. Moreover, when a burst of noise corrupts three or four bits, we will still identify an error has occurred. We will wrongly conclude, however, that the second codeword is the correct codeword. More generally, to correct d single-bit errors, we need a Hamming distance of $2d + 1$ between codewords.

Other types of codes can be used to detect and correct errors in memory (see, e.g., Fujiwara and Pradhan 1990). Many computer systems use Hamming code–based chips, however, to support fast, inexpensive single-bit error correction and double-bit error detection in memory (codewords separated by a Hamming distance of three).

Access Controls

Early computer systems required real memory to be allocated contiguously to a single user. For the period of processing, only the user's application program and the operating system resided in memory. To prevent the user's program from corrupting the operating system, a single boundary register was implemented in hardware in the central processing unit (Figure 13–3). Each time the user's program referenced a memory location, the processor checked to ensure that the memory cell was not within the locations assigned to the operating system. When a user program needed to access operating system facilities—for example, input/output facilities—a supervisor call instruction was issued.

For two reasons, most computer systems now allow multiple jobs to reside in real memory. First, single-user systems use machine resources inefficiently. For example, if a user program is waiting for disk input/output operations to be completed, both the central processor and the user program will be idle. The disk input/output operations will be under the control of the disk controller, and the

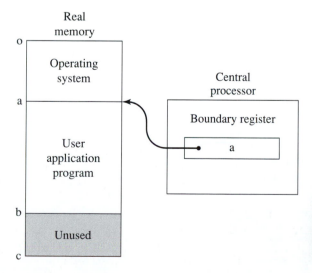

FIGURE 13–3. Real memory protection in a single-user, contiguous storage allocation system.

operating system will be waiting for an interrupt from the controller to indicate when input/output operations are complete. To overcome these inefficiencies, many computer systems now allow multiple jobs to reside in real memory at any one time. One job can then take advantage of the time when another job is idle.

Second, many personal computer systems allow only one job to be executed at any time, but nevertheless they still allow multiple jobs to be present in real memory at the one time. Users want to be able to switch rapidly from one application to another. For example, they might want to transfer work completed in a graphics application package to a word-processing application package.

If a computer system allows multiple jobs to reside in real memory at the one time, real memory can be assigned to jobs on a contiguous or noncontiguous basis. If real memory is allocated contiguously, a set of boundary registers can be used to protect the operating system and the various jobs. In Figure 13–4, for example, one boundary register contains the lower memory boundary of the active job, and another contains the upper memory boundary. Alternatively, one boundary register can store the lower memory boundary, and another can store an offset to indicate the size of the memory partition assigned to the active job. Hardware protection mechanisms in the processor ensure that any memory reference by the active program is confined to its allocated partition.

FIGURE 13–4. Real memory protection in a multiuser, contiguous storage allocation system.

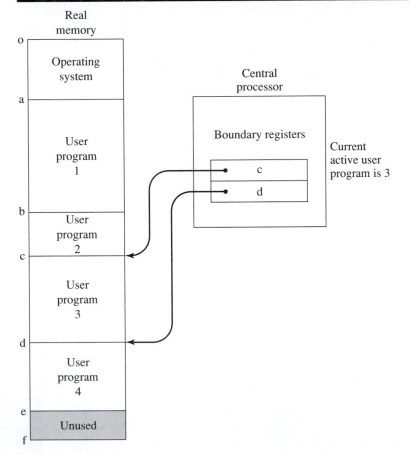

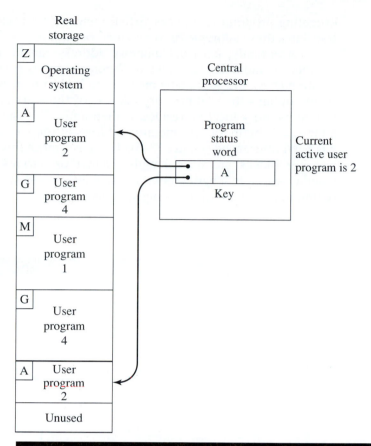

FIGURE 13–5. Real memory protection using locks and keys in a multiuser, noncontiguous storage allocation system.

If a noncontiguous storage allocation system is used, lock-and-key mechanisms can be employed to protect the areas of real memory assigned to a program. In Figure 13–5, for example, the operating system assigns user program 2 a key called A to unlock the various areas of real memory assigned to the program. Without the key, a program cannot access a memory location in the area. Sometimes a hierarchy of keys can be used whereby some keys can unlock several different areas of memory. For example, the operating system can be assigned a key called Z that will unlock any area of memory.

Control can be extended to each memory location if a location is "tagged" with extra descriptive information. For example, the tag can be used to indicate that the location contains data and not an instruction, or that data is an integer and not a real number. In this way, the processor avoids errors because it does not treat data as an instruction or vice versa, or it does not attempt to undertake arithmetic operations in mixed mode.

VIRTUAL MEMORY CONTROLS

Virtual memory exists when the addressable storage space is larger than the available real memory space. To achieve this outcome, a mechanism must exist that maps virtual memory addresses into real memory addresses. When an executing program references virtual memory addresses, the mechanism then translates these addresses into real memory addresses.

Conceptually, a virtual memory address can be represented as a block number, b, and a displacement, d. When programs reference a virtual memory location (b,d), the addressing mechanism looks up an address translation table. It first obtains the real memory address of the start of the block in which the virtual memory location resides. It then adds the displacement to this starting address to obtain the real memory address of the virtual memory location that has been referenced (Figure 13–6). This basic mechanism is used irrespective of whether blocks are fixed length (pages) or variable length (segments) or whether variable length blocks are broken up into several fixed length blocks (combined segmentation/paging systems).

FIGURE 13–6. Virtual memory address translation.

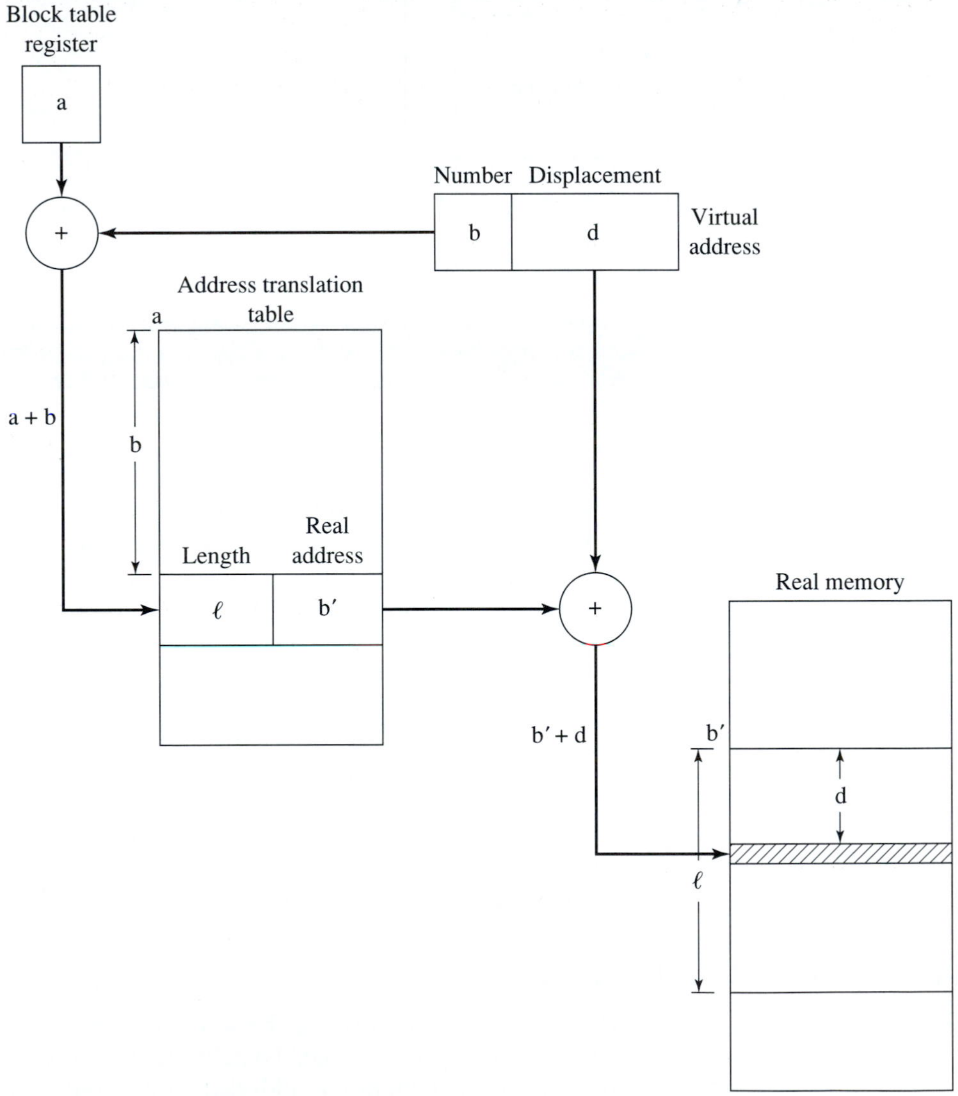

Two types of controls should be exercised over blocks of virtual memory. First, when an executing process references a virtual memory location, (b,d'), the addressing mechanism should check the displacement, d', is within the block boundaries—that is, $d' \leq d$. Thus, the process should not be able to reference a memory location outside the block. Second, an access control mechanism should check that the action the process wants to undertake on the block is within its allowed set of privileges. For example, if the process is only allowed to read the block and it issues a write instruction, the access control mechanism must prevent the instruction from being executed.

Either a ticket-oriented approach or a list-oriented approach can be used to control the actions a process wants to undertake on a virtual memory block (see Chapter 10). Figure 13–7 shows a ticket-oriented access control system. The access control mechanism starts out with a capability that allows it to access a secure password table. If Smith provides the correct password, she will be assigned a process that allows her to access her catalog. Within the catalog is a list of identifiers for each virtual memory block that she is allowed to access and the action privileges she has with respect to each block. Each virtual

FIGURE 13–7. Simple capability access control system.

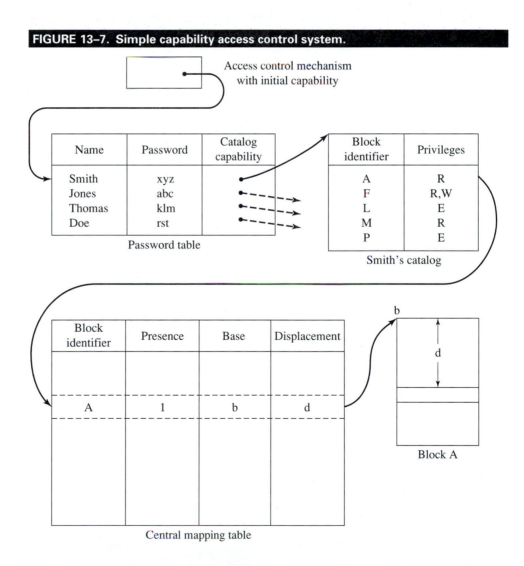

memory block identifier is contained in a central mapping table that provides the base address and displacement for the block and an indicator to show whether the block is in real memory or in auxiliary memory—that is, whether the block has been paged in or paged out.

Figure 13–8 shows a list-oriented access control system. Each virtual memory block has associated with it a list of processes that can access the block and the action privileges that each process has with respect to the block. When a process wants to access a virtual memory block, it specifies the unique identifier of the block and the actions it wishes to undertake on the block. A central mapping table points to the access controller for the block. The access controller, in turn, contains the address of the block, the list of processes authorized to access the block, and lists of action privileges assigned to each process. Unless an identifier for the process is contained in the access controller and the action requested is in the list of authorized action privileges for the process, the process can proceed no further. In essence, the addressing mechanism establishes a protective wall around the virtual memory block. Access to the block then can be obtained only through a single, guarded door in the wall.

Unfortunately, not all systems that manage virtual memory force a process to access a block through a secure door. They might have loopholes that allow processes to alter a displacement value after it has been checked such that $d' > d$, thereby allowing unauthorized access to another block. Moreover,

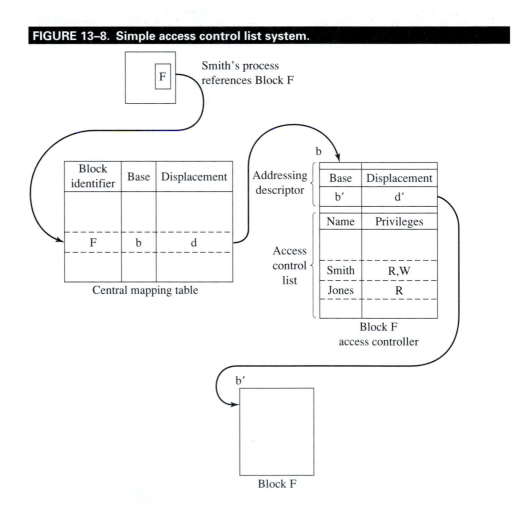

FIGURE 13–8. Simple access control list system.

some systems might not protect the capability lists that designate the action privileges which processes have with respect to a block. As a result, processes can illegally change their capabilities. In this light, holes exist in the protective wall, and the integrity of the block may be corrupted as a result. Confidential data in the block could be released to unauthorized parties, for example, or illegal copies could be made of proprietary programs.

OPERATING SYSTEM INTEGRITY

The operating system is the set of programs implemented in software, firmware, or hardware that permits sharing and use of resources within a computer system. The primary resources to be shared are processors, real memory, secondary memory, and input/output devices. To enhance usability, the operating system must manage these resources so they are available to each user. Moreover, each user must be able to execute a job without regard to other users.

Auditors often have paid little attention to the evaluation of operating system controls. Many auditors have considered the likelihood of operating system compromises to be low. Moreover, many have lacked the expertise to conduct a competent evaluation of operating system controls. Many also have considered operating system flaws to be endemic; consequently, they have focused on compensating controls.

Auditors cannot continue to ignore operating system controls. There are now many well-publicized cases in which serious losses have occurred through breaches of operating system controls (see, e.g., Spafford 1989). Auditors need, therefore, to have a basic understanding of the fundamental issues surrounding operating system integrity. In this light, the following subsections provide an overview of the goals that must be achieved if operating systems are to be reliable, the nature of threats to operating system reliability, the types of operating system flaws that sometimes undermine reliability, and the types of controls that can be exercised to try to ensure the operating system functions reliably.

Nature of a Reliable Operating System

Long ago, Stepczyk (1974) identified five goals that must be achieved if an operating system is to function reliably. These goals are still pertinent today:

1. The operating system must be protected from user processes. A user process must not be able to bring a computer system to a halt, destroy essential information, take control of the system, or change the system in an unauthorized way.
2. Users must be protected from each other. The operating system must prevent one user corrupting another user's processes or data.
3. Users must be protected from themselves. A user process might comprise several distinct modules or subprocesses, each with its own memory area and files. One module or subprocess should not be able to corrupt another module or subprocess.
4. The operating system must be protected from itself. As with user processes, one module or subprocess in the operating system should not be able to corrupt another module or subprocess.
5. When environmental failures occur, the operating system should be robust. For example, if a power failure occurs or the environment becomes too hot, the operating system should be able to bring operations to an orderly halt.

Whether operating systems achieve these goals depends on the access controls they enforce and how well they have been designed, implemented, verified, and tested.

Operating System Integrity Threats

Threats to operating system integrity can be accidental or deliberate. Accidental threats include hardware, software, and environmental failures that cause the operating system to crash or to process erroneously. A user also might undertake some unexpected procedure that the operating system cannot handle or handles incorrectly. If you are a frequent user of microcomputers, for example, you might have experienced operating system crashes when you have done something a little unusual. Most likely you will have been forced to reboot the microcomputer you are using to restart your work.

Deliberate threats to operating system integrity usually aim at unauthorized removal of assets (e.g., sensitive data files), breaches of data integrity (e.g., corruption of important data), or disruption of operations (e.g., causing an operating system to malfunction periodically). They occur in four ways. First, privileged personnel abuse their powers. For example, field engineers or local area network administrators use special utilities provided to them to circumvent operating system controls. Second, a would-be penetrator deceives privileged personnel, thus giving the penetrator access to the operating system. Third, special devices are used to detect electromagnetic radiation, emit electromagnetic radiation (jam the system), or wiretap communication lines. Fourth, a would-be penetrator interacts with the operating system to determine and exploit a flaw in the system.

To illustrate how deliberate threats might be manifested, the following techniques have been used in the past to successfully circumvent operating system controls:

Penetration Technique	*Explanation*
Browsing	Involves searching residue to gain unauthorized access to information. The residue could be in real memory or secondary memory. In this way, sensitive information like a password is obtained.
Masquerading	Involves carrying out unauthorized activities by impersonating a legitimate user of the system or impersonating the system itself. In the latter case, the penetrator sends a message to an operator that looks like a system-generated message (e.g., a request to change a password). The operator undertakes some action that results in a penetration. (See also the subsequent entry on "spoofing.")
Piggybacking	Involves intercepting communications between the operating system and the user and modifying them or substituting new messages. A special terminal is tapped into a communication line.
Between-lines entry	A penetrator takes advantage of the time during which a legitimate user still is connected to the system but is inactive. As with piggybacking, the penetrator connects a special terminal to a communication line.
Spoofing	A penetrator fools users into thinking they are interacting with the operating system. For example, a penetrator duplicates the logon procedure, captures a user's password, simulates a system crash, and requests the user to repeat the logon procedure. The

Penetration Technique	*Explanation*
	second time the user actually logs on to the operating system. See, also, Chapter 10.
Backdoors/ Trapdoors	A backdoor or trapdoor allows a user to employ the facilities of the operating system without being subject to the normal controls. For example, it might be possible to use certain services provided by the operating system without providing a password (see, e.g., Klaus 1997).
Trojan horse	Users execute a program written by the penetrator. Unbeknown to the user, the penetrator's program undertakes unauthorized activities. For example, it makes a copy of sensitive data and writes the data to a file in the penetrator's directory. (See also Chapter 10.)

Note that all these penetration techniques rely on legitimate techniques for communication between processes: writing files, sending messages, and sharing memory. Some types of penetration techniques employ channels that were not intended for interprocess communication, however. In short, they rely on *covert channels* to leak information from one process to another (Lampson 1973). These can be categorized in two ways: *(1)* covert storage channels, whereby one process communicates confidential information to another process by changing the values of system state variables, and *(2)* covert timing channels, whereby one process communicates confidential information to another process by changing the time period that a system takes to perform some function.

To illustrate a covert *storage* channel, assume any process can read any file name in any directory. One process can then communicate with another process by either writing or not writing a file name (or deleting a file name). Only one bit of information can be communicated at a time. If file names can be written or deleted quickly, however, enough sensitive information might be leaked to make the penetration worthwhile. Other types of file attributes besides names can be used to leak information—for example, file length or latest modification date and time. Providing the receiving process can read the file attribute, the sending process can alter the attribute to leak sensitive information to the receiving process.

To illustrate a covert *timing* channel, assume a process measures how long it takes to execute a loop. This length of time will vary, depending on the load imposed by other processes that are being executed. Thus, one process can communicate a bit of information to another process simply by increasing or decreasing the workload demands it makes on the central processor. The latter process checks to see whether the time it takes to execute its loop is higher than or lower than some threshold level. Covert timing channels have proved to be especially hard to eliminate in operating systems (Karger et al. 1991).

Operating System Integrity Flaws

Operating system penetrations result when integrity flaws exist in operating systems. These flaws arise for two reasons. First, the access control policy designed for the operating system is defective. Recall that in Chapter 10 we examine the requirements of a secure access control policy. Second, even if a secure access control policy is designed for the operating system, it might be implemented incorrectly in the operating system. We return to this issue subsequently. Some major types of implementation flaws that have been discovered in operating systems, however, are the following (see, further, Abbott et al. 1976; Landwehr et al. 1994; O'Shea 1991, pp. 130–131):

Integrity Flaw	Explanation
Incomplete parameter validation	The system does not check the validity of all attributes of a user's request. For example, the user requests an address outside the area allocated to the user's program. The system fails to reject the request.
Inconsistent parameter validation	The system applies different validation criteria to the same construct within the system. For example, the user is able to create a password containing blanks but is unable to change or delete the password because the system regards it as invalid. Ultimately the password is compromised because it is never changed.
Implicit sharing of data	The operating system uses a common area to service two or more user processes. Moreover, the operating system does not prevent user processes accessing data in this common area. If the operating system places sensitive data in this common area, it will be exposed. For example, one user process might be able to access the passwords belonging to another user process.
Asynchronous validation	If the operating system permits asynchronous processes, users take advantage of timing inadequacies to violate integrity. For example, a user process requests an input/output operation, and the operating system validates the user parameters. The system finds the channel needed is busy and issues an interrupt. The user process then changes the address for the input/output operation to an address outside its valid work space. The system returns control to an illegal address.
Inadequate access control	The operating system performs incomplete checking, or one part of the system assumes another part has performed the checking. For example, a user loads a program with the same name as a system routine, and the operating system does not check to see the program is from the system library. Thus, a user routine supplants a system routine (a Trojan horse exists).
Violable limits	System documentation states limits, e.g., the maximum size of a buffer. The system does not check to see if these limits are exceeded, however, and runs erroneously when they are exceeded.

When auditing an operating system, auditors should check to see what integrity flaws have been discovered and documented. In some cases, strategies to correct these flaws might also have been devised (see, e.g., Bruce et al. 1997; Curry 1992; Klaus 1997). Alternatively, ways of reducing expected losses from these flaws might be known. Auditors can then check the specific system audited to determine what actions have been undertaken in relation to the flaws. Unfortunately, known flaws are not always made public. Moreover, penetrators are unlikely to reveal flaws that they are exploiting.

Reference Monitors and Kernels

Historically, the controls that an operating system uses to safeguard assets and maintain data integrity have been dispersed throughout its various parts. Inevitably this approach has led to inconsistencies and omissions and the consequent integrity weaknesses discussed previously.

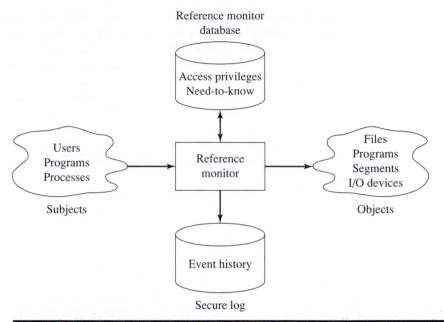

FIGURE 13–9. Reference monitor abstraction.

In an attempt to remedy these problems, some operating systems have now been designed based upon the concept of a *reference monitor*. A reference monitor is an abstract mechanism that checks each request by a subject (user process) to access and use an object (e.g., file, device, program) to ensure that the request complies with a security policy (Figure 13–9). It also maintains a history of all security-related events. A reference monitor is implemented via a *security kernel*, which is a hardware/software/firmware mechanism.

The motivation for following the reference-monitor approach to operating system design is that it concentrates all the security-relevant features of the operating system into a single component. The kernel that implements the reference monitor can then be separated from all other processes in the operating system and should be made tamperproof. In addition, the kernel might be small enough to prove formally that it accurately and completely implements the security policy embodied within the reference monitor. Auditors therefore, can have more confidence in the reliability of operating systems that have been designed based upon the reference-monitor approach.

From a security perspective, a critical aspect of a kernel is the set of *trusted processes* that it provides. Trusted processes are those that are not bound by all the security rules implemented in the kernel. They are provided to allow a trusted person, such as a system administrator, to tailor a security policy to the specific needs of an organization. For example, system administrators need access to a trusted process so they can maintain the secure table used by the kernel to determine the access privileges that each user possesses. Because trusted processes can be used to corrupt the integrity of a system, auditors need to evaluate them carefully to determine the reliability of the controls exercised over their use.

Design and Implementation Considerations

Because an operating system is complex, critical software, auditors should be concerned about the approach used to design and implement it. The top-down design, structured programming principles discussed in Chapter 5 should have been followed. Basically, the system should have been designed and specified as a hierarchy of layers corresponding to different levels of abstraction of the functions to be performed. For example, from a controls viewpoint, the top level should contain a formal specification of the security policy to be enforced. Various intermediate levels should then contain progressively more detail showing the operating system features that will be used to enforce the security policy. The lower levels should provide formal specifications for the programming language to be used to implement the controls in the operating system. To the extent that the operating system has been designed and implemented using this layered approach, auditors can have more confidence in its reliability.

Certification of Operating Systems

In an effort to improve operating system integrity, several different organizations and countries have developed criteria that can be used as a basis for designing, implementing, and evaluating operating system integrity (O'Shea 1991). Perhaps the best known, however, is the U.S. National Computer Security Center's Trusted Computer System Evaluation Criteria (TCSEC). These criteria were first published in 1983. In 1985, revised criteria were published in a document that became known as the "Orange Book" (reflecting the color of the covers used on the document) (U.S. Department of Defense 1985). Modifications and extensions to these criteria have subsequently been proposed to address such issues as open systems interconnection and distributed operating systems.

The TCSEC define a rating scale reflecting increasingly rigorous requirements to maintain system integrity (see, further, Chokhani 1992):

Division	*Requirements Overview*
D	Assigned to systems that fail to meet the criteria for any higher division.
C	Supports *discretionary* access control, object reuse, identification, authentication, and auditing. Two classes exist: C1, Discretionary Security Protection, which requires accountability only at the *group* level; and C2, Controlled Access Protection, which requires accountability at the *individual* level and improved audit trail and login control procedures.
B	Supports *mandatory* access control. Three classes exist: B1, Labelled Security Protection, which requires that all storage objects be labeled and subject to mandatory access control based on an *informal* security model; B2, Structured Protection, which requires that all system resources be protected based on a *formal* security model, that covert channels have been eliminated or their bandwidth limited, and that security-critical components be separated from other operating system components and reviewed and tested; and B3, Security Domains, which requires that security-critical components be engineered to minimize complexity.
A	Requires use of formal methods in the specification, design, modelling, and analysis of the system. Two classes exist: A1, Verified Design, which requires formal verification of the correspondence between the Top-Level Specification and the Formal Security Policy Model; and A2, Beyond Class A1, which extends formal verification to other system features (e.g., source code against specifications).

Operating system vendors can ask the National Computer Security Center to undertake an evaluation of their products (see, e.g., Calabrese 1991; Kaplan and Kovara 1993). This evaluation process is conducted concurrently with the design and implementation of the system. It provides a basis for improving the integrity-related features of the operating system. Eventually, the system will be assigned a final rating. If, therefore, auditors encounter a National Computer Security Center-rated operating system, they should be able to determine the strengths and weaknesses of the system on the basis of the rating assigned to the system. Moreover, they can be confident that the system has been subjected to rigorous reviews to derive the rating assigned to the system.

APPLICATION SOFTWARE CONTROLS

In the processing subsystem, application software computes, sorts, classifies, and summarizes data specific to an application system. It should perform validation checks to identify processing errors when they occur. Furthermore, it should be designed in such a way that processing errors are avoided in the first place.

Validation Checks

Processing validation checks primarily ensure that computations performed on numeric fields are authorized, accurate, and complete. The processing associated with alphabetic or alphanumeric fields typically is minimal: An existing field value is replaced (modified); or data is inserted in a field when a new record is created.

Because the types of processing performed on data vary considerably, it is difficult to provide a comprehensive description of the validation checks that should be undertaken. Nevertheless, the following might be used:

Level of Check	*Type of Check*	*Explanation*
Field	Overflow	Overflow can occur if a field used for computations is not zeroized initially, some error in computation occurs, or unexpected high values occur. In COBOL, for example, a special overflow clause is available.
	Range	An allowable value range can apply to a field.
Record	Reasonableness	The contents of one field can determine the allowable value for another. For example, after an employee's allowable deductions have been calculated for payroll, they can be checked to see if they fall within a valid range of values, given the employee's position within the organization.
	Sign	The contents of one field—for example, the record type field—might determine which sign is valid for a numeric field.
File	Crossfooting	Separate control totals can be developed for related fields and crossfooted at the end of a run. For example, for payroll, control totals can be calculated for gross pay, deductions, and net pay. At the end of processing, net pay should equal gross pay less deductions.
	Control totals	Run-to-run control totals can be developed and compared with the results of a run. For example, if the current balance of an accounts receivable file is $100,000 and the incoming transactions total $10,000 debit and $8,000 credit, the new balance of the file should be $102,000. The last record on the transaction file used as input to the master file update program may be a control record showing the totals for the debit and credit entries. The master file update program can use these control totals to check the accuracy of its computations.

The field and record validation checks described here now are often performed in the database subsystem. If a database management system is used to support the database subsystem, it may enforce the field and validation constraints rather than application programs. Migrating these checks from application programs to the database management system helps ensure that they are applied consistently across applications (see Chapter 14).

Some Matters of Programming Style

Auditors should be aware of some common programming errors that can result in incomplete or inaccurate processing of data. These errors can be avoided through good programming style. The experienced analyst and programmer specifically designs test data to create the underlying conditions for these errors and to check that the program handles these conditions correctly. The following subsections briefly describe some elements of good programming style that help avoid these errors.

Handle Rounding Correctly

Rounding problems occur when the level of precision required for an arithmetic calculation is less than the level of precision actually calculated. For example, the interest on a bank account might be calculated to five decimal digits. Only two are required, however, to record the lowest monetary amount—that is, a cent. If the remaining three decimal digits are simply dropped, an interest calculation made on the grand total of account balances might not agree with the sum of the individual interest calculations. Thus, it is unclear whether the interest calculation routine has performed its processing accurately.

An algorithm for handling this problem is well known. Auditors should check to see the algorithm has been used for two reasons. First, it might not be known by inexperienced programmers. Second, a minor modification to the algorithm provides an easy means to perpetrate a fraud. Figure 13–10 shows the algorithm for handling the rounding problem. To illustrate how the algorithm works for an interest rate of 3.25 percent, consider the following three examples:

1. Existing accumulator balance   −.00815
   Old account balance   1,351.62
   Interest calculated   43.92765
   New account balance   1,395.54765
   Rounded account balance   1,395.55
   New accumulator balance   −.0105 (−.00235 − .00815)
   Final account balance   1,395.54
   Final accumulator balance   −.0005

2. Existing accumulator balance   .00917
   Old account balance   650.23
   Interest calculated   21.13248
   New account balance   671.36248
   Rounded account balance   671.36
   New accumulator balance   .01165 (.00248 + .00917)
   Final account balance   671.37
   Final accumulator balance   .00165

3. Existing accumulator balance   .00002
   Old account balance   2,911.20
   Interest calculated   94.614
   New account balance   3,005.814
   Rounded account balance   3,005.81
   New accumulator balance   .00402 (.004 + .00002)
   Final account balance   3,005.81
   Final accumulator balance   .00402

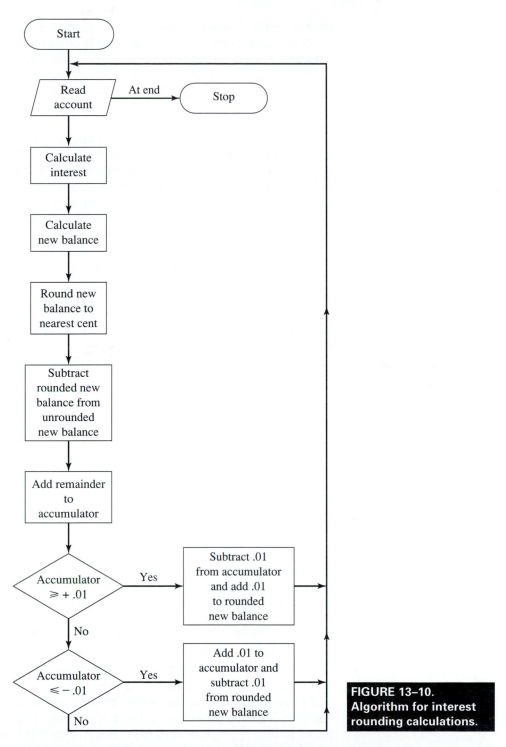

**FIGURE 13–10.
Algorithm for interest
rounding calculations.**

Depending on the balance in the accumulator, some accounts are rounded up and others are rounded down. By using this algorithm, the interest calculated on the grand total of the old account balances plus the grand total of the old account balances will equal the sum of the new account balances.

To perpetrate a fraud, a programmer simply modifies the algorithm as follows: when the condition occurs such that a cent should be added to the rounded new account balance (i.e., accumulator ≥ +.01), this cent is added to another accumulator. After processing is complete, this second accumulator is then added to an account created by the programmer to facilitate the conduct of the fraud. The amounts are small. Nonetheless, if several hundred thousand accounts exist, over a year the fraud can amount to a reasonable sum.

Print Run-to-Run Control Totals

Periodically in online programs, or at each major stage during the processing of data in batch programs, control totals should be printed. These control totals provide evidence that all input data has been processed accurately and completely. For example, an accounts receivable master file update program should show the total value of input transactions it has processed during some time interval or after a batch run, the total value of accounts on the input master file, and the total value of accounts on the output master file. Moreover, even if the data is nonnumeric, hash totals can be developed and summed to produce control totals. These control totals can then be checked against user-prepared control totals to determine whether the correct files were used as input, whether all data entered the program, whether the program dropped a record, and so on. Sometimes control totals are supplied as input parameters to a program. For example, the current value of accounts on the master file might be submitted as input so the program can check whether it has read the correct input file.

Minimize Human Intervention

Sometimes programs are written in such a way that they require human intervention to determine the types of processing they should undertake. For example, at the start of processing a user or operator might have to input a parameter value to indicate whether a program is to undertake end-of-month or end-of-quarter procedures.

Because human intervention is error-prone, users or operators can make mistakes when providing input parameter values. Thus, programs that minimize user or operator intervention to determine the nature of the processing they will undertake are less likely to perform their processing incorrectly. In some cases, however, it might be impossible to avoid some level of human or operator intervention. In these situations the program must provide clear instructions and clear feedback to the person who provides the input. Where possible, it also should check the validity of the input provided.

Understand Hardware/Software Numerical Hazards

In some applications, complex mathematical calculations must be performed. The accuracy of the results might be a function of the arithmetic idiosyncrasies of the machine on which the computation is done and the accuracy and precision of the results obtained from subroutines called to perform various parts of the calculation. In these situations, auditors might check to determine whether programmers who implemented the application are aware of *(1)* the specific ways the machines they used handle fixed point, floating point, and double precision arithmetic and *(2)* the level of accuracy and precision provided by the subroutines called in the programs they wrote. Certain types of round-off or truncation, for example, can produce unacceptable results. Similarly, a mathematical subroutine library needs to be calibrated so a user can determine whether the level of accuracy achieved by the algorithms is acceptable.

Use Redundant Calculations

The computations performed in some programs can be complex and error prone. For example, Hatton and Roberts (1994) compared the results produced by nine widely-used seismic application packages when they processed the same set of input data. They commented that the discrepancies and errors they found painted a "deeply disturbing picture." They observe (p. 794): "Put simply, they (the errors and discrepancies) could lead to a $20 million well being drilled in the wrong place!"

If complex mathematical calculations must be performed, programmers should consider whether redundant calculations should be implemented in the software used to perform the calculations. Often, two different sets of equations can be used to calculate a result, or an additional calculation can be undertaken to check a result. If programmers are uncertain about the arithmetic idiosyncrasies of the machines they are using or the accuracy and precision of subroutines they call in their programs, redundant calculations can provide some assurance that the results obtained are acceptable.

Avoid Closed Routines

Closed routines exist in a program whenever values are assumed to exist because tests for all other values have failed. For example, if only four values supposedly occur in a field, a program has a closed routine if it tests for three values only and then assumes the existence of the fourth value when tests for the other three values fail.

Programs always should check for all possible values in a field rather than assume the existence of a particular value if tests for all other values fail. This strategy avoids carrying out incorrect processing on the basis of assumed values that do not, in fact, exist because some type of error or irregularity has occurred.

AUDIT TRAIL CONTROLS

The audit trail in the processing subsystem maintains the chronology of events from the time data is received from the input or communication subsystem to the time data is dispatched to the database, communication, or output subsystems.

Accounting Audit Trail

The accounting audit trail should allow auditors to trace and to replicate the processing performed on a data item that enters the processing subsystem. If auditors are to accomplish this objective, they must be able to identify uniquely the processes executed on the data item and to understand these processes. Process identification is facilitated by recording the process identifier (name and version number) on any output reports or storing it in an audit trail record. Process understanding requires that up-to-date documentation be available for reference.

In some cases, the execution of processes leads to the creation of triggered transactions. Triggered transactions arise when a process identifies that some condition has occurred and, as a result, it generates a new transaction. For example, a process might generate a purchase order for a stock item when it determines that the quantity on hand of the stock item has fallen below a certain level. When triggered transactions occur, the processing subsystem should write the identity of the process that initiated the triggered transaction and the conditions that resulted in the triggered transaction to the audit trail.

If auditors are to be able to replicate the results of complex processes, the processing subsystem sometimes must record intermediate results, the values of any standing data items used, and the input and output data item values. For example, a program might perform a set of complex calculations to determine the average cost of inventory items. The calculations might be complex because stock movements are frequent and currency conversions are required (overseas suppliers are used). An audit trail of intermediate results and the values of standing data items used (for example, currency conversion factors) should assist auditors to verify the accuracy and completeness of the computations performed.

Operations Audit Trail

Of all the application subsystems, perhaps the most extensive operations audit trail data is maintained in the processing subsystem. Data from the operations audit trail is often critical to effective management of shared system resources. Moreover, data for the operations audit trail often is easy to collect because many operating systems provide facilities to create a comprehensive log of events that occur during application system execution. These facilities are often parameter driven. Users specify what data should be logged for each application system. The operating system will then store these requirements as parameters. During execution of each application system, it will invoke the necessary logging facilities depending on the parameter values provided (Figure 13–11).

Unfortunately, the flexibility provided by logging facilities in the processing subsystem can be their downfall. Users might be tempted to log too much data. As a consequence, the system overheads incurred can be high. Some operating systems will suspend user processes if the amount of data to be logged exceeds the throughput capability of their logging facility or threatens to exhaust the resources (e.g., disk space) available to their logging facility (Holden 1993). Auditors need to evaluate the user decisions in relation to the data they want logged. In this light, auditors must understand the types of data that can be stored in the operations audit trail. Moreover, they must understand how it can be retrieved and used.

FIGURE 13–11. Parameter-driven operating system logging facility for operations audit trail.

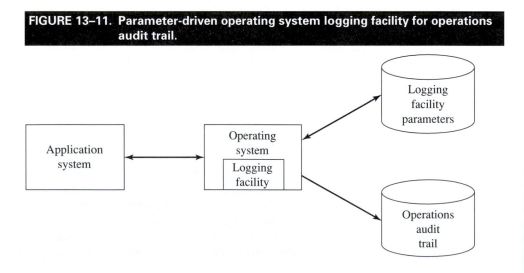

Content of the Operations Audit Trail

Four types of data are collected in the operations audit trail. The first is *resource consumption* data. This data identifies which user consumed a resource, what process consumed a resource, and when a resource was consumed. The following types of resource consumption are monitored:

Resource Category	*Examples*
Hardware	Central processing unit time used, peripherals used, primary memory used, secondary storage space used, communication facilities used.
Software	Compilers used, subroutine libraries used, file management facilities used, communication software used.
Data	Files accessed, frequency of access to data items, ways data used, number of backups made.
Personnel	Number of operator interventions required—e.g., to mount or dismount a magnetic tape for an application.

Users often can specify whether they want this data collected at the level of the application system, an individual program, an individual subroutine, or sometimes even a lower level (such as a program instruction). The lower the level specified for collection of the data, however, the more data that will be generated and the more overhead that will be added to system execution.

Resource consumption data can be used for many management and audit purposes. For example, it may be used as follows:

1. *Billing.* Resource consumption data provides the basis for charging users for the resources they consume. It also can form the basis for an organization's lease or rental payments for some resources. Auditors can use the data to check the accuracy and completeness of billings, lease payments, or rental payments.
2. *Performance evaluation.* Resource consumption data provides a basis for determining whether resources have been used efficiently. For example, the time required for an application program, subroutine, or system software program to process a transaction can be calculated. The result could indicate the logic in the program or subroutine needs to be restructured or more efficient system software needs to be purchased. Hardware utilization also can be examined. A particular input/output channel could be the cause of a bottleneck. The hardware platform might have to be reconfigured to reduce the amount of traffic on the channel. Chapter 21 discusses these matters in more detail.
3. *Potential integrity breaches.* Resource consumption data also can be used to identify potential system integrity violations. For example, checks can be made on when a program was executed, how many times the program was executed, the duration of its execution, and who initiated its execution. Any variations in the norms for these factors could indicate that unauthorized activities are being undertaken. Data also can be extracted to determine who accessed files, who copied files, and who renamed files. This data can be examined to evaluate whether the users of the files and the activities they undertook were authorized.

The second type of operations audit trail data that can be collected relates to *security-sensitive events*. The logging facility can be used to create audit trail entries for all changes to password or access privileges files or attempts to use resources that failed. These entries subsequently can be extracted from the log to determine whether they are authorized or whether they manifest threats to the integrity of the system. If the logging facility identifies an attempted integrity violation that represents an immediate and serious threat to the system, however, it might send a message that triggers an alarm at a terminal that is monitored continuously by a security administrator.

The third type of operations audit trail data that can be collected is *hardware malfunctions*. For example, processor or memory parity errors could be recorded by the logging facility. An abnormal number could indicate that a processor or memory component needs to be replaced. This data is important in designing an appropriate hardware/software platform and devising a suitable program of preventive maintenance for the platform.

Finally, the operations audit trail can be used to record *user-specified events*. The logging facility might allow users to write their own programs to collect operations data. It will invoke these programs when the user-specified event occurs. For example, the completion of a program step or the occurrence of a particular transaction type may be recorded. This capability is also useful in auditors' work. It allows them to embed audit evidence collection modules in the logging facility and to collect data on the state of controls in an application system at the same time as application system processing occurs. Careful control must be exercised over this facility, however, as user-specified routines might also be employed to modify or to delete data that is accessed or written by an application system while it is running. In this way, integrity breaches can occur. (These matters are discussed further in Chapter 18.)

Interrogating the Operations Audit Trail

Interrogating the operations audit trail maintained by an operating system involves four major steps:

1. Specifying audit objectives,
2. Extracting data from the operations audit trail that will allow auditors to meet these objectives,
3. Sorting the data extracted into the required order, and
4. Formatting and presenting the results.

Historically, auditors have experienced some difficulty in interrogating the operations audit trail. The log could contain many different types of data items and record types, voluminous data spanning multiple tapes, disks, or cartridges, data that has been encoded and compacted to reduce storage space requirements, and data that requires some editing before it is in a form suitable for use.

To help overcome these problems, several vendors have developed generalized packages that can be used by both management and auditors to interrogate the operations audit trail. These packages produce a set of standard reports using operations audit trail data. Users of the packages simply have to specify as parameters what reports they require. The packages then extract the necessary data, sort the data into the required order, and format and present the results. Typical reports that can be obtained automatically follow:

1. System user billing report,
2. Hardware utilization report,
3. Program resource consumption report,
4. Hardware malfunction report,
5. Program run schedule report,
6. Programmer resource consumption report, and
7. Report on programs abnormally terminated.

Even if generalized software that has been designed specifically to interrogate the operations audit trail of a particular machine or operating system is not available, other software can provide the necessary functions. For example, auditors might be able to use generalized audit software to interrogate the operations audit trail, providing the encoding and compaction routines used in the operations audit trail are not too complex (see Chapter 16).

Some Control Issues

The existence of software that records data for the operations audit trail sometimes poses control problems. This software can permit users to modify or delete records accessed by an application system during production running, or to modify or delete records written to the operations audit trail. For example, if the software allows users to declare a run-time exit that will allow them to invoke a subroutine, they can use the subroutine to carry out unauthorized activities on data, especially if the subroutine can be executed in the operating system's privileged mode.

There are various ways of detecting and preventing unauthorized use of the logging software. For example, users might be prevented from writing their own subroutines without special authority. Moreover, use of user subroutines can be monitored with the logging software to detect any unauthorized activity.

EXISTENCE CONTROLS

We have examined earlier in the chapter some existence controls that are important in the processing subsystem. For example, recall that we discussed how component replication can be used to mitigate losses associated with processor failure.

In this section we examine an important existence control called a checkpoint/restart facility. This is a short-term backup and recovery control that enables a system to be recovered if failure is temporary and localized.

Nature of Checkpoint/Restart Controls

If programs fail for some reason before they reach normal termination, some of the processing they have carried out might still be accurate and complete. Ideally, this processing should not have to be repeated during a recovery process, especially if a failed program has already consumed substantial resources up to the point of failure. To avoid having to restart failed programs from scratch, checkpoint/restart facilities have been developed that allow programs to be reestablished at some prior, valid intermediate point in their processing and restarted from that point.

Checkpoint/restart recovery cannot be undertaken for all types of program failure. In some cases, completely redoing the processing might be the only means of recovery. For example, if a program contains a serious logic error, the error has to be corrected and all processing redone. The following three examples show where a checkpoint/restart facility is useful, however, as a means of recovering from localized damage or abnormal termination of a program:

1. A hardware error occurs that is not expected to recur if processing is repeated. For example, a processor, bus, or memory error occurs that is transient.
2. An operator makes an error that means partial reprocessing of transactions is necessary. With a multi-cartridge file, for example, an operator might load the

incorrect version of the third cartridge. Because the first two cartridges have been processed correctly, the error can be corrected simply by restarting processing at the beginning of the third cartridge.

3. A program might be terminated abnormally for some reason. For example, it might have to be rolled out of main memory to allow a higher-priority program to operate, or its execution might be stopped because an automated operations facility recognizes an impending hardware failure.

Checkpoint/restart facilities cannot guard against long-term or global failure, however, such as the physical destruction of the data processing facility by fire. Other existence controls have to be invoked to effect recovery of the processing subsystem—for example, the backup and recovery controls described in Chapter 7.

Functions and Architectures of Checkpoint/Restart Facilities

To illustrate the functions and architectures used in checkpoint/restart facilities, consider two schemes (see, further, Bowen and Pradhan 1993). The first is a *processor-based scheme*, which, when a transient fault occurs, rolls the processor back a small number of instructions and then restarts the processor. The scheme distinguishes between the *active state* of the system, which is the state of the system represented in the central processor, registers, and cache memory, and the *checkpoint state*, which is the state of the system represented in main memory (Figure 13–12).

As the processor executes instructions, the registers and cache memory will be updated. At some point, an instruction will reference an address that is not in cache memory. If the cache memory is full, one of the cache "lines" or "slots" will have to be written back to main memory to make room for a new cache entry. When main memory must be updated as a result of the cache line being displaced, the checkpoint/restart facility initiates a checkpoint. Two actions occur upon a checkpoint: *(1)* the central processing unit registers are saved to a special area in main memory and *(2)* all cache lines or slots that have been modified (indicated via a bit that is set) are written to main mem-

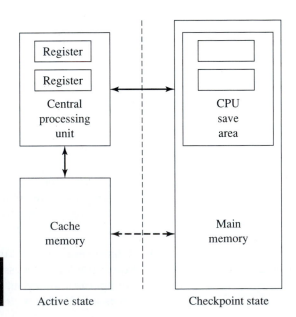

FIGURE 13–12. Processor-based checkpoint/restart facility.

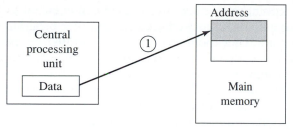

(a) First write to memory

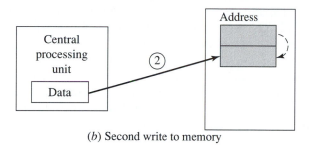

(b) Second write to memory

FIGURE 13–13. Memory-based checkpoint/restart facility.

ory. This last action must occur so main memory reflects the current state of the cache.

Assume, now, that a parity error occurs in the processor. Recovery is effected by *(1)* loading the central processing unit registers from the special save area in main memory and *(2)* marking any modified lines or slots in cache memory as invalid (in other words, a subsequent reference to these lines will result in main memory having to be accessed). In effect, the processor has been rolled back to the previous checkpoint. It can then be restarted in the hope that the parity error reflected a transient problem in the processor.

The second checkpoint/restart scheme we will consider is a *memory-based* scheme. The scheme relies on having two memory banks for each address (Figure 13–13). The processor first writes data to the first memory bank. If the write operation is successful, the data from the first memory bank is then copied to the second memory bank. If the write operation is not successful, however, roll back occurs by copying the contents of the second memory bank into the first memory bank. The write operation is then repeated, again in the hope that the failure is transient.

Other checkpoint/restart schemes exist. In Chapter 14, for example, we consider a scheme that allows us to recover a database when failure occurs before update of a database has been fully effected. The general notion underlying a checkpoint/restart facility, however, is that from time to time the state of a system must be preserved by flushing the contents of registers, buffers, working storage, and so on to a log. When failure occurs, the system is rolled back to one of these prior preserved states and restarted.

Audit of Checkpoint/Restart Facilities

Auditors should have four concerns about checkpoint/restart facilities. First, checkpoint/restart information written to a log must be secure; that is, it must be impossible for programmers to access this information and to change it. Otherwise, the memory access controls described earlier in this chapter could be circumvented. For example, programmers could change an address offset in a checkpoint/restart log after it has been checked by an access control mechanism to gain unauthorized access to another program's memory block.

Second, checkpoint/restart facilities must be effective and efficient. They should be adequate for the organization's needs. Moreover, from the viewpoint of programmers, users, or operators, they should be transparent. Alternatively, if human intervention is required, checkpoint/restart facilities must be flexible, easy to use, and not error prone. The facility also must be capable of setting checkpoints and recovering and restarting systems at high speeds.

Third, checkpoint/restart facilities should be well documented. From the documentation, auditors should be able to determine easily their functions, architecture, and the controls implemented to preserve their integrity. Auditors should also be able to determine whether the facility is likely to meet the needs of the organization they are auditing.

Fourth, checkpoint/restart facilities should work reliably. Auditors should be able to obtain evidence on their having effected accurate and complete recovery when temporary failures have occurred. Alternatively, auditors should see evidence of their having been tested periodically to evaluate whether they effect accurate and complete recovery.

SUMMARY

Processing controls prevent, detect, and correct errors from the time data is received from the input subsystem or the communication subsystem to the time data is dispatched to the database, communication, or output subsystems. They seek to enhance the reliability of the central processor on which programs are executed, the real or virtual memory in which instructions and data are stored, the operating system that manages system resources, and the application programs that execute instructions to meet specific user requirements.

Controls over the central processor seek to detect and correct errors that occur, restrict the instructions that can be executed depending on the system state (supervisor state or problem state), prevent application processes from getting into an endless loop, and provide fault tolerance through component replication. Controls over real and virtual memory are primarily concerned with detecting and correcting errors in a memory cell, restricting access to a memory cell to authorized processes, and allowing only those actions on a memory cell that have been assigned to the process.

The extent to which an operating system can protect its own integrity and the integrity of the resources it manages is a function of the security policy it enforces, the way it has been designed and implemented, and the way it has been verified and tested. Threats to operating system integrity arise from abuse of powers by privileged personnel, deception of privileged personnel by a would-be penetrator, use of special devices to detect electromagnetic radiation, emit electromagnetic radiation, or wiretap communications lines, and interaction with the system by a would-be perpetrator to detect and exploit a flaw. Operating system integrity can also be breached by using covert storage channels and covert timing channels. Integrity is improved if operating systems are designed based upon a reference monitor and implemented via a security kernel. Some organizations and countries have also published criteria whereby operating systems can be evaluated and certified in terms of their ability to maintain system integrity.

Application programs protect the integrity of data in the processing subsystem by exercising a set of validation checks on the data they process and the actions they perform. The reliability of the application programs themselves can be enhanced by ensuring that they conform to certain principles of programming style. In particular, they should handle rounding correctly when the level of precision required for an arithmetic calculation is less than the level of precision actually calculated, print run-to-run control totals, minimize human intervention in providing parameter values that determine the nature of the processing they will undertake, avoid hardware/software numerical hazards, use redundant routines to check the accuracy of complex calculations, and not use closed routines.

Audit trail controls in the processing subsystem should allow the set of processing performed on a data item to be traced and replicated. In addition, operating systems often provide a facility to maintain a comprehensive operations audit trail of resource consumption in the processing subsystem. This audit trail can be used to log resource consumption data, security-critical events, hardware malfunctions, and user-specified events.

Besides component replication, the primary existence control exercised in the processing subsystem is a checkpoint/restart facility. If temporary and localized failure occurs, a checkpoint/restart facility allows an application program to be restarted at some intermediate point in its processing. It does not have to be restarted from scratch to recover from the effects of the failure.

Review Questions

13–1 What are the major *functions* of the processing subsystem? What are the major *components* of the processing subsystem?

13–2 What factors can cause a central processor to fail? What controls can be used to detect and correct errors that occur in the central processor?

13–3 How does the existence of a multiple-state machine enhance control within the central processing unit?

13–4 What is the purpose of timing controls within the central processing unit?

13–5 Briefly distinguish between a multicomputer architecture and a multiprocessor architecture. What is the primary purpose of using these types of architectures when machines are built?

13–6 What factors cause errors in a real memory cell? How are errors often detected?

13–7 Distinguish between the real memory protection mechanisms used in a multiuser contiguous storage-allocation system and a multiuser noncontiguous storage-allocation system.

13–8 How does a "tagged" architecture enhance control over real memory cells?

13–9 Briefly explain the nature of virtual memory. How does the addressing mechanism work in a virtual memory system?

13–10 Briefly distinguish between a ticket-oriented and a list-oriented approach to access control over a virtual memory block.

13–11 List the five goals that a secure operating system must achieve.

13–12 Briefly explain the nature of the following types of operating system penetration techniques:
   a Browsing
   b Piggybacking
   c Trojan horse

13–13 Briefly explain the nature of:
   a Covert storage channels
   b Covert timing channels

13–14 Briefly explain the nature of the following types of operating system integrity flaws:
   a Incomplete parameter validation
   b Implicit sharing of data
   c Asynchronous validation

13–15 Briefly explain what is meant by a reference monitor. What is the relationship between a security kernel and a reference monitor?

13–16 Briefly explain the nature of trusted processes within a security kernel. Why do trusted processes need special attention during the audit of an operating system?

13–17 What approach should be followed to the analysis, design, and implementation of an operating system?

13–18 Outline the nature of the four rating divisions described in the U.S. National Computer Security Center's Trusted Computer System Evaluation Criteria.

13–19 Briefly explain the nature of the following types of application program validation checks in the processing subsystem:
   a Overflow check
   b Range check
   c Reasonableness check
   d Sign check
   e Crossfooting check
   f Control total check

13–20 What is the purpose of minimizing human intervention during application system processing?

13–21 What are hardware/software numerical hazards? In what types of application systems should auditors be concerned about hardware/software numerical hazards?

13–22 Why is it sometimes useful to employ redundant calculations in a program? In what types of programs would redundant calculations be most useful?

13–23 What data must be available in the accounting audit trail so auditors can uniquely identify the process that has been executed on an input data item and the functions performed by that process?

13–24 What is a triggered transaction? What implications do triggered transactions have for the accounting audit trail in the processing subsystem?

13–25 What component in the processing subsystem usually collects data for the operations audit trail? How is this component activated to collect particular kinds of data?

13–26 List the *four* categories of events that are recorded on the operations audit trail. Which category is likely to have the most entries? Briefly explain why.

13–27 What interest do auditors have in the way in which resource consumption data is used to bill users?

13–28 List two types of events that auditors might wish to monitor using the exit facilities in the operations audit trail logging facility. Briefly explain why these events are of interest to us as auditors.

13–29 Outline the control problems posed by the existence of an operations audit trail logging facility that allows user exits. Give *two* strategies for overcoming these control problems.

13–30 Briefly explain the nature of checkpoint/restart controls. What situations can arise where checkpoint/restart controls are needed?

13–31 From an audit perspective, what are the important requirements of a check-point/ restart facility? How can auditors determine the adequacy of check-point/restart facilities?

Multiple-Choice Questions

13–1 Which of the following faults in a central processing unit is *most likely* to be detected by a parity check?

  a Corruption of data in a register by electromagnetic interference

  b Failure of a computational process in the arithmetic unit through component fatigue

  c Fetch of an instruction that is not within the valid set of instructions

  d Incorrect execution of an instruction because of a design error in the logic unit

13–2 A multiple-state machine is one that provides:

  a Multiple types of computational and logic validity checks in a single state

  b A mechanism for executing different processes in different partitions

  c Different execution states as a basis for assessing the legitimacy of an instruction

  d Different levels of capability to allow the machine to run in degraded mode

13–3 Which of the following statements about multicomputer and multiprocessor architectures is *true*?

  a Only one copy of the operating system exists in a multicomputer architecture

  b Voting procedures are used only in a multiprocessor architecture

  c Timing controls can only be used in a multicomputer architecture

  d Memory and input/output devices in a multiprocessor architecture are shared

13–4 Real memory errors primarily are detected through:

  a Valid character checks

  b Read-after-write checks

  c Boundary register checks

  d Parity-based Hamming code checks

13–5 In which type of real memory access control system is a lock-and-key mechanism *most likely* to be used?

  a Single-user, contiguous storage allocation system

  b Single-user, noncontiguous storage allocation system

  c Multiple-user, contiguous storage allocation system

  d Multiple-user, noncontiguous storage allocation system

13–6 Which of the following types of checks is *not* likely to be performed by a virtual memory addressing mechanism?

  a The address translation table is examined to determine the real memory address for the block number of the virtual memory address

  b The real memory address that corresponds to the virtual memory address is checked to see that it contains zeros

  c The displacement is checked to see that it is within the boundaries of the block

  d The actions to be undertaken on the block are checked to determine whether they are within the allowed set of actions

13–7 Which of the following is *not* likely to be a goal of a reliable operating system?

  a The operating system must protect the environment from user processes

  b The operating system must protect user processes from each other

  c The operating system must be protected from itself

  d The operating system must protect user processes from themselves

13–8 Which of the following operating system penetration techniques takes advantage of the time during which a legitimate user is still connected to the system but is inactive?

  a Between lines entry

  b Piggybacking

  c Trojan horse

  d Spoofing

13–9 Which of the following is *unlikely* to be a technique used to implement a covert storage channel whereby one process can communicate sensitive information to another unauthorized process?

  a Changing the name of a file in a world-readable directory

  b Changing the workload demands placed upon the central processor

  c Changing the date at which a file was last modified

  d Changing the number of files deleted from a directory

13–10 If an operating system uses a subset of the memory allocated to a user program for a work space, this integrity flaw is called:

  a Violable limits

  b Asynchronous validation

  c Implicit sharing of data

  d Browsing

13–11 The difference between a security kernel and a reference monitor is that:

  a A security kernel is a component implementation of a security policy, whereas a reference monitor is an abstract representation of a security policy

  b A reference monitor is the component in a security kernel that handles access to the resources to be protected

  c A reference monitor is used to protect resources in a single-state machine, whereas a security kernel is used to protect resources in a multiple-state machine

  d A reference monitor enforces a discretionary security policy, whereas a security kernel enforces a mandatory security policy

13–12 Which of the following statements about trusted processes is *false*?

  a Only trusted personnel, such as security administrators, should be authorized to use them

  b They are not bound by all the security rules implemented within the kernel

  c They are used to tailor a security policy to the specific needs of an organization

  d They are needed only if a security kernel implements a discretionary access control policy

13–13 Which of the following statements about Division C2 certification according to the U.S. National Computer Center's Trusted Computer Evaluation Criteria is *true*?

  a Mandatory access control at the group level must be supported

  b Discretionary access control at the individual level must be supported

  c The correspondence between the top-level specification and the formal security model must be verified

  d Objects must be protected based on a formal security model

13–14 Match the following:
   I   Field check
   II   Record check
   III   File check

   A   Control total
   B   Sign test
   C   Overflow check
   D   Crossfooting check

   a III-C; II-D; I-B; II-A
   b I-C; II-B; III-A; III-D
   c II-A; III-B; I-C; I-D
   d III-D; I-C; II-B; II-A

13–15 In the processing subsystem, hardware/software numerical hazards are *most likely* to arise because of:
   a Incorrect program design relating to subroutines called in a computation
   b Transient memory errors in the registers of the arithmetic unit of the central processor
   c Arithmetic idiosyncrasies of the machine on which the computation is done
   d Use of closed routines when undertaking floating-point arithmetic

13–16 Which of the following application program controls is *most likely* to mitigate expected losses associated with rounding errors in a calculation?
   a Avoidance of closed routines when arithmetic instructions must be executed
   b Minimization of human intervention in providing parameter values
   c Calling two or more subroutines that perform the same calculation using different algorithms
   d Printing run-to-run control totals to allow the accuracy and completeness of computations to be checked

13–17 Which of the following events is *most likely* to be included in the *accounting* audit trail for the processing subsystem?
   a Program start time
   b Attempted integrity violation
   c A hardware malfunction
   d A triggered transaction

13–18 Which of the following would *not* be a report that typically could be produced by generalized software that is available to interrogate the operations audit trail in the processing subsystem?
   a Hardware utilization report
   b Account implosion report
   c Program run time report
   d Report on programs abnormally terminated

13–19 The logging software used to maintain the operations audit trail in the processing subsystem can cause control problems because:
   a It can be used to modify or delete records accessed by an application system during production running of the system
   b It often is complex and error-prone
   c It is powerful yet easy to use even by a computer novice
   d Empirical evidence shows it is often the target of fraud

13–20 Checkpoint/restart facilities would *not* permit recovery from which of the following problems?
   a Loading the wrong tape reel in a multireel file
   b A temporary hardware error
   c Loading the wrong version of the update program
   d A power loss

Exercises and Cases

13–1 You are an information systems auditor in a public accounting firm that has just taken over the audit of a medium-sized manufacturing company from another firm. The hardware/software platform used by the company is quite old. Two microcomputers are connected to a server via a local area network (all the same type of machine). The manufacturing and accounting application software used was written specifically for the company by a firm of external consultants. Apart from minor modifications, the software has been relatively stable for some seven years. Each machine has multiple users. For example, a warehousing clerk and the production manager both use the same machine to record raw material receipts, releases of raw materials into production, and completions of finished goods. Similarly, several accounting clerks use the same machine to carry out various accounting functions.

When you question the general manager about the age of the hardware and software, he explains that he does not see information systems as being central to the strategic success of the company. For the past 10 years, the size and operations of the company have remained about the same. As a result, he argues that the need to upgrade software during this period has been minor, and the hardware has been replaced only once or twice as best he can recollect. In his opinion, the hardware/software platform used by the company has been an excellent workhorse.

As you collect evidence on the reliability of controls in the hardware/software platform, you obtain the following findings in relation to the hardware used by the company:

a The central processing unit in the three machines uses a single parity bit to detect errors in its registers.

b The central processing unit recognizes a supervisor state and a problem state, but this capability is not used by the operating system; the hardware effectively acts as a single-state machine.

c There are no timing controls to recognize application system loops, nor are there replicated components to provide fault tolerance.

d Memory errors are detected via a single parity bit.

e Memory is allocated to programs on a non-contiguous basis. No access controls are exercised, however, to ensure that programs reference a memory cell only within their allocated memory areas.

Required: What are the implications of these findings for the conduct of the remainder of the audit? Be sure to discuss how they will affect the tests of controls you might undertake and the substantive tests you might undertake.

13–2 Bull and Bear Ltd. is a new, aggressive, Boston-based, medium-sized brokerage firm. It specializes in offering high-quality, personalized service to clients who have a relatively high level of wealth. It is managed by a few individuals who are young, highly motivated, highly educated, and dynamic.

You are an information systems auditor in a firm of public accountants that has just taken over the audit of Bull and Bear from another firm. During an interview with the managing director of Bull and Bear, she emphasizes the extensive use that the company makes of information technology to support its operations. She states that systems within the company have been designed to allow individual professionals to offer a full range of services to each client. Clients do not have to be passed to different individuals to obtain the advice they need on various aspects of their portfolio of investments. The managing director also points out that the previous auditors had not been reappointed because they had failed to come to grips with how Bull and Bear uses information technology to support its operations.

When you ask about the reliability of controls over Bull and Bear's information systems, the managing director boasts that the Board has total commitment to control over the company's operations. In particular, she points out that the operating system used on Bull and Bear's main computer has been certified at level C1 by the National Computer Security Center. She remarks, however, that other controls have been implemented in the operating system in addition to those required for a C1 rating.

The requirements that an operating system must meet for it to be given a C1 rating (discretionary security protection) are as follows:

a A discretionary access control policy must be supported.

b Identification and authentication must be implemented on the basis of individual persons or groups of persons. In other words, identification and authentication can occur at the level of groups rather than individuals. Authentication data must be protected from unauthorized access.

c Security-relevant events do not have to be recorded in a protected audit trail.

d Objects that are reused (e.g., memory) might not be cleared prior to their assignment to another user. Thus, browsing or scavenging can occur.

e The operating system must be developed using principles of modularity, layering, data abstraction, and information hiding. It must be tested by qualified persons.

f The kernel of the operating system must be protected from other processes to ensure its integrity is maintained.

g The design of the operating system must be documented, especially its security features. Test documentation also must be available.

h There are no requirements to be met in terms of covert channel analysis, design verification, separation of duties relating to system operators and security administrators, configuration management, correct operation of security features after a system failure, and prevention of unauthorized modifications when the system is distributed to the customer by the vendor.

Required: Outline how the C1 rating for the operating system is likely to affect the conduct of the audit. In particular, what are the likely implications for the design of tests of controls and substantive tests?

13–3 Sunshine Credit Union is a small credit union based in San Diego. In the past financial year, it has moved from using a microcomputer-based package to using the services of a computer service bureau to carry out its data processing (outsourcing its data processing). The bureau provides a popular generalized package to support the data processing needs of credit unions. Individual credit unions access this package via microcomputer terminals located in their offices. In addition, the service bureau machine has access to various financial networks. Thus, with the move to the service bureau, Sunshine has been able to offer an expanded range of services to its members.

Since the move to the bureau, the directors of the credit union have appointed a new director of financial services, Timothy Swan, with a view to improving the services offered to members. At the outset, Swan undertook a thorough review of Sunshine's accounting systems with the objective of streamlining the systems and improving control. In particular, he took advantage of the access controls provided within the credit union package and set up a system of passwords to restrict the action privileges of each employee to those commensurate with their responsibilities.

Swan still had some doubts about controls within the credit union package used by Sunshine, although the system appeared to provide good controls and to restrict the activities of credit union staff to their assigned action privileges. Because he had little technical knowledge of computer systems, however, he hired an information systems audit consultant, Helen Webb, to examine controls within the service bureau's system.

At their first meeting, Webb indicated that she was familiar with the operating system used by the service bureau, although she was not familiar with the package used to carry out the basic data processing. Nevertheless, as an initial step she asked Swan to sign on at a terminal and to show her the system. Once he had signed on, she asked him to attempt to call up the system editor. Swan indicated that he did not understand what she meant by the editor as he had never used the program before. She described the nature of the editor and gave him the command to invoke the editor. Swan noted her concern when the editor was successfully activated.

Next she asked him to attach the editor to a specific file, and she gave him the command to carry out the action. Again, he noted her concern when the system indicated the command had been successfully executed. When he queried her about her obvious concerns, she indicated that the editor had been successfully attached to the password file.

Finally, Webb asked Swan to attempt to invoke two other programs. She gave him the commands to use, and again the system indicated that the programs were available for use. When Swan asked Webb about the nature of these two programs, she indicated they were the copy and delete utilities provided by the operating system.

Required: Why is Webb concerned about the results obtained so far? What exposures does Sunshine face? Given that Sunshine is using a service bureau for its data processing activities, what actions would you recommend be taken to overcome the problems that exist?

13–4 Wombat Ltd. is a Sydney-based company that specializes in gathering and processing seismic data. It is employed by oil companies all over the world to undertake work in support of their exploration activities.

You are an information systems auditor in the chartered accounting firm that undertakes the statutory audit of Wombat's financial affairs. During your firm's year-end audit work, a major dispute arises between Wombat and one of its occasional customers. The customer has indicated it will sue Wombat to recover $50 million that it has expended in sinking several oil wells that turned out to be dry. The customer alleges that the output provided by one of Wombat's seismic data analysis systems is incorrect. The calculations undertaken by the system are erroneous. As a result, it has sunk oil wells in the wrong location.

When the impending law suit is revealed, your partner becomes concerned about the likelihood of its success and the size of the damages that might be awarded. Aside from the statutory requirement to disclose contingent liabilities in Wombat's financial statements, she is worried that Wombat may be unable to continue as a going concern if sizeable damages are awarded to the customer.

Required: Your partner asks you to prepare a confidential report that provides an opinion on the reliability of the controls exercised over the development, implementation, and operation of the application system that is the subject of the dispute. Outline a work plan that will enable you to gather the kinds of information you will need to form an opinion.

13–5 The information systems department in your organization has recently purchased a checkpoint/restart facility to support their batch processing operations. Although batch systems are only a small part of the applications portfolio in your organization, nevertheless there are several systems run overnight that consume substantial resources. Furthermore, these systems must meet tight production schedules. The checkpoint/restart facility was purchased in light of problems caused by power fluctuations. The utility company has indicated that periods of unstable power supply are likely to continue because of heavy demands that continue to be imposed upon them by several new industrial plants that have recently opened in the area.

As the internal auditor within your organization, you decide to investigate the reliability of the checkpoint/restart facility. In a series of tests that you conduct, the facility performs according to specifications. As you are about to conclude your tests, however, you find that you can easily access the contents of the log file maintained by the facility using the editor provided within the operating system.

Required: What exposures exist in light of the flaw that you have discovered in the facility? Given that you cannot prohibit use of the facility, what control recommendations would you make to try to reduce the likelihood of losses from the exposure?

Answers to Multiple-Choice Questions

13–1	a	**13–6**	b	**13–11**	a	**13–16**	c
13–2	c	**13–7**	a	**13–12**	d	**13–17**	d
13–3	d	**13–8**	a	**13–13**	b	**13–18**	b
13–4	d	**13–9**	b	**13–14**	b	**13–19**	a
13–5	d	**13–10**	c	**13–15**	c	**13–20**	c

REFERENCES

Abbott, R. P., J. S. Chin, J. E. Donnelley, W. L. Konigsford, S. Tokubo, and D. A. Webb (1976), *Security Analysis and Enhancements of Computer Operating Systems.* Washington, DC: Institute for Computer Sciences and Technology, National Bureau of Standards, Report No. NBSIR-76-1041.

Bowen, Nicholas S., and Dhiraj K. Pradhan (1993), "Processor- and Memory-Based Checkpoint and Rollback Recovery," *IEEE Computer* (February), 22–31.

Bruce, Glen, and Rob Dempsey (1997), *Security in Distributed Computing: Did You Lock the Door?* Upper Saddle River, NJ: Prentice-Hall.

Calabrese, Christopher J. (1991), "A Brief Introduction to the Unix® Operating System," *The EDP Auditor Journal*, III, 25–30.

Castano, Silvana, Maria Grazia Fugini, Giancario Martella, and Pierangela Samarati (1995), *Database Security.* Reading MA: Addison-Wesley.

Chokhani, Santosh (1992), "Trusted Products Evaluation," *Communications of the ACM* (July), 64–76.

Curry, David A. (1992), *Unix ™ System Security: A Guide for Users and Administrators.* Reading, MA: Addison-Wesley.

Denning, Dorothy E. (1976), "A Lattice Model of Secure Information Flow," *Communications of the ACM* (May), 236–243.

Denning, Peter J. (1976), "Fault-Tolerant Operating Systems," *Computing Surveys* (December), 359–390.

Fujiwara, Eiji, and Dhiraj K. Pradhan (1990), "Error-Control Coding in Computers," *IEEE Computer* (July), 63–72.

Gasser, Morrie (1988), *Building a Secure Computer System*. New York: Van Nostrand Reinhold.

Hatton, Les, and Andy Roberts (1994), "How Accurate is Scientific Software?" *IEEE Transactions on Software Engineering* (October), 785–797.

Henderson, Stuart (1997), "Trends in MVS Security," *EDPACS* (February), 1–10.

——— (1997), "How to Audit Windows NT Security," *IS Audit & Control Journal*, III, 30–32, 34–36.

Holden, Donald B. (1993), "Open VMS VAX Security Architecture," *The EDP Auditor Journal*, I, 38–45.

Kaplan, Ray, and Joe Kovara (1993), "Technical Implementation of VAX/VMS Security," *The EDP Auditor Journal*, I, 47–53.

Karger, Paul A., Mary Ellen Zurko, Douglas W. Bonin, Andrew H. Mason, and Clifford E. Kahn (1991), "A Retrospective on the VAX VMM Security Kernel," *IEEE Transactions on Software Engineering* (November), 1147–1165.

Klaus, Christopher (1997), "An Introduction to Backdoors," *EDPACS* (December), 1–9.

Lampson, Butler W. (1973), "A Note on the Confinement Problem," *Communications of the ACM* (October), 613–615.

Landwehr, Carl E., Alan R. Bull, John P. McDermott, and William S. Choi (1994), "A Taxonomy of Computer Program Security Flaws," *Computing Surveys* (September), 211–254.

Linden, Theodore A. (1976), "Operating System Structures to Support Security and Reliable Software," *Computing Surveys* (December), 410–445.

Nelson, Victor P. (1990), "Fault Tolerant Computing: Fundamental Concepts," *IEEE Computer* (July), 19–25.

O'Shea, G. (1991), *Security in Computer Operating Systems*. Oxford: NCC Blackwell.

Pfleeger, Charles P. (1997), *Security in Computing*, 2d ed. Upper Saddle River, NJ: Prentice-Hall.

Schell, Roger R., and Harold J. Brinkley (1995), "Evaluation Criteria for Trusted Systems," in Marshall D. Abrams, Sushil Jajodia, and Harold J. Podell, eds., *Information Security: An Integrated Collection of Essays*. Los Alamitos, CA: IEEE Computer Society Press, 137–159.

Siewiorek, Daniel P. (1990), "Fault Tolerance in Commercial Computers," *IEEE Computer* (July), 26–37.

Silberschatz, Abraham, and Peter B. Galvin (1998), *Operating System Concepts*, 5th ed. Reading, MA: Addison-Wesley.

Spafford, Eugene H. (1989), "The Internet Worm: Crisis and Aftermath," *Communications of the ACM* (June), 678–687.

Stallings, William (1996), *Computer Organization and Architecture: Designing for Performance*, 4th ed. Upper Saddle River, NJ: Prentice-Hall.

——— (1998), *Operating Systems: Internals and Design*, 3d ed. Upper Saddle River, NJ: Prentice-Hall.

Stepczyk, F. M. (1974), "Requirements for Secure Operating Systems," in *Data Security and Data Processing Volume 5 Study Results: TRW Systems, Inc.* New York: IBM Corporation, 75–205.

Tanenbaum, Andrew S. (1990), *Structured Computer Organization*, 3d ed. Upper Saddle River, NJ: Prentice-Hall.

——— (1992), *Modern Operating Systems*. Upper Saddle River, NJ: Prentice-Hall.

U.S. Department of Defense (1985), *DoD Trusted Computer System Evaluation Criteria*. Washington, DC: Department of Defense. DOD 5200.28-STD. U.S. Government Printing Office Number 008–000–00461–7.

Weissman, Clark (1995), "Penetration Testing," in Marshall D. Abrams, Sushil Jajodia, and Harold J. Podell, eds., *Information Security: An Integrated Collection of Essays*. Los Alamitos, CA: IEEE Computer Society Press, 269–296.

CHAPTER 14

Database Controls

Chapter Outline

Chapter Key Points

■ The database subsystem is responsible for defining, creating, modifying, deleting, and reading data in an information system. It maintains declarative data, relating to the static aspects of real-world objects and their associations, and procedural data, relating to the dynamic aspects of real-world objects and their associations. The major components in the database subsystem are the database management system used to manage data, the application programs that perform operations on data, the central processor and primary storage in which operations are performed, and the storage media that maintains the permanent or semipermanent copy of the database.

■ Access controls are used in the database subsystem to prevent unauthorized access to and use of data. A discretionary access control policy can be used, which allows users to specify who can access the data they own and what action privileges they have with respect to the data. A mandatory access control policy requires a system administrator to assign security aspects to data that cannot be changed by database users.

■ Under a discretionary access control policy, users who are not owners of data can be subjected to four types of access restriction: (a) name-dependent access control, which permits or denies access to a named data resource; (b) content-dependent access control, which permits or denies access depending on the content of the data item; (c) context-dependent restriction, which permits or denies access depending on the context (e.g., revelation of a specific data item value versus access for statistical purposes); and (d) history-dependent access, which permits or denies access depending on the history of prior accesses to the database. These types of restrictions can be implemented via views of the database.

■ Under a mandatory access control policy, classification levels can be assigned to specific data items/attributes in a record/relation and to records/relations as a whole. The value of the classification level is then compared against the user's clearance level to determine whether the data item/attribute or record/relation will be made available to the user.

■ A good database management system will enforce various types of integrity constraints to maintain the accuracy, completeness, and uniqueness of instances of the constructs used within the conceptual modelling or data modelling approach used to structure data in the database. For example, if the entity-relationship model is used, the database management system should ensure that each instance of an entity is unique and that the value of an attribute falls within an allowed set of values; if the relational data model is used, the database management system must ensure that key values uniquely identify each instance of a relation and that primary keys never have a null value; if the object data model is used, the database management system must ensure that each object is assigned a unique identifier and that subtypes comply with all the integrity constraints they inherit from their supertype.

■ When application programs use the database, they should follow certain update and report protocols to protect the integrity of the database. The update protocols include (a) sequence checking the order of the transaction file and master file during batch updates, (b) ensuring correct end-of-file procedures are followed so that records are not lost, (c) processing multiple transactions for a single record in the correct order, (d) and posting monetary transactions that mismatch a master file record against a suspense account. The report protocols include (a) printing control data for internal tables/standing data to ensure it remains accurate and complete, (b) printing run-to-run control totals, and (c) printing suspense account entries.

■ Data integrity can be violated when two processes are allowed concurrent access to a data item. One process could read and update a data item at the same time as another process reads and updates the data item. The effect of one update operation can be lost. Locking out one process while the other process completes its update can lead to a situation called deadlock in which two processes are waiting for each other to release a data item that the other needs. A widely accepted solution to deadlock is two-phase locking, in which all the data items needed to propagate the effects of a transaction are first obtained and locked from other processes. The data items are not released until all updates on the data items have been completed.

■ Concurrency controls in a distributed database environment can be complex. In a replicated database, one solution to the concurrency problem is to designate one replica of the database as the primary copy. Before accessing a data item, a transaction must acquire the lock for the primary copy. In a partitioned database, a transaction must first find the scheduler for the data item it is seeking to access.

■ Cryptographic controls can be used to protect the integrity of data in the database. The primary means of encrypting data is block encryption, because use of stream encryption would mean other blocks of data have to be retrieved to decrypt the required data. In the case of portable storage media, encryption can be carried out by a cryptographic device in the controller. The privacy of data is protected if the media is stolen, but one user's data is not protected from access by another user. To protect one user's data from access by another user, cryptographic keys must be assigned to the owner of the data and those users allowed to access the data.

■ File handling controls are used to prevent accidental destruction of data contained on a storage medium by an operator, user, or program. They include internal labels, generation numbers, retention dates, control totals, magnetic tape file protection rings, read-only switches, and external labels.

■ The accounting audit trail in the database subsystem maintains the chronology of events that occur to the database definition or the database itself. It must permit either an implosion operation or an explosion operation. Under implosion, a data item can be traced from its source to the data item it affects. Under explosion, the sequence of events that have occurred to a data item in the database definition or the database can be reconstructed. It is difficult to achieve the implosion and explosion requirements when certain types of changes occur within the database definition—for example, the database definition changes or the coding system changes, and a user query transcends the period before the change and the period after the change.

■ The operations audit trail in the database subsystem maintains the chronology of resource consumption events that affect the database definition or the database. Data administrators and database administrators can use the operations audit trail to determine when the database needs to be reorganized or when the processes that access the database need to be rewritten to improve their efficiency.

■ Existence controls are needed to recover the database from five types of failure: (a) application program error, (b) system software error, (c) hardware failure, (d) procedural error, and (e) environmental failure. Existence controls encompass both a backup strategy and a recovery strategy. All backup strategies require maintenance of a prior version of the database and a log of transactions or changes to the database. Recovery strategies take two forms: (a) rollforward, whereby the current state of the database is recovered from a previous version, and (b) rollback, whereby a previous state of the database is recovered from the current state.

■ The grandfather, father, son backup and recovery strategy involves maintaining the previous two versions of a master file and the previous version of the transaction file. If the current (son) version of the master file is lost, it can be recovered by processing the current transaction file against the previous version of the master file (father). If the previous version of the master file is lost during recovery, it too can be recovered by using the grandfather version of the master file and the previous version of the transaction file.

■ The dual recording or mirroring backup and recovery strategy involves maintaining two completely separate copies of the database (preferably, at two different locations) and updating both simultaneously. Dual recording/mirroring assists a recovery from environmental failure, processor failure, or storage medium failure, but it does not protect the database against software error or procedural error.

∎ Dumping involves copying the whole or a portion of the database to some backup medium. Recovery involves rewriting the dump back to the primary storage medium and reprocessing transactions that have occurred since the time of the dump. Either physical dumps or logical dumps can be taken. Physical dumping involves reading and copying the database in the serial order of the records on the storage medium. It facilitates global recovery of the database. Logical dumping involves reading and copying the database in the serial order of the logical records in a file. It facilitates selective recovery of the database.

∎ Logging involves recording a transaction that changes the database or an image of the record changed by an update action. Three types of logs can be kept: (a) transaction logs to allow reprocessing of transactions during recovery; (b) beforeimage logs to allow rollback of the database; and (c) afterimage logs to allow rollforward of the database.

∎ Residual dumping involves logging records that have not been changed since the last database dump. The database is recovered by going back to but not including the second last residual dump and rolling forward the database using the residual dump log. Residual dumping reduces the overheads associated with dumping because records that have been changed and recorded on the log are not then dumped.

∎ The differential file/shadow paging backup and recovery strategy involves keeping the database intact and writing changes to the database to a separate file. In due course these changes are written to the database. If failure occurs before the changes are applied, the intact database constitutes a prior dump of the database. Providing a log of transactions have been kept, these transactions can then be reprocessed against the database.

INTRODUCTION

The database subsystem provides functions to define, create, modify, delete, and read data in an information system. Historically, the primary type of data maintained in the database subsystem has been *declarative* data—that is, data that describes the static aspects of real-world objects and associations among these objects. For example, a payroll file and a personnel file store information about the pay rates for each employee, the various positions within an organization, and the employees who have been assigned to each position. The database subsystem might also be used, however, to maintain *procedural* data—that is, data that describes the dynamic aspects of real-world objects and the associations among these objects. For example, the database might contain a set of rules describing how an expert portfolio manager makes decisions about which stocks and bonds to choose for investment purposes. When both declarative and procedural data are stored, the database is sometimes called a *knowledge base* to reflect the greater "power" of the data maintained in the database subsystem.

The database subsystem is also being used increasingly to store *(1)* data about designs (e.g., manufacturing designs), in which the focus is design objects that can be composed or decomposed into other design objects, and *(2)* images, graphics, audio, and video, which can be used to support a multimedia application. In this light, substantial work is now being undertaken on *object-oriented* database management systems to support these types of applications. Moreover, with the emergence of huge databases and increasing use of decision support systems and executive information systems, there has been renewed interest in how databases should be structured to allow recognition of patterns among data, thereby facilitating knowledge discovery by decision makers. Huge databases that contain integrated data, detailed and summarized data, historical data, and metadata are sometimes called *data warehouses* (Inmon 1996). Databases that contain a selection of data from a data warehouse that is intended for a single function or department are called *data marts*. The process of recognizing patterns among data in data warehouses or data marts is sometimes called *data mining* (Brachman 1996).

Initially, the major components in the database subsystem were the application programs that defined, created, modified, and deleted data, the operating system that performed the basic input/output operations to move data to and from various storage media, the central processor and primary storage in which these activities were performed, and the storage media that maintained the permanent or semipermanent copy of the data. To achieve the objectives of database management outlined in Chapter 6, however, and to provide effective and efficient processing of procedural data, some important changes have occurred to the components used by the database subsystem. For example, the activities previously performed by application programs and operating systems have been migrated to database management systems; special database machines have been developed to support the database subsystem; expert systems have been developed to support the processing of procedural data.

In this chapter we examine controls over the database subsystem. We begin by discussing the policies and mechanisms needed to prevent unauthorized access to and use of the database. Next we examine the various types of integrity constraints that a database management system should maintain over a database. We then discuss the various controls that can be used within application software to maintain the integrity of data, the controls that must be exercised to prevent integrity violations when multiple programs have concurrent access to data, the ways in which data privacy can be preserved via cryptographic controls in the database subsystem, and the ways in which files must be processed to prevent integrity violations. Finally, we examine audit trail controls and existence controls within the database subsystem.

ACCESS CONTROLS

Access controls in the database subsystem seek to prevent unauthorized access to and use of data. As with all subsystems, access controls are implemented by first specifying a security policy for the subsystem and then choosing an access control mechanism that will enforce the policy chosen.

Recall that in Chapter 10 we examined security policies that enforce *discretionary* access control and security policies that enforce *mandatory* access control. In the database subsystem, the former allow users to specify who can access data they own and what action privileges they have with respect to that data. The latter require a system administrator to assign security attributes to data that cannot be changed by database users. In the following two subsections, we examine how both types of security policy might be applied within the database subsystem. In the third subsection, we discuss some implementation issues relating to the access control mechanisms that are used in the database subsystem.

Discretionary Access Controls

In the database subsystem, discretionary access controls can vary considerably. For example, if a relational database management subsystem is used to support the database subsystem, a user may be authorized to do the following:

- Create a schema;
- Create, modify, or delete views associated with the schema;
- Create, modify, or delete relations associated with the schema;
- Create, modify, or delete tuples in relations associated with the schema; and
- Retrieve data from tuples in relations associated with the schema.

These privileges often are given to users who are designated as the "owners" of a particular schema and its associated views and relations. Nevertheless, some might be assigned to users even if they are *not* the owners of a schema and its associated views and relations. For example, nonowner users might be allowed to create relational tuples or to delete tuples.

If users are *not* the owners of a schema and its associated views and relations, however, often they will be assigned more restricted privileges than those assigned to owners. These restrictions can be many and varied. Some important types of restrictions, however, are the following:

1. *Name-dependent restrictions.* Users either have access to a *named* data resource or they do not have access to the resource. If users have access to a data resource, the action privileges they have must also be specified. In the personnel database shown in Figure 14–1, for example, the payroll clerk

FIGURE 14–1. Name-dependent access control.

Personnel database

Name	Location	Salary	Home address	Performance rating
Smith	Production	56000	16 Park St., Anytown	2
Jones	Accounting	44000	2 Odd St., Anytown	4
Brown	Marketing	64000	26 Small Lane, Somewhere	1
Thomas	Research	68000	84 March St., Anytown	1

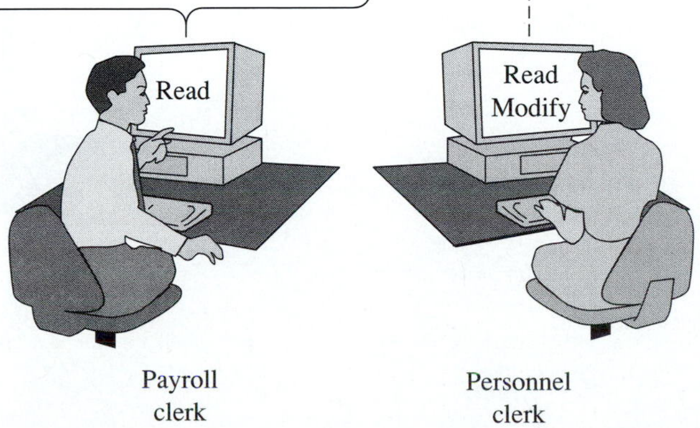

Read

Read
Modify

Payroll
clerk

Personnel
clerk

can read only the names of persons, their location, and their salary. On the other hand, the personnel clerk can read and modify the names of persons, their salary, their location, and their home address. Neither the payroll clerk nor the personnel clerk can access a person's work performance rating. This type of access control is also known as content-independent access control.

2. *Content-dependent restrictions.* Users are permitted or denied access to a data resource depending on its contents. In the personnel database shown in Figure 14–2, for example, the personnel clerk is not permitted to access the salary of an employee if it exceeds $60,000.

3. *Context-dependent restrictions.* Users are permitted or denied access to a data resource depending on the context in which they are seeking access. In the personnel database shown in Figure 14–3, for example, personnel clerks are not permitted access to the names of employees whose salaries exceed $60,000 unless they are seeking to execute some type of statistical function (such as calculating the average) on the salary data item values.

4. *History-dependent restrictions.* Users are permitted or denied access to a resource depending on the time series of accesses to and actions they have undertaken on data resources. For example, payroll clerks might not be permitted to read the names of employees who have salaries over $60,000. They might not be prevented from reading salaries, however, if they do not access the employee name data item. To circumvent the restriction, clerks could access the location and salary data and print the values for both data items. Next, they could access the location and name data items and print their values. If the sequence in which both requests were executed was the same, the names and salaries of employees could then be matched easily. History-

---

FIGURE 14–2. Content-dependent access control.

Personnel database

Name	Location	Salary	Home address	Performance rating
Smith	Production	56000	16 Park St., Anytown	2
Jones	Accounting	44000	2 Odd St., Anytown	4
Brown	Marketing	64000	26 Small Lane, Somewhere	1
Thomas	Research	68000	84 March St., Anytown	1

Read
Modify

Personnel
clerk

Personnel database

Name	Location	Salary	Home address	Performance rating
Smith	Production	56000	16 Park St., Anytown	2
Jones	Accounting	44000	2 Odd St., Anytown	4
Brown	Marketing	64000	26 Small Lane, Somewhere	1
Thomas	Research	68000	84 March St., Anytown	1

Statistical Function

Personnel clerk

FIGURE 14–3. Context-dependent access control.

dependent access controls would prevent this type of unauthorized action from occurring.

One way in which these four types of restriction are sometimes enforced is via the implementation of *views* (or *subschemas*). Recall from Chapter 6 that a view presents only a subset of the database to a user. Views simply might enforce name-dependent restrictions; in other words, certain named data items might not be available to a user via the view. The data presented to a user via a view can also be restricted using some type of conditional expression, thereby enforcing content-dependent, context-dependent, and history-dependent restrictions.

An important type of privilege we have not considered so far is a user's ability to grant their privileges (or some subset of their privileges) to another user. If the owner of, say, a view grants privileges to another user who in turn grants these privileges to another user, the privileges are said to *propagate* through the user community. Different types of controls might need to be exercised over the *extent* of propagation that occurs. One type is a *horizontal propagation* control, which limits the number of users to whom a user can assign privileges (Figure 14–4a). Another type is a *vertical propagation* control, which limits the depth of propagation or number of users in a sequence who can be granted privileges (Figure 14–4b).

If propagation of privileges is permitted, auditors should also check that it is possible to revoke the privileges. If, for example, owners discover they have assigned privileges to a user who acts improperly, they might wish to cancel the privileges. Moreover, they also might wish to cancel any privileges obtained by another user as a result of propagation. Otherwise, it might be difficult if not impossible to limit expected losses from irregularities that occur as a result of misuse of privileges.

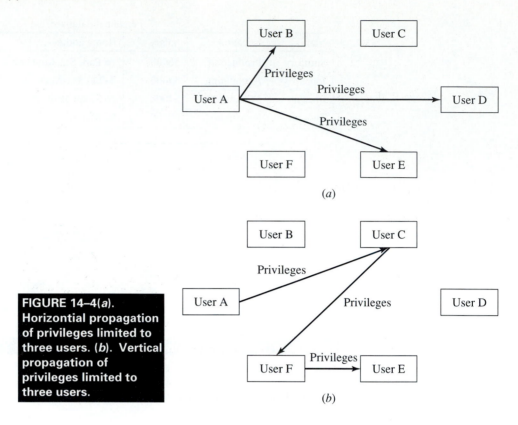

FIGURE 14–4(a). Horizontial propagation of privileges limited to three users. (b). Vertical propagation of privileges limited to three users.

Mandatory Access Controls

Recall from Chapter 10 that the U.S. Department of Defense has proposed an approach to establishing mandatory access controls. Under this approach, resources are assigned a *classification* level and users are assigned a *clearance* level. User access to a resource is then governed by a security policy, such as that specified in Bell and LaPadula's model or Biba's model (see Chapter 10). For example, users are not allowed to read a resource unless their clearance level is greater than or equal to the resource's classification level.

In the database subsystem, one way to implement this approach is to assign a classification level to each data item/attribute in a record/relation. Access to a data item/attribute is then governed by the rules specified in Bell and La-Padula's model and Biba's model. A classification level might also be assigned to a record/relation as a whole. The value of the classification level assigned to each record/relation should be equal to the highest classification level assigned to a data item/attribute in the record/relation.

In effect, the security and integrity rules present a *view* of the database to a user. Users are not permitted to see or to update all data in the database. One way to implement the view is by *filtering* data in a record/relation tuple or instance. Using this approach, a single tuple is stored. Conditional statements are then applied to determine what data in the tuple will be available to a user. A second approach is to create multiple tuples that satisfy the security and integrity rules applicable to each clearance level. This approach is known as *polyinstantiation*. The two approaches have different strengths and weaknesses, but we will leave these issues for further study.

Some Implementation Issues

A major factor affecting the reliability of the access control mechanism is the extent to which it is located in a single component or multiple components. As discussed in Chapters 10 and 13, the reliability of an access control mechanism can be increased if it is embedded within a single, secure, verified component—the kernel of the operating system. Moreover, access control rules are more likely to be applied consistently if they are exercised by a single component.

Unfortunately, practical constraints often dictate that the access control mechanism be distributed across several components. As the functions to be performed by the access control mechanism increase, the size and complexity of the kernel increase correspondingly. Thus, devising efficient implementations of the kernel is more difficult to achieve. Moreover, it becomes more difficult to verify the accuracy and completeness of the functions performed by the kernel and to maintain the security and integrity of the kernel.

For these reasons, access control rules in the database subsystem are often exercised by both the operating system and the database management system components. For example, to be granted access to the database, users might first have to be given access to the database management system. The operating system might restrict who has access to the database management system. If users are given access to the database management system, however, they then might have to identify and authenticate themselves again to the database management system to obtain access to data and to be given certain action privileges on the data. Providing users can gain access to the database only through the database management system, there is little risk of inconsistent access control rules being applied under this approach. If users can gain access to the database without having to go through the database management system, however, there is a risk that the access control rules applied by the database management system and those applied by, say, the operating system will be inconsistent.

When a database is distributed, it is even more difficult to ensure that the security and integrity of the access control mechanism is maintained and that a complete and consistent set of access control rules is enforced throughout the database subsystem. Regardless of whether the database is replicated at multiple sites or partitioned with different parts being distributed to different sites, efficiency considerations dictate that multiple access control mechanisms must often be used to support each replication or partition. If the database is replicated, the same access control rules must be enforced by the access control mechanism at each site. If the database is partitioned, user requests must be routed accurately and completely to the access control mechanism that mediates access to the data resource that has been requested. In each case, a complex set of functions have to be performed whose accuracy and completeness are difficult to verify and whose security and integrity are difficult to protect.

INTEGRITY CONTROLS

A good database management system will enforce various types of *integrity constraints* within the database subsystem. Integrity constraints are established to maintain the accuracy, completeness, and uniqueness of instances of the constructs used within the conceptual modelling or data modelling approach used to represent the real-world phenomena about which data is to be stored in the database subsystem.

The specific types of constraints provided by the system will depend to some extent on the conceptual modelling and data modelling approaches it supports. To illustrate the nature of integrity constraints that might be enforced, however, the following subsections provide an overview of some types of constraints associated with the entity-relationship model, relational data model, and object data model.

Entity-Relationship Model Integrity Constraints

The fundamental constructs in the entity-relationship model are entities, relationships between entities, and attributes of entities (see Appendix 4.3). *Entities* constitute the basic types (classes) of things (objects) in the real world to be modelled. Within the database subsystem, the following integrity constraints might be applied to entities:

Integrity Constraint	*Explanation*
Uniqueness	Each instance of an entity must be unique.
Maximum cardinality	Specifies the maximum number of instances of an entity that can exist in the database.
Minimum cardinality	Specifies the minimum number of instances of an entity that can exist in the database.
Entity identifier	Specifies the attribute(s) whose value(s) uniquely identify each instance of an entity.
Value type of identifier	Specifies the allowed value types for the attributes that comprise an entity's identifier—e.g., real number, integer, alphanumeric string.
Value set of identifier	Specifies the allowed set of values for the attributes that comprise the entity's identifier.

In the entity-relationship model, *relationships* reflect that two or more entities are coupled in some way. For example, a relationship might be shown between a student entity and a university entity to indicate that students attend universities. Within the database subsystem, a major type of integrity constraint that applies to relationships is a *cardinality* constraint. A cardinality constraint specifies either *(1)* the *maximum* number of instances of an entity that can be associated with an instance of another entity (or tuple of instances of multiple entities) or *(2)* the *minimum* number of instances of an entity that can be associated with an instance of another entity (or tuple of instances of multiple entities) (Figure 14–5).

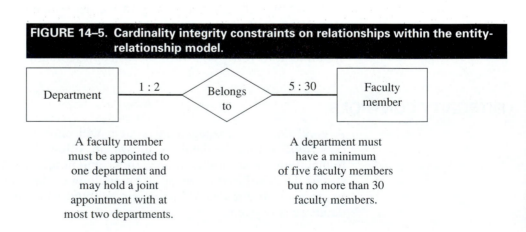

FIGURE 14–5. Cardinality integrity constraints on relationships within the entity-relationship model.

In the entity-relationship model, *attributes* reflect the properties possessed by entities. For example, two attributes of a person entity are age and gender. Within the database subsystem, the following integrity constraints might be applied to attributes:

Integrity Constraint	*Explanation*
Value type of attribute	Specifies the allowed value types for an attribute—e.g., real number, integer, alphanumeric string.
Value set of attribute	Specifies the allowed set of values for an attribute.
Transition law	Specifies the relationship between an attribute's previous value and its new value.

Relational Data Model Integrity Constraints

The fundamental construct in the relational data model is a relation (see Appendix 4.4). Within the database subsystem, the following integrity constraints might be applied to relations:

Integrity Constraint	*Explanation*
Key	Key constraints specify the candidate keys of a relation. Candidate key values must uniquely identify each tuple of a relation.
Entity	Entity integrity constraints are established to ensure that primary keys never have a null value.
Referential	Referential integrity constraints are established to maintain consistency among tuples in relations. If a tuple in a relation refers to data in another tuple of the relation or a tuple of another relation (via a foreign key), referential integrity contraints ensure that the referenced tuple must exist.

Object Data Model Integrity Constraints

The fundamental constructs in the object data model are objects and relationships among objects (see Appendix 4.2). *Objects* possess structural properties (attributes), which reflect the static characteristics of the object, and dynamic properties (methods or procedures), which reflect how the state of an object can change. Within the database subsystem, the following integrity constraints might be applied to the *structural properties* of objects:

Integrity Constraint	*Explanation*
Unique identifier	Each object must be unique. The database system can generate an object identifier that uniquely identifies the object throughout its life.
Unique key	Object keys are distinct from object identifiers. The former are system generated; the latter are user generated. Different constraints can apply to object keys. For example, keys might have to be unique within an object type or within all subtypes of a type. They might not have to be unique, however, across different object types.
Value type of attribute	Specifies the allowed value types for an attribute of an object—e.g., real number, integer, alphanumeric string, sets, lists, and arrays.

(cont.)

Integrity Constraint	*Explanation*
Value set of attribute	Specifies the allowed set of values for an attribute of an object. The values of an attribute might be defined procedurally (via a method) as a function of the values of other attributes of the object.
Types and inheritance	Ensures that an object of a subtype complies with all the integrity contraints associated with its supertype.

In the object data model, *dynamic properties* are the procedures that operate on objects. Dynamic properties facilitate encapsulation, whereby the structural characteristics of an object (or most of them) are kept hidden and only the procedures or methods (or at least a subset of them) are made public. Within the database subsystem, methods or procedures must comply with the syntactic and semantic rules of the language used to express them.

In the object data model, *relationships* among objects indicate that the property values of at least one of the objects depend on the property values of other objects in the relationship or that an object is a component of another object (aggregation or composition). Within the database subsystem, the following integrity constraints might be applied to relationships:

Integrity Constraint	*Explanation*
Referential	If one object refers to another object, the second object must exist and be of the correct type.
Composition	Specifies the actions to be undertaken upon insertion or deletion of objects that participate in composite relationships. For example, if an assembly is deleted from the database, all its subassemblies also must be deleted.
Cardinality	Specifies the minimum or maximum number of objects of particular types that can participate in a relationship.

APPLICATION SOFTWARE CONTROLS

As with the processing subsystem, the integrity of the database subsystem depends in part on controls that have been implemented in any application programs that use the database. Even though the database management system rather than the application software should directly access and update the database, nevertheless the database management system still depends on the application software to pass across a correct sequence of commands and update parameters and to take appropriate actions when certain types of exception conditions arise. Accordingly, the following subsections describe various update and report protocols that might be implemented in application software to protect the integrity of the database.

Update Protocols

Update protocols in application software seek to ensure that changes to the database reflect changes to the real-world entities and associations between entities that data in the database is supposed to represent. We briefly examine some of the more important protocols in the following subsections.

Sequence Check Transaction and Master Files

In a batch update run, the transaction file is often sorted prior to the update of the master file or the tables in the database. In some cases, the master file or tables to be updated might also be sorted into a particular order. It might seem superfluous, therefore, for the update program to then check the sequence of the transaction file (and perhaps the master file or tables) as it processes each record. Nevertheless, sometimes situations arise that result in records on the transaction file (or master file) unexpectedly getting out of sequence. First, some "patching" of the file can occur because of a previous error. If the patching is done incorrectly, the file could get out of sequence. Second, an erroneous program could insert records in the incorrect sequence on the file. Third, on rare occasions a sort utility incorrectly sorts a file, or a hardware/system software error that corrupts the sequence of a file goes undetected. Fourth, undetected corruption of data might have occurred when the file was sent across a communication line.

Ensure All Records on Files Are Processed

If a master file is maintained in sequential order, correct end-of-file protocols must be followed in an update program to ensure records are not lost from either a transaction file or a master file. Common errors are to close the transaction file upon reaching the end of the master file or to close the master file upon reaching the end of the transaction file. In the former case, the transaction file might contain new records for insertion after the last record on the old master file. In the latter case, existing master file records could be lost because an end-of-file marker is placed at the point of closure. Designing and implementing correct end-of-file protocols can be an especially complex task if multiple sequential transaction files and multiple sequential master files are to be processed concurrently.

Process Multiple Transactions for a Single Record in the Correct Order

Multiple transactions can occur for a single master record (tuple). For example, several sales orders plus a change-of-address transaction might have to be processed against a customer master record. The order in which transactions are processed against the master record can be important. Otherwise, several types of error can occur. For example, a customer might be billed at a wrong address, an employee might be paid after termination, or a person might receive welfare payments to which they are not entitled. Different types of transactions must be given transaction codes that result in their being sorted in the correct order before being processed against a master record.

Maintain a Suspense Account

Whenever monetary transactions must be processed against a master file (tables), the update program should maintain a suspense account. The suspense account is the repository for monetary transactions for which a matching master record cannot be found at the time an update is attempted. Mismatches can occur for several reasons; for example, an account number might be coded incorrectly in a transaction, a new account might not have been inserted correctly on the master file (table), or a transaction for a master record (tuple) might arrive before the master record (tuple) has been created. If monetary transactions for which a corresponding master record cannot be found are not charged to a suspense account, they can be lost because someone fails to correct the mismatch. Suspense accounts that have a nonzero balance provide a reminder that errors have occurred which still have to be corrected.

Report Protocols

Report protocols in application software have been designed to provide information to users of the database that will enable them to identify errors or irregularities that have occurred when the database has been updated. We briefly examine three such protocols.

Print Control Data for Internal Tables (Standing Data)

Many programs have internal tables that they use to perform various functions. For example, a payroll program might have an internal table of pay rates that it uses to calculate gross pays; a billing program might have an internal table of prices that it uses to prepare invoices; an electronic data interchange program might have a table that it uses to route orders to various suppliers; or an interest payment program might have a table of interest rates that it uses to pay customers interest on their bank accounts. Sometimes multiple versions of a table could be stored within the program. Different versions can take effect during different time periods, or perhaps a new version is prepared carefully over some time period to take effect after a certain date.

Maintaining the integrity of these tables is critical because the effects of errors in them can be substantial. For example, an error in a table of prices could mean a large number of customers are underbilled for merchandise they have received. It might be too costly to recover the monies lost. Furthermore, an organization might not want the error to be known publicly because of an adverse reaction by shareholders, creditors, and so on. In this light, access controls over the tables should be implemented to prevent unauthorized changes to them. Moreover, any changes made to internal tables (e.g., updating a pay rate) should be checked carefully for authenticity, accuracy, and completeness. One report protocol for standing data, therefore, is to print out internal tables after they have been changed to allow the changes made to be evaluated for authenticity, accuracy, and completeness.

Even if no changes are made to standing data, internal tables might still be printed periodically. Unauthorized changes could have been made to a table, or the table might have been corrupted in some way. Alternatively, if the table is large, it might not be printed and instead some type of control total (such as a hash total) could be calculated and reported. Users can then check this control total to determine whether it differs from the previous control total.

Print Run-to-Run Control Totals

Sometimes the execution of an application system involves running multiple programs that pass files between each other. (Chapter 13 discusses the need to calculate and print run-to-run control totals as a basis for identifying errors in the processing subsystem in these situations.) Run-to-run control totals are also a useful means of identifying errors or irregularities that occur in the database subsystem. For example, they could signal that a record (tuple) has been dropped erroneously from a master file (table) that has been updated.

Print Suspense Account Entries

As mentioned previously, monetary update transactions that mismatch a master record must be written to a suspense account. To ensure that these transactions are ultimately cleared to their correct accounts, a suspense account report must be prepared periodically showing the transactions that were posted to the suspense account. The mismatches must also be written to an error file and removed as they are corrected. The suspense account report should remind users that they must take action to clear the errors if they are not removed from the error file promptly.

CONCURRENCY CONTROLS

Recall from the objectives of database management examined in Chapter 6 that a major goal was to allow users of the database to share the same data resources. Otherwise, multiple versions of the same data items must be maintained to support different users. As a result, inconsistencies inevitably arise among different versions of the data resource.

Unfortunately, sharing data resources produces a new set of problems that must be handled by the database subsystem if data integrity is to be preserved. In the following subsections we examine the nature of these problems and the various strategies that can be used to overcome them. Note that these problems are general in nature. Although we focus on shared *data* resources, they arise with any resource that might be shared.

Nature of the Shared Data Resource Problem

The best way to understand the problems that arise when we share data resources is via an example. Consider, then, an inventory application in a company in which a sales clerk and a receiving clerk have online access to the inventory master file. Assume, also, that they have *concurrent* access to the file; in other words, both can access the inventory master file at the same time.

Figure 14–6 shows a time sequence of events that can occur which results in data integrity being violated. First, a supplier delivers 100 units of good XYZ. As a result, the receiving clerk accesses the record for XYZ to update it. Input/output routines then copy an image of the existing record into the

FIGURE 14–6. Concurrent processes as a threat to data integrity.

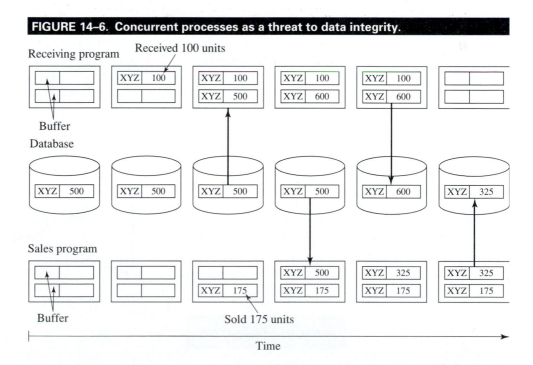

receiving program's buffer. The program next commences to update the image of the record. At the same time a customer places an order for 175 units of XYZ. As a result, the sales clerk accesses the record for XYZ to update it. Input/output routines copy an image of the record into the program's buffer. In the meantime, the receiving program completes its update and writes its buffer image of the record to the master file. The sales program also carries out its update and writes its buffer image to the master file. Instead of the inventory record showing 425 units, it shows only 325 units.

We can see, therefore, that uncontrolled concurrent access to data can cause problems for data integrity. In this example, the inventory record now understates the true value of inventory on hand by 100 units. As a result, the company might now reorder excessive inventory. Moreover, additional costs could be incurred associated with extra storage space that will be needed for inventory, higher levels of obsolescence that might occur, and lost interest on cash that would otherwise be available.

Data integrity problems caused by concurrent processes are not confined to update programs. Read-only programs also can produce erroneous results if they operate concurrently with an update program. For example, a read-only program might be producing a trial balance for an accounts file. If an update program is concurrently posting debit and credit entries to the accounts, a situation might arise in which only one side (e.g., the debit) of a double-entry transaction is posted prior to the read-only program accessing the records to be updated. Thus, the trial balance will not balance.

The obvious solution to the data integrity problems caused by concurrent processes is to lock out one process from a data resource while it is being used by another process. Unfortunately, this solution leads to another set of problems. It can cause a system to come to a halt because of a situation called *deadlock* or the "deadly embrace."

The Problem of Deadlock

Figure 14–7 shows the problems that can arise when one process is allowed to lock out another process from a resource. At time *t,* process *P* acquires exclusive control of data resource 1, and process *Q* also acquires exclusive control of data resource 2. At time *t* + 1, process *P* makes an additional request for data resource 2, and process *Q* also made an additional request for data resource 1. Neither process can continue until the other releases control of the data resource that it has acquired at time *t*. A deadlock situation results.

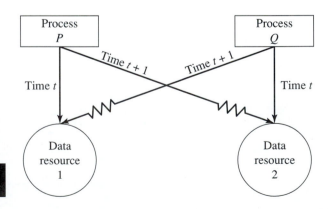

FIGURE 14–7. A deadlock situation.

The necessary and sufficient conditions for deadlock to occur follow:

Condition	Explanation
Lockout	A process can exclude another process from using a resource. Note that a read-only process might not wish to exclude other read-only processes. It might want to exclude other update processes, however.
Concurrency	Two or more processes can compete concurrently for exclusive control of two or more resources.
Additional request	While holding exclusive control of a resource, a process can request exclusive control of another resource.
No preemption	One process cannot force another process to release a resource prior to the process finishing with the resource.
Circular wait	A circular chain of processes exists. Each process in the chain holds a resource needed by the next process in the chain.

Solutions to Deadlock

How can a deadlock situation be resolved? At first thought we might believe the situation in Figure 14–7 can be overcome by simply forcing either process *P* or process *Q* to release the data resource over which it has exclusive control. This approach could indeed be a solution in some cases. Unfortunately, however, it does not always resolve the problem.

Consider the following simple example. Salesperson 1 receives a request from a customer for a certain set of parts—say, 80 units of Part A and 90 units of Part B. The customer is unwilling to take the order unless all the parts requested can be supplied. Salesperson 2 receives a similar request from another customer—say, 50 units of Part A and 100 units of Part B. Both salespersons initially query the database to determine whether sufficient inventory exists for all the parts requested (a read-only process). Recognizing that inventory could be depleted in the meantime because of other orders, they both commence to place their orders.

Figure 14–8 shows the situation that could result. Assume part A and part B are required in both salesperson's orders. Salesperson 1 acquires exclusive control of part A's record first and decreases the existing stock of 100 units by 80 units. At the same time, salesperson 2 acquires exclusive control of part B's record and decreases the existing stock of 150 units by 100 units. At time $t + 1$ a deadlock situation results. Consider what would happen if salesperson 1's program was allowed to preempt salesperson 2's program. After accessing part B's record, salesperson 1's program would find only 50 units (150 – 100) of part

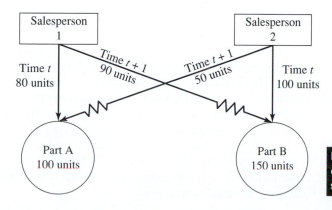

FIGURE 14–8. Inventory example of a deadlock situation.

B available because salesperson 2's program has already updated part B's record. Thus, salesperson 1's order would have to be canceled in its entirety because 90 units of part B are required.

The same situation results if salesperson 2's program is allowed to preempt salesperson 1's program. Unless one program's updates are undone before the other program continues, both customer orders are lost, whereas only one order need be lost.

Problems arise because the database is in an inconsistent state when the preemption occurs. The updates of one program, therefore, need to be undone. Unfortunately, in some cases rolling back the actions that have been undertaken by a program can be difficult. Shipping notices, invoices, and so on might have been prepared and transmitted by the program that is preempted. The locations of these outputs have to be identified, and they then have to be canceled. The degree of complexity associated with the preemption, therefore, is affected by how far the program needs to be rolled back. Moreover, a decision must also be made on which program should be preempted.

Preventing Deadlock

Over the years, a number of solutions have been proposed to resolve the problem of deadlock. The most widely accepted solution now, however, is called *two-phase locking*. It applies to a *transaction* that is being processed against the database. A transaction constitutes a sequence of interactions with the database that represents some meaningful unit of activity to a user. For example, in the context of the inventory application we examined previously, it would represent the sequence of operations needed to retrieve the relevant inventory records that satisfy the customer's request and to update them with the amounts ordered. Similarly, in the context of the trial-balance run discussed previously, it would represent the entire run from start to finish.

More precisely, however, a transaction must have four properties—the so-called ACID properties:

1. *Atomicity.* All actions taken by a transaction must be indivisible. Either all actions undertaken by a transaction are manifested in the current state of the database, or nothing is allowed to occur.
2. *Consistency.* A transaction must preserve the consistency of the database. The effects of a transaction are not reflected in the database until it *commits* its results. That is, all changes are first made in a temporary workspace until they can be written permanently, as an indivisible unit, to the database. Commitment is a two-phase process. During the first phase, the system writes the changes in the temporary workspace created for the transaction to some type of secure storage. If failure occurs during this phase, no harm has been done because the changes have not been applied to the database. During the second phase, the system copies the changes from secure storage to the database. If failure occurs during this phase, the new values of the database are recovered from secure storage. In either case, the transaction leaves the database in a consistent state.
3. *Isolation.* The events that occur within a transaction must be transparent to other transactions that are executing concurrently. In other words, no type of interference among transactions can be permitted.
4. *Durability.* When the results of a transaction have been committed, the system must guarantee that the changes survive any subsequent failure of the database. Existence controls, which we consider later in this chapter, are needed to achieve transaction durability.

Two-phase locking handles a transaction using the following protocol. First, before a transaction can read a data item, it must "own" a "read-lock" on the data item. Similarly, before a transaction can write a data item, it must own a "write-lock" on the data item. Second, different transactions are not allowed to own "conflicting" locks simultaneously. This rule means that two transactions can own read-locks on the same data item, but a read-lock and a write-lock or two write-locks are not permitted to occur simultaneously. Recall that inconsistent results can be obtained if two processes concurrently read and write a data item or two processes concurrently write a data item. It does not matter, however, if two processes concurrently read a data item. Third, when a transaction releases ownership of a lock, it cannot obtain additional locks. Release of a lock gives another transaction the opportunity to obtain control over the data item, and the consistency of results can no longer be guaranteed. Thus, a transaction should commit its database changes before it releases its locks.

Two-phase locking, therefore, has a growing phase and a shrinking phase. During the *growing phase*, the transaction acquires locks without releasing locks. When the transaction releases a lock, it enters the *shrinking phase*, and it must proceed irrevocably to release all its locks. Locks could be released because *(1)* the transaction has committed its updates or *(2)* it has been unable to acquire all the locks it needs.

Distributed Database Concurrency Controls

When databases are distributed, their contents are stored at multiple sites. Various distribution strategies are used. At one extreme, a *replicated* copy of the database can be stored at all sites. At the other extreme, the database can be *fragmented* into nonoverlapping *partitions*. Each partition is then stored at exactly one site. Between these extremes are strategies where some data is replicated and stored at some subset of sites and other data is partitioned and stored at one site only.

Concurrency and deadlock problems can become a major threat to distributed database integrity unless the database management system has suitable controls. In the case of a *replicated* database, the system must somehow ensure that all versions of a data item are kept in a consistent state. In this light, some concurrency and deadlock strategies for replicated databases require that all instances of the data item needed must be locked before update operations can proceed. In the case of a *partitioned* database, the location of the data item requested must be identified. Its lock then must be activated.

The locking task for both replicated and partitioned databases conceptually might seem straightforward. Implementing it efficiently and reliably, however, is another matter. To illustrate how concurrency controls might work for a distributed database, consider the two-phase locking scheme examined previously for a centralized database. First, a two-phase *scheduler* must be constructed to process and to enforce the locking protocols. Next, in a *replicated* database, one of the following two strategies might be implemented:

1. Schedulers are replicated and stored with each version of the data item. If a read-lock is requested, the transaction need only request the lock at the most convenient scheduler. If a write-lock is requested, however, the transaction must request the lock of all replications of the scheduler for the data item needed. Alternatively, voting schemes might be used whereby a transaction is granted the lock if it acquires the lock from the majority of the data item's

schedulers. It then notifies all of the data item's schedulers that it has been granted the lock. The voting method seeks to improve throughput, but it is more complex and error prone.

2. One version of the data item and its associated scheduler is designated as the primary copy. Before accessing a data item, a transaction must acquire the lock for the primary copy. The location of the primary copy is chosen to try to optimize system throughput. Transactions access a directory to determine the location of the primary copy. Alternatively, primary copies are all located at a central site. Under both approaches, difficulties arise if primary copies are lost or corrupted. Moreover, if primary copies are stored at a single site, they could all be lost if the site fails or is destroyed. For these reasons a second copy of the data item and its associated scheduler might be made, stored at a different site to the primary copy, and designated as the backup copy.

In a *partitioned* database, a transaction must acquire a read-lock or write-lock by first locating the scheduler for the data item requested. It must then activate the lock. Difficulties arise if the scheduler is lost or corrupted. As with a replicated database in which a primary-copy scheme is used, a second copy of the scheduler might be made and stored at another site as a backup copy.

Other strategies exist for handling concurrency and deadlock problems in distributed systems. Unfortunately, the area is complex. It could be difficult for auditors, therefore, to determine whether the concurrency controls implemented in a distributed database management system will maintain the integrity of data under all situations in which data resource conflicts arise.

CRYPTOGRAPHIC CONTROLS

Recall that we discussed the use of cryptographic controls in the boundary subsystem in Chapter 10 and the communications subsystem in Chapter 12. Cryptographic controls can also be used to protect the integrity of data stored in databases.

The primary means of protecting stored data is block encryption (see Chapter 12). Recall that block encryption operates on individual blocks of data. It differs from stream encryption, in which the cryptographic value of one block of data depends on the cryptographic value of another block of data. Clearly, users who want to access a record or a data item in a record usually are unwilling to wait while the cryptographic mechanism decrypts all prior records or data items in the file. This outcome would occur under stream encryption. In short, stream encryption is useful for transferring entire files between two users, but block encryption should be used when users require access to only part of a file.

Data stored on portable storage media, such as tapes, diskettes, and cartridges, can be protected by implementing a secure encryption device in the device controllers for the media. Data is encrypted automatically each time it is written and decrypted automatically each time it is read. Although this type of encryption protects the privacy of data should the storage medium be stolen, it does not protect one user's data from another user because the cryptographic key used for encryption/decryption purposes is common to all users.

If little or no sharing of data among users occurs, individual users can protect their own files using a personal cryptographic key. They must present this key to the system when they wish to perform operations on their files. This system is unsatisfactory, however, when data is shared. File owners must make their keys known to other users who require access to their file. As a result, encryption keys can become widely known, and the risk of key compromise increases.

Alternative cryptographic schemes have been devised when data must be shared. By way of illustration, however, consider the following scheme (see, further, Davies and Price 1989, pp. 150–151):

1. Each owner of a file is assigned a *file key* to perform cryptographic operations on the file.
2. A *secondary key* is assigned to encrypt/decrypt the file keys for the files owned by a particular user. Secondary keys create a protection domain that applies to a number of files, each of which has its own key. The file keys encrypted under the secondary key can be stored in the header records of the files to which they apply so they can be retrieved easily each time the file needs to be accessed. The file keys are secure because they are encrypted under the secondary key.
3. A *master key* is used to encrypt the secondary keys. Thus, the master key can be changed without having to reencrypt all data in the database. Only the secondary keys have to be decrypted and reencrypted.
4. To read and write a file, users must have access to the secondary key for the file so the file key in turn can be accessed and used for cryptographic purposes. Access to the secondary key can be protected using the standard types of access controls described in Chapter 10. Note the value of the secondary key is not revealed to users; they simply are permitted or denied access to it for cryptographic purposes.

Use of cryptographic controls in the database subsystem becomes more complex when the database is distributed. If the database is replicated, a decision must be made on whether the same keys will be maintained with each replication of the database. If a replica is lost or destroyed and the same keys are used, it is then relatively straightforward to make a copy of another replica to restore the lost replica. Moreover, it is also relatively easy to route a user transaction to another site if one site has a work overload and load balancing is being attempted. Several disadvantages arise, however, with this strategy: *(1)* The keys must be distributed in a secure way; *(2)* they reside at more sites so the risk of compromise is higher; and *(3)* changes to keys at one site mean keys at all other sites must also be changed. Alternatively, if each site has its own set of keys, the keys will be more secure. It is more difficult to use replicas for backup purposes, however, and it is also more difficult to process transactions at sites other than the ones where they were initiated.

If the database is partitioned, in some cases data owned by a user could be located at multiple sites. If the same keys are assigned to a user across all sites where the user's data is located, gaining access to the user's data is fairly straightforward. When a user transaction has been given the keys, it can access data at any site. Because the keys must be maintained at multiple sites, however, the disadvantages described above again apply. Alternatively, if different sites have different keys, data at each site is more secure, but higher processing overheads are incurred when transactions must access data at multiple sites.

FILE HANDLING CONTROLS

File handling controls are used to prevent accidental destruction of data contained on a storage medium. They are exercised by hardware, software, and the operators or users who load and unload storage media (e.g., tapes, diskettes, cartridges) used for the database, dumps of the database, transaction files, work files, logs, and audit trails.

Several types of data can be stored in a file's header and trailer records so that a program can determine whether it is accessing the correct file:

Internal Data Item	Nature
Internal label	Specifies the name of the file, table, or database. Used by the program to check that it has accessed the correct file, table, or database.
Generation number	With removable storage media like tapes, diskettes, or cartridges, several versions of a file, table, or database can exist, all with the same name. Used by the program accessing the file, table, or database to check it is accessing the correct version.
Retention date	Prevents the contents of a file, table, or database being overwritten before a specified date.
Control totals	A record within each file, table, or database may contain control totals that can be checked. This record is updated at the end of each run, and the control totals are reported. On the next update run, users provide these control totals as parameters to the update program. The program then checks that they match the control totals on the file, table, or database that is to be updated as a basis for ensuring the correct file is being accessed.

Several hardware controls are also used to prevent accidental erasure of information on storage media. File protection rings are used to protect data on magnetic tapes. To enable data to be written to a tape, a plastic ring must be inserted into the recess at the back of the reel. If the ring is removed, data cannot be written to the tape. Similarly, disks can be protected by activating a read-only switch on a disk drive, and diskettes can be protected by sliding a plastic tab on the diskette so that the hole the tab covers is open. If multiple files are stored on a disk or diskette, individual files can also be locked by setting a flag to prevent erasure of data.

To assist users or operators in loading the correct files, external labels can be stuck on the outside casing of storage media. These labels can contain the name of the file, its creation date, and a code to indicate whether the file is a master file, a transaction file, a work file, or a backup file. External labels are not a substitute for internal labels, however, because labels can become detached from the storage media, or they might not be updated to reflect the current contents of the storage medium.

AUDIT TRAIL CONTROLS

The audit trail in the database subsystem maintains the chronology of events that occur either to the database definition or the database itself. In many cases, the full set of events must be recorded: creations, modifications, deletions, and retrievals. Otherwise, it might be impossible to determine how the database definition or the database attained its current state, or who, via a retrieval transaction, relied on some past state of the database definition or the database.

Accounting Audit Trail

To maintain the accounting audit trail in an application system, the database subsystem must undertake three functions. First, it must attach a unique time stamp to all transactions applied against the database definition or the database. This

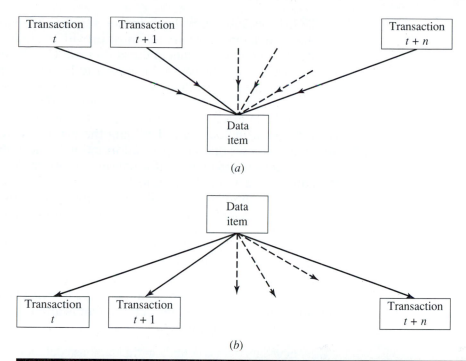

(a)

(b)

**FIGURE 14–9(a). Implosion purpose of an accounting audit trail. (b). Explosion
purpose of an accounting audit trail.**

time stamp has two purposes: *(1)* It confirms a transaction ultimately reached the
database definition or the database and *(2)* it identifies a transaction's unique position in the time series of events that has occurred to a data item in the database
definition or the database. As a result, the audit trail can be either imploded or
exploded (Figure 14–9). Under *implosion,* each transaction can be traced from its
source to the data item it affects: The transaction's source identifier enables its
origin to be traced unambiguously; its destination identifier designates the data
item it affects; and the time stamp inserted in the transaction confirms it ultimately took effect on the database definition or the database. Under *explosion,*
the time stamp can be sorted within the destination identifier for a set of transactions to enable the chronological sequence of events that has occurred to a data
item in the database definition or the database to be reconstructed.

Second, the database subsystem must attach beforeimages and afterimages
of the data item against which a transaction is applied to the audit trail entry
for the transaction. If the transaction modifies an existing data item value, the
value of the data item before it is updated and the value of the data item after it
is updated must be stored in the transaction's audit trail entry. When insertion,
deletion, and retrieval transactions occur that do not change existing data item
values, a flag can be set to indicate the beforeimage and afterimage are the
same. These beforeimages and afterimages have two purposes: *(1)* They facilitate inquiries on the audit trail because the effects of the transaction on the
database definition or the database can be determined immediately from the
audit trail entry and *(2)* they provide redundancy for the time stamp because
fraudulent deletion of an audit trail entry or fraudulent alteration of a time
stamp can be detected via a mismatch between the afterimage of a transaction
and the beforeimage of the subsequent transaction.

Third, because audit trail entries require permanent or semipermanent storage, the database subsystem must provide facilities to define, create, modify, delete, and retrieve data in the audit trail. Usually the audit trail should not have to be modified because it is meant to be a true history of what happened to the database. Two situations can arise, however, in which modifications to the audit trail are necessary. First, the application system updating the database processes data erroneously. As a result, the audit trail is a history of incorrect operations on the database. Undoing the erroneous results is not sufficient if someone accesses the erroneous information in the audit trail and makes incorrect decisions based on this information—for example, sues a customer for supposedly unpaid accounts. Second, the processes that create the audit trail could be flawed. In this case, the audit trail is not a true history of what happened to the database. Again, incorrect decisions might be made on the basis of the erroneous audit trail. In both cases, it might be best to modify the audit trail so later decisions made on the basis of data contained in the audit trail are not affected by the erroneous data.

Perhaps the most difficult problems encountered in supporting the audit trail arise from having to accommodate the effects of changes that occur within an application system. Consider the implications of the following types of changes on the audit trail:

1. A new data item is defined in the database definition and data collected to populate the database.
2. An existing data item is deleted from the database definition, and data is no longer collected for that data item.
3. The name used for a data item is changed.
4. A change of measurement scale occurs for a data item—for example, conversion from pounds to kilograms.
5. The coding system used for a data item changes—for example, conversion from a numeric to an alphanumeric code.
6. The key used to encrypt a data item is changed.

All these changes affect the various operations that have to be performed on the audit trail. For example, the addition or deletion of data items from the database definition mean the audit trail's data definition also has to be changed. In this light, problems can arise when users want to retrieve data from the audit trail that pertains to a time period during which some change has occurred that has affected the audit trail. For example, suppose users wish to examine all transactions that have updated an account during a particular financial period but the code used for that account has changed during the period. If they are not aware of the change of code for the account, they might retrieve only a subset of transactions for the account. Ideally, the system that supports the audit trail will automatically identify that a change has occurred and provide users with the full set of transactions. Alternatively, it should at least alert users to the change that has invalidated their query specification.

An important decision to be made is the length of time that an audit trail will be retained. In some cases, government regulations (e.g., taxation) mandate that an audit trail will be retained for a fixed period of time. Organizations might need to retain an audit trail, however, for longer periods than those dictated by regulations. In these cases, auditors must confirm that organizations have taken steps to ensure their audit trails remain readable and intelligible for the periods they must be retained. In this regard, Rothenberg (1995) points out how changes to hardware and software can quickly make digital records obsolete and inaccessible. He notes several cases in which the U.S. Federal Government has nearly lost significant data because the storage media used for this data became obsolete faster than expected.

Operations Audit Trail

The operations audit trail in the database subsystem maintains the chronology of resource consumption events that affect the database definition or the database. On the basis of the operations audit trail, data administrators or database administrators can make two decisions. First, in light of response times or the amount of resources consumed when transactions are applied against the database, the need for database reorganization might become clear. Reorganization might involve establishing new access paths via indexes or pointers, clearing overflow areas, assigning data to faster storage devices, and so on. Second, resource consumption data could indicate that the processes which apply transactions to the database definition or the database need to be restructured or to be rewritten. For example, a database administrator might determine that a new database management system would better meet the needs of their organization, given the types of updates that occur to the database and the types of queries made on the database.

EXISTENCE CONTROLS

The whole or portion of a database can be lost (destroyed or corrupted) through five types of failure:

1. *Application program error.* An application program can update data incorrectly because it contains a bug. Usually only localized damage occurs to the database because the program updates only a small subset of data in the database.
2. *System software error.* System software, such as an operating system, database management system, telecommunications monitor, or utility program, could contain a bug. The bug might lead to erroneous updates of the database, corruption of data, or a system crash. Whether local or global damage occurs to the database depends on the nature of the bug.
3. *Hardware failure.* In spite of the high reliability of most hardware components, failure can still occur. The failure might be minor and transient, and as a result only localized damage occurs to the database. The failure might be serious and permanent, however, in which case extensive damage could occur to the database; for example, a disk crash destroys the contents of a disk.
4. *Procedural error.* An operator or user could make a procedural error that damages the database. For example, operators might undertake an incorrect action when recovering from a system crash, or a user might supply incorrect parameters to an update run. Whether the damage is local or global depends upon the nature of the error made.
5. *Environmental failure.* Environmental failure, such as flood, fire, or sabotage can occur. Often extensive damage to the database occurs. Off-site storage of files is essential to restoring the database after many types of environmental failure (see Chapter 7).

Existence controls in the database subsystem must restore the database in the event of loss. They encompass both a backup strategy and a recovery strategy. All *backup strategies* involve maintaining a prior version of the database and a log of transactions or changes to the database. If an update program creates a new *physical* version of a file, the previous version and the file of transactions used during the update can be used for backup purposes. If update occurs in place, however, periodically a dump of the database must be taken, and a log of changes to the database since the dump also must be maintained.

Recovery strategies take two forms. First, the current state of the database might have to be restored if the entire database or a portion of the database is lost. This task involves a *rollforward operation* using a prior version or dump of the database and a log of transactions or changes that have occurred to the database since the dump was taken. Second, a prior state of the database might have to be restored because the current state of the database is invalid. This task involves a *rollback operation* to undo the updates that have caused the database to be corrupted. A log of changes to the database are used to restore the database to a prior, valid state.

In the following subsections, we examine the various forms of backup and recovery that can be used to restore a damaged or destroyed database. Auditors should have two concerns: *(1)* that a damaged or destroyed database can be restored in an authentic, accurate, complete, and timely way and *(2)* that the privacy of data is protected during all backup and recovery activities.

Grandfather, Father, Son Strategy

The grandfather, father, son strategy is one of the earliest backup and recovery strategies to have been developed. It evolved in the era when magnetic tapes were the dominant storage medium. Nonetheless, it can be used with other forms of storage media such as disks. It also applies to storage media that can be written to only once (e.g., some types of optical disks).

When the current version of a master file (the son) is lost or damaged, recovery is effected by using the previous version of the master file (the father) and the log of the transactions that updated it to recreate the current version of the master file (Figure 14–10). In the event that the previous version of the master file (the father) is damaged during the recovery process, the next oldest

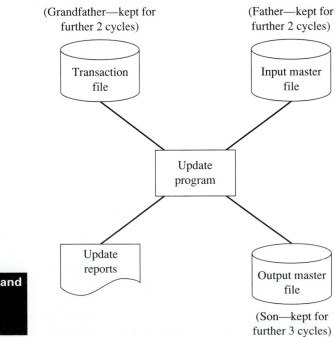

FIGURE 14–10. Father and son in a grandfather, father, son backup strategy.

version of the master file (the grandfather) is kept together with the log of transactions that updated it. The father version of the file can be restored therefore by using the grandfather version and its log of updates, and the son version of the file can be restored by using the father version and its log of updates.

Two conditions must be met before the grandfather, father, son strategy can be used. First, the input master file to an update run must be kept physically intact; that is, both changed and unchanged records must be written to a new file. Second, the transaction file used to effect updates also must be kept. These requirements are easily met when master files are kept on magnetic tapes. When master files are kept on disk, however, in-place (*in situ*) update is precluded because the prior version of the master file will be overwritten.

The major advantage of the grandfather, father, son strategy is its simplicity. There are several disadvantages, however. First, it is not well suited to situations in which concurrent processes are updating the database in place. Nevertheless, we shall see later that strategies like the differential file strategy, which are suited to these types of situations, are really a form of the grandfather, father, son strategy. Second, recovery is expensive when damage to the database is localized. In this situation, the entire update run has to be redone to recover a few damaged records. Third, the damaged file often is not available to other processes during recovery. Even though the damage might be localized, access to the son could be precluded (although users might be permitted access to the damaged son at their own risk while recovery is being effected).

Dual Recording/Mirroring Strategy

The dual recording or mirroring strategy involves keeping two completely separate copies of the database and updating both simultaneously (Figure 14–11). Ideally, the two copies are maintained at different physical locations. One copy

FIGURE 14–11. Dual recording/mirroring strategy with remotely located frontend processor, primary processor and primary database, and remotely located duplicate processor and duplicate database.

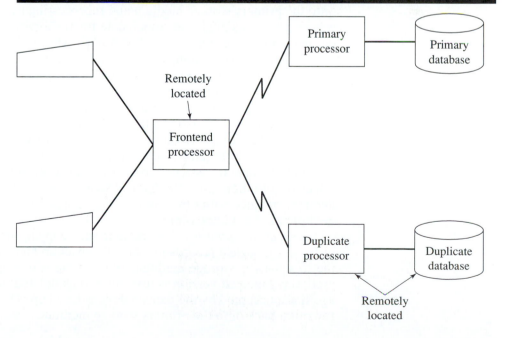

should be stored remotely to protect against environmental failure. Otherwise, dual recording protects only against a disk failure. Moreover, if processor failure is a concern, a second processor must be used. When failure occurs, the secondary database and processor become the primary database and processor.

The ease with which recovery can be effected under a dual recording strategy depends on *(1)* the length of time during which the database is unavailable and *(2)* the number of update transactions that have occurred during that period. Two recovery strategies can be used. First, a copy of the intact database can be taken at a convenient time. Update processes must be denied access to the database while the copy is made. The copy must be performed, therefore, during an off-peak period. Second, a log of transactions that have been processed against the intact database can be kept and processed against a previous dump of the damaged database. This strategy is used if fast recovery of the damaged database is important and it will be some time before an off-peak period occurs during which a copy can be made of the intact database.

The primary advantage of the dual recording strategy is that it permits the database to be available continuously. In some types of online reservation systems and online banking systems, for example, downtime is intolerable. The losses that arise when the database becomes unavailable exceed the costs of maintaining duplicate resources.

Dual recording has two major disadvantages, however. First, it is costly to maintain duplicate resources, although the costs decrease as hardware prices continue to decrease. Second, dual recording affords little protection against a procedural error, a system software error, or an application program error. These errors corrupt both the primary and secondary databases. Thus, a second backup and recovery strategy must be used to recover from these types of errors.

Dumping

Dumping involves copying the whole or a portion of the database to some backup medium (e.g., cartridge). Recovery involves rewriting the dump back onto the primary storage medium and reprocessing transactions since the dump was taken. Users might be responsible for resubmitting transactions that have occurred since the time of the last dump. Alternatively, a log of transactions may be kept between dumps. Errors and irregularities are less likely to occur if recovery is effected automatically via a log as opposed to having users resubmit transactions for processing.

Either a physical dump or a logical dump may be taken. A *physical dump* involves reading and copying the database in the serial order of the physical records on the storage medium—for example, track by track on a disk. In some cases, physical boundaries define the space occupied by a file—for example, only one file may be assigned to a particular disk. In this light, dumping can be selective. In other cases, the file is dispersed across multiple physical locations and intermingled with other files. In this case, selective dumping of the file may be difficult, if not impossible.

Logical dumping involves reading and copying the database in the serial order of the logical records in a file. The backup facility simply writes a named file to a backup storage medium. When a file is damaged and must be recovered, the damaged version is first marked as deleted; in other words, the storage space occupied by the damaged file is freed up. The dump of the file is then rewritten back onto the primary storage medium.

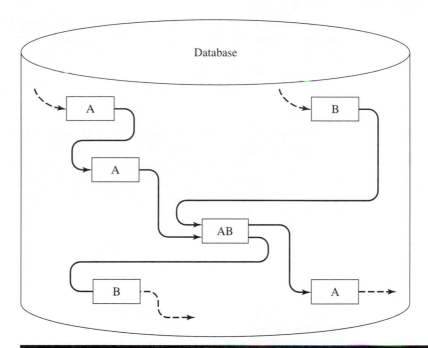

FIGURE 14–12. Multilist to illustrate some problems with a logical dump backup strategy.

Logical dumping becomes complex when data is shared and the records in a file are also members of other files. For example, consider the problems posed by the multilist file organization shown in Figure 14–12. Note that record AB is a member of two lists, A and B. Assume, now, that an erroneous program updates list A and damages record AB. Recovering AB using only a logical dump of list A will not effect accurate and complete recovery unless record AB is written back to its previous physical location. Otherwise, list B contains a corrupted record. Furthermore, two copies of record AB now exist on the database. For logical dumping purposes, therefore, the two lists must be considered as a single file.

Care must be exercised if the database is stored on multiple physical volumes and the database is then reorganized subsequent to a physical dump. Selective recovery of a single damaged volume then might no longer be possible. The reorganization might have resulted in records being assigned to different volumes. Moreover, pointers in records on the damaged volume that contain the addresses of related records on other volumes might have been updated. If only the damaged volume is then recovered, the restored volume might contain neither the correct records nor the correct pointer addresses for records on other volumes. To avoid these problems, a physical dump should be undertaken, therefore, immediately after a reorganization of the database.

Dumping can consume substantial time and resources, especially when large databases are involved. Physical dumping is faster to undertake than logical dumping, providing the same data is to be dumped. Logical dumping can be used selectively, however, to make copies of only those files that have been changed since the last dump. Physical dumping, on the other hand, makes copies of files even when they have not been changed since the last dump. In this light, it might consume more resources than logical dumping.

Whether recovery is faster from a physical dump or logical dump depends on the nature of the damage to the database. Physical dumping facilitates global recovery of the database. It is useful when the database is damaged globally because of, say, some type of environmental failure or failure of a physical storage device. Logical dumping facilitates selective recovery of the database. It is useful when the database is damaged locally because of, say, an erroneous program.

Dumping is usually straightforward to undertake, but it is only a partial backup and recovery strategy. It restores the database to a valid state prior to the time of failure. The effects of transactions after the dump up to the point of failure must still be recovered, however, through either users resubmitting data or the system maintaining a log of transactions or changed images of records on the database. Recovery can be complex when several different update programs are authorized to update the record. Recovering the record when failure occurs means transactions from multiple sources must be recaptured or several programs must be rerun to restore the database.

Logging

Logging involves recording a transaction that changes the database or an image of the record changed by an update action. The log can then be used to recover the database to the point of failure. The alternative strategy, which is to require users to resubmit transactions to recover the database to the point of failure, might not be viable for several reasons. First, the downtime required for users to resubmit all transactions might be unacceptable. Second, recovering the database could require transactions to be resubmitted in a specified order. For example, if a bank account fluctuates between a debit and a credit balance and interest is charged on debit balances, the time sequence for the resubmission of transactions to the account is important. If users have not recorded transactions in a time sequence or multiple sources of input exist, obtaining the required time sequence for resubmission of transactions might be impossible. Third, transaction data might not be received directly from a user. Instead, it might be generated automatically by a program or received from another computer (perhaps another organization's computer). In these cases, some form of logging must occur.

There are three logging strategies:

1. Logging input transactions,
2. Logging beforeimages of the record changed, and
3. Logging afterimages of the record changed.

In the following subsections, we examine the nature of each strategy and their relative strengths and limitations.

Logging Input Transactions

Using this strategy for recovery involves reprocessing update transactions from the time of the last dump up until the time the database was damaged. To effect recovery, information such as the time and date of processing, file updated, and program that performed the update must be stored with the transaction.

A problem with this strategy is to determine how the input transactions should be reprocessed during recovery. One approach is to have a special recovery update program that reads the log and updates the database in the same way the various application programs perform their updates. This program would be stripped of much of the logic contained in the application update programs. For example, it would not incorporate functions to handle the user interface, generate reports, or process transactions that did not change the database. Nevertheless, the program most likely will be large and error prone if it has to replicate the logic of many application update programs. Moreover, someone must ensure ongoing correspondence between the application update programs and the recovery program.

A second method of recovery is to have a program read the log and call the relevant application update program as a transaction for that program is encountered. A program identifier must be stored, therefore, with each transaction on the log so the appropriate application update program can be invoked. Moreover, if this strategy is used, Everest (1986, p. 435) suggests that a recovery flag be set to modify the normal operations of the application update programs. The flag would cause the programs to suppress generation of reports, error messages, and so on. Instead, special control total reports could be produced that enable the authenticity, accuracy, and completeness of the recovery process to be verified.

In some cases, recovery can be effected more quickly by sorting like transactions together. For example, all the transactions for a particular record can be sorted together, their effects summed, and a single update processed against the database. Sorting cannot be undertaken, however, if a particular time sequence of transactions is important to database integrity—for example, as with the interest calculation on a bank account.

If users submit transactions from an online terminal, a message must be displayed to tell them the last transaction recovered successfully from the transaction log. This feedback is important if they have to resubmit transactions because only partial recovery can be accomplished. It is important, also, if the input transactions are buffered before they are written to the log. The contents of the buffer could be lost upon failure. As a result, several transactions that have been processed successfully but which are stored in the buffer might not have been written to the log. For this reason, log files often are not buffered. Indeed, recall from the previous discussion on deadlock that changes to the database that arise because of a transaction are often made in temporary storage. These changes are committed to permanent storage only after the log file has been written. We discuss this issue further in the following subsection.

A decision also must be made on *when* to log transactions. All transactions input to the system can be logged. Or, only those transactions processed successfully can be logged. If the first strategy is adopted, the effects of unsuccessful transactions (for example, those that fail a validation test) must be suppressed or users warned when a recovery process is to be undertaken. Otherwise, displaying error messages associated with recovery of unsuccessful transactions might confuse them. These problems do not arise if only successful transactions are logged. This strategy is deficient, however, in terms of providing a complete audit trail. One solution is to log successful and unsuccessful transactions on separate files and to process only the file containing the successful transactions during recovery (Figure 14–13).

Logging Beforeimages

Logging beforeimages of the database is a strategy designed to facilitate rollback of the database. Each time a record is to be updated, its image before the update is logged. If a transaction fails before it commits all its changes to the database (i.e., it fails in flight and the database is therefore in

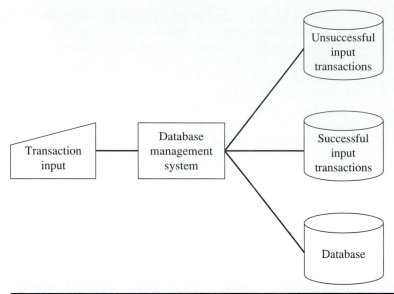

FIGURE 14–13. Separate logging of successful and unsuccessful input transactions for recovery and audit purposes.

an inconsistent state), the database can be rolled back to the last commit point. The log is read backward. Beforeimages are used to replace the existing records on the database. Similarly, if an erroneous program updates the database, rollback occurs to the point where the erroneous program commenced processing. As the log is read backward, the last beforeimage read for an updated record up to the point where the erroneous program commenced processing is the state of that record just prior to the program having commenced processing (Figure 14–14).

If the database is lost because of, say, a disk crash, beforeimages also can be used for a rollforward operation by applying them to a previous dump of the database. For those records that have been changed since the dump, their status is recovered up to the point where the last transaction for these records has not been processed. Some other recovery strategy must then be used to recover the effects of the last transaction; for example, users must resubmit the last transaction. For those records that have *not* been changed since the last dump, their status is current upon recovery because the dump contains their most-recent status.

The overheads associated with beforeimage logging can be substantial. Consider, for example, a database that uses a multilist structure. In a multilist structure, recall that records are chained to other records via pointers. For each list in the multilist structure, therefore, the addition or deletion of a record involves updating pointers in the record immediately before and perhaps the record immediately after the record to be added or deleted. For example, Figure 14-15 shows a multilist file where one record within the multilist is to be deleted. This record is a member of three lists: A, B, and C. The pointers in the lists go only in one direction. Deleting the record means a beforeimage of the deleted record must be taken. Also, beforeimages of the records that contain pointers to the deleted record also have to be taken because their pointer addresses must be updated to reflect the record has been deleted. Four beforeim-

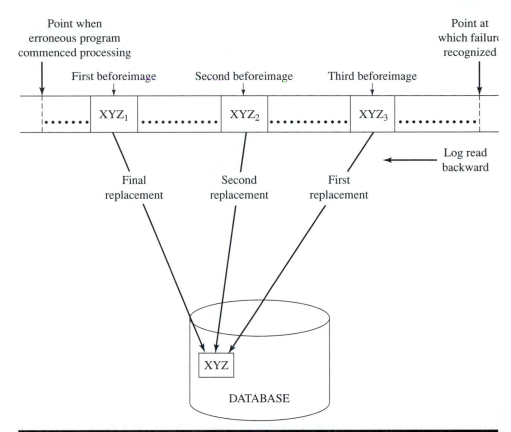

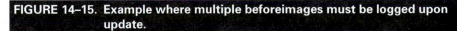

FIGURE 14–14. Removing the effects of an erroneous program using beforeimages.

FIGURE 14–15. Example where multiple beforeimages must be logged upon update.

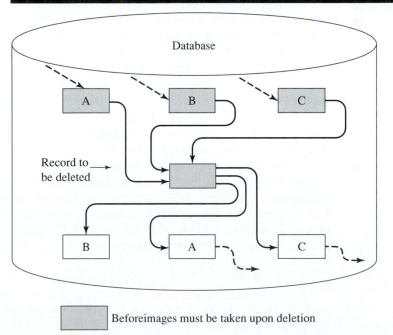

ages are needed, therefore. If the pointers were bidirectional, beforeimages of records that pointed back to the deleted record would also have to be taken because their pointer addresses must be changed too.

Adding or deleting records also can cause some reorganization of a file—for example, moving an overflow record to the home address if a record occupying the home address is deleted. Again, multiple beforeimages must be taken for all records changed. Similarly, if indexes have to be updated through addition or deletion of a record or a changed value in the field of a record, multiple beforeimages will be needed.

As with transaction logging, difficulties can arise with recovery if the beforeimage log is buffered. If the log is to be used to effect recovery from the damage done by an erroneous program, the contents of the buffer must be flushed to the log before rollback is commenced. Otherwise, records that have been updated only once since the erroneous program commenced processing and have their beforeimage stored in the buffer will not be rolled back. If, on the other hand, the beforeimage log is used to effect rollforward, the contents of the memory must again be flushed to the log. Otherwise, updated records that have their beforeimage stored in the buffer will not be restored to their penultimate state. Unfortunately, flushing the contents of the buffer to the log might not be possible if rollforward is needed because the system has crashed. The contents of the buffer will have been lost as a result of the crash.

Because of these difficulties, a protocol called *write-ahead logging* is often used to maintain log files. We examined this protocol previously when we studied concurrency and deadlock controls. Using this protocol, changes to the database are first made in a temporary storage area. When all changes are made, the log is then written. Only after the log has been successfully written are the changes then made to the database proper. A "commit" indicator is then written to the log. If, say, a transaction fails and the last record on the log is not a commit record, the log is read backwards up to the last commit point. The beforeimages read are used to replace database records. When the first commit point is reached, the database is again in a consistent state.

If some time passes before it is recognized that an erroneous program has entered the system, rollback can be difficult. Other processes could have updated the corrupted records in the interim period. Their updates must be redone when the corrupted records are corrected. Alternatively, the effects of erroneous actions they have undertaken because of corrupted data must be undone. Similarly, other processes could have read the corrupted records and taken unwanted actions on the basis of the corrupted values. For example, inventory might have been reordered because corrupted inventory records showed incorrectly that inventory was low. In some cases, therefore, it can be difficult, if not impossible, to determine the extent of damage that has resulted or to limit the damage that has occurred.

After rollback has been accomplished to undo the effects of an erroneous program, transactions still must be reprocessed using the corrected program. For this reason, storing transactions along with the beforeimages of the records changed facilitates recovery. The corrected program accesses the log and reprocesses the transactions that previously it had processed erroneously.

Logging Afterimages

Logging afterimages of the database is a strategy designed to facilitate rollforward of the database. After a record has been updated by a transaction, its image is copied onto the log. If, for example, a disk then fails, recovery is accomplished by rolling forward using the latest dump of the database and replacing the dump version of the record with afterimage versions from the log. The log is read forward, and the latest afterimage version read for a record constitutes the status of the record before the database was damaged. The unique location of each record must be stored with its afterimage on the log so that replacement of the dump version can be accomplished.

As with beforeimage logging, recovery is facilitated if all afterimages associated with a transaction are written to the log *before* the associated updates are applied permanently to the database. When failure occurs, rollforward is then undertaken up to the last commit point written on the log. Any afterimages stored on the log after the last commit point represent the effects of transactions that were still in flight at the time of failure. If these afterimages were to be restored, the database might be in an inconsistent state after recovery because one or more transactions may not have completed their updates.

If an erroneous program updates the database, rollback also can be accomplished using afterimages, though the logic involved is somewhat complex. The log must be read backward, and each afterimage must then be used to replace the database version of the record. Rollback continues until the last afterimage of each record taken *before* the erroneous program commenced processing has been obtained. These afterimages must be rewritten to the database because they represent the latest intact version of the database before the erroneous program commenced processing. If a record is updated infrequently, however, obtaining these afterimages could require extensive search back through the log or alternatively obtaining these images from a prior dump. Because of these complexities, using afterimages for rollback should be avoided.

The overheads associated with afterimage logging can be high. As with beforeimage logging, the addition or deletion of a record on the database may require multiple records to be updated because pointers must be changed, indexes must be maintained, and so on. As a result, multiple afterimages must be written to the log to record the subsequent state of each record changed on the database.

Residual Dumping

As an alternative to logging and taking a periodic full dump of the database, Everest (1986) suggests a backup strategy that he calls *residual dumping*. The primary motivation for residual dumping is the overhead involved in taking a full dump of the database. A log is insufficient for complete backup protection. If only a log were to be available for recovery, the possibility exists of having to examine all the entries on the log since the creation of the database. A dump avoids this problem by making it unnecessary to look back at the log prior to the dump. Nevertheless, dumps are costly in three ways: *(1)* They can take substantial time to accomplish; *(2)* the database is unavailable during the dump; and *(3)* dumps waste resources in that they are not selective. (A record could be logged and dumped within a short period, resulting in redundant backup.)

Residual dumping involves logging records that have *not* been changed since the last residual dump. Thus, records that have *not* been subject to an update action and therefore not logged since the last residual dump are logged. Residual dumping is used in conjunction with a beforeimage and afterimage logging strategy. Residual dump records are flagged to show that their beforeimage and afterimage are the same.

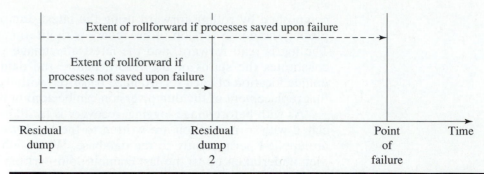

FIGURE 14–16. Rollforward recovery for a residual dump backup strategy.

Both rollforward and rollback operations are straightforward with a residual dump. With a rollforward operation, recovery involves going back to (but not including) the second last residual dump taken. The recovery process starts with an empty database. It progressively fills the database by writing afterimages to the database taken since the second last residual dump. How far the database must be rolled forward depends on whether the status of all processes that were executing could be saved at the point of failure. Consider Figure 14-16 to see why this is the case. If the status of all processes could be saved at the point of failure, recovery starts immediately after residual dump 1 and continues up to the point of failure. Between residual dump 1 and residual dump 2, the database is populated with the afterimages of changes made to the database during this period. Just prior to residual dump 2, the database contains the latest state of all records that have been changed during the period (some records may have been changed multiple times). Some "empty slots" still remain in the database, however, because not all records will have been changed and therefore logged. These slots will be filled when residual dump 2 is written to the database. After residual dump 2's records have been written to the database, therefore, a complete copy of the database will exist. If the status of processes could not be saved at the point of failure, a checkpoint exists at which all processes can be restarted when residual dump 2 has been written back to the database. If the status of all processes could be saved at the point of failure, the rollforward operation continues up to the last database commit point before failure occurred.

The situation with rollback operations is more straightforward. Residual dumping has no impact on a rollback operation. Beforeimages are used in the normal way to effect recovery. Residual dump records are simply ignored.

Rather than lock out concurrent update processes while residual dumping takes place, a residual dump can be undertaken as a background activity. Thus, residual dumping takes place over an interval while concurrent update processes are running. Again, a rollback operation is no different. What now constitutes the backup interval, however, for a rollforward operation? Consider Figure 14–17 to help resolve this issue. If the first residual dump extends over time period R_1 to S_1, should records not changed since R_1 or S_1 be logged when the second residual dump commences at R_2? It turns out that both strategies are viable. With strategy 1, if records older than S_1 are logged, the backup interval is from S_1 to S_2. With strategy 2, if records older

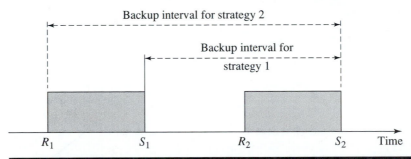

FIGURE 14–17. Residual dumping as a background operation.

than R_1 are logged, the backup interval is from R_1 to S_2. For strategy 2, note that the backup interval is longer but fewer records are dumped. With strategy 1, a record that has not been updated between the two residual dumps will still be dumped again during the second residual dump, thereby resulting in duplicate backup. With strategy 2, a record that has not been updated between residual dumps will not be dumped again during the second residual dump. Thus, inactive records will be dumped every alternate residual dump.

Everest (1986) discusses five advantages of a residual dump strategy relative to a traditional dump and log strategy:

1. Concurrent update processes are not excluded from the database during residual dumping. For large databases that take substantial time to dump, residual dumping may be the only feasible backup strategy.
2. Residual dumping results in less duplicate backup because a record will be logged only once unless it has been updated more than once.
3. Residual dumping offers greater flexibility in leveling system workloads. It can take place as a background operation. Moreover, the time of and period of residual dumping can be varied.
4. Residual dumping simplifies the recovery process because only a single log file is needed. A dump file is not required.
5. If residual dumping occurs on a logical basis, reorganization of the database can occur without having to take physical dumps before and after the reorganization.

Differential Files/Shadow Paging

A differential file is a file of changes made to the database (see, e.g., Severance and Lohman 1976; Aghili and Severance 1982). Rather than apply the changes to the database, however, the database is kept intact. Records that are updated are treated as new record additions and written instead to the differential file. When a record must be accessed, its location either on the database or differential file must be determined. Various strategies can be used to reduce access times. For example, the differential file can be stored on a separate device and channel to maximize instruction overlap and minimize access times (Figure 14–18). As the size of the differential file grows and the overheads of maintaining and accessing it become excessive, the changes should be applied to the database.

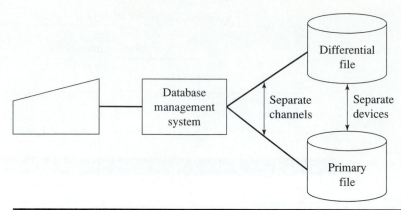

FIGURE 14–18. Differential file strategy for backup and recovery.

There are several advantages of a differential file, some of which relate to backup and recovery:

Advantage	Explanation
Reduces database dumping costs	Because the primary file remains unchanged, only the differential file need be dumped.
Facilitates incremental dumping	If additions to the differential file can be allocated sequential addresses on secondary memory and still be accessed (e.g., via an index or hashing algorithm), only the physical section of the device containing these changes to the differential file need be dumped for backup.
Permits realtime dumping and reorganization with concurrent updates	By building a differential-differential file (i.e., a second differential file), dumping the first differential file or reorganization of the primary file and first differential file can occur concurrently with update. The differential-differential file can be held in main memory if the time for dumping is short.
Facilitates rollback	The primary file constitutes beforeimage versions of updated records.
Facilitates rollforward	More frequent dumping can be undertaken because it is inexpensive to dump a differential file.
Reduces the risk of serious data loss	The small critical area of the differential file can be stored on a highly reliable device or duplexed.

A variation on the differential file strategy is the shadow paging strategy. With shadow paging, the database is divided into a number of pages (blocks). A page table is created, which contains pointers to the database pages. Provided the page table is not too large, it is kept in main memory. In addition, a shadow page table exists, which is stored on disk.

When the system begins to process a transaction, it first copies the contents of the current page table to the shadow page table. If the transaction then updates the database, the new page is written to a new area on disk. Note that the old page is not overwritten. The current page table entry for the updated page is modified to point to the address of the updated page (Figure 14-19). If the transaction then fails, the database can be rolled back by copying the contents

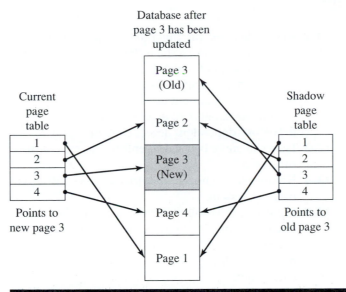

FIGURE 14–19. Shadow page strategy for backup and recovery.

of the shadow page table to the current page table. If the transaction commits, the shadow page table is discarded.

The advantage of the shadow paging strategy is its simplicity. It facilitates rollback in the event of transaction failure. It is not a complete backup and recovery strategy, however. Dumps and afterimage records must be kept to enable recovery if the database is lost through a disaster. Similarly, transactions and beforeimage records must be kept if more extensive rollback is required and transactions must be reprocessed because an application program was in error.

SUMMARY

The database subsystem provides functions to define, create, modify, delete, and read data in an information system. Several major types of controls must be implemented in the database subsystem to improve the reliability of its components and to protect the integrity of data stored in the database. Access controls restrict the actions that users can undertake on the database and the database definition to the authorized set of actions. Integrity constraints maintain the accuracy, completeness, and uniqueness of instances of the constructs used within the conceptual modelling or data modelling approach used to design the database. Application programs should use certain update and reporting protocols to prevent and to detect data integrity violations. When data is shared among multiple users, concurrency controls must exist to prevent inconsistent updating or reading of the database. Cryptographic controls can be used to preserve the privacy of data in the database. File handling controls reduce the likelihood of accidental erasure of data. Audit trail controls maintain a chronology of all events that occur in the subsystem. Finally, existence controls must be implemented to restore the database in the event of loss.

Review Questions

14–1 Briefly describe the functions of the database subsystem.

14–2 Distinguish between the following discretionary access control policies that are exercised in the database subsystem:
  a Name-dependent access control
  b Content-dependent access control
  c Context-dependent access control
  d History-dependent access control

14–3 How can *views* be used to enforce access controls in the database subsystem?

14–4 Briefly explain how mandatory access controls can be enforced in the database subsystem.

14–5 For *each* of the following constructs in the entity-relationship model, give *one* integrity constraint that might be exercised:
  a Entity
  b Relationship
  c Attribute

14–6 What is meant by *referential integrity* within *(a)* the relational data model, and *(b)* the object data model?

14–7 Why should application programs that update monetary data items in the database maintain a suspense account?

14–8 Why should application programs that use standing data print control totals to allow users to determine whether any changes have been made to standing data?

14–9 Briefly describe the data integrity problems that can be caused by concurrent update processes. Why might a read-only process want to exclude a concurrent update process?

14–10 How can lockout lead to deadlock? What problems can arise if preemption is used to break deadlock without rolling back the preempted processes?

14–11 Briefly describe the nature of two-phase locking. If two-phase locking is used to prevent a deadlock situation, what properties must the transactions have if two-phase locking is to be successful?

14–12 Briefly describe a strategy that can be used to implement concurrency controls in a distributed database subsystem when the database is
  a Replicated
  b Partitioned

14–13 Why is block encryption more likely to be used than stream encryption in the database subsystem?

14–14 What problems arise when cryptography is used as a control in a shared database environment? How can these problems be overcome, at least to some extent, using a hierarchy of cryptographic keys?

14–15 Briefly describe the nature of file handling controls. What control objectives are accomplished using a(n):
  a Internal file label
  b Retention date
  c File protection ring
  d External file label

14–16 Distinguish between the implosion and the explosion purposes of an accounting audit trail for the database subsystem. Use an accounts payable system to illustrate your answer.

14–17 Briefly explain why a change to the database definition might present difficulties for a user who wants to access data contained in the accounting audit trail that extends over a long period of time.

14–18 How might a database administrator use the operations audit trail maintained for the database subsystem?

14–19 Distinguish between a rollforward and a rollback recovery operation. For each type of operation, give *one* example of a failure that would lead to the operation being undertaken.

14–20 What conditions must exist before a grandfather, father, son backup strategy can be used? Briefly discuss the advantages and disadvantages of the strategy.

14–21 The dual recording/mirroring backup strategy does not allow recovery of the database from all types of failure. Briefly describe the situations where recovery can *not* be accomplished.

14–22 Briefly explain the differences between logical dumping and physical dumping. What are the relative advantages and disadvantages of each method of dumping?

14–23 Why is dumping only a partial backup strategy?

14–24 Briefly describe the various types of logs that can be used for recovery purposes. Why might a combination of logging strategies be used for recovery purposes?

14–25 When logging input transactions, why is it necessary to distinguish between transactions that have been processed successfully and those that have been processed in error? If this distinction is not made, during the recovery process what actions must be taken?

14–26 Briefly explain the process of rolling back the database using beforeimages of the records in the database. Why is it necessary to take beforeimages of records in a list file that are moved because of a physical reorganization to the file?

14–27 Explain the problems of using afterimages to roll back the database. Why might a decision have been made not to log beforeimages, even though the problems of rolling back the database were recognized at the outset?

14–28 Briefly explain the residual dump backup and recovery strategy. Is it necessary to log both beforeimages and afterimages of records changed using a residual dump strategy?

14–29 Briefly explain the concept of a differential file. What advantages does a differential file have for backup and recovery purposes?

14–30 Briefly explain the shadow paging backup and recovery strategy. Give one advantage and one disadvantage of the shadow paging strategy.

Multiple-Choice Questions

14–1 Which of the following types of database access control will prevent personnel clerks from accessing the names of employees whose salaries exceed $30,000 unless they are seeking to perform some type of statistical function?

a Content-dependent access control
b History-dependent access control
c Context-dependent access control
d Name-dependent access control

14–2 Which of the following types of database access control is the most difficult to enforce?
  a Name-dependent access control
  b Context-dependent access control
  c Content-dependent access control
  d History-dependent access control

14–3 The purpose of horizontal propagation controls is to:
  a Restrict user views of the database only to relations that are used in multiple application systems
  b Limit the number of users to whom a user can assign action privileges
  c Permit users to carry the action privileges they have been assigned from one application system to another application system
  d Limit the number of users who can pass on the action privileges they have been given to other users

14–4 Which of the following statements about polyinstantiation as a means of implementing mandatory access controls in the database subsystem is *true*?
  a Conditional statements are applied to a single tuple of a relation to determine what data the user can access
  b Different access controls mechanisms are established to handle different clearance levels
  c Multiple tuples of a relation are created to satisfy the security and integrity rules applicable to each clearance level
  d Classification levels are applied to different data items in a tuple rather than the tuple as a whole

14–5 If a minimal cardinality constraint applies to an entity in the entity-relationship model, it specifies:
  a The minimum number of relationships that the entity can have with other entities in the database
  b The smallest value that can be assigned to the primary key that uniquely identifies the entity
  c The minimum number of instances of the entity that can exist in the database
  d The minimum number of attributes of the entity that are permitted to have non-null values

14–6 Which of the following statements best describes the meaning of a referential integrity constraint in the relational data model?
  a The primary key of tuple in a relation must uniquely identify the tuple in the database
  b Users cannot reference a tuple of a relation unless they have been assigned the appropriate action privileges
  c The primary key value of a tuple of a relation cannot have a null value
  d If a data item in a tuple of one relation references the key of a tuple of another relation, the latter tuple must exist in the database

14–7 Incorrect end-of-file protocols in an application update program tend to result in:
  a Transaction file records not being processed
  b Standing data being corrupted
  c Programs getting into loops
  d The incorrect internal label being inserted into the header record on a file

14–8 An application program that updates monetary data items should maintain a suspense account to:

a Act as a repository for monetary transactions that mismatch the master file

b Allow postings if a forward invoicing facility is provided for customers

c Signal when end-of-period processing can be carried out

d Store the control total for the monetary value of the master file

14–9 Which of the following data items is *most likely* to have its integrity protected by controls over standing data?

a A raw material issue

b A pay rate

c A customer's address

d A quantity sold

14–10 Which of the following is *not* a condition for deadlock to arise?

a Additional request

b Circular wait

c Lockout

d Preemption

14–11 Which of the following properties of a transaction is *not* required for two-phase locking to work?

a Isolation

b Atomicity

c Consistency

d Temporality

14–12 Which of the following statements about concurrency controls in a distributed database environment is *true*?

a Isolation of transactions is not required to effect two-phase locking

b In a replicated database, two-phase schedulers may be stored with each version of the data item

c In a partitioned database, it is easier to enforce concurrency control when there is some overlap of partitions

d Voting schemes are more likely to be used to resolve concurrency problems in a partitioned database rather than a replicated database

14–13 Which of the following statements about cryptographic controls in the database subsystem is *false*?

a If little or no sharing of data among users occurs, each user can protect their own data using a personal cryptographic key

b Block encryption is more likely to be used to protect stored data than stream encryption

c One user's data can be protected from another user by implementing a secure encryption device in the controller for the storage medium

d If a hierarchy of keys is used to protect stored data, file keys are encrypted under secondary keys, which in turn are encrypted under a master key

14–14 Which of the following is *least likely* to be an objective of file handling controls?

a To prevent data items from being accidentally overwritten

b To ensure the correct file has been loaded for a program

c To prevent inefficient access by programs to data

d To ensure data is retained for a certain period

14-15 Which of the following objectives will require an *explosion* operation in terms of the accounting audit trail in the database subsystem?

    a To determine whether a transaction entered by one user updated an account before a transaction entered by another user

    b To determine whether a transaction updated the correct account in the database

    c To determine whether sufficient funds exist in an account to sustain a withdrawal

    d To determine whether an order transaction triggered in an electronic data interchange system was transmitted to the correct supplier

14-16 Which of the following objectives is *least likely* to be served by the operations audit trail in the database subsystem?

    a To determine whether a new index needs to be established in the database

    b To determine whether a more secure encryption key should be installed to protect the privacy of data

    c To determine whether a program that updates the database needs to be restructured

    d To determine whether faster storage devices need to be purchased to support the database

14-17 Which of the following is *not* a disadvantage of the grandfather, father, son backup and recovery strategy?

    a Precludes update in place

    b Consumes substantial resources to effect global recovery

    c File is unavailable during recovery

    d Cannot be used where concurrent processes update the file

14-18 Dual protection/mirroring affords protection against:

    a A procedural error

    b A system software error

    c An application program error

    d A power loss

14-19 Relative to physical dumping, logical dumping:

    a Is a faster backup strategy

    b Is slower when localized recovery is needed

    c Causes fewer problems with multilist file organizations

    d Is more appropriate when concurrent update of the database is permitted

14-20 Which of the following is *not* a purpose of logging?

    a To obviate the need for a dump

    b To provide a record of transactions in the time sequence in which they occurred

    c To reduce the downtime needed for resubmission of the transactions

    d To facilitate both rolling forward and rolling back the database

14-21 Which logging strategy facilitates rollforward of the database?

    a Logging input transactions

    b Logging beforeimages

    c Logging valid transactions only

    d Logging afterimages

14-22 A purpose of separating successful input transactions from unsuccessful input transactions on a log is to:

    a Avoid control total problems when the data must be reprocessed for recovery

    b Facilitate preserving the time series of the successful transactions only c Avoid duplicate error messages that might cause confusion as recovery occurs

    d Allow both a rollforward and a rollback operation to occur

14–23 Which of the following is *not* a problem when rollback is needed as a means of recovery and concurrent update processes have altered the damaged database?

    a All processes that update the corrupted data items must be identified so they can be locked out when an error is discovered

    b It might be difficult to determine the consequences of error so the effects of the damage can be undone

    c Rollback cannot be accomplished if afterimages have been damaged

    d Rollback may be pointless if too many other processes have accessed the data in error before the error has been discovered

14–24 Residual dumping involves logging records that have not been changed since the:

    a Last residual dump

    b Second-last residual dump

    c Last full dump

    d Second-last full dump

14–25 If a rollforward operation takes place using a residual dump, recovery involves:

    a Going back to but not including the second-last residual dump

    b Going back to and including the last residual dump

    c Going back to the last full dump because a residual dump does not facilitate rollforward

    d Going back to but not including the last residual dump

14–26 Which of the following is a disadvantage of residual dumping?

    a There is less flexibility in leveling system workloads

    b There is more duplicate backup

    c It cannot take place as a background operation

    d Recovery is more complex than with a physical dump

14–27 A differential file facilitates rollback because:

    a Record changes and beforeimages can be assigned to a high-speed storage device

    b The primary file constitutes beforeimage versions of the updated records

    c The differential file constitutes beforeimage versions of the updated records

    d It is easier to identify which users of the database have been affected by the corrupted records

14–28 Which of the following statements about shadow paging is *true*?

    a When processing of a transaction commences, the current page table is deleted

    b Rollback involves overwriting the shadow page table with the current page table

    c When a transaction updates the database, a new page is written to a new area on the storage medium

    d The current page table is discarded just before the transaction commits

Exercises and Cases

14–1 Barrel Roll Ltd. is a major Perth-based manufacturer of equipment and clothing for water sports—for example, bodyboards, surfboards, water skis, bikinis, wetsuits, and T-shirts. It sells its products throughout Australia, New Zealand, and Southeast Asia.

       You are an information systems auditor in the firm of external auditors that has just taken over the audit of Barrel Roll. Your partner has asked you to undertake an evaluation of the access controls used by Barrel Roll to protect its database. The company uses a major, widely sold relational database management system to manage its database. The database is maintained on a mainframe computer, and it can be accessed from a large number of microcomputers that are scattered throughout the various departments of the company. Most of the company's significant application systems are maintained using the database management system.

The audit procedures you undertake and the findings you obtain are as follows:

1. *Audit procedure:* Interview the system administrator and obtain the operating system user profiles to determine who has access to the database management system.

   Finding: Four hundred twenty-two users have access to the mainframe. Of these, 356 have access to the database management system.

2. *Audit procedure:* Select a sample of 20 users from the list of users who have access to the database management system, determine their position and role within Barrel Roll, and evaluate whether they should have access to the database management system.

   Finding: It is reasonable that each of the 20 users you investigate should have access to the database management system.

3. *Audit procedure:* The database management system maintains the list of authorized users, their authentication information, and the action privileges they have been assigned in its data dictionary. Select a sample of 50 users, evaluate whether their authentication information is likely to be secure, and check whether the action privileges they have been assigned are appropriate given their position and role within the organization.

   Finding: The database management system forces users to choose passwords that are at least five characters long and that do not match words in a dictionary. The system also forces users to change their passwords every month and not to resubmit one of the last 10 passwords they have used. Interviews with users indicate they are aware of the importance of password security and that they take password security seriously. Except for two people, the action privileges assigned to users seem to be appropriate: *(a)* a long-tenured clerk in the personnel department has access to payroll data, which he should not be able to access, and *(b)* a production supervisor has access to inventory records, which she should not be able to access. When you discuss these two cases with the database administrator, she is surprised because her records indicate these privileges were not assigned to the personnel clerk and the production supervisor at the outset.

4. *Audit procedure:* Select a sample of 20 tables and 20 views from the data dictionary. For the tables, evaluate whether the level of access granted to them is appropriate. For the views, evaluate whether they have been implemented correctly.

   Finding: The level of access granted to the tables seems reasonable. Some of the views are complex, but they appear to have been implemented correctly.

5. *Audit procedure:* Determine whether the database audit trail is activated and whether it is reviewed regularly.

   Finding: The database audit trail has not been activated. The database administrator indicates that response times degrade to unacceptable levels when the audit trail facility is invoked.

   Required: In light of your findings, how will you advise your partner to proceed with the remainder of the audit?

14–2 You are the manager of internal audit in a large, centralized manufacturing company that is currently using a relational database management system to support the company database. The company has used this system successfully for many years as a foundation for all its major application systems. The system has a large worldwide user base.

One day you are approached by the vice president of information systems to provide advice on a proposal that he has received from his systems analysis manager, his programming manager, and his database administrator. In the proposal, they argue that the company should cease use of the relational database management system and acquire an object database management system. They give three major reasons for the proposed change. First, they argue that the system will allow them to develop better conceptual models of application domains and that these models will provide the company with a competitive advantage in the marketplace. Second, they argue that the system will provide support for the company's engineers in the product design work they undertake. They point out that this work cannot be supported by the company's relational database management system. Third, compared with the relational database management system, they argue that the object database management system provides faster recovery of the database in the event of failure. They believe this advantage to be important in light of the large number of online users of the database.

The vice president of information systems is concerned about the significance of such a move for the company. In this light, he asks you to examine the specifications of the object database management system, especially from a controls viewpoint, and to comment on the proposal he has received.

When you examine the specifications of the object database management system, you note that it appears to provide high-quality controls in terms of access controls, concurrency controls, audit trail controls, and backup and recovery controls. It provides only weak support for a distributed database environment, but you are not concerned in light of the centralized operations of your company. You note, however, that the system appears to enforce few integrity constraints. It assigns a unique identifier to each object, but it is unclear from the specifications what other integrity constraints it enforces.

Required: What advice will you now provide to the vice president of information systems in light of your findings? Be sure to indicate the likely impact on application systems from a controls viewpoint if the system enforces few integrity constraints. Be sure, also, to indicate any likely impact on the way you would conduct your audits if the system were to be implemented. In both cases, try to be as specific as possible in the advice you provide.

14–3 As the manager of internal audit for Streaker Products, a manufacturer of running shoes and related athletic goods, you are called one day to a meeting with the controller, the information systems manager, and the accounts branch manager. The information systems manager is furious. He explains that the accounts receivable master file update program has been erroneously deleting records from the master file progressively over the past six months. The error has only just been discovered. He complains that reconstructing the master file to recover the erroneously deleted records is going to be costly. Furthermore, the company has lost revenue because the accounts receivable records have been lost. He is upset because the accounts branch has failed to identify the error on a timely basis.

The accounts branch manager is equally upset. She complains that her branch has suffered from high staff turnover, and thus her staff lack training and experience. Moreover, her branch is also understaffed and, as a result, her clerks have had little time to check anything or to follow up properly on errors they have identified. Furthermore, she argues the error occurred because a change to the online update program used by her staff was not tested properly by information systems personnel. Her view is that responsibility for the problem lies with the information systems manager, not her.

Required: The controller asks you to write a brief report for her explaining the following:

a What controls should have been present to identify the error and why, if they were present, they might have failed;

b How the lost accounts receivable master records might be recovered;

c How the revenue lost from failure to bill customers might be recovered; and

d How this event can be prevented in the future.

14–4 Pieces and Parts, Ltd. is a diversified manufacturing company with five large manufacturing plants located in upstate New York. To date, the company has maintained a centralized information systems facility at its biggest plant. All plants have had online access to this facility.

In the hope that response times and customer service will improve, the company has decided to decentralize its information systems facility. In this light, the information systems manager has prepared a plan to effect decentralization of information systems functions. One part of his plan deals with how the database will be distributed. He proposes that some data in the company's database will be replicated at some or all of the five plants. Other data will be partitioned and located at the plant where it will be used most frequently. Overall, he is seeking to minimize the amount of data communications traffic between the five plants.

You are an information systems auditor in the external audit firm that audits Pieces and Parts. A copy of the information systems manager's plan has been sent to the partner in charge of the audit for her comments. After perusing the plan, she is especially concerned about the possibility of data being corrupted because of concurrency problems. On average, inventory constitutes about 80 percent of Pieces and Parts' current assets, and many high-value inventory items exist. It is unclear whether Pieces and Parts' information systems and, in particular, its database management system can maintain data integrity when data is distributed and concurrent access to data occurs. Pieces and Parts' information systems manager insists, however, that concurrent access to data will not be a problem under his scheme for distributing data.

Required: The partner in charge of the audit asks you to prepare an audit plan for the coming year's audit to determine whether concurrency controls are in place and working. Because Pieces and Parts intends to let the audit out for tender at the end of the next financial year, the partner asks that you be mindful of selecting the most effective and efficient set of audit procedures in your plan. What audit procedures will you recommend your firm follow to determine whether concurrency controls are in place and working?

14–5 You are an internal auditor participating in the design phase of a new online accounts receivable system. Customer accounts will be updated automatically with data captured using point-of-sale devices. The customer service department will have terminals to create new accounts, debit customer accounts, inquire as to the status of accounts, and make alterations to adjust any errors identified in accounts.

When you review the design of the audit trail, you notice that the system designer has not provided for storing beforeimages and afterimages of the account balance with transaction records. When you ask him about this omission, he explains that he has made this choice to save storage space. Because of the large number of transactions that the system must process, he argues that the overheads incurred by the system will be too high if careful control is not kept over the amount of audit trail data that is recorded. In addition, he argues that beforeimages and afterimages of all records changed are written to the log used for backup and recovery purposes. He wants to minimize the amount of duplicate data maintained for audit trail purposes and backup and recovery purposes.

You explain to the designer that the customer service department will need to know the status of an account balance at various points in time to answer customer queries. He answers that all transactions for an account are chained to the account. Obtaining an account balance, therefore, is simply a matter of adding up all transactions associated with the account that is subject to the inquiry and subtracting this amount from the current account balance. He explains that this algorithm will be in the retrieval program that the customer service department will use. Moreover, in a worst-case scenario, he argues that the account balance at some point in time could be obtained for the backup and recovery log.

Required: Evaluate the designer's answer from an audit viewpoint. Can you think of any reasons why beforeimages and afterimages still should be stored with the transaction in spite of the designer's arguments?

14-6 The Convict Savings Bank is a large bank based in Sydney with branches scattered throughout Australia. The bank uses an online real-time update system for its customer accounts system. The branches are connected via a telecommunications network to a centralized database in the head office. The bank uses a relational database management system to maintain its database.

As a member of the firm that undertakes the external audit of the bank, you are reviewing the adequacy of backup and recovery procedures for the customer accounts system. During an interview with the database administrator, you ask her about the actions undertaken upon a system crash. She explains to you that operators attempt to restart the system immediately upon a system crash because downtime within the system has such an adverse impact on the level of customer service that the bank can provide. You are aware that the relational database management system used by the bank to support the system establishes relationships between records (tuples) via pointers. In this light, you ask whether the database is rolled back to the last commit point before the system is restarted. The database administrator indicates that this action is not taken for two reasons. First, she explains that commit points are made fairly infrequently to reduce the overheads associated with logging and to improve response times. She indicates that reducing the frequency with which commit points are made is unlikely to lead to a deadlock situation. Different tellers are unlikely to want to access a customer's account at the same time. Second, at peak periods during the day she argues that the time required to roll back the system to a commit point would be unacceptable. Customers will react adversely if they have to stand in a line for more than a few minutes. Moreover, the bank has a policy that customers will be served within five minutes or the bank will deposit ten dollars within their account.

You express your concern to her about the possibility of pointers in the database not having been updated when the crash occurs and, as a result, the database being in an inconsistent state. The database administrator concedes this point. Nevertheless, she argues that the existence of an inconsistency is a relatively minor problem. When the system is restarted, tellers are supposed to check whether the last transaction they submitted was posted. If it was not posted, they simply resubmit the transaction. In addition, an inquiry transaction will identify inconsistent or corrupted pointers. Even if the database is in an inconsistent state, the database administrator argues that it will have little effect because further transactions for the customer are unlikely to occur that day. Recovery of the database to a consistent state can then be left until a quiet time during the night shift.

Required: Write a brief report for the partner in charge of the audit commenting on the adequacy of backup and recovery procedures for the customer accounts system. Make any suggestions that you feel would improve the adequacy of backup and recovery procedures for the system. Comment, also, on any changes you believe should be made to the audit approach in light of your findings on backup and recovery controls in the online system.

Answers to Multiple-Choice Questions

14–1	a	14–8	a	14–15	a	14–22	c
14–2	d	14–9	b	14–16	b	14–23	c
14–3	b	14–10	d	14–17	b	14–24	a
14–4	c	14–11	d	14–18	d	14–25	a
14–5	c	14–12	b	14–18	d	14–26	d
14–6	d	14–13	c	14–20	a	14–27	b
14–7	a	14–14	c	14–21	d	14–28	c

REFERENCES

Aghili, Houtan, and Dennis G. Severance (1982), "A Practical Guide to the Design of Differential Files for Recovery of On-Line Databases," *ACM Transactions on Database Systems* (December), 540–565.

Bernstein, Philip A., and Nathan Goodman (1981), "Concurrency Control in Distributed Database Systems," *Computing Surveys* (June), 185–221.

Brachman, Ronald J., Tom Khabaza, Willi Kloesgen, Gregory Piatetsky-Shapiro, and Evangelos Simoudis (1996), "Mining Business Databases," *Communications of the ACM* (November), 42–48.

Castano, Silvana, Maria Grazia Fugini, Giancario Martella, and Pierangela Samarati (1995), *Database Security*. Reading MA: Addison-Wesley.

Cattell, R. G. G. (1994), *Object Data Management: Object-Oriented and Extended Relational Database Systems*, rev. ed. Reading, MA: Addison-Wesley.

Clarke, Rodney, Simon Holloway, and William List, eds. (1991), *The Security, Audit and Control of Databases*. Aldershot, England: Avebury Technical.

Davies, D. W., and W. L. Price (1989), *Security for Computer Networks: An Introduction to Data Security in Teleprocessing and Electronic Funds Transfer*, 2d ed. New York: John Wiley & Sons.

Elmasri, Ramez, and Shamkant B. Navathe (1994), *Fundamentals of Database Systems*, 2d ed. Redwood City, CA: Benjamin/Cummings.

Everest, Gordon C. (1986), *Database Management: Objectives, System Functions, & Administration*. New York: McGraw-Hill.

Gray, Jim, and Andreas Reuter (1993), *Transaction Processing: Concepts and Techniques*. San Mateo, CA: Morgan Kaufmann.

Haerder, Theo, and Andreas Reuter (1983), "Principles of Transaction-Oriented Database Recovery," *Computing Surveys* (December), 287–317.

Inmon, W. H. (1996), "The Data Warehouse and Data Mining," *Communications of the ACM* (November), 49–50.

Jajodia, Sushil, Shashi K. Gadia, and Gautam Bhargava (1995), "Logical Design of Audit Information in Relational Databases," in Marshall D. Abrams, Sushil Jajodia, and Harold J. Podell, eds., *Information Security: An Integrated Collection of Essays.* Los Alamitos, CA: IEEE Computer Society Press, 585–595.

———— and Ravi S. Sandhu (1995), "Toward a Multilevel Secure Relational Model," in Marshall D. Abrams, Sushil Jajodia, and Harold J. Podell, eds., *Information Security: An Integrated Collection of Essays.* Los Alamitos, CA: IEEE Computer Society Press, 460–492.

Kingsley, Dean, Sandee Carrier, and Douglas Feil (1993), *Security & Control in an Oracle® Environment.* Chicago: The EDP Auditors Foundation, Inc.

Lunt, Teresa F. (1995), "Authorization in Object-Oriented Databases," in Won Kim, ed., *Modern Database Systems: The Object Model, Interoperability, and Beyond.* Reading, MA: Addison-Wesley, 130–145.

Meadows, Catherine, and Sushil Jajodia (1995), "Integrity in Multilevel Secure Database Management Systems," in Marshall D. Abrams, Sushil Jajodia, and Harold J. Podell, eds., *Infor-mation Security: An Integrated Collection of Essays.* Los Alamitos, CA: IEEE Computer Society Press, 530–541.

Notargiacomo, LouAnna (1995), "Architectures for MLS Database Management Systems," in Marshall D. Abrams, Sushil Jajodia, and Harold J. Podell, eds., *Information Security: An Integrated Collection of Essays.* Los Alamitos, CA: IEEE Computer Society Press, 439–459.

Rothenberg, Jeff (1995), "Ensuring the Longevity of Digital Documents," *Scientific American* (January), 24–29.

Sandhu, Ravi S., and Sushil Jajodia (1995), "Integrity Mechanisms in Database Management Systems," in Marshall D. Abrams, Sushil Jajodia, and Harold J. Podell, eds., *Information Security: An Integrated Collection of Essays.* Los Alamitos, CA: IEEE Computer Society Press, 617–634.

Severance, Dennis G., and Guy M. Lohman (1976), "Differential Files: Their Application to the Maintenance of Large Databases," *ACM Transactions on Database Systems* (September), 167–195.

Smith, G. W. (1991), "Modeling Security-Relevant Data Semantics," *IEEE Transactions on Software Engineering* (November), 1195–1203.

Verhofstad, J. S. M. (1978), "Recovery Techniques for Database Systems," *ACM Computing Surveys* (June), 167–195.

Weber, Ron (1982), "Audit Trail System Support in Advanced Computer-Based Accounting Systems," *The Accounting Review* (April), 311–325.

CHAPTER

Output Controls

Chapter Outline

Chapter Key Points

■ The output subsystem provides functions that determine the content of data that will be provided to users, the ways data will be formatted and presented to users, and the ways data will be prepared for and routed to users.

■ Inference controls are used in the output subsystem to prevent compromise of statistical databases—databases from which users can obtain only aggregate statistics rather than the values of individual data items. They are used to prevent four types of compromise: (a) positive compromise, whereby users determine that a person has a particular attribute value; (b) negative compromise, whereby users determine that a person does not have a particular attribute value; (c) exact compromise, whereby users determine the precise value of an attribute possessed by a person; and (d) approximate compromise, whereby users determine within some range the attribute value possessed by a person.

■ One form of inference controls is restriction controls, which limit the set of responses that will be provided to users to try to protect the confidentiality of data about persons in the database. They can take various forms. For example, they might not provide a response to users if their query on the database results in smaller than a certain number of persons having attribute values that satisfy the query. Unfortunately, it is difficult to devise a set of restriction controls that cannot be compromised in fairly straightforward ways.

■ A second form of inference controls is perturbation controls, which introduce some type of noise into the statistics calculated on the basis of records retrieved from the database. They can be exercised on the records used as input to a statistical function. For example, statistics might be calculated on the basis of a sample of records that satisfy the query levied by the user. Alternatively, they can be exercised on the results obtained after a statistical function has been computed. For example, results can be rounded up and down to the nearest integer multiple of a fixed rounding base—say, multiples of five.

■ Batch output is output that is produced at some operations facility and subsequently distributed to the custodians or users of the output. Controls need to be established over the production and distribution of batch output to ensure that accurate, complete, and timely output is provided only to authorized custodians and users.

■ Controls can be exercised over various phases in the production and distribution of batch output—for example, securing the storage of any special stationery used to produce batch output, ensuring that only authorized users are permitted to execute batch report programs, ensuring that the contents of spooling/printer files cannot be altered, preventing unauthorized parties from viewing the contents of confidential reports as they are printed, collecting reports promptly to prevent their loss, having client services staff review batch output for obvious errors prior to its distribution to users, ensuring that batch output is distributed to the correct user, having end users review output for errors or irregularities, storing batch output securely, determining an appropriate retention period for batch output, and shredding batch output when it is no longer required.

■ Batch output reports can be designed to facilitate exercising effective and efficient controls over them. For example, the title page of a batch output report should show the distribution list for the report and the person to contact if operational problems are encountered in producing the report. Similarly, the detail pages should contain page numbers so loss of or unauthorized removal of pages from the report can be detected.

■ Online output is output that is delivered electronically to the terminal employed by a user to gain access to a system. As with batch output, controls need to be established over the production and distribution of online output to ensure that accurate, complete, and timely output is provided only to authorized users.

■ Controls can be exercised over various phases in the production and distribution of online output—for example, ensuring that the output that can be accessed online is authorized, accurate, and complete, ensuring that online output is distributed to the correct network address, preserving the integrity of and privacy of online output transmitted over a communication line, checking that data has been received by the intended user, determining whether the intended user has read and considered properly the contents of online output, ensuring that the disposition of the online output is appropriate, determining an appropriate retention period for online output, and deleting online output completely when it is no longer required.

■ Audit trail controls in the output subsystem maintain the chronology of events that occur from the time the content of output is being assimilated until the time users complete their disposal of output because it no longer should be retained.

■ The accounting audit trail in the output subsystem shows what output was assimilated for presentation to users, what output was then presented to users, who received the output, when the output was received, and what actions were subsequently taken with the output. It permits the state of output and the events that occurred to output to be determined at each point in its life.

■ The operations audit trail in the output subsystem maintains the record of resources consumed by components in the output subsystem to assimilate, produce, distribute, use, store, and dispose of various types of output. It can be used to improve the effectiveness and efficiency of the output subsystem.

■ Existence controls are needed to recover output in the event that it is lost or destroyed. If output is written to spool files or report files and the files have been kept, recovering the output is straightforward. A new copy of the output can be generated from the files. If output that shows the state of some item at a point in time needs to be recovered, beforeimages and afterimages will have to be kept. If output that shows events needs to be recovered, a log of transactions must be kept. Checkpoint/restart facilities also might be important to effecting partial recovery of output—for example, recovery when a hardware problem causes a program that prints customer invoices to abort in midstream.

INTRODUCTION

The output subsystem provides functions that determine the content of data that will be provided to users, the ways data will be formatted and presented to users, and the ways data will be prepared for and routed to users. The major components of the output system are the software and personnel that determine the content, format, and timeliness of data to be provided to users, the various hardware devices used to present the formatted output data to users (e.g., printers, terminals, voice synthesizers), and the hardware, software, and personnel that route the output to users.

Many changes have occurred and are continuing to occur in the output subsystem. Much output that previously was produced as hard copy (printed output) is now produced as soft copy (displayed on a screen). With improvements in database technology, communications technology, and reporting software, users are better able to obtain the output they want directly rather than having to go through some intermediary. In this regard, printers are now often dispersed widely throughout organizations rather than being located in a single facility as they were in the past (the computer room). Output is now more varied—for example, relative to the 1980s, today much greater use is made of sound, video, and images as forms of output. Laser printers have become ubiquitous as the means of producing the reports, graphs, and drawings that previously were produced on impact printers and plotters. With the widespread availability of cheap, high-density storage devices such as CD-ROMs, greater use is now made of imaging software to read, store, and present images as output. Many organizations now seek to enable public access to information about them; for example, they establish pages on the World Wide Web that provide textual, video, image, and sound (multimedia) output to users who access these pages.

In this chapter we examine controls in the output subsystem. We begin by examining how inference controls can be used to filter the output that users are permitted to see. These controls are especially important when users are given access to statistical databases. We then discuss controls over the production and distribution of batch output. Next we consider how the design of batch reports can contribute to effective control over batch output. Subsequently we discuss controls over the production and distribution of online reports. Finally, we examine the audit trail and existence controls that should be implemented in the output subsystem.

INFERENCE CONTROLS

The access control models examined in previous chapters permit or deny access to a data item based on the name of the data item, the content of the data item, or some characteristic of the query or time series of queries made on the data item (see, for example, Chapter 14). In some cases, however, it might be desirable to grant access to a data item but to restrict the type of information that can be derived from accessing the data item. This situation arises especially with statistical databases—databases from which users can obtain only aggregate statistics rather than the values of individual data items. In statistical databases, sensitive and confidential data items, such as medical history data items, are maintained. Moreover, access to each data item is needed to provide statistical summaries of the information contained in the database. Users must not be able to deduce information about specific data item values, however, on the basis of a query.

Inference controls over statistical databases seek to prevent four types of compromise that can occur:

1. *Positive compromise.* Users determine that a person has a particular attribute value—for example, the person called John Doe is an alcoholic.
2. *Negative compromise.* Users determine that a person does *not* have a particular attribute value—for example, the person called John Doe is not an alcoholic.
3. *Exact compromise.* Users determine the precise value of an attribute possessed by a person—for example, the person called Mary Doe has a salary of exactly $120,000 per annum.
4. *Approximate compromise.* Users determine within some range the value of an attribute possessed by a person—for example, the person called Mary Doe has a salary in the range $100,000 to $140,000.

Note that a compromise must be either positive or negative, and it also must be either exact or approximate. Thus, there are four combinations: positive and exact (Doe's salary is $120,000); positive and approximate (Doe's salary is in the range $100,000 to $140,000); negative and exact (Doe's salary is not $120,000); and negative and approximate (Doe's salary is not in the range $100,000 to $140,000).

When encountering statistical databases, auditors need to be concerned about the quality of inference controls in the output subsystem for three reasons. First, if data privacy is violated, the organization that owns the database could be sued by the people who supplied the data in confidence. The organization could be liable for any damages that arise. Moreover, in serious cases the organization's viability as a going concern could be at risk. Second, data privacy violations can also cause substantial damage to an organization's goodwill. For example, a government's reputation might be seriously impaired if one of its departments releases confidential information. Likewise, a private organization might no longer be able to offer a statistical database service because people refuse to provide it with further information. Third, data privacy violations can be the basis for other irregularities that are perpetrated in an organization. For example, knowledge gained improperly about a customer's wealth could allow an employee to initiate fraudulent transactions that are unlikely to be detected by the customer.

In the following subsections we will examine some conceptual foundations underlying the inference problem in statistical databases. These foundations will enable us to understand better the nature of the problem and the approaches we can use to try to overcome the problem. We then examine two major types of inference controls used to prevent these compromises from occurring: (1) restriction controls and (2) perturbation controls. Our goal is to try to understand inference controls well enough to be able to develop ways of testing them and ultimately to evaluate their reliability.

Conceptual Foundations

One way that we conceptualize the inference problem is in terms of tables that contain statistics about the entities in a database. For example, assume we have a database about people and that we are interested in only two attributes of the individuals in the database—namely, their gender and their salary. Assume, also, that we are interested in only one statistic associated with these attributes—namely, the *count* of individuals who possess particular values of these attributes.

Figure 15–1 shows how the count statistics for the database can be represented in tabular form. The table shows, for example, that 12 females receive a salary of $90,000 and zero males receive a salary of $110,000. Note, the table does not show the *structure* of the database. Rather, it shows a *view* of the database—specifically, the number of persons in the database who possess certain attribute values or combinations of attribute values.

When we query the database, we specify the individuals we want by using Boolean operators (AND, OR, NOT) to indicate the particular combination of attributes values we want satisfied. For example, if we want to retrieve the set of females who earn either $100,000 or $110,000, we would use the following expression: Gender = Females AND (Salary = $100,000 OR Salary = $110,000). Having retrieved this data, we could then calculate various statistics—for example, *count* the number of individuals we have retrieved or calculate their *average* salary. Note, if we are interested in counting the number of persons who satisfy the expression, we can think in terms of operations on the table shown in Figure 15–1. Specifically, we would select the female row in the table and then select the two cells for the salaries $100,000 and $110,000. We would then add these two cells together to get the result we want—namely, four females have a salary of either $100,000 or $110,000.

In the jargon of inference controls, the expression that represents the attribute values linked by Boolean operators is called the *characteristic formula*, and it is represented by the symbol C. The set of records that satisfy

Gender	Salary		
	$ 90,000	$ 100,000	$110,000
Female	12	1	3
Male	8	4	0

FIGURE 15–1. Two-table of counts of individuals having a particular gender and salary.

the characteristic formula is called the *query set*, and it is represented by the symbols *X(C)*. We are especially interested in the *size* of the query set, represented by the symbols $|X(C)|$. As the size of the query set *decreases*, the risk of compromising the database *increases*. For example, if we determine that only one female earns $100,000, it might be easy for us to determine the name of this female based on other attributes we know about her—for example, her position in the organization.

Intuitively, therefore, we would like to prevent users employing a characteristic formula that would give them access to the cell (female, $100,000) in Figure 15–1 because positive compromise of the database might occur. Similarly, we would like to prevent users employing a characteristic formula that would give them access to the cell (male, $110,000) in Figure 15–1 because negative compromise of the database might occur. One approach we can use to try to prevent these compromises occurring is to *aggregate* the cells to a higher level. For example, in Figure 15–2, we have taken the table T_{GS} shown in Figure 15–1 and added the rows and columns to produce two new tables T_G (rows added) and T_S (columns added). We permit users to employ characteristic formulas that will allow access to T_G or to T_S but not to T_{GS}. In short, users cannot employ a characteristic formula that includes some combination of the gender and salary attributes.

Unfortunately, this approach has two limitations. First, from the users' viewpoint, clearly the database has lost information content. For example, users can no longer determine how many females earn a salary of $90,000—a query that is unlikely to lead to compromise of the database. Second, sometimes a cell statistic in a lower-level table can still be determined based on the set of statistics provided in all higher-level tables. We must leave this issue for further study. Briefly, however, the set of higher-level and lower-level tables

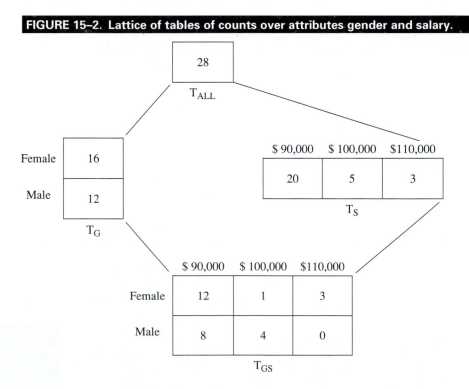

FIGURE 15–2. Lattice of tables of counts over attributes gender and salary.

can be conceived as a mathematical structure called a *lattice* (Figure 15–2). One of the properties of the lattice of tables is that a linear relationship exists between the statistics in the various tables. Unfortunately, a perpertrator can exploit this linear relationship, and inference problems can then occur.

Restriction Controls

Restriction controls limit the set of responses that will be provided to users to try to protect the confidentiality of data about persons in the database. The output subsystem responds, therefore, to only a proper subset of the queries that might be made against the database.

Restriction controls can take various forms. To illustrate their nature, however, consider the simple database shown in Figure 15–3. Assume that the salary information of individual employees is considered confidential. Nonetheless, statistical analyses of salary information are to be allowed. Furthermore, assume the query language that operates on the database allows the full range of Boolean operators to be used (AND, OR, NOT). In addition, assume it provides an extensive set of statistical functions—for example, count, sum, average, standard deviation, and skewness.

In the absence of inference controls, compromise is easy. We can use the following queries to determine Jones's salary:

> *Question:* How many employees are female and a consultant?
> *Answer:* 1.
> *Question:* What is the average salary of all employees who are female and a consultant?
> *Answer:* $62,000.

Because Jones is the only person in the database who is female and a consultant, we now know her salary.

A simple restriction control might be used to try to prevent the compromise. For example, assume the output subsystem enforces the following

Name	Sex	Position	Salary
Brown	M	Manager	70,000
Charles	F	Manager	70,000
East	M	Secretary	32,000
Gordon	M	Clerk	34,000
Harris	M	Consultant	58,000
Jones	F	Consultant	62,000
Long	F	Secretary	30,000
Martin	M	Consultant	64,000
Proud	F	Clerk	36,000
Reid	F	Manager	68,000

FIGURE 15–3. Payroll database where salary is confidential.

rule: Do not respond to a query if fewer than k records satisfy the query. Suppose that $k = 2$. Responses to the set of queries used previously to determine the salary of Jones now would no longer be provided by the output subsystem.

Even with this restriction, unfortunately, we can still easily compromise the database. Consider the following queries:

> *Question:* How many employees are consultants or *not* consultants?
> *Answer:* 10.
> *Question:* How many employees are *not* (female and a consultant)?
> *Answer:* 9.
> *Question:* What is the total salary paid to all employees who are consultants or *not* consultants?
> *Answer:* $524,000.
> *Question:* What is the total salary paid to all employees who are *not* (female and a consultant)?
> *Answer:* $462,000.

We can now determine Jones's salary by subtracting $462,000 from $524,000. Clearly, then, the restriction imposed on the query set size is inadequate as a means of preventing compromise of the database.

To counteract this compromise, a further restriction might be imposed on the query set size. Suppose the following rule is enforced by the output subsystem: Do not respond to a query if greater than $n - k$ records satisfy the query. The output subsystem now would no longer respond to the set of queries used above because it is subject to the rule $k \leq |X(C)| \leq n - k$.

Unfortunately, this restriction is still inadequate as a means of preventing compromise of the database. Using a technique called the "tracker," we can still determine Jones's salary. Assuming that $k = 2$, consider the following queries:

> *Question:* How many employees are consultants?
> *Answer:* 3.
> *Question:* How many employees are males and consultants?
> *Answer:* 2.
> *Question:* What is the total salary paid to all employees who are consultants?
> *Answer:* $184,000.
> *Question:* What is the total salary paid to all employees who are male and consultants?
> *Answer:* $122,000.

With these queries, we have satisfied the rule that $2 \leq |X(C)| \leq 8$. Again, however, we can determine Jones's salary easily by subtracting $122,000 from $184,000. Thus, the two restrictions imposed on the query set size are still inadequate as a means of preserving the integrity of the database.

The basic idea behind a tracker is to pad the original query with a set of auxiliary attributes so the restrictions on query set size can be circumvented. By eliminating the effects of the auxiliary attributes from the answer, the result for the original query can then be determined. Formally, the tracker can be represented as follows (see Schlörer 1975). Let C be a characteristic formula defined over the database. Recall that C represents a query expressed as a combination of data item names and Boolean operators. Suppose, now, that someone undertaking interrogations on the database knows that a person P

can be uniquely characterized by the formula C. Suppose, further, that C can be decomposed into two other formulas, $C1$ and $C2$, such that $C = C1$ AND $C2$. The *individual tracker, T,* of person P can now be represented by the formula $C1$ AND NOT $C2$. The database can be compromised using the following formula:

$$\text{Count}(C) = \text{Count}(C1) - \text{Count}(C1 \text{ AND NOT } C2)$$

provided that the query set size restrictions are not violated—that is:

$$k \leq \text{Count}(C1 \text{ AND NOT } C2) \leq \text{Count}(C1) \leq n - k$$

To illustrate how the tracker works, consider the Venn diagram shown in Figure 15–4. The set $C1$ comprises all persons who are consultants. The set $C2$ comprises all persons who are females. The intersection of the sets $C1$ and $C2$ comprise the persons who are consultants and females. In this case we know that this set comprises only one person, namely, Jones. Thus, the set ($C1$ AND NOT $C2$), the shaded area in Figure 15–4, identifies the persons who are consultants and males (not females). If we subtract the set of consultants who are males from the set of all consultants, the set of consultants who are females can be identified. In other words, we can select the record for Jones. Because the set of consultants who are males comprises two persons and the set of all consultants comprises three persons, note we have not violated the query set size restrictions.

The problem with individual trackers is that a new tracker must be found for each person in the database. Schlörer (1975) has shown, however, that we can construct a *general tracker* that will work for anyone in the database. Moreover, in one medical database he discovered that 98 percent of the records could be identified using no more than ten attributes. Thus, trackers often can be constructed fairly quickly. As a result, query set size restrictions provide only limited protection against database compromise.

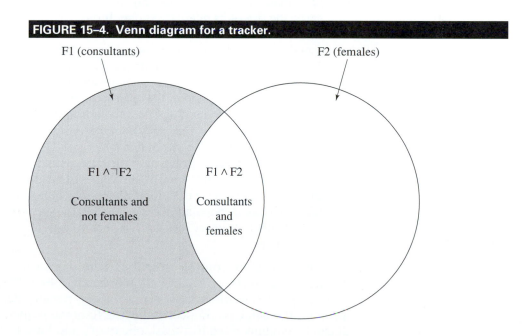

FIGURE 15–4. Venn diagram for a tracker.

F1 (consultants) F2 (females)

$F1 \wedge \neg F2$

Consultants and not females

$F1 \wedge F2$

Consultants and females

Still other types of restriction controls have been proposed (see Denning and Schlörer 1983, Adam and Wortmann 1989, Castano et al. 1994). For example:

1. *Order control.* A query, C, is not permitted if it involves more than d attributes. Assume that $d = 1$. In Figure 15–2, access to the count statistics in T_{GS} would be prevented because a query to determine these statistics involves two attributes. Thus, only the statistics in T_{ALL}, T_G, and T_S could be obtained.

2. *Relative table size control.* A query, C, is not permitted if its effect is to access a table of statistics whose relative size s_m/N is greater than some threshold value $1/k$. The size of the table is calculated by taking the product of the number of elements of each dimension of the table (the product of the domain sizes). For example, the two-dimensional table, T_{GS}, in Figure 15–2 has three elements in one dimension and two elements in the other dimension. Thus, $s_m = 3 \times 2 = 6$. The total number of records in the database is $N = 28$. Assume that we choose $k = 5$. The control means that a table can be accessed only if the average number of records falling in each cell exceeds k. The average number of records per cell in table T_{GS} is 28/6, which is less than 5. As a result, the table cannot be accessed. On the other hand, the average number of records in each cell of table T_S is 28/3, which means it can be accessed.

3. *Query set overlap control.* If the query sets associated with two queries contain a large number of common records, compromise may be possible. For example, in the two queries used previously to illustrate the notion of a tracker, one query set was a *subset* of the other query set; that is, the former query set was completely overlapped by the latter query set. A query set overlap control must keep track of different queries made by each user to determine whether the size of the overlap with two query sets exceeds some threshold level.

4. *Cell suppression.* The basic idea behind cell suppression is to restrict access to any cells in a table that contain sensitive statistics as well as access to any cells that allow the contents of sensitive cells to be deduced. For example, Figure 15–5 shows that four cells in table T_{GS} have been suppressed. Consider the cell for female, salary = \$100,000. Figure 15–1 shows that this cell is sensitive because the size of its query set is one. If only this cell were suppressed, however, its value can easily be deduced by taking the sum of the remaining cells in the female row in table T_{GS} from the value for the female cell in table T_G (16 – 15 = 1). Thus, the cell for female, salary = \$110,000 in Figure 15–2 has been suppressed, also, to prevent the compromise occurring. Similar considerations apply to the suppression of the corresponding cells for males in table T_{GS}.

5. *Grouping or rolling up.* To prevent compromise of the database, this control merges cells together when they contain sensitive statistics. For example, Figure 15–6 shows how the attributes, salary = \$100,000 and salary = \$110,000, have been merged to form a new attribute, namely, salary $\geq$ \$100,000.

6. *Partitioning.* Using this control, the values of all attributes are used to partition the database into a set of mutually exclusive, nonoverlapping atomic populations. No atomic population can comprise a single record. A query, C, is permitted only if its query set, $X(C)$, is an atomic population or the union of atomic populations.

The restriction controls described here work with varying levels of effectiveness (see, further, Adam and Wortmann 1989). Perhaps one of the most difficult problems arises, however, when two persons decide to collude to compromise the database. If a control exists to prevent query overlap, for example, it can be circumvented if you ask one query and I ask the other query. We then

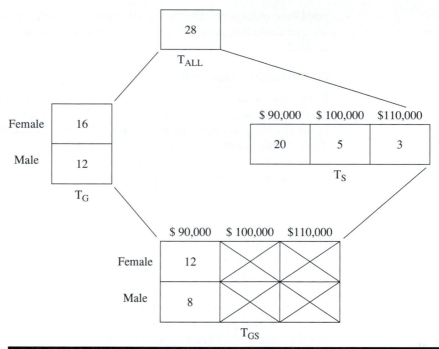

FIGURE 15–5. Preventing compromise using cell suppression.

FIGURE 15–6. Preventing compromise using grouping or rolling up.

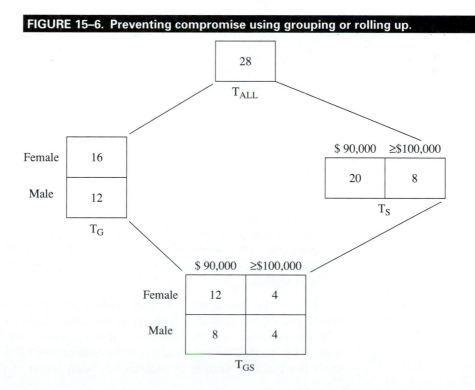

pool our results to determine the sensitive statistic. Unless the system knows we are colluding, our efforts to compromise the database are likely to be successful.

Perturbation Controls

Perturbation controls introduce some type of *noise* into the statistics calculated on the basis of records retrieved from the database. Compared with restriction controls, they seek to allow more statistics to be calculated on the database. They result in an information loss, however, associated with the variance of the perturbed statistic around the true value. This information loss is manifested as a bias or inconsistency in the results obtained. *Bias* refers to the difference between the average value of the perturbed statistic and the value of the true statistic. It should be zero or a small value. *Inconsistencies* arise when different statistics contradict each other or some type of nonsense value is returned as a result of the query. For example, the value obtained from row addition of a table might not equal the value obtained from column addition, or the query might return a real number when only integers are possible—for example, 3.62 people satisfy the query.

Perturbation controls can be exercised on either the *records* used as input to a statistical function or the *results* obtained after a statistical function has been computed. Three types of *record-based* perturbation controls that have been proposed follow:

1. *Query set sampling.* When the set of records that satisfies the query has been obtained, a sample of the records in the set is taken as the basis for calculating the statistics requested by the user. For example, a fixed proportion of records might be chosen randomly from the query set. Ideally, this proportion should be high so the statistic calculated on the basis of the sample is close to the statistic calculated on the basis of the query set. If the query set size is small, however, a high proportion might mean that most if not all the records in the query set are included in the sample. As a result, compromise of the database might be possible.

2. *Data perturbation.* With data perturbation, the values chosen to compute the statistic are first perturbed by error values that are chosen randomly from a distribution that has an expected value of zero. Thus, $x_i' = x_i + e_i$, where x_i' is the perturbed value, x_i is the original value, and e_i is the error value chosen from the distribution of error values with a mean of zero. Choosing a distribution of error values with a large variance enhances security, but it also increases the information loss associated with the calculated statistic. Data perturbation can also lead to inconsistencies—for example, negative counts.

3. *Data swapping.* With data swapping, records in the original statistical database are replaced with randomly generated records that will produce the same *t*-order statistics as the original database. Note that *t* is the number of attributes on which the statistic is based. As *t* becomes larger, the query set size becomes smaller, and thus there is greater risk of compromise. For higher values of *t*, therefore, the calculated statistic is more likely to differ from the true statistic.

Under the query set sampling or data perturbation approaches, the same result must be returned if a query is repeated. Otherwise, users will be faced with inconsistent results. Moreover, if the same result is not returned when a query is repeated, the database can be compromised through an *averaging attack*. If a random sample of records has been taken or the error term has been generated with a zero mean, database users simply repeat the query a large number of times and take the average of the results to obtain the true value (or a close approximation of the true value).

Results-based perturbation controls introduce an error term *after* the true statistic has been calculated; that is, the statistic is first computed on the basis of all records that satisfy the query, and the result is perturbed with some error term. Results-based perturbation controls differ primarily in terms of the ways they generate the error used to inoculate the results. For example, some systematically round the result to the nearest integer multiple of a fixed rounding base. If, say, the result is 28 and the fixed rounding base is 5, the result presented to the user would be 30. Other schemes randomly round the results to the next highest or next lowest integer multiple of a fixed rounding base. Again, the different schemes vary in terms of their abilities to protect the privacy of data, the information loss they produce, and their relative cost to operate.

BATCH OUTPUT PRODUCTION AND DISTRIBUTION CONTROLS

Batch output is output that is produced at some operations facility and subsequently distributed to or collected by the custodians or users of the output. It can take many forms—for example, a hard-copy management control report; pages containing tables, graphs, or images; negotiable instruments such as checks for distribution to employees, clients, or vendors; film or 35mm slides; a CD-ROM containing images and sound; microfiche containing document images; and a cartridge containing data for archival storage.

Production and distribution controls over batch output are established to ensure that accurate, complete, and timely output is provided only to authorized custodians or users. If the output is lost or corrupted, severe disruption can occur to the operations of the organization. For example, if customer bills are destroyed and the organization does not have backup, cash flow difficulties can arise. Likewise, if the privacy of output is violated, the organization can suffer losses in several ways: Unauthorized persons could use the information to gain access to the organization's information systems; confidential information, such as trade secrets, patents, marketing information, and credit information could be lost to a competitor; a criminal could blackmail the organization by threatening to expose confidential information about customers or clients.

We can structure our discussion on controls over batch output if we consider the different phases through which batch output must pass to be produced for and distributed to authorized custodians or users. As perhaps our most important example of batch output, consider batch reports. (We can use our discussion on batch reports also to illustrate controls that might be applied to other types of batch output.) Figure 15–7 shows the phases through which batch reports may pass in the output subsystem. Not all batch reports necessarily pass through each phase; for example, a report might be printed directly rather than queued or spooled. Moreover, what controls are exercised within each phase will depend on costs and benefits; more sensitive reports ought to be subjected to more controls. In the following subsections, however, we consider illustrative controls within each phase.

Stationery Supplies Storage Controls

Historically, when organizations used impact printers, they often had large amounts of preprinted stationery; for example, their invoice or customer statement stationery had a preprinted logo, address, and telephone number for the

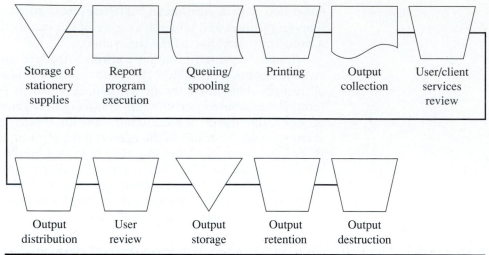

FIGURE 15–7. Stages in the production and distribution of batch output.

organization. It was more visually appealing to have these items preprinted (perhaps in color) rather than having them printed by an impact printer when output was produced. With widespread use of laser printers, however, use of preprinted stationery has declined. Many laser printers allow templates or masks of logos, addresses, telephone numbers, and so on, to be stored in them and printed (perhaps in color) on the plain-paper stationery they use. Alternatively, these templates or masks can be stored in programs (e.g., word processing programs) and printed on laser printers.

For several reasons, however, many types of preprinted stationery are still used. First, for some applications the preprinted features or the special paper on which the preprinting is done mitigate against forgeries. For example, negotiable instruments like checks are still used by some organizations, and they are likely to be prepared using preprinted stationery. Second, an organization might deem that preprinted stationery is still more visually appealing than printing constant output (e.g., the organization's logo) via a laser printer on plain-paper stationery. Various types of shading and dropout colors, for example, cannot be produced easily via laser printers. Third, printing speeds decrease and the costs of printing increase (e.g., because of increased consumption of toner) as larger amounts of information must be printed by a laser printer. In high-volume output applications, using preprinted stationery for output might be faster and cheaper.

Whenever preprinted stationery is used, auditors should check to determine whether the organization exercises careful controls over the stationery. For example, the following controls might be used:

Control	*Explanation*
Stationery suppliers should produce preprinted stationery only under proper authorization and provide preprinted stationery only to authorized persons	Prevents unauthorized parties from obtaining copies of an organization's preprinted stationery to use improperly.
Maintain an inventory system for preprinted stationery	Helps account for all purchasing, receipt, and use of preprinted stationery.

Control	*Explanation*
Store preprinted stationery securely	Prevents unauthorized destruction or removal of stationery.
Control access to preprinted stationery	Only authorized persons should be able to gain direct access to stationery supplies.
Prenumber preprinted stationery	Facilitates control over use of preprinted stationery
Store signature stamps and preprinted stationery for negotiable instruments at separate physical locations	Reduces the exposure if either preprinted stationery for negotiable instruments or signature stamps are stolen.

In the absence of these controls, losses can arise. For example, check stationery might be stolen, and word processing software might then be used to print fraudulent details on the check. Moreover, authorized signatures can also be scanned and then subsequently printed on the check, perhaps to appear like a signature stamp or to give the impression of a valid written signature. Similarly, if an organization's customer database is stolen along with the organization's preprinted invoice stationery, a competitor can produce and distribute fraudulent invoices to the organization's customers to destroy the organization's goodwill.

Report Program Execution Controls

Auditors should have three concerns in relation to the execution of report programs. First, only authorized persons should be able to execute them. Otherwise, confidential data could be divulged. For example, a bank would want to restrict the execution of the program that prints personal identification numbers (PINs) for customers to only a few trusted employees. Likewise, most organizations would seek to restrict access to programs that print negotiable instruments like checks and authorization images like signatures to only a few trusted employees. During an audit, auditors should determine what report programs are sensitive. They should then check to see which users have access to these programs. They should also check whether high-quality identification and authentication controls are in place and working to ensure that only authorized users access the programs.

Second, the action privileges assigned to authorized users of report programs should be appropriate to their needs. For example, an organization might wish to limit the number of copies of a report that a user can produce or to limit production of a report to certain times of the day or certain days within a month. Auditors should check to see whether the access control mechanism used by the organization can enforce these types of restrictions. If it can enforce this type of restriction, auditors should then evaluate the ways in which action privileges have been assigned to users.

Third, report programs that produce a large amount of output should include checkpoint/restart facilities. Recall from Chapter 13 that checkpoint/restart facilities can reduce the amount of work that has to be redone when some type of system failure occurs. From the viewpoint of our evaluating controls in the output subsystem, however, auditors should be concerned to see that checkpoint/restart facilities are not misused. For example, they should not be invoked to produce an unauthorized copy of a report. If auditors are concerned about this exposure, they can examine the operating system log for evidence of unauthorized use of checkpoint/restart facilities associated with sensitive report programs.

Queuing/Spooling/Printer File Controls

If a report program cannot write immediately to a printer, the output is queued or spooled. System software causes the report program to "think" it is writing to the printer when actually it is writing a printer file to disk storage. When the printer becomes available, spooling software reads the file and produces the report.

The presence of an intermediate file in the printing process leads to two control problems. First, printer files provide opportunities for unauthorized modifications to and copying of reports. For example, software can be used to change the value of a data item in a printer file, perhaps to prevent disclosure of some irregularity. Similarly, a copy of the printer file can be made and transmitted to an off-site location. Second, spooling software might be used inappropriately. For example, to recover from a printer malfunction, spooling software might allow operators to return to some prior intermediate point and to restart printing of a report. Unauthorized copies of the report might be produced in this way. Likewise, spooling software might allow operators to request more copies of a report than the number requested by the person who initiated printing of the report. Again, unauthorized copies of the report might be made.

Auditors must evaluate how well their client organizations achieve the following control objectives in relation to queuing or pooling of printer files:

1. The contents of printer files cannot be altered.
2. Unauthorized copies of printer files cannot be made.
3. Printer files are printed only once.
4. If copies of printer files are kept for backup and recovery purposes, they are not used to make unauthorized copies of reports.

Printing Controls

Controls over printing have three purposes: *(1)* to ensure that reports are printed on the correct printer; *(2)* to prevent unauthorized parties from scanning sensitive data that are printed on reports; and *(3)* to ensure that proper control is exercised over printing of negotiable forms or instruments.

Reports can be printed either intentionally or unintentionally on the wrong printer. If users have access to multiple printers, probably they will select which printer they wish to employ by making choices from a screen menu (Figure 15–8). Some printers that users can access might be secure because they are kept behind locked doors. Others might be insecure because they are located in public areas. Users who seek to perpetrate an irregularity could intentionally direct a sensitive report to a printer that is not in a secure location to provide a copy to an unauthorized user or to facilitate unauthorized removal of a copy themselves to an off-site location. Printing might also occur on the wrong printer, however, simply because *(1)* users forget to change their menu selection from a printer that is not in a secure location to one that is in a secure location or *(2)* a fault in the communications subsystem sends output to an incorrect device address.

Several steps might be undertaken to try to ensure that sensitive reports are printed only on a secure printer. First, users might be permitted to activate printing of sensitive reports from workstations that can access only secure printers. Second, users might be trained to check that they have selected the correct printer before they print sensitive reports. Third, software controls might be implemented to trap sensitive reports before they are printed on a printer that is not in a secure location.

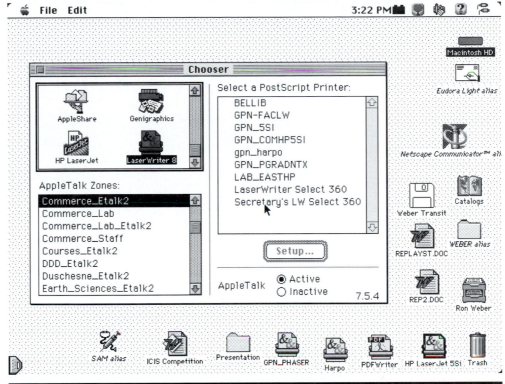

FIGURE 15–8. Making a printer selection.
Courtesy of Apple Computer, Inc.

Even when reports are printed at a secure location, it still might be necessary to limit disclosure of the report contents. For example, the report might contain PINs or confidential pay information that the operators or users who produced the report should not see. In these situations, special stationery sometimes can be used to hide the contents of the report. For example, Figure 15–9 shows the special multipart stationery that is sometimes used to print pay advice slips. Employees simply tear off the unreadable top copy to reveal their pay details on the second copy. A similar type of stationery is sometimes used to print PINs (see Figure 10–13). Users tear off the unreadable top copy to reveal their PIN on the second copy.

When impact printers are used, new printer ribbons are also a means of obtaining unauthorized copies of at least sections of a sensitive report. On the first cycle of a printer ribbon, it will contain a clear imprint of the data that has been printed. It might reveal, for example, the PINs printed out on PIN mailers. When sensitive data must be printed on an impact printer, therefore, controls must be in place to ensure that either old printer ribbons are used on the printer or new printer ribbons are not removed before they have gone through multiple cycles of printing. In some cases, also, the printer ribbon might be removed from the printer. For example, often no printer ribbons are used in the impact printers that print PIN mailers. Instead, the top copy of a PIN mailer has a carbon backing that results in the PIN being printed only on the second (confidential) copy of the PIN mailer.

Careful control must be exercised when negotiable instruments such as checks are printed. If preprinted stationery is used, the number of forms generated should be reconciled against the number of forms received from stationery

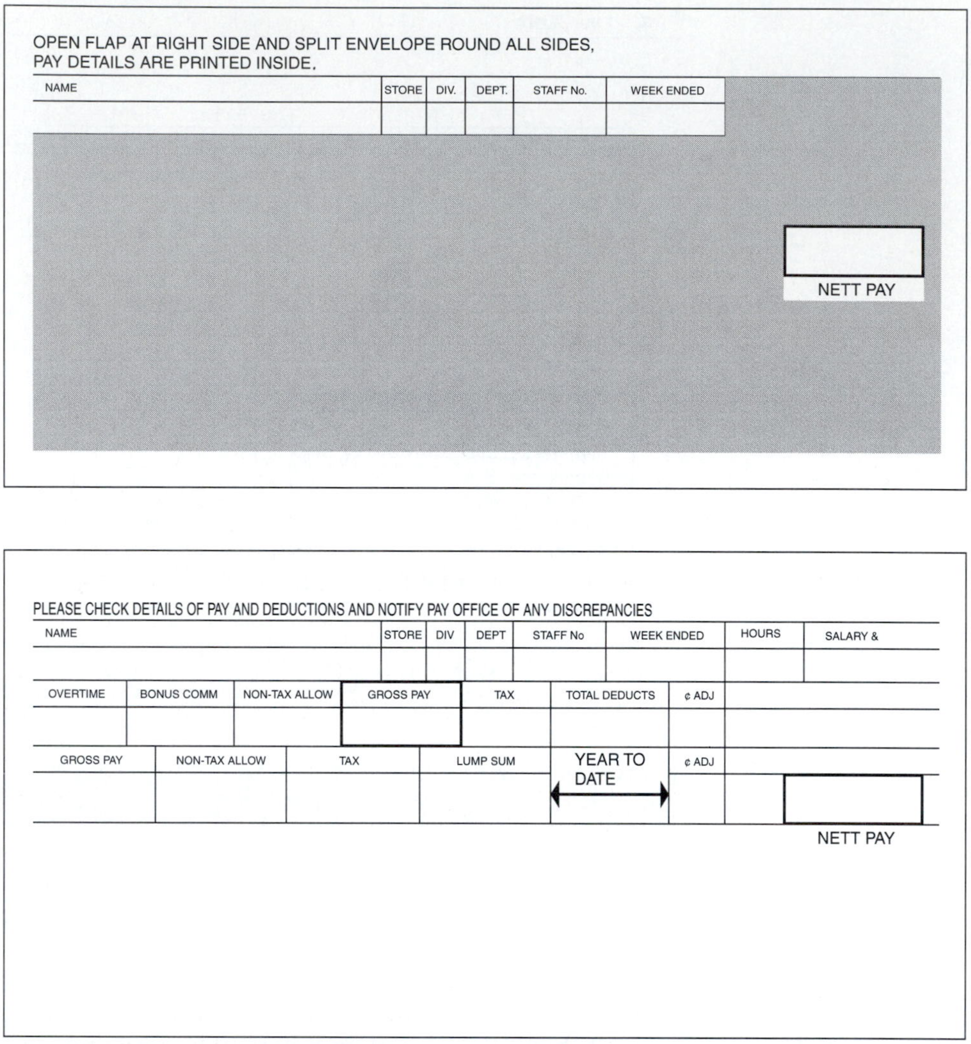

OPEN FLAP AT RIGHT SIDE AND SPLIT ENVELOPE ROUND ALL SIDES,
PAY DETAILS ARE PRINTED INSIDE.

NAME	STORE	DIV.	DEPT.	STAFF No.	WEEK ENDED

NETT PAY

PLEASE CHECK DETAILS OF PAY AND DEDUCTIONS AND NOTIFY PAY OFFICE OF ANY DISCREPANCIES

NAME	STORE	DIV	DEPT	STAFF No	WEEK ENDED	HOURS	SALARY &

OVERTIME	BONUS COMM	NON-TAX ALLOW	GROSS PAY	TAX	TOTAL DEDUCTS	¢ ADJ	

GROSS PAY	NON-TAX ALLOW	TAX	LUMP SUM	YEAR TO DATE	¢ ADJ	
				◄——►		

NETT PAY

FIGURE 15–9. Protecting data privacy with multipart forms. (Moore Paragon Australia Ltd.)

supplies. In this regard, prenumbering the forms assists the reconciliation process. Even if preprinted stationery is not used, however, the number of forms generated should still be reconciled against some type of control total. Any rejections, exceptions, or mutilations that occur during the print run should be controlled and accounted for properly.

Report Collection Controls

When output has been produced, it should be secured to prevent loss or unauthorized removal, especially if the output contains negotiable instruments. For example, user/client services group employees might collect output reports, film, or cartridges and hold them pending collection by users. They should collect the output promptly and store it securely. Alternatively, if users direct output to an unattended device—say, reports to a laser printer—they should be responsible for prompt collection of the output, especially if the device is in a public area.

If user/client services group representatives have responsibility for collecting output, they should maintain records of the output they handle. For example, they should note the date and time when each output item was collected and the state of the output when it was received—for example, whether all output was intact (see the next section). The identity of the user/client services group representative who collected the output should also be recorded.

Controls should exist to identify when output is not collected promptly and secured. For example, the manager in charge of information systems operations should have a system in place to indicate when any output has not been collected promptly from a production facility. Similarly, someone should have responsibility for removing and securing output that has not been collected promptly from output devices that are in public areas.

User/Client Services Review Controls

Before output is distributed to users, a user/client services representative might check it for obvious errors. The following types of checks could be undertaken: *(1)* whether pages in a printed report are illegible because, say, a laser printer is low on toner; *(2)* whether the quality of film output is satisfactory; *(3)* whether tape cartridges or CD-ROMs have been labeled properly; *(4)* whether any pages in a printed report are missing; and *(5)* whether any pages in a report have been printed askew. This type of checking has two purposes. First, it provides a higher level of service by the information systems function to users. Users should obtain higher-quality output than they might otherwise receive. Second, if errors or irregularities in output are subsequently detected, it may be easier to detect their likely source. If pages in a report are missing, for example, responsibility can be assigned to user staff rather than to the information systems personnel who are responsible for production of the report.

Report Distribution Controls

If user/client services group representatives have responsibility for collecting output, they must ensure that it is distributed securely and promptly to the correct users. Distribution can occur in various ways:

1. Output might be placed in locked bins that users clear periodically.
2. Output might be delivered directly to users.
3. Output might be mailed to users, either via internal mail or via the normal postal service.
4. Output might be handed over to users or user representatives who present themselves to collect the output.
5. Output might be dispatched to users via a courier service.
6. Output might be given to a mail distribution organization; for example, customer invoices might be given to the organization to be stuffed in envelopes and dispatched.

To exercise control over output distribution activities, records should be kept of the date and time at which output was distributed and the identity of the person who received the output. Likewise, if output is given to a mail distribution organization, control totals should be kept and checked to ensure that all output is given to the organization and that the organization dispatches all output. These records provide a basis for identifying the nature and source of output errors or irregularities if they occur.

Controls must be in place to ensure that output is dispatched on a timely basis. If mailing of invoices is delayed, for example, an organization might experience cash flow difficulties. Similarly, managers could make wrong decisions if they do not promptly receive reports that notify them of important changes in, say, their organization's financial position. Regular reviews should be undertaken, therefore, to ensure that output has been collected or distributed on a timely basis. These reviews should extend to third parties, such as mail distribution organizations, who distribute batch output.

Special care must be taken when a large number of copies of a report have to be distributed. A recipient name-and-address file should be maintained. To facilitate distribution of the report, the file then might be printed on gummed labels that are attached to individual copies of the report. If the user population changes frequently, the number of copies of the report required could vary from run to run. In these situations, maintaining the integrity of the name-and-address file is critical. If an unauthorized party were to insert their name and address on the file, a gummed label would be produced for them. They would then receive a copy of the report.

In some cases, many different users collect output from a user/client services group. Alternatively, the collection is undertaken on behalf of users by a third party (e.g., a courier). Where users or third parties are unknown to the user/client services group, they should be asked to identify and authenticate themselves. Either prior authorization must have been given to hand over the output to the unknown user or third party. Alternatively, the users or third party should produce evidence to show they are authorized to collect the output.

User Output Controls

Users should perform reviews similar to those carried out by user/client services representatives in the information systems function to detect problems with output. Because users are more familiar with the application area, however, they are better placed to detect errors and irregularities in output. Moreover, periodically they should undertake an in-depth review of output to evaluate its quality. For example, they might perform test calculations to check the accuracy of extensions or control totals shown in an output report, or they might undertake a physical count of some inventory items to check whether the amounts on hand correspond to those shown in an inventory listing.

Procedures must be established to allow complete and timely reporting of output problems identified by users to someone who has overall responsibility for the quality of the application system that generated the output. Moreover, users must be properly informed of these procedures. If reporting procedures have not been established or users are unaware of these procedures, output problems that manifest important errors or irregularities in the application system might be overlooked or not identified promptly.

Controls should be in place to ensure that users review output on a timely basis. There is little point to providing users with prompt, accurate, and complete output if they then fail to attend to it within an appropriate time interval. Serious losses might arise as a result of users' tardiness in examining the output provided to them. For example, an organization might fail to adjust its portfolio of investments in light of important changes in the stock market. To ensure that output is used promptly, management might undertake periodic reviews. In this light, employees might be required to endorse batch reports with the time and date of their review.

Storage Controls

Three major controls should exist in relation to storage of output. First, output should be stored in an environment that will allow it to be preserved for the period it is required. In this regard, various output media have different requirements in terms of the environments in which they should be kept. For example, although cartridges and CD-ROMs are fairly robust, nonetheless to maximize their lives they should be stored in environments that have a constant temperature and are dust free. Some laser-printed output will also deteriorate quickly if it is stored in hot, humid environments. Microfiche and microfilm should also be stored in cool, dry, dust-free environments.

Second, output must be stored securely. Stored output might contain confidential data that would lead to serious exposures if it fell into the hands of unauthorized parties. In some cases the stored output could be negotiable instruments, and an organization would incur direct financial losses if the instruments were stolen. Stored output might also contain data that is essential to the ongoing operations of an organization. If it were lost, damaged, or destroyed accidentally, the organization could suffer severe disruptions.

Third, appropriate inventory controls must be kept over stored output. For example, records must be kept of what output is in storage, where it is stored, and who has removed or returned output. To reduce the likelihood of loss or damage, the output should also be stored tidily in proper facilities. Periodically, checks should be made to ensure that the output that is actually stored matches the records of what is supposedly stored. If the output is kept by a third party, assurances must be obtained (perhaps from the third party's auditor) that the third party maintains adequate controls over storage.

Retention Controls

A decision must be made on how long each type of output will be retained. This decision can affect the choice of output medium and the way in which the output is stored. For example: reports produced by a laser printer deteriorate faster than reports produced by an impact printer; images stored on CD-ROMs deteriorate faster than those stored on microfiche; reports stored in warm, humid environments will deteriorate faster than those stored in cool, dry environments.

The decision on a retention period also affects how stored output must be managed. For example, output that has to be stored on magnetic media for long periods of time occasionally must be rewritten to ensure that it can still be read accurately and completely. Magnetic media will deteriorate because of stray magnetic fields, oxidation, or other types of material decay. Storage media also can become unreadable because they depend on old technology that becomes obsolete sooner than expected. For example, Rothenberg (1995) reports that the 1960 U.S. Census data was nearly lost because it was stored on magnetic tapes using formats that had been superseded by new, incompatible formats. Likewise, documents that were created using word processors or spreadsheet packages at some time in the past—say, ten years ago—might no longer be readable because storage formats have changed. Recognition of such exposures requires careful management of stored output.

A retention date should be determined for each output item produced. The output item must then be kept until its retention date expires. Various factors affect the retention date assigned to an output item—for example, the need for archival reference of a report, backup and recovery needs, taxation legislation specifying a minimum retention time for data, and privacy legislation specifying a maximum retention time for data.

Destruction Controls

When output is no longer needed, it should be destroyed. Report destruction can be accomplished easily using a paper shredder. As retention dates expire, reports should be transported in a secure manner to the shredding facility. Partially printed reports from aborted report runs and discarded stationery also should be shredded to prevent any unauthorized use.

Output stored on magnetic media also needs to be destroyed or deleted when its retention date has expired. In the case of disks or cartridges, the data can be overwritten. Special programs are available to ensure that all traces of the data or residue from the data are removed from the disk or cartridge. These programs should be used in particular when confidential data is to be destroyed. In the case of write-once media, such as CD-ROMs, the media might have to be physically crushed so it is no longer readable. Some types of shredders can also be used to destroy CD-ROMs. They shred the CD-ROMs in the same way that paper is shredded. In the case of microfiche or microfilm, they might have to be burned in a high-temperature furnace. Alternatively, special microfiche and microfilm shredders are available that reduce the microfiche and microfilm to powder. If microfiche and microfilm were to be shredded like paper, much of the content could still be read.

BATCH REPORT DESIGN CONTROLS

An important element in the effective execution of production and distribution controls over batch output reports is the quality of their design. Good report design facilitates the orderly flow of reports through the various output phases examined in the previous section. Good management ensures that users employ these design features to comply with the control procedures laid down for batch reports during the output process.

Table 15–1 shows the information that should be included in a well-designed batch report to facilitate its flow through the output process and the execution of controls as it passes through each phase. The title page contains information that assists operators and user/client services personnel to perform their work. In an environment where large numbers of reports are produced, this information is especially important. If the same report is produced several times a day, or a report program has to be rerun for some reason, confusion can arise if each instance of a report is not identified uniquely.

The title page should also contain details about the person to contact in the event that operational problems have occurred in the production of the report; for example, the print might be too light, or some pages might have been printed askew. This person can then take control over the defective report; for example, they might ensure that a confidential report is destroyed securely and authorize the production of another copy of the report. The title page should also contain details of the person to contact in the event that errors or irregularities are discovered on the basis of information contained within the report. Recall that we discussed previously the need for organizations to ensure that employees know the procedures they should follow when they discover errors and irregularities as a result of their examination of reports.

TABLE 15–1 Control Information to Be Included in a Well-Designed Report

Control Information	Position in Report	Purposes
Report name	Title page	Permits immediate identification of report.
Time and date of production	Title page, detail pages	Prevents confusion when report is produced several times per day or when for some reason the report has to be produced again, e.g., an error in the report program.
Distribution list (including number of copies)	Title page	Facilitates distribution of the correct number of copies of the report to authorized users. Helps to ensure that unauthorized copies of the report are not produced.
Processing period covered	Title page	Users can see what data/time period has been covered by the report.
Program (including version number) producing the report	Title page	Permits immediate identification of originating system/program.
Contact persons	Title page	Indicates who should be contacted in the event that the report has been produced defectively and who should be contacted in the event that errors or irregularities are discovered on the basis of the report.
Security classification	Title page, detail pages	Alerts operators and user/client services representatives to the sensitivity of data contained in report.
Retention date	Title page	Indicates date before which the report should not be destroyed.
Method of destruction	Title page	Indicates whether special procedures need to be followed to dispose of the report.
Page heading	Detail pages	Shows content of report pages and perhaps security classification of data contained in report.
Page number	Detail pages	Prevents undetected removal of a report page.
End-of-job marker	Immediately after last entry, last page of report	Prevents undetected removal of last page of the report.

The information on the detail pages of a report prevents the unauthorized removal of data from the report. A person wishing to prevent a fraud from being discovered might remove a page containing exception information. Certain pages of a report might be especially valuable to a competitor. Page numbering and end-of-job markers are used, therefore, to prevent the unauthorized removal of a report page.

ONLINE OUTPUT PRODUCTION AND DISTRIBUTION CONTROLS

Historically, production and distribution controls over online output were fairly straightforward. The primary concerns were ensuring that only authorized parties could obtain online output, protecting the integrity of output as it was transmitted over communications lines, ensuring that online output could not be viewed by unauthorized parties when it was displayed at a terminal, and preventing unauthorized copying of online output when it was distributed to a terminal. These control concerns still remain.

Three factors, however, have had a major impact on the nature and extent of exposures associated with online output and the controls needed over online output. First, for several reasons the amount of online output has increased substantially. For example, rather than exchange paper documents, many organizations now use electronic data interchange (EDI) to exchange information. As a result, output of paper-based orders, invoices, customer statements, and so on, has decreased considerably. Instead, these documents are produced as online output and transmitted to their recipients electronically. Similarly, with the growth of the Internet, the amount of online output that is available has increased substantially. For example, many organizations have established pages on the World Wide Web (Web) that give information about the products and services they provide. These pages can be accessed easily by anyone on the Internet who has a Web browser.

Second, the variety of online output and the ways in which online output can be manipulated have increased substantially. For example, online output has shifted from primarily text and graphics to include photographs, images, movies, and sound. These newer forms of output can be modified with powerful editors, however, such that the integrity of the real-world things or events that they purportedly represent cannot be assumed. For example, photographs can be altered to show things or events that never existed (Mitchell 1994). Likewise, checks, stocks, bonds, and currency can be scanned, altered with image-editing and font-manipulation programs, and printed on a color printer for fraudulent purposes (Schwartz 1994).

Third, the growth of the Internet has resulted in changed perceptions of the nature of online output. Online output is no longer conceived as something to be confined and directed to a well-known set of authorized users. Rather, it is intended to be available broadly and to be accessible by a largely undefined, substantial user community.

As with batch output, we can structure our discussion on controls over online output by considering the various phases through which online output must pass (Figure 15–10): establishing the output at the source, distributing the

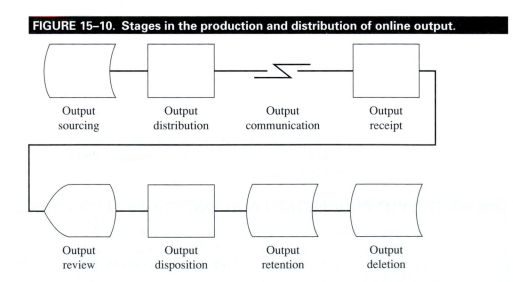

FIGURE 15–10. Stages in the production and distribution of online output.

Output sourcing — Output distribution — Output communication — Output receipt

Output review — Output disposition — Output retention — Output deletion output; communicating the output; receiving and viewing the output, retaining the output, and deleting the output. As always, the specific controls established within each phase will depend on the costs and benefits of establishing, operating, and maintaining them.

Source Controls

Source controls are needed to ensure that output which can be generated or accessed online is authorized, accurate, complete, and timely. The types of source controls used vary depending on the way users obtain output. In this regard, four major ways of obtaining online output exist:

1. Online output can be generated as a result of some event that necessitates an exchange of information with some organization. For example, inventory might be depleted below its reorder point, which results in automatic generation of an order that is then transmitted electronically to a supplier via an EDI system. Similarly, an accounts payable clerk might authorize payment to a supplier, which results in electronic funds transfer transactions being generated.
2. Users invoke a program to access a database and to prepare output; for example, users employ a high-level language like SQL to access a relational database, undertake computations, and prepare reports.
3. Users invoke some kind of file transfer program or browser program to access output that has already been prepared and exists somewhere in a file; for example, users employ a browser to access some organization's pages on the Web or to access postings on a bulletin board or news group.
4. Users transmit output or receive output via e-mail. They might send e-mail to or receive e-mail from a specific person or group. Alternatively, they might send e-mail to a list server so it is broadcast to all persons who have their e-mail addresses on the distribution list maintained by the list server. They may also receive e-mail because they have their e-mail address on the distribution list of a list server.

Consider controls over each of these methods in turn. In the case of events occurring that necessitate exchange of information with another organization, the primary control objectives are that *(1)* authorized, accurate, complete, and timely transactions are generated and *(2)* these transactions are generated and transmitted once only. If employees initiate the transactions, we would be concerned that appropriate access controls and input controls are in place to ensure that these objectives are achieved (see Chapters 10 and 11). If the transactions are initiated automatically, we would be concerned that programs that generate the transactions are functioning correctly.

In the case of users invoking a program to access a database and to prepare output, four control objectives are pertinent. First, data in the database that provides the basis for generating online output must be authorized, accurate, complete, and timely. We have already discussed controls to ensure that these objectives are achieved in the previous chapter on the database subsystem (Chapter 14). Second, the program used to prepare the online output must work in an authorized, accurate, and complete manner. Providing a standard package like SQL is used and we are confident the package has not been modified inappropriately, we might conclude the exposure associated with this control objective is low. Third, only authorized users should be able to gain access to the database and to the program that prepares output. Our focus here would be on the access controls that have been established. Recall that we discussed access controls when we considered the boundary subsystem in Chapter 10. As an example, however, Web pages might be encrypted and accessible only by persons who have the correct cryptographic key. Fourth, users must understand how to employ correctly the program that prepares output. Users who do not properly understand the program might obtain results that look plausible but nevertheless are wrong. Recall that we discussed this issue in Chapter 11 when we examined various kinds of user interfaces to a database.

In the case of users who employ some type of file transfer or browser program to access output that has already been prepared and is stored somewhere in a file, we need to consider four control objectives. The first is that the online output which is made available should be authorized, accurate, complete, and timely. If the organizations audited are *providing* the online output, they should have controls in place to ensure the output does not misrepresent them in some way—for example, by displaying incorrect or out-of-date prices for their goods or services (Miller 1996). Likewise, they will want to ensure that the output is appropriate to their mission, goals, and objectives. Some universities have had problems with students, for example, who have set up Web pages that contain data that the universities deem to be inappropriate (such as assignment answers and pornographic material) or files that have undesirable properties (such as program files containing viruses) (see, e.g., Bethke 1996). With respect to the accuracy and completeness of the output, various tools might be used to check the veracity of output that is made available on, say, the Web. For example, software is available to verify links established among a collection of Web pages (Press 1995). If, on the other hand, the organizations audited are *accessing* output provided by another organization, they will again want to ensure that the output is authorized, accurate, complete, and timely. They will not want to enter contracts, for example, on the basis of incorrect output they have obtained via a browser program or to download program files that contain viruses. Accordingly, they will need to educate employees about the dangers of accessing or downloading information from an unknown source and to establish policies to govern the types of remote access that are permitted.

The second control objective is to ensure that online output that can be accessed by a browser program is not used improperly. For example, an organization might store copyrighted images like maps or photographs or a proprietary database in Web pages. It will make the images or database available to anyone who will pay a fee. The difficulty the organization faces, however, is that purchasers could then improperly use the images or data they extract from the Web pages. For example, purchasers might copy maps, modify them in some way, and in turn then make them available for sale on the Web. It might be difficult to establish that some type of copyright violation or violation of contractual terms has occurred. Organizations need to give careful thought, therefore, to the online output they will make available to browser programs. They might incur losses because they are unable to exercise cost-effective controls over the ways online output is used. Similarly, if the organization's employees are themselves users of online output provided by another organization, controls should be in place to ensure that output obtained via a browser is not used improperly.

The third control objective is to ensure that the source of the output is authentic. Otherwise, an organization might obtain online output that is erroneous, or it might provide information to obtain the online output that results in it sustaining losses. For example, a retailer might regularly access industry sales data made available in some marketing organization's Web pages. A competitor might masquerade on the Web as the marketing organization, however,

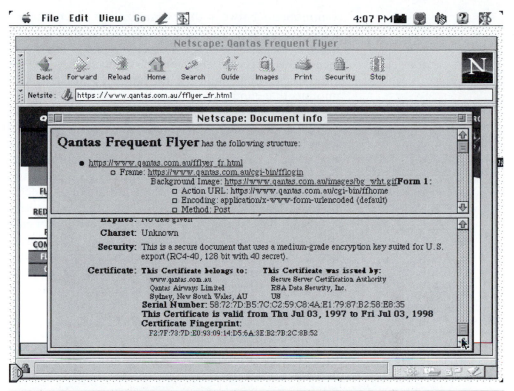

FIGURE 15–11. Using public-key cryptography to provide assurance about Web site authenticity.
Courtesy of Qantas Airways Limited and Netscape Corporation.

and provide erroneous sales data to the retailer, resulting in the retailer making wrong decisions. Likewise, customers might transmit credit card information to an organization that sells its goods or services via the Web. Customers need to ensure that they are transmitting the credit card information to the authentic seller of the goods or services. One way to ensure the authenticity of organizations that provide online output is to use public-key cryptography and digital signatures (see Chapter 10). In this light, some Web browsers provide digital-signature capabilities (Figure 15–11).

The fourth control objective is that the online output obtained by the employees of an organization should be appropriate to the goals and objectives of the organization. For example, many organizations have encountered problems when their employees became addicted to "surfing" the Internet or exploring the World Wide Web. Aside from the waste of computing resources that results, substantial losses in employee productivity can occur. Moreover, if employees are pursuing their own personal interests, the online output obtained could reflect unfavorably on the organization if it became public. For example, employees might be active contributors to or users of information from news groups about pet animals or tasteless jokes. Organizations need to establish policies on what output will be deemed appropriate.

In the case of users who receive e-mail either directly from a sender or indirectly via a list server, three control objectives exist. The first is that users must understand that e-mail can represent official correspondence sent on behalf of their organization to another organization or received by their organization from another organization. Thus, e-mail can be the basis for legally binding commitments between their organization and other organizations. In this light, management must establish guidelines so that users know what content they are authorized to transmit via e-mail and what actions they must undertake for each type of e-mail they might receive. A policy should exist, also, as to whether personal mail can be sent electronically and, if so, the nature and amounts that can be sent.

The second control objective is that users should conform to rules of etiquette (or *netiquette*, which stands for net etiquette) when they transmit internal or external e-mail. It has been found that recipients of an electronic message often take unintended offence at the content of a message or at having received a message they do not want (e.g., a sales message). As a result, care must be taken in formulating the contents of an electronic message and choosing the recipients of an electronic message. When recipients take offence as a result of a message they have received, a situation called "flaming" sometimes arises. The recipient might send back a strongly worded or abusive message (a flame) that in turn offends the sender of the message. The sender replies in kind with a flame, and the aggression escalates. Electronic messages that do not conform to netiquette can reflect unfavorably on both senders and their organizations. Table 15–2 shows some widely accepted rules of netiquette.

The third control objective is that the sender of any message deemed to be material must be known. It must not be possible for the sender of a material message to forge another person's identifier or address or to send the message

---

TABLE 15–2   Some Rules of Net Etiquette (Netiquette)

1. Be courteous when constructing a message. Avoid arrogance, aggression, sarcasm, and satire.
2. Use humor carefully. What is humorous to one person can be offensive to another.
3. Do not include the entire contents of a previous message sent to you in your reply. Be selective and include only those parts that will assist the recipient to understand your reply. In particular, delete information that is likely to be irrelevant, such as message routing information. At the same time, do not delete information that results in part of a message being misunderstood or giving offence because it is out of context.
4. DO NOT CAPITALIZE ALL WORDS IN A MESSAGE. A message that uses only uppercase is harder to read than a message that uses both lower- and uppercase. Some net users also perceive senders who use only uppercase in their messages to be arrogant.
5. Minimize the frequency with which you post messages to a list server. Furthermore, make sure your message is likely to have wide appeal to the users of a list server. If you post too frequently and your messages are of limited value, you could be perceived to be engaged in some form of self-aggrandizement and possibly be flamed.
6. When replying to a message sent to you via a list server, make sure your message is not copied to all users of the list server. In most cases (if not all), your reply should be directed only to the sender of the message.
7. Do not seek information from members of a list server or news group that can be obtained easily via other means. You will be perceived as lazy and wasting other people's time.
8. Be careful about posting questionnaires to members of a list server or news group. Many users of a list server or news group perceive that the primary purpose of posting messages should be to disseminate information rather than to solicit information.
9. Do not post messages that say something like "Why doesn't someone say something about (a topic)?" or "Who wants to talk about (a topic)?"
10. Don't post replies to messages sent via a list server that say "Me too!" or "Ditto!"

anonymously. Digital signatures provide one way of verifying the source and authenticity of the sender of a message (see Chapter 10).

Distribution Controls

When online output is distributed to persons or organizations, controls should exist to ensure that only the correct persons or organizations receive the output. Recipients' electronic addresses should be kept current. Access controls also might need to be established over distribution lists to ensure that unauthorized parties do not insert their addresses on the list. Substantial losses might be incurred, for example, if an unauthorized person received confidential information about customers or electronic payments were made to an unauthorized trading partner in an EDI system. Periodically, distribution lists might be checked, therefore, to see that only authorized addresses exist on the list.

Controls also must exist to ensure timely distribution of online output. If transactions are not dispatched promptly to a trading partner in an EDI system, for example, an organization's operations might be severely disrupted. Similarly, losses can be incurred if decision makers fail to act promptly because they have not received online output on a timely basis. Logs that contain online output need to be checked regularly to ensure that the online output is being cleared promptly.

In some cases, distribution of electronic messages is controlled by an intermediary. For example, some list servers will not distribute a message until it has been authorized by a moderator. The sender of a message who wants the message distributed to the list dispatches it to the list server. The list server notifies the moderator that a request has been made to distribute a message. The moderator then examines the message and either approves or rejects the distribution of the message. Messages usually are accepted or rejected on the basis of whether they are congruent with the objectives of the list and whether they conform to netiquette. The moderator also might not permit anonymous messages to be distributed. This control tries to prevent "spamming" of the network—in other words, posting of a message (such as an advertising message) to a large number of users by sending the message to as many list servers as possible. To prevent spamming, some list servers will only allow an authorized member of the list server to post messages to other members of the list server.

Within an organization, policies might be needed to define the allowed recipients of messages. For example, subordinates might not be permitted to send messages directly to senior management. Instead, messages first might have to be sent to their immediate superiors, who then decide whether to forward the message to their immediate superiors. In this way, proper lines of authority, responsibility, and communication are maintained.

Likewise, policies might be needed to govern forwarding of messages, "carbon" copying of messages, and "blind" copying of messages. Inappropriate use of these capabilities in electronic message systems can undermine authority and responsibility structures, create behavioral problems within an organization, and lead to a breakdown in controls.

Communication Controls

We examine communication controls at length in Chapter 12. Recall that they are established to reduce exposures from active attacks (e.g., message insertion, deletion, and modification) and passive attacks (e.g., release of message contents) on the communication subsystem.

When the list of the senders and receivers of online output is well defined and stable, conventional symmetric cryptographic methods can be used to protect the integrity of data. Senders and receivers share a common cryptographic key. When the list of senders and receivers is not well defined or stable, however, use of symmetric cryptography becomes problematical. It is difficult to keep cryptographic keys up-to-date and to maintain their secrecy. For this reason, asymmetric (public key) cryptography is sometimes used. For example, a server on the Web might have a public key and a private key. It might encrypt all output using its private key. Any recipient can then decrypt the output using the server's public key. Thus, the authenticity of the source of the message can be assured because the server signs any message it transmits. Moreover, only passive attacks, not active attacks, can be undertaken on the message. If signed, secret messages are needed, however, the server will require the public keys of any recipients. It will first encrypt the message using its private key to sign the message. It will then encrypt the message again using the recipient's public key to protect the secrecy of the message (see Chapter 10).

Receipt Controls

Controls can be exercised on receipt of output to evaluate whether the output should be accepted. For example, users might have downloaded a program file with a Web browser or received a program file as an attachment to an e-mail message. The program could contain a virus. Before the file is accepted, therefore, it should be scanned for viruses. Similarly, an e-mail message could contain a *letter bomb*—a file containing a huge amount of output designed to swamp the receiving computer's storage capacity. Controls might be established to reject any message that exceeds a certain size.

Review Controls

Even though output might be transmitted to a valid address and received intact, it might remain unread or it might not be acted upon promptly. The intended recipient might be on vacation, for example, or they might be preoccupied with other tasks. In an EDI system, defects in a trading partner's computer system can result in orders not being filled promptly. Controls must be in place to ensure important output is acted upon on a timely basis by intended recipients. In light of this concern, some e-mail systems will automatically notify a sender if recipients are unavailable to read their mail for a period. Recipients also might be asked or required to acknowledge that they have examined output that has been sent to them and that they understand and have acted upon its contents. The operations audit trail also might be used to record the time and date at which online output reports were accessed and the length of the time interval during which they were reviewed. Periodically, this data should be reviewed by management.

A major difficulty now facing many users is information overload caused by the volume of online output they are receiving. Much of this output is unsolicited. It is a cost of their being a member of news groups or on the distribution lists of list servers. Many users deal with this overload by scanning the message headers of the output they receive and immediately deleting the output they deem irrelevant. Some users now employ intelligent agents (software tools) that scan the output they receive and select the output that is likely to be useful to them for further examination. A consequence of this overload, however, is that important messages can be missed or given only cursory attention. Intelligent agents can also miss messages that are important because they have inadequate search criteria. Some organizations might need to formulate policies for their employees to follow in relation to the amount of output they receive to ensure that important output is treated appropriately. For example, restrictions could be placed on employees' memberships of news groups or list servers. Alternatively, they might be required to give priority to output they receive from certain sources and to attend to output from other sources only if they have time.

When confidential output is distributed to users, it is important to ensure that it is not viewed by other people. Terminals can be positioned physically such that display output cannot be viewed by a passerby. Hoods can also be placed on terminals to prevent casual viewing of screens. Confidential output can be displayed at a lower light intensity so it is visible only within close proximity of the terminal screen.

There is also little point to ensuring secure distribution of output to a terminal if the output is then not secure at the terminal. For example, many users have no access controls implemented in their microcomputers. It is easy for someone to enter their room, switch on their microcomputer, and access any online output (e.g., e-mail) they have received. Intruders can even forward copies of output to their own machines. Terminals need to be physically secure. Moreover, access controls need to be in place and working reliably to ensure that confidential output cannot be accessed by unauthorized parties.

Disposition Controls

An organization might need policies to provide guidance to their employees on when online output they receive should be forwarded or copied to other people. Consider, for example, the case of e-mail. Historically many organizations had a central mail facility. All mail was opened at the facility and distributed to the appropriate person within the organization. Through experience or written instructions, a small number of people knew where the mail that came into the organization should be dispatched. E-mail, however, is received at many points within the organization. Employees need to be aware that mail they receive could be important to another person, even if it appears to be of little value to them. Moreover, employees who receive the mail might not be the appropriate persons to take actions in light of its contents. The recipients must know, therefore, the lines of disposition that should be followed.

After online output is distributed to a terminal, it is difficult to exercise control over subsequent disposition of the output. For example, users might copy the output to a diskette or cartridge and remove the output to another location. They can also easily electronically forward the output to another site or make it available for access by other sites. Policies must be established to ensure that employees understand what actions they can take with respect to online output they receive. Enforcement of these policies is difficult, however, because actions taken by employees cannot be scrutinized continuously. Primary reliance must be placed on the integrity of employees. It also might be possible to keep some type of secure log to record the actions taken by employees in relation to confidential output. If these logs are to be useful as controls, however, they must be examined periodically by management for evidence of irregularities.

Retention Controls

With the substantial volume of online output that many users and organizations now receive, there is a tendency to want to dispose of it quickly. Much of the online output might be unsolicited. Much of it also might have little value to the ongoing operations of an organization. Nonetheless, some online output that users or organizations receive could be important—for example, EDI output. In this light, appropriate retention controls must be in place and working reliably.

Two factors affect how long online output should be retained. First, statutory requirements might exist that specify the retention period. For example, the output might have to be kept to comply with taxation laws. Second, the output might describe the states of things or events that have occurred that have important implications for an organization. For example, it might describe contractual obligations agreed upon by the organization and one of its customers or transactions they have undertaken with each other. Guidelines must exist, therefore, to assist employees to determine when online output is likely to be important to their organization and when it is likely to be unimportant and therefore can be culled.

Because online output is likely to be kept in electronic form, access controls must be established to maintain its integrity. Only authorized persons should be allowed to access retained online output. Moreover, backup and recovery controls must also be established. Retained online output can be lost as a result of some type of disaster that befalls an organization. Loss of retained online output could severely impair the operations of an organization. Adequate records must also be maintained describing any online output that has been retained and any other pertinent information about the output such as the nature and location of its backup.

Deletion Controls

When the useful life of online output has expired, it should be deleted. Usually this task is straightforward. An operating system utility can be used to delete files. This utility might be executed regularly to search for online output files whose retention date has expired and to then delete these files.

Additional precautions might have to be taken if the deleted files still contain information that could create exposures for the organization. Recall that deletion of a file often means that the storage space occupied by the file is simply released for other programs to use. The data in the deleted file is not actually destroyed. Persons who seek to act improperly can use their programs to try to read data contained in freed-up storage space. In this light, special utilities might need to be executed to overwrite data in retained online output files whose retention date has expired before the storage space occupied by these files is released for use by other programs.

AUDIT TRAIL CONTROLS

Audit trail controls in the output subsystem maintain the chronology of events that occur from the time the content of output is determined until the time users complete their disposal of output because it no longer should be retained.

Accounting Audit Trail

The accounting audit trail shows *what* output was presented to users, *who* received the output, *when* the output was received, and what *actions* were subsequently taken with the output. This information can be used for various purposes. For example, as discussed previously, it might be required to fulfill statutory obligations. Because of these obligations, an organization can be called to account for past events that have occurred. The accounting audit trail can provide the data needed to respond to any statutory request for information.

If an erroneous data item is discovered in an organization's output, the accounting audit trail also can be used to determine those users who might have relied on the output to make a decision. These users can then be notified to enable them to determine whether they need to take any actions to mitigate their exposure. If users who relied on the erroneous output are internal to the organization, it might be fairly straightforward to notify them promptly of the situation. If the erroneous output has been placed in a page on the Web, however, the situation is often problematic. The output might have been accessed by a large number of persons who are external to the organization. The organization must then determine what responsibilities it has, if any, to notify these users. Likewise, if an organization broadcasts erroneous output via a list server, it might be impossible to track down all the people who have relied on the output. The output might have been transmitted to other list servers and rebroadcast multiple times. For this reason, organizations that make output publicly available often place a disclaimer with the output notifying people that they use the output at their own risk. Nevertheless, even if the disclaimer can be sustained in all cases of erroneous output, an organization might still want to notify users who have obtained erroneous output to reduce losses of goodwill that may arise.

The audit trail can also be used to determine whether unauthorized users have gained access to or unauthorized activities have occurred in the output subsystem. In this light, periodically management could examine the audit trail to determine whether the contents of output provided to users reflect improper access or improper activities. As a deterrent to irregularities, some organizations warn users that their activities are being logged. For example, an external user who gains access to an organization's Web pages via a browser might be informed that they should act appropriately and that all actions they take will be recorded.

Unfortunately, perhaps more than any other subsystem, efficiency considerations in the output subsystem dictate how complete the audit trail should be and how long it should be kept. Internal and external users of an organization's output subsystem can generate large amounts of batch and online output. The costs to store all this output for long periods of time can be excessive. Moreover, the exposures associated with much of this output could be low. Accordingly, organizations must evaluate the exposures associated with different types of output. A decision can then be made on what output will be stored in the audit trail and the retention period that will apply to the different types of output.

Operations Audit Trail

Activities in the output subsystem can consume substantial resources; for example, expensive output devices might be required to produce graphs and images, consumption of costly, high-quality preprinted stationery could be high, large amounts of machine time might be required to produce image output, substantial storage space might be required to archive output, and a costly communications infrastructure might have to be implemented and maintained to support online access to output by both internal and external users.

The operations audit trail maintains a record of the resources consumed to produce the various types of output. For example, it can be used to record the number of report pages printed or the volume of output requested by external users. In addition, it might record data that enables print times, response times, and display rates for output to be determined. This data can then be analyzed to determine whether an organization should continue to provide different types of output to users. It can also provide information that enables the organization to improve the timeliness of output production and reduce the amount of resources consumed in producing output.

EXISTENCE CONTROLS

Output can be lost or destroyed for a variety of reasons; for example, a report can go astray in the mail, customer invoices can be stolen, online output can be dispatched to a wrong network address, or reports can be destroyed in a fire. In some cases, recovery of the output is simple to accomplish; in other cases, it is difficult or impossible.

One factor that affects the ease with which batch output recovery can be accomplished is the availability of report files. Recall that earlier in this chapter we discussed the fact that many computer systems do not write output directly to an output device. Instead, they write the output to a magnetic file, and the file is later dumped to the output device. This strategy, called "spooling," allows more efficient use of output devices because the devices can be driven at maximum speed (they are not slowed down by other types of processing that a report program must undertake). Furthermore, spooling creates *virtual* output devices; for example, programs can write simultaneously to multiple printers via spool files when, in fact, only one printer exists.

Spool files also facilitate backup and recovery of batch output. If batch output is lost or destroyed, obtaining a new copy of the output is straightforward, providing the spool file for the output is still available. The spool file simply has to be written once again to the output device. Using spool files for backup and recovery purposes, however, usually requires active intervention by the person responsible for backup and recovery. Spooling systems keep output files only for a limited period. Moreover, many work with a fixed size spool file. When the spool file is full, the system returns to the start of the file and begins to overwrite the existing information. Spool files often fill up quickly; consequently, they might be available only for a limited time as a backup and recovery resource.

Two strategies that can be employed to enhance batch output existence controls are to *(1)* use larger spool files so they are overwritten less frequently or *(2)* retain the spool files for longer periods. Unfortunately, many information systems operations facilities produce large volumes of batch output. Thus, the overheads incurred in having larger or retaining more spool files to facilitate infrequent recovery of lost or destroyed output might be unacceptable. In this light, spool files might be used *selectively* to facilitate recovery of lost or destroyed output. Batch output might be assigned a criticality rating, and the period for retention of spool files could be based on this criticality rating.

A second factor that affects the ease with which backup and recovery can be accomplished is the nature of the report to be recovered. Batch or online reports show either *status* information—for example, the quantity on hand of various inventory items—or *transaction* information—for example, customer purchases throughout a given period. Of course, a single report can show both types of information. From the viewpoint of recovering output, however, the two types of information pose different problems. On the one hand, status information can be constantly changing—for example, the quantity on hand of an inventory item is frequently updated as stock is received or sold. If a stock report must be recovered, therefore, the prior values of different data items have to be retrieved. Some type of beforeimage or afterimage and a time stamp for the data item values must be kept. On the other hand, transaction information usually is not updated. Consequently, recovering a batch or online report that contains transaction information often is easier to accomplish. Nonetheless, storage costs preclude indefinite retention of transaction data, so the time period for easy recovery usually is limited.

A related issue is that recovery of batch or online output is more difficult when in-place updates occur. Consider, for example, a simple batch processing run in which master files are updated with transaction files and prior versions of the master files are not overwritten. Recovery of report output is straightforward. Status information can be obtained from the prior versions of master files, and transaction information can be obtained from the period transaction files. In some cases, combined status and transaction information might have to be obtained by redoing the update run. If in-place update occurs, however, prior versions of status information are overwritten. Beforeimages and afterimages of status information must be kept, therefore, if recovery is to be accomplished. Moreover, status information at a point in time and transaction information for a period often are not collected together conveniently on the one file. Instead, a time stamp must be attached to data, and recovery of report output will involve selecting and sorting data on the basis of time stamps.

Recovery of batch or online output is easier if the data on which the output is based is not volatile. For example, much of the information that an organization might place in its pages on the Web might remain constant over long periods. If users lose a report they have generated based on this information, they can simply use their browser to access the pages again to reproduce their report. Many organizations indicate the date on which their pages have last been updated. Accordingly, users can check whether an update has occurred subsequent to when they first prepared their report.

Use of a checkpoint/restart facility can be important to effecting partial recovery of output. For example, consider the implications for recovery if a hardware error causes a program that prints customer invoices to abort. In the absence of a checkpoint/restart facility, the entire invoice production run might have to be redone. This action can be costly if large volumes of printed stationery have to be discarded and destroyed and prior versions of master files have to be recovered to restart the run. If a checkpoint/restart facility is used, however, recovery can be accomplished by returning to a prior checkpoint and restarting the run from that checkpoint (see Chapter 13).

Finally, recovering the output subsystem accurately, completely, and promptly can be critical to the survival of many organizations. If an organization participates in an EDI system, for example, its operations could cease quickly if it loses its output subsystem. It might not be possible to handle critical transactions like orders for raw materials using a manual ordering system.

SUMMARY

The output subsystem provides functions that determine the content of data that will be provided to users, the ways data will be formatted and presented to users, and the ways data will be prepared for and routed to users.

Five sets of controls are exercised over these functions. First, inference controls are used to filter the output that users are permitted to see. They are especially important in regulating access to statistical databases where users are allowed to obtain summary information about data but the privacy of persons about whom data is stored must be preserved. Inference controls work by either restricting query set sizes or perturbing the input or output of a statistical function.

Second, batch output production and distribution controls seek to ensure that batch output is not lost or corrupted or that the privacy of data is not violated during its preparation and routing to users. They are exercised at different phases in the production and distribution of output—for example, over withdrawal of specially prepared preprinted stationery from an inventory of this stationery to retention and destruction of batch output.

Third, high-quality design of batch reports facilitates controls being exercised over batch output as it passes through the various production and distribution phases. For example, the title page can be used to show important control information like the authorized recipients of the report, the security classification of information contained in the report, and the period of time during which the report must be retained.

Fourth, online output production and distribution controls seek to ensure that online output is not lost or corrupted and that the privacy of data is not violated during its preparation and routing to users. As with batch output, controls are exercised during various phases of the production and distribution process—for example, during the creation of online output at its source to deletion of the output when it is no longer required.

Finally, like all other subsystems, the output subsystem requires a set of audit trail controls and a set of existence controls. Audit trail controls maintain the chronology of events from the time the content of output is determined to the time the output is presented to users. Existence controls enable either batch or online output to be recovered in the event of loss.

Review Questions

15–1 Briefly describe the functions of the output subsystem.

15–2 Briefly describe the nature of inference controls. What are the *four* types of compromises of statistical databases that inference controls seek to prevent?

15–3 What is a characteristic formula? Why are auditors often interested in the size of the query set that satisfies the characteristic formula?

15–4 Briefly describe the nature of restriction controls. Why is a restriction on the minimum size of the query set an inadequate means of preventing a compromise of privacy in the database?

15–5 Briefly describe the nature of a "tracker." What is the distinction between an individual tracker and a general tracker?

15–6 Briefly describe the nature of each of the following types of restriction controls:
  a Order control
  b Relative table size control
  c Query set overlap control
  d Cell suppression
  e Grouping or rolling up
  f Partitioning

15–7 Briefly describe the nature of perturbation controls. How do perturbation controls differ from restriction controls?

15–8 Briefly distinguish between record-based perturbation controls and results-based perturbation controls. What are the relative strengths and limitations of record-based perturbation controls versus results-based perturbation controls?

15–9 Briefly describe the nature of each of the following types of record-based perturbation controls:
   a Query set sampling
   b Data perturbation
   c Data swapping

15–10 What are the purposes of batch output production and distribution controls? What factors affect the choice of the batch output production and distribution controls used in an application system?

15–11 Briefly describe the major elements of an inventory system for preprinted computer stationery. Give *three* advantages that will accrue from having the inventory system you describe.

15–12 Give *three* concerns that auditors should have in relation to the execution of batch report programs.

15–13 Outline some controls that could be instituted to prevent alteration of fields on a printer file produced as a result of spooling. What controls could be used to ensure a printer file is printed only once?

15–14 Give *three* purposes to controls over printing of batch reports.

15–15 What controls can be implemented to ensure that sensitive reports are printed only on a secure printer?

15–16 Give *two* purposes to controls over batch report collection. Briefly describe *two* controls that can be established to ensure these objectives are achieved.

15–17 Briefly describe the nature and purposes of user/client services review controls in relation to batch output.

15–18 Give *three* controls that can be implemented to ensure batch reports are distributed securely and promptly only to authorized users.

15–19 Give *two* purposes of user output review controls for batch reports.

15–20 Briefly describe the nature and purposes of output storage controls in relation to batch output.

15–21 How do obsolescence concerns affect the decision on how long batch output can be retained on a storage medium?

15–22 Give *two* control objectives that relate to destruction of batch output.

15–23 Why should each page in a batch report have a page heading and a page number? What is the purpose of printing an end-of-job marker on the last page of a batch report?

15–24 Why are source controls needed in relation to online output? Briefly describe the nature and purposes of *four* source controls that might be used over output that can be obtained via a Web browser program.

15–25 What are the nature and purposes of netiquette? Give *four* rules of netiquette.

15–26 Give *two* controls that might be used to ensure online output is received on a timely basis.

15–27 In electronic messaging systems, why do organizations need policies to govern forwarding, "carbon" copying, and "blind" copying of messages?

15–28 If online output is obtained via the Internet, how can asymmetric cryptography be used to gain assurance about the authenticity of the source of the output?

15–29 Give *two* controls that might be exercised to determine whether online output should be accepted.

15–30 Why do organizations need policies to govern the disposition of electronic mail that their employees may receive?

15–31 Give *two* exposures that an organization faces in relation to unauthorized removal of online output.

15–32 What is the nature of the accounting audit trail in the output subsystem? Give *two* ways in which the accounting audit trail might be used.

15–33 Give *two* uses of the operations audit trail in the output subsystem.

15–34 How are spool/printer files useful for backup and recovery purposes? From a backup and recovery viewpoint, what factors determine how long a spool file should be kept?

15–35 The ease with which backup and recovery of output can be accomplished depends upon whether the output shows status information or transaction information. Briefly explain.

Multiple-Choice Questions

15–1 With respect to statistical databases, inference controls seek to prevent:

   a Unauthorized addition, modification, or deletion of a data item

   b Incorrect deductions by users based on the contents of the database

   c Privacy violations in relation to data about persons in the database

   d Access to detailed data when summary data is available

15–2 Which of the following statements about trackers is *false*?

   a They pad the original query so the restrictions on query set size can be circumvented

   b Privacy violations obtained via trackers can be prevented by specifying *both* a minimum query set size and a maximum query set size

   c General trackers can be constructed that will work for anyone in the database

   d Trackers often can be constructed fairly quickly

15–3 Which of the following restriction controls merges cells that contain sensitive statistics?

   a Rolling up

   b Relative table size control

   c Partitioning

   d Order control

15–4 Compared with restriction controls, perturbation controls:

   a Allow fewer statistics to be calculated on the data contained in the database

   b Eliminate biases or inconsistencies that arise as a result of implementing inference controls

   c Are not subject to averaging attacks

   d Result in an information loss associated with the variance of the perturbed statistic around the true value

15–5 Which of the following statements about *record-based* perturbation controls is *false*?

   a They calculate a statistic on the basis of a random sample of records that satisfy the query

   b They calculate a statistic after some type of error term has been added to the data in the records that satisfy the query

   c They can be compromised through an averaging attack if the error term has been generated from a distribution with a zero mean

   d They introduce an error term after the true statistic has been calculated on the basis of the data in the records that satisfy the query

15–6 Preprinted stationery causes special control problems because it:

    a Can be used in an unauthorized way to embarrass the organization

    b Is usually handled by only a few people so the risk of collusion is higher

    c Is easier to forge than negotiable instruments

    d Undermines the usefulness of spooling software as a means of providing backup and recovery controls

15–7 Which of the following is *not* an objective of batch report program execution controls?

    a Only authorized persons should be able to execute batch report programs

    b Batch report programs should be allowed to use preprinted stationery only if they are executed by operations staff

    c The action privileges assigned to users of batch report programs should be appropriate to their needs

    d Batch report programs that produce large amounts of output should have checkpoint/restart facilities

15–8 A control problem that arises with spooling software is that:

    a Relative to normal reporting software it is easier to carry out unauthorized modifications to spooling software

    b It is error prone because the software is highly complex

    c It can be used to obtain an unauthorized copy of a report

    d Encryption functions are rarely available to protect the integrity of the software

15–9 Which of the following is *unlikely* to be a control objective for batch report printing controls?

    a To ensure that reports are printed on the correct printer

    b To ensure that printed reports are collected promptly by authorized parties

    c To prevent unauthorized parties from scanning sensitive data on reports as they are printing

    d To ensure that impact printer ribbons are not used to disclose sensitive data

15–10 With respect to batch report output, which of the following is *not* a function that should be performed by a user/client services group?

    a Scanning batch reports for obvious errors or omissions

    b Detection of missing print positions because a laser printer is low on toner

    c Detailed checking of report contents to ensure accuracy and completeness

    d Checking whether pages in a batch report have been printed askew

15–11 Which of the following controls is likely to be *most* cost-effective as a means of ensuring that a mail distribution organization dispatches printed invoices on a complete and timely basis?

    a Control totals and a log should be kept and checked by both the organization that prints the invoices and the mail distribution organization

    b The invoices should be given only to a courier who acts on behalf of the mail distribution organization

    c The mail distribution organization should establish a review group to check the quality of the invoices they receive

    d The mail distribution organization should maintain a customer name-and-address file in case some invoices have to be reprinted

15–12 Which of the following statements about the user output review phase in the production and distribution of batch reports is most likely to be *false*?

  a Users should not waste resources by performing quality checks on reports if the user/client services group also performs quality checks

  b Users should sign and date batch reports so management can establish whether users have reviewed reports on a timely basis

  c Periodically users should undertake an in-depth review of output to check its authenticity, accuracy, and completeness

  d Users may not report output problems unless procedures have been established to notify someone who has overall responsibility for output quality

15–13 Which of the following statements about the storage, retention, and destruction of batch output is most likely to be *false*?

  a Legislation could specify both a maximum period of retention and a minimum period of retention for batch output

  b Output retained on magnetic media should be rewritten periodically in case storage formats become superseded by new, incompatible formats

  c Inventory controls exercised by a third party should be checked periodically if batch output is stored with the third party

  d The operating system should set the delete flag on confidential files as soon as their retention date expires so the storage space occupied by the file is released to other programs

15–14 On a batch report, the control information that prevents undetected removal of the last page of the report is the:

  a Page number

  b End-of-job marker

  c Security classification

  d Page title

15–15 Which of the following exposures in relation to online output production and distribution is *least likely* to be covered by *source* controls?

  a Inappropriate use of information obtained from a bulletin board

  b Lack of authenticity in relation to files that can be accessed publicly via the Internet

  c Unauthorized modification of a distribution list kept on a list server for online output

  d Unauthorized placement of copyrighted information in Web pages

15–16 Which of the following is *not* a rule of netiquette?

  a When replying to a message, do not include the full contents of the message you have received in your reply.

  b Avoid soliciting information from the users of a list server via questionnaires sent to the list server.

  c When replying to a message sent to you via a list server, ensure that a copy is sent to all other users of the list server.

  d Do not send a message that is completely in upper case text.

15–17 One objective of *distribution* controls in relation to online output is to:

  a Prevent online messages from being routed first through an intermediary

  b Prevent inappropriate use of blind copies of messages

  c Obviate the need for users to acknowledge receipt of messages

  d Allow electronic messages to circumvent traditional lines of authority and communication

15–18 Which of the following controls is likely to offer most protection over online output when it is transmitted through the Internet?
   a Asymmetric cryptography
   b Message routing protocols
   c Symmetric cryptography
   d File compression algorithms

15–19 Which of the following exposures associated with online output is *least likely* to be covered by *receipt* controls?
   a Acceptance of a letter bomb from an anonymous source
   b Downloading of a program file containing a virus
   c A user's failure to read a message because they are absent on vacation
   d Improper forwarding of a message to another party

15–20 Which of the following is *least likely* to be an exposure covered by *disposition* controls over online output?
   a Forwarding of confidential e-mail to unauthorized parties
   b Unauthorized copying of online output to diskettes and removal of the diskettes off site
   c Failure to forward e-mail received in a general mailbox to persons charged with addressing the matters mentioned in the mail
   d Unauthorized viewing of confidential data displayed on a screen by a passerby

15–21 Which of the following information is *least likely* to be stored in the *accounting* audit trail in relation to online output?
   a The persons who received the online output
   b The resources consumed to produce the online output
   c The time at which the online output was received
   d The contents of the online output

15–22 Which of the following factors makes the output recovery process *easier*?
   a Lack of use of spooling or printer files
   b Transaction data to be recovered instead of status data
   c In-place update rather than batch update is used
   d Avoidance of use of checkpoint facilities

Exercises and Cases

15–1 You are an external auditor with the federal government audit office responsible for undertaking audits of all federal government departments. In this capacity you conduct audits not only to determine whether government agencies have expended public funds in accordance with government directives but also to evaluate whether public funds have been expended effectively and efficiently.

   Recently, one of the large government departments has established a statistical database containing substantial amounts of information on social welfare recipients. For example, the database contains health information, pension entitlements information, and financial status information. Much of the information is considered by the federal government to be confidential. The database has been established, however, under authority from the federal government to allow high-quality research to be undertaken on social-welfare recipients. The federal government has pointed to its burgeoning expenditures on social welfare. It argues that it wishes to expend monies where they are most needed and that research is needed, therefore, to plan expenditures, especially in light of an aging population. Moreover, it is concerned about an apparent rise in social-welfare fraud, and it believes that better research might enable losses to be controlled more successfully.

You are a member of the audit team undertaking the first examination of the system as it progresses through its design phases. When you ask the project manager about the controls to be built into the system to preserve the privacy of information about people, she indicates that query-set size controls will be used. When you ask about the nature of these query-set size controls, she indicates that the query set size must be greater than three records or less than $n - 3$, where n is the size of the database, before a response will be provided to users.

After some reflection, you express concern that a minimum query-set size of three and a maximum query-set size of $n - 3$ could allow compromise of the database. The project manager responds, however, that the decision on query-set size has been chosen only after extensive consultation with researchers who are likely to use the database. They have argued strongly that the information loss will be too great if the minimum query-set size is increased or the maximum query-set size is decreased. When you ask the project manager whether any other controls will be implemented to preserve the privacy of data about people who have their records stored in the database, she indicates that no other controls will be used. She comments that the government has allocated only limited funds for the project. As a result, the controls chosen must be cheap to implement, operate, and maintain.

Required: Write a brief report for your manager outlining any exposures you believe should be brought to the attention of the government. If you believe any serious exposures exist, provide some brief recommendations to help overcome them. In this regard, be mindful of the tight budget imposed upon the project.

15–2 Southern Cross Securities Limited (SCS) is a large Melbourne-based financial institution offering a wide ranging of financial services to investors. One of SCS's most popular services is portfolio management for people who have moderate to high levels of wealth. SCS's financial analysts have consistently obtained high returns for their clients. Moreover, SCS has invested substantial amounts in training its analysts so they can provide high levels of personal service to their clients. As a result, clients have continued to comment favorably on their dealings with the company.

You are a member of the external audit firm that has just taken over the audit of SCS from another audit firm. As part of the audit, your partner has asked you to review output controls in the system used to provide portfolio management services for people. During your review, you note that SCS prepares monthly statements for its customers. In an interview with SCS's manager of information systems operations, you obtain the following information about the system:

a The monthly customer statement print run is initiated by the manager in charge of the portfolio management section. He often prints the statements on a laser printer located in his section. If this printer is unavailable for some reason, however, he will direct output to another laser printer that is available somewhere else within the organization. No special preprinted stationery is used for the statements; instead, the company's logo, and so on, are stored as a template within the print program that produces the statements. About 500 statements are printed each month.

b When you ask whether customer statements have ever been lost, the operations manager indicates he believes there have been a few occasions in the past in which statements for a few particular customers have gone missing. On these occasions, the manager in charge of the portfolio management section had printed the statements at a location outside his department. He had then been delayed and had not been able to collect the statements promptly. When the statements had gone missing, he simply printed another copy for the customers whose statements were missing.

c The monthly statements plus address labels are given to a small mail distribution organization located in the same building as SCS. The manager in charge of portfolio management simply leaves the statements and address labels on his desk at the end of each month, and a clerk from the mail distribution organization picks them up off his desk at some time.

d From time to time, customers will complain about not receiving their monthly statements or receiving their statements late. Sometimes work overload pressures in the mail distribution organization lead to errors in dispatch (e.g., the wrong statement being sent to customers) or delays in dispatching statements. Customers have been willing to accept these problems, however, because of the high level of service provided by the analysts.

e Complaints about customer statements are directed to the analyst responsible for the customer's portfolio. Customers have instructions on their statements to contact their analysts in the event of problems or complaints.

f A copy of the customer statements is written to a cartridge. The statements are kept for five years before they are deleted. Deletion occurs automatically when the operating system detects the retention date has expired. Cartridges are kept on site in case they are needed to respond to a query.

Required: In light of this information, what recommendations would you make to your partner in terms of how the audit should now proceed? Remember that your primary focus is on whether assets have been safeguarded and whether errors or irregularities have occurred that have resulted in a material misstatement of SCS's accounts.

15–3 Farm Equipment Supplies Limited (FESL) is a major manufacturer of equipment to support primary producers based in Cleveland, Ohio. To control its overall manufacturing costs, FESL uses a just-in-time inventory system in conjunction with a material requirements planning system. Although stockouts of component parts have occurred occasionally in the past, overall the system has been very successful. It has enabled FESL to gradually expand its share of the market for farm equipment by containing its costs, even through the slow-growth periods associated with depressed prices for primary production.

Fundamental to the success of FESL's just-in-time and material requirements planning systems has been an EDI system that FESL has established with its component suppliers. Long-term contracts have been written with several suppliers, and a private EDI network has been established with the suppliers to enable exchange of information. The reliability of this network is critical to FESL being able to meet its manufacturing schedule and to satisfying its customers, demands on a timely basis.

As the manager of internal audit for FESL, one day you are called to a meeting with the president of FESL, the vice-president of manufacturing, and the vice-president of information systems. A major problem has arisen as a result of program maintenance work being carried out on the EDI system. An error was introduced into one of the reordering programs that transmits orders to suppliers to replenish the kanbans (inventory bins) on the production floor. As products were completed, backflush transactions were initiated to increase finished goods inventory and to reduce raw materials and work-in-process inventories. The program did not correctly identify when some of the kanbans needed to be replenished, however. As a result, orders on suppliers were submitted late. Moreover, some orders were transmitted to the wrong supplier. Significant losses have now been incurred. The production process has come to a standstill because inventory has not been delivered on time to some kanbans. The president is also concerned about lost sales that may occur because finished goods now cannot be delivered on time to some of FESL's major customers.

The vice-president of information systems indicates that she has now put in place some additional controls to further reduce the likelihood of errors being introduced into programs as a result of the maintenance process. She points out, however, that the EDI system is now very complex and that maintenance of the system is becoming an increasingly difficult task. She believes it is unrealistic to expect that errors will not occur again at some time in the future.

Required: The president asks you to prepare a report describing some controls that could be put in place to identify (a) when EDI output (e.g., orders on suppliers) is not being dispatched on a timely basis, and (b) when the output has been dispatched to the wrong recipient. He asks you to assume that programming errors may once again occur, and he wants to know, therefore, whether any cost-effective compensating controls can be implemented. Write a brief report outlining any controls you think might be put in place to reduce the exposures that concern the president. Remember, your recommendations should include only controls that are likely to be cost-effective.

15–4 You are the vice-president of internal audit for Kids-Want-Em Ltd. (KWEL), a large, Atlanta-based manufacturer and distributor of high-quality children's toys and games. Your company prides itself on the scientific way in which it designs children's toys and games to foster their intellectual and physical development. Indeed, several of KWEL's computer games have won awards from various parents' and teachers' associations for their novel approaches to teaching children important but difficult mathematical constructs.

One day you are called to a meeting with the president of KWEL, the vice-president of marketing, and the vice-president of information systems. The president reports that she has just been given advance notice by a friend of an article being prepared for a national weekly newspaper about one of KWEL's employees. As best the president can determine, the employee was a member of a "humor" news group on the Internet. Apparently the employee posted a fairly offensive joke to the news group, and several members of the news group then reacted angrily. They responded by posting messages to the news group severely criticizing the posting made by KWEL's employee. Indeed, some members of the news group posted responses that made a personal attack on the employee. The employee in turn responded angrily, and a flame war commenced. The language used within the flame war was highly vitriolic.

The identity of the employee who posted the joke that started the flame war is not known. Apparently the person had used a pseudonym as their identifier. Moreover, until recently it was not known that the source of the message was one of KWEL's computers. The employee had managed to disguise the source of the message with some clever hacking that masked the true address of the source computer. KWEL's name came to light, however, when the employee supposedly sent a letter bomb to one of his or her protagonists. The letter bomb crashed the protagonist's computer system, which belonged to the protagonist's company. As a result, operations within the protagonist's company were severely disrupted because the company had inadequate backup. Thus, they had difficulties effecting recovery of the system. When the president of the protagonist's company discovered the reason for the crash, he was incensed. He called in a computer security consultant to sort out the mess and to try to identify the source of the letter bomb. During the first meeting with the consultant, apparently he indicated he would sue for damages. During the consultant's investigation, he supposedly discovered that one of KWEL's computers was the source of the letter bomb. A reporter from the national weekly newspaper heard about the story and commenced carrying out her own investigations. The results of her investigations were brought to the attention of the president of KWEL's friend, who immediately called the president to inform her of the events.

Required: The president of KWEL asks you to prepare a report outlining (a) the exposures now faced by KWEL, (b) the immediate actions that should be undertaken to mitigate these exposures, and (c) the controls that should be put in place to try to prevent this type of event occurring in the future.

15–5 First South Australian State Bank recently has installed a new network for teller operations in its 500 branches throughout the state. Teller machines in each branch are connected to a branch controller. The controllers, in turn, are connected to the head-office machine. Although some processing has been distributed to the controllers, the customer accounts master file still remains centralized.

Unfortunately, the new network is unreliable. Furthermore, the problems are not being solved quickly because the bank's information systems staff are blaming the machine vendor. The machine vendor has responded by arguing that the problem lies with the bank's information systems staff who have not undergone sufficient training to acquire adequate competence with the system that has been installed. On a number of occasions, the machine vendor claims it has had to respond to problems that could have been fixed quickly if the bank's information systems staff had been properly trained to use the system.

One consequence of the unreliable network is that tellers sometimes submit duplicate transactions. The network often goes down for only a few minutes. When the network goes down, tellers are supposed to check whether the last transaction they submitted was posted to the account by submitting an inquiry when the network comes up. Unfortunately, customer lines are long because the network is unreliable, and tellers often simply resubmit the last transaction to save time rather than initiate an inquiry. Thus, the same transaction sometimes is processed twice.

Required:.   Assuming the unreliability of the network continues, what exposures does the bank face if transactions are processed twice? What controls would you recommend be implemented to prevent duplicate transaction processing?

Answers to Multiple-Choice Questions

15–1	c	15–7	b	15–13	d	15–19	d
15–2	b	15–8	c	15–14	b	15–20	d
15–3	a	15–9	b	15–15	c	15–21	b
15–4	d	15–10	c	15–16	c	15–22	b
15–5	d	15–11	a	15–17	b		
15–6	a	15–12	a	15–18	a		

REFERENCES

Adam, Nabil R., and John C. Wortmann (1989), "Security-Control Methods for Statistical Databases: A Comparative Study," *Computing Surveys* (December), 515–556.

Bethke, Barney (1996), "Home Page Security Risks," *EDPACS* (July), 14–17.

Castano, Silvana, Mariagrazia Fugini, Giancarlo Martella, and Pierangela Samarati (1994), *Database Security*. Reading, MA: Addison-Wesley.

Comer, Douglas E. (1995), *The Internet Book: Everything You Need to Know About Computer Networking and How the Internet Works*. Upper Saddle River, NJ: Prentice-Hall.

Denning, Dorothy E., and Jan Schlörer (1983), "Inference Controls for Statistical Databases," *Computer* (July), 69–82.

Jajodia, Sushil, and Catherine Meadows (1995), "Inference Problems in Multilevel Secure Database Management Systems," in Marshall D. Abrams, Sushil Jajodia, and Harold J. Podell, eds., *Information Security: An Integrated Collec-* *tion of Essays*. Los Alamitos, CA: IEEE Computer Society Press), 570–584.

Miller, Nigel (1996), "Establishing Web Sites—Legal Issues and Risks," *Computers & Security*, 15(3), 198–202.

Mitchell, William J. (1994), "When is Seeing Believing?" *Scientific American* (February), 44–49.

Press, Larry (1995), "The Internet is Not TV: Web Publishing," *Communications of the ACM* (March), 17–23.

Rothenberg, Jeff (1995), "Ensuring the Longevity of Digital Documents," *Scientific American* (January), 24–29.

Schlörer, Jan (1975), "Identification and Retrieval of Personal Records from a Statistical Database," *Methods Information Mediation* (January), 7–13.

Schwartz, Robert J. (1994), "Detecting Forgeries in a Desktop Publishing Environment," *IS Audit & Control Journal*, I, 55–58.

PART
IV

Evidence Collection

To evaluate the quality of an application system, auditors need to collect evidence. Various tools and techniques have been developed to aid their evidence collection activities. Some primarily gather data on how well a system safeguards assets or on how well it protects data integrity. Others are more useful for collecting evidence on whether a system is effective or whether it is efficient. Some even have eclectic capabilities. The problem is not a shortage of evidence-collection techniques to use. Rather, it is becoming skilled in using the different techniques and knowing what technique or set of techniques can provide most assistance in a particular set of circumstances.

The next five chapters describe the various evidence-collection tools and techniques that have been developed to gather data on whether systems safeguard assets, maintain data integrity, achieve their objectives effectively, and process data efficiently. Our focus is on the nature of the tools and techniques, methodologies for using the tools and techniques, and the relative advantages and disadvantages of the tools and techniques.

Chapter	Overview of Contents
16 Audit Software	Discusses generalized audit software, industry-specific audit software, high-level languages, utility software, expert systems, neural network software, specialized audit software, and other software that is useful for evidence-collection purposes.
17 Code Review, Test Data, and Code Comparison	Discusses where program defects occur and the nature and use of program source code review, test data, and program code comparison.
18 Concurrent Auditing Techniques	Discusses the nature of concurrent auditing techniques, the need for concurrent auditing techniques, the major types of concurrent auditing techniques (Integrated Test Facility, Snapshot/Extended Record, System Control/Audit Review File, Continuous and Intermittent Simulation), and how to implement concurrent auditing techniques.
19 Interviews, Questionnaires, and Control Flowcharts	Discusses the nature, design, and use of interviews, questionnaires, and control flowcharts.
20 Performance Monitoring Tools	Discusses the objects of performance measurements, the characteristics of performance monitors, the nature of hardware, software, firmware, and hybrid performance monitors, how to present performance measurement results, and the risks to maintenance of data integrity when performance monitoring is undertaken.

Audit Software

Chapter Outline

Review Questions

Multiple-Choice Questions

Exercises and Cases

Answers to Multiple-Choice Questions

References

Chapter Key Points

■ Various types of software can be used to assist auditors in evidence collection. Some can be purchased off the shelf. Others must be developed specifically to address audit needs.

■ A major tool that auditors can use to collect evidence on the quality of application systems is generalized audit software. Generalized audit software provides a means to gain access to and manipulate data maintained on computer storage media. It was developed to allow auditors to (a) undertake their evidence-collection work in a variety of hardware/software environments, (b) develop an audit capability quickly, and (c) minimize the technical knowledge auditors need to be able to retrieve data from and manipulate data in computer-based information systems.

■ Generalized audit software provides the following major sets of functions: (a) file access functions that permit different types of file structures, record formats, and data formats to be read; (b) file reorganization functions that allow files to be sorted and merged; (c) selection functions to extract data that satisfies certain conditional tests; (d) statistical functions to allow sampling to be undertaken and the results of sampling to be evaluated; (e) arithmetic functions to enable computations to be performed on data; (f) stratification and frequency analysis functions to allow data to be categorized and summarized in different ways; (g) file creation and updating functions to allow work files to be created and updated; and (h) reporting functions to allow results to be formatted and output in flexible ways.

■ The functional capabilities of generalized audit software can be used to accomplish four major audit tasks: (a) examine the existence, accuracy, completeness, consistency, and timeliness of data maintained on computer storage media; (b) examine the quality of processes embedded within an application system; (c) examine the existence of the entities the data purports to represent by facilitating physical observation and counting of these entities via statistical sampling; (d) undertake analytical review to monitor key audit indicators such as trends in working capital ratios over time.

■ Generalized audit software has three functional limitations: (a) evidence collection is not always timely because it can be used to gather evidence on the state of an application system only some time after data has been processed; (b) it can perform only limited tests to verify the authenticity, accuracy, and completeness of processing logic; and (c) it can be used in only a limited way to determine the propensity of an application system to make errors.

■ Sometimes auditors will want to use generalized audit software to access data maintained on another machine. There are several ways auditors can transfer data from the other machine to the machine on which the generalized audit software package resides: The file can be written to a cartridge, tape, or diskette that can be read by the machine on which the generalized audit software package resides; the data can be transferred via a modem and a file transfer utility; or the data can be transferred via a gateway to a local area network to which the machine where the generalized audit software resides is connected.

■ Generalized audit software applications must be managed properly like the development and implementation of any piece of software. The following phases should be managed carefully: (a) feasibility analysis and planning for the generalized audit software application; (b) design of the generalized audit software application; (c) coding and testing of the generalized audit software application; and (d) operation, evaluation, and documentation of the results obtained from the generalized audit software application.

■ Industry-specific audit software is audit software that has been designed to provide high-level commands that invoke common audit functions needed within a particular industry. It might run only on a limited set of hardware/software platforms. Moreover, it might have been developed to access data maintained by a specific application package that is used widely within the industry.

■ Auditors might sometimes use high-level languages, such as fourth-generation programming languages and statistical software, to gain access to data and manipulate it. In some cases, fourth-generation languages could be more user friendly and better supported than generalized audit software. They might also perform functions that cannot be performed using generalized audit software. Statistical software might be used because it provides more powerful statistical functions than those provided in generalized audit software.

■ Utility software is software that performs fairly specific functions that are needed frequently, often by a large number of users, during the operation of computer systems. Auditors can use utility software to (a) facilitate assessment of security and integrity, (b) facilitate gaining an understanding of an application system, (c) assess data quality, (d) assess program quality, (e) facilitate program development, and (f) facilitate assessing operational efficiency.

■ Expert systems are programs that encapsulate the knowledge that human experts have about a particular domain and possess capabilities to reproduce this knowledge when presented with a particular problem. They have four major components: (a) a knowledge base that contains facts about the domain of interest and rules that represent the heuristics that experts use to solve problems in the domain; (b) an inference engine that uses some type of logic to reason about problems in the domain; (c) a tutorial component or explanation facility to provide information to users about a line of reasoning used to reach a particular conclusion; and (d) a knowledge acquisition component that can be used to elicit new information about the domain so the system can improve its capabilities.

■ Audit expert systems have been developed to assist with risk analysis, internal control evaluation, audit program planning, and provision of advice on various technical aspects of the audit (such as the adequacy of doubtful debts provision).

■ Neural network software has been designed to function like neurons in the brain. It is used primarily for pattern recognition, learning, and classification purposes. For example, it can be used to recognize patterns in data that manifest fraud has occurred. Neural networks are "trained" by presenting them with a large number of cases where the outputs (or results) for a given set of inputs are known. The network learns by adjusting internal weights among its components until it can predict the output based on the input pattern.

■ Specialized audit software is software written in a procedure-oriented or problem-oriented language to fulfill a specific set of audit tasks. The software might have extensive functionality, but it has been developed for specific audit users to achieve specific audit goals.

■ Specialized audit software can be developed in three ways. First, auditors can take total responsibility for developing and implementing the software themselves. Second, internal auditors can ask programmers in their own organization to develop and implement the software. Third, auditors could ask an outside software vendor to prepare the software. Whatever the approach used, auditors must exercise careful control over the development and implementation process to ensure that the software meets their needs and the integrity of the software is preserved.

■ Over the years, other types of audit software have been developed. For example, software has been developed to simulate the operations of internal control systems, to generate questions to elicit internal control weaknesses, to allow description of an internal control system and questioning about the state of the internal control system, and to represent the complex interrelationships that sometimes exist between internal controls so system vulnerabilities can be assessed. Much of this software is experimental in nature. Nevertheless, auditors should be aware of it so they can obtain insights that might improve their audit practice.

■ Whenever auditors use audit software for evidence-collection purposes, they should evaluate the level of control they are able to exercise over the software. To the extent that the software is controlled by another party or auditors must rely on another party to execute the software, they run the risk of the integrity of the software or the results produced by the software being undermined either intentionally or unintentionally. Auditors should seek to maintain a library of audit software that they can control and execute themselves.

INTRODUCTION

In this chapter we begin our discussion of various tools that auditors can use to collect evidence on the reliability of controls within an application system. Specifically, we focus on different types of software that auditors can employ to facilitate their evidence-collection work. A wide range of software now exists that auditors might find useful during an audit. In this light, we must have an understanding of the nature of this software, the functions it can perform, where it might be used within an audit, and its inherent strengths and limitations.

In the following discussion, we focus first on four types of off-the-shelf software that auditors often use during the evidence-collection phase of an audit: generalized audit software, industry-specific audit software, high-level languages, and utility software. We then examine two types of audit software that have their roots in artificial intelligence—namely, expert systems and neural networks. Next, we discuss specialized software that auditors sometimes must develop and implement to address needs that cannot be met satisfactorily using off-the-shelf audit software. We then briefly examine some other types of audit software that have been developed over the years but have not enjoyed widespread use. By having an appreciation of this software, we can gain insights into how auditors use other audit software in innovative ways. Finally, we examine the approaches they can use to exercise control over audit software so that they have confidence in the integrity of the results they obtain using the software.

GENERALIZED AUDIT SOFTWARE

Generalized audit software is off-the-shelf software that provides a means to gain access to and manipulate data maintained on computer storage media. Auditors can obtain evidence directly on the quality of the records produced and maintained by application systems. In turn, their judgments on the quality of the records will enable them to make judgments about the quality of the application system that processes these records.

Generalized audit software packages first appeared in the mid-1960s. They were developed by several large public accounting firms to facilitate the audit work they needed to carry out on mainframe computers. Enhanced versions of these mainframe generalized audit software packages are still available and still used. Today, however, microcomputer-based generalized audit software packages are available. Data is often transferred from a mainframe to a microcomputer to enable auditors to work with a generalized audit software package. Over the years, the extent of usage of generalized audit software by auditors has been monitored (e.g., Tobinson and Davis 1981; Reeve 1984; Garsombke and Tabor 1986; Lovata 1988). It has remained the most frequently used computer-assisted auditing tool.

Motivations for Generalized Audit Software Development

The primary motivation for developing generalized audit software is the set of problems caused by the diversity of computerized information processing environments that auditors might confront. The characteristics of information systems can vary considerably: different hardware and software environments, different data structures, different record formats, different processing functions. With resource constraints, it is often impossible to develop specific programs for every system that will extract, manipulate, and report data required for audit purposes. Generalized audit software has been developed specifically to accommodate a wide variety of different hardware and software platforms. The trade-off is a loss of processing efficiency for the ability to develop quickly a program capable of accomplishing audit objectives in a new environment. In many cases, however, the loss in processing efficiency is more than compensated by savings in the labor hours required to develop audit software capabilities for specific computer systems.

A second major motivation for developing generalized audit software is the need to develop quickly an audit capability in light of changing audit objectives. Both external and internal auditors often face situations in which new audit objectives must be developed or existing audit objectives change. For example, the volume of transactions processed through an application system might increase markedly such that the system becomes a high-materiality system rather than a low-materiality system. Generalized audit software allows us to adapt quickly when these types of changes occur.

A third major motivation for developing generalized audit software is the need to provide audit capabilities to auditors who might be relatively unskilled in the use of computers. In the past, few auditors had extensive training and experience in computers. Today, many auditors have a broad, general understanding of computer systems. They might lack the specific knowledge and experience needed, however, to be able to cope with the different types of hardware and software platforms they confront. Most generalized audit software packages can be used by auditors who are not computer audit specialists. In this light, the computer audit capabilities of these auditors can be extended.

Functional Capabilities of Generalized Audit Software

Table 16–1 shows the major sets of functions that auditors can perform using generalized audit software. These functions can be executed using some type of high-level user interface, such as a graphical user interface. For example, Figure 16–1 shows how one major generalized audit software package allows some

TABLE 16–1 Major Sets of Functions Performed by Generalized Audit Software

Set of Functions	Examples
File access	Capabilities to read different data coding schemes, different record formats, and different file structures.
File reorganization	Sorting and merging files.
Selection	Boolean and relational operators available: e.g., A AND (B OR C); A EQ 2500; A GT 3000.
Statistical	Varies from sampling every nth item to support of attributes and variables sampling.
Arithmetic	Full set available: addition, subtraction, multiplication, division, exponentiation.
Stratification and frequency analysis	Capabilities to classify data into categories according to certain criteria.
File creation and updating	Capabilities to create and update work files based on an organization's production files.
Reporting	Editing and formatting of output.

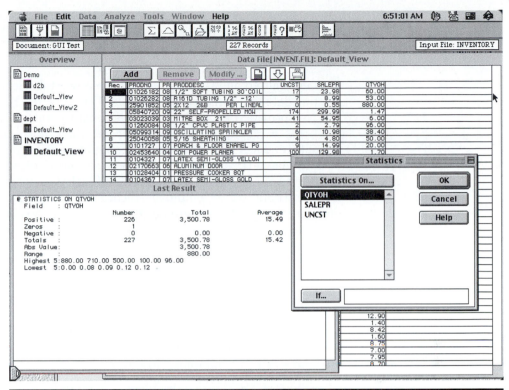

FIGURE 16–1. Statistical functions in a generalized audit software package.
Courtesy of ACL Services Ltd.

statistical functions to be invoked on an inventory file and the results produced. In the following subsections, we examine each set of functions listed in Table 16–1 in more detail.

File Access

The file access functions enable files having different data coding schemes, record formats, and file structures to be read. Coding schemes like ASCII, EBCDIC, zoned, packed, and binary often can be read. Records can have fixed or variable formats. Typically, the file structures that can be accessed are sequential, index sequential, and random, although some packages provide access to more complex structures such as trees and networks. Some generalized audit software packages allow several files to be read simultaneously. Some also provide direct access to files created by several popular database management systems, accounting packages, spreadsheet packages, and word processing packages.

File Reorganization

The file reorganization functions allow data to be sorted into different orders and data from different files to be merged onto one file. Sorting capabilities are necessary for a variety of purposes—for example, reporting data in a specified order or comparing data on two files. Merging capabilities are needed if data from separate files is to be combined on a separate work file. Functions can then be executed on this work file—for example, statistical functions or various kinds of calculations.

Selection

Generalized audit software provides powerful selection capabilities for extracting data that satisfies certain tests. Typically, the Boolean operators AND, OR are provided as well as the relational operators EQ, GT, LT, NE, GE, LE—that is, equal to, greater than, less than, not equal to, greater than or equal to, and less than or equal to. Complex queries containing nested tests can be formulated (Figure 16–2). Brackets establish precedence. For example, the query (PAY GT 24000 AND (OVERTIME GE 6000 OR ALLOWANCES EQ 6)) would extract employee records in which pay is greater than $24,000 per year and overtime is greater than or equal to $6,000 per year, or employee records in which pay is greater than $24,000 and the allowances classification is category 6.

Statistical

The statistical capabilities of generalized audit software vary from moderately powerful to sophisticated. At a basic level, every *n*th record can be selected or records can be selected at random. Some packages also provide comprehensive attributes sampling, variables sampling, combined attributes/variables sampling, discovery sampling, stratified sampling, and dol-

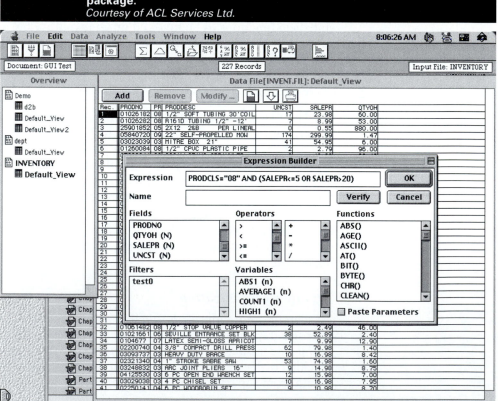

FIGURE 16–2. Formulating complex expressions within a generalized audit software package.
Courtesy of ACL Services Ltd.

lar-unit sampling capabilities. Some also provide functions to support analytical review procedures—for example, regression and financial ratio analysis capabilities. Selected data and key analytical review results from prior years can be saved and brought forward to facilitate analytical review in subsequent years. Generalized audit software also can be designed to provide input to separate statistical and financial modelling software where more powerful capabilities are required.

Arithmetic

Generalized audit software provides the full set of arithmetic operators enabling work fields to be computed, the arithmetic accuracy of data to be checked, control totals to be produced, and so on. For example, net pay calculations for a payroll file can be recomputed, or files can be crossfooted. Often the calculations can be made based on data from more than one input record. Calculated fields can be stored and then used in subsequent calculations. With some packages, calculated fields can also be used to develop tables for look-up purposes.

Stratification and Frequency Analysis

Generalized audit software packages often provide good capabilities with respect to stratification and frequency analysis (Figure 16–3). Different types of stratification, frequency analysis, and aging analysis can be undertaken. For example, the frequency of accounts receivable balances in certain classes can be determined: $0–$200, $200.01–$400, $400.01–$600, and so on. The distribution

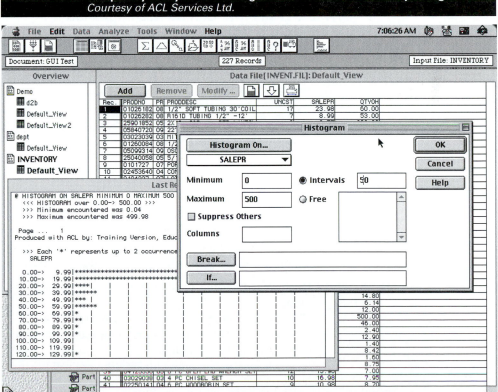

FIGURE 16–3. Frequency analysis within a generalized audit software package.
Courtesy of ACL Services Ltd.

of accounts receivables balances could be an important determinant of the type of sampling method chosen or the substantive audit procedures chosen.

File Creation and Updating

Some generalized audit software packages allow work files to be created and updated. For example, the output could contain samples of input file records or user-defined records that include fields extracted from input records or calculated fields. In some cases, the output files can be written in formats that are suitable for input into widely used database management software, spreadsheet software, or word processing software. Auditors can use generalized audit software to extract the data needed for audit purposes from the application system files. By using the work file instead of the application system files, auditors then cause minimum interference to normal application system processing.

Reporting

Comprehensive reporting facilities are often available in generalized audit software packages. For example, free-form reports can be produced that allow auditors to control the title of the report, content of column headings, width of columns in the report, levels of subtotals, number of detail lines, page footers and page headers, and formatting of fields (such as zero suppression and the addition of dollar signs). Some reports that contain data that most auditors will require during an audit are produced automatically—for example, reports containing control totals, record counts, negative amounts, and blank or zero fields. Special-purpose reports also may be available—for example, those that will be sent to outside parties for confirmation purposes.

Audit Tasks that Can Be Accomplished Using Generalized Audit Software

Auditors can combine the functional capabilities of generalized audit software to accomplish several audit tasks:

1. Examine the quality of data,
2. Examine the quality of system processes,
3. Examine the existence of the entities the data purports to represent, and
4. Undertake analytical review.

In the following subsections, we briefly examine the ways in which these tasks can be accomplished.

Examine the Quality of Data

Auditors can use the functional capabilities of generalized audit software to examine the existence, accuracy, completeness, consistency, and timeliness of data maintained on computer storage media. Consider the following examples:

1. Records for various fixed assets can be retrieved to see if, in fact, the records exist.
2. The calculation of sales discounts can be checked for accuracy.
3. The address field for customers in an accounts receivable file can be examined to see if it contains blanks.
4. Records on the personnel file and the payroll file can be compared for consistency.
5. A file of share prices can be checked to determine the last time it was updated.

Auditors might examine the quality of data maintained in application system files or in an organization's database for two reasons. First, the quality of the data reflects the quality of the application system that processes the data. For example, if the address field in a debtor's records is blank, we should question the adequacy of the validation processes contained in the system. Second, the quality of data reflects the quality of the personnel who developed and maintain the application system and the quality of the personnel who use the system. If the data is low in quality, the application system processing the data could be poorly designed, poorly implemented, or poorly maintained. If this situation has been allowed to continue, the quality of the personnel who use the system also must be questioned. Moreover, even if the system is well designed, implemented, and maintained, the data supplied by users might still be low in quality.

Examine the Quality of System Processes

Even though the quality of the data in an application system might be high, the quality of system processes still could be low from the viewpoint of achieving the objectives of an organization. For example, the data in an accounts receivable file might be accurate, complete, consistent, and timely. A substantial number of overdue accounts might exist, however, which reflects adversely on both the accounts receivable application system and the personnel who use the system. The system might not be producing adequate management reports to enable timely collection of receivables. Alternatively, the system might be producing adequate reports. Nonetheless, accounts receivable personnel may not be using the reports or not properly following up on collections.

Besides examining the quality of data, auditors can use generalized audit software to examine the quality of system processes in other ways. For example, in our accounts receivable example, auditors could use it to age the accounts receivable file to determine whether debtors were paying their accounts on a timely basis. Similarly, auditors could use generalized audit software to calculate inventory turnover statistics as a basis for identifying obsolete inventory. If they identified substantial amounts of obsolete inventory, auditors should then question the adequacy of system processes for managing inventory. Moreover, auditors should also question whether inventory is overvalued.

Still another way of using generalized audit software to examine the quality of the processes in an application system is via a technique called *parallel simulation* (Mair 1975). It involves auditors writing a program to replicate those application processes that are critical to an audit opinion and using this program to reprocess application system data. The results produced via the simulation program are then compared with the results produced by the application system. Any discrepancies identified form the basis for follow-up work by the auditor.

Figure 16–4 shows a parallel simulation program reprocessing transaction data against a master file and producing a new master file. Generalized audit software then compares the master file produced by the parallel simulation program with the master file produced by the application system and generates a report of discrepancies. The parallel simulation program can be written in any programming language—preferably a high-level programming language to allow fast development of the simulation program. Because some generalized audit software packages provide sufficient functionality, however, they are often used to develop the simulation program in preference to other high-level programming languages. The program written using generalized audit software

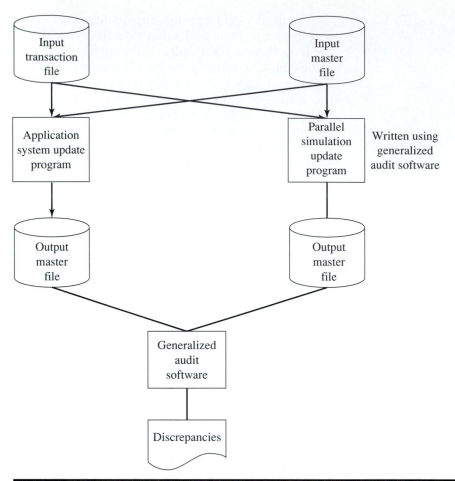

FIGURE 16–4. Example use of the parallel simulation technique.

might not execute efficiently. Processing efficiency usually is not a major consideration, however, when parallel simulation is used as an evidence-collection method.

Whenever a parallel simulation program is developed, note that auditors might not include all the functionality of the application system program to be simulated in the simulation program. Rather, they should focus on those functions that are critical to their audit opinion and develop and implement their parallel simulation program to include only those functions.

Examine the Existence of the Entities the Data Purports to Represent

Data could exist and be accurate, complete, and consistent. It might not represent an object in the real world, however. For example, it might represent a bogus insurance policy or an inventory item that no longer exists. Auditors must determine, therefore, whether the entities that the data purports to describe really exist.

The statistical sampling capabilities of generalized audit software provide an important means of doing this. For example, auditors can use these capabilities to select a sample of debtors for confirmation or a sample of inventory for physical observation. The powerful reporting capabilities of generalized audit software can then be used to print confirmations in the form required for mailing to debtors or to sort and print inventory data in a way that will facilitate auditors' physical counts of inventory. They can then input the results obtained from their confirmations or physical inventory work to generalized audit software to obtain probabilistic statements about the number of errors or the size of the dollar error that is likely to exist in the accounts.

Undertake Analytical Review

Analytical review is the process of obtaining key ratios and totals from an organization's data for comparison with previous years' ratios and totals or industrywide ratios and totals. The information obtained from analytical review is used to support or question preliminary audit conclusions based on system reviews and other substantive tests. For example, a decline in the working capital ratio of an organization might be used to support a preliminary audit conclusion that the ongoing viability of the organization is at risk.

Auditors can use generalized audit software to support analytical review work in several ways. First, they can use generalized audit software to extract data required for analytical review from an organization's database or an outside database and to prepare various ratios and totals. Second, if generalized audit software provides regression analysis capabilities, auditors can use the software to examine firm and industry trends. Alternatively, they can use generalized audit software to prepare data in a format suitable for input to another package that provides regression capabilities or other kinds of modelling capabilities required. Third, auditors can use generalized audit software to maintain a database of key data and key indicators across time. For example, auditors might want to store key indicators from the current year's audit for future years so trends across years can be identified.

Functional Limitations of Generalized Audit Software

To use generalized audit software effectively and efficiently, auditors must understand both its capabilities and its limitations. The following subsections examine three limitations that undermine its usefulness as a means of collecting evidence on the reliability of information systems:

1. Generalized audit software permits auditors to undertake only *ex post* auditing and not concurrent auditing.
2. Generalized audit software has only limited capabilities for verifying processing logic.
3. It is difficult for auditors to determine the application system's propensity for error using generalized audit software.

Ex Post Auditing Only

Generalized audit software enables evidence to be collected only on the state of an application system after the fact. In other words, the software examines the quality of data after it has been processed. Even if auditors use generalized audit software to undertake parallel simulation, the results produced by the parallel simulation program are checked against a set of existing results produced by the application system. Thus, some time lag will occur between an application system error occurring and its possible identification using generalized audit software. In some cases this elapsed time could be substantial if the application system is not audited on a regular basis.

For some types of systems, timely identification of errors could be critical. For example, consider a situation in which multiple online users access a shared database. Unless an error that occurs in a data item is discovered quickly, it could permeate the database and cause several incorrect decisions to be made by users. Timely identification and correction of the error is therefore critical. In this light, Chapter 18 discusses the use of concurrent auditing techniques that permit evidence to be collected, and sometimes evaluated, at the same time as application system processing occurs. Auditors must use specialized rather than generalized audit software, however, to implement concurrent auditing techniques.

Limited Ability to Verify Processing Logic

Often the tests performed with generalized audit software involve "live" data—that is, data captured and processed by the application system during the normal course of business. The limitations of using live data to test application systems, however, are well known. The data might not manifest the exceptional conditions that occur occasionally within the application. As a result, the application system's capability to handle these exceptional conditions accurately and completely is not tested. To overcome this problem, test data must be designed specifically to determine how the application system handles exceptional conditions. (Chapter 17 discusses this issue in more detail.)

Limited Ability to Determine Propensity for Error

Systems can be designed and implemented in ways that allow them, at least to some extent, to accommodate change (see Chapters 4 and 5). For example, database management systems can be used to isolate certain types of changes to the database design from the application systems that access the database. Alternatively, application systems can be designed and implemented in ways that cause them to degenerate quickly when change occurs. Perhaps they are written in this way to allow them to process data efficiently.

Auditors must be concerned with whether application systems have been designed appropriately to accommodate change. Otherwise, there are higher inherent risks associated with application systems because errors are more likely to result when changes to the systems must be undertaken. Unfortunately, auditors can obtain little evidence using generalized audit software on an application system's capability to accommodate change. Instead, the evidence must be obtained in other ways—for example, reviewing the management control framework, examining the ways application systems are designed, and examining the ways program code is written.

Accessing Data with Generalized Audit Software

The way auditors access data with generalized audit software will depend on whether the data they need to access resides on the same machine as the generalized audit software package they are using. If the data they need to access resides on the same machine as their package—for example, they are using a mainframe-based generalized audit software package—access usually is straightforward. They simply define the file, record, and data formats of the file they wish to access. Their generalized audit software package then should be able to access the file. In some situations, the file might be stored using a format that cannot be read by their generalized audit software package. They then might have to use some type of utility to convert the file into a format that can be read by their generalized audit software package.

Often, however, the file they wish to access and the generalized audit software package do not reside on the same machine. For example, they might be using a microcomputer-based generalized audit software package that, for

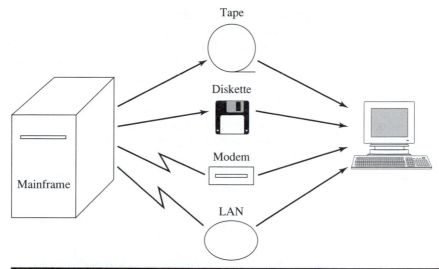

FIGURE 16–5. Transferring data from mainframe to microcomputer for generalized audit software use.

security reasons, they keep on a machine reserved solely for audit use. In these circumstances, they must then transfer the file from the machine on which it resides (another mainframe computer, mid-range computer, or microcomputer) to the machine on which their generalized audit software package resides.

To illustrate how auditors might undertake a file transfer, assume that the file resides on a mainframe and the generalized audit software package resides on a microcomputer. Several methods can be used to undertake the file transfer (Figure 16–5):

1. If the file to be transferred is large, it can be written to a cartridge or perhaps a tape. Before transfer, it might be useful to sort the file in the order that will be most useful to the generalized audit software application. It might also be useful to select only certain fields in records for transfer or certain records for transfer. These actions will reduce processing time on the microcomputer. The microcomputer on which the generalized audit software package resides must have a device that can read the cartridge or tape.
2. If the file to be transferred is small, it can be written to a diskette. The diskette can then be transported to the microcomputer on which the generalized audit software resides.
3. A modem plus some type of file transfer utility can be used to transfer the file from the mainframe computer to the microcomputer.
4. The mainframe can be connected via a gateway to a local area network. The microcomputer on which the generalized audit software resides is also connected to this network. A file transfer utility can then be used to transfer the file to be accessed from the mainframe to the microcomputer.

Similar methods can be used to undertake other types of file transfers that auditors might require. For example, if auditors need to upload a file from a microcomputer to a mainframe, they could transfer it via a modem and some type of file transfer facility or transfer it via a local area network through a gateway to the mainframe. Likewise, if auditors need to transfer a file from one microcomputer to another, they might use a diskette or transfer it over a local area network.

When accessing a file using generalized audit software, auditors must take steps to ensure they are accessing the authentic, accurate, complete, and latest version of the file. If the file accessed is on the same machine as the generalized audit software package, it is easier to ensure that the file accessed is the production file. Auditors should be given authorization to access the file like any other authorized user. Nonetheless, they might still undertake checks, such as calculating control totals, to ensure that they have the correct file. If the file is to be transferred from one machine to another, however, auditors face the risk that unauthorized modifications to the file might be made before it is transferred. Auditors need to gain assurances that the file is transferred intact. Again, they might execute procedures like calculating control totals on the file received and comparing them with control totals calculated on the file that was transferred. These procedures are unlikely to be foolproof, however, so auditors need to recognize that they lose some independence and control whenever another party is involved in file transfer procedures.

Managing a Generalized Audit Software Application

Whenever auditors develop a generalized audit software application, they should follow the steps discussed in Chapter 5 to ensure that the work is managed properly. In some cases, the application will be simple and require few resources. Accordingly, project management concerns will be minimal. In other cases, however, the application will be complex and costly. Careful control will have to be exercised, therefore, to ensure that the development work is carried out effectively and efficiently. In the following subsections, we briefly examine the work that should be undertaken during the major phases of developing and implementing a generalized audit software application.

Feasibility Analysis and Planning

Certain types of generalized audit software applications are costly to develop, implement, and operate. Auditors should take care to estimate the costs and benefits of a generalized audit software application whenever it has some or all of the following characteristics:

1. The application will access large data files such that the execution time required will be substantial.
2. The application is complex such that the development and testing time required will be substantial.
3. The application system to be evaluated using generalized audit software is poorly documented and poorly understood.
4. The application system to be evaluated using generalized audit software is subject to frequent changes that will require the generalized audit software application to be modified frequently.
5. The application is to be run frequently; it is not a one-off or occasional use of generalized audit software.
6. The audit staff are not skilled users of computer systems, or they lack knowledge of and experience with the generalized audit software package.
7. The audit objectives to be accomplished with the generalized audit software application are unclear or still evolving.

When auditors estimate the costs associated with a generalized audit software application, they must ensure that they take into account all the material costs that are likely to be incurred. Many different types of costs can arise—for example, labor costs associated with understanding, developing, implementing, and operating the application; labor costs associated with application systems staff and technical and administrative staff who must provide assistance; computing costs associated with the development, testing, and execution of the application; supply costs such as those associated with the special stationery used for confirmation letters; and costs of disruption if errors are introduced into the application system as a result of their using generalized audit software. Similarly, many different types of benefits can accrue from using generalized audit software—for example, reductions in the amount of time to perform the audit, improved detection of errors and irregularities, and improved feedback to the users of application systems on the quality of controls. Again, auditors must be sure that they take all material benefits into account when determining whether a generalized audit software application will be worthwhile.

Having estimated the costs and benefits associated with a generalized audit software application, auditors should then prepare a budget to determine whether the benefits of the application are likely to exceed the costs. The budget will also form the basis for controlling the development, implementation, and operation of the application. Auditors also need to prepare a timetable for development to ensure that the application can be developed within the required timeframe.

Application Design

During the application design phase, auditors undertake detailed design of the generalized audit software application. The amount of work done during this phase will depend on such factors as the size, complexity, and criticality of the application. For example, if the application is large and will consume substantial amounts of machine time to execute, auditors should take substantial care to ensure that the logic is correct from the outset and that the generalized audit software package will perform the functions required as efficiently as possible. On the other hand, if the application is small and requires few machine resources, auditors might use a prototyping approach when preparing the application. For example, auditors might prepare a quick, preliminary design with a view to obtaining a working version of the application that they can use on an experimental basis.

Some of the important design steps to be undertaken during this phase are as follows:

Design Step	Explanation
Obtain detailed understanding of application system to be audited	Auditors can obtain this understanding by reviewing application system documentation, flowcharting the application, preparing decision tables, and so on.
Design output reports required	The output reports constitute some of the working papers for the audit. Auditors must ensure that the information they require for the audit is output in a convenient form.
Prepare file definitions	Auditors must define any files to be accessed and any work files to be created.
Define the logic of the audit software program	Auditors must determine what functions they want the generalized audit software application to perform. The logic of the application should be documented in some way—e.g., flowcharts or decision tables.

(cont.)

Design Step	*Explanation*
Define any supplementary data needed	Additional data, such as reference (look-up) tables, may need to be defined.
Prepare a test plan	Testing can be undertaken using a test deck or live data. Chapter 17 discusses various techniques for testing programs.
Desk check logic	When the logic of the generalized audit software application has been defined, auditors should undertake desk-checking to determine whether their audit objectives will be met.

When auditors have completed the design phase, they might need to review and to evaluate the design against the budget and timetable prepared during the feasibility analysis phase. In light of the design prepared, it might be clear that they cannot achieve the outcomes required of the generalized audit software application within the budget or timetable prepared. More resources or additional time might have to be allocated to the application. Alternatively, the application might have to be scrapped or modified in some way.

Coding and Testing

After the design has been completed, the application must be coded and tested. In some cases, auditors simply input commands to the generalized audit software package and observe the outcome as each command is interpreted and executed. They are likely to follow this approach if the results from each command can be obtained quickly. In other cases, however, auditors might write a series of commands and store them in a command file that is subsequently read and executed by the generalized audit software package. They are likely to follow this approach if the commands take substantial time to execute. The command file might be read and invoked at some time during the night when the load on the machine used to execute the generalized audit software application is low. Because online and batch execution of commands is often needed, some packages allow a command file to be created for subsequent use as auditors input each command and observe its outcome (Figure 16–6). Thus, auditors can develop the application iteratively and store the final version for subsequent execution as a command file.

Auditors should ensure that the results produced by a generalized audit software application are correct and complete. For example, they might select a few input records from the application system's files and validate the output produced by the generalized audit software program in light of these input records. In this regard, some packages provide a facility to select a small number of records from a file to enable testing of the generalized audit software application to be undertaken before the entire file is accessed. If the generalized audit software program will consume substantial resources during its execution, testing the application becomes especially critical before production running is undertaken.

Operation, Evaluation, and Documentation of Results

As discussed previously, sometimes operation of a generalized audit software application simply involves submitting input commands to the package that are interpreted and executed immediately. If auditors prepare batch command files for delayed execution, however, they might need to establish a processing schedule with the operations manager. Furthermore, if some time has

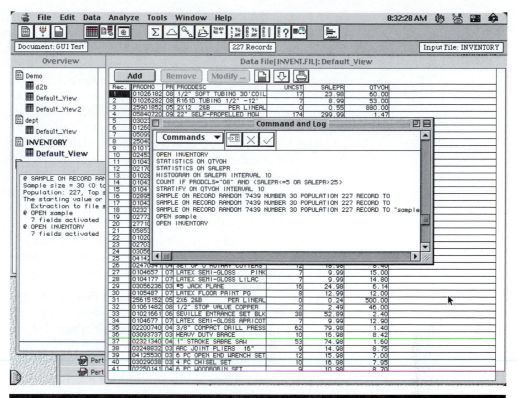

FIGURE 16-6. Command file in a generalized audit software package.
Courtesy of ACL Services Ltd.

elapsed since the audit software application was last run, auditors should check to see that no changes have been made to the application system that would impact its completeness and correctness. For example, a change to a record format could cause the application to produce erroneous output.

Upon obtaining the reports produced by the audit software application, auditors should review the output to check for any errors, derive a set of audit conclusions, and determine whether audit objectives have been attained. Respecification and rerunning of the application might be necessary. The output must be incorporated into the audit working papers along with audit conclusions and any suggestions for improvements in future use of the application. In this regard, some packages prepare output and an audit trail to facilitate preparation of audit working papers. The costs and benefits of the application also should be compared with the budget. Finally, any files created by the application that might be needed for future use should be secured.

INDUSTRY-SPECIFIC AUDIT SOFTWARE

Some types of audit software packages are now available that are oriented toward specific industries—for example, the financial services, health care, and insurance industries. The packages are still *generalized* because they provide auditors with high-level languages that can be used to invoke a wide range of functions. They differ from the types of audit software examined previously, however, in two ways. First, because they are oriented toward a particular industry, they provide high-level commands that invoke common audit functions needed within the industry. For example, in the banking industry, they might use a single command to invoke logic that would check for account kiting. If generalized audit software were to be used to check for kiting, several commands might be required to express the logic needed to execute the various tests. Second, industry-specific audit software could have been developed to access data maintained by a specific generalized application package that is used extensively within the industry. Accordingly, the file, record, and field definitions used by the application package could be built into the audit software package; that is, auditors do not have to provide these definitions each time they want to run the package.

The CAPS package developed by Brisbane-based Kendalls Chartered Accountants is an example of an industry-specific audit software package. It has been designed for auditors of financial institutions (primarily auditors of credit unions and building societies). As such, it provides high-level commands to invoke functions that they will need. In addition, CAPS has been written to access the data maintained by two widely used generalized application packages within the finance industry. Indeed, CAPS cannot be used unless auditees employ one of these two packages for their basic application processing. If the auditee uses one of those packages, however, CAPS provides nine major sets of audit capabilities:

1. *Loan arrears audit.* CAPS can be used to evaluate the movements in loan arrears on a member's loan balance throughout a specified period. For example, a report is provided showing any case in which a new disbursement has occurred in spite of the loan being in arrears. Using this type of information, auditors could assess the auditee's controls over loan arrears.

2. *Interest audit.* This module recalculates all interest on member loans and savings accounts to provide an independent check on calculations carried out by the application system.

3. *Term deposit interest audit.* This module recalculates total term deposit interest to a specified date to provide an independent check on calculations carried out by the application system.

4. *Member ledger balances audit.* This module provides several functions that assist auditors to evaluate the veracity of member ledger balances. For example, it provides summarized information on each loans, savings, and investments ledger; it allows stratified sampling of member ledger balances for confirmation purposes; and it provides routines to statistically evaluate the results of a confirmation of members.

5. *Member ledger transactions audit.* This module examines ledger transactions for evidence of unusual circumstances. For example, it identifies transaction values outside a specified range; it identifies when a disproportionate number of a particular transaction type has occurred; and it selects transactions randomly for audit scrutiny.

6. *Member biographical audit.* This module examines the reasonableness of various demographic and personal data held about a member. For example, it looks for member names without vowels (unusual names); it tests for post codes (zip codes) outside a particular range; and it tests for members who have a post office box number as a primary address.

7. *Dormancy audit.* This module identifies member accounts that are dormant and that, as a consequence, bear a greater risk of fraudulent or unauthorized transactions remaining undetected for some time. The module retains a separate file of dormant accounts and provides a report on changes to the file when subsequent dormancy audits are conducted.

8. *Incompatible duties audit.* This module allows the set of transactions that different operators (tellers) are allowed to execute to be defined. It will then

check transaction log files to determine whether any operators are executing transactions that manifest inadequate separation of duties.

9. *Legislative compliance audit.* This module determines whether the financial position of an organization complies with legislative requirements. For example, a credit union might have to ensure that the proportions of its loans maturing within 3 months, 6 months, 9 months, 12 months, and greater than 12 months fall within certain ranges. Otherwise, it will be in breach of legislation.

The primary advantages of industry-specific audit software over generalized audit software are that it runs more efficiently and that it is easier to use because it incorporates higher-level functions. The primary disadvantage is that it has a more limited domain of application than generalized audit software. As such, it tends to be more useful for internal auditors or external auditors who perform a large number of audits within a specific industry.

HIGH-LEVEL LANGUAGES

Besides generalized audit software, auditors can often use a high-level language to gain access to data and manipulate this data. In particular, many auditors now use fourth-generation programming languages, such as SQL and QBE, and generalized statistical software, such as SPSS™ and SAS®, to collect evidence on system reliability (Higgins 1997).

Fourth-generation languages have proved useful to auditors' work for several reasons. First, most functions incorporated within generalized audit software packages are also included within fourth-generation languages. For example, auditors can use fourth-generation languages to select data from files that satisfy certain criteria and to format this data for reporting purposes. They might have weaker capabilities in a few areas—for example, statistical sampling capabilities. Often auditors can overcome these difficulties, however, by using "macros," which allow them to write programs (perhaps using the high-level language) to perform particular functions and then to invoke these programs with a single command. Furthermore, some vendors of fourth-generation languages have adapted their software to produce specialized versions for auditors that contain, for example, statistical sampling functions.

Second, for the types of functions auditors might want to perform, fourth-generation languages could be more user friendly than generalized audit software. For example, a fourth-generation language might provide them with more flexible reporting capabilities. Auditors might also be able to avoid difficult downloading of data from one computer to another computer or troublesome conversion of one file or data format to another file or data format.

Third, if auditors use a fourth-generation language that is employed extensively throughout the organization audited, they are likely to be able to get good support to overcome any difficulties they might encounter. For example, if the organization uses a relational database and SQL, many persons within the organization should be able to assist auditors if they have problems using SQL to access and manipulate data in the database.

Many auditors have also become more frequent users of statistical packages because they now place increased reliance on analytical review as a diagnostic tool in the conduct of audits. In some generalized audit software packages, the statistical capabilities provided are fairly basic. They are oriented primarily toward support of statistical sampling activities. Analytical review often relies on using other statistical models, however, some of which are complex and require substantial computational support. For example, if auditors undertake time series modelling, they need various types of linear and nonlinear regression models; if auditors develop bankruptcy prediction models, they need discriminant analysis models. Statistical packages often offer very powerful modelling capabilities, and these capabilities are continually being enhanced. Moreover, the user interfaces are friendly, and high-quality help functions and documentation exist to support their users.

As with generalized audit software, the widespread deployment of microcomputers has contributed significantly to auditors' increased use of fourth-generation languages and generalized statistical packages. With suitable utility software, auditors can download or transfer a copy of the data they need from another computer. The microcomputer versions of fourth-generation languages and statistical packages can then be employed to access and manipulate the data and prepare reports. In this way, auditors can work in a standardized environment rather than having to deal with multiple hardware/software platforms.

UTILITY SOFTWARE

Utility software is software that performs fairly specific functions that are needed frequently, often by a large number of users, during the operation of computer systems. For example, they include copy programs, sort programs, disk search programs, and disk formatting programs. They often come as part of the suite of programs provided with major system software, such as operating systems, database management systems, fourth-generation languages, or data communications software. Much independent utility software has now been developed, however. It can be purchased to undertake functions that cannot be accomplished using the utility programs provided with system software or alternatively to undertake functions more effectively and efficiently than the utility programs provided with system software. Some also exists as freeware or shareware (although free use might be restricted only to personal use rather than business use). It might be downloaded, for example, from a site on the Internet.

Auditors use utility software for *five* reasons:

1. Utility software might have been developed to perform a specific security- or integrity-related function. For example, auditors might use a utility program to check for viruses on a disk.
2. Before auditors can use generalized audit software or other types of audit software, they might need to format and download data using utility software.
3. Utility software might perform functions that cannot be performed using generalized audit software or other audit software available. For example, auditors might use a utility program to try to recover a damaged disk file that contains data that is material to the audit. It is unlikely that audit software will be able to perform this function.
4. Utility software might accomplish audit tasks more effectively and more efficiently than audit software. For example, it might be possible to select certain kinds of data and print a report using generalized audit software. Utility software might perform the same functions but consume fewer resources and prepare better-formatted reports.
5. Auditors might use utility software to assist with the development of new audit software. For example, they might seek to develop audit modules that they can embed in application systems to collect evidence at the same time that application system processing occurs (see Chapter 18). Auditors might use utility

software to help test whether the modules work accurately and completely before they release the modules into production.

Because many utility software packages are now available, auditors might often have difficulty identifying what software exists, where it is located, how it can be obtained, and what functions it performs. Some operating system vendors have produced documentation that describes utility software that they and other organizations have developed which can assist auditors in their work (e.g., Lamb et al. 1991). Various Usenet groups on the Internet will also provide information about utility software that might be useful. It will help, also, if auditors understand the major types of utility software that exist so they can perhaps pinpoint better the software they need. In this light, the following subsections briefly describe major categories of utility software that are available.

Utility Software to Facilitate Assessing Security and Integrity

Some utility software has been developed specifically to implement, operate, maintain, and test various aspects of security and integrity within the information systems function. For example, several security- or integrity-related utilities have been developed with system administrators in mind. In other words, they have been designed to assist those people who are responsible for managing operating system security and integrity. In this light, the utilities often are provided by the vendor of the operating system that system administrators are required to manage. Other utilities have been developed, however, as part of a package of utilities that many users will find useful (see, e.g., Leibsla 1991) or as standalone utilities that perform some specific security- or integrity-related function.

The following utilities illustrate those auditors might find useful from time to time:

Utility	*Function*
Virus scanner	Checks to determine whether a virus has corrupted a disk (Figure 16–7).
Damaged disk recovery	Diagnoses and attempts to repair damaged disks. Disk can be recovered in part or in total.
Unerase	Searches for and recovers erased files. Can be useful if data has been deleted to hide an irregularity.
Undo format	Recovers data if it has been lost because disk has been reformatted.
Software inventory manager	Identifies illegal software that is being used on microcomputers or local area networks. Can prevent installation of illegal software. Reduces exposures from software copyright and licensing violations. See Stocks et al. (1997).
Static security analyzer	Analyzes the security-relevant parts of a computer's file system. Detects whether the computer's security state and configuration files have changed in undesirable ways.
Dynamic security analyzer	Detects anomalous behavior on the part of users or patterns of events that are known to reflect misuse of a system.
Dial-up access risk analyzer	Detects unauthorized dial-up nodes in a network.
Access control analyzer	Analyzes how well access controls have been implemented and maintained within an access control package.
Invalid Social Security Numbers	Detects invalid U.S. Social Security Numbers.

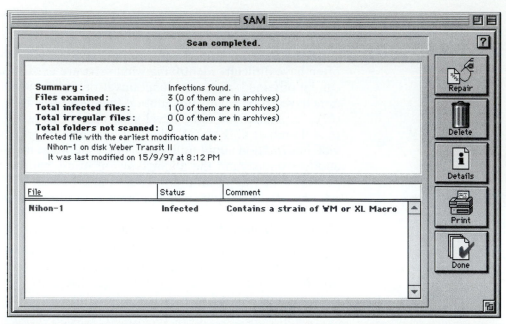

FIGURE 16–7. Output of a virus scanner.
Courtesy of Symantec Corporation.

Utility Software to Facilitate System Understanding

A major problem often confronted during the evidence-collection phase of an audit is how to gain quickly an understanding of the programs and data being audited. Understanding program logic has always been a problem. As organizations undertake more complex modelling of real-world phenomena, however, understanding the data associated with application systems also has become increasingly difficult. If the organization audited uses a CASE tool to document its systems, auditors can use various facilities incorporated within the tool to assist them to understand the systems—for example, the diagramming/charting and data dictionary facilities. In addition, from time to time the following utilities, designed primarily to assist programmers to maintain documentation on systems, can also assist auditors to understand application system programs and data. They should allow auditors to better direct their use of other evidence-collection techniques:

Utility	*Function*
Configuration analyzer	Provides information on the system configuration. For example, a listing is provided of hardware and software in use, network topology, memory usage, disks available and their utilization, and operating systems in use.
Flowcharter	Produces flowcharts from program source code or structured English.
Hierarchy charter	Produces hierarchical function charts from structured code. A module and its associated lower-level modules are diagrammed. The interfaces between modules are shown on the hierarchy chart.
Execution path mapper	Shows all the execution paths through a program by referencing paragraph names.
Cross-reference lister	Provides cross-reference listings for programs showing where a label (field) is referenced in a program.

Utility	*Function*
Data structure charter	Produces charts from the database definition showing the structure of data within the database. Useful if tree or network databases are used.
Transaction profile analyzer	Analyzes the characteristics of data updating the database, e.g., volume of a particular transaction type.
Text manager/Help system	If system documentation is stored on magnetic media or CD-ROM, allows selective retrieval of text (based on key words) from the documentation. Some systems have excellent online documentation based on hypertext facilities.

Utility Software to Facilitate Assessing Data Quality

Utility software that facilitates testing the quality of data can assist auditors in two ways. First, some utilities allow auditors to test the quality of data directly. For example, a pointer validation utility will check to see that the links between records in a database have not been corrupted. Second, some utilities facilitate use of other evidence-collection tools. For example, a sort package can be used to order data for reporting purposes. Auditors from time to time might make use of the following utilities:

Utility	*Function*
Find file	Searches magnetic media to find lost files, directories, and data.
Query facility	Allows selected retrieval of data from a variety of data structure types.
Rule validation	Independently discovers both known and unknown rules that govern database contents. Identifies possible errors in the database by detecting records that deviate from the rules.
Data structure conversion	Maps one data structure into another, e.g., a tree or network data structure into a flat (sequential) file.
Pointer validation utility	Searches storage structures that use pointers for invalid pointers, e.g., child nodes in a network that do not point back to their parent node.
Data manipulation utilities	Perform sundry functions, e.g., sort, merge, copy (selective copy), create, modify, delete, reorganize, format conversion, rename.
Dump/lister	Printing (sometimes with partial editing) of file contents.
Data comparison utility	Compares two sets of data and lists the differences.

Utility Software to Facilitate Assessing Program Quality

These utilities allow auditors to test a program's ability to maintain data integrity. The testing takes two forms. First, the validity of existing program logic is assessed. Second, the capability of the program to withstand abnormal conditions is assessed; for example, data input with severe outlier values can be submitted to the program. From time to time, the following utilities, developed primarily for programmers, might also assist auditors to assess program quality:

Utility	Function
Test data generator	Automatic generation of test files with data having specified attributes.
Trace	Monitors the status of programs as they step through various execution paths.
Online debugging facility	Permits online changes to object code and activation of programs at selected start points.
Execution path monitor	Indicates whether test data has traversed all execution paths within a program.
Output analyzer	Examines test output for various conditions, e.g., differences between output produced and a prior version of output.
Network simulator	Simulates performance in a communications network without having to use the network platform or have the network platform in place.
Terminal simulator	Allows simulation of online programs so testing can proceed without the hardware/software platform having to be available.
Test manager/driver	Manages the overall testing process for a program or set of programs.
Concurrent monitor	Captures selected events as application systems are running.
Source/object code comparison	Compares two versions of the source/object code of a program and lists differences.
Change tracker	Monitors changes to program source code libraries. Can be a facility within a librarian package.

Utility Software to Facilitate Program Development

To accomplish audit work, sometimes auditors need to write their own programs. For example, in some cases the costs of executing generalized audit software to collect the evidence auditors need might be prohibitive. They might have to process large data files, and they might also have to execute the program frequently. To reduce the costs associated with the audit, therefore, auditors might write specialized programs to obtain the evidence they need.

Whenever auditors develop software, they have the same objectives as a programmer—namely, fast, accurate preparation of a program that effectively and efficiently performs its required functions. Once again, CASE tools can be used to assist auditors to develop their own software. In addition, from time to time the following utilities can assist auditors in their work:

Utility	Function
Shorthand preprocessor	Allows source code to be written in an abbreviated form.
Macro	Inserts standard code into a program.
Decision-table preprocessor	Converts decision tables into source code.
Library copy	Copies source code from a library into a program.
Tidy	Formats source code so it is more readable.
Report generators	Simplifies coding of reports.
Language subset facility	Restricts source code used to an efficient subset.
Code optimizer	Operates on the source or object code of a program to remove inefficient code.
Volume test facility	Shows the performance of a program under stress.

Utility Software to Facilitate Assessing Operational Efficiency

One area where generalized audit software is likely to be of little help to evidence-collection efforts is in terms of evaluating systems efficiency. Often auditors need to use specialized utilities that have been developed to gather data on and report on how efficiently hardware and software resources are being used. These utilities perform three types of functions. First, they gather the necessary data on resource consumption. Second, they use this data to calculate statistics that reflect various aspects of operating efficiency. Third, they report these statistics in various forms: tables, bar charts, pie charts, histograms, frequency distributions, graphs, and so on. (Chapter 20 discusses these issues further.) Some major types of performance data that can be collected via these utilities, however, follow:

- Central processing unit utilization
- Real-memory utilization
- Secondary storage utilization
- Channel utilization
- Communication line utilization
- Peripheral utilization
- Task rates
- Response times
- Queue lengths
- Input/output (I/O) buffer excesses and deficiencies
- I/O concurrency
- Direct access seek times
- Paging rates/thrashing
- Frequency of checkpoints/recovery
- Storage media read/write errors
- Effects of changes in memory allocations to tasks
- Effects of changes in task priorities
- Deviations from transaction profiles
- Need for database restructuring/reorganization
- Performance of hashing algorithms/indexes

Interpreting these types of performance data is often difficult. Auditors might have to rely on performance-monitoring experts to explain the implications of the data they have obtained for the judgments they must make on efficiency-related issues.

EXPERT SYSTEMS

Expert systems are programs that encapsulate the knowledge that human experts have acquired about a particular domain and possess capabilities to reproduce this knowledge when presented with a particular problem. Throughout the 1980s, several audit firms, internal audit groups, and independent vendors expended substantial resources to develop expert systems to assist with audit work. In light of the success enjoyed with these expert systems, development work has continued. As a result, auditors can now use expert systems to assist them with both evidence-collection and evidence-evaluation activities.

Motivations for Using Expert Systems

There are three major reasons why auditors might develop, maintain, and use expert systems:

1. Expert systems make available to many auditors the knowledge typically possessed by only a few auditors. By definition, expertise is a scarce resource. When expertise is embodied in an expert system, however, it can be accessed and used widely without the expert having to be present. Thus, expert systems provide a mechanism for effectively disseminating and operationalizing expertise in the audit domain.

2. Because computer technology evolves rapidly, it is difficult for auditors to remain knowledgeable across the range of technologies they are likely to confront in an audit. They might attempt to handle this complexity by designating certain audit colleagues as having responsibility for remaining current in a particular technology, embodying their expertise in an expert system, and disseminating their expertise via the expert system.

3. Expert systems provide a mechanism for increasing consensus and consistency in auditors' evaluation judgments. Because expert systems can be used to guide auditors through a series of judgmental steps, they help ensure that (a) important judgments are not omitted; (b) auditors are aware of significant information that may affect their judgment; (c) auditors are alerted to judgmental inconsistencies; (d) auditors are aware of alternative judgments that might be made on the basis of the evidence available; and (e) auditors maintain a proper record of documentation to support their decision making.

In light of these motivations, potentially expert systems might affect both the effectiveness and efficiency of audits. Research conducted by Baldwin-Morgan (1993) indicates, however, that the primary impact of expert systems has been and is likely to continue to be on audit *effectiveness* rather than audit efficiency. Auditors should not hope, therefore, to reduce the costs of audits via expert systems.

Components of an Expert System

To emulate human expertise, an expert system has at least two major components (Figure 16–8). First, domain knowledge elicited from an expert is stored in a *knowledge base*. The knowledge base contains well-established facts about the domain of interest and rules that represent the heuristics used by experts to solve problems in the domain. Second, an *inference engine* uses the knowledge

FIGURE 16–8. Major components in an expert system.

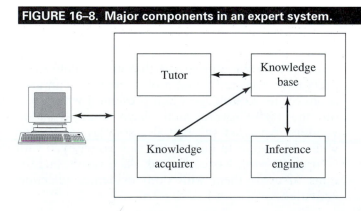

TABLE 16–2   Example Rules within Knowledge Base of an Expert System for Accounts Receivable Application

1. IF   (a) batch controls are not used over input data
   THEN   unauthorized changes can be made to cash receipts transactions
2. IF   (a) batch controls are used over input data
             (b) batch controls are not checked
   THEN   unauthorized changes can be made to cash receipts transactions
3. IF   (a) batch controls are used over input data
             (b) batch controls are checked
             (c) a batch register is not maintained
   THEN   unauthorized changes can be made to cash receipts transactions
4. IF   (a) unauthorized changes can be made to cash receipts transactions
             (b) bank deposits and cash receipts transactions are not independently reconciled
   THEN   an accounts receivable fraud can occur
5. IF   (a) an accounts receivable fraud can occur
   THEN   allowance for doubtful debts may be understated
6. IF   (a) adequate control is not exercised over credit granting
   THEN   allowance for doubtful debts may be understated

base to solve particular problems presented to the expert system. It employs some type of logic to establish interrelationships among facts and rules to reach a conclusion about a problem in the domain of interest.

In some cases, two other components are also present in an expert system (Figure 16–8): *(1)* a *tutorial component* or *explanation facility* might be used to provide information to the user of the system about the line of reasoning employed to reach a particular conclusion and *(2)* a *knowledge acquisition component* might be used to elicit new knowledge from users so the expert system can progressively expand its capabilities.

The ways in which knowledge bases and inference engines are implemented in expert systems can vary considerably. Nevertheless, to provide a basic understanding of how expert systems can assist their evaluation judgment, Table 16–2 shows some data auditors might store within the knowledge base of an expert system they use to assist their evaluation judgment on accounts receivable systems. Note the peculiar form of this data when compared with the data stored in traditional data processing systems. The form is called a "production rule," and it is characterized by the "if . . . then" representation of the data. Production rules are not the only way of storing knowledge in an expert system. For example, knowledge might be stored as cases and retrieved to support case-based reasoning—that is, reasoning on the basis of the similarity between the current problem situation and prior problem situations (see, e.g., Kolodner 1993). Nonetheless, production rules are commonly used to store knowledge that characterizes the audit domain.

To illustrate how the rules in the production-rule based expert system are used, assume we present two findings to the expert system based on evidence collected about a particular accounts receivable system: *(1)* batch controls are used but not checked within the accounts receivable system and *(2)* bank deposits and cash receipt transactions are not independently reconciled. Assume, also, that the inference engine in the expert system employs a "forward chaining" strategy to reach conclusions. Using this strategy, the system attempts to deduce new facts about the accounts receivable system by matching the existing facts with the antecedent parts of the production rules. When a match occurs, the consequent part of the production rule is added to the knowledge base as a new fact. The pattern matching activities then continue until no new conclusion can be reached.

Given the rules in Table 16–2, the inference engine would proceed sequentially until it reached Rule 2. At this point, some of the facts presented to the expert system match the antecedent part of the rule—the "if" part of the rule. The consequent—the "then" part of the rule—provides a new fact about the accounts receivable system—namely, that unauthorized changes can be made to cash receipts transactions. The inference engine proceeds further looking for a match between the antecedent part of some rule and the facts it now has available within the knowledge base. It would find a match at Rule 4. As a result, it would add a new fact to the knowledge base—namely, that an accounts receivable fraud could occur within the system. Further search would produce a match with Rule 5. The system would conclude that the allowance for doubtful debts could be understated within the accounts receivable system. Note from Table 16–2 that this conclusion could also be reached on the basis of other facts presented to the system.

Types of Audit Expert Systems

Most audit expert systems that have been developed can be assigned to one of four categories:

1. *Risk analysis.* The expert system will evaluate materiality and various types of risk associated with the auditee—for example, the likelihood that the auditee's management will prepare fraudulent financial statements.
2. *Internal control evaluation.* Based on the reliability evaluations of individual internal controls, the expert system will identify likely exposures that exist.
3. *Audit program planning.* The expert system will recommend a set of audit procedures to be conducted on the basis of the characteristics of the auditee and perhaps the results of a preliminary review or internal control evaluation.
4. *Technical advice.* The expert system assists by providing advice on various technical issues that are often encountered during the audit—for example, evaluating the adequacy of the doubtful debts provision, or determining whether the financial statements comply with various statutory disclosure requirements.

If auditors' need for expert advice falls outside these areas, they might have difficulty identifying an expert system that they can employ. Of course, over time, other types of expert systems will be developed that auditors will be able to use. Because expert systems are costly to develop and often require long periods of testing before they are deemed reliable, however, the range of choice is likely to remain limited.

NEURAL NETWORK SOFTWARE

Neural networks were developed within the field of artificial intelligence as tools primarily to undertake pattern recognition, learning, and classification. Their name derives from the fact that their architecture is based on the structure and functioning of the neurons in our brains. For example, Figure 16–9 shows the structure of a neuron and a multilayered neural network. Roughly,

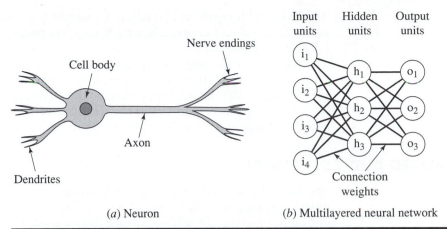

Input   Hidden   Output
units   units   units

Connection
weights

(a) Neuron   *(b)* Multilayered neural network

FIGURE 16–9. Brain neurons and neural networks.

the input units in the network represent the dendrites in the neuron, the hidden units represent the cell body, and the output units represent the axon (or perhaps the nerve endings).

To gain a basic appreciation of how neural networks function, consider a learning application that is relevant to auditors' work. Assume that we want to train a neural network to recognize patterns in data that manifest irregularities in a sales application. To train the network, ideally we will have a large number of cases, some in which irregularities are present and others in which irregularities are absent.

We first have to decide on the inputs we will provide to the neural network, which is a critical decision itself. In our sales application, we might have inputs like the number of sales over the past 12 months, cash balances over the past 12 months, the level of bad debts over the past 12 months, and so on. For each pattern or profile of inputs, we must know whether an irregularity is present. We train the network by submitting each pattern of inputs to the network plus the known outcome; that is, for the pattern, an irregularity does or does not exist.

Basically, the network functions as follows. The impact of the values of an input unit on a hidden unit will depend on the *weight* assigned to the connection between the input unit and the hidden unit. Whether each hidden unit "fires" depends on some function of the input unit values and the connection weights. In turn, the impact of a hidden unit firing on an output unit depends on the weight assigned to the connection between the hidden unit and the output unit. Whether the output unit fires depends on some function of the hidden units' firings and the connection weights.

In our example, assume that we have just one output unit in our neural network. It fires when it "believes" an irregularity exists, and it does not fire when it believes irregularities are not present. At the outset, the weights assigned to the connections might be random values. We submit our first case as input to the neural network. According to the vector of weights used in the network, it indicates whether an irregularity is present. We also "tell" the network the correct outcome. If it has made an incorrect decision, it uses various sorts of learning algorithms to adjust the weights assigned to its connections (see, e.g., Rich and Knight 1991). Learning is simply the process of adjusting weights within the network. And so the process goes on. We continue to provide cases to the network, and it continues to adjust its weights. In due course, the neural network should detect accurately whether an irregularity is present based on patterns in the input data.

Like expert systems, neural networks are not in widespread use among auditors. Nonetheless, their use is increasing. A number of retail banks, for example, are now using data mining systems developed using neural network shells to detect suspicious credit card transactions as a means of controlling credit card fraud (see, e.g., Brachman et al. 1996).

SPECIALIZED AUDIT SOFTWARE

Specialized audit software is software written in a procedure- or problem-oriented language to fulfill a specific set of audit tasks. The term "specialized" does not mean the software performs only a narrow range of functions. Indeed, in some cases the software has extensive functionality. Rather, specialized means auditors have developed and implemented the software where the purposes and users of the software are well-defined before the software is written. On the other hand, with generalized software, the specific tasks to be undertaken by the software and the identity of users will not be known at the outset.

Reasons for Developing Specialized Audit Software

There are six reasons auditors might develop specialized audit software:

1. *Unavailability of alternative software.* Occasionally, auditors might encounter situations in which no generalized software is available to perform audit procedures. For example, the auditee might have developed or purchased some type of specialized hardware platform on which only a minimal suite of software will run.

2. *Functional limitations of alternative software.* Even if auditors have generalized software available to perform an audit task, its functionality might be limited. For example, government auditors sometimes undertake complex information processing activities to check for errors and irregularities. They match data from tax returns, bank accounts, share transactions, welfare payments, and so on, to identify whether citizens are defrauding their government. The generalized software available to government auditors might not be capable of processing the large number of files that must be matched concurrently nor handling the complex data formats and file structures that have been used.

3. *Efficiency considerations.* In some cases, the audit tasks to be undertaken consume substantial resources, perhaps because auditors have to access large databases or have to perform audit tasks frequently. For example, in the complex matching task sometimes undertaken by government auditors examined previously, processing efficiency is often a primary objective. The matching task can be very costly because large, complex data files have to be processed. In this light, government auditors often develop specialized audit software because it will perform the matching task more efficiently than generalized software.

4. *Increased understanding of systems.* Sometimes the systems to be audited are complex. Nonetheless, it is important that auditors gain a proper understanding of the system as a basis for conducting the audit. One way that they might seek to gain this understanding is to prepare program specifications and to write the source code for specialized audit software. In the case of the computer matching example examined previously, government auditors might gain

valuable insights into the application systems that process the files used in the matching task if they participate in the development and implementation of the specialized software used to carry out the matching task.

5. *Opportunity for easy implementation.* Opportunities sometimes exist to develop and implement specialized audit software quickly and easily. For example, auditors might be able to insert a few instructions in an application system that gathers data that is critical to a judgment on the reliability of controls in an application system.

6. *Increased auditor independence/respect.* To the extent that auditors develop their own software and are not reliant on the auditee to provide software or staff support, they are more independent in the conduct of their audit. Moreover, auditors have an opportunity to demonstrate professional competence to the auditee. As a result, the auditee might have increased respect for their work. In the case of the government matching example examined previously, this respect and confidence in the auditor's abilities could be essential to obtaining support by the legislature to continue matching work. If the legislature loses confidence in its auditors, it might deem that the rights of individual persons overrule the need to search out fraud. As a result, it might order that the matching activities be stopped.

One important area where auditors often have to prepare specialized audit software is in the development and implementation of concurrent auditing techniques. Concurrent auditing techniques collect audit evidence at the same time as the application system is processing production data. They require audit hooks, modules, or routines to be embedded in the application system to select the evidence required. These are often implemented via specialized program code. (We return to this topic in Chapter 18.)

Development and Implementation of Specialized Audit Software

Specialized audit software can be developed and implemented in three ways. First, auditors can take total responsibility for developing and implementing the software themselves. This approach allows auditors to exercise a high level of control over the software. To produce high-quality software, however, auditors must possess good analysis, design, and programming skills. Second, internal auditors can ask programmers in their own organization to develop and implement the software. Alternatively, external auditors can ask programmers in the client organization to develop and implement the software. Third, auditors could ask an outside software vendor to prepare the software. Auditors might adopt this approach if the software is especially sensitive. Though the costs might be higher, using the services of an independent third party provides extra assurance that integrity violations have not occurred during the development and implementation process.

Whatever approach auditors use to develop and implement specialized audit software, they must exercise careful control over the development and implementation process to ensure that the software meets their objectives and the integrity of the software is preserved. Auditors can exercise most control when they prepare the software themselves. If auditors use other personnel to prepare the software, however, they should still take responsibility for preparing program specifications, managing the programming process, performing acceptance testing, and preparing user documentation. Unless auditors perform these tasks, they must be circumspect about placing reliance on the integrity of the program.

OTHER AUDIT SOFTWARE

Over the years, other types of software have been developed to assist auditors in their audit work. The following examples illustrate the varied nature of this software:

1. Burns and Loebbecke (1975) have shown how software can be written to simulate the operations of an internal control system. This software can be used to estimate the dollar error that might occur in accounts as a result of weaknesses in the internal control system.
2. Garner and Tsui (1985) have developed questionnaire generator software. Users indicate potential weaknesses in an internal control system. The software then suggests questions and issues that might be pursued to tease out the nature and extent of the internal control weaknesses.
3. Bailey et al. (1985) have developed a system that allows users to describe the characteristics of an internal control system. The system produces, as output, a model of the internal control system. It also allows users to ask questions about various characteristics of the internal control system to make an assessment about whether various internal control objectives are being met.
4. Hansen and Messier (1984) have proposed the use of a relational database management system to represent the complex interrelationships among controls, their locations, vulnerabilities that result if they are absent, and possible exposures. This data can be incorporated into a decision support system that will assist users to make decisions about where they should collect evidence on the reliability of controls.

We will not discuss this software any further because it has not achieved widespread use. Often it has been developed on an experimental basis by researchers who work in the auditing area. Nonetheless, we need to be aware that such software exists. We might encounter audits in which use of the software potentially will give us high payoffs. Moreover, we should strive constantly to improve our audit practice. Even if we cannot use the software directly, we might obtain insights from reading about it that help us to undertake more cost-effective audits.

CONTROL OF AUDIT SOFTWARE

When using audit software for evidence-collection purposes, auditors should evaluate the level of control they are able to exercise over the software. If auditors have to employ software controlled by other parties, they run the risk that the software might have been modified improperly (either deliberately or unintentionally). The results produced using the software, therefore, might not be accurate or complete. Similarly, if auditors must rely on other parties to execute software on their behalf, they run the risk that the results obtained will lack integrity. The execution of the software might have been compromised in some way. Alternatively, a mistake might have been made when executing the software.

If auditors have to employ software controlled by other parties, there are two ways they can determine whether the software has been modified:

1. *Hash total.* At a prior time, auditors might have been able to obtain or calculate a hash total of the object code for the software. They can then calculate the hash total for the object code of the program provided and compare the result obtained with the previous hash total calculated. If auditors are to be able

to rely on the results, they need to have control over the program that computes the hash total.

2. *Test data.* Auditors can develop test data to test out those functions in the software on which they intend to rely. Unless auditors are confident that the software has not been modified since they last used it, they will need to execute the test data each time they employ the software for evidence collection purposes.

If auditors rely on other parties to execute software on their behalf, they must carefully examine the results provided for evidence of any errors or irregularities. Auditors might desk check a sample of computations performed by the software, for example, to satisfy themselves that the software has been executed properly.

If auditors maintain an independently controlled library of audit software, unauthorized modifications to the software are less likely to occur. Auditors can protect the library via access controls. Moreover, they might be able to maintain the software on a machine that they control. For external auditors, maintaining an independent library on their own machine has an additional advantage: Providing they can download data to their own machine, they are less constrained in carrying out audit work by the availability of software on the client platform audited.

SUMMARY

There is a variety of software available to auditors to assist in evidence collection. For a start, auditors can use generalized audit software, which has been designed specifically to allow them to gain access to and manipulate data maintained on computer storage media. It provides powerful functions that enable access to files maintained in a variety of formats, sorting and merging of files, selection of data that satisfy certain conditions, statistical sampling and evaluation of data, arithmetic operations on data, stratification and frequency analysis of data, file creation and updating, and flexible reporting of results obtained.

Sometimes auditors also might be able to use industry-specific audit software, which has been designed to provide audit functions that they will find useful during the conduct of audits in specific industries. Auditors can also use high-level languages, such as those provided in fourth-generation software or statistical software, whenever they provide easier access to data or a more comprehensive range of functions than generalized audit software. From time to time, auditors might use utility software to assess security and integrity within an application system, facilitate their understanding of the application system to be audited, assess data quality, assess program quality, facilitate the development of other software that they might need to conduct an audit, and assess the operational efficiency of an application system.

Various types of decision support software are also available. For example, expert systems have been developed to undertake risk analysis, internal control evaluation, and audit program planning. Some expert systems also provide advice on different technical issues that are often encountered during an audit—for example, evaluating the adequacy of doubtful debts provision.

At times, auditors might have to develop specialized audit software when no other software is available to perform an audit function or the other software is functionally limited or operationally inefficient. Other advantages might also accrue from developing specialized audit software—for example, increased understanding of the application system to be audited and improved independence because they are no longer reliant on other parties to assist them in the conduct of the audit.

When auditors use audit software for evidence-collection purposes, they must exercise careful control over the software to ensure it has not been modified improperly and that the results produced using the software have integrity. If they have to employ software controlled by other parties, they can use hash totals and test data to detect any modifications that might have been made to the software. If auditors rely on other parties to execute software on their behalf, they should carefully examine the results produced to determine whether they are accurate and complete. If auditors can maintain an independent library of audit software on a machine they control, they can have more confidence in the integrity of the results produced using audit software.

Review Questions

16–1 Briefly discuss the motivations for developing generalized software specifically for audit purposes. Even though generalized retrieval software already existed before audit software was developed, why did auditors prefer to develop their own software packages?

16–2 What is a generalized audit software package?

16–3 Without using the examples provided in the chapter, give *two* examples of how auditors might use each of the following functional capabilities of audit software:
a File reorganization
b Statistical
c Arithmetic
d Stratification and frequency analysis

16–4 Briefly explain the difference between a Boolean operator and a relational (conditional) operator used in a selection expression for generalized audit software. Be sure to explain their different purposes from an audit perspective.

16–5 What purposes might auditors seek to achieve in using generalized audit software to examine the quality of data maintained on an application system files?

16–6 Briefly explain the parallel simulation technique. What is the purpose of using parallel simulation? Outline some of the advantages and disadvantages of using this technique for audit purposes.

16–7 How can auditors use generalized audit software to examine the existence of entities that the data purports to represent?

16–8 How can auditors use generalized audit software to assist the conduct of analytical review?

16–9 Why does generalized audit software have only limited capabilities for verifying the processing logic within an application system and the propensity of the application system for error?

16–10 Give *two* reasons why auditors might wish to download data from another machine onto the machine on which their generalized audit software package resides.

16–11 Give *two* ways in which auditors might transfer data from a mainframe computer to a microcomputer so that they can use a microcomputer-based generalized audit software package to access and manipulate the data.

16–12 Briefly describe the major phases that must be managed during the development and implementation of a generalized audit software application.

16–13 Briefly describe the nature of industry-specific audit software. How does it differ from generalized audit software?

16–14 What are the relative advantages of industry-specific audit software versus generalized audit software?

16–15 Briefly explain the nature of a high-level programming language. How are high-level programming languages useful to auditors?

16–16 Briefly explain the nature of utility software. Give *two* locations where auditors might find utility software that could assist them.

16–17 Briefly describe *two* utilities that auditors can use to assist their evaluation of information system security and integrity.

16–18 How might auditors use the following utilities during the evidence-collection phase of an audit?
  a Configuration utility
  b Pointer validation utility
  c Trace
  d Report generator

16–19 Give *three* ways in which utility software might be used to facilitate auditors' assessment of operational efficiency in an application system.

16–20 Give *three* major reasons why auditors might develop, maintain, and use expert systems.

16–21 How might an expert system assist auditors in the following tasks:
  a Analyzing the inherent risk associated with an audit
  b Evaluating the reliability of an internal control system
  c Planning an audit program.
  d Evaluating the adequacy of doubtful debts provision

16–22 Briefly explain the nature of a neural network. What are its major components? How can neural networks assist auditors?

16–23 Briefly explain the nature of specialized audit software. Give *three* reasons why auditors might develop specialized audit software.

16–24 Why is it important that auditors maintain careful control over any software they use during the conduct of an audit? If the software they use is controlled by other parties, give *two* ways in which auditors might attempt to determine whether the software has been modified since they last used it.

Multiple-Choice Questions

16–1 Which of the following was not a motivation for developing generalized audit software?
  a Need to develop an audit capability quickly in light of changing audit objectives
  b Provide an audit capability for auditors relatively unskilled in the use of computers
  c Provide certain functional capabilities specific to the auditor's needs
  d Unavailability of any other form of generalized interrogation software that could undertake audit functions

16–2 What type of functional capabilities of generalized audit software do auditors use when they instruct the software to read a zoned field?
  a Arithmetic capabilities
  b File reorganization capabilities
  c File access capabilities
  d File creation and updating capabilities

16–3 The expression PRICE LE 20 OR (PRICE GT 50 AND DISCOUNT LE 5) OR PRICE EQ ZEROS would extract products from a file that have a price:

a Less than or equal to 20, or a price greater than 50 and at the same time a discount less than 6, or a price equal to zero

b Less than 20 or greater than 50 and in either case a discount less than 5, or a price equal to zero

c Less than or equal to 20 and discount less than or equal to 5, or a price greater than 50 and discount less than or equal to 5, or a price equal to zero

d Less than 20, or a price greater than 50 and at the same time a discount less than 5, or a price equal to zero

16–4 A functional capability that is likely to exist in generalized audit software but is unlikely to exist in many other generalized interrogation languages is a:

a Boolean expression capability

b Statistical sampling capability

c File reorganization capability

d Merge capability

16–5 Parallel simulation involves the auditor:

a Writing a program to completely replicate the processing logic of an application program

b Using the random number capabilities of generalized audit software to simulate financial transactions for a period

c Writing a program to replicate those application processes that are material to an audit opinion and using this program to reprocess application system data

d Using generalized audit software to perform a parallel run during the implementation of a new application system

16–6 Which of the following functional capabilities in generalized audit software are auditors *most likely* to use to examine whether the entities that the data purports to represent do, in fact, exist?

a Statistical sampling capability

b Stratification and frequency analysis capability

c Analytical review capability

d Arithmetic capability

16–7 Which of the following is *not* a functional limitation of generalized audit software?

a Permits *ex post* auditing only and not concurrent auditing

b Difficult to determine an application system's propensity for error using generalized audit software

c Limited capabilities for verifying processing logic

d Limited capabilities for recomputing material arithmetic expressions

16–8 Which of the following is *most likely* to be a reason for wanting to transfer a file from a mainframe computer to a microcomputer on which generalized audit software resides?

a Auditors can process the file faster on the microcomputer and thereby achieve audit objectives more efficiently

b Auditors can exercise better control over use of generalized audit software

c There is less likelihood that the file will be subject to unauthorized modifications

d Auditors avoid working with error-prone data format conversions when they work with the file on the mainframe

16–9 During the feasibility analysis and planning stage of a generalized audit software application, which of the following factors is *least likely* to affect the decision on whether to proceed with the application?

a The application system to be audited is large and complex

b The application system to be audited has large data files

c The application to be audited is poorly documented

d The application to be audited has been programmed using a third-generation language

16–10 Compared with generalized audit software, which of the following is *unlikely* to be true of industry-specific audit software?

a It will be most useful for external auditors who perform a small number of audits within a particular industry

b It will perform its functions more efficiently than generalized audit software

c Commands will be easier to specify using industry-specific audit software

d It is more likely to include functions that check for legislative compliance within an industry

16–11 Which of the following is *least likely* to be a reason why auditors use high-level languages instead of generalized audit software to perform evidence-gathering functions?

a They contain more functions that are useful to auditors than generalized audit software

b They provide a more user-friendly interface than generalized audit software

c They will be better supported by the organization that is being audited

d They allow auditors to avoid difficult downloading of data from one computer to another computer

16–12 Which of the following is *most likely* to be a reason for using utility software rather than generalized audit software during the conduct of an audit?

a Independence will be breached if both external auditors and internal auditors use the same generalized audit software package

b There are functional limitations to generalized audit software in terms of the audit tasks to be accomplished

c Utility software to accomplish the auditor's task is more widely available than generalized audit software

d The instructions for using utility software are often better documented than the instructions for using generalized audit software

16–13 Which of the following functions is performed by a dial-up access risk analyzer?

a Analyzes how well dial-up access controls have been implemented within an access control package

b Counts the number of times incorrect passwords have been submitted at dial-up nodes

c Detects the existence of unauthorized dial-up nodes in a network

d Determines whether password controls have been implemented over dial-up nodes

16–14 Which of the following tasks probably would be most difficult to perform using utility software?

a Merging data on two files

b Dumping several records in a database to check their format

c Selecting a dollar unit sample for confirmation

d Converting one data format to another data format

16–15 A hierarchy charter primarily would be useful in helping auditors to:
a Assess data quality in an application system
b Evaluate the efficiency of an application system
c Understand an application system
d Develop and implement specialized audit software

16–16 Which of the following utilities can be used to directly examine the quality of data in a database?
a Tidy facility
b Test manager/driver
c Trace
d Pointer validation utility

16–17 Which of the following utilities can be used to directly examine the authenticity, accuracy, and completeness of program logic?
a Transaction profile analyzer
b Output analyzer
c Prompter
d Text manager

16–18 Which of the following is *least likely* to be an outcome of auditors' use of expert systems?
a Increased consensus in evaluation judgments
b Better dissemination of expertise in relation to new technology
c Better documentation in support of audit judgments made
d Improved efficiency in the conduct of an audit

16–19 The component in an expert system that provides information to auditors about the line of reasoning used to reach a conclusion is the:
a Inference engine
b Knowledge acquirer
c Knowledge base
d Tutor

16–20 Which of the following is *not* true about the production rules that are used in expert systems developed to assist auditors?
a They are used to represent the heuristics sometimes employed by auditors to make judgments
b They are the only technique currently available for storing the knowledge that characterizes the audit domain
c The antecedent part of a production rule specifies the condition that leads to a particular action
d They are stored in the knowledge base of an expert system

16–21 Which of the following components of a neural network designed to assist auditors to detect fraud will be altered during its training period?
a Input components
b Output components
c Hidden components
d Connection weight components

16–22 Which of the following is *not* a reason for having client personnel instead of auditors develop and implement specialized audit software?
a Auditors might lack the expertise to write effective and efficient software
b The software might also be useful to client personnel
c Communications between auditors and client personnel are improved
d The time-consuming task of preparing program specifications is alleviated

16–23 Which of the following is *least likely* to be a reason for auditors wanting to exercise control over any audit software that they use?

  a To ensure excessive resources are not consumed when executing the software

  b To prevent intentional compromise of the software

  c To try to avoid mistakes being made when executing the software

  d To ensure the results obtained via the software are complete

Exercises and Cases

16–1 Livalife Insurance is a large insurance company with offices scattered throughout the United States and more than 1,000 independent agents. You are a member of the external audit team. During the year-end work, you are called to a meeting with your manager. He explains that he is concerned about the activities of one agent who seems to have submitted an abnormal number of change-of-address forms for her clients. All the change-of-address forms give a single new address—namely, the agent's home address. On many of the policies taken out by the agent's clients, personal loans have been obtained. Your manager explains that he is concerned that the agent might be illegally obtaining policy loans on her clients' policies, unbeknown to her clients.

Required: Explain how you could use generalized audit software to find out whether the agent has been illegally taking out policy loans on her clients' policies. Assuming that the agent has been acting illegally, what controls would you recommend instituting to prevent this type of fraud happening again?

16–2 The following data items are maintained in a company's database for each inventory item that it holds in stock:

  part number
  part name
  part description
  bin location
  unit price
  unit cost
  unit measure
  quantity on hand
  quantity on order
  item activity
  special prices allowed

Required: List the audit objectives that you could accomplish by using generalized audit software to access and manipulate these data items. Briefly explain how you would use generalized audit software to accomplish these objectives. *Hint:* You might wish to consult a standard auditing textbook to find typical audit objectives and a typical audit program (set of audit procedures) for inventory. You should then try to work out how generalized audit software could be used to assist you in the execution of this program.

16–3 The following data items are maintained in a company's database for each fixed asset item that it owns:

  fixed asset number
  fixed asset description
  fixed asset classification
  location

responsible manager
maintenance schedule
purchase price
purchase date
vendor information
depreciation method
current depreciated value
salvage value
depreciation amount
taxable value
insured value
insurance vendor

Required: List the audit objectives that you could accomplish by using generalized audit software to access and manipulate these data items. Briefly explain how you would use generalized audit software to accomplish these objectives. *Hint*: You might wish to consult a standard auditing textbook to find typical audit objectives and a typical audit program (set of audit procedures) for fixed assets. You should then try to work out how generalized audit software could be used to assist you in the execution of this program.

16–4 The following data items are used to submit payroll time data to a payroll system:

employee number
regular hours
overtime hours
expenses
commission payments
sick time
vacation time
leave time without pay

Required: List the audit objectives that you could accomplish by using generalized audit software to access and manipulate these data items. Briefly explain how you would use generalized audit software to accomplish these objectives. *Hint*: You might wish to consult a standard auditing textbook to find typical audit objectives and a typical audit program (set of audit procedures) for payroll. You should then try to work out how generalized audit software could be used to assist you in the execution of this program.

16–5 This exercise requires that you have a knowledge of the high-level language called SQL. SQL has been implemented in many database management systems as a means of defining, creating, updating, and querying data. If you are not familiar with the language, you are likely to find a description provided in many books on database management (e.g., Elmasri and Navathe 1994). In addition, you will find it helpful if you have a basic knowledge of database normalization (see Appendix 4.4 in this book).

You are the senior information systems auditor in the internal audit group of Baccus Bathrooms Ltd. (BBL), a major manufacturer and distributor of bathroom equipment, fittings, and accessories. BBL sells its products in both the domestic market and international markets.

One day, you are called to a meeting with your boss, who is the manager of internal audit for BBL. He indicates that he has become increasingly concerned about the quality of controls over BBL's inventory. There have been various indicators of problems with the inventory system; for example, some unexpected stockouts have occurred, erroneous and missing data has been found in several inventory reports, and inventory update programs have had to be aborted occasionally because of error conditions that have been encountered.

BBL uses a major database management system to support its database. In this light, your boss asks you to use the SQL query capabilities provided in the system to evaluate the quality of the data in the inventory database. In particular, he asks you to focus initially on raw-materials inventory because he suspects that significant problems exist in this area. He wants you to report back to him quickly as he is concerned that material losses might occur because of the apparent problems in the inventory system.

As an initial step, you obtain the definition of five major relations in the raw-materials database. The relations are in (3NF) to mitigate problems that occur with possible update anomalies. The attributes (fields) in each of the five relations are as follows:

Item-Table

itemno	character (10)	identifier for raw-material item
descript	character (40)	description of the inventory item
vendno	number (5)	identifier of the vendor who supplies item
unitprice	number	unit price of item
qoh	number	quantity of item on hand
qoo	number	quantity of item on order
rlev	number	reorder level
eoq	number	economic order quantity
reorderdate	date	date of reorder

Vendor-Table

vendno	number (5)	identifier of the vendor who supplies item
vendname	character (20)	name of vendor who supplies item
street	character (20)	street address of vendor
city	character (20)	city address of vendor
state	character (5)	state address of vendor
country	character (20)	country address of vendor
postcode	character (8)	postcode/zipcode address of vendor

Issues-Table

jobno	number	identifier for production job
itemno	character (10)	identifier for raw-material item
issuedate	date	date of issue of raw material to production job
qtyissue	number	quantity issued to production job

Returns-Table

jobno	number	identifier for production job
itemno	character (10)	identifier for raw-material item
returndate	date	date item returned to inventory
qtyreturn	number	quantity returned to inventory
qtydefect	number	quantity returned because defective

Receipts-Table

receiptno	number	receiving report number
itemno	character (10)	identifier for raw-material item
receiptdate	date	date item received
receiptqty	number	quantity received
runitprice	number	unit price of item received

To examine the quality of data in the database, you decide to commence with the following queries on the database:

1. Find any inventory items without an item description or a unit price.
2. Find any items that have the same item description.
3. Find any items where the quantity on hand exceeds the reorder level plus the reorder quantity.
4. Find any items where the quantity on hand is less than the reorder level but the reorder date field is blank.
5. Find any items where the total quantity received is greater than twice the quantity on hand.
6. Find any items where the quantity returned as defective is more than 10 percent of the total quantity returned.
7. Find any items where the unit price in receipts is not equal to the unit price in inventory.
8. Find any item where the number of the item returned does not match the number of any item in inventory.
9. Find any item for which the quantity issued over the last month exceeds the quantity on hand plus the quantity on order.
10. Find any item for which no vendor entry exists in the vendor table.

Required: For each of these queries, state the audit objective(s) you are trying to achieve. Also provide an SQL command(s) that will satisfy the query. *Hint:* If you have access to a database management system that provides an SQL interface, you might find it useful to define these relations in the database, populate the relations with some test data, and try the SQL commands on the database you have created. You will then be able to identify any syntactic or semantic errors you have made in formulating the queries.

16–6 You are an information systems auditor in an external audit firm that undertakes a large number of audits of financial institutions, especially banks and credit unions. One day your partner requests a meeting with you to discuss ways in which information technology might be used to improve the effectiveness and efficiency of your firm's audits. She is concerned about the possibility of losing clients unless audit costs are reduced to meet competitive moves by other audit firms. She is also concerned that the risks faced by many of the firm's clients are increasing as they face a more aggressive market for consumer loans. She wonders whether clients are now making adequate provision for bad consumer loans in their financial statements. She fears that some clients might eventually fail because, in her view, they have been making inappropriate loans. She also fears that her audit staff sometimes lack the experience and knowledge to recognize high-risk conditions and adjust their audit approach accordingly.

Your partner asks you about the possibility of building an expert system to help her staff in their audit work. She believes that sufficient expertise exists within the firm in relation to making consumer loans that an expert system could be constructed to assist audit staff evaluate the reliability of controls over consumer loans and the adequacy of client provisions for bad loans. Her view is that her audit staff could take the expert system with them on laptop computers to client premises and obtain the required input to the system during conversations with client staff. The system would then provide them with evaluations that they could use as the basis for planning their audit work.

As an initial step toward determining the feasibility of the expert system, she asks you to evaluate whether it is likely the contents of the knowledge base can be sufficiently well specified to build an expert system. She suggests that you consider the types of knowledge that would be relevant to the following factors when considering a consumer loan:

1. Customer's collateral,
2. Stability of the customer's employment record,
3. Amount and stability of the customer's income stream,
4. Customer's credit worthiness, and
5. Customer's existing obligations and spending patterns.

Required: For each of these factors, briefly describe some information that would need to be obtained to assist in an evaluation of the factor. Also, briefly describe how this information might bear upon the evaluation judgment (in other words, think about how this knowledge might be incorporated into, say, the production rules that would be implemented in the knowledge base of an expert system).

16–7 You are the manager of internal audit for a large bank. Over the past few years, you have become increasingly concerned about the extent of bad commercial loans that have had to be written off the bank's books. Competition in the marketplace for commercial loans has been intense. As a result, the bank has been forced to make loans to corporate customers that previously it would have declined. You are concerned, however, that at times the bank's commercial lending department acts imprudently. You fear that some of the department's decisions ultimately could lead to cash-flow difficulties and a run on the bank's deposits.

When you have raised these matters with the bank's Board of Directors, you have been met with skepticism. Some members of the Board have argued that the bank has had to take on riskier loans simply because it has to face the harsh realities of the marketplace. They argue that it is your job to evaluate whether adequate controls are in place over lending operations and to determine whether the provision for bad loans is adequate. They question you about whether these, in fact, are your concerns.

To obtain more evidence on whether your concerns are justified, you decide to have some specialized audit software written for you and your staff to use. You conclude that the purpose of the software should be to calculate various financial ratios and trends based upon the customer's financial statements. The software should then use these ratios and trends to provide a rating on a scale of 1 to 100 of the risk associated with a loan (in short, you are seeking to have a decision support system built). This rating should then be considered along with other information, such as the likely integrity of the customer's management, to reach an overall conclusion on the risk associated with the loan. You can then compare your assessment of the risk of the loan against the lending staff's assessment of the risk of the loan.

Required: Outline the specifications for the software that you want written. In particular, identify the ratios and trends that you will want calculated. *Hint:* You might want to consult a text on financial statement analysis to identify the ratios and trends that are likely to be important.

Answers to Multiple-Choice Questions

16–1	d	16–7	d	16–13	c	16–19	d
16–2	c	16–8	b	16–14	c	16–20	b
16–3	a	16–9	d	16–15	c	16–21	d
16–4	b	16–10	a	16–16	d	16–22	d
16–5	c	16–11	a	16–17	b	16–23	a
16–6	a	16–12	b	16–18	d		

REFERENCES

Baldwin-Morgan, Amelia Annette (1993), "The Impact of Expert Systems Audit Tools on Auditing Firms in the Year 2001: A Delphi Investigation," *Journal of Information Systems* (Spring), 16–34.

Brachman, Ronald J., Tom Khabaza, Willi Kloesgen, Gregory Piatetsky-Shapiro, and Evangelos Simoudis (1996), "Mining Business Databases," *Communications of the ACM* (November), 42–48.

Brown, Carol E., and David S. Murphy (1990), "The Use of Auditing Expert Systems in Public Accounting," *Journal of Information Systems* (Fall), 63–72.

———— and M. Phillips (1991), "Expert Systems for Internal Auditing," *Internal Auditor* (August), 23–28.

Capuder, Sr., Lawrence F. (1994), "Implementing Micro-Computer Based Audit Techniques," *EDP Auditing*. Boston: Auerbach Publications, Portfolio 73–02–26, 1–15.

Doo, Alan (1990), "Mainframe to Microcomputer File Transfer Techniques," *The EDP Auditor Journal*, IV, 81–87.

Elmasri, Ramez, and Shamkant B. Navathe (1994), *Fundamentals of Database Systems*, 2d ed. Redwood City, CA: Benjamin/Cummings.

Garcia, Marc A. (1990), "Microcomputer Audit Software: Uses and Comparisons by Dresser Industries Internal Audit," *The EDP Auditor Journal*, IV, 65–71.

Garsombke, H. P., and Tabor, R. H. (1986), "Factors Explaining the Use of EDP Audit Techniques," *Journal of Information Systems* (Fall), 48–66.

Gillevet, Joe (1995), "Utilizing CAATs to Determine the Possibility of Input Errors in Automated Systems," IS *Audit & Control Journal*, IV, 17–24.

Higgins, H. Ngo (1997), "SQL Language for Accounting Auditors," IS *Audit & Control Journal*, V, 22–24.

Kolodner, Janet (1993), *Case-Based Reasoning*. San Mateo, CA: Morgan Kaufmann.

Lamb, Jason, Stanley R. Jarocki, and Ana M. Seijas (1991), *NetWare Security: Configuring and Auditing a Trusted Environment*. Provo, UT: Novell, Inc.

Leibsla, Mel (1991), "Audit Use of Norton Utilities," *The EDP Auditor*, IV, 69–72.

Lovata, Linda M. (1988), "The Utilization of Generalized Audit Software," *Auditing: A Journal of Practice & Theory* (Fall), 72–86.

———— (1990), "Audit Technology and the Use of Computer Assisted Audit Techniques," *Journal of Information Systems* (Spring), 60–68.

Mair, William C. (1975), "Parallel Simulation—A Technique for Effective Verification of Computer Programs," *EDPACS* (April), 1–5.

Newman, Carolyn J., and Keagle W. Davis (1990), "Buyers' Guide in Microcomputer-Based Generalized Audit Software," *The EDP Auditor Journal*, IV, 25–49.

Olson, David L., and James F. Courtney (1992), *Decision Support Models and Expert Systems*. New York: Macmillan.

Reeve, R. C. (1984), "Trends in the Use of EDP Audit Techniques," *Australian Computer Journal* (May), 42–47.

Rich, Elaine, and Kevin Knight (1991), *Artificial Intelligence*, 2d ed. New York: McGraw-Hill.

Smaha, Stephen E., and Jessica Winslow (1994), "Software Tools for Detecting Misuse on UNIX Systems," *EDP Auditing*. Boston: Auerbach Publications, Portfolio 75–01–71, 1–11.

Stapleton, Donald C. (1992), "Auditing for Unauthorized Microcomputer Software," *EDP Auditing*. Boston: Auerbach Publications, Portfolio 73–01–40, 1–13.

Stocks, Morris H., Brian J. Reithel, Tommie Singleton, and Robert K. Robinson (1997), "An Empirical Investigation of Information Systems Audits and Software Piracy," *IS Audit & Control Journal*, VI, 32–40.

Tobinson, Gary L., and Gordon B. Davis (1981), "Actual Use and Perceived Utility of EDP Auditing Techniques," *EDP Auditor* (Spring), 1–22.

Van Dijk, J. C., and Paul Williams (1991), *Expert Systems in Auditing*. New York: Macmillan.

Williams, Paul, and Michael P. Cangemi (1990), "Microcomputer-Based Audit Tools," *The EDP Auditor Journal*, IV, 53–63.

CHAPTER
17

Code Review, Test Data, and Code Comparison

Chapter Outline

Chapter Key Points

■ Three evidence-collection techniques auditors can use primarily during substantive testing are (a) program code review, (b) test data, and (c) code comparison. Program code review involves reading source-code listings with a view to identifying defective program code. Test data involves executing a program using a sample of data to determine whether the program is defective. Code comparison involves using software to compare a source-code version or object-code version of a program against another version of the program that has known characteristics (e.g., auditors believe it to be error free).

■ Program code review, test data, and code comparison can be used as independent evidence-collection techniques. Sometimes, however, auditors might use them in a coordinated way. First, they can undertake code review to generate hypotheses about defects in the program. Next, they can use test data to determine whether their flaw hypotheses are confirmed. They can then have the defects in the program corrected to produce a "blueprint." Finally, auditors can use code comparison to compare production versions of the program against this blueprint to identify undocumented changes that have been made to the program.

■ On the basis of a few empirical studies, we can draw some tentative conclusions about where defects are likely to occur in programs: (a) a small number of modules will have a large number of faults, and a large number of modules will have none or a small number of faults; (b) requirements specification and design errors are just as likely to occur as coding errors; (c) design errors seem to relate primarily to the user interface, input/output devices, and the database; (d) coding errors seem to related primarily to incorrect computation, incorrect indexing, and incorrect control flow; and (e) defects relating to data management are more common than defects relating to computation.

■ The objectives of program source-code review are to identify erroneous code, unauthorized code, ineffective code, inefficient code, and nonstandard code. Source-code review involves seven steps: (a) on the basis of materiality and risk, selecting the source code to be examined; (b) reviewing the organization's programming standards to develop expectations about the characteristics of the code and likely defects in the code; (c) obtaining an understanding of the program's specifications as a basis for determining whether the program has the correct functionality; (d) obtaining an up-to-date listing of the source code; (e) reviewing the programming language used to implement the code to develop expectations about where defects are likely to occur in the code; (f) reviewing the source code in a systematic way to identify program defects; and (g) formulating flaw hypotheses that form the basis for further testing of the program.

■ The primary benefit of program source-code review is that it provides a level of detailed knowledge about a program that is difficult to acquire using other evidence-collection techniques.

The primary disadvantages are that it is time consuming and often difficult and costly to undertake.

■ Test data is reliable if it reveals a defect in a program when the program contains a defect. Unfortunately, we know of no way to ensure that reliable test data has been designed. Auditors should use a systematic approach to the design of test data, however, to achieve high levels of reliability in their test-data designs.

■ Two types of systematic approaches to the design of test data exist. Black-box, or specification-based testing methods, view the program to be tested as a black box. Test data is designed on the basis of the program's specifications rather than its internal control structure. White-box, or program-based testing methods, rely on the internal control structure of the program. Test data is designed on the basis of a direct examination of the program's source code.

■ Two types of black-box test-data design methods that auditors might use are equivalence partitioning and boundary value analysis. With equivalence partitioning, auditors divide the input domain of the program into classes where each element of a class is treated identically to all other members of the class, at least according to the specifications. Auditors can use decision tables and decision trees to help them identify the equivalence classes in a program's input domain. They then choose one element from each of the material equivalence classes to include within their test-data design. Providing a program is not defective in terms of its treatment of this element, auditors assume it is not defective in terms of its treatment of other elements in the equivalence class. With boundary value analysis, auditors again focus on the equivalence classes in a program's input domain. They choose test data items, however, that test how the program treats the boundary values of each material equivalence class. For example, if a program tests whether a value is greater than a certain amount, auditors will choose a test data value that is equal to the amount, just above the amount, and just below the amount. They will also test the boundary values for any material output of the program.

■ There are three objectives that auditors might seek to achieve when they undertake white-box test-data design. First, they can seek to achieve full statement coverage of a program, whereby they try to ensure that each statement in a program is executed at least once. Second, they can seek to ensure full branch coverage, whereby they seek to ensure that each statement is executed at least once and each branch is executed at least once. Third, they can seek to achieve full path coverage, whereby every logic path in the program is executed at least once. Full statement coverage is the easiest objective to achieve. For moderately complex programs, achieving full path coverage is often practically impossible.

■ Two types of white-box test-data design methods that auditors might use are basis path testing and loop testing. Basis path testing is an approach designed to achieve full branch coverage in a program. Auditors first convert the program into a flowgraph and then design test data to traverse each of the independent paths in the flowgraph. An independent path is one that introduces at least one node in the flowgraph that has not been traversed by another path. The number of independent paths in a program can be determined by calculating a measure called McCabe's cyclomatic complexity number which, as its name implies, is also a measure of the complexity of the program. Loop testing seeks to test whether the material loops in a program have any defects. Because the number of paths through a loop or a set of nested loops can be large or practically infinite, loop testing focuses on those aspects of a loop or set of loops that are likely to be defective.

■ Creating test data is often difficult and time-consuming. One approach auditors can use is to rely on existing production data and to modify this data so it complies with test-data design. Another approach auditors might use is to rely on test data that has been designed by the organization they are auditing and again modify this test data so it complies with test-data design. If auditors cannot obtain high-quality test data using either of these two methods, they will have to create all the test data themselves. Whatever approach auditors use, a number of automated aids are now available that facilitate their design, creation, and use of test data—for example, test data generators to assist with the creation of test data that complies with their test-data design.

■ The major benefit of using test data as an evidence-collection technique is that it allows auditors to examine the quality of program code directly. They do not infer the quality of the code based on other evidence, such as the quality of production output. The major disadvantage of using test data is that it is often time-consuming and costly.

■ Auditors use program code comparison for two reasons. First, it gives them some assurance that they are auditing the correct version of the software. Second, it gives them some assurance that any software they use as an audit tool is the correct version of that software.

■ Software is available to undertake two types of code comparison: (a) source-code comparison and (b) object-code comparison. With source-code comparison, auditors should be able to obtain a meaningful list of any discrepancies between two versions of a program's source code. They need to determine, however, whether the version of the source code they are evaluating is the one used to prepare the production object code. With object-code comparison, it is unlikely that auditors will be able to identify the nature of any discrepancies found between two versions of a program's object code. They can better determine, however, whether changes have been made to the current version of a program's production object code.

■ Source-code and object-code comparison are often most effective when they are used in conjunction with one another. First, auditors compare the audit version of a program's source code with the version that the organization they are auditing contends is the source code used to compile the production version of the object code. Any discrepancies identified between the two versions of the source code must be reconciled. Second, auditors compile either the audit version or the organizational version of the source code to produce the production version of the object code. Third, auditors compare the object code produced via this compilation with the production object code in use to identify whether discrepancies exist.

■ The primary benefit of code comparison is that it is easy to undertake. The software used to perform code comparison is neither costly to purchase nor difficult to use. The primary limitation of code comparison is that it does not provide evidence directly on the quality of the code being compared.

INTRODUCTION

In this chapter, we examine three evidence-collection techniques used during substantive testing to determine primarily whether *(1)* programs meet their functional requirements and *(2)* program code is defective because it is unauthorized, inaccurate, incomplete, ineffective, or inefficient. The first technique is *program code review*, whereby we obtain program source-code listings and read these listings to evaluate the quality of the program code. The second

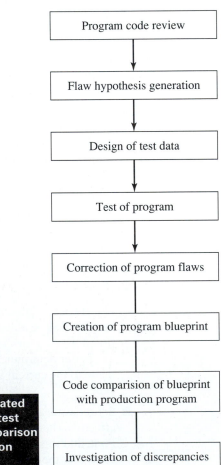

FIGURE 17–1. Integrated use of code review, test data, and code comparison for evidence-collection purposes.

technique is *test data*, whereby we design a sample of data to be executed by the program and then examine the output produced to reach a judgment on the quality of the program. The third technique is *code comparison*, whereby we compare two versions of a program's source or object code. One version—the blueprint—has known attributes, and we seek to determine whether the other version has the same attributes.

Each of these techniques can be used independently. Sometimes, however, we might choose to use them in a coordinated way (Figure 17–1). First, we undertake program code review to generate hypotheses about deficiencies in the program code—for example, errors or inefficiencies. Next we design and execute test data to test these hypotheses. We can then ask that any deficiencies we confirm using the test data be corrected. These two steps might be carried out iteratively until we are satisfied with the quality of the program code. The resulting version of the program then becomes a blueprint. At a later time, we then compare production versions of the program against this blueprint to determine whether any discrepancies exist.

In the subsequent discussion, we first examine where we are likely to identify defects in a program. By knowing this we can better focus our efforts during program code review and test-data design and execution. We then discuss the nature of program code review, test data, and code comparison, their use in our evidence-collection work, and their strengths and weaknesses.

WHERE DO PROGRAM DEFECTS OCCUR?

Code review and test data can be time-consuming evidence-collection techniques to use. Auditors should apply them, therefore, where they will have most effect. In this light, it would be useful if we knew those program locations where defective code is most likely to occur.

In spite of the enormity of the programming effort worldwide, unfortunately, few rigorous studies of where the problem areas in programs lie have been reported. The bibliography at the end of this chapter contains references for several of these studies. Here are a few tentative conclusions, however, that we can draw based on the studies conducted so far:

1. Pareto's law seems to apply in programming: A small number of program modules will have a large number of faults, and a large number of modules will have none or only a few faults. Moreover, a small number of faults affect a large number of modules, and a large number of faults affect only a small number of modules.
2. Requirements specification and design errors are just as prominent, if not more prominent, than coding errors. Auditors should be careful, therefore, if they rely on the accuracy and completeness of the program requirements or program design in their evidence-collection work.
3. Design errors seem to relate primarily to interface problems with users, input/output devices, and the database. Many design errors also reflect that the programmer has failed to implement part of the specifications—in other words, logic has been omitted.
4. Coding errors seem to relate primarily to incorrect computation, incorrect indexing, or incorrect control flow.
5. Defects relating to management of data seem to be more common than defects relating to computation.

The extent to which defects exist in a program is also likely to depend on the age of the program. The more times a program has been used for production purposes, the more likely it is that defects will have been identified and corrected. Thus, auditors often should be able to limit the extent of the testing undertaken with older programs. In some cases, however, organizations have learned to live with defective older programs, in which case auditors might need to expand the extent of their testing.

PROGRAM SOURCE-CODE REVIEW

Auditors will use program source-code review when they are unwilling to treat a program as a black box. In other words, they decide that they are not prepared to make inferences about the quality of a program's code based only on an examination of the program's input and output. Instead, they wish to look at the internal workings of the program to evaluate its quality.

Objectives of Code Review

When undertaking code review, it is important that auditors have the objectives they wish to accomplish clearly fixed in their minds. The code review task is complex, and they can be distracted easily if they do not have clear goals. The objectives auditors might seek to accomplish are the following:

1. *Identify erroneous code.* The use of code review to identify erroneous code is well established. Recall that we discuss this purpose in Chapter 5 under various headings: desk checking, structured walkthroughs, and design and code inspections. The empirical evidence we examined earlier in the chapter indicates that coding errors are still a major cause of low-quality programs. Thus, auditors can use code review to determine whether program code complies with its specifications.

2. *Identify unauthorized code.* Without directly examining a program's source code, auditors are unlikely to identify unauthorized code in a program. Unauthorized code often is triggered by a specific data value or combination of data values. For example, a fraudulent programmer might modify a program so it does not print out details of his or her own account when it is overdrawn. Similarly, he or she might modify a program to exclude transactions having certain account number and date values from normal data validation processes. Unless auditors submit test data having these specific values and have a way of checking that the test data has traversed all execution paths in the code that is their focus, they are unlikely to detect this unauthorized code.

3. *Identify ineffective code.* Auditors can examine whether code is ineffective in two ways. First, they can evaluate whether the code meets the documented program specifications. Second, they can examine whether the code meets user requirements. Recall, the empirical evidence discussed earlier in the chapter suggests that documented program specifications and user requirements often do not correspond. Moreover, assuming the program specifications are correct, design errors that result in the program not complying with specifications are also prevalent.

4. *Identify inefficient code.* Code review also can allow auditors to identify inefficient segments of code. For example, in a sequence of tests of transaction types, the tests might not have been ordered according to their frequency of occurrence. As a result, the program executes more of its code than it would have to if the tests were reordered. Auditors might also use code review to identify the existence of instructions that execute inefficiently on the hardware/software platform used.

5. *Identify nonstandard code.* Nonstandard code takes a variety of forms. For example, it could be code that does not comply with organizational standards covering data item names or internal documentation. Alternatively, it could be code that does not employ structured programming control structures. What-

ever the nature of the nonstandard code, often it manifests other defects in the code—for example, unauthorized code or erroneous code.

Which of these objectives should be emphasized within code review will depend on the objectives auditors have for the audit and the nature of the material exposures they conclude exist. For example, if their primary concern in the audit is the integrity of the data in the financial statements, their focus will be on whether unauthorized or erroneous code exists. If auditors conclude, however, that there are few opportunities for defalcations associated with the code they are examining, they will probably narrow their focus to determining whether erroneous code exists.

Source-Code Review Methodology

A review of program source code involves seven steps:

1. Select the source code to be examined.
2. Review the organization's programming standards.
3. Obtain an understanding of the program specifications.
4. Obtain the source-code listing.
5. Review the programming language used to implement the code.
6. Review the source code.
7. Formulate flaw hypotheses.

The following subsections briefly discuss each of these steps.

Source-Code Selection

Program source-code review can be a time-consuming evidence-collection technique to use. In this light, auditors should select source code for review that is material to their audit objectives. Risk assessment techniques can be applied to determine the level of materiality associated with the source code. For example, Sherer and Paul (1993) describe a methodology for identifying high-risk program modules. It involves five major steps:

1. The hazards (e.g., errors or irregularities) that can occur with a program are identified.
2. The expected losses associated with the occurrence of each hazard are estimated.
3. The exposure associated with each program module is estimated by relating factors like the module's functions and frequency of use to the hazards and their financial consequences.
4. A software reliability model is used to determine the expected number of failures that will occur in each module as a result of software faults.
5. The expected losses of failure in each module are estimated based on the likelihood of it failing, the hazards that will arise as a consequence, and the expected losses associated with these hazards.

The source code must be not only material but also readable. Otherwise, it will be difficult for auditors to identify defects in the code. If an organization has not enforced rigorous programming standards, unfortunately the code produced by its programmers might be unreadable (unless the programmers act professionally and apply their own standards). Providing programmers adhere to the structured programming conventions examined in Chapter 5, however, program code should be readable. Moreover, to the extent that programmers use high-level languages to write code, the readability of the code will be enhanced even further. Nonetheless, before embarking on use of code review as an evidence-collection technique, auditors need to assess its feasibility.

Review Programming Standards

By reviewing the organization's programming standards, auditors develop a set of expectations about the characteristics of the code they will review—for example, the way labels will be assigned to variables and constants, the way programs will be structured, and the way comments will be placed throughout the program. Deficiencies in the standards might also indicate where defects are likely to occur in the code. For example, the standards might not place a limit on the size of program modules. In this light, auditors might expect that some modules will be large, inherently complex, and therefore error prone.

Besides the organization's overall programming standards, additional standards also might have been established for particular application systems. For example, the program modules in a real-time application system may be highly complex. As a result, programmers might have been required to include more extensive in-line documentation in the code they wrote. If they have not complied with these additional documentation standards and the code has been modified frequently, auditors might expect that erroneous code will exist. Because the documentation is defective, maintenance programmers might not always have properly understood the code they were modifying.

Understand the Program Specifications

By understanding the program specifications, auditors can address the question, Does the program do what it is supposed to do? Here they must make a choice about how they will obtain an understanding of the program specifications. One alternative is to review the documented program specifications—those used by the programmer as the basis for constructing the code. By reviewing these specifications, auditors can check the correspondence of the code with the specifications. Using this approach, deficiencies in the specifications might also become apparent; for example, auditors might identify an important control that is missing in the specifications.

A second alternative is for auditors to attempt to understand the purposes of the program by consulting wider sources of information. For example, auditors can interview users of the program to check their understanding of what the program is supposed to do. They can then determine whether the functions manifested in the code comply with the user's understanding of the functional requirements for the program. This alternative is often more costly to undertake than the first alternative. As we discussed earlier in the chapter, however, errors often exist in program specifications. We might not identify these errors if we rely only on the specifications to check for defects in program code.

Obtain Source Code

When auditors obtain the source code that they wish to review, they must take steps to ensure that it is the current version and not outdated. Otherwise, auditors might not identify important defects in the source code—for example, unauthorized code that has been introduced to enable a defalcation to be perpetrated.

If the source code is controlled via a configuration management system (see Chapter 5), auditors can have greater confidence that they have obtained the current version of the source code. If controls over maintenance of source and object code are weak, however, auditors might conclude that they cannot undertake code review because they cannot rely on the currency of the source code that information systems personnel have provided to them. Alternatively, auditors might take steps to determine whether they have the current version of the source code. For example, they might compile the source code and then compare the object code produced with the production object code (using the code comparison software discussed later in this chapter). Again, auditors must be confident in the currency of the production object code provided to them for comparison purposes.

Review Programming Language Used

From the auditors' viewpoint, unfortunately a large number of programming languages now exist. They might often encounter a situation, therefore, in which they are not familiar with the programming language used to implement the source code they want to review. In these situations, auditors must either acquire familiarity with the programming language or rely on someone else to undertake the code review on their behalf. If auditors must rely on someone else to undertake the review and they conclude they cannot be confident in the integrity of the information that will provided to them, they must choose a technique other than code review to gather evidence.

The programming language used to implement the source code is often determined on the basis of policies or standards that have been implemented within the organization. For example, programmers might be required to use COBOL or a particular type of fourth-generation language to implement any accounting or administrative applications. These policies and standards can be useful in mitigating the problems associated with a diversity of programming language use within an organization. From time to time, however, they might also result in the choice of a programming language that is not well suited to the application's needs. For example, COBOL is well suited to applications that have extensive file manipulation or report generation requirements, but it is not a good language for high-performance, real-time applications. In this latter case, languages like Ada and C are a better choice. Similarly, FORTRAN is well suited to applications that have extensive computational requirements, but it is not a good language where complex data structures must be manipulated. In this latter case, a language like PASCAL would be a better choice.

If the programming language chosen is not well suited to an application's needs, the source code auditors encounter is likely to be complex. Thus, the probability of defects existing in the code is likely to be higher. Moreover, the cost of undertaking code review is likely to be higher. In these situations, auditors should evaluate whether they wish to rely on the code even if they were not to identify any defects in the code during the conduct of their review. They should also consider whether other evidence-collection procedures might be more cost-effective.

During their review of the programming language used for an application system, auditors should also determine whether the particular version of the language used by the organization contains any nonstandard features. For example, some COBOL compilers include verbs that are not American National Standards (ANS) COBOL verbs to assist programmers to debug programs. Unfortunately, use of some of these nonstandard features often leads to programmers writing defective code. In this light, auditors should determine what nonstandard features exist in the programming language used to implement the code they are reviewing and whether any of these features are known to be error-prone.

Similarly, auditors should determine whether some features in the particular version of the programming language used by the organization are obsolete. For example, several standards have now been issued for the COBOL programming language. The 1974 standard included the ALTER verb, which permitted programmers to change the point to which control was transferred in a program using the GO TO statement. The ALTER verb made it difficult, if not impossible, to determine the actual execution sequence of the program. Moreover, it could be used to activate unauthorized code. The 1985 standard did not include the ALTER verb. Nonetheless, subsequent to 1974, many organizations continued to use older versions of COBOL. Furthermore, some post-1985 COBOL compilers continued to support features included in the 1974 standard that were omitted in the 1985 standard. Features in a programming language that are made obsolete have usually been found to be problematical for some reason. Accordingly, if auditors see them still used by an organization, they should pay special attention to those parts of the code they are reviewing that use them.

Review Source Code

Currently, we have little theory or empirical evidence to help us choose the most effective and efficient way of reviewing program code. Many questions remain unanswered. Do some ways of reviewing code identify more errors than others? Are some ways of reviewing code faster than others? Does the best way depend on how the code is written (structured)? Should code be reviewed differently if, say, efficiency is the main concern rather than, say, data integrity? Does the effectiveness and efficiency of a code review technique depend upon our psychological and demographic characteristics?

One way to commence code review is to draw a structure chart for the code we are reviewing. Recall from Chapter 5 that a structure chart is a diagrammatic representation of the hierarchy of modules within a program and the interfaces among the modules. If the code we are reviewing is well documented, a structure chart might exist already for the code. We need to then check, however, that the structure chart is up to date.

Figure 17–2 shows a program structure chart and a few ways that auditors might use the structure chart to systematically cover the code they are reviewing. First, auditors can cover the code from the top-level modules through to the bottom-level modules. The advantage of this approach is that they first build a broad understanding of the code and progressively increase their detailed understanding as they proceed through the levels. The disadvantage is that auditors become overwhelmed because they end up considering all the details of processing only toward the end of the review. Second, auditors can cover the code by using a preorder traversal of the structure chart; that is, they cover the leftmost branch of the structure chart first and proceed across to the rightmost branch. The advantage of this approach is that auditors progressively build an appreciation of the details of processing. The disadvantage is that a preorder traversal of modules might not result in auditors selecting sets of modules in the order that best facilitates their understanding of the code. In this light, the third approach has auditors traverse branches in the structure

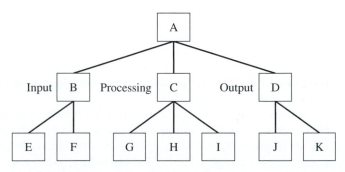

Coverage by level: A; B, C, D; E, F, G, H, I, J, K

Coverage by preorder: A, B, E, F, C, G, H, I, D, J, K

Coverage by input, output, processing: A, B, E, F; D, J, K; C, G, H, I

FIGURE 17–2. Structured approaches to code review of program modules.

chart in the order that they believe best facilitates their understanding of the code. For example, auditors might conclude that they need to understand the input modules first, then the output modules, and then the processing modules. Figure 17–2 shows the sequence of modules they would traverse using this approach.

In any programming language, certain reserved words (statements or commands) are error prone and inefficient. Some are also more likely to be used to implement unauthorized code. Still others can be used to prevent errors or irregularities occurring during the execution of a program or to enhance efficient execution of the program. For example, when auditors review the input/output modules in a COBOL program, they should pay special attention to how the following reserved words are used:

COBOL Reserved Word	*Audit Concerns*
SELECT	Relates a file to an input/output device. Can be checked to see the program processes only authorized files.
REDEFINES	Permits alternative record formats to be defined for the one file. Selection of a specific format often is triggered by an IF clause. Can be checked to see the data items redefined are authorized data items. Its use is often associated with error-prone code.
OPEN/CLOSE	Makes a file available and unavailable for processing. Multiple OPEN/CLOSE verbs in a program may mean a file is being made available for unauthorized processing.
FILE STATUS	Places file status (e.g., record does not exist) in a data name that the program can access so recovery can be effected when an error occurs.
INVALID KEY	Traps exception conditions associated with record keys so recovery can be effected.
ACCEPT	Program stops and awaits the input of data from a peripheral, e.g., the console. Can be used to input a code that will cause a conditional test to branch to unauthorized code.
DISPLAY	Can be used to breach the privacy of data by having the contents of a record displayed on a particular output device, e.g., the console.
COPY	Used to copy standard sections of code from a library—e.g., code associated with the ENVIRONMENT DIVISION and DATA DIVISION—to reduce the likelihood of coding errors occurring and to enforce standard error-recovery routines.
COPY. . . REPLACING	Used to change the definition of data items copied into a program from a library. Can be checked to see the changes are authorized. Its use is often associated with error-prone code.

Similarly, when auditors review the control structure within the processing modules in a COBOL program, they should pay special attention to how the following reserved words are used:

COBOL Reserved Word	*Audit Concerns*
IF	Typically the major conditional statement used in a program. Can be used to activate an unauthorized section of code when a certain condition is true or false. Nested IFs with many levels are also error prone.

(cont.)

COBOL Reserved Word	*Audit Concerns*
GO TO	Allows an unconditional branch of control. Use should be restricted to branch of control within the same paragraph.
GO TO . . . DEPENDING ON	The GO TO with DEPENDING is a way of implementing the CASE control structure. It allows a conditional branch of control depending on the value in a specified data item. The branch could be to an unauthorized section of code. The GO TO . . . DEPENDING ON is also error prone.
PERFORM . . . UNTIL	The UNTIL statement permits a conditional branch to be carried out with the PERFORM. The branch could be to an unauthorized section of code.
SEARCH/SEARCH ALL	SEARCH undertakes a sequential search of a table. SEARCH ALL undertakes a binary search of a table. They are simpler and more efficient to use than, say, a search implemented via a PERFORM . . . UNTIL structure.
INSPECT	Used to replace certain occurrences of a given character in a field with another character. Can be inserted before and after a validation test so a specific transaction passes the test. The first instance changes the data item value so it passes the test. The second restores the data item to its original value. The INSPECT statement is complex and error prone.
EVALUATE . . . WHEN	Used to implement the CASE structure. One of the cases could be a branch to an unauthorized section of code.
CALL	Used to call a subprogram (subroutine). The subprogram could contain unauthorized code.

When auditors encounter computations within a COBOL program, again, they should pay special attention to how the following reserved words are used:

COBOL Reserved Word	*Audit Concerns*
ROUNDED	Prevents truncation of significant digits that are needed in a computation.
OVERFLOW	Allows the program to effect recovery when data will not fit into the receiving field.
ON SIZE ERROR	Allows the program to effect recovery when data is truncated or division by zero occurs.
COMPUTE	Allows many arithmetic operations to be specified at once. Often results in more efficient code than using ADD, SUBTRACT, and so on. Nonetheless, its use is often associated with error-prone code.

Sometimes publications are available to help auditors identify the problematical features of a programming language. For example, Vesely (1989) provides an extensive treatment of those features of the COBOL programming language that should not be used by a programmer. He also discusses why these features should not be used.

A tool that is often useful during the conduct of code review is a *cross-reference lister*. For example, auditors can use it to show what data item names are used within a program and where they are used. Similarly, auditors can use it to identify where the different reserved words in the programming language are used within the program. Thus, they can more easily pinpoint the location of the material data items and the problematical reserved words within the code.

Formulate Flaw Hypotheses

If auditors do not identify any defects in the source code that they review, most likely they can conclude that they can place reliance on the code to meet control objectives. In this light, auditors should be able to conclude also that they can reduce the extent of subsequent substantive testing they undertake.

If auditors believe they have identified a defect in the code they have reviewed, however, two alternatives are then available. First, auditors might conclude that they do not wish to place reliance on the code in meeting control objectives. Accordingly, auditors should expand the extent of subsequent substantive tests to determine how the defect they believe exists has impacted the attainment of control objectives. Second, auditors might conclude that they need to investigate the presumed defect further. They should then formulate flaw hypotheses that predict the impact of the defect on control objectives. Auditors can then use some other evidence-collection technique to determine whether the predicted defect has the anticipated effect on control objectives. For example, they can design and use test data to test their flaw hypotheses.

Benefits and Costs of Code Review

The primary benefit of reviewing program source code is that it provides a level of detailed knowledge about a program that auditors will find difficult to acquire using other evidence-collection techniques. With other evidence-collection techniques, inferences must be made about the quality of the code on the basis of some test result. With program source-code review, however, auditors examine the code directly. In this light, they can obtain high levels of assurance about the quality of the code if they cannot identify any defects. Alternatively, if auditors do identify a defect, they can often make fairly precise predictions about the impact of this defect on the financial statement assertions or effectiveness and efficiency assertions made by management.

As discussed previously, a major disadvantage of program code review is its cost. We have examined some of the factors that can impact this cost—for example, the readability of the code, auditors' knowledge of the programming language used, the extent to which the programming language used contains nonstandard features, and the complexity of the application functions that are implemented in the code. Before undertaking program code review, therefore, auditors must carefully evaluate whether alternative evidence-collection techniques might be a cheaper means of obtaining the information they require.

Unfortunately, the evidence on whether code review is an effective means of detecting defects in a program is also equivocal. Using an experimental approach, for example, Basili and Selby (1987) and Lauterbach and Randall (1989) found that code review was more effective than some forms of test data use. On the other hand, Myers (1978) found that test data outperformed code review as a means of identifying program defects when the test results obtained by two programmers working independently were then pooled. Interestingly, Basili and Selby (1987) found that code review was more effective than test data when it was used by more expert programmers.

TEST DATA

The use of a sample of data to assess the quality of a program is fundamental to many evidence-collection techniques. It is based on the premise that it is possible to generalize about the overall reliability of a program if it is reliable for a set of specific tests.

As with program code review, it is unlikely that auditors will be interested in testing an entire program. Rather, they will focus on testing those parts of a program that they deem to be material and on which they intend to rely. Like program code review, test data can be an expensive evidence-collection procedure. Auditors need to focus their efforts, therefore, on those parts of a program where the payoffs will be highest.

In the following subsections, we first examine the nature of reliable test data. We then discuss some major approaches to the design of test data that auditors might employ. Finally, we examine some ways that auditors can create test data and how they might use various automated tools to assist them in the design, creation, and use of test data.

Nature of Reliable Test Data

As background to our discussion on test data techniques, let us examine first the nature of reliable test data. Perhaps the most widely accepted notion of reliable test data has been proposed by Gerhart and Goodenough (1975) and Howden (1976). They argue as follows. Suppose we have a program, P, for computing a function, F, whose domain (input) is a set, D. Let $T \subset D$ be the test data used to determine whether P contains any defects. T is deemed to be a reliable set of test data for P if:

$$P(x) = F(x) \forall x \in T \Rightarrow P(x) = F(x) \forall x \in D$$

In other words, T is reliable if it reveals an error in P whenever P contains an error. The fact that P has no defects when it processes every element in the set of test data is sufficient to ensure that P will have no defects when it processes *any* element in its input domain.

Although the notion of a reliable set of test data helps us to clarify our ideas about test data, Weyuker and Ostrand (1980) have shown why it is difficult, if not impossible, to establish that a set of test data is reliable. Basically, their reasoning is as follows. Suppose we have a program that processes every element in its domain correctly except one. Unless this element is included in the test data, we will not detect the program defect. How, then, can we ensure that this element is included in the test data set? Unfortunately, we know of no way.

In any event, even if we could design reliable test data, human error might still undermine the conclusions we reached about the program. A test data element might reveal a program defect, but the person who undertakes the testing might not realize an error has occurred. In short, using test data for evidence-collection purposes is always problematical. We need to take care if the benefits are to exceed the costs.

Approaches to Designing Test Data

Because we cannot automatically generate a reliable set of test data, test data therefore must be designed. To improve the quality of the test-data design, we should use a systematic approach. Otherwise, important defects in the program might be missed. Moreover, excessive test data might be designed and used. We must avoid the tendency to believe that more comprehensive testing will result when a larger amount of data is designed, created, and executed through a program. Unfortunately, a larger amount of test data ensures neither that a program's critical features will be tested, nor that testing will be carried out in the most economical manner. Auditors are often subject to severe cost constraints. In this light, their use of systematic approaches to the design of test data, therefore, is essential.

Two types of systematic approaches to the design of test data exist (Figure 17–3): (a) black-box or specification-based testing methods and (b) white-box or program-based testing methods. Black-box methods view the program to be tested as a black box; that is, they do not rely on any knowledge of the internal

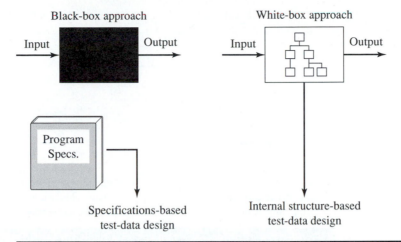

FIGURE 17–3. Approaches to test-data design.

workings of the program. Instead, test data is designed on the basis of the program's functional specifications. White-box methods rely on the internal control structure of the program to be tested. Test-data design is undertaken after the program listing has been examined. We examine some examples of each of these two approaches in more detail.

Black-Box Test-Data Design Methods

Auditors use black-box test-data design methods whenever their primary focus is on whether some part of an application system meets its functional requirements. Besides functional defects, however, black-box testing might also help to identify other types of defects in programs: *(1)* user interface errors, *(2)* errors in interfacing with external systems or databases, *(3)* efficiency problems, *(4)* initialization errors, and *(5)* termination errors.

When auditors use black-box testing, they must first seek to determine what an application, program, or section of a program is supposed to do. They can try to elicit this information from knowledgeable users. Alternatively, they can try to obtain it by examining and evaluating the program's specifications. When auditors have a clear understanding of the functional requirements for the program, they can then commence to design the test data they need to evaluate compliance by the program with these requirements.

Although there are many black-box test-data design methods (Roper 1994), in the following subsections we examine just two of them: equivalence partitioning and boundary value analysis. These two techniques provide good illustrations of the nature of black-box techniques. Moreover, they are techniques we are likely to use frequently if we undertake black-box testing.

Equivalence Partitioning

The intuitive idea behind equivalence partitioning is straightforward and appealing. The input domain of a program (or set of programs or a module) is partitioned into classes where each element of a class is treated identically to all other members of the class, at least according to the specifications (Figure 17–4). The objective during test-data design is to select a test-data design element that falls *within* the class and one that falls *outside* the class. Because the test-data design element that falls within the class is supposed to be representative of all other members in the class, we assume the program logic for all other members of the class is correct if it is correct for the chosen element. Similarly, because the test-data design element that falls outside the class is

Input domain

Output domain

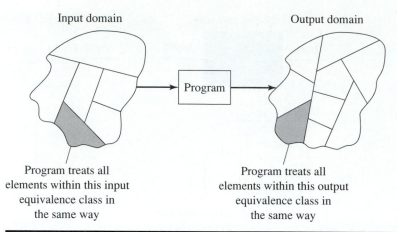

Program

Program treats all
elements within this input
equivalence class in
the same way

Program treats all
elements within this output
equivalence class in
the same way

FIGURE 17–4. Equivalence classes as a basis for test-data design.

supposed to be representative of all other members that fall outside the class, we assume the program logic is correct for all other members that fall outside the class if it is correct for the chosen element.

Two tools that auditors can use to help them identify the equivalence classes in the input domain of a program are decision tables and decision trees. Consider the *decision table approach* first. Assume we interview a payroll clerk about the payment of sales commissions. We are told that most salespersons are paid a base salary plus 3 percent of sales if more than 100 units of the product are sold and 4 percent of sales if more than 125 units of the product are sold. A salesperson can elect to sign a special contract called a Type A contract, however, whereby no sales commission is paid until sales exceed 125 units of the product. With a Type A contract, sales commission is then paid at the rate of 6 percent of sales.

Assume that we deem sales commission expense to be a material item and that we intend to rely on controls over the calculation of sales commission with a view to reducing the extent of our substantive testing. In this light, we decide to test whether that section of the program that calculates sales commissions is working reliably.

We construct an initial version of a decision table to test the sales commission logic using the following steps:

1. List all the conditions that apply to the calculation of sales commission. Place these conditions in the condition stub of the decision table.
2. List all the actions that apply to the calculation of sales commission. Place these actions in the action stub of the decision table.
3. Construct the rules for the decision table by constructing all combinations of condition values. If there are n conditions in the decision table, each of which can take on a "yes" or "no" value, the number of conditions will be 2^n.
4. Show what actions will be undertaken under what combination of condition values.

Table 17–1a shows the result of following these steps. Note that we have three conditions; therefore, we have $2^3 = 8$ rules. Two of these rules turn out to have impossible condition values (intrarule inconsistencies): we cannot have sales that are greater than 125 but not greater than 100 (rules 2 and 6). These rules are shown in the Table 17–1a as having error actions.

The rules in the table show us the equivalence classes for the input domain of the sales commission logic. All we now have to do is design a set of test data by choosing one piece of test data that satisfies each rule of the decision table

TABLE 17–1A   Unreduced Decision Table

Sales Commissions	Rules 1	2	3	4	5	6	7	8
Condition stub								
Type A contract	Y	Y	Y	Y	N	N	N	N
Sales > 125	Y	Y	N	N	Y	Y	N	N
Sales > 100	Y	N	Y	N	Y	N	Y	N
Action stub								
Salary = base			X	X				X
Salary = base + 3% sales							X	
Salary = base + 4% sales					X			
Salary = base + 6% sales	X							
Error		X				X		

(except rules 2 and 6). We will then have covered each of the equivalence classes in the input domain.

A further step we might want to undertake is to *reduce* the decision table. We leave the process of reducing decision tables for further study (Hurley 1983). To get an intuitive feel for the reduction process, however, consider rules 3 and 4 in Table 17–1a. Note that they have the same action values and that they differ only on the basis of the response to one condition—namely, the sales > 100 condition. Because this condition does not affect the outcome of the actions undertaken, the two rules can be combined in a reduced form of the decision table. In Table 17–1b, the two rules are represented as rule 3. Note that a "–" has been used in the response to condition 3 to show the value of this condition has no effect on the actions to be undertaken. The reduction process can be continued iteratively. Rules can be combined whenever they have the same set of action values and their conditions differ only in terms of one condition value.

Note that we have five equivalence classes in Table 17–1b, whereas we have six equivalence classes in Table 17–1a. Whether we choose the unreduced form of the decision table or the reduced form of the decision table as the basis for our test-data design depends on the assumptions we are willing to make about how the program is written. Programmers who have written efficient code should have constructed the conditional tests according to the reduced form of the deci-

TABLE 17–1B   Reduced Decision Table

Sales Commissions	Rules 1	2	3	4	5	6	7
Condition stub							
Type A contract	Y	Y	Y	N	N	N	N
Sales > 125	Y	Y	N	Y	Y	N	N
Sales > 100	Y	N	–	Y	N	Y	N
Action stub							
Salary = base			X				X
Salary = base + 3% sales						X	
Salary = base + 4% sales				X			
Salary = base + 6% sales	X						
Error		X				X	

TABLE 17-2   Reduced Decision Table with Associated Test Data and Test Results

	Rules						
Sales Commissions	**1**	**2**	**3**	**4**	**5**	**6**	**7**
Condition stub							
Type A contract	Y	Y	Y	N	N	N	N
Sales > 125	Y	Y	N	Y	Y	N	N
Sales > 100	Y	N	–	Y	N	Y	N
Action stub							
Salary = base			X				X
Salary = base + 3% sales						X	
Salary = base + 4% sales				X			
Salary = base + 6% sales	X						
Error		X			X		
Test data stub							
Contract Type	A	A	A	B	B	B	B
Sales	126	–	125	126	–	101	100
Results stub							
Expected Result	17,560	–	10,000	15,040	–	13,030	10,000
Confirmed	√	–	√	√	–	X	√

sion table. To illustrate why this is the case, consider rule 3 in the reduced form of the decision table in Table 17-2. If the programmer has written efficient code, only the first and second conditions should be tested before the relevant actions are invoked. If the program has been poorly written, however, the third condition might be tested even though its outcome is irrelevant to the actions to be invoked. The superfluous code could contain an error, which we might not detect if we design test data based on the reduced form of the decision table.

By adding two extra parts (stubs) to a decision table, we can enhance them to facilitate our test-data design and documentation of our test results. The test data stub shown in Table 17–2 shows the test data we have chosen to test each of the equivalence classes. The results stub shows some hypothetical results we might have obtained from our testing efforts. Note that the expected results

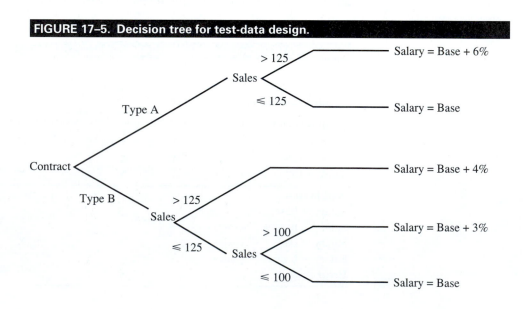

FIGURE 17–5. Decision tree for test-data design.

were obtained in the tests of rules 1, 3, 4, and 7 (confirmed). The expected result for rule 6, however, was not confirmed.

The *decision tree approach* to the design of test data relies on the same underlying principles as the decision table approach. The major difference is in the way the logic to be tested is documented. Figure 17–5 shows a decision tree for our sales commission example. To design test data, we follow each branch of the decision tree. We can use a colored pen to mark off a branch when we have completed the test-data design for that branch.

Boundary Value Analysis

Boundary value analysis is an extension of the equivalence partitioning test-data design technique. It has been motivated by the empirical finding that logic errors often occur at the boundaries of equivalence classes rather than elsewhere within the class.

As with equivalence partitioning, the intuitive idea behind boundary value analysis is straightforward and appealing. Consider the three conditions shown in the decision table in Table 17–2. The first condition asks whether we have a Type A contract. We automatically test the boundary of this condition whenever we use one piece of test data that contains a Type A contract and one that does not contain a Type A contract. The second condition asks whether sales are greater than 125. To test the boundary of this condition, we need two pieces of test data: one that is just above the boundary and one that is just below the boundary. For this condition, we should use a piece of test data that has sales equal to 125 and another that has sales equal to 126. If the condition had been sales greater than or equal to 125, note that we would have needed a third piece of test data to test the boundary of this condition—namely, one that had sales equal to 125. With the third condition in the decision table, again two pieces of test data are needed to test the boundary: one with sales equal to 100 and another with sales equal to 101.

Boundary value analysis also applies these requirements to *output* values. For example, assume that the maximum compensation a salesperson can earn is $16,000. We would then have to choose sales values for a Type A contract and a Type B contract that would lead to compensation of both $16,000 and $16,001. In some cases it might be impossible to obtain the exact output values we require, in which case we should obtain the output values that are closest to the boundary.

Decision tables are again a useful tool in helping us undertake boundary value analysis test-data design. As we discovered previously, the rules in the decision table represent the input domain equivalence classes. If we then examine the conditions that define the equivalence classes, we have the basis for choosing the boundary values for our test-data design.

White-Box Test-Data Design Methods

Auditors use white-box test-data design methods whenever their primary focus is on whether defective execution paths exist in a program. The underlying assumption is that significant information about any defects in a program can be obtained by systematic execution of different logic paths through the program. Furthermore, when auditors use white-box test-data design methods, they are recognizing that predicting the actual behavior of a program is still difficult even when they have substantial prior information about the program.

As with black-box testing, auditors begin white-box testing by choosing those parts of a program that they deem to be material from the viewpoint of their audit. Next auditors study a source-code listing of the program to identify where these parts have been implemented within the program code. Their primary goal is to identify the *control structure* underlying the code because the control structure indicates the different execution paths through the program. Having identified the critical sections of source code and the control structure, auditors can then proceed to design test data to traverse this code.

When auditors design test data using white-box methods, they must specify a test completion criterion. Three criteria can be used. The first is *full statement coverage* (Figure 17–6). Under this criterion, the test-data design is deemed to be sufficient if each program statement is exercised at least once during the test run. Of the three test completion criteria, full statement coverage testing provides the least information about whether the program contains defects. The reason is that many paths through a program will remain untested when the program includes a large number of branches and loops. For example, consider the following program statements:

IF AGE LESS THAN 18

MULTIPLY AMOUNT BY DISCOUNT GIVING DEDUCTION.

Providing auditors use test data with age less then 18, they will achieve full statement coverage as both statements will be executed. They will not know, however, whether the program executes correctly for values of age that are 18 or greater. Nonetheless, test data that achieves this criterion is the least costly to design. Moreover, in some cases it will successfully identify the most important defects in a program.

The second white-box test-data design test completion criterion is *full branch coverage*. Under this criterion, the test-data design is successful if each statement is executed at least once and each branching path is executed at least once (Figure 17–6). Although branch testing provides more information about whether a program has defects than statement testing, unfortunately it still has limitations. For example, branch testing will not identify an error in a program that results in an incorrect sequence of branches being tested—in other words, a set of tests have been executed *after* another set of tests when they should have been executed *before* the other set of tests. In addition, it might not identify an incorrect predicate when the branch in-

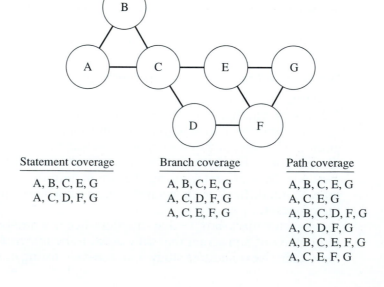

FIGURE 17–6. White-box test completion criteria.

Statement coverage	Branch coverage	Path coverage
A, B, C, E, G	A, B, C, E, G	A, B, C, E, G
A, C, D, F, G	A, C, D, F, G	A, C, E, G
	A, C, E, F, G	A, B, C, D, F, G
		A, C, D, F, G
		A, B, C, E, F, G
		A, C, E, F, G

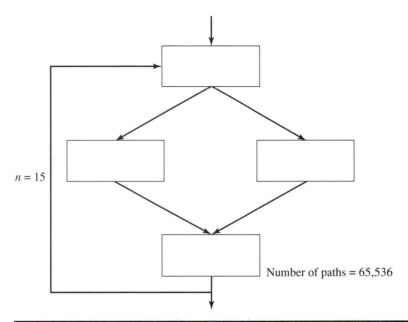

$n = 15$

Number of paths = 65,536

FIGURE 17–7. Program loop with large number of alternative paths through loop.

volves compound conditions. For example, consider the following two program statements:

IF TRANTYPE EQ "1" OR TRANTYPE EQ "3"

MULTIPLY AMOUNT BY RATE GIVING DISCOUNT.

Providing that test data with transaction type equal to one is input to the program, the branch will be traversed. The program could still be in error, however, because the conditional test statement perhaps should have been for a transaction type equal to one or four and not one or three.

The third white-box test-data design test completion criterion is *full path coverage*. Under this criterion, every logic path through the program is executed at least once (Figure 17–6). Unfortunately, full path coverage is a theoretical ideal because, for all practical purposes, some programs have an infinite number of paths through them. The simple program segment represented by Figure 17–7, for example, has 65,536 possible paths through the segment (there are two paths through the loop, and depending on the results of a conditional test the loop can be executed once, twice, and so on). Whenever loops are used in programs, the number of possible execution paths through the program explodes combinatorially. For this reason, some programming researchers have been seeking to develop ways to undertake formal proofs of program correctness. In practice, only limited path coverage testing can be accomplished.

As with black-box test-data design techniques, there are many white-box test-data design techniques (Roper 1994). In the following subsections, however, we briefly examine just two of these techniques that might be useful in audit work: basis path testing and loop testing.

Basis Path Testing

Basis path testing is a test-data design method that provides a way to achieve full branch coverage of the program or section of code auditors want to test. Many black-box testing techniques in essence are variations on basis path testing.

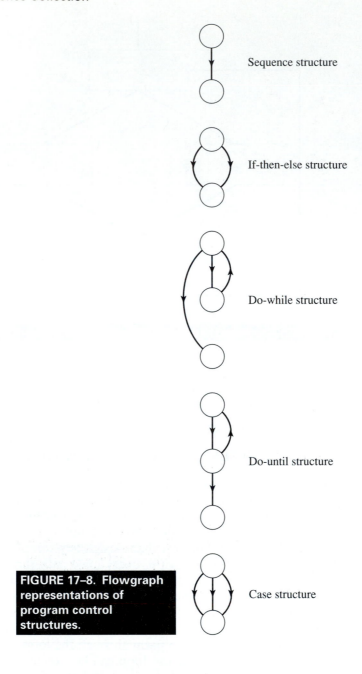

Sequence structure

If-then-else structure

Do-while structure

Do-until structure

FIGURE 17–8. Flowgraph representations of program control structures.

Case structure

To use basis path testing, auditors first convert the code they want to test to a flowgraph. This conversion often is straightforward. Figure 17–8 shows the subgraphs used to represent various program control structures in a flowgraph. Figure 17–9a then shows a conventional flowchart for a section of code we might encounter, and Figure 17–9b shows the corresponding flowgraph. If we are skilled at flowgraphs, we can convert code directly to a flowgraph. Otherwise, we might use the intermediate step of constructing a flowchart first. Basically, however, the steps we use to construct a flowgraph are as follows:

1. Proceed statement by statement through the program code (or flowchart).
2. Ignore any sequence statements (e.g., MOVE A TO B).
3. Whenever any of the control structures shown in Figure 17–8 are encountered, substitute the appropriate subgraph.

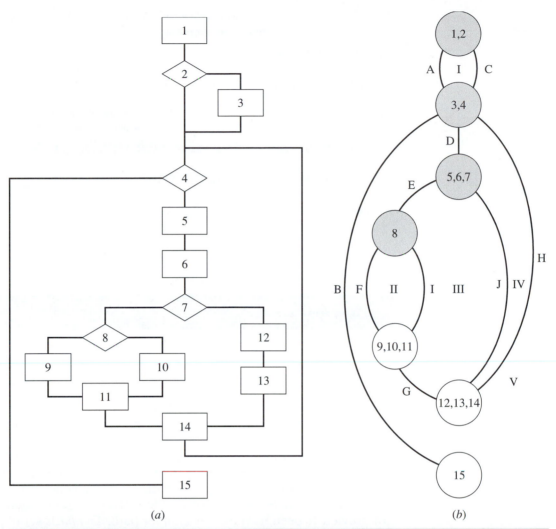

FIGURE 17–9(a). Flowchart representation of program control structure. (b). Flowgraph representation of program control structure. °

4. If a compound conditional statement is encountered, the number of conditions is deemed to be $b + 1$, where b is the number of Boolean operators in the conditional statement (Figure 17–10).

The important feature of flowgraphs is that they allow auditors to calculate a metric called McCabe's cyclomatic complexity number (McCabe 1976). This number is intended to be a measure of the logical complexity of a program. (Indeed, McCabe argues that program modules that have a cyclomatic complexity number greater than 10 should be restructured.) It is calculated as follows:

$$V(G) = e - n + 2$$

where e is the number of flowgraph edges and n is the number of flowgraph nodes. An alternative way to calculate V(G) is to count the number of "regions" in the flowchart. With one exception, a *region* is simply an enclosed area in the plane of the subgraph. The exception is the area outside the subgraph, which also counts as a region. V(G) can also be calculated as follows:

$$V(G) = p + 1$$

where p is the number of predicate nodes in the flowgraph.

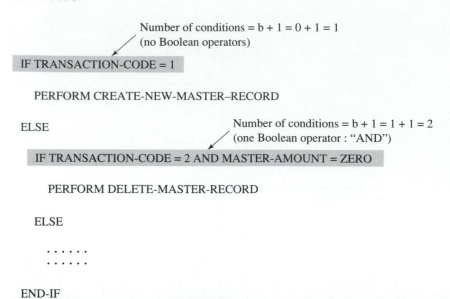

Number of conditions = b + 1 = 0 + 1 = 1
(no Boolean operators)

IF TRANSACTION-CODE = 1

PERFORM CREATE-NEW-MASTER–RECORD

ELSE

Number of conditions = b + 1 = 1 + 1 = 2
(one Boolean operator : "AND")

IF TRANSACTION-CODE = 2 AND MASTER-AMOUNT = ZERO

PERFORM DELETE-MASTER-RECORD

ELSE

· · · · · ·
· · · · · ·

END-IF

FIGURE 17–10. Counting the number of conditions via the number of Boolean operators.

Consider, then, our flowgraph in Figure 17–9*b*. There are 10 edges and 7 nodes. Thus, $V(G) = 10 - 7 + 2 = 5$. Similarly, there are 4 enclosed regions, I, II, III, and IV, plus the fifth region, V, for the area outside the subgraph. As a final check, there are 4 predicate nodes (the shaded nodes in Figure 17–9*b*), so $V(G)$ is again 5.

From our viewpoint of seeking to test a section of program code, the important point to McCabe's cyclomatic complexity number is that it defines the number of independent paths in the basis set of the code. An *independent* path is one that introduces at least one node (set of program statements) that has not previously been traversed by another path. The *basis* set of paths is the set of paths that form the "basis" for constructing all possible paths through the flowgraph. We can construct the paths via a linear combination of the paths in the basis set.

To illustrate these concepts, again consider Figure 17–9*b*. The independent paths in the basis set are as follows:

Path 1:	A, B
Path 2:	C, B
Path 3:	A, D, E, F, G, H, B
Path 4:	A, D, E, I, G, H, B
Path 5:	A, D, J, H, B

Note that the basis set is not unique. For paths 3, 4, and 5, for example, we could have started out with the path C, D. When we have a basis set, however, any other path through the flowgraph—for example, A, D, J, H, D, E, F, G, H, B—is simply composed from the paths in this basis set.

Designing the test data is now straightforward. We simply prepare test data that will traverse each path in the basis set. For example, if we prepare test data to traverse Path 3, we will execute the program statements represented by the following numbered flowchart components in Figure 17–9*a*: 1, 2, 4, 5, 6, 7, 8, 9, 11, 14, 4, 15. When we have designed test data to traverse the other four paths in the basis set, we know we will have achieved full branch coverage.

Loop Testing

A major type of control structure often encountered in programs is a loop. Loops will be tested as part of a basis path testing strategy. Remember, however, that basis path testing achieves only branch coverage. If loops form a critical part of the program code on which auditors wish to rely, they might wish to undertake more comprehensive testing of loops to confirm that their reliance on the code is appropriate.

Providing that we have a well-structured program—one that uses the structured programming control structures discussed in Chapter 5—we might encounter two types of loops whenever we test a program (Figure 17–11). *Simple loops* have no other loops embedded within their control structure. If n is the maximum number of iterations of the loop, the following set of tests have a good chance of detecting any errors in the loop:

1. Check the loop at its lower boundary by exercising zero, one, and two passes through the loop.
2. Check the loop at its upper boundary by exercising iterations $n - 1, n, n + 1$ through the loop.
3. Exercise some intermediate number of passes through the loop, m, where $m < n$.

As the name implies, *nested loops* have other loops embedded within their control structure. As the number of embedded loops increases, the number of possible paths through the code increases exponentially. In this light, if possible, deep levels of nesting should be avoided (the program code should be restructured). Whenever nesting exists, however, Beizer (1990) recommends that the following testing approach be used to limit the number of tests executed yet gain reasonable assurance about the quality of the code:

1. Commence with the innermost loop. Set the counters for all other loops to their minimum values.
2. Undertake simple loop tests for the innermost loop.
3. Work outwards, keeping inner loop counters at typical values but retaining outer loop counters at their minimum values.
4. Continue with this pattern until all loops have been tested.

Programs are often built by concatenating loops—that is, placing one loop after another. Provided the loops are independent of each other, auditors

FIGURE 17–11. Types of program loops.

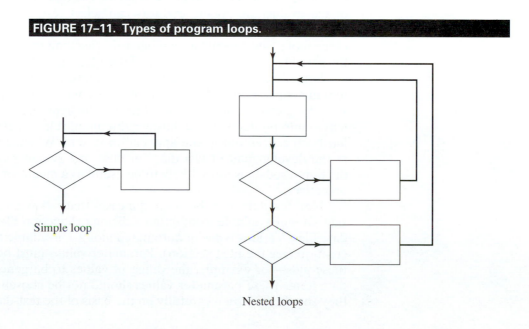

Simple loop

Nested loops

can test the loops independently using the approaches outlined previously. Sometimes the loops are not independent, however, because the counter for the subsequent loop starts at the terminating value of the previous loop. Essentially, dependent loops of this nature are like nested loops. The procedures for testing nested loops described previously can then be followed.

If auditors encounter program code in which the loops are not well structured, they should be circumspect about relying on the code and therefore undertaking tests to confirm that it is appropriate for them to rely on the code. Instead, it is probably more appropriate that auditors decide not to rely on the code and to expand the extent of substantive testing accordingly.

Creating Test Data

When auditors have designed the test data they need for evidence-collection purposes, their next step is to create test data that complies with the design. This task can be difficult and time-consuming to complete, especially when auditors must prepare a large number of test cases.

One approach auditors can use to reduce the amount of resources required to create test data is to rely on existing production data. They should not simply select a random sample of this production data and execute it through the code on which they intend to rely. This approach is unlikely to lead to effective and efficient testing. Rather, auditors should select instances of production data that comply with their test-data design. In this light, they might use generalized audit software, for example, to select cases off the production files that satisfy their design. If there are no production cases that satisfy the design, auditors might still select cases that almost comply with the design and modify them appropriately.

Whenever auditors use production data as the basis for test data creation, however, they must take care that they do not overlook logic that is exercised infrequently by production data and therefore might be missing from the production files they use as the basis for creating their test data. By ensuring that they check the correspondence between test-data design and the production data they have selected, auditors reduce the chances of failing to exercise important logic when they use production data.

Auditors might also be able to use test data prepared by the auditee to assist in the creation of their own test data. The auditee's information systems personnel should have prepared test cases to test the program that is the focus of the evaluation. Again, auditors can select test cases off the auditee's test data files that comply with their design using, say, generalized audit software. Once more, auditors must be diligent in checking the correspondence between the set of test cases they choose and their test-data design.

Sometimes, also, the auditee will prepare test data for an application system in cooperation with the auditor. The objective is to prepare a comprehensive "base case" that can be used to test the application system before it is released into production and during subsequent releases after maintenance work has been carried out to the application system. Whenever auditors participate in the development of test data for *base case system evaluation* (BCSE), production test data is more likely to be useful as a means of accomplishing testing objectives.

New test data must be created if cases that satisfy an auditor's test-data design are not available from either existing production files or the auditee's test data files. Various types of automated aids are available to assist with test data creation (see the next section). Parameter values must be provided as input to these aids—for example, the range of values to be generated for a particular data item. These parameter values should not be chosen haphazardly. Rather, they should be chosen carefully on the basis of the test-data design.

Automated Aids to Support Design, Creation, and Use of Test Data

Because design, creation, and use of test data are often time-consuming, re-source intensive, and error prone, various automated aids have been developed to assist in the completion of these tasks (see, e.g., Varsegi 1993). Auditors might find the following aids to be valuable when undertaking evidence-collection work using test data:

Automated Aid	*Overview*
Test data/file generators	These tools allow test cases and test files to be generated automatically. For example, auditors can specify the boundary value for a conditional statement, and a test data generator will generate three test cases: one with a value equal to the boundary value, one with a value just exceeding the boundary value, and one with a value just less than the boundary value.
Test capture/playback tools	These tools capture live transactions and allow auditors to reuse them for testing. They were developed to assist programmers, because it is often difficult to re-create the conditions that lead to failure in an online system. Auditors can use them to capture streams of data that often lead to program failure—for example, high-volume, stress conditions. The input test streams can also be edited to examine the performance of the program under changed conditions.
Test coverage/execution path monitor tools	These tools take source code as input and insert flags in the source code to indicate which statements and branches have been traversed by test data. The instrumented program is then compiled, and test data is then executed using the compiled program. At the completion of a test run, the instrumented program will print a report showing which statements or branches have or have not been executed.
Test drivers/harnesses	These tools facilitate the overall testing process. They act as an intermediary between the operating system and the program to be tested. If the program being tested terminates abnormally, they will capture and print useful diagnostic information. At the same time they will prevent disruption to or termination of the operating system. They also facilitate top-down testing by allowing modules that have not yet been written to be called. They will print a message showing the module has been called and perhaps pass parameter values back to the calling module. When a program reaches a certain point in its execution, they will either halt the program conditionally or unconditionally and permit programmers to access useful data (e.g., the contents of a record).
Test output comparators	These tools allow the results obtained from executing one set of test data to be compared with the results obtained from executing another set of test data. Differences between the two sets of results are highlighted. Comparisons can also be made between the results obtained from executing the same production data through two versions of a program.
Static analyzers	These tools assist in the design of test data. They will read program source code and identify alternative ways of reaching different sections of code. Test data can then be designed to traverse each of these alternative paths. They will also identify sections of code that cannot be reached.

To illustrate how these tools might be used, assume auditors have employed decision tables to facilitate their design of test data using the equivalence partitioning approach. Recall that equivalence partitioning is a black-box testing approach; that is, it is based on the program's specifications rather than direct examination of the program's source code to identify its control structure. The risk with equivalence partitioning, therefore, is that auditors will not execute sections of code because they are not documented in the specifications.

After auditors have designed and created the test data, they might then instrument the program using an execution path monitor tool. They can then execute the instrumented program using the test data they have created. If the execution path monitor identifies sections of code they have not tested, three possibilities exist: *(1)* their test data is erroneous or incomplete; *(2)* the program code is erroneous; *(3)* the program code does not comply with the specifications. Whatever the reason, auditors can then go back and either modify their test data or investigate the program further to detect the source of the discrepancy.

Benefits and Costs of Test Data

The major benefit of using test data as an evidence-collection technique is that it allows auditors to examine the quality of program code directly. Well-designed test data specifically addresses the question of whether the code complies with specifications. The quality of the code need not be inferred from the quality of production data that the program has processed. Well-designed test data also specifically addresses the question of whether defective execution paths exist in the code.

Some people claim that a major benefit of using test data arises from auditors needing little technical competence with computers to use the technique. For a simple batch system or an undisciplined approach to the use of test data, this claim could be true. As we have seen in this chapter, however, the design and creation of high-quality test data and the use of automated tools to support the test data approach require auditors to have substantial knowledge of information technology.

The primary disadvantage of using test data as an evidence-collection technique is that it is often time-consuming and costly. As the theory underlying test-data design improves and automated tools to support test-data design, implementation, and use become more widely available, this disadvantage might become less important. As the quality of code improves and more code is implemented via high-level languages, use of test data also becomes more feasible.

Unfortunately, little research has been undertaken comparing the effectiveness of different test data strategies. Moreover, the results obtained so far have been mixed. For example, Howden (1978) and Basili and Selby (1987) found that programmers using some types of black-box testing strategies outperformed programmers using some types of white-box testing strategies. Myers (1978) found no difference in performance, however, between programmers using black-box testing and programmers using white-box testing. Lauterbach and Randall (1989) found that white-box testing outperformed black-box testing. In short, auditors have little guidance on whether black-box testing is likely to be more effective than white-box testing and under what circumstances it is likely to be more effective. Moreover, auditors have little guidance in choosing a particular test-data design strategy from the large number of test-data design strategies that have now been developed.

In our discussion of the benefits and costs of code review, recall, also, that we examined briefly the results of some experimental research on the effectiveness of code review versus test data as a means of detecting defects in programs. We saw that the results reported were equivocal. Several studies found test data to be more effective than code review; others obtained the opposite finding. Some of the more interesting research undertaken by Myers (1978), concludes that the most effective testing strategy will occur when two knowledgeable persons work independently to conduct testing and their results are then combined. He also found that the effectiveness and efficiency with which test data is employed seems highly dependent on the capabilities of the persons who use the technique.

PROGRAM CODE COMPARISON

Auditors use program code comparison for two reasons. First, it provides some assurance that they are auditing the correct version of software. For example, they might wish to undertake code review of the material parts of a program. They need to determine, therefore, whether the source code provided to them for review purposes corresponds to the source code used to compile the production object code. Using program code comparison, auditors can determine whether the two versions of the source code are the same. We discuss this use of code comparison next.

Second, it provides some assurance that any software used as an audit tool is the correct version of the software. For example, assume an organization has used specialized audit software to collect audit evidence throughout some period of time. Auditors need to determine whether they can rely on the evidence as a basis for forming their audit judgments. In this light, auditors might wish to compare an audit version of the specialized audit software (one that they have tested comprehensively at a prior time and one that they have judged to be free of material defects) with the organization's version of the software. If auditors find correspondence between the audit version and the organization's version of the software, they might then conclude they can rely on the evidence collected by the specialized audit software as the basis for the audit judgments they make.

Types of Code Comparison

Software is available to undertake two types of program code comparison: *(1)* source-code comparison and *(2)* object-code comparison. With source-code comparison, the software should provide a meaningful listing of any discrepancies between two versions of a program's source code. Nevertheless, often auditors must obtain further assurance that the source-code version they are evaluating is the one used to compile the production object code.

With object-code comparison, auditors will have difficulty identifying the *nature* of any discrepancies found between two versions of object code. Recall that few people can read and understand object code. Thus, a report of discrepancies is unlikely to provide much assistance. Instead, object-code comparison is better used to obtain an answer to the following simple question: Are there any discrepancies between two versions of object code? If discrepancies are identified, other techniques must be used to identify the nature of and cause of the discrepancies.

Using Code Comparison

Source-code and object-code comparison are often most effective as audit techniques when auditors use them in conjunction with each other. Figure 17–12 shows an overall approach we can follow. First, we compare the audit version of a program's source code with that version that the organization we are auditing contends is the source code used to compile the production object code. Any discrepancies identified between the source-code versions must be reconciled. Second, we compile either the audit or organizational version of the source code with the compiler used to produce the production object code. Third, we compare the object code produced via this compilation with the

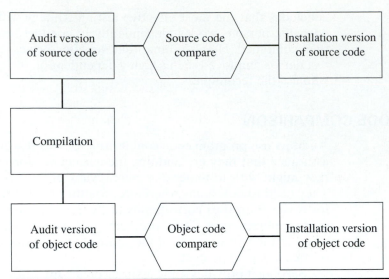

FIGURE 17–12. Use of code comparison for evidence gathering.

production version of the object code. Any discrepancies identified mean either the wrong compiler has been used or the organization has supplied us with the wrong version of the source code or production object code.

Benefits and Costs of Code Comparison

The code comparison technique is an easy way of identifying changes made to programs. The software that performs code comparison usually is neither costly to purchase nor to execute. Furthermore, auditors require little technical skill to be able to use the software.

Identifying the implications of any discrepancies found in the code, however, requires some knowledge of programming and the programming language used. Auditors must be able to determine whether a discrepancy reflects a material change to the program or a minor change. They must also be able to read and understand the program code if they are to be capable of making an informed judgment on the materiality of the discrepancy.

A limitation of the technique is that it does not provide any evidence directly on the quality of the code being compared. Auditors do not know, for example, whether the code safeguards assets or is efficient. They must first thoroughly evaluate one version of the code against audit objectives and then use this version as a blueprint for comparison purposes. If auditors identify discrepancies between another version of the code and this blueprint version, they must then be able to judge whether the changes made have undermined the quality of the code.

Code comparison programs also differ in terms of the quality of their output. For example, assume two versions of code differ because a block of documentation text in the program has been shifted from one position in the program to another position in the program. Some code comparison programs will show that the entire block has been changed. They will print out the entire block as having been deleted from one part of the code. They will also print out the entire block as having been inserted in another section of the code. Other code comparison programs will show that the block of text simply has been shifted in terms of its position in the program. If auditors were to frequently use the former type of code comparison program, eventually, they might become careless and miss a material change that was made in a block of code that had also been shifted within the program they are evaluating.

SUMMARY

Three evidence-collection techniques used primarily to evaluate the quality of program logic are code review, test data, and code comparison. Each can be used independently. Each can also be used in conjunction with the other two, however, to perform an integrated test of whether defects exist in a program. Code review provides a basis for auditors to generate flaw hypotheses about program logic. Test data enables auditors to test these hypotheses. Code comparison allows auditors to test whether the production version of a program used is the tested version.

A major decision auditors must make when using code review or test data is how they will determine the requirements that the program they will examine must fulfill. Empirical evidence shows that documented program specifications are often defective. Thus, if auditors rely on these specifications as the basis for the code review or test-data design, they could reach erroneous conclusions about the quality of the program being examined. Similarly, empirical evidence shows that program designs are often defective. Thus, if auditors rely on the design (perhaps as manifested in the code), they again might reach erroneous conclusions about the quality of the program code they are examining.

Code review involves seven steps: *(1)* selecting the source code to be examined on the basis of materiality and risk; *(2)* reviewing the organization's programming standards to develop expectations about the nature of and quality of the code that is likely to be encountered; *(3)* obtaining an understanding of the program specifications; *(4)* obtaining the source code listing; *(5)* reviewing the programming language used to implement the code to develop expectations about the likely strengths and weaknesses of the code; *(6)* reviewing the source code to identify defects in the code; and *(7)* formulating hypotheses about the effects of these defects.

The black-box approach to developing test data uses the program specifications as the basis for test-data design. Two black-box approaches are *(1)* equivalence partitioning, which divides the input domain of a program into a number of equivalence classes that will be tested, and *(2)* boundary value analysis, which tests the boundary conditions of the equivalence classes of the input domain. The white-box approach to developing test data uses the internal structure of the program as the basis for test-data design. Two white-box approaches are *(1)* basis testing, which aims to achieve full branch coverage in testing the program, and *(2)* loop testing, which aims to identify defective program loops.

Software is available to perform either source-code comparison or object-code comparison. Source-code comparison provides a meaningful description of discrepancies between two versions of a program. Auditors need to obtain assurance, however, that the source code examined is the version used to compile the production object code. Object-code comparison often does not allow auditors to interpret meaningfully any discrepancies they identify between two versions of object code. Nevertheless, if one version of the object code is the production version, auditors can determine directly whether unanticipated and perhaps unauthorized modifications have occurred to the production program.

Review Questions

17–1 Briefly explain the nature of the code review, test data, and code comparison evidence-collection techniques. Explain how they can be used as an interrelated set of techniques to examine the quality of a program.

17–2 Briefly outline the findings of the limited empirical research that has been undertaken on where errors occur in programs. What implications do these findings have for auditors' use of various audit evidence-collection techniques?

17–3 Briefly explain how code review can be used to identify ineffective code and nonstandard code in a program.

17–4 On what criteria should auditors select the source code to be examined during program source code review?

17–5 What are the purposes of examining an organization's programming standards in preparation for reviewing a program's source code?

17–6 What are the purposes of examining the choice of programming language used when undertaking a review of program source code?

17–7 Briefly explain the purpose of auditors first reviewing input/output instructions when undertaking code review of a program.

17–8 What concerns arise when auditors encounter a CALL statement during code review of a COBOL program?

17–9 Give three COBOL verbs that can be used to violate the privacy of data. Explain briefly how they can be used. How would auditors go about detecting the use of these verbs?

17–10 In a COBOL program, what verbs would auditors review to check any computations performed in the program? What verbs do you think would be the most error-prone?

17–11 Give one strength and one limitation of program code review as an audit evidence-collection technique.

17–12 What is meant by reliable test data? Practically, is it possible to establish whether a set of test data is reliable? Why or why not?

17–13 Briefly explain the difference between the black-box approach to test-data design and the white-box approach to test-data design.

17–14 Briefly explain the nature of equivalence partitioning as a black-box test-data design method.

17–15 How can decision tables and decision trees help auditors to undertake the equivalence-partitioning approach to test-data design?

17–16 What factors affect whether auditors use a reduced form or an unreduced form of a decision table to design test data for audit evidence-collection purposes? If auditors base their test-data design on the reduced form of a decision table, why is it then important to use an execution path monitor in conjunction with their program test?

17–17 Briefly explain the nature of boundary value analysis as a test-data design method. Why was boundary value analysis developed?

17–18 If a white-box approach to test-data design is used, briefly explain the difference between the objectives of full statement coverage, full branch coverage, and full path coverage. In practice, which objective do you think auditors will usually have when they design test data?

17–19 Briefly explain the nature of basis path testing as a test-data design method. What type of program coverage does basis path testing assist auditors to achieve?

17–20 Briefly explain the nature of McCabe's cyclomatic complexity number. How is it useful to auditors in their work?

17–21 Briefly explain the nature of loop testing as a test-data design method. List the steps auditors should undertake to test whether there are errors in a simple loop.

17–22 Briefly explain how auditors can use production data to create test data. Is production data sometimes still useful even though it does not meet exactly the test-data design specifications?

17–23 How would a test driver/harness help auditors to undertake testing of a program for audit purposes?

17–24 Briefly explain the difference between an execution path monitor and a static analyzer. Which type of tool is likely to be more useful to auditors? Why?

17–25 "Auditors require limited technical knowledge to use test data effectively as an evidence-gathering tool." Discuss briefly.

17–26 Why might auditors use program code comparison when evaluating the quality of a program?

17–27 Briefly explain the difference between program source-code comparison and program object-code comparison. What are the relative advantages and disadvantages of each type of code comparison?

17–28 List two reasons why differences can arise between two object-code versions of a program.

17–29 Briefly explain one strength and one limitation of code comparison as an audit evidence-collection technique.

Multiple-Choice Questions

17–1 Based on a limited number of empirical studies of where problems occur in programs, which of the following statements is *false*?
  a Requirements specification and design errors are just as prominent as coding errors
  b Coding errors seem to relate primarily to incorrect indexing, incorrect computation, and incorrect control flow
  c Defects relating to computation are more common than defects relating to data management
  d A small number of program modules will have a large number of faults

17–2 Which of the following is *most likely* to be the motivation for auditors to use program source-code review?
  a Generalized audit software is unavailable as an evidence-collection tool
  b The auditor believes the program to be reviewed contains inefficient code
  c The program processes only small quantities of data so only a small amount of code needs to be reviewed
  d The auditor is unwilling to treat the program as a black box

17–3 When using risk assessment techniques to assess the materiality of source code, a software reliability model can be used primarily to:
  a Determine the hazards that are associated with each module
  b Estimate the expected losses associated with the occurrence of each hazard
  c Estimate the exposures associated with each module's use
  d Determine the expected number of failures that will occur in each module as a result of software faults

17–4 Which of the following is *most likely* to be the auditor's purpose in reviewing an organization's programming standards during the conduct of code review?
  a To develop expectations about the characteristics of the code that will be reviewed
  b To better understand the program's specifications when they are evaluated
  c To identify those areas where non-standard code is most likely to occur in a program
  d To determine the material modules in a program so they can be selected for review

17–5 During the conduct of code review, which of the following strategies is most likely to identify defects in the program's specifications?
  a Evaluating the code for compliance with the organization's coding standards
  b Evaluating the documented program specifications in light of interviews conducted with users
  c Evaluating the code for compliance with the documented program specifications
  d Evaluating the complexity of the control structures that are used within the program

17–6 Which of the following is *unlikely* to be a reason for auditors to review the programming language used to implement the code they are reviewing?

a To determine whether they must have someone else undertake the code review on their behalf

b To evaluate whether the program's specifications are likely to be defective in light of the programming language chosen

c To evaluate whether the choice of programming language used is well suited to the application's needs

d To determine whether the programming language used contains any non-standard features

17–7 Which of the following COBOL computational verbs is likely to be the *most* error-prone?

a MULTIPLY

b SUBTRACT

c COMPUTE

d DIVIDE

17–8 For which of the following COBOL reserved words are coding errors *most likely* to be made?

a INSPECT

b ON SIZE ERROR

c PERFORM . . . UNTIL

d FILE STATUS

17–9 A reliable set of test data is one that:

a Reveals an error in a program whenever the program contains an error

b Traverses all conditional execution paths in the program that it tests

c Requires no change even when modifications are made to the program that it tests

d Produces consistent results across various executions of the program that it tests

17–10 Which of the following statements *best* describes the difference between the black-box and the white-box approaches to test-data design?

a The black-box approach relies on knowledge of the functional specifications of the program to be tested, whereas the white-box approach relies on knowledge of the program's internal structure

b The black-box approach emphasizes reliable test-data design, whereas the white-box approach emphasizes cost-effective test-data design

c The black-box approach is oriented toward automatic test data generation, whereas the white-box approach is oriented toward automatic theorem proving

d The black-box approach is oriented toward unit testing, whereas the white-box approach is oriented toward system testing

17–11 Which of the following statements about equivalence partitioning as a test-data design method is *false*?

a One test data element should be selected that falls within each equivalence class, and one should be selected that falls outside each equivalence class

b The primary basis for the test-data design using equivalence partitioning is the set of program specifications

c The objective of equivalence partitioning is to achieve full path coverage of the program to be tested

d The equivalence classes for the program to be tested are identified via the set of conditional tests undertaken by the program

17–12 The purpose of the results stub in a decision table used for test-data design purposes is to:

a Document the conditions that lead to a particular action

    b Shows the expected and actual outcomes for the test data associated with each rule

    c Shows the rules for different conditional values

    d Shows the actions to be undertaken when a rule is satisfied

17–13 Which of the following statements about boundary value analysis is *true*?

    a It cannot be used to design test data to test the boundaries of output values

    b It leads to smaller amounts of test data being designed than equivalence partitioning

    c It is easier to undertake if decision trees rather than decision tables are used as the basis for test-data design

    d It is motivated by the empirical finding that logic errors often seem to occur at the boundaries of equivalence classes

17–14 Achieving full statement coverage during testing of a program means that:

    a Every branching statement in the program is traversed at least once during the test run

    b All execution paths in the program are traversed at least once by the test data

    c For any statement that is traversed by test data, both the "true" and "false" values are tested

    d Each program statement is executed at least once during the test run

17–15 Which of the following statements about basis path testing is *false*?

    a The number of paths in the basis set can be calculated using McCabe's cyclomatic complexity number

    b Basis path testing is an approach to achieving full branch coverage of the code auditors are seeking to test

    c Basis path testing is an inappropriate test-data design technique when the code contains compound conditional statements

    d Test data must be designed to traverse each path in the basis set

17–16 Which of the following statements about McCabe's cyclomatic complexity number is *false*?

    a It is equal to the number of predicate nodes in a flowgraph plus one

    b It sets a lower limit on the complexity of program code that is suitable for basis path testing

    c It defines the number of independent paths in the basis set of a section of program code

    d It is designed to be a measure of the logical complexity of a piece of program code

17–17 Which of the following statements about loop testing is *false*?

    a It supplements basis path testing because loops will not be traversed with test data designed using basis path testing

    b With nested loops, testing should commence with the innermost loop and work outwards to the outermost loop

    c With simple loops, the loop should be checked at its lower boundary by exercising zero, one, and two passes through the loop

    d Providing concatenated loops are independent of one another, they can be tested using the strategies developed for simple loops and nested loops

17–18 Which of the following statements about creating test data is *true*?

    a Test data should never be created using live production data

    b The approach used to create test data will affect the approach used to design test data

    c Test data to exercise the paths executed most frequently in a program should be designed first

    d Generalized audit software can be used to select test data off an auditee's test data files that comply with the auditor's test-data design

17–19 Which of the following pairs of automated testing tools identify sections of code that cannot be reached during execution of a program?
  a Test output comparators and test data generators
  b Execution path monitors and static analyzers
  c Test harnesses and output comparators
  d Static analyzers and test harnesses

17–20 Which of the following statements about the costs and benefits of using test data as an audit evidence-collection tool is *true*?
  a Black-box testing tends to be a more effective test-data design strategy than white-box testing
  b A major advantage of using test data to collect evidence is that auditors require little technical competence with computers to use it effectively
  c The most effective test-data design strategy might be to have two auditors work independently to conduct testing and to pool their results than to have them work together during testing
  d Use of test data to collect audit evidence will take less time than code review, but it is less effective at identifying program defects

17–21 Which of the following is *least likely* to be a reason for audit use of code comparison software?
  a To identify production object code that is ineffective or inefficient
  b To identify unauthorized changes that have been made to production source code
  c To determine whether reliance can be placed on the integrity of software provided to auditors for evidence-collection purposes
  d To determine whether source code that was reviewed during the previous audit needs to reviewed again

17–22 Which of the following should *not* cause a discrepancy to be identified when object-code comparison is undertaken between an audit blueprint of a program and a production version of the program?
  a The wrong version of the source code has been used to compile the production object code
  b A block of documentation text has been shifted in the production version of the source code
  c Different versions of a compiler have been used to compile the blueprint and production code
  d A direct fix has been made on one version of the object code

Exercises and Cases

17–1 As the auditor responsible for examining the accounts receivable system within an information systems facility, you decide to undertake code review of a COBOL program that prints out a list of customers who have exceeded their allowed credit limit. Because the source code is stored in a library and online facilities are available, you use an editor to retrieve all instances of various key words in the program. One of the "IF" statements you retrieve runs as follows:

```
IF ACBAL LE ALLOWBAL OR ACNUM EQ C105–6A
     NEXT SENTENCE
ELSE
     PERFORM PRINT-ROUTINE
END-IF
```

You are perplexed by this piece of code. None of the employees within the organization has an account with the company numbered C105-6A. Moreover, you cannot find any customer to whom this account number has yet been issued.

Required: Try to identify why you should be concerned with this piece of code. When you have identified the reason why you should be concerned, outline how you would then proceed with the audit. Note, you will require a basic knowledge of COBOL (or some programming knowledge) to be able to answer this question.

17–2   You are the auditor in charge of the audit of the payroll system for an organization. One of your staff performs a code review of the input validation program for timecard data. She brings the following section of COBOL code to you because she is unable to understand the purpose of the code:

```
INSPECT HRS-WORKED TALLYING UNTIL FIRST 9
    REPLACING BY 4.
IF HRS-WORKED LT ZERO OR HRS-WORKED GT 60
    PERFORM ERROR-ROUTINE
    GO TO READ-NEW-CARD.
IF TALLY EQ 1
    INSPECT HRS-WORKED UNTIL FIRST 4
    REPLACING BY 9.
GO TO SALARY-CALC.
```

Required: Briefly outline the advice you would give to her. In particular, explain the meaning of the code and indicate the way in which you believe the audit should now proceed. Note, you will require an intermediate knowledge of COBOL to be able to answer this question.

17–3   Yatalee Yoghurt Ltd. is a major Brisbane-based firm that sells dairy foods throughout Australia. It is also a major exporter of dairy foods to the Southeast Asian region.

Your audit firm has just taken over the external audit of Yatalee. As the partner in charge for the first-time audit of Yatalee, one day you are called to mediate in a dispute that has arisen between the manager on the audit and the senior information systems auditor from your firm who has been asked to consult to your audit team.

On the basis of the senior information systems auditor's review and testing of general/management controls, she has concluded that a high level of reliance can be placed upon these controls. Accordingly, she has advised that the extent of substantive testing can be reduced. In this light, she and the manager on the audit have been planning the substantive tests to be undertaken in the remainder of the audit. A dispute has arisen between them over the substantive tests that now should be undertaken in relation to production costs. The calculation of some production costs is complex, and they constitute a material item in Yatalee's financial statements.

Because the program code to calculate production costs has been written in COBOL, the manager is arguing that the senior information systems auditor should undertake program source-code review to determine whether material errors or irregularities are likely to exist in the production cost figures. The senior information systems auditor is arguing, however, that she should use the firm's generalized audit software package to perform parallel simulation to determine whether material errors or irregularities are likely to exist in the production cost figures. She points out that Yatalee uses structured walkthroughs to examine the quality of code in any of its major programs before they are released from testing into production use. During her tests of the structured walkthrough process, she concluded that a high level of reliance could be placed upon these controls. In her opinion, therefore, program source-code review is unlikely to identify any defects in the program code because the code has already been reviewed by a team of programmers. She argues that it would be more cost effective to test for defects in the code using parallel simulation.

Required: What advice would you give to the manager and the senior information systems auditor to try to help them to resolve their dispute?

17–4 You are the auditor responsible for evaluating an organization's invoicing program. You decide to use test data to test that section of the program relating to sales discounts. During an interview with the sales manager, you make the following notes about how the program is supposed to operate:

Providing customers pay within 30 days, they are entitled to a sales discount. If the sales amount is more than $5,000, a 1 percent discount applies. If sales are more than $10,000, a 1.5 percent discount applies. For new customers, however, a salesperson is allowed to override the standard discount. For sales less than or equal to $5,000, the salesperson can give a 1 percent discount; more than $5,000, a 1.5 percent discount; and more than $10,000, a 2 percent discount. If the customer is the federal government, a 4 percent discount always applies, providing payment is still received within 30 days.

Required: Use a decision table to design test data that complies with the equivalence partitioning approach. Be sure to check that your decision table and test data design are complete.

17–5 The specifications for a fixed-assets program include the following paragraph.

Straight-line depreciation is to be charged on fixed assets at the following rates:

Code no.	Rate
100–199	10%
200–299	15%
300–399	20%

If the fixed asset is located in Alice Springs, however, a further 5 percent is to be added to the depreciation rate to allow for the higher deterioration that results from the more severe climate. Moreover, any asset in the 200–299 code category that produces more than 10,000 units per year is to have an extra 2 percent added to the depreciation rate to allow for the higher deterioration that occurs when the asset produces at above normal output.

Required: Use a decision table to design test data that complies with the boundary value analysis approach. Be sure to check that your decision table and test data design are complete.

17–6 Boon Lay Trading (Pte) Ltd. is a medium-sized import-export business based in Singapore. As the information systems auditor working on the audit team that is undertaking an audit of Boon Lay, you conclude that you cannot rely on controls over the programming function within Boon Lay. Accordingly, you decide to expand the extent of substantive testing you will undertake to determine whether material errors or irregularities exist in Boon Lay's accounts.

One of the major expense items within Boon Lay's accounts is freight costs. During analytical review work that the audit team has undertaken, freight costs were identified as having grown significantly more than the volume of turnover. During your review work of management controls over the information systems function within Boon Lay, you also noted that significant maintenance work had been undertaken on the application system where freight costs are calculated.

You decide to test a section of code in this application system that undertakes some of the freight cost calculations. The system is written in COBOL, and the program module you are currently examining contains the following code:

```
    IF FREIGHT-REGION EQUALS "A" OR "B"
        MOVE RATE (1) TO FREIGHT-COST
        PERFORM FREIGHT-COST-EXPENSE
    ELSE
        IF FREIGHT-REGION EQUALS "C"
            MOVE RATE (2) TO FREIGHT-COST
            PERFORM FREIGHT-COST-EXPENSE
        ELSE
            IF FREIGHT-REGION EQUALS "D"
                MOVE RATE (3) TO FREIGHT-COST
                PERFORM FREIGHT-COST-EXPENSE
            ELSE
                MOVE RATE (4) TO FREIGHT-COST
                ADD 1 TO PENALTY-COST-SHIPMENTS
                PERFORM FREIGHT-COST-EXPENSE
            END-IF
        END-IF
    END-IF
    IF GROSS-FREIGHT-AMOUNT GT 2500.00
        COMPUTE NET-FREIGHT-AMOUNT = GROSS-FREIGHT-
        AMOUNT – (GROSS-FREIGHT-AMOUNT * DISCOUNT (1))
    ELSE
        IF GROSS-FREIGHT-AMOUNT GT 2000
            COMPUTE NET-FREIGHT-AMOUNT = GROSS-
            FREIGHT-AMOUNT – (GROSS-FREIGHT-AMOUNT *
            DISCOUNT (2))
        ELSE
            IF GROSS-FREIGHT-AMOUNT GT 1500 AND
            CUSTOMER-TYPE EQUALS "GOOD"
                COMPUTE NET-FREIGHT-AMOUNT = GROSS-
                FREIGHT-AMOUNT – (GROSS-FREIGHT-
                AMOUNT * DISCOUNT (3))
            ELSE
                COMPUTE NET-FREIGHT-AMOUNT = GROSS-
                FREIGHT-AMOUNT
            END-IF
        END-IF
    END-IF
```

Required: Draw a flowgraph representation of the code. Identify a basis set of paths for the module. Calculate McCabe's cyclomatic complexity number to check you have the correct number of paths in the basis set. On the basis of reading the code, comment on any concerns you have about its quality.

17–7 You are a partner with information systems audit expertise in a firm of external auditors. Because of your scintillating personality, you win the audit of a medium-size manufacturing firm that has just gone public.

Subsequent to the controls review and during the planning of the substantive tests, the manager on the job approaches you about his intention to use test data to determine whether the accounting software used by the manufacturing firm contains any material defects. The manager is concerned because he has encountered problems with the manufacturing firm's information systems manager. When he informed the information systems manager that he intended to use test data to test the accounting software, she ridiculed him, claiming that he was proposing a pointless exercise. She argued that all the accounting software had been purchased as generalized packages from several well-known software vendors. She also argued that the manufacturing firm did not carry out any software development, implementation, and maintenance work. Indeed, she was the only information systems professional employed by the firm, and her job was to keep the firm's systems running smoothly. In short, she had responsibility for planning and operations. Thus, there was no risk that the software had been modified. She threatens that she will inform her managing director that the auditors are wasting money if your manager proceeds with using test data.

Required: To avert an impending disaster with your client, how would you now proceed? In particular, address the question of whether the audit manager should proceed with using test data for evidence-collection purposes. Explain your reasons for your recommendation.

17–8 You are the senior information systems auditor in a public accounting firm. At the start of this financial year, your firm took over the audit of a major bank that has a full range of wholesale and retail banking services. Your firm was successful in winning the tender for the provision of external audit services.

Interest on corporate loans is a highly material revenue item for the bank. During the conduct of analytical review activities at the start of this financial year, the audit team has noticed some aberrations in the size of corporate loan interest earned. Specifically, when the audit team built a model to predict the amount of interest that should have been earned, the reported amount turned out to be substantially higher than the predicted amount. The team has checked its model carefully, and the members of the team cannot find a reason for the variance.

The partner in charge of the audit subsequently met with the president of the bank to indicate that substantive tests would have to be increased. Additional work would be needed to determine whether the variation between the reported amount of interest and the predicted amount of interest reflected errors or irregularities in the bank's accounts or an error in the analytical model. The partner informed the president that the additional substantive testing might lead to a 5 percent increase in the cost of the audit. The president reacted angrily. She indicated to the partner that your firm would not have won the audit tender if the bank had known that audit fees would be increased in this way. The partner and the president agreed to take a few days to reflect on the situation.

A day after this meeting, the president called the partner to inform him that last year the previous audit firm had undertaken extensive testing of the program that calculates interest revenue on corporate loans. When the audit firm had completed its tests, it had taken a copy of the source code. The president informs your partner that no changes have been made to the program since that time. She asks whether you might not compare the current program against the version obtained by the previous audit firm to confirm that there are no defects in the program's calculation of interest.

Your partner has contacted the previous audit firm. The partner in that firm who was responsible for the bank's audit confirms that the interest program was tested, that his firm was happy with the results, and that they indeed made a copy of the source code. He indicates that he will send a cartridge containing a copy of the source code to your firm.

Upon receipt of the cartridge, the partner in your firm who is in charge of the bank's audit contacts you to request your assistance by your undertaking the code comparison tests. When you use a code-comparison program to compare the source code provided by the previous audit firm against the production source code provided by the bank, you find no discrepancies. Using the bank's compiler, you then compile the source code provided by the previous audit firm. Next you use the code comparison program to compare the object code you generate against the production object code provided to you by the bank. Again, you find no discrepancies.

Required: Write a brief report to the partner in your firm who is in charge of the bank's audit advising him on how you think he should now proceed. If you have any concerns about the reliability of your findings, you should mention these concerns in your report, together with their implications for how the remainder of the audit should be conducted.

Answers to Multiple-Choice Questions

17–1	c	**17–7**	c	**17–13**	d	**17–19**	b
17–2	d	**17–8**	a	**17–14**	d	**17–20**	c
17–3	d	**17–9**	a	**17–15**	c	**17–21**	a
17–4	a	**17–10**	a	**17–16**	b	**17–22**	b
17–5	b	**17–11**	c	**17–17**	a		
17–6	b	**17–12**	b	**17–18**	d		

REFERENCES

Basili, V.R., and B.T. Perricone (1984), "Software Errors and Complexity: An Empirical Investigation," *Communications of the ACM* (January), 42–52.

——— and R.W. Selby (1987), "Comparing the Effectiveness of Software Testing Strategies," *IEEE Transactions on Software Engineering* (December), 1278–1296.

Beizer, B. (1983), *Software Testing Techniques.* New York: Van Nostrand Reinhold.

Clapp, Judith A., Saul F. Stanten, W.W. Peng, D.R. Wallace, Deborah A. Cerino, and Roger J. Dziegiel, Jr. (1995), *Software Quality Control, Error Analysis, and Testing.* Park Ridge, NJ: Noyes Data Corporation.

Coburn, Edward J. (1988), *Advanced Structured COBOL.* San Diego: Harcourt Brace Jovanovich.

De Millo, Richard A., Richard J. Lipton, and Alan J. Perlis (1979), "Social Processes and Proofs of Theorems and Programs," *Communications of the ACM* (May), 271–280.

Elshoff, James L. (1976), "An Analysis of Some Commercial PL/1 Programs," *IEEE Transactions on Software Engineering* (June), 113–120.

Endres, Albert (1975), "An Analysis of Errors and Their Causes in System Programs," *IEEE Transactions on Software Engineering* (June), 241–252.

Gerhart, Susan L., and John B. Goodenough (1975), "Toward a Theory of Test Data Selection," *IEEE Transactions on Software Engineering* (June), 156–173.

Glass, R. L. (1981), "Persistent Software Errors," *IEEE Transactions on Software Engineering* (March), 162–168.

Hetzel, Bill (1988), *The Complete Guide to Software Testing,* 2d ed. Wellesley, MA: QED Information Sciences.

Howden, William E. (1976), "Reliability of the Path Analysis Testing Strategy," *IEEE Transactions of Software Engineering* (September), 208–215.

——— (1978), "Theoretical and Empirical Studies of Program Testing," *IEEE Transactions on Software Engineering* (July), 293–298.

Hurley, Richard B. (1983), *Decision Tables in Software Engineering.* New York: Van Nostrand Reinhold.

Lauterbach, L., and W. Randall (1989), "Experimental Evaluation of Six Test Techniques," *Proceedings of Compass 89.* New York: ACM Press, 36–41.

Marrick, Brian (1995), *The Craft of Software Testing: Subsystem Testing Including Object-Based and Object-Oriented Testing.* Upper Saddle River, NJ: Prentice-Hall.

McCabe, T.J. (1976), "A Complexity Measure," *IEEE Transactions on Software Engineering* (December), 308–320.

Myers, Glenford J. (1978), "A Controlled Experiment in Program Testing and Code Walkthroughs/Inspections," *Communications of the ACM* (September), 760–768.

——— (1979), *The Art of Software Testing*. New York: John Wiley & Sons.

Newcomer, Larry R. (1995), *Programming with Modern Structure COBOL*, 2d ed. New York: McGraw-Hill.

Ostrand, T.J., and E.J. Weyuker (1984), "Collecting and Categorizing Software Error Data in an Industrial Environment," *The Journal of Systems and Software* (November), 289–300.

Pressman, Roger S. (1997), *Software Engineering: A Practitioner's Approach*, 4th ed. New York: McGraw-Hill.

Roper, Marc (1994), *Software Testing*. London: McGraw-Hill.

Rubey, Raymond J., Joseph A. Dana, and Peter W. Biche (1975), "Quantitative Aspects of Software Validation," *IEEE Transactions on Software Engineering* (June), 150–155.

Schneidewind, N.F., and M. Hoffman (1979), "An Experiment on Software Error Data Collection and Analysis," *IEEE Transactions on Software Engineering* (May), 276–286.

Sherer, Susan A., and Jack W. Paul (1993), "Focusing Audit Testing on High Risk Software Modules: A Methodology and an Application," *Journal of Information Systems* (Fall), 65–84.

Varsegi, Alex (1993), *MVS COBOL Application Developer's Toolbox*. New York: McGraw-Hill.

Vesely, Eric Garrigue (1989), *COBOL: A Guide to Structured, Portable, Maintainable, and Efficient Program Design*. Upper Saddle River, NJ: Prentice-Hall.

Weyuker, E.J., and T.J. Ostrand (1980), "Theories of Program Testing and the Application of Revealing Subdomains," *IEEE Transactions on Software Engineering* (May), 236–246.

CHAPTER 18

Concurrent Auditing Techniques

Chapter Outline

Chapter Key Points

- Concurrent auditing techniques are used to collect audit evidence at the same time as an application system undertakes processing of its production data. They comprise two basic components. First, special audit modules are embedded in application systems or systems software to collect, process, and print audit evidence. Second, in some cases, special audit records are used to store the audit evidence collected.

- If concurrent auditing techniques identify a critical error or irregularity, they can notify auditors immediately by transmitting the audit evidence to a printer or screen that auditors should examine continuously. Alternatively, the evidence can be stored and printed or displayed at a later time.

- Five factors have motivated the use of concurrent auditing techniques. First, the paper-based audit trail in application systems is progressively disappearing. Concurrent auditing techniques provide a way for auditors to capture the evidence that previously existed in this paper-based audit trail. Second, errors or irregularities in advanced computer systems can propagate quickly to other systems and cause material losses. Concurrent auditing techniques allow auditors to monitor these systems on a timely basis. Third, performing transaction walkthroughs in advanced computer systems is often difficult. Concurrent auditing techniques provide a means of tracing transactions as they follow different execution paths in an application system. Fourth, all systems have entropy, which is their tendency to move toward internal disorder and eventual collapse. Concurrent auditing techniques provide early warning of the presence of and effects of entropy in application systems. Fifth, outsourced and distributed information systems pose problems for auditors because it is difficult for them to be physically present at information systems facilities to gather evidence. The embedded audit routines used with concurrent auditing techniques provide a way of collecting audit evidence when application system processing is carried out at remote locations.

- Integrated test facility (ITF) is a concurrent auditing technique that involves establishing a dummy entity on an application system's files and processing audit test data against this dummy entity. In this way, auditors can verify the application system's processing authenticity, accuracy, and completeness.

- The test data used with ITF might be live production transactions that are tagged so the application system knows they must also be processed against the dummy entity. Alternatively, the test data used could be designed specifically by auditors according to a test plan and submitted as part of the normal production data for the application system.

- The presence of ITF transactions in an application system affects the results obtained—for example, the control totals produced by the application system. Auditors can inform users that output has been affected by ITF transactions. Alternatively, they can try to remove their effects in some way. For example, auditors can modify the application system so it does not include the effects of ITF transactions in any output it produces.

■ The snapshot concurrent auditing technique involves having embedded audit modules take pictures of a transaction as it flows through various points in an application system. The snapshots are either printed immediately or written to a file for later printing. Auditors must determine where they want to place the snapshot points in an application system, which transactions will be subject to snapshot, and how and when the snapshot data will be presented for audit evaluation purposes.

■ A modification to the snapshot technique is the extended record technique. Whereas snapshot writes a record for each snapshot point, the extended record technique appends data for each snapshot point to a single record. All the data relating to a transaction is kept, therefore, in the one place.

■ The system control audit review file (SCARF) concurrent auditing technique involves embedding audit modules in an application system to provide continuous monitoring of a system's transactions. The data collected via these routines includes errors and irregularities, policy and procedural variances, system exceptions, statistical samples, and snapshots and extended records. It is written to a special SCARF file for immediate or subsequent audit evaluation.

■ The continuous and intermittent simulation (CIS) concurrent auditing technique can be used whenever application systems use a database management system. Transactions that are of interest to auditors are trapped by the database management system and passed to CIS. CIS then replicates the application system's processing, and the two sets of results are compared. If CIS's results differ from the application system's results, data about the discrepancy is written to a special audit file. If the discrepancies are material, CIS can instruct the database management system not to perform the updates to the database on behalf of the application system.

■ When auditors implement concurrent auditing techniques, they should follow the same steps necessary to achieve any well-implemented system. Auditors must (a) perform a feasibility study; (b) seek the support of persons who will be affected by use of concurrent auditing techniques; (c) ensure that they have sufficient expertise to develop, implement, operate, and maintain concurrent auditing techniques effectively and efficiently; (d) ensure that they have the commitment of key stakeholders including management, information systems staff, and application system users; (e) make the necessary technical decisions; (f) plan the design and implementation; (g) implement and test the techniques; and (h) carry out a postaudit of costs and benefits after concurrent auditing techniques have been used for some time.

■ The major strengths of concurrent auditing techniques are that they provide a (a) viable alternative to *ex post* auditing and auditing around the computer, (b) surprise test capability for auditors, (c) test vehicle for information systems staff, and (d) training vehicle for new users.

■ Surveys of audit use of concurrent auditing techniques indicate limited but stable use over many years. In addition, these surveys have found that concurrent auditing techniques are more likely to be used if (a) the audit is conducted by internal auditors instead of external auditors, (b) auditors are involved in the development work associated with a new application system, (c) auditors are employing other types of computer-assisted audit techniques, and (d) the incidence of automatically generated transactions in application systems goes up.

■ The major limitations of concurrent auditing techniques are (a) the costs of developing, implementing, operating, and maintaining them can be high; (b) they are unlikely to be used effectively and efficiently unless auditors have substantial knowledge of and experience with information systems auditing; and (c) they are unlikely to be effective unless they are implemented in application systems that are relatively stable.

INTRODUCTION

The previous two chapters discuss techniques that auditors can use to collect evidence *after* an information system has processed its production data. In some cases, however, this *ex post* collection of evidence for evaluation purposes is unsatisfactory from the viewpoint of achieving audit objectives. Instead, auditors need to identify problems that can occur in an information system on a more timely basis. For this reason, a set of audit techniques has been developed to collect evidence at the same time as an application system undertakes processing of its production data. These techniques are called *concurrent auditing techniques*.

In this chapter, we examine the basic nature of concurrent auditing techniques, the reasons why they were developed, their relative advantages and disadvantages, and some methods of implementing concurrent auditing techniques. A large number of different concurrent auditing techniques have now been developed. A close examination, however, reveals that they are all variations on a theme. For this reason, here we cover just a few of the major techniques that have been used. If we understand the nature of these few techniques, we should then be able to adapt them in various ways to suit the particular needs of any audit we might wish to undertake.

BASIC NATURE OF CONCURRENT AUDITING TECHNIQUES

Concurrent auditing techniques use two bases for collecting audit evidence. First, special audit modules are embedded in application systems or system software to collect, process, and print audit evidence. Second, in some cases, special audit records are used to store the audit evidence collected so auditors can examine this evidence at a later stage. These records can be stored on application system files or on a separate audit file.

Though evidence collection is concurrent with application system processing, the timing of evidence reporting is a decision that auditors can make. If a concurrent auditing technique identifies a critical error or irregularity, auditors might program the embedded audit routines to report the error or irregularity immediately. In this light, the evidence could be transmitted directly to a printer or terminal in the auditor's office (Figure 18–1a). In other cases, however, immediate reporting of the error or irregularity might not be essential. Auditors can then store the evidence for reporting at some later time (Figure 18–1b).

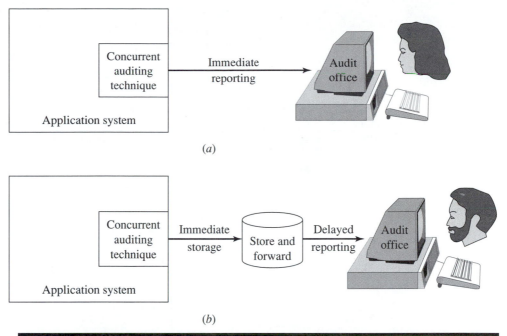

FIGURE 18–1(a). Immediate reporting of event with concurrent auditing. (b). Delayed reporting of event with concurrent auditing.

NEED FOR CONCURRENT AUDITING TECHNIQUES

Concurrent auditing techniques were developed in the late 1960s and early 1970s to address a set of problems that were arising as computer-based information systems became more widespread. Moreover, several recent trends provide further impetus to deploy concurrent auditing techniques more extensively. We examine these factors briefly in the following subsections.

Disappearing Paper-Based Audit Trail

Historically, auditors have placed substantial reliance in evidence-collection work on the paper trail that documents the sequence of events that have occurred within an information system. This trail has provided a means of determining whether material errors or irregularities have occurred in an information system.

Paper-based audit trails have been progressively disappearing, however, as computer systems have replaced manual systems and as source documents have given away to screen-based input and output. A paper audit trail is no longer left automatically as the outcome of an event in an application system. Instead, the existence of an adequate audit trail depends on purposeful design and implementation of processes to record events in computer systems.

Auditors might choose not to rely on the audit trails implemented within an application system; for example, they might doubt the authenticity of the data collected in the application system's audit trail. In such circumstances, auditors can use concurrent auditing techniques to record the events in which they are interested. In essence, auditors can use concurrent auditing techniques to ensure that they have an adequate audit trail in an information system and to obtain a higher level of assurance in the veracity of the data collected in the audit trail.

Continuous Monitoring Required by Advanced Systems

A common characteristic of advanced information systems is that they are tightly coupled; that is, an event in one application system leads to an event in another application system. For example, consider the set of systems shown

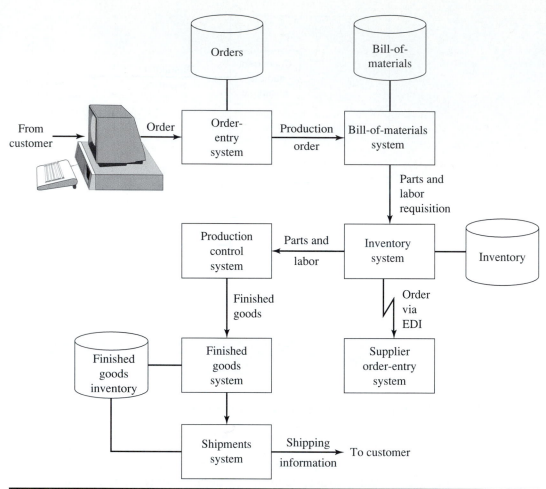

FIGURE 18–2. Example of tightly coupled application systems.

in Figure 18–2. The receipt of an order from a customer leads automatically to the issuance of a production order. This order is then exploded via a bill-of-materials application system to determine the parts and labor needed to fulfill the order. An inventory system next checks the availability of inventory, reserves the inventory if it is available, and places an order on a supplier via an electronic data interchange system if any part is in short supply. A production scheduling system then schedules the order for production. When production is to be started, a production control system initiates the issue of materials and labor requisitions and collects production performance and costing data as the order progresses through the production system. When production of the goods is completed, a finished goods system updates inventory. Finally, a shipments system initiates dispatch of the goods to the customer.

When systems are tightly coupled, errors or irregularities in one system can quickly propagate to other systems and cause material losses. For example, assume an order-entry program corrupted data in an order in the set of systems described previously. If the corrupted data resulted in an overstatement of the quantity required by the customer, the bill-of-materials system would in turn overstate the quantities of materials and labor required. Excessive raw materials might then be ordered as inventory falls below reorder levels, and additional labor might be hired unnecessarily. Subsequent orders might be lost because the inventory system indicates insufficient materials and labor are available to fill these orders on a timely basis. Limited production capacity might be wasted as goods are produced that no one has ordered. Further costs might be incurred as excessive goods are shipped to the customer and presumably eventually returned by the customer.

To mitigate losses when systems are tightly coupled, timely identification of errors or irregularities is essential. For this reason, auditors might use concurrent auditing techniques to report any event that could manifest an error or irregularity immediately it occurs. They can then follow up on the event to determine whether it represents a material exposure.

Increasing Difficulty of Performing Transaction Walkthroughs

Auditors often gain an understanding of an application system by taking typical transactions and tracing them through the various execution paths that can be traversed within the system. Walking typical transactions through a system also helps to identify the system's strengths and weaknesses and plan subsequent audit tests.

Advanced information systems make the walkthrough process more difficult because they often have a large number of complex execution paths. As demonstrated previously, extensive coupling between different application systems also complicates matters. For example, understanding how a parts master file is updated might mean auditors must examine processes in the production scheduling system, inventory reordering system, purchasing system, receiving system, and warehousing system.

Concurrent auditing techniques facilitate our understanding of advanced systems by collecting all the information normally obtained from a walkthrough in the one place. They can be used to capture images of a transaction as it traverses a particular execution path. These images then can be written to a file for subsequent examination. When auditors then attempt to understand a system and to identify its strengths and weaknesses, all the information associated with the different execution paths in the system exists in the one place.

Presence of Entropy in Systems

All systems have a characteristic called *entropy*, which is the tendency of systems toward internal disorder and eventual collapse. In information systems, entropy arises in a variety of ways. One form occurs because user information requirements change as the business they undertake changes. As a result, existing information systems become less effective at meeting their needs. A second form occurs through increases in the numbers of transactions that must be processed. The existing hardware and software eventually becomes unable to handle the workload satisfactorily. Errors then occur, for example, because transaction queues exceed their maximum allowed length. A third form arises through having to maintain existing systems. Knowledge about existing systems gradually degrades over time as the personnel who developed these systems leave to take other positions. As a result, errors creep into systems during maintenance work because maintenance staff do not fully understand the systems on which they are working.

Concurrent auditing techniques provide a means of identifying increasing entropy in information systems at an early stage. They can be used to gather data on error and exception frequencies and to give advance warning of stresses being placed on systems. Thus, they facilitate auditors' understanding of a system's evolution. They also assist the stakeholders in an information system to mitigate the consequences of errors by providing feedback that allows them to undertake timely modifications in light of changing circumstances.

Problems Posed by Outsourced and Distributed Information Systems

Sometimes it is difficult for auditors to be physically present at an information systems facility to gather audit evidence. For example, a company's data processing might be performed by an outsourcing vendor located elsewhere, or its data processing might be distributed over many different physical locations. This presents two difficulties for auditors. First, they cannot collect valuable audit evidence because they cannot directly observe activities at remote sites, nor can they easily interview personnel who work at remote sites. Second, it is often more difficult for auditors to use computer-based evidence collection tools like generalized audit software or test data because they cannot easily access program and data files, or they encounter operational difficulties in running these tools at remote sites.

Concurrent auditing techniques provide a partial solution to these problems. By embedding audit routines into physically remote application systems deemed material, auditors can collect evidence that will increase the chances of identifying errors or irregularities that occur. In some cases, auditors might also be able to obtain evidence on ineffective or inefficient processing that is occurring—for example, system response times that are abnormally long.

Problems Posed by Interorganizational Information Systems

Many organizations now must rely on the quality of data processing carried out in other organizations to achieve asset safeguarding, data integrity, system effectiveness, and system efficiency objectives. For example, in an electronic data interchange system (EDI) system, errors or irregularities in one organization's information systems can propagate to another organization's information systems.

Auditors can use concurrent auditing techniques in two ways to monitor the quality of information processing carried out within interorganizational information systems. First, auditors can use them to monitor the quality of data received from other organizations. For example, in an EDI system, auditors might use a concurrent auditing technique to detect significant changes in the patterns of transactions received from a customer or vendor. Auditors can then investigate these changed patterns to determine whether they manifest an error or irregularity. Second, auditors might use concurrent auditing techniques in cooperation with auditors in the other organizations that participate in an interorganizational information system to monitor the quality of the overall system. For example, auditors might initiate test transactions that will propagate to another organization's information systems. These transactions in turn will be monitored by auditors in this organization using concurrent auditing techniques.

TYPES OF CONCURRENT AUDITING TECHNIQUES

Although many concurrent auditing techniques have been developed, Mohrweiss (1988) argues that they all fall into three categories: *(1)* those that can be used to evaluate application systems with test data while they undertake production processing, *(2)* those that can be used to select transactions for audit review while application systems undertake production processing, and *(3)* those that can be used to trace or map the changing states of application systems as they undertake production processing. With this classification in mind, we examine four major concurrent auditing techniques in the following subsections:

1. Integrated test facility (ITF),
2. Snapshot/extended record,
3. System control audit review file (SCARF), and
4. Continuous and intermittent simulation (CIS).

The ITF technique can be used to test an application system with test data during normal production processing. The snapshot/extended record technique can be used to trace the changing states of an application system as it undertakes production processing. The SCARF and CIS techniques can be used to select transactions during production processing for audit review.

Integrated Test Facility

The ITF technique involves establishing a minicompany or dummy entity on an application system's files and processing audit test data against the entity as a means of verifying processing authenticity, accuracy, and completeness. For example, auditors could use ITF in the following ways: If the application is a payroll system, they might set up a fictitious person in the database; if the application is an inventory system, they might set up a fictitious stock item in the database; if the application is an EDI system, they might work cooperatively with auditors in other organizations and set up dummy entities in the database of their own organization or client organization as well as the databases of other organizations with which their own organization or client organization interacts. Auditors would then use test data to update the fictitious entities. This test data would be included with the normal production data used as input to the application system.

Using ITF involves two major design decisions:

1. What method will be used to enter test data?
2. What method will be used to remove the effects of ITF transactions?

In the following subsections, we consider the choices available when auditors have to make these decisions and the advantages and disadvantages of each choice.

Methods of Entering Test Data

Test data can be posted against an ITF dummy entity using two methods. The first involves tagging transactions submitted as production input to the application system to be tested (Figure 18–3a). The application system must be programmed to recognize the tagged transactions and have them invoke two

FIGURE 18–3(a). Tagging live transactions for ITF processing. **(b).** Using test transactions for ITF processing.

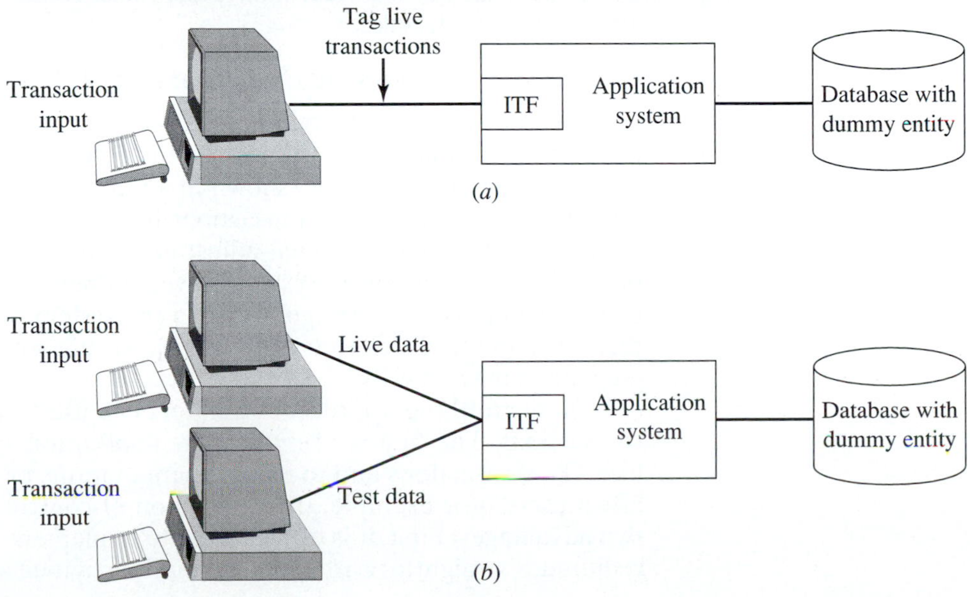

updates: one for their designated application system master file record and one for the ITF dummy entity.

Several strategies can be used to choose and to identify ITF transactions. First, auditors can include a special identifier field in a source document or a screen layout to denote that a transaction is to be treated as both a normal transaction and an ITF transaction. Somehow auditors must choose which transactions they wish to tag; for example, they select a transaction that has characteristics that are congruent with a test-data design, or they use some type of sampling plan. Second, auditors can embed audit software modules in the application system's programs to recognize transactions having certain characteristics that are of interest to them. These modules then select and tag the transactions as ITF transactions. Third, auditors can embed sampling routines in the application system programs. These routines tag transactions as ITF transactions according to a sampling plan. Whatever the strategy used, the application system must be programmed to treat the tagged transactions in a special way.

Tagging live transactions as ITF transactions has two advantages: *(1)* ease of use and *(2)* testing with transactions representative of normal system processing. It has two major disadvantages. First, using live data could mean that the limiting conditions within the system are not tested. Second, the extraneous code included within the application system to recognize the tagged transactions and to treat them in a special way could interfere with production processing; for example, it could degrade system response time or undermine data integrity because it contains errors.

The second method of entering test data involves designing new test transactions and entering them with the production input into the application system (Figure 18–3*b*). If auditors use this approach, they should first develop a test-data design as the basis for choosing the characteristics of the test data they will use (see Chapter 17). Auditors then create the test data and insert the dummy entity's unique identifier in the key field (identifier) of the data to denote that it is an ITF transaction.

This approach has two advantages. First, test data can be created based on a test-data design. Thus, the test data is likely to achieve more complete coverage of the execution paths in the application system to be tested than selected production data. Second, the application system does not have to be modified to tag the ITF transactions and to treat them in a special way. Instead, the test transactions are treated like any other transaction. The primary disadvantage of the approach is that test data design and creation can be time-consuming and costly to undertake.

Methods of Removing the Effects of ITF Transactions

The presence of ITF transactions within an application system affects the output results obtained—for example, the control totals produced by the application system and the errors shown in an input validation report. Unless auditors inform users that ITF transactions have been entered into the application system and then make manual adjustments to the system's output, the effects of the ITF transactions must be removed. Otherwise, users could become concerned about errors or irregularities in the system, which might cause them to then expend resources to try to track down the source and nature of the discrepancies they identify.

There are three approaches auditors can use to remove the effects of ITF transactions. The first is to modify the application system programs to recognize ITF transactions and to ignore them in terms of any processing that might affect users—for example, the calculation of control totals. This approach has two advantages. First, it is often simple to implement because the programming required is straightforward. Second, audit activities are transparent to users of the application system. Thus, auditors can carry out covert testing of the application systems. Nevertheless, the method has three disadvantages. First, costs are incurred to develop, maintain, and operate the software that recognizes the ITF transactions and treats them in special ways. If the system is stable or few modifications are made that affect ITF transactions, this cost could be relatively low. Second, the presence of extraneous code in the application system increases the risk of errors or irregularities in the system. The code inserted in the application system might be defective, or the programmer who implements the code might use the opportunity to perpetrate an irregularity. Third, in some cases it is difficult to make the ITF transactions transparent to the users. If auditors enter erroneous transactions to test the error validation routines within the application system, for example, they are seeking to determine whether the errors are correctly reported. Unless auditors print the ITF results on a separate report that is not provided to users or display them on a screen that is not viewed by users, it will be hard to mask audit activities.

The second approach to removing the effects of ITF transactions is to submit additional input that reverses the effects of the ITF transactions. This approach has the advantage of simplicity because the application system does not have to be modified. Nevertheless, it has several disadvantages. First, if auditors seek to act covertly, they must submit the reversal entries within a time frame that prevents the ITF transactions having an effect on the system's output—for example, before the display or printing of balances in accounts. Second, if auditors are to maintain data integrity within the system, they must ensure that the reversals are carried out correctly. Unfortunately, determining the correct reversal entries to submit can sometimes be difficult because it is hard to ascertain all the records that have been affected by a transaction. Third, some output is still likely to be affected by ITF transactions—for example, control totals for the number of transactions processed and the contents of input validation reports. Fourth, reversal entries can cause problems in a shared database environment. For example, consider a company that borrows and lends daily on the short-term money market and that has a computer-based decision support system for its money-market managers. The managers could use the decision support system frequently to access the cash accounts master file to determine monies that are available for investment purposes. If auditors affect monetary balances with ITF transactions and the reversal entries have not been processed before managers access the balance (the lag might only be a matter of milliseconds), costly investment errors can result.

The third approach to "removing" the effects of ITF transactions is to submit trivial entries so the effects of the ITF transactions on output are minimal. Clearly, the effects of the transactions are not really removed; rather, their impact on users should be reduced. This approach has the advantage of simplicity because the application system does not have to be modified. It has several disadvantages, however. First, users will still have to be informed about the existence of ITF testing. Even though the transactions submitted are trivial, users might become concerned about control totals that do not balance. As a result, they might expend resources needlessly on trying to identify the nature and source of the error. Moreover, the transactions might be evident in other ways, such as errors printed on input validation reports. Second, having to use trivial transactions precludes auditors from testing the limits of the system. These limiting values might be a primary concern in audit work. Third, in a shared data environment, even trivial transactions can have critical consequences. For example, a small adjustment to a balance might still be sufficient to cause some costly and erroneous action to be taken.

In light of the difficulties associated with removing the effects of ITF transactions, therefore, it is a moot point whether auditors should try to hide audit activities from users. It might be better to disclose that audit testing is being conducted but not to indicate the nature, extent, and timing of testing. In this way, users will be apprised of audit work and follow up if they have concerns about discrepancies in their output. Costly and needless investigative work can then be avoided.

Snapshot/Extended Record

For application systems that are large or complex, tracing the different execution paths through the system can be difficult. If auditors wish to perform transaction walkthroughs, therefore, they could face a difficult or impossible task. A simple solution to the problem is to use the computer to assist with performing transaction walkthroughs.

The snapshot technique involves having software take "pictures" of a transaction as it flows through an application system. Typically auditors embed the software in the application system at those points where they deem material processing occurs. The embedded software then captures images of a transaction as it progresses through these various processing points. To validate processing at the different snapshot points, auditors usually have the embedded software capture both beforeimages and afterimages of the transaction. They then can assess the authenticity, accuracy, and completeness of the processing carried out on the transaction by scrutinizing the beforeimage, the afterimage, and the transformation that has occurred on the transaction. Figure 18–4 shows how the technique might be used to obtain audit evidence at various points in a simple batch system.

Implementing the snapshot technique requires auditors to make three major decisions. First, they must decide where to locate the snapshot points within the application system that is the focus of the audit. Auditors should make this decision on the basis of the materiality of the processing that occurs at each point in the application system. In some circumstances, however, auditors might have to temper their desire to capture snapshots in light of demands placed on the application system. For example, a processing point might be material, but efficiency considerations might be paramount. If auditors embed software to capture snapshots at this point, they might produce an unacceptable degradation in response times when the system is under load.

The second decision auditors must make is when they will capture snapshots of transactions. Auditors might have the embedded software always make snapshots for certain high-exposure transactions—for example, transactions in a financial institution that alter the terms of major loans. Alternatively, they might choose particular transactions for scrutiny via snapshot before they are entered into the application system. They must then tag these transactions in some way, and the embedded software must recognize that the transactions are tagged for snapshot purposes. Auditors might also program the embedded software to make snapshots of various transactions based on some type of sampling plan. Whatever the approach auditors use, they must be careful to obtain sufficient, reliable evidence but not to capture so much evidence that they suffer from information overload.

The third decision auditors must make relates to reporting of the snapshot data that is captured. The embedded software must provide sufficient identification and timestamp information for each transaction to enable auditors to determine the transaction to which the snapshot data applies, the sequence of state changes that has occurred as the transaction has passed through the various snapshot points, the processing points for which the snapshot data has been captured, and the time and date at which the snapshot data for each processing point was captured. A reporting system must also be designed and implemented to present this data in a meaningful way.

A modification of the snapshot technique is the *extended record technique*. Instead of having the software write one record for each snapshot point, auditors can have it construct a single record that is built up from the images cap-

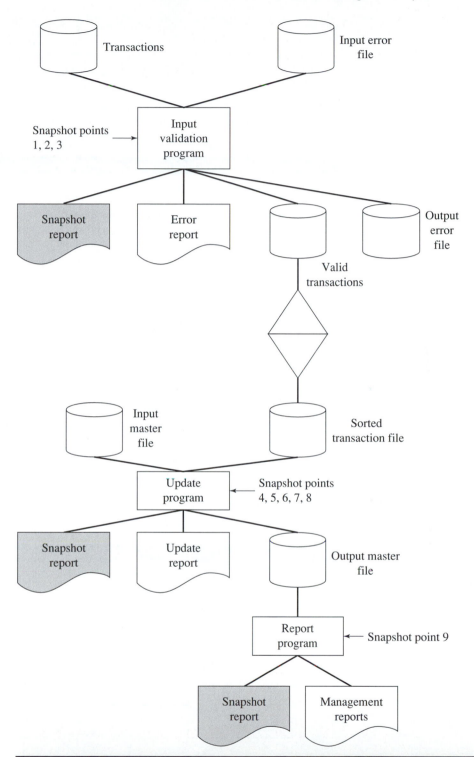

FIGURE 18–4. Collecting audit evidence at various points in an application system using the snapshot technique.

tured at each snapshot point. This record is progressively built as the transaction that is of interest to auditors traverses the various snapshot points in the application system (Figure 18–5). Extended records have the advantage of collecting all the snapshot data related to a transaction in one place, thereby facilitating audit evaluation work.

	Snapshot point 1	Before-image	After-image	Snapshot 2	Before-image	After-image		Snapshot point n	Before-image	After-image	

FIGURE 18–5. An extended record used with the snapshot technique.

The snapshot and extended record techniques can be used in conjunction with the ITF technique to provide an extensive audit trail. ITF provides a master record against which auditors can post various types of transactions. The snapshot and extended record techniques provide an audit trail as instances of each of these transaction types progress through the application system that auditors are testing.

System Control Audit Review File

The system control audit review file (SCARF) technique is the most complex of the four concurrent auditing techniques we will examine. It involves embedding audit software modules within a host application system to provide continuous monitoring of the system's transactions. These audit modules are placed at predetermined points to gather information about transactions or events within the system that auditors deem to be material. The information collected is written onto a special audit file—the SCARF master file. Auditors then examine the information contained on this file to see if some aspect of the application system needs follow-up. Figure 18–6 illustrates the method as applied to a master file update program.

FIGURE 18–6. Use of SCARF with a master file update program.

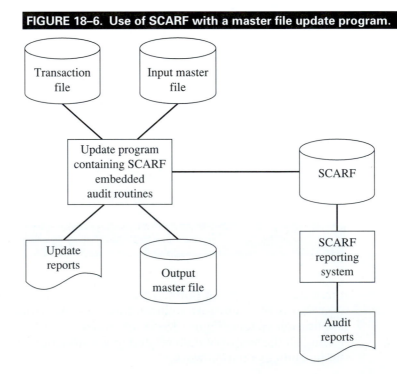

In many ways, the SCARF technique is like the snapshot/extended record technique. Indeed, the SCARF embedded software can be used to capture snapshots and to create extended records. We see subsequently, however, that other types of data can be collected via the SCARF embedded modules—for example, system exceptions deemed material. Moreover, we also see subsequently that the SCARF technique uses a more complex reporting system than the snapshot and extended record techniques.

Using SCARF involves two major design decisions:

1. Determining what information will be collected by SCARF embedded audit routines, and
2. Determining the reporting system to be used with SCARF.

We examine each of these decisions in the two subsections that follow.

Information to be Collected by SCARF

The nature of and placement of SCARF embedded audit routines within an application system depend on the types of evidence auditors want to collect. Auditors might use SCARF to collect the following types of information:

Information Captured	*Explanation*
Application system errors	Ideally, an application system contains all the logic necessary to prevent and to detect errors that occur. Nevertheless, design and programming errors might exist from the start, or errors could creep into the system as it is modified and maintained. SCARF audit routines provide an independent check on the quality of system processing.
Policy and procedural variances	Organizations often have technical and administrative policies and standards to guide staff in their work. For example, a company might require one of its products to be sold in certain size lots. Industries also have accepted policies and standards to which members of the industry are expected to adhere. SCARF audit routines can be used to check when variations from these policies and standards occur.
System exceptions	SCARF can be used to monitor different types of application system exceptions. For example, certain errors might be allowed within the system provided they are within a specified tolerance. Nonetheless, auditors might wish to examine the frequency with which these errors occur. Similarly, salespersons might be given some leeway in the prices they charge to customers. SCARF can be used to see how frequently salespersons override the standard price. To detect fraudulent use of policyholder's funds by insurance agents, auditors might capture funds withdrawal transactions that exceed a certain amount and occur within a few days of a change-of-address transaction (presumably to the agent's address).
Statistical samples	Some embedded audit routines might be statistical sampling routines. SCARF provides a convenient way of collecting all the sample information together on one file.
Snapshots and extended records	Printing snapshots and extended records during normal application system processing may be inconvenient. The snapshots and extended records can be written onto the SCARF file and printed when required.
Profiling data	Auditors can use embedded audit routines to collect data that allows them to build profiles of system users. They can then use the embedded audit routines to detect deviations from these profiles that may manifest errors or

(cont.)

Information Captured	*Explanation*
	irregularities. For example, some banks use profiling data to detect check kiting that their customers undertake via automated teller machine systems. Similarly, some telephone companies use profiling data to detect unusual patterns of telephone calls that their customers are placing (perhaps manifesting telephone fraud). The profiling data collected via embedded audit modules can also be used in intrusion detection systems (see Chapter 10).
Performance measurement data	Auditors can use embedded routines to collect data that is useful for measuring or improving the performance of an application system. For example, the frequency of occurrence of certain kinds of transactions can be monitored. Application programs can then be modified to test for the most frequently occurring kinds of transactions first.

Because the integrity of the SCARF embedded audit routines is critical to the reliability of the evidence auditors collect via SCARF, they must give careful consideration to protecting the content and integrity of the routines. Several steps might be undertaken. Application programs should not contain the source code of the embedded audit routines. Call statements, only, should exist. The source code for the routines should be maintained in a special library file that can be accessed only by authorized parties. The documentation supporting the routines should also be kept securely. When maintenance work has to be carried out on the routines, careful thought needs to be given to how the maintenance work will be conducted. If auditors have the knowledge and the programming skills, they might undertake the maintenance themselves. If auditors must rely on others, however, they might seek the assistance of an independent third party.

Structure of the SCARF Reporting System

Determining the structure of the SCARF reporting system involves several design decisions: *(1)* determining how the SCARF file will be updated, *(2)* choosing sort codes and report formats to be used, and *(3)* choosing the timing of report preparation. If SCARF is to be used in conjunction with ITF and the snapshot/extended record techniques, care must be taken to ensure that these decisions are congruent with design decisions made in relation to these other techniques.

With respect to the method of updating the SCARF file, one alternative is to have each application system create a temporary SCARF work file that is copied in due course to a SCARF master file (Figure 18–7a). This method has the advantage of simplicity. It has the disadvantage, however, of fragmented SCARF data existing until the individual SCARF work files are copied to the master file. In some cases, data fragmentation might undermine SCARF's effectiveness as an audit technique because it prevents timely analysis of SCARF data across application systems. For example, it might be important to know quickly that salespersons are overriding prices and giving substantial discounts on an inventory item that is experiencing severe production problems. To overcome data fragmentation problems, auditors might have individual SCARF systems concurrently update a single SCARF master file (Figure 18–7b). In some ways, this approach is more complex than using individual work files because the problems of concurrent access to a single file discussed in Chapter 14 must be managed. These problems can be mitigated, however, if the file is managed by a database management system.

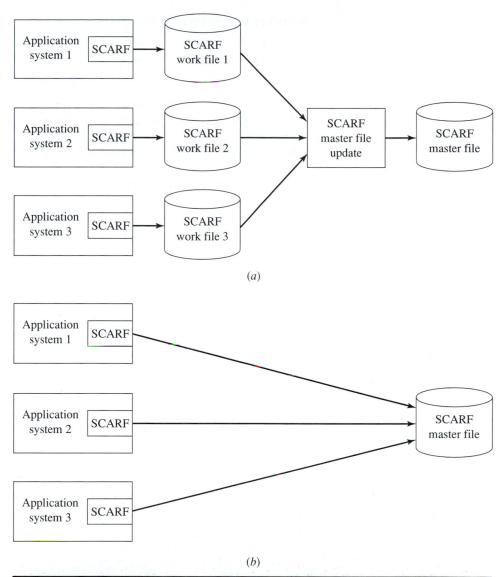

FIGURE 18–7(a). Indirect updating of SCARF master file via work files. **(b).** Direct updating of SCARF master file.

Careful thought must be given to the sort codes and report formats used with SCARF data. Without adequate sort codes, it will be impossible to organize the SCARF data usefully for audit purposes. For example, auditors might have difficulty identifying the nature of the exception that the SCARF system has captured and the location where the exception has occurred. Without adequate report formats, auditors might find it difficult to interpret the data that the SCARF system has provided to them. A SCARF system can collect large amounts of data. If the data is not carefully organized and summarized, data that manifests errors and irregularities, for example, might be missed.

The decision on the length of the reporting period depends primarily on the importance of the audit evidence collected and the costs of generating the SCARF reports. If the SCARF system identifies a high-materiality exception, auditors might have the reporting system notify them immediately. In most cases, however, auditors must choose an interval over which SCARF data will be collected before it is then organized, summarized, and reported.

Continuous and Intermittent Simulation

Koch (1981, 1984) has proposed a variation on the SCARF concurrent auditing technique, which he has called *continuous and intermittent simulation* (CIS). This technique can be used whenever application systems use a database management system. Whereas SCARF requires auditors to embed audit modules within an application system to trap exceptions that are of interest to them, CIS uses the database management system to trap these exceptions. The application system is left intact. Instead, when the application system invokes the services provided by the database management system, the database management system in turn indicates to CIS that a service is required. CIS then determines whether it wants to examine the activities to be carried out by the database management system on behalf of the application system (Figure 18–8).

During application system processing, CIS executes in the following way:

1. When the database management system reads an application system transaction, it invokes CIS and passes the transaction across to CIS. CIS then determines whether it wants to examine the transaction further. This decision is made in the same way that SCARF embedded audit routines decide whether to examine a transaction further. For example, the transaction might be selected by CIS on the basis of statistical sampling criteria, or it might be selected because it has unusual characteristics. If the transaction is selected, the next three steps are executed; otherwise, CIS waits for a new transaction.

2. The database management system provides CIS with all data requested by the application system to process the selected transaction. Using this data, CIS also processes the transaction. In other words, CIS replicates application system processing in the same way that a parallel simulation program replicates application system processing (see Chapter 16).

3. Every update to the database that arises from processing the selected transaction will be checked by CIS to determine whether discrepancies exist between the results it produces and those the application system produces. If discrepancies exist and they are a serious concern, CIS might prevent the database management system from carrying out the updates requested by the application system. Otherwise, CIS notes the exception, and the application system processing then continues.

4. Exceptions identified by CIS are written to a log file in the same way that SCARF uses an exception log. Like SCARF, CIS also requires a reporting system for the log file to report exceptions in a meaningful and timely way.

When Koch initially proposed CIS, he concluded that the database management system used by an application system would have to be modified to trap the exceptions. This requirement reduced the likelihood that CIS could be implemented in a cost-effective way. Today, however, many current database management systems provide "exit" facilities that allow users to write their own modules and have them invoked by the database management system. Thus, CIS can be implemented using these facilities.

The primary advantage of CIS over the SCARF and snapshot/extended record techniques is that CIS does not require modifications to the application system. Instead, the audit routines are called by the database management system. The primary disadvantage is that auditors might wish to collect evidence at processing points other than those that invoke the services of the database management system.

Koch (1984) also provides a detailed comparison of the relative advantages and disadvantages of CIS versus parallel simulation. The primary advantages of CIS over parallel simulation are *(1)* like other concurrent auditing techniques, CIS provides an online auditing capability, whereas parallel simulation

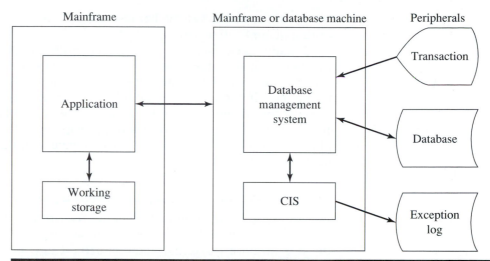

FIGURE 18–8. Environment for continuous and intermittent simulation
(From Koch 1981; Reprinted by permission of the MIS Quarterly, Vol. 5, No. 1, March 1981. Copyright 1981 by the Society for Information Management and the Management Information Systems Research Center.)

provides a batch auditing capability; *(2)* the number of program instructions needed to implement CIS usually will be less than the number needed to implement parallel simulation; and *(3)* the input/output overheads associated with CIS will be less because CIS creates no files aside from an exception log. Relative to parallel simulation, the primary disadvantage is that CIS often will be more difficult to implement because it executes in an online real-time environment rather than a batch environment.

IMPLEMENTING CONCURRENT AUDITING TECHNIQUES

When auditors implement concurrent auditing techniques, they should follow the same steps necessary to achieve any well-implemented system. Because these steps have been described extensively in Chapters 4 and 5, the following sections provide only a brief overview and highlight those aspects having special relevance for concurrent auditing.

Perform a Feasibility Study

Concurrent auditing techniques result in overheads for application systems because special audit records and audit routines must be embedded within them. Sometimes these overheads can be minor. For example, response times and turnaround times increase only marginally. Sometimes they can be unacceptable. For example, system response times degrade to the point where users are seriously impaired in carrying out their work.

Auditors must always consider carefully the costs and benefits of using concurrent auditing techniques. The costs include development costs, implementation costs, maintenance costs, and operations costs. When determining operations costs, auditors must take into account the externalities caused by concurrent auditing techniques, such as the overhead costs imposed on the host application system and the resulting impact on users. When determining benefits, auditors should recognize that the work carried out by several groups of stakeholders might be facilitated by the existence of concurrent auditing techniques. Beside the benefits obtained for the audit, information systems staff, for example, might benefit because concurrent auditing techniques facilitate testing of application systems.

If auditors can implement concurrent auditing techniques when an application system is first developed, the costs are likely to be lower. The system can then be designed from the outset to accommodate the concurrent auditing techniques. If auditors have to modify an existing application system to accommodate concurrent auditing techniques, however, often the costs will be high. In this light, auditors should seek to participate in the development of new application systems to determine whether concurrent auditing techniques should be incorporated in them.

Seek the Support of Groups Affected by Concurrent Auditing

Because concurrent auditing techniques require ongoing support, they are typically the responsibility of an organization's internal audit staff. Nevertheless, the organization's external auditors should also be contacted as they might have requirements that can be met by concurrent auditing techniques. In any event, they must be apprised of how concurrent auditing techniques are used within the organization. Use of concurrent auditing techniques might mean that external auditors can place greater reliance on the work carried out by internal auditors. Moreover, if the techniques are used properly, external auditors are likely to assign a lower control risk to the organization and decrease the extent of substantive testing accordingly.

Information systems staff will also be affected by the use of concurrent auditing techniques. If auditors lack the expertise to implement and maintain concurrent auditing techniques, they may have to rely on information systems staff to assist them. Moreover, information systems staff might be users of concurrent auditing techniques. As discussed previously, concurrent auditing techniques could prove to be a useful test vehicle for information systems staff when they conduct their own evaluation of an application system.

Auditors must also work hard to establish good communications with the information systems staff. In the past, a major reason why concurrent auditing techniques have failed is neglect in communicating to the audit staff changes in the application system that affect the concurrent auditing techniques that have been implemented in the system. Information systems staff need to appreciate how their maintenance work might affect concurrrent auditing techniques that are embedded in an application system.

Application system users also must be informed if concurrent auditing will affect their work. For example, we saw how use of ITF might result in discrepancies to control totals in an application system. Users need to be apprised of how use of concurrent auditing techniques might impact their work. Users also might be interested in concurrent auditing techniques as a training vehicle for new staff.

Ensure that the Relevant Expertise Is Available

If auditors are to use concurrent auditing techniques successfully, they must have a reasonable level of expertise in information systems audit and control. For a start, auditors must be able to identify where material processing points occur within application systems. Otherwise, they will not be able to determine where embedded audit modules are best placed. Auditors must also be able to make astute decisions in relation to such matters as the record structures and reporting systems that concurrent auditing techniques will use. Otherwise, they might not collect the evidence they require, or they might not be able to obtain the evidence in a form that is useful to them. Finally, auditors need the expertise either to implement, operate, and maintain concurrent auditing techniques or to evaluate the work of others who undertake these tasks on their behalf.

Ensure the Commitment of Stakeholders

Concurrent auditing techniques require resources to develop, implement, operate, and maintain. Auditors require management's commitment, therefore, if the resources needed to support concurrent auditing techniques are to be available on an ongoing basis. Management should be committed if they can see clear payoffs from using concurrent auditing techniques. The onus is on auditors, therefore, to use concurrent auditing techniques effectively and to demonstrate clearly that benefits exceed costs.

Information systems staff must also be committed to their organization's use of concurrent auditing techniques. If they are not committed, they might directly sabotage the techniques or contribute to their downfall through neglecting to communicate application system changes that affect the techniques to audit staff. As discussed previously, auditors might also have to rely on them to support development, implementation, operation, and use of the techniques.

The existence and operation of concurrent auditing techniques are unlikely to remain transparent to users. Recall that we discussed previously some of the ways in which users might be affected—for example, via discrepancies in reports and degradation in response times. Users are unlikely to tolerate these disruptions in the long run unless they, too, see the benefits to using concurrent auditing.

Make the Necessary Technical Decisions

When auditors implement concurrent auditing techniques, recall that they must make several key technical design decisions. For ITF, they must choose the test data method to be used and the method of removing the effects of the ITF transactions. For snapshot/extended records and SCARF, they must decide on those points in the system where data will be captured and the type of data that will be captured. In the case of SCARF, they must also determine the structure of the reporting system. For CIS, they must choose the transactions whose application system processing will be simulated.

These design decisions cannot be made lightly. They can have a substantial impact on the costs and benefits of using concurrent auditing techniques. Where they lack expertise or they have doubts about the choices to make, therefore, they should seek the counsel of other information systems auditors who have experience with concurrent auditing techniques or information systems professionals who are experienced with information system design decisions.

Plan the Design and Implementation

When the necessary technical decisions have been made, auditors can proceed with the specific design for the concurrent auditing techniques. They can also plan the implementation of the concurrent auditing techniques. Decisions must be made, for example, on the data structures to be used, the programming language to be used, the ways in which audit modules will be embedded within the host application systems, and the methods to be used to protect the integrity of the audit modules.

Auditors must also carefully plan how they will use the concurrent auditing techniques. For example, auditors need to consider the procedures they will use for follow-up of detected variances, the approaches they will employ to maintain the concurrent auditing techniques, and the standards they will enforce in terms of documenting the techniques, their associated support procedures, and the results produced. The techniques might provide auditors with high-quality audit evidence. If auditors do not use this evidence effectively and efficiently, however, the impact of the techniques will be lost.

Implement and Test

The procedures discussed in Chapters 4 and 5 for orderly and controlled implementation of an application system should be used when implementing concurrent auditing techniques. If auditors implement these techniques when the host application system is first built, they can take advantage of the project management procedures that are used throughout the various phases of the system development life cycle. If auditors implement these techniques after the host application system has been built, however, they must employ the project management procedures used for maintenance and modifications to application systems.

The implementation of concurrent auditing techniques will be facilitated if high-level software is available to support use of concurrent auditing. For some types of hardware/software platforms, for example, software has been developed to initiate calls to a library of concurrent auditing routines, receive information back from these routines, and process and present the information in a form that facilitates audit work (see, e.g., Hageman 1996).

Great care must be taken when testing concurrent auditing techniques. An error in a concurrent auditing technique may cause an error in the application system. Poor design and implementation work can affect the host application system's performance adversely. The continuing support of management, information systems staff, and application system users requires that any deleterious effects of using concurrent auditing techniques should be minimized.

Postaudit the Results

After concurrent auditing techniques have been running for some time, auditors should evaluate their costs and benefits, particularly in light of the estimates of costs and benefits they made during the feasibility phase. This postaudit identifies defects that possibly can be corrected or ways in which the techniques can be used more effectively and efficiently. It also can lead to the conclusion that concurrent auditing techniques should be scrapped.

A postaudit also formalizes the experience gained with concurrent auditing techniques and establishes guidelines for their design and implementation in other application systems. Auditors are then better placed to make decisions on whether the techniques should be implemented elsewhere and, if so, how they should be implemented.

STRENGTHS/LIMITATIONS OF CONCURRENT AUDITING TECHNIQUES

Concurrent auditing techniques provide the following benefits to auditors, information systems staff, and application system users:

Advantage	*Explanation*
Viable alternative to ex post auditing and auditing around the computer	Concurrent auditing techniques allow auditors to collect more comprehensive and more timely evidence. Furthermore, auditors need not infer the quality of application system processing through examining only a system's input and output. In addition, concurrent auditing techniques can be used to collect evidence at intermediate points in an application system's processing.
Surprise test capability	Using concurrent auditing techniques, auditors can gather evidence relatively unobtrusively. Thus, information systems staff and application system users often are not aware that evidence is being collected.

Advantage	*Explanation*
Test vehicle for information systems staff	Information systems staff should have the same concerns as auditors about whether application systems meet asset safeguarding, data integrity, effectiveness, and efficiency objectives. Concurrent auditing techniques should be useful to information systems staff, therefore, as a test vehicle to be used in evaluating whether an application system meets these objectives. Auditors must consider trading off some independence for the benefits to be obtained by allowing information systems staff to enhance their test capabilities using concurrent auditing techniques.
Training vehicle for new users	Some organizations use ITF as a training vehicle for new staff. Training need not proceed by simulating the preparation of input data and its entry into the application system. Instead, with batch systems, new staff can prepare data on the system's source documents, submit the data to the application system, and obtain feedback on any mistakes they make via the system's error reports. Similarly, with online systems, they can key the data in using the system's data-entry screens and obtain feedback on errors they make.

In spite of the apparent advantages of concurrent auditing techniques, their use has not been widespread. Periodically, surveys have been undertaken of the extent of their use. The results of these surveys are problematical for several reasons. First, they have not used common definitions for the different types of concurrent auditing techniques. Second, in some cases, data on a particular technique has not been collected. Third, different types of auditors have been surveyed. Nonetheless, a common theme emerges: Use of concurrent auditing techniques has been fairly stable and limited over many years. The following table summarizes the results of several of these surveys, where the percentages in the table reflect the number of respondents who indicated they had used the concurrent auditing technique:

Technique	*Study* IIA (1977)	Perry and Adams (1978)	Tobinson and Davis (1981)	Langfield-Smith (1987)	Mohrweis (1988)	IIA (1991)
Integrated Test Facility	5.0%	15.0%	13.3%	22.7%	12.2%	11.0%
Embedded Audit Modules/SCARF	15.8%	20.0%	13.3%	2.1%	11.9%	11.0%
Snapshot/Extended Records	18.4%	20.0%	4.4%	—	9.9%	—

The results of these surveys also indicate that several factors affect the use of concurrent auditing techniques:

1. Internal auditors are more likely to use concurrent auditing techniques than external auditors. This situation occurs because internal auditors should be able to obtain the resources required from their organizations to support the development, implementation, operation, and maintenance of concurrent auditing techniques.
2. Concurrent auditing techniques are more likely to be used if auditors are involved in the development work associated with a new application system. As discussed previously, it is easier to install concurrent auditing techniques at the outset rather than to retrofit an application system with these techniques.

3. Concurrent auditing techniques are more likely to be used if auditors employ other computer-based audit techniques. In short, auditors need the knowledge and experience of working with computer systems to be able to use concurrent auditing techniques effectively and efficiently.
4. Concurrent auditing techniques are more likely to be used as the incidence of automatically generated transactions in application systems goes up. The audit trail is less visible for these types of transactions, and the costs of errors and irregularities associated with them can be high.

We have already examined some of the major limitations of concurrent auditing techniques. In short, however, the following seem to be important:

1. The costs of developing, implementing, operating, and maintaining concurrent auditing techniques can be high. For this reason, the benefits of using concurrent auditing techniques must be clear to all stakeholders. Otherwise, the needed resources and support will not be forthcoming.
2. Unless we have substantial knowledge of and experience with information systems auditing, it is unlikely that we will be able to use concurrent auditing techniques effectively and efficiently. Moreover, we must have a good understanding of the target application system if we are to be capable of placing concurrent auditing techniques at strategic points within it.
3. Concurrent auditing techniques are unlikely to be effective unless they are implemented in application systems that are relatively stable. If the host application system is changing frequently, the costs of maintaining concurrent auditing techniques are likely to be high. We might be able to justify these costs on the basis of the high exposures associated with the high levels of volatility in the application system. Nonetheless, we must be aware of the increased difficulties we are likely to face.

In summary, assessing the benefits and costs of using concurrent auditing techniques can be difficult. For a start, identifying all the benefits and costs associated with their use is hard. Because several different sets of stakeholders exist, we must take care in assessing how concurrent auditing techniques affect each of them. Valuing the benefits and costs is also difficult. Again, we need to consider value from the viewpoints of all the different stakeholder groups.

SUMMARY

Concurrent auditing techniques collect audit evidence at the same time as application system processing occurs. This evidence can be written to a file and periodically printed for auditors to analyze and evaluate. Alternatively, auditors can print or display the evidence immediately so they can determine whether to take some type of immediate action—for example, commence investigation of a potential irregularity.

Four major concurrent auditing techniques are integrated test facility (ITF), snapshot/extended record, system control audit review file (SCARF), and continuous and intermittent simulation (CIS). ITF involves establishing a dummy entity in an application's system files and processing audit test transactions against the dummy entity. The snapshot/extended record technique involves embedding audit modules in an application system and capturing images of the transaction as it passes through the system. SCARF also involves embedding audit modules within an application system and capturing variances and exceptions that are of interest to auditors. CIS replicates application system processing for transactions that are of interest to auditors. It is invoked by the database management system used by the application system that processes the transactions.

The design, implementation, and maintenance of concurrent auditing techniques should follow well-known system development standards that facilitate development and use of effective and efficient application systems. These standards require auditors to interact with groups who will be affected by their use of concurrent auditing techniques, to perform a feasibility study, to plan the implementation and testing, and to undertake a postaudit. Several key design decisions must be made, including the method of entering test data in ITF and removing its effects, the points where audit modules will be embedded in an application system to take snapshots and create extended records, the types of variances and exception data to be collected by SCARF, and the processing to be replicated by CIS.

The major advantages of using concurrent auditing techniques are that they provide auditors with a viable alternative to using *ex post* auditing and auditing around the computer, they allow auditors to implement a surprise testing capability, they facilitate testing of application systems by information systems staff, and they provide a training vehicle for application system users. The major limitations are that they are often costly to develop, implement, operate, and maintain; they require auditors to have a fairly extensive knowledge of information system audit and control if they are to use them effectively and efficiently; and they are unlikely to work satisfactorily if their host application system must be frequently modified and maintained.

Because the costs associated with developing, implementing, operating, and using concurrent auditing techniques can be high, they are more likely to be used by internal auditors than external auditors. They are also more likely to be used when they are implemented as part of the development of a new application system, when auditors are also using other types of computer-assisted evidence-collection tools, and when the incidence of automatically generated transactions in an application system is high.

Review Questions

18–1 Briefly explain the nature of concurrent auditing techniques.

18–2 Why has the disappearance of paper-based audit trails motivated the implementation and use of concurrent auditing techniques?

18–3 Why is there often a need for continuous monitoring of advanced information systems? How do concurrent auditing techniques facilitate continuous monitoring of advanced information systems?

18–4 Why has it become more difficult for auditors to perform transaction walkthroughs with application systems? How can concurrent auditing techniques assist auditors to perform transaction walkthroughs?

18–5 What is entropy? Information systems staff often have a very high rate of turnover in their jobs. Is this a form of entropy in information systems? If so, how can concurrent auditing techniques be used to help mitigate the effects of this form of entropy?

18–6 How can auditors use concurrent auditing techniques to monitor application systems that are developed, implemented, operated, and maintained on behalf of an organization by an outsourcing vendor?

18–7 Why are concurrent auditing techniques useful in monitoring the authenticity, accuracy, and completeness of transaction processing in distributed application systems?

18–8 Briefly describe the nature of ITF.

18–9 Describe *two* methods of entering test data for an ITF application and discuss the relative advantages and disadvantages of each method.

18–10 Describe *two* methods of removing the effects of ITF transactions and the relative advantages and disadvantages of each method.

18–11 Outline the difference between the snapshot and extended record concurrent auditing techniques.

18–12 What are three major design decisions auditors must make when implementing the snapshot/extended record concurrent auditing technique?

18–13 Briefly describe the nature of the SCARF concurrent auditing technique. Discuss how snapshot and SCARF might be integrated with one another.

18–14 A properly written input program for an application system should contain the program code needed to undertake comprehensive validation of input data. Why might auditors still be interested in using SCARF embedded audit modules to check whether input data is valid?

18–15 Briefly describe *three* types of evidence that auditors might collect using the SCARF concurrent auditing technique.

18–16 What decisions must auditors make in determining the structure of the reporting system to be used with the SCARF concurrent auditing technique?

18–17 Briefly describe the nature of the CIS concurrent auditing technique.

18–18 Briefly describe each of the major steps that must be undertaken during the execution of the continuous and intermittent simulation (CIS) technique.

18–19 Give *one* advantage and *one* disadvantage of continuous and intermittent simulation with respect to *(a)* SCARF and *(b)* parallel simulation.

18–20 What are *two* types of cost externalities that auditors impose on other groups when using a concurrent auditing technique?

18–21 Why do auditors need to consult with other groups whenever they implement a concurrent auditing technique?

18–22 Do auditors need high levels of expertise with information systems audit and control to be able to use concurrent auditing techniques successfully? Why or why not?

18–23 Why do auditors need to seek the support of other groups whenever they implement a concurrent auditing system? In particular, why do they need the support of management?

18–24 Give one major design decision that auditors must make whenever they implement:
  a Integrated test facility
  b Snapshot/extended record
  c System control audit review file
  d Continuous and intermittent simulation

18–25 In our planning of the design and implementation of a concurrent auditing technique, give *two* factors we must consider in deciding how we will use a concurrent auditing technique once it is implemented.

18–26 Why must auditors take great care in testing a concurrent auditing technique before they release it into production use?

18–27 Give *two* purposes of carrying out a postaudit on the use of a concurrent auditing technique.

18–28 Give *two* advantages of using concurrent auditing techniques in an organization.

18–29 Are concurrent auditing techniques used extensively in practice? Based on empirical research that has been conducted, give *three* factors that seem to affect whether a concurrent auditing technique will be used within an organization.

18–30 Give *two* limitations of using concurrent auditing techniques within an organization.

Multiple-Choice Questions

18–1 Which of the following is *not* a justification for using concurrent auditing techniques?
a Cheaper to implement, operate, and maintain than ex post auditing techniques
b Increasing difficulties of performing walkthroughs
c More timely identification of errors and irregularities needed in advanced systems
d Increasing difficulties of gathering evidence as the number of distributed systems grows

18–2 Entropy, the tendency of a system toward disorder, is present in:
a Only systems with weak controls
b All systems
c Only advanced systems that are complex
d Only systems with a high level of coupling

18–3 Relative to designing new test data, tagging live transactions in an ITF has the advantage that:
a Special audit routines do not have to be embedded in the host system
b The limiting conditions in the system are more likely to be tested
c Source documents and data-entry screens do not have to be redesigned
d Test transactions are more likely to be representative of normal application system processing

18–4 Which of the following advantages is common to submitting reversal entries and submitting trivial transactions as two means of removing the effects of ITF transactions?
a The limiting values in the host system can be tested
b ITF activities are transparent to users
c No costs and risks are involved with program modification
d Control totals are not affected by ITF transactions

18–5 The snapshot technique involves:
a Recording the state of an application system's working storage at a point in time
b Taking pictures of a transaction as it flows through a system
c Evaluating the afterimages of all data items changed for accuracy and completeness
d Providing a filter in the input program through which selected transactions must pass

18–6 The difference between the snapshot technique and the extended record technique is:
a With the extended record technique, record images that are collected at different points in an application system are stored contiguously, whereas with snapshot they are stored separately
b More audit evidence is collected with the extended record technique, especially in terms of material processing relating to asset safeguarding and data integrity objectives
c Printing of audit reports in snapshot is immediate upon evidence being collected, whereas printing of records with extended records is delayed
d Only afterimages of transactions are collected using the snapshot technique, whereas both beforeimages and afterimages are collected with extended records

bank transaction types in the table would be your primary focus when you examine the use of ITF by NHKCBC's internal auditors? Briefly explain why you would seek evidence on how well the internal auditors have used ITF to test these transaction types. Also, briefly outline the criteria you would use to determine how well the internal auditors have used ITF to carry out their testing.

18-3 Finer Furnishings Limited is a Vancouver-based company that makes an extensive range of furniture for sale throughout North America. While it produces a wide range of standard lines of furniture, many of its products are also custom designed in light of extensive discussions conducted with its retailer customers. These custom designs are then produced in batches to satisfy the retailer's anticipated demand.

The costing system used to assign costs to batches of furniture and to individual pieces of furniture manufactured by Finer Furnishings is relatively complex. Moreover, it is highly computerized. Production personnel enter various inputs into the system to calculate costs—for example, their labor time, the machines used and the durations of their use, the materials requisitioned, scrap and wastage quantities, scheduling delays, and small tools use. The system also takes into account an extensive range of overhead costs in determining a final product cost. To add to the complexity, the costing system is tightly integrated with other systems used by Finer Furnishings—for example, a sales forecasting system, an order entry system, a bill-of-materials system, a material requirements planning system, and an inventory system. Moreover, these systems rely extensively on electronic data interchange for exchange of critical data between Finer Furnishings and its customers and suppliers.

The market in which Finer Furnishing operates is intensely competitive. As a result, its products have little profit margin. The accuracy of the costings performed within the costing system, therefore, is critical to the survival of the company. The system is also a high-exposure system because it has to be maintained frequently. It is a legacy system; it is old, extensively modified, poorly structured, and not well documented.

Because of the high exposures associated with the system and the lack of a visible audit trail, the internal audit staff have implemented snapshot/extended records as a concurrent auditing technique within the system. They spend considerable time using the snapshots and extended records to check the accuracy of costings within the system. On several occasions in the past, costing errors have severely undermined the company's financial position. In this light, senior management has charged internal audit with the responsibility for timely detection of costing errors or irregularities.

You are the senior information systems auditor for an external audit firm that has just taken over the audit of Finer Furnishings. During discussions that your partner has had with the manager of internal audit, he has been told that Finer Furnishings expects the extent of substantive testing associated with the costing system will be minimal because reliance can be placed on the work performed by the internal audit group via the snapshots and extended records.

Required: Your partner asks you to advise him on the merits of the arguments made by the manager of internal audit with Finer Furnishings. Write a brief report outlining your recommendations. If you believe further information needs to be obtained from Finer Furnishings in relation to the internal audit staff's use of the snapshot/extended record technique, indicate what information you believe should be sought.

18-4 Swagmans Banking Corporation is a large Australian bank based in Melbourne. It offers a wide range of services to customers in Australia through an extensive network of branches.

Swagmans has decided to offer its customers a share trading service. Customers can call a toll-free number 24 hours a day, seven days a week, to give instructions for the purchase of or sale of shares. Between 8:00 AM to 8:00 PM, Monday to Friday, the call will be taken by an agent. Outside these times, customers must leave their instructions as a recorded message. These instructions will then be executed as soon as possible on the next working day.

Senior management believes the service will be popular with the bank's customers. Providing the transaction is more than $6,000, the brokerage fee levied by the bank will be cheaper than stockbrokers or any other financial institutions that offer share trading services. The bank will offer no advisory services to its customers, however. It will only execute trades according to their instructions.

You are Swagmans's manager of internal audit. One day you are called to a meeting with the manager in charge of customer services. She explains that the Board of Directors has expressed some concerns about the exposures Swagmans might face as a result of introducing the share trading system. The bank has an image as a carefully managed, conservative financial institution within the marketplace. The Board is anxious to preserve that image because it believes it is a major reason why so many of the bank's customers have remained loyal over extended periods. Moreover, it believes it is the reason for the high quality of its customer base.

You are aware that during the systems development process for the share trading system, the analysts responsible for the system gave extensive consideration to ways of preventing and detecting errors or irregularities within the system. You wonder, however, whether it might be worthwhile implementing embedded audit modules within the system to support the use of SCARF as a concurrent auditing technique. Exceptions that potentially manifested high-exposure errors or irregularities could then be reported immediately to the internal audit group.

Required: Briefly describe five events or sets of events that you might want to monitor using the SCARF concurrent auditing technique. Briefly describe why you wish to monitor these events. What data would you collect via the SCARF embedded audit modules to allow your staff to check whether a material error or irregularity has occurred in the share trading system?

18–5 You are the manager of internal audit for a large North America–based financial institution. One day your staff report to you that they have discovered an error in the amount of interest paid to a significant number of depositors. Your institution has overpaid several million dollars of interest as a result of an error that was made during the maintenance of a program. The error was not discovered before the program was released again into production.

You call an urgent meeting to discuss this finding with your institution's president, controller, vice president (information systems), and vice president (customer relations). The five of you canvass the actions you must now take. One possibility is to try to recover the interest from the customers' accounts. The vice president (customer relations) believes this action is fraught with problems, however. Because the overpayment occurred several weeks ago, he points out that some customers might have "spent the interest" already. He also argues that substantial damage to customer goodwill might occur if the interest is now deducted from customer accounts. Moreover, he is concerned about how he will deal with customer inquiries and complaints that are likely to arise. He is certain that some customers will dispute the deduction, and some might even take legal action.

The president is concerned about how the error will affect the share price of the financial institution if it becomes public knowledge. The competence of the whole management team will come under scrutiny. He considers what information he must also provide to the Board of Directors and the external auditors.

The vice president (information systems) contemplates the actions she must now undertake to prevent such an error occurring again. She believed that the procedures used to test programs before they were released into production were highly reliable. Clearly, some breakdown has occurred. She wonders whether she must now establish a quality-assurance group to prevent a major software error occurring again.

The meeting is adjourned so everyone can give the matter further consideration. For your part, you begin to wonder whether you might use CIS as a concurrent auditing technique to detect material errors and irregularities that could occur in deposits, loans, and investments application systems. A significant exposure for your financial institution is that it offers a wide range of products and services. For example, many kinds of fixed deposit accounts and investment accounts exist, and many different types of loans are offered to customers in an effort to tailor the loans to their circumstances and needs. Your institution also offers various equity trusts, property trusts, and combined equity-property trusts in which customers can invest. Transactions associated with these products and services can lead to some complex calculations—for example, those associated with penalties that customers incur if they withdraw monies early from fixed deposit accounts, and those associated with the payout values of loans if customers decide to pay off a loan early.

On the one hand, you feel that CIS might be fairly straightforward to implement. Your institution uses a database management system to maintain its database, and all application systems use the database management system to gain access to and maintain the database. Indeed, the integrated nature of the customer database is considered to be one of your institution's major competitive advantages because it allows a very high level of customer service to be provided. On the other hand, you recognize that the development, implementation, operation, and maintenance costs associated with replicating all interest receipts or payments via CIS is prohibitive. You wonder what calculations should be the focus of your efforts if you were to implement CIS.

Required: Assume you decide to implement CIS for a trial period of a year. You decide to limit its use, however, to three types of interest payment that your financial institution makes to customers. What types would you choose? Briefly explain why you would choose these types. Would you have CIS simulate every instance of each of the three interest payment types? Why or why not? Briefly explain the approach you would use.

Answers to Multiple-Choice Questions

18–1	a	**18–5**	b	**18–9**	d	**18–13**	a
18–2	b	**18–6**	a	**18–10**	b	**18–14**	c
18–3	d	**18–7**	c	**18–11**	c	**18–15**	c
18–4	c	**18–8**	d	**18–12**	a	**18–16**	d

REFERENCES

Clark, R., R. Dillon, and T. Farrell (1989), "Continuous Auditing," *Internal Auditor* (Spring), 3–10.

Groomer, S. Michael, and Uday S. Murthy (1989), "Continuous Auditing of Database Applications: An Embedded Audit Module Approach," *Journal of Information Systems* (Spring), 53–69.

Hageman, Willem (1996), "Controlling the Online Environment," *IS Audit & Control Journal*, II, 36–40, 42–43.

Institute of Internal Auditors (1977), *Systems Auditability and Control Study: Data Processing Audit Practices Report*. Altamonte Springs, FL:

The Institute of Internal Auditors Research Foundation.

——— (1991), *Systems Auditability and Control: Module 2: Audit and Control Environment.* Orlando, FL: The Institute of Internal Auditors Research Foundation.

Koch, Harvey S. (1981), "Online Computer Auditing Through Continuous and Intermittent Simulation," *MIS Quarterly* (March), 29–41.

——— (1984), "Auditing On-Line Systems: An Evaluation of Parallel Versus Continuous and Intermittent Simulation," *Computers & Security* (February), 9–19.

Langfield-Smith, Kim (1987), "The Use of Computer-Assisted Audit Techniques in Australian Internal Audit Departments," *The EDP Auditor Journal*, II, 28–40.

Leinicke, L. M., W. M. Rexroad, and J. D. Ward (1990), "Computer Fraud Auditing: It Works," *Internal Auditor* (August), 26–33.

Mohrweis, L. C. (1988), "Usage of Concurrent EDP Audit Tools," *The EDP Auditor Journal*, III, 49–54.

Munson, James E. (1973), "We Tried ITF—We Like ITF," *EDPACS* (December), 1–3.

Perry, William E. (1974a), "Concurrent EDP Auditing: An Early Warning Scheme," *EDPACS* (January), 1–7.

——— (1974b), "Concurrent EDP Auditing: An Implementation Approach," *EDPACS* (February), 1–6.

——— (1974c), "Snapshot—A Technique for Tracing and Tagging Actions," *EDPACS* (March), 1–7.

——— and Donald R. Adams (1978), "Use of Computer Audit Practices," *EDPACS* (November), 3–18.

Reeve, Robert C. (1984), "Trends in the Use of EDP Audit Techniques," *The Australian Computer Journal* (May), 42–47.

Skudrna, Vincent J., and Frank J. Lackner (1984), "The Implementation of Concurrent Auditing Techniques in Advanced EDP Systems," *EDPACS* (April), 1–9.

Tobinson, Gary L., and Gordon B. Davis (1981), "Actual Use and Perceived Utility of EDP Auditing Techniques," *The EDP Auditor Journal* (Spring), 1–22.

Woda, Alex (1995), "Continuous Audit Process Tools and Techniques: Part 1," *EDP Auditing*. Boston: Auerbach, Portfolio 73–02–35, 1–12.

——— (1995), "Continuous Audit Process Tools and Techniques: Part 2," *EDP Auditing*. Boston: Auerbach, Portfolio 73–02–35, 1–15.

CHAPTER

19

Interviews, Questionnaires, and Control Flowcharts

Chapter Key Points

■ Interviews, questionnaires, and control flowcharts are three techniques that auditors use primarily to collect evidence that allows them to (a) come to an understanding of an organization and its application systems, (b) make a judgment on the level of inherent risk associated with an organization and its application systems in light of this understanding, (c) come to an understanding of an organization's control structure, (d) make a judgment on the level of control risk associated with each application system in light of this understanding, and (e) undertake tests of the reliability of controls on which they intend to rely.

■ Auditors can use interviews to obtain both qualitative and quantitative information during evidence-collection work. Ultimately their objective is to elicit frank, complete, and honest answers from a respondent who has more information about a particular topic than themselves.

■ A respondent's motivation to reply to questions asked during an interview is a function of the extent to which they perceive the interview is a means of attaining their own goals. As auditors undertake interviews that are more stressful on respondents, they will need to increase respondents' motivation to respond to their questions by showing the relevance of their questions to respondents' own goal attainments. Alternatively, auditors can reduce the stress associated with interviews by limiting the number of questions asked, making stressful interviews shorter, and attempting to alleviate any fears that respondents might have before the interview commences.

■ Undertaking interviews involves three phases: (a) preparing for the interview, (b) conducting the interview, and (c) analyzing the interview. When auditors prepare for interviews, they should perform background research to ensure that an interview is the best way to obtain the evidence required, identify the respondents, prepare the interview content, schedule the time and place of the interview, and check the background of their respondents. When they conduct an interview, they should seek to establish rapport with respondents, observe certain rules of protocol to ensure they obtain most information from the interview (e.g., minimize digressions from the interview content), and maintain records of the interview. When auditors analyze interviews, they should prepare a report promptly because their recall of the interview deteriorates quickly, try to separate fact from opinion, and evaluate what the interview responses mean for their audit objectives.

■ Auditors can use questionnaires to gather factual data, such as whether a control exists within an application system. They can also use questionnaires to gather attitudinal data, such as whether an applications system has had detrimental effects on users' quality of working lives.

■ The development of a questionnaire involves four main phases: (a) design of questions, (b) design of response scales, (c) design of the layout and structure, and (d) ensuring the questionnaire is valid and reliable. The design of questions must take into account respondents' knowledge and ability and whether auditors will administer the questionnaire or whether respondents will complete the questionnaire by themselves. The questions must also be designed to evoke valid and reliable responses. The type of response scale associated with each question depends on the nature of the question asked. Factual questions will require a different type of response scale from attitudinal questions. The layout of a questionnaire should be clear, simple, logical, and visually appealing. Questionnaires are reliable if, assuming no other factors have changed, respondents give the same answers over repeated administrations of the questionnaire. Questionnaires are valid if their items scores or composite score successfully predict some outcome, contain items that are meaningful in terms of the construct auditors are seeking to measure via the questionnaire, and successfully tap the construct auditors are seeking to measure via the questionnaire.

■ Auditors must take care to use questionnaires effectively. They must know when to use questionnaires, what types to use, how to use them, and what the responses mean. Auditors might use questionnaires when they wish to obtain information from physically dispersed locations or they wish to structure an interview or review process. The type of questionnaire auditors use should depend on its validity and reliability relative to alternative questionnaires. They must administer questionnaires carefully so responses are valid and reliable. In the case of standardized questionnaires, auditors must follow the instructions provided with them on how they should be administered. Interpreting the results obtained from using a questionnaire often requires knowledge and experience with the questionnaire. In the case of standardized questionnaires, instructions might be provided detailing how the results should be interpreted.

■ Control flowcharts show *what* controls exist in a system and *where* these controls exist in the system. They have three major audit purposes: (a) comprehension—the construction of a control flowchart highlights those areas where auditors lack understanding of either the system itself or the controls in the system; (b) evaluation—experienced auditors can use control flowcharts to recognize patterns that manifest either control strengths or control weaknesses in a system; and (c) communication—auditors can use control flowcharts to communicate their understanding of a system and its associated controls to others.

■ Many types of control flowchart can be constructed. Auditors commonly use four types of control flowchart, however, in their audit work. First, document control flowcharts show the controls over the flow of documents through the manual components of a computer system. Second, control data flow diagrams can be used to show controls over the data flows through a system. Third, system control flowcharts show the controls exercised over the physical components in a system. Fourth, program control flowcharts can be used to show the controls exercised internally to a program.

■ Constructing a control flowchart involves four steps: (a) choosing the primary flowchart technique to use to allow particular features of a system to be highlighted and better understood; (b) choosing the appropriate level of detail at which to work so auditors are not overwhelmed with content but nonetheless they do not miss important control strengths or weaknesses; (c) preparing the primary flowchart so the system features can be easily understood; and (d) preparing the control flowchart based on the primary flowchart so control strengths and weaknesses become manifested.

■ In spite of their widespread use, information on the relative strengths and weaknesses of control flowcharts is meager. Document control flowcharts are useful as a means of showing controls in manual systems, but their usefulness continues to decline as fewer manual activities are carried out in information systems. Control data flow diagrams are a useful means of communicating and understanding controls over flows of data within a system. System control flowcharts help auditors to understand controls over the physical components of an information system. Research conducted on program flowcharts has produced mixed evidence on their usefulness. Nonetheless, they might assist auditors to understand controls over a limited set of logic in an application system that they might want to investigate during the conduct of their audit work.

■ A major limitation of control flowcharts is that they can be time-consuming to develop and difficult to modify and maintain. To some extent this limitation has been overcome as computer packages to support development and maintenance of different types of flowcharts have become more widespread. A further limitation of control flowcharts is that they require auditors to be skilled in audit work before they are likely to be able to interpret them effectively.

INTRODUCTION

In this chapter we examine three techniques that auditors use primarily to collect evidence that allows them to *(1)* understand an organization and its application systems, *(2)* make a judgment on the level of inherent risk associated with an organization and its application systems in light of this understanding, *(3)* understand an organization's control structure, *(4)* make a judgment on the level of control risk associated with each application system in light of this understanding, and *(5)* undertake tests of the reliability of controls on which they intend to rely. The three evidence-collection techniques are interviews, questionnaires, and control flowcharts. Each was widely used when auditors conducted audits of manual systems. Their importance has not diminished now that the primary focus is the audit of computer systems. Instead, we see in this chapter that their form has simply changed over the years to accommodate evidence-collection needs in a computer systems environment.

INTERVIEWS

When conducting an audit, auditors use interviews for a variety of reasons. Consider each of the following examples:

1. Systems analysts and programmers who designed and implemented an application system can be interviewed so auditors can obtain a better understanding of the functions and controls embedded within the system.
2. Clerical staff can be interviewed to determine how they correct input data that the application system identifies as inaccurate or incomplete.

3. Users of an application system can be interviewed to determine their perceptions of how the system has affected the quality of their working life.
4. If an error is discovered in an application system, personnel can be interviewed to understand better the nature of the error and to try to track down its cause.
5. Operations staff can be interviewed to determine whether any application systems seem to consume abnormal amounts of resources when they are executed.
6. An organization's controller can be interviewed to identify the critical systems that she or he believes exist within their organization.

Note the different ways in which auditors can use interviews. In the first example, their primary focus might be to gain an understanding of an organization's control structure. In the second example, their primary focus might be to test some input controls on which they intend to rely. In the third, fifth, and sixth examples, their primary focus might be to reach a judgment on the level of inherent risk associated with different application systems. In the fourth example, their primary focus might be to reach a judgment on the level of control risk associated with an application system.

Auditors can use interviews to obtain both qualitative and quantitative information during evidence-collection work. Ultimately, their objective is to elicit frank, complete, and honest answers from a respondent who has more information about a particular topic than they do. In this regard, auditors need to distinguish between interviews and interrogations. The motivation for an interrogation is some type of wrongdoing. The respondent often might be antagonistic and uncooperative—possibly the suspected culprit. When auditors conduct an interview, however, respondents should bear no antagonism toward them. Auditors undertake interviews frequently. Interrogations, however, require special skills (see, e.g., Krauss and MacGahan 1979). Although auditors might participate in a team that investigates some type of wrongdoing (Bologna 1995), they should leave interrogations to people who possess the requisite skills.

Some Conceptual Issues

If auditors are to conduct interviews effectively, they must have a basic understanding of what motivates a person to respond to questions asked during an interview. This knowledge will allow them to design and undertake better interviews and to identify why problems sometimes arise during the conduct of interviews.

A respondent's motivation to reply to questions asked during an interview is a function of the extent to which they perceive the interview to be a means of attaining their own goals (Figure 19–1). If respondents see the interview as

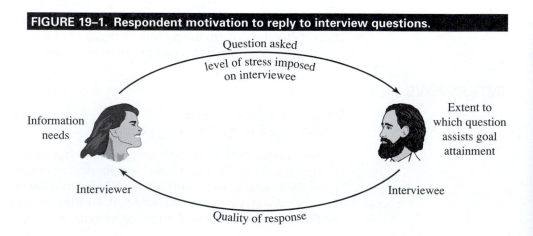

FIGURE 19–1. Respondent motivation to reply to interview questions.

Question asked

level of stress imposed on interviewee

Information needs

Extent to which question assists goal attainment

Interviewer

Interviewee

Quality of response

helping them attain their goals, they will respond positively to the questions asked. If they see the interview as hindering their goal attainment, they might be unhelpful and even antagonistic toward the interviewer.

Different interviews require different levels of respondent motivation if they are to be accomplished successfully. The reason is that the questions asked during different interviews vary in terms of the amount of stress they place on respondents. For example, interviews differ in terms of the amount of time required to answer questions, the recall effort required to answer questions, and the threats and fears generated by the questions. More stressful interviews require higher levels of respondent motivation. Auditors can control the level of stress caused by an interview by limiting the number of difficult questions asked, making more stressful interviews shorter, and attempting to alleviate any fears that may arise as a result of the interview before the interview is commenced.

In any interview, auditors must be aware that two forces arise that sometimes conflict—namely, the interviewer's desire to obtain answers to questions about a problem and the respondent's desire to pursue topics that interest them if they perceive the interviewer to be a responsible person. The auditors' task is to try to foster the respondent's interest in the topic of the interview. Auditors must clearly communicate the purpose of the interview to respondents, show them empathy, and promote a spirit of mutual trust and respect.

Preparing for the Interview

Conducting successful interviews requires careful preparation. The following subsections outline some major tasks that auditors must accomplish during the preparation phase.

Perform Background Research

Before auditors undertake an interview, they must ensure that the information they require is not readily available elsewhere. Otherwise, respondents might become upset if they consider the interview to be a waste of their time. Auditors should be convinced that an interview is the best way to obtain the evidence they need. By performing background research, auditors become familiar with the organization's policies and terminology relating to the interview topic. Auditors might also identify other issues to be pursued during the interview. Alternative sources of the information they require might also be found.

Identify the Respondents

Auditors must take time to identify those personnel within an organization who can provide them with the best information on an interview topic. Interviews can be costly and time-consuming. In this light, auditors must strive to avoid interviewing the wrong person, thus wasting time and effort.

Organization charts often are a first source of information on the appropriate respondents. Auditors might also seek the help of senior management in identifying the best respondents. By enlisting the help of senior management, auditors also make them aware of the interviews to be carried out within their areas of responsibility. Furthermore, senior management can introduce auditors to the respondents (perhaps at a group meeting) prior to the conduct of the interviews. In this way, respondents have advance notice of the reasons for the interview. They might also assign auditors more legitimacy in their role as interviewer.

Prepare the Interview Content

During the preparation phase, auditors should identify clearly the objectives of the interview and make a list of the information to be sought during the interview. If several auditors are conducting interviews, the interview process must be coordinated so respondents are not asked the same question by different auditors.

After the information to be sought has been identified, it can be structured in a time sequence for the interview. General information should be requested at the beginning and end of interviews. Specific information should be requested toward the middle of interviews. Information requested at the beginning of interviews should be neither controversial nor sensitive. Otherwise, the respondent might not relax, and the remainder of the interview might be spoiled. Respondents often leave significant points they wish to make to the end of interviews. In this light, information requested at the end of interviews should give respondents an opportunity to express opinions on central issues.

After the information sought has been structured, the questions to be asked during the interview can be prepared. Formally preparing questions does not mean the interview must be inflexible. If necessary, auditors must be willing to adapt and diverge from the formal structure. Respondents might digress from the questions auditors ask but nevertheless provide them with important audit evidence.

Either closed or open questions can be used. A closed question requires a yes or no response. Thus, closed questions should be used infrequently and only toward the middle of interviews when specific information is requested. Most often, open questions should be asked, especially at the beginning and end of interviews. Open questions can lead to closed questions. For example, the open question, "What types of controls do you exercise over the preparation of batches of input transactions?" can lead to the closed question, "Do you prepare hash totals on document numbers?" This technique of asking open questions and then using the responses to proceed to questions with a more limited set of responses is sometimes called a *funnel* (Burns, 1994, p. 350).

The types of questions formulated for interviews depend on the tasks performed by the respondent and the respondent's seniority within the organization. The tasks performed determine the nature of the information requested. The level of seniority determines whether the questions focus on operational issues or policy issues.

After an interview has been structured and the questions prepared, auditors should review its content to determine whether it is satisfactory. It might be too long, ask too many difficult questions, require too much respondent recall, ask too many sensitive questions, omit questions that need to be asked, and so on. The opinions of other auditors on the quality of the interview content also might be solicited. This review can lead auditors to restructure or to modify questions or to break the interview into two or more interviews.

Schedule Time and Place of Interview

When auditors have finished preparing interview content, respondents can be contacted to schedule the time and place of their interviews. By scheduling interviews in advance, respondents have time to prepare; they can think about the interview and, if necessary, collect material relevant to the interview.

Lunchtime and late afternoon interviews should be avoided. Respondents are hungry, tired, or concerned with terminating the interview. Midmorning interviews often work well. Respondents are fresh. Moreover, they have had time to clear any urgent business.

If possible, interviews should be conducted at respondents' work places. Respondents are familiar with the surroundings. Moreover, they have access to any materials needed during the interview. A different venue should be chosen, however, if there is a high risk of distractions occurring (e.g., frequent telephone calls) or there is insufficient privacy.

Check the Background of the Respondent

Before conducting interviews, auditors should check the background of respondents. This check can cause them to avoid certain topics during an interview because they might evoke antagonistic responses. For example, auditors might not pursue questions on the quality of controls over a particular function if the respondent has been censured by their superior for improperly exercising controls over the function.

If auditors know a respondent's biases before an interview, they can better direct the interview to obtain objective responses. They also might be able to couch the interview in terms of the respondent's interests so he or she is more motivated to answer questions. For example, through background checking, auditors might know that a respondent believes controls over some function are weak. Rather than asking her whether she believes controls are weak or strong, auditors can focus their questions on why the respondent believes controls are weak, what exposures she thinks exist, and how she would improve the reliability of controls.

Conducting the Interview

At the start of the interview, auditors should reiterate its purpose to confirm with respondents that the interview to occur corresponds with the arranged interview. Respondents also might have some questions about the objectives of the interview. At this time, it is especially important that auditors seek to establish rapport with the respondent. Auditors can facilitate establishing rapport by "mirroring" the respondent in terms of their posture, voice tonality, rate and volume of speech, extent of eye contact, and gestures (Figure 19–2).

The interview should follow basically the structure established during the preparation phase. During the interview, auditors should apply certain rules of protocol:

1. Minimize digressions from the main purpose of the interview.
2. For the most part, be a listener.
3. Allow respondents some thinking time.
4. Avoid condescension and criticism; be polite.
5. Avoid sarcasm, and be careful of humor.
6. Avoid jargon and buzzwords; clearly state the questions.
7. Be attentive and interested.
8. Avoid disagreements and confrontations.
9. Answer courteously the respondent's questions.
10. Maintain a relaxed formality; avoid familiarity.

FIGURE 19–2. Establising rapport during an interview.

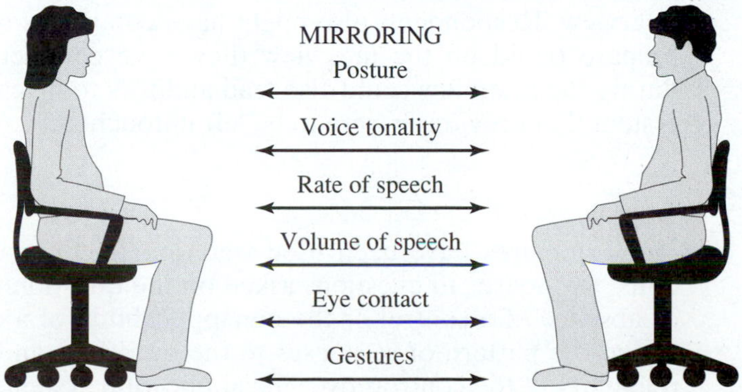

MIRRORING

Posture

Voice tonality

Rate of speech

Volume of speech

Eye contact

Gestures

To facilitate recalling the content of interviews, auditors might have to maintain records. Either notes can be taken or a tape recorder used. Tape recorders often make respondents nervous. Their advantage, however, is that they relieve auditors of notetaking so they can focus better on the interview. On the other hand, notetaking keeps an auditor's mind on the interview, especially the items that he or she records. Auditors should minimize the time spent on notetaking, however, because it could distract respondents and interrupt the flow of an interview. Whatever recording method auditors use, they should first ensure its acceptability to respondents at the start of an interview. Respondents also should have the right to review the transcript of interviews, notes taken during interviews, and questionnaires completed during interviews to assess their accuracy.

In some cases, an auditor might conduct an interview jointly with another auditor—a tandem interview. Tandem interviews have several advantages. First, they allow more efficient use of time. One interviewer can ask questions, while the other makes notes. Second, because respondents have one interviewer's complete attention, increased rapport often results. As a result, auditors obtain higher-quality information from an interview. Third, the questioning, recording, and analysis of interviews are more in depth, complete, and accurate. Nonetheless, tandem interviews place greater stress on respondents. Thus, they are best used with people whose time is at a premium.

At the end of the interview, auditors should review the material covered with respondents. During the review, auditors should endeavor to clear up ambiguities or omissions. Similarly, respondents might wish to clear up ambiguities and omissions that they believe have occurred. Auditors should conclude interviews promptly but not abruptly. They should also request respondents to make time available at a later stage to pursue matters arising from the interview or to obtain further information from them.

Analyzing the Interview

As soon as possible after the termination of interviews, auditors should prepare a report. Recall of events usually deteriorates rapidly within a few hours of an interview. During the preparation of interview reports, auditors should have two major objectives. First, they should attempt to separate fact from opinion. If they doubt the factual content of some of the information provided, they might need to seek independent verification of the information. Where opinion is involved, for verification purposes, auditors might need to show respondents a copy of the interview write-up. Second, auditors should attempt to assimilate the information they obtain during an interview and determine what it means for their overall audit objectives. Is the process well controlled? Has the system decreased the quality of the respondent's working life?

As discussed previously, some follow-up might be required after interviews have been conducted. Auditors might need to contact respondents to obtain further information or to clarify some issues that have arisen as a result of the interview. Respondents also might have comments on the report that auditors prepare based on the interview they have conducted. Information obtained during the interview could also lead auditors to investigate other aspects of the system that previously were to be left untouched.

QUESTIONNAIRES

Questionnaires have been used traditionally to evaluate controls within systems. Responses to questions asked on the questionnaire indicate the presence or absence of a control or the nonapplicability of a control. Auditors then examine the pattern of responses to the questions and reach a judgment on the reliability of the controls over the application system.

Auditors can use questionnaires for other purposes, however, as evidence-collection tools. For example, auditors can use questionnaires to assess users' overall feelings about an information system as an indicator of the system's effectiveness. Similarly, they can use questionnaires to identify areas within an information system where potential inefficiencies exist. For example, auditors might survey clerical staff who supply input to an application system to determine whether they think procedures for data entry can be streamlined.

Design of Questionnaires

Extensive research has been carried out on questionnaire design. For the most part, however, successful questionnaire design is still an art. In the following three sections, we focus briefly on some major aspects of questionnaire design: *(1)* design of questions, *(2)* design of response scales, and *(3)* design of the layout and structure of the questionnaire.

Question Design

Three major factors affect the design of the questions to be used in a questionnaire. The first is the characteristics of the respondent group. The respondent group can be either the auditors or the users of a system. For example, auditors often complete the well-known internal control questionnaire as they undertake evidence-gathering tasks. If auditors are attempting to elicit attitudes on various attributes of system quality, however, the respondent group will be the system's users. For example, customers could be surveyed to determine their levels of satisfaction with a system, or analysts and programmers could be asked their opinions on how easy the system is to maintain and modify.

If auditors are the respondent group, questions can be specific, terms can be left undefined, and instructions for completing the questionnaire can be minimized. They should have been trained to use the questionnaire. Alternatively, they could have designed the questionnaire themselves. In this light, auditors should require minimal help to complete the questionnaire. If other stakeholders in a system are the respondent group, however, these liberties usually cannot be taken. Questions must be spelled out clearly, terms must be defined, and instructions for completing the questionnaire must be clear.

The second factor affecting design of questions is the nature of the information sought. Auditors can use questionnaires to elicit either facts or opinions. A factual question would be: "Is there a fire extinguisher in the computer room?" An opinion question would be: "Do you feel the members of the information system staff are competent?" Sometimes the distinction between a factual question and an opinion question, however, is blurred.

The primary problem in designing factual questions is to ensure the respondent group understands precisely the facts required. Thus, the questionnaire designer might provide different kinds of information (some redundant) on the questionnaire to try to ensure that respondents understand what facts are required. Question clarity is also important with opinion questionnaires. Perhaps the primary problem in designing opinion questions, however, is to ensure that the wording of the question does not bias the response either by leading respondents or by being argumentative. For example, consider this question: "Shouldn't the system's response time be faster?" User responses to this question could be biased positively. The question is clearly communicating an expectation that the system response time should be faster.

The third factor affecting question design is the way in which the questionnaire is to be administered. This factor affects the extent to which questions need to be self-explanatory. If auditors are completing, say, an internal control questionnaire, the questionnaire designer can assume they have substantial prior knowledge of the questionnaire. Moreover, if they administer questionnaires to users, the questionnaire designer might assume auditors will answer any questions or clarify any ambiguities that arise. If a questionnaire is self-administered by a user group, however, the questionnaire designer must word the questions carefully. Respondents might not be able to ask auditors for assistance. For example, auditors might be measuring the effect of a distributed online real-time system on job satisfaction. Users might be dispersed physically over wide areas. As a result, auditors might have to use a mail questionnaire to assess users' opinions on how the system has affected their job satisfaction.

Though the question design depends on the factors described previously, some general design guidelines can be given:

1. *Ensure that questions are specific.* The question, "Are controls over input adequate?" is too general to be useful. The question, "Are hash control totals for batches calculated?" is much more specific. It provides respondents with a frame of reference to answer the question.

2. *Use simple language and avoid jargon.* In some cases, technical terms have a precise meaning, and expert users in the domain will understand them—for example, auditors should know what the term *encryption* means when it is used on an internal control questionnaire. If respondents are users of an interactive language, however, the question, "Are the semantics of the language sufficient for you to be able to perform your job?" could cause confusion. Users might or might not know what the term *semantics* means.

3. *Avoid ambiguous questions.* The question, "Does the system allow you to perform your job faster and improve your job satisfaction?" is ambiguous. What does a "no" answer mean? There are several possibilities: The job might be performed faster but job satisfaction remains unchanged; the job might be performed faster but job satisfaction decreases; both the speed with which the task is performed and job satisfaction remain unchanged; job satisfaction might increase but the speed with which the job is performed is unchanged, and so on. Questions should focus on a single item; they should be clear and unambiguous.

4. *Avoid leading questions.* Leading questions suggest the answers respondents should give. For example, suppose a manager is asked about his or her use of an interactive system. The question, "Does your secretary use the system to obtain the information for you?" is unlikely to be answered truthfully. The question might be taken to imply something bad about managers who do not directly use the system themselves.

5. *Avoid presumptuous questions.* Questions should not presume anything about respondents. The question, "How often do you use the system?" presumes respondents use the system. Respondents might or might not use the system.

6. *Avoid hypothetical questions.* The question, "Would you like the system to provide a faster response time?" is likely to evoke a positive response. Most users would not object to having a faster response time in an interactive system. Whether they would be willing to pay for a faster response time, however, is another issue.

7. *Avoid embarrassing questions.* At times auditors might use questionnaires to obtain information that is personal, delicate, or controversial. Care must be taken to formulate questions in such a way that they do not embarrass respondents. For example, suppose auditors are exploring the quality of the system design process that an organization uses. If they ask system designers, "Do you consider the impact of the systems you design on the quality of their users' working life?" a positive response is likely to be obtained. To answer otherwise implies system designers engage in socially unacceptable behavior.

8. *Avoid questions that involve extensive recall.* Factual questions involve respondents recalling information. The accuracy of their responses depends on the extent of recall needed. The question, "How many times did you use the system in January?" is unlikely to produce an accurate response if it is asked the following December, unless respondents maintain a diary of use.

9. *Avoid questions about which respondents have little or no knowledge.* Respondents tend to answer questions on a questionnaire, even when they have little or no knowledge about the subject matter covered by a question. If responses to factual questions are being elicited, auditors might be able to detect that respondents lack knowledge of the domain covered by a question. Where questions elicit a respondent's opinion, however, his or her ignorance of a domain could go undetected.

Choosing a Response Scale

The type of response scale associated with each question on a questionnaire depends on the nature of the question asked. If questions require a factual response, the choice of response scale usually is straightforward. For example, Figure 19–3 shows three types of response scale that might be used. Typically the scales involve checking a yes or no response or inserting some piece of information into a response space: for example, a make of machine.

FIGURE 19–3(*a*). Excerpt from internal control questionnaire. (*b*). Excerpt from fire protection checklist. (*c*). Excerpt from hardware configuration questionnaire.

Disposal of Output:

	Yes	No	N/A
1 Are sensitive reports shredded?			
2 Is disposal of carbon paper secure?			
3 Is disposal of waste paper from computer room secure?			

(*a*)

Fire Protection:

_____ 1 Fire exits marked clearly

_____ 2 Portable fire extinguishers placed at strategic points

_____ 3 Fire drills conducted regularly

(*b*)

Hardware Configuration:

Vendor:

_____ Intel

_____ Sun   _____ Hewlett Packard

_____ IBM   _____ Macintosh

_____ Fujitsu   _____ Tandem

_____ Silicon Graphics   Other _____

Model: _____

Number of disk drives: _____   Number of tape drives: _____

(*c*)

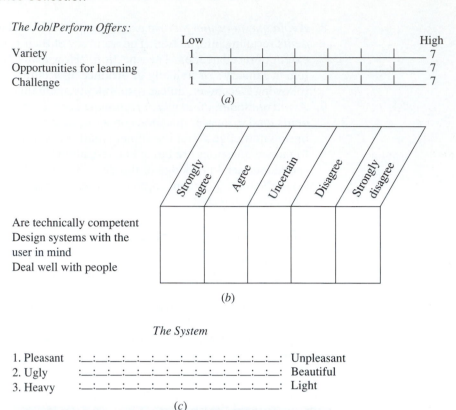

The Job/Perform Offers:

	Low						High
Variety	1						7
Opportunities for learning	1						7
Challenge	1						7

(*a*)

Strongly agree | Agree | Uncertain | Disagree | Strongly disagree

Are technically competent
Design systems with the user in mind
Deal well with people

(*b*)

The System

1. Pleasant :___:___:___:___:___:___:___:___:___: Unpleasant
2. Ugly :___:___:___:___:___:___:___:___:___: Beautiful
3. Heavy :___:___:___:___:___:___:___:___:___: Light

(*c*)

FIGURE 19–4(a). Seven-point scale used to assess users' attitudes about the jobs they perform. (*b*). Likert scale used to assess users' feelings about the information system staff. (*c*). Semantic differential scale used to assess users' attitudes about the system.

When auditors use questions to elicit opinions or attitudes, however, the choice of a response scale is a more complex decision. Figure 19–4 shows three types of scales that might be used for questions on various aspects of system effectiveness. Figure 19–4a shows a common seven-point scale. Figure 19–4b shows a Likert scale. Responses to individual items on a Likert scale are summed and the average calculated. Figure 19–4c shows a semantic differential scale used to assess respondents' attitudes toward an information system.

The choice of an appropriate response scale to measure attitudes or opinions sometimes requires substantial expertise. For example, if users have the same opinion or attitude about the subject addressed in a question, auditors need to ensure that the response scale used elicits consistent responses. Unless auditors are well trained in psychometrics, therefore, they should seek the advice of psychometrician whenever a new questionnaire must be designed.

Sometimes auditors might ask respondents to answer a question by providing a ranking. Rankings are useful whenever respondents have difficulty assigning precise values to a response. For example, auditors might ask respondents to rank a set of data files according to the cost of reconstructing them. The ranking they give might be factual, although the precise costs of reconstruction might be difficult to determine. Similarly, auditors might ask respondents to rank a list of threats according to their likelihood of occurrence. In this situation, the ranking might be subjective but nevertheless useful as a basis for designing or evaluating controls.

Choice of Layout and Structure

The layout and structure of a questionnaire affect how accurately the questionnaire will be completed. If the questionnaire is used in mail surveys, layout and structure also affect the response rate. The objective is to achieve a layout and structure that is clear, simple, logical, and visually appealing.

The length of a questionnaire affects the morale of respondents. If questionnaires are too long, respondents become fatigued. They either refuse to answer the questionnaire or the answers they give toward the end of the questionnaire become more unreliable.

If respondents have not been trained to complete a questionnaire, care must be taken to show clearly the flow of questions through the questionnaire. This design issue is especially important if responses to some questions cause branches to other questions. The questionnaire should appear uncluttered; the questions and various sections of a questionnaire should be spaced adequately.

Questions placed at the beginning of questionnaires should be general in nature and place little stress on respondents. More difficult questions—for example, those that require extensive recall or are controversial—should be placed toward the middle and end of the questionnaire.

Reliability and Validity Issues

Questionnaires must be *reliable*. Conceptually, we deem them to be reliable if, assuming no other factors had changed, respondents were to give the same answers over repeated administrations. In other words, assuming a respondent's views, perceptions, attitudes, or opinions had not changed and that we administered the questionnaire to the respondent on different occasions, we would achieve the same outcome at each administration of the questionnaire.

Unfortunately, we will encounter difficulties if we try to evaluate the reliability of questionnaires by having respondents complete them multiple times. At subsequent administrations, respondents might remember the responses they gave on previous administrations. Thus, the administrations are not independent. Moreover, other factors could change between administrations of the questionnaire. For example, a control might start to malfunction, or the quality of a respondent's working life could decrease. Even if the questionnaire were reliable, therefore, the ratings given by the respondent would change.

Various ways of assessing the reliability of questionnaires have been developed. We leave these methods of assessment for further study. To give some intuition behind the measures, however, one way we assess reliability is to see whether different respondents who give, say, high ratings on a particular subset of questions give, say, low ratings on another subset of questions. In other words, we evaluate whether respondents who have similar patterns of responses on certain questions also exhibit similar patterns of responses on other questions.

Another way we evaluate reliability is to include multiple questions on a questionnaire relating to the same construct we are seeking to measure. For example, assume we are interested in measuring the quality of a respondent's working life and we need a measure of job satisfaction. We could use a questionnaire that had multiple questions that asked about the respondent's job satisfaction in different ways. If the ratings to the different questions were highly correlated, we could then have greater confidence in the reliability of our measure of job satisfaction.

Reliability is important, irrespective of whether we seek factual responses or attitudinal responses. For example, assume auditors ask respondents whether message authentication codes are used to protect the integrity of data traversing data communications lines. Even though the question requires a

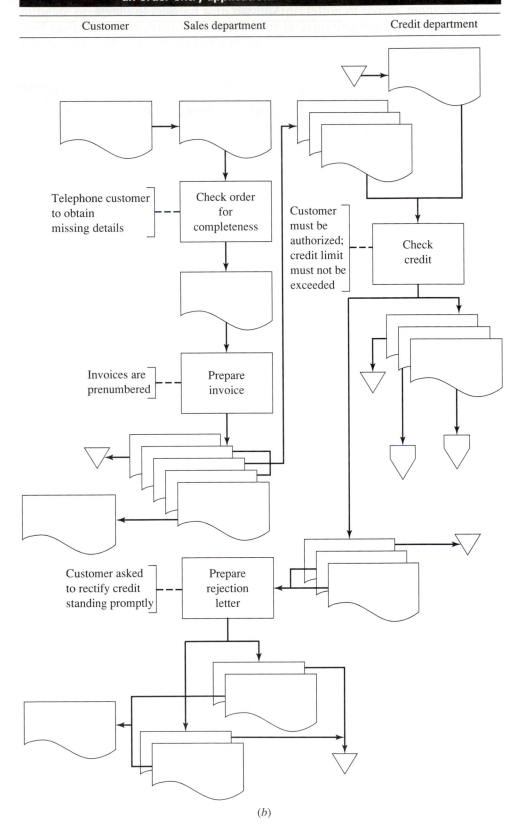

FIGURE 19–5(b). Section of a control flowchart based on a document flowchart for an order-entry application.

(b)

physical or resource level in a system. For example, a data flow diagram does not show controls exercised by central processors to prevent or detect malfunctions.

Third, we can use a *system flowchart* to show the controls exercised at the physical or resource level in a system. Because a system flowchart primarily illustrates the flow of data among the major components of a system—the programs, storage media, processors, communication networks, and so on—it can be narrated to show the controls exercised to ensure the correct functioning of these components. Unlike a data flow diagram, therefore, it is not especially useful in understanding the controls exercised at the logical level in a system. Nonetheless, it shows how component failure can undermine data integrity within the system. Figure 19–7a shows a portion of a system flowchart for a payroll system. Figure 19–7b shows the corresponding control flowchart.

Fourth, we can use a *program flowchart* to show the controls exercised internally to a program. If we are attempting to understand the detailed workings of a program, especially those modules within the program that are used to preserve the integrity of data processed by the program, a program flowchart can

FIGURE 19–6(a). Section of a data flow diagram for an order-entry application.

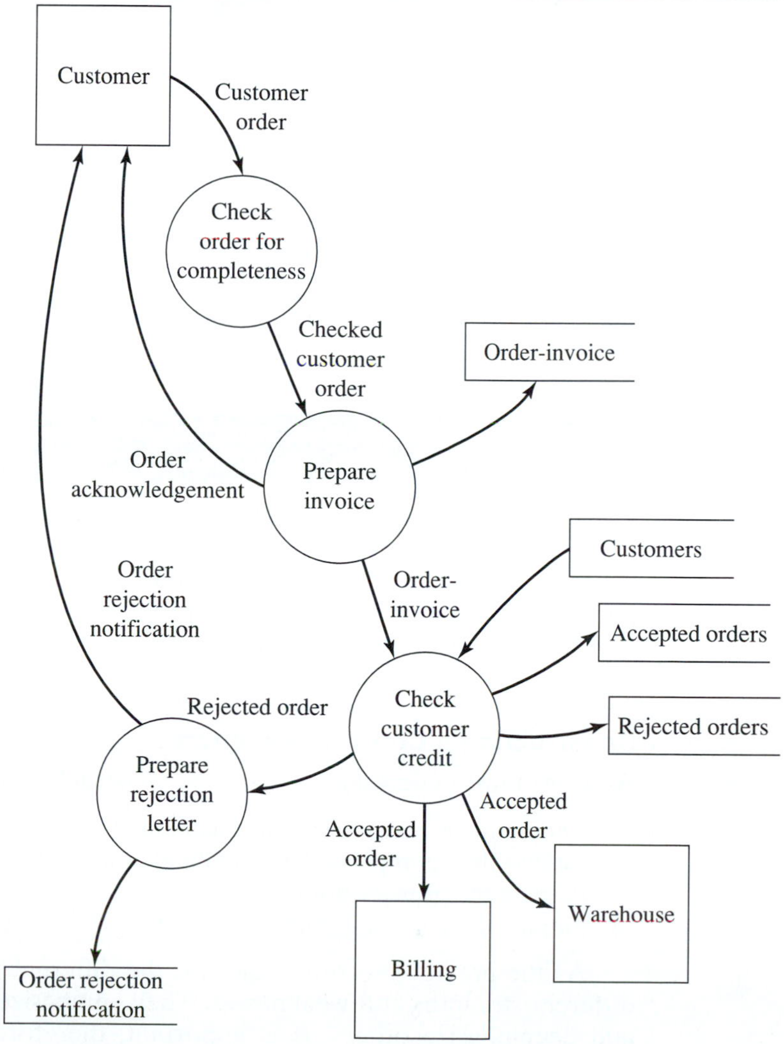

(a)

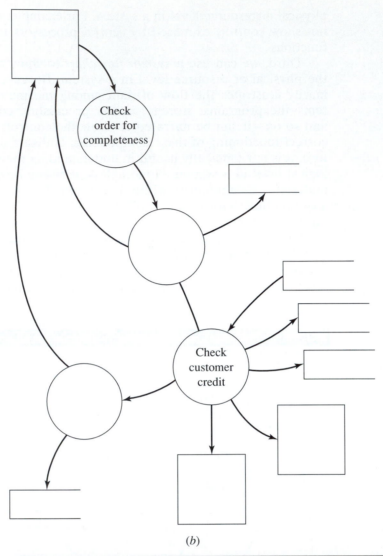

(b)

FIGURE 19–6(*b*). Section of a control flowchart based on a data flow diagram for an order-entry application.

facilitate our understanding of the controls exercised. Figure 19–8*a* shows a portion of a program flowchart for a program that validates time card data submitted to a payroll system. Figure 19–8*b* shows the corresponding control flowchart.

Constructing a Control Flowchart

Auditors must undertake four steps to construct a control flowchart:

1. Choose the primary flowchart technique to use.
2. Choose the appropriate level of detail at which to work.
3. Prepare the primary flowchart.
4. Prepare the control flowchart.

As the previous section indicates, the different flowchart techniques have different strengths and weaknesses. They emphasize some aspects of a system and deemphasize others. It is important, therefore, for auditors to identify those aspects of a system that are their main concern and to choose the appropriate charting technique to highlight them.

The preparation of a flowchart can take substantial time. The effort involved should be commensurate with the benefits auditors anticipate they will gain from using the flowchart. On the one hand, a flowchart must contain sufficient detail to enable auditors to judge the quality of controls employed within the system being described. On the other hand, too much detail can obfuscate matters and detract from auditors spending time on other more productive evidence-gathering activities. Unfortunately, an auditor's ability to choose the right level of detail tends to come only with experience in using the various types of flowcharting methods. Few formal guidelines exist to help auditors

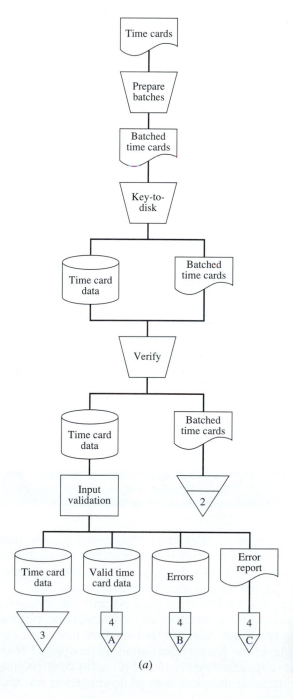

(a)

FIGURE 19–7(a). Section of a system flowchart for a payroll application.

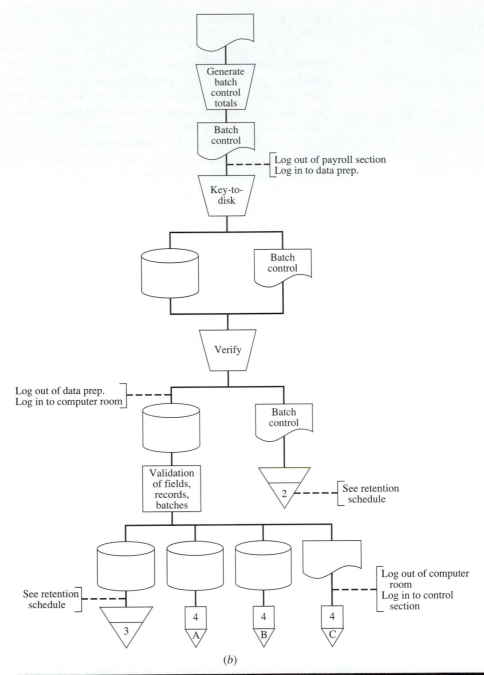

Generate batch control totals

Batch control

Log out of payroll section
Log in to data prep.

Key-to-disk

Batch control

Verify

Log out of data prep.
Log in to computer room

Batch control

Validation of fields, records, batches

2   See retention schedule

See retention schedule

Log out of computer room
Log in to control section

3   4
     A   4
          B   4
               C

(b)

FIGURE 19–7(b). Section of a control flowchart based on a system flowchart for a payroll application.

with this decision. Simpson (1993) recommends, however, that auditors use various levels of flowcharts to document a system and its controls. High-level flowcharts should show the major functions performed within a system. Low-level flowcharts should then show the details.

When the flowcharting method and the level of detail at which to work have been chosen, auditors can construct the primary flowchart. Each flow-charting technique has standard symbols that must be used and basic rules for preparing a flowchart. Unless auditors have good reasons, they should comply with these standard symbols and rules for constructing a flowchart. Otherwise, they undermine the usefulness of flowcharts as a vehicle for communicating in-

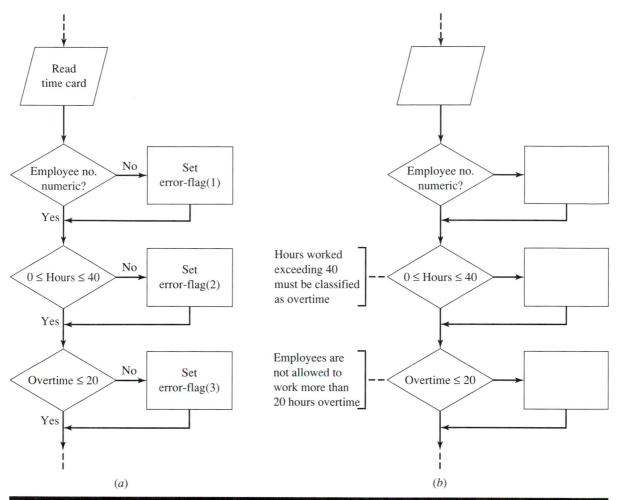

FIGURE 19–8(a). Section of a program flowchart for a payroll application. (b). Section of a control flowchart based on a program flowchart for a payroll application.

formation to others. Moreover, the flowchart could become difficult to modify in subsequent audits because others cannot understand the nonstandard symbols and rules that have been used to prepare the flowchart.

When auditors have prepared the primary flowchart, they can then construct the control flowchart. Recall that the control flowchart usually should show only the controls exercised within the system. Other information about the system should be narrated on the primary flowchart. The major reason for separating controls from other information about the system is to reduce the level of detail on a single flowchart. If the primary flowchart is sparse, however, it might be simpler to show controls on the primary flowchart. Moreover, in the absence of a well-drawn primary flowchart, understanding the nature of the controls narrated on the control flowchart will be difficult. Often auditors can obtain a full understanding of the system only if the primary and the control flowcharts are placed side by side. Deficiencies in the primary flowchart inhibit auditors' understanding of the details on the control flowchart.

Strengths and Limitations of Control Flowcharts

Unfortunately, the information available on the strengths and weaknesses of the various types of control flowcharting techniques is meager. Given that auditors have used document control flowcharts extensively over many years, we

Review Questions

19–1 Give *five* ways in which interviews, questionnaires, and control flowcharts can assist auditors during the conduct of an audit.

19–2 Briefly explain the difference between interviewing and interrogation. Why should auditors be careful about becoming involved in an interrogation?

19–3 Why do people respond to questions in an interview? Why is it important auditors have an understanding of what motivates a person to respond to questions they might ask during an audit interview?

19–4 Why do different types of interviews require varying levels of respondent motivation? Give two examples of audit interviews that auditors might conduct, one that requires a high level of respondent motivation, and one that requires a low level of respondent motivation.

19–5 In the structure of an interview, where should general questions be placed? Where should specific questions be placed? Why is placement of questions during an interview important?

19–6 Briefly explain the difference between a closed and an open question. What factors affect whether auditors use a closed or an open question during an audit interview?

19–7 Briefly outline the factors that auditors should consider when choosing a time and place for an audit interview.

19–8 What is meant by establishing rapport with the interviewee during the conduct of an audit interview? Why is establishing rapport important during the conduct of an audit interview? Briefly describe *four* techniques auditors might use to try to establish or maintain rapport during an interview.

19–9 What can auditors do if a confrontation situation arises during an audit interview?

19–10 Briefly explain what is meant by a tandem interview. What are the advantages and disadvantages of a tandem interview? Give an example of where auditors might use a tandem interview during the conduct of an audit.

19–11 What tasks must auditors perform during the analysis of an audit interview? When should auditors carry out these tasks?

19–12 Why must auditors consider who will be the respondent group in the design of an audit questionnaire? What impact does the type of respondent group have on the design of an audit questionnaire?

19–13 During the conduct of an audit, how will the characteristics of a self-administered questionnaire differ from the characteristics of a questionnaire that auditors administer to auditees themselves? When should a self-administered questionnaire be used? When should a questionnaire that auditors administer to auditees themselves be used?

19–14 How do response scales differ for questions asked via an audit questionnaire to obtain factual information versus questions asked to obtain attitudes or opinions?

19–15 What is meant by the reliability and validity of a questionnaire? Why must auditors be concerned about reliability and validity issues when they administer questionnaires during an audit?

19–16 What advantages do standardized questionnaires offer to auditors in the conduct of their audit work? Does their use have any disadvantages?

19–17 One problem with using the same audit questionnaire on a routine basis is the problem of "cheating." Explain briefly.

19–18 Give three problems of mail questionnaires. Outline some techniques that auditors can use to overcome these problems when they employ mail questionnaires during the conduct of an audit.

19–19 What is a control flowchart? What are the purposes of a control flowchart?

19–20 Briefly describe the nature and purposes of *four* types of control flowchart that auditors might construct during their audit work.

19–21 Outline the steps that must be undertaken when constructing a control flowchart. Be sure to indicate the critical decisions that must be made at each step.

19–22 For *each* of the four types of control flowcharts described in the chapter, give a strength and a limitation.

19–23 How might the availability of flowcharting software assist auditors to prepare and maintain control flowcharts they construct during the conduct of an audit?

19–24 A major advantage of control flowcharts is that they can be prepared and used effectively by auditors who have little knowledge of data processing controls. Discuss briefly.

19–25 To what extent is the hypothesized usefulness of flowcharts supported by empirical research results?

Multiple-Choice Questions

19–1 Which of the following statements about interviews versus interrogations is *true*?
  a An interrogation requires fewer skills to conduct than an interview because the need to establish rapport with respondents is not as important
  b A respondent in an interview is more likely to be uncooperative than a respondent in an interrogation because interviews generate higher levels of stress
  c Interrogations require a shorter period of time to conduct than an interview because they cover fewer topics and the questions asked can be more focused
  d Interrogations are more likely to be used than interviews to elicit information from an employee who is suspected of perpetrating a fraud

19–2 In which of the following situations would an interview *not* be appropriate?
  a Determining the impact of an application system on a user's quality of working life
  b Obtaining advice from operations personnel on which applications are inefficient
  c Obtaining the opinions of management on the material systems within the organization
  d Determining from managers how they colluded to carry out a defalcation

19–3 A respondent's motivation to reply to the questions asked during an interview is *primarily* a function of:
  a Whether the respondents perceive the questions asked during the interview to be complex or simple
  b The stress placed on respondents by having to answer the questions asked during the interview
  c The extent to which respondents perceive the interview to be a means of achieving their own goals
  d The extent to which respondents perceive the questions asked during the interview are interesting

19–4 A tandem interview is an interview conducted:
  a With one respondent and two interviewers
  b With two or more respondents
  c On two or more separate occasions
  d On a regular rotating basis

19–5 In an interview, closed questions should be asked:
   a Toward the beginning of an interview
   b Toward the middle of an interview
   c When a complex topic is being examined
   d When a controversial topic must be addressed

19–6 Which of the following is *most likely* to be the best time to conduct an interview?
   a Outside normal working hours when respondents will not be distracted by the pressures of work
   b Over a meal or break so respondents can relax and attend better to the interviewer's questions
   c Midmorning when respondents have had time to clear their urgent work but they are still fresh
   d Just after respondents arrive at work before they have time to be distracted by immediate work demands

19–7 Which of the following is *not* a rule of protocol to follow when conducting an interview?
   a For the most part, be a listener rather than a talker
   b Use technical terms whenever possible to communicate more effectively
   c Answer all the respondent's questions courteously
   d Avoid familiarity, and maintain a relaxed formality

19–8 Tape recorders should be used in an interview *only if*:
   a The prior permission of respondents has been obtained
   b Nonsensitive material is to be covered in the interview
   c Respondents do not appear to be nervous
   d Respondents' time is at a premium

19–9 Which of the following guidelines is *most likely* to result in the high-quality analysis of an audit interview?
   a It should be left until some time after the interview so auditors have a chance to reflect on the information obtained
   b Auditors should show their report to the interviewee to obtain their comments on accuracy and completeness
   c The auditor's interpretations of the respondent's opinions should be deferred until a global evaluation judgment must be made
   d The analysis should be undertaken by someone other than the auditor who conducted the interview to improve objectivity

19–10 Which of the following types of questionnaires probably would require the most explanatory information to be included with the questionnaire?
   a An internal control questionnaire completed by auditors
   b A questionnaire completed by auditors during an interview
   c A self-administered questionnaire mailed to dispersed application system users
   d A questionnaire requiring factual answers from respondents

19–11 Which of the following is *not* a general design guideline for questions to be included in a questionnaire?
   a Avoid having more than a few responses to each question
   b Avoid using questions that involve extensive recall
   c Avoid using hypothetical questions
   d Avoid using embarrassing questions

19–12 Which of the following types of response scales typically is *not* likely to be used on a questionnaire when opinions are solicited?
   a Multi-point scale
   b Semantic differential scale
   c Likert scale
   d Yes/no scale

19–13 In a questionnaire, more difficult questions should:
   a Be placed toward the middle and end of the questionnaire
   b Require a yes or no response to reduce complexity
   c Leave little room for opinion to increase response objectivity
   d Be placed toward the beginning of a questionnaire

19–14 The representativeness of the sample items on a questionnaire in terms of the domain of interest is a measure of its:
   a Construct validity
   b Predictive validity
   c Face validity
   d Content validity

19–15 A reliable questionnaire is one that:
   a Measures what it is supposed to measure in terms of its underlying construct
   b Has only a limited number of questions that the respondent must answer
   c Obtains the same responses across repeated administrations of the questionnaire
   d Predicts the values of other constructs to which the construct it measures is related

19–16 A primary problem with internal control questionnaires used by auditors is:
   a They are prone to high response error rates
   b They are completed mechanically after repeated use
   c They often have low predictive validity
   d They allow no scope for respondents to offer an opinion

19–17 Which of the following flowcharting techniques is *most likely* to form the basis of a control flowchart that shows controls exercised at the logical or functional level in an application system?
   a Document flowchart
   b Data flow diagram
   c System flowchart
   d Program flowchart

19–18 In the preparation of a control flowchart, the *most difficult* decisions are usually associated with:
   a Choosing the appropriate level of detail at which to work
   b Preparing the primary flowchart
   c Narrating controls on the primary flowchart
   d Choosing the primary flowcharting technique to use

19–19 In the preparation of a control flowchart, computer-assisted software engineering tools are *most unlikely* to assist in:
   a Determining the correct position to narrate controls on the control flowchart
   b Reducing the amount of time required to prepare the control flowchart in the first place
   c Undertaking subsequent modifications to the control flowchart in light of changes in the application system
   d Narrating controls on the control flowchart so the meaning of each control is clear

19–20 Which of the following aspects of control flowcharts requires the *most* audit experience for their effective use?
   a Choosing the right primary flowcharting technique to describe the features of interest in the application system
   b Correctly modifying the control flowchart in light of changes that occur to the application system
   c Correctly narrating controls on the primary flowchart to reflect their underlying reliability
   d Recognizing patterns on the control flowchart that signal control strengths and weaknesses

performance measurement data. It can measure the occurrence of more macroscopic events than hardware monitors, such as a program's access to a record in a database. Its major limitation is that it introduces artifact into the target system.

■ Firmware monitors use microcode in the target system to measure events. Because the execution time for a microinstruction is shorter than a normal program instruction, firmware monitors produce less artifact than software monitors. Moreover, they can access some hardware indicators that cannot be accessed by software. Thus, their domain overlaps both hardware monitors and software monitors. Microcode has a constrained space, however, and thus only a limited number of probes can be inserted for monitoring purposes.

■ A hybrid monitor has hardware, software, and perhaps firmware components. These components can be configured in many different ways. For example, software or firmware probes can detect events and write them to a hardware interface. An external device then reads, processes, stores, and presents the data written to the hardware interface. Thus, hybrid monitors can detect both software- and hardware-related events. They are sometimes difficult to use, however, because measurements taken by the software component and measurements taken by the hardware component must be coordinated.

■ Performance measurement data can be presented using either tables or charts. Two types of charts that are often used to present performance measurement data are Gantt charts and Kiviat graphs. Gantt charts use horizontal bars to show the percentage utilization of a resource and the extent of overlap of resource utilization among a number of resources. Kiviat graphs present performance measurement results so problems with performance can be recognized easily. They use radial axes in a circle to plot various performance measurement results. The shape of the resulting plot can be used to determine the extent to which the system is balanced in terms of its resource utilization.

■ Auditors should have two concerns about data integrity whenever performance monitors are used. First, they should determine whether the monitor has been installed correctly in the target system. They must evaluate the integrity of the measurements made by the monitor and the integrity of the target system processes after instrumentation. Second, auditors must try to determine whether a monitor has been used to violate data integrity. They should evaluate whether unauthorized use of the monitor has occurred to breach data privacy.

INTRODUCTION

Performance measurement tools enable auditors to obtain evidence on factors relating to system efficiency. Auditors can use the measurements taken in two ways. First, for systems that already are operational, the measurements provide the basic data for diagnosis of problems and construction of tuning therapies.

For example, data on the frequency of page faults can be used to select a paging algorithm in a virtual storage system. Second, the measurements can be used to estimate the values of parameters in analytical and simulation performance evaluation models of computer systems. For example, to evaluate the effects of a changed hardware configuration on throughput, auditors might construct a simulation model. Auditors can use performance measurement tools to estimate the characteristics of existing workloads (e.g., service demands) for input to the simulation model. Similarly, auditors can use them to estimate important system parameters (e.g., service times at a communications controller) so they can determine how the system will handle the workload demands placed upon it. (We return to these matters again in Chapter 23.)

In this chapter we take a brief look at the nature, characteristics, and relative advantages and disadvantages of different types of performance measurement tools. Our goal is not to obtain in-depth knowledge of these tools. Indeed, if we are to be capable of using these tools effectively, we will need to undertake substantial study elsewhere and to gain extensive experience with the tools. Rather, our goal is to obtain sufficient knowledge of the tools so that we know how they might fit into the audit work we wish to undertake in an organization. Moreover, auditors need to know enough about the tools so they can interact intelligently with skilled users of the tools. When we have a need, therefore, to undertake performance measurements in our audit work, we will be able to state our requirements in ways that can be understood by performance measurement specialists. Moreover, we will be able to understand and evaluate the work they undertake on our behalf.

The chapter proceeds as follows. First, we briefly examine some of the objects of measurement—that is, those phenomena we use to gauge whether a system is efficient and those factors that affect overall system efficiency. Next, we discuss some general characteristics of performance measurement tools. We then examine some specific types of tools we can use to obtain performance measurement data. Following our examination of performance measurement tools, we briefly consider some ways of presenting performance measurement data so it can be interpreted easily. Finally, we consider some implications of using performance measurement tools for asset safeguarding and maintenance of data integrity.

THE OBJECTS OF MEASUREMENT

Auditors might wish to measure many characteristics of an information system to facilitate evaluating its performance. Nonetheless, all characteristics that auditors can measure fall into three classes:

1. *Performance indices.* Performance indices are the output measures auditors can use to judge whether a system is performing satisfactorily. For example, in an online system auditors are likely to be interested in response times. In a batch system, however, auditors are likely to be interested in turnaround times.

2. *Workload parameters.* Workload parameters are used to characterize the resource demands that will be placed on a system. For example, in an online system auditors might be interested in such factors as the arrival rate of users at terminals, the amount of disk storage space that each will require, and the amount of central processor time that each will need to service their jobs. In a batch system, auditors might be interested in such factors as the number of transactions in a batch run, the percentage of database records that will be modified by these transactions, and the central processor time required to service each transaction.

3. *System parameters.* System parameters are used to characterize those factors that affect a system's capability to deal with the workload demands placed on it. For example, auditors might be interested in the average time it takes for a remote processor to respond to a request, the average number of transmission errors that occur on a data communications line, the number of terminals available for input, and the average time it takes for a cryptographic device to encrypt/decrypt a message.

Note that these classes of measures are overlapping. Depending on their objectives, auditors might classify some measures differently. For example, if auditors are trying to improve the performance of the central processor, throughput might be the performance indice that is their focus. If they are trying to determine how long it will take to process particular jobs, however, auditors might consider throughput to be a given system parameter. Accordingly, they will estimate turnaround times based on average throughput. In summary, however, auditors need to be able to characterize the workload demands placed upon a system, its capability to service these workload demands, and the performance that the system ultimately achieves. (We return to these issues in Chapter 23.)

GENERAL CHARACTERISTICS OF PERFORMANCE MEASUREMENT TOOLS

It will help our understanding of performance measurement tools if we first examine their general structural, functional, and operational characteristics. We will then be in a better position to be able to compare and contrast the different types of performance measurement tools.

Performance measurement tools have five basic components (Figure 20–1):

1. *Sensor.* The sensors (or probes) detect the occurrence or nonoccurrence of events and the magnitude of events.
2. *Selector.* The selector designates the subset of events to be monitored from the set of all events that the tool can detect.

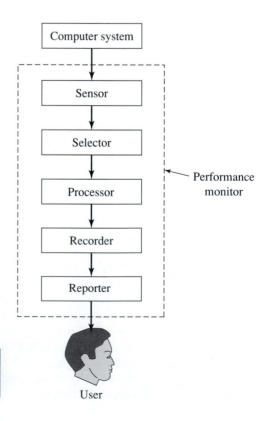

FIGURE 20–1. Structural elements of a performance monitor.

3. *Processor.* The processor transforms the data collected into a form suitable for storage and output. For example, it might count how many instances of an event have occurred during a particular time interval.
4. *Recorder.* The recorder writes the processed data to the permanent storage medium.
5. *Reporter.* The reporter summarizes the information stored and presents it to users.

As we shall see subsequently, the way these components are implemented in different kinds of performance measurement tools varies considerably. Moreover, the way these components are implemented affects the basic capabilities of the performance measurement tool. Nonetheless, the components provide us with a way of understanding the structure of the tool and some of its likely functional and operational characteristics.

Auditors can use performance measurement tools to undertake five types of measurements of resource consumption events:

Type of Measurement	*Explanation*
Trace	Recorded sequence of occurrence of events. For example, auditors might record the time when a seek on a disk begins and the time when the seek on a disk ends, or they might record the times when data communication packets arrive at a controller.
Event duration	Real time consumed by event. For example, auditors might record the real time consumed on the central processing unit by a batch job.
Relative duration	Ratio of total real time for the event over total elapsed time. For example, auditors might record the percentage of time that a disk channel is busy during the elapsed time it takes to write a record to a database.
Event frequency	Number of times the event occurs over a given time period. For example, auditors might record the number of page faults that occur during a one-minute interval.
Distribution of event	Distribution of event times over some elapsed time period. For example, auditors might record the average response times for an online system during several one-hour intervals throughout a day.

Not all performance measurement tools are capable of making these measurements equally well. For example, some are designed primarily to measure a small set of resource consumption events with high accuracy. Others are designed to measure a larger set of resource consumption events but with less accuracy. The more expensive tools usually have greater measurement capabilities.

The overall capabilities of a performance measurement tool are a function of seven attributes of the tool:

Attribute	*Explanation*
Artifact (interference)	Extent to which presence of the tool causes overheads and interferes with the normal operations of the system. For example, the measurement activities undertaken by the tool might consume central processor time or storage space.
Domain (scope)	Number of different classes of events that the tools can detect.
Resolution (input rate)	Maximum frequency at which events can be detected and recorded correctly. Two input resolutions can be specified: the *burst-mode rate* specifies the rate at which events can be measured for a short period, and the *sustained rate* specifies the rate at which events can be measured over a longer period.

(cont.)

Attribute	Explanation
Input width	Number of bits of input data that a tool can extract and process when an event occurs.
Data reduction capabilities	Extent to which data can be summarized before it is stored.
Data storage capabilities	Amount of permanent storage available for recording data.
Precision	Number of digits available to represent data.

Other factors also affect the usefulness of a performance measurement tool. For example, external auditors will be concerned with the tool's portability—that is, the extent to which they can use the tool on several different hardware/software platforms. Auditors would be also concerned about the amount of time it would take them to set up and use the tool when they are dealing with relatively unfamiliar hardware/software platforms and the quality of the documentation provided with the tool.

TYPES OF PERFORMANCE MEASUREMENT TOOLS

Performance measurement tools can be classified in several ways. For example, we can focus on the way the tool is activated. If its measurement activities are triggered by the occurrence of a certain type of event, it is an *event-driven* tool. Such tools are useful when the frequency with which an instance of the event type occurs is low. They do not impose overheads on the system unless an instance of the event type occurs. If instances of the event types occur frequently, however, event-driven tools can impose high artifact on the system being measured.

For this reason, *sampling* tools might be used instead. Sampling tools are activated by some type of timing mechanism. They undertake measurement activities when they receive a signal from the timing mechanism. They cease measurement activities after a fixed interval or when they receive another signal from the timing mechanism. They might also cease measurement activities after a particular type of event has occurred. By varying the sampling rate, the artifact imposed on the system can be controlled. For example, to decrease the artifact, the sampling rate can be reduced. The sampling error will increase, however, so our sample statistics will be less precise in terms of estimating the population characteristics that interest us.

Performance measurement tools can also be classified in terms of when they present their results. *Online* tools display their results continuously or after short time periods have elapsed. They are useful, for example, when real-time observation of certain types of events could give insights into the nature of a performance problem that is being experienced. *Batch* tools store their mea-

TABLE 20–1 Attributes of Different Types of Performance Measurement Tools

Attribute	Type of Monitor			
	Hardware	Software	Firmware	Hybrid
Monitor artifact	Zero–small	Moderate–high	Moderate–high	Small–moderate
Monitor domain	Moderate	Large	Moderate	Moderate–large
Resolution	High	Low–moderate	Moderate	Moderate–high
Input width	Moderate	High	Moderate	Moderate–high
Data reduction capabilities	Moderate–substantial	Substantial	Low–moderate	Moderate–substantial
Data storage capabilities	Moderate–large	Large	Large	Moderate–large
Precision	High	Low–moderate	Moderate	Moderate–high
Portability	Moderate–high	Low–moderate	Low	Low–moderate
Difficulty of installation/use	High	Moderate	Moderate	High

surement data for presentation at a later time, perhaps using a separate analysis program for presentation purposes. They are useful, for example, in the regular, day-to-day monitoring of a system's performance.

Perhaps the most common way to classify performance measurement tools is based on the nature of the components that make up the tool. Four types of tool usually are identified on this basis: hardware monitors, software monitors, firmware monitors, and hybrid monitors. For each type of tool, Table 20–1 provides an overview of the attributes that affect their usefulness to auditors. In the following subsections, we discuss in more detail the nature of each type of tool and their relative strengths and limitations.

Hardware Monitors

A hardware monitor is a device connected to a target computer (the computer to be measured) that detects signals in the target computer's electronic circuitry. It can tell us the state of various hardware components in the target system, such as registers, channels, buses, and memory locations. Auditors can use a hardware monitor to obtain the following types of data:

1. Whether a central processing unit (CPU) is busy or idle,
2. Whether a channel is busy or idle,
3. Whether a memory location has been referenced by a read or write operation (via a signal on a memory bus),
4. Whether a page fault has occurred in a virtual memory system (because the page required resides on disk rather than in main memory),
5. Whether a memory reference has been satisfied by cache memory rather than main memory,
6. Whether a particular instruction operation code (opcode) has been issued (to count the frequency with which each opcode is used),
7. The start and finish of program module executions when the modules reside at known memory locations,
8. Program execution when the program resides at known memory addresses, and
9. Which device (e.g., disk drive) attached to a channel has been referenced via an input/output operation.

Structure and Functions of Hardware Monitors

Figure 20–2 shows the basic structure of a hardware monitor. *Probes* are connected to the target system. The *concentrator* reduces the number of cables from the host system to the monitor. The *comparator* performs a test on two or

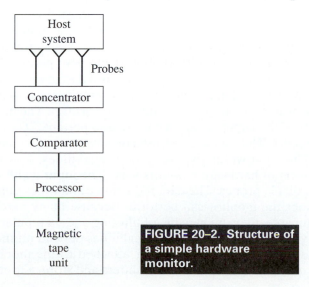

FIGURE 20–2. Structure of a simple hardware monitor.

more registers and outputs a signal depending on the result of the test. The *processor* has three major components: *(1)* a logic unit allows different kinds of tests to be specified; *(2)* counters are available to count either event occurrences or the time interval between events; and *(3)* a clock generates timing signals. The final component of the monitor is the *storage unit* used to record the measurement data.

To illustrate how auditors might use a hardware monitor, assume they are interested in the extent of overlap between the operations of a CPU and two channels. Furthermore, assume they wish to distinguish between problem state and supervisor state operations in the CPU. Using a hardware monitor, auditors would need to keep track of four flip-flops (devices that can be in one of two states) in the target computer: the CPU busy/idle flip-flop; the busy/idle flip-flop for channel 1; the busy/idle flip-flop for channel 2; and the problem/supervisor flip-flop for the CPU. Using logical AND combinations of the states of the flip-flops, auditors can obtain 12 measurements via the hardware monitor:

1. CPU busy in problem state only,
2. CPU busy in supervisor state only,
3. Channel 1 busy only,
4. Channel 2 busy only,
5. CPU in problem state and channel 1 busy,
6. CPU in problem state and channel 2 busy,
7. CPU in problem state and both channels busy,
8. CPU in supervisor state and channel 1 busy,
9. CPU in supervisor state and channel 2 busy,
10. CPU in supervisor state and both channels busy,
11. Both channels busy only, and
12. CPU busy only.

Note that measurement 12 is simply the addition of measurements 1 and 2. The measurements can be printed out as counts or perhaps displayed graphically to illustrate better the overlap that occurs.

Strengths of Hardware Monitors

Because hardware monitors measure the state of a system electronically, they can detect very short duration events in a computer system—for example, a change of the CPU from a busy to an idle state. Thus, they are high-resolution tools. They also are able to monitor several events simultaneously, even events occurring on independent hardware units.

Hardware monitors usually have a broad domain. Many types of resource consumption activities can be monitored. Nonetheless, the size of the monitor domain is affected by the target system's architectural design. If the system does not provide access to important measurement points, then the domain of hardware monitors is restricted. Architectural design to facilitate measurement is important because large-scale integrated circuits are now used extensively.

Hardware monitors cause little or no artifact. The monitor functions independently of the target system. They are also portable. They simply recognize signals in circuitry. Thus, they can be used on any system that has suitable probe points.

The input width, data reduction capabilities, data storage capabilities, and precision of hardware monitors vary. The input width depends on the number of available probes. The data reduction capabilities depend on what logical operations the monitor can perform. Because many hardware monitors are programmable, they are capable of filtering and manipulating the data collected in many ways. The data storage capabilities depend on the size of secondary storage devices incorporated into or attached to the monitor. Precision is a function of the word length of the counters and storage used by the monitor.

Effective use of hardware monitors requires substantial expertise. Probes can be connected to incorrect points. Also, care must be taken to ensure stress is not placed on the probe points so that damage does not occur to the hardware. To assist with the placement of probes, machine vendors might provide documentation on probe points for their hardware, particularly if they have taken monitoring requirements into account in the design of the hardware. Similarly, the vendors of hardware monitors sometimes provide libraries of probe points for the common types of machine architectures.

Limitations of Hardware Monitors

Perhaps the major limitation of hardware monitors is their inability to trace software-related events. For example, a hardware monitor cannot detect a program's access to a data structure because it is unable to monitor directly the contents of random access memory. Likewise, it is unable to determine whether a program variable has been modified. These types of capabilities become important when the performance of an individual program must be evaluated. Unless the sequence of state changes that occur within the program can be traced, it is difficult to determine those parts of the program that are executed most frequently and those parts that consume the most resources.

The use of hardware monitors has declined progressively. As discussed previously, the use of large-scale integrated circuits has reduced the number of probe points on many computers. As a result, it has become increasingly difficult to use hardware monitors. Moreover, software-related events have become the focus of many efforts to improve performance in computer systems. Nonetheless, hardware monitors still have their place. With the continuing growth of networks and distributed systems, hardware monitors could again be used extensively because of the need to measure very short-interval events.

Software Monitors

A software monitor is a program (subroutine, instruction) inserted into the code of a system or another program to collect performance measurement data. If the monitor is incorporated into the operating system, usually the intent is to examine the performance of systemwide functions. If the monitor is incorporated into an application program, however, usually the intent is to gather performance data on that specific program.

Auditors can use a software monitor to obtain the following types of data:

1. The arrival of a transaction from a terminal at a terminal controller,
2. The length of a transaction queue for an online program,
3. Which records have been accessed during an inquiry on a database,
4. A request by a program to use an operating system module,
5. The start time and completion time for a program module,
6. The frequency with which a particular program module is used,
7. The response time at a terminal,
8. The length of a transaction queue at a laser printer connected to a local area network, and
9. The elapsed time for the operating system to service an input/output request.

Structure and Functions of Software Monitors

Figure 20–3 shows the steps we must follow to set up a software monitor. First, instrumentation must be added to a target program—either the operating system, an application program, or some other system or utility software. We can use either source or run-time instrumentation. If we use source instrumentation, we must manually add probe points to the target program. Alternatively, we might be able to use a preprocessor that reads the source code of the target

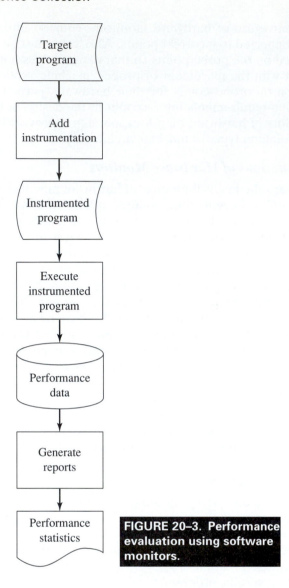

FIGURE 20–3. Performance evaluation using software monitors.

program and inserts the probe points automatically. If we use run-time instrumentation, a probe monitor routine is added to the run-time environment of the target program. Unlike source instrumentation, run-time instrumentation does not require that the target program be recompiled. After instrumentation, we execute the target program to allow the probes to collect performance data. We then must analyze this data and produce performance reports.

To illustrate how software monitors might be used, first consider an *operating system monitor*—that is, a monitor built into the operating system. The measurements undertaken by an operating system monitor are often triggered by an operating system interrupt. For example, assume auditors are concerned about the length of time taken to undertake input/output operations. The monitor could be used, therefore, to record the time when different jobs request an input/output operation (as signaled by an interrupt). It can also be used to record the time when an input/output operation is finished (also as signaled by an interrupt). Auditors could then analyze statistics for the elapsed times between the start and finish of input/output operations to try to determine whether their concerns are justified.

As a second example, consider a *program analyzer*—that is, a monitor incorporated into a program to determine its resource consumption patterns. For example, assume auditors want to assess the efficiency with which an interactive application program executes different decision models that users call selectively to aid their decision-making processes. Their goal might be to focus first on those models that are used most frequently and consume most time. The following code is an excerpt from the interactive program (written in COBOL) and the software monitoring instructions that auditors might insert in the program:

```
WHAT-DEC-MOD.

_____

_____

IF DECNO IS EQUAL T0 6
CALL CLOCKTIME USING STARTTM
PERFORM DEC-MOD6
CALL CLOCKTIME USING ENDTM
PERFORM STATS.
```

The instructions execute in the following way. First, when the interactive program identifies that the user has requested decision model 6 (DECNO = 6), it calls a subroutine that accesses the system clock to obtain the start time of the execution of the subroutine that performs the processing related to decision model 6. Second, the program performs the subroutine that executes the decision model. Third, when the subroutine returns control, the program again accesses the system clock to determine the finish time of the event. Finally, the program executes a subroutine that writes away to some storage device the decision model number, the start time, and the finish time. At the end of the measurement period, auditors can access this data, determine the number of times a particular decision model was used, plot the distribution of execution times, and calculate relevant statistics such as the mean and variance of execution times for each decision model.

Types of Software Monitors

In their performance measurement work, auditors can use two types of software monitors. The first type is an *event-driven software monitor*, which undertakes measurements when some type of event occurs internally to the system or program. A common event-driven software monitor auditors will encounter is the *accounting system* incorporated into multiuser operating systems. These monitors capture resource-consumption data associated with users and their jobs—for example, the start and end times for user program execution, the amount of CPU time consumed, the number of input/output operations undertaken, and the amount of primary and secondary memory consumed. The major purpose of the accounting system is to provide the data required to bill users for resource consumption. Nonetheless, this data is often useful to auditors for performance evaluation purposes. Auditors need to check the ways the accounting system collects resource-consumption data, however, to ensure they are congruent with their performance evaluation needs. For example, the accounting system might smooth resource consumption levels across users to mitigate the effects of different multiuser workloads on the time taken to run each application program. This smoothing of resource-consumption patterns might mask information auditors need to evaluate the efficiency of an application program.

The advantage of using event-driven software monitors is that auditors obtain data on each instance of the type of event that interests them during the measurement period. Therefore, they should make good predictions about the population parameters that interest them—for example, the time taken for input/output operations. The disadvantage of using these types of monitor is that measurement overheads become high as the frequency of the event being monitored increases.

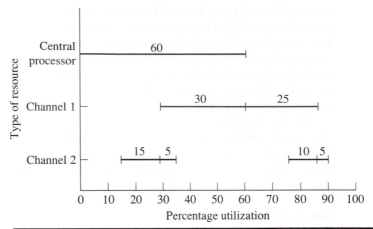

FIGURE 20–6. Gantt chart showing resource utilization.

busy but the central processor is idle. We use a similar procedure to show when only channel 2 is busy, when channel 1 and channel 2 only are busy concurrently, when channel 2 and the central processor only are busy concurrently, and when all three resources are busy concurrently.

We can then extract various information from the Gantt chart. For example, we can see that the central processor is busy 60 percent of the time during our measurement time interval. Similarly, we can see that channel 1 is busy 55 percent of the time during our measurement time interval. We might note, also, that channel 1 is busy for half the time that the central processor is busy (30/60 = 0.5). We must then evaluate this data to determine whether we have a bottleneck resource and whether the three resources are being used efficiently.

Kiviat Graphs

Kiviat graphs were first developed in the 1970s. Their purpose is to present performance measurement results so problems with resource usage can be recognized easily. Particular types of performance problems are manifested in Kiviat graphs having a particular shape.

To illustrate their nature and functions, consider the Kiviat graph shown in Figure 20–7. Note, first, that the basis for the graph is a circle with four axes that

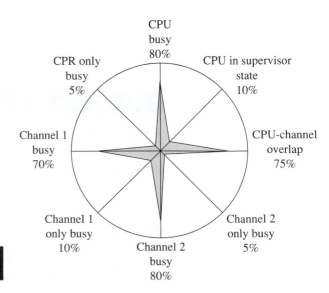

FIGURE 20–7. Kiviat graph for a balanced system.

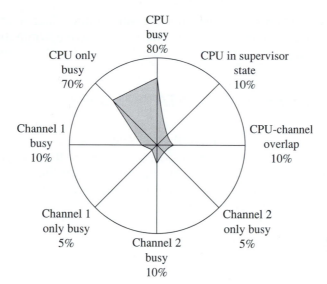

FIGURE 20–8. Kiviat graph for a processor-bound system.

divide the circle into eight equal segments. Each of the eight radii of the circle is used to measure the level of some performance variable. The center represents the zero point on the scale used to measure the performance variable. The maximum value of the performance variable is where the radius intersects the circumference of the circle.

The performance variables shown in Figure 20–7 are those often used in the earliest Kiviat graphs. They reflect a concern with optimizing use of the CPU and the input/output channels. If we proceed counterclockwise around the radial axes of the graph, note that we alternate between having a goal of a higher value and a goal of a lower value. For example, we want the central processor to be busy for a reasonably high percentage of the time (not too high). We do not want it to be busy, however, by itself. Our goal is to have an overlap of central processor and channel operations. To the extent we see a symmetric star plotted on the graph, we can conclude we have a reasonably balanced system. In this light, Figure 20–7 represents a balanced system. Figure 20–8, on the other hand, represents an unbalanced, central processor-bound system.

Other types of performance variables can be plotted on Kiviat graphs. For example, Figure 20–9 shows a Kiviat graph for an online system where we have

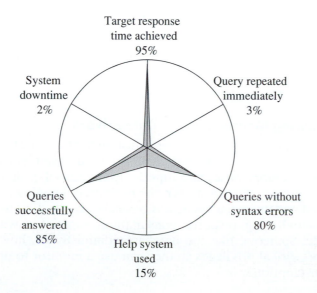

FIGURE 20–9. Kiviat graph for an online system.

focussed on six performance measures rather than eight performance measures. Again, our concern is with whether we have a symmetric star emerge when we plot the values of the performance variables on the graph.

PERFORMANCE MEASUREMENT AND DATA INTEGRITY

Auditors should have two concerns about data integrity whenever performance monitors are used. First, they should determine whether the monitor has been installed correctly in the target system. Here the concern is with the integrity of the measurements made by the monitor and the integrity of the target system processes after instrumentation. Second, auditors must try to determine whether a monitor has been used to violate data integrity. Here the concern is with unauthorized use of the monitor to breach data privacy. The following two subsections briefly discuss each of these concerns.

Ensuring Correct System Instrumentation

The proper placement of a hardware monitor's probes and a software monitor's checkpoints is sometimes a difficult task. With hardware monitors, auditors can use test programs to check proper placement of probes. Sometimes these test programs are provided by the monitor vendor. If they are not, auditors might need to prepare their own test programs. When these programs have been developed, they can then calculate the resource utilization that should occur with them and compare the results with the resource utilization results obtained via the monitor. If serious discrepancies exist between the two sets of results, auditors must question whether they have correctly instrumented the target system using the hardware monitor.

Auditors can facilitate proper placement of a software monitor's checkpoints if they use a software monitor that automatically inserts checkpoints at user-specified locations in the target system. In this regard, some software monitors can be used interactively to instrument the target program. The monitor automatically inserts the checkpoints that issue calls to either standard predefined measurement routines already included in the monitor or user-coded measurement routines. Furthermore, the monitor checks that checkpoints are not inserted at locations in the host system where they might cause errors—for example, at locations referenced in the program as data and not instructions.

Some software monitors also validate any user-supplied measurement routines. These monitors impose various restrictions on the code supplied by users. For example, the monitor will check that the code does not *(1)* contain illegal or privileged instructions, *(2)* modify itself or other measurement routines, *(3)* store data in or branch into the target system, and *(4)* contain backward branches. Still other types of checks might be applied. For example, the monitor might check whether a probe would cause intolerable interference, thereby destroying the integrity of a time-critical target system process.

Ensuring Maintenance of Data Privacy

Use of performance monitors must be controlled carefully. Because monitors have access to lower-level elements within the hierarchy of system resources (e.g., memory buses and input/output channels), they can be used to breach data privacy. For each user, the permitted domain of the monitor must be defined and enforced via access controls. Application users should be restricted to monitoring resource consumption associated with their own processes only. Someone like the database administrator, however, might be granted more global privileges so they can use a monitor to optimize overall resource consumption.

In the case of hardware monitors, physical access to the monitor must be restricted. In the case of software monitors, access to the monitor should be controlled via password controls—for example, those implemented in the operating system's access control mechanism. A log of users of a software monitor also can be kept and reviewed periodically to determine whether unauthorized actions have occurred.

Software monitors themselves also must be protected. Because they are sometimes assigned powerful privileges to allow them to collect performance measurement data, they are attractive targets for Trojan horses (see Chapter 13). Access controls therefore must be implemented to prevent unauthorized modification of the functions they perform.

SUMMARY

Performance measurement tools enable auditors to obtain evidence on hardware and software resource consumption. They can use this evidence to decide how to improve resource utilization.

Four types of performance measurement tools are available: *(1)* hardware monitors, *(2)* software monitors, *(3)* firmware monitors, and *(4)* hybrid monitors. Hardware monitors take measurements through probes attached to the circuitry of the target system's hardware. Software monitors take measurements through checkpoints inserted into the target system. Firmware monitors take measurements through the microcode inserted in the target system. Hybrid monitors use an external hardware device to process data collected by an internal software/firmware component. The different types of monitors have varying capabilities with respect to their scope, resolution, input width, data reduction and storage capabilities, precision, portability, and the artifact they produce.

When auditors obtain performance measurement data, they must consider carefully how they will present the data. They might use tables or charts. Whatever the presentation method used, auditors must ensure that the data can be interpreted accurately and completely. They should conform to the rules and heuristics for good design of tables and charts.

Two types of graphs that are often used to present performance measurement data are Gantt charts and Kiviat graphs. Gantt charts use horizontal bars to show the percentage utilization of a resource and the extent of overlap of resource utilization among several resources. Kiviat graphs use radial axes in a circle to plot the values of performance variables. The variables alternate between those for which a higher value is the goal and those for which a lower value is the goal. A balanced system will be reflected in a symmetric star-shaped plot on the Kiviat graph.

When using a performance monitor, auditors must ensure that the monitor is installed correctly. Otherwise, the measurements taken could be invalid, or the integrity of the target system might be corrupted. When auditors use a hardware monitor, test programs should be run to determine whether the probes have been placed correctly. If possible, auditors should use a software monitor that automatically inserts user-specified checkpoints into the target program. Alternatively, they should use a software monitor that will carry out various types of validation tests on the probes they wish to place in the target system.

Access to performance monitors also must be controlled because they can be used to breach data privacy. Hardware monitors must be subject to physical access controls. Software monitors must be subject to logical access controls. Software monitors themselves also must be protected against unauthorized modifications because they are suitable targets for Trojan horses.

Review Questions

20–1 How can auditors use the measurements taken via performance measurement tools to assist them in improving efficiency in a system?

20–2 Give three classes of characteristics of a computer system that might be measured by a performance measurement tool. Briefly explain why instances of each of these classes of characteristics may be measured.

20–3 What is the function of the sensor in a performance measurement tool?

20–4 Briefly explain why it might be necessary to carry out some form of reduction on data collected by a performance measurement tool before it is stored.

20–5 Briefly explain why auditors might be interested in obtaining the distribution of disk seek times for an online real-time program when attempting to improve the efficiency of the program.

20–6 What is meant by *artifact*? Why is it important for auditors to know the extent of artifact that a performance measurement tool may produce? Is it possible to control for artifact? Briefly explain.

20–7 What is meant by the resolution of a performance measurement tool? Why is the level of its resolution important?

20–8 Briefly explain the difference between an event-driven performance measurement tool and a sampling measurement tool. What are their relative advantages and disadvantages?

20–9 Briefly explain the nature of a hardware monitor.

20–10 Why does a hardware monitor have greater resolution than a software monitor?

20–11 Give two factors that limit the domain of a hardware monitor. Briefly explain how they limit the domain.

20–12 Briefly explain the nature of a software monitor.

20–13 Briefly explain the difference between an operating system monitor and a program analyzer.

20–14 Briefly explain the difference between an event-driven software monitor and a sampling software monitor. What are the relative advantages and disadvantages of each type of monitor?

20–15 Why is the accounting system incorporated into an operating system considered to be a software monitor? Give one strength and one limitation of using the accounting system for performance evaluation purposes.

20–16 How do the domains of hardware and software monitors differ? Give an example of an event that most likely would be only in the domain of a hardware monitor, one that most likely would be only in the domain of a software monitor, and one that most likely would be in both domains.

20–17 Theoretically, the input width of a software monitor is unlimited. Practically, however, it is limited by the extent of interference it produces. Explain.

20–18 Briefly explain what is meant by time and space artifact.

20–19 Are hardware monitors more portable than software monitors? Why?

20–20 Briefly explain the nature of a firmware monitor. How does a firmware monitor differ from a software monitor?

20–21 Give two advantages that firmware monitors have over software monitors. What problems could arise because of the high resolution capabilities that firmware monitors possess?

20–22 Briefly explain the nature of a hybrid monitor.

20–23 Why do hybrid monitors produce a lower artifact than software monitors but a higher artifact than hardware monitors?

20–24 How are Gantt charts used to present performance measurement results?

20–25 What is a Kiviat graph? How are Kiviat graphs used to present performance measurement results?

20–26 What is meant by instrumenting a system for performance measurement? Why is it desirable for vendors to consider instrumentation during the design stages of a computer system?

20–27 What problems arise during performance measurement if a system is incorrectly instrumented? How can incorrect instrumentation be detected in a hardware monitor and a software monitor?

20–28 Give two advantages of using a software monitor that instruments a system automatically.

20–29 Why is it important to control who gains access to a performance monitor? Why is a performance monitor a likely target for someone wishing to carry out unauthorized activities in a computer system?

Multiple-Choice Questions

20–1 Which of the following is *least likely* to be a purpose of using a performance measurement tool with a computer system?
a Developing a tuning therapy to improve performance
b Estimating the value of parameters in an analytical model
c Detecting the most error-prone modules in a program
d Estimating the characteristics of a workload model

20–2 Which of the following is *most likely* to be considered a performance indice when undertaking performance measures in a computer system?
a Arrival rate of users at terminals
b Average number of errors on a data communications line
c Throughput of a batch system
d Average amount of disk storage consumed by each user

20–3 The structural element of a performance monitor that determines the subset of activities to be measured is the:
a Selector
b Processor
c Sensor
d Recorder

20–4 The type of measurement whereby the real time consumed by an event is monitored is called:
a An event frequency measurement
b A trace measurement
c A relative frequency measurement
d An event duration measurement

20–5 Monitor artifact is:
a The noise present in the set of measurements taken when the system is under load
b The extent to which the presence of the monitor interferes with the normal system operations
c The extent to which the measurements collected must be recorded in summary form
d The extent to which low-level activities that the monitor cannot detect must be accounted for by an average resource consumption measure

20–6 The set of resource consumption activities that the monitor can detect is called the:
a Monitor resolution
b Monitor precision
c Monitor input width
d Monitor domain

Required: You are the internal audit manager for the organization. Top management has directed the controller to resolve the problems, and he has asked your assistance because he knows you have expertise in computer system performance evaluation. Write a brief report indicating how you will approach the task, the possible causes of the problem, the type of performance data you will gather, and the tools you will use to gather the performance data.

20–5 The following performance measurement data pertains to two systems, A and B:

System A

System State	Percent of Time
CPU busy	90
CPU only busy	85
CPU channel overlap	5
Channel only busy	5
Any channel busy	10
CPU wait	10
CPU in problem state	85
CPU in supervisor state	5

System B

System State	Percent of Time
CPU busy	15
CPU only busy	5
CPU channel overlap	10
Channel only busy	75
Any channel busy	85
CPU wait	85
CPU in problem state	10
CPU in supervisor state	5

Required: Draw Gantt charts and Kiviat graphs to show the performance measurement data for the two systems. What conclusions would you reach about the two systems on the basis of the data you have displayed graphically? How are they similar? How are they different?

20–6 You are the manager of internal audit for a large financial institution that uses advanced computer systems: distributed systems, online real-time update systems, database management systems, and so on. The top managers of your company have decided that computer operations are sufficiently material that it is worthwhile employing a full-time person with expertise in computer performance evaluation. This person will be responsible for setting up and carrying out a program of regular performance reviews of all major information systems within your company.

The top managers recognize that the person responsible for performance evaluations at times will be in a position to breach the integrity of systems. They are concerned that the powers vested in the person not be abused. They are concerned, also, about the impact of this person's activities on the conduct of the external audit.

Required: The top managers ask you to write a brief report recommending some controls that might be implemented and exercised over the person to ensure proper performance of duties. In addition, they ask you to advise them on any changes they should expect to the work undertaken by your company's external auditors in light of their appointing a person to undertake performance evaluation of the company's major systems. In particular, they are interested in whether the external auditors are likely to increase or decrease the extent of the audit work they undertake.

Answers to Multiple-Choice Questions

20–1	c	**20–7**	a	**20–13**	b	**20–19**	a
20–2	c	**20–8**	c	**20–14**	d	**20–20**	b
20–3	a	**20–9**	b	**20–15**	c	**20–21**	b
20–4	d	**20–10**	a	**20–16**	b	**20–22**	d
20–5	b	**20–11**	a	**20–17**	c		
20–6	d	**20–12**	d	**20–18**	d		

REFERENCES

Anderson, Gordon E. (1984), "The Co-ordinated Use of Five Performance Evaluation Methodologies," *Communications of the ACM* (February), 119–125.

Cady, J., and B. Howarth (1990), *Computer Systems Performance Management and Capacity Planning.* Upper Saddle River, NJ: Prentice-Hall.

Jain, Raj (1991), *The Art of Computer Systems Performance Analysis: Techniques for Experimental Design, Measurement, Simulation, and Modeling.* New York: John Wiley.

McKerrow, Phillip (1988), *Performance Measurement of Computer Systems.* Reading, MA: Addison-Wesley.

Menascé, Daniel, Virgilio A. F. Almeida, and Larry W. Dowdy (1994), *Capacity Planning and Performance Monitoring: From Mainframes to Client-Server Systems.* Upper Saddle River, NJ: Prentice-Hall.

Evidence Evaluation

Having collected evidence on how well a system meets its objectives, auditors then must evaluate the evidence. The evaluation process involves weighting and combining the piecemeal evidence they have collected to make a global decision. When auditors make this global evaluation decision, they must determine whether they believe controls are in place and operating reliably to ensure the system safeguards assets, maintains data integrity, achieves organizational goals effectively, and consumes resources efficiently.

Auditors make most use of their judgment capabilities when they make the global evidence evaluation decision. In spite of substantial research, we are only just beginning to understand how the various pieces of evidence that auditors collect should be weighted and combined to make the decision and the types of judgment pitfalls they must seek to avoid. To a large extent, auditors still must rely on their intuition and experience when assessing the impact of a system's strengths and weaknesses on the likelihood of it achieving its asset safeguarding, data integrity, effectiveness, and efficiency objectives.

The next three chapters examine the evidence evaluation process for the four major decisions that auditors must make: whether the system to be evaluated safeguards assets, whether it maintains data integrity, whether it achieves its goals effectively, and whether it consumes resources efficiently. Until we know more about the evaluation process, the chapters can provide only some guidelines to assist making high-quality evaluation decisions. Currently, it is this area that requires some of the most intensive research to better understand the decision-making process that auditors must use.

Chapter	*Overview of Contents*
21 Evaluating Asset Safeguarding and Data Integrity	Measures of asset safeguarding and data integrity; qualitative and quantitative techniques for evaluating asset safeguarding and data integrity; cost-effectiveness guidelines.
22 Evaluating System Effectiveness	Measures of system effectiveness relating to task accomplishment goals, quality of working life goals, operational effectiveness goals, technical effectiveness goals, and economic effectiveness goals; techniques for evaluating system effectiveness.
23 Evaluating System Efficiency	Performance indexes as measures of system efficiency; evaluation of system efficiency using workload models and system models.

CHAPTER

Evaluating Asset Safeguarding and Data Integrity

Chapter Outline

Chapter Key Points

■ To make a decision on how well assets are safeguarded, auditors need a measure of asset safeguarding. The measure they use is the expected loss that will occur if the asset is destroyed, stolen, or used for unauthorized purposes. Similarly, to make a decision on how well data integrity is maintained, auditors need a measure of data integrity. The measure of data integrity they use will depend on their audit objectives and the nature of the data item on which they focus. Three measures they can use are (a) the size of the dollar error that might exist, (b) the size of the quantity error that might exist, and (c) the number of errors that might exist.

■ When auditors make the global evaluation decision, they seek to determine the overall impact of individual control strengths and weaknesses on how well assets are safeguarded and how well data integrity is maintained. They make this decision at various stages during the conduct of an audit: (a) after having undertaken preliminary audit work and gained an understanding of the control structure, (b) after having undertaken tests of controls, and (c) after having undertaken substantive tests.

■ The determinants of auditor judgment performance can be usefully grouped into four categories: (a) the auditor's cognitive abilities, which are subject to various biases that can arise from the heuristics that auditors use to help them make judgments; (b) the auditor's knowledge, which has been developed on the basis of education, training, and experience; (c) the environment in which the auditor must make his or her decision, which depends on factors like the technology available to assist the auditor, the extent to which group judgment processes are used during the audit, the auditor's prior involvement with the audit, and the extent to which the auditor will be held accountable for his or her work; and (d) the auditor's motivation, which will depend on factors like how accountable the auditor will be held for his or her work.

■ One form of technology that can be used to assist auditors to make the global evaluation judgment is a control matrix. In a control matrix, we list the exposures that can occur in the columns of the matrix and the controls we use to reduce expected losses from these exposures in the rows of the matrix. In the elements of the matrix, we might indicate, for example, how effectively a particular control reduces expected losses from a particular exposure.

■ A second form of technology that can be used to assist auditors to make the global evaluation judgment is a deterministic model. Deterministic models simply involve estimating the size of each error or loss and multiplying it by the number of times the error or loss has occurred. These models are most useful when errors and irregularities occur deterministically, which is often the case in computer systems (e.g., a program either makes an error or it does not make an error). Even if errors or irregularities occur stochastically, the size of the error or loss can still be estimated on the basis of the most likely value of the error or loss or the extreme values of the error or loss.

∎ Software reliability models use statistical techniques to estimate the likelihood that an error will be discovered during some time period based on the pattern of past errors that have been discovered in the system. Three types of models have been developed. Time-between-failures models are based on the assumption that the time between successive failures of a system will get longer as errors are removed from the system. Failure-count models are used to predict the number of errors that are likely to occur during a time interval on the basis of the number of errors that occurred during previous time intervals. Fault-seeding models make estimates of the number of errors that exist in a system based on the number of seeded errors that are discovered during a testing process and the number of new errors that are discovered during the testing process.

∎ Engineering reliability models allow auditors to estimate the overall reliability of a system as a function of the individual components and individual internal controls that make up the system. They are based on three fundamental parameters: (a) the probability that a process in the system will fail, (b) the probability that a process will correctly signal an error or irregularity when one occurs, and (c) the probability that the error or irregularity will be corrected when one occurs.

∎ Bayesian models provide auditors with a formal method of revising prior estimates of the reliability of an internal control system on the basis of new evidence gathered during the conduct of an audit. Prior research has shown that humans perform poorly when they must revise the probability of an event occurring in light of new information they receive. Bayesian models help to overcome these limitations of humans as statistical decision makers.

∎ Whenever possible, auditors should use analytical models to help them make the global evaluation judgment. They are usually the cheapest to develop and use. Sometimes, however, the assumptions that underlie analytical models are too restrictive, or the analytical models are not mathematically tractable. In these situations, simulation models might be used to help auditors make the evaluation judgment. A program must be constructed to capture the important characteristics of the system to be evaluated, and the program must then be run to study the behavior of the system it is intended to model. From the auditors' viewpoint, their focus will be the likely error or loss that can arise from errors or irregularities in the system that is being modeled by the simulation program.

∎ Expert systems are another means that auditors can use to help make the global evaluation judgment on whether a system safeguards assets and maintains data integrity. They might provide auditors with insights on the way in which control strengths and weaknesses compound and compensate to affect the overall reliability of the system. Auditors can also use them as a reasonableness check on their evaluation judgments. The performance of many expert systems is brittle, however, outside the domain in which they have been developed. In this light, auditors must ensure that they have been developed to provide assistance in the specific domain where they must make the global evaluation judgment.

■ There are five costs associated with implementing and operating controls in a system: (a) initial setup costs that must be incurred to design and implement the controls; (b) costs to execute the controls; (c) costs to search for errors and irregularities when they are signaled, determine whether they exist, and correct them when they are found; (d) costs associated with errors and irregularities that are not discovered or errors and irregularities that are discovered but not corrected; and (e) costs associated with maintaining the controls. The benefits of having a control system relate to the reduction in expected losses that will occur because fewer errors and irregularities arise.

■ The design, implementation, operation, and maintenance of a control system produce a stream of benefits and costs over its life. In this light, whether to establish a control system should be considered as a capital investment decision. Thus, standard net present value criteria can be used to help make the decision. Auditors will have to estimate the size of the benefits and costs during each period of the control system's life. In addition, they will have to estimate the discount rate to use. Unfortunately, given the nature of a control system, determining the appropriate discount rate to use might be difficult.

INTRODUCTION

When auditors evaluate how well assets are safeguarded, they attempt to determine whether assets could be used or have been used for unauthorized purposes and the losses that could occur or have occurred as a result. When auditors evaluate how well data integrity is maintained, they attempt to determine whether material errors could occur or have occurred in data and the size of the error and subsequent losses that could occur or have occurred as a result.

In this chapter, we examine both the decision on how well assets are safeguarded and the decision on how well data integrity is maintained. We consider these decisions jointly because substantial overlap exists in terms of the evaluation methodologies that auditors can use for each decision.

The chapter proceeds as follows. In the first section, we discuss various measures of asset safeguarding and data integrity that auditors can use as the basis for their judgment process. Next, we examine the nature of the global evaluation decision they must make. We then discuss those factors that audit research has shown are major determinants of the quality of auditors' judgments when they make the global evaluation decision. In the subsequent section, we examine various tools that have been developed to assist auditors make the global evaluation decision. Finally, we discuss how auditors might evaluate the cost-effectiveness of controls.

MEASURES OF ASSET SAFEGUARDING AND DATA INTEGRITY

To evaluate how well assets are safeguarded and data integrity is maintained, auditors need some kind of measurement scale. Asset safeguarding and maintenance of data integrity are not all-or-nothing affairs; assets are safeguarded and systems maintain data integrity to varying degrees. Auditors need to be able to evaluate the *extent* to which assets have been safeguarded and data integrity has been maintained.

A measure of *asset safeguarding* that auditors can use is the *expected loss* that occurs if the asset is destroyed, stolen, or used for unauthorized purposes. Auditors can assign different probabilities to the different losses that could occur—that is, if there is uncertainty surrounding the size of the dollar losses that result if assets are not safeguarded, the losses can be described via a probability distribution. Auditors can then calculate the expected loss if the asset is not safeguarded.

For example, assume that there is a .3 probability of losing $900,000 if an asset is destroyed (in, say, lost revenues generated via the asset), a .6 probability of losing $1,000,000, and a .1 probability of losing $1,200,000. The expected loss can then be calculated using this formula:

$$
\begin{aligned}
EL &= \Sigma_i p_i L_i \\
&= (900{,}000 \cdot .3) + (1{,}000{,}000 \cdot .6) + (1{,}200{,}000 \cdot .1) \\
&= 990{,}000
\end{aligned}
$$

The measure of *data integrity* that auditors use during an audit depends on their audit objectives and the nature of the data item on which they focus. Their overall concern is the extent to which a system of internal control permits errors to occur. External auditors' focus is likely to be on whether a material *dollar error* exists in the financial statements. The measure of data integrity will be the size of the dollar error that external auditors estimate exists in the accounts as a result of internal control weaknesses. Internal auditors are also likely to be concerned about dollar errors that might exist already or that might arise at some time in the future. In addition, they might also be concerned about the existing or potential size of *quantity errors* and the existing or potential *number of errors*. For example, they might be evaluating the quantities-on-hand for inventory where their focus is whether the recorded quantities-on-hand are accurate. Similarly, they might be evaluating the accuracy and completeness of name-and-address records, where their focus is the number of records that are in error. External auditors might also be concerned about quantity errors and the number of errors, but perhaps only to the extent that they are related to dollar errors in the accounts.

If internal controls can fail stochastically, an auditor's estimate of data integrity must be made in terms of a *probability distribution of error* that might arise. For example, from time to time a clerk might enter a wrong amount at a terminal that an input validation program is unable to detect. If this error occurs randomly, the impact of data integrity will depend on factors like the nature and seriousness of the input error made, the timing of the error, and the ways it compounds or compensates with other errors that might be made. A single point estimate of the resulting error, therefore, is unlikely to suffice. Instead, auditors need to determine the shape of the probability distribution of the error that might result and the various moments of that distribution (the mean, variance, skewness, and kurtosis).

To illustrate these concepts, Figures 21–1a, 21–1b, and 21–1c show examples of probability distributions of errors that might arise. Figure 21–1a shows a probability distribution of error for a dollar data item. Note how the distribution is skewed to the right, which means that most possible errors are small but a few nevertheless are large. Figure 21–1b shows a probability distribution of error for a quantity data item. Note how the distribution is skewed to the left, which means that a few possible errors are small but most are large. Figure 21–1c shows a probability distribution of error for the number of data items that could be in error. Note the flatness (kurtosis) of the distribution, which indicates that possible errors are spread more evenly between small errors and large errors relative to the distributions shown in Figures 21–1a and 21–1b.

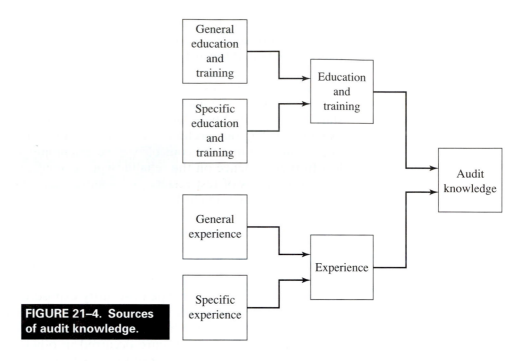

FIGURE 21–4. Sources of audit knowledge.

As we might expect, both general and specific knowledge play a part in determining the quality of audit judgments. For many audits, the level of general knowledge could be an important determinant of the decision quality when making asset safeguarding and data integrity judgments. For example, the organization we are auditing might not be complex, and it might also be representative of many other types of organizations we have encountered. As the level of specificity associated with the organization we are auditing increases, however, the complexity associated with the judgments we must make also increases. As a result, we need to have more specialized knowledge if we are to make high-quality judgments.

Whenever auditors make the asset safeguarding and data integrity evaluation judgment, therefore, they should evaluate whether their knowledge is appropriate for the judgments they must make. They will require some level of general knowledge to be competent to make a judgment. In some cases, however, auditors might also require a high level of specialized knowledge to be able to make a competent judgment. Moreover, auditors must recognize that the knowledge they need has to be specialized in terms of the particular audit they are undertaking. Many research studies have shown that humans are often expert only in a fairly narrow domain. When experts move outside their domain, they perform no better than novices. If auditors conclude they do not have the appropriate knowledge to make the evaluation judgment, they must seek to find someone who is competent to make the judgment. Alternatively, somehow they must endeavor to acquire the knowledge quickly (which could be impossible in the time frame during which they must make the decision). To some extent, it might also be possible to mitigate the effects of inadequacies in their knowledge base by using judgment tools to assist them.

Audit Environment

The audit environment describes the context in which auditors must make their evaluation judgment. Potentially, many characteristics of the environment might bear on auditor judgment processes. Libby and Luft (1993) identify four characteristics, however, that seem to be especially important.

The first is the *audit technology* that auditors can use to guide and support their audit judgment. We are using the term here in a broad sense. It includes elements like the internal control questionnaires used to structure the evaluation of internal controls, the audit standards and policies used to guide the conduct of audits, the expert systems used to help in evaluations, the way we structure audit teams to try to improve the quality of the audit, and the ways we document our findings to try to facilitate our making a final judgment. Auditors use this technology to try to overcome some of the deficiencies in their judgment processes and to extend their cognitive abilities. Later in the chapter, we discuss in more detail some of the audit technologies specifically designed to assist auditors in undertaking an evaluation of the extent to which systems safeguard assets and maintain data integrity.

The second environmental characteristic is *group processes*. One of the interesting features of the audit profession is that it uses groups extensively during the conduct of an audit; it does not rely on individual persons to make judgments. Unfortunately, research in auditing is only just beginning to provide us with some understanding of why group processes in auditing might be useful and why, therefore, auditors are likely to have incorporated group processes into their work. For example, interactions within a group might enable the members of the group to recall better the audit evidence that has been collected and to better evaluate the importance of this evidence. Group processes, like audit review, also seem to reduce the likelihood of errors and omissions in the conduct of an audit. Nonetheless, in some cases, groups can undermine the quality of judgments that are made. For example, a phenomenon called *group think* has been identified whereby individual persons in a group make more risky decisions because they perceive they are less accountable for their decisions.

The third environmental characteristic is *prior involvement* in an audit. On the one hand, prior involvement with an audit (say, in a previous year) might enhance the knowledge that auditors bring to the evaluation judgment. In this light, it might improve the quality of their judgment. On the other hand, prior involvement might cause auditors to be less critical of the audit work they examine as it represents some of their own work. Thus, prior involvement might undermine the quality of their evaluation judgment. Again, audit research is only just beginning to provide us with insights on the effects of prior involvement on judgment quality.

The fourth environmental characteristic is *accountability*. Auditors are accountable for their work in many different ways. For example, they are accountable to their supervisors and their clients, and they will also be held accountable for their work under the law. The positive aspect of accountability is that it should motivate auditors to try to make high-quality judgments whenever they evaluate asset safeguarding and data integrity. A potential downside, however, is that auditors might become too concerned with accountability issues (like keeping extensive documentation). As a result, auditors might become exhausted and devote insufficient attention to the cognitive processes they need to exercise to make a high-quality evaluation decision.

Auditors must be mindful, therefore, of how various characteristics of the audit environment can either facilitate or inhibit their judgments on how well a system safeguards assets and maintains data integrity. Auditors should try to employ audit technology to enhance their decision-making processes. They should also try to employ group processes at appropriate points in their judgment processes to improve the quality of their decision making. To the extent that they have had prior involvement with an audit, auditors should recognize that this involvement can have both positive and negative effects. Accordingly, they should seek actively to mitigate the negative effects of prior involvement.

Similarly, auditors should recognize that the different ways in which they are held accountable for their work can have positive and negative effects on the quality of their judgment processes. As with prior involvement, auditors should seek actively to mitigate the negative effects of any accountability requirements to which they are subjected.

Auditor's Motivation

The motivation auditors have to perform an audit task can affect *(1)* the effort they exert to perform the task and *(2)* the cognitive processes associated with the task. For example, if auditors are making a judgment about whether material errors exist in financial statements, the loss function they face is likely to affect the amount of effort they exert to make this judgment. If a large number of people rely on the financial statements and auditors make a poor judgment, they could be sued for substantial amounts. This potential for loss is also likely to affect the *salience* of certain evidence to the evaluation judgment. For example, auditors might be more sensitive to evidence that suggests the possibility of top-management fraud when many people rely on their audit opinion.

We have also seen previously how factors like prior involvement with the audit and accountability considerations might *decrease* auditors' motivation to exert effort in performing activities that are critical to their making a high-quality evaluation decision. For example, auditors might place too much faith in the quality of the work they have performed during a prior year's audit. Likewise, auditors might expend so much effort documenting their work because of accountability concerns that they are then too exhausted to expend the resources needed to consider carefully the evidence they have collected as the basis for their evaluation judgment.

In short, as with the other factors discussed previously that affect judgment performance, auditors need to be mindful of how their level of motivation can affect the quality of their decision-making processes. In some cases, auditors are likely to have appropriate levels of motivation to exert the effort required to make a high-quality judgment. In other cases, however, various factors could be at work to undermine their level of motivation and thus to mitigate against their making high-quality decisions. In these cases, auditors need to have sufficient self-awareness to take steps to increase their level of motivation to an appropriate level.

AUDIT TECHNOLOGY TO ASSIST THE EVALUATION DECISION

In this section, we examine some of the technology that has been developed to assist auditors to make the global evaluation decision on how well a system safeguards assets and protects data integrity. By *technology*, recall from the previous discussion that we are interpreting this term in a broad sense. It is not just confined to computer technology; it also applies to any tool, structure, policy, or approach developed to facilitate undertaking the audit. Given the complexity of the evaluation judgment auditors must make, this technology can help by structuring and perhaps in part automating the evaluation decision. It also might provide auditors with insights that help them to understand the evaluation decision better.

Control Matrices

One of the earliest technologies developed to assist with the evaluation decision are control matrices (see, e.g., Mair, Wood, and Davis 1976). Control matrices can be prepared in various ways. Table 21–1 shows a common approach, however, using the example of the data capture activities associated with the input subsystem belonging to an application system.

TABLE 21–1 Input Subsystem Evaluation for Customer Order Transaction Class					
Controls / *Errors/irregularities*	*Unauthorized customer*	*Unauthorized terms and credit*	*Incorrect quantity*	*Incorrect price*	*Untimely processing*
Order-entry operator					
well-trained	M	M	M	M	M
Input screen layout (quality)					
screen organization			M	M	M
field captions and entry fields			M	M	M
field alignment, justification, spacing			M	M	M
headings and messages			M	M	M
Input program					
valid customer check	H				
authorized credit		H			
inventory available			M		
Sales manager					
override report	M	M		L	L

Note: H = high reliability; M = moderate reliability; L = low reliability.

Note the structure of the controls matrix shown in Table 21–1. The columns of the matrix show causes of loss—in this case, circumstances that would cause a loss to occur if they arose during the data capture stage of an application system's processing. The rows of the matrix are controls exercised over the causes of loss to reduce expected losses from the causes. The elements of the matrix might be some rating of the effectiveness of each control at reducing expected losses from each cause, the reliability of the control with respect to each control in light of tests of controls that have been conducted, or the marginal benefits and costs of exercising the control. In Table 21–1, the elements show a simple rating of whether a control is likely to have high, medium, or low reliability in reducing losses from a particular exposure.

To undertake the evaluation decision using the control matrix, conceptually we first examine each column of the matrix and ask the following question: For a given cause of loss, do the controls over the cause reduce the expected loss from the cause to an acceptable level? For each cause of loss, we must somehow weigh up the effect of the various controls and determine whether the exposure that remains is at an acceptable level. We must consider the columns in total to determine whether a material loss could still arise.

A control matrix can be prepared at various levels of aggregation in our evaluation decision. In Table 21–1, we see it used at the application subsystem level. It can also be used, however, at the system level, cycle level, and overall accounts level. Basically, it is a way of bringing together some of the important factors auditors must consider when making the evaluation decision.

Deterministic Models

Deterministic models can be useful when evaluating part of a system of internal control or obtaining a first approximation of how well a computer system safeguards assets and maintains data integrity. For example, consider the access control mechanism in an operating system. Assume we discover an integrity flaw in the system that allows hackers, under certain conditions, to violate the privacy of a data file. In other words, the flaw can be exploited so the data file (asset) is no longer safeguarded against unauthorized use.

To determine the consequences of the flaw, we might access the system log to determine how many times the flaw has been exploited, assuming, of course, that the integrity of the log has been preserved. Calculating the loss that has resulted because of the flaw involves estimating the loss on each occasion that the flaw was exploited and summing the losses. Thus, the model used in this example is deterministic, provided there is no uncertainty about the losses involved.

Consider, also, a batch computer system. Any errors that we identify in the programs within the system are deterministic. In other words, if we discover that a program processes a data item incorrectly, it will always process the data item incorrectly. We simply have to determine the frequency with which the data item occurs and the magnitude of the error that then arises. We might use audit software to retrieve all instances of the data item from the audit trail so the total error for the data item can be determined. The ways in which different errors compound and compensate, however, still must be considered.

Even if the system to be evaluated contains stochastic elements (for example, some errors made by a data input clerk might not be detected by an input validation program), auditors might still find a deterministic model to be useful when they make their evaluation decision. For example, they can construct a *mean value* deterministic model by replacing each probabilistic element with its average value. To obtain some idea of the probability distribution of errors that can result, auditors might also construct an *extreme value* deterministic model. In these types of models, they would replace the probabilistic elements with their lowest and highest values.

Deterministic models are relatively simple to construct. Auditors might use them to perform a pencil-and-paper analysis of how well a system safeguards assets and maintains data integrity. The models provide only limited information, however, about the forms of the probability distribution of error that can be produced when a system contains stochastic elements. In these circumstances, auditors must exercise caution when they interpret the results they obtain using them.

Software Reliability Models

Software reliability models use statistical techniques to estimate the likelihood that an error will occur during some time period on the basis of the patterns of past errors that have been discovered in the system. The models assume that the number of errors discovered over time increases at a decreasing rate (Figure 21–5). This assumption seems reasonable. When a system is first tested,

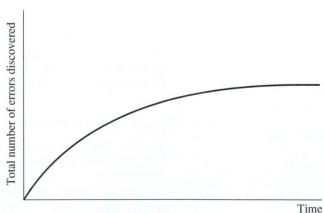

FIGURE 21–5. Pattern of error discovery in systems over time.

errors are found relatively quickly. As testing proceeds, however, each additional error is harder to find. Provided that records are kept of the error discovery process, the shape of the function that relates the probability that an error will occur to the age of the system can be estimated and predictions made about the likelihood that future errors will occur. Note that the age of the system might need to be measured in terms of the number of times it has been executed rather than elapsed time. Substantial elapsed time might have occurred, but a system might be executed infrequently and after variable intervals during this period. As a result, errors might not surface because only a few execution paths through the system have been exercised.

The software reliability models that have been developed fall into three main classes:

Class of Model	*Nature of Model*
Time-between-failures models	These models are based on the assumption that the time between successive failures of a system will get longer as errors are removed from the system. The time between failures is predicted to follow a distribution whose parameters depend on the number of errors that remain in the system during the interval between failures.
Failure-count models	These models attempt to predict the number of failures that will occur during a fixed testing interval. As errors within the system are corrected, the models predict that the number of errors discovered during the next time interval will be less.
Fault-seeding models	In these models, errors are introduced into a system that has an unknown number of "indigenous" errors. The system is then tested, and the seeded and indigenous errors discovered are counted. On the basis of the proportion of seeded and indigenous errors discovered, estimates can be made of the total number of indigenous errors in the system.

Software reliability models potentially are powerful tools that auditors can use when they must assess how well a system safeguards assets and maintains data integrity. The models require minimum data to make predictions about the likelihood of errors remaining in a system—often only the length of the interval of system execution time that occurs between the discovery of successive errors and a classification of the errors that are discovered as to their materiality. Furthermore, they do not rely on evidence gathered about the strengths and weaknesses of individual internal controls within the system, except as a basis for classifying the materiality of the errors that are discovered. The models also can be easily implemented via computer programs.

In this light, auditors can use these models in two ways. First, if they have sufficient confidence in the predictive powers of the model, they can make an evaluation judgment without having to rely solely on the difficult task of assimilating piecemeal evidence on the strengths and weaknesses of the individual internal controls within a system. Second, they might use the models as analytical review tools. If a model predicts that the likelihood of further errors occurring in a system is high, auditors might decide to adopt a substantive test approach to an evaluation of the system. If a model predicts that the likelihood of further errors occurring in a system is low, however, auditors might proceed with tests of controls to evaluate the system in the hope that they can conclude that they can rely on controls and reduce the extent of substantive testing of the system.

Engineering Reliability Models

Engineering reliability models allow auditors to estimate the overall reliability of a system as a function of the reliability of the individual components and individual internal controls that make up the system. In this respect they mirror the auditor's traditional approach to assessing the overall reliability of a system based on evidence collected about the reliability of individual internal controls within the system. In some ways the assumptions underlying the models are restrictive. Moreover, their practical usefulness is still questionable. Nevertheless, the models provide important insights into how control strengths and weaknesses can compensate and compound to affect the overall reliability of a system. As such, they help auditors to understand how the overall evaluation of internal control should be made.

The fundamental ideas behind using engineering reliability theory to model internal control systems were introduced into the accounting literature by Cushing (1974). To illustrate his approach, consider, first, a simple system where there is one process, a single control, and a single error correction procedure (Figure 21–6a). Assume, also, that only one type of error or irregularity occurs within the system. The reliability of the system—that is, the probability the system will not have an error or an irregularity after execution is completed—is calculated as follows:

$$R = p + (1 - p)P(e)P(c)$$

where:

R = system reliability
p = probability the process executes correctly
$P(e)$ = probability the control detects an error or irregularity when one exists
$P(c)$ = probability an error or irregularity is corrected when the control detects an error or irregularity and one exists

In other words, the reliability of the system equals *(1)* the probability the process executes correctly plus *(2)* the probability the process executes

---

FIGURE 21–6(a). System with one process and one control. (b). System with one process and two controls.

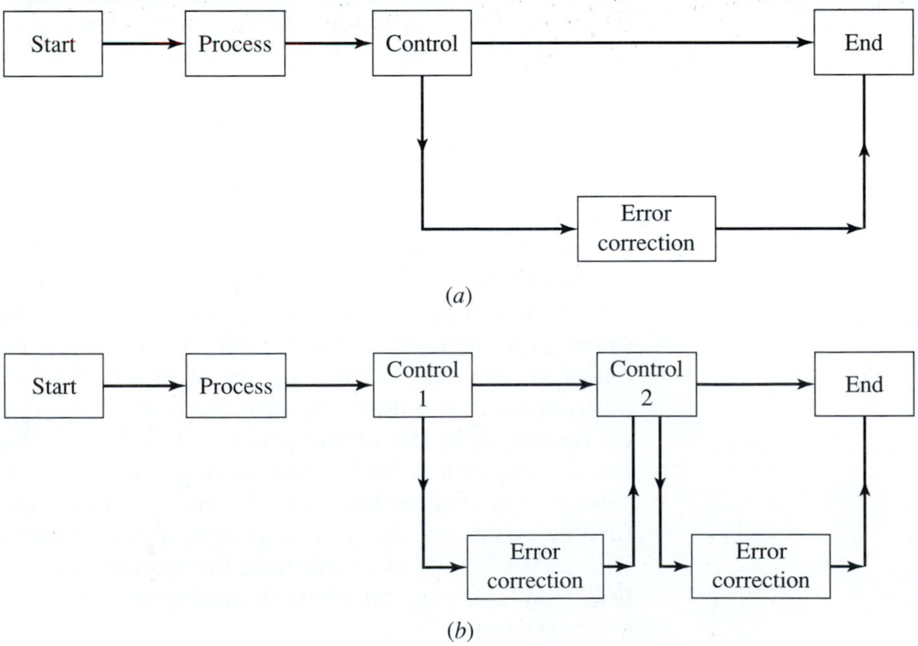

(a)

(b)

incorrectly but the control identifies the error or irregularity and the error or irregularity is corrected.

Consider, first, how auditors can use the model to assess how well an asset is safeguarded. We will assume the system to be assessed is a fire detection and extinguisher system. Furthermore, we will assume that the probability $(1 - p)$ of a fire occurring is .005. In other words, the probability of the "process" executing correctly—that is, there is no fire—is .995. Further assume that the probability $P(e)$ of the fire system signaling a fire when one occurs is .95. Assume, also, that the probability of the fire system correctly activating the extinguisher and putting the fire out when a fire is signaled and one exists $P(c)$ is .90. Thus, the reliability of the fire system is as follows:

$$R = .995 + (.005)(.95)(.90)$$
$$= .999275$$
$$(1 - R) = .000725$$
$$(R - p) = .004275$$

Note that the probability of a fire occurring even with the detection and extinguisher system is $(1 - R)$, which is equal to .000725. This probability is not zero because the detection system might fail to signal a fire when one exists or the extinguisher might fail to put a fire out when one is correctly signalled. Nonetheless, with the use of the fire system, the probability of a fire causing destruction is reduced by .004275—that is, $R - p$.

Now consider how the model can be used to assess how well a system maintains data integrity. Assume, for example, that the "system" to be evaluated is the keying operation in an application system. The control process is verification of the data that has been keyed. The probability of data being keyed correctly is .9. Thus, the probability of incorrect keying $(1 - p)$ is .1. $P(e)$ is the probability .9 that the verifier operator detects a keying error when one exists. $P(c)$ is the probability .95 that the verifier operator corrects a detected error. The reliability of the process R is as follows:

$$R = .9 + (.1)(.9)(.95)$$
$$= .9855$$
$$(1 - R) = .0145$$
$$(R - p) = .0855$$

Note that the probability of an error occurring even with verification is .0145. The reasons are, for example, that the verifer operator might omit verifying some incorrectly keyed data, the verifer operator might make the same mistake as the initial keyboard operator, and the wrong character might be keyed during the correction process. The verification control improves the overall reliability of the process, however, by $R - p$—that is, by .0855.

This example involves assuming only one type of error or irregularity occurs within the system. For more than one error or irregularity type, the parameters in the formula can be suitably subscripted. Thus, R_i the reliability of the system for the ith error or irregularity type can be computed as follows:

$$R_i = p_i + (1 - p_i)P(e_i)P(c_i)$$

The overall reliability of the system for all error or irregularity types is as follows:

$$R = \prod_{i=1}^{n} R_i$$

For example, if $R_1 = .9$ and $R_2 = .8$, then $R = (.9)(.8)$—that is, .72. In other words, there is a .72 probability that no type of error or irregularity will occur within the system.

Figure 21–6b shows the case of a simple system in which only one error or irregularity type occurs, a single process exists, and two controls operate. For example, extend the previous key-preparation system example and assume that an input program executed during the initial keying of data automatically checks batch totals. Verification as a second control, however, still would identify compensating errors that were not detected by the batch total check. After the second control point, the reliability of the system is as follows:

$$R^2 = R^1 + (1 - R^1)P(e_2)P(c_2)$$

Thus, the reliability of the system after the second control point, R^2, depends on the reliability of the system after the first control point, R^1. Note that, in this case only, $P(e_2)$ and $P(c_2)$ are probabilities associated with the second control point and not the second error type.

More generally, in a single system where $i = 1, n$ error or irregularity types can occur and $j = 1, r$ controls exist, the reliability of the system after the jth control for the ith error or irregularity type is as follows:

$$R_i^j = R_i^{j-1} + (1 - R_i^{j-1})P(e_{ij})P(c_{ij})$$

To illustrate the application of this formula, Table 21–2 shows the reliability calculations for a single process system in which there are two controls and two error or irregularity types. Note that the second control is unable to identify any of the first error or irregularity type—thus, $R_1^2 = R_1^1$.

By itself, a reliability (probability) figure is not especially meaningful to auditors. Instead, they need to know what dollar or quantity error a system can produce or how many data items are likely to be in error. For example, if auditors are assessing data integrity and they are dealing with monetary or

---

TABLE 21–2   Reliability Calculations for System with Single Process, Two Controls, and Two Error Types

$p_1 = .8$	$p_2 = .85$
$P(e_{11}) = .85$	$P(e_{21}) = .85$
$P(c_{11}) = .95$	$P(c_{21}) = .90$
$P(e_{12}) = 0$	$P(e_{22}) = .80$
	$P(c_{22}) = .95$

$$\begin{aligned}
R_1^1 &= p_1 + (1 - p_1)P(e_{11})P(c_{11}) \\
&= .8 + (.2)(.85)(.95) \\
&= .9615 \\
R_2^1 &= p_2 + (1 - p_2)P(e_{21})P(c_{21}) \\
&= .85 + (.15)(.85)(.90) \\
&= .96475 \\
R_1^2 &= R_1^1 + (1 - R_1^1)P(e_{12})P(c_{12}) \\
&= .9615 + (.0385)(0) \\
&= .9615 \\
R_2^2 &= R_2^1 + (1 - R_2^1)P(e_{22})P(c_{22}) \\
&= .96475 + (.03525)(.8)(.95) \\
&= .99154 \\
R &= (R_1^2)(R_2^2) = (.9615)(.99154) = .953366 \\
p &= (p_1)(p_2) = (.8)(.85) \qquad = .68 \\
R - p &= .953366 - .68 = .273366
\end{aligned}$$

quantity error types, the effect of error type i on a data item can be calculated by the following:

$$A_i = Ne_{ir} \cdot Ve_i \cdot T_r$$

where:

A_i = dollar or quantity error produced

Ne_{ir} = average number of errors of type i that remain undetected after r control processes

Ve_i = estimated average dollar or quantity effect of an undetected type i error

T_r = frequency with which the set of r controls is performed

The expected total dollar or quantity error is simply the sum of the individual error effects—that is:

$$A = \sum_{i=1}^{n} A_i$$

If auditors are attempting to estimate the *number* of data items that are likely to be in error, the formula is as follows:

$$H = \sum_{i=1}^{n} H_i$$

where $H_i = Ne_{ir} \times T_r$.

Note that A and H are expected (mean) values. Thus, auditors still must estimate the probability distributions of these variables. The distributions of A and H are a function of the distributions of Ne_{ir}, Ve_i, and perhaps T_r if T_r is stochastic.

The model described so far also needs further refinement if it is to be used in practice to evaluate how well a system safeguards assets and maintains data integrity. It must be extended to handle the multiple-process case. It also must be extended to handle redundant processes and redundant controls.

Bayesian Models

Bayesian models provide auditors with a formal method of revising prior estimates of the reliability of an internal control system on the basis of new information obtained from evidence gathering activities that they undertake during the course of the audit. Conceptually, we can consider the evaluation decision as a sequential process in which we start out with prior estimates of whether the internal control system is reliable and revise these estimates progressively as new evidence comes to hand. At some stage, auditors must cease evidence gathering and reach a decision on the overall reliability of the system.

Bayesian models have been advocated for some time as a means to assist auditors to make evaluation decisions. Auditing researchers have been motivated to examine these models because they are aware of long-standing research results obtained elsewhere that show that humans perform poorly when they must revise prior estimates of the probability of an event in light of new information received (see, e.g., Slovic and Lichtenstein 1971). Thus, they have sought ways of improving the judgment process. The models that have been formulated apply equally well in a manual or a computerized environment.

To illustrate the nature of the Bayesian approach, consider Figure 21–7, which shows the overall evaluation decision that auditors face. The internal control system is either reliable or unreliable, and we can reach a decision either to accept the system as reliable or to reject it as unreliable. Clearly, we want to reach an accept decision when the system is reliable and a reject

State of the internal control system

	Reliable	Unreliable
Accept	Correct decision	Incorrect decision
Reject	Incorrect decision	Correct decision

Auditor's decision

FIGURE 21–7. Decision problem faced by the auditor.

decision when the system is unreliable. Unfortunately, in the absence of perfect information, we might make a wrong decision; in other words, we might make an accept decision when the system is unreliable and a reject decision when the system is reliable. Both types of wrong decision can be costly. In the former case, we could be sued if the unreliable internal control system leads to the organization we are auditing entering liquidation or bankruptcy. In the latter case, we perform superfluous audit work, face conflict with the client, and have fewer resources available to undertake more productive auditing work.

Assume, then, at the outset of the audit that we believe (subjectively) there is a .9 probability of the internal control system being reliable and therefore a .1 probability of the internal control system being unreliable. These probabilities could have been determined in various ways; for example, they might reflect our prior experience with the system or a judgment we make on the basis of our preliminary review of the system. Assume, further, that the estimated cost of accepting an unreliable internal control system is $1,000,000 (e.g., lawsuits), and the cost of rejecting a reliable internal control system is $50,000 (e.g., unproductive audit work). In the absence of further information, the appropriate decision to make can be determined on the basis of the expected losses under both decisions. In the case of the accept decision, it would be (.9)(0) + (.1)(1,000,000)—that is, $100,000. In the case of the reject decision, it would be (.9)(50,000) + (.1)(0)—that is, $45,000. In the absence of further information, we would minimize our losses by making a reject decision.

Assume, now, that we undertake some type of test to evaluate the reliability of controls in the system. For example, suppose we execute a set of test data through the system and evaluate the test results obtained. The test results indicate that the system is reliable. Because the test data cannot test the system comprehensively, however, we recognize there is some risk that the test results are favorable even though the system might be unreliable. We need to take this possibility into account when making our judgment. Using a Bayesian approach, we must first estimate the probability of *(1)* getting a favorable result given that the system is reliable and *(2)* getting a favorable result given that the system is unreliable. These estimates require that we have some knowledge about the reliability of the test; for example, we might have prior experience with the particular test data approach we have used.

Assume, now, that we conclude the following estimates apply to the reliability of the test:

Probability (favorable|reliable) $= P(F|R) = .8$
Probability (favorable|unreliable) $= P(F|U) = .2$

Using Bayes' rule, the probability of the system being reliable *given* the favorable test results and the probability of the system being unreliable *given* the favorable test results can be calculated as follows:

$$P(R|F) = \frac{P(F|R)P(R)}{P(F)}$$

$$= \frac{P(F|R)P(R)}{P(F|R)P(R) + P(F|U)P(U)}$$

$$= \frac{(.8)(.9)}{(.8)(.9) + (.2)(.1)}$$

$$= .97$$

$$P(U|F) = 1 - P(R|F)$$

$$= 1 - .97$$

$$= .03$$

In light of these revised probabilities, we can now calculate the new expected losses for the accept and reject decisions. For the accept decision, the expected loss is $(.97)(0) + (.03)(1,000,000) = \$30,000$. For the reject decision, the expected loss is $(.97)(50,000) + (.03)(0) = \$48,500$. Thus, the decision now is to accept the system as reliable—a change from the previous decision.

Note that the expected loss under the revised probabilities is \$48,500, whereas the expected loss under the prior probabilities is \$100,000. Thus, if the test costs more than \$51,500 (\$100,000 – \$48,500), we should not undertake it. On the other hand, if the costs are less than \$51,500, it is worthwhile for us to undertake the test. If the test costs us exactly \$51,500 to undertake, we will be indifferent about proceeding with the test.

As new evidence is gathered on the reliability of the system, auditors can continue to revise the probabilities of the system being reliable and unreliable using Bayes' rule. At some stage, of course, the costs of acquiring more evidence will exceed the benefits. At that point, auditors must terminate their evidence collection activities and make the evaluation judgment.

Simulation Models

Whenever possible, auditors should use analytical models to help them make the evaluation judgment. With analytical models, usually auditors can evaluate the value of the dependent variables that interest them at low cost over a wide range of variations in the independent variables and the structure of the model. The deterministic models and probabilistic models examined previously, for example, often can be developed and solved quickly and cheaply.

Sometimes, however, analytical models are not appropriate to use when auditors make the global evaluation judgment. For a start, they might conclude that the assumptions underlying the models are too restrictive and thus do not mirror reality sufficiently well. In addition, analytical models might not be mathematically tractable because the appropriate equations to use to model the system are not obvious or the equations appear to be insolvable. In these cases, auditors might consider using simulation models to assist their making the global evaluation judgment.

When auditors use a simulation model, they can evaluate the behavior of a system over time. For example, consider how we might use a simulation model to evaluate asset safeguarding. We might be evaluating a security system in which there is some probability that a guard will fail to detect an intruder, some probability that a surveillance system also might fail to detect the intruder, some probability that the intruder can crack a password system, and so on, and

FIGURE 21–8. Flowchart for pricing simulation.

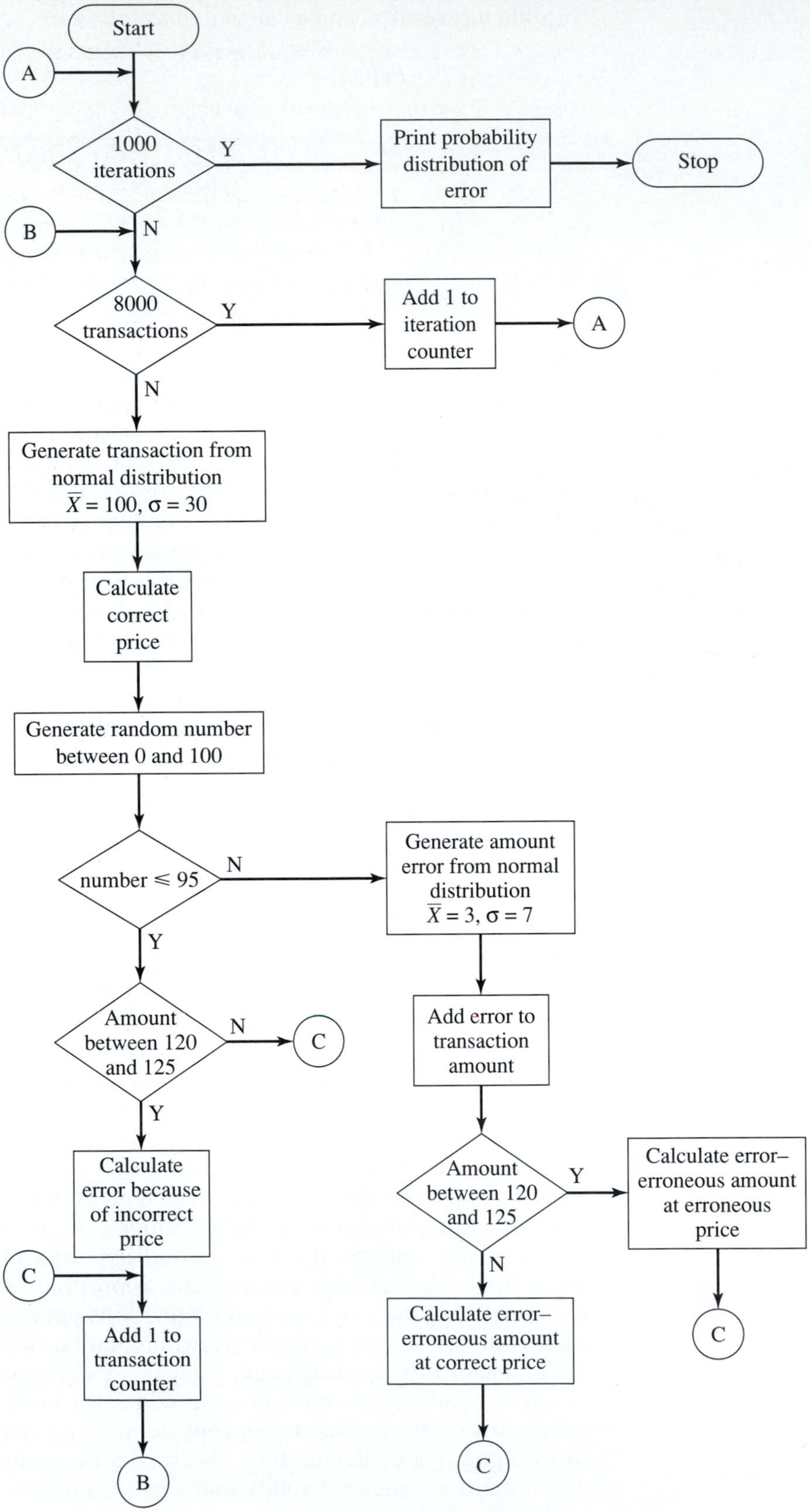

eventually the intruder gains access to and steals sensitive data files. Often an analytical model can be used to determine the probability of all controls failing. Nevertheless, if controls compound and compensate in different ways, we might need to use a simulation model to obtain the needed insights for us to be confident in our evaluation of the reliability of the system of controls. Moreover, we can study how the security system responds over time as it is subjected to various types of threats. We are not basing our decision, therefore, on a one-off situation in which the security system might or might not detect the intruder.

Auditors can also use a simulation model to evaluate how well a system maintains data integrity. Indeed, this use was suggested long ago by Burns and Loebbecke (1975). To illustrate its use, assume that a clerk uses a desktop computer to perform complex pricing calculations relating to a product. A counter maintained by the computer shows that in the past year 8,000 calculations were performed. During the evidence collection phase, assume that we find the amount data item within the transactions follows a normal distribution, with a mean of 100 units and a standard deviation of 30 units.

Assume, also, that we discover that two errors have occurred during the pricing process. First, an estimated 5 percent of the time the clerk types the wrong transaction amount as input to the program. The clerk sometimes overstates the amount and sometimes understates the amount. The best description we can give of the error is that it appears to be distributed normally, with a mean of 3 units and a standard deviation of 7 units (overstatements occur more often than understatements). Second, the program contains an error. It gives the incorrect price if the transaction amount is between 120 and 125 units.

Figure 21–8 shows the flowchart for a simulation program written to estimate the dollar error that could have occurred. Note that the program simulates the year's transactions a thousand times. At the end of the simulation, the program prints out the probability distribution of total error that might have resulted because of the stochastic error (the clerk typing in the wrong amount) and the deterministic error (the incorrect pricing routine). This probability distribution gives us an indication of the risk associated with our judgment. For example, the mean error might be a small amount, but the distribution might be skewed positively in light of some large errors that can occasionally occur if a particular combination of circumstances arise. We need to take this possibility into account when we make our judgment on how well the system has maintained data integrity.

Of course, in practice the simulation program needed to evaluate how well a system maintains data integrity usually would be more complex than the program needed to implement the flowchart shown in Figure 21–8. High-level simulation languages are now available, however, that auditors can use to implement simulation programs quickly and to obtain user-friendly output. Some of these languages provide animation capabilities to help their users better understand the dynamics of the system they are modeling.

Expert Systems

Recall in Chapter 16 that we examined the nature and use of expert systems as a tool that auditors could employ to assist their evidence collection and evaluation. We defined expert systems as programs that encapsulated the knowledge that human experts have about a particular domain and that could reproduce this knowledge when presented with a particular problem.

Given the complexity that auditors often face when making the global evaluation judgment, expert systems can be especially useful if they have been developed for the domain in which the judgment must be made. Auditors might find them useful in two ways. First, they could provide auditors with insights into the way various control strengths and weaknesses compound and compensate with one another. Provided the expert system that auditors use has an explanation capability, they can ask queries of it that give them feedback about how it has reached a conclusion based on a particular configuration of control strengths and weaknesses that they have presented to it. This feedback should help auditors come to a better understanding of the overall reliability of the system. Second, auditors can use the output of the expert system as a "reasonableness test" for their own global evaluation judgment. To the extent that they have reached a similar conclusion to the expert system, they can have more confidence in the quality of their judgment. If the output of the expert system differs substantially from their own judgment, however, auditors might need to reconsider carefully the bases on which they have reached their judgment.

Perhaps the most important issue auditors need to consider when using an expert system to assist with the global evaluation judgment is the particular domain for which it has been developed. The performance of many expert systems is "brittle" after they are used outside the specialized domain for which they have been developed. In other words, the quality of the advice they provide deteriorates quickly as the circumstances of the domain in which they are applied differs from the circumstances of the domain for which they have been developed. At the outset, therefore, auditors should take care to ensure that the expert system is well matched to the domain where they are making their evaluation judgment.

COST-EFFECTIVENESS CONSIDERATIONS

So far our discussion has proceeded without our considering the costs of safeguarding assets or maintaining data integrity. Reliable systems can be achieved, however, only at a cost. Whenever we invest in making a system more reliable, we must consider whether the benefits we expect to obtain exceed the costs we expect we will incur.

In the following subsections, we briefly examine some aspects of the judgment auditors must make on whether the controls in place are cost-effective. We deal with this decision only at a reasonably intuitive level. Some of the approaches that have been developed to help us to make this decision, however, are somewhat complex. We will leave these approaches for further study (see, e.g., Cushing 1974).

Costs and Benefits of Controls

Implementing and operating controls in a system involves five costs:

1. Initial setup costs must be incurred to design and implement controls. For example, a security specialist might have to be employed to design a physical security system, and a systems analyst might be assigned the task of designing the validation routines for an input program. When these design tasks are completed, costs will then be incurred, for example, to install magnetic card door locks and to write programs.
2. Costs associated with executing controls will be incurred. For example, the wages of a security officer must be paid, and the costs associated with using a processor to execute input validation routines must be met.
3. When a control signals that some type of error or irregularity has occurred, costs will be incurred to search for the error or irregularity, to determine whether one exists (that is, the control has operated reliably in signalling an error or irregularity), and to correct any errors or irregularities that are found.

4. Costs arise because controls do not detect some errors or irregularities (the control might malfunction or it might not have been designed to detect the error or irregularity that has occurred), and costs arise because the control system fails to correct errors and irregularities properly when they are discovered. These undetected or uncorrected errors or irregularities then cause losses. For example, an uncorrected error or irregularity could allow a defalcation to occur.

5. Maintenance costs are incurred to ensure the controls are kept in correct working order. For example, periodically a security guard must be retrained, and input validation routines might have to be rewritten as the format of input data changes.

The first cost described here is the outlay for a system of controls. The remaining four costs are the ongoing operational costs of a control system.

The benefits derived from having a control system relate to a reduction in the incidence of errors or irregularities and the losses associated with these errors or irregularities. In some cases, errors or irregularities would occur routinely without the control. For example, transposition errors most likely will be made by a clerk responsible for input data, and these errors might remain undetected unless a check digit is used. In other cases, the control acts as a deterrent. For example, a burglar alarm might discourage would-be intruders from attempting unauthorized entry to a computer center. The benefits of a control system are calculated by determining the reduction in expected losses that will occur from errors and irregularities by virtue of the existence of the control system.

To determine whether a control is cost-effective, therefore, auditors must compare the reduction in expected losses that will occur by virtue of having the control with the costs of designing, implementing, operating, and maintaining the control (Figure 21–9). Unfortunately, determining the size of these parameters is not straightforward. For example, a control might reduce losses that are expected to occur from several types of errors and irregularities. The extent of the loss reduction, however, might depend on what controls are in place already and how reliably these controls are operating. Similarly, the costs associated with designing, implementing, operating, and maintaining a control might depend on what controls are in place already. Economies of scale might occur, for example, in relation to the costs of operating and maintaining similar types of controls.

A Controls Matrix View of the Cost-Effectiveness of Controls

Earlier in the chapter we examined the use of control matrices to evaluate whether a set of controls had reduced exposures to an acceptable level. Control matrices can also be used to help us to characterize the decision on whether controls are cost-effective.

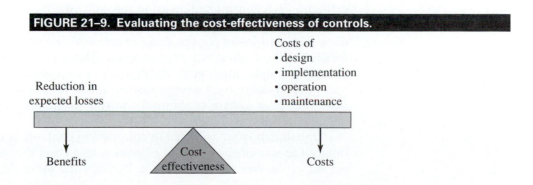

FIGURE 21–9. Evaluating the cost-effectiveness of controls.

When we examine a column of a control matrix, recall that we are seeking to determine whether a set of controls reduces an exposure to an acceptable level. In essence, we are asking whether the reduction in expected losses exceeds the costs of designing, implementing, operating, and maintaining the set of controls. To determine whether we should put additional controls in place, we also need to consider whether the marginal reduction in expected losses from the exposure from having additional controls will exceed the marginal costs of the controls.

Even if a control is not cost-effective in terms of a *single* exposure, however, it might be cost-effective in terms of *all* the exposures where it acts to reduce expected losses. In this light, we must also consider each *row* of the controls matrix. As we work across each of the rows in Table 21–1, for example, we are considering the reduction in expected losses that occurs for each of the exposures listed in the columns with regard to the particular control in the row we are considering. In other words, we focus on a particular control by choosing a row in the controls matrix, and we consider the impact of this control on all exposures by working across the row in the controls matrix.

The *global* evaluation question involves our asking this question: What is the optimal set of controls for the organization? The answer to this question somehow involves our undertaking a joint evaluation of the columns and rows in the controls matrix. Whereas from a columnar perspective, it might not be worthwhile to have a control, from a row perspective the benefits of the control when it is exercised over *all* exposures might exceed its cost.

Unfortunately, there are two complicating factors when auditors seek to make this global evaluation decision. First, as discussed previously, the marginal benefits and costs of exercising a control might depend on what controls are in place already and the reliability of these controls. In other words, the benefits and costs of a control are *conditional* parameters. Second, there is an overriding constraint on how many controls should exist in a system. This constraint applies when for all controls that still might be exercised the marginal benefits of any one control exceed the marginal costs of that control. In short, although auditors might understand conceptually the nature of the global evaluation decision on controls, the pragmatics associated with making this decision are difficult.

Controls as an Investment Decision

The design, implementation, operation, and maintenance of a control produces a stream of benefits and costs over its life. As discussed previously, at the outset, costs are incurred associated with designing and implementing the control. Each year, benefits are then obtained in the form of reduced expected losses from exposures. Each year, costs are also incurred associated with operating and maintaining the control. In this light, we should conceive of a control as a form of investment. At least conceptually, we should calculate the net present value for each control and invest in the control if its net present value is greater than or equal to zero. Where there are competing controls (controls that reduce expected losses for the same exposures), we should invest in that control which has the highest net present value. Because the costs of evaluating each control we might implement are likely to be excessive, we will probably need to focus our evaluation on a *set* or *system* of controls. In other words, we will consider the set or system of internal controls as the investment rather than individual controls as the investment.

One difficulty we will face in considering controls as an investment is to estimate the size of the stream of benefits and costs that will occur during each period of the control system's life. Perhaps the more difficult decision we will have to make, however, is to determine the appropriate discount rate to use in our net present value calculations. Current finance theory tells us that the discount rate, k, that we should use should be calculated as follows:

$$k = k_f + \beta(\bar{k}_m - k_f)$$

where:

k_f = risk-free rate of return
$\bar{k}_m$ = expected rate of return on the market portfolio
β = beta coefficient of a security

The β coefficient of a security indicates the riskiness of returns on the security relative to returns on the market portfolio. The value of β can be obtained by regressing the returns on the security to returns on the market portfolio.

What is the β we should use, however, for an investment in a control system? Conceptually we need to find a firm that operates in the market that invests only in the control system we are seeking to evaluate. Of course, practically we know that such firms are unlikely to exist. In this light, we might use the β of the firm that is seeking to design, implement, operate, and maintain the control system we are evaluating and make some adjustment to β (upwards or downwards) depending on our estimate of the risk associated with the control system relative to the overall risk associated with the firm.

SUMMARY

When evaluating asset safeguarding and data integrity, auditors attempt to determine whether assets could be destroyed, damaged, or used for unauthorized purposes, and how well the completeness, soundness, purity, and veracity of data are maintained. The evaluation process involves auditors making a complex global judgment using piecemeal evidence collected on the strengths and weaknesses of an internal control system.

To evaluate how well an internal control system safeguards assets and maintains data integrity, measures of asset safeguarding and data integrity are needed. Common measures are the expected dollar loss for asset safeguarding and the dollar error, quantity error, and number of errors a system can produce for data integrity.

When auditors make the global evaluation judgment, they seek to determine the impact of individual control strengths and weaknesses on the overall reliability of a system. They make this judgment at the conclusion of their preliminary evaluation of the internal control system and after they complete their tests of controls and substantive testing.

The primary factors that appear to affect the quality of auditors' global evaluation judgments are their cognitive abilities, their knowledge, various environmental factors such as the audit technology they have available to assist them, and their level of motivation to make the judgment well. In this chapter, we have focused on the audit technology auditors can use to help them make the global evaluation decision. This technology takes the form of control matrices, deterministic models, software reliability models, engineering reliability models, Bayesian models, simulation models, and expert systems.

The evaluation of an internal control system must be considered within a cost-effectiveness framework. Auditors must estimate the stream of benefits and costs associated with the design, implementation, operation, and maintenance of an internal control system. They must also estimate the discount rate they will use for this stream of benefits and costs. Auditors can then calculate the net present value of the system to determine whether it is a worthwhile investment.

Review Questions

21-1 List three measures of data integrity and give an example where each measure would be used. Briefly explain why measures of data integrity often need to be expressed probabilistically.

21-2 Why should auditors consider the variance of the probability distribution of error that a system could produce?

21-3 Briefly explain the nature of the global evaluation decision on whether a system safeguards assets or maintains data integrity.

21-4 At what points during an audit do auditors have to make the global evaluation decision?

21-5 List *four* categories of factors that are likely to affect auditors' performance when making the global evaluation decision.

21-6 Briefly describe some heuristics that auditors might use, perhaps unknowingly, to make the global evaluation decision. How might these heuristics undermine the quality of global evaluation judgment?

21-7 Briefly explain the different effects that *general knowledge* and *specific knowledge* can have on the quality of auditors' global evaluation judgments when they undertake an audit.

21-8 Briefly explain how the following *two* characteristics of the audit environment can have an impact on the quality of auditors' global evaluation judgments:
 a Technology
 b Group processes

21-9 Briefly explain how prior involvement in an audit could affect auditors' motivation to undertake the audit.

21-10 How does the level of motivation auditors have during the conduct of an audit affect (a) the effort they exert to perform an audit task and (b) the cognitive processes they use to perform the audit task?

21-11 Briefly explain the nature of a control matrix. How can auditors use a control matrix to assist making the global evaluation judgment on whether a system safeguards assets and maintains data integrity?

21-12 Briefly explain the nature and purpose of deterministic models designed to assist auditors to make the evaluation decision on how well a system safeguards assets and maintains data integrity. Outline the major strengths and limitations of deterministic models.

21-13 During the test of a program, an auditor discovers that the program incorrectly calculates the discount given for certain types of customers. Outline how the total amount of dollar error that results because of the incorrect calculation could be determined.

21-14 Briefly explain what is meant by a mean value and an extreme value deterministic model for evaluating data integrity. Under what circumstances might auditors use each type of model?

21-15 Briefly explain the nature of the following types of software reliability models:
 a Time-between-failures models
 b Failure-count models
 c Fault-seeding models

21-16 How can auditors use *software* reliability models to help them make the global evaluation judgment on how well a system maintains data integrity?

21-17 In the context of *engineering* reliability models of internal control systems, briefly explain *in words* what is meant by the overall reliability of a system of internal control.

21-18 How are engineering reliability models useful to auditors? What problems are auditors likely to encounter if they use them in practice?

21–19 In engineering reliability models, define the following terms:
   a R_i
   b $P(e_{ij})$
   c $P(c_{ij})$
   d $(1-p_i)$
   e Ne_{ir}
   f T_r
   g Ve_i

21–20 Briefly describe the nature of a Bayesian decision-making model as it applies to the evaluation of an internal control system. Can the Bayesian approach be used to evaluate the reliability of a single control, a set of controls, or both?

21–21 If $P(F|R)$ is the probability of a favorable test result given an internal control system is reliable and $P(F|U)$ is the probability of a favorable test result given an internal control system is unreliable, give the formula for determining the probability of having a *reliable* internal control system if a *favorable* test result is obtained.

21–22 The flowchart in Figure 21–8 shows the simulation program iterating 1,000 times. Why is it necessary to iterate 1,000 times through the year's transactions? Outline one method auditors might use to determine whether 1,000 iterations is enough.

21–23 What circumstances would lead auditors to construct a simulation model rather than use an engineering reliability model to evaluate whether an internal control system safeguards assets and maintains data integrity?

21–24 Give *two* ways in which expert systems might be used to assist auditors when they have to make the global evaluation judgment on how well a system safeguards assets and maintains data integrity.

21–25 What do we mean by expert systems often being *brittle*? What implications does their brittleness have when auditors use them to assist making the global evaluation judgment on how well a system safeguards assets and maintains data integrity?

21–26 Why must maintenance of asset safeguarding and data integrity be considered within a cost-effectiveness framework?

21–27 Briefly explain the major *costs* involved in implementing and operating an internal control system. How are the *benefits* of an internal control system assessed?

21–28 How can a controls matrix be used to assist auditors to determine whether a cost-effective internal control system is being used to safeguard assets and to maintain data integrity?

21–29 Briefly explain how the implementation and operation of an internal control system can be characterized as an *investment* decision. What discount rate should auditors use if they evaluate an internal control system as an investment?

Multiple-Choice Questions

21–1 The shape of the probability distribution of error that an internal control system could produce is important because it indicates the:
   a Risk auditors face when they make a decision about the materiality of the error the system could produce
   b Size of the error that the system could produce
   c Number of internal controls in the system that are failing stochastically
   d Level of materiality that should be used to evaluate the error that the system could produce

21–2 Which of the following statements about the global evaluation judgment on maintenance of asset safeguarding and data integrity is *most likely* to be *false*?

  a It must be made at both the subsystem and system levels during the conduct of an audit

  b The possibility of both past and future material losses or misstatements having occurred must be considered

  c It must be made only after tests of management controls and application controls have been conducted

  d It will affect the level of substantive testing that auditors undertake during their audit work

21–3 When auditors make a global evaluation judgment, they might unconsciously use the *availability heuristic*, which means that they will:

  a Adjust their initial estimate of the likelihood of an event occurring based on the amount of new information that is presented to them

  b Assess the probability of one thing occurring based on its similarity to another event that has occurred

  c Anchor their initial estimate of an event occurring based on the availability of prior information about the event

  d Assess the probability of an event occurring based on their ability to remember instances of the event occurring

21–4 Which of the following is *least likely* to require specialized knowledge to make a high-quality audit judgment?

  a The evaluation of cutoff transactions associated with a sales system to determine whether there is evidence of earnings manipulation

  b The evaluation of the reliability of input controls that are important to maintaining data integrity in an order-entry application system

  c The evaluation of output produced by a utility used to examine a database log for evidence of exposures that arise from breaches of access controls

  d The review of output produced by generalized audit software used to undertake ratio analysis during analytical review conducted near the close of an audit

21–5 Our prior involvement with an audit is *most likely* to affect:

  a The extent of effort we are likely to exert during the audit

  b Whether we use group processes during the audit

  c Whether we focus on asset safeguarding or data integrity during the conduct of the audit

  d The extent to which we use technology to support the audit

21–6 In a matrix conceptualization of the evaluation judgment in which the rows are controls and the columns are causes of loss, the *row* evaluation judgment involves determining:

  a Whether each control objective has been achieved

  b Whether each potential loss has been reduced to an acceptable level

  c Whether the most cost-effective set of controls has been determined to reduce expected losses to an acceptable level

  d Whether the benefits of each control exceed its costs

21–7 Deterministic models for evaluating the overall reliability of internal control systems are *most likely* to be useful when:

  a The systems comprise more manual components than computer-based components

  b They are used to obtain a first approximation of how well a system safeguards assets and maintains data integrity

  c They are used to evaluate asset safeguarding concerns rather than data integrity concerns

  d The internal control components vary considerably in terms of their reliability

21–8 A software reliability model that attempts to predict the number of failures that will occur in a system during a fixed testing interval is a:
a Fault-seeding model
b Mean-error-time model
c Time-between-failures model
d Failure-count model

21–9 What is the variable *P(e)* in the following reliability formula:

$$R = p + (1 - p)P(e)P(c)$$

a Probability of an error
b Probability of a control signaling an error or irregularity
c Probability of a control signaling an error or irregularity when one exists
d Probability that an error discovered is corrected

21–10 Given that a system can only experience two error and irregularity types and that $R_1 = .7$ and $R_2 = .9$, the overall reliability of the system is:
a .63
b .9
c .7
d .16

21–11 Given the following values:

$$
\begin{array}{ll}
p_1 = .8 & p_2 = .9 \\
P(e_{11}) = .9 & P(e_{21}) = .8 \\
P(c_{11}) = .7 & P(c_{21}) = .9 \\
P(e_{12}) = .7 & P(e_{22}) = .8 \\
P(c_{12}) = .9 & P(c_{22}) = .7
\end{array}
$$

The reliability of the system is (to three decimal places):
a .963
b .961
c .980
d None of the above

21–12 What is the variable T_r in the following formula that calculates the dollar error produced?

$$A_i = Ne_{ir} \cdot Ve_i \cdot T_r$$

a Tolerance of the *r*th control
b Number of errors of type *r*
c Frequency with which the set of *r* controls is executed
d Total cost of executing the *r*th control

21–13 Which of the following is *most likely* to be the major reason for using Bayesian models to evaluate the reliability of an internal control system?
a They are the cheapest and most reliable analytical model to use
b They provide more information on the reliability of an internal control system than a software reliability model
c They provide more accurate results than a simulation model
d They provide a formal means of revising the auditor's assessment of the reliability of an internal control

21–14 Assume that an auditor is evaluating the reliability of a control. The auditor's prior probability of the control being reliable is .95. A test is undertaken, however, and the test result indicates the control is unreliable. Previous experience with the test has shown that the probability of the test producing an unfavorable result when the control is, in fact, reliable is .15, and the probability of the test producing an unfavorable result when the control is, in fact, unreliable is .9. In light of the test result, the auditor should now assess the probability of the control being reliable as:

a .24

b .76

c .8125

d None of the above

21–15 Which of the following is *most likely* to be the reason for auditors to use a simulation model instead of an analytical model to assist them to evaluate how well a system safeguards assets or maintains data integrity?

a Simulation models are cheaper to design, implement, and execute

b The analytical model needed is not mathematically tractable

c Evaluation costs are reduced over a wide range of values of the independent variable and changes in the structure of the model

d A simulation model allows the mean and variance of the probability distribution associated with the reliability of the internal control system to be calculated

21–16 Which of the following is *not likely* to be the reason for auditors to use an expert system to assist them to evaluate how well a system safeguards assets or maintains data integrity?

a The quality of the advice it provides is robust across a wide range of different types of internal control system

b It allows them to ask questions about how it reached a particular conclusion on the reliability of an internal control system

c It provides them with insights into how the various internal control strengths and weaknesses compound and compensate

d It provides them with a reasonableness check when they are evaluating the quality of their own judgments

21–17 Which of the following is an *implementation cost* for an internal control system?

a Wages of a specialist employed to maintain physical security

b Cost of an undetected error in a communications line

c Costs of testing a modification to an access control routine

d Programming labor costs involved in writing an input validation routine

21–18 Which of the following is *most likely* to be a difficulty when using a controls matrix to evaluate whether the most cost-effective set of controls has been used in an internal control system?

a Not all types of exposures and not all types of control objectives can be evaluated using a controls matrix

b A control matrix focuses only on costs and not benefits, and it focuses only on the operational and maintenance costs associated with controls

c Choosing values for the elements of the matrix might be difficult because the costs of a particular control might depend on what controls are in place already

d The order in which controls should be listed in the rows and exposures should be listed in the columns might not be clear until the benefits of the controls have been assessed

21–19 When evaluating whether an investment in a control system is worthwhile, the term β in the formula used to calculate the discount rate is:

a The risk-free rate of return

b Weighted cost of capital of the firm investing in the control system

c The coefficient obtained when the returns on the security of a firm that designs and implements similar types of control systems are regressed against returns on the market

d The coefficient obtained when returns on the market portfolio are regressed against the risk-free rate of return

Exercises and Cases

21-1 The Singapura Lion Development Bank (SLDB) is a medium-sized bank that is based in Singapore. It has grown rapidly over the past five years, largely because of the efforts of a young, aggressive management team who have focused on trying to obtain high levels of customer satisfaction with services and using information technology extensively to provide a wide range of services. Management has been supported fully by a four-person board of directors, one of whom is the managing director of SLDB.

You are a partner in a medium-sized accounting firm (25 personnel, including three partners). Recently, you have been approached by the managing director of SLDB, who is an old acquaintance from your university student days. He indicates that the current auditors (a large audit firm) are likely to be dismissed at the forthcoming annual general meeting of shareholders. The managing director informs you that disputes have arisen between management, the board of directors, and the auditors about some of the current procedures being used and the directions being followed by SLDB. He indicates that the current auditors are too conservative and not well matched to the aggressive, customer-oriented culture of SLDB.

The managing director asks whether he can nominate your firm as the new auditors. He points out that you and your firm would be a good match for SLDB because you, too, have a reputation for young, high-quality, innovative staff. He also points out that you and he have known each other for many years. In addition, a year ago you carried out a major controls evaluation of the electronic funds transfer controls within SLDB. Management of SLDB engaged you to undertake the task because you are well known as an expert in the area of computer-based information systems control and audit. Again, they were unhappy with the quality of the work undertaken by their existing auditors. Because of disputes with them, they asked you to do the job. In this light, the managing director indicates that you have a good knowledge of SLDB already.

Because of some concerns you have, you ask the managing director for several days to think about your answer. As you contemplate the answer you will give, you think about the pros and cons of accepting the engagement. On the one hand, SLDB will be your biggest client by far, and it is likely to increase the likelihood of your obtaining other large clients, especially within the financial services sector. On the other hand, neither you nor any of your colleagues has experience in the conduct of audits of financial institutions. Your client base primarily consists of medium-sized manufacturing and import-export businesses. The scope of the controls evaluation you conducted previously for SLDB was quite restricted in that it addressed only computer controls and not broader management controls. As you think about having to make the global evaluation judgment at the end of the next financial year on whether there are material errors or irregularities in SLDB's financial statements, you become increasingly uncertain about what you should do.

Required: To help you make the decision, you decide to try to list out the factors that might affect your decision. Make a list of these factors. When you have considered your list, what decision will you make? Why?

21-2 You are the partner-in-charge of the external audit of H'ani Diamond Mines Ltd. (HDML), a medium-sized South African diamond mining company with its head office in Johannesburg. Because there has been significant turnover of management during the past year at one of HDML's major mining sites (some of the management have been fired because of irregularities that have been discovered and disputes with the miners on the site that they have been unable to resolve satisfactorily), you are conducting an audit of some of the material application systems at the site.

During your planning of the audit of the payroll system at the site, two of the control objectives you agreed on with the manager responsible for the conduct of the audit were as follows:

a All and only those changes to employee data that meet management's criteria should be made accurately and promptly.

b All and only those requests to hire employees that satisfy management's criteria should be approved.

A review of internal controls has now been conducted. During an examination of working papers prepared for the audit, you note the following controls are supposedly in place at the mine site over the computerized payroll system:

1 Documents that initiate changes to employee data are approved by management before they are entered into the payroll system.

2 A report of all changes made to employee data is printed by the payroll system, and this report is reconciled against management-approved changes by an independent clerk.

3 Batch totals are prepared for all data to be entered into the payroll system by a control clerk who is not authorized to access the system. The control clerk then uses a report of data entered into the system to check that data has been submitted on a timely, complete, nonredundant, and accurate basis.

4 Hours-worked fields and overtime-hours worked fields are validated for reasonableness by the payroll system.

5 Employment applicants are interviewed by the personnel manager and the senior foreman on the site to evaluate whether the applicants have suitable qualifications and experience.

6 Any revision to an existing union agreement or any new union agreement is reviewed by HDML's lawyers.

7 Employees complete sign-in sheets to indicate which personnel are working on site.

Required: Prepare a controls matrix. In the columns, list the exposures that HDML faces if it does not achieve the above two control objectives. List the controls listed here in the rows of your controls matrix. For each exposure you list, indicate with a tick mark in the elements of the matrix whether you believe each control will reduce losses that would be incurred if the exposure were to eventuate. How well do you think the controls listed here reduce expected losses from failure to safeguard assets or maintain data integrity to an acceptable level?

21–3 Ferngoods Ltd. is a large Auckland-based white goods manufacturer (e.g., refrigerators, washing machines, stoves) that sells its products throughout the Southeast Asian market. It employs about 1,500 people, and it has large inventories of raw materials, work in process, and finished goods that it stores at its Auckland facility. Ferngoods's operations have grown rapidly over the past five years. It has quickly gained a reputation for producing high-quality products. Management has had substantial difficulties expanding the capabilities of the company at a rate that is sufficient to meet the increased demand for Ferngoods's products.

From the outset, Ferngoods has been a sophisticated user of computers to support all aspects of its operations. At times, however, these systems have barely been able to cope with the expansion in activities caused by the rapid increase in sales. In particular, major problems have arisen with Ferngoods's systems to support their manufacturing operations. Because of this, three years ago, Ferngoods employed an international consulting firm to try to find manufacturing software that would be suitable for its operations. After an extensive study, the consultants recommended that Ferngoods write its own software because the costs of adapting the then-available off-the-shelf software would have been substantial. As a result, over a two-year period, a large team of Ferngoods's information systems staff, together with consultants, have been involved in the development and implementation of the software.

Over the past ten months, the manufacturing software has been operational. Although no major crises have arisen, both users and the information systems staff who are responsible for maintaining the software are still coming to grips with its capabilities and, in particular, its strengths and limitations. Many of the consultants involved in developing the software are no longer under contract to the company.

You are the partner responsible for information systems audit in a large firm of accountants that has just taken over the audit of Ferngoods from a small-medium size accounting firm. At this time you are trying to plan how you will undertake the audit of the manufacturing system. During discussions with the information systems manager responsible for the system, she indicates that you might wish to rely on the statistical models they are using to evaluate the reliability of the system. These models were developed by one of the consultants employed to develop the manufacturing system. In particular, they are using a time-between-failures model, which predicts the length of the interval of time before the next failure occurs based on the history of past failures. She shows you some computer output from their model and points to a number that she says indicates the model's prediction that it will be another four months before a system failure will be experienced. On this basis, she argues that the system is now stable and reliable. She argues that you should adjust your audit work accordingly.

During a subsequent conversation with the manager of inventories at Ferngoods, you ask him for his impressions of the system. He indicates that he thinks the system is working reliably, although he is still not certain. He comments that two months ago some material discrepancies were found between the system's records and physical stocktake records. The reasons for these discrepancies were never discovered, although several senior production people were suspected of fraud. Because they knew they were under suspicion (though nothing could be proved), they subsequently left Ferngoods. Apart from this event, he is still trying to come to a good understanding of the system himself.

Required: You are mindful of the fact that it is important for your firm to contain costs on this first audit of Ferngoods. Indeed, your firm won the audit of Ferngoods in a competitive tendering process in which audit costs were a major factor in the decision. What is your preliminary evaluation of the manufacturing system on the basis of the evidence you have collected so far? How do you think you will now proceed with the audit of the system?

21–4 You are an auditor examining the data-entry process for a large Toronto-based mail-order retail firm that dispatches goods to customers on behalf of about 30 clients. You are currently focusing on two error types that can occur: *(1)* the data-entry clerk can enter a wrong amount ordered for an order placed by a customer and *(2)* the data-entry clerk can enter a wrong product code for an order placed by a customer. Sometimes the first error will be identified by a reasonableness check exercised by the program. Sometimes the second error will be identified by a product-code check digit, although not all product codes have check digits. Moreover, sometimes the wrong product code might still be a valid product code anyway.

In light of evidence you collect during interviews and examination of documentation on the likelihood of the data-entry clerk making these errors, the errors being discovered by the controls, and the errors then being corrected properly by the data-entry clerk, you prepare the following table:

$$p_1 = .7 \quad p_2 = .85$$
$$P(e_{11}) = .8 \quad P(e_{21}) = .9$$
$$P(c_{11}) = .9 \quad P(c_{21}) = .95$$
$$P(e_{12}) = .75 \quad P(e_{22}) = .8$$
$$P(c_{12}) = .6 \quad P(c_{22}) = .75$$

Required: Using the engineering reliability formulas provided in the chapter, calculate the reliability of the input program in relation to these two errors. What do you conclude about the reliability of the program? How would you now proceed with the audit in light of your conclusions about the reliability of the program?

21–5 Electronic Connections Ltd. (ECL) is a major supplier of computer network-related services. It was started by two young programmers in 1963 who purchased a (then) large secondhand mainframe computer to provide time-sharing services to customers. ECL expanded it services throughout the 1960s and 1970s. In particular, it developed large, complex commercial, scientific, and engineering software, initially to meet the specific needs of particular customers and then to address the needs of a wider customer base. Early in the 1980s, it established a hardware and software infrastructure to provide electronic funds transfer services to financial institutions. Because of its innovative, high-quality support, its electronic funds transfer services were a major success, particularly with small- to medium-sized financial institutions. In the late 1980s, it began to provide a range of electronic data interchange services and electronic mail services. In the early 1990s, it entered the Internet market aggressively by providing a wide range of relatively cheap services to support its customers' use of the World Wide Web. ECL's management had a view that having customers use their Internet services in due course could be used to leverage their use of other, more profitable services that ECL provided.

About 18 months ago, senior management of ECL initiated a major study of physical security controls and logical access controls. Senior management had increasingly recognized that there were some significant exposures in relation to the facilities and systems that ECL operated. Since the early 1980s, ECL has had in place a small but effective internal audit function. The problem that senior management has perceived, however, is that changes to the control system have been unable to keep pace with changes to the hardware-software platform that ECL uses to support its customers. Because of this, they asked a firm of external consultants who offered a "packaged" physical security and logical access controls solution to evaluate its feasibility within ECL.

You are the manager of internal audit for ECL. You were appointed about 12 months ago to fill the vacancy created by the retirement of the previous manager of internal audit (who had filled the position since it was created). Previously you were a manager in a major public accounting firm. Senior management has asked your advice on the recommendations provided by the external consultants who have been examining physical security and logical access controls within ECL. Basically, their report recommends that ECL purchase and implement their packaged controls solution to reduce exposures to acceptable levels.

You are concerned, however, because you also have a report prepared independently by your two most senior staff auditors on the work undertaken by the external consultants. Each has been with ECL for more than ten years, and they know the company well. In one part of their report, they have undertaken a discounted cash flow analysis of the packaged solution proposed by the consultants. In addition to basing their analysis on information provided by the consultants, they have also collected their own data on the likely benefits and costs of the control system. Their most optimistic estimate of the net present value (NPV) of the control system over its estimated six-year life is –$325,000 (that is, the NPV is negative). Their most pessimistic figure is –$2,063,700. In calculating the NPV, they have used discount rates that vary between 10 percent and 15 percent. Unfortunately, the consultants' report provides no discounted cash flow analysis. Indeed, the hard quantitative data they provide on costs and benefits is sketchy.

Required: Make a list of issues you feel you should take into account in preparing your report for senior management. You need to consider the situation carefully because some of the issues you identify could have a significant impact on the recommendations you ultimately make to senior management.

Answers to Multiple-Choice Questions

21–1	a	**21–6**	d	**21–11**	b	**21–16**	a
21–2	c	**21–7**	b	**21–12**	c	**21–17**	d
21–3	d	**21–8**	d	**21–13**	d	**21–18**	c
21–4	b	**21–9**	c	**21–14**	b	**21–19**	c
21–5	a	**21–10**	a	**21–15**	b		

REFERENCES

Ashton, Robert H., and Alison Hubbard Ashton, eds. (1995), *Judgment and Decision-Making Research in Accounting and Auditing.* New York: Cambridge University Press.

Burns, David C., and James K. Loebbecke (1975), "Internal Control Evaluation: How the Computer Can Help," *Journal of Accountancy* (August), 60–70.

Cushing, Barry E. (1974), "A Mathematical Approach to the Analysis and Design of Internal Control Systems," *The Accounting Review* (January), 24–41.

Goel, Amrit L. (1985), "Software Reliability Models: Assumptions, Limitations, and Applicability," *IEEE Transactions on Software Engineering* (December), 1411–1423.

Libby, Robert, and Joan Luft (1993), "Determinants of Judgment Performance in Accounting Settings: Ability, Knowledge, Motivation, and Environment," *Accounting, Organizations and Society*, 18(5), 425–450.

Mair, William C., Donald R. Wood, and Keagle W. Davis (1976), *Computer Control & Audit*, 2d ed. Altamonte Springs, FL: The Institute of Internal Auditors, Inc.

Pressman, Roger S. (1997), *Software Engineering: A Practitioner's Approach*, 4th ed. New York: McGraw-Hill.

Slovic, Paul, and Sarah Lichenstein (1971), "Comparison of Bayesian and Regression Approaches to the Study of Information Processing in Judgment," *Organizational Behavior and Human Performance* (June), 649–744.

Trotman, Ken T. (1996), *Research Methods for Judgment and Decision Making Studies in Auditing.* Melbourne: Coopers & Lybrand.

Tversky, Amos, and Daniel Kahneman (1974), "Judgment Under Uncertainty: Heuristics and Biases," *Science* (September), 1124–1131.

CHAPTER 22

Evaluating System Effectiveness

Chapter Outline

Chapter Key Points

■ The purpose of evaluating system effectiveness is to determine how well a system meets its objectives. The evaluation involves six steps: (a) identify the objectives of the information system, (b) select the measures to be used, (c) identify the data sources, (d) obtain *ex ante* values for measures, (e) obtain *ex post* values for measures, and (f) assess the system impact by comparing *ex ante* and *ex post* measures.

■ To be able to evaluate system effectiveness and understand why a system is either effective or ineffective, auditors need a model of how the various factors that potentially impact system effectiveness are interrelated. One useful model posits that the quality of the system and the quality of the information it produces have an impact on users' perceptions about the usefulness of the system and the ease with which the system can be used. These two perceptions are also affected, however, by users' beliefs about their abilities to use computers competently—their self-efficacy. Users' perceptions about the usefulness and ease of use of the system in turn affect how they use the system—for example, the frequency with which they use the system and the ways in which they use it. How they use the system then affects their performance in their organizational role and ultimately the overall performance of the organization. How they use the system also affects their satisfaction with it.

■ There are many characteristics of the hardware and software components of an information system that might affect users' perceptions of the usefulness and ease of use of the system—for example, response time, ease of interaction with the system, and quality of documentation and help facilities. Auditors might also need to evaluate factors that are somewhat opaque to users but nonetheless affect system quality—for example, the extent to which the hardware platform is efficient, the extent to which the software platform has to be maintained, the operational efficiency of the system, and the extent to which hardware-software components are independent of one another so they can be adapted quickly in light of changing needs.

■ There are several aspects of information quality—for example, authenticity, accuracy, completeness, timeliness, and relevance. The importance of these characteristics will vary, depending on the nature of the system. For example, accuracy will be more important in an operational control system and less important in a strategic planning system. The perceptions of these characteristics can also vary across users. For example, one user might perceive some information to be more relevant than another user.

■ Users will judge the usefulness of an information system in terms of whether they perceive it will enable them to improve their job performance. Users will judge the ease of use of an information system in terms of the amount of effort they will have to expend to employ the functionality provided in the system. Both perceived usefulness and perceived ease of use will affect how users work with the system.

■ Computer self-efficacy is a construct that describes a user's perceptions about him- or herself in terms of ability to use a computer. It is not confined to straightforward skills like copying files and entering data into spreadsheets. Rather, it applies to broader tasks like using a spreadsheet effectively to undertake financial statement analysis. Computer self-efficacy is likely to affect users' perceptions of the usefulness and ease of use of an information system.

■ Auditors must be careful when evaluating how information systems are used. First, they need to determine whether use of a system is voluntary or involuntary. If use is involuntary, the amount and frequency of use are not likely to be good indicators of the effectiveness of an information system. Second, they need to examine the nature of the use made of an information system. For certain types of systems (e.g., decision support systems), it might be important to see that the information system has produced fundamental changes in the ways users perform their jobs before auditors can judge the system to be effective. Third, auditors might need to determine who uses a system to determine its effectiveness. In some cases it might be best if users work directly with a system themselves. In other cases it might be best if they use intermediaries to work with the system on their behalf.

■ Two important ways that auditors can evaluate the effects of an information system on users are to examine task-accomplishment impacts and quality-of-working-life impacts. To evaluate the impact of an information system on users' task accomplishment, auditors must first determine the ways in which task accomplishment should be measured. These will vary, depending on the nature of the information system. To evaluate the impact of an information system on users' quality of working life, often auditors must look for suitable proxies or surrogate measures of the impact. For example, they might not be able to reliably assess directly whether a system has improved users' opportunities for growth and security in their workplace. Auditors might get an indication of this impact, however, through changes in factors like the absenteeism rate and sick rate associated with users who employ the system.

■ Information system satisfaction has been a frequently used measure in research that has been undertaken to determine whether an information system is effective. It is widely believed that users will be satisfied with an information system that they deem to be effective. Information system satisfaction measures address issues like user relationships with information system staff, the quality of information provided by the system, and the reliability of the system. Substantial overlap exists, however, between information system satisfaction measures and perceived usefulness and ease-of-use measures.

■ To evaluate the organizational impact of an information system, auditors need to understand the goals of an organization. The overall effectiveness of an information system can then be evaluated in terms of how well it enables an organization to achieve its goals.

■ Unfortunately, it is often difficult to determine the goals of an organization. Organizational theorists have argued that the goals of an organization must be considered from multiple, sometimes conflicting perspectives. For example, auditors might try to determine goals from the mission statement of an organization and evaluate how well an information system helps the organization achieve these goals. Different stakeholders in the organization, however, might have goals that are different from the formally stated goals. For example, some managers might be more concerned to acquire the resources that they will need to enable their departments to function properly. They might evaluate the effectiveness of an information system in terms of how well it allows them to acquire the resources they believe they need to operate their departments successfully.

■ Management often is likely to ask auditors to evaluate the economic effectiveness of an information system. In this light, auditors need to be aware of the "productivity paradox" surrounding investments in information systems. This paradox pertains to the phenomenon that organizations are continuing to invest substantial amounts of money in information systems, sometimes without any apparent payoffs from this investment. It now appears that the payoffs have occurred in terms of improved productivity and improved value for consumers but not improved profitability. The gains in profitability are quickly competed away by other firms who copy the information systems innovations.

■ There are four steps that auditors need to undertake to evaluate the economic effectiveness of an information system. First, they need to identify the benefits associated with the information system. Both tangible and intangible benefits are likely to have occurred. Different stakeholders in the system are also likely to have experienced different types of benefits. Second, they need to identify the costs associated with the information system. As with benefits, both tangible and intangible costs are likely to have occurred, and the costs are likely to differ across different stakeholder groups. Third, they need to value the benefits and costs they have identified. This task can be difficult, especially when they are attempting to value intangible benefits and costs. Different stakeholders also might place different values on the same benefits and costs. Fourth, they need to discount the benefits and costs to obtain a net present value for the investment in the information system. The most difficult aspect of this task is likely to be determining an appropriate discount rate to use.

INTRODUCTION

After a system has been operational for some time, it might be subjected to a postimplementation review. A postimplementation review has a twofold purpose. First, it can be used to determine how well the system is meeting the objectives established for it, whether it should be scrapped or continued, and, if it is to be continued, whether it should be modified in some way to meet its objectives better. Second, the review can be used to evaluate the adequacy of the system development process used to design and implement the system. In light of this evaluation, system development standards might be changed or system development personnel might be provided with feedback on how to improve the tasks they undertake.

In this chapter, we focus primarily on the first objective of a postimplementation review—namely, evaluating systems to determine how well they meet their objectives. The first section will provide an overview of how we undertake an evaluation of system effectiveness. Next, we examine a model that has been developed to show the major factors that are believed to affect information system effectiveness. We then discuss the influence of each of these factors on information system effectiveness. Our goal is to develop an understanding of the nature of each of these factors, the ways they are interrelated, and the approaches we might use to measure them and their impact.

OVERVIEW OF THE EFFECTIVENESS EVALUATION PROCESS

Ideally, all information systems should be subjected periodically to a postimplementation review to assess how well they are meeting their objectives. Empirical research has shown, however, that only certain systems undergo postimplementation evaluations (see, e.g., Hamilton and Chervany 1981a, 1981b). Several factors appear to affect which information systems are selected for review. For example, if top managers have few doubts about the success of a system, they might not request a postimplementation review. Conversely, if they have substantial doubts about the success of the system, they may commission a review.

Reviews also can be undertaken for political reasons. For example, managers might request that a review be undertaken on a system for which they are responsible even when they know the system is a success. By having someone independent confirm its success, they might be seeking to enhance their standing with senior management. They might have an expectation that they can then extract more resources from the organization for their own purposes. Whenever auditors are requested to undertake a postimplementation review, therefore, they should be circumspect about the underlying motivations for the evaluation.

An evaluation of system effectiveness involves six steps:

1. *Identify the objectives of the information system.* Sometimes the objectives might have been stated clearly when the system was first developed. Sometimes, however, the objectives might be vague and ill defined. Different stakeholders in the information system also might have different objectives for the system. Somehow auditors must tease out the objectives that each stakeholder group has for the system so they can determine which of these objectives have been achieved.
2. *Select the measures to be used.* Auditors need to be able to measure the extent to which each objective they identify for the system has been achieved. In some cases, they might use quantitative measures that they obtain via, say, questionnaires administered to users or statistics relating to productivity. In other cases, auditors might use qualitative measures obtained via, say, interviews with and observations of users.
3. *Identify data sources.* Having chosen the measures they wish to obtain, auditors must then identify the best sources of data for these measures. In some cases, it might be various types of users. In other cases, it might be, for example, manufacturing records on productivity, wastage, spoilage, and so on that are maintained routinely by an organization.
4. *Obtain* ex ante *values for measures.* When auditors have identified the measures and the best sources of data for these measures, they must attempt to determine the values of these measures before the system they are evaluating was implemented. Auditors need a basis for establishing the impact of the system. Unless these *ex ante* values were collected prior to the implementation of the system, it could be difficult to obtain them after the system is operational.

5. *Obtain* ex post *values for measures.* After the system is implemented, auditors then must collect data on the measures they have chosen to evaluate effectiveness. One difficulty they face is determining what time period should elapse before the measures should be taken. It might take some time before the effects of an information system on an organization begin to stabilize. It might also be important to collect data on these measures over time if they are interested in the patterns of changes that are occurring.

6. *Assess the system impact.* When auditors have values for the *ex ante* and *ex post* measures, they can then assess the impact of the system by comparing the values for the two sets of measures. It is important that they try to look beyond the measures to understand the reasons for any changes they observe. Their report will be more useful to management if they can account for the changes they have identified.

Auditors might find the execution of these steps somewhat more difficult to undertake if an organization has had no prior information system in place that can be used to provide a basis for comparison with the current information system. If a previous information system existed, the bases for evaluating the current information system are often clearer. Indeed, the new system might have been developed to overcome some specific limitations of the previous system. The focus of an auditor's evaluation then can be on whether the limitations of the old system have been mitigated by the new system. When no previous information system has existed, however, auditors might find it more difficult to identify the stakeholders' intentions for the information system and the areas of impact of the information system.

A MODEL OF INFORMATION SYSTEM EFFECTIVENESS

For many years, researchers in the information systems discipline have attempted to understand what we mean by information system effectiveness, to develop valid and reliable measures of information system effectiveness, and to identify the major factors that affect information system effectiveness. Unfortunately, these goals have proved especially difficult to achieve. Although we have made some progress, much research is still needed if we are ever likely to obtain a thorough understanding of the nature of information system effectiveness and the factors that impact information system effectiveness.

Figure 22–1 shows a model of information system effectiveness that is intended to be an amalgam of work that has been carried out by several researchers (e.g., Davis et al. 1989; DeLone and McLean 1992; Ferguson 1997; Seddon and Kiew 1994; and Seddon 1997). We examine each of the components of this model in the following sections. In summary, however, the model manifests a set of hypothesized relationships among factors that are thought to have an impact ultimately on whether an information system is effective. First, the quality of the system and the quality of the information it produces are hypothesized to affect whether users perceive the system to be both useful and easy to use. These two perceptions are also affected, however, by users' beliefs about their abilities to use computers competently (self-efficacy). Users' perceptions about the usefulness and ease of use of the system in turn affect how they use the system—for example, the frequency with which they use the system and the ways in which they use the system. How they use the system then affects their performance in their organizational role and ultimately the overall performance of the organization. How they use the system also affects their satisfaction with the system. There is also an hypothesized two-way relationship between satisfaction and individual impact. To the extent users are more satisfied with a system, it is likely to have a greater effect on them. Similarly, to

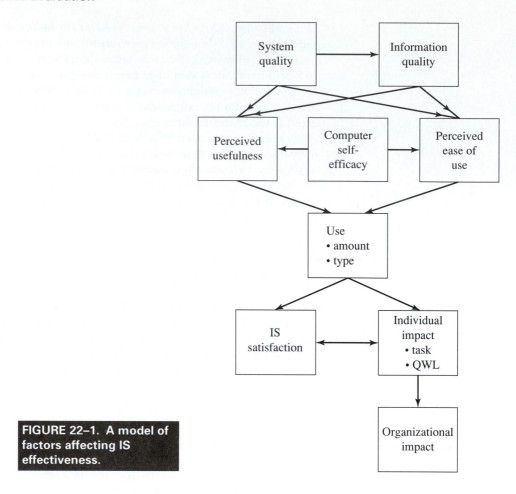

FIGURE 22–1. A model of factors affecting IS effectiveness.

the extent the system has a greater positive (negative) effect on them, they are more (less) likely to be satisfied with the system.

Auditors can use the model shown in Figure 22–1 in two ways. First, they can use it to structure their approach to the collection of the data they will need to make a judgment about whether a system meets its objectives effectively. Each component in the model indicates the types of evidence auditors must collect to be able to reach a global evaluation about the effectiveness of the system. Second, auditors can use the model to help them understand why a system might be effective or ineffective. In some ways they could approach the evaluation of system effectiveness by simply collecting evidence about the individual and organizational impacts that arise as a result of implementing and operating a system—the final components in the model. If auditors do not collect data on the preceding components, however, they will not have a sound basis for determining why a system is effective or ineffective. For example, if auditors find a system has not had the desired individual and organizational impacts, management might ask them to provide the reasons why the desired impacts have not occurred and the remedial actions they should take. Auditors can use the model to help them think about potential causes and to provide a basis for their making recommendations to try to improve the effectiveness of the system.

We must remember, however, that all models are simplifications of the complex phenomena that inevitably we will encounter in practice. For example, from Chapter 4 we know that information systems can have a significant impact on power structures within organizations. If users perceive from the outset that they will lose power when a particular information system is implemented, their perceptions of the usefulness and ease of use of the system are likely to be affected adversely. In short, the model shown in Figure 22–1 does not capture all factors and relationships that might be important to auditors in a specific context. Nonetheless, when auditors must undertake the task of evaluating system effectiveness, they can use the model shown in Figure 22–1 to structure their thinking about the task and to structure their approach to the task. We simply need to remember that auditors might need to modify the model to better suit the circumstances. In the following sections, therefore, we examine in more depth each of the major components in the model to help us come to a better understanding of the nature of information system effectiveness and the ways auditors might carry out audits to evaluate information system effectiveness.

EVALUATING SYSTEM QUALITY

Potentially many characteristics of the hardware and software components of an information system might affect users' perceptions of the usefulness and ease of use of the system. One set of characteristics will be fairly apparent to users after they have interacted with the system for only a short period of time. It includes the following:

1. Response time (online system),
2. Turnaround time (batch system),
3. Reliability (stability) of the system,
4. Ease of interaction with the system,
5. Usefulness of the functionality provided by the system,
6. Ease of learning,
7. Quality of documentation and help facilities, and
8. Extent of integration with other systems.

We have examined the importance of these factors in previous chapters, and we will examine some of them again in the next chapter. From the viewpoints of the users of a system, however, these factors tend to have a somewhat immediate impact on their attitudes toward the system. If users find it difficult to interact with a system, for example, they are unlikely to have favorable perceptions about the usefulness of the system and the ease with which they can use the system to accomplish their goals.

Another set of factors associated with system quality tends to be somewhat opaque to the users of a system. Nonetheless, ultimately these factors affect other factors that have a more direct impact on users. Some are associated with hardware effectiveness. For example, a system's response time or turnaround time might be unsatisfactory if the hardware platform used to support the system is poorly configured or has inadequate resources. Chapter 20 discusses the sorts of evidence auditors need to collect to make a judgment about the effectiveness of the hardware platform, and Chapter 23 discusses how they can make this evaluation judgment.

Some of these factors are also associated with software effectiveness. To assist auditors to make a judgment about software effectiveness, they should examine four attributes of the software used to support the system:

1. *History of repair maintenance.* The history of program repair maintenance indicates the quality of a program's logic. Recall that repair maintenance is carried out to correct logic errors. Extensive repair maintenance means inappropriate design, coding, or testing technologies have been used to implement the program.

2. *History of adaptive maintenance.* Adaptive maintenance is carried out to alter a program to accommodate changing requirements. There are two reasons why it occurs. First, program designers might have formulated incorrect specifications in the first place. As a result, the specifications have to be changed and the program logic altered. Incorrect program specifications mean they should examine the approaches used to develop the specifications. Second, user requirements might change. As a result, the program has to be altered to meet these new user requirements. Nonetheless, frequent modifications to meet changes in user needs might mean the program is inflexible; in other words, it has not been designed to accommodate change.

3. *History of perfective maintenance.* Perfective maintenance is carried out to improve program resource consumption—that is, to make the program execute more efficiently. Large amounts of perfective maintenance might mean that the program has been designed poorly. Alternatively, perhaps the hardware platform on which the program runs is being changed frequently and the program has to be constantly tuned to adapt to the new platform.

4. *Run-time resource consumption.* If at run time an application program consumes resources inefficiently, it could mean that it is poorly designed or that the programming language or compiler used is inappropriate for the task to be performed. Auditors should examine the technology used to support these aspects of software implementation.

The designers and programmers responsible for carrying out program modification and repair maintenance and the operators responsible for running programs can provide auditors with information on the appropriateness of the software technology used to support an application system. Designers and programmers can make judgments on the overall quality of programs. For example, they know whether a program is easy to modify or repair. Operators often can make judgments on whether a program consumes abnormal amounts of resources at run time.

Finally, some of the factors that are somewhat opaque to users are associated with the level of independence that has been implemented in the hardware-software platform used to support the system. An important objective in choosing the technology to support an information system should be to attain independence within and among the major resources that support the system: hardware, software, and data (Figure 22–2). Independence is a desired goal for three reasons. First, it allows a system to be adapted more readily to a future environment. Second, it allows a system to be adapted more readily to multiple existing environments. Third, it allows a system to be adapted more readily to a backup environment. Many organizations now strive to implement "open

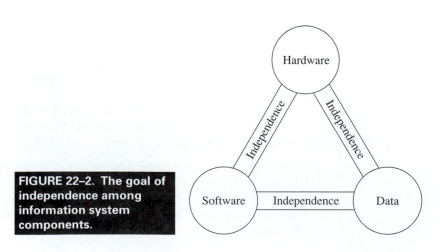

FIGURE 22–2. The goal of independence among information system components.

system" technologies—that is, technologies that have been designed specifically to meet independence goals. Some organizations still use proprietary technologies, however, which means that independence goals are unlikely to be achieved.

EVALUATING INFORMATION QUALITY

The quality of the information produced by an information system can have important effects on users' perceptions of the usefulness of the system and ease of use of the system. Throughout this book, the quality of information has been our ongoing concern. Some of the attributes of information quality that auditors might seek to measure are the following:

1. Authenticity,
2. Accuracy,
3. Completeness,
4. Uniqueness (nonredundancy),
5. Timeliness,
6. Relevance,
7. Comprehensibility,
8. Precision,
9. Conciseness, and
10. Informativeness.

When auditors evaluate the quality of information produced by a system, note that they are basically trying to assess how well the information enables users to undertake their jobs. Nonetheless, auditors should be sensitive to the fact that the information provided by a system can have other impacts on users' lives. For example, users might have a negative view of the quality of information provided by a system if they perceive that the information is used by management to gain increased power over them.

Auditors must also recognize that different users might have different perceptions about the quality of information produced by a system. Information provides a *representation* of phenomena that are occurring in the real world (Figure 22–3). The problem is that our perceptions of the world are shaped by the models we use to understand the world. One person's model of the world might not be the same as another person's. If the information system has been designed primarily on the basis of the first person's conception of the world, the second person might not perceive the quality of the information it produces to be high.

Auditors must recognize, therefore, that the attributes of information quality are not always "objective." The ratings provided by users can vary depending on how well the information represents the ways they conceive the real world. Auditors should be circumspect, therefore, if they obtain widespread variations among users about the quality of information produced by a system. On the one hand, it might reflect that auditors have not obtained valid and reliable measurements. On the other hand, it might reflect that users have quite different perceptions of the world that the information system is seeking to represent.

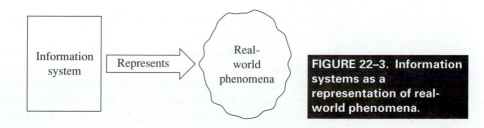

FIGURE 22–3. Information systems as a representation of real-world phenomena.

EVALUATING PERCEIVED USEFULNESS

Davis et al. (1989, p. 985) define perceived usefulness as "the prospective user's subjective probability that using a specific application system will increase his or her job performance within an organizational context." They point out that users are likely to be rewarded for good job performance. In this light, perceived usefulness is linked to whether users will ultimately gain rewards from their use of an information system and therefore the attitudes they have toward using the system. If their attitudes are favorable, they are likely to use the system more frequently and more effectively. If their attitudes are unfavorable, however, they are not likely to use the system.

Several items have been used to measure the perceived usefulness of an information system. Davis (1989) has found the following items to be valid and reliable, however:

1. Users perceive that the information system enables them to accomplish tasks associated with their job more quickly.
2. Users perceive that the information system enables them to improve their job performance.
3. Users perceive that the information system enables them to increase their productivity.
4. Users perceive that the information system enables them to increase their effectiveness on the job.
5. Users perceive that the information system makes it easier for them to undertake the tasks associated with their job.
6. Users perceive the information system to be useful in their job.

If auditors are seeking to evaluate the perceived usefulness of an information system, therefore, they might wish to use these items in a questionnaire or as the basis for any interviews they conduct with users.

Again, auditors should be mindful that other factors might affect users' perceptions of the usefulness of an information system. If a system produces unfavorable effects on the quality of users' working lives, for example, they might view the system negatively even though it has the potential to enhance their job performance.

EVALUATING PERCEIVED EASE OF USE

Davis et al. (1989, p. 985) define perceived ease of use as "the degree to which the prospective users expect the target system to be free of effort." As with perceived usefulness, perceived ease of use shapes users' attitudes toward a system. Again, if their attitudes are favorable, they are likely to use the system more frequently and more effectively. If their attitudes are unfavorable, however, they are not likely to use the system.

Several items have been used to measure the perceived ease of use of an information system. Davis (1989) has found the following items to be valid and reliable, however:

1. Users perceive that it is easy for them to learn to operate the information system.
2. Users perceive that it is easy for them to get the information system to do what they want it to do.
3. Users perceive that they can interact with the system in a clear and understandable way.
4. Users perceive that interaction with the information system is flexible.
5. Users perceive that they can quickly become skilful with the information system.
6. Users perceive that the information system will be easy to use.

If auditors are seeking to evaluate the perceived ease of use of an information system, as with perceived usefulness they can use these items in a questionnaire or as the basis for any interviews they conduct with users. Moreover, as with perceived usefulness, auditors should be mindful of other factors (like quality-of-working-life effects) that might affect users' perceptions of the ease with which an information system can be used.

EVALUATING COMPUTER SELF-EFFICACY

Compeau and Higgins (1995, p. 192) define computer self-efficacy as "a judgment of one's ability to use a computer." They point out that this judgment is future oriented; in other words, it reflects a person's perceptions of their ability to use computers in the future rather than their perceptions about how they have used computers in the past. Presumably, however, a person's past experiences in using computers affects their perceptions about how they will use computers in the future. Moreover, Compeau and Higgins indicate that computer self-efficacy is intended to reflect broad task competence in using computers rather than straightforward skills competence. In other words, people must not only be able to perform simple tasks like copying files and entering data into spreadsheets, they must also be able to apply these skills to broader tasks such as using a spreadsheet to undertake financial statement analysis.

Several researchers believe that computer self-efficacy is an important variable in accounting for the likely effectiveness of an information system (see, e.g., Ferguson 1997). In this regard, Figure 22–1 shows that computer self-efficacy is predicted to affect users' perceptions of the usefulness of and ease of use of an information system. If users have a poor perception of themselves in terms of their competence to use computers, it is unlikely that they will perceive the output provided by a system to be useful or that the system will be easy to use.

If auditors wish to measure users' computer self-efficacy, they will need some kind of measurement instrument. In this regard, Compeau and Higgins (1995) have developed a questionnaire designed to measure computer self-efficacy. Initial research conducted using the questionnaire indicates that it is valid and reliable. It first asks respondents to consider a new software package designed to assist them with their work. Under various conditions, it then asks them whether they think they could complete their job using the software package and, if they answer yes, how confident they feel in their judgment. Examples of conditions are no one being available to tell users what to do, only the software manuals being available for reference, and the respondent having used a similar package before.

In some cases, computer self-efficacy might not be a major concern in terms of whether an information system is likely to be effective. For example, auditors might be dealing with users who have extensive experience with similar sorts of computer systems to the one they are evaluating. Where such conditions do not exist, however, auditors should be mindful of the impact that users' perceptions of computer self-efficacy might have on the effectiveness of an information system.

EVALUATING INFORMATION SYSTEM USE

If people perceive that an information system is useful and that it is easy to use, research indicates that they will have positive attitudes toward the system. These positive attitudes in turn will translate into favorable intentions toward using the system. Intentions have been shown to be a good predictor of actual use of the system (Davis et al. 1989).

In the interests of simplicity, however, Figure 22–1 does not show the link between perceived usefulness and perceived ease of use of an information system and a user's attitude toward the system, nor does it show the link between attitude and behavioral intention. Rather, we focus instead on how the information system is used. In this regard, the concept of information system usage turns out to be problematical. In the following subsections, we briefly explore various notions of usage.

Voluntary Versus Involuntary Use

Whenever auditors measure information system use, they must be careful to determine whether use is voluntary or involuntary (Figure 22–4). In some systems, users can choose whether they employ a system to help them with the tasks they are performing. In other systems, reports are generated on a routine basis, and users receive the reports unsolicited. Users might also be compelled by management to use the output provided by the information system.

If system use is voluntary, auditors can build monitors into the system to determine unobtrusively how often the system is invoked by users to perform different tasks. If use is involuntary, however, auditors must then attempt to determine whether use is "real" or "apparent." Auditors can try to obtain evidence, for example, on whether system output has actually been employed to undertake a task. Alternatively, they might use interviews or questionnaires to gauge employees' real use of the system. Auditors should take care, however, if they use interviews or questionnaires to obtain data about system use from employees. The results they obtain might not be reliable. Users might not accurately recall how frequently they use a system, for example, or they might overstate frequency of use to gain favor with management.

Amount and Frequency of Use

Auditors can employ amount of use and frequency of use of an information system as a means of trying to establish "how much" the system is used. There are various measures of amount of use that might be helpful. For example, auditors could use the following:

1. Duration of connect time to the system,
2. Number of inquiries made,
3. Number of functions invoked in the system,
4. Number of records accessed in database,
5. Number of reports generated, and
6. Size of chargeout costs for system use.

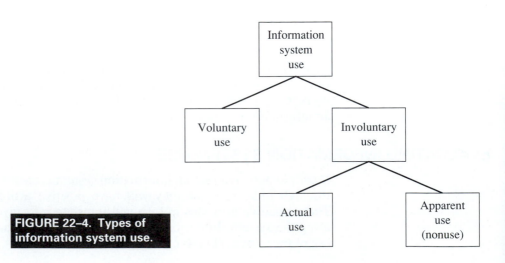

FIGURE 22–4. Types of information system use.

Problems exist with all these measures, however, in terms of establishing the impact of an information system on users. For example, system connect time might be high, but the system might be idle for much of the time that the connection exists. Likewise, connect time might be high because users have little competence in using the system. As a result, they consume excessive resources to produce the output they require.

In light of these problems, frequency of use is sometimes employed as a measure of system use. Frequency of use might be a good indicator of a user's reliance on an information system. If users frequently invoke a system's functionality, presumably they find the system useful in performing their tasks. Indeed, the amount of use (as measured by, say, connect time) might be low because users can quickly accomplish their tasks. Fast but frequent access of the system, however, might still indicate that the system is effective.

Nature of Use

Ginzberg (1978b) has argued that frequency of use is often an inappropriate measure to evaluate system effectiveness. He points to situations in which a system is used infrequently yet it is considered to be successful. For example, the act of building a decision support system could provide important insights into how an ongoing problem should be approached. In this light, users might consider the system to be successful even though their day-to-day use of the system may be low.

As a consequence, Ginzberg (1978b) argues that the overall success of a system must be evaluated in terms of the *way* it is used and not just the frequency of use. The way a system is used evokes different types of change in a user's actions. He identifies four different levels of individual change that can occur:

Level of Change	Explanation
Management action	Users simply treat the system as a black box and use the information or solution to the problem provided by the system.
Management change	Users must have an elementary understanding of the system. They treat the system as a tool that can be applied to find answers to specific problems.
Recurring use of the management science approach	Users develop a fundamental appreciation of the analytical approach used by the system to solve problems. They attempt to apply this analytical approach to other problems.
Task redefinition	The system causes users to rethink their view of the job, the way in which they perform the job, and so on. Users employ the system to help redefine tasks.

Ginzberg (1978a) argues that different types of systems require different types of change (levels of adoption) if they are to be successful. For example, at one extreme, a clerical replacement system such as a payroll system requires only a "management change" level of adoption. At the other extreme, a decision support system for portfolio managers requires a "task redefinition" level of change. Furthermore, he argues that attempting to adopt a level of change other than the one appropriate to the type of system at hand is a waste of effort. In essence, Ginzberg's argument is based on a contingency theory of implementation; namely, successful systems require different levels of adoption depending on the nature of the system (Figure 22–5). He has found evidence to support his argument (Ginzberg 1978a).

Auditors should be careful, therefore, not to conclude that a system has high operational effectiveness solely on the basis of its amount or frequency of

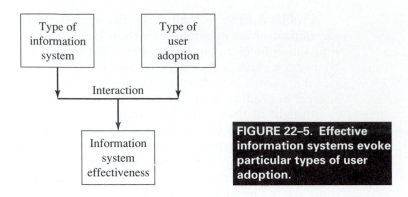

FIGURE 22–5. Effective information systems evoke particular types of user adoption.

use. Ginzberg's research suggests that the level of change brought about by the system also must be examined. In this light, auditors also need to examine the way in which a system is being used to assess its effectiveness.

Source of Use

Auditors might also need to determine *who* uses an information system when they assess its effectiveness. In some cases, users themselves might interact directly with the information system. In other cases, an intermediary might act on their behalf. For example, for some decision support systems that have been developed to facilitate group work, a person called a "chauffeur" is often needed to assist users to work with the system. The chauffeur is an expert in the group decision support system who helps users to "drive" the system. If users interact infrequently with the system, they might need assistance from someone who is familiar with the system to deal with its complexities.

Direct use of a system could be either effective or ineffective. For example, if users need to interact frequently with a system and the user interface is fairly straightforward, auditors might have cause for concern if users employ intermediaries (e.g., secretaries) to undertake their work. This situation might signal that users have not fully come to grips with the system and that they have not properly integrated the system into the work they undertake. On the other hand, if users interact infrequently with a system and a fair level of expertise is required to properly employ the functionality of the system, auditors might be concerned if users are attempting to interact directly with the system themselves. Because of their lack of expertise with the system, they might be wasting time trying to understand how the interface and the system work. Moreover, they might be unable to employ the full power of the system because of their lack of understanding of its functionality.

EVALUATING INDIVIDUAL IMPACT

The impact of an information system on users can be manifested in several ways. Two major types of impacts that auditors need to consider when they assess a system's effectiveness, however, are task accomplishment impacts and quality-of-working-life impacts. In particular, auditors need to remember that an interaction most likely will exist between the two (Figure 22–6). If a system improves users' task accomplishment, it might also improve their quality of working life. For example, they might be more satisfied with their jobs. Similarly, if a system improves users' quality of working life, it may also improve their task accomplishment. For example, if a system allows users greater opportunities to use their abilities on the job, it might improve their task accomplish-

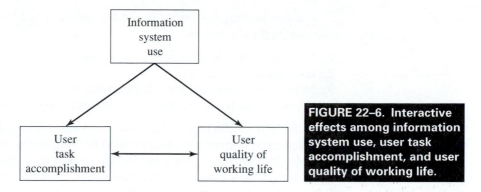

FIGURE 22–6. Interactive effects among information system use, user task accomplishment, and user quality of working life.

ment. On the other hand, if a system produces a negative impact on one, the interaction effects might produce a negative impact on the other. In the following subsections, therefore, we will seek to obtain a better understanding of these two types of outcome.

Task Accomplishment Impacts

An effective information system improves the task accomplishment of its users. The following are some general measures that auditors can use to try to determine whether a user's task accomplishment has improved:

1. Decision accuracy,
2. Time to make decision,
3. Decision confidence,
4. Effectiveness of decision,
5. Quality of product or service produced,
6. Customer satisfaction with product or service produced, and
7. Time to undertake task.

Often, however, auditors need to identify specific measures of task accomplishment to determine whether an information system is effective. Unfortunately, performance measures for task accomplishment differ considerably across applications (and sometimes across organizations).

To illustrate this problem, consider the ways task accomplishment might be assessed for a manufacturing control system, a sales system, and a welfare system that supports counselors in their work. Some measures of task accomplishment that auditors might use for the manufacturing control system follow:

1. Number of units output,
2. Number of defective units reworked,
3. Number of units scrapped,
4. Amount of waste produced,
5. Amount of downtime, and
6. Amount of idle time.

For the sales system, some measures of task accomplishment that auditors might use follow:

1. Dollar value of sales made,
2. Changes in customer satisfaction ratings,
3. Amount of doubtful/bad debts that arise,
4. Average time for delivery of goods to customer,
5. Number of new customers acquired, and
6. Number of sales made to old customers.

For the welfare system, some of the measures of task accomplishment that auditors might use follow:

1. Number of clients successfully counseled,
2. Average cost per client,
3. Number of clients returning for counseling, and
4. Client satisfaction ratings of counseling service provided.

A further problem auditors will encounter when evaluating task accomplishment is to choose a measure that is neither too global nor too detailed. For example, in light of the implementation of a new information system, auditors might decide to monitor whether customers are more satisfied with the services provided by the employees who use the system. They might find, for example, that customer satisfaction has increased. Unfortunately, however, the measure might be too global to provide auditors with insights into why this outcome has occurred. They must take care to choose a measure of customer satisfaction that will allow them to determine why customers are more satisfied and how the system appears to have affected employee task accomplishment to produce high levels of customer satisfaction.

It might also be important for auditors to trace task accomplishment over time. Task accomplishment might improve after the system has been implemented, but it might not persist (Figure 22–7). If system designers have not carried out the process of refreezing (see Chapter 4), for example, users of the system might revert to their old behavior patterns. As a result, the level of task accomplishment might decline, perhaps to levels lower than before the implementation of the system.

Quality of Working Life Impacts

Besides affecting task accomplishment, an information system can also affect its users' quality of working life (see, e.g., Hirschheim 1986; Kraut et al. 1989). Auditors must be mindful of this impact, because important relationships appear to exist between the quality of working life of people and their physical and mental health. For example, research has found associations between the characteristics of work and the incidence of heart disease, peptic ulcers, arthritis, psychosomatic illness, alienation, and suicide among employees. In many countries, the direct and indirect costs of employee ill health are substantial (Greenberg et al. 1995).

FIGURE 22–7. Monitoring task accomplishment over time.

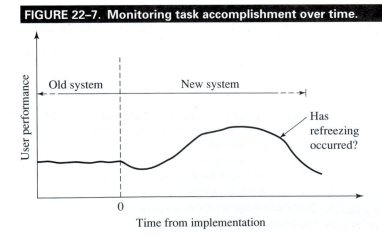

What are the factors that contribute to a high quality of working life? The following are often listed:

Quality of Work Life Attribute	Explanation
Adequate and fair compensation	The income received from work should meet social standards of sufficiency and bear an appropriate relationship to the income received from other work.
Safe and healthy working conditions	The physical work conditions should minimize the risk of illness and injury. There should be limitations on hours worked.
Opportunity to use and develop human capacities	Jobs should provide autonomy, involve both planning and implementation activities, allow use of multiple skills, and be meaningful. Employees should obtain feedback on their actions.
Opportunity for continued growth and security	There must be ongoing opportunities to develop and use new skills. Employment and income security should exist.
Social integration in the work organization	The workplace should be free of prejudice, allow interpersonal openness, and encourage a sense of community.
Constitution in the work organization	The workplace should preserve personal privacy, allow free speech, provide equitable treatment, and allow due process when disputes arise.
Balanced work role and total life space	Work should be integrated with the total life space; e.g., it should not place unreasonable demands on leisure and family time.
Social relevance of work life	Employees should perceive the workplace to be socially responsible.

If auditors try to use these factors to assess the impact of an information system on the quality of working life of its users, they will encounter two problems. First, they will find that different users have different perceptions of what constitutes a high quality of working life. For example, some will consider the quality of working life from a productivity perspective, some from a physical conditions and wages perspective, and some from an alienation perspective. In this light, auditors should recognize the limitations of overall measures of the quality of working life as opposed to measures tailored specifically for individual persons.

Second, it is often difficult to find valid and reliable measurement instruments to assess the quality of working life. One problem that the designers of these instruments face is that somehow their measures must take into account the variation in responses by persons to the same environment. For example, a person who has had several jobs is likely to have a higher level of satisfaction with a particular job than a person who is employed for the first time. The time span for measurement also must be chosen. Employees who are subject to poor working conditions might report a high quality of working life if they have high expectations of better things to come. The measures also must be verifiable and not subject to manipulation. Otherwise, responses could be biased intentionally by a particular person or interest group to further their cause.

Because of these problems, one approach auditors can adopt to assess the quality of working life is to use surrogate measures—that is, measures that act as indicators of the level of the quality of work life existing instead of directly measuring attributes of the quality of working life. Some surrogate measures that have been widely used follow:

$$\text{Absenteeism rate} = \frac{\text{total absent days}}{\text{total working days}}$$

$$\text{Tardiness rate} = \frac{\text{total incidents of tardiness}}{\text{total working days}}$$

$$\text{Strike rate} = \frac{\text{total strike days}}{\text{total working days}}$$

$$\text{Work ban rate} = \frac{\text{total work bans}}{\text{total working days}}$$

$$\text{Stoppage rate} = \frac{\text{total stoppages}}{\text{total working days}}$$

$$\text{Grievance rate} = \frac{\text{total grievances}}{\text{average work force size}}$$

$$\text{Turnover rate} = \frac{\text{total turnover incidents}}{\text{average work force size}}$$

$$\text{Accident rate} = \frac{\text{total accidents}}{\text{total working days}}$$

$$\text{Sick rate} = \frac{\text{total sick days}}{\text{total working days}}$$

$$\text{Theft/sabotage rate} = \frac{\text{total theft/sabotage incidents}}{\text{average work force size}}$$

Changes in these measures manifest changes in the quality of working life. For example, a lowered quality of working life can cause increased turnover of employees or a greater number of strikes. Thus, to assess the effectiveness of an information system, the focus is on how these measures change after the system has been implemented.

There are three advantages of using surrogate measures to assess the quality of working life. First, the measures are objective, verifiable, and difficult to manipulate. If auditors can obtain agreement among stakeholders that they are reasonable indicators of the quality-of-working-life changes that are associated with an information system, they are not likely to then encounter problems with disputes about their accuracy and reliability. Second, the data required for the measures is relatively easy to obtain. Most of the data should be maintained routinely by an organization. For example, the personnel department of the organization should keep records on sickness, absenteeism, and strikes. Third, the cost of changes in the measures can be assessed. For example, the cost of absenteeism can be measured by calculating the cost of wages and fringe benefits of replacement workers, the opportunity cost of profit lost during the replacement process, and the cost of the personnel department's time in dealing with the absenteeism.

The major disadvantage of using surrogate measures is that auditors will not always know why the quality of working life has been lowered or raised by an information system. What attributes of the quality of working life have been affected by the implementation of a system still must be determined. Otherwise, if the quality of working life has been lowered, there is little basis for corrective action. Use of surrogate measures does not alleviate an auditor's need, therefore, to investigate cause-effect relationships.

EVALUATING INFORMATION SYSTEM SATISFACTION

Information system satisfaction has been a widely used measure in research that has been undertaken to try to determine those factors that affect the success of an information system (see, further, DeLone and McLean 1992). The underlying assumption has been that users will be satisfied with a system that is effective. Figure 22–1 indicates, however, that the relationships between information system effectiveness and information system satisfaction sometimes might be complex. Presumably, information system satisfaction will be affected by the amount of and nature of information system use. Users' interactions with a system are likely to affect how they feel about the system. If they feel positively about the system, presumably they will be more motivated to use the system to improve their task accomplishment. They will also consider their quality of working life to have improved. At the same time, the direct effects of an information system on users' task accomplishment and quality of working life are likely to affect their satisfaction with an information system. If the system undermines their quality of working life, for example, they are unlikely to have favorable attitudes toward the system.

Several instruments to measure information system satisfaction have been developed that auditors might use during an audit to evaluate the effectiveness of an information system (see, e.g., Ives et al. 1983; Doll and Torkzadeh 1988; and Seddon and Yip 1992). Some examples of the types of items included in these instruments are the following:

1. Relationships with information system staff,
2. Processing of system change requests,
3. Timeliness of information,
4. Level of information system training provided to users,
5. Relevance of output,
6. Amount of output,
7. Quality of documentation provided, and
8. Dependability of the information system.

The users of an information system are then asked to rate how satisfied or dissatisfied they are with these items.

Whenever auditors use an instrument to measure information system satisfaction, however, they need to consider whether they should tailor the instrument to the specific type of information system they are evaluating. Instruments that have been developed for a batch general ledger system, for example, might not provide valid and reliable measures of user satisfaction with a decision support system. Although questions about user satisfaction with the interactive features of the latter system are likely to be important, these same questions most likely will be irrelevant in the context of user satisfaction with the former system.

Auditors should note, also, that the distinction between information system satisfaction and other measures like perceived usefulness and perceived ease of use of an information system is not clear-cut. Some of the items included in published instruments for measuring information system satisfaction are similar to those included in instruments to measure perceived usefulness and perceived ease of use of an information system. When auditors evaluate the effectiveness of an information system, therefore, they need to be circumspect about the potential overlap between measures.

EVALUATING ORGANIZATIONAL IMPACT

If an information system has a positive impact on the people who use it, presumably it will also have a positive impact on the organization in which these people are members. The relationship between the impact on people and the impact on their organization, however, is not straightforward. People might become more efficient in performing their jobs, for example, but they still might not contribute significantly to the attainment of the organization's overall goals.

In the following subsections we examine the potential impact of an information system on an organization from two perspectives: first, from the viewpoint of its impact on the overall effectiveness of the organization; and second, from the viewpoint of its impact on economic effectiveness. The latter impact is simply one aspect of the former impact. However, often auditors will be asked to give particular attention to the economic impacts of an information system. Moreover, some difficult issues arise when evaluating the economic impact of an information system.

Organizational Effectiveness

What are (should be) the goals of a high-quality information system? This question turns out to be a frustrating and difficult one to answer. One possible response is that the overall objective of an information system is to increase the effectiveness of the organization it services. This response simply shifts the problem, however, for the next question we must ask is this: What are the goals of an effective organization? The goals of an information system and the goals of the organization it serves are inextricably intertwined. Information systems are developed to help an organization meet its goals. Thus, whether or not a system is effective must be assessed in terms of organizational goals.

Unfortunately, little consensus exists on what constitute the goals of an organization. When Steers (1977) undertook a review of the literature on organizational effectiveness, for example, he found that many different types of indicators had been used to measure goal accomplishment. They included measures of profitability, growth, turnover, absenteeism, job satisfaction, stability, flexibility, morale, and readiness. We might debate whether some of these indicators measure goal accomplishment or the state of factors that affect goal accomplishment. For example, economists might argue that ultimately the effectiveness of organizations is solely a function of their profitability. Factors like turnover, stability, readiness, and absenteeism all affect profitability. An organizational theorist might argue, however, that profitability is too gross a measure of effectiveness for it to be especially useful. Managers need to understand how well their organizations are performing on the factors that ultimately could affect profitability, such as the ability of the organization to adapt to changes in its environment and the quality of working life of its employees.

Long ago, organizational theorists recognized that the effectiveness of an organization could be evaluated from multiple, sometimes conflicting, perspectives. For example, in the 1970s, Cunningham (1977) identified seven different approaches to evaluating organizational effectiveness, all of which are still widely accepted today (see, e.g., Daft 1995):

Evaluation Approach	*Explanation*
Rational goal model	Evaluates the organization's ability to achieve its formally stated goals.
Systems resource model	Evaluates how well the organization distributes resources to meet the needs of its various subsystems.

Evaluation Approach	*Explanation*
Managerial process model	Evaluates the organization's ability to perform various managerial functions that facilitate achieving the overall goals.
Organizational development model	Evaluates how well the organization allows members to model their own goals and how well it facilitates their working as a team.
Bargaining model	Evaluates how well decision makers within the organization can obtain the resources they need to accomplish the tasks they deem important.
Structural functional model	Evaluates how well the organization can respond to a variety of situations and events.
Functional model	Evaluates the usefulness of the organization's activities from the viewpoint of its stakeholder groups.

An important model of organizational effectiveness, however, has been proposed by Quinn and Rohrbaugh (1983) and Quinn and Cameron (1983). This model, called the *competing values model*, has two dimensions of organizational effectiveness: a focus dimension and a structure dimension (Figure 22–8). In terms of *focus*, organizations can pursue goals that address either *external concerns*, such as pressure from shareholders and environmental lobbyists, or *internal concerns*, such as the well-being of employees and the level of morale within the organization. In terms of *structure*, organizations can pursue goals that address either *flexibility concerns*, such as environmental monitoring and maintaining readiness for change, or *stability concerns*, such as maintaining control over operations.

The competing values model underscores the difficulties that exist in terms of how organizations often have to pursue different goals to survive.

FIGURE 22–8. Competing values model of organizational effectiveness.

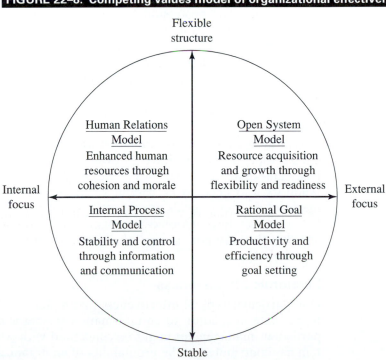

Somehow, management must balance these goals so that pursuit of one does not substantially undermine another to the point where the organization is unable to survive. Indeed, Cameron (1986) argues that an important characteristic of effective organizations is the way they manage paradox. Somehow they achieve goals concurrently that are in conflict with one another—for example, high specialization of roles to achieve efficiencies and at the same time high generalization of roles to achieve flexibility. Moreover, the emphasis that management needs to give to one set of goals versus another set might vary throughout the life of an organization. For example, a young organization might place more emphasis on flexibility and innovation and less emphasis on profitability. A mature organization, on the other hand, might place more emphasis on profitability and control and less emphasis on human-resource issues.

When auditors evaluate the effectiveness of an information system, therefore, they need to frame their evaluation in the context of the goals that the stakeholders in the information system are seeking to pursue. It will not be helpful, for example, if auditors evaluate an information system on the basis of how much it has contributed to productivity when its stakeholders' goals are more oriented toward promoting flexibility and openness within an organization. Such an evaluation could be misleading, if not useless.

Auditors need to recognize, also, that the goals held by stakeholders in relation to an information system may be both overt and covert. In other words, they might be stated formally or at least discussed openly and perhaps agreed upon by the stakeholders in the system. Alternatively, they might not be articulated formally or discussed openly, perhaps because of the political damage that might accrue. For example, management might have a covert goal to gain more control over employees, which might cause major difficulties with a union if it were to be articulated openly.

The importance of different goals among different stakeholder could also vary, and in some case the goals might even conflict with one another. For example, a group of donors to a charitable organization might view the effectiveness of an information system in terms of how well it permits efficient use of scarce funds. The professionals who work within the charitable organization, however, might be more concerned with how well the information system permits them to provide services to their clients.

In summary, whenever auditors evaluate the impact of an information system on an organization, they have to take great care at the outset to reach a good understanding of the important stakeholders in the information system and the goals they have for the system (both overt and covert). If auditors do not have a sound understanding of the stakeholders and their goals, the usefulness of their effectiveness evaluation will be undermined. Auditors need to recognize that they could have to evaluate an information system on multiple bases and that sometimes these bases might be incongruous with one another. Auditors also need to be careful whenever they make judgments about the merits of one set of goals over another set of goals. These judgments might reflect that they have adopted the perspective of one group of stakeholders only and that they are not "seeing" the system from the viewpoints of other groups of stakeholders.

Economic Effectiveness

One particular type of effectiveness that management is likely to ask auditors to evaluate in relation to an information system is economic effectiveness. In particular, management might be concerned with whether an information system has contributed to the profitability of an organization.

Evaluating the economic effectiveness of information systems has proved to be an especially difficult task. During the late 1980s and early 1990s, for example, several researchers pointed to a phenomenon that they called the "productivity paradox" (see, e.g., Brynjolfsson 1993). They observed that organizations were continuing to invest large sums of money in information technology. When they tried to identify the payoffs that organizations were obtaining from this investment, however, they were unable to determine whether any had materialized. The question they asked, therefore, was why organizations were continuing to undertake seemingly irrational behavior—namely, investing in information technology when little or no payoffs were evident.

Hitt and Brynjolfsson (1996) have pointed out how the productivity paradox might be resolved. Whenever we evaluate the impact of investments in information technology, they argue we must address three separate but interrelated questions:

1. Has an investment in information technology increased *productivity* within an organization?
2. Has an investment in information technology increased *profitability* within an organization?
3. Has an investment in information technology created *value for consumers*?

Hitt and Brynjolfsson (1996) present evidence that investments in information technology often produce payoffs in terms of productivity and value for consumers but not in terms of organizational profitability. In other words, the benefits of using information technology can be captured in terms of outcomes like employees performing their tasks more efficiently and customers being provided with higher-quality products and services. An organization might have no increase in profitability, however, as a result of its investments in information technology. The reason is that profitability gains from improved productivity and increased consumer value are quickly competed away. When one organization uses information technology in innovative ways, other organizations often can quickly copy these innovations. As a result, the profitability payoffs obtained from the use of information technology by the innovating organization are short-lived. Nonetheless, if an organization were not to invest in information technology, it might find that its competitive position is eroded. Eventually, it could go out of business. In short, management might have no option but to invest in information technology if they want to stay in business, even though these investments might produce no improvement in profitability.

Auditors must be careful, therefore, when approaching the evaluation of economic effectiveness for an information system. In particular, they need to address the three questions asked previously. They might have to point out to management why investments in information technology are important, even though there is no payoff in terms of improved profitability.

In principle, however, there are four steps auditors should seek to undertake when they evaluate the economic effectiveness of an information system:

Step 1: Identify the benefits of the information system

In light of our previous discussion, identifying the benefits of an information system can be a difficult task. Are the benefits manifested in improved productivity, improved profitability, or improved value for consumer? To some extent, also, the benefits will depend on the nature of the information system. For example, some of the benefits derived from an information system developed to support welfare counselors would be different from those

TABLE 22–1 Some Tangible Benefits and Costs of an Information System

Benefits	*Costs*
Cost savings	Implementation costs
Labor	Hardware/software purchases
Fewer needed	System development costs
More productive	Labor: System analysis and programming
Machines	Hardware usage and supplies
Fewer needed	Documentation
More productive	Overhead
Overhead	Ongoing operational costs
Revenue increases	Hardware usage and supplies
More sales of existing	Labor
products	Program maintenance
Expanded markets	Operations personnel
	Clerical support
	Overhead

derived from an information system developed to support a manufacturing process. Likewise, some of the benefits derived from implementing a strategic information system would be different from those derived from implementing a transaction-based information system (see, for example, Weill and Olson 1989).

The benefits obtained from implementing an information system also might be tangible (see Table 22–1) or intangible. For example, the system might reduce production costs (a tangible benefit), or it might enhance employee morale (an intangible benefit). In particular, auditors need to attend to the externalities or spillover effects that sometimes can occur with information systems. For example, assume an organization implements an advanced information system. It might then be able to hire better information systems staff because people are attracted to the job challenges that arise in having to work with the advanced system.

To facilitate identifying benefits, auditors might classify users according to whether they are considered to be primary or secondary users of the system and internal or external to the organization. Figure 22–9 shows this approach, for example, with an order-entry system. Auditors might then try to identify the tangible and intangible benefits for each type of user.

FIGURE 22–9. Classification of information system users for an order-entry system.

		Location of user	
		Internal	External
Type of user	Primary	e.g., Order-entry clerk	e.g., Customer
	Secondary	e.g., Marketing manager	e.g., Taxation authority

Step 2: Identify the costs of the information system

Two major types of costs arise with information systems: implementation costs and ongoing operational costs. Implementation costs include the cost of any new hardware and software that must be purchased, labor costs associated with system development work, hardware usage and supply costs associated with program compilations and tests, and documentation costs associated with the preparation of user help facilities. The ongoing operational costs include charges for computer time and supplies, system maintenance costs, and clerical support costs associated with data capture, data preparation, and operational running of the system.

As with benefits, costs might be tangible (see Table 22–1) or intangible. For example, the cost of having to purchase additional hardware is tangible, whereas the costs of any increased stress placed on users because of their interactions with the system is an intangible cost. Moreover, to assist auditors to identify costs, again they might find it useful to divide users into primary or secondary users and internal or external users. As with benefits, externalities or spillovers could also be important. For example, because of the demands placed on clerical support staff by an information system, they might be less able to support another system within an organization.

Step 3: Value the benefits and costs of the information system

When the individual benefits and costs have been identified, auditors must then value them. In some cases, valuing benefits and costs is straightforward. For example, reductions in the costs of producing a good or providing a service might be easy to determine, or the costs of operating a system might be readily apparent from the invoices submitted by the outsourcing company that operates the system. In some cases, however, valuing benefits and costs may be difficult. For example, auditors might find it hard to value the benefits associated with the increased organizational flexibility that the system has provided or the costs associated with additional stresses that the system has placed upon employees.

Often auditors must rely on the users of an information system to assist them with valuing the benefits and costs of the system. If users cannot estimate the value of a benefit or cost directly, several techniques can be used to assist them with the valuation. First, auditors might attempt to break the benefit or cost down into smaller components. Users might be able to value the smaller components more easily, and the overall valuation can then be determined as a function of the valuation of these smaller components. Second, auditors might attempt to simulate a market situation and ask users how much they would be willing to pay an outside vendor to obtain the benefit or to alleviate the cost. A market analogy might help them estimate the value of the benefit or cost. Third, auditors might provide users with a listing of both tangible and intangible benefits and costs and ask users to rank order the benefits and costs according to their value. Because values can then be attached to the tangible benefits and costs, it might then be possible to estimate values of the intangible benefits and costs more easily. Fourth, auditors might ask users for a range of value estimates—for example, the most optimistic value, the most pessimistic value, and the most likely value. A simulation approach might then be used to determine whether the decision on the economic effectiveness of the system changes under the different values. Finally, it is sometimes worth deferring the valuation of intangibles until after the tangibles have been valued. For some systems, it might become clear that the decision on the economic effectiveness of the system will not be affected by the value of the intangibles.

Step 4: Determine the net present value of the information system

When the benefits and costs of an information system have been estimated, auditors can then determine the net present value of the system using the formula:

$$NPV = \sum_{t=0}^{n} \frac{B_t - C_t}{(1 + k)^t}$$

where B_t = benefits of the information system in period t
C_t = costs of information system in period t
n = life of information system in periods
k = required rate of return

As discussed in Chapter 21, k is determined using the formula:

$$k = k_f + \beta(\bar{k}_m - k_f)$$

where k_f = risk-free rate of return
$\bar{k}_m$ = expected rate of return on the market portfolio
β = beta coefficient of an "appropriate" security

Estimating β is a problem. Recall from Chapter 21 that conceptually it is estimated by regressing the returns on a security of an organization involved in designing, implementing, and marketing information systems of the type being considered with the returns on the market portfolio. Of course, it is probably impossible for us find such an organization. In this light, we have to estimate β using other means.

Remember that the net present value auditors estimate using these formulas is an *expected* value. Because the benefits and costs of the information system are uncertain, the net present value is also uncertain. The variance of the probability distribution over the net present values is an important indicator of the risk involved in investing in the information system.

SUMMARY

The evaluation of system effectiveness involves determining how well a system meets its objectives. The process involves six steps: *(1)* identifying the objectives of the information system, *(2)* selecting the measures to be used, *(3)* identifying data sources, *(4)* obtaining *ex ante* values for the measures, *(5)* obtaining *ex post* values for the measures, and *(6)* assessing the impact of the system by comparing the *ex post* and *ex ante* values of the measures.

To structure our approach to the evaluation of system effectiveness and to help us to understand why a system might be effective or ineffective, we need a model of the factors that are thought to affect system effectiveness and the relationships among these factors. In this chapter, we have used one such model and studied the nature of, measurement of, and relationships among its components. In this model, the quality of a system and the quality of the information it produces are hypothesized to affect whether users perceive the system to be both useful and easy to use. In addition, users' perceptions about their self-efficacy with computers will also affect whether they perceive the system to be both useful and easy to use. Users' perceptions about the usefulness and ease of use of the system will in turn affect how they use the system—for example, their frequency of use and nature of use. The ways in which users use the system will affect their performance in their organizational roles and the overall performance of the organization. Their use of the system will also affect the satisfaction they have with the system, which in turn will have an impact on their performance in using the system.

When undertaking an evaluation of the components of this model, auditors must recognize that different stakeholders in an information system will have different perspectives on how well each component is being achieved. For example, different users might have different views on how well a system is enabling them to undertake their organizational role, depending on the particular task objectives they have for the system and their perceptions of how the system has affected their quality of working life. Similarly, different managers might have different views of how well a system is helping their organization to achieve its objectives, depending on what objectives they see as being most relevant for their organization.

Auditors must also recognize that it is sometimes difficult to identify where the benefits and costs from implementing an information system have occurred. For example, information systems often have no payoffs in terms of improved profitability for an organization. The organization might be more productive, however, and consumers might capture more value from the products and services produced by the organization. The difficulty faced by the organization is that any profitability gains from the information system are quickly competed away. If it does not invest in the information system, however, it might go out of business because it is not competitive.

Review Questions

22-1 Not all information systems are subjected to a postimplementation review. Identify one factor that *increases* the probability of a system undergoing postimplementation review and one factor that *decreases* the probability of a system undergoing postimplementation review. Briefly justify your answer.

22-2 List the *six* major steps to be undertaken when evaluating an information system to assess its effectiveness.

22-3 In the model of information system effectiveness we have used in this chapter, which components are affected by the following components?
  a System quality
  b Perceived ease of use
  c Computer self-efficacy
  d Individual impact
  e Information system satisfaction

22-4 From an auditor's viewpoint, what are the *two* major purposes of the model of system effectiveness described in the chapter?

22-5 Give *four* measures of system quality.

22-6 How might the history of adaptive maintenance for a system affect our assessment of its quality?

22-7 How does the level of resource independence in an information system affect our assessment of its quality?

22-8 Give *four* measures of information quality. Why might different users of an information system have different perceptions about the quality of the information provided by the system?

22-9 What is meant by the perceived usefulness of an information system? Give *four* measures of perceived usefulness.

22-10 How is perceived usefulness distinguished from perceived ease of use of an information system? Give *four* measures of perceived ease of use of an information system.

22-11 What is meant by computer self-efficacy? Is computer self-efficacy always likely to be a concern when assessing information system effectiveness?

22-12 Why is it important that auditors distinguish between voluntary and involuntary use when assessing the effectiveness of an information system? How might they identify involuntary use of an information system?

22–13 Is frequency of use always a good measure of the effectiveness of an information system? Briefly explain.

22–14 Briefly explain why auditors should assess the nature of the use made by different users of an information system when seeking to evaluate the effectiveness of the information system. What type of change (level of adoption) should the following systems evoke if they are to be operationally effective:

a Inventory reordering system

b Accounts receivable system

c System designed to assist short-term money market operators with their investment decisions

22–15 How might the source of use of an information system impact an auditor's evaluation of its effectiveness?

22–16 Give *four* general measures that auditors might use to assess the impact of an information system on the task accomplishment of its users. Why might auditors have to adapt these measures in light of the particular type of information system whose effectiveness they are evaluating?

22–17 Why might auditors need to trace task accomplishment over time when they evaluate the effectiveness of an information system?

22–18 "Auditors are concerned with controls, not the quality of working life in an organization! That should be left to the personnel people in the organization." Briefly discuss.

22–19 Briefly explain why different groups in an organization might assess their quality of working life differently. When evaluating the effectiveness of an information system, whose viewpoint on the quality of working life should auditors adopt when evaluating the effectiveness of the system?

22–20 Briefly explain the meaning of the following attributes of the quality of working life:

a Opportunity to use and develop human capacities

b Social integration in the work force

c Constitution in the work organization

22–21 Why might auditors have to use surrogate measures to assess the impact of an information system on the quality of working life of its users? Give three surrogate measures that auditors might employ and explain briefly how they might be useful.

22–22 Give *one* major advantage of using a surrogate measure of the quality of working life. Give *one* major disadvantage.

22–23 Briefly explain how user information system satisfaction and user task accomplishment might be related when auditors evaluate the effectiveness of an information system.

22–24 Briefly explain the nature of each of the following approaches to evaluating organization effectiveness:

a Rational goal model approach

b Systems resource model approach

c Managerial process model approach

d Organizational development model approach

e Bargaining model approach

f Structural functional model approach

g Functional model approach

22–25 Briefly explain the nature of the competing values model approach to assessing organizational effectiveness. What relevance does this model have in terms of an auditor's assessment of the effectiveness of an information system?

22–26 What is meant by the "productivity paradox" in relation to investment in information systems?

22–27 Why is it important that auditors evaluate the economic effectiveness of an organization's information system in terms of:
  a Changes in productivity in the organization
  b Changes in the organization's profitability
  c Changes in the value of products and services to the organization's customers

22–28 Briefly describe two techniques that auditors might use to identify the benefits and costs associated with an information system.

22–29 Briefly describe two techniques that auditors might use to value the benefits associated with an information system.

Multiple-Choice Questions

22–1 Which of the following steps *most likely* will be undertaken first when evaluating the effectiveness of an information system?
  a Identify the objectives of the information system
  b Identify the sources of effectiveness data
  c Select the effectiveness measures to be used
  d Obtain the *ex ante* values of effectiveness

22–2 Which of the following is *least likely* to be an important association that auditors would find when conducting an evaluation of information system effectiveness?
  a Between computer self-efficacy and perceived ease of use
  b Between perceived system quality and perceived usefulness
  c Between system quality and computer self-efficacy
  d Between perceived usefulness and type of use

22–3 Which of the following is *least likely* to be used as a measure of system quality during the conduct of an evaluation of information system effectiveness?
  a Turnaround time
  b Extent of adaptive maintenance
  c Ease of interaction
  d Authenticity of information

22–4 Which of the following is *least likely* to be used as a measure of information quality during the conduct of an evaluation of information system effectiveness?
  a Timeliness
  b Comprehensibility
  c Usefulness of functionality
  d Precision

22–5 The perceived usefulness of an information system has been defined as the prospective user's subjective probability that using the system will increase his or her:
  a Job performance within an organizational context
  b Quality of working life within an organizational context
  c Satisfaction within a job context
  d Computer self-efficacy within a job context

22–6 Which of the following is *least likely* to affect users' perception of the ease of use of an information system?
  a Time required for them to learn to operate the system
  b Level of effort required for them to become skilful with the system
  c Increased ease with which they can undertake the tasks associated with their job
  d Ability to interact with the system in a clear and understandable way

22-7 Which of the following statements about computer self-efficacy is *least likely* to be *true*?
  a It manifests a person's judgment of his or her ability to use a computer
  b A person's judgment of his or her computer self-efficacy is primarily future oriented
  c It is less likely to be important when people are experienced users of an information system
  d It pertains primarily to a person's ability to undertake simple tasks using a computer

22-8 Frequency of use is *most likely* to be a more reliable indicator of information system effectiveness than amount of use when:
  a The ratio of idle time to connect time is low
  b Users have a high level of competence in using the system
  c Users can accomplish their tasks quickly
  d System use is voluntary rather than involuntary

22-9 Which of the following levels of change will a decision support system developed to facilitate top management's strategic decision making have to evoke for it to be successful:
  a Management action
  b Management change
  c Recurring use of the management science approach
  d Task redefinition

22-10 The management change level of adoption requires users of an information system to:
  a Treat the system as a black box and use the information or solution to the problem provided by the system
  b Have an elementary understanding of the system so it can be used as a tool to find answers to specific problems
  c Rethink their view of their job and the way in which they perform their job
  d Develop a fundamental appreciation of the analytical approach used by the system to solve a problem

22-11 Which of the following is *least likely* to be a valid and reliable measure of task accomplishment for the users of a system?
  a User satisfaction with a decision
  b Time required to undertake a decision
  c Accuracy of a decision
  d Effectiveness of a decision

22-12 Which of the following is *least likely* to be a problem when measuring changes to the quality of working life subsequent to the implementation of an information system?
  a Different groups within an organization have a vested interest in how the quality of working life is defined
  b Users are unlikely to be forthcoming in terms of how an information system has affected their quality of working life
  c Few instruments with high validity and reliability are available to be able to measure changes to the quality of working life
  d Employees could inflate their ratings of the quality of working life if they have expectations of better things to come

22-13 Which of the following is used as a surrogate measure when attempting to evaluate the level of the quality of working life?
  a Strike rate
  b Adequacy of compensation provided
  c Level of safety in the workplace
  d Level of opportunities for personal growth

22–14 A disadvantage of using a surrogate measure to assess the level of the quality of working life is that:

    a The measure is neither objective nor verifiable

    b The data supporting the measure is difficult to obtain

    c The underlying reasons for any changes to the level of the quality of working life identified via the measure are difficult to determine

    d Surrogate measures are not available for every direct measure

22–15 Which of the following best describes the "productivity paradox" associated with information technology?

    a Organizations have continued to invest large amounts of money in information technology without any apparent payoffs

    b Returns from investments in information technology appear to be monotonically increasing over time

    c The highest returns from investments in information technology do not always go to the first users of the technology

    d Unlike many other types of investments, few externalities seem to be associated with investments in information technology

22–16 Payoffs from investments in information technology are *least likely* to occur in relation to:

    a Profitability

    b Value for consumers

    c Productivity

    d Cost reductions

22–17 Which of the following is an operational cost of an information system?

    a Purchase of system software

    b Perfective maintenance on programs

    c Preparation of user manuals

    d System analysis time devoted to information requirements analysis

22–18 Spillover effects are:

    a The extra overhead costs incurred because the limits on the size of a direct access file have been exceeded

    b The unanticipated costs that arise in other information systems by virtue of the implementation of a particular information system

    c Any intangible benefit that arises as a result of using an information system

    d The error introduced into the cost-benefit analysis of an information system when the cost of capital is not taken into account

22–19 Which of the following strategies is *more likely* to facilitate a user estimating the value of intangible benefits?

    a Lump all intangible benefits together and try to come up with an overall value

    b Try to identify a similar system that has already been implemented and determine the value of intangible benefits in that system

    c Group similar tangible and intangible benefits together and estimate the value of the group

    d Provide users with a listing of both tangible and intangible benefits and ask users to rank order the benefits according to their value

22–20 The net present value of an information system must be determined by discounting the benefits and costs by the required rate of return. To determine the required rate of return, the parameter, β, must be estimated by:

    a Determining the mean of the risk-free rate of return

    b Determining the variance of the rate of return on the market portfolio

    c Regressing the return on the security of an organization that designs and implements systems of the type being considered with the returns on the market portfolio

    d Regressing the return on the security of the organization designing and implementing the system with the return on the market portfolio

Exercises and Cases

22–1 You have recently been appointed as the manager of internal audit for a large private university. One of the important tasks you have been asked to undertake is a regular, periodic evaluation of the effectiveness of the major information systems used within the university.

A critical system within the university is the student records system. It was one of the first online real-time update systems developed about 15 years ago by the university's administrative information systems department. It is used frequently by many staff within the university.

During your evaluation of the system, you are perplexed by some seemingly contradictory findings. On the basis of your examination of the system, you conclude that the quality of the system is low. The system provides a reasonable response time, and it is reliable and stable. Moreover, users comment that it provides good functionality. The user interface seems very unfriendly, however, and virtually no documentation and help facilities are provided with the system. The system is also poorly integrated with other systems, and it is based on proprietary rather than open-systems technology. Given the age of the system, the maintenance costs associated with the system are also relatively high.

When you interview users to determine the quality of information provided by the system, they indicate that it is high; the information is accurate, complete, timely, relevant, and so on. When you measure users' perceptions of the usefulness of the system, they again give the system a high rating. They give only a moderate rating, however, when you measure their perceptions of how easy the system is to use. Nonetheless, you are surprised even by this rating because you would have rated ease of use to be very low based on your observations of the system.

Required: You have been asked to work with the manager of the university's administrative information systems department to determine those systems that need to be redesigned and rewritten. On the basis of the information you have collected, what do you think your recommendations will be in relation to the student records system? Can you explain some of the seemingly contradictory findings that you have obtained in relation to the system?

22–2 The Hi-Strung Manufacturing Company (HSM) is a large manufacturer of a range of specialized products to support the electricity industry. It has 27 departments, each of which is given substantial autonomy to manage its financial affairs.

To date, HSM has used a batch financial reporting system for its departments. At the end of each week, the departmental managers receive financial reports from the information systems department. There reports are intended to assist the departmental managers to exercise control over their own departments.

HSM is about to implement a new computer system that will allow departments to input their own financial data and to obtain various reports that can be used to assist in running a department. The project team is intending to cease operation of the old financial system at the end of the next two months and to commence operation of the new system immediately at the changeover date.

A major task now facing the project team is to undertake training of HSM's departmental staff who will operate and use the new computer system. While some managerial level personnel will be involved, most direct users of the system will be clerical staff. About 100 staff will require training with the new system.

To conduct the training, the project team plans to carry out five group training sessions, each of which will involve about 20 users of the new system. Each group will receive two days of training: one day prior to the system coming online; and a second day after the system has been operational for one month. The first day's training will introduce users to the basic functionality provided within the system. It will also show them the online help facilities that are available within the system. The second day's training will introduce users to some of the more advanced features of the system after they have gained basic familiarity with the system. It will also allow them to address any concerns they have in light of their first month's experience with the system.

For the first two months' operation of the system, the project team also plans to set up a special help desk in the information systems department to assist users with any difficulties they encounter with the system. Users will be able to phone this help desk to get assistance when they encounter difficulties in using the system.

You are the manager of internal audit with HSM. In light of the impending implementation of the new financial system, you receive a visit from HSM's controller. She expresses concern about the adequacy of training proposed for the new system. She points out that many of the clerical staff who will be involved with the new system have little or no experience with computers. She also perceives that many are reluctant to use computers. In this light, she asks your opinion on whether you believe the training proposed for the system will lead to effective use of the system.

Required: Write a brief report indicating any concerns you have about the proposed training approach for the new system. Briefly indicate some ways in which you believe these concerns could be mitigated.

22–3 Two years ago, the director-general (chief executive officer) of a large state government department in Australia took a decision to introduce executive information systems (EISs) within her department. With major cutbacks to funding of her department having occurred, she was searching for ways to improve the effectiveness and efficiency of her management team and thereby to improve the overall performance of her department.

To develop and implement the EISs, she engaged a consulting firm who specialized in EISs. For the first 12 months, the consultants worked closely with her management team. They started out with just two managers who were excited about the potential of EIS within the department. Initially they built small EISs to support the most pressing needs of these managers. Using a prototyping approach, they gradually modified these EISs in light of feedback from the managers. They then expanded the capabilities of these EISs as the two managers become more comfortable with using an EIS to support their daily work.

The consultants then took a fairly low-key approach to introducing additional EISs into the department. They relied on the two managers who had first gained experience with an EIS to "sell" the concept of EIS to their colleagues. Over the course of the first year, almost all the other members of the senior management team requested that an EIS be built for them. At the outset the take-up was slow, and there were also a few "laggards." Eventually, however, all the managers requested that an EIS be built for them.

You are the manager of internal audit in the state government department where the EISs have been introduced. The director-general has now asked you to undertake an evaluation of how effective the implementation of EISs has been within her department. She is particularly concerned to determine whether the EISs have improved the effectiveness of her senior management team.

Required: Briefly describe the critical data you believe you need to collect to allow you to prepare a report for the Director-General. Outline the approach you would use to reach a judgment on whether the EISs have been effective. Be sure to point out any areas where you believe special care will be needed in determining whether the EISs have been effective.

22–4 Pacific Networking Links Ltd. (PNL) is a large Brisbane-based developer of advanced networking software for the worldwide market in open-system architectures. The company is divided into ten major departments, based around particular products and services that it offers to customers. Over its 15-year life, the success of the company has varied considerably. It is generally agreed by market analysts that PNL operates a high-risk business. Nonetheless, the returns provided to shareholders on average have compensated them for the risks they take.

At a recent meeting of the senior management team, the managing director has pointed out a concern raised by a member of the board of directors about the increasing levels of hardware investment within PNL. The board member had asked why the increased investments in hardware had not been accompanied by increased levels of profitability for PNL. He asked the managing director to determine the reasons why the extra investments in hardware were necessary and to prepare a report for the board.

When the managing director undertook an investigation to try to find out the reasons for the hardware investments, he found out that they were motivated primarily by the need to service the exponential growth of e-mail use and World Wide Web use by PNL's employees. In addition, PNL had established an extensive set of Web pages about its own operations, and these pages were receiving a high number of hits from Web users who were scattered throughout the world.

When the board received the managing director's report, several members immediately expressed grave concerns about the effectiveness of PNL's use of e-mail and the World Wide Web. For example, they asked whether employees were over-communicating among themselves and with people outside PNL and whether they were spending too much time "surfing the Web" for no real gain. The board also asked whether the Web pages that PNL had established had produced any payoffs in terms of additional sales of products and services. In this light, the board has now asked the managing director to prepare a report on the effectiveness of PNL's use of e-mail and the World Wide Web. Some members of the board have already indicated that they believe that e-mail and World Wide Web access should be restricted and perhaps limited to only one or two hours in the day.

At the meeting of the senior management team, several managers have expressed their alarm about the possibility of the board restricting use of e-mail and World Wide Web use within PNL. They argue that the activities of their staff will be severely impaired. The managing director points out, however, that beliefs will not be enough to convince the board. Several members of the board are astute users of computer technology themselves, and they want hard facts on whether PNL's use of e-mail and World Wide Web services is effective.

You are an external consultant engaged by PNL's managing director to investigate the issue of whether PNL's use of e-mail and World Wide Web services is effective. You have a substantial reputation for your high-quality work and your independence in terms of examining the effectiveness of information systems. Your report will be presented to the board. In this light, the managing director has asked you to focus in particular on the impact of PNL's use of e-mail and World Wide Web services on the overall effectiveness of the organization.

Required: Outline the major areas that will be the focus of your investigation of the effectiveness of PNL's use of e-mail and World Wide Web services. In discussing your approach, be sure to remember that effectiveness can be evaluated from multiple perspectives.

22–5 Australasian Life Insurers Ltd. (ALI) is a large Melbourne-based life insurance company that sells life insurance throughout Australia, New Zealand, and Southeast Asia. Four years ago, a new chief executive officer (CEO) was appointed to ALI. He had previously been a senior executive with many years of experience in another life insurance company, and he had acquired a reputation for foresight and innovativeness. The Board of ALI had directed him specifically to change the image of ALI and to improve ALI's profitability as quickly as possible. Over the years, ALI had acquired the image of a conservative insurance company that was a follower rather than a leader. There also had been little change in the return on investment provided to shareholders. Given the increasing competitiveness of the insurance industry, ALI's Board felt that this situation could no longer continue.

The new CEO immediately embarked upon some major business process reengineering projects. In particular, he argued that customers wanted to be able to contact ALI and to deal with only one person who could service all their needs. He spoke vehemently against the existing arrangements whereby employees specialized in various areas of insurance and, as a result, customers were passed around to those employees who knew most about the insurance product or service they required.

When the CEO described the changes he wanted to undertake, there was fierce resistance from many employees. They argued that ALI had a market niche because it could provide highly specialized life insurance to the market. They contended that products and services could be delivered satisfactorily to customers only if employees who were specialists dealt directly with customers. The CEO responded by arguing that information technology could be used to help employees service the specialized needs of customers.

In light of the CEO's beliefs, he authorized major investments in developing and acquiring new information systems. For example, several expert systems were developed to assist employees to deal with the sometimes complex inquiries made by customers. The whole point to these systems was to allow customers to have a single point of contact with ALI.

The reengineered processes and supporting information systems have now been operational for about six months. Some of the changes that have occurred within ALI have been dramatic. Others have been subtle. The following are some examples:

a Over the past 18 months, staff turnover has been approximately 40 percent. Many senior specialist employees have been unwilling to accept the changes, and they have gone elsewhere. A large number of retrenchments have also occurred.

b Surveys of customers indicate that they like the changes that have occurred. In particular, they favor the streamlined way that they can now deal with ALI.

c In spite of customers' improved satisfaction with ALI's products and services, surprisingly, a slow drift away of ALI's customers to other insurance companies seems to have begun. The reasons are unclear.

d ALI's profitability has jumped sharply. It seems that the new processes and systems have improved employee productivity. Interestingly, however, the capital markets have been lukewarm about ALI's improved profitability. To the surprise of the board and the CEO, the increase in the price of ALI's shares has been lower than they expected.

e The culture of ALI has clearly changed. One market analyst has recently commented that ALI is now more of a marketing organization rather than a life insurance organization.

Required: Do you consider the changes brought about by the CEO to have been successful? In particular, on the basis of the limited data provided here, what is your judgment on the effectiveness of the information systems that have been implemented? Provide brief arguments in support of your judgment.

Answers to Multiple-Choice Questions

22–1	a	**22–6**	c	**22–11**	a	**22–16**	a
22–2	c	**22–7**	d	**22–12**	b	**22–17**	b
22–3	d	**22–8**	b	**22–13**	a	**22–18**	b
22–4	c	**22–9**	d	**22–14**	c	**22–19**	d
22–5	a	**22–10**	b	**22–15**	a	**22–20**	c

REFERENCES

Cameron, Kim S. (1986), "Effectiveness as Paradox: Consensus and Conflict in Conceptions of Organizational Effectiveness," *Management Science* (May), 539–553.

Compeau, Deborah R., and Christopher A. Higgins (1995), "Computer Self-Efficacy: Development of a Measure and Initial Test," *MIS Quarterly* (June), 198–211.

Cunningham, J. Barton (1977), "Approaches to the Evaluation of Organizational Effectiveness," *Academy of Management Review* (July), 463–474.

Daft, Richard L. (1995), *Organization Theory & Design*, 5th ed. Minneapolis/St. Paul, MN: West Publishing Company.

Davis, Fred D. (1989), "Perceived Usefulness, Perceived Ease of Use, and User Acceptance of Information Technology," *MIS Quarterly* (September), 319–340.

Davis, Fred R., Richard P. Bagozzi, and Paul R. Warshaw (1989), "User Acceptance of Computer Technology: A Comparison of Two Theoretical Models," *Management Science* (August), 982–1003.

Davis, Louis E., and Albert B. Cherns, eds. (1975), *The Quality of Working Life: Volume I—Problems, Prospects, and the State of the Art*. New York: The Free Press.

DeLone, William H., and Ephraim R. McLean (1992), "Information System Success: The Quest for the Dependent Variable," *Information Systems Research* (March), 60–95.

Doll, William J., and G. Torkzadeh (1988), "The Measurement of End-User Computing Satisfaction," *MIS Quarterly* (June), 259–274.

Ferguson, Colin (1997), "The Effects of Microcomputers on the Work of Professional Accountants," *Accounting and Finance* (May), 41–67.

Ginzberg, Michael J. (1978a), "Redesign of Managerial Tasks: A Requisite for Successful Decision Support Systems," *MIS Quarterly* (March), 39–52.

———— (1978b), "Finding an Adequate Measure of OR/MS Effectiveness," *Interfaces* (August), 59–62.

Greenberg, Paul E., Stan N. Finkelstein, and Ernst R. Berndt (1995), "Economic Consequences of Illness in the Workplace," *Sloan Management Review* (Summer), 26–38.

Hamilton, Scott, and Norman L. Chervany (1981a), "Evaluating I.S. Effectiveness—Part I: Comparing Evaluating Approaches," *MIS Quarterly* (September), 55–69.

———— and ———— (1981b), "Evaluating I.S. Effectiveness—Part II: Comparing Evaluation Viewpoints," *MIS Quarterly* (December), 79–86.

Hirschheim, Rudy A. (1986), "The Effect of A Priori Views on the Social Implications of Computing: The Case of Office Automation," *Computing Surveys* (June), 165–195.

Hitt, Lorin M., and Erik Brynjolfsson (1996), "Productivity, Business Profitability, and Consumer Surplus," *MIS Quarterly* (June), 121–142.

Ives, Blake, Margrethe H. Olson, and Jack J. Baroudi (1983), "The Measurement of User Information Satisfaction," *Communications of the ACM* (October), 785–793.

Kraut, Robert, Susan Dumais, and Susan Koch (1989), "Computerization, Productivity, and Quality of Work-Life," *Communications of the ACM* (February), 220–238.

Lawler, Edward E. (1975), "Measuring the Psychological Quality of Working Life: The Why and How of It," in Louis E. Davis and Albert B. Cherns, eds., *The Quality of Working Life: Volume I—Problems, Prospects, and the State of the Art*. New York: The Free Press, 123–133.

Macy, Barry A., and Philip H. Mirvis (1976), "A Methodology for Assessment of Quality of Work Life and Organizational Effectiveness in Behavioral-Economic Terms," *Administrative Science Quarterly* (June), 212–226.

Mohrman, Susan A., and Edward E. Lawler III (1984), "Quality of Work Life," in Kendrith M. Rowland and Gerald R. Ferris, eds., *Research in Personnel and Human Resources Management, Volume 2*. Greenwich, CT: JAI Press, 219–260.

Quinn, Robert E., and Kim Cameron (1983), "Organizational Life Cycles and Shifting Criteria of Effectiveness: Some Preliminary Evidence," *Management Science* (January), 33–51.

—— and John Rohrbaugh (1983), "A Spatial Model of Effectiveness Criteria: Towards a Competing Values Approach to Organizational Analysis," *Management Science* (March), 363–377.

Seashore, Stanley E. (1975), "Defining and Measuring the Quality of Working Life," in Louis E. Davis and Albert B. Cherns, eds., *The Quality of Working Life: Volume I—Problems, Prospects, and the State of the Art*. New York: The Free Press, 105–118.

Seddon, Peter B. (1997), "A Respecification and Extension of the Delone and McLean Model of IS Success," *Information Systems Research* (September), 240–253.

—— and Min-Yen Kiew (1994), "A Partial Test and Development of the DeLone and McLean Model of IS Success," in Janice I. DeGross, Sid L. Huff, and Malcolm C. Munro, eds., *Proceedings of the Fifteenth International Conference on Information Systems*. Vancouver, 99–110.

—— and Siew-Kee Yip (1992), "An Empirical Evaluation of User Information Satisfaction (UIS) Measures for Use with General Ledger Accounting Software," *Journal of Information Systems* (Spring), 75–92.

Steers, Richard M. (1977), *Organizational Effectiveness: A Behavioral View*. Santa Monica, CA: Goodyear Publishing Company.

Weill, Peter, and Margrethe H. Olson (1989), "Managing Investment in Information Technology," *MIS Quarterly* (March), 3–17.

Evaluating System Efficiency

Chapter Outline

Chapter Key Points

■ There are two reasons why auditors might become involved in evaluating system efficiency. First, management might ask them to evaluate an existing operational system to determine whether its performance can be improved. Second, management might ask them to evaluate alternative systems that they are considering for purchase, lease, rental, or development.

∎ There are eight major steps to be undertaken during the efficiency evaluation process: (a) formulate the objectives of the study, (b) prepare the budget for the evaluation, (c) define performance indices, (d) construct a workload model, (e) construct a system (configuration) model, (f) run experiments, (g) analyze results, and (h) provide recommendations.

∎ A performance index is a measure of system efficiency. It expresses quantitatively how well a system achieves some type of efficiency criterion. There are four types of performance indices: (a) timeliness indices, which measure how quickly a system is able to provide users with the output they require; (b) throughput indices, which measure how much work is done by a system over a period of time; (c) utilization indices, which measure the proportion of time a system is busy; and (d) reliability indices, which measure the availability of a system to process a user's workload.

∎ A system workload is the set of resource demands or service demands imposed on the system by the set of jobs that occur during a given time period. During the evaluation of system efficiency, auditors often must use a model of the workload rather than the real workload itself. It might be too costly to conduct experiments using the real workload. Alternatively, the system to be evaluated might not yet be operational, in which case the real workload is not available for evaluation purposes. The workload model auditors use should be representative of the real workload and generate the kinds of resource requests that are appropriate for the system or the component of the system under study.

∎ Two important dimensions on which workload models differ are (a) the source of the data on which they are based and (b) whether they can be executed on a real system. Natural workload models are based on either a content or time subset of the real workload. Artificial workload models are based on estimates of the characteristics of the real workload, often because the real workload is not available. If the workload model can be executed on the system to be evaluated, it is an executable workload model. Otherwise, it is a nonexecutable workload model.

∎ Workloads need to be characterized in some way. One approach is to use the average or mean value of a characteristic, such as the arrival rate of transactions at a processor. Another way is to group similar workload components together and describe the characteristics of the group. Sometimes correlations between the different characteristics of a workload model will need to be taken into account.

∎ There are various types of workload models. Traces are executable workload models constructed by taking some subset of the real workload or generating them via some tool. Instruction mixes specify the frequency with which different instructions occur or are expected to occur within an application. Kernel programs are programs or subroutines that have been coded as a representative job that will be executed on the system to be evaluated. They focus on the processor-intensive parts of the job rather than the input/output parts of the job. A synthetic job is a job or set of jobs that is coded and executed on the system to be evaluated. It differs from a kernel in that it exercises the input/output capabilities of the system to be evaluated. Benchmarks are executable workload models composed of traces, kernels, or synthetic jobs that are deemed to be standards against which the performance of different computer systems can be evaluated. Probabilistic workload models describe resource demands via a probability distribution. Specific workload requests are generated by sampling from a distribution.

■ To determine whether a system can be changed to improve its efficiency, the system itself must be modeled. The modeling process involves specifying the system components, the interfaces between the components, how the system operates, and the functional relationships between outputs and inputs.

■ Auditors can use three major types of system models to evaluate efficiency. Analytical models describe the relationships among performance indices, workload parameters, and system parameters via mathematical formulas. The major types of analytical model used to evaluate system efficiency are queuing models. Simulation models are used to emulate both the static and the dynamic properties of the system to be evaluated. They allow systems to be studied in more detail than analytical models. Empirical models can be used when the system to be evaluated is operational. Auditors obtain values for the performance indices, workload parameters, and system parameters that are of interest to them. They then use a statistical model, such as an analysis of variance model, a regression model, or an analysis of covariance model, to determine whether there are statistically significant relationships between the performance indices and the workload and system parameters.

■ Analytical models are often the cheapest and fastest way to undertake evaluations of system efficiency. Simulations often provide more accurate results than analytical models. They are sometimes used to validate and calibrate analytical models, which are then used to carry out experiments because they are cheaper. Empirical models often are the most expensive model to develop, implement, and use. Nonetheless, they often provide the most accurate results. They are sometimes used to validate and calibrate analytical or simulation models, which are then used to carry out experiments because they are cheaper.

■ There are several stages in the development and use of a system model. First, the model must be formulated. The relationships among the performance indices and the workload and system parameters must be specified. Second, the model must be implemented. In the case of analytical models and simulation models, programs might have to be written. Third, the model must be validated and calibrated. Fourth, experiments must be conducted during which the values of the workload and system parameters are varied and their impact on the performance indices determined.

■ Only certain types of workload models and system models can be used in combination with one another. For example, a trace workload model can be used with a simulation model or an empirical model but not an analytical model. Auditors must consider carefully how the workload and the system model will interact, therefore, before choosing the performance evaluation methodology to use.

INTRODUCTION

The need to evaluate the efficiency of computer systems is often a contentious issue. On the one hand, several factors have undermined the importance of efficiency evaluations. For example: hardware is cheap relative to labor, so it is often more cost-effective to buy extra hardware instead of spending time to improve the efficiency of systems; a substantial amount of computing is now done on single-user microcomputers where efficiency is often a minor consideration; to reduce complexity, many large-scale systems have now been broken up into smaller systems and the work assigned to minicomputers or microcomputers where, again, efficiency is less a concern.

On the other hand, however, several countervailing trends have underscored the ongoing importance of efficiency evaluations. For example: microcomputers are often components in large-scale local area networks where efficiency is a major issue; users of computing systems have become increasingly reliant on national and international data communication systems that need to provide fast response times (e.g., access to pages on the World Wide Web); to resolve difficulties in some computing systems, it is unclear just what type of hardware should be acquired to alleviate bottlenecks. For some types of computer systems, therefore, efficiency evaluations are needed. Management somehow has to recognize when acquisition of more hardware is not a panacea for unsatisfactory system performance.

In this chapter we discuss some methodologies that auditors can use to evaluate whether a system is efficient—that is, whether it achieves its objectives in the least-cost manner. The methodologies we will discuss have been developed within the area usually called "computer performance evaluation" or more recently "capacity planning." As we discussed in Chapter 20, however, our goal is not to be experts in this area. Rather, we will seek to have sufficient understanding so we can recognize when performance evaluations might be needed and we can interact successfully with individuals who specialize in performance monitoring.

The chapter proceeds as follows. The first section provides an overview of the efficiency evaluation process. In the second section we examine some of the major performance indices used to assess system efficiency. The third section discusses various approaches that we can use to model the workloads that are placed on computer systems. In the fourth section we consider various ways of modeling the computer system to be evaluated so that we can assess the efficiency of the system either analytically or empirically. Finally, we briefly examine the interrelationships that exist between the workload model we choose and the system model we can then use.

THE EVALUATION PROCESS

There are two reasons why auditors might become involved in evaluating system efficiency. First, top managers might ask them to evaluate an existing operational system to determine whether its performance can be improved. For example, it might be possible to decrease the response time of an interactive system by increasing the size of the memory partition allocated to each active user in the system. Second, top managers might ask auditors to evaluate

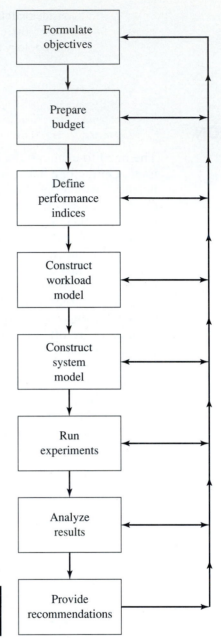

FIGURE 23–1. Major steps in the evaluation of system efficiency.

alternative systems that they are considering for purchase, lease, rental, or development. For example, management might be attempting to choose between two generalized accounting systems that are available in the marketplace. Auditors might be requested to provide advice on which system is better able to process the organization's workload.

Whatever the reasons for the evaluation, Figure 23–1 shows eight major steps auditors must undertake during an evaluation of system efficiency. At each step, note that one outcome might be the revision of work done at prior steps. For example, the formulation of a suitable workload model might be more costly than anticipated at the outset of the evaluation process. Thus, initial estimates of the costs and benefits of the evaluation process might have to be revised. One possible consequence of this revision might be that the evaluation is terminated because the expected benefits of the evaluation no longer exceed the costs.

Following is an overview of the work to be performed at each step in the evaluation process:

1. *Formulate the objectives of the study.* As with all evaluation studies, it is important to define clearly the objectives of the study at the start. This step can take considerable time. The objectives determine the boundaries of the system to be evaluated. Furthermore, they indicate the nature of the performance indices that will be required to assess the efficiency of the defined system and the types of models that will be formulated to help evaluate system efficiency. The objectives could be global—for example, to improve the performance of the online registration system. They could be specific—for example, to improve a processor's utilization. The objectives also should specify the constraints that apply—for example, to improve the response time of the interactive system without purchasing any more hardware resources.

2. *Prepare the budget for the evaluation.* Efficiency evaluations can be costly to carry out. The benefits obtained should exceed the costs of the evaluation and the costs of any changes needed to achieve the benefits. Estimating the costs of the evaluation usually is reasonably straightforward. Unfortunately, estimating the benefits of the evaluation and the costs of changes needed to achieve these benefits often is difficult. Only after the evaluation is complete will auditors know whether efficiency can be improved, what benefits can be expected from the improved efficiency, and the cost of the changes necessary to achieve the improved efficiency. Ultimately, experience in carrying out efficiency evaluations is a major determinant of quality decisions when the budget for the evaluation is prepared.

3. *Define performance indices.* The performance indices provide the basis for evaluating the level of efficiency attained within the system. What performance indices are chosen for an evaluation study will depend on the objectives of the study. For example, if the objective of the study is to improve the timeliness of the output of an interactive system, clearly an index of performance is response time. Response time now must be defined, however. There could be some debate as to whether response time ends upon receipt of the first character of output or the last character of output. If the system is overloaded, it could take some time for the output to print or to be displayed. As a result, the latter definition might be used.

4. *Construct a workload model.* Figure 23–2 shows a structural model of a computer system. The performance of a system is some function of the workload the system must process. When evaluating system efficiency, auditors must construct a workload model that is representative of the real system workload. If the system to be evaluated is operational, the workload model might be based on the real workload. If the system to be evaluated is in the design stages, an artificial workload model must be constructed—that is, one based on the expected characteristics of the workload to be processed.

5. *Construct a system (configuration) model.* The performance of the system to be evaluated is studied using a model of the system. Again, if the system is operational, the workload can be processed and the values of various performance

FIGURE 23–2. Structural model of a computer system.

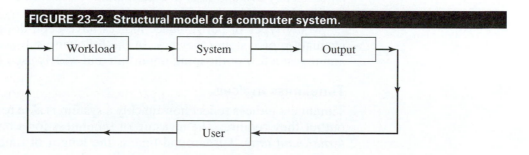

indices calculated. If the effects of a changed hardware/software platform are to be determined or the purchase of a new system is to be considered, however, some type of artificial model of the changed or new system must be constructed. In essence, the system model maps the attributes of the workload into values of the performance indices chosen.

6. *Run experiments.* When the workload and system models have been constructed, auditors can run experiments to determine the values of the performance indices. Sensitivity analyses can be carried out by varying both the characteristics of the workload and the system.

7. *Analyze results.* When evaluating efficiency, auditors hypothesize certain relationships between the values of the performance indices and the characteristics of the workload and system models. For example, they might hypothesize that varying the time quantum allocated to each job in an interactive system will have a major impact on response times, or that changing the device-to-channel assignment of a system's disk drives will cause a marked change in throughput. When experiments have been run with these changed parameters and the values of the performance indices determined, the data can be analyzed to determine whether the relationships hypothesized do, in fact, exist.

8. *Provide recommendations.* After auditors analyze the data from the experiments, they can then make recommendations on how system efficiency can be improved. The recommendations will depend on whether (a) the data supported the hypotheses they formulated about relationships between performance indices and the system and workload characteristics, and (b) the benefits are likely to exceed the costs of changes to improve system efficiency.

PERFORMANCE INDICES

A performance index is a measure of system efficiency. It expresses quantitatively how well a system achieves some type of efficiency criterion. Performance indices have several functions: They allow users to decide whether a system will meet their needs, they permit comparison of alternative systems, and they show whether changes to a hardware/software platform have produced the desired effect.

Performance indices often must be expressed as a probability distribution. For example, the response time in an online system might have considerable variation—perhaps from one second to one minute or more. If a performance index is expressed only as a mean value, it could hide important information from users. In the case of an online system, users might be unaware that at certain times of the day effective problem solving using a decision model might be inhibited by the system's slow response time. The mean, variance, and shape of the distribution alert users to the possibility of these types of difficulties occurring.

Performance indices also must be expressed in terms of a workload. The response time of an interactive system will vary depending on the number and the nature of the jobs in the system. Often one of our major objectives during an efficiency evaluation is to determine how the values of performance indices vary as the workload on the system is varied.

Many types of performance indices have been developed to facilitate the evaluation of system efficiency. In the following subsections, however, we examine just a few of the more important and widely used indices.

Timeliness Indices

Timeliness indices reflect how quickly a system is able to provide users with the output they require. The measure of timeliness for a batch system typically is *turnaround time*. Turnaround time is the length of time that elapses between submission of a job and receipt of the completed output. For interactive systems, the measure of timeliness is the *response time*. Typically the response time is defined as the length of time that elapses between submission of an input transaction to the system and receipt of the first character of output. The elapsed time between submission of a request by a user and the execution of the request is the *reaction time*. The elapsed time between completion of one transaction and submission of a new transaction is called the *think time* (reflecting the amount of time that users think about their work between transactions).

Timeliness indices must be defined in terms of a unit of work and the priority categorization given to the unit of work. In a batch system, the unit of work usually is a job. In an interactive system it might be a job (multiple transactions) or a single transaction. Higher priority units of work are given access first to available computing resources. Thus, these units of work should have faster turnaround and response times. The ratio of the value of the timeliness index at a given load to the value of the timeliness index at minimum load is called the *stretch factor*. The stretch factor is a measure of how a system performs under load.

Timeliness indices also are user-oriented performance indices because they reflect the primary concerns of the system user. Other indices discussed subsequently are system-oriented indices because they are more likely to be the concern of information systems personnel.

Throughput Indices

Throughput indices are measures of the productivity of a system; that is, they indicate how much work is done by the system over a period of time. The *throughput rate* of a system is the amount of work done per unit time period. For a central processor, for example, throughput is often measured in millions of instructions per second (MIPS). For an online transaction processing system, throughput is often measured in transactions per second (TPS). For a communications network, throughput is often measured in packets per second (pps) or bits per second (bps).

The *nominal capacity* or *nominal capability* of a system is the maximum achievable throughput rate. In some cases, we might not want to achieve the nominal capacity when a system operates. If we achieve the system's nominal capacity, the response time that results, for example, might be too fast for users; the display of output might have occurred so quickly that users may be unaware the system has responded. The capacity that we can use effectively is called the *usable capacity*. The ratio of the usable capacity to the nominal capacity is called the system's or the component's *efficiency*.

It is often useful to plot the value of a throughput index against different load values. Initially, when the system is under a light load, the throughput rate may increase rapidly. At some point, however, the rate of increase in throughput will begin to decrease (Figure 23–3). The throughput at this point is often

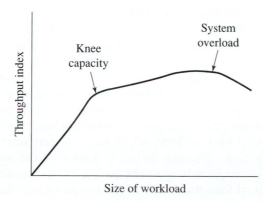

FIGURE 23–3. Typical relationship between throughput and workload.

called the *knee capacity*. At some higher point, the throughput will begin to decrease. The system is then overloaded.

Again, throughput indices must be defined in terms of some unit of work—a job, a task, an instruction, and so on. Note, also, the interdependencies between timeliness indices and throughput indices: More responsive systems often have a greater throughput.

Utilization Indices

Utilization indices measure the proportion of time a system resource is busy. For example, a processor utilization index is calculated by dividing the amount of time the processor is busy by the total amount of time the system is running. Similarly, channel utilization is defined to be the amount of time the channel is busy divided by the amount of time the system is running. Utilization indices may be defined for any hardware, software, or data resource within the system.

The period during which a resource is not utilized is called its *idle time*. Idle time is not necessarily an undesirable outcome, providing it is within reasonable bounds. In well-balanced systems, idle time is often spread fairly evenly across system resources so that resources are neither too busy nor too slack.

Reliability Indices

The reliability of a system is often defined in terms of its availability to process users' work or the absence of failures or errors in processing. The percentage of time that the system is available for processing is called the *uptime*. The percentage of time the system is not available for processing is called the *downtime*. The average time that elapses between some type of failure or error is called the *mean time between failure* (MTBF). Often we might be interested in the distribution of times between failure. The MTBF might be relatively low, but a large right skew in the distribution indicates the time between failures on some occasions is long. On these occasions, the costs of downtime could be high.

WORKLOAD MODELS

A system workload is the set of resource demands or service demands imposed on the system by the set of jobs or transactions that occur during a given time period. Conceptually, the workload can be characterized as a matrix. The rows in the matrix are the set of jobs/transactions that occur for the time period under consideration. The columns in the matrix are the hardware, software, and data resources belonging to the system or the services provided by the system. The elements of the matrix are the amounts of each resource or service demanded by each job/transaction. System performance (efficiency) must be defined in terms of a given workload.

Purposes of Workload Models

When evaluating system efficiency, a workload model might be formulated for several reasons. First, using the real workload of the system for evaluation purposes could be too costly. To measure efficiency for a representative workload, the time period for evaluation may be long. Second, the real workload cannot be used if the system to be evaluated is not operational. If auditors are evaluating competing systems (say, proposed hardware/software platforms for a system yet to be implemented), an artificial workload must be created for purposes of the evaluation. Third, auditors might want to carry out sensitivity analyses when evaluating system efficiency. If the behavior of the system is to be examined under varying workloads, it might be easier to change the characteristics of a workload model than the real workload to carry out these sensitivity analyses.

Desired Properties of Workload Models

The workload model auditors select when they evaluate the efficiency of a system should have two properties: *(1)* it should be representative of the real workload and *(2)* it should generate requests for services that are appropriate to the system or the components of the system under study. In the following subsections, we briefly examine each of these goals.

Representativeness

If the workload model is to be useful, it must be *representative* of the real workload. A representative workload model is one that produces the same values of the performance indices as the real workload. For example, if a single performance index, throughput rate, is used for the evaluation, the throughput rate values for the workload model and the real workload should be equal. Recall that performance indices often are stochastic variables, so the mean, variance, and higher moments of the distributions of the performance indices for the workload model and the real workload should be compared.

This notion of representativeness is conceptually useful, but it is not always practically useful. For a system that is not operational, the real workload is not yet known. Thus, determining the representativeness of the workload model is difficult if not impossible. Even if the values of performance indices for the real workload and the workload model are known, there is the problem of determining whether the workload model will remain representative when the system structure is changed. A workload model is devised to provide a cheaper means of undertaking sensitivity analysis than the real workload. The costs of inaccurate performance measurements, however, must not exceed the cost savings obtained by using a model. Ideally, the model's representativeness will be invariant across system structures.

If a workload model is to be representative, it must remain current. Workload patterns sometimes change quickly. For example, the installation of certain types of workstation software might substantially change the demands placed on a mainframe, or changed customer demands for goods and services might alter the types of input submitted to an application system. Workload models must be updated to reflect these changed patterns of resource demands.

If a real workload exists, one way to increase the representativeness of the workload model is to base it on a larger sample of jobs from the real workload. The costs of developing, using, and maintaining the workload model increase, however, and in some cases the workload model might become less compact. If a real workload does not exist, the representativeness of the workload model can be increased by devoting more resources to predicting the likely characteristics of the resource demands that will be placed on the system. Again, the costs of developing, using, and maintaining the workload model increase.

Appropriateness of Resources Requested

The purpose of the workload model is to generate resource demands on the system or the component of the system under study. The nature of the resource demands generated via the workload model must be appropriate to the services provided by the system or the component under study.

For example, at the system level, the service requested might be processing of transactions. The focus of performance measurement might be the average response time per transaction. If auditors are interested in the performance of a central processing unit, however, it will not be appropriate to have the workload model generate transactions. The service provided by the central processor is execution of instructions. In this light, the workload model must generate a request for instruction execution rather than a request for transaction processing. Auditors might begin with the types of transactions that the system will process and then work out the sorts of instructions that will have to be executed to process the transactions. Ultimately, however, the workload model must generate a demand for execution of various types of instructions.

To facilitate determining the types of resource demands that auditors will need to generate via a workload model, it is often useful to think about a system in terms of a hierarchy of components. For example, a computer can be conceived in terms of a processor, a main memory unit, an input/output unit, and a bus that connects the processor, main memory, and input/output components. The types of services provided by each of these components differ. As discussed previously, the execution of instructions is likely to be the primary focus with the processor. If auditors are evaluating the performance of the bus, however, their focus will be how fast it carries bits of information among the other components. Thus, the workload model will have to generate requests to carry bits of information that vary in size and frequency.

Types of Workload Models

Two important dimensions on which workload models differ are *(1)* the source of the data on which they are based and *(2)* whether they can be executed on a real system (Figure 23–4). In this light, two factors have a major impact on the type of workload model to be used: *(1)* whether a real workload exists already to provide the basis for the workload model and *(2)* the type of system model to be used to carry out the performance evaluation.

Natural Workload Models

Natural workload models are constructed on the basis of some subset of the real workload. There are two methods of obtaining the subset required. First, time subsets can be chosen. The start and finish times should be chosen so as to maximize representativeness and to minimize construction and use costs. Unfortunately, these objectives conflict. Longer time intervals increase representativeness, but also they could increase the costs of constructing and using the workload model.

Second, content subsets can be chosen. A random sample of jobs from the real workload might be selected. Alternatively, jobs might be partitioned into classes, and a random sample of jobs can then be chosen from each class to form the basis for constructing the workload model. The size of the sample chosen depends on the trade-off made between representativeness and

	Source of data	
	Real workload	Estimated workload
Yes	Natural, executable workload model	Artificial, executable workload model
No	Natural, nonexecutable workload model	Artificial, nonexecutable workload model

Can it be executed?

FIGURE 23–4. Types of workload model.

workload model construction and use costs. Smaller samples are less representative, but they enable cheaper workload models to be constructed and used.

Natural workload models have two major strengths. First, because they are constructed from jobs in the real workload, their representativeness can be high. Second, the cost to construct a natural workload model usually is low. This cost increases, however, as the representativeness of the model increases. Natural workload models can only be used, however, if a real workload already exists.

Artificial Workload Models

If a workload model is not constructed from jobs in the real workload, it is an artificial workload model. We might base an artificial workload model on estimates we make of the characteristics of the real workload. Alternatively, we might identify workload models that have already been constructed by other parties (perhaps based on real workloads that exist in other organizations) that we believe are representative of the real workload that currently exists or will exist when the system to be evaluated is operational.

Auditors might use an artificial workload model for two reasons. First, a real workload might not be available because the system to be evaluated has not been constructed. Second, even if a real workload exists, they might conclude it is cheaper to construct and use an artificial workload model than a natural workload model. Whenever auditors use artificial workload models, however, the risk they run is that it will not be representative of the real workload.

Executable Workload Models

An executable workload model is one that can be executed on the system to be evaluated. It can be prepared on the basis of the real workload (an executable, natural workload model). For example, a sample of jobs can be selected from the real workload. Alternatively, it can be prepared on the basis of the anticipated characteristics of jobs in the real workload (an executable, artificial workload model). For example, a workload modeling tool might be used to create jobs that request certain types of services.

Executable workload models often have high representativeness. Moreover, complex system models do not have to be built if the real system can be used to execute the model. Executable workload models have several disadvantages, however. Modifications to them are not always easy to make because the characteristics of the jobs themselves have to be changed. Thus, sensitivity analyses using the model might be difficult to carry out. The operational costs of using the model also could be high because they are often less compact than artificial workload models.

Nonexecutable Workload Models

A nonexecutable workload model cannot be executed on the system or a model of the system to be evaluated. Like an executable workload model, it might be based on the real workload (a nonexecutable, natural workload model). For example, its parameters, like the mean and standard deviation of job arrival times, might be calculated on the basis of the real workload. Alternatively, it might be based on the anticipated characteristics of the real workload (a nonexecutable, artificial workload model). For example, its parameters might be based on the anticipated characteristics of the real workload.

Nonexecutable workload models are usually more flexible and compact than natural workload models. They facilitate sensitivity analyses and are less costly to use. These advantages are attained only at a cost, however. Nonexecutable workload models often are more costly to construct, less representative, and less portable than executable workload models.

Workload Characterization

A workload has various characteristics (sometimes called *parameters* or *features*). For example, auditors might describe a workload in terms of different types of transactions, the arrival rates of the transactions, and the sources of the transactions. Their goal is to characterize a workload using those properties of the workload that have the greatest impact on the performance indices they use to evaluate the system or component under study.

Auditors need to be able to describe the characteristics of the workload in some way. One approach is to use the average or mean value of the characteristic. For example, they might calculate the average number of transactions per minute that are entered into an online transaction processing system. If necessary, auditors can give a more detailed description of the characteristic by determining other values like the standard deviation and the median (assuming the characteristic is subject to variability).

Sometimes the values of several characteristics of a workload will be related in some way. For example, when the average number of transactions submitted from one cluster of terminals goes up, the average number of transactions submitted from another cluster of terminals might also go up. Similarly, if a particular type of transaction is submitted, it is likely that another type of transaction will then be submitted. Various types of mathematical techniques can be used to take these relationships into account when a workload model is being developed—for example, factor analysis and Markov analysis.

At times auditors also might need to partition the workload into several relatively homogeneous components and to describe these components rather than the individual items on which they are based. For example, it might be useful to group batch jobs with common characteristics together and to characterize the workload in terms of typical jobs within the group. Statistical techniques like cluster analysis can sometimes be used to find workload components that have common characteristics.

Some Examples of Workload Models

A large number of different types of workload models have been constructed. They vary widely in their capabilities with respect to representativeness, cost, compactness, and so on. To illustrate the diversity that exists, the following subsections provide an overview of some of the major types that have been used. As we study this material, however, we need to be aware that the distinction between some types of workload model is not always clear and that the terminology is not always used consistently.

Traces

Traces are executable workload models. They are constructed by taking some subset of the real workload or generating jobs using some type of tool. A content subset of the real workload can be taken: Particular types of jobs or transactions are sampled. Alternatively, a time subset can be chosen: All the jobs or transactions that occur during particular time intervals are chosen.

Traces are used as input to simulation models of computer systems. Alternatively, they can be used as input to the computer system itself where empirical models are then used to evaluate the impact of variations in the trace on system efficiency. Traces often have high representativeness. They are also portable, but they are not compact.

Instruction Mixes

An instruction mix specifies the frequency with which different instructions occur (natural workload) or are expected to occur (artificial workload) within an application. The average execution time for a system is then computed using the following formula:

$$\bar{t} = \sum_i p_i\, t_i$$

where $\bar{t}$ = average execution time

        p_i = probability of the ith instruction being executed

        t_i = execution time of the ith instruction

Often the speed of a processor is quoted using the inverse of the average instruction time—for example, millions of instructions per second (MIPS) or millions of floating-point instructions per second (MFLOPS).

The relative frequencies of the different types of instructions in the mix can be determined in three ways: First, if the system is operational, a trace of instructions in the real workload can be taken and the incidence of the different types of instructions counted; second, standard instruction mixes such as the Gibson mix can be used (see Jain 1991); and third, the frequencies of the different types of instructions can be estimated on the basis of the expected workload.

An instruction mix is a very limited workload model. Its primary strength is that it provides a basis for quickly comparing the speeds of different central processors. Also, it is cheap to use. Obtaining a representative instruction mix, however, can be difficult. A set of representative programs must be chosen and the frequencies of instructions used estimated or counted. Instruction mixes also might not take into account instruction overlap, nor do they include input/output instructions. A further limitation is that instruction mixes often will differ across systems. For example, the instruction set of a complex instruction set computer (CISC) will differ substantially from a reduced instruction set computer (RISC). The latter type of computer is likely to have a much higher MIPS rating than the former type of computer. Each instruction executed on a RISC, however, accomplishes less work than each instruction executed on a CISC. Thus, instruction mixes permit only a partial system evaluation to be carried out.

Kernel Programs

A *kernel program* is a program or subroutine that has been coded as a representative job within the system to be evaluated. Nonetheless, kernel programs focus on the processor-intensive parts of the job and not the input/output requirements. For example, in a scientific installation the kernel may be a matrix inversion routine. From the list of instructions in the kernel and the execution times of the instructions in the system being evaluated, the total execution time of the kernel can be calculated. Thus, the execution times of two competing systems can be estimated. If an operational system is available, a kernel might also be executed on the system and the system's performance measured empirically.

Instruction mixes and kernel programs have similar strengths and weaknesses. Kernel programs usually contain more representative instructions because they are based on jobs that are likely to be executed within an organization. Like instruction mixes, however, they provide only a first approximation of system efficiency, and they are a limited form of workload model.

Synthetic Jobs

A *synthetic job* is a representative job (or set of jobs) that is coded and executed on the system to be evaluated. Unlike kernels, they also seek to exercise the input/output capabilities of the system to be evaluated. Providing a synthetic job used is representative of the real workload, therefore, it will allow more accurate estimates to be made of system efficiency than instruction mixes or kernel programs.

Synthetic jobs are less compact than instruction mixes and kernel programs. Thus, they are more costly to develop and use. Nonetheless, they can be constructed so they are flexible to use. For example, the resources consumed by a synthetic job can be changed by altering some of its parameters, such as the number of demands it makes on the processor and the frequency of disk accesses it initiates.

Care must be taken if a synthetic job is used to evaluate alternative hardware/software platforms. Erroneous decisions can be made if synthetic jobs are not written so they execute efficiently on the hardware/software platforms they use.

Benchmarks

Benchmarks are executable workload models composed of traces, kernels, or synthetic jobs that are deemed to be standards against which the performance of different computer systems can be evaluated. *Natural benchmarks* are based on an organization's real workload. *Artificial benchmarks* are based on the expected characteristics of an organization's real workload.

Often artificial benchmarks are developed to be representative of the typical workloads that are experienced within particular industries or on particular types of hardware/software platforms. Jain (1991) describes some of the early benchmarks that were developed, such as the Whetstone, Dhrystone, and Debit-Credit benchmarks. Table 23–1 provides an overview of some more recent, widely used artificial benchmarks and benchmarking tools.

Probabilistic Workload Models

In a probabilistic workload model, resource demands are described by a probability distribution. Various types of distributions can be used—for example, the Poisson distribution, the exponential distribution, and the normal distribution. A time series of work demands is generated by sampling from the probability distribution.

Probabilistic workload models are used extensively in analytical and simulation studies of computer system performance. The system model used can impose constraints on how the workload model is formulated. For example, if auditors use a queuing model to evaluate system efficiency, it is difficult to obtain a tractable model if the workload model takes into account correlations between service times.

Probabilistic workload models differ in their representativeness of the real workload. To the extent the workload model is not constrained by tractability requirements imposed by the system model, the workload model has high potential for representativeness. Probabilistic workload models are also compact and flexible. Resource demands are described easily by a probability distribution. Changing the workload simply involves changing the parameters of the distribution. Development costs also are often low. Usage costs, however, depend on how many samples are taken from the distribution when system efficiency is evaluated.

TABLE 23–1 Some Benchmarks and Benchmarking Tools

System Performance Evaluation Cooperative (SPEC) Benchmarks

The Standard Evaluation Performance Corporation is a nonprofit corporation that was formed to develop a standard set of benchmarks developed for high-performance computers. The SPEC benchmark suites comprise *(1)* SPEC Release 1, which is a set of processor-intensive benchmarks intended to be representative of scientific and engineering environments; *(2)* SPEC SDM 1, which is a set of benchmarks intended to exercise processor, memory, disk input/output, and operating system services representative of a commercial software development environment; *(3)* SPEC CINT92 and CFP92, which are sets of integer and floating point benchmarks that extend SPEC Release 1 to take into account faster hardware and smarter optimizing compilers; and *(4)* System File Server Release 1.0, which is a set of benchmarks designed to allow file server performance across different vendor platforms to be evaluated.

Transaction Processing Performance Council (TPC)

The TPC is a nonprofit corporation that was formed to develop a standard set of data processing and database benchmarks. The TPC produced two early benchmarks called Debit/Credit and TP1 that were used widely. In due course, however, they proved to be problematic for several reasons; for example, they did not require full disclosure of the test system's details. The current TPC benchmarks measure transaction processing performance and database performance in terms of the number of transactions that the system and the database can process per second. Some of the TPC benchmarks are *(1)* TPC Benchmark™ A, which is a benchmark designed to measure performance in online transaction processing, update-intensive database environments; *(2)* TPC Benchmark™ B, which is a benchmark designed to measure performance in the host/server computer via a database stress test characterized by significant input/output but moderate processor execution; *(3)* TPC Benchmark™ C, which is designed to measure performance in a complex database environment where many transaction types exist; *(4)* TPC Benchmark™ D, which is designed to measure performance in decision support environments; and *(5)* TPC Benchmark™ E, which is designed to measure performance in large, complex, enterprisewide online transaction-processing environments.

Performance Awareness Corporation

Performance Awareness Corporation has produced a toolkit called preVue™, which can be used to generate a workload appropriate for the system under test. Utilities allow the workload to be "recorded" and then "played back" to the system under test, and the results obtained then "evaluated."

Neal Nelson & Associates

Neal Nelson & Associates have produced two benchmarking tools. The first is the Business Benchmark®, a program that generates workloads with increasing levels of multitasking to undertake stress-testing of various subsystems in a target system. It provides reports to show how the target system slows down as it performs different tasks at different load levels. The second is the Remote Terminal Emulator, which is used to create and play back scripts of keystrokes that users produce as they interact via terminals with the target system. Standard scripts also exist for different types of workload, such as office automation, database, and transaction processing workloads.

AIM Technology

AIM Technology has produced a suite of benchmarks to evaluate UNIX™ system performance. For example, the benchmarks provide performance ratings of the target system under peak performance, increasing workloads, and execution of standard UNIX™ utilities.

IBM's Large Systems Performance Reference (LSPR) Method

IBM's LSPR method is designed to measure relative processor capacity in IBM and IBM-compatible System/370 and System/390 processor architectures. LSPR measurements allow users to assess the change in performance that is likely to occur if they change processors. The measurements assume that "external" resources, such as the number of channels and input/output devices and the amount of secondary storage, are adequate. The processor, therefore, is deemed to be the limiting factor in performance. Different LSPR workloads have been developed to cover different types of applications—for example, engineering and scientific batch workloads, commercial batch workloads, and online workloads.

Business Applications Performance Corporation (BAPCo)

BAPCo produces benchmarks for popular applications and industry-standard operating systems. For example, its benchmarks are used to produce a performance rating for widely used personal computers that are used to run wordprocessing, spreadsheet, database, desktop graphics, desktop publishing, and software development applications.

SYSTEM MODELS

To determine whether a system can be changed to improve efficiency, the system itself must be modeled. The modeling process involves specifying the system components, the interfaces between the components, how the system operates, and the functional relationships between outputs and inputs.

When the system has been modeled, various parameters in the model can be changed to determine their impact on system efficiency. For example, auditors might investigate the impact of changes in the priority assigned to different jobs, the size of the time slice allocated to a job, the amount of memory allocated to a job, the device-to-channel assignment, the paging algorithm used, the number of users allowed to access the system simultaneously, and the maximum allowed paging rate. Using the performance indices discussed earlier in the chapter, auditors can run experiments to determine the effects of changes in a particular workload or system parameter when the other parameters are held constant.

One of the more difficult problems in constructing a system model is knowing how to decompose the system into subsystems so the evaluation problem can be conceptualized. Kobayashi (1978) points out that often subsystem boundaries can be identified when we observe major differences in the time interval between events in the components. For example, to evaluate cache memory algorithms, we must work with a subsystem having time intervals of nanoseconds. In contrast, if we evaluate input/output scheduling by the operating system, the time interval usually can be expressed in milliseconds. Note that a single event in the latter subsystem can be represented by multiple events in the former subsystem. To evaluate performance of the input/output subsystem, the model should not be defined at the level of the cache memory subsystem; otherwise, it is unlikely that a tractable model will result.

The following three subsections provide an overview of the three major types of system models that auditors can use to evaluate efficiency: *(1)* analytical models, *(2)* simulation models, and *(3)* empirical models. If you wish to be a proficient user of these models, you will need to undertake further study (see the bibliography at the end of this chapter). The following discussion, however, should provide a fundamental understanding of these models.

Analytical Models

A variety of analytical models have been developed to evaluate system efficiency. Queuing models, however, have received the most widespread use. Perhaps the major reasons are the availability of a substantial theoretical base to support use of queuing models and the capability of queuing models to represent complex probabilistic phenomena in computer systems.

It is easy to conceive of a computer system within a queuing framework. Jobs or transactions (customers) make demands on various computer resources (servers). For example, a transaction submitted by a user at an online terminal will request processor time, memory, input/output devices, a communications line, and so on. As resource contention among transactions arises, queues result. There will be a queue of jobs waiting for processor service, another waiting for service from an input/output device, another waiting for service from system software, and so on.

The output of queuing models includes the timeliness, throughput, and utilization indices discussed previously in the chapter, as well as measures like the mean waiting time in a queue, mean waiting time in the system, mean number of jobs waiting for service, and mean number of jobs in the system. Auditors can also use queuing models to identify the bottleneck resource in a computer system. Thus, queuing models enable them to evaluate system efficiency and to devise strategies for improving system efficiency. Often, auditors can use queuing models to focus on a specific resource management problem—for example, hierarchical memory management, channel scheduling, network routing, and buffer allocation.

In the following subsections we briefly examine the major steps to be undertaken when we construct a queuing model to evaluate system efficiency. The subsections assume basic familiarity with queuing theory. Moreover, because the use of queuing theory to model computer systems has now been developed extensively, in a few pages we can only treat the subject superficially. Nonetheless, detailed treatments of the topic can be found elsewhere (e.g., Menascé et al. 1994).

Model Formulation

The first step when using a queuing model to evaluate system efficiency is to formulate the model. This step involves choosing the type of queuing model to be used to represent the system.

The earliest queuing models constructed to evaluate computer systems were simple single-server models. The model consists of a single process (server) and a single queue of jobs (Figure 23–5). Jobs are described by a distribution of arrival times and requested service times. The underlying assumptions of the model are restrictive; for example, the interarrival times and service times are statistically independent, all interarrival times are distributed identically, and all service times are distributed identically. Because only one resource queue exists, auditors have to consider the entire system as a black box. In computer systems in which one resource dominates (for example, the processor), the model might be appropriate. In multiple resource systems, however, its usefulness is limited. As a result, many computer systems are now modeled as a network of single resource models (Figure 23–6). Substantial advances have been made in the theory supporting these models (see, e.g., Denning and Buzen 1978).

The queuing model used can be a closed model, an open model, or a mixed model. In a *closed* model, for all classes of jobs, the number of jobs in that class is fixed and constant. New jobs are generated internally to the model. Auditors use this type of model when they have terminal jobs (jobs in which a new job starts after the completion of the previous job and some think time has to elapse) and batch jobs (jobs in which a new job starts immediately on completion of the previous job). In an *open* model, for all classes of jobs, an external source of jobs exists. Auditors use this type of model when jobs arrive at a rate that is independent of the system's response time or turnaround time. For example, transactions might arrive from other computer systems over a data communications line. *Mixed* models have some job classes that are closed and some that are open.

Open models usually are easier to solve mathematically than closed models. Closed models, however, are sometimes more representative of real systems. For example, assuming an infinite population source (open model) is unrealistic for an interactive system where a finite number of terminals exists.

FIGURE 23–5. Single process/single queue model of a computer system.

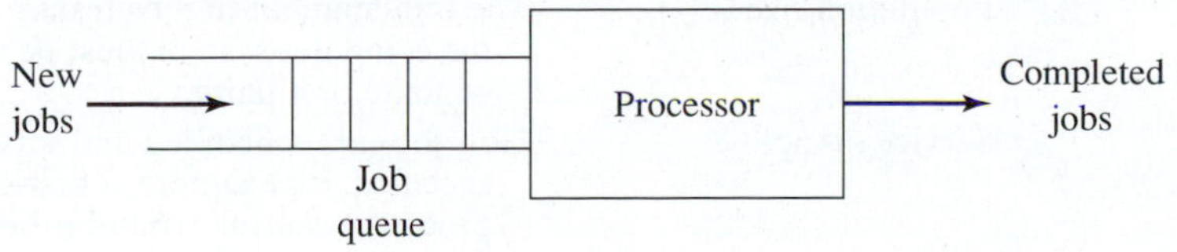

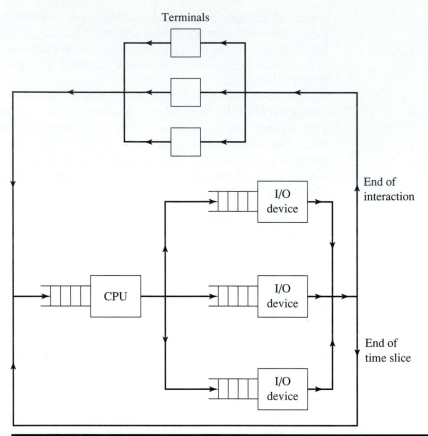

FIGURE 23–6. Queuing network model of a computer system.

Estimating Model Parameter Values

When the queuing model has been formulated, the values of the parameters in the model must be estimated. If the system to be modeled is operational, the parameter values can be estimated from data obtained using a performance monitoring tool. Otherwise, the expected parameter values must be used.

Some of the major input parameters used in queuing models follow:

Parameter	*Explanation*
Arrival pattern	The distribution of interarrival times for each job/transaction class must be specified; for example, an exponential distribution is often used.
Service time distribution	The distribution of service time for each server (e.g., processor and input/output device) must be specified; for example, an exponential distribution is often used.
Number of servers	The number of each class of server must be specified; for example, number of processors and number of laser printers.
System capacity	The maximum number of jobs/transactions that the system can accommodate must be specified. This number includes those being serviced as well as those in queues. The number can be finite (closed system) or infinite (open system).
Population size	The total number of jobs/transactions that can ever arrive at the computer system must be specified. This number might be finite or infinite.
Service discipline	How jobs are scheduled and served by the processor must be specified; for example, a first-come-first-served basis or a processor sharing (round robin) basis may be used.

Parameter	*Explanation*
Input/output device routing frequencies	Jobs are processed alternately by either a processor or an input/output device. The routing frequency for an input/output device is the proportion of total input/output operations executed that apply to that device.
Number of job classes	The jobs in the system must be categorized; for example, as either batch or time-sharing or into different priority classes.

Sometimes queuing systems are specified using a shorthand method called the Kendall notation. It takes the form *A/B/c/K/m/Z*, where *A* is the interarrival time distribution, *B* is the service time distribution, *c* is the number of servers, *K* is the system capacity, *m* is the population size, and *Z* is the service discipline. For example, a specification of the form M/M/5/50/5,000/FCFS means that both the arrival times and service times are described via an exponential distribution (M is the symbol used to designate an exponential distribution because of its "memoryless" or Makovian property, which means that the probability of an arrival does not depend on the history of the arrival process), the number of servers in the system is 5, the system capacity is 50, the population size is 5,000, and the service discipline is first-in-first-out. Often only the first three parameters are specified—*A/B/c*—when the population size is infinite and the service discipline is first-come-first-served.

Solving the Model

The point to using the Kendall specification is that the formulas needed to solve queuing models have been determined for the different types of models. When the Kendall specification for the type of queuing model appropriate for describing a computer system is determined, the formulas that can be used to solve the model are then known. Denning and Buzen (1978) provide a survey of these formulas. The solutions can be obtained using *exact analysis* or *approximate analysis*. Exact analysis is used when the assumptions underlying the model are satisfied. Because some queuing model assumptions are restrictive and often might be violated, however, approximate analysis can be used to solve the model. Approximate analysis also can be used if exact analysis will be too expensive to undertake or alternative, more credible models such as simulation will be too expensive to use.

To illustrate how queuing models can be solved, assume auditors are dealing with a small firm that has one terminal connected to a single computer. The terminal provides access to the computer for 12 hours per day. The 15 employees in the firm arrive randomly at the terminal throughout the day. Thus, this arrival process can be described via a Poisson distribution. Further assume that the distribution of service times at the terminal is exponential with a mean of 40 minutes.

A simple open queuing model, with the Kendall notation M/M/1, can be used to model this system approximately (note that we use M for the first parameter because the interarrival times for an arrival process that can be described via a Poisson distribution are exponentially distributed, and the model is approximate because we are assuming the number of employees is infinite). To solve the model, we first set up the relevant parameter values. Let $E(s)$ be the expected (mean) service time and $E(t)$ be the expected (mean) interarrival time. Then:

$E(s)$ = 40 minutes

$E(t)$ = 48 minutes ((12 hours/15 employees) $\times$ 60 minutes)

Next we calculate a measure called the traffic intensity, u, which indicates the number of servers needed to keep up with the incoming stream of jobs (employees). For the simple queuing model we are using, it is defined as follows:

$$u = E(s)/E(t)$$

Thus, in our example, $u = 40/48$, which is 5/6.

We can then calculate some standard performance measures. The average time an employee will spend in the queue for the terminal is determined by the following formula:

$$W_q = (uE(s))/(1-u)$$

For our example, this value is 200 minutes.

Similarly, we can calculate the average time an employee spends waiting for and using the terminal via the following formula:

$$W = E(s)/(1-u)$$

For our example, this value is 240 minutes (equivalently, 200 minutes waiting and 40 minutes using the terminal).

Using a law called Little's Law (named after its founder), we can also calculate the number of employees in the queue using the following formula:

$$L_q = (1/E(t))/W$$

For our example, this value is 4.167.

Clearly, then, the performance of the current system is problematical. Queue lengths and queue waiting times most likely are unacceptable. We can then use queuing models to determine the number of additional terminals that need to be purchased to bring queue lengths and queue waiting times down to an acceptable level. Note that as we acquire additional terminals, the processor could then become a bottleneck. As a result, we might have to modify our model to take into account multiple processors as well as multiple terminals.

Model Validation and Calibration

When a queuing model has been constructed, it should be validated to determine how accurately it predicts the values of the various performance indices. If the system to be evaluated is operational, auditors can compare the results of the queuing model with those obtained using performance monitoring tools. The robustness of the model over changing workloads and changing system parameters also can be examined. If the system to be evaluated is not operational, however, auditors must examine the model and its output for face validity. In addition, they might construct a simulation model and compare the output of the queuing model with the output of the simulation model.

Validation allows the size of the error in the output of the queuing model to be determined. If the size of the error is unacceptable, auditors will have to calibrate the model. Calibration reduces the size of the output error by reducing or eliminating model formulation inaccuracies, inaccuracies caused by the use of approximate solution methods, and inaccuracies caused by incorrect estimates of parameter values.

Simulation Models

Simulation models are constructed to emulate both the static and dynamic properties of a system. They enable auditors to study systems in more detail than analytical models. As a result, they often produce more accurate results. Too much detail can be included in simulation models, however, which can make them costly to develop, use, and maintain.

Auditors might use a simulation model to evaluate system efficiency for several reasons. First, they might not be able to construct a tractable analytical model. The system to be modeled might be too complex, or the assumptions they have to make might be too restrictive. Second, the system to be evaluated may not be operational. Thus, empirical performance measurement cannot be carried out. Third, the simulation model could be used to validate the analytical model. This objective could be especially important when auditors have made simplifying assumptions in the analytical model and they are unsure about their impact on the validity of the results produced via the model. Fourth, simulation could be cheaper to use than empirical performance measurement, especially when auditors wish to vary workload and system parameters to determine their impact on overall performance.

In the following subsections, we briefly examine the steps we follow when we construct a simulation model to evaluate system efficiency. Again, our goal is not to be an expert in building simulation models. Rather, we are seeking to gain an understanding of the overall process we must use to develop, operate, and maintain simulation models.

Model Formulation

At the start of the design of a simulation model, it is essential for auditors to determine how the model will be used for performance evaluation purposes. These objectives affect the design of a simulation model in several ways. They determine the input (workload) parameters, internal (system) parameters, and output variables needed in the model. The output variables to be measured are the performance indices of interest in the evaluation. The input and internal parameters included in the model reflect decisions auditors must make on what variables will be manipulated to determine their impact on the performance indices.

The objectives also determine the level of system detail to be included in the model. Simulations can be expensive to implement and run. Therefore, the model should focus only on those variables of interest. Moreover, the level of detail included in the model should be sufficient simply to produce results that contain an acceptable level of error. If the system to be modeled is the central processor, the simulation must be sufficiently detailed to study instruction execution. If the system to be modeled is an application system, however, the simulation must be formulated at a more macroscopic level.

Simulation models differ in their structure depending on whether we focus on processes or events. If auditors focus on processes, time is incremented by constant intervals (quasi-continuous simulation). If auditors focus on events, time is incremented when the simulation changes its state (discrete-event simulation). When auditors model a computer system to evaluate efficiency, they usually formulate a discrete-event simulation model because their focus is the state changes in the system that occur when some type of event occurs.

For example, the following would be a typical structure that auditors might use in a discrete-event simulation of a simple online transaction processing system in which they use a probabilistic workload model (Figure 23–7):

1. *Initiate a transaction from a terminal.* This event occurs as a function of the time when the last job was completed and the think time we allocate. Auditors determine the think time by sampling from a probability distribution that describes the time users spend working on their jobs between submission of transactions.
2. *Assign the transaction to the central processor.* If the processor is busy, the transaction will have to be allocated to a queue. If the processor is idle, work on the transaction can commence immediately.

FIGURE 23–7. Structure of a typical discrete-event simulation model used for efficiency evaluation purposes.

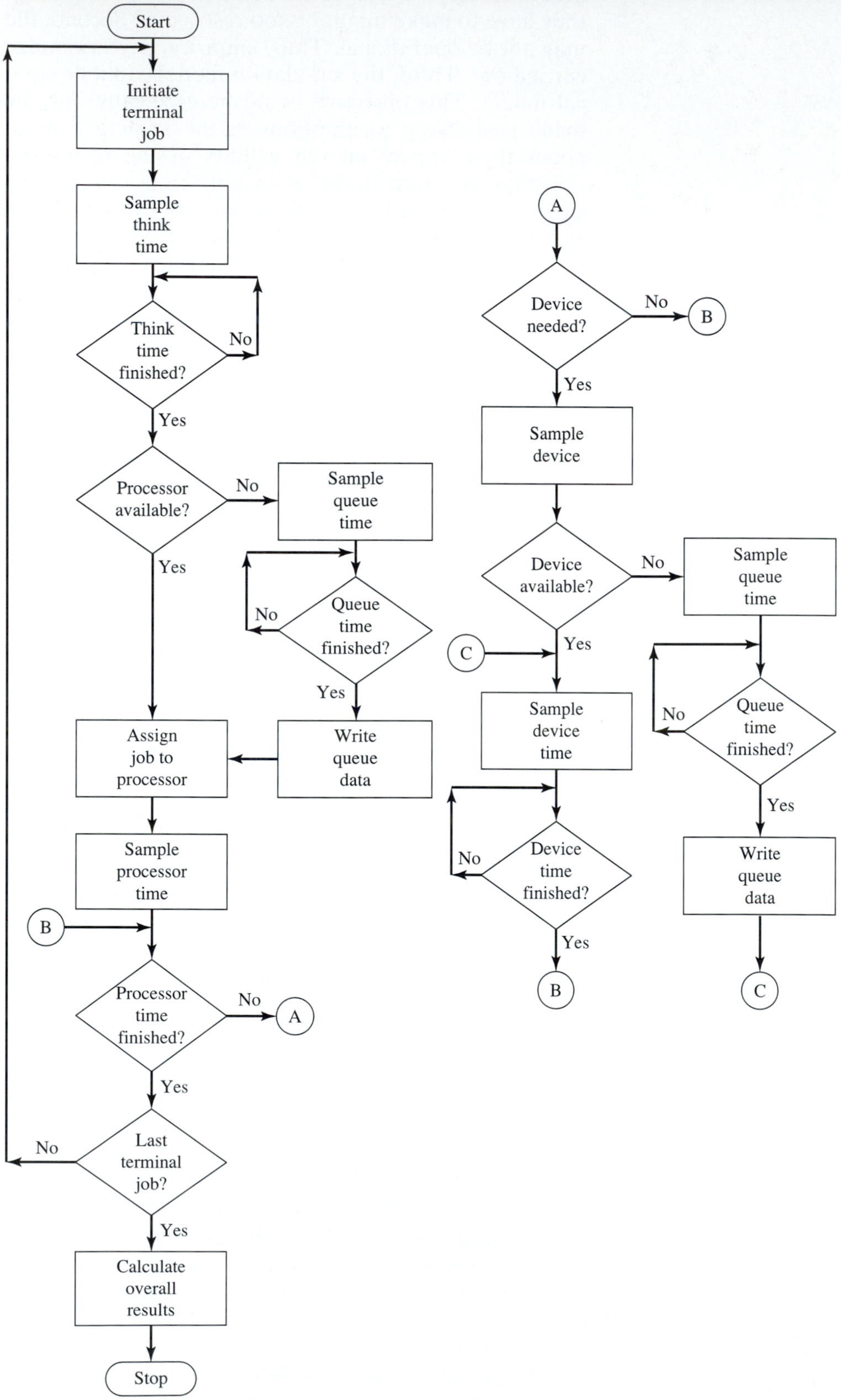

3. *Determine the amount of processor time to be spent on the transaction by sampling from a probability distribution.* This time might be broken up into fixed time slices to reflect a multiprogramming environment. Periodically, requests for services from other devices (e.g., a disk device) will be issued. The timing of the requests for services from other devices might be obtained by sampling from a probability distribution. The choice of which device is requested might also be based on sample values drawn from a probability distribution, although at times the choice of the current device might depend upon the choice of the previous device; for example, the choice of a printer must be preceded by the choice of a disk.

4. *Determine the time required for a device to service a transaction.* When a device is chosen, the request for service might have to be assigned to a queue if the device is busy. Otherwise, the request can be serviced immediately if the device is free. The amount of time requested might be obtained by sampling from a probability distribution.

5. *Write results to a log for subsequent analysis.* When the time interval assigned for the services provided by a device has elapsed, the simulation again returns control to the central processor. The sequence of processor servicing and device servicing continues until the simulation determines that processing is complete for the transaction. Processing of a new transaction then commences. Data pertaining to the completed transaction must be written to a log for subsequent analysis—for example, total response time for the transaction, queue lengths for the central processor and various devices, and total waiting time in various queues.

6. *Calculate overall results and terminate the simulation.* When a sufficient number of transactions has been processed (as indicated, say, by stability in the overall results), the performance indices can be calculated and the simulation terminated. For example, the mean and standard deviation might be determined for the response time, lengths of different queues, and waiting times in different queues. The distributions of these performance indices also might be plotted. The simulation can then be terminated.

When auditors formulate a simulation model, therefore, they follow steps that are similar to those they use when we formulate an analytical model. Auditors must identify jobs, service centers, queues, arrival times, service times, and so on. In addition, however, they must determine the sequence of events that occur and understand the interrelationships that exist among the various components in the system. The value of a simulation model arises from auditors' ability to represent these dynamics in their model and to better understand how these dynamics affect the performance of the system they are evaluating.

Model Implementation

When auditors implement a simulation model, they must make a choice on how the workload model will be implemented and how the system model will be implemented. They must also choose the programming language they will use to implement the simulation model.

The workload model can be implemented using a probabilistic workload model or a trace. If auditors choose a probabilistic workload model, resource requests are generated as random samples from specified distributions. If auditors choose a trace, the time series of resource requests for an artificial or operational system must be kept. Trace-driven simulations usually produce more accurate results. The correlations between resource requests by jobs can be preserved, and a more detailed description of the workload is possible. Traces often are more costly to construct and run, however, than probabilistic models. Furthermore, the simulation results tend to be less accurate when sensitivity

23–7 Which of the following is *most likely* to be an advantage of a natural workload model?

a Its representativeness is high

b It is easy to modify

c It is cheap to execute

d It is compact

23–8 Which of the following workload models is *most likely* to have the highest level of representativeness?

a A kernel program

b A cycle count

c An instruction mix

d A synthetic job

23–9 Which of the following is a *disadvantage* of a probabilistic workload model?

a Lack of compactness with respect to workload characterization

b Inflexibility when workload characteristics change

c Tractability requirements sometimes lower representativeness

d High development costs relative to benchmarks

23–10 When modeling a computer system, the boundaries between subsystems can be identified by:

a The physical differences between the components that make up each subsystem

b The presence of some form of communication channel between the subsystems

c A major difference in the time interval between events in each subsystem

d A switch in the nature of the processor, e.g., hardware to software to microcode

23–11 In a queuing model of a computer system, which of the following is *least likely* to be a server?

a A processor

b An input/output device

c Memory

d A user

23–12 A problem with using queuing theory to model computer systems is:

a Closed models, which are often more representative of real systems than open models, are harder to solve mathematically

b Queuing models are not useful when the computer system under study has multiple processors

c Only a limited set of performance indices can be investigated using a queuing model of a computer system

d Queuing models cannot represent the complex probabilistic phenomena that occur in computer systems

23–13 A queuing model in which all jobs are generated internally to the model is called:

a An internal model

b A closed model

c A mixed model

d An open model

23–14 A round robin strategy describes:

a An arrival pattern at a server

b A processor service discipline

c An input/output device routing strategy

d An approach to building a natural workload model

23–15 The *most likely* reason that approximate analysis will be used to solve a queuing model is:

    a The system to be modeled does not involve online, interactive input

    b An open queuing model has been used to model the computer system

    c A natural workload model has been used

    d Restrictive modeling assumptions have been violated

23–16 With a queuing model of a computer system, calibration is the process of:

    a Determining the size of the error in the values of the performance indices provided by the queuing model

    b Making the results of an open queuing model approximate the results of a closed queuing model

    c Reducing the size of the output errors by reducing or eliminating various forms of inaccuracies

    d Undertaking sensitivity analyses to determine the most important workload and system parameters

23–17 Which of the following is *least likely* to be a reason why auditors use a simulation model to evaluate the efficiency of a computer system?

    a Cheaper than a queuing model

    b Used to validate the analytical model

    c The system to be evaluated may not be operational

    d An analytical model may not be tractable

23–18 If auditors focus on *processes* in the design and implementation of a simulation model, time is incremented:

    a When the system changes its state

    b By constant intervals

    c By random intervals

    d When the system invokes a new process

23–19 Which of the following is *least likely* to be true of a trace-driven simulation model?

    a It produces more accurate results than a simulation based on a probabilistic workload model

    b It is more costly to construct and run than a probabilistic model

    c It is less accurate when sensitivity analyses involving major modifications to the workload or system structure are carried out

    d Compared with a probabilistic workload model, it is more difficult to preserve correlations between resource requests

23–20 Which of the following is *least likely* to be a way of validating a simulation model?

    a Plotting the means of the distribution of arrival times and service times associated with a probabilistic workload model

    b Examining the values of the performance indices produced by the simulation model for reasonableness

    c Comparing the results produced by the simulation model with the results produced by a queuing model

    d Evaluating the reasonableness of the results produced by the simulation when workload and system parameters are altered

23–21 The major empirical model used in performance evaluation is:

    a The general linear model

    b Regression

    c Analysis of variance

    d Analysis of covariance

23–22 If auditors wish to evaluate the effects on system response time of a changed processor service discipline, a changed channel allocation, and the number of logons that occur each minute, it is *most likely* that the empirical model they will use is:

a Analysis of variance

b Factor analysis

c Analysis of covariance

d Regression

23–23 Which of the following workload models cannot be used with a simulation system model?

a Benchmark

b Instruction mix

c Synthetic job

d Probabilistic

23–24 Which of the following workload models cannot be used with an analytical system model:

a Probabilistic

b Instruction mix

c Trace

d Kernel program

Exercises and Cases

23–1 Van Dieman's Banking Corporation (VDBC) is a large, Hobart-based bank with branches scattered throughout Australia and New Zealand. It was first established during the convict days in Tasmania, and over the past 100 years it has grown to offer a wide range of wholesale and retail banking services.

You are an information systems audit specialist in the accounting firm that has just taken over the external audit of the bank. During interim audit work, your partner asks you to examine controls over capacity planning associated with the bank's computer systems. From discussions with the previous auditor, she is aware that the bank's computer systems have experienced problems in the past because they have been overloaded. As a result, the bank's employees have sometimes taken shortcuts in terms of controls to try to reduce response-time and turnaround delays that they would otherwise experience. To reduce the load on the computer systems, top managers have also requested that various reports (including those used for capacity planning and control purposes) not be produced. During the previous audit, VDBC's management was asked to design and implement a reporting system that would allow them to identify information systems capacity problems on a timely basis.

When you interview senior management in the information systems division about capacity management, you are told that weekly reports are now produced showing values for the following four performance indices for each of the bank's major systems:

● Turnaround time,

● Reaction time,

● Throughput rate, and

● Processor utilization.

When you ask how these indices were selected, you are told that they were chosen by the operations manager. When you ask how the reports are used, you are told that they are reviewed by the operations manager who is responsible for then alerting the manager of the information systems division to any problems that exist.

Required: In light of these findings, what conclusions would you draw about the reliance you would place on the reporting system as a means of identifying capacity planning problems with VDBC? What recommendations would you now give to your partner as to how you should now proceed? Also, what are you initial conclusions in relation to the implications of your findings for the conduct of the remainder of the audit?

23–2 Briefly explain how resource demands are generated in a probabilistic workload model. If the demand for processor time by transactions is distributed normally with a mean of 5 microseconds and a variance of 2.5 microseconds and the random number generator you use for your workload model is functioning correctly, what percentage of the transactions generated should request more than 7 microseconds of processor time? How could you check that, in fact, this is the case with your workload model? (*Hint:* You will need to remember material taught to you in your introductory statistics course to be able to answer this question.)

Assume, now, that the amount of processor time demanded by transactions varies considerably throughout the day. Assume, also, that the probabilistic workload model is to be used as input to a simulation model of a hardware/software platform that your organization is considering purchasing. As the manager of internal audit for your organization, how would you recommend that the substantial variations in processor time demanded by transactions throughout the day be taken into account in terms of the design and implementation of the workload model?

23–3 During the design of a new motor vehicle registration system for a state highway department, the systems analysts must decide on the number of terminals that are needed for the clerks who serve customers at the front desk. Customers can come to the counter, pay their registration renewals, and receive their stickers for the coming year. The system also provides answers to queries about registration rates for the different types of motor vehicles, the status of registration on a particular vehicle, the insurance category to which the vehicle belongs, and so on.

The systems analysts believe that one terminal will serve two clerical staff adequately. They are not sure, however, whether it will serve three without a queue developing, especially during peak periods (for example, around lunchtime).

Required: Outline how you would construct a queuing model to help the analysts with their problem. When you design your model, you should consider different ways that customers might queue for service and different ways in which they might be served by the clerks. Indicate whether you would use an open model or a closed model and the reasons for your choice. How would you validate and calibrate your model? Note that you should assume there is excess capacity with the central processor, disks, and so on.

23–4 Spreaditround Ltd., is a large fertilizer company with offices scattered throughout the United States. A communications network links the various offices to the head office in Detroit. The offices have online real-time update capabilities to several centralized databases.

Response times in the network have been deteriorating. After an investigation into the possible reasons for the increase in response times, the system programming group suggests two alterations to the network that they believe could remedy the situation. The first is to purchase a new model of network controller. They are uncertain, however, as to which of two models of controller to purchase. The second option is to change the method of polling terminals in the system from roll-call to hub polling.

The system programming group constructs a simulation model of the network and runs the model for 2,000 iterations. The first 1,000 iterations allow the simulation to stabilize. During the second 1,000 iterations, response times for a particular controller-method of polling configuration are measured. The experiment is run four times, one for each controller-method of polling combination.

As the manager of internal audit for Spreaditround, you receive a report from the system programming group on their simulation runs that contains the following table:

Mean Response Times in Seconds for 1,000 Iterations of Each Controller-Method of Polling Combination			
	Type of Controller		
Method of Polling	*Type 1*	*Type 2*	*Row Mean*
Roll-call	5.0020	4.1570	4.5794
Hub	5.0010	3.0620	4.0315
Column Mean	5.0015	3.6095	4.3055

Required: On the basis of the simulation results, what do you conclude about the proposed changes? If a statistical analysis (ANOVA) of the results were undertaken, what variables do you think would be statistically significant? What kinds of concerns might you have about the validity of the results obtained using the simulation model?

23–5 We obtain the following results for a regression model used to assess the impact of the number of jobs per hour that request over 5 microseconds of central processor time (X_1) and the number of jobs per hour that require more than one work space in main memory (X_2) on the response time of a system (measured in seconds):

$$Y = .106 + .371X_1 + .402X_2 \ (R^2 = .16)$$

Required:

a What is the expected impact on response time of introducing two more jobs into the system that request more than 5 microseconds of processor time?

b What is the impact on response time of introducing one more job that requests more than 5 microseconds of processor time and four jobs that require more than one work space?

c What is the expected response time if there are no jobs in the system requiring more than 5 microseconds of processor time or more than one work space?

d What kinds of concerns might we have about the validity of the estimations made using this model?

23–6 Your organization uses an online real-time update system for several of its application systems. Recently, there has been concern over increasing response times with the system. The workload has been growing. Nevertheless, because two of the online real-time update systems are used by clerical staff who deal directly with customers, customer goodwill depends on fast response times being maintained. The information systems manager has suggested decreasing response times by seeing whether the introduction of job priority classes and an increase in the time slice allocated to jobs would improve system throughput.

You are the internal auditor in your organization having expertise in performance evaluation. Management asks you to evaluate the changes proposed by the information systems manager. You decide to evaluate the changes using an experiment.

Required: Outline how you would set up the experiment. Describe how you would determine whether the changes proposed are worthwhile. Be sure to describe the sorts of steps you would undertake to try to ensure your results are valid and reliable.

23–7 Chuckle and Sue is a medium-sized, Perth-based firm of solicitors who specialize in providing advice to the yachting industry. Twelve months ago the partners decided to install their first computer system to help them process a rapidly increasing volume of accounting transactions and to obtain better management information on the state of their practice. The system that the firm chose comprised a local area network of six workstations connected to a 5 gigabyte hard disk. The software obtained was all off-the-shelf packages.

Since the system was installed, the six workstations have been used in the following way: One has been used as an update terminal to process transactions against the various ledgers and client files; one has been used as an inquiry terminal by the receptionist/secretary to answer questions from clients; and the other four have been used by the partners to inquire on client files and to print information they need for billing purposes.

Because transaction volumes have been increasing rapidly, the partners decided to add a seventh workstation to the network to act as an update terminal. As soon as one of the accounts clerks began to use the workstation to update files, however, response time in the network degraded significantly. As a consequence, Gloria Chuckle, the senior partner in the firm, approached the computer company that had sold the system to her firm to determine the cause of the problem. A salesperson from the vendor informed her that the local area network configuration was an inappropriate configuration to use if the seventh workstation was to be used as an update terminal. He advised her to sell off the workstations and the network and to purchase a minicomputer system that would drive seven terminals.

Required: You are an information systems consultant in the firm of accountants that has Chuckle and Sue as their client. Gloria has approached your partner to seek his advice on the veracity of the information provided by the vendor's salesperson. She is clearly upset by the prospective costs of converting to a new system and the associated disruption that will occur. Your partner asks you to prepare a brief report outlining how you will determine the cause of the problems in the current system as a basis for then deciding on an appropriate solution to these problems.

Answers to Multiple-Choice Questions

23–1	d	**23–7**	a	**23–13**	b	**23–19**	d
23–2	a	**23–8**	d	**23–14**	b	**23–20**	a
23–3	d	**23–9**	c	**23–15**	d	**23–21**	a
23–4	b	**23–10**	c	**23–16**	c	**23–22**	c
23–5	b	**23–11**	d	**23–17**	a	**23–23**	b
23–6	c	**23–12**	a	**23–18**	b	**23–24**	c

REFERENCES

Anderson, Gordon E. (1984), "The Coordinated Use of Five Performance Evaluation Methodologies," *Communications of the ACM* (February), 119–125.

Anonymous (1993), "The World of Benchmarks," *Capacity Management Review* (July), 9, 12.

Cady, J., and B. Howarth (1990), *Computer Systems Performance Management and Capacity Planning*. Upper Saddle River, NJ: Prentice-Hall.

Cao, Xiren (1993), "Some Common Misperceptions about Performance Modeling and Validation," *Performance Evaluation Review* (December), 11–15.

Chandy, K. Mani, and Charles H. Sauer (1978), "Approximate Methods for Analyzing Queuing Network Models of Computing Systems," *Computing Surveys* (September), 281–317.

Denning, Peter J., and Jeffrey P. Buzen (1978), "The Operational Analysis of Queueing Network Models," *Computing Surveys* (September), 225–261.

Ferrari, Domenico (1978), *Computer Systems Performance Evaluation*. Upper Saddle River, NJ: Prentice-Hall.

Fleming, Philip J., and John J. Wallace (1986), "How to Lie with Statistics: The Correct Way to Summarize Benchmark Results," *Communications of the ACM* (March), 218–221.

Huck, Shuyler W., William H. Cormier, and William G. Bounds, Jr. (1974), *Reading Statistics and Research*. New York: Harper & Row.

Jain, Raj (1991), *The Art of Computer Systems Performance Analysis: Techniques for Experimental Design, Measurement, Simulation, and Modeling*. New York: John Wiley.

Kobayashi, Hisashi (1978), *Modeling and Analysis: An Introduction to System Performance Evaluation Methodology*. Reading, MA: Addison-Wesley.

McKerrow, Phillip (1988), *Performance Measurement of Computer Systems*. Reading, MA: Addison-Wesley.

Menascé, Daniel, Virgilio A. F. Almeida, and Larry W. Dowdy (1994), *Capacity Planning and Performance Monitoring: From Mainframes to Client-Server Systems*. Upper Saddle River, NJ: Prentice-Hall.

Neter, John, William Wasserman, and Michael Kutner (1985), *Applied Linear Statistical Models: Regression, Analysis of Variance, and Experimental Designs*, 2d ed. Homewood, IL: Irwin.

Raatikainen, Kimmo E. E. (1993), "Cluster Analysis and Workload Classification," *Performance Evaluation Review* (May), 24–30.

Information Systems Audit Management

This last part of the book contains one chapter that deals with how we need to manage the information systems audit function. As with any organizational function, good management is essential if the function is to perform its role effectively and efficiently.

In the chapter, we examine how traditional management functions—planning, organizing, staffing, leading, and controlling—need to be applied within an information systems audit context. In particular, we focus on certain features of the information systems audit function that make it somewhat different from other organizational functions—for example, the limited prospects for career advancement internally to an information systems audit group because of its small size. We need to understand how traditional managerial functions must be adapted to cater for these differences.

We also need to be aware of the professional context in which an information systems audit function ought to operate. In particular, we focus on the significant role that the Information Systems Audit and Control Association now plays in terms of providing a common body of knowledge for information systems auditors, developing and maintaining standards of competency for information systems auditors, conducting the Certified Information Systems Auditor (CISA) examination to assess the competency of information systems auditors, and formulating and enforcing a code of ethics among information systems auditors.

Finally, we close the chapter and the book by canvassing some possible futures of information systems auditing. In particular, we focus on the impact that various forms of technological change might have on the conduct of information systems auditing within organizations. As managers, we need to be alert to and plan for the changes that might ensue.

Managing the Information Systems Audit Function

Chapter Outline

Chapter Key Points

■ Managing the information systems audit function involves traditional management functions: planning, organizing, staffing, leading, and controlling. Furthermore, information systems audit managers must take into account two other factors: the impact of professionalism and the impact of changing technology.

■ We need to formulate two types of plans when we manage the information systems audit function: long-run plans and short-run plans. Our goals with long-run planning are to provide an overall direction for the information systems audit function and to ensure we have adequate resources available to discharge our responsibilities effectively and efficiently. Our goal with short-run planning is to put in place a risk-management program that will enable us to systematically evaluate exposures that face the organization we are trying to assist.

■ Organizing the information systems audit function involves our addressing four issues: (a) establishing formally the legitimacy of the information systems audit function within an organization, (b) determining whether the information systems audit function should play a staff role or a line role within an organization's overall audit function, (c) determining whether the information systems audit function should be centralized or decentralized, and (d) determining how the information systems audit function should be resourced.

■ The legitimacy and role of the information systems audit function should be established via an audit charter. If information systems auditors play a staff role, they will assist general staff auditors by providing specialist advice on technologically complex matters associated with computers. If they play a line role, however, they will be an integral part of any audit team. Many factors affect the decision on whether the information systems audit function should be centralized or decentralized. Probably the most important factor, however, is whether the organization in which the information systems audit function is placed is itself centralized or decentralized. How well the information systems audit function is resourced will depend in part on how well long-run and short-run planning activities are undertaken.

- ◼ The staffing function involves sourcing and recruiting information systems audit staff, appraising and developing information systems audit staff, and determining suitable career paths for information systems audit staff. In terms of sourcing and recruitment, a long-standing issue is whether it is better to recruit staff who primarily have an information technology background or staff who primarily have an auditing background. Careful staff appraisal and development is critical within the information systems audit function because staff need to remain proficient in technical, social, and managerial skills. Providing suitable career paths for information systems auditors is often difficult because many organizations employ only a small number of information systems auditors.

- ◼ When we lead an information systems audit group, we need to achieve harmony of objectives at three levels. First, the actions taken by individual auditors need to be congruent with the overall objectives of the specific audits in which they participate. Second, each audit needs to be undertaken in such a way that its outcomes are congruent with those established under the short-term plan for the information systems audit function. Third, the activities of the information systems audit function overall must help the organization to achieve its mission and goals and in some cases to shape its mission and goals. To achieve harmony of objectives, leadership processes must be adjusted to take into account the needs of individual information systems auditors. For example, at times information systems audit managers might need to be somewhat autocratic; at other times they might need to lead using a democratic style.

- ◼ Control needs to be exercised at the level of individual audits and the level of the overall information systems audit function. At the level of individual audits, some important control strategies are to state and document clearly the objectives of an audit, to monitor and evaluate progress, to subject the audit work performed to independent review, to report carefully the results of an audit, and to obtain feedback from the stakeholders in an audit on their views about the quality of the audit. At the level of the overall information systems audit function, some important control strategies are to undertake periodic detailed reviews of selected audits, to regularly review information systems audit standards, policies, and procedures, and to use benchmarking to evaluate how well the information systems audit function is performing relative to information systems audit functions within other organizations.

- ◼ The leading international professional organization for information systems auditors is the Information Systems Audit and Control Association (ISACA). The ISACA has more than 14,000 members in more than 100 countries. It has local chapters in more than 50 countries.

- ◼ The five hallmarks of a profession are (a) existence of a common body of knowledge, (b) existence of standards of competency, (c) conduct of a valid and reliable examination to assess competency, (d) existence of a code of ethics, and (e) enforcement of the code of ethics through a disciplinary mechanism. The ISACA has sought to put in place all five hallmarks. It has worked to define a common body of knowledge for information systems auditors. This body of knowledge has been articulated and published in *COBIT: Control Objectives for Information and Related Technology*. ISACA has also defined standards of competency in relation to information systems audit independence, technical competence, work performance, audit reporting, audit follow-up, and audit charter. An examination of competency called the Certified Information Systems Audit examination is conducted internationally by the ISACA. The ISACA has also formulated a code of professional ethics and put in place a disciplinary mechanism for its members.

■ The Internet has had and will continue to have a major impact on the conduct of the information systems audit function. Some control and audit issues that have arisen in light of the Internet are greater exposure to data integrity and privacy violations, increased problems with copyright of information made available on the Internet, wasted resources with ineffective and inefficient use of the Internet (especially the World Wide Web), a greater incidence of computer viruses, and greater exposure to the effects of erroneous information and programs.

■ Electronic commerce involves the use of computer-based data communications technologies to facilitate execution of commercial transactions. It is relatively easy to secure the conduct of electronic commerce when *private* data communications networks are used. When *public* data communications networks are used to carry out electronic commerce, however, problems arise in relation to establishing the identity and authenticity of parties to transactions, protecting the privacy and integrity of messages exchanged, and effecting secure exchange of monies for goods and services provided. Most controls to secure electronic commerce conducted over public networks are based on public-key cryptographic methods.

■ Business process engineering involves organizing the activities conducted within businesses on the basis of processes rather than functions. The goal is to make these activities more effective and efficient. A problem with business process engineering, however, is that traditional controls (such as separation of duties) are often compromised in the hope of gaining improved effectiveness and efficiency. Information systems auditors need to be mindful, therefore, of how business process reengineering can undermine controls and to work toward mitigating the effects of any increased exposures that occur.

■ Many information systems activities are now being outsourced to allow organizations to concentrate better on their core functions. Some short-term and long-term risks are associated with information systems outsourcing, however. For example, organizations that outsource must rely on the outsourcing vendor to protect the integrity and privacy of their data. Information systems auditors must play a role in the decision to outsource, design of the outsourcing contract, monitoring performance under the contract, and termination of the contract.

■ Protection of data privacy has remained an enduring issue within the information systems audit discipline. Traditional data privacy safeguards have been founded on the principle of Fair Information Practices whereby people are given rights such as knowing whether information has been stored about them, requiring the existence of personal data systems to be registered publicly, and requiring erroneous data about themselves to be corrected. With increasing use of the Internet and the existence of large numbers of networked personal computers, however, our ability to enforce the rights given under the Fair Information Practices principle is breaking down. Protection of data privacy remains a major concern, however. In this light, information systems auditors must seek out ways to preserve data privacy in spite of the increasing exposures that are occurring as a result of the impacts of new information technology.

■ Data mining techniques enable us to detect patterns that can manifest errors and irregularities in huge databases. They rely on such tools as statistical models, expert systems, and neural networks. Data mining techniques facilitate our processes of knowledge discovery—that is, assessing whether assets have been safeguarded, data integrity has been maintained, and systems are operating effectively and efficiently.

■ Increasingly, the boundaries of traditional organizations are beginning to blur. Interorganizational information systems and virtual organizations are being established that allow individuals and organizations to work together, regardless of their physical location or time zone. In these types of environments, information systems auditors must place greater reliance on the work of other auditors and the existence and enforcement of standardized information systems controls and audit procedures.

INTRODUCTION

In the last chapter of this book, we examine how we might manage the information systems audit function. Our focus primarily is on the management of an internal audit group. Nonetheless, much of what we shall consider will apply, also, to the management of an external audit group.

We organize our discussion around traditional management functions: planning, organizing, staffing, leading, and controlling (see also Chapter 3). Within each of these primary functions, we discuss the sorts of activities we are likely to carry out if we have overall responsibility for an organization's information systems audit function. We then discuss ways in which moves toward professionalism have affected and are likely to continue to affect the information systems audit function. Finally, we conclude this book by considering how current environmental developments are likely to influence the future conduct of information systems auditing.

PLANNING FUNCTION

We need to formulate two types of plans when we manage the information systems audit function: long-run plans and short-run plans. In the following subsections, we briefly examine the nature of, purposes of, and preparation of each type of plan.

Long-Run Planning

When we undertake long-run planning in relation to the information systems audit function, our goals are twofold: *(1)* to provide an overall direction for the function and *(2)* to try to ensure we will have adequate resources to discharge the responsibilities associated with the function effectively and efficiently. Our determination of the former goal will have a marked influence on our deliberations in relation to the latter goal.

Overall, the long-run goal of the information systems audit function should be to support the mission of the organization in which it is placed. We must determine, therefore, how critical the goals of asset safeguarding, data integrity, system effectiveness, and system efficiency are to the host organization. Clearly, these four goals will be important to some extent in all organizations. We must recognize, however, that their relative importance will vary across organizations. For example, asset safeguarding and data integrity are likely to be of paramount importance to financial institutions. In a consulting firm, however, asset safeguarding and data integrity often will be a minor concern. The firm is likely to have few information systems assets to safeguard and little data that is critical to its operations. Instead, the primary assets are likely to be the firm's consultants. Moreover, the critical data is likely to be the knowledge possessed by these consultants.

In short, we need to adopt a contingency perspective on the nature of and amount of long-run planning we undertake in relation to the information systems audit function. In this regard, McFarlan et al.'s (1983) strategic grid might help us make this determination (Figure 24–1). Recall from Chapter 3 that they focus on the importance of existing information systems and the importance of future information systems in determining the nature of and extent of information systems planning that should be undertaken within an organization. The extent of planning needs to increase as the importance of existing and future information systems to an organization increases. Similarly, more long-run planning needs to be undertaken as the importance of future information systems to an organization increases.

In the context of the information systems audit function, we would expect that asset safeguarding, data integrity, effectiveness, and efficiency will become more critical as the importance of existing and future information systems to an organization increases. Accordingly, we will need to undertake more planning in relation to the information systems audit function. Similarly, as the importance of future information systems to an organization increases, we will need to undertake more long-run planning in relation to the information systems audit function.

FIGURE 24–1. Information systems audit planning within a contingency perspective.
Adapted by permission of the Harvard Business Review. From "The Information Archipelago—Plotting a Course," by F. Warren McFarlan, James L. McKenney, and Philip Pyburn, January–February 1983. Copyright © 1983 by the President and Fellows of Harvard College; all rights reserved.

	Importance of future systems	
	Low	High
Importance of current systems — Low	Only small amounts of IS audit planning	Extensive long-run IS audit planning
Importance of current systems — High	Extensive short-run IS audit planning	Extensive short-run and long-run IS audit planning

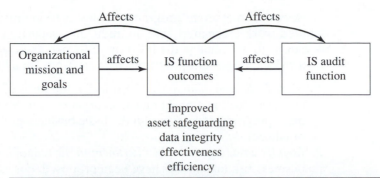

FIGURE 24–2. **Having an impact on an organization's missions and goals via an IS audit function.**

We must recognize, also, that it might be possible to turn the goals of asset safeguarding, data integrity, effectiveness, and efficiency into a source of competitive advantage for an organization. In this light, planning for the information systems audit function should not always be secondary to the overall planning undertaken on the organization's mission and goals. In some organizations, it might be possible to use the activities of the information systems audit function to affect the determination of the organization's mission and goals (Figure 24–2). To the extent that the information systems audit function allows new levels of asset safeguarding, data integrity, effectiveness, and efficiency to be achieved, the organization might be able to undertake strategic initiatives—for example, that lead it to compete in new markets.

Short-Run Planning

The major feature of short-run planning associated with the information systems audit function should be the risk-management program that management adopts. The purpose of this program is to identify those areas within an organization that need to be audited with a view to reducing the exposures faced by the organization to an acceptable level. Risk management needs to be proactive rather than reactive.

We have already examined some of the important elements that underlie a risk-management program in Chapters 2 and 7. In Chapter 2, recall that we discussed three types of risk that have an important impact on audit work: inherent risk, control risk, and detection risk. Initially, we try to assess the risk associated with not meeting our asset safeguarding, data integrity, effectiveness, and efficiency objectives by virtue of the nature of the organization or business processes with which we are dealing (inherent risk). We then examine the reliability of the controls in place to reduce exposures from this risk. If we believe our control objectives have still not been met (control risk), we design tests to confirm our suspicions. There is a risk, however, that these tests will still not detect a failure to meet control objectives (detection risk). We try to control the overall audit risk that we face, which is a function of the inherent, control, and detection risks.

In Chapter 7, recall, also, that we examined the important steps we undertake in a security program: *(1)* preparation of a project plan, *(2)* identification of assets, *(3)* valuation of assets, *(4)* threats identification, *(5)* threats likelihood assessment, *(6)* exposures analysis, *(7)* controls adjustment, and *(8)* report preparation. Our goal with a security program is to reduce expected losses from exposures to an acceptable level. We will continue to implement controls up to the point where the reduction in expected losses from having the control equals the costs of designing, implementing, operating, and maintaining the control.

A risk-management program enables us to identify where we should do the detailed work associated with an audit or a security program and how overall we can begin to manage the level of audit risk associated with an organization. Most risk-management programs are variations on a few basic steps:

1. *Identify the unit of analysis.* Historically, the focus of a risk-management program was the functional units in an organization. Now, however, risk-management programs often focus on the basic business processes associated with an organization.

2. *Identify a set of generic risks pertinent to the unit of analysis.* Several different business-risk taxonomies have been proposed. For example, Erickson (1996) divides risks into financial risks (e.g., risks that a customer will not pay, risks that assets will decline because of interest rate rises) and system risks (e.g., ease with which hardware can be replaced, the processing logic complexity); Arthur Andersen divides risks into environment risks, process risks, and information for decision-making risks (Dahlberg 1996) and Kanter and Pitman (1997) list 11 risk factors, including the size of the unit of analysis, the complexity of operations, and the liquidity of assets.

3. *Determine a risk weighting for each unit of analysis.* The importance of each generic risk must be evaluated in the context of each unit of analysis. Often, some type of weighting is assigned to each generic risk factor (e.g., a rating on a ten-point scale). A materiality weighting might also be assigned to the unit of analysis. Some type of global risk weighting can then be calculated as a function of the individual generic risk ratings and perhaps the materiality weighting. Table 24–1 shows one approach whereby the risk weightings for the generic risk factors are summed and then multiplied by a materiality factor (on a scale of zero to ten) to determine an overall risk weighting for the unit of analysis.

4. *Prioritize audits (security evaluations) based on risk weightings.* When an overall risk weighting has been determined for each unit of analysis, a priority list can be prepared for the different units. This priority list forms the basis for the conduct of audits over, say, the coming year.

5. *Determine the resources needed to support the program of audits to be conducted.* When the audits to be undertaken have been determined, the resources required to support these audits can be estimated. In particular, personnel needs (which are the most significant resources required in the conduct of audits) can be resolved. If resource requirements exceed those that are likely to be available, some iteration must occur to either (a) gain management approval

---

TABLE 24–1   Prioritizing Audit Areas Using Risk Weightings

Business Process	RF1	RF2	RF3	RF4	RF5	RF6	Materiality	Overall Weighting
			Risk Factors					
Order Entry	7	7	3	5	5	6	8	264
Invoicing	7	7	2	4	3	6	7	203
Accounts Receivable	7	7	1	2	3	6	7	182
Merchandise Returns	2	2	1	2	2	4	5	65
Bad Debt Recovery	3	4	1	3	2	4	5	85

RF1 = Operational impact
RF2 = Business impact
RF3 = Rate of change
RF4 = Complexity
RF5 = Size
RF6 = Risk of fraud
Overall weighting = $\Sigma RF_i \times$ Materiality

for more resources or (b) make stakeholders aware that some exposures are unlikely to be addressed in the audit program to be pursued in the current year.

Short-run planning based on risk management is unlikely to be successful unless the unit of analysis's stakeholders are actively involved in the risk-management process. Stakeholders should have an intimate knowledge of their unit of analysis. Accordingly, they are often in a better position than auditors to determine the risks they confront and the potential impact of these risks. For this reason, many organizations now use a process of *control self-assessment*, which basically is a formal, documented process whereby the stakeholders in a unit of analysis evaluate the likelihood of their unit achieving the goals of asset safeguarding, data integrity, effectiveness, and efficiency (West and Khan 1997).

ORGANIZING FUNCTION

When we organize the information systems audit function within an organization, we need to establish *(1)* the formal legitimacy of its place within the organization, *(2)* its role within the organization's overall audit function, *(3)* whether it should be centralized or decentralized, and *(4)* how it should be resourced. We will examine each of these issues in the following subsections.

Need for an Audit Charter

An information systems audit group usually operates within the overall internal audit function in an organization. The legitimacy and role of the internal audit function (and hence the information systems audit function) should be expressed in an *audit charter*. Cangemi (1996, pp. 9–11) notes that this charter should address three primary issues:

1. *Audit function's place within the organization.* The charter should formally establish the place of the audit function within an organization and describe the ways in which it is intended to contribute to the organization's overall mission and goals.
2. *Audit function's authority.* The charter should state the auditor's rights to have access to records, facilities, and personnel in the conduct of their work. The charter should also establish the internal audit manager's right to have direct access to the Board of Directors' audit committee or to the Board itself.
3. *Audit function's scope.* The charter should establish the audit function's responsibilities in relation to providing advice to management about how well the organization is attaining asset safeguarding, data integrity, effectiveness, and efficiency objectives. At the same time, it should state that management has primary responsibility for controls within an organization and undertaking corrective actions in light of advice that the audit function provides.

Unless an audit charter exists, the rights and responsibilities of both the internal audit function and the information systems audit function within an organization will not be clear. As a result, disputes over the mandate of both functions could arise, and their effectiveness and efficiency will be undermined.

Staff Versus Line Function

A long-standing debate about how to organize the information systems audit function relates to the question of whether information systems audit specialists should play a staff role or a line role within external or internal audit groups (see, e.g., Mullen 1993). If information systems audit specialists play a staff role, they advise and assist financial auditors on technologically complex matters relating to computers (Figure 24–3a). If they play a line role, however,

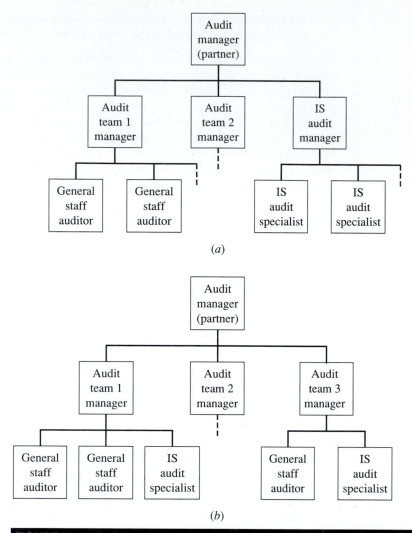

FIGURE 24–3(a). Information systems auditing as a staff function. (**b**). Information systems auditing as a line function.

they are an integral part of an audit team, and they assume responsibility for those parts of an audit that involve the computer (Figure 24–3b).

Several arguments are given in support of having information systems audit specialists play a *staff* role:

1. *Better use of information systems audit resources.* Maintaining an effective and efficient information systems audit group requires substantial commitment to ongoing education and training. Furthermore, skilled information systems auditors are often difficult to hire. In a staff capacity, information systems auditors focus on only those parts of the audit that involve the computer. Better use is made, therefore, of a scarce resource.
2. *Greater work satisfaction for information systems auditors.* Information systems auditors working in a staff capacity will focus only on the computer-related parts of an audit. This more intensive use of their skills could give them greater job satisfaction.
3. *Greater organizational commitment to information systems auditing.* In a staff capacity, the information systems audit group has a separate existence. Thus, senior management are less likely to overlook the information systems audit function. They should be more committed, therefore, to its support.

4. *Facilitates co-ordination and control among information systems auditors.* If information systems auditors are placed within a separate group having their own manager, their activities might be easier to coordinate and control.
5. *Facilitates increased information systems audit specialization.* If a separate information systems audit group is established, different members of the group can specialize in different aspects of computer technology and use (e.g., databases, networks, and end-user computing). These specializations can then be deployed to those audits where they are needed.

These arguments have motivated some organizations to establish information systems audit *competency centers*, which essentially perform information systems audit service bureau functions. Financial auditors can send data files to a competency center to be processed. Center staff also provide specialist consulting advice to financial auditors. The center could also be responsible for developing and maintaining information systems audit standards, refining information systems audit methodologies, and purchasing, developing, implementing, testing, operating, and maintaining computer-assisted audit techniques.

Several arguments have been given, however, for having information systems audit specialists play a *line* role rather than a staff role:

1. *Greater goal congruence.* As an integral member of an audit team having full responsibility for an audit, information systems audit specialists should have a better understanding of the overall audit objectives. Moreover, they should be more committed to its successful completion.
2. *Facilitates communications within the audit function.* The existence of a separate information systems audit group sometimes causes friction between information systems audit specialists and financial auditors. The information systems auditor sees the financial auditor as being technically deficient and resistant to change. The financial auditor sees the information systems audit specialist as being more interested in technology than accomplishing the audit's objectives. If the two types of auditors are placed within the same work group, they might have a better appreciation of and greater empathy for each other's role.
3. *Improves overall audit expertise of both financial and information systems auditors.* If information systems auditors perform a staff function, financial auditors tend to abrogate responsibility for those parts of the audit involving computers. At the same time, information systems auditors tend to abrogate responsibility for those parts of the audit that do not involve computers. If information systems auditors perform a line function, however, both financial auditors and information systems auditors have to accept greater responsibility for each other's performance. Financial auditors have incentives, therefore, to improve their information systems audit skills. Similarly, information systems auditors have incentives to improve their financial audit skills.
4. *Better coordination in planning and executing an audit.* When information systems auditors perform a staff function, sometimes the planning and execution of an audit are poorly coordinated. Financial auditors and information systems auditors might undertake their work at different times. As a result, they might address different audit objectives, duplicate each other's work, or omit to undertake important audit work in the belief that it will be undertaken by the other. They might undertake too much audit work because they fail to appreciate that compensating controls exist in areas they do not audit. Additional overheads are also incurred in the maintenance of two management structures. These types of problems might be mitigated if the two groups are integrated.

The adoption of a staff versus a line role for information systems auditors has some important implications for several other aspects of managing the audit function within an organization—for example, the career paths that can be pursued by information systems auditors and the education and training they should receive.

Centralization versus Decentralization

In large organizations, a decision must sometimes be made on whether the internal audit group and thus the information systems audit group should be centralized or decentralized. Similarly, in an external audit firm, a decision must sometimes be made about whether the information systems audit group will be located in only some of the firm's offices or decentralized to all the firm's offices.

The question of whether an information systems audit group should be centralized or decentralized has no clear-cut answer. The following factors are representative of those that influence the decision:

1. If information systems audits are to be performed in locations that are dispersed physically, a tendency exists toward decentralization to overcome communication and control problems.
2. If the audit group has a shortage of information systems audit expertise, a tendency exists toward centralization to make more effective use of the limited expertise that is available.
3. If financial auditors have basic competence in information systems auditing, a tendency exists to have a centralized group of information systems audit specialists performing a staff function.
4. If implementation of computer-assisted audit techniques at physically dispersed locations is difficult, a tendency exists to establish a centralized information systems audit group that performs service bureau type functions.
5. Newly formed information systems audit groups tend to be centralized. Decentralization occurs as the group matures.

Perhaps the most important factor affecting the centralization-decentralization decision is whether the organization in which the information systems audit group is located is centralized or decentralized. As we saw in Chapter 3, the information systems function is likely to be more successful if the way it is structured is congruent with the way its host organization is structured. Similarly, the information systems audit function is likely to be more successful if the way it is structured is congruent with the way its host organization is structured.

Resourcing the Information Systems Audit Function

If information systems audits are to be undertaken effectively and efficiently, adequate resources must be available. Provided proper long-term and short-term planning is undertaken, the nature and amount of resources needed can be estimated. For example, short-term plans for the information systems audit function should enable us to predict the number of staff we will need over the coming year, the skills these staff must have, the types of computer-assisted audit techniques we will need to collect and evaluate evidence, the support we will require from other employees (e.g., programmers), and the demands we will have to make on auditees during the conduct of our audit work. As managers in charge of the information systems audit function, we must acquire and schedule the availability of these resources as they are needed. Otherwise, the conduct of information systems audits will be impaired.

STAFFING FUNCTION

The staffing function associated with the information systems audit staff is similar to any other staffing function that must be carried out in an organization: Staff must be hired, developed, and supported, and voluntary and involuntary termination of staff must be managed (see Chapter 3). In the following subsections, we examine a few staffing issues that are especially pertinent to managing information systems audit personnel.

Sourcing and Recruitment of Information Systems Audit Staff

A long-standing issue within the information systems audit discipline has been the question of whether it is better to recruit staff with an information technology background or staff with an audit background. Those who favor recruiting staff with an information technology background give several reasons. First, they argue that well-trained computer professionals already have a solid grounding in computer controls. Systems analysts and programmers, for example, should already have experience in the design and implementation of controls in the systems they have built. Second, they argue that the technical knowledge and insight required to evaluate a computer-based information system can only be obtained through practical experience in systems design and implementation. Third, they argue that information systems auditors need more knowledge of information technology than auditing to perform their function well. Moreover, the auditing knowledge required can be obtained more easily than the information technology knowledge.

Those who favor recruiting staff with an audit background contend, first, that gaining an appreciation of the overall control philosophy needed to be an effective and efficient information systems auditor is best obtained through initial education and training in accounting and auditing. Second, they argue that ultimately the objective of many audits is to make some judgment about the state of the accounting records. Information systems auditors who have more in-depth training in accounting and auditing are best placed to make this judgment. Third, they argue that information technology knowledge is volatile. It constantly changes as the technology itself changes. Accounting and auditing knowledge, on the other hand, is more stable. Thus, it provides a better basis from which to work as an information systems auditor.

Rittenberg (1977) tried to find a resolution to this debate. He asked a large number of auditors whether they perceived data processing knowledge or auditing knowledge to be more difficult to acquire. Interestingly, those who had a data processing background thought auditing knowledge was more difficult to acquire. Those who had an auditing background, however, thought data processing knowledge was more difficult to acquire. Clearly, both types of knowledge are important to information systems auditors' work. Moreover, no easy answer exists to the question of whether we are better off if we are educated first in information technology or educated first in accounting and auditing.

Whenever we recruit information systems auditors, however, we need to identify the education, training, experience, and skills we will want appointees to possess. These requirements should be an outcome of our planning efforts. Our short-run plans should identify our immediate needs in terms of staff capabilities—in particular, those needs that are essential and those that are desirable in terms of the audits we need to undertake over, say, the next 12 months. Our long-run plans should provide the foundation for staff development as well as recruitment. Hiring of information systems staff must be based on how well applicants satisfy both these short-run and long-run needs.

Appraisal and Development of Information Systems Audit Staff

As with any staff, information systems audit staff should undergo a regular cycle of review and appraisal. Both staff and management must prepare thoroughly for the appraisal. Each should reflect carefully on the staff member's strengths and weaknesses. Each should also try to reach agreement with the other on their assessment of the staff member's strengths and weaknesses. Management must then affirm the staff member's strengths and provide constructive feedback on weaknesses. In addition, development goals must be set and a plan prepared to facilitate the staff member's attaining these goals.

Information systems auditing is a demanding profession because it requires practitioners to be proficient in technical skills associated with computers and auditing, management and organizational skills, written and oral communication skills, interpersonal skills, and leadership skills. People are highly unlikely to have all these skills at the outset of their careers. Rather, they will have to be acquired (often slowly and painfully) over time. In this light, staff development plans must foster the acquisition of these skills in a way that is congruent with the information systems auditor's level of authority and responsibility in their organization.

For example, in certain roles, information systems auditors might not have to possess high levels of technical skills to perform their function effectively. They might need to be accomplished *users* of computer-assisted audit techniques, but they might not have to possess the skills needed to *develop* these techniques themselves. Provided they have a moderate understanding of the technology and a good understanding of and experience with auditing, the application domain, and "soft" skills like oral communications, they might be in a strong position to perform a competent audit. In other roles, however, information systems auditors might require high levels of technical skills. For example, they might have to act as consultants to audit teams that are operating in complex database and data communications environments. The training programs they attend, therefore, might focus more on providing knowledge and experience with technology and less on interpersonal skills.

Bruno (1994) argues that three trends underscore the importance of ongoing education and training for information systems auditors. First, the technology that underlies systems is undergoing constant and rapid change. Information systems auditors must be provided with the education and training that allows them to remain competent in the technology. Second, many organizations have adopted total quality management (TQM) practices. In this light, all personnel are subject to constant benchmarking and appraisal. At the same time, they are being empowered so they have greater control over their work. Third, organizations are continuing to downsize and re-engineer their processes. Unless information systems auditors are well educated, well trained, and experienced, they might not be able to cope effectively with the consequences of these trends.

Career Paths for Information Systems Audit Staff

Finding a suitable career path for information systems auditors can present a problem. Often organizations have only a small number of information systems auditors (sometimes only one). They are a specialist group among the general staff auditors within an internal audit group or an external audit firm. Thus, information systems auditors have few promotional opportunities.

In some internal information systems audit groups, a few levels in a hierarchy might exist—for example, assistant information systems auditor, information systems auditor, and manager of information systems audit. Given organizational trends toward downsizing and flattening of management structures, however, the number of levels is likely to shrink rather than grow. In some external audit firms, a clear path to partner might exist for individuals who wish to specialize in information systems audit—junior, senior, manager, and partner. The information systems audit groups within external audit firms are also likely to be larger than the information systems audit group that forms part of an organization's internal audit group.

Some information systems auditors might not look to an extensive range of promotional opportunities as the basis for obtaining satisfaction from their jobs. Instead, they might seek the intrinsic rewards they obtain from practicing as an information systems auditor—for example, the variety of work they encounter, and the challenge they face in remaining competent as information technology changes rapidly. An information systems auditor's aspirations need to be addressed during appraisal meetings. Persons who seek extensive promotional opportunities must be counseled on the realistic set they face if they continue their careers in information systems auditing. Persons who seek intrinsic rewards, however, should be given an opportunity to articulate the ways in which they can be given the experience, education, and training to provide them with a satisfying career.

A career in information systems auditing is often viewed as a useful stepping stone for other careers—for example, data or database administration, information systems consulting, information systems management, quality assurance management, security administration, and financial management. Like all auditing positions, incumbents obtain a wide, diverse range of experience that stands them in good stead for many other positions within organizations. Information systems auditing also has the added advantage of providing incumbents with excellent grounding in information technology, which is now critical to many organizations' strategy and operations.

LEADING FUNCTION

Recall in Chapter 3 that we recognized the objective of the leading function was to achieve harmony of objectives. In other words, managers seek to exercise the leadership function effectively to try to ensure that persons or groups within their organization work toward achieving the organization's goals. Managers seek to achieve the purpose of leadership via the processes of motivating, providing direction to, and communicating with their subordinates. In the following two subsections, we discuss leadership objectives and processes as they apply to the information systems audit function.

Leadership Objectives

The manager of an information systems audit group needs to be concerned about achieving harmony of objectives at three levels (Figure 24–4). First, the actions taken by individual information systems auditors or teams of information systems auditors need to be congruent with the overall objectives of specific audits in which they participate. Effective leadership is required to ensure that individual information systems auditors or teams of information systems auditors do not deliberately or unintentionally work at cross-purposes with one another.

Second, each audit needs to be undertaken in such a way that its outcomes are congruent with those established under the short-term plan that should have been prepared for the information systems audit function. Recall from our previous discussion that the major purpose of the short-term plan is to enact an organization's risk-management strategy—that is, to identify those areas within an organization that need to be audited with a view to reducing

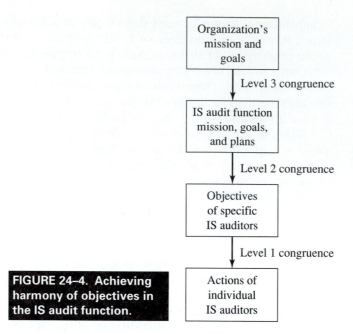

FIGURE 24–4. Achieving harmony of objectives in the IS audit function.

the exposures faced by the organization to an acceptable level. Effective leadership is required to ensure that each audit contributes in the ways intended to an overall reduction in exposures.

Third, the activities of the information systems audit function overall must assist the organization to achieve its mission and goals and, in some cases, to *shape* its mission and goals. Effective leadership is required to ensure that the aggregate efforts of all who work in the information systems audit function contribute effectively and efficiently to the organization's mission and goals.

In our discussion of whether information systems auditors should perform either a staff function or a line function, we have already canvassed some of the difficulties that arise in achieving harmony of objectives within the information systems audit function. If information systems auditors perform a staff function, for example, effective leadership will be required to ensure that they do not pursue their own agenda (e.g., acquiring experience in the audit of new technology) rather than contributing to achieving the objectives of the audits in which they participate. Similarly, effective leadership will be required to ensure that information systems auditors and financial auditors coordinate the work they undertake.

Leadership Processes

Recall from Chapter 3 that contingency theories of motivation predict the factors which best motivate people will vary depending on the nature of the person. Managers of an information systems audit function, therefore, will have to understand the needs of each of their subordinates if they are to motivate them effectively. They gain this understanding through *(1)* observation of and reflection on their behaviors as they perform their information systems audit role and *(2)* feedback obtained from them, especially when managers undertake personal appraisal interviews with them. If information systems auditors have a technical career orientation, managers might be able to accommodate their needs by providing them with work experiences that cover a variety of technologies. If auditors have a managerial career orientation, however, managers might only be able to provide them with limited opportunities. As discussed previously, information systems audit groups are usually small with few managerial layers. In this light, managerial career advancement often must be sought outside the information systems audit group.

Like motivation, contingency theories of leadership indicate that the approaches to providing direction used also must vary depending on the needs of the people being managed. At one extreme, directions can be provided using an authoritarian style. At the other extreme, directions can be discerned via democratic, participative processes. The former approach is likely to be more successful when undertaking routine information systems audit work in which auditors have extensive knowledge of and experience with audit objectives and audit procedures. The latter approach is likely to be more successful when undertaking audit work where high uncertainty exists.

The conduct of high-quality audits requires that managers communicate effectively with their staff. Recall from Chapter 3 that good communicators must have certain personal attributes—for example, awareness, objectivity, a capacity for empathy, and self-knowledge. Managers must seek to foster these attributes in themselves and in their subordinates. In addition, managers must put in place certain routine forms of communication. For example, managers must ensure that long-term and short-terms plans for the information systems audit function are documented and disseminated and that the objectives of each audit are clearly understood by the audit team that must undertake the work. Otherwise, routine, day-to-day information systems audit work is likely to be undermined.

CONTROLLING FUNCTION

Exercising control over the information systems audit function needs to be conceived in the context of exercising total quality management and continuous improvement within the organization in which the information systems audit function is located. Like all other personnel within an organization, information systems auditors must strive continuously to ensure that work meets quality standards and to identify ways to improve the quality of their work.

At the level of an individual audit, control can be exercised in several ways:

1. At the beginning of an audit, objectives should be clearly stated and documented. Moreover, the resources required to conduct the audit should be determined. The overall conduct of the audit needs to be planned and documented. Spreadsheet and project management software might be used to assist with these tasks.
2. During the conduct of the audit, progress needs to be monitored and evaluated. Material variances from the audit plan should be investigated. The quality of the work performed also needs to be evaluated. Furthermore, the audit work that has been conducted must be documented properly. Automated tools, such as software to support workpaper completion and internal controls evaluation, can be used to ease the documentation task.
3. Throughout an audit and near the end of an audit, the work conducted must be subjected to independent review. This review should evaluate whether the working papers are complete, the work conducted has been properly planned and supervised, the appropriate audit procedures have been used, the outcomes of the audit support the audit conclusions reached, and the audit work has been done effectively and efficiently. It is essential that this work be done before the audit manager signs off on an audit.
4. Substantial care must be taken with reporting the results of the audit. The audit report must be clear, cogent, and factual. Readers must see how the conclusions reached can be attributed to the audit findings. Good practices should

be affirmed in the audit report; poor practices and control weaknesses should be pointed out objectively. The potential consequences of poor practices and control weaknesses should be articulated. Recommendations for improvement should be provided.

5. Subsequent to the completion of the audit, stakeholders (e.g., the audit committee of the Board of Directors and management of the function that has been audited) should be consulted to determine their satisfaction with the audit work conducted. This consultation might involve stakeholders completing questionnaires to rate their perceptions about the quality of the audit work undertaken (see, e.g., Levine 1993).

At the level of the information systems audit function overall, various types of controls can be exercised. On a regular basis throughout a year, a detailed review should be carried out on selected audit assignments that have been undertaken to ensure the work done meets quality standards. On an annual basis, information systems standards, policies, and procedures need to be evaluated to ensure their currency and appropriateness. Every few years, an external, independent party might be asked to review the information systems audit function to assess its effectiveness and efficiency.

We can also use *benchmarking* to evaluate how well the information systems audit function is performing. Recall that benchmarking is the process of using key performance indicator values to compare the performance of a function or process within an organization with similar functions or processes in other organizations. In the case of information systems auditing, the sorts of key performance indicators we might use are the activities performed by the information systems audit group, the resources expended on information systems audits, the time taken to complete information systems audits, the levels of stakeholder satisfaction with the information systems audit function, and the level of turnover of information systems audit staff. Recall from our discussions in Chapter 3, however, that we must be cautious in our use of benchmarking. Relative to other organizations, for example, the environmental circumstances surrounding our own organizations might differ considerably. Moreover, strategically we might wish to pursue information systems audit directions that are different from those that other organizations pursue.

TOWARD INFORMATION SYSTEMS AUDIT PROFESSIONALISM

One of the hallmarks of a profession is that a professional association exists to service the needs of its members. These needs are often defined in terms of five conditions that must be satisfied if an occupational group is to call itself a profession: *(1)* existence of a common body of knowledge, *(2)* existence of competency standards, *(3)* conduct of a valid and reliable examination to assess competency, *(4)* existence of a code of ethics, and *(5)* enforcement of the code of ethics through a disciplinary mechanism.

Professional Associations

Since the mid-1960s, many existing professional associations of accountants have sought to address the needs of their members who work in the area of information systems auditing. For example, the American Institute of Certified Public Accountants (AICPA) and the Institute of Chartered Accountants in Australia (ICAA) have had task forces and produced publications that have focused on control and auditing in computerized environments. Various associations of computing professionals have also sought to cater for the needs of their members who have an interest in information systems audit and control. For example, the Association for Computing Machinery (ACM) and the

Institute of Electrical and Electronic Engineers (IEEE) both have special interest groups that deal with computer security-related matters.

In 1969, however, the EDP Auditors Association (EDPAA) was founded in Los Angeles as a professional organization that was intended to address specifically the needs of information systems auditors. The Association started out with approximately 100 members. Today it has more than 14,000 members in more than 100 countries. It also has local chapters in more than 50 countries scattered around the world. The membership of its task forces comprise persons from its many chapters. Its international presidents have also been chosen from different countries. In 1994, the Association changed its name to the Information Systems Audit and Control Association (ISACA). More information about the ISACA can be obtained at its World Wide Web site: http://www.isaca.org.

Common Body of Knowledge

Early in its existence, the EDPAA sought to articulate a common body of knowledge for information systems auditors. In this light, in 1976 it established the EDP Auditors Foundation (EDPAF). The EDPAF was charged with the responsibility for education and research within the Association. As one of its first tasks, it undertook a major survey of information systems managers, information systems auditors, and information systems and audit educators to try to identify and obtain consensus on the types of and levels of knowledge that competent information systems auditors should possess.

A major outcome of the survey was the production of a publication called *Control Objectives*. This publication set out control objectives for various types of organizational activities, a list of controls that might be used to achieve these objectives, and a list of audit procedures that might be used to determine whether these controls were in place and operating reliably. *Control Objectives* was revised periodically to reflect the changing information systems audit environment. Members of the Association were expected to be able to demonstrate that they possessed a competent level of knowledge of *Control Objectives*. In essence, it documented the common body of knowledge that the then-EDPAA believed competent information systems auditors should possess.

In 1996, *Control Objectives* was replaced with a multi-volume publication called *COBIT: Control Objectives for Information and Related Technology* (Information Systems Audit and Control Foundation 1996). In 1998, the ISACA produced a second edition of *COBIT*. The focus of *COBIT* is on *business processes*. For each business process, *COBIT* has a listing of control objectives, controls that can be used to achieve these objectives, and audit procedures that can be used to determine whether the controls are in place and operating reliably. Again, *COBIT* essentially articulates a common body of knowledge for information systems audit professionals.

The ISACA seeks to promulgate knowledge about information systems audit and control in various ways. For example, each of its local chapters offers regular technical sessions for its members. The ISACA also has an active research and publication agenda. Research monographs on different information systems audit and control topics are available through its bookstore, and it publishes a quarterly journal called the *IS Audit & Control Journal*. The ISACA has also developed model undergraduate and postgraduate curriculums for information systems auditing.

Competency Standards

In 1985, the EDPAA established a Standards Board to develop and promulgate standards that would guide the work of information systems auditors. The Board was asked to develop standards that would apply internationally. In

June 1987, the EDPAA published the "General Standards for Information Systems Auditing." These initial standards have since been updated and expanded to cover new areas. The standards address the following:

1. Audit charter
2. Independence
   - Professional independence
   - Organizational relationship
3. Professional ethics and standards
   - Code of professional ethics
   - Due professional care
4. Competence
   - Skills and knowledge
   - Continuing professional education
5. Planning
   - Audit planning
6. Performance of audit work
   - Supervision
   - Evidence
7. Reporting
   - Reporting content and form
8. Follow-up activities
   - Follow-up

Subsequent to the issuance of the General Standards, several Statements on Information Systems Auditing Standards have been issued to tease out the implications of the General Standards for various aspects of information systems audit practice. These cover the following areas:

No.	Title	Content of Statement on IS Auditing Standards
1.	Independence: attitude and appearance; organizational relationship	Information systems auditors must have an independent attitude toward an audit. They should also appear to be independent. They must be independent of the organizational unit they are evaluating.
2.	Independence: involvement in the systems development process	Information systems auditors should independently review the system development process being followed by a project team. They should not become actively involved in the development and implementation of an application system. They can recommend controls and system enhancements, however, without impairing their independence. Moreover, they can be involved in the design and implementation of audit tools and techniques without impairing their independence.
3.	Performance of work: evidence requirement	Information systems auditors should obtain sufficient, relevant, and reliable evidence to support their findings and conclusions. This evidence should be properly organized and documented.
4.	Performance of work: due professional care	In the conduct of their work, information systems auditors should exercise a level of skill that is commensurate with that possessed by their colleagues.
5.	Performance of work: the use of risk assessment in audit planning	Information systems auditors should use risk assessment techniques to develop an overall audit plan and to plan specific audits. They should document the risk-assessment technique they have adopted.
6.	Performance of work: audit documentation	Information systems auditors should maintain documentation that shows their audit plan, audit scope and objectives, audit program, audit steps, evidence gathered, audit findings and conclusions, audit report, and auditee's responses to recommendations.

No.	Title	Content of Statement on IS Auditing Standards
7.	Reporting: audit reports	Information systems auditors should issue reports that communicate the objectives of the audit, the auditing standards used, the audit scope, and the findings and conclusions. The report should be organized and presented logically, issued on a timely basis, identify the auditee, and indicate an issue date.
8.	Performance of work: audit considerations for irregularities	Information systems auditors should assess the risk of occurrence of irregularities when they undertake an audit. They should design audit tests that might reasonably be expected to detect material irregularities. When irregularities are detected, their impact on the audit objectives and evidence collected must be considered. Their existence should be communicated to management in an appropriate and timely manner.
9.	Performance of work: use of audit software tools	Information systems auditors should obtain reasonable assurance about the integrity and usefulness of any audit software they are intending to use in an audit. When they use audit software to access production data, they must seek to protect the integrity of the production system and its data.

The ISACA has also issued a set of information systems auditing guidelines. The purpose of the guidelines is to provide practical assistance when applying information systems auditing standards.

Members of the ISACA must comply with the standards under their Code of Professional Ethics (see the next section). Noncompliance could result in loss of certification for a member who holds the Certified Information Systems Auditor certificate (see the next section) or loss of membership of the Association.

Competency Examination

In 1978, the EDPAA announced officially that it would establish an examination and certification process as a means of assessing whether people who claimed membership of the profession had achieved a certain level of competency. In conjunction with the Educational Testing Center of Princeton, New Jersey, the EDPAF developed the Certified Information Systems Auditor (CISA) Examination. The Foundation had several goals: *(1)* to develop and maintain a valid and reliable instrument that could be used to test a person's competence in information systems auditing, *(2)* to motivate people to improve and maintain their competence as information systems auditors, *(3)* on an ongoing basis to monitor the competence of individuals who claimed themselves to be information systems auditors, and *(4)* to assist management with personnel selection and development. After an initial "grandfather period" for those experienced in information systems auditing, on 10 April 1981 the examination became a requirement for those who wished to obtain CISA designation.

CISA is now widely accepted internationally as a yardstick to evaluate an information systems auditor's competence. Each year the examination is administered in multiple languages at many testing centers throughout the world. Responsibility for maintaining the test is vested in the ISACA's Test Enhancement Committee (TEC). TEC solicits and evaluates examination questions from persons who are interested in writing questions for the examination.

The CISA Examination covers five job domains:

1. Information systems audit standards and practices and information systems security and control practices;

2. Information systems organization and management (e.g., strategy, policies and procedures, organizational structures);
3. Information systems process (e.g., hardware and software platforms, communications network infrastructures);
4. Information systems integrity, confidentiality, and availability (e.g., logical and physical controls, data validation); and
5. Information systems development, acquisition, and maintenance.

The number of questions in each job domain varies to reflect the relative importance of the domain in the conduct of the information systems auditor's job function. The relative weightings were established after a large-scale survey of information systems auditors to establish the importance of each domain.

To obtain the CISA designation, information systems auditors must pass the CISA examination and have a minimum of five years' information systems audit and control experience. Some waivers can be obtained in relation to the experience requirement—for example, two years if a university bachelor's degree has been earned. This experience must have been gained within the ten-year period prior to the candidate's sitting for the examination.

Retaining the CISA designation is not automatic. Information systems auditors who have obtained the CISA certification must fulfil the following conditions:

1. Report that they have earned a minimum of 20 contact hours continuing professional education each year;
2. Pay the continuing education maintenance fee in full;
3. Comply with ISACA's Code of Professional Ethics (see the following section); and
4. Report that they have earned a minimum of 120 contact hours of continuing professional education during each three-year certification period.

Code of Ethics

Members of the ISACA and holders of the CISA designation must comply with a Code of Ethics. This code covers the following matters:

1. Support for the establishment of and compliance with information systems standards, procedures, and controls;
2. Compliance with standards promulgated by the ISACA;
3. Trustworthy service to stakeholders in the audit process, and avoidance of participation in improper acts;
4. Maintenance of the confidentiality of audit evidence obtained;
5. Maintenance of independence;
6. Maintenance of competence through participation in appropriate professional development activities;
7. Use of due care when conducting audits, and acquisition and documentation of sufficient evidence to support audit conclusions and recommendations;
8. Communication of audit outcomes to the appropriate stakeholders in the audit process;
9. Support for the education of stakeholders in the audit process to enhance their understanding of information systems and information systems auditing; and
10. Maintenance of high standards of conduct at both a professional and a personal level.

Disciplinary Mechanism

As discussed previously, the ISACA will take disciplinary action against its members if they violate its Code of Professional Ethics. For example, if members do not comply with the General Standards, their membership will be revoked. A member who holds the CISA designation will also lose their certification.

Given the international nature of the ISACA, it is difficult to provide legal backing for the disciplinary mechanism. Within the international information systems audit community, however, the role of the ISACA is now well understood. Moreover, the CISA designation is well accepted and held in high regard by many employers of information systems auditors. Disciplinary actions by the ISACA will have force, therefore, in the sense that they can substantially impact an information systems auditor's job opportunities.

SOME FUTURES OF INFORMATION SYSTEMS AUDITING

In the final section of this book, we briefly examine some major factors that are likely to have a significant, ongoing impact on the future work of information systems auditors. Some have been enduring (e.g., privacy); others have been more recent (e.g., the Internet). As managers of the information systems audit function within an organization, we need to remain knowledgeable about these factors and to plan for the ways in which they might affect us.

Internet

In the early 1980s, a major development that occurred in the information systems domain was the emergence of the Internet. The Internet is the vast collection of computers that are interconnected worldwide via their use of interlinked communication networks and a common communication protocol called TCP/IP (Transmission Control Protocol/Internet Protocol). A typical configuration for Internet computers is a local area network of personal computers connected via a router to a wide area network that in turn is connected to other wide area networks (Figure 24–5).

The Internet provides important services to information system users—for example, the World Wide Web (which is a collection of multimedia resources that have been implemented in a standardized way and which are accessible via programs called browsers), e-mail, and user groups. Because these services

FIGURE 24–5. Typical Internet configuration.

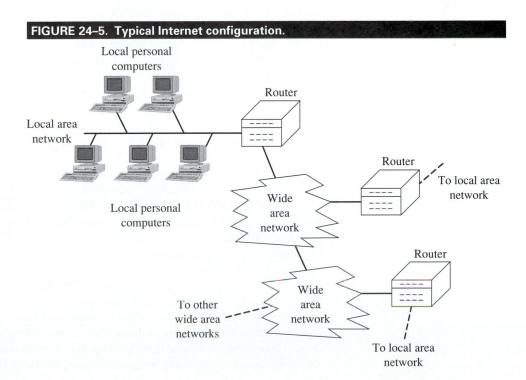

have proved to be very popular, the Internet has experienced phenomenal growth. Between January 1993 and July 1996, for example, it is estimated that the number of host computers grew from 1.3 million to 12.9 million; and between June 1993 and January 1997, it is estimated that the number of World Wide Web (Web) sites grew from 130 to 650,000 (Lynch 1997).

The Internet has now been with us for many years. Like personal computers, however, we are still trying to understand the eventual impacts that it will have on our lives and on the nature of and activities conducted within organizations. As we begin to assimilate and understand one type of impact, yet another opens up. As with personal computers, multiple waves of impacts are occurring that look as if they will continue for many years.

From an information systems audit perspective, some concerns that arise with an organization's use of the Internet are the following:

1. The primary purposes of the Internet are to facilitate communication and to enable sharing of resources. As a result, protecting the privacy and integrity of resources that can be accessed via the Internet is sometimes difficult. Hostile intruders might seek to exploit the open nature of the Internet to gain improper access to resources (see, e.g., Vacca 1996). Consequently, data privacy might be violated, or data integrity might be corrupted. As different types of exposures become apparent, controls over the Internet continue to improve. Nonetheless, management must recognize that privacy and integrity risks accrue whenever computers are connected to the Internet.

2. The privacy and integrity of data transmitted over the Internet cannot always be assured. Messages often pass through many computers, some of which might not be well-protected. Controls will only be as good as those of the weakest link in the chain of computers through which messages pass. Unless the sorts of cryptographic controls described in Chapters 10 and 12 are in place, therefore, the contents of messages could be exposed or altered during transit from one computer to another.

3. Copyright issues arise that relate to both material that organizations can retrieve via the Internet and material that they make available via the Internet. On the one hand, the organization's management must ensure that any information their employees download via the Internet is not copyrighted material. On the other hand, they must also ensure that any information their employees make available via the Internet is not copyrighted material. Copyright issues are especially a concern with multimedia information provided via the Web.

4. Many organizations continue to grapple with the problem of making effective use of the Internet (see, e.g., Nieuwenhuizen 1997). For example, organizations have undertaken costly Web page development, but they have had little improvement in sales or profitability. Some organizations have proscribed use of the Internet by their employees, except between certain hours of the day. They have argued that productivity has been undermined severely by their employees' excessive use of e-mail, user groups, and the Web.

5. The quality of resources that an organization makes available via the Internet needs to be controlled carefully. If an organization's employees make wrongful information or an erroneous program available via the Internet, for example, the organization might become liable for losses incurred by another organization that relied on the wrong information or erroneous program. Similarly, controls over e-mail need to be exercised. Employees must understand that the messages they send can affect the organization's image in the marketplace or commit it legally to the provision of goods and services.

6. If an organization downloads information or programs via the Internet, it should take steps to ensure that the information and programs are reliable. The information and programs need to be authentic, accurate, and complete,

and they need to be free of copyright restrictions. An organization also needs to ensure that downloaded programs are free of irregularities like viruses or Trojan horses that might undermine the integrity of its information systems.

Information systems auditors need to continue to monitor ongoing developments with the Internet. They must be aware of the different exposures that arise through Internet use and the controls that can be put in place to reduce expected losses from these exposures. These exposures and controls continue to change as new impacts occur on organizations as a result of their use of the Internet.

Electronic Commerce

McConnell (1996, p. 22) defines *electronic commerce* as "use of technology to enhance the processes of commercial transactions among a company and its customers and business partners." This definition is very broad. In the context of this definition, we have been engaging in electronic commerce since we began to use computers to facilitate the conduct of business processes (e.g., debtors processing). Narrower definitions of electronic commerce tend to focus on the use of data communications technologies to facilitate the execution of commercial transactions. They require parties to a commercial transaction to interact with each other via data communication technologies.

Perhaps the first form of electronic commerce to emerge was electronic data interchange (EDI). In EDI systems, many problems surrounding the authenticity and privacy of transactions are mitigated because the parties to the transactions are defined from the outset. Often they interact with each other via private data communication networks. To the extent that they use public networks, however, they can employ private-key cryptography to establish the authenticity of any transactions in which they engage and to protect the privacy of these transactions. Moreover, they can establish a means of payment for goods and services at the outset—for example, direct debiting of bank accounts.

Relative to EDI, however, the growth of public networks like the Internet has changed the way in which two parties can interact with one another. For a start, they might not know each other prior to the transaction. As a result, they might have little or no knowledge about each other's true identity, address, creditworthiness, reliability, and so on. For example, an Internet user might contact a company that advertises using the Web to purchase some particular service that the company offers. The user might have never contacted the company before. Moreover, after the first transaction occurs, subsequent transactions could be nonexistent or infrequent.

When electronic commerce occurs via public networks like the Internet, therefore, three fundamental problems arise:

1. How do the parties to a transaction establish each other's *identity* and *authenticity*?
2. How do the parties to a transaction protect the *privacy* of their dealings?
3. How do the parties to a transaction effect a secure *exchange* of money for any goods and services provided?

In Chapter 10, we saw how public-key cryptography can be used to address some of these problems. Recall that public-key cryptography can be used to send signed, secret messages. Accordingly, the type of protocol that might be used for an electronic transaction is the following:

1. The customer sends a message to the vendor with the customer's public key.
2. The vendor replies by sending the customer the vendor's own public key.
3. To protect the privacy of their message, the customer first encrypts their message using the vendor's *public* key. Thus, only the vendor should be able to decrypt the message using their *private* key. In this way, the customer can send

confidential credit card information or a one-time password that the vendor can use to initiate a transfer of funds from the customer's bank account to their own bank account.

4. The customer then encrypts the message again using their *private* key. This round of encryption effectively attaches a digital signature to the message.

5. On receipt of the customer's message, the vendor first decrypts the message using the customer's *public* key and then decrypts the message again using their own *private* key. Only if the message makes sense can the vendor have a fairly high level of assurance of the customer's identity.

This protocol provides no assurance, however, about the vendor's or customer's authenticity or their trustworthiness in terms of delivering goods and services or paying for goods and services. For this reason, various kinds of certification arrangements are being used increasingly to support electronic commerce. For example, a customer can send his or her public key to a certification authority. The certification authority takes steps to ensure the customer's authenticity (and perhaps other attributes like creditworthiness). The certification authority then uses its own *private* key to attach its digital signature to the customer's public key. Customers then send their public key to a vendor under the certification authority's digital signature. When the vendor sees the certification authority's identity, they then consult some kind of public directory of public keys belonging to certification authorities and use the appropriate public key to verify the authenticity of the customer's public key (Figure 24–6). Similarly,

FIGURE 24–6. Use of certification authority in electronic commerce.

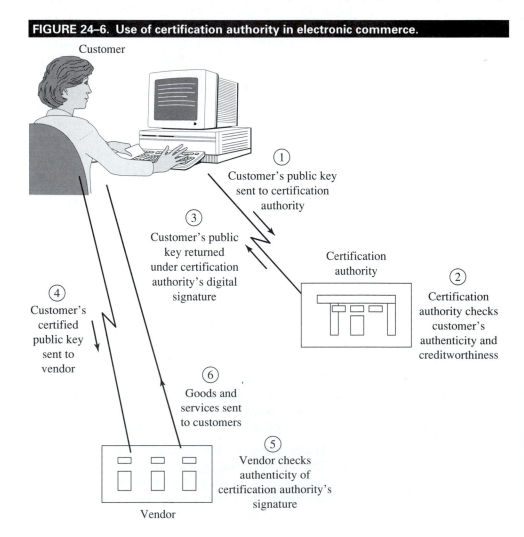

vendors can have their public keys certified to provide evidence of their authenticity to customers.

Arrangements to facilitate electronic commerce will continue to evolve. For example, systems to permit use of digital cash, electronic checks, and credit card transactions over public networks will continue to improve (see, e.g., Tibaldeo and Buben 1996). Auditors must remain current with this technology and assist their organizations or clients to adapt effectively and efficiently to its use. In this regard, McConnell (1996) underscores the need for well-developed business plans. Moreover, auditors must be aware of the exposures that exist with various types of systems to support electronic commerce and the controls that can be put in place to reduce losses from these exposures.

Business Process Reengineering

In the early 1990s, influential work by researchers/consultants like Hammer and Davenport motivated many organizations to reexamine the procedures they used to deliver goods and services to their customers (see, e.g., Hammer 1990 and Davenport 1993). This work, which went under the rubric of business process reengineering (BPR), produced major changes in many organizations. Interest in BPR peaked in the mid-1990s, but the basic notions espoused are likely to influence organizational design for many years to come.

BPR encompasses several fundamental design notions. A central idea, however, is to organize activities on the basis of *processes* rather than *functions*. For example, if customers wished to purchase different kinds of insurance, historically they often would have had to deal with many persons in an insurance company. Someone might have had responsibility for life insurance, someone else might have had responsibility for house and contents insurance, still someone else might have had responsibility for automobile insurance, and so on. Moreover, the person who handled the sales function might not have been the same person who handled subsequent servicing of the insurance policies or collection or payment of funds associated with the insurance policies.

The inefficiencies caused by this phenomenon of "hand-off" in organizations were a major target for BPR efforts. Procedures were redesigned so that one or a small number of people handled entire processes. For instance, in our insurance company example, salespeople might have been trained to handle sales for all types of policies that a customer might wish to purchase. In addition, they might have been trained to handle subsequent servicing of the policies and perhaps subsequent collection of or payment of funds associated with the policies.

The claimed benefits of BPR were improved effectiveness and efficiency. For instance, in our insurance company example, customers presumably would have been happier dealing with a single person who responded to their insurance needs rather than multiple people. The costs of hand-off procedures associated with one employee giving work to another employee also would have been eliminated or reduced. Many organizations also found that they could use BPR to facilitate their downsizing efforts.

BPR also had its costs, however, some of which initially were not apparent to the organizations that used it. For example, in some organizations, BPR wrought substantial behavioral problems. Employees sometimes had difficulty adjusting to the new work demands placed on them. For example, they had to expand their range of competencies quickly to be able to cope effectively and efficiently with customer needs. The associated downsizing that often accompanied BPR also produced uncertainty and stress.

Interestingly, auditors were slow to realize and to point out that BPR often had significant implications in terms of undermining controls and increasing the exposures faced by organizations. For example, a major reason why hand-off procedures were often employed within organizations was to enforce separation of duties. When hand-off was eliminated, separation of duties no longer existed. As a result, organizations faced higher exposures from errors and irregularities that might occur. These types of problems were often exacerbated because business process reengineering efforts were usually accompanied by organizational downsizing. For example, when downsizing occurred, organizations had fewer staff available to enforce separation of duties.

Competitive forces will compel organizations to continue to examine the effectiveness and efficiency of their work processes. Information systems auditors, therefore, must be vigilant in *(1)* examining the implications of proposed work process changes for the controls used by an organization and the exposures that it faces and *(2)* pointing out to management any detrimental effects that might occur with proposed work process changes. Our experiences with BPR are a reminder that often tensions exist between effectiveness and efficiency needs and asset safeguarding and data integrity needs (Sia and Neo 1997). The rapid and widespread acceptance of BPR was a signal that many managers no longer believed the costs of controls could be justified. We cannot assume that the need for controls is obvious, especially to management. In this light, we must continually subject control systems to BPR analysis in the same way that other work systems within the organization will be scrutinized for opportunities to improve their effectiveness and efficiency.

Outsourcing

Concurrent with the BPR movement in the early 1990s, interest in outsourcing was also high. *Outsourcing* is the use of parties who are external to an organization to provide goods or services to the organization. Like BPR, outsourcing is now perceived as an important means of improving an organization's competitiveness. It allows an organization to focus more on its own core competencies and likewise to take advantage of other organizations' core competencies. Like BPR, the basic notions that underlie outsourcing are likely to influence organizational design for many years to come.

Outsourcing can be applied to any organizational function. For example, it can be used to obtain the legal services needed by an organization or the component parts that it needs for some type of product that it manufactures. Historically, however, the information systems function has always been a primary target for outsourcing. For example, the early use of service bureaus by organizations to obtain some or all of their information systems services was a form of outsourcing. Moreover, since the early 1990s, for three reasons the information systems function has become a particular focus for outsourcing activities (see, e.g., Gurbaxani 1996).

First, management often perceives they will be able to exercise greater *control* over the information systems function if it is outsourced. When reliance is placed on an outside vendor, management believes that *(1)* the information systems function will become more responsive to user needs, *(2)* a reduction in information systems costs will occur through economies of scale that the vendor obtains and passes on to its customers, and *(3)* users will exercise greater care in their consumption of information systems resources because they will have to pay for them directly.

Second, management often perceives that the information systems function will become more *innovative* if it is outsourced. When reliance is placed on an outside vendor, management believes that *(1)* their organization will be better able to divest old technology and gain access to new technology, *(2)* greater information systems expertise will be available through staff employed by the outsourcing vendor, and *(3)* the limitations of existing staff will be overcome because they can be transferred to the outsourcing vendor where they will have more opportunities to develop their skills.

Third, management often perceives that they will be better able to *exploit* information systems assets that they have developed internally if they make these assets available for sale via the outsourcing vendor. Thus, the outsourcing vendor provides a means of tapping markets for these internally developed information systems products and services.

From the viewpoint of information systems auditors, however, outsourcing of information systems services poses some difficult problems. Auditors have a role to play at four different stages of outsourcing:

1. *Decision to outsource.* We must assist management to determine what information systems services, if any, should be outsourced. In particular, we must identify those information system activities that are strategic to the organization. These activities are the least likely candidates for outsourcing (McFarlan and Nolan 1995). If they are outsourced, great care must be taken because they will be more difficult to control. We must also assist management to identify whether suitable outsourcing vendors exist that have the skills, experience, and reputation required for the long-term relationship needed when information systems services are outsourced to be successful.

2. *Contract design.* Scott (1996) points out that auditors need to evaluate the suitability of outsourcing contract provisions in relation to (a) finances—e.g., fixed costs, variable costs, and invoice verification, (b) audit rights—e.g., the scope and timing of audit activities in relation to the outsourcing vendor, (c) performance—e.g., the criteria to be used to evaluate whether the outsourcing vendor is discharging their duties under the contract, (d) vendor relations—e.g., the outsourcing personnel who will deliver the information systems services and the nature and frequency of reporting by the outsourcing vendor, and (e) control—e.g., the outsourcing vendor's responsibilities in terms of maintaining data integrity and providing suitable backup and recovery.

3. *Contract monitoring.* During the contract period, information systems auditors might be responsible for monitoring compliance with the terms of the contract. We must continually evaluate whether our own organization or client and the outsourcing vendor are discharging their duties properly under the contract.

4. *Contract termination.* Major difficulties can arise when an outsourcing contract is to be terminated. For example, an organization might have lost its ability to provide internal information systems services. Furthermore, effecting a smooth transition to another outsourcing vendor or to internal provision of information systems services may be a complex task.

The decision to outsource, therefore, can have a critical impact on an organization's ability to attain asset safeguarding, data integrity, effectiveness, and efficiency objectives. On the one hand, the outsourcing vendor can provide capabilities that allow an organization to better achieve these objectives. On the other hand, an outsourcing relationship has features that undermine the attainment of these objectives. Information systems auditors must seek to ensure that their ability to collect and evaluate evidence in relation to the attainment of these objectives is not inhibited when their organization or client enters into an information systems outsourcing arrangement.

Data Privacy

Data privacy refers to the right to have stored or transmitted data protected from *(1)* inadvertent or unauthorized disclosure or *(2)* unauthorized use. Inadvertent disclosure occurs when data is revealed because some type of error or irregularity occurs. Unauthorized disclosure occurs when a person having a right to access certain data uses these rights to allow unauthorized persons examine the data. Unauthorized use occurs when a person having a right to access certain data uses this right for unintended purposes.

For several reasons, data privacy concerns have remained an enduring issue in the information systems field. First, as the cost of information technology decreases and its power increases, the risk of privacy violations increases. For example, the existence of large, diverse databases containing information about individuals and the emergence of sophisticated data mining and data matching technologies enable would-be privacy violators sometimes to easily create detailed profiles about individuals. Second, international regulatory regimes associated with data privacy are not uniform. Actions that violate privacy which are proscribed in one jurisdiction might not be proscribed in another jurisdiction. It may be easy to circumvent privacy laws simply by shifting data from one jurisdiction to another jurisdiction. Third, some researchers now argue that existing privacy legislation is based on outdated principles that require persons to possess information they are unlikely to have. They claim, therefore, that privacy laws based on these principles will become increasingly ineffective. We briefly return to this issue subsequently.

Nature and Scope of Privacy Legislation

Since the beginning of the 1970s, the need to protect the privacy of data has been recognized increasingly. As a result, many countries have now enacted privacy laws that impose codes of "fair information practice" on organizations (see below). In some cases, the laws apply only to the public sector. In other cases, however, they apply to both the public and private sectors.

Regulatory regimes differ considerably. Some directly impose statutory obligations on organizations that handle personal data. Others establish a statutory framework. They delegate the implementation and operational details, however, to a supervisory body like a privacy commissioner. Some establish statutory codes of conduct for particular industry sectors or for particular classes of activities or records (e.g., health records). Others encourage industries to establish self-regulatory codes with some level of supervision by a government agency.

Perhaps the most widely respected set of privacy-protection principles on which many existing regulatory regimes are based are those proposed by the Organisation for Economic Co-operation and Development (OECD) (1980). These principles provide the foundation for a regulatory regime called Fair Information Practices (FIP):

1. *Collection limitation principle.* Limitations to the collection of personal data should exist. Such data should be obtained by fair and lawful means and with the knowledge and consent of the subject.
2. *Data quality principle.* Personal data should be relevant, accurate, complete, and timely.
3. *Purpose specification principle.* Personal data should be collected only for specified purposes. Its use should be limited to those purposes.
4. *Use limitation principle.* The consent of the subject or the authority of law should be required before personal data is disclosed or used for purposes other than those initially specified when the data was collected.
5. *Security safeguards principle.* Reasonable controls should be exercised to protect the existence, integrity, and privacy of personal data.
6. *Openness principle.* People should be able to establish the nature, existence, and ownership of personal data systems.

7. *Individual participation principle.* People should be able to establish whether data exists about them in a personal data system. If such data exists, they should be able to examine it and correct or delete data about themselves that is inaccurate, incomplete, out of date, or irrelevant.

8. *Accountability principle.* People who exercise control over personal data systems should be held accountable for ensuring that measures are in place and working to give effect to the above principles.

Some believe that the OECD guidelines now need updating to take into account technologies that have become increasingly invasive. Others, like Laudon (1996), argue that FIP is breaking down because it is becoming increasingly difficult to enforce the underlying privacy principles. For example, he points out that people conceivably might have known about all databases that contained information on them in an era when mainframe computers with little interconnectivity were the dominant forms of information technology. In an era in which networked personal computers have replaced mainframes to a large extent, however, people are unlikely to know what databases contain information about them and where these databases are located. For this reason, Laudon (1996) argues that people should be given property rights to information about themselves and allowed to trade this information in information markets.

From the viewpoint of information systems auditors, we need to recognize, therefore, that laws which are based on FIP are becoming increasingly problematic. Most likely, new FIP-based laws will continue to be enacted. Their efficacy, however, could be limited. If we wish to preserve privacy in our own organizations or our clients' organizations, increasingly we will have to rely on controls we put in place and ethical principles that guide behavior in relation to information use rather than the protection provided by privacy laws.

Implications for Information Systems Auditing

The impact of privacy legislation on our work as information systems auditors will depend on the particular forms of legislation existing in the country and state in which we work or the forms of the legislation applying to the organizations we audit. Nonetheless, privacy legislation is likely to have five broad implications for our work as information systems auditors:

1. *Need to be familiar with statutes.* Auditing standards require auditors to be familiar with statutes affecting the organizations they audit. In the case of privacy statutes, the laws that are relevant to our work may have both domestic and foreign origins. If the organizations we audit collect personal data in other countries and transfer this data across international boundaries, for example, we will need to identify and understand the implications of any foreign laws that pertain to this data.

2. *Need to audit for legislative compliance.* Because penalties could arise for noncompliance with a privacy act, information systems auditors might be given responsibility for ensuring that the organizations they audit comply with the statutes. Internal auditors might also be responsible for preparing a privacy impact statement and constructing a comprehensive privacy plan. In some cases, external auditors might have to determine whether contingent liabilities have arisen because their clients have failed to comply with a privacy act.

3. *Auditor as user of personal data.* As users of personal data, information systems auditors could be subject to the provisions of a privacy act. For example, organizations might have to identify their auditors and the ways in which their auditors will use personal data in advance. Approval might have to be obtained for any deviations from these stated purposes.

4. *Auditor as maintainer of personal data.* In the course of an audit, we might extract personal data from files to include in our working papers. Under a privacy act, we might then be responsible for ensuring that adequate security exists over our own files, in the same way that we are responsible for evaluating whether adequate security exists over files belonging to the organizations we audit. Indeed, under a privacy act, the organizations we audit could be prevented from providing us with personal data unless we can show that our files are secure.

5. *Need to evaluate fairness of information practices.* Although privacy legislation might not apply to a specific information practice in which an organization we audit engages, we must still be mindful that many people now expect organizations to evaluate their actions for compliance with privacy principles. As information systems auditors, therefore, we need to continually evaluate how information technologies are used in the organizations we audit in case unfavorable implications arise for personal privacy. For example, the organizations we audit might engage in some type of computer matching activities that are legal. Nonetheless, if these activities were to become public, they might lead to a substantial loss of organizational goodwill. Accordingly, we might assist a client organization to prepare a *privacy policy document* to provide guidance to management and employees on the practices that need to be undertaken to preserve privacy within the organization (Jerksey et al. 1996).

Some external audit firms have now established specialized practices in the area of data privacy. In some countries, also, the Data Privacy or Data Protection Commissioner will also provide guidance on the nature and conduct of privacy audits.

Data Mining and Knowledge Discovery

Information systems auditors are concerned about errors that might cause a material misstatement of the financial statements. In some countries (e.g., the United States), external auditors also have a responsibility to design an audit to provide reasonable assurance that fraud has not caused a material misstatement of the financial statements. Detecting fraud will always be a concern for internal auditors irrespective of the responsibilities that external auditors might have to discharge.

A technique that is becoming increasingly important as a means of detecting errors and irregularities is *data mining*. A problem we now face is that we are sometimes confronted with huge databases. Somehow we must determine whether errors or irregularities are likely to exist in these databases. Alternatively, we might wish to use the data contained in these databases to provide information about errors and irregularities that occur in the businesses we are auditing. Data mining techniques are designed to detect patterns among data that might signal, for example, the presence of errors or irregularities (see, e.g., Brachman et al. 1996). They rely on various tools like statistical packages, expert systems, and neural networks to tease out patterns that exist in data. The process of using these patterns to determine new knowledge is called *knowledge discovery*. From the viewpoint of auditors, knowledge discovery means that they are better able to assess whether assets have been safeguarded, data integrity has been maintained, and systems are operating effectively and efficiently. For example, they might use data mining techniques to try to determine whether the characteristics of transactions undertaken with stolen credit cards differs from those undertaken with legitimate credit cards (Casarin 1997). Auditors are likely to have to place increasing reliance on data mining techniques to assess audit risk and to collect and evaluate audit evidence.

Interorganizational Systems and Virtual Organizations

Increasingly, organizational boundaries are beginning to blur. In the late 1980s, for example, interorganizational information systems began to emerge (Konsynski and McFarlan 1990). The forerunners of these systems were EDI systems. Organizations started to use computer technologies to effect greater cooperation with one another, however, even when they were in direct competition with one another. For example, two suppliers might allow a customer to directly access their production databases to determine which supplier was in a better position to provide component parts to satisfy a rush order that the customer had received. Each supplier might even divert orders to the other when it was not in a position to satisfy the orders. The then-new computer technologies (e.g., open systems) seemed to facilitate the arrival of a new era where paradoxically competition and cooperation could walk hand in hand.

In the mid-1990s, virtual organizations began to emerge (Gallegos and Powell 1997). These organizations transcended boundaries within and across organizations. Again, the then-new computer technologies (e.g., cooperative work systems) allowed people and organizations to break the constraints imposed by physical location and time. The goal was to assemble the best people and the best organizations to meet a marketplace need—for example, to design and bring a new product to market.

Interorganizational information systems and virtual organizations pose major challenges for our work as information systems auditors. For example, increasingly we must rely on standards if effective and efficient communications among the parties in an interorganizational information system or a virtual organization are to occur. Also, we face the exposure of having to rely on controls in multiple locations that are sometimes remote and sometimes not within our domain of influence. Often, we might have to rely on the work of other auditors. In this light, we need to support efforts toward greater standardization of information systems controls and audit procedures (e.g., the Information Systems Audit and Control Foundation's COBIT).

SUMMARY

Effective management of the information systems audit function requires traditional management tasks to be performed well: *(1)* planning, *(2)* organizing, *(3)* staffing, *(4)* leading, and *(5)* controlling. *Planning* involves preparing long-run plans to ensure that the work of the information systems audit function is congruent with the mission and goals of the organization in which it is located. It also involves preparing short-run plans to ensure that audits are undertaken that will lead to effective risk management within an organization. *Organizing* involves formulating an audit charter to establish the information systems audit function's role and legitimacy within an organization, deciding whether information systems auditors will perform a staff or a line role, determining whether the information systems audit function will be centralized or decentralized, and ensuring that adequate resources are available to carry out information systems audits. *Staffing* involves sourcing and recruiting information systems audit staff, appraising and developing them, and establishing suitable career paths for them. *Leading* involves determining and using an appropriate leadership style that will motivate information systems audit staff to act in a way that is congruent with the overall mission and goals of the organization in which they arc employed. *Controlling* involves undertaking continuous quality improvement and benchmarking to ensure that high-quality audits are undertaken and the work performed by the information systems audit function is congruent with the mission and goals of the organization in which it is located.

If an occupational group is to call itself a profession, it must *(1)* have a common body of knowledge, *(2)* have defined standards of competency, *(3)* conduct a valid and reliable examination of its members to assess competency, *(4)* have a code of ethics, and *(5)* enforce the code of ethics via a disciplinary mechanism. In the information systems audit discipline, the Information Systems Audit and Control Association is the organization that has done most to ensure these conditions are satisfied. It has produced publications that in essence seek to define a common body of knowledge for information systems auditors. It has issued general standards that address critical aspects of an information systems auditor's work—independence, technical competence, work performance, and reporting. In addition, it has issued various statements on auditing standards that provide more detailed interpretations of the general standards. It conducts the Certified Information Systems Auditor examination to assess competency in information systems auditing. It has also established a code of ethics for its members that it seeks to enforce via various disciplinary mechanisms—for example, revocation of membership for non-compliance with the code of ethics.

Various environmental and technological changes have had and will continue to have an impact on information systems auditors' work. The *Internet's* widespread use has caused several concerns relating to preserving the privacy and integrity of information, maintaining copyright of information that is stored on and disseminated via the Internet, and making effective and efficient use of Internet resources. The conduct of *electronic commerce* via public data communication networks has led to concerns about establishing the identity and authenticity of parties to an electronic exchange, preserving the privacy of electronic exchanges, and effecting secure exchange of monies for goods and services provided. *Business process reengineering* and *downsizing* have enabled business processes to be redesigned so they are more effective and more efficient (according to some measures), but often important controls like separation of duties have been compromised as a result. *Outsourcing* has been undertaken to allow an organization to focus on its core competencies and improve its competitiveness. Substantial risks arise with outsourcing, however, relating to whether the outsourcing vendor discharges their duties effectively and efficiently. *Data privacy* issues have been an enduring concern in the information systems audit discipline. While the cost of information technology decreases and its power increases, the risk of privacy violations increases. The increasing development, implementation, and use of huge databases makes it more difficult for us to discover errors and irregularities in data. In the future, it is likely that we will have to place more reliance on *data mining* techniques to identify patterns in data that could manifest errors or irregularities and to enhance our processes of *knowledge discovery*. Increasingly, the boundaries of traditional organizations are beginning to blur as *interorganizational systems* and *virtual corporations* allow people and corporations to work with one another without being constrained by physical location and time zone. They motivate greater concern with standardized information systems control and audit procedures.

Review Questions

24–1 Briefly explain the purposes of long-run planning in relation to the information systems audit function. How might the nature and extent of long-run planning for the information systems audit function differ depending upon where an organization is placed in McFarlan et al.'s (1983) strategic grid?

24–2 Briefly explain the purposes of short-run planning in relation to the information systems audit function.

24–3 Outline the major steps in a risk-management program.

24–4 What is an audit charter? What are the major components of an audit charter? Why does the information systems audit function need an audit charter?

24–5 Briefly explain how the information systems auditor's role within an organization will differ depending on whether they are performing a staff function or a line function.

24–6 Give *two* advantages of the information systems auditor performing a staff-function role within an organization and *two* advantages of their performing a line-function role.

24–7 Give *three* factors that most likely will affect whether the information systems audit function within an organization will be centralized or decentralized.

24–8 What are the primary bases used to organize the resources to support the information systems audit function within an organization?

24–9 Is it better to hire persons who primarily have a computing background or persons who primarily have an auditing background as information systems auditors?

24–10 Briefly outline the steps to be undertaken during appraisal of information systems audit staff. Why is it important to use the appraisal process to determine the development needs of information systems audit staff?

24–11 What difficulties exist with finding suitable career paths for information systems auditors? Give two alternative career paths that an information systems auditor might pursue.

24–12 Give *three* objectives of leadership within the information systems audit function.

24–13 Briefly outline *two* leadership processes we need to put in place if we manage the information systems audit function.

24–14 How can we exercise control over individual audits and the information systems audit function overall?

24–15 What are the *five* conditions that must be satisfied if an occupational group is to call itself a profession?

24–16 Briefly explain the nature of the Information Systems Audit and Control Association.

24–17 How has the Information Systems Audit and Control Association addressed the need for information systems auditors to share a common body of knowledge?

24–18 What are *four* categories of general standards developed by the Information Systems Audit and Control Association?

24–19 Why did the Information Systems Audit and Control Association issue their Statements on Auditing Standards?

24–20 What mechanism has been set up by the Information Systems Audit and Control Association to assess the competency of information systems auditors?

24–21 What are the *five* domains that are tested within the CISA examination?

24–22 What are the *four* conditions that an information systems auditor must fulfil to retain the CISA designation?

24–23 Give *five* matters covered by the Information Systems Audit and Control Association's Code of Ethics.

24–24 What is the primary disciplinary mechanism used by the Information Systems Audit and Control Association in relation to its members? Do you think this disciplinary mechanism is effective? Why?

24–25 Give *three* ways in which organizational use of the Internet has affected the information systems auditor's function.

24–26 What is meant by *electronic commerce*? Give *three* control problems that arise when electronic commerce is conducted via public data communications networks.

24–27 How is public-key cryptography useful in the context of electronic commerce conducted via public data communications networks?

24–28 What is business process reengineering? From a control viewpoint, what unfavorable impacts have arisen when business process reengineering has been used within organizations?

24–29 What is information systems outsourcing? How should an information systems auditor be involved when an organization decides to undertake information systems outsourcing?

24–30 Why has data privacy remained an enduring concern within the information systems audit and control discipline?

24–31 Give *four* principles that underlie the regulatory regime called FIP. Why are the principles underlying FIP becoming increasingly difficult to enforce?

24–32 Give *three* implications of data privacy legislation for the work carried out by information systems auditors.

24–33 What is data mining? How might data mining techniques facilitate the work of information systems auditors?

24–34 What is an interorganizational information system? What is a virtual organization? How might interorganizational information systems and virtual organizations impact the work of information systems auditors?

Multiple-Choice Questions

24–1 Which of the following is *least likely* to be a major focus when undertaking long-run planning for the information systems audit function?
  a Identifying the sequence in which material application systems within the organization in which the information systems audit function is located will be audited
  b Determining the relative weightings to be given to asset safeguarding and data integrity goals within the organization in which the information systems audit function is located
  c Providing an overall direction for the information systems function in light of the goals of the organization in which the information systems audit function is located
  d Ensuring that the information systems audit function has adequate resources to discharge its responsibilities effectively and efficiently

24–2 In a risk management program, the unit of analysis is:
  a The exposure on which the audit team is focusing
  b The business process or function to be audited
  c The weighting assigned to a generic risk
  d The type of resource being considered to support the conduct of the audit

24–3 The *primary* purpose of control self-assessment is to:
  a Educate stakeholders about the reliability of different types of controls
  b Make stakeholders aware of the differences between inherent risk, control risk, and detection risk
  c Force stakeholders to reflect on the weighting assigned by the information systems audit team to different risks
  d Take advantage of stakeholders' knowledge in determining the exposures faced

24–4 Which of the following is *not* likely to be covered within an audit charter prepared for an organization's information systems audit function?
  a Information systems audit function's place within the organization
  b Scope of the work to be performed by the information systems audit function

    c Audit approach to be adopted by the information systems audit function

    d Information systems audit function's rights to have access to records, facilities, and personnel

24–5 Which of the following arguments is *most likely* to be used in terms of having information systems auditors perform a staff role within an organization:

    a Makes better use of scarce information systems audit resources

    b Promotes greater goal congruence between financial auditors and information systems auditors

    c Improves the overall audit expertise of both financial auditors and information systems auditors

    d Facilitates communications between financial auditors and information systems auditors

24–6 Which of the following arguments is *most likely* to be used in support of decentralizing the information systems audit function within an organization:

    a A shortage of skilled information systems audit staff exists

    b Information systems audits must be performed in many locations that are dispersed physically

    c Financial auditors have basic competence in information systems auditing

    d The information systems audit group has been newly established within the organization

24–7 Which of the following has been a finding of prior research that has examined whether information systems audit staff should be recruited with an information technology background or an audit background:

    a Programmers make better information systems auditors than systems analysts or system designers

    b Information systems auditors who have an information technology background have higher turnover than those who have an audit background

    c Information systems professionals believe that information technology knowledge is easier to acquire than audit knowledge

    d It is easier to recruit more senior auditors than information technology professionals to the information systems audit function

24–8 Which of the following is *least likely* to be a purpose of a yearly staff appraisal meeting conducted between an information systems auditor and his/her manager?

    a To determine the interpersonal skills that the information systems auditor needs to develop more fully

    b To affirm the information systems auditor's accomplishments during the preceding period

    c To evaluate the information systems auditor's performance against benchmarks

    d To resolve disagreements about the information systems auditor's performance on a particular audit

24–9 Which of the following is *least likely* to be a reason why the career paths available to information systems auditors are often limited?

    a Many organizations have only a few information systems audit positions available

    b Information systems audit skills are too narrow and specialized for many other jobs

    c Promotional opportunities have been affected by trends toward downsizing and flattening organizational structures

    d Information systems auditors must compete with general staff auditors for the higher-level positions that are available.

24–10 If information systems auditors perform a staff function, which of the following aspects of leadership is likely to be *most difficult* to accomplish?

    a Motivating information systems auditors to undertake audit work in technical domains where they have little experience

    b Ensuring that information systems auditors achieve the objectives of the audit in which they participate rather than pursuing their own agenda

    c Motivating information systems auditors to compare their performance against benchmarks they establish for themselves

    d Ensuring that information systems auditors maintain a commitment to maintaining their professional competence

24–11 Which of the following statements about exercising leadership processes with information systems auditors is *most likely* to be *false*?

    a An authoritarian leadership style will be most successful when information systems auditors are undertaking audits involving high uncertainty

    b Leadership styles need to be altered depending on whether information systems auditors have a managerial career orientation or a technical career orientation

    c Leadership styles need to be varied throughout an information systems auditor's career

    d The effectiveness of leadership styles is highly dependent on information systems audit managers' ability to communicate with their staff

24–12 Employing an independent consultant to evaluate the information systems audit function every few years is likely to provide *most* assistance in which of the following areas?

    a Evaluating the quality of work performed on individual information systems audits

    b Determining whether information systems audit reports communicate the findings of audits in a clear, unambiguous fashion

    c Choosing the set of benchmarks that should be used to determine the effectiveness and efficiency of the information systems audit work conducted

    d Evaluating the appropriateness of the audit policies and procedures used to govern the conduct of information systems audit work

24–13 Which of the following is *least likely* to be a criterion for defining a profession?

    a Existence of a code of ethics

    b Existence of a disciplinary mechanism

    c Government-mandated requirement for registration of practitioners

    d Defined common body of knowledge

24–14 A major purpose of the Information Systems Audit and Control Foundation's publication called *COBIT: Control Objectives for Information and Related Technologies* is:

    a To establish a basis for a disciplinary mechanism within the information systems audit profession

    b To provide benchmarks for the conduct of information systems audits in medium- to large-size organizations

    c To provide a common body of knowledge for the information systems audit profession

    d To provide the conceptual foundations for the development of information systems audit standards

24–15 A major purpose of the Information Systems Audit and Control Association's Statements on Information Systems Auditing Standards is to:

    a Cover temporary gaps in the General Standards for information systems auditing

    b Show how the General Standards for information systems auditing relate to one another

    c Explain the General Standards for information systems auditing in the context of the Association's Code of Ethics

    d Tease out the implications of the General Standards for information systems audit practice

24–16 Which of the following was *not* a major goal when the EDP Auditors Foundation established the CISA examination?

    a Providing a basis for a disciplinary mechanism within the information systems audit and control profession

    b Motivating people to develop and maintain their competence as information systems auditors

    c Assisting management with personnel selection and development in relation to information systems auditors

    d Providing an ongoing basis to monitor the competence of people who claimed to be information systems auditors

24–17 Which of the following matters is *not* covered in the code of ethics of the Information Systems Audit and Control Association?

    a The need to comply with standards promulgated by the Information Systems Audit and Control Association

    b Support for stakeholders in the audit process to enhance their understanding of information systems auditing

    c The disciplinary action to be taken by the Information Systems Audit and Control Association when members violate the code of ethics

    d The need to communicate audit outcomes to appropriate stakeholders in the information systems audit process

24–18 Organizations' increasing use of the Internet has had *least* impact on:

    a The overall structure of the approach used to conduct an information systems audit

    b Exposures associated with the quality of information systems resources that an organization makes available to other parties

    c The incidence of virus-related problems that an organization encounters with information systems resources

    d Their ability to ensure that their employees focus primarily on their core job functions

24–19 The *primary* purpose of using a certification authority in electronic commerce is to:

    a Ensure both the vendor and customer choose secure private keys

    b Provide a banking facility for both the vendor and the customer

    c Ensure that both the vendor and customer comply with the terms of contracts

    d Provide a means of ensuring the authenticity of both the vendor and the customer

24–20 A major way in which business process engineering has undermined controls in organizations is that it has:

    a Reduced the effectiveness of data communications controls

    b Reduced separation of duties among employees

    c Reduced the quality of staff needed to perform various tasks

    d Reduced the efficiency with which functional controls can be operated

24–21 Information systems auditors should be *most concerned* about management's decision to undertake outsourcing of the information systems function when:

    a A long-term contract with the outsourcing vendor is being contemplated

    b The information systems function plays a strategic role within the organization

    c Reliance will have to be placed on other auditors to evaluate the ongoing financial position of the outsourcing vendor

    d The outsourcing vendor is large in size relative to the organization

24–22 Which of the following is *not* a principle under the regulatory regime for protection of data privacy called FIP?

    a People should be able to determine the existence of and to delete data about themselves that is irrelevant

    b Personal data should be collected only for specified purposes

    c Data should be collected about people only with their knowledge and consent

    d A higher level of control should be exercised over stored data relative to transmitted data

24–23 Which of the following statements about the implications of privacy legislation for auditors *most likely* is *false*?

    a As users of personal data, auditors will be exempt from privacy legislation because of their statutory obligations to audit an organization's accounts

    b Internal auditors must evaluate their organization's practices in relation to protecting data privacy to ensure compliance with any legislation

    c Both domestic and foreign privacy statutes may be relevant to our work as information systems auditors

    d Auditors should evaluate the fairness of information practices in relation to privacy protection even if their organizations are not subject to privacy statutes

24–24 If auditors are seeking to detect whether fraud has caused material misstatements in the accounts, data mining *most likely* will be used to assist them to:

    a Extract data from an object-oriented database that can be used as input to a statistical program for analytical review purposes

    b Undertake audit procedures that will reduce the inherent risk associated with the organization they are auditing

    c Recognize patterns among data in large databases that might signal the presence of fraud

    d Reduce the reliance they must place on compliance test procedures to determine whether controls are in place and working

24–25 Which of the following is *not* an implication of interorganizational information systems and virtual organizations for the conduct of audit work?

    a Processing controls become more important than boundary controls

    b Greater reliance must be placed on the work of other auditors

    c Control and audit standards become more important

    d The inherent risk associated with the audit increases

Exercises and Cases

24–1 Southern Aurora Limited (SAL) is a large Sydney-based financial institution that operates internationally. It has also established strategic alliances with a number of financial institutions based in Singapore, New York, and London. Because of the extensive range of products and services that it offers, it faces high exposure in some markets and low exposure in other markets.

Although SAL relies heavily on its computer-based information systems, nonetheless to date the approach taken to the audit and control of these systems has been somewhat piecemeal. To some extent the problem has been that the internal audit function was managed by someone who was a very conservative, traditional financial auditor. SAL's board of directors and senior management were also conservative, and they placed few demands on the internal audit function for change.

Recently, however, significant turnover of board positions and senior management positions has occurred. The new management have been aggressive in seeking out additional market opportunities for SAL. Moreover, they have asked that all functions within the organization begin a comprehensive review process to find ways to improve effectiveness and efficiency.

As a result of the changes occurring, the previous manager of internal audit has resigned, and a new manager has been appointed. He has received increased funding from senior management because they see the internal audit function as being important in their efforts to seek out ways to improve effectiveness and efficiency within SAL. The new manager of internal audit has used some of this funding to provide redundancy payouts to several existing financial auditors. In addition, he has employed three information systems audit specialists with a view to undertaking more effective and efficient audit work within SAL. You are one of these information systems auditors, and you have been asked to manage the information systems audit group.

In light of the responsibilities you have been given, the manager of internal audit shows you an outline of a strategic plan that he is preparing for the audit group. In its current draft form, the plan has the following goals:
1. To perform high-quality audits,
2. To provide timely reporting and advice to management to allow them to discharge their responsibilities,
3. To maintain a client focus to fulfill management's expectation of the audit function better,
4. To provide full audit coverage of all material functions within SAL on a regular rotating basis,
5. To ensure the effectiveness and efficiency of the internal audit function,
6. To ensure that internal audit staff maintain a high level of competence,
7. To foster and operate within a quality-management philosophy in SAL,
8. To foster and operate within an ethical culture in SAL, and
9. To foster and maintain an image of professionalism within the internal audit function.

He asks you to reflect on each of these goals and to identify two or three objectives for each goal that you believe you and the other two information systems auditors will need to achieve if the goal is to be met. In deliberating on these objectives, he asks you to remember the new environment in which the internal audit function is now operating.

Required: For each goal, list the two or three objectives you believe you and your colleagues within the information systems audit group need to achieve. Briefly explain why these objectives must be achieved if the goal is to be met.

24-2 You are the manager of internal audit for the Department of Transport, which is a major government department within your state. You have an internal audit staff of five professionals. Two are senior auditors, and three are junior auditors. Two of the juniors were hired less than 12 months ago in the last round of college recruitment. The other was hired two years ago.

You are preparing to undertake your yearly round of staff appraisal interviews. In this light, one of your seniors has come to discuss the performance of one of the juniors who was hired less than 12 months ago. The junior has been working under his supervision.

Your senior indicates that the junior has outstanding information systems audit skills. She has a bachelor's degree in computer science and a masters of business administration degree (with specialization in accounting and auditing). Technically, her work has been of the highest quality. Moreover, she is highly motivated, she works hards, and she is keen to learn new audit skills. Her downfall, however, is her interpersonal skills. She is aggressive and abrupt, and she does not "suffer fools gladly." As a result, your senior has frequently been contacted by managers within the department who have been unhappy about their interactions with the junior. Recently, one manager called to indicate she would not allow the junior to undertake audit work in her section again. During a meeting with the junior, she felt the junior had virtually accused her of incompetence because of some control weaknesses that the junior had discovered. The tone of the meeting had quickly degenerated, and no productive outcomes had been achieved.

Your senior also indicates that the problems extend to the junior's relationships with the other two juniors and the other senior. The other two juniors feel they are constantly being "put down" in relation to the audit work they have undertaken and, in particular, their lack of computer knowledge. The other senior feels he is given little respect. (He has had long experience as a financial auditor, and he is nearing retirement.)

At various times over the past six months, your senior indicates he has attempted to counsel the junior on the problems that have emerged. He had told her directly about the complaints made by audit clients and the attitudes of her colleagues within the audit group toward her. The junior had dismissed his counsel summarily, however. She had retorted that she was dismayed by the level of incompetence shown by some managers with the department and some of her audit colleagues. At one point she shouted angrily: "If they can't stand the heat in the kitchen, they should get out." She made it clear that nobody would stand in her way of getting the "right" job done.

Your senior indicates that he believes the situation now cannot be retrieved. He recommends that you fire the junior immediately. He is no longer prepared to work with her nor, he argues, will the other auditors work with her. In addition, he cannot assign her to certain audit work because of her poor relationships with several clients. He expresses his regret, however, about the resulting loss of her very high level of information systems audit technical skills. He believes it is most unlikely that someone with her level of technical skills can be hired again.

Required: Although you have been aware that problems were being encountered with the junior auditor, you are somewhat taken aback by the severity of these problems (as now described to you by the senior). Your meeting with the junior is scheduled for 10:30 AM tomorrow. How do you plan to approach the conduct of the meeting? What outcomes do you wish to achieve?

24–3 You have recently been employed as the manager of internal audit for a large multinational financial services company. It is clear to you that you have been given the job because of your reputation as a troubleshooter, your extensive experience with financial institutions, and your widely acknowledged expertise in information systems audit and control. You have attained a high profile, for example, because of the excellent work you undertook when you were president of the local chapter of the Information Systems Audit and Control Association.

The company has just been through the most difficult 12-month period of its history, and the company's management is still striving to turn the company around. The primary source of the difficulties has been a major fraud that was discovered 14 months ago. The nature of the fraud is complex, but basically it involved collusion among several senior managers and financial traders to use investors' funds improperly. The fraud was "accidentally" uncovered by the company's external auditors. When federal officials began to investigate the activities of the company in detail, they also discovered other irregularities—for example, evidence of insider trading by senior personnel within the company.

When the federal investigation was complete, it was damning of the company's management and, in particular, the performance of internal audit staff. The federal investigators found that some critical internal controls were weak or nonexistent. They focused especially on the poor state of controls in some of the company's major computer systems.

The chair of the board of directors reacted immediately to the report by asking that the manager of internal audit (your predecessor) be fired. A number of senior personnel within the company were also fired, and some have been charged with criminal offences. Many of the company's long-standing clients and customers took their business elsewhere. As a result, the company's share price plummeted. Angry shareholders demanded the resignation of the chair of the board of directors. After substantial pressure, she resigned, along with half the other board members.

You have a good understanding of the situation you now face. You believe you have the full support of the new chair of the board of directors. Indeed, she has met with you several times to discuss various problems with you and to assure you of the board's support in discharging your responsibilities. She underscores the need to establish a vibrant, effective, efficient internal audit group within the company and to rectify deficiencies in the company's internal control systems, especially those associated with the company's computer systems.

The internal audit staff, however, are demoralized. Since the departure of the previous internal audit manager, they have been reporting to a temporary manager who has accounting skills but few audit skills. Most of the audit group have tried to leave the company, but they have been unable to find jobs elsewhere. The criticisms levied against the internal audit group by the federal investigators are now widely known in the marketplace. As a result, the internal auditors cannot find other positions because their reputations are tarnished. Moreover, the one internal auditor who has expertise in information systems audit and control resigned shortly after the fraud was discovered to take up work as a full-time musician. (She plays clarinet in an up-and-coming jazz quartet.) Attempts were made to replace her, but it seems that good information systems auditors now are not willing to join the company because of its poor reputation.

You have also found that the company's managers now have a high level of mistrust of the internal audit group. They, too, have had their reputations tarnished by the events that have occurred. Moreover, with the company's downturn, their compensation has been affected adversely. They blame the internal audit group for many of the problems they now face.

Required: Outline your strategies to revitalize the internal audit group within the company. In particular, discuss the leadership strategies you will use with the internal audit group to restore morale and motivate staff, the ways in which you will build up information systems audit and control expertise within the group, and the approach you will use to try to reestablish good relationships between the internal audit group and the managers who will be the group's clients.

24–4 You are the manager of internal audit of a large multinational foodstuffs company. One day, you meet with one of your audit seniors at her request. She has primary responsibility for information systems auditing within your company, and she has eight staff members that report to her.

At the beginning of the meeting, she reports that she has encountered some problems with one of her staff. During a detailed review of an audit that he has recently conducted of the company's personnel and payroll systems, she has discovered several aspects of his work that concern her. First, it appears that he has "borrowed" program code from a colleague who works with a competitor organization to develop certain specialized software that he needed to conduct the audit. In addition, he has made an unauthorized copy of a commercial audit software package that is used to evaluate the reliability of controls in the local area network platform that your company uses.

Second, he has been careless in protecting the privacy of some sensitive information contained in the personnel files that he was examining. He had used the specialized software he had developed to undertake some sophisticated computer matching of data in different company files as a means of detecting any payroll irregularities that might exist. Unfortunately, he had copied some of these files to a diskette and left the diskette on a desk in the payroll department where he was working temporarily. Another employee had discovered the diskette when she was working late one evening, and she read the contents of the file using software on her own machine. She thought it might be interesting to see the sorts of data that the auditor was examining. The diskette contained sensitive personnel performance data and medical data. The employee had disclosed some of this data to a colleague, who in turn had disclosed it to other colleagues. As a result, a distressed employee had made a complaint to the personnel manager when he discovered that confidential information about his drug dependency problems and work performance problems were circulating among company employees. The personnel manager in turn had made a complaint to your audit senior.

Third, the audit documentation prepared by the auditor was of mixed quality. Some parts of the audit were well documented. Other parts were poorly documented, however, especially those relating to use of the "borrowed" software and the commercial software that had been copied and those relating to the computer data matching that had been undertaken. The auditor had reached some worrisome conclusions about the reliability of controls in the personnel and payroll areas and the existence of irregularities in these areas. During a meeting with the vice president responsible for these areas, however, he had been evasive about the basis for his conclusions when he was questioned aggressively by the vice president. (The vice president was clearly upset about the conclusions that had been reached.) The auditor reacted negatively to the questioning, however, and insisted that his conclusions were valid. He retorted that the vice president would be culpable if she did not attend immediately to the matters he had raised in his report. A stand-off situation now exists.

Your audit senior asks what steps you and she should now take to try to mitigate the problems that have occurred. She points out that she and all her staff are CISAs and members of the Information Systems Audit and Control Association. In light of the level of professionalism that exists within her group, she is distressed that the current situation has arisen.

Required: On the basis of the information provided to you by your senior auditor, outline the steps you now propose to undertake.

24-5 You are the manager of internal audit for a large Australian city council. The council is responsible for all the normal services—for example, water, sewerage, roads, waste disposal, parklands, and animal licensing. By world standards, the council's operations are extensive, and its annual budget is large.

One day you are approached by the mayor. He wishes to discuss the responses that the council has received to a tender document which it issued three months ago. The tender relates to the provision of and installation of an extensive series of sewerage and water pipes that are to be located in several new suburbs that the council wants to open up for development.

A large number of replies to the tender were received from companies all around the world. By far, the cheapest tender, however, was received from a joint venture company that calls itself Virtual Pipelines. The mayor is concerned about the nature of the tender. He explains that in essence Virtual

Pipelines (VP) comprises nine companies. Company A has taken responsibility for preparing the final tender document. It is also slated to manage the overall provision of and installation of the pipes and related components (e.g., valves). It has contracted with Company B, however, which has a design for the pipes and related components required for the project. The design requires certain modifications, however, to meet the needs of the council. Company A has contracted with Company C, therefore, which is a specialist in design modifications for sewerage and water pipes and their related components. Company C has in turn contracted with Company D to undertake an engineering analysis of the modified design and to prepare manufacturing plans on the basis of the design. Company C has also contracted with Company E to convert the files created by its computer-aided design package into the format used by Company D's computer-aided design package. Company A has also contracted with Company F to undertake the actual fabrication of the pipes and their related components. Company F has contracted with Company G, however, to undertake certain die-making and casting. Company A has also contracted with Company H to provide a set of standard documentation for all aspects of the project. Finally, Company A has contracted with Company I to provide archiving and backup services for all documentation and computer files.

When the council first received VP's tender document, most members of the tender evaluation team quickly dismissed it because of VP's "outlandish" governance structure. One member of the team argued the proposal was "outstanding," however, from an engineering viewpoint. She also argued that no other tenders would beat VP's price. On the latter point, she was right. After the first-pass evaluation of the large number of tender documents received, VP's price was significantly below the next lowest. As a result, the tender evaluation team looked at VP's tender document more closely. They concluded that it was indeed the best proposal from an engineering viewpoint—one that would probably set a standard for future work.

Because the council had had no experience with any of the companies involved in VP's tender, however, several members of the tender evaluation team sought out background information on the companies. Some were old, well-established companies; others were new, high-technology companies. They were located all over the world. Surprisingly, none had worked with any of the others before they came together to prepare the tender document. Company A, which was one of the new, high-technology companies, had clearly been the driving force, however, behind the ethos that had arisen with the consortium. It had searched the Internet extensively to find the companies with which it wanted to contract. In turn, it had encouraged and assisted its partners to find other partners in the same way. Indeed, in the preparation of VP's tender document, little face-to-face interaction had occurred among employees in the different companies in the joint venture. Most work had been done electronically across the Internet.

Required: The tender evaluation team have now advised the council that they should accept VP's tender. During discussions in council, however, a number of councilors have expressed major reservations about VP's viability as an organization. In this light, the council has instructed the mayor to seek your advice and opinion on how the council should now proceed. In particular, because the work associated with the tender will have to be carried out over a four-year period, they value your opinion on any control and audit issues that you perceive to be associated with the project.

Answers to Multiple-Choice Questions

24–1	a	24–7	c	24–13	c	24–19	d
24–2	b	24–8	d	24–14	c	24–20	b
24–3	d	24–9	b	24–15	d	24–21	b
24–4	c	24–10	b	24–16	a	24–22	d
24–5	a	24–11	a	24–17	c	24–23	a
24–6	b	24–12	d	24–18	a	24–24	c
						24–25	a

REFERENCES

Atkinson, Randall J. (1997), "Toward a More Secure Internet," *IEEE Computer* (January), 57–61.

Bhimani, Anish (1996), "Securing the Commercial Internet," *Communications of the ACM* (June), 29–35.

Borenstein, Nathaniel (1996), "Perils and Pitfalls of Practical Cybercommerce," *Communications of the ACM* (June), 36–44.

Brachman, Ronald J., Tom Khabaza, Willi Kloesgen, Gregory Piatetsky-Shapiro, and Evangelos Simoudis (1996), "Mining Business Databases," *Communications of the ACM* (November), 42–48.

Bruno, Paul R. (1994), "Skill Enhancement for the EDP Auditor," *EDP Auditing*. Boston: Auerbach Publication, Portfolio 72–02–20.

Cangemi, Michael P. (1996), *Managing the Audit Function: A Corporate Audit Department Procedures Guide*, 2d ed. New York: John Wiley & Sons.

Casarin, Paul (1997), "Using Data Mining Techniques in Auditing," *The IS Audit & Control Journal*, V, 43–46.

Dahlberg, Patricia (1996), "Q&A on New Model for Information Technology Risk Management," *IS Audit & Control Journal*, III, 22–26.

Davenport, T. H. (1993), *Process Innovation: Reengineering Work Through Information Technology*. Boston: Harvard Business School Press.

Erickson, John (1996), "Integrated Risk Assessment: Part Two: Coverage Scenarios, Yearly Review Plan and Linkage," *IS Audit & Control Journal*, I, 44–48.

Finne, Thomas (1997), "What Are the Information Security Risks in Decision Support Systems and Data Warehousing," *Computers & Security*, 16(3), 197–204.

Gallegos, Frederick, and Stephen R. Powell (1997), "Telecommunications Networks and Virtual Corporations," *The IS Audit & Control Journal*, III, 26–28.

Gurbaxani, Vijay (1996), "The New World of Information Technology Outsourcing," *Communications of the ACM* (July), 45–46.

Hammer, Michael (1990), "Reengineering Work: Don't Automate, Obliterate," *Harvard Business Review* (July-August), 104–112.

Information Systems Audit and Control Foundation (1996), *COBIT: Control Objectives for Information and Related Technology*. Rolling Meadows, IL: The Information Systems Audit and Control Foundation.

Jerskey, Pamela, Ivy Robyn Dodge, and Sanford Sherizen (1996), "A Privacy Audit Primer," *EDPACS* (March), 1–7.

Kalakota, Ravi, and Andrew B. Whinston (1996), *Frontiers of Electronic Commerce*. Reading, MA: Addison-Wesley.

———— and ———— (1997), *Electronic Commerce: A Manager's Guide*. Reading, MA: Addison-Wesley.

Kanter, Howard, and Marshall K. Pitman (1997), "Audit Risk Assessment: A Renaissance Approach," *IS Audit & Control Journal*, I, 34–35, 38–39.

Klur, David (1996), "Take My Key, Please: Certification Authorities and Electronic Commerce," *IS Audit & Control Journal*, VI, 28–31, 33.

Konsynski, Benn R., and F. Warren McFarlan (1990), "Information Partnerships—Shared Data, Shared Scale," *Harvard Business Review* (September–October), 114–120.

Lacity, Mary C., Leslie P. Willcocks, and David E. Feeny (1996), "The Value of Selective IT Sourcing," *Sloan Management Review* (Spring), 13–25.

Laudon, Kenneth C. (1996), "Markets and Privacy," *Communications of the ACM* (September), 92–104.

Levine, Constance (1993), "How TQM Worked for One Firm," *Journal of Accountancy* (September), 73–79.

Lynch, Clifford (1997), "Searching the Internet," *Scientific American* (March), 44–48.

McConnell, Michael J. (1996), "Strategic Considerations in Electronic Commerce," *IS Audit & Control Journal*, VI, 22–26.

McFarlan, F. Warren, James L. McKenney, and Phillip J. Pyburn (1983), "The Information Archipelago—Plotting a Course," *Harvard Business Review* (January–February), 145–156.

McFarlan, F. Warren, and Richard L. Nolan (1995), "How to Manage an IT Outsourcing Alliance," *Sloan Management Review* (Winter), 9–23.

McNamee, David (1996), "Developing an IS Risk Assessment Process," *IS Audit & Control Journal*, III, 14, 17–18.

Mowshowitz, Abbe (1997), "Virtual Organization," *Communications of the ACM* (September), 30–37.

Mullen, Jack B. (1993), "The Integrated Audit Approach," *EDP Auditing*. Boston: Auerbach Publication, Portfolio 72–01–60.1.

Nieuwenhuizen, John (1997), *Asleep at the Wheel: Australia on the Superhighway*. Sydney: Australian Broadcasting Commission.

Organisation for Economic Co-operation and Development (OECD) (1980), "Guidelines on the Protection of Privacy and Transborder Flows of Personal Data," available at http://www.oecd.org.

Rice, Anita L. (1993), "Global Standards for EDP Audit," *EDP Auditing*. Boston: Auerbach Publication, Portfolio 72–01–10.

Rittenberg, Larry E. (1977), *Auditor Independence and Systems Design*. Altamonte Springs, FL: The Institute of Internal Auditors.

Scott, S. Yvonne (1996), "Audit and Control of Information Systems Outsourcing," *IS Audit & Control Journal*, VI, 46–51.

Sia, Siew Kien, and Boon Siong Neo (1997), "Reengineering Effectiveness and the Redesign of Organizational Control: A Case Study of the Inland Revenue Authority of Singapore," *Journal of Management Information Systems* (Summer), 69–92.

Smith, H. Jeff, Sandra J. Milberg, and Sandra J. Burke (1996), "Information Privacy: Measuring Individuals' Concerns about Organizational Practices," *MIS Quarterly* (June), 167–196.

Tibaldeo, Glen, and Don Buben (1996), "Cashing in on Technology: A Primer on Electronic Payment Systems," *IS Audit & Control Journal*, VI, 14–15, 17–20.

Vacca, John (1996), *Internet Security Secrets*. Foster City, CA: IDG Books.

West, Sally, and Andrea Khan (1997), "The Client as Participant: IS Audit and Control Self-Assessment," *IS Audit & Control Journal*, I, 20–23.

Zabura, Donald V. (1993), "The CISA Examination," *EDP Auditing*. Boston: Auerbach Publication, Portfolio 72–20–10.

Index

Job titles (cont.)
    librarian, 82
    network administrator, 81
    operational specialist, 82
    operator, 82
    quality assurance specialist, 82
    security administrator, 81
    systems analyst, 81
    systems programmer, 81
    workstation specialist, 82

K

Kaizen, 346
Kendall notation, 945
Kernel programs, 939
Kernels
    security kernel, 535
    and trusted processes, 535
Kernel state, 522
Keyboarding, 421
Keys. *see* Cryptographic controls
Kiviat graphs, for performance
        measurement data, 836–838
Knee capacity, 934
Knowledge base, expert systems, 688,
        689
Knowledge discovery, meaning of, 998

L

Languages. *see* Programming
        languages
Language subset facility, 686
Large Systems Performance Reference
        (LSPR) Method, 941
Lattice, 619
Leadership style, 85
    adaptation of, 85
Leading function, 84–86
    audit management, 981–983
    communication function, 86
    contingency theories of leadership,
        85, 982–983
    leadership styles, 85
    motivation function, 84–85
    objectives of, 981–982
    purpose of, 84
Legal aspects
    hacking, 266
    proprietary database, 264
Letter bombs, e-mail, 642
Lexical validation, 453
Librarian
    documentation librarian, 313–314
    position description, 82
    role of, 179, 312
Library copy, 686
Library software, 165
Life-cycle approach, 107–109
    components of, 108
    phases in, 108–109
Line error correction, 484–485
    forward error correcting codes, 485
    retransmission, 485
Line error detection
    cyclic redundancy checks, 484
    loop check, 483–484
    parity checking, 484
Line switching, 483
Link controls, 487
    Asynchronous Transfer Mode
        (ATM), 487

International Organization for
        Standardization Higher-level
        Data Link Control (SDLC),
        487
    Synchronous Data Link Control
        (SDLC), 487
Link encryption, 494–495
List-oriented access control,
        529–530
List-oriented authorization, 389–390
Little's Law, 946
Local area network controls,
        299–301
    auditor activities, 301
    cable scanners, 300
    file server functions, 299–300
Local area networks
    bus topology, 488
    control factors, 488, 489, 490, 491
    features of, 487
    hybrid topology, 491
    ring topology, 488–490
    star topology, 490
    tree topology, 488
Location, of information systems
        function, 83
Lockout, and deadlock, 577
Logging, 590–595
    afterimages, 594–595
    beforeimages, 591–594
    input transactions, 590–591
    write-ahead logging, 594
Logical batches, 439
Logical dumping, 588–590
Long-key systems, 374
Loop check, 483–484
Loop testing, 733–734
    nested loops in, 733
    simple loops in, 733

M

Macros, 681, 686
Mainframes, backup options, 269
Maintenance
    adaptive maintenance, 177
    auditor concerns related to, 177–178,
        296–297
    configuration management systems,
        177
    controls for computer operations,
        295–297
    perfective maintenance, 177
    performance monitoring software,
        296
    preventive maintenance, 295
    repair maintenance, 177, 295
    reports, 296
    of storage media, 310–311
Management controls, 44–45
    data resource management controls,
        68
    elements of, 49–50
    operations management controls,
        68
    programming management controls,
        68
    quality assurance management
        controls, 68
    systems development management
        controls, 68
    top management controls, 68
    See also Top management controls

Management subsystems, 38–39
    lawful and unlawful events,
        identification of, 40–41
    types of, 39
    See also Audit management
Mandatory access controls, 385–388,
        569
    types of, 568
Market price, transfer pricing, 91
Masquerading, meaning of, 532
Master key, 581
Mean-time-between failure (MTBF),
        483, 934
Memory
    real memory controls, 524–527
    virtual memory controls, 527–531
Memory-based scheme,
        checkpoint/restart, 547
Menu bars, 446
Menu system, 446–448
    efficiency issues, 448
    error reduction with, 447–448
    types of menus, 446
Mesh topology, 491
    control factors, 491–492
Message authentication codes, 498
Message sequence numbers, 498
Message switching, 483
Metadata
    meaning of, 223
    uses of, 223
Methods standards, elements of, 90
Mirroring strategy, 587–588
    pros/cons of, 588
Modems, 479, 481
    functions of, 481
Modular approach, coding, 168–169
Monitoring
    Gantt charts, 163
    program evaluation and review
        technique (PERT), 163–165
    quality assurance, 336–349
    work breakdown structures, 163
Motivation, theories of, 84–85
Motivator-hygiene theory, 84
Multiple execution states, 521–522
Multiple-state machine, 522
Multiplexing, 482
    asynchronous multiplexing, 482
    efficiency factors, 483
    frequency-division multiplexing, 482
    synchronous multiplexing, 482
    time-division multiplexing, 482
Multipoint topology, 488

N

NAK signal, 485
Name-dependent access control,
        565–566
National Computer Security Center,
        536–537
Natural benchmarks, 940
Natural languages, 450–452
    limitations of interfaces, 451–452
Natural workload models, 936–937
Neal Nelson & Associates,
        benchmarking tools, 941
Negotiated price, transfer pricing, 91
Nested loops, 733
Netiquette, rules of, 640
Network administrator, position
        description, 81